understanding computers:
today and tomorrow
2003 enhanced edition

understanding computers: today and tomorrow

2003 enhanced edition

CHARLES S. PARKER

DEBORAH MORLEY

BRETT MIKETTA

THOMSON

COURSE TECHNOLOGY

Australia • Canada • Mexico • Singapore • Spain • United Kingdom • United States

Understanding Computers: Today and Tomorrow 2003 Enhanced Edition
is published by Course Technology.

Managing Editor:
Rachel Crapser

Senior Product Manager:
Kathy Finnegan

Product Manager:
Karen Stevens

Technology Product Manager:
Amanda Young Shelton

Associate Product Manager:
Brianna Germain

Editorial Assistant:
Emilie Perreault

Marketing Manager:
Rachel Valente

Production Editor:
Jennifer Goguen, Dee Josephson,
TSI Graphics, Melissa Panagos

Development Editor:
Pam Conrad

Composition:
TSI Graphics
Gex Publishing Services

Text Designer:
Bill Brammer

Cover Designer:
Julie Malone

The best way for students to learn about technology is to use it. **Understanding Computers: Today and Tomorrow, 2003 Enhanced Edition,** provides a truly interactive approach to learning about computers with a text that is fully integrated with a completely updated, multimedia-enhanced Web site. This nontechnical, introductory text explains in straightforward terms the importance of learning about computers, types of computer systems and their components, principles by which computer systems work, practical applications of computers and related technologies, and ways in which the world is being changed by computers. The goal of this text is to provide the reader with a solid knowledge of computer basics and with a framework for using this knowledge effectively in the workplace.

KEY FEATURES

Like previous editions, *Understanding Computers: Today and Tomorrow, 2003 Enhanced Edition* is current and comprehensive. Flexible organization and an engaging presentation combine with learning tools in each chapter to help the reader master important concepts. Numerous marginal notations lead students to highly interactive multimedia tutorials, exercises, and TechTV video clips on the *Understanding Computers* Web site. Boxed features on a variety of topics provide insight on current issues of interest.

Currency
The state-of-the-art content of this book and its multimedia support package reflect the latest technologies, trends and classroom needs. Throughout the writing and production stages, enhancements were continually being made to ensure that the final product would be as current as possible.

Comprehensiveness and Depth
Accommodating a wide range of teaching preferences, *Understanding Computers: Today and Tomorrow, 2003 Enhanced Edition* provides comprehensive coverage of traditional topics while covering hot topics such as the Internet; portable PCs and mobile devices; wireless and mobile communications; Internet searching, online shopping, downloading music, and other online activities; multimedia technology and design; e-commerce and e-business; object-oriented programming; Web databases; global computing issues; and security, privacy, and other timely social issues.

Readability
We remember more about a subject if it is presented in a straightforward way and made interesting and exciting. This book is written in a conversational, down-to-earth style—one designed to be accurate without being intimidating. Concepts are explained clearly and simply, without the use of overly technical terminology. Where complex points are presented, they are made understandable with realistic examples from everyday life.

Chapter Learning Tools

1. **Outline, Learning Objectives, and Overview:** For each chapter, an Outline of the major topics to be covered, a list of student Learning Objectives, and a chapter Overview helps instructors put the subject matter of the chapter in perspective and lets students know what they will be reading about.

2. **Boldfaced Key Terms and Running Glossary:** Important terms appear in boldface type as they are introduced in the chapter. These terms are defined at the bottom of the page on which they appear and in the end-of-text glossary.

3. **Chapter Boxes:** In each chapter, a **Trend box** provides students with a look at current and upcoming developments in the world of computers; an **Inside the Industry box** provides insight into some of the personalities and practices that have made the computer industry unique and fascinating; and a **How It Works box** explains how a technology or product works in more detail than covered in the chapter. Periodic **Campus Close-Up boxes** take a look at how computers and technology are being used at colleges or other educational facilities.

4. **Illustrations and Photographs:** Instructive, current full-color illustrations and photographs appear throughout the book to help illustrate important concepts. Figures and screen shots are carefully annotated to convey important information.

5. **Summary and Key Terms:** This is a concise, section-by-section summary of the main points in the chapter. Every boldfaced key term in the chapter also appears in boldface type in the summary. A matching exercise of selected key terms helps students test their retention of the chapter material.

6. **Review Activities and Projects:** End-of-chapter activities allow students to test themselves on what they have just read. A **Self-Quiz** (with the answers at the end of the text) consists of true-false and completion questions. Five additional easily graded matching and short-answer **Exercises** are included for instructors who would like to assign graded homework. End-of-chapter **Projects** require students to extend their knowledge by doing research beyond merely reading the book. Organized into five types of projects (Short Answer/Research, Hands On, Writing About Computers, Presentation/Demonstration, and Interactive Discussion), a special icon denotes projects that are written as group projects.

7. **Web Tutors, Further Explorations, and Interactive Exercises:** Throughout the text, students are directed to the *Understanding Computers* Web site to complete multimedia-enhanced Web Tutors. The Further Exploration section of the Web site gives students easy access to a variety of Web resources containing more in-depth information on a given topic. Each chapter concludes with a multimedia-rich capstone interactive exercise. These online activities allow students to interact with the concepts discussed in the text and test their knowledge of chapter materials.

8. **Art and Photo Program:** Chapters include fully annotated illustrations integrated with the text material, as well as numerous screen shots that showcase the latest applications. Many illustrations are rendered in a photorealistic style so that you can see the details of computer components close up. In addition, current full-color photographs appear throughout to help illustrate important concepts.

Updated Windows

Three modules contain a special foldout Window containing helpful information or a photo-essay. The updated Windows included with the full text include a "The History of Computers" timeline, a "Web Guide" containing links to useful Web site resources, and a "Ubiquitous Computing" window that takes a look at the ways computers affect our lives.

End of Text Glossary

The Glossary at the end of the book defines all boldfaced key terms in the text with a page reference indicating where the term is discussed.

NEW TO THIS ENHANCED EDITION

2003 Update section

A 40-page 2003 Update section has been added after Chapter 16 and contains the following elements:

- ▼ **Chapter-by-Chapter Update Guide**—An easy-to-use two-page spread for each chapter provides students with currency updates for the content contained in the chapter, as well as an overview of related new and emerging technology trends. Illustrative color photographs and several new Chapter Boxes are included in the update.

- ▼ **Expanded Computer History Coverage**—Students also have the opportunity to learn more about computer history, specifically about the different computer generations, through a two-page Inside the Industry Computer History boxed feature.

- ▼ **Tech News Video Projects**—Eight new exciting Tech News Video Projects direct students to watch relevant Tech TV news clips available through the Online Companion Web site and prepare for a class discussion or written opinion paper.

Updated Windows

The three special foldout Windows have been updated for currency. All three foldout Windows contain new photos and updated information, and the Web link URLs on the Web Guide window have been checked and updated as needed.

STUDENT AND INSTRUCTOR SUPPORT MATERIALS

Understanding Computers: Today and Tomorrow, 2003 Enhanced Edition is available with a complete package of support materials for instructors and students. Included in the package are the comprehensive Understanding Computers Web site, an Instructor's Resource Kit on CD-ROM, and a full-content online course.

web tutor

further
exploration

tech news
video project

THE UNDERSTANDING COMPUTERS WEB SITE

The Understanding Computers Web site located at:

   http://www.course.com/parker2002

provides media-rich support for students, including the following resources:

▼ **Web Tutors**—a series of multimedia-enhanced tutorials that allow students to interact with the concepts discussed in the text.

▼ **Further Exploration**—links to Web sites with more in-depth information on a given topic from the text.

▼ **Tech News Video Projects**—links to TechTV news clips.

▼ **Interactive Exercises**—multimedia-rich capstone exercises that allow students to test their knowledge after completing each chapter.

▼ **Web Guide**—provides students with categorized and regularly updated links to the Web's most useful sites.

Instructor's Resource Kit CD-ROM

All of the teaching tools available with this book are provided to the instructor on a single CD-ROM. Please note that the Instructor's Manual and ExamView Testbank are also available online at www.course.com.

Electronic Instructor's Manual

The Instructor's Manual is written to provide instructors with practical suggestions for enhancing classroom presentations. For each of the 16 chapters of the text, the Instructor's Manual provides the following components:

▼ A complete, three-level **Chapter Outline.**

▼ A list of **Learning Objectives.**

▼ **Summary,** oriented to the instructor, with teaching suggestions.

▼ A list of the **Key Terms** in the chapter and their definitions.

▼ **Teaching Tips,** with recommended topics for class discussion, important points to cover in class, and mention of additional instructor resources.

▼ A **Teaching Outline** that gives a detailed breakdown of the chapter, with all major headings and subheadings as well as points to cover under each. References to all textbook figures are also included in this outline.

▼ **Lecture Anecdotes** providing additional stories, news items, and information specific to chapter content to liven up lectures.

▼ **Answers to Exercises** that appear at the end of the chapter.

▼ **Suggestions for Projects** that appear at the end of the chapter.

ExamView

This textbook is accompanied by ExamView, a powerful testing software package that allows instructors to create and administer printed, computer (LAN-based), and Internet exams. ExamView includes over 2,400 questions that correspond to the topics covered in this text, enabling students to generate detailed study guides that include page references for further review. The computer-based and Internet testing components allow students to take exams at their computers, and also save the instructor time by grading each exam automatically.

PowerPoint Presentations

This book comes with Microsoft PowerPoint slides for each chapter. These are included as a teaching aid for classroom presentation, to make available to students on the network for chapter review, or to be printed for classroom distribution. Instructors can customize these presentations to cover any additional topics they introduce to the class.

Guide to Using the 2003 Update

Available online at www.course.com, a Guide to Using the 2003 Update includes suggestions for how to incorporate the material new to the 2003 Enhanced Edition into your course, a chapter-by-chapter teaching outline for the new material, and suggestions for solutions for the video projects.

Tabbing Guide

The tabbing guide can be used to show how and where this textbook has been updated for this edition from the 2000 edition. Page references are included to make planning a class easier for the instructor.

UNDERSTANDING COMPUTERS TODAY AND TOMORROW ONLINE COURSE

For instructors who want to add a richer online component to their courses, Course Technology is proud to present the *Understanding Computers: Today and Tomorrow* Online Course in WebCT and BlackBoard. This new, full-content online course correlates with the text and can be used in a variety of ways: to supplement the text in a traditional classroom setting or as a virtual classroom for distance learning students. Students learn technology by interacting with the content in this dynamic, interactive multimedia environment. Each chapter of the course is filled with interactive activities such as the Web Tutors and Interactive Exercises, links, animations, demonstrations, collaborative classroom activities, critical thinking exercises, and self-tests. For more information on how to bring online content to your course, contact your local Course Technology sales representative.

ACKNOWLEDGMENTS

The following past and present reviewers of this text deserve a special word of thanks for their thoughtful suggestions that have helped to define and improve the quality of this text over the years.

2003 Enhanced Edition – Educational Reviewers

Beverly Amer, Northern Arizona University
Cesar Marron, University of Wyoming
David Womack, University of Texas, San Antonio

2003 Enhanced Edition – Industry Expert Reviewers

Jeremy Bates, Multimedia Developer, R & L Multimedia Developers
Charles Hayes, Product Marketing Manager, SimpleTech, Inc.
Rick McGowan, Vice President & Senior Software Engineer, Unicode, Inc.
Russell Reynolds, Chief Operating Officer & Web Designer, R & L Multimedia Developers
Dave Stow, Database Specialist, OSE Systems Inc.

2002 Edition – Educational Reviewers

Beverly Amer, Northern Arizona University
Chris Brown, Bemidji State University
Joann C. Cook, College of DuPage
Terry Felke, WR Harper College
Janos T. Fustos, Metropolitan State
Jim Hanson, Austin Community College
Richard Kiger, Dallas Baptist University
James Lasalle, University of Arizona
Paul Lou, Diablo Valley College
Kent Lundin, Brigham Young University-Idaho
Donna Madsen, Kirkwood Community College
Randy Marak, Hillsboro CC
Joseph D. Oldham, University of Kentucky
Lisa B. Perez, San Joaquin Delta College
Delores Pusins, Hillsborough CC
Mike Rabaut, Hillsborough CC
Tim Sylvester, Glendale Community College
Semih Tahaoglu, Southeastern Louisiana University
Merrill Wells, Red Rocks Community College
George Woodbury, College of the Sequoias
Nan Woodsome, Araphoe Community College
Israel Yost, University of New Hampshire
Vic Zamora, Mt. San Antonio College

2002 Edition – Industry Expert Reviewers

New to this edition are individuals working in the computer industry who reviewed parts of the textbook in their area of expertise, to insure the timeliness and technical accuracy of the information contained in the text. Special thanks to the following individuals:

Alan Charlesworth, Staff Engineer, Sun Microsystems
Khaled A Elamrawi, Senior Marketing Engineer, Intel Corporation
Timothy D. O'Brien, Senior Systems Engineer, Fujitsu Software
John Paulson, Manager, Product Communications, Seagate Technology
Omid Rahmat, Editor in Chief, Tom's Hardware Guide www.tomshardware.com

Previous Editions

Beverly Amer, Northern Arizona University; James Ambroise Jr., Southern University, Louisiana; Virginia Anderson, University of North Dakota; Robert Andree, Indiana University Northwest; Linda Armbruster, Rancho Santiago College; Michael Atherton, Mankato State University; Gary E. Baker, Marshalltown Community College; Richard Batt, Saint Louis Community College at Meremec; Luverne Bierle, Iowa Central Community College; Jerry Booher, Scottsdale Community College; Frederick W. Bounds, Georgia Perimeter College; James Bradley, University of Calgary; Curtis Bring, Moorhead State University; Brenda K. Britt, Fayetteville Technical Community College; Cathy Brotherton, Riverside Community College; Janice Burke, South Suburban College; James Buxton, Tidewater Community College, Virginia; Gena Casas, Florida Community College, Jacksonville; Thomas Case, Georgia Southern University; John E. Castek, University of Wisconsin-La Crosse; Mario E. Cecchetti, Westmoreland County Community College; Jack W. Chandler, San Joaquin Delta College; Jerry M. Chin, Southwest Missouri State University; Edward W. Christensen, Monmouth University; Carl Clavadetscher, California State Polytechnic University; Vernon Clodfelter, Rowan Technical College, North Carolina; Laura Cooper, College of the Mainland, Texas; Cynthia Corritore, University of Nebraska at Omaha; Sandra Cunningham, Ranger College; Marvin Daugherty, Indiana Vocational Technical College; Donald L. Davis, University of Mississippi; Robert H. Dependahl Jr., Santa Barbara College, California; Donald Dershem, Mountain View College; John DiElsi, Marcy College, New York; Mark Dishaw, Boston University; Eugene T. Dolan, University of the District of Columbia; Bennie Allen Dooley, Pasadena City College; Robert H. Dependahl Jr.; Santa Barbara City College; William Dorin, Indiana University Northwest; Jackie O. Duncan, Hopkinsville Community College; John W. Durham, Fort Hays State University; Hyun B. Eom, Middle Tennessee State University; Michael Feiler, Merritt College; J. Patrick Fenton, West Valley Community College; James H. Finger, University of South Carolina at Columbia; William C. Fink, Lewis and Clark Community College, Illinois; Ronald W. Fordonski, College of Du Page; Connie Morris Fox, West Virginia Institute of Technology; Paula S. Funkhouser, Truckee Meadows Community College; Gene Garza, University of Montevallo; Timothy Gottleber, North Lake College; Dwight Graham, Prairie State College; Wade Graves, Grayson County College; Kay H. Gray, Jacksonville State University; David W. Green, Nashville State Technical Institute, Tennessee; George P. Grill, University of North Carolina, Greensboro; John Groh, San Joaquin Delta College; Rosemary C. Gross, Creighton University; Dennis Guster, Saint Louis Community College at Meremec; Joe Hagarty, Raritan Valley Community College; Donald Hall, Manatee Community College; Sallyann Z. Hanson, Mercer County Community College; L. D. Harber, Volunteer State Community College, Tennessee; Hank Hartman, Iowa State University; Richard Hatch, San Diego State University; Mary Lou Hawkins, Del Mar College; Ricci L. Heishman, Northern Virginia Community College; William Hightower, Elon College, North Carolina; Sharon A. Hill, Prince George's Community College, Maryland; Fred C. Homeyer, Angelo State University; Stanley P. Honacki, Moraine Valley Community College; L. Wayne Horn, Pensacola Junior College; J. William Howorth, Seneca College, Ontario, Canada; Mark W. Huber, East Carolina University; Peter L. Irwin, Richland College, Texas; Nicholas JohnRobak, Saint Joseph's University; Elizabeth Swoope Johnson, Louisiana State University; Jim Johnson, Valencia Community College; Mary T. Johnson, Mt. San Antonio College; Susan M. Jones, Southwest State University; Amardeep K. Kahlon, Austin Community College; Robert T. Keim, Arizona State University; Mary Louise Kelly, Palm Beach Community College; William R. Kenney, San Diego Mesa College; Richard Kerns, East Carolina University, North Carolina; Glenn Kersnick, Sinclair Community College, Ohio; Gordon C. Kimbell, Everett Community College, Washington; Mary Veronica Kolesar, Utah State University; Robert Kirklin, Los Angeles Harbor Community

College; Judith A. Knapp, Indiana University Northwest; James G. Kriz, Cuyahoga Community College, Ohio; Joan Krone, Denison University; Fran Kubicek, Kalamazoo Valley Community College; Rose M. Laird, Northern Virginia Community College; Robert Landrum, Jones Junior College; Shelly Langman, Bellevue Community College; James F. LaSalle, The University of Arizona; Linda J. Lindaman, Black Hawk College; Chang-Yang Lin, Eastern Kentucky University; Alden Lorents, Northern Arizona University; Paul M. Lou, Diablo Valley College; Deborah R. Ludford, Glendale Community College; Barbara J. Maccarone, North Shore Community College; Donna Madsen, Kirkwood Community College; Wayne Madison, Clemson University, South Carolina; Donna L. Madsen, Kirkwood Community College; Kathryn A. Marold, Ph.D., Metropolitan State College of Denver; Randy Marak, Hill College; Gary Marks, Austin Community College, Texas; Ed Martin, Kingsborough Community College; Vickie McCullough, Palomar College; James W. McGuffee, Austin Community College; James McMahon, Community College of Rhode Island; William A. McMillan, Madonna University; Don B. Medley, California State Polytechnic University; John Melrose, University of Wisconsin—Eau Claire; Mary Meredith, University of Southwestern Louisiana; Marilyn Meyer, Fresno City College; Carolyn H. Monroe, Baylor University; William J. Moon, Palm Beach Community College; Marilyn Moore, Purdue University; Marty Murray, Portland Community College; Don Nielsen, Golden West College; George Novotny, Ferris State University; Richard Okezie, Mesa Community College; Dennis J. Olsen, Pikes Peak Community College; Bob Palank, Florissant Community College; James Payne, Kellogg Community College; Robert Ralph, Fayetteville Technical Institute, North Carolina; Herbert F. Rebhun, University of Houston-Downtown; Arthur E. Rowland, Shasta College; Kenneth R. Ruhrup, St. Petersburg Junior College; John F. Sanford, Philadelphia College of Textiles and Science; Carol A. Schwab, Webster University; Larry Schwartzman, Trident Technical College; Benito R. Serenil, South Seattle Community College; Tom Seymour, Minot State University; John J. Shuler, San Antonio College, Texas; Gayla Jo Slauson, Mesa State College; Harold Smith, Brigham Young University; Willard A. Smith, Tennessee State University; Timothy M. Stanford, City University; Alfred C. St. Onge, Springfield Technical Community College, Massachusetts; Michael L. Stratford, Charles County Community College, Maryland; Karen Studniarz, Kishwaukee College; Sandra Swanson, Lewis &Clark Community College; William H. Trueheart, New Hampshire College; Jane J. Thompson, Solano Community College; Sue Traynor, Clarion University of Pennsylvania; James D. Van Tassel, Mission College; James R. Walters, Pikes Peak Community College;\Joyce V. Walton, Seneca College, Ontario, Canada; Diane B.Walz, University of Texas at San Antonio; Joseph Waters, Santa Rosa Junior College, California; Liang Chee Wee, University of Arizona; Fred J. Wilke, Saint Louis Community College; Charles M. Williams, Georgia State University; Roseanne Witkowski, Orange County Community College; James D. Woolever, Cerritos College; Patricia Joann Wykoff, Western Michigan University; A. James Wynne, Virginia Commonwealth University; and Robert D. Yearout, University of North Carolina at Asheville.

We would also like to thank the people on the Course team—their professionalism, attention to detail, and enormous enthusiasm makes working with them a pleasure. In particular, Rachel Crapser, Amanda Young Shelton, and Pam Conrad were instrumental in developing the format for this update, and Pam, Amanda, and Jennifer Goguen were invaluable during the writing, rewriting, and production of this book. Thanks also to Rachel Lucas for her video research; Anne Leuthold at TechTV for helping us secure the Tech TV video clips; Brianna Germain for managing the Instructor's Resources package and Online Companion; Emilie Perreault for all of the work that she has done; and Rachel Valente for her efforts on marketing this text. Thanks also to Kristen Duerr, Greg Donald, Melissa Panagos, Donna Gridley, and Kathy Finnegan.

We are also very appreciative of Elizabeth Boyd for her excellent work on the Test Bank and her helpful suggestions for text updates, as well as the numerous organizations that were kind enough to supply information and photographs for this text. Special thanks goes to Elizabeth Hayes for her hard work on behalf of this book for the past several editions, as well as her great job creating the PowerPoint slides that accompany this text.

Charles S. Parker
Deborah Morley

We sincerely hope you find this book interesting, informative, and enjoyable to read. If you have any suggestions for improvement, comments, or corrections that you'd like to be considered for future editions, please send them to deborah.morley@course.com

BRIEF CONTENTS

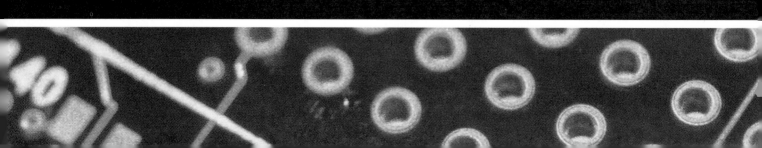

CONTENTS

Web Guide Window

Ubiquitous Computing Window

understanding computers:
today and tomorrow
2003 enhanced edition

INTRODUCTION

We live in an age of computers. Businesses, government agencies, and other organizations use computers and related technologies to handle tedious paperwork, provide better service to customers, and assist managers in making good decisions. Individuals use computers for such activities as paying bills, shopping, managing investments, preparing their taxes, playing games, researching products, communicating with others, and exchanging electronic photos and greeting cards. Because of their growing prominence in our society, it is essential to know something about computers and how they are used today.

This module introduces you to computers and some of their uses. Chapter 1 helps you understand what computer systems are, how they work, how people use them, and presents key terminology that you will encounter repeatedly throughout the text. Chapter 2 delves into how to turn a computer on and use it to access resources on the Internet and World Wide Web. Though the Internet and World Wide Web are covered in more detail in Chapter 9, Chapter 2 is intended to give you the knowledge, skills, and tools necessary to access the World Wide Web for research purposes and to complete the online exercises and activities that accompany this textbook.

INTRODUCTION

CHAPTER 1

OUTLINE

Introduction to the World of Computers

LEARNING OBJECTIVES

After completing this chapter, you will be able to:

1. Explain why it's essential to learn about computers today.

2. Describe several uses for computers in business or personal life.

3. Identify some of the major components of a computer system and explain their relationships to one another.

4. Define terms that commonly arise in reading about or discussing computers.

5. Describe the purpose of a network and what the Internet is.

6. List the five major categories of computers, giving at least one example of what the computers in each category might be used for.

7. Discuss the social impact of computers and some issues that arise from their prominence in our society.

Overview

As you've probably already discovered, computers and other forms of technology have a big impact on our lives. Computer systems keep track of bank transactions and credit-card purchases. They are the cornerstones of the airlines' massive reservations systems. Computers perform the billions of computations needed to send equipment to distant places like Mars and to operate it once it's there. Computers direct production in factories and provide business executives with the up-to-date information they need to make decisions. They also allow us access to the Internet, which has had a tremendous impact on the way people work and live. In addition to the general-purpose computers already discussed, there are special-purpose, *embedded computers* found in watches, televisions, phones, fax machines, kitchen appliances, exercise equipment, and many other everyday devices. In short, computers are used in virtually an endless number of ways.

Fifty years ago, computers were part of an obscure technology that interested a handful of scientists. Today, they are part of daily life. Experts call this trend *pervasive computing,* in which few aspects of daily life remain untouched by computers and computer technology. Because of its prominence in our society, it is important to understand what a computer is, a little about how it works, and the implications of living in a computer-oriented society.

This book is a beginner's guide. If you're considering a career as a computer professional in business, it will give you a comprehensive introduction to the field and provide you with a solid foundation for future study. If not, it will give you the basic knowledge you need to understand and use computers in school, on the job, and in your personal life. Today, many jobs depend heavily on computer-based information, and your success in the workplace may depend on your ability to manage that information and to use it to make effective decisions.

This chapter first examines what computers do and how they work. You will learn the correct terminology to use when discussing computers and computer components, including input, output, memory, storage, hardware, software, and computer networks. A later section looks at the various sizes of computers that today's users may encounter. Most of the computer concepts introduced in this chapter are discussed in more detail in subsequent chapters of this text. ■

COMPUTERS IN YOUR LIFE

Why Learn About Computers?

Prior to 1980, it was not essential for the average person to know how to use a computer in his or her job and it was uncommon to have a computer at home. Computers were large and expensive, and few people had access to them. Furthermore, the use of computers generally required a lot of technical knowledge. Most computers used in organizations were equipped to do little but carry out high-volume paperwork processing, such as issuing bills and keeping track of customer and product balances. Most ordinary working people were afraid of computers and there were few good reasons for getting familiar with them.

Suddenly things began to change. *Microcomputers*—inexpensive personal computers or PCs that you will read about later in this chapter—were created and computer use increased

web tutor

For a tutorial on the various uses of computers, go to www.course.com/ parker2002/ch1

dramatically. This increased use of computers has affected our personal lives, as well as changed the way many companies do business and the skills they seek in the people they hire.

Today we are living in the midst of a computer revolution, where many jobs heavily depend on the creation, collection, use, and dissemination of information. What's more, this revolution is showing no signs of slowing down; if anything, it's accelerating. Whether you become a teacher, lawyer, doctor, professional athlete, executive, or skilled tradesperson, your performance will largely depend on information and your use of it. Today's computers, with their almost dizzying speeds and high level of accuracy and reliability, are continually taking on new roles in our society.

Now, just like with a car, you don't need to know everything about a computer to use it effectively. You can learn to drive a car without knowing much about internal combustion engines, and you can learn to use a computer without a complete understanding of the technical details of how a computer works. Yet, a little knowledge gives you a big advantage. Knowing something about cars can help you to make wise purchases and save money on repairs. Likewise, knowing something about computers can help you buy the right one for your needs, use it for maximum benefit, and give you a much higher level of comfort and confidence along the way. Therefore, *computer literacy*—knowing and understanding computers and their uses—is essential today for everyone. The next few sections illustrate how computers are used in the home, the workplace, and other places in our society.

For a historical look at the development of computers, see the History of Computers window located within this module.

Computers in the Home

The proliferation of traditional and new types of computers in the home has increased home computing dramatically over the last few years. The home office has taken on greater importance since more and more people are doing some type of work at home. Use of the Internet at home to exchange e-mail, shop online, download music and software, and so forth has also led to special *Internet appliances*—easy to use devices designed for specific tasks, such as accessing the Internet or checking e-mail. These appliances commonly incorporate the roles of more than one traditional appliance, such as the telephone or television, in addition to their computing capabilities. This trend is called *convergence.*

It is also becoming more common to have a *smart home* in which household tasks (such as watering the lawn, turning on and off the air conditioning, and making coffee) can be controlled by a main home computer. *Smart appliances*—traditional appliances with some type of computer technology or connectivity built in—are expected to be even more prominent in the future. Figure 1-1 provides several examples of computer use in the home.

> **FIGURE 1-1**

Computer use in the home.

HOME OFFICE
An increasing number of individuals find the need to have a home office to work from home on a part-time or full-time basis.

COMMUNICATIONS
Most households today have access to the Internet and e-mail, either through a regular PC or through an Internet appliance, as shown here.

ENTERTAINMENT
Gaming, interactive TV, music downloads, and other entertainment activities performed using a computer or set-top box are becoming increasingly popular.

REFERENCE
The vast amount of reference software and reference Web sites have made the PC a very useful reference tool.

Computers in the Workplace

Though computers have been used in the workplace for years, their role is continually evolving. Originally just a research tool for computer experts and then a productivity tool for office workers, the computer today is used by all types of employees in all types of businesses. From the CEO of a multinational corporation, to the check-out clerk at the grocery store, to the package delivery person, the computer is a universal tool for decision making, productivity, and communications (see Figure 1-2).

Some of the most common uses of computers in the workplace—such as productivity software, source data automation, point-of-sales systems, electronic data exchange, and e-commerce—are discussed in later chapters of this book.

FIGURE 1-2

Computer use in the workplace.

MULTIPURPOSE WORKSTATION
Most business professionals today require their own desktop computer in the office or at home to prepare budgets and reports, exchange electronic mail, organize their work, and share information with other computer users.

PRESENTATION TOOL
Increasingly, computers are being used to make presentations in front of an audience. The content of the presentation might be stored on a portable computer or on the Internet or other computer network.

COMMUNICATIONS
Handheld PCs and other types of mobile devices are commonly used by employees who work out of the office to keep in touch with others and to access data located on the company network.

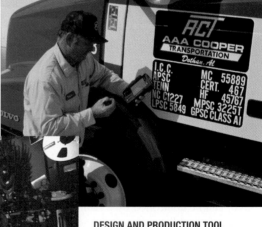

DESIGN AND PRODUCTION TOOL
The computer has become a vital creative tool in fields such as advertising, art, architecture, engineering, and movie/multimedia production. Affordable computers can quickly produce stunning photorealistic renderings and animation sequences, such as the creation of the *Toy Story* movies, as shown here.

trend

Ready-to-Wear PCs

We all know that like practically all other electronic devices, computing devices are shrinking. We can fit the computing power of a computer that used to fill an entire room into one that fits in the palm of a hand today. And that's just the beginning.

As PC components get smaller, the possibility of creating PCs that can be worn on the body or embedded in clothing becomes more plausible. Already we have watches that can perform some of the functions found on handheld PCs; some also can check e-mail, give GPS navigational readings, take digital pictures, or play MP3 files.

Going a step further is the truly wearable PC, such as the ones made by Xybernaut (see photo). These computers come in different forms, but typically the CPU and hard drive are contained in a small unit worn on a belt. The screens are attached to the belt or fitted into glasses or goggles. Because the display is so close to the eye, the screen gives the impression of a 15-inch monitor even though it's tiny. Instructions can be entered into the PC by using icons on the screen or through voice recognition. At present, the widest applications are for warehouse workers, map-makers, police and fire personnel, delivery people, and other applications where hands-free computing increases productivity.

The biggest disadvantage to wearable PCs today is the batteries needed to run them. The choice at the moment is between limited battery life with a lighter unit, or a bulkier, heavier, longer-life battery pack. For example, half of the Xybernaut's two-pound weight is the battery that lasts four to six hours.

The potential uses for wearable computers are virtually unlimited. Already, there is talk about integrating PCs into vests and other clothing. In fact, Philips and Levi's have paired up to create the ICD+ jacket that contains an MP3 player, a cell phone, a microphone, and earphones built in. As PC components continue to shrink and technology improves, we all may end up with a ready-to-wear PC.

Computers in Our Society

In addition to being found in the home and the workplace, many people encounter and use computers in day-to-day life, such as when shopping, running errands, dining in a restaurant, getting a car repaired, and so forth. As they become more and more integrated in our society, computers are also becoming more invisible and easy to use. Kiosks featuring screens that you touch with your finger are commonly found in hotels, conference centers, retail stores, and other public locations to allow you to easily look up information. Computers and devices for accessing the Internet are found in virtually all schools and public libraries, as well as in many airports, health clubs, hotel rooms, taxis, and restaurants. Many service professionals, such as waiters, auto technicians, and delivery people, use computers to keep track of customers.

It is also becoming increasingly common for individuals to carry Web-enabled cell phones, pagers, handheld computers, or similar portable devices to remain in touch with others and obtain stock quotes, driving directions, airline flight updates, and other needed information while on the go. Some computers are even small enough to be embedded in clothing or worn as a watch or other accessory, as discussed in this chapter's Trend box.

web tutor

For a tutorial on the various components in a computer system, go to www.course.com/parker2002/ch1

WHAT IS A COMPUTER AND WHAT DOES IT DO?

A **computer** is a programmable, electronic device that accepts **input,** performs operations or **processing** on the data, and **outputs** and **stores** the results. Because it is *programmable,* the instructions—called the *program*—tell the computer what to do. The relationships between these four main computer operations (input, processing, output, and storage) are shown in Figure 1-3.

To illustrate these operations, look at a comparable device you probably have in your home—a stereo system. A simple stereo system might consist of a compact disc (CD) player, a receiver, and a pair of speakers. To use the system, a CD is inserted into the CD player and the power to the system is turned on. The CD player then converts the patterns stored on the CD into electronic signals and transmits them to the receiver. The receiver receives the signals, strengthens them, and transmits them to the speakers, which play the corresponding music. In computer terms, the CD player reads *data* (music) from the *storage media* (the CD) and sends the appropriate *input* to the receiver. The receiver *processes* the data and sends it to the speakers, which produce musical *output.* Though these operations resemble the operations a computer system performs, there is one important difference: The stereo system is not

◆ FIGURE 1-3

Input, processing, output, and storage.

These tasks require an interactive dialog between the user and computer.

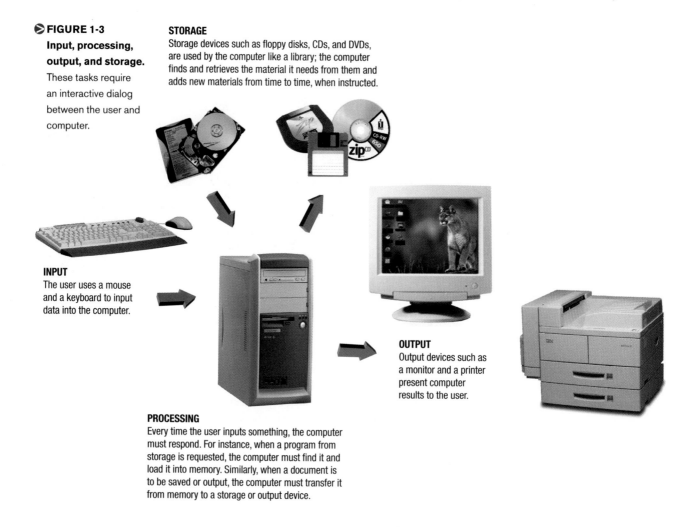

STORAGE
Storage devices such as floppy disks, CDs, and DVDs, are used by the computer like a library; the computer finds and retrieves the material it needs from them and adds new materials from time to time, when instructed.

INPUT
The user uses a mouse and a keyboard to input data into the computer.

OUTPUT
Output devices such as a monitor and a printer present computer results to the user.

PROCESSING
Every time the user inputs something, the computer must respond. For instance, when a program from storage is requested, the computer must find it and load it into memory. Similarly, when a document is to be saved or output, the computer must transfer it from memory to a storage or output device.

>**Computer.** A programmable, electronic device that accepts data input, performs operations on that data, and presents and stores the results. >**Input.** What is supplied to a computer to process. >**Processing.** The conversion of input to output. >**Output.** The results of computer processing. >**Storage.** Saving data, results, or programs for future use.

a versatile, *programmable* system, like a computer system is. A computer can perform an enormous variety of processing tasks, as well as support a much greater variety of *peripheral equipment* (input, output, and storage devices), than can a stereo system.

Traditional and Multimedia Hardware

A *computer system* consists of a computer and its peripheral equipment. It includes the instructions and facts that the computer processes, as well as the operating manuals, procedures, and people who use the computer. In other words, all the components that contribute to the computer functioning as a useful tool can be said to be part of a computer system. The physical machinery in a computer system (see Figure 1-4) is collectively referred to as **hardware;** the various hardware devices in a computer system are discussed next. The instructions or programs used in a computer system—called *software*—are discussed in a later section.

Virtually all computer systems sold today are *multimedia computer systems* that contain traditional hardware for working with text and graphics, plus additional hardware for use with other types of media, such as sound and video. Multimedia hardware includes speakers, microphones, and video cameras. Chapter 10 of this text includes a more complete discussion of multimedia.

Input Devices

An *input device* is any piece of equipment that supplies material (input) to the computer. The most common input devices are the keyboard and mouse (see Figure 1-4). Other possibilities include image and bar-code scanners, joysticks, touch screens, digital cameras, electronic pens, fingerprint readers, and microphones. Input devices for a stereo system might be a CD player and antenna. Input devices are discussed in more detail in Chapter 5.

Processing Devices

At the heart of any computer system is the **central processing unit (CPU),** located inside the computer's main box or *system unit.* The CPU in a computer system is the equivalent of a stereo system's receiver. Like its counterpart, the CPU can't do anything useful without peripheral equipment for input, output, and storage functions, as well as storage media to hold the data it needs to process. A computer system, of course, is not a stereo system. A CPU can be *programmed,* or given new instructions. Consequently, a computer system can perform an amazing variety of tasks, such as mathematical calculations, writing letters, accessing the Internet, composing music, and creating animation sequences. Programming, processing, and the CPU are all discussed in more detail in later chapters of this text.

Output Devices

An *output device* accepts processed materials from the computer, similar to the way the speakers in a stereo system output sound processed by the stereo receiver. Most computer systems also have a monitor and a printer as output devices, as shown in Figure 1-4. Output devices are covered in more detail in Chapter 5.

Storage Devices

Storage devices include the disks and other storage media used to store data, as well as the drives and other devices used to access those media. The storage devices featured in Figure 1-4 are a hard disk drive, a floppy disk drive, a Zip drive, removable disks, a CD or

---

>**Hardware.** Physical equipment in a computer system, such as the computer and its peripheral devices. >**Central processing unit (CPU).** The chip located inside the system unit of a computer that performs the processing for a computer and communicates with its peripheral devices.

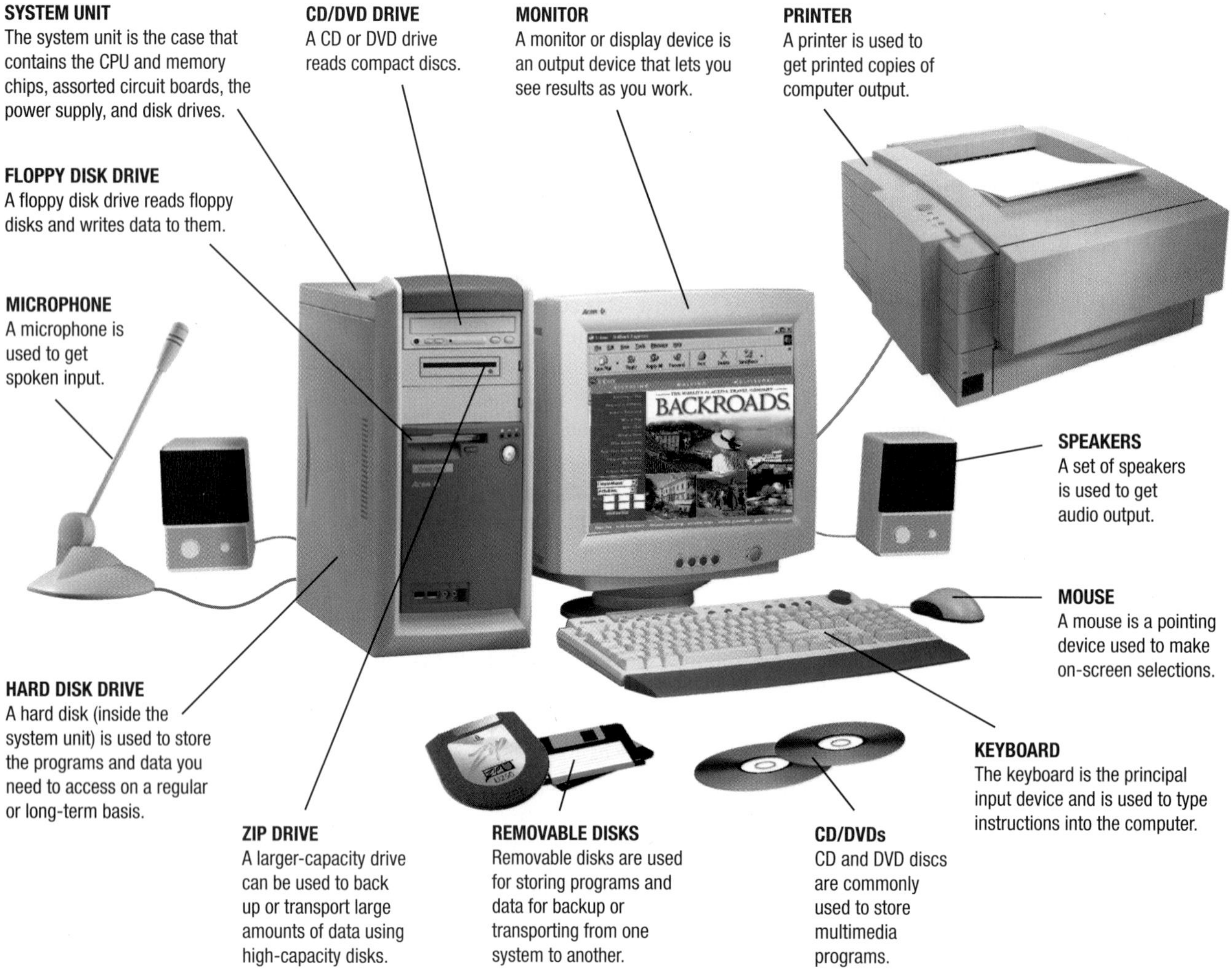
SYSTEM UNIT
The system unit is the case that contains the CPU and memory chips, assorted circuit boards, the power supply, and disk drives.
CD/DVD DRIVE
A CD or DVD drive reads compact discs.
MONITOR
A monitor or display device is an output device that lets you see results as you work.
PRINTER
A printer is used to get printed copies of computer output.
FLOPPY DISK DRIVE
A floppy disk drive reads floppy disks and writes data to them.
MICROPHONE
A microphone is used to get spoken input.
BACKROADS
SPEAKERS
A set of speakers is used to get audio output.
MOUSE
A mouse is a pointing device used to make on-screen selections.
HARD DISK DRIVE
A hard disk (inside the system unit) is used to store the programs and data you need to access on a regular or long-term basis.
KEYBOARD
The keyboard is the principal input device and is used to type instructions into the computer.
ZIP DRIVE
A larger-capacity drive can be used to back up or transport large amounts of data using high-capacity disks.
REMOVABLE DISKS
Removable disks are used for storing programs and data for backup or transporting from one system to another.
CD/DVDs
CD and DVD discs are commonly used to store multimedia programs.

FIGURE 1-4
The hardware of a computer system.

DVD drive, and CD or DVD discs. This type of storage—which stores the data and programs that people need from session to session—is sometimes more specifically referred to as *secondary storage.* Storage devices can either be installed inside the computer or attached to the computer as an external device.

A second type of storage is **memory** (sometimes called *primary storage*). This type of storage is *volatile,* which means that the data is only there while the power to the computer is turned on and while it is needed for processing. Memory is located within the system unit that houses the CPU and other components. Since turning off the power to the computer erases any data left in memory, storage devices are used instead of memory to save any work that may be needed at a later time. Memory is discussed in more detail in Chapter 3; storage is covered in Chapter 4.

Software

As already mentioned, the term **software** refers to the programs or instructions used to tell the computer hardware what to do. Software is generally purchased in some sort of a physical package (see Figure 1-5). Such a *software package* may consist of the program, as

>Memory. A temporary holding place for the computer to store data and program instructions awaiting processing, intermediate results, and processed output. **>Software.** Computer programs.

well as instructional and help materials, on CD or DVD discs, printed operating instructions and user manuals, and a printed license to use the software—all or some of which are inside a shrink-wrapped box or plastic case. The programs on the disks have been written in a programming language, though you virtually never need to learn a programming language to use the software. You can buy software in a store, through mail order, or over the Internet. If you download the software from the Internet, you won't receive a physical package. Instead, the components (program, license, user's manual, and so forth) are downloaded directly to your computer in an electronic format.

The most widely used software programs are revised every year or so to keep up with changes in technology, such as higher-capacity disk drives and faster computer chips, as well as users' demands for more exciting and multimedia-oriented programs and games. Each revision is commonly assigned a number—for instance, Windows 98, Office 2000, and WordPerfect 9. Occasionally, a version is identified by a name instead of a number, such as Windows Me or Office XP.

Computers use two basic types of software: Application software and systems software. The differences between these types of software are discussed next.

further exploration

For links to further information about software and software vendors, go to www.course.com/parker2002/ch1

Application Software

Application software is designed to perform specific tasks or *applications,* such as computing bank-account interest, preparing bills, creating letters, building and analyzing budgets, managing files and databases, playing games, scheduling airline flights, and diagnosing hospital patients' illnesses. Most people have specific types of application software in mind when they acquire a computer system. Some examples of application software are illustrated in Figure 1-6; application software is discussed in greater detail in Chapter 7.

Systems Software

The programs that allow a computer to operate, as well as run application software, are called **systems software.** One of the most important pieces of systems software is the *operating system,* a set of programs that supervise the computer system's work. Without the operating system, none of the application programs on your computer system can run; in fact, the computer would not function. Chapter 6 of this text is dedicated to systems software.

Data, Information, and Programs

To produce results, a computer uses *data* and *programs.* The program inputs data and processes it; the result—the output—is referred to as *information.*

Data

Data is essentially raw, unorganized facts. Almost any kind of fact or set of facts can become computer data—the words in a letter to a friend, the text and pictures for a book,

☞FIGURE 1-5

Software package. A typical software package consists of one or more program disks, a printed user's guide, and a printed user's license inside a shrink-wrapped box.

>Application software. Software programs that enable users to perform specific tasks or applications on a computer. **>Systems software.** Programs, such as the operating system, that control the operation of a computer and its devices, as well as enable application programs to run on the computer system. **>Data.** Raw, unorganized facts.

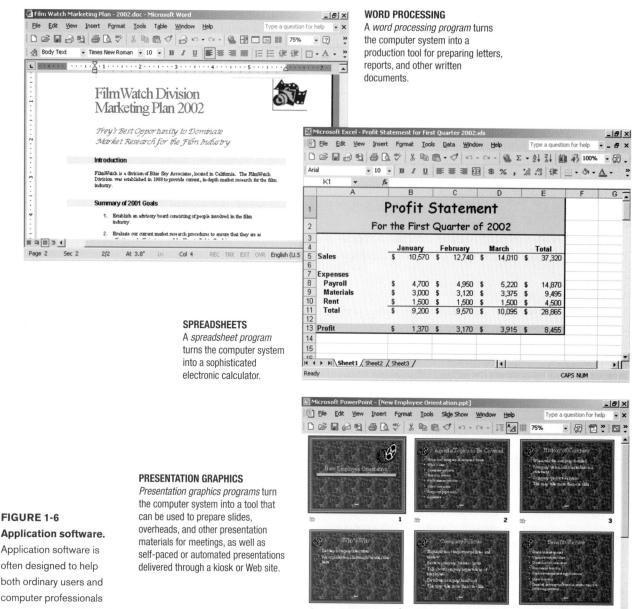

WORD PROCESSING

A *word processing program* turns the computer system into a production tool for preparing letters, reports, and other written documents.

SPREADSHEETS

A *spreadsheet program* turns the computer system into a sophisticated electronic calculator.

PRESENTATION GRAPHICS

Presentation graphics programs turn the computer system into a tool that can be used to prepare slides, overheads, and other presentation materials for meetings, as well as self-paced or automated presentations delivered through a kiosk or Web site.

▶ **FIGURE 1-6**

Application software.
Application software is often designed to help both ordinary users and computer professionals work more productively at their tasks, as well as for education and entertainment.

a budget, a photograph, or the facts stored in a set of employee records. Data can exist in many forms. Computer systems commonly handle four types of data: text, graphics, audio, and video.

▼ *Text* data consist of standard alphabetic, numeric, and special characters—that is, the type of data one normally sees in a simple word-processed letter, a budget, or a printed report.

▼ *Graphics* data consist of still pictures, such as drawings, graphs, and photographs. Graphics data require more processing power and storage capacity than text, because graphics are more complicated and usually use multiple colors.

DATABASE MANAGEMENT

A *database management system* turns the computer system into an electronic research assistant, capable of searching through mounds of data to prepare reports and answer questions, as well as maintain inventory and other important records.

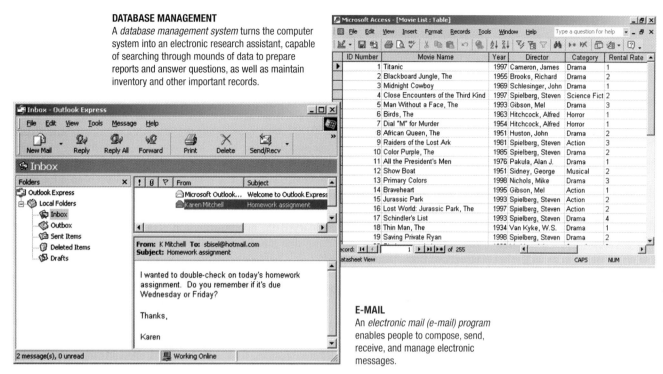

E-MAIL

An *electronic mail (e-mail) program* enables people to compose, send, receive, and manage electronic messages.

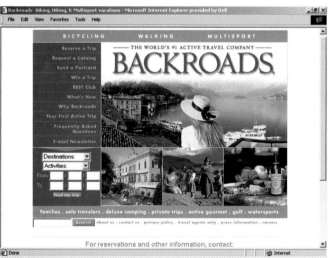

WEB BROWSER

Web browsers enable people to view information located on any of the millions of sites on the Internet's World Wide Web.

▼ *Audio* data include any type of sound, such as music and voice. Modern computers can store sounds in *machine-readable form,* just as they store any other type of data. Like graphics data, audio data require a much larger amount of storage space than textual data.

▼ *Video* data consist of motion pictures, such as a movie clip, a feature-length film, or live video from a videoconference. Two common types of video are computer animation and full-motion video. Computer animation consists of a series of images displayed one right after another to produce the illusion of motion, like you see in an animated TV cartoon, show, or movie, such as *The Simpsons* or *Toy Story.* Full-motion video is usually a series of photographic frames that capture real movement as it occurs, such as in most motion pictures. As you might imagine, video data require the most amount of processing power and storage capability.

Information

When users input data into a computer system, they usually don't want to receive the same data back without changes. Instead, they want the system to process the data into new, useful information. **Information,** in the language of computers, refers to data that has been processed into a meaningful form.

Information from a computer is frequently for the purpose of answering some type of question. A computer user might want to know, for example, how many of a firm's employees earn more than $100,000, how many seats are available on a particular flight from Los Angeles to San Francisco, or what Mark McGwire's home-run total was during a particular baseball season. The difference between data and information lies in the word *meaningful*. Mark McGwire's home-run total may be meaningful to a baseball fan, because it could enhance the experience of watching baseball games. Someone who doesn't follow this sport, however, may regard Mark McGwire's home-run total as completely meaningless—just ordinary data, not information. Thus, information is a relative term; it identifies something that has significance to a specific person in a specific situation. Like beauty, the difference between data and information is strictly in the eye of the beholder.

Of course, you don't need a computer system to process a set of facts and produce information. Anyone can go through an employee file and make a list of people earning a certain salary. By hand, however, this work would take a lot of time, especially for a company with thousands of employees. Their high speeds allow computers to perform such tasks almost instantly with accurate results. Conversion of data into information is called by a variety of terms, one of which is *information processing*.

Information processing has become an especially important activity in recent years because the success of many businesses depends heavily on the wise use of information. Because better information often improves employee decisions and customer service, many companies today regard information as among their most important assets and consider the creative use of information to be a key competitive strategy.

Programs

As already discussed, a **program** is a set of instructions that tells the computer how to process data into information. Computers cannot yet run programs written in ordinary English. Instead, specialists (called *programmers,* as discussed in the next section) create programs in a *programming language*—a set of codes or commands that the computer system can read and use. As discussed in the Inside the Industry box, computers follow the commands specified in a computer program exactly, even if those instructions contain errors or were not precisely what the programmer intended.

Programming languages come in many varieties—BASIC, Visual Basic, Pascal, COBOL, C++, and Java are a few you may have heard about. Some languages are traditional programming languages for developing applications; others are designed for use with Web pages or multimedia programming. Millions of people now use computers without ever writing programs, leaving that task largely to professional programmers. Programming languages are discussed in detail in Chapter 13.

Users and Computer Professionals

In the early days of computing, a clear distinction separated the people who made computers work from those who used them. This distinction remains, but as computers become more available and easier to use, the distinction is blurring.

>**Information.** Data that have been processed into a meaningful form. >**Program.** A set of instructions that command a computer system to perform specific actions.

inside the industry

Programs That Run Amok

More Embarrassing Evidence That Computers Do Only What They're Told

Computers sometimes do the craziest things. A litany of stories has been reported in the press throughout the years to remind us of this.

Heard the one about the company computer that sent reminders out to every customer—even if the total owed came to $0.00? This mishap resulted because a programmer failed to consider all of the possibilities and code them into the applicable program. Or how about the one where a borrower was paying on installment and tricked the computer by prematurely sending in the final coupon with the final monthly payment? The computer erroneously concluded that when a last coupon was successfully paid it should close the corresponding account. The programmer had failed to instruct it to first check for any unpaid balance.

In the early days of computing, it was the programmers who seemed to make all of the mistakes telling the computer what to do. Today, users are getting in on the act and catching up fast.

One interesting story surfaces from the Pacific Northwest. An office worker instructed his e-mail software—the program enabling him to correspond with colleagues via electronic mail—to generate an automatic "out of office" reply to every message he received while he was out traveling on business. Or so he thought. Instead, he had inadvertently instructed his e-mail program to send messages to all 2,000 people in his departmental address book for each message he received. And not only that; he also requested a return receipt (a return e-mail notifying that the message was received) for each message.

Within a few hours, the network was clogged with more than 150,000 messages. Trained computer personnel had to step in and temporarily pull the plug on the offender's system. But perhaps not before they had something to say to him in their own e-mail message.

Help! My computer has gone insane. Computers precisely follow instructions laid out in programs, whether those instructions were intended or not.

Users, or *end users,* are the people who use a computer system to obtain information. They include the accountant who needs a report on a client's taxes, the secretary who uses a word-processing program to create a letter, and the shop-floor supervisor who needs to know whether workers have met the day's quotas. Children playing computer games and people bidding at an online auction over the Internet are also considered end users.

Programmers, on the other hand, are people whose primary job responsibility is to write the programs that computers use. Although a few users may do small amounts of programming to customize the software on their desktop computers, the distinction between an ordinary user and a professional programmer is based on the work that the person has been hired to do.

>**User.** A person who uses a computer system. >**Programmer.** A person whose job it is to write, maintain, and test computer programs.

further exploration

For links to further information about computer certification programs, go to www.course.com/parker2002/ch1

In addition to programmers, organizations may employ other computer professionals. For instance, *systems analysts* design computer systems within their companies. *Computer operations personnel,* in contrast, are responsible for the day-to-day operations of large computer systems. Computer personnel are also often employed to help train users or assist them with their desktop computer systems, and to troubleshoot user-related problems.

COMPUTER NETWORKS AND THE INTERNET

A **computer network** ties computers together so that users can share hardware, software, and data, as well as electronically communicate with each other (see Figure 1-7). As illustrated in this figure, many networks use a *network server* to manage the data flowing through the network devices. Chapter 8 illustrates networks in much greater detail.

Computer networks exist in many sizes and types. For instance, a home network might connect two computers inside the home to share a single printer and Internet connection. A small office network of five or six desktop computers might enable workers to share an expensive printer and a common bank of files on a very-high-capacity disk drive, both of which are also connected to the network. A large corporate network, which can connect all of the offices or retail stores of a corporation, is an example of a much larger network, as is the Internet, which ties together thousands of networks and millions of users throughout the world.

The Internet

The **Internet** is the largest and most well known computer network in the world. It is technically a network of networks, since an individual user connects to a network set up by their *access provider* or *Internet service provider (ISP),* which in turn is connected to a larger network, which may be connected to an even larger network. All together, this network of networks is referred to as the Internet. Since all the networks on the Internet are interconnected, any computer with Internet access can communicate with any other computer on the Internet, regardless of the ISP used.

Millions of computers of all sizes, millions of people from all walks of life, and thousands of organizations worldwide are connected to the Internet. The two most common Internet activities today are exchanging *e-mail*—electronic messages—and accessing the *World Wide Web (WWW).* The World Wide Web consists of a huge collection of *Web pages* that are available over the Internet. There are Web pages for virtually any topic. You can access product information, current news and weather, airline schedules, government publications, music downloads, and so forth, as well as shop, bank, buy and sell stock, and other types of online financial transactions.

The basics of using the Internet and World Wide Web are covered in the next chapter; a more detailed discussed of the Internet is reserved for Chapter 9.

Accessing Networks

To access a computer network, you need a *modem* (which sends and receives data over telephone or cable lines) or some other type of *network adapter* to physically connect your computer to the network. You will also need a software program that lets you connect to and use the facilities of the network. As already discussed, an Internet service provider (ISP) is needed to gain access to the Internet.

To *log on* to a network, an identification number or name (often called a *user ID* or *login ID*) and a password are usually required. Once your PC has been set up with the proper ID

>**Computer network.** A collection of computers and devices that are connected together to share hardware, software, and data, as well as to electronically communicate with one another. >**Internet.** The largest and most widely used computer network in the world, linking millions of computers all over the world.

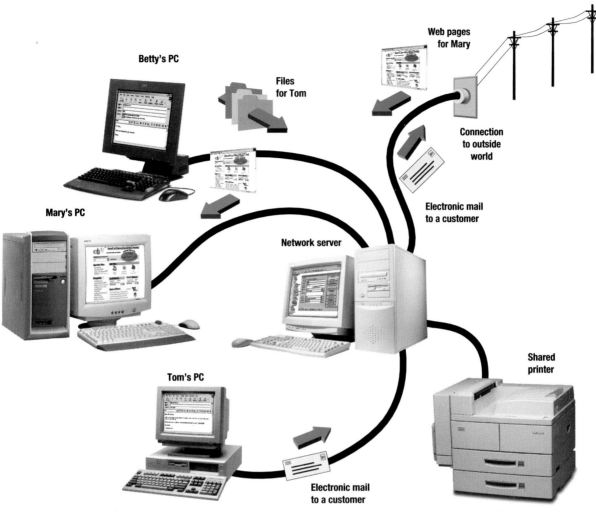

Betty's PC

Files
for Tom

Web pages
for Mary

Connection
to outside
world

Electronic mail
to a customer

Mary's PC

Network server

Shared
printer

Tom's PC

Electronic mail
to a customer

▶ FIGURE 1-7

Computer networks.

Computer networks meet
users' needs to share hardware, software, and data—
as well as to communicate
with each other—both within
a company and with the
outside world.

and password, connecting to the network is very simple. For a home or office network, you will usually be asked for your user ID and password each time you turn the computer on. After providing the correct information, you will have access to the appropriate network resources and you can select whatever type of application you want to run, just as you would with a *stand-alone* (nonnetworked computer). Accessing networks is discussed in more detail in Chapter 8 of this text.

To access the Internet, you need to open the appropriate program or programs (usually a *Web browser* or special program supplied by your provider). With some types of Internet connections, your computer also needs to dial an appropriate telephone number in order to complete the Internet connection.

Network Servers

As illustrated in Figure 1-7, it is common for networks to use a network server. *Network servers* are computers—often powerful PCs, or, in large networks, *midrange* or *mainframe* computers (discussed shortly)—that manage the resources on a network. For example, they might control access to shared printers and other hardware, as well as to shared programs and data. A server connected to the Internet to store Web pages is called a *Web server.*

Computer users often hear the terms *online* and *offline* in reference to computer networks and servers. Any computer (or other device) in a condition that allows it to send data to or receive data from a computer network is said to be online to the network. If a device isn't online, it's offline.

Some companies may keep their stores or regional offices online to the central computer system at all times during business hours to receive real-time data about sales and other important business transactions. Other companies may leave stores and regional offices offline to their headquarters' computers most of the time, connecting to them only as needed to transmit and receive data.

Online and *offline* are also used to describe the readiness of peripheral devices. For instance, when your printer is ready to receive signals from your computer system, it is online; otherwise, it is offline. Another common application of the word *online* refers to tasks performed over the Internet, such as *online banking, online stock trading,* and just being "online to the Internet."

COMPUTER SYSTEMS TO FIT EVERY NEED

web tutor

For a tutorial on the various computer configurations, go to www.course.com/parker2002/ch1

The computer market offers a great variety of systems to serve computer users' needs. This section considers two important ways computers differ from one another: size and capability.

Computer systems are generally classified in one of four categories: small, or *microcomputers;* medium-size, or *midrange computers;* large, or *mainframe computers;* and super powerful *supercomputers.* An emerging category on the small end of this continuum is the *mobile device* category. In practice, classifying a computer into one of these five categories by size alone is not always completely accurate. Large midrange computers, for example, often are bigger than small mainframes. In addition, the types of computers that fit into each category are continually changing as technology changes, so these categories cannot be defined precisely and are instead used as general guidelines.

As a rule of thumb, larger computers have greater processing power. For example, big computers can usually process data faster than small computers. Big computers can also accommodate larger and more powerful peripheral devices. Naturally, more powerful computers and peripheral equipment have higher prices. A computer system can cost anywhere from a few hundred dollars to several million dollars.

Mobile Devices

A **mobile device** is loosely defined as a very small device usually based on a wireless phone, pager, or similar communications device (see Figure 1-8). If the device is based on a wireless phone, it is sometimes referred to as a *smart phone; smart pagers* are pagers with other capabilities built in.

▶ **FIGURE 1-8**

Mobile devices. Smart phones, pagers, and other mobile devices have assumed some of the tasks traditionally performed on a PC, such as viewing Web pages and exchanging e-mail. Many smart phones and pagers can only display text, not images.

>**Mobile device.** A very small device, usually based on a wireless phone or pager, that can perform a limited amount of computing.

Voice-Activated Internet

Well, it was bound to happen. When it comes to accessing the Web using a phone or portable PC, fingers are about to become obsolete.

Speech recognition can now be used to replace the touch or pen interface used with portable PCs, as well as the annoying "Press 1 for..." touch-tone interface used with many automated services. For Web access, this enables users to request information or retrieve their e-mail hands-free—an especially appealing feature for drivers. Hands-free Web access can be performed using a portable PC or mobile device with speech recognition abilities built in, a voice-operated car navigation and communications system, or a *voice portal*.

Fairly new on the scene, voice portals are typically Web-by-phone services that allow you to request information and exchange e-mail and instant messages using a regular phone, cell phone, or wireless mobile device. These services use speech recognition to interpret requests for information (stock quotes, driving directions, restaurant reviews, flight information, e-mail, etc.) and text-to-speech technology to read e-mail and other written information back to the individual over the phone. Some of these services, such as TellMe and ShoutMail, were free at the time of this writing, supported by short ads. Though still very limited, this type of Web access has vast potential, since it can be accessed without a PC or special device—only a telephone is required.

Voice-activated Internet isn't limited to mobile users, however. Using standard speech-recognition software, such as Dragon's NaturallySpeaking, conventional PC users can also get into the action, surfing the Web and dictating e-mail using only their voice. Though the keyboard won't be retired anytime soon, it may someday go the way of the dinosaur.

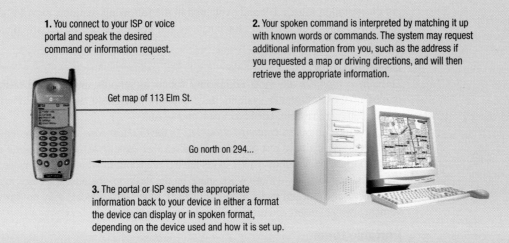

1. You connect to your ISP or voice portal and speak the desired command or information request.

2. Your spoken command is interpreted by matching it up with known words or commands. The system may request additional information from you, such as the address if you requested a map or driving directions, and will then retrieve the appropriate information.

Get map of 113 Elm St.

Go north on 294...

3. The portal or ISP sends the appropriate information back to your device in either a format the device can display or in spoken format, depending on the device used and how it is set up.

Mobile devices generally perform a limited amount of computing. They are usually designed to allow wireless access to the Web and e-mail, in addition to their regular telephone or paging capabilities. Currently a mobile device's small screen usually displays 11 lines or less of text-only data. This limitation makes mobile devices most appropriate for individuals desiring occasional updates on stock prices, weather, directions, and other text-based data, rather than general Web browsing. Because they often don't contain a keyboard—at best, a very small one—mobile devices are also better for receiving e-mail than responding to e-mail.

Some mobile devices allow voice-activated dialing, and voice-based Web navigation and e-mail composition are beginning to become available (see the How It Works box). As voice-input systems and wireless Internet both continue to improve in the future, mobile device use is expected to increase tremendously, especially in countries that already have a huge installed wireless phone base.

further exploration

For links to further information about PCs and PC vendors, go to www.course.com/parker2002/ch1

Personal Computers

A technological breakthrough in the early 1970s allowed the circuitry for an entire CPU to fit on a single silicon chip smaller than a dime. These computers-on-a-chip, or *microprocessors,* could be mass-produced at a very low cost. Microprocessors were quickly integrated into all types of products, leading to powerful handheld calculators, digital watches, electronic toys, and sophisticated controls for household appliances such as microwave ovens and automatic coffeemakers.

Microprocessors also created the possibility of building inexpensive computer systems small enough to fit on a desktop, inside a briefcase, or even inside a shirt pocket (see Figure 1-9). These small computer systems, designed to be used by one person at a time, are called **microcomputers** or **personal computers (PCs).**

PCs are widely used in small and large businesses. A small business might use its PCs for all of its computing tasks, including tracking merchandise, preparing correspondence, billing customers, and completing routine accounting chores. A large business might use microcomputers as productivity tools for office personnel and as analysis tools for decision makers, to name just two important applications. PCs are also commonly connected to a company network to provide access to company files, as well as the network's Internet connection. Portable computers are absolutely essential for many workers, such as salespeople who need to make presentations or take orders from clients off-site, agents who need to collect data at remote locations, and managers who need computing and communication resources as they travel.

Sizes of PC Systems

As illustrated in Figure 1-9 and explained in the following sections, most PC systems currently available to individuals for business and home use can be classified as *desktop* or *portable* units.

Desktop Units

Desktop computers are most commonly found in schools, homes, and businesses. The names of these computer systems have become household words—HP Pavilion, Apple iMac, Compaq Presario, IBM NetVista, and so on.

Desktop computers come in two styles. In the *desktop-case style,* the system-unit case is designed specifically to rest on a desk. In the *tower-case style,* the system-unit case usually stands upright on the floor. Tower cases have more room in which to mount secondary storage units, and they leave more work space on the desktop. Because the cases may be farther from the user or tucked under a desk, however, tower-case models may not provide as convenient a way to insert and remove disks from drives.

Portable Units

Portable PCs come in a variety of sizes, including notebook, tablet, handheld, and pocket computers.

Notebook computers (sometimes called *laptop computers*) are designed for users who need access to a fully-functioning computer at remote sites. Today's units are light and small enough to fit into a briefcase or small carrying case. Although many notebooks provide just about the same power as their desktop cousins, they tend to cost more, and have smaller screens and denser keyboard arrangements. Despite these disadvantages, the portability of notebook PCs has made them extremely popular. A newer type of PC that is similar to a notebook but that usually doesn't fold shut is the tablet PC. *Tablet PCs* also commonly don't have a keyboard—they usually are touched with the finger or special pen instead.

Handheld computers (sometimes called *palmtop computers*) are about the size of a paperback book or pocket calculator. These computers usually look like a miniature

>**Microcomputer.** A computer system based on a microprocessor, designed to be used by one person at a time.
>**Personal computer (PC).** Another name for microcomputer.

FIGURE 1-9
A variety of PCs.

DESKTOP COMPUTERS
Desktop PCs can use (left to right) a tower-style case, a desktop-style case, or an integrated all-in-one unit consisting of a monitor and system unit.

PORTABLE COMPUTERS
Portable computers include (left to right) pocket, handheld, tablet, and notebook PCs.

notebook and are held in one hand while entering data with the other. The even smaller *pocket computers* usually don't have keyboards; instead—like tablet PCs—the screen is touched with the finger or special pen. Sometimes these devices are referred to as *personal digital assistants,* or *PDAs,* since they provide personal organizer functions such as a calendar, appointment book, and address book, as well as messaging, electronic mail, and other communications functions. For a look at how these types of PCs are used by medical students, see the Campus Close-Up box.

To share information between a portable computer and desktop computer, a variety of options are available. Some handheld or pocket PCs come with a cradle that attaches to a desktop computer. After inserting the handheld PC into the cradle, the two computers synchronize the data entered since the last synchronization. Other portable PCs come with infrared capabilities that allow you to "beam" data from the device to your PC. To use a notebook or tablet computer as a desktop computer, special *docking stations* are available. After plugging the notebook or tablet PC into the docking station, you can access the contents of that computer using the keyboard, mouse, and monitor attached to the docking station—a more comfortable working setup for many people.

Network Computers, Thin Clients, and Internet Appliances

Most PCs sold today are equipped with disk drives and other types of secondary storage. An exception to this standard is a relatively new class of PCs optimized for accessing networks. Instead of having their own local disk drives or other storage hardware on the unit itself, these PCs typically rely on the network for storage. Because they can often use the network

campus close-up

Wired Med Students

From Stanford University to the University of Florida, medical students are going high-tech. Though some medical schools strongly recommend that their first-year students acquire a handheld PC, others—such as Stanford Medical School—incorporate their use in classroom and learning activities.

Med students at Stanford use PDAs to access electronic "flashcards," class-specific study materials, and lecture schedules, as well as to contact classmates, instructors, and administrators. Students can also view electron micrographs (pictures of cells taken with an electron microscope), CT-scans and X-rays that have been converted to a high-resolution format readable by the PDA device. Phyllis Gardner, senior associate dean for education and student affairs at Stanford Medical School, believes that doctors will increasingly rely on the mobility of PDA-type devices. "Instead of the notebook that physicians traditionally carried around, future doctors will have PDAs to access patient histories, results of physicals, other electronic medical records, and laboratory information. We're training students for that."

Though a little slow to embrace handheld PCs, the medical community is quickly catching up. Scores of new applications, such as medical calculators, patient record systems, drug reference systems, and diagnostic software, are rapidly changing the practice of medicine. In addition to saving a physician time and alleviating errors due to misreading a doctor's handwriting, handheld PCs can also automatically check patient records for such things as previous symptoms, drug interactions, and insurance coverage when the physician enters in a diagnosis or prescription. When doing rounds in the hospital, for example, chart information can be entered into the portable PC and simultaneously transmitted wirelessly to the hospital's computer. At the end of the day, the same information can also be uploaded to the main computer at the physician's office to update records located there.

Other intriguing possibilities include exchanging information with patients via a secure Web site. For example, there are asthma and blood pressure monitors that can upload readings to a Web site for the patient's doctor or nurse to access. One step further is the physician-patient communications system, such as the Healinx system used by Blue Shield and Kaiser Permanente. This system allows patients to store their medical profile online and have online consultations with their physician, as well as request appointments and prescription renewals 24 hours a day.

Despite the late start, handheld use in the medical community is likely to explode in the near future. The portability factor, along with the trend of hospitals, pharmaceutical companies, and other organizations handing out free or low-cost devices to doctors, all point to massive increased growth in this area. Thanks to handheld PCs and prescription software, even one of the oldest standing doctor jokes—illegible handwriting—may become outdated.

server for some processing tasks, they also tend to have less memory and processing power than regular PCs. All these characteristics make these types of computers less expensive than regular PCs. **Network computer (NC)** is the original term for this type of computer; **thin client** is a term that is more common today.

As discussed in a later chapter about networking, an advantage to these types of PCs is that software is accessed from the network server, so changing or upgrading software involves

>**Network computer (NC).** A PC designed to access a network for processing and data storage, instead of performing those tasks locally.
>**Thin client.** Another name for network computer.

only updating the server, not the software on the individual PCs. Disadvantages include having no local storage and not being able to function as a stand-alone computer when the network isn't working. Despite the disadvantages, the low price of network computers/thin clients has made them a growing sector of the desktop PC market.

Network computers designed primarily for browsing the World Wide Web and exchanging e-mail are called **Internet appliances,** *information appliances,* or *Web pads* (see Figure 1-10). Their ease of use and low cost have made these devices a fast-growing area in home computing sales—especially for individuals who don't want or need a traditional home PC. Though they often have no other function than Internet access, usually require a monthly fee for Internet and e-mail access, and frequently have no local storage devices, their popularity is growing. Many of these devices are intended to be located in the kitchen or other convenient location and automatically log on to the Internet to check your e-mail on a regular basis and let you know when new e-mail arrives. Others are designed to be connected to your TV.

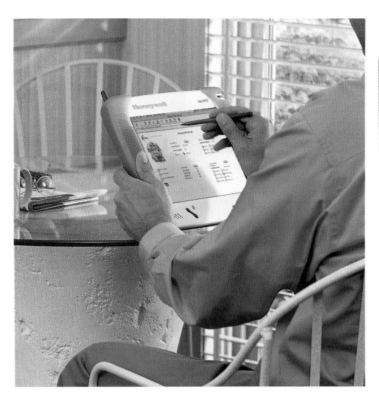

FIGURE 1-10
Network computers and Internet appliances. The Internet appliance shown here can be used to view Web pages and exchange e-mail.

PC Compatible or Macintosh?

Most users choose between two major computer *platforms*—PC compatible or Macintosh—when they buy a microcomputer. The movement toward the two major standards started over a decade ago, when the IBM PC and the original Apple Macintosh were the two front-running microcomputer systems.

Most vendors followed IBM's lead, building their systems around Intel microprocessor chips and (later) catering to Microsoft Windows applications. Such computer systems are known as **PC compatibles.** Though Apple sales have picked up in recent years, the vast majority of computers are PC-compatible devices. Among the largest vendors of these machines are Compaq, IBM, Dell, Hewlett-Packard, NEC, and Gateway. Today, PC-compatible computers are also commonly referred to as the *Windows platform, Wintel* machines, or *IBM-compatible PCs.*

Macintosh computers—frequently just called *Macs*—are made by Apple Corporation. Because of their reputation for advanced graphics capabilities, Macs are often the platform of choice for artists and designers. The modern look of Apple's iMac desktop computer and iBook notebook computers has also appealed to young computer buyers. Because there are virtually no Macintosh-compatible computers out there to bring the price down, expect to pay more than for a PC-compatible computer for comparable hardware.

Midrange Computers

Midrange computers—sometimes called *minicomputers* or *minis*—are medium-size computers (see Figure 1-11). Most of them fall between PCs and mainframes in processing power, although the very smallest midrange computers are virtually indistinguishable from the most powerful PCs, and the largest closely resemble small mainframes. Midrange computers usually cost far more than microcomputers, which is more than most individuals can afford.

◉ **FIGURE 1-11**

Midrange system. In a midrange system, several display workstations or PCs are connected to the same computer. A midrange computer is commonly used to run a small business, such as a healthcare facility or medical office.

Any of several factors might lead an organization to choose a midrange system over a PC or mainframe. Often, midrange buyers need computer systems that can interact with multiple users and run several large programs simultaneously. Many microcomputer systems lack sufficient power to handle such complex applications. Mainframes, discussed in the next section of this chapter, can handle these applications with ease, but they are much larger and generally much more expensive than midrange computers.

Midrange computers are commonly used as servers, with several PCs or other devices networked to access the midrange computer's resources. These types of computers are frequently referred to as *midrange servers.*

Mainframe Computers

The **mainframe computer** (see Figure 1-12) is a standard choice for almost any large organization. It often operates 24 hours a day, serving thousands of users interacting through PCs or other devices during regular business hours and processing large jobs late at night, such as payroll and billing. Some large organizations need several mainframes to complete their computing workloads. Typically these organizations own or lease a variety of computer types—mainframes, midrange computers, and PCs—which collectively meet all of their processing needs. Increasingly, these organizations are linking together various sizes of computers into networks.

Most mainframes are assigned to handle the high-volume processing of business transactions and routine paperwork. For a typical business, this workload includes tasks such as tracking customer purchases and payments, sending out bills and reminder notices, and paying employees. These operations were some of the earliest applications of computers in business and have been the responsibility of mainframes since the 1950s. IBM, Sun, and Unisys are three of the leading mainframe computer manufacturers. Today's mainframes are sometimes referred to as *high-end servers* or *enterprise servers.*

>**Mainframe computer.** A large computer that performs extensive business transaction processing.

FIGURE 1-12

Mainframe computer.
Today's mainframes are physically smaller than the original mainframes and are used by large businesses, schools, and hospitals to maintain records and other types of shared data. Display workstations and PCs may both be used to access mainframe resources.

Supercomputers

Some organizations, such as large scientific and research laboratories, have extraordinary information processing needs. Applications such as sending astronauts into space, testing safety and aerodynamic features on cars and aircraft, controlling missile guidance systems, and weather forecasting, for example, require extreme accuracy and immense speed to perform the needed extensive computations. To meet such needs, a few vendors offer very large, sophisticated machines called **supercomputers.** One recent trend is for large businesses to use supercomputers for hosting extremely complex Web sites and decision-support systems for executives. Applications expected to be more prominent in the future include using supercomputers to facilitate three-dimensional applications, such as 3D medical scans, 3D architectural modeling, and holograms.

Supercomputers can cost several million dollars each. During the past few years, innovators have tried to build less-expensive supercomputers by linking together hundreds of smaller computers or thousands of microprocessor chips. The resulting class of super-computers is often referred to as *massively parallel processors (MPPs)*. For example, one of the fastest supercomputers in the world, ASCI White (see Figure 1-13), contains a total of 8,192 CPUs and can perform 12 trillion calculations per second. Put another way, it would take an individual with a calculator 10 million years to do the calculations ASCI White can do in one second. The entire system costs $110 million, requires the floor space of two basketball courts, and is used primarily to simulate nuclear weapons tests.

COMPUTERS AND SOCIETY

The ability of computers to sort through massive amounts of data and quickly produce useful information for almost any kind of user—from teenager to payroll clerk to corporate president—makes them indispensable tools in our society. Without computers, businesses could

>**Supercomputer.** The fastest, most expensive, and most powerful type of computer.

FIGURE 1-13

Supercomputers. Super-computers are used for specialized situations that require immense processing tasks. While mainframe computers often execute many programs at one time, super-computers generally run one program at a time, as fast as possible.

never function at the level they do today. Banks would be overwhelmed by the job of tracking all the transactions they process. Familiar airline and telephone services would be impossible. Moon exploration and the space shuttle would still belong to science fiction, and scientific advances such as DNA analysis and gene mapping would be nonexistent.

The Information Age and the New Information Revolution

The prominence of information technology over the last few decades has resulted in this time period being referred to as the *information age.* Now, according to many experts, we are entering a new *information revolution.* Many believe that the last major information revolution was the invention of the printing press in the mid-1450s; today's information revolution is usually thought of as being tied to the vast amount of information accumulated and distributed via the Internet. As discussed next and throughout this text, the availability of this huge collection of information has a great deal of advantages, but it has some disadvantages, as well.

Benefits of a Computer-Oriented Society

The benefits of having such a computer-oriented society are numerous, as touched on throughout this chapter. The speed, accuracy, and reliability of computers have changed the way we do business—not just at a management level as initially projected, but on day-to-day operations. The capability to design, build, and test new buildings and other structures before the actual construction begins has led to safer buildings and a more efficient development cycle. The ability to have beginning medical students perform virtual surgery using a computer instead of performing actual surgery on a patient is obviously a better option. The ability to shop, pay bills, do product research, and look up the vast amount of information available through the Internet from home or wherever you happen to be at the time is a huge convenience that few would have even dreamed about even a decade ago. And the ability of businesses to be open for business 24 hours a day, 7 days a week, 365 days a year via the Internet and operate more efficiently, as well, is a distinct advantage.

Impact of Computers, the Internet, and a Networked Economy

Along with the benefits of a computer-oriented society, computers have brought a variety of problems ranging from health concerns to personal security and privacy issues to ethics. Many businesses are feeling pressured to quickly become prepared to do business via the Internet or risk being left behind. Many jobs have also evolved with the emergence

further exploration

For links to further information about technology publications, go to www.course.com/parker2002/ch1

of the computer, such as including tasks previously performed by a secretary or an assistant, simply because the worker can now have a computer on his or her desk, briefcase, or pocket.

As far as privacy is concerned, individuals need to be aware of the vast amount of information that can be accumulated about them and distributed to others. Such information can be obtained from their online and offline buying history, as well as available public information, such as home purchases. The accumulation and distribution of information are important factors of our new networked economy, but it is one area of great concern to many consumers.

These issues are serious and worthy of much more discussion. Since this chapter can only mention them briefly, subsequent parts of this book explore more of the social benefits and problems created by computers.

INT

SUMMARY

Chapter Objective 1:
Explain why it's essential to learn about computers today.

Computers appear almost everywhere in today's world. They're embedded in consumer products, they help managers run businesses, and they direct production in factories, to name just a few applications.

COMPUTERS IN YOUR LIFE

Chapter Objective 2:
Describe several uses for computers in business or personal life.

Computers abound in today's workplace largely because we are living in an era when most jobs heavily depend on the collection, use, creation, and dissemination of information. Computers are also becoming increasingly indispensable in the home and our personal lives for such tasks as working at home, shopping online, and exchanging e-mail.

WHAT IS A COMPUTER AND WHAT DOES IT DO?

Chapter Objective 3:
Identify some of the major components of a computer system and explain their relationships to one another.

Four words summarize the operation of a **computer** system: **input, processing, output,** and **storage.** The input and output functions are performed by peripheral equipment, called *input devices* and *output devices.* Just as your stereo receiver couldn't play CD music without a CD player or speakers, the computer would be helpless without peripheral devices. The processing function is performed by the **central processing unit,** or **CPU.**

Some types of peripheral equipment read from and write to storage media using *storage devices.* Storage media, such as disks, CDs, and DVDs, keep programs and data indefinitely. A temporary type of storage called **memory** holds the programs and data that the system is currently processing.

People who talk about computers commonly distinguish between hardware and software. **Hardware** refers to the actual physical equipment that makes up the computer system, such as the CPU, memory, and input, output, and storage devices. **Software** refers to computer programs. Software comes in two basic forms: **application software** and **systems software.**

Chapter Objective 4:
Define terms that commonly arise in reading about or discussing computers.

A computer's input takes two forms: data and programs. **Data** are the raw, unorganized facts on which the computer carries out its processing; **programs** are sets of instructions that explain to the computer what to do with certain data. A program must be written in a *programming language* that the computer can understand. Data that the computer has processed into a useful form are called **information.**

Users are the people who use the computer system. Within a computing environment, many types of computer professionals help users to meet their computing needs; for example, **programmers** are responsible for writing computer programs.

COMPUTER NETWORKS AND THE INTERNET

Chapter Objective 5:
Describe the purpose of a network and what the Internet is.

To allow users to share hardware, software, and data and communicate with one another, **computer networks** tie individual computers and related devices together. Many networks use a network server to host common files and programs and to manage the traffic on the network. To access most computer networks, you need some type of *modem* or *network adapter* and appropriate software. To access the **Internet,** the largest network in the world, you also need the services of an *access provider* or *ISP.*

COMPUTER SYSTEMS TO FIT EVERY NEED

Small computers are often called **microcomputers** or **personal computers (PCs).** Most microcomputer systems today are either desktop or portable computers, and they fall within either the **PC-compatible** or **Macintosh** platform. Even smaller PCs, usually based on a cell phone or pager, are referred to as **mobile devices** and are commonly used for accessing World Wide Web data and e-mail, in addition to their regular phone or pager functions. **Network computers** (also called **thin clients**) are special-purpose PCs designed to access a network, instead of doing independent processing, and usually use the network for storage, instead of storing data locally. A type of network computer called an **Internet appliance** is designed specifically for accessing the World Wide Web and e-mail.

Medium-size computers are called **midrange computers,** and large computers are called **mainframe computers.** The very largest computers, which run applications that demand the most speed and power, are called **supercomputers.**

While categories of computers based on size can provide helpful distinctions, in practice it is sometimes difficult to classify computers that fall on the borders of these categories, and the computers that fit in each category are continually changing as technology improves.

Chapter Objective 6:
List the five major categories of computers, giving at least one example of what the computers in each category might be used for.

COMPUTERS AND SOCIETY

Although computer systems have become indispensable tools for modern life, their growing use has created troubling problems, ranging from health concerns to personal security and privacy to ethics. The new networked economy has added benefits and problems stemming from our computer-oriented society. Because of the vast amounts of information now available through the Internet, this era is sometimes referred to as the *information age.*

Chapter Objective 7:
Discuss the social impact of computers and some issues that arise from their prominence in our society.

Instructions: Match each key term on the left with the definition on the right that fits best.

1. application software

2. central processing
   unit (CPU)

3. computer

4. computer network

5. hardware

6. input

7. Internet

8. Internet appliance

9. memory

10. microcomputer

11. mobile device

12. output

13. processing

14. program

15. software

16. storage

17. systems software

_____ A collection of computers and devices that are connected together to share hardware, software, and data, as well as to electronically communicate with one another.

_____ A computer system based on a microprocessor, designed to be used by one person at a time.

_____ A programmable, electronic device that accepts data input, performs operations on that data, and presents and stores the results.

_____ A set of commands that instruct a computer system to perform specific actions.

_____ A specialized network computer designed primarily for Internet access and e-mail exchange.

_____ A temporary holding place for the computer to store data and program instructions awaiting processing, intermediate results, and processed output.

_____ A very small device, usually based on a wireless phone or pager, that can perform a limited amount of computing.

_____ Computer programs.

_____ Physical equipment in a computer system, such as the computer and its peripheral devices.

_____ Programs, such as the operating system, that control the operation of a computer and its devices, as well as enable application programs to run on the computer system.

_____ Saving data, results, or programs for future use.

_____ Software programs that enable users to perform specific tasks or applications on a computer.

_____ The chip located inside the system unit of a computer that performs the processing for a computer and communicates with its peripheral devices.

_____ The conversion of input to output.

_____ The largest and most widely used computer network, linking millions of computers all over the world.

_____ The results of computer processing.

_____ What is supplied to a computer to process.

REVIEW ACTIVITIES

Answers for the self-quiz appear at the end of the book.

Self-Quiz

True/False

Instructions: Circle **T** if the statement is true or **F** if the statement is false.

T F **1.** Software includes all the physical equipment in a computer system.

T F **2.** Because memory is volatile, it is erased when the power to the computer is turned off.

T F **3.** A word processing program is an example of application software.

T F **4.** Computer programs are usually written in conversational English.

T F **5.** Hardware is a term that only applies to storage devices.

Completion

Instructions: Answer the following questions.

6. Devices such as a printer and monitor would be classified as _____ devices.

7. Devices such as a floppy-disk or DVD drive would be classified as a _____ device.

8. A desktop-style PC that does not usually have any local storage or processing power and is designed to access a network is called a(n) _____.

9. Data that have been processed into a meaningful form are called _____.

10. Another name for microcomputer is _____.

Exercises

1. For the following list of computer hardware devices, write the *principle* function of each device in the space provided. Choices include input device (I), output device (O), storage device (S), and processing device (P).

   a. CPU _____
   b. Mouse _____
   c. Monitor _____
   d. CD drive _____
   e. Keyboard _____

2. Match each term with the best description.

   a. Word processing program
   b. Operating system
   c. Spreadsheet program
   d. Web browser

   _____ Allows access to resources located on the Internet.
   _____ Supervises the running of all other programs on the computer.
   _____ Helps prepare written documents like letters and reports.
   _____ Turns the computer into a sophisticated electronic calculator and analysis tool.

3. Would text data or video data require more processing power and storage space?

4. List two reasons why a business may choose to network its employees' computers.

5. By writing the numbers 1 to 5 in the blanks at the left of each of the following types of computer systems, order them by size from the least powerful to the most powerful (1 represents the least powerful).

 —————— Notebook computer
 —————— Mainframe computer
 —————— Supercomputer
 —————— Mobile device
 —————— Network server

1. **Shopping for a Basic System** If you were to purchase a basic computer system this weekend, what would you purchase? Most individuals who have not yet completed an entry-level computer concepts course or who don't work with computers on a daily basis would have to rely on the knowledge of the salesperson to make the selection. For this project, visit a computer retailer in your area and ask the salesperson what computer system you should purchase. Do not purchase the system—the goal is to determine your level of comfort with the terminology and explanations presented by the salesperson. At the conclusion of your research, prepare a one-page summary of your findings and submit it to your instructor.

   Note: Keep a copy of this summary. You may want to review and reflect on its contents as you learn the concepts of computers throughout this course. If you need to purchase a PC prior to the end of the course, be sure to read Chapter 16 of this text first for some helpful guidelines and other PC-buying information.

2. **This Week's Special** It seems as though most large retail stores that carry computer products have one model or another on sale for a special price every week. Sometimes these products may be limited to stock on hand. What might explain this sales strategy? Can we compare computers to the clothing industry and attribute this behavior to seasonal changes or shifts in consumer fashion? For this project, research this issue and answer the two questions posed. At the conclusion of your research, prepare a one-page summary of your findings and submit it to your instructor.

3. **24 Hours** Computers have a tremendous impact on our daily lives. They can be used to generate information, or embedded in devices or appliances to make them work. For this project, take notice of all encounters you have with computing devices for the next 24 hours. You should note both positive and negative impacts of these devices, and what your daily routine might be like without them. At the conclusion of the 24 hours, prepare a one-page summary of your encounters and submit it to your instructor.

Hands On

4. **The Internet** The Internet and World Wide Web are both handy tools that can help you to research topics covered in this textbook and to complete many of the projects. Chapter 2 explains the functions of the Internet and the World Wide Web, but you may wish to learn how to use these tools now. To accomplish this, it's just a matter of finding an Internet-enabled computer on your campus, at home, or at your public library, and then logging on, typing in an address for a specific information site, and choosing among the onscreen selections. For this project, follow the directions provided by your instructor or lab aide to access the Understanding Computers 2002 Web site at: www.course.com/parker2002. Once you are at the site, note the types of information and activities that are available to you as a student and browse through a few of them. (To see information beyond the initial page, use the mouse to click on *hyperlinks*—usually underlined or otherwise highlighted text or graphical buttons.) At the conclusion of this task, prepare a one-page summary describing the resources available through this Web site and submit it to your instructor.

Writing About Computers

5. **Great Expectations** It is often said that learning about computers is essential in today's information-based society. Some students take a computer literacy course to meet the requirements of a certificate, transfer program, or degree program. Others take such a course for personal enrichment, job skill requirements, or job advancement. If you are reading this textbook as part of a computer course, what goals do you hope to meet by taking this course? For this project, identify your objectives for taking the course (or your objectives for reading this text, if you are reading this book on your own), as well as any expectations you have of the instructor or the content of the course, and what you hope to have learned by the time the course is completed. Submit this project to your instructor in the form of short paper, not more than two pages in length.

6. **Computers as Tools** Students make use of many tools during the course of their studies in order to accomplish or facilitate the learning process. Some of these tools, such as writing implements, calculators, and recording devices, are relatively inexpensive, but limited in terms of the functions they can perform. In the past few years, computer prices have dropped enough that many students are now purchasing them as educational tools. For this project, identify the educational functions a computer could be used for and give several examples of ways you could use a PC as a tool to help you with your studies. Submit this project to your instructor in the form of short paper, not more than two pages in length.

7. **The Purpose of Software** Software is often referred to as the set of instructions that make the computer work. It is generally categorized as systems software (if its purpose is to run the computer system), and application software (if its purpose is to enable the user to perform some type of task). For this project, form a group to discuss software. The group should identify three of the

leading microcomputer operating systems, and six categories of application software with two example programs for each category. Be sure to find out the manufacturer, version, system or hardware requirements, function or purpose, current cost of each package, and draw some conclusions about the dominance of one or more manufacturers in either or both of these software categories. Your group should submit the results of your research and discussions to your instructor in the form of short paper, not more than three pages in length.

Presentation/ Demonstration

8. **Price and Power** The price of computers continues to drop as processing ability and memory size continue to double about every 18 months. This pattern of achievement is unprecedented and continues today. For this project, visit your school or local library and research the available archive of newspapers, computer journals, and other periodicals for empirical evidence of this trend. Share your findings with the class in the form of a short presentation. This presentation should not exceed 5 minutes and should make use of one or more presentation aids such as the chalkboard, handouts, overhead transparencies, or computer-based slide presentation format. You may be asked to submit a summary of the presentation to your instructor.

9. **Make or Assemble** Most computer companies do not manufacture the entire machine themselves. Instead, they assemble a line of computers under a brand name. In the process of assembling a computer, these companies select components from a wide range of potential manufacturers. As a result, the quality or reliability of the computer system you purchase is based on the quality or reliability of the company that manufactured the individual components selected during the assembly process. For this project, form a group to research the major components of a computer system and who actually manufactures them. You must include an analysis of one complete computer system you found in an ad in the newspaper, computer journal, or on the Web. Be sure to state the brand of the PC plus the manufacturers of the various hardware components in the system. (You may need to call the manufacturer or research the product on the Internet or in person to determine the various component manufacturers.) Your group will present its findings to the class in the form of a short presentation. This presentation should not exceed 10 minutes and should make use of one or more presentation aids such as the chalkboard, handouts, overhead transparencies, or computer-based slide presentation format. Your group may be asked to submit a summary of the presentation to your instructor.

    Hint: Here is a partial list of companies that manufacture computer system components: 3COM, Intel, Microsoft, Maxtor, Iomega, Imation, Logitech, US Robotics, Hewlett Packard, Creative Labs, Toshiba, Advanced Micro Devices (AMD), Seagate, and Sony.

10. **Off-The-Shelf System** An off-the-shelf computer system is generally one that is in stock and ready to use right after you purchase the system. It already has the operating system software and an assortment of application software installed on the hard drive. You may be required to connect the mouse, keyboard, monitor, and telephone cord, but you are generally relieved of having to accomplish any detailed installation or setup procedures. These systems are sometimes referred to as "turn-key" systems, which means that all you are required to do is turn the computer on and start using it. For this project, form a group to identify the characteristics of a current "off-the-shelf" system. Compare a number of these systems using ads in the newspaper or computer journals. Be sure to discuss what software comes preinstalled with the system, the total price of the system including the monitor, the warranty, and whether you would recommend purchasing the system "as is," or with additional upgrades. Your group will present the findings to the class in the form of a short presentation. Be sure to include both PC- and Macintosh-based systems in the presentation. The presentation should not exceed 10 minutes and should make use of one or more presentation aids such as the chalkboard, handouts, overhead transparencies, or computer-based slide presentation format. Your group may be asked to submit a summary of the presentation to your instructor.

Interactive
Discussion

11. **Computer Literacy** It has been suggested that computer literacy should be one of the basic requirements of a high school or college education. The definition of computer literacy varies but is generally consistent with the knowledge and understanding of computers and their uses. Many schools are still dealing with this issue. There is some reluctance to adopt computer literacy as a formal requirement since students already have so many requirements to complete before graduation.

   Select one of the following positions or make up your own and express your point of view on the subject. Your instructor will indicate whether your response is to be posted to a class bulletin board, discussed in a class chat room, or discussed as an in-class activity. You may also be asked to submit a summary of your position and point of view to your instructor.

   a. Computer literacy is important, but not as important as reading, writing, or arithmetic, and should not be a basic requirement for graduation from high school or college.
   b. Computer literacy is an essential skill and should be required for graduation at either the high school or college level.

12. **A Computer-Oriented Society** Consider the following statement and establish your position, or point of view, on the subject. Your instructor will indicate whether your response is to be posted to a class bulletin board, discussed in a class chat room, or discussed as an in-class activity. You may also be asked to submit a summary of your position and evaluation of the statement.

   > Computers are becoming an integral part of our society. Individuals and organizations are using them to help accomplish everything from tedious paperwork to testing and manufacturing life-saving drugs. As they continue to become more powerful and drop in price, computers will become even more widespread in our society. As discussed in the preface to this text, we will soon reach a point where the key to success in virtually every profession will depend on them and we will have no choice but to integrate them into every aspect or our business and personal lives. It seems as though, no matter who you are or what you do for a living, it is likely that computers will somehow impact both the way you work and your success at your work. Even as this text is being written, companies are producing computer-based androids and robotic pets to assist, entertain, and perhaps replace us in the workforce. Have we reached a point in time where portions of Stanley Kubrick's and Arthur C. Clarke's movie *2001: A Space Odyssey* will no longer be a just a great science fiction movie?

   Note: If you have not seen the movie *2001: A Space Odyssey,* reviewing the dialog titled "Good afternoon, Hal" between "Hal," a 9000 series computer and Mr. Amer, an astronaut on the spacecraft, at http://www.underview.com/2001/haltrans.html would provide you with sufficient background to develop a point of view on the subject.

Interactive
Exercise

Understanding the World of Computers. It's time to review basic PC concepts and components. Go to the Interactive Exercise at www.course.com/parker2002/ch1 to complete this exercise.

Using Your PC, Windows, and the Web

LEARNING OBJECTIVES

After completing this chapter, you will be able to:

1. Explain what happens when you start up a computer.

2. Identify common elements of the Windows graphical user interface (GUI) and their functions.

3. Demonstrate how to open a program and manipulate open program windows.

4. Explain what the Internet and World Wide Web are and how computers, people, and Web pages are identified on the Internet.

5. Demonstrate how to access a Web page on the Internet and discuss how to search for Web pages containing specific information.

6. Explain how e-mail can be used to send and receive messages to and from other Internet users.

7. Describe how plug-ins and other types of files can be downloaded from the Internet and installed on a computer.

Not too long ago, most computers were difficult to use and very intimidating. Some users had to program their computers to get them to perform the necessary functions. If an appropriate application program was available, the user still had to type the correct sequence of somewhat cryptic text-based commands to get the program started and then to control the program's actions.

This situation has radically changed over the last decade or two. Desktop systems with easy-to-use graphical interfaces and sophisticated multimedia capabilities have emerged as the standard. These systems, used in conjunction with the vast amount of useful and exciting software applications available today, enable even novice users to take advantage of current technology.

In order to use application software, however, you first need to know how to start up the computer and instruct it to start the appropriate program. You also need to be a little familiar with the commands and mouse actions that may be needed to tell the program what you want it to do. This is the purpose of this chapter. It will get you up and running enough so that you can use a computer to perform any computer-based assignments for this course, such as starting a word processing program to type a paper or completing an exercise or tutorial located on the textbook's Web site.

Chapter 2 begins by introducing the basic features of the Windows operating system, including how to start up a PC and how to start an application program. It covers the wide variety of menus, windows, and icons you are likely to encounter, and it explains how to open, close, resize, and otherwise manipulate the windows that appear on your screen when programs and documents are open. The chapter also explains how Internet addresses work and how to gain access to Web pages. Remember when reading this chapter that it's just an overview; operating systems, application software, the Internet, and the World Wide Web are covered in much more detail in later chapters. Selecting and purchasing a PC is discussed in Chapter 16. If you need to buy a computer during this course, be sure to read through that chapter beforehand. ■

STARTING YOUR COMPUTER: THE BOOT PROCESS

The first thing a new computer user needs to know about using a PC is how to turn the power on and start it up, assuming that the computer is already out of the box and the cables are correctly connected (refer to Figure 3-16 in Chapter 3 for cable illustrations and setup descriptions). To turn on a PC, the power switch (usually located on the front of the system unit) is used. Once the power switch is activated, an indicator light on the front of the system unit lights up. If the power indicator light is on but the computer doesn't appear to be active, the unit may be *asleep*—a low power standby mode designed to save energy and wear-and-tear on the computer. Sleeping computers can usually be awakened by moving the mouse or pressing a key on the keyboard.

Problem	Steps to try to remedy the solution
Power indicator light on the system unit is not on.	1. Make sure the system unit's power cable is securely connected to both the power supply and system unit. 2. Make sure the power supply is turned on. 3. Press the power button located on the computer to turn it on.
Power indicator light on the system unit is on, but there is no picture on the screen.	1. Move the mouse or press a key on the keyboard to wake up the computer if it is asleep. 2. Make sure the monitor's power cable is securely connected to both the power supply and the monitor. 3. Make sure all the switches on the power supply are turned on. 4. Make sure the cable from the monitor to the system unit is securely connected. 5. Press the power button located on the monitor to turn it on. 6. Check to make sure the monitor's brightness and contrast levels are not turned all the way down.
"Non-system disk" error message is displayed on screen.	1. Remove the disk from the floppy drive and press any key to continue.
Computer boots up, but the keyboard won't work.	1. Check to make sure the keyboard cable is securely connected to the system unit.
Computer boots up, but the mouse won't work.	1. Check to make sure the mouse cable is securely connected to the system unit. 2. Reboot the computer if the mouse was unplugged, but still doesn't work now that it is connected. 3. If using a wireless mouse, replace the batteries located inside the mouse.

> **FIGURE 2-1**

Common problems encountered while booting up a PC.

After the power button is pressed, the **boot** process begins. During the boot procedure, part of the computer's **operating system**—the type of systems software that manages a computer's activities—is loaded into memory. The computer also does a quick diagnostic on the computer and may run special utilities, such as checking for computer viruses. You may hear beeps and whirling noises as these procedures take place and some characteristics of the PC (such as amount of memory, the number of attached drives, and the operating system being used) may be quickly displayed on the screen.

There are several things that can prevent a computer from booting up properly. Some of the most common and easy to fix problems are listed in Figure 2-1 with some suggested remedies.

USING THE WINDOWS OPERATING SYSTEM

After a PC is booted up, the computer waits to receive input from the user regarding what activity he or she would like to perform first. The manner in which an operating system or any other type of program interacts with its users is known as its *user interface.* Older software programs used a *text-based user interface,* which required the user to type precise instructions indicating exactly what the computers should do. Most programs today use a

web tutor

For a tutorial on using Windows, go to www.course.com/ parker2002/ch2

>Boot. To start up a computer. **>Operating system.** The main piece of systems software that enables the computer to manage its activities and the resources under its control, run application programs, and interface with the user.

graphical user interface or **GUI** (pronounced "goo-ey"), which uses graphical objects (such as icons and buttons) and the mouse to much more easily tell the computer what the user wants it to do.

GUIs became the standard once hardware became sufficient to support it. Older systems could not adequately deliver the necessary *WYSIWYG* (*what you see is what you get,* pronounced "wizzy-wig") displays in which screen images resemble printed documents, since the output wasn't of acceptable quality. And later, when screen outputs started to look acceptable, it just took too long to display the graphics on the computer to be worthwhile. These days, of course, most computers can rapidly display WYSIWYG displays, as well as other types of text and graphics.

The Windows Interface

One of the most widely used GUIs is **Microsoft Windows**—also known as just *Windows.* Windows is the most common operating system for PCs today and has come in a variety of versions over the years, such as Windows 95, Windows 98, Windows 2000, Windows Me, and Windows XP. One of the advantages of using Windows is that application software written for any version of the Windows operating system has a similar appearance and works essentially the same way as Windows does. Thus, if you are comfortable using the Windows interface and some Windows software, all other Windows software should seem familiar. The next few sections describe what the Windows interface looks like and how to use it. Other graphical operating systems, such as Mac OS (used on Macintosh computers) and graphical versions of Linux (used on some PC computers) look and act similarly to Windows.

The Desktop

The Windows **desktop** appears on the screen after a computer using the Windows operating system has completed the boot process. The desktop is where documents, folders, programs, and other objects are displayed when they are being used, similar to the way documents and file folders are laid on a desk when they are being used. Though the appearance of the Windows desktop can be customized, all desktops contain common elements, such as desktop icons, the taskbar, the Start button, windows, and task buttons (see Figure 2-2).

▼ *Desktop icons* are used to open programs, documents, or Web pages.

▼ The *taskbar* is located along the bottom of the desktop. It houses the *Start button* at the left edge, *toolbars* and *task buttons* in the center, and a clock and other indicators at the far right edge.

▼ The *Start button* is used to display the *Start menu,* the main menu for Windows that is used to start programs.

▼ *Toolbars* (groups of icons that can be used to quickly invoke commands) may be displayed on the Windows taskbar.

▼ *Windows* are rectangular objects displayed on the screen that contain programs, documents, and other content. Windows are discussed in more detail shortly.

▼ A *task button* appears on the taskbar for each window that is currently open, though the window may not be visible on the desktop at all times. As discussed later, these task buttons can be used to select which windows are visible on the screen.

>**Graphical user interface (GUI).** A graphically-based interface that allows a user to easily communicate instructions to the computer.
>**Microsoft Windows.** The most common operating system for IBM and IBM-compatible PCs. >**Desktop.** The background work area displayed on the screen when using Microsoft Windows.

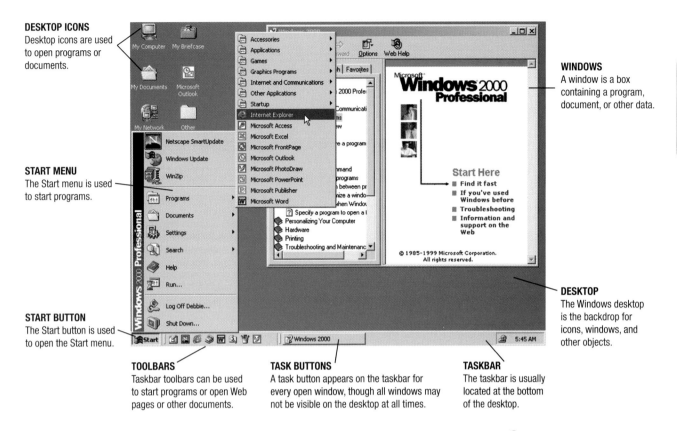

DESKTOP ICONS
Desktop icons are used to open programs or documents.

START MENU
The Start menu is used to start programs.

START BUTTON
The Start button is used to open the Start menu.

WINDOWS
A window is a box containing a program, document, or other data.

DESKTOP
The Windows desktop is the backdrop for icons, windows, and other objects.

TOOLBARS
Taskbar toolbars can be used to start programs or open Web pages or other documents.

TASK BUTTONS
A task button appears on the taskbar for every open window, though all windows may not be visible on the desktop at all times.

TASKBAR
The taskbar is usually located at the bottom of the desktop.

◆ **FIGURE 2-2**
The Windows desktop.

Windows

The principle component of the GUI is the window. As mentioned earlier, a **window** is a rectangular area of information that is displayed on the screen. These windows can contain programs and documents, as well as *menus, dialog boxes, icons,* and a variety of other types of data, as discussed next.

Menus

A **menu** is a set of options—usually text based—from which the user can choose to initiate a desired action in a program. At the top of many windows is a *menu bar* showing the main menu categories (see Figure 2-3). *Pull-down menus* (also called *drop-down menus*) display on the screen when the user selects an item on the menu bar. As shown on the right-most screen in Figure 2-3, in some Microsoft programs (such as Windows and some versions of Microsoft Office) a feature called *personalized menus* can be used. With personalized menus, only the options that were most recently used are initially displayed on the menu. Waiting a moment or clicking on the down arrow symbol at the bottom of the menu displays all items that belong on that menu.

Options on pull-down menus either display another, more specific, menu; open a *dialog box* to prompt the user for more information; or execute a command. These options are discussed in the following sections along with other conventions that pull-down menus typically follow.

>**Window.** A rectangular area appearing on the screen of a computer using a GUI operating system such as Windows; windows can contain icons, documents, and other information. >**Menu.** A set of options (usually text-based) that can be displayed on the screen to enable the user to issue commands to the computer.

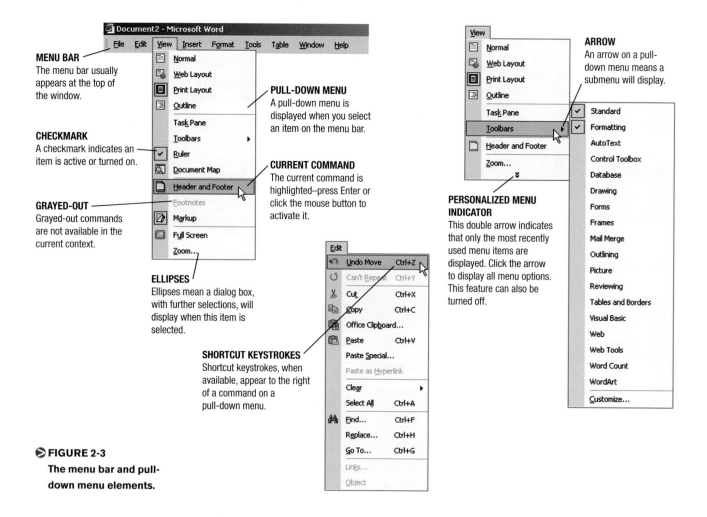

MENU BAR
The menu bar usually appears at the top of the window.

CHECKMARK
A checkmark indicates an item is active or turned on.

GRAYED-OUT
Grayed-out commands are not available in the current context.

PULL-DOWN MENU
A pull-down menu is displayed when you select an item on the menu bar.

CURRENT COMMAND
The current command is highlighted–press Enter or click the mouse button to activate it.

ELLIPSES
Ellipses mean a dialog box, with further selections, will display when this item is selected.

SHORTCUT KEYSTROKES
Shortcut keystrokes, when available, appear to the right of a command on a pull-down menu.

ARROW
An arrow on a pull-down menu means a submenu will display.

PERSONALIZED MENU INDICATOR
This double arrow indicates that only the most recently used menu items are displayed. Click the arrow to display all menu options. This feature can also be turned off.

FIGURE 2-3
The menu bar and pull-down menu elements.

Current Command

The *current command,* such as the Header and Footer option on the top left screen of Figure 2-3, is the command that can be activated by either pressing the Enter key or by clicking the mouse button while still pointing to that item. To select a choice other than the current one, move the mouse pointer to that item and click or move the current command using the appropriate arrow key on the keyboard and then press the Enter key. To close a menu without making a selection, press the Escape (Esc) key on the keyboard.

Checkmarks

An item on a menu with a *checkmark* to the left of it means that the associated option is turned on. For instance, the checkmark by the Ruler option on the top left screen of Figure 2-3 means that the ruler for this program is displayed on the screen. If this menu item was not checkmarked, the ruler would not appear on the screen. You can *toggle* between checking and unchecking a checkmark item by clicking the item with the mouse. Sometimes on a menu only one item in a group of items can be selected. When this is the case, another symbol—a dot or circle called a *radio button*—is used instead to indicate the selected item. Radio buttons will be discussed in more detail shortly.

Grayed-out Type

On the View pull-down menu at the top left of Figure 2-3, the Footnotes command is shown in faded or *grayed-out* type. This means that this particular choice is unavailable in the context of what you're currently doing. For example, if you haven't created any footnotes in a document, viewing them is impossible at this time.

Arrows

An *arrow* ▶ to the right of a menu option—such as Toolbars in the right-most screen in Figure 2-3—means that this menu item will display another menu containing more specific options when selected. For example, when you position the mouse pointer over the Toolbars choice as in the figure, the pull-down menu showing all possible toolbars is displayed.

Ellipses

On menus, *ellipses* (. . .) are often displayed to the right of a command—such as next to the Zoom option on the View menu shown in Figure 2-3. Ellipses mean that selecting the menu item will display a dialog box. As discussed shortly, a *dialog box* is displayed when additional information needs to be supplied; once the dialog box has been completed, the appropriate command will be carried out.

Shortcut Keystrokes

Some menu items display shortcut keystrokes next to them, such as Ctrl+Z (performed by holding down the Ctrl key while tapping the Z key) for Undo and Ctrl+C for Copy on the Edit menu shown at the bottom of Figure 2-3. Shortcut keystrokes are used when the menu is not currently open to execute that command.

Icons and Other Navigational Objects

In addition to menus, other navigational objects can typically be used to allow the user to select the desired option or command. Figure 2-4 shows a variety of navigational objects you may find on the desktop or in Windows programs. These objects are described in more detail next.

◗ FIGURE 2-4
Icons and other
navigational objects.

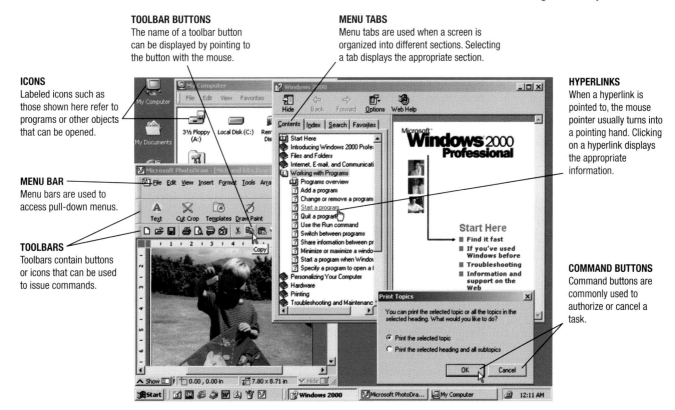

TOOLBAR BUTTONS
The name of a toolbar button can be displayed by pointing to the button with the mouse.

MENU TABS
Menu tabs are used when a screen is organized into different sections. Selecting a tab displays the appropriate section.

ICONS
Labeled icons such as those shown here refer to programs or other objects that can be opened.

MENU BAR
Menu bars are used to access pull-down menus.

TOOLBARS
Toolbars contain buttons or icons that can be used to issue commands.

HYPERLINKS
When a hyperlink is pointed to, the mouse pointer usually turns into a pointing hand. Clicking on a hyperlink displays the appropriate information.

COMMAND BUTTONS
Command buttons are commonly used to authorize or cancel a task.

Icons

Icons are small pictures that represent such items as a computer program or document. When you select an icon with the mouse, the software takes the corresponding action, often starting or opening the appropriate program or document. Programs are commonly represented as *program icons* displayed on the Windows desktop. To start a program or anything else represented by a desktop icon, the mouse is used. Depending on how Windows is set up, either a single click or a double-click of the left mouse button opens the program or document. (Using the mouse is discussed in more detail in Chapter 5.) Icons can also be located on *toolbars*, as discussed next.

Toolbars

A **toolbar** consists of a set of icons or buttons called *toolbar buttons* and usually stretches horizontally across the screen. Each toolbar button has a name, which is displayed if you point to the button (see Figure 2-4). In a software suite, such as Microsoft Office or Corel WordPerfect Office, the toolbar buttons that can be used to save a document, print a document, or perform other common tasks have the same appearance in all programs within the suite. As shown in Figure 2-2, there can also be toolbars displayed on the Windows taskbar.

Command Buttons

A *command button* is an icon that represents a basic command, such as the OK and Cancel buttons shown on the dialog box in Figure 2-4 that allow users to approve or cancel the dialog box settings. A grayed-out command button represents an action that is unavailable for current operation.

Menu Tabs

Some programs or program elements contain *menu tabs*, such as on the Help screen in Figure 2-4. Menu tabs, such as Contents, Index, Search, and Favorites in the figure, organize a screen into file-folder-type tabs. By clicking any of the tabs, the information corresponding to that tab is displayed. For example, in Figure 2-4, the Contents tab on the Help screen is currently selected.

Hyperlinks

Both image-based hyperlinks and text-based hyperlinks (referred to as *hypertext*) are an increasingly common control option. Though initially found just on Web pages, hyperlinks now more frequently appear on other types of Windows applications, such as on the Help screen in Figure 2-4. Icons on the Windows desktop (see Figure 2-5) that are underlined, as well as underlined and/or different colored text on a Web page or Help screen, generally indicate hyperlinks. When you move the mouse pointer to a hyperlink, the pointer's shape usually changes to a pointing hand. Clicking the hyperlink opens the appropriate program or document or displays some other type of new information on your screen. Hyperlinks found on Web pages are discussed in more detail later in this chapter.

Dialog Boxes

After selecting a menu item with an ellipses (. . .) next to it, a **dialog box** appears on the screen. Dialog boxes are windows that prompt the user to provide further information. Such information can be supplied by a variety of means, several of which are covered in the following sections and illustrated in Figure 2-6.

Radio Buttons

Radio buttons, also known as *option buttons,* are round buttons that work like the push buttons on old radios—only one choice in the group of radio buttons can be selected at any

HYPERLINK
Single-click to open icon.

NOT A HYPERLINK
Double-click to open icon.

FIGURE 2-5
Desktop icons and hyperlinks. Depending on how Windows is set up, desktop icons may look and act like hyperlinks.

>**Icon.** A small picture or other type of graphical image that represents a program or document and invokes some action when selected.

>**Toolbar.** A set of icons or buttons displayed horizontally or vertically on the screen that can be used to issue commands to the computer.

>**Dialog box.** A box that requires the user to supply information to the computer about the task being requested.

RADIO BUTTONS
Radio buttons work like the push buttons on old radios in that only one button in a group of radio buttons can be selected at one time.

CHECK BOXES
When a check is placed in a check box, the associated action is selected. Several, none, or all boxes in a group of check boxes can be checked at one time.

TEXT BOXES
Text boxes require you to enter information into the computer—such as a page number.

SPIN BOXES
A spin box controls a fixed set of numeric values. You click an up or down arrow to the right of a value to make the value higher or lower.

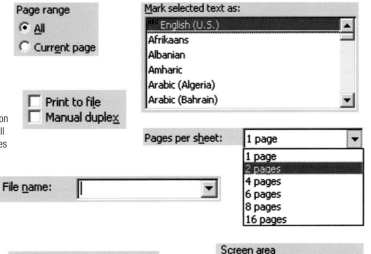

SIMPLE LIST BOXES
In a list box, you make a choice by clicking it with a mouse or by reaching it by using the arrow keys and pressing Enter. A vertical scroll bar lets you access choices not currently viewable.

DROP-DOWN LIST BOXES
A drop-down list box has a down-facing arrow to the right of the first choice in the list. When you click on the arrow, other choices appear.

SLIDERS
A slider lets you select a value from a range.

MESSAGE BOXES
A message box pops up on the screen when a potential problem is unfolding.

▶ **FIGURE 2-6**
Dialog-box elements.

one time. When you click a radio button, that button becomes filled in to mark the currently selected option; all other radio buttons in the group become deselected.

Check Boxes

To make an option preceded by a *check box* active, you must place a checkmark in the box by clicking it with the mouse. Check boxes differ from radio buttons in that you can select any number of check boxes on the dialog box. To deactivate (uncheck) any check box, click on its checkmark again.

Text Boxes

Text boxes provide spaces for you to type information, such as a number, or the name of a particular document or folder. After you enter the appropriate information into the text box, pressing the Tab key generally moves you to the next section of the dialog box. A *spin box* lets you either enter a number in the text box or tweak a numeric value up or down by clicking the up-arrow or down-arrow buttons located at the edge of the spin box.

List Boxes

Two kinds of list boxes appear in Figure 2-6. Like a pull-down menu, a *simple list box* presents a list of options, allowing you to choose the desired option. Often, the list exceeds the size of its window, and a vertical scroll bar allows you to see parts of the list currently off the screen. To save even more space, a *drop-down list box* can be used. This type of list box displays only one selection initially, allowing you to see the others by clicking the drop-down arrow button located on the right edge of the box.

Sliders

A *slider* can be dragged with the mouse to select a value from a range of values. Sliders are commonly used for adjusting audio volume, changing the monitor resolution, and setting the difficulty level for a computer game.

DESKTOP ICONS
Click any desktop icon that looks like a hyperlink; double-click any desktop icon that doesn't to start that program.

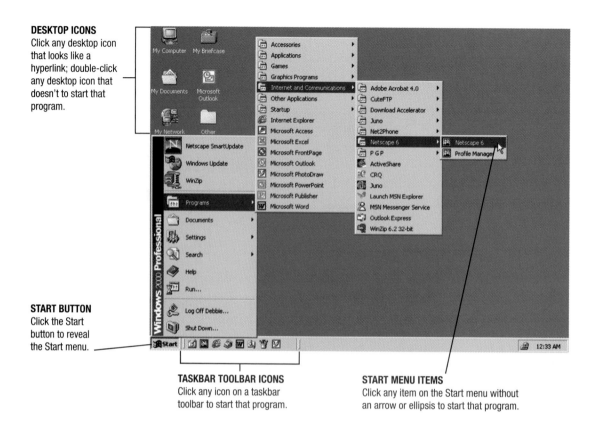

START BUTTON
Click the Start button to reveal the Start menu.

TASKBAR TOOLBAR ICONS
Click any icon on a taskbar toolbar to start that program.

START MENU ITEMS
Click any item on the Start menu without an arrow or ellipsis to start that program.

● **FIGURE 2-7**

Starting a program.

Desktop icons, taskbar toolbar icons, or the Start menu can be used to start a program.

Message Boxes

A *message box* pops on the screen when the program needs to provide status information or when a potential problem is unfolding. You may see such a message when you attempt to execute an improper command or select a command that requires verification (such as formatting a disk or deleting a document from a disk). In any type of message box, the user must acknowledge the message by choosing one of the displayed command buttons (such as Retry or Cancel in Figure 2-6) before proceeding further.

Opening Windows and Starting Programs

To start a program (or open any other type of window) in Windows, desktop or toolbar icons or the Start menu are used. To open a window or start a program, you can use any of the following methods (refer to Figure 2-7).

▼ Click a taskbar toolbar icon.

▼ Click a desktop icon if it looks like a hyperlink.

▼ Double-click a desktop icon if it doesn't look like a hyperlink.

▼ Click the Start button and then select the desired program from the Start menu.

As on any pull-down menu, an item on the Start menu with an arrow to the right of it ▶ means that the choice will display another menu, and an item with an ellipsis (. . .) next to it will display a dialog box when selected. Any item without an arrow or ellipsis starts a program; to start the program, simply click the item. Alternatively, if the desktop has a taskbar toolbar—such as the Quick Launch toolbar shown in Figure 2-7—clicking a toolbar icon also opens the appropriate program.

MAXIMIZED WINDOW
A maximized window covers the entire desktop.

SIZING BUTTONS
These buttons can be used to minimize, maximize, restore, and close windows.

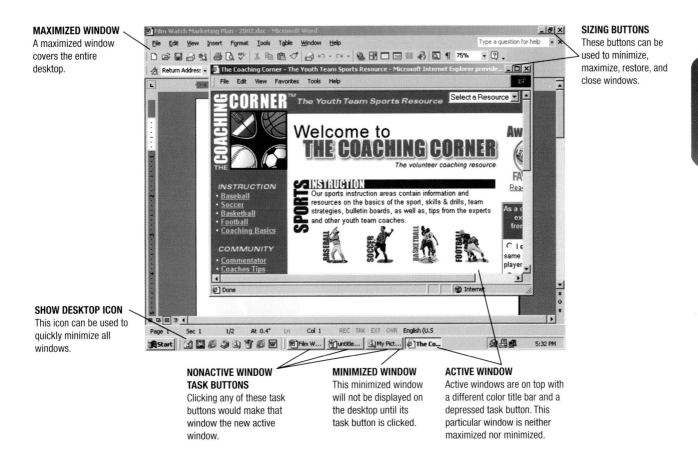

SHOW DESKTOP ICON
This icon can be used to quickly minimize all windows.

NONACTIVE WINDOW TASK BUTTONS
Clicking any of these task buttons would make that window the new active window.

MINIMIZED WINDOW
This minimized window will not be displayed on the desktop until its task button is clicked.

ACTIVE WINDOW
Active windows are on top with a different color title bar and a depressed task button. This particular window is neither maximized nor minimized.

> **FIGURE 2-8**
>
> **Minimizing and maximizing windows.**

Manipulating Windows

Open windows may occasionally need to be resized or otherwise manipulated in order to work efficiently. Several ways to do this are described next.

The Active Window

When more than one window is open at one time, only one can be the *active window*— the window on which commands will be executed. To identify the active window, look for the window that is on top of the others, has a different colored *title bar* (the top border of the window containing the name of the window), and has a task button with a depressed appearance (see Figure 2-8).

Only one window can be active at a time. To make any onscreen window active, click the mouse pointer on the window. You can also click the window's task button located on the taskbar at the bottom of the Windows desktop to make that window the new active window.

Minimizing and Maximizing Windows

Windows can be minimized to just a task button on the taskbar or maximized to fill the entire screen by clicking the appropriate sizing button with the mouse. The buttons to perform these tasks are located at the top right of most windows (such as those in Figure 2-8) and are described next.

▼ The *Minimize button* ▬ hides a window, leaving only its task button on the taskbar. A program that has been minimized is still running and can be displayed on the screen again by clicking its button on the taskbar.

▼ The *Maximize button* ▢ enlarges the window as much as possible, usually filling the entire screen.

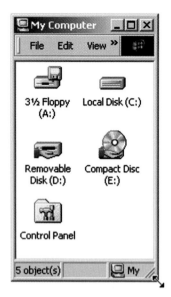

◈ FIGURE 2-9

Resizing a window. You can change both the width and height of a window together by dragging a corner sizing handle.

▼ The *Restore button* 🗗 is displayed instead of the Maximize button when a window is currently maximized. Clicking the Restore button reduces a maximized window to its previous size.

▼ The *Close button* ☒ at the far upper-right corner of the window closes a window and exits you out of the program. To reopen the window at a later time, the program must be started again using a desktop or taskbar toolbar icon, or the Start menu.

When it is necessary to access an icon on the desktop hidden behind open windows, you don't need to minimize each open window. Instead, it is faster to click the Show Desktop button 🗔 on the Quick Launch taskbar toolbar (as shown in Figure 2-8), if that toolbar is displayed on the screen. Clicking the Show Desktop button again restores the desktop to its previous appearance.

Resizing and Moving Windows

Resizing windows (making them larger or smaller) allows you to view more than one window on the desktop at a time. The active window can be resized using the window's *border* (the edge of the window). When the mouse pointer is moved over a window border, it looks like a double-pointed arrow and the window width or height can be adjusted by holding down the mouse button and moving the mouse to the desired location. To adjust the width of the window, move the left or right border; to size the height, move the top or bottom border. To adjust the window's width and height simultaneously, point the mouse to the *sizing handle* at the window's corner, hold down the button, and move the corner of the window to the desired location (see Figure 2-9). Resizing can only be performed on nonmaximized windows.

When you resize a window or perform work within individual windows, the mouse pointer often changes its appearance in a *context-sensitive* manner. In other words, the shape of the pointer changes automatically based on the operation you are performing. For example, when you resize a window (as in Figure 2-9), the pointer resembles a double-pointed arrow. Also, as mentioned earlier, when you move the pointer over hypertext, the pointer changes to a pointing hand. Figure 2-10 shows some of the mouse pointer shapes that you may see on your screen from time to time.

In addition to resizing windows, you can further customize your screen by moving a nonmaximized window from one part of the screen to another. To move a window:

1. Point to the window's title bar with the mouse.

2. Hold down the mouse button.

3. Drag the window to the desired location.

4. Release the mouse to complete the move of the window to the new location.

◈ FIGURE 2-10

Context-sensitive mouse pointer shapes. Most software programs cause the mouse pointer to be context sensitive, changing its shape with respect to the operation the user is performing.

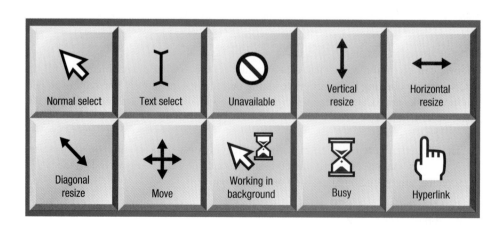

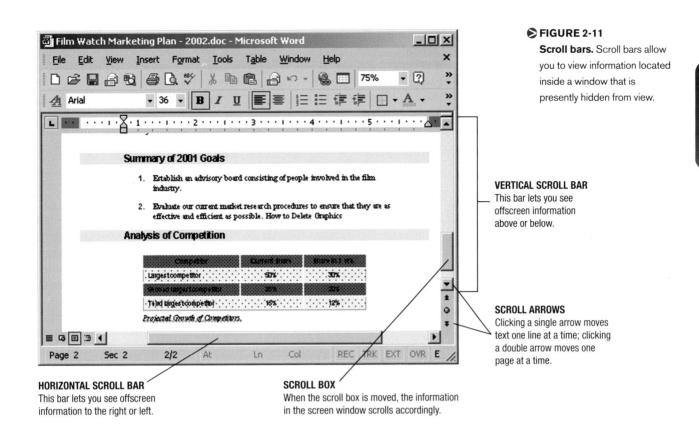

INT

● **FIGURE 2-11**

Scroll bars. Scroll bars allow you to view information located inside a window that is presently hidden from view.

VERTICAL SCROLL BAR
This bar lets you see offscreen information above or below.

SCROLL ARROWS
Clicking a single arrow moves text one line at a time; clicking a double arrow moves one page at a time.

HORIZONTAL SCROLL BAR
This bar lets you see offscreen information to the right or left.

SCROLL BOX
When the scroll box is moved, the information in the screen window scrolls accordingly.

This same move procedure can be used to move a desktop icon or an object or block of text in many application programs.

Scroll Bars

Often, a screen window is not big enough to display all the contents of the window. When this happens, **scroll bars** appear at the bottom and/or right edge of the window (see Figure 2-11). Using a scroll bar, you can *scroll* to see the rest of the information located in the window. Scrolling moves information up, down, and sideways within the window. When you scroll down, for example, lines disappear from the top of the window as new ones appear at the bottom. Ways to use scroll bars are listed next.

▼ Click one of the two *scroll arrows* at the edge of the scroll bar to move a small amount in the direction of the arrow, exposing information that was out of view.

▼ Click an empty spot on the scroll bar on either side of the scroll box to move about one screen at a time in that direction.

▼ Drag the *scroll box* (the rectangle located between the two scroll arrows) with the mouse to quickly move to a specific location in the document. If you move the scroll box from the top of the scroll bar to the middle, for example, the middle part of the document will be displayed.

▼ Use the special scroll wheel or button located on the top of your mouse, if one exists.

>**Scroll bar.** A horizontal or vertical bar that appears along an edge of a window when the window is not large enough to display the entire content contained within the window; the scroll bar can be used to view the rest of the information in the window.

Scroll boxes are usually sized in proportion to the percentage of information currently displayed. Therefore, a large scroll box indicates that most of the information within the window is displayed, while a small scroll box indicates that most information is hidden from view. For example, in Figure 2-11 the scroll box is about one-fourth the size of the scroll bar, which indicates that about one-fourth of the document is currently displayed within the window.

Instead of the scroll bars, you can also often use the keyboard's cursor-movement keys, such as PageUp (PgUp) to scroll up and PageDown (PgDn) to scroll down.

Shutting Down the Computer

At the end of a work session, you usually leave your PC on if you will be using it again later that day. To reduce power consumption, most computers can be put to sleep (into *standby mode*) by using the Standby option on the Shut Down dialog box (discussed next) or a special sleep key on the keyboard. When a computer is in standby mode, the monitors and hard drive are generally turned off to save power and wear-and-tear on the computer. Many PCs can also be set up to automatically go to sleep after a set period of inactivity.

When you are finished working with a computer for the day, you may want to turn it off. Before doing so, it is important to *shut down* the computer. Shutting down a computer properly gives you the opportunity to make sure all the work you have done has been saved and allows Windows to save any information it needs, delete temporary files, and close programs. Turning off a computer without shutting it down can leave extra data and files on your computer that can eventually take up valuable storage space and cause problems with your computer in the future.

To shut down a computer when necessary, follow these steps.

1. Click the Start button to display the Start menu.

2. Select the Shut Down option at the bottom of the Start menu.

3. Make sure the Shut Down option is selected on the Shut Down Windows dialog box, then click the OK button.

4. If you see a message stating that it is safe to turn off the computer, press the power button on the computer. If your computer automatically turns the power off instead, you don't need to do anything further.

As mentioned earlier, other options are usually available on the Shut Down dialog box. The Standby option can be used to put the computer into standby mode; the Restart option can be used when the computer stops responding or is otherwise acting strangely; and the Log Off or Restart as a New User options can be used to log off a network so another user can log on.

USING THE INTERNET AND WORLD WIDE WEB

What Is the World Wide Web?

As discussed in Chapter 1, the **Internet** is a collection of networks that connects millions of computers all over the world. The **World Wide Web** or *Web* is one part of the Internet. It is a collection of documents—called **Web pages**—that are accessed through the Internet. Web pages are connected to each other by hyperlinks and commonly contain a variety of text, images, and animated objects; they can contain music and video clips, as well.

>**Internet.** The largest and most widely used computer network in the world, linking millions of computers all over the world. >**World Wide Web (WWW).** The collection of Web pages available through the Internet. >**Web page.** A document, usually containing hyperlinks to other documents, located on a Web server and available through the World Wide Web.

A group of related Web pages belonging to an individual or organization is called a **Web site.** Today, most medium-size to large companies in the United States maintain one or more Web sites, and millions of individuals and small firms have them too. A computer that hosts one or more Web sites is called a **Web server.**

A Web site can contain anywhere from 1 to 2,000 or more pages. Your visit to a Web site often begins at the site's **home page.** A home page typically acts like a table of contents for the site, containing hyperlinks that enable visitors to access other main pages on the site. You can freely navigate among Web pages by selecting hyperlinks, in any order you wish. In addition to allowing you to access other Web pages on the same site, hyperlinks on a Web page can also be used to jump around within a Web page, display Web pages from entirely different Web sites, and download files, such as images, music files, or programs.

What Is a Browser?

To view Web pages, you need a **Web browser** program. The two most common browsers—*Microsoft Internet Explorer* and *Netscape Navigator*—are illustrated shortly; a few alternative browsers are shown in Figure 2-12. Though originally designed to display Web pages,

further exploration

For links to further information about Web browsers and browser applications, go to www.course.com/parker2002/ch2

FIGURE 2-12

Web browsers. In addition to Netscape Navigator and Microsoft Internet Explorer (illustrated in Figure 2-15), other possible browsers include (top to bottom) MSN Explorer, Opera, and the browser used with America Online.

>**Web site.** A related group of Web pages usually belonging to an organization or individual. >**Web server.** A computer that hosts Web pages so they can be accessed through the Internet. >**Home page.** The main starting page for a Web site. >**Web browser.** A program used to view Web pages.

how it works

Internet Appliances

An *Internet appliance*, also known as a *Web pad* or *e-mail station*, is a device designed for easy access to the Internet. It typically doesn't allow you to perform any other computing tasks, and often cannot be connected to a printer or hard drive. The primary market for these devices is either individuals who have no use for a more conventional PC (such as those individuals who just want to be able to exchange e-mail), or busy families who want a convenient e-mail station for the kitchen or other common location.

Usually the back of an Internet appliance contains ports for a power supply and phone cord. If the device can support a printer or other type of peripheral, there will be other ports (such

as serial or USB), as well. Typically after connecting the necessary cables and turning it on, the station is ready to go.

It is important to realize that some Internet appliances can only be used with one specific provider, either a conventional ISP (such as MSN) or a proprietary service for that particular Internet appliance. Many devices are set up to access the Internet on a regular basis to check for new e-mail; a blinking light typically indicates that new e-mail has arrived. Features and capabilities vary with the device. For example, some devices can download and play MP3 files. Others use storage cards so that downloads and e-mails can be saved for future use. Expect built-in video cameras for video phone calls—reminiscent of the Jetson's—to be common in the near future.

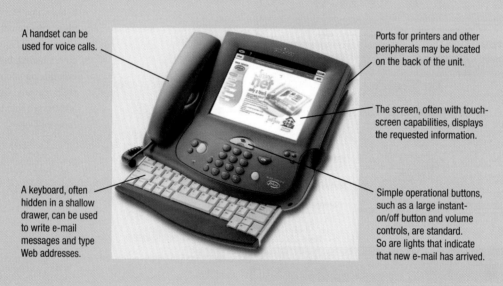

A handset can be used for voice calls.

Ports for printers and other peripherals may be located on the back of the unit.

The screen, often with touch-screen capabilities, displays the requested information.

A keyboard, often hidden in a shallow drawer, can be used to write e-mail messages and type Web addresses.

Simple operational buttons, such as a large instant-on/off button and volume controls, are standard. So are lights that indicate that new e-mail has arrived.

many browsers can also be used for other Internet applications, such as sending and receiving e-mail and downloading files.

The remainder of this chapter is dedicated to introducing how to use a Web browser to access Web pages, exchange e-mail, and perform the most common Internet tasks. The examples and directions are for the Internet Explorer 5.5 and Navigator 6 browsers. If you are using a different version of one of these browsers or are using a different browser altogether, the screens will probably look a little different than yours, but they should be close enough for you to understand how to perform these tasks using your browser. Chapter 9 covers the Internet and the World Wide Web in greater detail.

In addition to using a PC to access the Internet, other devices—such as smart phones or Internet appliances—can be used to access certain Web-based information. For a brief look at how an Internet appliance works, see the How It Works box.

Accessing the Internet

In order to access the Internet, your computer needs to be connected to a computer that is continually connected to the Internet. Your computer can always be connected to that computer (called a *direct* or *always-on connection*), or your PC can dial up and connect to that computer only when needed (referred to as a *dial-up connection*). In either case, the computer to which you connect belongs to an **Internet service provider (ISP)**—often called a *service provider* or *access provider* for short.

ISPs function as a gateway or onramp to the Internet. Typically, they are continually connected to a larger network, called a *regional network,* which, in turn, is connected to the major high-speed networks within each country called *backbone networks.* Backbone networks within a country are connected to each other and to backbone networks in other countries. Together they form one enormous network of networks—the Internet.

Many ISPs charge a monthly fee for Internet access. Free Internet access is available; it is usually supported by onscreen advertising. If you connect to the Internet using a school or company network, the school or company acts as the ISP. If you connect using a smart phone, PDA, or other handheld device, your wireless provider typically acts as your ISP.

The Web browser you use to access the Internet may be determined by your ISP. For example, users of America Online—one of the largest ISPs in the world—use the special America Online browser shown in Figure 2-12. Most other ISPs allow you to use the browser of your choice.

The various types of direct and dial-up Internet connections are discussed in Chapter 8. Choosing and getting set up with an ISP are discussed in Chapter 9. Assuming you are already set up with an ISP, to begin using your browser, open it using the appropriate desktop icon or Start menu item. With some dial-up connections, you may also need to start your dialing program. You may also be asked to enter your user name and password before being connected to the Internet; these will have been assigned or chosen during your ISP set-up procedure. Once you are connected, your computer can retrieve and display Web pages, as discussed shortly.

Internet Addresses

Before taking a look at how to use a Web browser, it is important to know how Internet addresses work. An **Internet address** performs the same function as a residential or business address. It identifies the location of something on the Internet, namely a particular computer, person, or Web page. Addresses on the Internet are unique; each one is assigned to one and only one person or resource.

IP Addresses and Domain Names

IP addresses and **domain names** are used to identify computers available through the Internet. IP (short for *I*nternet *p*rotocol) addresses are numeric, such as *206.68.137.41.* If the computer hosts information available through the Internet (such as Web pages), the computer usually also has a unique text-based domain name, such as *microsoft.com,* that corresponds to the computer's IP address. IP addresses and their corresponding domain names are unique for the entire Internet. To ensure this, a nonprofit organization called the *Internet Corporation for Assigned Names and Numbers* or *ICANN* is responsible for coordinating the assignment of IP addresses and domain names, and there is a central registration system for domain name registration.

A domain name identifies the location of a computer. It can include such information as the name of the computer, and the name, type, and geographic location of the organization. The rightmost part of a domain name is called the *top-level domain (TLD).* Top-level domains—such as *.com* (for *commercial*), *.edu* (for *education*), *.gov* (for *government*), and *.mil* (for *military*)—indicate the type of organization the domain name represents. TLDs can also represent the the country of origin. For instance, the domain name

www.fs.fed.us

suggests a government computer in the United States and belongs to a computer at the USDA Forest Service.

Because of the high demand for domain names, new top-level domains are periodically proposed and approved. Two of the newest domain names—*.biz* and *.info*—became available for use in 2001.

E-Mail Addresses

People are most often identified on the Internet through their e-mail addresses. An individual's **e-mail address** usually consists of a **user name** (an identifying name that is unique for that person's ISP's domain name), followed by the @ symbol, followed by the ISP's domain name. For example,

jsmith@course.com

marias@course.com

are the e-mail addresses of two hypothetical mailboxes at Course Technologies, the publisher of this textbook, respectively assigned to jsmith (John Smith) and marias (Maria Sanchez). People with e-mail addresses can be reached either through private company networks, over the Internet, or both. Using e-mail addresses to send e-mail messages is discussed later in this chapter.

Web Page Addresses

Web pages are most commonly identified on the Internet through **uniform resource locators,** or **URLs.** Every Web page has a unique URL (sometimes pronounced "earl"). If you know a page's URL, you can type it in the specified area on your Web browser's screen and the page will be displayed, as illustrated shortly.

As shown in Figure 2-13, Web page URLs almost always begin with *http://* (for *hypertext transfer protocol,* the protocol or standard being used to display most Web pages). The

▶ FIGURE 2-13

How URLs work.

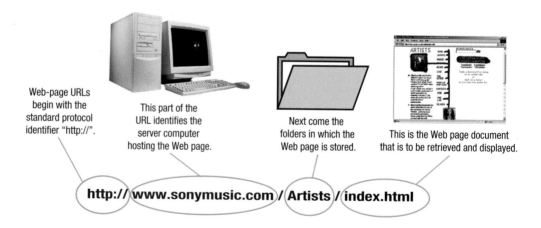

Web-page URLs begin with the standard protocol identifier "http://".

This part of the URL identifies the server computer hosting the Web page.

Next come the folders in which the Web page is stored.

This is the Web page document that is to be retrieved and displayed.

http:// www.sonymusic.com / Artists / index.html

---

second part of an URL identifies the computer where the Web page is located—frequently *www* and then the domain name of the computer. If needed, the third and fourth parts of an URL identify the location of the Web page on that computer, with folder names and the appropriate filename for the Web page separated by forward slashes. For example, the home page for Microsoft Corporation, the University of Virginia, and the Yahoo! search site, respectively, only need the first two parts and have the following URLs:

http://www.microsoft.com

http://www.virginia.edu

http://www.yahoo.com

The URL shown in Figure 2-13, however, requires all four parts to identify the Artists section of Sony Music's Web site. To the right of the computer and domain name (www.sonymusic.com), the URL identifies the folder (Artists) that must be opened in order to find the specified Web page file (index.html).

As you have probably already noticed, URLs can become lengthy and take time to type. Fortunately, you don't always need to type URLs to reach desired Web pages. If the page you are viewing contains a hyperlink to the desired page, you can simply click it to display the page, as illustrated shortly. These are also ways to revisit pages you've been to previously. These are discussed later in this chapter.

Pronouncing Internet Addresses

Because Internet addresses are frequently given verbally, it is important to know how to pronounce them. A few guidelines are listed next (see Figure 2-14 for a few pronunciation examples).

▼ If a portion of the address forms a recognizable word or name, it is spoken; otherwise it is spelled out.

▼ The @ sign is pronounced *at*.

▼ The period (.) is pronounced *dot*.

▼ The forward slash (/) is pronounced *slash*.

Address	Pronunciation
berkeley.edu	berkeley dot e d u
president@whitehouse.gov	president at whitehouse dot gov
microsoft.com/IE/Intro.htm	microsoft dot com slash i e slash intro dot h t m

◉ FIGURE 2-14
Pronouncing Internet addresses.

Surfing the Web

Once your Web browser is open and you are connected to the Internet, the page currently designated as your browser's starting page or home page will be displayed within the browser window. (Usually this page is the home page for your browser's, school's, or ISP's Web site, but it can usually be changed to any page using your browser's Options or Preferences dialog box.)

All browsers have navigational tools to help you move forward or backward through the pages viewed in your current Internet session, as well as buttons or menu options to print Web pages when necessary. Figure 2-15 illustrates the most common components of the Microsoft Internet Explorer and Netscape Navigator browsers.

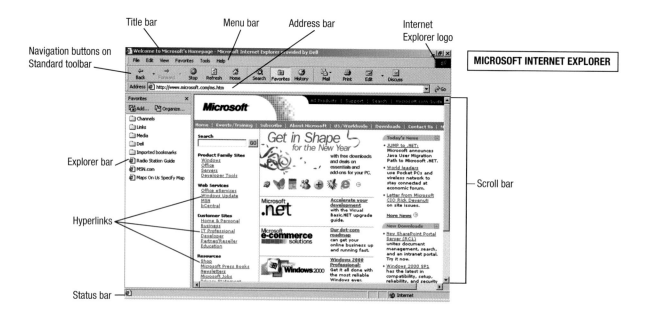

Title bar   Menu bar   Address bar   Internet Explorer logo

Navigation buttons on Standard toolbar

MICROSOFT INTERNET EXPLORER

Explorer bar

Hyperlinks

Status bar

Scroll bar

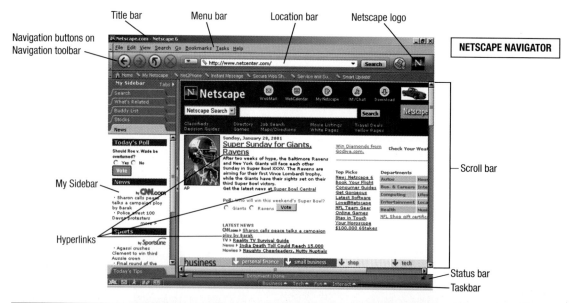

Title bar   Menu bar   Location bar   Netscape logo

Navigation buttons on Navigation toolbar

NETSCAPE NAVIGATOR

My Sidebar

Hyperlinks

Scroll bar

Status bar

Taskbar

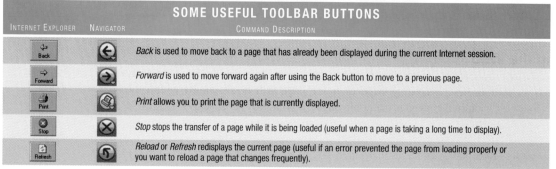

SOME USEFUL TOOLBAR BUTTONS

INTERNET EXPLORER	NAVIGATOR	COMMAND DESCRIPTION
Back	(back icon)	*Back* is used to move back to a page that has already been displayed during the current Internet session.
Forward	(forward icon)	*Forward* is used to move forward again after using the Back button to move to a previous page.
Print	(print icon)	*Print* allows you to print the page that is currently displayed.
Stop	(stop icon)	*Stop* stops the transfer of a page while it is being loaded (useful when a page is taking a long time to display).
Refresh	(reload icon)	*Reload* or *Refresh* redisplays the current page (useful if an error prevented the page from loading properly or you want to reload a page that changes frequently).

▶ **FIGURE 2-15**

Browsers. Microsoft Internet Explorer and Netscape Navigator have emerged as the two most widely used browsers. Both use similar interfaces and commands.

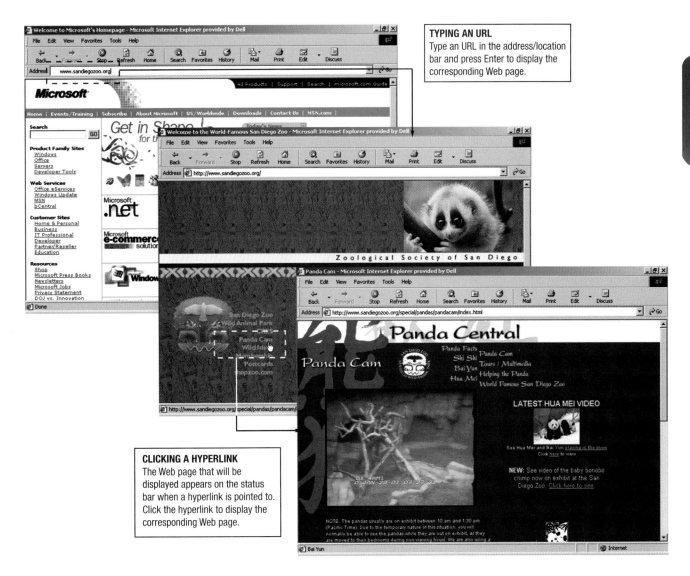

TYPING AN URL
Type an URL in the address/location bar and press Enter to display the corresponding Web page.

CLICKING A HYPERLINK
The Web page that will be displayed appears on the status bar when a hyperlink is pointed to. Click the hyperlink to display the corresponding Web page.

FIGURE 2-16

Using URLs and hyperlinks. Typing an URL in the address/location bar or clicking a hyperlink are the two most common ways to display a new Web page.

Using URLs and Hyperlinks

To change from the starting Web page to a new Web page, you can type the appropriate URL in the browser's *address bar* or *location bar* and press Enter (see Figure 2-16). You can either edit the existing URL or delete it and type a new one. Be sure to match the spelling, capitalization, and punctuation exactly. If you don't know the appropriate URL to type, you can search for an appropriate page, as discussed shortly.

If there is a hyperlink displayed for the page you would like to go to, simply click on the link. Remember, hyperlinks can be either text or image-based. If you are not sure if something on a page is a link or not, rest the mouse pointer on it for a moment. If it is a hyperlink, the pointer should change to indicate that it is a link, as shown in Figure 2-16. The URL for the new page is also displayed on the browser's status bar. Once you click the hyperlink, the appropriate page is displayed. To return to a previous page, click the Back button on your browser's toolbar. To print the current Web page, use the browser's Print button or select Print from the browser's File menu.

Things You May Encounter on a Web Page

You will encounter a variety of different objects on Web pages as you explore the World Wide Web. Though we can't go into an in-depth discussion on the various possible Web-page components here, it is good to be a familiar with the most common ones so you'll

web tutor

For a tutorial on using a Web browser, go to www.course.com/parker2002/ch2

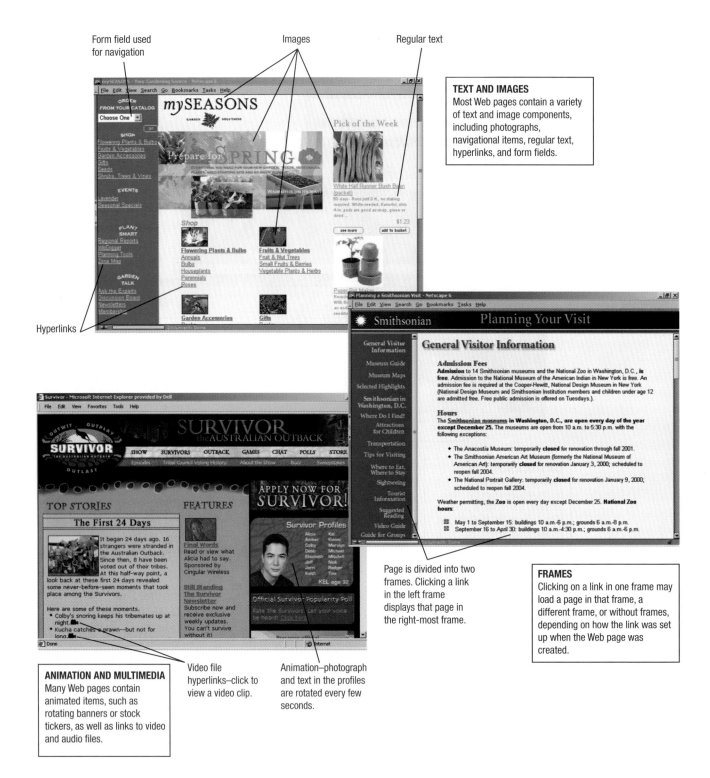

Form field used for navigation

Images

Regular text

TEXT AND IMAGES
Most Web pages contain a variety of text and image components, including photographs, navigational items, regular text, hyperlinks, and form fields.

Hyperlinks

Page is divided into two frames. Clicking a link in the left frame displays that page in the right-most frame.

FRAMES
Clicking on a link in one frame may load a page in that frame, a different frame, or without frames, depending on how the link was set up when the Web page was created.

ANIMATION AND MULTIMEDIA
Many Web pages contain animated items, such as rotating banners or stock tickers, as well as links to video and audio files.

Video file hyperlinks–click to view a video clip.

Animation–photograph and text in the profiles are rotated every few seconds.

▶ **FIGURE 2-17**
Common things that you may encounter on a Web page.

know how to deal with them as you encounter them. Some common things you may run into are listed next and illustrated in Figure 2-17.

▼ *Text and images.* Most Web pages contain text and text-based links. Images can include photographs, logos, navigational buttons and icons, and images to be downloaded. A single image that has specific areas individually linked to different Web pages is called an *image map*.

▼ *E-mail hyperlinks.* Hyperlinks to an e-mail address start an e-mail message to the person specified in the link. Sending e-mail using these types of links is discussed a little later in this chapter.

▼ *Form fields.* Many Web pages contain forms used to submit questions, feedback, registration, or order information. To complete a form, fill in the blanks and then click the Submit button that is usually located at the bottom of the form. Some Web pages contain a single form field for navigational purposes—choose the desired topic and then click the Go button or other navigation button next to the field, if necessary.

▼ *Frames.* Frames divide the browser window into separate areas, each containing a different Web page that scrolls individually. Frames are often used to keep a navigation bar always visible in one frame while the content of the other frames change as you click on hyperlinks in the navigation frame. The frame a new page will load in when a hyperlink is clicked is determined when the Web page is created. You can often resize the frames by dragging the frame borders with the mouse.

▼ *Animation.* The most common types of animation on a Web page are *animated GIFs* (a series of small images displayed one after another to simulate movement), *Java applets* (small programs executed by your browser, such as a scrolling marquee or stock ticker), and *Shockwave* or *Flash* applications (commonly used for games, interactive items, and other types of animation). Animation is discussed in more detail in Chapter 10.

▼ *Multimedia links.* Web pages can contain links to play or download audio and video files, in addition to downloadable images. Downloading files from a Web page is discussed later in this chapter. Multimedia is discussed more in Chapter 10.

Using Bookmarks and the History List

Once you have visited a Web page, the URL for that page is recorded in your browser's *history list.* To revisit a page, you can open the history list and select the page. How long a page stays in the history list depends on your browser settings. To more easily revisit pages on a regular basis, virtually all browsers include a *bookmark* or *favorites* feature, which lets you save the addresses of specific Web pages. Once a bookmark has been added (usually by selecting the appropriate option from your browser's Bookmark or Favorites menu when the desired page is displayed), the page can be redisplayed at future sessions by simply selecting the bookmark from the Bookmark or Favorites list. Figure 2-18 illustrates how to use bookmarks and the history list. Some browsers, such as Internet Explorer, can display the bookmark or favorites list in a separate pane on the screen so it is always available.

Searching the Web

While casual surfing is a popular Web pastime, people often turn to the Internet to find specific types of information. When you know generally what you want but don't know where to find it, one of your best options is to perform an *Internet search.* There are a number of special Web pages, called *search sites,* available to help you locate what you are looking for on the Internet, as well as *reference sites* to look up addresses, ZIP codes, maps, and other information. Many recent browsers also contain built-in search and reference capabilities.

further exploration

For links to further information about Internet search methods and strategies, go to www.course.com/parker2002/ch2

ADDING BOOKMARKS
If you are currently viewing a page for which you want to add a bookmark, select Add to Favorites or Add Current Page from the Favorites or Bookmarks pull-down menu to add the entry to the bottom of your bookmark list.

BOOKMARKS
A bookmarking feature lets you save the locations of your favorite Web sites so that you can easily return to them.

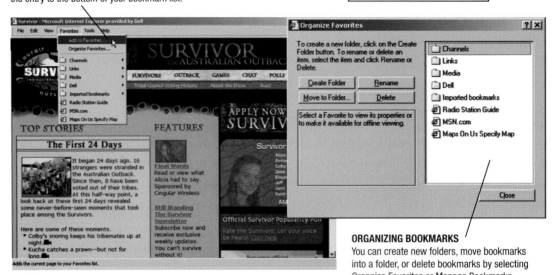

ORGANIZING BOOKMARKS
You can create new folders, move bookmarks into a folder, or delete bookmarks by selecting Organize Favorites or Manage Bookmarks from the Favorites or Bookmarks menu.

HISTORY LIST
A history-list feature displays the names and descriptions of sites you've most recently visited.

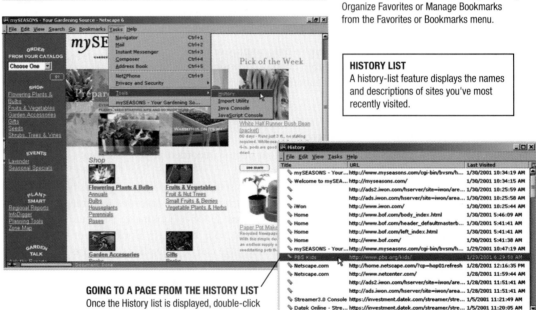

GOING TO A PAGE FROM THE HISTORY LIST
Once the History list is displayed, double-click a page to redisplay it in your browser.

> ◆ **FIGURE 2-18**
> **Using bookmarks and a history list.** In Internet Explorer, bookmarks are called favorites.

Browser Search Capabilities

To perform a simple search, type the name of the topic, company, or product you are looking for in your browser's address/location bar and press Enter (Internet Explorer users) or click the Search button (Netscape users), as illustrated in Figure 2-19. Most newer browsers then start their built-in search function, search for the terms that you typed, and display a list of possible Web pages (for browsers without built-in search capabilities, follow the steps in the next section to search using a search site instead). You can also open the browser's search function by selecting the Search tab on Netscape's My Sidebar or clicking Internet Explorer's Search button. Once the Search feature is open, type the key terms you'd like to search for in the appropriate box on the search pane.

KEYWORDS
Type keywords here and click the
Search button or press Enter.

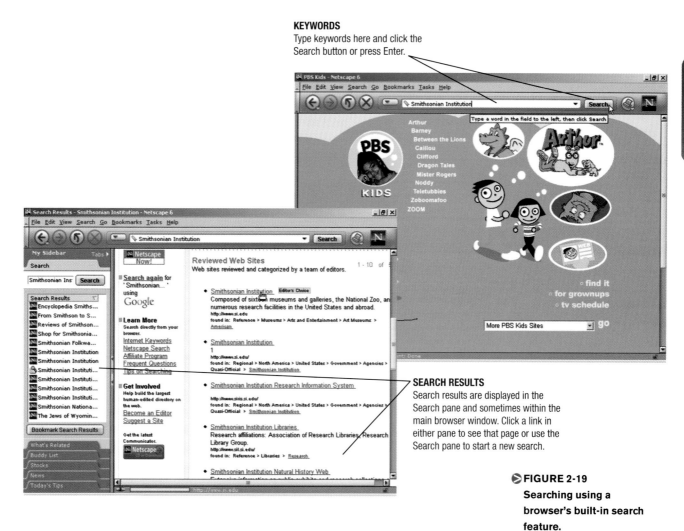

SEARCH RESULTS
Search results are displayed in the
Search pane and sometimes within the
main browser window. Click a link in
either pane to see that page or use the
Search pane to start a new search.

FIGURE 2-19
**Searching using a
browser's built-in search
feature.**

Search Sites

Though a browser's search function may be adequate for simple searches, for more complex searches you may want to use a **search site.** Most search sites use a *search engine*—a special software program—in conjunction with a huge database of Web pages to help visitors find Web pages that contain the information that they are seeking. These databases are usually updated automatically, though some use human editors to manually classify the Web pages according to content. To begin a search using a search site, type the URL for the desired search site in the address/location bar; most search sites—such as Yahoo!, Excite, Ask Jeeves, and Go.com—are available for use free of charge. These sites are also often referred to as *portal pages;* that is, pages that would like to be the starting page for your browser. Search sites usually allow two types of search operations: (1) typing in keywords or (2) selecting categories (see Figure 2-20).

The first type of search operation—using keywords—is similar to typing keywords in the browser's address/location bar. Once you type a keyword in the appropriate location and press Enter, the site's search engine returns a list of matching pages that can be viewed by clicking on the appropriate page's hyperlink. Just as with a browser search, you can usually type more than one keyword—most sites list the pages containing all of the words that you typed higher in the list of matching sites displayed. You can also usually use special operators, such as the plus key (+), minus key (−) and quotation marks (" ") for a

>**Search site.** A Web site that allows users to search for Web pages that match supplied keywords or fit in particular categories.

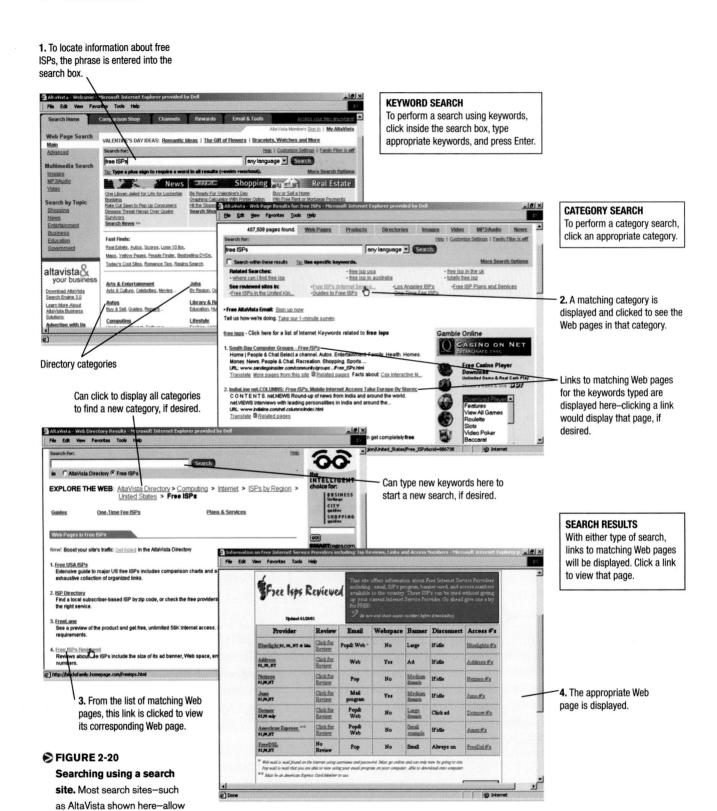

1. To locate information about free ISPs, the phrase is entered into the search box.

KEYWORD SEARCH
To perform a search using keywords, click inside the search box, type appropriate keywords, and press Enter.

CATEGORY SEARCH
To perform a category search, click an appropriate category.

2. A matching category is displayed and clicked to see the Web pages in that category.

Links to matching Web pages for the keywords typed are displayed here—clicking a link would display that page, if desired.

Directory categories

Can click to display all categories to find a new category, if desired.

Can type new keywords here to start a new search, if desired.

SEARCH RESULTS
With either type of search, links to matching Web pages will be displayed. Click a link to view that page.

3. From the list of matching Web pages, this link is clicked to view its corresponding Web page.

4. The appropriate Web page is displayed.

▶ **FIGURE 2-20**
Searching using a search site. Most search sites—such as AltaVista shown here—allow you to search by typing keywords, selecting categories, or using a combination of both.

more specific search, such as to indicate that you want to see only pages containing all of the keywords or see pages containing one keyword but not another. Usually search tips are available on each search site to explain the various search options for that site; look for a search help or search tips hyperlink on the site's home page. Further search techniques are covered in Chapter 9 of this text.

With the second type of search—selecting categories—a list of categories is displayed on the screen. After clicking on a category hyperlink, you are presented with a list of more specific subcategories for the main category that you selected, plus a list of matching Web pages. To reach more specific subcategories and matching Web pages, keep selecting categories. Whenever a list of appropriate Web pages is displayed, clicking a link displays that page. This type of search site is frequently called a *directory*.

As illustrated in Figure 2-20, many search sites allow you to use a combination of keywords and category selections. Often, starting with keywords and then selecting categories if appropriate Web pages are not immediately listed is an efficient way to utilize a search site.

Reference Sites and Web Site Searches

Many search sites include some reference functions to help you easily locate maps, addresses, and other reference information. There are also many specialty sites for these purposes, including online telephone directories, atlases, dictionaries, thesauruses, encyclopedias, mapping services, and so forth. To find such sites, check out the Web Guide window in the NET module or type the category of reference guide you are looking for (such as "ZIP code lookup" or "topographical maps") in a search site's search box.

A final type of searching to mention here is searching within a particular Web site. Many sites include a search option to allow visitors to locate documents on the site regarding a particular topic, or to locate particular products. Effective Web site search capability is becoming increasingly important as more and more buyers are shopping online for products—if visitors can't find a product on a site, they can't buy it.

When you are searching for products to buy online, special *shopping bots* or *shopping agents* can be used. These and other types of *intelligent agents* are discussed in the chapter Trend box. Online shopping and other types of popular Internet activities are covered in more detail in Chapter 9.

E-MAIL

Electronic mail, or **e-mail,** was one of the first applications to appear on the Internet and it remains the most widely used—Americans alone send billions of e-mail messages daily. If you are connected to the Internet, you can send an e-mail message to anyone who has an Internet e-mail address, regardless of whether or not they are on the Internet at the time you send the message. As illustrated in Figure 2-21, e-mail messages are routed from the sender's PC to his or her ISP, and then through the Internet to the receiver's ISP. When the receiver logs on to the Internet and requests his or her mail, the message is sent to that PC. To indicate what e-mail should be retrieved, the mail server being used and the appropriate e-mail address are specified in the browser's Options or Preferences screen. Some browsers allow multiple e-mail accounts (such as both a personal and school account) to be set up at one time. Others support only one, so the settings must be changed to check a different e-mail account when necessary.

Web-based e-mail—such as HotMail and Yahoo! Mail—works a little differently. Instead of specifying the e-mail settings in your browser, with Web-based e-mail you type your user name and password in the designated boxes on the mail service's Web site. This feature makes Web-based e-mail more flexible, since a user's e-mail can be accessed from any computer without changing the browser settings. Instead of being sent to your PC, Web-based e-mail is typically stored on the e-mail server and just viewed through the mail service's Web site. Web-based e-mail is a popular option for travelers, students, and other users who switch between computers frequently.

>**Electronic mail (e-mail).** Electronic messages sent from one user to another over the Internet or other network.

trend

Shopping Bots and Other Types of Intelligent Agents

Benevolent Servants or Potential Social Problem?

Imagine arriving at work each morning to find your PC booting up as soon as you walk in your office building. On the screen, you see today's agenda, a list of phone calls and e-mails that came in since you left your desk last night, and a file of news items culled from the morning paper neatly organized in a folder. These events show intelligent agents have been busy to save you time and attention that you can devote to more useful tasks.

Intelligent agents (often called *bots,* which is short for "ro*bots*") are small programs that perform such tasks for a computer user as retrieving and delivering information and automating repetitive tasks. Put another way, intelligent agents are digital servants. The concept of intelligent agents is not new; it originated in the 1950s with the evolution of the field of artificial intelligence (AI). What's more, you are probably using agent software today without even knowing it. Intelligent agents are often built into operating systems, e-mail programs, Web browsers, and other products.

Today's agents are commonly used to search the contents of multiple databases. One example is the *shopping bot* or *shopping agent* available on the Web, such as mySimon (see image). These bot programs search through thousands of online stores to find the best price on the product that you specify. Other bots found on the Web include those that search for stocks that meet the buying criteria you specify, those that search through news to retrieve news items of interest to you, those used to create customized automated replies to e-mails, and those used by search sites to locate and classify new Web pages.

Today's use notwithstanding, the golden age of intelligent agents lies in the future. Newer and upcoming applications for bots include bots that recognize natural spoken language, such as a car stereo bot that can under-

stand and correctly respond to the direction "I'd like to listen to some classical music, please." Another exciting use is in association with a three-dimensional animated image on a Web site, such as a virtual salesperson or customer service representative. These type of bots—sometimes referred to as *virbots* (for "*vir*tual ro*bot*")—will be able to respond both verbally and with appropriate physical gestures to simulate having a conversation with a human.

The potential vast use of intelligent agents leads to some very important social concerns. Will companies regularly rely on intelligent agents to monitor every action or keystroke employees perform? How many types of workers might intelligent agents eventually replace? Will the use of agents to adjust pricing of products to reflect the price at competitors' Web sites lead to price fixing? Should agents be allowed to automatically carry out tasks like supplying intravenous medicine to hospital patients? Can sensitive databases protect their contents from hostile agents? Questions like these are sure to merit serious debate as the twenty-first century unfolds.

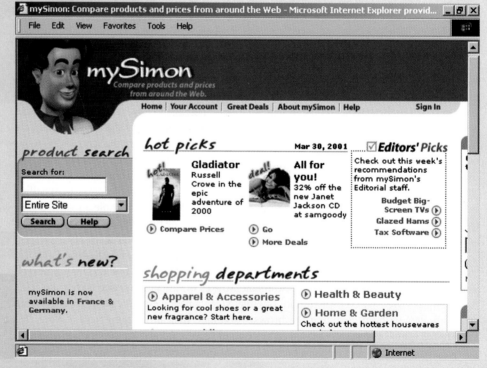

Okay, but where can I buy . . . ? Agent sites like mySimon will search the Web to find the lowest price on items for sale online.

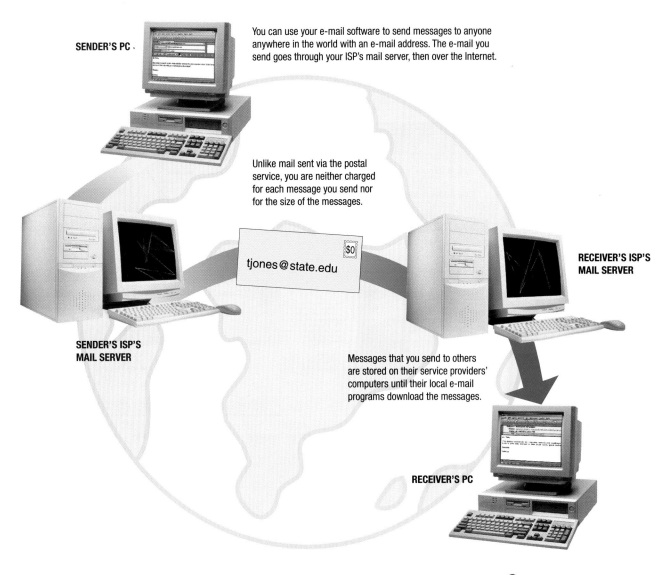

You can use your e-mail software to send messages to anyone anywhere in the world with an e-mail address. The e-mail you send goes through your ISP's mail server, then over the Internet.

SENDER'S PC

Unlike mail sent via the postal service, you are neither charged for each message you send nor for the size of the messages.

tjones@state.edu

$0

SENDER'S ISP'S MAIL SERVER

RECEIVER'S ISP'S MAIL SERVER

Messages that you send to others are stored on their service providers' computers until their local e-mail programs download the messages.

RECEIVER'S PC

FIGURE 2-21
How e-mail works.

Sending E-Mail

Virtually all browsers today have a built-in e-mail program that you can use to send and receive e-mail messages. Businesses sometimes use a different e-mail program, such as *Eudora* or *Pegasus Mail,* but most e-mail programs closely resemble each other. Internet Explorer users often use *Microsoft Outlook* or *Microsoft Outlook Express;* Netscape users typically use *Netscape Mail.*

If there is an appropriate e-mail hyperlink (such as sales@abc.com) displayed on a Web page, just click it to launch your e-mail program and begin an e-mail message to that person. If not, follow these steps to send an e-mail message (refer to Figure 2-22).

1. Open the mail program (Netscape users: Click the envelope icon 📧 on the left edge of the taskbar to open the Netscape Mail window, then click on the New Msg toolbar button; Internet Explorer users: Click the Mail toolbar button and select New Message).

2. At the Compose or New Message window, type the e-mail address of the person you are writing in the To: box.

3. Type a short title of the message in the Subject: box.

FIGURE 2-22
Sending and receiving e-mail.

SENDING E-MAIL
E-mail messages can be started either by using an e-mail hyperlink or by opening your e-mail program and clicking New Message, New Mail, or New Msg.

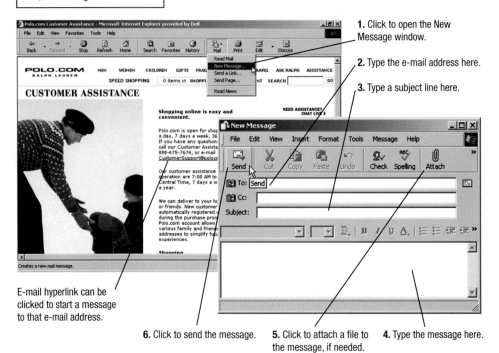

1. Click to open the New Message window.

2. Type the e-mail address here.

3. Type a subject line here.

E-mail hyperlink can be clicked to start a message to that e-mail address.

6. Click to send the message.   **5.** Click to attach a file to the message, if needed.   **4.** Type the message here.

RECEIVING E-MAIL
E-mail messages are retrieved to your Inbox where they can be read, replied to, printed, filed or deleted.

Available mail folders; the Inbox folder is selected.

1. The e-mail window was opened by clicking the Mail button and selecting Read Mail.

2. Click a message to display it.

3. Selected message is displayed here.

4. Type the message itself in the message area.

5. If you want to attach a digital photograph, Word document, or any other type of file to your e-mail message, click the Attach button and select the appropriate file.

6. Click on the Send button to send the message.

When sending a message, you can send the message to more than one person by typing more than one e-mail address in the To: or Cc: boxes. Another common feature used when sending mail is an *address book*. An address-book feature lets you store the e-mail addresses of friends and associates along with a short nickname for each person. Once someone is in your address book, you can type his or her name or nickname instead of their full e-mail address; their e-mail address will automatically be filled in for you. To add someone who sent you an e-mail message to your address book, you usually can right-click on the message and choose "Add Sender to Address Book" from the displayed menu.

Receiving E-Mail

To check for new e-mail messages or to reread an old e-mail message (refer again to Figure 2-22):

1. Open your mail program (Netscape users: Click the envelope icon ✉ on the left edge of the task bar; Internet Explorer users: Click the Mail toolbar button and select Read Mail).

2. Type your e-mail password, if requested.

3. Click the Get Msg or Send/Recv toolbar button, if necessary.

When you check your mail, your new e-mail messages are retrieved and placed in your Inbox folder. Clicking a message displays it in the message area, as shown in Figure 2-22. To display an e-mail message in a new window instead of at the bottom of the screen, you can usually double-click the message. Once an e-mail message is displayed, it can be printed, replied to, forwarded to someone else, filed into a different folder, or deleted using your e-mail program's toolbar buttons.

Managing E-Mail

When you send e-mail, copies of the messages that you send are stored in a folder named Sent, Sent Items, or something similar so that you can read them or resend them, if necessary. These messages remain there, and your retrieved e-mail messages remain in your Inbox folder, until you delete them or move them into a different folder (you can create new folders in either program using the mail program's File menu and then drag messages into the desired folder). Once an e-mail message is deleted, it is moved into a special folder for deleted items (called Trash in Netscape Mail and Deleted Items in Outlook Express)—you should clean out these folders periodically by selecting Empty Trash from Netscape's File menu or Empty 'Deleted Items' Folder from Outlook Express' Edit menu to free up space on your hard drive.

Mailing Lists, Newsgroups, Chat, and Instant Messaging

Variations of conventional e-mail include mailing lists, newsgroups, chat, and instant messaging. A *mailing list* is a topical discussion group that communicates through shared e-mail messages. To participate, an individual needs to sign up or *subscribe* to the list. Then, when an e-mail message is sent to the mailing list, it is automatically sent to all subscribers. Some mailing lists are set up to distribute information in just one direction (such as news or product information from a company or organization); these mailing lists are sometimes called *newsletters*. Other mailing lists can be set up so that subscribers can both send and receive messages to and from the mailing list; a common example is a mailing list set up for a college class so that class members can easily communicate and participate in online discussions.

A *newsgroup* is similar, but the messages are not sent to each individual's e-mail address. Instead, the messages are sent to the newsgroup and arranged by topic or *thread*. Newsgroup messages (which usually look similar to e-mail messages) can be viewed when a subscriber opens their *newsreader* (often incorporated into e-mail programs with a special

further exploration

For links to further information about newsgroups, go to www.course.com/parker2002/ch2

inside the industry

Emoticons: Expressing Yourself with Your PC

One disadvantage of written communication as compared to spoken or in-person conversations is that the emotions of the individuals are not easily conveyed. When someone makes a derogatory comment while smiling, you can tell that the person is joking. When someone writes a derogatory comment in an e-mail or newsgroup message, it is likely to be taken seriously.

To overcome this, *emoticons*—short for *emotional icons* and also called "smileys"—are used. These symbols are created with keyboard symbols and are used to represent a smiling face (hence the name), a wink, a sad face, and so on. In addition, shorthand acronyms have also come into common use. A sampling of some of the most common of these that you may want to include in your e-mail messages is listed next (turn your head to the side when viewing the emoticons.)

Emoticons		Acronyms	
Symbol	**Meaning**	**Acronym**	**Stands For**
:-)	Smile	ROTFL	"Rolling on the floor laughing"
:-(	Frown	LOL	"Laughing out loud"
;-)	Wink	BTW	"By the way"
:-D	Laugh	IMHO	"In my humble opinion"
:-P	Sticking out	TTFN	"Ta ta for now"
	tongue	BTDT	"Been there, done that"
:->	Sarcastic	BRB	"Be right back"
>:-<	Angry		

folder designed to contain the newsgroup messages) or opens the appropriate newsgroup Web page. Participants can either start a new thread by sending a new message to the newsgroup, or can reply to a message to have their response grouped with the other responses for that thread.

Chat refers to a facility that enables people to engage in interactive conversations over the Internet. Most chat sessions are typed on the keyboard, but—unlike e-mail and newsgroups—chat participants must be online at the same time and read each other's messages in *real time* (at the same time they are written). Chat sessions can be private and reserved only for users who know the proper password to participate, or open to anyone. Growing applications of chat include live online product support and chatting with celebrities.

Internet telephony is a form of chat that is growing in popularity. This involves placing telephone calls over the Internet, usually either from your PC to the recipient's PC or from your PC to the recipient's telephone. Some systems allow only one person to speak at a time (similar to a family radio); other systems enable people to converse just as they would over their regular phones.

Instant messaging is a popular variation of chat in which you are informed when someone on your *buddy list*—a list containing the names of friends and associates that you specify—are online; when they are online, you can send them a message that immediately appears on their screen (see Figure 2-23). You can then have a real–time typed conversation.

As shown in Figure 2-23, some users like to use special smiley-faces and other symbols to spice up their e-mail and other online written communications. For a brief look at these and some frequently used abbreviations, see the Inside the Industry box.

▶ FIGURE 2-23

Instant messaging. Instant messages appear on the screen in real time and are usually sent to and received from people on your "buddy list."

Netiquette

A special etiquette—referred to as *netiquette*—has evolved on the Internet to guide online behavior. Most netiquette has to do with written communication, such as electronic mail,

A MINIGUIDE TO NETIQUETTE
Read the FAQs *FAQs* are frequently asked questions and answers to them. Reading a FAQ list will help you to avoid common mistakes in protocol that could disrupt a newsgroup or waste a company contact's time answering a question already covered in the FAQs.
Lurk, before you leap *Lurking* refers to observing a newsgroup's activities for a period of time to get the particular spin of the group, before actively participating.
Watch what you say Things that you say or write online can be interpreted as being sexist, racist, ethnocentric, xenophobic, or in just general bad taste. Also check spelling and grammar—nobody likes wading through poorly written materials.
Avoid flame mail While we're on the subject of being objectional, try to avoid *flame mail*—caustic or inflammatory remarks directed toward certain people in the group. That includes taking part in *flame wars*, in which several people participate in being jerks.
Avoid spam mail Don't send *spam mail*—unsolicated bulk e-mails—the Internet equivalent of junk mail.
Don't shout SHOUTING REFERS TO TYPING YOUR ENTIRE E-MAIL MESSAGE USING CAPITAL LETTERS. USE CAPITAL LETTERS ONLY FOR EMPHASIZING A FEW WORDS.
Choose good titles The first thing that people read in your e-mail message or newsgroup posting is what will catch their interest or turn them off. Titling messages appropriately (such as "Question regarding MP3 downloads") is much better than a vague choice (such as "Question").

◗ FIGURE 2-24
Netiquette guidelines.

newsgroups, and chat. A good rule of thumb is always to be polite, considerate of others, and nonoffensive. This holds true whether you are asking a question via a company's e-mail address, posting a newsgroup message, or chatting with a friend. When the communication involves business, you should also be careful with your grammar and spelling to avoid embarrassing yourself. Many users are much more casual with e-mail than with more formal communications, but you should be professional. Some more specific guidelines are listed in Figure 2-24.

DOWNLOADING AND INSTALLING PLUG-INS AND OTHER FILES

When you explore the Web, it is common to run across a Web page that contains a hyperlink for **downloading** (copying) a file to your computer. Common types of files downloaded from the Internet include *zipped* (compressed) files; *PDF (Portable Document Format)* files; image files; music and video files; executable program files; files in a common application format, such as Microsoft Word or Excel; and *browser plug-ins*.

A **browser plug-in** is a program that updates your browser with features that it currently lacks. One widely used plug-in package, Adobe Acrobat Reader, enables your browser to view pages that have been formatted as Adobe Acrobat PDF files. PDF files display documents more or less exactly the way they appear in print and cannot be edited with the Acrobat Reader program. They are frequently used for financial statements, government forms, and other published documents. Other popular types of plug-in packages include those that allow you to view video and hear audio files downloaded from Web pages, and those used to view Web page animation. If the page you are viewing requires a plug-in that you lack, a message is usually displayed containing a link to download the plug-in file. A list of some widely used browser plug-ins appears in Figure 2-25. Most plug-ins are available free of charge.

web tutor

For a tutorial on downloading files, go to www.course.com/ parker2002/ch2

>**Downloading.** The process of copying a file from one computer to another over the Internet or other network. >**Browser plug-in.** A program that supplies a browser with additional capabilities.

⊚ **FIGURE 2-25**
Common browser
plug-ins.

Plug-In	Publisher	Description
Acrobat Reader	Adobe Systems	View documents similar to the way they appear in print.
Beatnik Player	Beatnik	Listen to high-quality interactive Web audio in a variety of audio formats.
Cosmo Player	Cosmo Sotware	Experience interactive, animated 3D virtual reality applications written in VRML.
Download Acelerator Plus	SpeedBit	Download files faster with resumable download support.
Flash Player	Macromedia	Experience Flash animations.
Internet Postage	Stamps.com	Print postage directly on your envelopes or mailing labels.
Liquid Player	Liquid Audio	Play CD-quality music over the Internet. Includes support for MP3 files.
Live3D	Netscape	Experience 3D virtual-reality worlds writtem in VRML.
Net2Phone	Net2Phone	Make inexpensive long-distance phone calls from your PC.
Quick Time	Apple	View QuickTime videos and other types of multimedia.
RealPlayer	RealNetworks	Play streaming audio and video files, as well as live audio and video events presented over the Web.
Shockwave	Macromedia	Experience Shockwave animations.

further exploration

For links to further information about plug-ins, go to www.course.com/ parker2002/ch2

Downloading Files

To download a file from a Web page, just click the appropriate hyperlink (see Figure 2-26) and indicate where you would like the file to be stored (usually it's on your desktop or in an easy-to-find folder, such as My Documents or My Download Files, on your hard drive). Depending on the size of the file and the speed of your computer and Internet connection, downloading a file can take anywhere from a few seconds to several hours. If the file you are downloading is to be viewed with a plug-in and the appropriate plug-in is installed, some files open automatically in your browser instead of being downloaded to your hard drive first, as discussed in the next section.

Using Downloaded Files

After a file has finished downloading, you need to find the file and open it. Usually one of the Windows file management programs—My Computer or Windows Explorer—is used to open downloaded files. The My Computer program is shown in Figure 2-26; using this program is covered in more detail in Chapter 6.

Once the downloaded file has been located and opened, if it is a plug-in file or other executable (program) file, the installation process usually starts automatically (see Figure 2-26). Once the file has been installed, it is usually fine to delete the downloaded installation file from your hard drive. If the downloaded file is not a program or plug-in file, it will be opened in the appropriate program; some possibilities are listed next.

▼ *Zipped (.zip)* files are compressed for faster downloading and are opened with a de-compression program, such as WinZip.

▼ *PDF (.pdf)* files are opened using the *Adobe Acrobat Reader* program or plug-in.

▼ *Image (.gif, .jpg, .tif, .bmp, etc.)* files are opened with either a browser, image viewer, or image editor, depending on the type of file and the programs available on your computer.

▼ *Music (.wav, .mp3, etc.)* files are opened with an appropriate media player, such as Windows Media player, or an appropriate plug-in, such as RealPlayer or WinAmp.

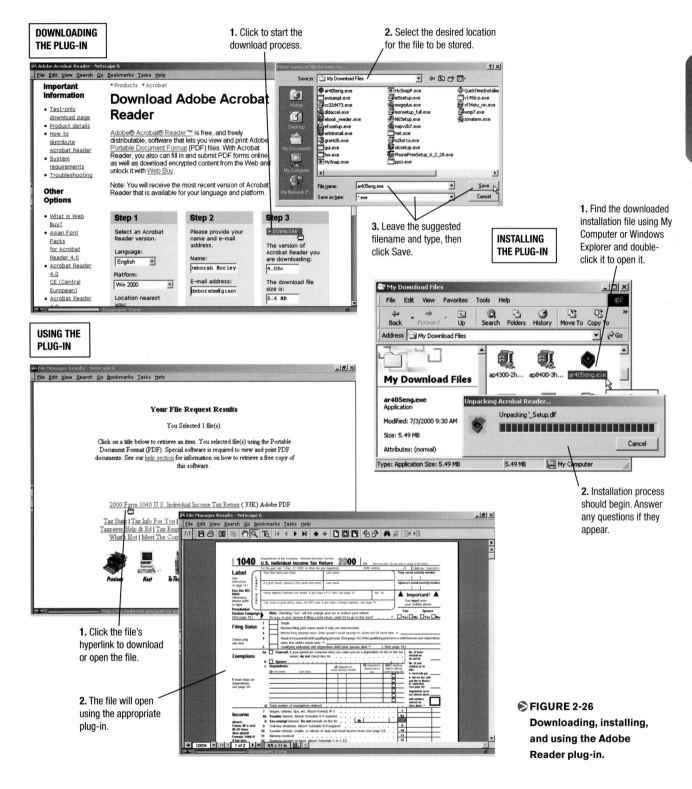

FIGURE 2-26
Downloading, installing, and using the Adobe Reader plug-in.

▼ *Video (.avi, .mov,* etc.*)* files are opened with an appropriate media player, such as Windows Media player or MusicMatch, or an appropriate plug-in, such as RealPlayer or QuickTime.

▼ *Executable (.exe)* automatically execute (run) when opened. They usually either start the program or start the installation process for the downloaded program.

▼ *Application (.doc, .xls,* etc.*)* files exist in a common application format, such as Microsoft Word *(.doc)* or Microsoft Excel *(.xls)* and are opened in their respective programs.

SUMMARY

Personal computers today are much more easy to use and less intimidating than in the past. Improvements such as graphical user interfaces have contributed to this trend. After learning how to start up and use a PC, the first application to be learned is frequently how to use a Web browser.

STARTING YOUR COMPUTER: THE BOOT PROCESS

Chapter Objective 1:
Explain what happens when you start up a computer.

The **boot** process occurs when a computer is powered up. During the boot process, quick diagnostics and other utilities may run, and then the computer's **operating system** is loaded into memory. The operating system is a collection of programs that manages a computer's activities.

USING THE WINDOWS OPERATING SYSTEM

Chapter Objective 2:
Identify common elements of the Windows graphical user interface (GUI) and their functions.

Microsoft Windows is the most common operating system for IBM and compatible PCs at the present time. As with most programs today, it uses a **graphical user interface (GUI).** GUIs typically display information in rectangular **windows** and more than one window can be displayed on the **desktop** at a time. Other common features are **menus** and **toolbars** from which commands may be selected; **icons** or small pictures that represent programs or documents; **dialog boxes,** which are used to supply necessary information before a command is executed; and **scroll bars,** which are used to move through the information available within a window.

Chapter Objective 3:
Demonstrate how to open a program and manipulate open program windows.

The *Start* menu is the main menu for the Windows operating system and can be used to start programs. Desktop icons can also be used to start programs. Once a window has been opened, it can be resized using the window's *border* or the *Minimize, Maximize,* and *Restore* buttons; moved using the window's *title bar;* and closed using the Windows *Close* button, as necessary.

After a short period of inactivity, many PCs automatically go into a standby mode. Computers can be shut down when necessary using the Shut Down option on the Start menu.

USING THE INTERNET AND WORLD WIDE WEB

Chapter Objective 4:
Explain what the Internet and World Wide Web are and how computers, people, and Web pages are identified on the Internet.

The **Internet** is a worldwide collection of networks. One resource available through the Internet is the **World Wide Web (WWW)**—an enormous collection of **Web pages** located on **Web servers.** The starting page for a **Web site** (a related group of Web pages) is called the **home page** for that site. Web pages are viewed with a **Web browser,** such as *Microsoft Internet Explorer* or *Netscape Navigator.*

To access the Internet, an **Internet service provider (ISP)** is used. After signing up with an ISP, you are assigned a **user name.** This name, used in conjunction with the ISP's **domain name,** determines your **e-mail address**—the address that others will use to send you e-mail messages. In addition to a unique domain name, computers available through the Internet also have a unique numerical **IP address.** One other type of **Internet address** is the **URL** or **uniform resource locator** used to identify Web pages. Most Web pages begin with *http://* and end with a top-level domain such as *.com, .edu,* or *.gov.*

Once you are connected to the Internet and have opened your browser, Web pages can be displayed either by clicking on a hyperlink or by typing the appropriate URL in the browser's address/location bar. You can also create *bookmarks* or use the *History List* to return to favorite Web pages more easily.

Chapter Objective 5:
Demonstrate how to access a Web page on the Internet and discuss how to search for Web pages containing specific information.

To locate specific information on the Internet, an *Internet search* can be performed using either your browser's built-in search capabilities or a **search site.** Search sites typically employ search engines to help you find appropriate Web pages by entering keywords or by selecting directory categories; they also frequently contain handy reference tools, as well.

E-MAIL

Electronic mail (e-mail) can be used to send electronic messages to other Internet users. Messages can be sent and received using your browser's e-mail program. Once e-mail messages are received, they can be printed, forwarded to another user, filed into an appropriate folder, or deleted. When messages are sent, they can include attached files in virtually any file format.

Tools related to e-mail include *mailing lists* (used to send e-mail messages to a specific predetermined group of people); *newsgroups* (locations where messages about a particular topic are posted and can be read online); and *chat* and *instant messaging* (for live, real-time message exchanges). Special etiquette rules for online behavior are referred to as *netiquette.*

Chapter Objective 6:
Explain how e-mail can be used to send and receive messages to and from other Internet users.

DOWNLOADING AND INSTALLING PLUG-INS AND OTHER FILES

Copying a file from an Internet computer to your PC is called **downloading** a file. When files are downloaded, they are either stored somewhere on your hard drive, or are opened automatically using a **browser plug-in** program. Plug-ins are commonly used to view video files, hear audio files, view PDF files, and display animated items.

To download a file, usually a hyperlink on a Web page is clicked. To install a downloaded file, the file is opened using a file management program, such as My Computer or Windows Explorer. If the downloaded file is not an installation program, it will be opened in the appropriate viewing program.

Chapter Objective 7:
Describe how plug-ins and other types of files can be downloaded from the Internet and installed on a computer.

KEY TERMS

Instructions: Match each key term on the left with the definition on the right that fits best.

1. desktop

2. electronic mail
(e-mail)

3. icon

4. Internet

5. Internet address

6. Internet service
provider (ISP)

7. menu

8. Microsoft Windows

9. operating system

10. search site

11. toolbar

12. uniform resource
locator (URL)

13. Web browser

14. Web page

15. Web site

16. window

17. World Wide Web
(WWW)

_____ A document, usually containing hyperlinks to other documents, located on a Web server and available through the World Wide Web.

_____ A program used to view Web pages.

_____ A rectangular area appearing on the screen of a computer using a GUI operating system such as Windows that can contain icons, documents, and other information.

_____ A related group of Web pages usually belonging to an organization or individual.

_____ A set of icons or buttons displayed horizontally or vertically on the screen that can be used to issue commands to the computer.

_____ A set of text-based options that can be displayed on the screen to enable the user to issue commands to the computer.

_____ A small picture or other type of graphical image that represents a program or document and invokes some action when selected.

_____ A Web site that allows users to search for Web pages that match supplied keywords or fit in particular categories.

_____ An address, usually beginning with _http://,_ that uniquely identifies a Web page on the Internet.

_____ An organization that provides access to the Internet.

_____ Electronic messages sent from one user to another over the Internet or other network.

_____ The background work area displayed on the screen when using Microsoft Windows.

_____ The collection of Web pages available through the Internet.

_____ The largest and most widely used computer network, linking millions of computers all over the world.

_____ The main piece of systems software that enables the computer to manage the activities and resources under its control, run application programs, and interact with the user.

_____ The most common operating system for IBM and IBM-compatible PCs.

_____ What identifies a computer, person, or Web page on the Internet. Can be an IP address, domain name, e-mail address, or URL.

Self-Quiz

True/False

Instructions: Circle **T** if the statement is true or **F** if the statement is false.

T F **1.** A box displayed when more information about the selected command is required is called a menu.

T F **2.** When the mouse pointer changes to a ⬉ , you are ready to resize the window.

T F **3.** The World Wide Web is the collection of Web pages available through the Internet.

T F **4.** An example of an IP address would be *microsoft.com.*

T F **5.** It isn't possible to tell if a word or image on a Web page is a hyperlink until you click it.

Completion

Instructions: Answer the following questions.

6. In most Windows applications, the Print command would be located on the _____ menu.

7. When a group of _____ appear in a dialog box, only one in the group may be selected.

8. The program used to display Web pages is called a(n) _____.

9. To save the URL for a page you might like to revisit, you should create a(n) _____ for that page.

10. A(n) _____ is a program used to supplement your browser to give it additional capabilities.

Exercises

1. Match each icon with the appropriate name.

a.   c. ▣

b. ▢   d.

_____ Toolbar button.
_____ Minimize button.
_____ Maximize button.
_____ Command button.

2. List three things that commonly are located on the Windows desktop.

3. On a dialog box, to ask which printer you would like to use when printing a document, which type of dialog box component would be the most appropriate? Why?

4. Assume that you need to find information about the history of the New York stock exchange for a research paper. List two sets of keywords you could use when using a search site to find appropriate Web pages.

5. If a computer manufacturer called Apex created a home page for the Web, what would its URL likely be? Also, supply an appropriate e-mail address for yourself, assuming that you are employed by that company.

Short Answer/ Research

1. **The Cold Boot** When you start a computer that has been shut down, it has to perform what is generally referred to as a "cold boot." This process is fairly straightforward and involves a few basic procedures. For this project, research what is involved in the boot process (beyond what is presented in the text) and observe what information is actually displayed on the screen during this process. In addition, determine what a "warm boot" is, and why you might prefer this option to a "cold boot" after a system error has occurred. At the conclusion of your research, prepare a one-page summary of your findings and submit it to your instructor.

2. **Gateway to the Internet** In order to access the Internet at home, you need to select an Internet service provider (ISP), a type of connection, and, perhaps, a level of service. For this project, research which providers service your area, what types of connections they support (such as conventional dial-up, ISDN, DSL, cable, or satellite), and what levels of service they offer. You may wish to start this research with your local telephone and cable-TV company, but don't overlook other local companies that may be listed in your telephone book or that advertise on TV or the radio. At the conclusion of your research, prepare a one-page summary of your findings and submit it to your instructor. Be sure to include the cost and speed for each service, any limitations on e-mail (such as number of e-mail addresses, mailbox size, or size of attachments), as well as indicate whether or not each service ties up your telephone line.

3. **Surf the Web** Once your Web browser is open and you are connected to the Internet, you can explore a sequence of Web pages by simply clicking hyperlinks, as described in the chapter. This form of exploration is often referred to as "surfing the Web." For this project, surf the Web and find a definition for each of the following Internet-related terms: *banner, cookie, spider, spam, hit, firewall, lurker, 404 error, shopping bot,* and *hit.* At the conclusion of your research, prepare a one-page summary of your findings and submit it to your instructor. Be sure to cite the source (Web page URL) of each definition in your summary.

   Hint: You may wish to use an online technical encyclopedia, such as webopedia.com or whatis.com.

Hands On

4. **Your E-Mail Counts** E-mail, short for electronic mail, allows you to send and receive messages and files over the Internet. This form of communication is one of the most popular and practical uses of the Internet. For this project, locate the e-mail address for each of your local congressional representatives and send one of them an e-mail message about a topic of concern to you. Some possible computer-related topics include the taxation of goods and services sold over the Internet, potential upcoming legislation that might regulate the content or your freedom of expression over the Internet, and criminal activities that occur over the Internet.

At the conclusion of this task, print a copy of the e-mail you sent to your local representatives as documentation of your efforts (look in your Sent or Sent Items folder), and submit it to your instructor.

> **Hint:** Web sites such as www.congress.org (see the following image) can be useful to look up your congressional representatives and e-mail addresses.

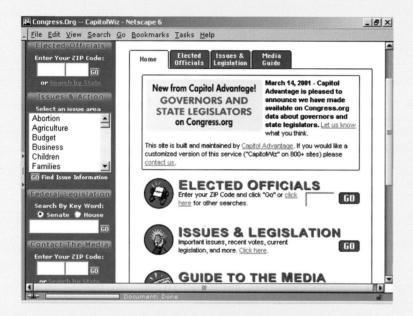

5. **A Customized Desktop** The Windows desktop is where Windows users interface with that operating system while using their computer. The appearance of the desktop can be easily customized to match the user's preferences. For this project, investigate what properties of the Windows desktop can be customized and select the configuration you like best. Submit this project to your instructor in the form of a short paper, not more than two pages in length.

> **Hint:** Open the Display icon in the Control Panel (accessible through the Settings option of the Start menu) and experiment with the options on the various tabs. Be sure to record the original settings before experimenting so you can return the desktop to its prior configuration when you have completed this project.

6. **Browser Plug-Ins** As discussed in this chapter, a browser plug-in is a program that extends the capabilities of your browser. Plug-ins can generally be downloaded for free and installed in your Web browser by simply clicking the appropriate link at the developer's Web site. Companies like Adobe, Macromedia, and RealNetworks have developed some of the most popular plug-ins. For this project, select one application that interests you that frequently requires a plug-in (such as listening to audio files, viewing video files, experiencing virtual reality (VRML) worlds, viewing animation, etc.) and investigate what plug-ins are available for your selected application. Be sure to identify the name of each plug-in, the URL where it can be downloaded, the price (if applicable), the company that developed the plug-in, and the advantages for using that plug-in. Submit this project to your instructor in the form of a short paper, not more than two pages in length. Be sure to include your recommendation for a plug-in for your selected application.

Writing About Computers

7. **The "Goo-ey" Interface** A program interface that takes advantage of a computer's graphical capabilities is generally referred to as a graphical user interface (GUI), pronounced "goo-ey." The first graphical user interface was designed in the 1970s and was offered as an alternative to text-based interfaces in the 1980s. The initial idea and evolution of this interface has been dominated by three major companies and involves some interesting stock options, accusations, and legal proceedings. For this project, form a group to research the history of the GUI interface, the result of the somewhat contentious legal proceedings surrounding it, the main GUI players today, and why this type of interface has become so popular on desktop computers. Your group should submit your findings to your instructor in the form of a short paper, not more than three pages in length.

Presentation/ Demonstration

8. **Netiquette** As discussed in the chapter, netiquette is essentially the etiquette of the Internet and World Wide Web. It is constantly evolving and generally describes the social conventions and guidelines for polite, inoffensive, written communications that take place over the Internet. For this project, research the topic of netiquette and present some of the rules or guidelines, and the most common netiquette errors. Be sure to include some examples from a newsgroup or other type of online discussion group and at least five additional emoticons or abbreviations not included in the chapter's Inside the Industry box. The presentation should not exceed 5 minutes and should make use of one or more presentation aids such as the chalkboard, handouts, overhead transparencies, or computer-based slide presentation format. You may be asked to submit a summary of the presentation to your instructor.

9. **Shareware, Freeware, Commercial, or Open-Source Software?** Downloading software, as described in the chapter, is as easy as clicking the appropriate hyperlink and indicating where you would like to store the software. The types of software you can download from the Internet are generally categorized as shareware, freeware, or commercial software. In addition, some software is labeled "open-source software." For this project, form a group to research downloadable software. Your group should prepare a short presentation of your findings, including an explanation of the guidelines or copyright protections that should be taken into consideration before using each type of software. Be sure to provide at least three examples of popular software in each category you discuss. Your presentation should also include a discussion of any potential risks associated with downloading software from the Internet. The presentation should not exceed 10 minutes and should make use of one or more presentation aids such as the chalkboard, handouts, overhead transparencies, or computer-based slide presentation format. Your group may be asked to submit a summary of the presentation to your instructor.

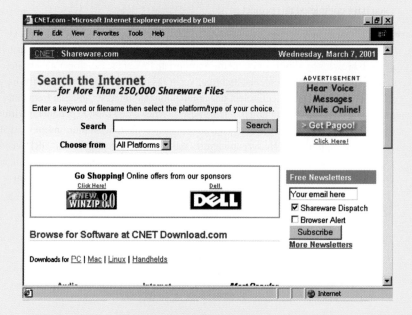

10. **E-Mail Options** If you have access to the Internet, you can exchange electronic messages, including files, with any other person on the Internet. This exchange of electronic correspondence can be accomplished using your computer equipment, or using a PC available through your school, public library, cybercafé, or other public location. For an e-mail account, you may have the option of using your home or school e-mail account, or a Web-based e-mail service such as HotMail or Yahoo! Mail. For this project, form a group to research what e-mail options are available for the students at your school and surrounding community. Your group should prepare a short presentation of your findings including a brief summary of the free Web-based e-mail services available, and the most common features used when sending, receiving, and managing your e-mail. In addition, your group should identify any potential benefits or limitations of using a free Web-based e-mail service. This presentation should not exceed 10 minutes and should make use of one or more presentation aids such as the chalkboard, handouts, overhead transparencies, or computer-based slide presentation format. You may be asked to submit a summary of the presentation to your instructor.

Interactive Discussion

11. **Digital-Only Materials** Traditional print media like newspapers, magazines, and books are costly to produce and distribute. In addition, by the time they are printed and distributed, the information they contain is hours, days, weeks, or even months old. Publishers that publish in a digital-only format are starting to capture some of the traditional market share, because the information they provide is more up-to-date. In order to deal with this issue, most publishers have started to produce and distribute some, or all, of their content in both traditional and electronic format. It is certainly possible that these publishers may decide to discontinue publishing content in the traditional format altogether and opt for the digital-only format.

Select one of the following positions or make up your own and express your point of view on the subject. Your instructor will indicate whether your response is to be posted to a class bulletin board, discussed in a class chat room, or discussed as an in-class activity. You may also be asked to submit a summary of your position and point of view to your instructor.

a. Traditional forms of printed communication will never be discontinued. We may have to pay more in order to read traditional newspapers, but they will always be available.

b. Traditional forms of printed communication will eventually complete the transition into a digital-only format. We will all have some sort of portable digital display or audio device that will replace traditional newspapers, books, and magazines.

12. **Human or Computer Contact Prevails?** Consider the following statement and establish your position, or point of view, on the subject. Your instructor will indicate whether your response is to be posted to a class bulletin board, discussed in a class chat room, or discussed as an in-class activity. You may also be asked to submit a summary of your position and evaluation of the statement to your instructor.

In this chapter you were introduced to the PC, the Windows operating system, and the World Wide Web. These topics are covered in more detail in later chapters in this text but were introduced early so that you could begin making use of the computer for lab work, research, and Web-based study materials that have been provided at the textbook's Web site. As you progress through the course, you will find that computers are very powerful tools. They can be used to search the Web and locate the information that you need to write a paper, which might have otherwise have taken several days to accomplish in a traditional library. They can be used to communicate via e-mail with your friends or instructor, which might have otherwise have taken place in person. They can be used to play video games, which might have otherwise been played at a video arcade with some of your friends. In fact, computers are becoming such powerful tools for communication, productivity, education, commerce, and entertainment that we may end up spending more time interacting with a computer than with other people.

Interactive Exercise

Using the Web. It's time to practice going online and exploring the World Wide Web! Go to the Interactive Exercise at www.course.com/parker2002/ch2 to complete this exercise.

HARDWARE

When most people think of computer systems, images of hardware fill their minds. Hardware includes all of the exciting pieces of equipment that you unpack from boxes when you buy a computer system. This module explores the rich variety of computer hardware available in today's marketplace. But as you'll see later in this book, hardware needs guidance from software to perform any useful function. Hardware without software is like a car without a driver or a canvas and paintbrush without an artist.

This module divides coverage of hardware into three subject areas. Chapter 3 describes the hardware located inside the main box of the computer called the system unit–the location where virtually all of the work of a computer is performed. Chapter 4 discusses the types of hardware that provide an indispensable library of resources for the computer–storage devices. Chapter 5 covers the wide variety of equipment that can be used for input and output.

HARDWARE

The System Unit:
Processing and Memory

LEARNING OBJECTIVES

After completing this chapter, you will be able to:

1. Understand how data and programs are represented to a computer and be able to identify a few of the coding systems used to accomplish this.

2. Explain the functions of the hardware components commonly found inside the system unit.

3. Explain how systems can be expanded in order to attach new peripheral devices or add new capabilities.

4. Describe how the computer system's CPU and memory components process program instructions and data.

5. Name and evaluate several strategies that can be used today for speeding up the operations of computers, and some strategies that may be used in the future.

The *system unit* of a computer is often thought of as a mysterious "black box" that makes the computer work, without much understanding of what happens inside it. In this chapter, we demystify that notion by looking inside the box and closely examining the functions of the parts inside. In doing so, the chapter will give you a feel for how the *CPU, memory,* and other devices commonly found within the system unit work together to process data into meaningful information.

To start, we discuss how a computer system represents data and program instructions. Here we talk about the codes that computers use to translate data back and forth from symbols that the computer can manipulate to symbols that people are accustomed to using. These topics lead into a discussion of how the CPU and memory are arranged with other processing and storage components inside the system unit, and how a CPU is organized and interacts with memory to carry out processing tasks. Finally, we look at strategies to speed up a computer that you can implement today, and some that may be used to speed up computers in the future.

While most of you reading this chapter will apply its principles to conventional personal computer systems—such as desktop and notebook PCs—keep in mind that the principles discussed in this chapter cover a broad range of computer products. These products include microprocessors embedded in appliances and other devices, as well as powerful mainframe and supercomputers. ■

DATA AND PROGRAM REPRESENTATION

In order to be understood by a computer, data and programs need to be represented appropriately. There are coding systems (also called coding schemes) that can be used to represent numeric, text, and multimedia data, as well as the programs themselves. These concepts are discussed in the next few sections.

Digital Data Representation

When we talk about computers today, most of us are referring to *digital computers* which understand only two states—off and on (typically represented by 0s and 1s). The mobile devices, microcomputers, midrange computers, mainframes, and supercomputers discussed in Chapter 1 are all digital computers. As you will learn in this chapter, digital computers do their processing by converting data and programs into strings of 0s and 1s, which they manipulate at almost unimaginable speed. Converting data to digital form so that a digital computer can use it is called *digital data representation.*

The electrical components of a digital computer system recognize just two states. For example, a circuit is either open or closed, a magnetic spot or depression on a storage medium is either present or absent, and so on. This two-state, or *binary,* nature of electronic devices is illustrated in Figure 3-1. For convenience, it is common to think of these binary states in terms of 0s and 1s. Computer people refer to such 0s and 1s as *bits,* which is a contraction of the term *bi*nary dig*its.* With their electronic components, computers do all processing and communications by representing programs and data in bit form—in other words, by using just 0s and 1s. Binary, therefore, can be thought of as the computer's "native language."

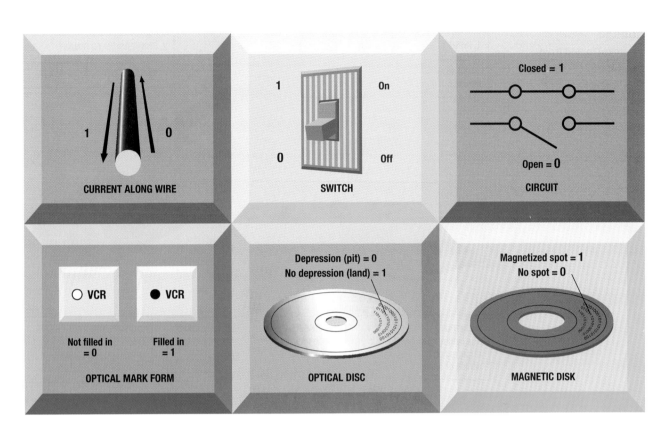

> ▶ **FIGURE 3-1**
>
> **The binary nature of electronics.** Circuits are either open or closed, a current runs one way or the opposite way, a charge is either present or absent, and so forth. The two possible states of an electronic component define bits, represented by computers as 0s and 1s.

People, of course, don't speak binary language. You're not likely to go up to a friend and say,

0100100001001001

which translates into the word "HI" using one binary coding system. People communicate with one another in *natural languages,* such as English, Chinese, Spanish, and French. For example, this book is written in English, which uses a 26-character alphabet and uses a number system with 10 possible symbols—0 through 9. As already mentioned, computers, however, understand only two symbols—0 and 1. For us to interact with a computer, a translation process from natural language to binary and then back again is required. When we type a message, the computer system translates the natural-language symbols in the message into 0s and 1s. After it completes processing, the computer system translates the 0s and 1s that represent the processed results back into natural language. This conversion process is illustrated in Figure 3-2.

Conversion from natural-language words and numbers to their binary equivalents and back again frequently takes place within an input or output device. When a user types a message, an encoder chip inside the keyboard usually translates this input into a series of 0s and 1s and sends it to the CPU. The output that the CPU sends to the monitor or some other output device is also in binary form; the output device—with the aid of a decoder chip—translates this code into understandable words and numbers. For example, if the CPU sends the message

0100100001001001

to your monitor, the word *HI* would appear on your screen.

Computers represent programs and data through a variety of binary-based coding schemes. The coding system used depends primarily on the type of data needing to be represented. Coding systems for numerical, text-based, and other types of data are discussed in the next few sections.

◆ **FIGURE 3-2**

**Conversion to and from
binary form.**

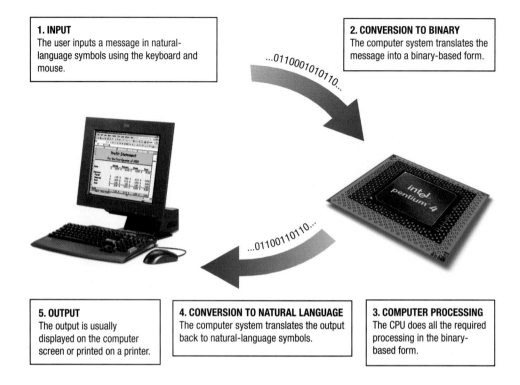

1. INPUT
The user inputs a message in natural-language symbols using the keyboard and mouse.

2. CONVERSION TO BINARY
The computer system translates the message into a binary-based form.

...0110001010110...

...01100110110...

5. OUTPUT
The output is usually displayed on the computer screen or printed on a printer.

4. CONVERSION TO NATURAL LANGUAGE
The computer system translates the output back to natural-language symbols.

3. COMPUTER PROCESSING
The CPU does all the required processing in the binary-based form.

The Binary Numbering System

A *numbering system* is a way of representing numbers. The system we most commonly use is called the decimal, or base 10, numbering system. It is called *decimal* or *base 10* because it uses 10 symbols—the digits 0, 1, 2, 3, 4, 5, 6, 7, 8, and 9—to represent all possible numbers. Numbers greater than nine, such as 21 and 683, are represented by combinations of these 10 symbols.

Because we are so familiar with the decimal numbering system, it may never have occurred to most of us that we could represent numbers in any other way. However, nothing says that a numbering system has to have 10 possible symbols. The **binary numbering system** (sometimes called the *base 2 numbering system* or the *true binary numbering system*), for example, uses just two symbols (0 and 1) instead of 10 symbols. Because of this, the binary numbering system is used extensively with computers to represent numbers.

Here's a quick look at how these numbering systems work. In both the binary and decimal numbering systems, the position of each digit determines the power, or exponent, that the base number (2 for binary or 10 for decimal) is raised to. In the decimal numbering system, going from right to left, the first position or column represents 10^0, or 1; the second position represents 10^1, or 10; the third position represents 10^2, or 100; and so forth. Thus, as Figure 3-3 shows, a decimal number such as 7,216 is understood as $7 \times 10^3 + 2 \times 10^2 + 1 \times 10^1 + 6 \times 10^0$. As illustrated in Figure 3-4, the binary number 1001 represents $1 \times 2^3 + 0 \times 2^2 + 0 \times 2^1 + 1 \times 2^0$ which, translated into the decimal system, is 9.

Another numbering system used with computers is the *hexidecimal numbering system,* which uses 16 different symbols. This numbering system, how computers can perform arithmetic using various numbering systems, and how to convert between numbering systems is illustrated in the appendix at the end of this text.

>**Binary numbering system.** The numbering system that represents all numbers using just two symbols (0 and 1).

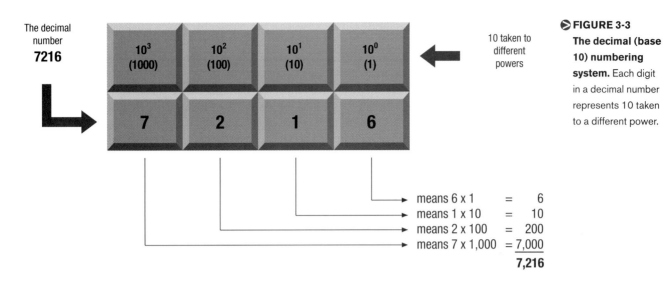

● **FIGURE 3-3**
The decimal (base 10) numbering system. Each digit in a decimal number represents 10 taken to a different power.

Coding Systems for Text-Based Data

While numeric data is represented by the true binary numbering system, text-based data is represented by fixed-length binary coding systems specifically developed for text-based data—namely, *ASCII, EBCDIC,* and *Unicode.* Such codes represent all characters on the keyboard that can appear in text data, such as numeric characters, alphabetic characters, and special characters such as the dollar sign ($) and period (.).

ASCII, EBCDIC, and Unicode

Among the most widely used coding systems for text-based data are **ASCII** (*A*merican *S*tandard *C*ode for *I*nformation *I*nterchange) and **EBCDIC** (*E*xtended *B*inary-*C*oded *D*ecimal *I*nterchange *C*ode). Virtually all microcomputers employ ASCII, developed largely through the efforts of the American National Standards Institute (ANSI). ASCII is also widely adopted as the standard for data communications systems. EBCDIC, developed by IBM, is used primarily on IBM mainframes.

further exploration

For links to further information about binary and other types of data representation, go to www.course.com/parker2002/ch3

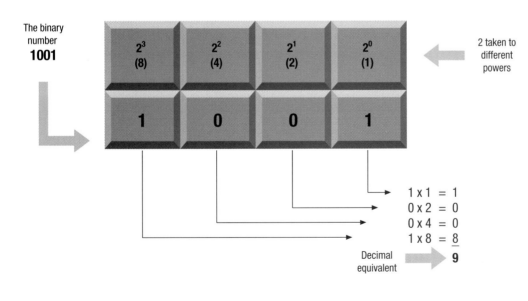

● **FIGURE 3-4**
The binary (base 2) numbering system. Each digit in a decimal number represents 2 taken to a different power.

>**ASCII.** A fixed-length, binary coding system widely used to represent text-based data for computer processing on many types of computers.
>**EBCDIC.** A fixed-length, binary coding system widely used to represent text-based data on IBM mainframe computers.

Both ASCII and EBCDIC represent each printable character as a unique combination of 8 bits (see Figure 3-5), though the original version of ASCII was a 7-digit code. A group of 8 bits allows 256 (2^8) different combinations, so an 8-bit code can represent up to 256 characters. This scheme leaves more than enough combinations to account for the 26 uppercase and 26 lowercase characters, the 10 decimal digits, and the other characters on the keyboard. Because of this, some special characters not on the keyboard—such as mathematical or drawing symbols—were also included in these codes. Many computer systems can accept data in either ASCII or EBCDIC and perform the necessary conversions to their native code.

A new code for text-based data that is gaining prominence is **Unicode.** Unicode is a universal coding standard designed to represent text-based data written in any language, including those with different alphabets, such as Chinese and Greek. Instead of an 8-bit code, like ASCII and EBCDIC, Unicode is a 16-bit code that can represent 65,536 (2^{16}) characters—sufficient for standard characters in all of the world's current languages, as well as many mathematical symbols and pronunciation marks.

Byte Terminology

The 8 bits that represent a character in ASCII or EBCDIC are collectively referred to as a **byte.** A byte traditionally represents a single character of data, though Unicode requires two bytes (16 bits) per character. Computer equipment capacity, such as memory and storage, are measured in bytes, based on the amount of data that they can hold. You may also have run across the terms *kilobyte, megabyte, gigabyte,* and *terabyte* before. In computer terminology, 1 **kilobyte (KB)** equals a little over 1,000 bytes (1,024, to be precise); 1 **megabyte (MB)** equals about 1 million bytes; 1 **gigabyte (GB)** equals about 1 billion bytes; and 1 **terabyte (TB)** equals about 1 trillion bytes. Therefore, 2 KB is about 2,000 bytes and 10 MB is approximately 10 million bytes.

FIGURE 3-5
ASCII and EBCDIC. These two common, fixed-length binary codes represent characters as unique strings of 8 bits.

Character	ASCII Representation	EBCDIC Representation	Character	ASCII Representation	EBCDIC Representation
0	00110000	11110000	I	01001001	11001001
1	00110001	11110001	J	01001010	11010001
2	00110010	11110010	K	01001011	11010010
3	00110011	11110011	L	01001100	11010011
4	00110100	11110100	M	01001101	11010100
5	00110101	11110101	N	01001110	11010101
6	00110110	11110110	O	01001111	11010110
7	00110111	11110111	P	01010000	11010111
8	00111000	11111000	Q	01010001	11011000
9	00111001	11111001	R	01010010	11011001
A	01000001	11000001	S	01010011	11100010
B	01000010	11000010	T	01010100	11100011
C	01000011	11000011	U	01010101	11100100
D	01000100	11000100	V	01010110	11100101
E	01000101	11000101	W	01010111	11100110
F	01000110	11000110	X	01011000	11100111
G	01000111	11000111	Y	01011001	11101000
H	01001000	11001000	Z	01011010	11101001

>**Unicode.** A coding system for text-based data in any written language. >**Byte.** A group of 8 bits that represents a single character of data. >**Kilobyte (KB).** 1,024 bytes. >**Megabyte (MB).** Approximately 1 million bytes. >**Gigabyte (GB).** Approximately 1 billion bytes. >**Terabyte (TB).** Approximately 1 trillion bytes.

The typical desktop computer sold today usually has about 128 megabytes of memory and a hard disk that can store many gigabytes of data. For comparison, one of the fastest supercomputers in the world has 6 terabytes of memory and more than 160 terabytes of hard disk space. With computer storage capacities ever increasing, some vendors of computer systems for large business and scientific applications have started to reach into the *petabyte (PB)* and *exabyte (EB)* ranges with their product offerings. A PB is about 1 quadrillion bytes; an EB is about 1 quintillion.

The Parity Bit

Sometimes, though rarely, something happens during transmission of data to the CPU and one of the pieces of data transmitted becomes inadvertently altered. For example, suppose you press the *B* key on your computer's keyboard. If the keyboard encoder supports ASCII coding, it will transmit the byte 01000010 to the CPU. If electrical interference on the line causes the sixth bit to change from 0 to 1, the CPU will receive the message 01000110. Unless something indicated the mistake to the CPU, it would wrongly interpret this byte as the letter *F.*

Detecting these types of transmission errors is the role of the *parity bit,* an additional bit position often automatically added to the end of each byte when a fixed-length coding system, such as EBCDIC and ASCII, is used. The parity bit is automatically set to either 0 or 1 to force the number of 1-bits in each byte to be either an even or an odd number. Computer systems support either even or odd parity. In an *odd-parity system,* the parity bit forces the number of 1-bits in a byte to be an odd number. In an *even-parity system,* it makes them be an even number. Figure 3-6 shows how the parity bit works for the ASCII representation of the word "HELLO" on an even-parity system.

The parity check is not foolproof. For example, if two bits are incorrectly transmitted in a single byte (a very rare occurrence), the errors will not be detected.

Coding Systems for Other Types of Data

So far, the discussion of data coding schemes has focused on numerical and text data, which consist of alphanumeric symbols and special symbols, such as the comma and semicolon. Graphics, audio, and video data must also be represented in binary form in the computer system.

Graphics Data

Graphics data consists of still pictures. One of the most common methods for storing graphics data is in the form of a bitmap. *Bitmap* graphics form images as a map of hundreds of thousands of dots. Each dot is assigned some combination of 0s and 1s that represents the appropriate shade or color. These dots are called *pixels.*

The simplest type of bitmap, a *monochrome* graphic, must differentiate between only a foreground color and a background color. Suppose that these colors are black and white and the 1 bit represents white, while the 0 bit represents black. The system can then translate any picture into a black-and-white bitmap, as shown in the top part of Figure 3-7, and store that bitmap using binary representation.

web tutor

For a tutorial on using binary representation and the parity bit, go to www.course.com/parker2002/ch3

FIGURE 3-6

The parity bit. If a system supports even parity, as shown here, the number of 1-bits in every byte must always be an even number. The parity bit is set to either 0 or 1 in each byte to force the number of 1-bits to be an even number.

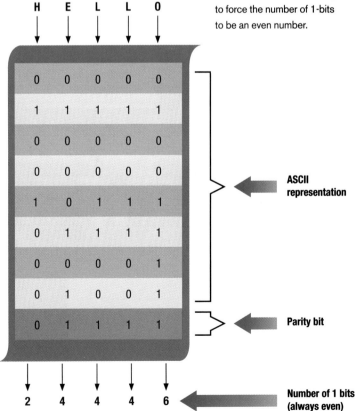

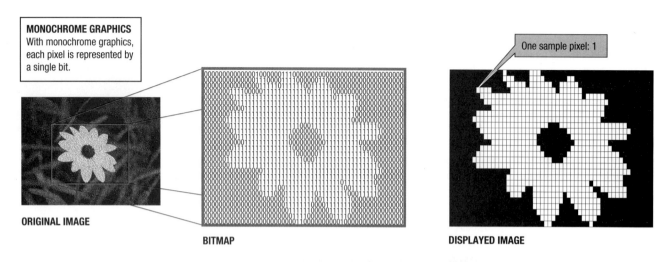

MONOCHROME GRAPHICS
With monochrome graphics, each pixel is represented by a single bit.

ORIGINAL IMAGE

BITMAP

DISPLAYED IMAGE

One sample pixel: 1

GRAYSCALE GRAPHICS
With 256-shade grayscale graphics, each pixel is represented by one byte. Different bytes represent different shades of gray.

One sample pixel: 01101110

One sample pixel: 1110

16-COLOR IMAGE
Each pixel is a half byte and each half byte represents a different color.

COLOR GRAPHICS
Color images can be 16-color, 256-color, or photographic quality. The more colors used, the better the image quality.

One sample pixel: 01110110

256-COLOR IMAGE
Each pixel is one byte and each byte represents a different color.

One sample pixel: 101001100100110111001011

PHOTOGRAPHIC-QUALITY (TRUE COLOR) IMAGE (16.7 million colors)
Each pixel is three bytes and each three-byte string represents a different color.

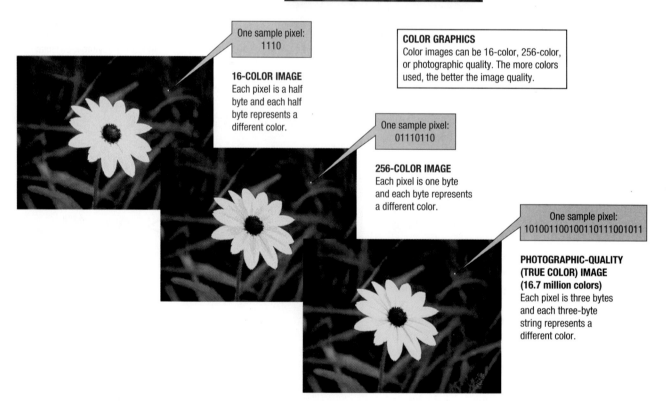

FIGURE 3-7

Bitmap graphics. With bitmapped images, each of the hundreds of thousands of pixels are assigned some combination of 0s and 1s to represent a unique shade or color. In color images, the more colors used, the better the image quality.

When color images are not appropriate but more realism is desired, *grayscale* images can be used. In grayscale images, each pixel can be not only pure black or pure white but also any of the 254 shades of gray in between. Thus, each dot or pixel could appear in any of 256 possible states. You may remember from an earlier discussion that a single byte (8 bits) can represent any of 256 (2^8) states. So, 11111111 could represent a pure white pixel, 00000000 a pure black one, and any byte pattern in between—such as 11001000 and 00001010—could represent some shade of gray (see the middle part of Figure 3-7).

Color coding works similar to grayscale graphics, in that the color of each pixel is represented by a specific pattern of bits. Computers often handle graphics with 16 colors, 256 colors, or 16,777,216 colors. A 16-color image assigns only one-half byte (4 bits) to each pixel (such as 0000, 1111, or some combination in between); a 256-color image assigns 1 byte (8 bits) for each pixel; and a 16.78-million-color (called photographic-quality or *true color*) image requires 3 bytes (24 bits) per pixel (see the bottom part of Figure 3-7).

Theoretically, the higher number of bits used in color coding, the higher-quality image. In practice, however, it is sometimes difficult for the human eye to tell much of a quality difference between low-end and high-end color images. Sixteen-color images, such as those you often see on Web pages, can actually be quite respectable looking. To save time in transmitting large graphics files over phone lines and other slow transmission media, Web developers often reduce 256-color images to 16 colors. The computer can do this by a process called *dithering*. Dithering produces colors not available on the limited color palette by coloring neighboring pixels with two available colors that appear to blend together to make a different color. For example, your eye will see a lime green color on the screen when several yellow and green pixels are placed adjacent to one another.

When images need to be resized or otherwise manipulated, bit-mapped images are not the best choice since they become distorted when resized. A better choice in this situation is *vector-based* images, which use mathematical formulas to represent images instead of a map of pixel colors; vector-based images can be resized without losing quality.

Audio Data

Computers often process audio data—such as the sound of someone speaking or a song from a CD—after it has been digitally encoded by a method called *waveform audio*. Waveform audio captures several thousand digital snapshots, called *samples*, of a real-life sound sequence every second. When the samples are played in order, they recreate the sound of the voice or music.

For example, audio CDs record sound sampled at a rate of approximately 44,000 times per second. Each 2-byte sample corresponds to a unique sound. As you can imagine, when these sounds are played back at a rate of about 44,000 samples per second, the human ear cannot distinguish them, and they collectively sound like real continuous voice or music. With so many samples per second, however, you can also understand why sound files take up a great deal of storage space.

Because of its potentially huge storage size, when audio data is transmitted over the Internet it is often compressed to shorten the download time. For example, files that are *MP3-encoded*—that is, compressed with the MP3 compression algorithm—are about 10 times smaller than on a CD, so they download 10 times faster and take up much less storage space. Technology used to encode and decode audio or video data into binary form is referred to as a *codec*. For an idea of how MP3 compression works, see the chapter How It Works box.

Video Data

Films that you see at the movies or on TV are displayed using a collection of frames, where each frame contains a still graphical image. When the frames are projected one after the other—typically at a rate of 30 frames per second—the illusion of movement is created. With so many frames, you can imagine that the amount of data involved in showing a two-hour feature film can be quite substantial. For instance, just a single 256-color image shown on a 640-by-480-pixel display requires 307,200 bytes. When you multiply that

how it works

MP3 Compression

The *MP3 format* is a compression system for music. The MP3 format helps reduce the number of bytes in a song without hurting the quality of the song. MP3 is officially MPEG Audio Layer-3, an *MPEG* (Moving Pictures Experts Group) compression standard. Each layer uses a different sampling rate to obtain different compression results. Layer 3–the norm for music today–typically compresses a CD-quality song by a factor of 10 to 12 while still retaining CD-quality sound. For example, the 51 MB Queen song shown in the accompanying illustration compresses to less than 5 MB after conversion to the MP3 format. Higher compression levels can be used, but the quality of the song is affected. For example, near-CD quality (with a 15:1 compression ratio) stores about 1 minute of music in 700 KB of space, instead of about 1 MB for 11:1 compression. Compressing it to the much lower FM radio quality (22:1) would store the same one minute of music in about 400 KB of space. Compared to the 10 MB required to store the one minute in the CD's native WAV format, MP3 compression is pretty impressive.

The MP3 format became widely used when downloading songs from the Internet began to become a popular pastime. MP3 files can be downloaded in minutes rather than hours, and the MP3 format lets you store hundreds of songs on a single storage medium.

To reduce the file size, MP3 compression Layer 3 uses *perceptual coding* techniques to remove all superfluous information (the parts of the song that the human ear wouldn't hear anyway). A coding scheme called *Huffman coding* is then used to substitute shorter strings of bits for frequently used larger strings. This process is typically repeated until an appropriate level of compression is reached. The result–saved with the extension .MP3– can then be played on a PC with MP3 software or using any MP3-compatible device (such as an MP3, CD, or DVD player).

1. CD version of song: 51 MB.

2. Software removes unnecessary parts of the song and codes the song in MP3 format.

3. MP3 version of song: 4.7MB.

Unnecessary data is removed

Huffman coding is applied

Queen - We will rock you.mp3

---

figure by 30 times per second, 60 seconds per minute, and 120 minutes you get more than 66 gigabytes of information for a two-hour movie. Fortunately, video data can be compressed so that computers can more readily handle them. For example, a two-hour movie can be compressed to fit on a 4.7-gigabyte DVD disc.

Machine Language

Just like data, which must be represented by 0s and 1s, programs also need to be represented and processed in binary form. Before a computer can execute any program instruction, such as reading the next group of data items in a file, moving a block of data from one place to another, or opening a new window on the screen, it must convert the instruction into a binary code known as **machine language.** An example of a typical machine-language instruction appears below:

01011000011100000000000100000010

>**Machine language.** A binary-based programming language that the computer can execute directly.

A machine-language instruction may look like a meaningless string of 0s and 1s, but it actually organizes bits into groups that represent specific operations and storage locations. The 32-bit instruction shown here, for instance, moves data between two specific memory locations on one type of computer system. Similar instructions transfer data from memory to other locations, add or subtract values in memory, and so on. The basic set of machine-language instructions that a CPU can understand is known as that CPU's *instruction set*.

Early computers required users to write all their own programs in machine language. Today, however, hardly anyone writes machine-language code. Instead, programming specialists rely on *language translators*—special programs that automatically convert instructions written in a more English-like programming language into machine language. The translation is so transparent that most people aren't even aware that it is taking place. Programming languages and language translators are discussed in more detail in Chapter 13.

Each computer platform has its own machine language. Machine-level code for an IBM microcomputer is incompatible with the Apple Macintosh. This fact explains why you must buy a program, such as a word processor or spreadsheet, in a form intended for your specific type of computer system.

INSIDE THE SYSTEM UNIT

The **system unit** is the box or case that houses the processing hardware for the computer, as well as a few other devices, such as disk drives used for storage, the power supply, and cooling fans. The inside of a system unit for a typical PC system is shown in Figure 3-8.

The system unit usually contains the CPU, memory (*RAM* and *ROM*) chips, boards onto which chips are mounted, *ports* that provide connections for external devices, a power supply, internal storage devices, and *buses* and other internal circuitry to connect everything together. As illustrated in Figure 3-8, all devices inside the system unit are connected in one way or another to a special board—called the **system board** or **motherboard**—inside the system unit. The system unit also typically has built-in *expansion bays*—open locations into which storage equipment, such as disk drives, can be mounted. There are also usually empty *expansion slots* on the motherboard into which additional *circuit boards* can be inserted to add new devices or capabilities. In the next few sections, we discuss all of these devices.

CPU

Every PC's system unit contains at least one primary, general-purpose, **microprocessor** or **CPU** chip (see Figure 3-9). This chip consists of a variety of circuitry and components and is mounted onto the motherboard (refer again to Figure 3-8). The key ingredient in the microprocessor is the *transistor*—a device made of semiconductor material that acts like a switch controlling the flow of electrons inside a chip. Today's CPUs contain tens of millions of transistors. A recent breakthrough reduced the size of the transistor by 30 percent, which will enable future microprocessors to contain a billion transistors. These microscopic transistors can turn on and off more than a trillion times per second and microprocessors created with these transistors could complete close to a billion calculations in the blink of an eye—a significant speed increase over current CPUs. How a CPU works is discussed in more detail a little later in this chapter.

web tutor

For a tutorial on the components found inside the system unit, go to www.course.com/parker2002/ch3

>**System unit.** The main box of a computer that houses the CPU, motherboard, memory, and other devices. >**System board.** Another name for motherboard. >**Motherboard.** The main circuit board of a computer, located inside the system unit, to which all computer-system components connect. >**Microprocessor.** Another name for CPU. >**CPU.** The chip located inside of the system unit of a computer that performs the processing for a computer and communicates with its peripheral devices.

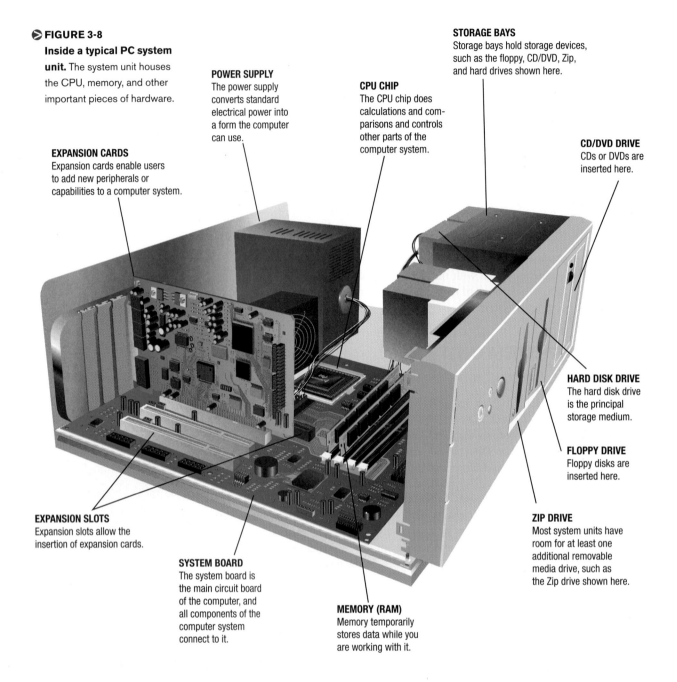

FIGURE 3-8

Inside a typical PC system unit. The system unit houses the CPU, memory, and other important pieces of hardware.

POWER SUPPLY
The power supply converts standard electrical power into a form the computer can use.

CPU CHIP
The CPU chip does calculations and comparisons and controls other parts of the computer system.

STORAGE BAYS
Storage bays hold storage devices, such as the floppy, CD/DVD, Zip, and hard drives shown here.

EXPANSION CARDS
Expansion cards enable users to add new peripherals or capabilities to a computer system.

CD/DVD DRIVE
CDs or DVDs are inserted here.

HARD DISK DRIVE
The hard disk drive is the principal storage medium.

FLOPPY DRIVE
Floppy disks are inserted here.

ZIP DRIVE
Most system units have room for at least one additional removable media drive, such as the Zip drive shown here.

EXPANSION SLOTS
Expansion slots allow the insertion of expansion cards.

SYSTEM BOARD
The system board is the main circuit board of the computer, and all components of the computer system connect to it.

MEMORY (RAM)
Memory temporarily stores data while you are working with it.

Most microcomputer systems made today use CPU chips manufactured by Intel, Advanced Micro Devices (AMD), or Motorola. Chips in the Intel line—such as the Celeron and Pentium 4—and the AMD line—such as the Athlon and Duron—appear in microcomputer systems made by IBM, Compaq, Hewlett-Packard, Dell, Gateway, and scores of other PC-compatible systems. Chips in the Motorola line are found primarily in Apple Macintosh computers, though the standard CPU for Macintosh computers today is the PowerPC chip—a chip that resulted from a cooperative effort from Apple, Motorola, and IBM. Some of the latest models in the PowerPC line are the 750 (G3) and G4. Other possible microprocessors include the low-power *Transmeta Crusoe* chips, typically found in portable PCs and mobile devices, and *Alpha* and *SPARC* chips, used with high-end servers and workstations. For a look at other uses for microprocessor chips, see the chapter Trend box.

The type of CPU chip in a computer's system unit greatly affects what a person can do with the system. Software is sometimes designed to work on a specific chip or chip

> **FIGURE 3-9**
> **CPU chips.** Shown here are the Intel Pentium 4 and AMD Athlon CPUs.

family, and a program that works with one chip may not function on a computer using a different chip. For instance, a program designed for a speedy Intel Pentium 4 chip may not work well, or even at all, on the earlier and far less-capable 80486 chip. A selection of the CPUs introduced over the years is summarized in Figure 3-10; the characteristics listed in Figure 3-10 are discussed next.

Processing (Clock) Speed

CPU *processing speed*—also known as its *clock speed*—is the speed at which a processor executes instructions. Clock speed is rated in *megahertz (MHz)*. The earliest CPU chips ran

> **FIGURE 3-10**
> **CPU chip characteristics.**

Year Introduced	CPU Name	Manufacturer	Clock Speed	Level 1 Cache	Level 2 Cache	Level 3 Cache	Word Size	System Bus Width	System Bus Speed
1978/1979	8086/8088	Intel	4.77–10 MHz	n/a	n/a	n/a	16 bit	8–16 bit	5–10 MHz
1982	80286	Intel	6–12.5 MHz	n/a	n/a	n/a	16 bit	16 bit	6–12 MHz
1985	80386	Intel	16–33 MHz	n/a	16 KB	n/a	32 bit	16–32 bit	16–33 MHz
1989	80486	Intel	16–100 MHz	8–16 KB	128–256 KB	n/a	32 bit	32 bit	16–50 MHz
1993	Pentium	Intel	60–233 MHz	16–32 KB	256 KB–1 MB	n/a	32 bit	32–64 bit	50–66 MHz
1995	Pentium Pro	Intel	150–200 MHz	16 KB	256 KB–1 MB	n/a	32 bit	64 bit	60–66 MHz
1997	Pentium II	Intel	200–450 MHz	32 KB	512 KB–2 MB	n/a	32 bit	64 bit	66–100 MHz
1997	K6	AMD	400–550 MHz	64 KB	256 KB	n/a	32 bit	64 bit	100 MHz
1997	PowerPC 750 (G3)	Motorola	200–400 MHz	32 KB	256 KB–1 MB	n/a	32 bit	64 bit	100 MHz
1998	Celeron	Intel	266–900 MHz	32 KB	0–128 KB	n/a	32 bit	64 bit	66–100 MHz
1999	Pentium III	Intel	450 MHz–1.1 GHz	32 KB	256 KB–2 MB	n/a	32 bit	64 bit	100–133 MHz
1999	Athlon	AMD	850 MHz–1.2 GHz	128 KB	256 KB	n/a	32 bit	64 bit	200–266 MHz
1999	Duron	AMD	750–850 MHz	128 KB	64 KB	n/a	32 bit	64 bit	200 MHz
1999	PowerPC G4	Motorola	400–800 MHz	32 KB	512 KB–2 MB	n/a	32 bit	64 bit	133 MHz
2000	Pentium 4	Intel	1.3 GHz and above	20 KB	256 KB	n/a	32 bit	64 bit	400 MHz
2001	Itanium	Intel	733 Mhz and above	32–64 KB	96 KB	2–4 MB	64 bit	64 bit	266 MHz

trend

Smart Bullets, Smart Tennis Shoes, High-Tech Pets, and Other Unusual Uses for Microchips

We all know that microchips can be used to build tiny computers and make household appliances work, but did you know they can also be used to steer bullets in combat, track runners in a race, and keep your pet safe? These are just a few of the more innovative uses for microchips.

In the first major update to the Army's M-16 rifle since 1967, prototypes of a new gun—called the Objective Individual Combat Weapon, developed by Alliant Techsystems—are being tested. Instead of relying on a soldier's perfect aim, this new gun uses a laser and smart bullets to hit its mark. Once the soldier marks the desired target with a red dot in his or her laser sights, a small (dime-size) stack of microprocessors inside the bullet determines how many times the bullet must revolve in flight to reach the marked destination. The gun can be fired from up to 1,000 meters away; the smart bullets explode a meter above the target's head, scattering shrapnel on the enemy.

A less lethal, but no less interesting, chip application is the smart tennis shoe. Used now for several years in races such as the Boston Marathon, New York Marathon, and Ironman competitions, the heart of the smart tennis shoe is the ChampionChip. This chip, typically attached to the runner's shoe, contains a transponder chip and energizing coil. When the chip passes a special antenna located at the start line, finish line, and selected locations in between, the athlete's ID number is transmitted to the timing computer. At any time during the race, the runner's status can be displayed on the race's Web site. Family and friends can also enter in a runner's ID number to immediately receive an update on the athlete's progress.

To keep tabs on your pet, pet identification systems, such as Home Again by Schering-Plough Animal Health and PETrac by AVID (the American Veterinary Identification Device), can be used. These systems register dogs, cats, and other pets with identifying microchips implanted just under the skin. Similar to tracking systems used by animal researchers, the pet ID chip and an antenna are encased in a tiny glass tube and injected under the skin. When the animal is scanned with a special scanner, its unique ID number is revealed. On implantation, this ID number is entered into a database along with the information about the pet, the owner, and sometimes the veterinarian. When lost pets are scanned at animal shelters, animal hospitals, and other locations with scanners that can read these chips, their owners can be quickly identified. Unlike physical tags, which can fall off or become unreadable, or bar code tattoos, which can wear off, chip identification lasts the entire life of the animal.

These are just a few examples of the new and exciting microchip applications becoming available today. With the continued decreasing price and size of chips, it is conceivable that more everyday items will become high-tech in the years to come.

ChampionChips provide a fast, accurate timing system for a variety of athletic events. Whenever an athlete passes over a mat containing a send antenna (as shown here), his or her ID number is broadcast to a receive antenna. The system allows start, split, and ending times to be instantaneously recorded.

at less than 5 MHz; today's CPUs run at more than 1,000 MHz or 1 *gigahertz (GHz)*. Though processing speed is an important factor in computer performance, other factors (such as *word size, RAM, cache memory, bus width,* and *bus speed,* discussed shortly) greatly affect performance, as well.

inside the industry

Moore's Law

Still applicable after all these years.
In 1965 Gordon Moore, the cofounder of Intel, observed that the number of transistors (the key ingredient in microprocessors) per square inch on integrated circuits (chips) had doubled every year since the integrated circuit was invented. At that time, Moore made a startling prediction. He predicated that this doubling trend would continue for the foreseeable future. Here we are, 35 or so years later, and, though the pace has slowed down a bit, transistor density still doubles about every 18 months (see the accompanying graph).

What is so amazing about Moore's prediction is that it is still applicable today. Eventually, there has to be a physical limit of the number of transistors crammed onto a chip. But the end is not yet in sight.

Other computer components also have their own "Moore's Laws." In general, the term is used to describe the amount of time it takes components to double in capacity or speed. For example, storage capacity doubles approximately every 20 months and chip speed doubles about every 24 months.

Moore originally predicted that the doubling trend would continue through 1975. Due to technological breakthroughs, it has been maintained for far longer and most experts, including Moore himself, expect it to hold for two more decades. In fact, Intel states that the mission of its technology development team is to continue to break barriers to Moore's Law.

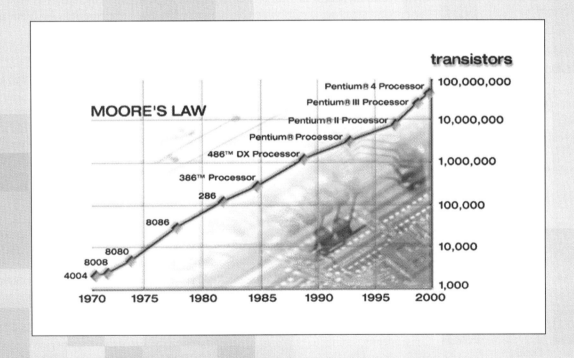

You may notice from Figure 3-10 that CPU speed seems to double about every two years. This phenomenon is related to a prediction made back in 1965—dubbed *Moore's Law*—as discussed in the Inside the Industry box.

Word Size
A computer *word* is the amount of data (measured in bits or bytes) that a CPU can manipulate at one time. Different CPUs may have different word sizes. Most newer CPU chips are designed for 64-bit words. This means that data move around within the CPU and from the CPU to memory in 64-bit (8 byte) chunks. Usually, a larger word size allows faster processing in a computer system.

further exploration

For links to further information about CPU chips, go to www.course.com/parker2002/ch3

Memory

When someone uses the term *memory* in reference to computers, they are almost always referring to the computer's main memory called *random access memory* or *RAM*. As discussed in Chapter 1, RAM is volatile and is the location where data and programs are temporarily stored until they are no longer needed. RAM is comprised of chips attached to the motherboard and used primarily by the computer. This is in contrast to *storage media* (discussed in Chapter 4), which are typically disk based and are used more actively by the user. It's important to be careful when using the terms *memory* and *storage* since they are frequently confused and misused. In general, "memory" refers to chip-based storage—usually the amount of RAM located inside the computer. In contrast, "storage" refers to the amount of permanent storage available to a PC—usually in the form of the PC's hard drive or removable storage media such as floppy disks and CDs, as discussed in the next chapter.

Though less commonly discussed than RAM, four other types of memory should be mentioned. Two of these—*cache memory* and *registers*—are volatile and used by the CPU, similar to RAM. Two other kinds—*read-only memory (ROM)* and *flash memory*—are non-volatile. These five types of memory are discussed next.

RAM

RAM (random access memory)—the computer system's main memory—is used to store the programs and data with which the computer is currently working. RAM is *volatile,* meaning that its content is erased when the computer is shut off. Data is also erased when it is no longer needed, such as when the program in which the data was created is closed. To save a document before closing the program and erasing the document from RAM, a storage device needs to be used, as discussed in the next chapter. The document can then be retrieved from the storage medium at a later time.

Like the CPU, RAM consists of circuits etched onto chips. These chips are arranged onto circuit boards called *single in-line memory modules (SIMMs), dual in-line memory modules (DIMMS),* or *Rambus in-line memory modules (RIMMs),* depending on the type of memory and type of circuit board used. These modules plug into the system board, as shown in Figure 3-8.

The amount of data that can be stored in RAM is measured in bytes. Most desktop PCs sold today have about 128 MB of RAM and allow the addition of more memory, if needed. For example, in the computer in Figure 3-8, there are two SIMM boards containing memory already installed and room to add an additional two boards, if necessary.

Types of RAM

Ordinary RAM is often referred to as *DRAM (dynamic RAM)* in technical literature. This name refers to its need for regular recharging as processing takes place. During recharge, DRAM cannot be accessed by the CPU. A faster type of RAM—called *SRAM (static RAM)*—does not need recharging. However, SRAM chips are more expensive than DRAM. Consequently, computer makers use them sparingly for main memory. A newer type of DRAM is *SDRAM (synchronous DRAM).* SDRAM is much faster than DRAM because it is synchronized to the *system clock*—the computer's built-in clock that synchronizes its operations, as discussed later in this chapter. *RDRAM (Rambus DRAM), PC133 SRAM,* and *double-data rate (DDR) SDRAM* are the newest, fastest types of RAM available at the time this book was published. Most computers today use either SDRAM, RDRAM, PC133 SRAM, or DDR SDRAM chips.

>**Random access memory (RAM).** Chips located on the motherboard that provide a temporary holding place for the computer to store data and program instructions while it is needed.

Memory Speed

Memory speed is typically measured in megahertz (MHz) like CPU speed, though some memory manufacturers measure speed in *nanoseconds* (billionths of a second), instead. Common maximum speeds in megahertz are 100 MHz for SDRAM, 133 MHz for PC133 SRAM, 266 MHz for DDR SDRAM, and 800 MHz for RDRAM. Memory manufacturers are continually working on ways to make memory faster. Having components, such as RAM or *buses* (discussed shortly), operate at a slower speed than the CPU has caused bottlenecks in the past, where the CPU sits idle while it waits for the appropriate component to finish what it needs to do first. Consequently, computer manufacturers are continually looking for ways to increase the speed of slower components to avoid this problem.

Memory Addressing

Once the CPU stores something in RAM, it must be able to find it again when needed. To accomplish this, each location in memory has an *address*. Whenever a block of data, instruction, program, or result of a calculation is stored in memory, it is stored into one or more consecutive addresses, depending on its size (see Figure 3-11). Computer systems automatically set up and maintain directory tables that provide the addresses of the first character of all data stored in memory, along with the number of addresses used, to facilitate the retrieval of the data, when necessary.

When the computer has finished processing a program or set of data, it frees up that memory space to store other programs and data. Thus, the content of each memory location constantly changes. This process can be roughly compared with handling of the mailboxes in your local post office: The number on each P.O. box (memory location) remains the same, but the mail (data) stored inside changes as patrons remove their mail and as new mail arrives.

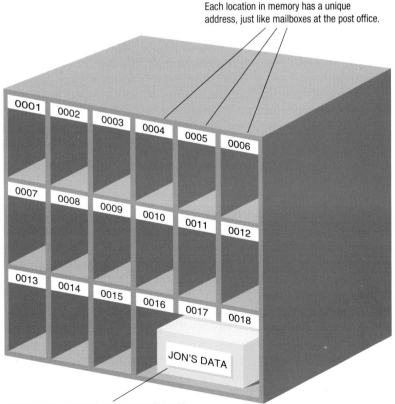

Each location in memory has a unique address, just like mailboxes at the post office.

Programs and blocks of data are usually too big to fit in a single address. A directory keeps track of where the first character of each program and data block can be found and the number of addresses it spans.

FIGURE 3-11
Memory addressing.

Cache Memory

Cache memory is a special group of fast memory chips located inside or close to the CPU chip to speed up processing. It works, in principal, similarly to the way you might work at a desk with file folders or documents that you need most often placed within an arm's length. Other useful materials might be placed somewhat farther away, but still within easy reach.

The computer works in a similar manner. Although it can access materials in RAM relatively quickly, it can work much faster if it places the most urgently needed materials into storage areas that allow even faster access. These storage areas—cache memory—contain the most frequently and recently used data and instructions. To make cache memory more effective, when the cache is full and the CPU calls for a new instruction, the system overwrites the data in cache that hasn't been used for the longest period of time. This way, the high priority information that's used continuously stays in cache, while the less frequently used information is overwritten.

Two types of cache memory appear widely in computers. The first is referred to as *internal cache* and is built right into the CPU chip. The second, *external cache,* is located on chips placed close to the CPU (refer ahead to Figure 3-12). A computer can have several different levels of cache memory. *Level 1 cache* is virtually always built into the chip. *Level 2 cache* used to be external cache but is now typically also built into the CPU like Level 1 cache. The level numbers refer to the distance from the CPU: Level 1 is closest, Level 2 is next closest, Level 3 (appearing now in newer computers as external cache) would be even further away, etc. The cache closest to the CPU is always faster but generally costs more and stores less data than other levels of cache. Typically all levels of cache memory are faster than the PC's RAM. As you might guess, the computer looks for data in the closest locations first—first in Level 1 cache, then in Level 2 cache, then in Level 3 cache (if it exists), and then in RAM. Typically a larger cache results in faster processing.

Registers

Another type of memory built into the CPU chip is the CPU's **register.** Registers are the locations within the CPU that each program instruction and piece of data are normally loaded into (either from RAM or cache memory) just before they are processed by the CPU. Registers are the fastest type of memory used by the CPU, even faster than Level 1 cache. Generally, the more data the register can contain at one time—usually 32 bits, though the newer 64-bit chips such as the Itanium use 64-bit registers—the faster the CPU is. Most CPUs contain several registers; registers are discussed in more detail later in this chapter.

ROM

Another type of memory that is usually of less concern to the user than RAM is **ROM** (for **read-only memory**). ROM consists of nonerasable chips into which data or programs have been permanently stored. Like RAM, these chips are mounted in carrier packages that are, in turn, attached to a board inside the system unit. An important difference, however, is that you can neither write over the data or programs in ROM (which is the reason ROM chips are called *read-only*), nor destroy their contents when you shut off the computer's power (that is, they're nonvolatile).

Important pieces of systems software are often stored in ROM chips. For instance, one of the computer's first activities when you turn on the power is to perform a power-on self-test or *POST.* The POST program is stored in ROM, and it produces the beeps you hear as your computer system boots up. POST takes an inventory of system components, checks each component for proper functioning, and initializes system settings.

>**Register.** A high-speed staging area within the CPU that temporarily stores data during processing. >**Read-only memory (ROM).** Nonerasable chips located on the motherboard that usually store program instructions.

Flash Memory

Flash memory (sometimes called *flash RAM*) is a type of nonvolatile memory that can be erased and reprogrammed in units of memory called *blocks*. Flash memory gets its name because a block is erased in a single action or *flash*. This type of organization makes flash memory faster than RAM, though it is more expensive than RAM and has to store data in block-size, not byte-size, pieces.

Flash memory chips are used in many newer computers for the PC's *BIOS* or *basic input/output system*. A computer's BIOS consists of the sequence of instructions the PC follows when it is started up. By storing this information in flash memory, instead of a ROM chip, the BIOS information can be updated as needed.

Flash memory chips are also frequently used in portable PCs and devices such as cell phones, printers, digital cameras, pagers, and so forth. In addition, they can be used as a storage medium for mobile devices when the flash memory chips are embedded into removable flash memory cards. Flash memory cards and storage are discussed in more detail in Chapter 4.

further exploration

For links to further information about memory chips, go to www.course.com/parker2002/ch3

Buses

A **bus** is an electronic path within a computer that ties the PC's components (such as the CPU, memory, and peripheral devices) together. You can picture a bus as a highway with several lanes. Data and instructions can enter a bus at the appropriate on-ramp (via a piece of hardware, such as the keyboard, printer, or CPU), and then they move down the bus, with the number of bits being transmitted at one time dependent on the size or width of the bus—each wire in the bus can transmit one bit at a time. Just as in a highway, the wider (or more lanes) a bus has, the more data that can be transferred at one time. For example, an eight-bit bus contains eight separate paths and can transmit eight bits—one byte—at one time. Sixteen-, 32-, 64-, and 100-bit buses can transfer 16, 32, 64, or 100 bits at one time, respectively. Consequently, a wider bus size can help speed up processing. An example of how the buses in a PC might be set up is shown in Figure 3-12.

Internal and System Buses

The bus that moves data around within the CPU is usually referred to as the PC's *internal bus,* while the bus that moves data back and forth between the CPU and memory is called the *system bus.* Today's computers typically have a specific system bus to connect the CPU to RAM called the *frontside bus (FSB).* The *backside bus (BSB)* transfers data between the CPU and external cache. Many CPUs today have 64-bit internal and system buses, though the speed of the system bus varies, as indicated back in Figure 3-10. Generally a faster system bus indicates a faster PC, and a faster frontside bus creates less of a bottleneck in the overall performance of the system.

Expansion Buses

Buses that connect the CPU to peripheral (typically input and output) devices are usually referred to as *expansion buses.* Expansion buses, typically 16 to 64 bits wide, are etched onto the motherboard, and connect the CPU to the *expansion slots* on the motherboard to which external devices may be connected. There are a variety of expansion bus standards. As illustrated in Figure 3-12, most CPUs today use a *chipset* of one or more chips that help bridge or connect the various buses to the CPU. Some of the most common types of expansion buses are discussed next.

>**Flash memory.** A type of nonvolatile memory that can be erased and reprogrammed; commonly implemented in the form of sticks or cards.
>**Bus.** An electronic path on the motherboard or within the CPU or other computer component along which bits are transmitted.

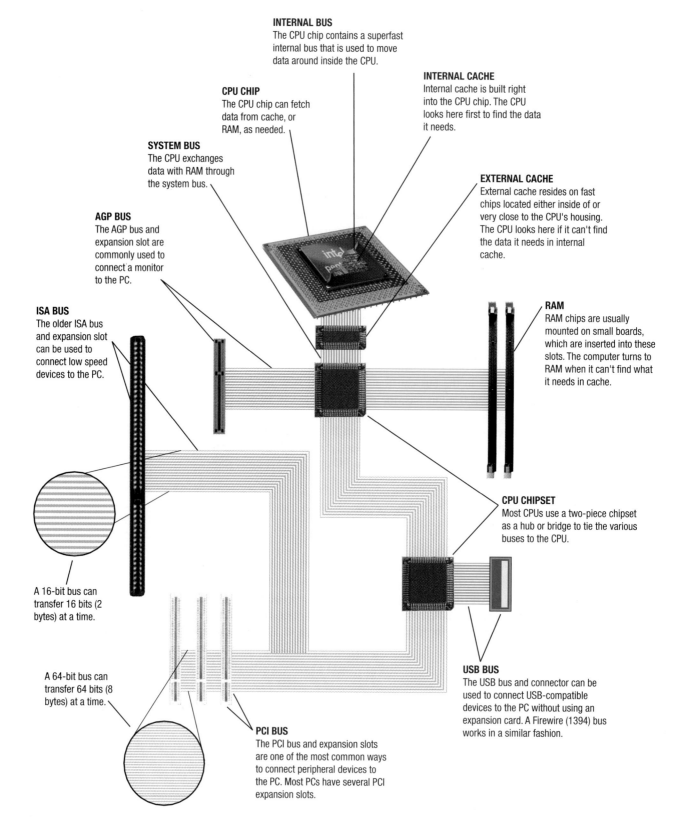

INTERNAL BUS
The CPU chip contains a superfast internal bus that is used to move data around inside the CPU.

CPU CHIP
The CPU chip can fetch data from cache, or RAM, as needed.

INTERNAL CACHE
Internal cache is built right into the CPU chip. The CPU looks here first to find the data it needs.

SYSTEM BUS
The CPU exchanges data with RAM through the system bus.

EXTERNAL CACHE
External cache resides on fast chips located either inside of or very close to the CPU's housing. The CPU looks here if it can't find the data it needs in internal cache.

AGP BUS
The AGP bus and expansion slot are commonly used to connect a monitor to the PC.

ISA BUS
The older ISA bus and expansion slot can be used to connect low speed devices to the PC.

RAM
RAM chips are usually mounted on small boards, which are inserted into these slots. The computer turns to RAM when it can't find what it needs in cache.

CPU CHIPSET
Most CPUs use a two-piece chipset as a hub or bridge to tie the various buses to the CPU.

A 16-bit bus can transfer 16 bits (2 bytes) at a time.

A 64-bit bus can transfer 64 bits (8 bytes) at a time.

PCI BUS
The PCI bus and expansion slots are one of the most common ways to connect peripheral devices to the PC. Most PCs have several PCI expansion slots.

USB BUS
The USB bus and connector can be used to connect USB-compatible devices to the PC without using an expansion card. A Firewire (1394) bus works in a similar fashion.

FIGURE 3-12

Buses. Buses transport bits and bytes from one computer-system component to another, including the CPU, cache, RAM, and peripheral devices.

ISA

The *ISA* (for *I*ndustry *S*tandard *A*rchitecture) bus has been around since 1984. Though it is still included on some new PCs (typically connected to the PCI bus, as shown in Figure 3-12), it is beginning to be phased out and replaced by the newer bus standards discussed next. The ISA bus is slow, transmitting 8 or 16 bits at one time. Consequently, when ISA buses are used, it is for slower devices—such as the system's mouse or sound card.

PCI

The *PCI* (*P*eripheral *C*omponent *I*nterconnect) bus is one of the most common types of expansion bus. It can transmit 32 bits at a time and is significantly faster than the ISA bus, delivering more than 100 *MBps* (*megabytes*—millions of bytes—*per second*). A newer, faster version of PCI introduced in 2000 is called *PCI-X*. PCI-X supports a 64-bit bus width and speeds of more than 1,000 MBps (1 GBps). In addition to connecting the CPU to the PCI expansion slots, the PCI bus is used to connect other buses to the CPU, such as the ISA and USB buses, as shown in Figure 3-12. Eventually, the PCI bus is expected to be replaced by a faster architecture, such as the new *InfiniBand* architecture, which offers data transfer speeds up to 2.5 GBps and can support up to 64,000 devices.

AGP

The *AGP* (*A*ccelerated *G*raphics *P*ort) bus is a relatively new bus standard that was developed in response to the trend toward greater performance requirements for graphics display. With the increasing demands of 3D graphics and full-motion video playback, both the processor and the video card need to process more information much more quickly than before. Though the PCI bus has been adequate for video displays in the past, it is reaching its performance limit. AGP provides a fast, 32-bit, direct interface between the video card and RAM, operating at over 2,000 MBps (2 GBps).

USB

One of the more versatile new bus architectures in recent years is the *universal serial bus (USB)*. The USB standard enables up to 127 devices to be connected to a computer's PCI bus through a single connector *(port)* on the computer's system unit. At 12 *Mbps* (*megabits per second)* or 1.5 MBps (megabytes per second), the original USB standard can transmit data at a much slower rate than both PCI and AGP. The newer *USB 2* standard supports data transfer rates of 480 Mbps (60 MBps)—still slower than PCI and AGP, but the convenience and wide support of USB have made it one of the most widely used standards for peripherals today.

Firewire/IEEE 1394

Firewire (also known as *IEEE 1394* and *Lynx*) is a new external bus standard developed by Apple. Like USB, Firewire can connect multiple external devices to the PCI bus via a single port. Firewire is very fast, supporting data transfer rates of up to 400 Mbps, and is commonly used with video cameras and other multimedia peripherals for both Apple and IBM-compatible computers. It is expected that USB and/or Firewire will eventually replace the ISA and other types of older buses.

System Expansion

Not everyone wants the same type of computer system. One person may be satisfied with 64 MB of RAM, while another may want 128 MB or 256 MB in the same model of computer. Similarly, while many people need only average sound capabilities from their computer systems, musicians and music buffs often desire top-of-the-line audio capabilities. To account for the wide variety of needs in the marketplace, most PC vendors enable you to customize your system. To attach a new device to your PC, it is typically plugged into an exterior connector called a *port,* as discussed in a later section. If the proper port is not available on your desktop PC, it can be added. Expansion for notebook and handheld PCs typically occurs a little differently. How system expansion is handled for these different types of PCs is explained next.

Expansion Cards for Desktop PCs

Expansion cards (also called by a variety of other names, such as *add-in boards, interface cards,* and *adapter boards*) expand the functions of desktop computers, as well as allow additional peripheral devices to be attached to the computer. These small circuit boards plug into *expansion slots* within the computer's system unit. As shown in Figure 3-12, there are a variety of expansion slots that can be located inside a PC, such as ISA, AGP, and PCI. These expansion slots are different sizes, use different types of cards, and are connected to the appropriate bus on the motherboard. As shown in Figure 3-13, most expansion cards have a *port* (connector) that is exposed through the case of the system unit; this port is where the appropriate external device (monitor, printer, scanner, etc.) is plugged in. The various ports that may be found on a system unit are covered shortly.

Computer systems often accept many types of expansion cards. For example, monitors are usually connected to their own *video-graphics boards,* which both translate output into a form the monitor can understand and temporarily store the output before it is displayed. Similarly, your computer system can communicate with the Internet or with remote fax machines through a *fax/modem board,* or with a local network using a *network interface card.* To use external speakers, a *sound card* is used. Instead of using expansion boards and tying up valuable expansion slots inside the system unit, some motherboards use *integrated sound* or *integrated video,* instead. In this case, these capabilities are built directly into chips on the motherboard. When an integrated feature is used, a special bus connects the chip to the appropriate port on the outside of the system unit so the appropriate device can be attached to the PC.

You usually buy a new PC with the desired peripheral equipment and corresponding expansions cards already installed, though you can add others at a later time, as new needs are identified. Before adding a new card, however, you should make sure that your system has room for that particular type of card. Though most PCs today come with several expansion slots on the motherboard, some are already filled up when the PC is purchased.

▶ FIGURE 3-13

Expansion cards and slots.

Types of Add-In Boards

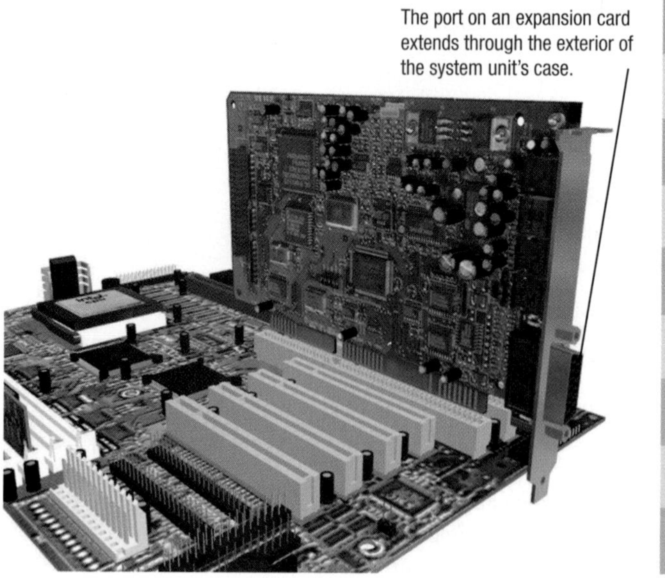

The port on an expansion card extends through the exterior of the system unit's case.

Board Type	Purpose
Accelerator board	Uses specialized processor chips that speed up overall processing
Disk controller card	Enables a particular type of disk drive to interface with the PC
Video-graphics board	Enables a particular type of display to interface with the PC
Fax/modem board	Provides communications capabilities
Memory module	Adds additional RAM to the PC
Network interface card	Enables computer to be connected to a network
Sound board	Enables users to attach speakers to a PC
TV-tuner card	Allows your PC to pick up television signals
Video capture board	Allows video images to be input into the computer from a video camera

>**Expansion card.** A circuit board that can be inserted into a slot on a PC's motherboard to add one or more functions or attach a peripheral device.

Remember that different types of expansion slots are not interchangeable: ISA slots are larger than PCI slots, and APG slots are a little smaller than PCI slots. If you don't have an available slot to add the necessary expansion card to attach a peripheral device, you may be able to purchase the device in a USB or Firewire version instead. With either types of port, a *hub* can be used to convert a single port into multiple ports as needed.

PC Cards: Expansion for Notebook and Other Portable Computers

For many years, notebook users were not able to do much system expansion. Most portable computers lack room inside their system units to accommodate either the standard desktop bus or conventional expansion boards. Then came PCMCIA. *PCMCIA*—which stands for *Personal Computer Memory Card International Association*—refers to the standard way to connect peripheral devices to notebook computers.

The PCMCIA standard uses a credit-card-size adapter card known as the *PCMCIA card,* or more commonly, the **PC card** (see Figure 3-14). PC cards typically plug into slots on the side of a notebook computer's case; these slots connect to the *PC card bus* inside the notebook or laptop computer.

PC cards come in three basic types. A Type I card, the thinnest of the lot, is often used to add memory. A Type II card typically adds networking or modem capabilities, or sound. Type III cards, the thickest type, often contain a removable hard drive. A notebook computer may have a multipurpose slot that can accommodate two Type I cards, two Type II cards, or a single Type III card. Often PC cards can be plugged in or unplugged while the computer is turned on as your needs change during a work session. Notebooks may also have a universal drive bay which can be used to alternate between a hard drive, CD or DVD drive, and floppy drive, as needed.

> **FIGURE 3-14**
> **PC cards.** PC cards allow notebook users to enhance their computing environments. The Type III card shown here has a built-in modem and separate ports for a phone jack and local-network connection.

Expansion for Handheld PCs and Mobile Devices

Most handheld PCs and mobile devices have a limited amount of expandability. Both the popular handheld *Palm PC* and the *Handspring Visor,* a Palm competitor, come with at least one built-in expansion slot designed to attach peripheral devices. For example, the Visor's expansion slot accepts its proprietary *Springboard modules* (see Figure 3-15). Available modules include modems, digital cameras, storage devices, bar-code scanners, telephone modules, GPS receivers, and MP3 players, as well as software and electronic book modules. In addition to its similar *Universal Connector System* port, recent Palm PCs also have postage-stamp-size slot that accepts *SD (Secure Digital) cards* and *MMCs (MultiMedia Cards).* Though used primarily for removable storage today (as discussed in Chapter 4), this slot will also accept the *Secure Digital Input/Output (SDIO)* devices— small devices, such as a digital camera or GPS receiver, attached to an SD card—expected to become available in the future.

Ports

Most system units feature exterior connectors or sockets—called **ports**—that enable you to plug in external hardware devices. Each port is attached to the appropriate bus on the motherboard so that the devices plugged into each port can communicate with the CPU.

As illustrated in Figure 3-16, there are unique connectors for each type of port on a computer system. If there is an available port for the device you want to add, simply plug it in (you usually need to shut down the computer first). If there isn't an available port, you need to insert the appropriate expansion card to create one, or use a USB or Firewire version of the device, if you have one of those two ports available on your PC.

> **FIGURE 3-15**
> The Handspring Visor's Springboard expansion slot allows a variety of expansion options, such as the addition of a digital camera, bar-code, or telephone module.

>**PC card.** A small card that fits into a slot on the exterior of a portable computer to provide new functions. >**Port.** A socket on the exterior of a PC's system unit to which a device may be connected.

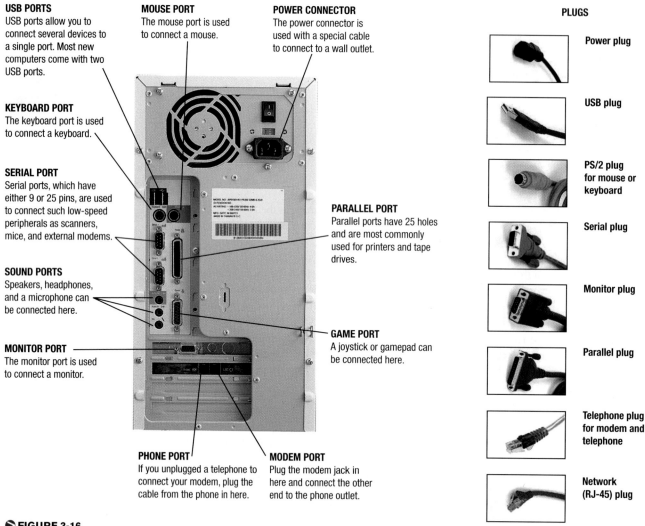

USB PORTS
USB ports allow you to connect several devices to a single port. Most new computers come with two USB ports.

KEYBOARD PORT
The keyboard port is used to connect a keyboard.

SERIAL PORT
Serial ports, which have either 9 or 25 pins, are used to connect such low-speed peripherals as scanners, mice, and external modems.

SOUND PORTS
Speakers, headphones, and a microphone can be connected here.

MONITOR PORT
The monitor port is used to connect a monitor.

MOUSE PORT
The mouse port is used to connect a mouse.

POWER CONNECTOR
The power connector is used with a special cable to connect to a wall outlet.

PARALLEL PORT
Parallel ports have 25 holes and are most commonly used for printers and tape drives.

GAME PORT
A joystick or gamepad can be connected here.

PHONE PORT
If you unplugged a telephone to connect your modem, plug the cable from the phone in here.

MODEM PORT
Plug the modem jack in here and connect the other end to the phone outlet.

PLUGS

Power plug

USB plug

PS/2 plug for mouse or keyboard

Serial plug

Monitor plug

Parallel plug

Telephone plug for modem and telephone

Network (RJ-45) plug

▶ FIGURE 3-16
Ports and connectors.

When connecting cables to the system unit, it is important to pay attention to the *gender* of the port, in addition to the shape and pin count and configuration. *Male* connectors have the pins extended and connect to *female* connectors with matching holes. If a port is of the proper type (such as serial), but is the wrong gender or has the wrong number of pins, adapters or special cables can typically be used to convert the connector to the desired configuration.

Because there are a limited number of ports on the system unit and adding expansion boards to a computer system can be time consuming and somewhat intimidating for many users, USB and Firewire ports are quickly gaining popularity. In fact, it is becoming common to see USB ports located on the front of a system unit for easier access. Some of the most common ports are discussed next. Several of the older ports, such as *serial* and *parallel,* are beginning to be referred to as *legacy ports* and are being eliminated on some PCs.

▼ *Serial ports* can transmit data only a single bit at a time. However, they use very inexpensive cables and they can reliably send data over long distances. Serial ports can be used for such devices as keyboards, mice, and modems, though most systems today come with dedicated ports to attach the mouse and keyboard, as shown in Figure 3-16. *Serial connectors* typically have 9 or 25 pins and are referred to as *DB-9* or *DB-25 connectors.*

▼ *Parallel ports* can transmit data one byte (8 bits) at a time—making data transfers several times faster than those through serial ports—but they require more expensive cables and cannot reliably send data across distances greater than 50 feet. Parallel ports typically connect nearby printers and scanners to a PC. Newer types of parallel ports include the *Enhanced Parallel Port (EPP)* and the *Extended Capabilities Port (ECP).* These ports look like conventional parallel ports and accept the same size and shape of plug as the conventional parallel port (a 25-pin connector), but are more than 10 times faster when used with an appropriate cable. When used with a regular parallel cable, the speed of these ports is similar to that of the conventional parallel port.

▼ *SCSI (Small Computer System Interface) ports* are high-speed parallel ports generally used to attach printers or scanners.

▼ *USB ports* are used to connect USB devices to the computer. Most new PCs come with two USB ports. A *USB hub*—a device that plugs in your PC's USB port to convert one port into several USB ports—can be used to connect multiple USB devices to a single USB port, when necessary. In addition, USB devices are also *hot swappable.* This means that as you add or unplug devices with the system power on, the computer system immediately recognizes the change so you don't have to reboot in order to have the system recognize which devices are currently available.

▼ *Firewire (IEEE 1394) ports* are used to connect Firewire devices to the computer. Similar to USB, a *Firewire hub* can be used to connect multiple devices to a single port and Firewire devices are hot-swappable.

▼ *Network ports* are used to connect a PC to a local area network. Most network cards contain a port that accepts an *RJ-45 connector,* which looks similar to a telephone connector but is larger. Coaxial cable or fiber optic connectors can be used for network connections, as well. Networks are discussed in more detail in Chapter 8.

▼ The *keyboard port* and *mouse port* typically use a *PS/2 connector* and are used to connect the keyboard and mouse to the system unit.

▼ The *monitor port* can be connected directly to the motherboard or can be located on an expansion card. In either case, it is used to connect the monitor to a PC. Monitor ports increasingly use the AGP bus.

▼ The *modem port* and *phone port* typically appear on a modem board. The modem port connects the modem card to your phone outlet. The phone port can be used to connect a telephone, if desired, so you don't lose the use of your phone outlet.

▼ A *MIDI port* is used to connect a *MIDI* (musical *instrument d*igital *i*nterface) device to the computer. MIDI devices include musical keyboards and other instruments that can be connected to the computer to compose music to be stored electronically. A MIDI port usually looks similar to a keyboard port.

▼ An *IrDA (Infrared Data Association)* port receives infrared transmissions from such devices as wireless keyboards, wireless mice, and portable devices. Consequently, the port does not use a plug. With infrared transmission, there cannot be anything blocking the infrared light waves, so newer wireless mice and keyboards tend to use radio wave transmission instead. However, IrDA ports are commonly used to "beam" data from a handheld PC or other portable device to another PC.

▼ A *game port* is used to connect a joystick, game pad, steering wheel, or other device commonly used to control computer game programs.

Notebook computers have ports similar to desktop PCs, but don't usually have as many. Some typical notebook ports are illustrated in Figure 3-17. Additional ports not shown in the figure that are commonly found on notebook computers include IrDA ports for infrared transmission and those used to connect the notebook to a docking station.

▶ FIGURE 3-17
Typical ports on a notebook computer.

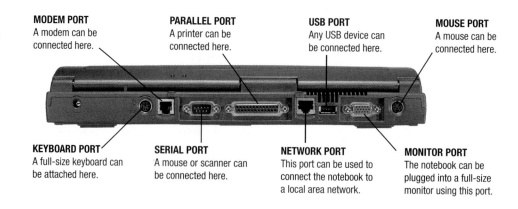

MODEM PORT
A modem can be connected here.

PARALLEL PORT
A printer can be connected here.

USB PORT
Any USB device can be connected here.

MOUSE PORT
A mouse can be connected here.

KEYBOARD PORT
A full-size keyboard can be attached here.

SERIAL PORT
A mouse or scanner can be connected here.

NETWORK PORT
This port can be used to connect the notebook to a local area network.

MONITOR PORT
The notebook can be plugged into a full-size monitor using this port.

HOW THE CPU WORKS

Regardless of size, every computer's CPU is basically a collection of electronic circuits and components. Electronic impulses from an input device pass through RAM and enter the CPU through a system bus. Within the CPU, these impulses move through the circuits and various components—as directed by the program—to create a series of new impulses. Eventually, a set of impulses leaves the CPU headed for an output device.

Typical CPU Components

To begin to understand this process, you need to know first how the CPU is organized and what components it includes. Then we can discuss how electronic impulses move from one part of the CPU to another to process data. The architecture and components included in a CPU (referred to as *microarchitecture*) vary from microprocessor to microprocessor. A simplified example of the principal components that may be included in a typical CPU is illustrated in Figure 3-18 and discussed next.

Arithmetic Logic Unit (ALU)

The **arithmetic/logic unit (ALU)** is the section of the CPU that performs arithmetic and logical operations on data. In other words, it's the part of the computer that computes. *Arithmetic* operations include addition, subtraction, multiplication, and division. *Logical* operations compare pairs of data items to determine whether they are equal and, if not, which is larger. The fact that the CPU can perform only basic arithmetic and logical operations might not seem very impressive, but when combined in various ways at tremendous speeds, these operations enable the computer to perform immensely complex and data-intensive tasks, in a very short period of time—a remarkable feat.

Control Unit

The **control unit** directs the flow of electronic traffic within the CPU. In other words, the control unit coordinates or manages the computer's operation, much like a traffic cop controls the flow of vehicles on a roadway. Based on the instructions received from the *decode unit* (discussed shortly), the control unit tells the ALU what to do and makes sure that everything happens at the right time in order for the appropriate processing to take place.

>**Arithmetic/logic unit (ALU).** The part of the CPU that contains circuitry to perform arithmetic and logical operations. >**Control unit.** The part of the CPU that coordinates its operations.

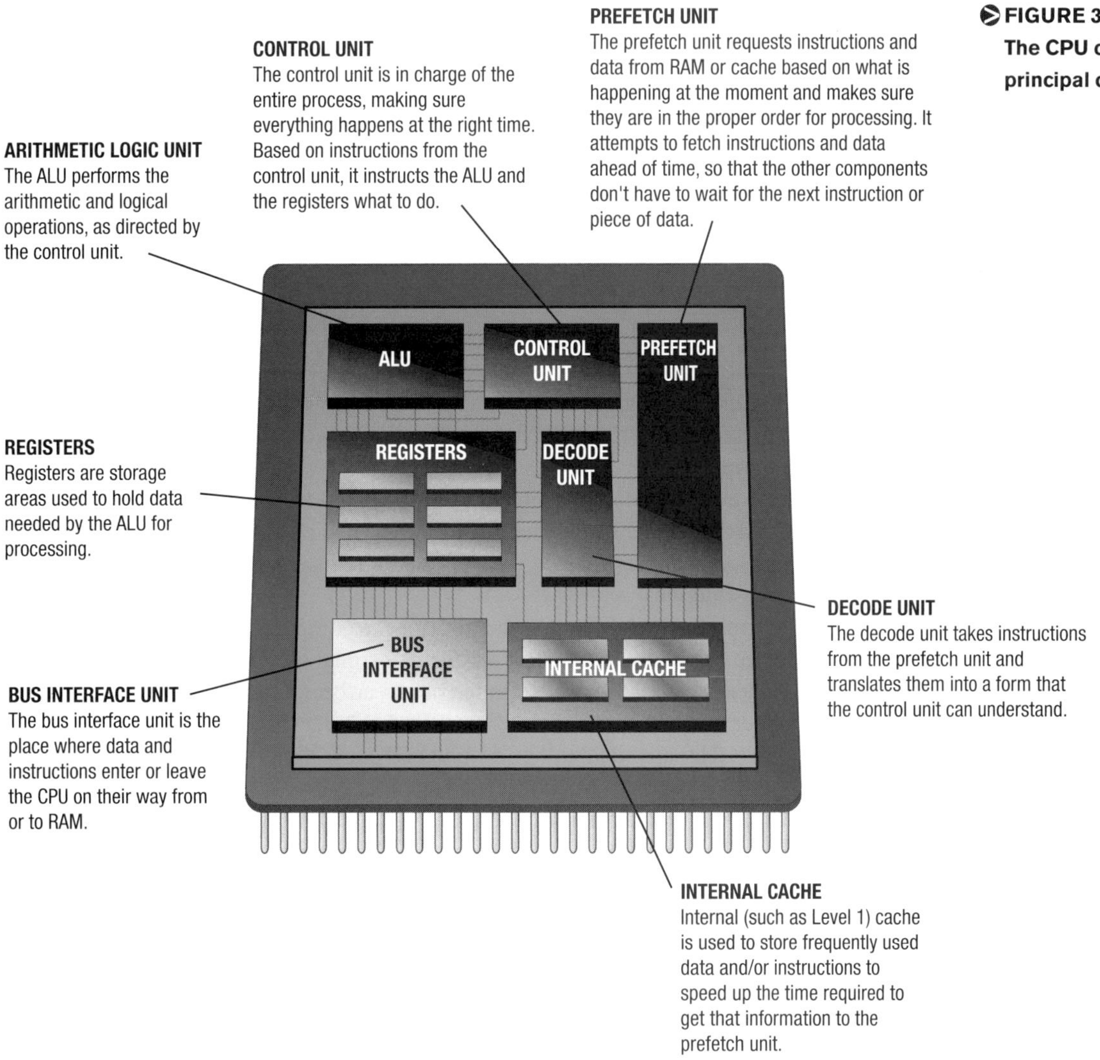

ARITHMETIC LOGIC UNIT
The ALU performs the arithmetic and logical operations, as directed by the control unit.

CONTROL UNIT
The control unit is in charge of the entire process, making sure everything happens at the right time. Based on instructions from the control unit, it instructs the ALU and the registers what to do.

PREFETCH UNIT
The prefetch unit requests instructions and data from RAM or cache based on what is happening at the moment and makes sure they are in the proper order for processing. It attempts to fetch instructions and data ahead of time, so that the other components don't have to wait for the next instruction or piece of data.

REGISTERS
Registers are storage areas used to hold data needed by the ALU for processing.

BUS INTERFACE UNIT
The bus interface unit is the place where data and instructions enter or leave the CPU on their way from or to RAM.

DECODE UNIT
The decode unit takes instructions from the prefetch unit and translates them into a form that the control unit can understand.

INTERNAL CACHE
Internal (such as Level 1) cache is used to store frequently used data and/or instructions to speed up the time required to get that information to the prefetch unit.

FIGURE 3-18
The CPU chip and its principal components.

Registers

As discussed earlier in this chapter, *registers* are the temporary holding places within the CPU into which data are transferred just before processing. The ALU uses registers to store data, intermediary calculations, and the final results of processing. A CPU may have a variety of registers for different purposes, such as an *instruction register* to hold instructions, and an *accumulator register* to hold intermediary processing results. One of Intel's most recent chips—the Itanium—has a total of 256 different registers.

Decode Unit

The *decode unit* translates instructions into a form that can be processed by the ALU and stored in the registers. After decoding, the instructions go to the control unit for processing.

Prefetch Unit

The *prefetch unit,* present in many recent microprocessors, orders data and instructions from cache or RAM based on the task at hand. By attempting to retrieve the necessary instructions and data ahead of time, the prefetch unit helps to avoid delays in processing. It also ensures that all instructions are lined up correctly to send off to the decode unit.

Internal Cache

As mentioned earlier, internal cache (such as Level 1 cache) is used to store frequently used instructions and data. If the necessary items are not in internal cache, they must be retrieved from external cache or RAM.

Bus Interface Unit

The *bus interface unit* is the place where instructions and data flow in and out of the CPU. It connects the CPU to the system bus to connect the CPU to RAM.

The System Clock and the Machine Cycle

As mentioned at the beginning of this chapter, every instruction that you issue to a computer—either by typing a command or clicking something with the mouse—is converted into machine language. In turn, each machine-language instruction in a CPU's *instruction set* (the collection of basic machine-language commands that the CPU can understand) is broken down into several smaller, machine-level instructions called *microcode*. Microcoded instructions, such as moving a single piece of data from one part of the computer system to another or adding the numbers located in two specific registers, are built into the CPU to provide its basic instructions.

The built-in **system clock** in a PC synchronizes the computer's operations. This clock typically resides on the motherboard and sends out a signal on a regular basis to all other computer components, similar to a metronome or a heartbeat. Each signal is referred to as a *cycle;* the number of cycles per second is measured in hertz (Hz): One megahertz (MHz) and one gigahertz (GHz) are equal to one million and one billion ticks of the system clock, respectively.

During each tick or clock cycle, the CPU executes a certain number of pieces of microcoded instructions. Consequently, a higher clock speed means that more instructions can be processed per second than the same CPU with a lower clock speed. Older computers may take more than one clock tick for each instruction; today's faster *superscaler* computers are able to perform multiple instructions per clock tick. Despite the number or fraction of clock ticks required per instruction, when the CPU processes a single piece of microcode, a *machine cycle* is completed.

A **machine cycle** consists of four operations separated into two parts: An *instruction stage* (I-stage) and an *execution stage* (E-stage). These operations are as follows (see Figure 3-19):

▼ I-Stage
  1. The program instruction or information about a needed piece of data is *fetched.*
  2. The instructions are *decoded* so the ALU can understand them.

▼ E-Stage
  3. The ALU *executes* the appropriate instruction.
  4. The result is *stored* either in a register or memory, depending on the instruction.

Because a machine cycle only processes a single instruction, many seemingly simple commands (such as adding two numbers) may require more than one machine cycle. When needed, the machine cycle is repeated as many times as necessary to complete the instructions. A simplified example of how a PC might input two numbers and com-

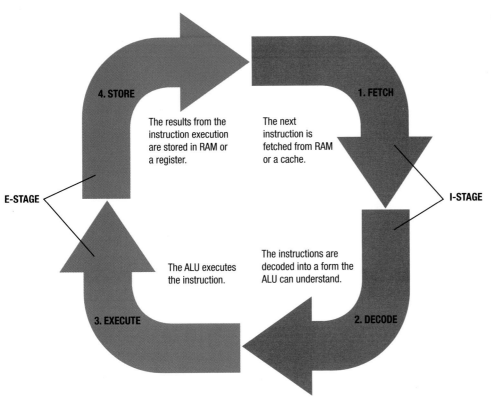

4. STORE

The results from the instruction execution are stored in RAM or a register.

1. FETCH

The next instruction is fetched from RAM or a cache.

E-STAGE

I-STAGE

The ALU executes the instruction.

The instructions are decoded into a form the ALU can understand.

3. EXECUTE

2. DECODE

▶ **FIGURE 3-19**

Machine cycle. The processing of a single machine-level instruction is accomplished in a four-step machine cycle. Some recent computers divide executing the instruction into two steps, resulting in a five-step machine cycle.

pute their sum is illustrated in Figure 3-20. In this example, four machine cycles are used, as follows:

1. The number 2 is input and stored in a register.

2. The number 3 is input and stored in a register.

3. The addition instruction is input and the control unit instructs the ALU to add the two numbers stored in the register.

4. The equal sign input is interpreted as a request to display the result of the previous instruction, and the ALU is directed to output the sum.

These steps may seem to define a tedious process, especially when a computer must go through thousands, millions, or even billions of machine cycles to complete a single program's processing. But computer hardware works at almost unimaginably high speeds and is continually getting faster. The slowest hardware performs an instruction in *milliseconds* (thousandths of a second) or *microseconds* (millionths of a second). In the fastest hardware, speeds are measured in *nanoseconds* (billionths of a second) or *picoseconds* (trillionths of a second).

Because different computers can process a different number of instructions per clock tick, for a more universal measurement computer processing speed can be measured in the number of instructions it can process per second, instead of the number of cycles per second. In this case, the terms *mips* (millions of instructions per second), *megaflops, gigaflops,* and *teraflops* (millions, billions, and trillions of floating-point operations per second, respectively) are used. For example, one of the fastest computers in the world—ASCI White, built for the federal government by IBM—operates at over 12 teraflops. In other words, it can process over 12 trillion operations per second.

Though originally used only with mainframe and supercomputers, today's microcomputers have become so fast that their speeds are now being quoted using this terminology. For example, Apple rates the speed of its PowerPC G4 CPU at over one gigaflop.

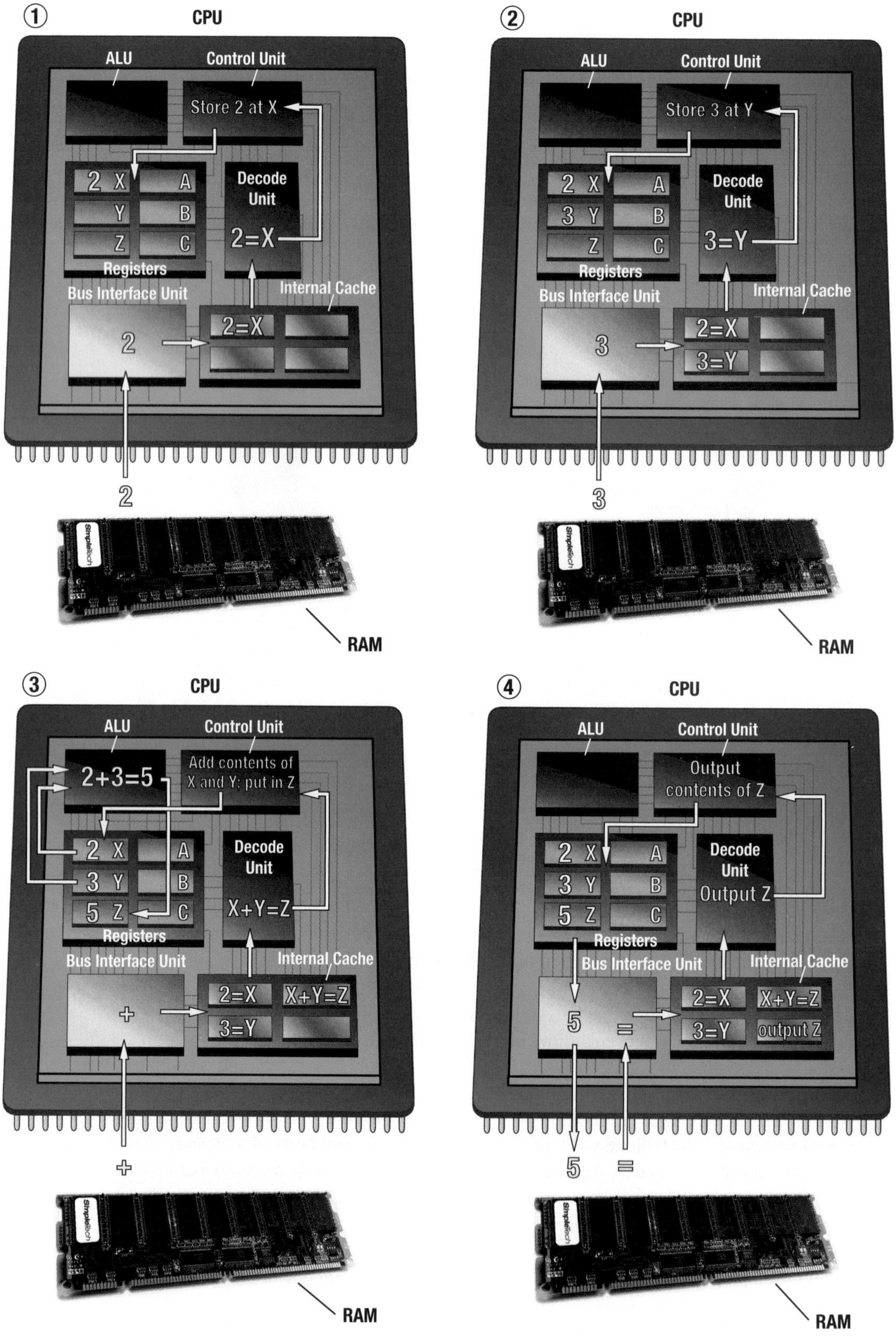

FIGURE 3-20

Sample machine cycles. Some tasks, such as adding up two numbers as shown here, may require more than one machine cycle. This example uses 4 machine cycles.

MAKING COMPUTERS FASTER NOW AND IN THE FUTURE

Over the years, computer designers have developed a number of strategies to achieve faster performance in their machines. Researchers are also constantly working on ways to speed up the computers of the future. This section discusses several of these methods. There are also some things that you can do to speed up your computer today, as discussed next.

Speeding Up Your System Today

Several strategies that may speed up your current computer are listed next.

Add More Memory

With today's graphic-intensive interfaces and applications, much more memory is required than was necessary even a couple of years ago. If you seem to have to wait too long when opening programs or saving documents and your CPU is relatively fast (it runs at over 600 MHz), you should consider adding more memory to your system to bring it up to a minimum of 128 MB.

Perform System Maintenance

As you work and use your hard drive to store and retrieve data, and as you install and uninstall programs, your PC gets less efficient. Part of the reason for this is as large files are stored and restored, they often become *fragmented*—that is, not stored in contiguous (adjacent) storage areas. Because the different pieces of the file are physically located in different places, it takes longer for the computer to retrieve or store it. Another reason a computer may become inefficient is that when programs are uninstalled, pieces of the program are sometimes left behind or references to these programs are left in operating system files. Yet another reason is that as a hard drive begins to get full, it takes longer to locate and manipulate the data stored there. All of these factors can result in a system performing more slowly than it should.

To alleviate some of these problems, regular *system maintenance* should be performed. Here are some ideas.

▼ Uninstall any programs that you no longer want on your computer to free up space on your hard drive. Be sure to use the designated removal procedure for your operating system such as the Add/Remove Programs icon in the Windows Control Panel or an "Uninstall" option for that program located on the Start menu to remove the program for Windows PCs.

▼ If you have large files (such as digital photos or other graphical images) archived on your computer, consider moving them to a removable storage device, such as a Zip disk or CD-R disc. Once copied onto the new medium, they can be deleted from your hard drive to free up space. If the files are important, you may want to make copies of the files on two different disks, just to be safe.

▼ Open the Recycle Bin (or similar location holding deleted files on your PC) and empty it. As long as you are sure that none of the files in the Recycle Bin needs to be restored, those files are taking up room on your hard drive needlessly.

▼ Use a utility program, such as Windows' Disk Cleanup, to delete unnecessary files left over from installing programs, uninstalling programs, and browsing the Internet. There are also a variety of utility programs that can be purchased to clean up your hard drive (see Figure 3-21).

FIGURE 3-21
Utility programs. There are a variety of utility programs available to help clean up your hard drive and speed up your system.

▼ Use a utility program, such as Windows' Disk Defragmenter, to arrange the files on your hard drive more efficiently. On large hard drives, defragmentation may need to be run during the night because of the length of time required. Defragmentation and other system maintenance activities are discussed in more detail in Chapters 6 and 16.

Buy a Larger or Second Hard Drive

As already mentioned, hard drives get less efficient as they get filled up. If your hard drive is almost full and you don't have any data or programs you can remove, you should consider buying and installing a second hard drive, assuming that you have an empty storage bay inside your computer. Some users can comfortably install a second hard drive themselves; others prefer to have the new drive installed for them. In either case, once the drive is installed, you can transfer your data to the new drive, uninstall a few of the larger programs and install them again on the new drive, and otherwise free up space on your first hard drive. Alternately, you can replace your existing hard drive with a larger one, though the data transfer process will be a little more complicated.

Upgrade Your Internet Connection

If your system primarily seems slow when you are on the Internet, the culprit might be your Internet connection. If you are using dial-up access, be sure you are using a 56K modem. If you use the Internet a great deal for work or multimedia purposes, consider switching to cable, satellite, or DSL Internet service. (The differences between these types of Internet connections are described in Chapters 8 and 9.)

Upgrade Your Video Card

If you're a gamer or otherwise use 3D-graphic-intensive applications, consider upgrading your video card to one that better supports 3D graphics. If you don't use 3D applications, upgrading your video card won't usually improve your speed.

Upgrade Your CPU

Upgrading your CPU used to be a popular choice, since the price difference between a new system and a new CPU was relatively high. With today's low computer prices and fast basic processor speeds, however, this upgrade is getting less common. If you have a fairly slow Pentium chip (less than 300 MHz), you might want to look into whether your motherboard would support a faster chip and the cost involved, but most of the time it would be better to put that money into a new system, when needed.

Strategies for Making Computers Speedier

There are several strategies that researchers and manufacturers are working on to build faster PCs. Some are described next.

Moving Circuits Close Together

As complex as computers seem, all must follow one intuitive natural law: Circuits that are physically located closer together require less time to move bits between them. During the past several decades, computer-chip makers have packed circuitry progressively closer and closer together. Today, they fit several million circuits on a single, fingernail-size chip. This remarkable achievement doesn't mean that chip makers can continue to shrink circuitry without constraint, however. When the circuits are in use, they generate heat, and circuits placed too close together can become hot enough to melt the chip. For this reason, virtually all CPUs today employ fans, *heat sinks* (small components typically made out of aluminum with fins that help to dissipate heat) or some combination of the two to cool the CPU. Low-power CPUs that run cooler than traditional CPUs (such as those made by Transmeta) may also be more common in the future.

Increasing Register Size

Until the year 2001, most CPU registers were 32-bit width or smaller. With the introduction of 64-bit CPUs, such as the Intel Itanium in 2001 and AMD's new 64-bit chip (code-named "Sledgehammer") expected out in 2002, computer processing speed is expected to increase dramatically.

Faster and Wider Buses

As discussed earlier, wider buses lead to faster processing. Buses also vary in speed; faster buses tend to result in faster processing. Buses are available now that run at 400 MHz.

Faster Memory

Memory also varies in speed—faster memory helps speed up processing. Fast memory today runs at over 100 MHz. One of the faster type of RAM available—Rambus RDRAM—runs at 800 MHz in hopes of more closely matching memory speed with CPU speeds to reduce or eliminate bottlenecks.

Improved Materials

Traditionally, CPU chips have used aluminum circuitry etched onto a silicon backing. However, because designers are quickly reaching limits on the number of aluminum circuits that they can pack onto a silicon chip without heat damage or interference, chip makers are always looking for better materials to use. The most recent trend is replacing the aluminum on silicon chips with copper. Copper is a far better electrical conductor, and it can produce chips containing more circuitry at a lower price (see Figure 3-22). Aluminum has been used on chips for more than 30 years; until IBM's breakthrough, copper bled into the chip's silicon backing. IBM is currently using copper wiring on Power PC chips, as well as for its mainframe and supercomputer lines, such as in one of the world's faster supercomputer—ASCI White—shown in Figure 1-13 in Chapter 1.

Another recent development is *SOI (silicon on insulator)*. SOI chips—used on IBM's AS/400 servers along with copper wiring—use a thin layer of insulating material over the silicon to reduce heat and power consumption. This results in being able to place the circuits closer together than is possible without the insulating material.

Improved Instruction Set Design

An earlier discussion in this chapter mentioned that each computer has its own *instruction set*. Traditionally, computers have been built under a design principle called *complex instruction set computing (CISC)*. A computer chip with CISC design contains a relatively large instruction set.

Starting in the mid-1970s, processors with instruction sets limited to only the most frequently used instructions became available. These devices follow a principle called *reduced instruction set computing (RISC)*. Experience has shown that computers using the RISC design work faster, unless the instruction is extraordinarily complex.

With the introduction of 64-bit CPUs, such as Intel's Itanium chip, a new design option—*explicitly parallel instruction computing (EPIC)* became available. The primary philosophy behind EPIC is *instruction–level parallelism (ILP)*. With ILP, individual operations are executed in parallel, significantly speeding up processing. ILP is made possible by increasing numbers of transistors on a chip to enable multiple operations to be performed at one time.

Pipelining

In older PC systems, the CPU had to completely finish processing one instruction before starting another. More recent PCs, however, can process multiple instructions at one time.

FIGURE 3-22
Copper chips. Copper chips conduct electricity far better than traditional aluminum-circuited ones and require less power. The portion of the fingernail-sized chip pictured here has six circuit layers, and each of the millions of circuits is 500 times thinner than a human hair.

Stages

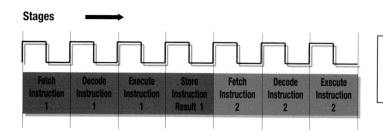

WITHOUT PIPELINING
Without pipelining, an instruction finishes an entire machine cycle before another instruction is started.

Stages

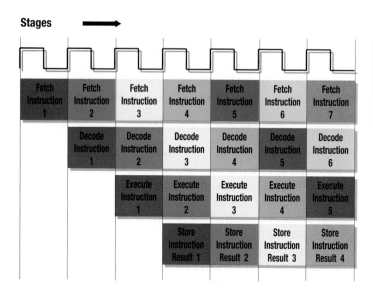

WITH PIPELINING
With pipelining, a new instruction is begun when the preceding instruction moves to the next stage of the machine cycle.

FIGURE 3-23

Pipelining. Pipelining streamlines the machine cycle by executing different stages of multiple instructions at the same time, so the different parts of the CPU are idle less often. In today's CPUs, 10- to 20-stage pipelines are typical.

One way this is accomplished is through **pipelining.** With pipelining, a new instruction begins executing as soon as the previous one reaches the next stage of the machine cycle. Figure 3-23 illustrates this process with a 4-stage pipeline. Notice that while the pipelined CPU is executing one instruction, it is simultaneously fetching and getting the next instruction ready for execution. Without a pipeline, the arithmetic part of the processor would be idle while an instruction is being fetched and decoded. CPUs today are commonly built with multiple pipelines, which can greatly increase the number of instructions performed per machine cycle.

Multiprocessing and Parallel Processing

Despite the astounding evolution of computer technology over the past half century, the vast majority of PCs are still driven by single CPUs. In the race to develop tomorrow's ever-faster computer systems, scientists have developed multiprocessing and parallel processing. In contrast to the instruction–level parallelism discussed earlier (where multiple operations are performed simultaneously within a single CPU), multiprocessing and parallel processing use two or more coordinated CPUs to perform operations simultaneously.

With **multiprocessing,** each CPU typically works on a different job. With **parallel processing,** the multiple processors work together to make one job finish sooner (see Figure 3-24). Two of the most common designs are *symmetric multiprocessing (SMP)* and *massively parallel processing (MPP).* With SMP, a single copy of the operating system is in charge of

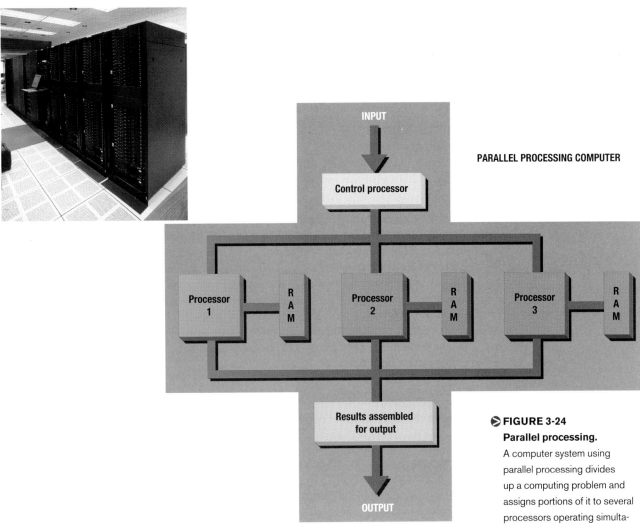

PARALLEL PROCESSING COMPUTER

> **FIGURE 3-24**
> **Parallel processing.**
> A computer system using parallel processing divides up a computing problem and assigns portions of it to several processors operating simultaneously. The NCSA supercomputer system shown is one of the fastest Linux clusters in the world and contains 512 dual-processor Pentium III servers linked together for a total of 1,024 processors.

all the processors and the processors share memory. Typically, SMP systems do not usually exceed 64 processors. MPP systems, in contrast, can use hundreds or thousands of microprocessors and each processor has its own copy of the operating system and its own memory (as in Figure 3-24). MPP systems are typically more difficult to program than SMP systems.

The trend in today's larger multiprocessing systems is using multiple SMP servers (called *nodes*) linked together to act as one computer. The resulting computer system is sometimes called a *cluster.* For example, the ASCI White supercomputer pictured in Figure 1-13 consists of 512 servers containing16 processors each, for a total of 8,192 processors. The Linux cluster shown in Figure 3-24 uses 512 dual-processor servers linked together for a total of 1,024 processors. These types of systems are generally *scalable*—meaning that the computer system can be made more powerful at any time simply by adding more nodes to it.

Multiprocessing can increase the number of calculations performed in any given time period astronomically, For example, ASCI White can perform at over 12 teraflops (trillion of operations per second). This amount of processing is estimated to be more data than one person with a calculator could do in 10 million years. When tremendous amounts of processing are required but access to a supercomputer is not feasible, one recent trend is to use the computing capabilities of a large collection of PCs to work together to process the necessary data. For instance, large businesses can use their employees' desktop workstations to process data overnight while the office is closed. These *distributed processing* systems can be as powerful as supercomputer. For example, one business that uses 5,000 workstations after their engineers go home at night has reached a combined computing speed of 6 teraflops. This type of multiprocessing can even occur with home computers connected through the Internet. Usually a small program or screen saver is downloaded and then, when the system is idle, the software puts it to work on a small piece of the current project. Usually the projects to which individuals donate their PC's processing time involve scientific research, such as the Human Genome Project or cancer research.

Future Trends

While some of the strategies discussed in the prior section are currently being implemented, some new ideas are further from being actualized. Selected trends we may see in the near future are discussed next.

Organic Computers

Biotechnology is the term commonly used to describe combining biology with technology. Biotechnology is involved with creating *organic computers*—computers containing organic matter. Biotechnology enables circuits to be grown and shaped as tiny molecules. Though some researchers estimate that it may be 10 years before a molecular computer is available to consumers, they feel it will be worth the wait. With estimates of ultra-tiny processors 100 billion times faster than the most powerful processors available today, and the possibility of microscopic sensors that can be embedded in paint, clothing, or medical diagnostic machines that are as small as the bacteria they analyze, organic computers hold great promise for the future.

Nanotechnology

Current computer technology—called *lithography*—allows for electronic circuits smaller than one micron (1,000 nanometers). A newer field of science—called *nanotechnology*—is working at the individual atomic and molecular levels to create computer chips that are thousands of times smaller than current technologies permit. (On nanometer is one-billionth of a meter.) Researchers at IBM, Motorola, Dow Chemical, Hewlett-Packard, and other organizations are working on nanometer-size products and materials. Some prototypes include a miniscule device (about one-fiftieth the width of a human hair) that can measure small amounts of electric charge; a single switch that can be turned on and off like a transistor but is made out of a single organic molecule; and a miniature hard drive that holds 20 GB of data and is read by heads only a few nanometers thick.

The implications of these technological breakthroughs could be widespread in the future, including microscopic robots that can enter the bloodstream and perform tests or irradiate cancerous tumors, molecular circuits, and much denser memory and storage than are currently possible. Nanotechnology may also lead to computers so small they can be woven into the fibers of clothing or embedded in practically any type of device or appliance.

further exploration

For links to further information about new processing trends, go to www.course.com/parker2002/ch3

New Materials

Silicon backing has traditionally been used for microprocessors for a number of reasons. First, as the main ingredient in beach sand, it is one of the most plentiful elements known. Second, it is lightweight. Third, it is a natural *semiconductor.* In contrast to both metal (which conducts electricity) and wood (which doesn't), silicon falls somewhere in between. The significance of this is that its properties may be altered to let electricity pass or prevent it from passing. Silicon-backed chips have been in wide use since the 1970s, when manufacturing techniques for microminiature circuitry became widely available.

Today, because designers may be approaching limits on the number of circuits that they can pack onto a silicon chip without heat damage, they are looking at alternative technologies to replace the standard CPU materials. As already discussed, copper is currently being used. One newer possibility is *optical processing,* which uses light waves instead of electrons. Optical chips emit less heat and can move data faster. The technology, however, is still in its infancy and optical chips are currently limited to a few applications. *Superconductive materials* are another approach. Superconductive materials—which resist heat buildup—can be used to pack a chip's circuitry closer together, resulting in speedier chips. Two possibilities being researched are ceramic superconductors and a new form of carbon consisting of 60 carbon atoms surrounding a hollow cluster. When one or more alkali metals are inserted into the empty space between the carbon atoms, the resulting compound—called a *fulleride*—often becomes a superconductor.

In Chapter 3 we looked inside of a typical PC system unit and examined the functions of the hardware found there. Most of this hardware is involved with processing.

DATA AND PROGRAM REPRESENTATION

Chapter Objective 1:
Understand how data and programs are represented to a computer and be able to identify a few of the coding systems used to accomplish this.

The electronic components of a digital computer work in a two-state, or binary, fashion. It is convenient to think of these binary states in terms of 0s and 1s. Computer people refer to such 0s and 1s as bits. Converting data to these 0s and 1s is called *digital data representation.*

Computers use the **binary numbering system** to represent numbers and perform numeric computations. Text-based data can be represented with one of several fixed-length binary codes. Two popular coding schemes are **ASCII** and **EBCDIC.** These systems represent single characters of data—a numeric digit, alphabetic character, or special symbol—as strings of eight bits. Each string of bits is called a **byte.** Computer systems allow for an additional bit position, called a *parity bit,* in each byte to reveal transmission errors. **Unicode** is another binary code used with text-based data that can represent text in all written languages, including those that use alphabets different than English and other Western European languages.

The storage capacity of computers often is expressed in **kilobytes (KB),** or thousands of bytes; **megabytes (MB),** millions of bytes; **gigabytes (GB),** billions of bytes; and **terabytes (TB),** trillions of bytes.

The binary system can represent not only text but graphics, audio, and video data, as well. **Machine language** is the binary-based code through which computers represent program instructions. A program must be translated into machine language before the computer can execute it.

THE SYSTEM UNIT

Chapter Objective 2:
Explain the functions of the hardware components commonly found inside the system unit.

Almost all PCs sold today are comprised of a variety of hardware components. For instance, chips are mounted onto circuit boards, and those boards are positioned in slots on the **motherboard** or **system board** located inside the **system unit.**

Every PC has a **microprocessor** or **CPU** chip attached to its motherboard that performs the processing for the computer. CPU chips differ in many respects; one difference is word size. A computer *word* is a group of bits or bytes that the processor can manipulate as a unit. A larger word size usually implies a more powerful processor. Another difference is the amount of *cache memory*—memory located inside or very close to the CPU chip to help speed up processing. Other important differences are the general architecture of the CPU, bus speed and width, and the CPU's *clock speed.*

The main memory chips for a PC are commonly referred to as **RAM,** for **random access memory.** RAM is volatile and used to temporarily store programs and data while they are needed. Memory chips that store nonerasable programs comprise the computer's **ROM,** for **read-only memory.** Nonvolatile memory that can be erased and reprogrammed in blocks is called **flash memory.** Flash memory chips can be found in PCs and mobile devices; flash memory chips mounted on small cards can be used for storage with portable PCs, digital cameras, and other smaller devices. Memory built into the CPU chip to hold instructions and data before or during processing are called **registers.**

A computer **bus** is an electronic path along which bits are transmitted. Common buses include *internal buses,* which move data around within the CPU; *system buses,* which move data between the CPU and RAM; and *expansion buses,* which connect the CPU to peripheral devices. Common buses include *PCI, APG, USB (universal serial bus),* and *Firewire.*

Many system units have external **ports** through which peripheral devices connect to the computer. Also, many desktop PCs contain limited numbers of internal *expansion slots,* into which users can insert an **expansion card** to give the computer added functionality. Owners of notebook computers normally expand their systems by adding **PC cards.** Handheld PC and mobile device users can use special cards or modules compatible with their particular type of device, such as *SD cards* and *Springboard modules.*

Chapter Objective 3:
Explain how systems can be expanded in order to attach new peripheral devices or add new capabilities.

HOW THE CPU WORKS

A PC's CPU has several major sections. The **arithmetic/logic unit (ALU)** performs arithmetic and logical operations on data. The **control unit** directs the flow of electronic traffic between memory and the ALU and also between the CPU and input and output devices. Registers—high-speed staging areas within the CPU that hold program instructions and data immediately before and during processing—are used to enhance the computer's performance. The *decode unit* decodes the instructions input into the CPU; the *internal cache* stores frequently used instructions and data; the *bus input unit* inputs data and instructions from RAM; and the *prefetch unit* requests data and instructions before or as they are needed.

Chapter Objective 4:
Describe how the computer system's CPU and memory components process program instructions and data.

The CPU processes instructions in a sequence called a **machine cycle** or *instruction cycle.* Each machine-language instruction is broken down into several smaller instructions called *microcode,* and each piece of microcode corresponds to an operation (such as adding two numbers located in the CPU's registers) that can be performed in the CPU's circuits. The computer system has a built-in **system clock** that synchronizes all of the PC's activities.

A machine cycle consists of four steps. During the *I-stage* (instruction stage), the instruction is fetched and decoded into a form the ALU can understand; during the *E-stage* (execution stage), the ALU executes the instruction under control-unit supervision and stores the result as instructed.

In addition to measuring a PC's speed byits CPU's clock speed (the number of machine cycles per second stated in *megahertz MHz* or *gigahertz GHz*), the more universal measurement of number of instructions processed per second can be used. The terms *mips* (millions of instructions per second), *megaflops* (millions of floating-point operations per second), *gigaflops* (billions of operations per second), and *teraflops* (trillions of operations per second) are commonly used.

MAKING COMPUTERS FASTER NOW AND IN THE FUTURE

There are several possible remedies for a computer that is performing too slowly including adding more memory, performing system maintenance to clean up the PC's hard drive, buying a larger or additional hard drive, and upgrading the computer's Internet connection, video card, or CPU, depending on the primary role of the computer and where the bottleneck appears to be.

Chapter Objective 5:
Name and evaluate several strategies that can be used today for speeding the operations of computers, and some strategies that may be used in the future.

To make computers work faster over all, over the years computer designers have developed a number of strategies, and researchers are continually working on new strategies. Some of the strategies already being implemented include moving circuits closer together, increasing register size, using faster buses and memory, building components out of better materials, using improved instruction set design (such as *RISC* and *EPIC*), using one or more **pipelines, multiprocessing,** and **parallel processing.**

Some possibilities for future computers include organic computers, microscopic computers using the field of nanotechnology, and new materials, such as optical processing and superconductive materials.

KEY TERMS

Instructions: Match each key term on the left with the definition on the right that fits best.

1. arithmetic/logic unit (ALU)

_____ 1,024 bytes.

2. ASCII

_____ A fixed-length, binary coding system widely used to represent text-based data for computer processing on many types of computers.

3. binary numbering system

_____ A group of eight bits that represents a single character of data.

4. bus

_____ A high-speed staging area within the CPU that temporarily stores data during processing.

5. byte

_____ A socket on the exterior of a PC's system unit to which a device may be connected

6. central processing unit (CPU)

_____ An electronic path on the motherboard or within the CPU or other computer component along which bits are transmitted.

7. control unit

_____ Approximately 1 billion bytes.

8. gigabyte (GB)

_____ Approximately 1 million bytes.

9. kilobyte (KB)

_____ Approximately 1 trillion bytes.

10. megabyte (MB)

_____ Chips located on the motherboard that provide a temporary holding place for the computer to store data and program instructions while they are needed.

11. motherboard

_____ The chip located inside the system unit of a computer that performs the processing for a computer and communicates with its peripheral devices.

12. port

_____ The main box of a computer that houses the CPU, motherboard, memory, and other devices.

13. random access memory (RAM)

_____ The main circuit board of a computer, located inside the system unit, to which all computer-system components connect.

14. register

_____ The numbering system that represents all numbers using just two symbols (0 and 1).

15. system clock

_____ The part of the CPU that contains circuitry to perform arithmetic and logical operations.

16. system unit

_____ The part of the CPU that coordinates its operations.

17. terabyte (TB)

_____ The timing mechanism within the computer system that synchronizes the transmission of instructions and data through the computer's circuits.

Self-Quiz

True/False

Instructions: Circle **T** if the statement is true or **F** if the statement is false.

T F **1.** A hard disk that can hold 5 GB can hold about 5 billion characters.

T F **2.** ASCII is one coding system widely used to represent numeric data to a computer.

T F **3.** The logical operations a CPU may perform could include such things as addition, subtraction, multiplication, and division.

T F **4.** A bus is a pathway, such as on the motherboard or inside the CPU, along which bits can be transferred.

T F **5.** Processing shared by two or more computers or processors working together can be called parallel processing.

Completion

Instructions: Answer the following questions.

6. The binary number 1101 is equivalent to the decimal number _____.

7. _____ memory is very fast temporary storage located close to or inside the CPU, where the computer stores the most frequently and recently used data and instructions.

8. The main board for the computer to which all hardware needs to be connected is referred to as the _____.

9. A(n) _____ is a socket on the exterior of a computer's system unit into which a peripheral device may be plugged.

10. With _____, the CPU is able to begin executing a new instruction as soon as the previous instruction has reached the next stage of the machine cycle.

Exercises

1. What does each of the following acronyms stand for?

    a. RAM _____

    b. ROM _____

    c. USB _____

    d. AGP _____

2. Number the following terms from 1 to 8 to indicate their size from smallest to largest.

    _____ Petabyte

    _____ Kilobyte

    _____ Gigabyte

    _____ Exabyte

    _____ Byte

    _____ Terabyte

    _____ Bit

    _____ Megabyte

3. Given the following ASCII character representations and the specified parity settings, indicate whether a 0 or 1 should be added to the end of the character to correctly follow the parity rule. Also state which character is being represented.

Byte Representation	Parity	0 or 1?	CHARACTER
00110101	even	_____	_____
01011010	odd	_____	_____

4. Match each of the following pictures with its appropriate name.

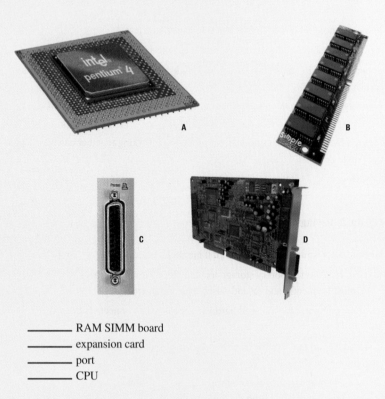

_____ RAM SIMM board
_____ expansion card
_____ port
_____ CPU

5. If your PC seems sluggish, list two things you could do to try to speed it up without resorting to purchasing an entirely new system.

1. **The Chips** The leading manufacturers of CPU chips are Intel, AMD, and Motorola. Each of these companies has at least one chip available on the market right now and likely has plans for the release of a new chip in the not too distant future. For this project, identify the current chip available from each manufacturer and research its characteristics and specifications. Be sure to look for any characteristics that make one chip different than the others. Discuss whether or not the chips use the same amounts of cache, how their clock speeds compare, and what role these factors have in the speed of the microprocessor. If you can locate benchmark test results for the chips (simulations that attempt to measure the true speed and performance of the chips), be sure to include those results and who ran the test (the manufacturer, a computer journal, etc.). At the conclusion of your research, prepare a one-page summary of your findings and submit it to your instructor.

2. **Observations** Gordon Moore (Intel's chairman emeritus), Bill Machrone (vice president of technology at Ziff Davis), and Arthur Rock (noted venture capitalist) have all made interesting observations about the capacity and costs associated with the microprocessor industry. For this project, discover their observations and how each one applies to the microprocessor industry. Does Gordon Moore's observation still hold true? If so, do you think it will remain true for the next 30 years? At the conclusion of your research, prepare a one-page summary of your findings and submit it to your instructor.

3. **In Review** You should always start the process of expanding or upgrading your computer by reading the hardware and software reviews provided by most traditional and online magazines like *Computerworld, PC Week, InfoWeek,* or *MacWeek.* These magazines do an excellent job of reviewing most computer-related components by category, providing you with the latest information about compatibility, performance, cost, reliability, and overall value. For this project, select a piece of hardware that you would like to upgrade on your PC or add to your computer system (if you don't have a computer, just assume that you do). Some possible options include adding a new video board, modem, sound card, scanner, digital camera, printer, or DVD, CD-R, or Zip drive. Research specific models of this product and select the one that would best suit your needs, noting why you selected the model you did over its competitors. In your findings, be sure to identify how the device will be connected to your PC. If an expansion card is required, identify which slot the card would be inserted into and make certain that there is an empty slot of that type on your PC. If there isn't an available slot, check whether the product can be connected in a different manner, such as by using a different type of card or a USB or Firewire port. At the conclusion of your research, prepare a one-page summary of your findings and submit it to your instructor.

4. **Inspecting a System Unit** The system unit contains many components, including the motherboard, CPU chip, RAM, expansion cards, power supply, fan, hard disk, floppy-disk drive, CD or DVD drive, etc. For this project, find a PC that you can open up and look inside of (be sure to ask permission first before opening up a school computer). Before opening up the system unit, turn off the computer and unplug the power cord. Remove the cover from the system unit and perform a system inspection. **Do NOT touch** any components inside the PC without first discharging the static electricity from your body by touching the outside of the power supply unit or by wearing an antistatic wristband. During the course of the inspection, sketch a diagram showing the location of each component listed above, plus any other important components that you recognize (annotate your diagram with any identifying marks found on each of these components). Be careful not to disturb any of the components during the course of the inspection and return the system cover to its original location before you plug the computer back into the power supply. Don't forget to include the name and location of any external ports on your sketch. At the conclusion of this task, submit a copy of the diagram to your instructor, as documentation of your efforts.

5. **The IC Story** The transistor is the basic building block of modern day integrated chips (ICs), and is often referred to as the most important invention of the 20th century. The story behind the invention of transistors and their eventual application to the development of microprocessors is filled with luck, mistakes, chances, the Apollo space mission, and pioneering engineers. For this project, investigate and summarize the major historical events leading to the development of microprocessors, as we know them today. Do you think we would have CPUs today if the U.S. government had not been in a race to put the first man on the moon? Submit this project to your instructor in the form of a short paper, not more than two pages in length.

6. **Faster Components** The question of who has more influence on the market between hardware manufacturers and software developers has been an issue since the first IBM PC computer. As soon as the hardware manufacturers figured out a way to process data faster, the software developers come out with a software package that met, or exceeded that additional capacity. In the early days of the IBM PC, hardware manufacturers simply increased the speed of the computer's system clock, which in turn caused the CPU, memory, and expansion bus to transfer data at a faster rate. This worked for a while, but it soon became apparent that individual components would have run at their own clock speeds in order to meet or exceed the increasing demands of the software developers. One of the newest improvements is a new type of RAM called Rambus DRAM; another has been the increase in speed in the system bus. For this project, investigate and summarize the how hardware manufacturers have successfully increased the processing ability of the computer by improving the architecture and processing components inside the PC. Do you think that the hardware manufacturers or software developers are the primary catalyst for improved performance in the computer industry? Have we reached a point at which the hardware for the home computer market now provides more processing power than we actually need? Submit this project to your instructor in the form of a short paper, not more than two pages in length.

7. **Competitive History** Both Intel and AMD have Web sites that provide a fairly detailed account of each company's historical events and achievements. These Web sites also include a significant amount of data about the founders of the company, where the companies are located, latest news events, and their visions for the future. For this project, form a group to review these two Web sites and prepare a summary that shows some of the major success and setbacks that each of these companies has experienced since they began. Don't forget to include some of the major historical events and people in your summary. Which of these two chip manufacturers do you think will have the most market share in the next five years? Do either of these manufacturers make any other products? Based on the information you have discovered, do you have a preference for a CPU made by one of these two manufacturers over the other? Your group should submit this project to your instructor in the form of a short paper, not more than three pages in length.

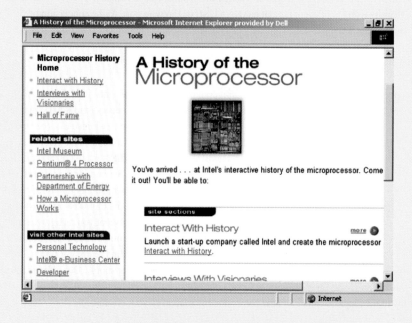

8. **True Binary** All numbers processed by the CPU must be represented in a binary format. The conversion from decimal (base 10) to and from true binary (base 2) format is a fairly straightforward process and can be accomplished with basic arithmetic. The conversion from true binary format to hexadecimal (base 16) format is also a fairly straightforward process, and is generally used to conserve memory whenever possible. For this project, present an example of how a three-digit decimal number can be converted to both binary and hexadecimal and back again, without the use of a calculator (you may wish to read the Numbering Systems Appendix located at the back of this text). Is there any relationship between true binary and ASCII, EBCDIC, or Unicode? Why does a computer use base 2 instead of base 10 like humans do? This presentation should not exceed five minutes and should make use of one or more presentation aids such as the chalkboard, handouts, overhead transparencies, or computer-based slide presentation format. You may be asked to submit a summary of the presentation to your instructor.

9. **Future Chips** Companies such as Intel, AMD, and Motorola are always developing new strategies to improve the performance of their chips. These strategies range from using more conductive materials, to new cooling strategies, to biotechnology. For this project, form a group to research the expected future microprocessors of these three companies. Your group should present a summary of the announced plans that each of these companies has for future chips, and how they will be faster, or more capable, than the models available now. Who do you think will lead the market in five years? Is there really that much of a difference in speed and capability between the top chips manufactured by each of these manufacturers? Is there a difference in strategy between the three companies? This presentation should not exceed 10 minutes and should make use of one or more presentation aids such as the chalkboard, handouts, overhead transparencies, or computer-based slide presentation format. You may be asked to submit a summary of the presentation to your instructor.

10. **A Memory Checklist** Adding additional RAM memory to your computer is a fairly straightforward process, but does require you to identify a few parameters before going to the store and making the actual purchase. The parameters include the number of available RAM slots on your motherboard, the type of RAM modules that can be used, speed requirements, whether or not the RAM boards need to be added in pairs or equal amounts, and so forth. Another consideration is whether or not the memory is proprietary—that is, only available from the PC's manufacturer—or whether RAM from other manufacturers is allowed. For this project, form a group to prepare a presentation that explains the various parameters listed above and identifies how average students would go about the process of upgrading the memory in their computer. Are there any warranty issues that should be taken into consideration? Have any of you had any personal experience upgrading the memory in a computer before? If so, was the task very difficult? Also be sure to discuss how you might go about comparison shopping for the best price, once the appropriate type of memory has been determined. This presentation should not exceed 10 minutes and should make use of one or more presentation aids such as the chalkboard, handouts, overhead transparencies, or computer-based slide presentation format. You may be asked to submit a summary of the presentation to your instructor.

11. **Latest and Greatest** It seems as though no matter what computer you purchase, it will be out of date in a couple of years. This assertion is based on the hardware, operating system, and memory requirements specified on the packaging of the latest and greatest programs that you need in order to remain productive at your job.

     Select one of the following positions, or make up your own, and express your point of view on the subject. Your instructor will indicate whether your response is to be posted to a class bulletin board, discussed in a class chat room, or discussed as an in-class activity. You may also be asked to submit a summary of your position and point of view.

     a. You don't need to purchase a new system every two years, because the hardware is upgradeable and allows for the replacement of the CPU and expansion of memory. Besides, the idea that someone would have to continually purchase the latest and greatest version of a program is absurd. In most cases, the increase in the marginal utility of these programs does not even justify the purchase price, let alone the cost of additional hardware upgrades required.

b. You will need to purchase new hardware approximately every two years since the processing ability of the CPU tends to double every 18 to 24 months, and the hardware is not as upgradeable as the vendors lead you to believe. It is not simply a matter of just plugging in few expansion boards. You will need to purchase a completely new motherboard, which of course will require a different type of memory. When you add up the cost involved in this process, it becomes less expensive to purchase a new system. From a software point of view, you must use the latest version, or risk not being compatible with the version of the program others are using.

12. **It's The Law** Consider the following statement and establish your position, or point of view, on the subject. Your instructor will indicate whether your response is to be posted to a class bulletin board, discussed in a class chat room, or discussed as an in-class activity. You may also be asked to submit a summary of your position and evaluation of the statement.

In 1956, Gordon Moore (Intel's chairman emeritus, shown in the accompanying photo) observed that the total transistor count on a microchip seemed to double every 18 to 24 months. This observation eventually became known as Moore's Law and appears to be accurate even today. Why Moore's Law has held true for such a long time is not entirely clear. It has been suggested that this trend is a self-fulfilling prophecy, rather than a natural progression of scientific efforts. This line of reasoning implies that the research and development efforts of each major chip manufacturer uses Moore's Law as a target to be achieved within the next 18 to 24 months and, when they achieve it, it simply reaffirms the law. In either case, if this trend continues, we will be using CPUs with one billion transistors in the year 2011, and one trillion transistors in the year 2030. The implications of this law holding true could mean that our already computer-dependent society could become even more dependent, as technologies related to virtual reality, voice recognition, robotics, and artificial intelligence become integrated into every part of our society. Furthermore, if Moore's Law does hold true until the year 2030, the microprocessor will surpass the processing power of the human brain, and ultimately cause humans to join the long list of antiquated processing devices that are no longer cost effective.

Interactive Exercise

Understanding the System Unit.   Let's review the basic components found inside the system unit! Go to the Interactive Exercise at www.course.com/parker2002/ch3 to complete this exercise.

OUTLINE

Storage

LEARNING OBJECTIVES

After completing this chapter, you will be able to:

1. Explain the difference between storage systems and memory.

2. Name several general properties of storage systems.

3. Identify the two primary types of magnetic disk systems and describe how they work.

4. Discuss the various types of optical disc systems available and how they differ from each other and from magnetic systems.

5. List at least three other types of storage systems.

6. Summarize the storage alternatives for a PC, including which storage systems should be included in all PCs and when the other systems would be appropriate.

In Chapter 3, we discussed the role of RAM, the computer's main memory. RAM *temporarily* holds program instructions, data, and output until they are no longer needed by the computer. However, as soon as the computer finishes with any given program and its data, it writes over that information in RAM with a new program and that program's data. Therefore, if programs, data, and processing results are to be preserved for future use, a computer system needs more permanent storage. **Storage** systems–also sometimes called *secondary storage systems* or *external storage*–fill this role. Although they provide slower access than memory, storage devices have a much greater storage capacity, are far less expensive per megabyte, and are *non-volatile* (the data is not erased when the power is turned off).

We begin this chapter with a discussion of characteristics common among storage systems. Then we cover one of the most important kinds of storage systems in use today–those based on magnetic disks. While this part of the chapter is primarily about floppy disk drives and hard disk drives, we also look at other common magnetic storage devices, such as SuperDisk, Zip, and Jaz drives. From there we study optical-disc storage systems and other types of storage systems, such as magnetic tape, on-line storage, smart cards, and flash memory. The chapter concludes with a summary and comparison of the storage devices covered in the chapter. ■

PROPERTIES OF STORAGE SYSTEMS

Several important properties characterize storage systems. In this section we consider several of them, including the two physical parts of a storage system, the nonvolatility property of storage, the ability to remove storage media from many storage devices, and the methods of accessing and representing data.

Physical Parts

All storage systems involve two physical parts: a *storage device* and a *storage medium.* A *floppy disk drive* and a *DVD drive* are examples of storage devices; a *floppy disk* and a *DVD disc* are types of storage media. The drives or other types of storage devices write data and programs onto, and read them from, storage media. A storage medium must be inserted into, or otherwise properly attached to, the appropriate storage device for data, programs, or other content to be stored on or retrieved from it.

Storage devices can be internal or external. *Internal devices*—such as a *floppy disk drive, hard disk drive,* and *CD* or *DVD drive*—typically come installed and configured within the system unit when you buy a PC. These devices can also be installed in empty bays inside the system unit at a later time, if necessary. *External devices* are stand-alone pieces of hardware that connect via cables to ports on the exterior of the system unit. Internal devices have the advantage of requiring no additional desk space and are often faster than the external counterparts, but external devices can more easily be moved to a new computer system, or added when there is no more room left inside the system unit.

>**Storage.** Saving data, results, or programs for future use.

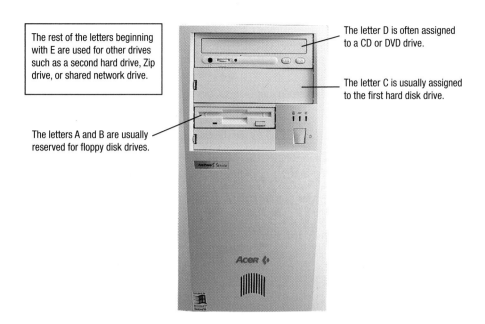

The rest of the letters beginning with E are used for other drives such as a second hard drive, Zip drive, or shared network drive.

The letters A and B are usually reserved for floppy disk drives.

The letter D is often assigned to a CD or DVD drive.

The letter C is usually assigned to the first hard disk drive.

FIGURE 4-1

Storage device identifiers.

To keep track of storage devices in an unambiguous way, the computer system assigns letters of the alphabet or names to each of them.

The computer system keeps track of disk drives and other storage devices in an orderly fashion by assigning letters of the alphabet or names to each of them. Letter designations, which are common in the PC-compatible world, are illustrated in Figure 4-1 (Apple computers more often use names to identify their drives). The device names or letters uniquely identify each device. Thus, if you declare you want to save a document to the *A* drive, it is clear to the computer system which drive you are referring to.

In most storage systems, the storage media must pass by *read/write heads* located inside its storage device in order for data to be read from or written to the media. For example, when you watch a videotaped movie on a home entertainment system, the videotape passes by the VCR heads, which can either play or record onto the tape. Disks, tapes, and other storage media used by computer systems work by similar principles. Some storage devices use a single read/write head; others may use multiple read/write heads.

Nonvolatility Property

Storage media are **nonvolatile.** This means that when you shut off power to the storage device, the data stored on the medium will still be there when you turn the device back on. This feature contrasts with RAM, which is **volatile.** As discussed in previous chapters, data held in volatile storage is erased once the power to the computer is turned off.

Removable vs. Fixed Media

In many storage systems, although the storage device is always connected to the computer, the associated storage medium must be inserted into the device before the computer can read from it or write to it. These are called *removable-media* storage systems. Floppy disks, CDs, and DVDs are examples of removable media. On the other hand, *fixed-media* storage systems, such as most hard disk drive systems, seal the storage medium (such as the hard disk) inside the storage device (such as hard disk drive) and users cannot remove it.

>**Nonvolatile.** Storage that retains its contents when the power is shut off. >**Volatile.** Storage whose contents are erased when the power is shut off.

Fixed-media devices generally provide higher speed and better reliability at a lower cost than removable-media alternatives. Removable-media devices have other advantages, however, including the following:

▼ *Unlimited storage capacity*—You can insert a new medium into the storage device once one becomes full.

▼ *Transportability*—You can easily share media between computers and people.

▼ *Backup*—You can make a duplicate copy of valuable data on the removable medium and store the copy away from the computer, for use if the original copy is destroyed.

▼ *Security*—Sensitive programs or data can be stored on removable media and stored in a secured area.

Virtually all desktop and notebook computer systems include both removable-media and fixed-media storage devices.

Random vs. Sequential Access

further exploration

For links to further information about removable storage devices and media, go to www.course.com/ parker2002/ch4

When the computer system receives an instruction requiring data or programs located in storage, it must go to the appropriate location and retrieve the appropriate data or programs. This procedure is referred to as *access.*

Two basic access methods are available: random and sequential. *Random access,* also called *direct access,* means that you can retrieve data directly from any location on the medium, in any order. With *sequential access,* however, you can retrieve the data only in the order in which it is physically stored on the medium. A computer system's tape drive (discussed later in this chapter) is an example of sequential access. Computer tapes work like cassette tapes or videotapes—to get to a specific song or place in a movie, you must play or fast-forward through all of the tape before it. Most all other types of computer storage devices—including the hard disk drives, floppy disk drives, and CD/DVD drives discussed in this chapter—are random access devices. They work like audio CDs or movie DVDs— you jump directly to a particular selection or location, as needed.

Media that allow random access are sometimes referred to as *addressable* media. This means that the storage system can locate each piece of stored data or each program at a unique *address,* which is automatically determined by the computer system.

Logical vs. Physical Representation

Anything (a program, letter, digital photograph, song, etc.) stored on a storage medium is referred to as a **file.** Data files are also sometimes called *documents.* When you save a document just created (such as a memo or letter in a word processing program), it is stored in a new file on the designated storage medium. During the storage process, the user is required to give the file a name, called a *filename;* that name is used when the user requests to see the document at a later time. Naming files and retrieving stored documents are discussed further in later chapters of this text.

To keep files organized, related documents are often stored inside **folders** (sometimes called *directories*) on the disk or other storage medium. For example, one folder might contain memos to business associates while another holds a set of budgets for a specific project (see Figure 4-2). Organizing data into documents and folders is natural for most individuals.

>File. Something stored on a storage medium, such as a program, document, or image. **>Folder.** A logical named place on a storage medium into which files can be stored to keep the medium organized. Sometimes called a directory.

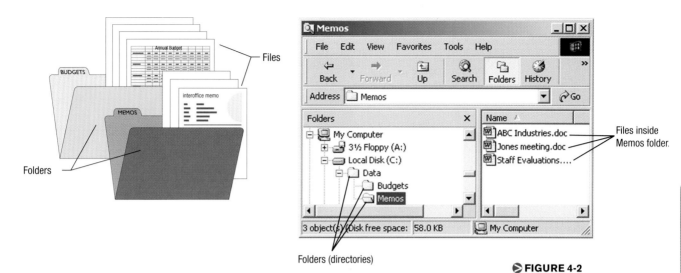

► **FIGURE 4-2**
Organizing data. Folders (directories) can be used to organize related items.

To further organize files, you can create *subfolders* (*subdirectories*) within a folder. Consequently, you might create a "Letters" folder that contains one subfolder for letters sent to friends and a second subfolder for letters sent to potential employers. A folder can contain a mixture of subfolders and documents.

Though documents are saved and retrieved using drive, folder, and filenames by both the user and the computer, the views of where a particular document are located is very different. The user's view of the way data is stored (what we have discussed so far in this section and what appears on the Windows Explorer screen in Figure 4-2) is referred to as *logical file representation.* We view a document file stored as one unit in a particular folder on a particular drive. In contrast, the physical way data is stored and organized on the storage media (as viewed by the computer) is called *physical file representation.* For example, the ABC Industries file shown in Figure 4-2 is *logically* located within the Data and Memos folders on the hard drive C, but it could be *physically* stored in many different pieces scattered across that hard drive. When this occurs, the computer keeps track of where the various locations used are and the logical representation (filename, folder names, etc.) that are being used to identify that file. Fortunately, users don't have to be concerned with how files are physically stored on a disk, since the computer keeps track of that and retrieves files for us whenever we request it.

MAGNETIC DISK SYSTEMS

Speedy access to data, relatively low cost, and the ability to erase and rewrite data make **magnetic disks** the most widely used storage media on today's computers. With magnetic storage systems, data are written by read/write heads magnetizing particles a certain way on a medium's surface. The particles retain their magnetic orientation so they can be read at a later time, and rewriting to the medium is possible (the magnetic orientation is changed, as necessary, to reflect the new content stored there). Storing data on a magnetic disk is illustrated in Figure 4-3. We discuss the most common types of magnetic disks next: Hard disks and floppy disks.

>**Magnetic disk.** A storage medium that records data using magnetic spots on disks made of flexible plastic or rigid metal.

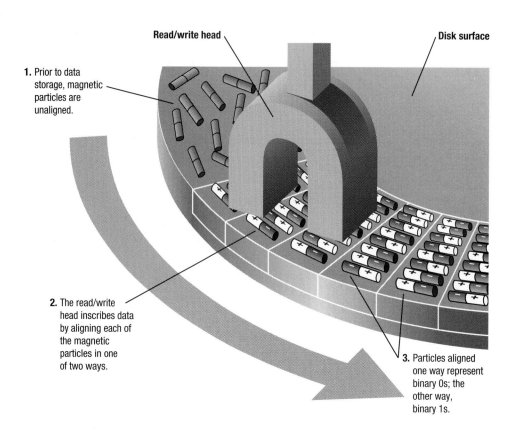

◈ FIGURE 4-3

Storing data on magnetic disks.

Read/write head

Disk surface

1. Prior to data storage, magnetic particles are unaligned.

2. The read/write head inscribes data by aligning each of the magnetic particles in one of two ways.

3. Particles aligned one way represent binary 0s; the other way, binary 1s.

Floppy Disks

Floppy disks—sometimes called *diskettes*—store data on small, round platters made of tough plastic. Floppy disks are a removable medium and very inexpensive, so they are handy for such tasks as backing up small amounts of data, sending small files to others, archiving rarely used files, and sharing data between two computers—such as a computer at home and one at school. Conventional floppy disks are written to and read by *floppy disk drives.*

Physical Properties

The physical properties of a floppy disk are illustrated in Figure 4-4. The actual surface of the floppy disk is made out of flexible plastic coated with a magnetizable substance. The disk is protected inside a square, rugged plastic cover lined with a soft material that wipes the disk clean as it spins. After being inserted into a disk drive, the drive mechanism engages the disk's hub and begins to spin the disk inside the jacket. The floppy disk's write-protect square can block writing operations to prevent users from accidentally erasing or overwriting data. To prevent the drive from writing to a floppy disk, slide the small piece of plastic to expose this square opening.

Most floppy disks in use today measure 3½ inches in diameter and can fit into a shirt pocket. Despite the small dimensions, a 3½-inch floppy disk can store a respectable amount of data. The most common capacity today is 1.44 megabytes—also called *high-density* floppy disks (density refers to how tightly bits of data are packed onto the floppy disk). Older 720-kilobyte floppy disks are called *double-density* or *low-density* floppy disks. A 1.44 MB (high-density) floppy disk has enough room to store between about 500 to 700 pages of double-spaced text created in a common word processing format.

>**Floppy disk.** A low-capacity, removable magnetic disk made of flexible plastic permanently sealed inside a hard plastic cover.

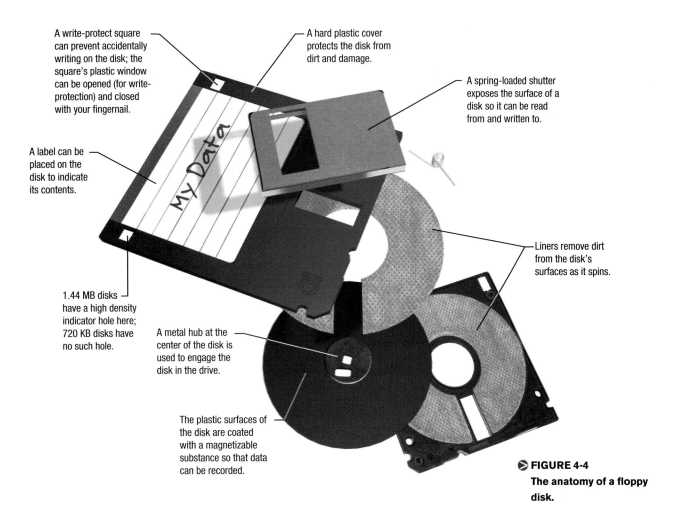

A write-protect square can prevent accidentally writing on the disk; the square's plastic window can be opened (for write-protection) and closed with your fingernail.

A hard plastic cover protects the disk from dirt and damage.

A spring-loaded shutter exposes the surface of a disk so it can be read from and written to.

A label can be placed on the disk to indicate its contents.

Liners remove dirt from the disk's surfaces as it spins.

1.44 MB disks have a high density indicator hole here; 720 KB disks have no such hole.

A metal hub at the center of the disk is used to engage the disk in the drive.

The plastic surfaces of the disk are coated with a magnetizable substance so that data can be recorded.

FIGURE 4-4
The anatomy of a floppy disk.

Tracks, Sectors, and Clusters

Each side of the actual surface of a floppy disk contains a specific number of concentric **tracks**—narrow rings which the read/write head encodes with 0s and 1s when it writes data and programs to the disk (see Figure 4-5). In order to work on a particular computer system, floppy disks must be *formatted.* Formatting divides the disk surface into pie-shaped **sectors,** and thereby prepares it for use with a particular operating system.

Most floppy disks sold today are already formatted for either IBM or Macintosh computers and, therefore, are ready to use. Formatting a disk containing data erases everything on the disk. Though floppy disks used to be reformatted in the past if they became unreliable, because of their low cost today (less than 50 cents each), floppy disks are usually just discarded when they become unreliable. The formatting process is sometimes used, however, to quickly erase a floppy disk for reuse.

On many PC systems, the part of a track that crosses a fixed number of contiguous sectors—anywhere from two to eight sectors is typical—forms a unit called a **cluster.** A cluster is the smallest addressable area on a disk; consequently, everything stored on a disk always takes up at least one cluster of space on the disk.

The computer system automatically maintains a floppy disk's *file directory* or *file allocation table (FAT),* which keeps track of the files stored on the disk. This directory shows

>**Track.** A concentric path on a disk where data are recorded. >**Sector.** A pie-shaped area on a disk surface. >**Cluster.** The part of a track on a disk that crosses a fixed number of contiguous sectors and the smallest addressable area of a disk.

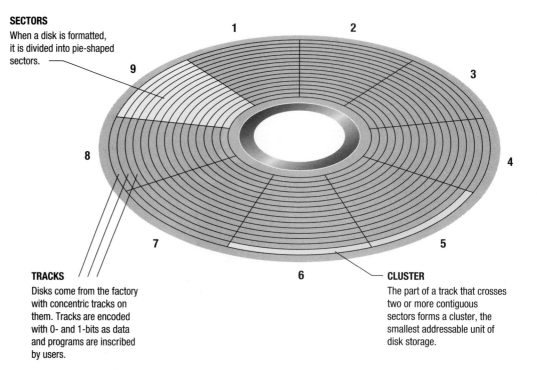

SECTORS
When a disk is formatted, it is divided into pie-shaped sectors.

TRACKS
Disks come from the factory with concentric tracks on them. Tracks are encoded with 0- and 1-bits as data and programs are inscribed by users.

CLUSTER
The part of a track that crosses two or more contiguous sectors forms a cluster, the smallest addressable unit of disk storage.

FIGURE 4-5

Tracks, sectors, and clusters. Any file stored on a disk takes up a least one cluster.

the name of each file, its size, and the cluster at which it begins, so the computer can retrieve the file when requested. If a file takes up more than one cluster of space, each cluster contains directions pointing to the next cluster used, so the computer can retrieve all pieces of the file in order when it is needed.

Using Floppy Disks

To use a floppy disk, you first must insert it into its floppy disk drive. There is only one correct way to insert the floppy disk into a drive—with the disk label facing up and the end containing the metallic shutter mechanism going in first (see Figure 4-6). The disk is fully inserted when the *eject button* on the front of the drive pops out—you hear a click when this happens. Because the drive openings for some other types of removable disks (such as *Zip disks,* discussed shortly) are similar in size and appearance to a floppy drive opening, be careful when inserting a floppy disk to ensure that you are using the proper drive. If the disk does not fit into or doesn't "click" into place inside the drive opening, you are likely inserting it into the wrong drive.

When the floppy disk needs to be accessed, the drive begins to spin the disk within its plastic cover, allowing the read/write heads access to all sectors on the disk through the opening in the metal shutter. The read/write heads also move in and out, allowing access to all tracks on the disk. If the drive's *indicator light* is on, meaning that the disk is spinning and the read/write heads are accessing the disk, you should not remove the floppy disk. After the light goes off, you can press the eject button to remove the disk.

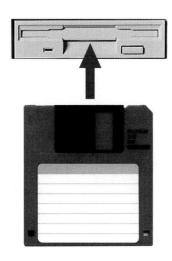

FIGURE 4-6

Inserting a floppy disk into a drive. Disks go into a drive only one way–label side up, with the disk shutter facing the drive door.

Superdiskettes

One drawback to floppy disks is their fairly low storage capacity. Not long ago, computer users considered 1.44 megabytes a reasonable amount of storage. Now, however, multimedia documents are rapidly increasing storage demands. Consequently, a number of higher-capacity removable storage products—sometimes called *superdiskettes*—have emerged in recent years, either as replacements for standard floppy disks or as supplemental storage solutions (see Figure 4-7).

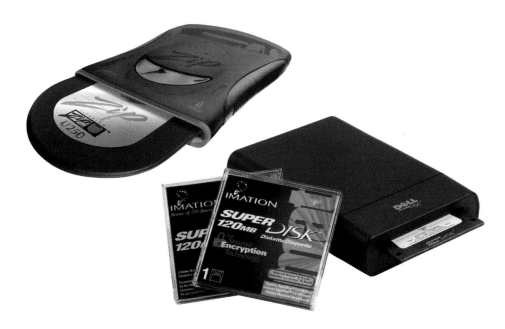

⬧ FIGURE 4-7

Superdiskettes. High-capacity floppy disks with capacities of 100 megabytes or more are commonly sold either as replacements for standard disks or as supplemental storage solutions. (Left: 250 MB Iomega Zip 250 drive and disk; right: 120 MB Imation SuperDisk drive and disk.)

Zip Drives

Introduced by Iomega Corporation in 1995, *Zip drives* are magnetic disk drives that accept removable *Zip disks* with a capacity of 100 or 250 megabytes; the newer Zip 250 drives can read and write to both sizes of Zip disks. Though similar in size and appearance to floppy disks, Zip disks cannot be used in a conventional floppy disk drive, and the Zip drive cannot read standard floppy disks. Since drives typically run less than $100 and disks cost about $10 each, they do, however, provide an affordable storage alternative. Zip drives are ideal for users who need to back up large files or transfer large files between systems or other users that have a Zip drive. Because Zip drives were one of the first high-capacity removable storage solutions, they enjoy widespread use. This decreases the problem of being a *proprietary system,* that is, a system incompatible with any other type of storage system.

SuperDisk Drives

SuperDisk drives, originally made by Imation (see Figure 4-7) and more technically called *laser servo drives,* are similar to Zip drives in that they accept disks with larger capacities (120 or 250 megabytes) than standard floppy disks. While SuperDisk drives are slower than Zip drives, they have the distinct advantage of being able to also read from and write to standard floppy disks. SuperDisk drives store data magnetically, like a conventional floppy disk, but use a laser to locate the tracks and position the read/write heads. Because optical (laser) positioning locates heads much more precisely than magnetic positioning, laser servo disks can have tracks closer together than conventional floppy disk drives can manage, and can therefore fit more data on the same physical size of disk.

HiFD Drives

A more recent alternative to the standard floppy drive is Sony's *HiFD* drive. HiFD disks have a capacity of 200 MB, the equivalent of approximately 140 conventional 1.44 MB floppy disks. HiFD drives are faster than Zip and SuperDisk drives and can also read conventional floppy disks.

It is expected that eventually Zip, SuperDisk, HiFD, or some new type of higher-capacity removable media will replace the conventional floppy disk drive as the low-end removable-disk standard. Even now some computers are coming with an internal SuperDisk or HiFD drive instead of a conventional floppy disk drive.

web tutor

For a tutorial on the various components of a hard drive, go to www.course.com/parker2002/ch4

Hard Disks

With the exception of computers designed to use only network storage devices (such as network computers and some Internet appliances), virtually all PCs come with a **hard disk system** designed to store your programs and much of your data. Such a system is located inside the system unit and is not designed to be removed, unless it needs to be repaired or replaced. In common practice, the terms *hard disk, hard disk drive, hard disk system,* and *hard drive* are used interchangeably to refer to this type of storage system.

Physical Properties

A typical hard disk system (Figure 4-8) consists of one or more rigid metal platters (hard disks) mounted onto a shaft and sealed along with an access mechanism inside a case (the hard drive). On most desktop PCs, hard disk platters measure 3½ inches in diameter; most notebook computers have 2½-inch hard disks. Even smaller hard disk systems are becoming available for systems requiring tiny drives. For example, IBM's Microdrive has a hard disk the size of a quarter and can hold one gigabyte of information.

Most PC hard drives are hermetically sealed units. This precaution keeps the disk surfaces completely free of contamination, enables the disks to spin faster, and limits causes of operational problems. Hard disks typically spin between 5,400 and 15,000 revolutions per minute (rpm). In addition to spinning faster than most other types of storage systems, the hard disk constantly rotates when your computer is turned on instead of only rotating

☉FIGURE 4-8

A hard disk drive. Hard disk systems for microcomputers usually hold several gigabytes of data.

MOUNTING SHAFT
The mounting shaft spins the disks at a speed of several thousand revolutions per minute while your computer is turned on.

SEALED PACK
The hard disk drive is hermetically sealed in a case to keep it free of air contamination.

HARD DISKS
There are usually several hard disk surfaces on which to store data. Most disks store data on both sides of the disk.

CIRCUIT BOARD
Below the disks is a circuit board that contains the disk controller. This board makes sure the disks rotate at a constant speed and tells the heads when to read and write.

ACCESS MECHANISM
The access mechanism moves the read/write heads in and out together between the disk surfaces to access required data.

READ/WRITE HEADS
There is a read/write head for each disk surface. On most systems, the heads move in and out together and will be positioned on the same track and sector on each disk.

>**Hard disk system.** A storage system consisting of one or more metal magnetic disks and an access mechanism typically permanently sealed inside its drive.

when it needs to be accessed as in other storage systems. This feature eliminates the delay of waiting for the drive to come up to the correct speed.

Like other storage devices, the capacity of hard disk systems is measured in megabytes or gigabytes. Most new PCs today have an internal hard drive of at least several gigabytes. An *internal* hard drive, such as the one in Figure 4-8, is located within the system unit. An *external* hard drive attaches to a port on the system unit and can be used to supplement the storage built into the computer system. External systems are often slightly slower and more expensive than their internal counterparts.

Hard Disk Addressing

Like floppy disks, hard disk surfaces are divided into tracks and sectors when formatted, but include many more of both. A new hard disk is typically formatted for use at the factory before it is sold, so it is ready for software and data to be installed. Because reformatting a disk erases everything on the disk, hard drives are rarely reformatted. This task is only performed if errors are preventing the hard drive from operating properly and there is no other option.

In addition to tracks and sectors, hard disk storage addressing uses the concept of a **cylinder.** A disk cylinder is the collection of one particular track on each disk surface, such as the first track or the tenth track on each disk surface. In other words, it's the area on all disks that can be accessed without moving the read/write arm, once the arm has been moved to the proper position. For example, the four-disk system in Figure 4-8 contains eight possible recording surfaces (using both sides of each disk), so a cylinder would consist of eight tracks, such as track 13 on all eight surfaces (see Figure 4-9). Hard drives are commonly organized into anywhere from a few hundred to a few thousand cylinders. The number of tracks on a single disk is equal to the number of cylinders in the disk system.

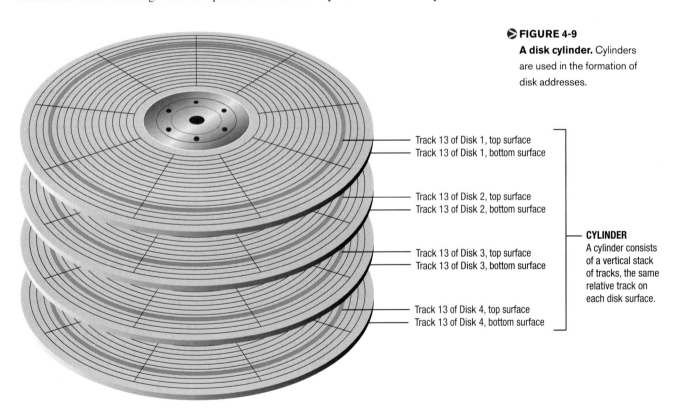

FIGURE 4-9

A disk cylinder. Cylinders are used in the formation of disk addresses.

Track 13 of Disk 1, top surface
Track 13 of Disk 1, bottom surface

Track 13 of Disk 2, top surface
Track 13 of Disk 2, bottom surface

Track 13 of Disk 3, top surface
Track 13 of Disk 3, bottom surface

Track 13 of Disk 4, top surface
Track 13 of Disk 4, bottom surface

CYLINDER
A cylinder consists of a vertical stack of tracks, the same relative track on each disk surface.

>**Cylinder.** The collection of tracks located in the same location on a set of hard disk surfaces.

Reading and Writing Data

Most hard drives have at least one read/write head for each recording surface. These heads are mounted on a device called an *access mechanism* (refer back to Figure 4-8). The rotating mounting shaft spins at thousands of revolutions per minute while the access mechanism moves the heads in and out between the disk surfaces (similar to a floppy drive) to access the required data. Such a *movable access mechanism* as described here is by far the most popular type of access mechanism for hard disks.

A read/write head never touches the surface of a hard disk platter at any time, even during reading and writing. The heads are located extremely close to the surface of the disk, however, often within a millionth of an inch above the surface. The presence of a foreign object the width of a human hair or even a smoke particle (about 2,500 and 100 millionths of an inch, respectively) on a hard disk's surface will damage the disk and heads. Such an event is known as a *head crash*. As Figure 4-10 shows, the results are like placing a huge boulder on a road and then trying to drive over it with your car. One never knows when a hard drive will crash—there may be no warning whatsoever—and this is a good reason for keeping the drive regularly backed up. Backing up a computer system is discussed in more detail in Chapter 16.

Disk Access Time

A hard drive with a movable access mechanism shifts the read/write heads in and out among the tracks together. It positions all the heads on the same cylinder when data is read from or written to any of the tracks on that cylinder. The following three events must be carried out in order to read or write data:

▼ *Seek time*—the time required for the read/write heads to move to the cylinder that contains (or will store) the desired data.

▼ *Rotational delay*—the time required for the mounting shaft to rotate the disks into the proper position.

▼ *Data movement time*—the time required for the system to read the data from the disk and transfer it to the RAM, or to transfer the data to be written to the disk from RAM and then store it on the disk.

◆ FIGURE 4-10

Obstacles on a hard-disk surface. A human hair or even a smoke particle on a fast-spinning hard-disk surface can damage both the surface and the read/write head.

The sum of the time it takes to perform these three events—*seek time, rotational delay,* and *data movement time*—is known as **disk access time.** Hard disk access times often run from 10 to 20 milliseconds. To minimize disk access time on a system with a movable access

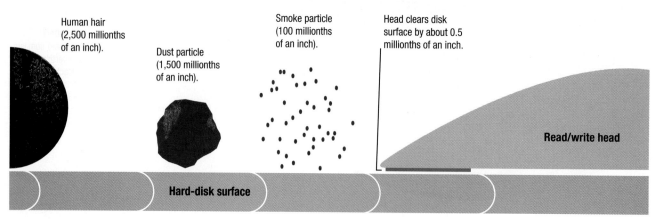

Human hair (2,500 millionths of an inch).

Dust particle (1,500 millionths of an inch).

Smoke particle (100 millionths of an inch).

Head clears disk surface by about 0.5 millionths of an inch.

Read/write head

Hard-disk surface

>**Disk access time.** The time it takes to locate and read data from (or position and write data to) a storage medium.

mechanism such as the one depicted in Figure 4-8, drives usually store related data on the same cylinder. This strategy sharply reduces the seek-time component and improves the overall access time.

Disk Cache

Disk caching refers to a strategy for speeding up system performance. When disk caching is being used, during any disk access the computer system also fetches program or data contents located in neighboring disk areas (such as the entire track) and transports them to a dedicated part of RAM known as a **disk cache.** The theory behind disk caching assumes that neighboring data will likely have to be read soon anyway, so the computer system can reduce the number of disk accesses by copying such data into RAM early. When the next piece of data is requested, the computer system checks the disk-cache area first, to see if the data it needs is already there. If it is, the data is retrieved for processing; if not, the computer retrieves the appropriate data from the disk (see Figure 4-11).

Disk caching saves not only time but also wear and tear on the disk. In portable computers, it can also extend battery life. Disk caching is frequently implemented through circuitry on the disk controller board (the circuit board that manages the hard disk).

Disk Standards

PC hard disk systems can use several different interface standards. These standards determine performance characteristics, such as the density with which data can be packed onto the disk, the speed of disk access, how large the disk can be, and the way the disk drive interfaces with other hardware.

Today, two standards dominate the market: *ATA/IDE,* for *AT a*ttachment/*i*ntegrated *d*rive *e*lectronics, and *SCSI,* for *s*mall *c*omputer *s*ystem *i*nterface. With ATA/IDE, the *controller*— the chip that controls the flow of data to and from the hard drive—is built into the drive; SCSI (pronounced "scuzzy") controllers are either built into the computer or located on a SCSI

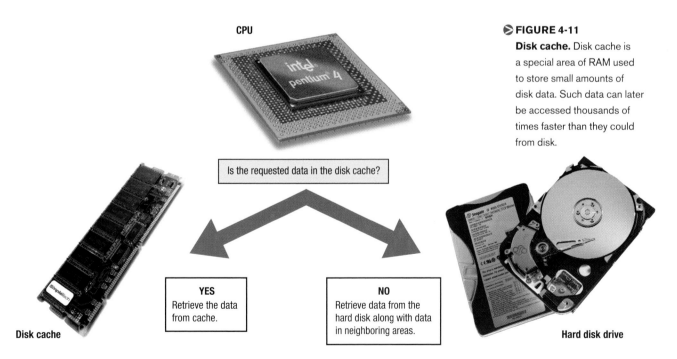

CPU

Is the requested data in the disk cache?

YES
Retrieve the data from cache.

NO
Retrieve data from the hard disk along with data in neighboring areas.

Disk cache

Hard disk drive

◗ **FIGURE 4-11**

Disk cache. Disk cache is a special area of RAM used to store small amounts of disk data. Such data can later be accessed thousands of times faster than they could from disk.

>**Disk cache.** A disk-management scheme that directs a drive to read additional data adjacent to the required data during a disk fetch to reduce the number of disk fetches. Also used to refer to the part of RAM used to store this data.

expansion card to which the drive would be connected. ATA/IDE drives are typically less expensive and easier to configure, but SCSI provides faster access, enables you to connect multiple devices to a single controller, and allows longer cable lengths. There are many versions of ATA/IDE and SCSI. Common versions include ATA/IDE, ATA-2/EIDE (*enhanced IDE*), Ultra-ATA, ATA/66, SCSI-2, SCSI-3, Wide SCSI, Fast SCSI, Ultra SCSI, Ultra2 SCSI, Wide Ultra2 SCSI, Ultra3 SCSI, and Ultra160 SCSI. When buying a new hard drive, it's important to check out which standards the drive supports and compare that with the standards your PC can support. In addition to being used with hard disk drives, SCSI interfaces can also be used with some scanners, CD drives, and DVD drives.

A newer storage standard that is expected to become widely used with storage systems shared over networks (such as *storage area networks,* discussed in Chapter 8), is *Fibre Channel*. Fibre Channel storage devices connect to the host computer using a special adapter card and have the advantage of reliability, flexibility, and very fast data delivery—up to two gigabits per second delivery time. Because it is more expensive than other standards and is geared for long-distance, high-bandwidth applications, Fibre Channel is not expected to be widely used with PCs and low-end servers, at least in the near future. It is, however, expected to eventually replace SCSI for high-end storage systems.

Partitioning and FAT32

Partitioning a hard drive enables you to logically divide the physical capacity of a single drive into separate areas called *partitions*. You can then treat each of the partitions as an independent disk drive, such as a C drive and a D drive, though they are physically still one drive. Though at least one partition is created when a hard drive is first formatted, you can change the number and sizes of the partitions at any time, although this action destroys any data in those partitions. Consequently, before you repartition a hard drive, you should transfer any affected data to another storage medium first and then copy the data back onto the repartitioned hard drive. Some operating systems have a limit to the number of partitions that can be used.

Because older operating systems allowed hard drives only up to 512 MB, hard drives larger than that used to have to use multiple partitions. Most newer operating systems allow larger drives, but partitioning a large drive can make it more efficient. This is because operating systems typically use a larger cluster size (the smallest addressable area on a disk, as already discussed) with a larger hard drive. When a large cluster size is used, disk space is often wasted because even tiny files have to use up one entire cluster of storage space. When a hard drive is partitioned, each logical drive uses a smaller cluster size, since the drive is smaller. To further cut down on wasted storage space, Windows computers using the *FAT32* file system are much more efficient than those using the original FAT system, since FAT 32 systems allow cluster sizes to be as small as 4 KB each.

One final reason for partitioning a hard drive is to be able to use two different operating systems on the same hard drive—such as Windows and Linux. You can then decide which operating system you will run each time you turn on your computer. Creating the appearance of having separate hard drives for file management, multiple users, or other purposes are other common reasons for partitioning a hard drive. Some users choose to install their programs on one hard drive (usually C) and store their data on a second drive (such as D). This system can make locating data files easier, as well as enable users to back up all data files simply by backing up the entire data drive (program files aren't typically backed up). Operating systems and backing up data are discussed in more detail in later chapters of this text.

Removable Hard Disk Systems

While most hard disk systems are *fixed,* meaning that you cannot separate the hard disks from their drives, hard disk systems that use *removable* hard disk cartridges are gaining popularity. One of the most widely used systems is Iomega's *Jaz drive* (see Figure 4-12). A Jaz cartridge, which can store up to two gigabytes, takes slightly longer to access than a conventional, fixed hard disk, but can be replaced when full and easily removed to be stored or transported to a different location. Jaz drives cost less than $300; cartridges cost about $80.

FIGURE 4-12

Removable hard disk systems. These drives, such as the Iomega Jaz (top right), Iomega Peerless (bottom right), and Castlewood ORB (left) shown here, work with removable cartridges to deliver performance close to a computer system's native fixed hard disk system. Most of these types of drives are available in both external and internal versions.

Iomega's newest hard drive, *Peerless,* is about twice as fast as a Jaz drive and holds up to 20 GB per disk. Peerless drives cost about $250; 20 GB disks cost less than $200.

A relatively new addition to the removable hard disk arena is the Castlewood's *ORB drive,* which uses 2.2 GB ORB disks. ORB drives cost about $150; ORB disks cost about $35 each. All three of these systems are proprietary, so their media can only be used with their respective drives and they are not compatible with each other.

Removable hard disk systems are useful for storing and backing up very large files—primarily by users working with large capacity audio, video, or graphics files. They are also commonly used for complete system backups.

Hard Disk Systems for Notebook Computers

Notebook computers can use internal fixed-media hard drives similar to a desktop PC, such as the top right image in Figure 4-13. They also can use removable hard drives specifically designed for notebook and other portable computers instead of, or in addition to, an internal hard drive. These drives can be inserted into the notebook when needed (see the leftmost image in Figure 4-13); PC card drives can also be used in some digital cameras and with desktop PCs using a special PC card adapter. External hard drives are also available for notebook computers and can be connected using a PC card adapter (see the bottom right image in Figure 4-13). A newer alternative for portable computer storage is flash memory cards, discussed later in this chapter.

Hard Disk Systems for Large Computer Systems

Large computer systems generally use hard disk systems for storage instead of floppy disk systems. Hard disk systems on large computers implement many of the same principles as PC-based hard drives. Instead of finding a single hard drive installed within the system unit, however, you are most likely to find an array of multiple hard drives that are placed

> **FIGURE 4-13**
>
> **Hard drives for notebook computers.** Hard disk drives for notebooks and other portable computers can be in the form of PC cards or removable drives (left), internal disk drives (top right), or external disk drives (bottom right).

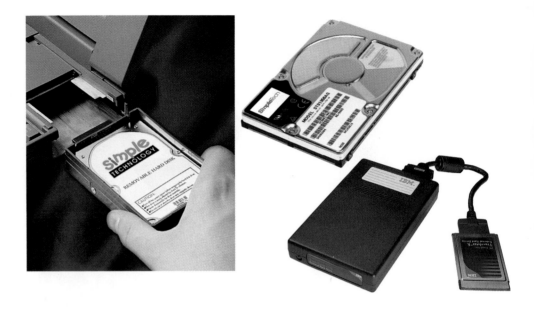

into a large unit that is separate from the system unit (see Figure 4-14). Because it comprises a sophisticated system within the computer system, this type of storage system is sometimes referred to as a *hard disk subsystem* or an *enterprise storage system*. Storage capacities on such disk systems can run from a few dozen gigabytes to several terabytes.

Not too long ago, hard disk systems for large computers stored data on very-large-diameter disks—14 inches or so across. This design created several problems. First, large disks cannot rotate at the high speeds that smaller ones can and larger disks require greater seek time. Also, as the diameter of a disk increases, so does the potential for wobble at its outer edge as the disk spins. More disk wobble forces the read/write heads to ride further away from the disk surface to prevent a head crash. This also detracts from performance.

Today's large-system hard drives employ smaller disks to avoid these problems, even though they may need more platters to store the same amount of data. This approach has another critical advantage over a single, larger disk—it allows the system to read from multiple disk surfaces at the same time.

> **FIGURE 4-14**
>
> **Hard disk system for larger computers.** Hard disk systems for larger computers often consist of arrays of hard disk drives.

Each drawer or array can usually hold several individual drives. These drives typically hold between 9 and 72 GB each.

A hard disk subsystem usually can contain multiple drawers of drives.

RAID

RAID (for *r*edundant *a*rrays of *i*ndependent—or *i*nexpensive—*d*isks) uses two or more relatively small hard drives in combination to do the job of a larger drive. This setup can increase performance, as well as increase *fault tolerance*—the ability of a system to recover from an unexpected hardware or software failure, such as a system crash. Because RAID usually involves recording redundant (duplicate) copies of information, that information can be used, when necessary, to reconstruct lost data.

There are six different RAID designs or levels (0 to 5) that use different combinations of RAID techniques. For example RAID level 0 uses *disk striping,* which spreads files over several disk drives (see the top part of Figure 4-15). Though striping improves performance,

FIGURE 4-15
RAID (*r*edundant *a*rray of *i*nexpensive *d*isks). The two main benefits of RAID are speed and the ability to easily recover from a disk crash.

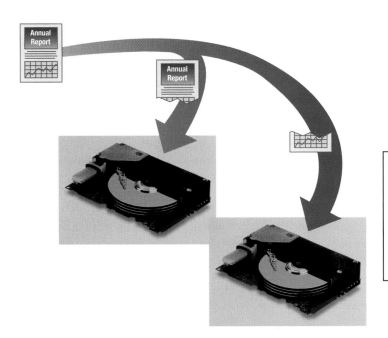

STRIPED DRIVE ARRAY
When a file is written to a striped array, it is split among all the drives in the array except the parity drive (not shown). The parity drive is instead sent data that can be used to recover in the event of a crash.

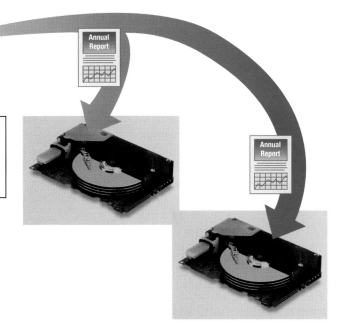

MIRRORED DRIVE ARRAY
When a file is written to a mirrored drive array, an identical copy of the file is sent to another drive in the array.

>**RAID.** A storage method that uses several small hard disks in parallel to do the job of a larger disk.

since the array can access multiple drives at a time to store or retrieve data, it doesn't provide fault tolerance.

Another common RAID technique is *disk mirroring,* in which data is written to two duplicate drives simultaneously (see the bottom part of Figure 4-15). The objective to disk mirroring is to increase fault tolerance—if one of the disk drives fails, the system can instantly switch to the other drive without any loss of data or service. RAID level 1 uses disk mirroring. Levels beyond level 1 use some combination of disk striping and disk mirroring, with different types of error correction provisions.

Because using RAID is significantly more expensive than just using a traditional hard disk storage system, it is most commonly used with network and Internet servers.

OPTICAL DISCS

web tutor

For a tutorial on reading and writing to optical discs, go to www.course.com/parker2002/ch4

Optical discs use laser beams to write and read data at densities many times finer than those of a typical magnetic disk. Consequently, their storage capacity is much higher than a floppy disk, from 650 MB up. Although fixed hard drive systems offer faster access and have a higher storage capacity than optical discs, optical disc systems use removable media—a distinct benefit. Optical discs—primarily *CDs* and *DVDs*—are much more widely used than removable hard drive systems. They are the standard today for software delivery, as well as commonly used for storing high-capacity music and video files. There are also versions of both CD and DVD drives available for home audio and home theater use. Optical discs are commonly referred to as *compact discs.*

CD and DVD discs are read by *CD* and *DVD drives.* The speed of a CD or DVD drive is rated as 24×, 32×, 36×, and so on. These labels describe how fast the drive is compared to the first version of that drive. For instance, a 36× drive is 36 times the speed of the baseline unit that was originally manufactured. Most optical discs have a title and other text printed only on one side and are inserted into the drive with the printed side facing up (the data is stored on the bottom, nonprinted side of the disc). When inserting such a CD or DVD, be careful not to get dirt, fingerprints, scratches, or anything else that might hinder light reflectivity on the disc's surface.

Though the most common PC use of optical discs is with a single-capacity PC optical drive, there are *optical libraries* or *optical jukeboxes* available for servers or large computers to offer access to multiple optical discs at one time. Like old phonograph-record jukeboxes, these optical data warehouses "play" selected platters from the collections when requested.

CDs

CD-ROM (*c*ompact *d*isc, *r*ead-*o*nly *m*emory) discs were the first optical discs of wide acceptance. Data on CD-ROMs are stored at the factory by burning tiny depressions (called *pits*) into the discs' surfaces with high-intensity laser beams. The CD-ROM drive's lower-intensity laser beam can then read the data, based on the reflection of light from the disc, as illustrated in the top part of Figure 4-16. Because the storage process permanently etches the surface of the CD-ROM, the data cannot be erased and no data can be added to the disc.

Newer **recordable (CD-R)** and **rewritable (CD-RW) CDs** both allow users to store data on compact discs, but only data on rewritable CDs can be erased and overwritten.

>**Optical disc.** A disc read and written to using a laser beam. >**CD-ROM.** A low-end optical disc that allows a drive to read data on the disc, but not write to it. >**Recordable CD (CD-R).** A type of CD that can be written to but not erased or rewritten to. >**Rewritable CD (CD-RW).** A type of CD that can be written to, as well as erased or rewritten to.

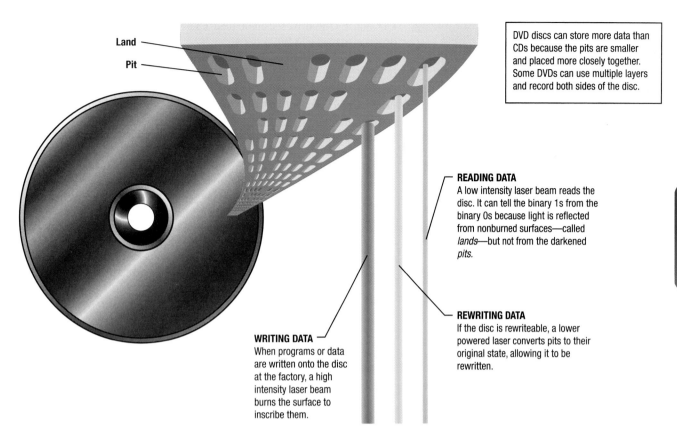

Land

Pit

DVD discs can store more data than CDs because the pits are smaller and placed more closely together. Some DVDs can use multiple layers and record both sides of the disc.

READING DATA
A low intensity laser beam reads the disc. It can tell the binary 1s from the binary 0s because light is reflected from nonburned surfaces—called *lands*—but not from the darkened *pits*.

REWRITING DATA
If the disc is rewriteable, a lower powered laser converts pits to their original state, allowing it to be rewritten.

WRITING DATA
When programs or data are written onto the disc at the factory, a high intensity laser beam burns the surface to inscribe them.

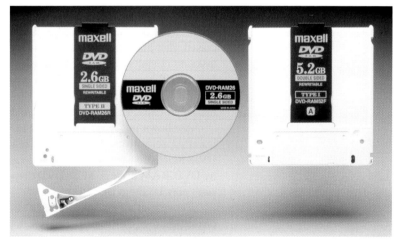

REWRITABLE CDs
CDs can be written to over and over if a special drive and CD are used.

DVDS
Because of their much higher storage capacity, DVDs are replacing CDs.

CD-R discs can only be written to once. Both types of discs look very similar to CD-ROM discs (see the bottom left image in Figure 4-16). Recordable CDs are commonly used to store music files, allowing home users to make high-quality personalized music CDs. CD-RW discs can be written to and erased similar to a floppy disk. Consequently, they are a good alternative for large file storage, as well as for creating a "master" disc before burning a CD-R disc (most CD-RW drives can write to both CD-RW and CD-R discs, but some

FIGURE 4-16

Optical discs. Because DVD technology can store data more closely together, in different layers on the disc, and sometimes on both sides of the disc, they have a greater capacity than CD discs.

FIGURE 4-17

Mini optical discs. Miniature optical discs, such as the DataPlay digital media disc, offer high-capacity removable storage that can be used with a PCs and a variety of mobile devices.

further exploration

For links to further information about DVD technology, go to www.course.com/parker2002/ch4

CD and CD-R drives cannot read CD-RW discs). CD-R and CD-RW drives also read CD-ROM discs.

Two specialty types of CD discs are *PhotoCD* and *PictureCD* developed by Eastman Kodak for storing photographic images in a digital format. These CDs are usually created instead of, or in addition to, photo prints when conventional film is developed. PictureCD is used by consumers and photos cannot be added to the CD after it is created. PhotoCD is used by professionals and additional photos can be added after it is created. A final optical alternative is one of the mini optical disc formats available. Some of these types of discs can be read by conventional optical drives; others, such as the quarter-size *DataPlay digital media* discs that can hold 500 MB (see Figure 4-17) require a proprietary reader or the capability to read the device built into the mobile device (cell phone, PDA, MP3 player, etc.) being used.

At 650 MB, all CDs have a much higher storage capacity than conventional floppies. It is expected, however, that CDs will be eclipsed by DVDs (the even higher capacity optical disc technology discussed next), once that technology becomes improved and standardized.

DVDs

The acronym *DVD* (for *digital versatile disc*) refers to a relatively new high-capacity optical storage format that can hold from 4.7 GB to 17 GB, depending on the number of recording layers and disc sides being used. The DVD was initially developed to store the full contents of a standard two-hour movie, but is now also used to store computer data and software. **DVD-ROM** technology is seen by many as the successor to music CDs, computer CD-ROMs, and prerecorded VHS videotapes that people buy or rent for home viewing—in other words, read-only products. **Rewritable DVDs** discs (called either **DVD-RAM** or **DVD+RW,** depending on the standard being used) can be recorded and erased, just like magnetic disks and CD-RW discs, though they currently perform these tasks more slowly than a conventional floppy disk. In a few years, it is likely that many people will be recording television programs at home on blank DVD-RAM discs, just as they do today on blank VHS tapes. They will also likely be using rewritable DVD discs as their high-capacity removable storage medium of choice.

As shown in Figure 4-16, DVD-RAM discs are located inside a cartridge; with some lower capacity discs, the disc can be removed from the cartridge so it can be inserted into a DVD-ROM drive (two-sided, higher-capacity DVD-RAM discs can currently be read only by DVD-RAM drives). Most DVD drives can play both computer and audio CDs, but you can't play DVDs in a CD drive.

Though, at a maximum storage capacity of 17 GB, DVD capacity offers a huge improvement over the original 360 KB floppy disks, the demand for even higher-capacity removable storage media is always present. For a look at some storage possibilities for the future, see the Inside the Industry box.

Magneto-Optical Discs

There are a few other types of storage systems that use a combination of magnetic and optical technology—the *magneto-optical (M-O) disc* is one of the most common. Magneto-optical drives read special M-O discs, which are usually optical discs inside a rectangular cartridge, similar in appearance to the DVD-RAM discs shown in Figure 4-16. M-O discs can store up to 5.2 GB per disk.

>**DVD-ROM.** A low-end optical disc that can be read from, but not written to, by the user. >**Rewritable DVD (DVD-RAM** or **DVD+RW).** A type of DVD that can be written to, as well as erased or rewritten to.

inside the industry

Holographic Storage

Three-Dimensional Storage Is Just About Here

Storing information in three dimensions is far from a new idea. DVDs use multiple layers to store more data on the same size disc as a CD. In November 1999, C3D introduced its *fluorescent multilayered disc (FMD)*, a storage medium with as many as 50 fluorescent layers. Though still in the development stages, C3D claims that the disc will be no larger than a CD and could hold 100 GB of data.

One very promising technology being researched by such companies as IBM, Lucent Technologies, and Imation is *holographic storage.* Unlike other methods that record data only on the surface of a disc, holographic data storage allows recording through the entire thickness of the material. Similar to other optical discs, lasers are used to record the data, but the data is stored in a "page" format, where all data on each page are stored and retrieved together.

Because a million or more bits can be located on each page and thousands of pages can be stored in material no larger than a small coin, holographic systems offer the possibility of compact devices holding many trillions of bytes of information. The additional advantages of no moving parts and simultaneous access of all information stored in a page give this technology the potential for very rapid access. Some predictions include a capacity of 1 trillion bits or more and a data-throughput rate of at least 1 billion bits a second.

Potential applications for holographic data storage systems include satellite communications, military operations, high-speed digital libraries, and image processing for medical, video, and military purposes.

InPhase Technologies–a development group of Lucent Technologies–was formed to research, develop, and market fast, high-capacity holographic storage.

OTHER TYPES OF STORAGE SYSTEMS

Other types of secondary storage systems include storing files on magnetic tape, on the Internet or another network, and new types of storage commonly used for multimedia and e-commerce applications. Some examples of these new types of storage systems are *smart cards* and various types of *flash memory* media.

Magnetic Tape Systems

Magnetic tape used to be a prominent storage alternative for computer systems. Because of its sequential-access property, however, it is used primarily today to back up the contents of other storage systems. Though slow, magnetic tape is a very inexpensive medium.

>**Magnetic tape.** A plastic ribbon with a magnetizable surface that stores data as a series of magnetic spots.

◑ **FIGURE 4-18**

Magnetic tape. Cartridge tapes are the most predominant type of magnetic tape at the present time. Since it is a sequential media, magnetic tape is used primarily for backup.

Magnetic tapes are made of plastic coated with a magnetizable substance that is polarized to represent the bits and bytes of digital data, similar to magnetic disks. Computer tapes differ in a number of respects, including the size of the reel or cartridge, tape width, and the formats and densities with which they record data.

The device that reads magnetic tape is called a *tape drive* or *tape unit*. It may be an internal or external piece of hardware. The tape drives for microcomputers are usually small enough for a person to hold in one hand, while the refrigerator-sized tape drives connected to large mainframes often occupy several square feet of floor space. Whatever its size or type, every tape drive contains one or more read/write heads over which the tape passes to allow the drive to read or write data. Just as with other magnetic storage technologies, the 1s and 0s stored on magnetic tape are represented by magnetization.

Most magnetic tapes today are in the form of *cartridge tapes* (see Figure 4-18). There are a variety of sizes and formats for cartridge tapes, such as *digital audio tape (DAT), quarter-inch-cassette (QIC), Travan, digital linear tape (DLT),* and *advanced intelligent tape (AIT)*. Sizes and formats of tapes are not generally interchangeable, but since magnetic tapes are most often used for backup with a specific tape drive, this incompatibility is usually not a problem. A single tape cartridge can hold anywhere from a few hundred megabytes of data to 50 or so gigabytes, and twice as much if you compress the data. The concept of data compression is discussed in Chapter 6.

Larger computer systems may use *detachable-reel tapes* (also called *open reel tapes*) instead of cartridge tapes. These tapes commonly measure one-half inch wide and are used with external tape drives. With a detachable-reel system, a *supply reel* contains the tape to be used or accessed; a *take-up reel* winds tape after it has been used. Because cartridges are easier to handle and provide far larger capacities than they offered only a few years ago, detachable-reel tape drives are rapidly losing popularity.

Online Storage

Though the term **online storage** can be used to refer to storage located on any network storage device, it is generally used today when referring to a hard drive located on a server accessible through the Internet. As illustrated in Figure 4-19, there are many Web sites dedicated to online storage—often for free. They vary from sites specializing in posting digital photographs, to sites geared mainly to file storage for either convenient remote access from any location or for backup purposes. Though some sites allow access to anyone, most online storage sites are set up to have file access only by password, if desired, to limit access to yourself and anyone else you give your password to. Some sites allow you to e-mail links to others to download just specific files in your online collection.

Though online storage is a convenient way for users with traditional PCs to share files with a group of others, it is also becoming more important as the use of information appliances, network computers, mobile devices, and other systems with little or no local storage become more prominent.

For businesses that need a large amount of secure storage for backing up their files, subscription online storage is available, with fees typically dependent on the amount of data and how long the data needs to be stored.

Smart Cards

A **smart card** is a credit-card-size piece of plastic that contains some type of computer circuitry, typically including a processor, memory, and storage (see Figure 4-20). This circuitry

further exploration

For links to further information about online storage, go to www.course.com/parker2002/ch4

>**Online storage.** Storage located on a network storage device, such as on a server accessible through the Internet. >**Smart card.** A credit-card-sized piece of plastic containing a chip and other circuitry into which data can be stored.

SIGN UP AND LOGIN

Online storage services require you to create an account first, then you log in each time you need to access your files. Without your user name and password, no one else can access your files, unless you have them set up as public files.

Online storage. Online storage services, such as xDrive shown here, allow you to upload and download files from any PC or device with Internet access. Some services allow you to specify files that can be accessed by anyone, or by anyone with an appropriate password, to facilitate sharing files between individuals.

ACCESSING FILES

Once you have logged in, you can upload files to the service's hard drive. The files can often be organized into folders and can be accessed from any PC or device with Internet access.

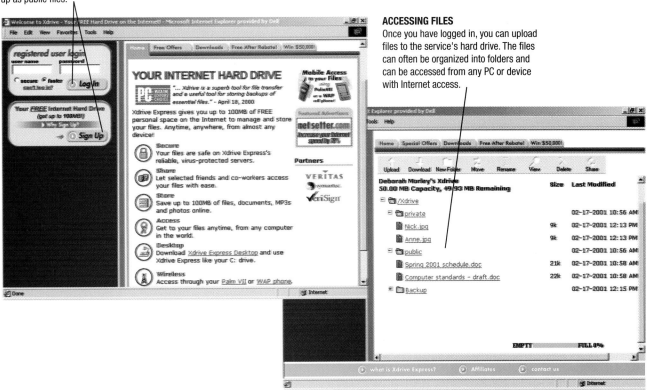

WHAT IS A SMART CARD?

A smart card looks like an ordinary credit card, but typically contains a wafer-thin chip and circuitry for processing and storage. When inserted into a reader, the information stored in the chip can be accessed.

Smart cards.

USES FOR SMART CARDS

Smart card applications abound, such as a replacement for cash in vending machines, toll booths, fast food restaurants, and parking lots, as well as for holding security or personal information.

how it works

Smart Cards

Smart cards look like ordinary credit cards on the outside, but are completely different on the inside. Built into the card are circuitry, memory, and a microprocessor. Essentially, a smart card is a wafer-thin computer.

Smart cards can contain both data and applications, but the storage capacity is very limited at present. Typical capacity is about 1 KB for data that can be changed and there is additional read-only memory to hold permanent information.

Common types of data stored in a smart card are digital cash values, digital signatures, banking and credit card information, health insurance information, and loyalty system information (frequent flyer points, for example). Smart cards are also frequently used to allow the card holder access to secure facilities and data on a computer network. Though these applications have used conventional magnetic stripe technology in the past, the microprocessor in a smart card protects the integrity of the data on the card, and data stored in the card's memory can be added or modified as needed.

To use a smart card, it is inserted into a card reader, as shown in the accompanying illustration. Alternatively, a wireless smart card (with an antenna built in) could send data to a wireless reader. Though some applications only require possession of the card to be able to use it, a trend likely to increase in the near future is pairing up a smart card with an authentication system. With such a system, biometric information (information about a particular feature of the card holder, such as a fingerprint or voice print) is also stored in the card and the card cannot be used unless a matching finger or voice print is entered into the reader.

Once a smart card has been accepted, the transaction—making a purchase, opening a door, digitally signing a document—can be completed.

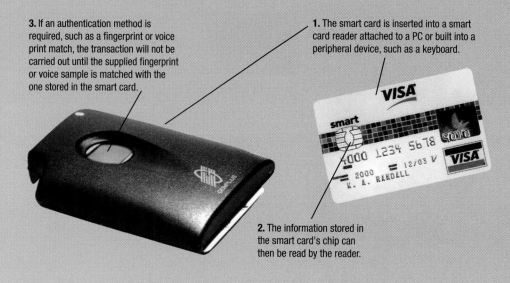

3. If an authentication method is required, such as a fingerprint or voice print match, the transaction will not be carried out until the supplied fingerprint or voice sample is matched with the one stored in the smart card.

1. The smart card is inserted into a smart card reader attached to a PC or built into a peripheral device, such as a keyboard.

2. The information stored in the smart card's chip can then be read by the reader.

can store electronic data and programs, but the storage capacity varies widely—usually from a few kilobytes to a few megabytes. Many smart cards used today store a prepaid amount of money for retail purchases via vending machines, gas stations, fast-food restaurants, toll booths, and online purchases using a smart cell phone or *smart card reader* (see the How It Works box). Every time the card is used, the available amount of money is reduced. To refill a reusable card, a kiosk that accepts cash, credit, or debit cards is usually used. Smart cards can also be loaded with identification data for accessing facilities or computer networks, as well as for housing an individual's medical history and insurance information for fast treatment and hospital admission in an emergency.

Smart card use with *e-commerce*—financial transactions over the Internet—is covered in more detail in Chapter 11.

Flash Memory Devices

While magnetic and optical storage systems use disks that spin, **flash memory** devices uses chips and other circuitry instead, similar to smart cards. While smart cards are generally used to store digital cash or small amounts of information that doesn't change, flash memory devices are used to store and transfer larger amounts of data on a more regular basis, similar to a floppy disk. Flash memory systems have no moving parts, are significantly smaller, and have a much lower power consumption rate than conventional drives. These characteristics make them highly appropriate for use with notebook computers, digital cameras, handheld PCs, and other portable devices. Today, flash memory is found in the form of sticks, cards, or drives.

Flash Memory Sticks

Flash memory sticks were introduced by Sony initially for use with their digital walkman and MP3 digital music players. Since then, however, their use has expanded to digital cameras, PCs, and other applications. Some newer computers come with a memory stick port built in; if not, a mouse or other peripheral device containing a memory stick port or a floppy disk or PC card adapter can be used (see Figure 4-21). Memory sticks are especially convenient for transferring audio or photo files back and forth from a computer to a digital camera, MP3 player, or other portable device with a memory stick port built in.

Memory sticks are about the size of a stick of gum and hold from 4 to 64 MB each; the 64 MB stick holds the equivalent of about 40 floppy disks and costs less than $100.

Flash Memory Cards

Flash memory cards (refer again to Figure 4-21) come in a variety of formats. They are available in PC card form, as well as other standards—such as *CompactFlash, SmartMedia, Secure Digital (SD),* and *MultiMedia Cards (MMC).* These cards can be directly inserted into any device (PC, digital camera, pocket PC, etc.) that supports that format. When an appropriate port is not built into the device, a *flash memory card reader* or adapter can be used. Common storage capacities for flash memory cards are from 2 to 512 MB.

Flash Memory Drives

Flash memory drives are referred to as *solid-state drives,* because they have no moving parts. Consequently, they are much more resistant to shock and vibration than conventional drives and so are appropriate for harsh environments. They also have a longer expected life than magnetic drives.

Miniature portable flash memory drives are also becoming available. For example, the keychain-size *Q Drive* shown in Figure 4-21 holds up to 64 MB and is recognized as an additional drive as soon as it is plugged into the computer's USB port.

COMPARING STORAGE ALTERNATIVES

Storage alternatives are often compared by weighing a number of product characteristics and cost factors. Some of these product characteristics include speed, compatibility, storage capacity, and the ability to remove the storage media. Keep in mind that each storage alternative normally involves trade-offs. For instance, usually you must sacrifice access speed to gain the convenience of removability. Also, although virtually everyone wants the fastest possible storage, higher speeds generally come at greater expense.

>**Flash memory.** A type of nonvolatile memory that can be erased and reprogrammed; commonly implemented in the form of sticks or cards.

► FIGURE 4-21

Flash memory. Common forms of flash memory include memory sticks, cards, and drives.

MEMORY STICKS

Memory sticks, designed for use with digital cameras and other portable devices, can be used in PCs with an appropriate adapter or peripheral device.

MEMORY CARDS

Memory cards are available in PC card form, as well as in a variety of formats, such as CompactFlash, SmartMedia, and MultiMedia cards. Memory card adapters are available for desktop and notebook PCs.

MEMORY DRIVES

In addition to drives designed to replace conventional magnetic disk drives, portable flash memory drives are available. This drive, which connects to a PC's USB port, holds up to 64 MB and behaves like any other drive on the PC when connected.

Storage Medium	Storage Capacity (in bytes)	Write Speed	Approximate Cost (each/per MB)*	Can Be Read by
Conventional 3 1/2-inch floppy disk	1.44 MB	Slow	$0.50/0.35	Conventional floppy drive, SuperDisk drive, HiFD drive
Zip 100 disk	100 MB	Medium	$10/0.10	Zip 100 and Zip 250 drives
SuperDisk	120 MB	Medium	$10/0.08	SuperDisk drive
HiFD disk	200 MB	Medium	$15/0.08	HiFD drive
Zip 250 disk	250 MB	Medium	$70/0.28	Zip 250 drive
CD-R disc	650 MB	Slow	$1/0.002	Most CD and DVD drives
CD-RW disc	650 MB	Slow	$5/0.01	CD-RW drives; some CD and DVD drives
Jaz II disk	2 GB	Fast	$125/0.06	Jaz II drive
Orb disk	2.2 GB	Fast	$35/0.02	Orb drive
DVD-RAM disc	5.2 GB	Slow	$32/0.01	Most DVD drives
DVD+RW disc	9 GB	Slow	$100/0.01	Most DVD+RW drives
Peerless	20 GB	Fast	$180/0.01	Peerless drive

*Cost as of 2001

FIGURE 4-22

Secondary storage alternatives compared. When comparing removable storage mediums, look at storage capacity, speed, cost, and device compatibility.

Today, most users need at least an internal hard disk system, some type of CD or DVD drive, and a floppy disk drive compatible with conventional 1.44 MB floppy disks. Hard disks have the advantage of large capacity, reasonable cost, and fast data access. They are used to store most data and virtually all programs not required to run directly from a CD or DVD disc. A CD or DVD drive is needed to run multimedia programs too large to be stored on the hard disk and for installing new software. Floppy disks, on the other hand, are commonly used for transferring small amounts of data between computer systems and for backing up small files, though their use for file transfer is decreasing as users are beginning to e-mail each other files instead, when possible.

Users who need to transfer data between systems or to back up greater amounts of data, and who don't already have a rewritable CD or DVD drive installed, will need to select a high-capacity, removable storage system, such as a superdiskette, removable hard disk, or rewritable optical disc system. Usually the type of system used depends on two factors: the needed storage capacity, and any required compatibility with another computer's storage systems. Some of the most common removable storage media are compared in Figure 4-22.

In addition, when comparing media with respect to their ability to back up your data, you may also want to look at how long each medium can reliably store data. The chapter Trend box examines this consideration.

How Many Tomorrows Will Today's Data Last?

The Answer May Shock You

As the computer age began to mature and high-capacity archival media became available to store information recorded on paper, many people saw these media as the way to preserve information forever. Paper degrades over time and eventually turns to dust. Many types of electronic media, by contrast, were far more durable—at least that's what the experts were saying.

Today, a far less rosy picture is emerging.

The problem is that digital tapes and optical discs are degrading far more quickly than anyone thought possible. Many experts are now warning that tapes can begin losing data in as few as five years, and CDs can start producing reading errors within the same time span. Tape breaks down with exposure to air, heat, and humidity, and contact with stray magnetic fields can rearrange the magnetized particles that store data on them. The surface of a CD can erode with exposure to ordinary light, causing the loss of data on the disk's surface; it can also be scratched.

The results of media degradation are already beginning to be felt. Approximately 20 percent of the information collected on tapes made during NASA's 1976 Viking mission to Mars has been lost due to deterioration. Thus, part of our nation's heritage is gone forever. Also, some drug companies have been getting reading errors when moving product-testing data from one computer system to another, due to degraded bits on the original storage medium. How sympathetic would a jury be if these companies try to claim in court that tests showed their products to be safe and effective, but their computers destroyed the data? Unfortunately, tapes and disks—unlike paper—usually do not show signs of degradation until it's too late.

And that's not the end of the bad news. A potentially more serious problem: The software needed to read a lot of archival data has long ago been tossed out and is no longer supported by anyone. Critical satellite data collected in the Amazon forest in the 1970s—data needed to establish deforestation trends—are trapped on magnetic tapes that no one can read. Also no longer accessible because of missing or outmoded software are some POW and MIA records from the Vietnam War as well as many records at one large eastern university. We will face the same problem if some new storage devices, such as the drives that read miniature optical discs and Zip disks, are eventually discontinued.

Close to three quarters of the data created today is in digital form. Much of this never makes it onto paper. Electronic data are accumulated so easily and quickly that many people don't think about holding on to it for the long run. At best, an incomplete legacy of the world today may be left for future generations; at worst, a disaster looms if critical pieces of information are lost.

Today, many organizations are taking steps to be more cautious in maintaining information. For example, the National Archives now requires the submission of technical information about how documents or records provided to them are created. The Securities and Exchange Commission has gone one step further; it makes companies filing electronic reports submit them in certain file formats only.

Digital media manufacturers are trying to help by developing new products that will be able to withstand the test of time. At this writing, however, if you want something to last at least 100 years or more, the top choice in media has been around before "computers" became a household word: paper.

Perishable commodities. Tapes and disks degrade over time, making unusable the programs and data stored on them.

Storage systems make it possible to save programs, data, and processing results for later use. They provide **nonvolatile** storage, so when the power is shut off, the data stored on the storage medium remain intact. This differs from *memory,* which is **volatile.** The most common types of storage media are magnetic disks and optical discs, which are read by the appropriate type of drive.

Chapter Objective 1:
Explain the difference between storage systems and memory.

PROPERTIES OF STORAGE SYSTEMS

All storage systems involve two physical parts: A storage device and a storage medium. In addition to being nonvolatile, storage devices can record data either on *removable media,* which provide access only when inserted into the appropriate storage device, or *fixed media,* in which the media is permanently located inside the storage device. Removable media provide the advantages of unlimited storage capacity, transportability, safer backup capability, and security. Fixed media have the advantages of higher speed, lower cost, and greater reliability.

Two basic access methods characterize secondary storage systems: Sequential and random access. *Sequential access* allows a computer system to retrieve the records in a file only in the same order in which they are physically stored. *Random access* (or *direct access*) allows the system to retrieve records in any order.

Files (sometimes called *documents*) stored on a storage medium are given a *filename* and can be organized into **folders** (sometimes called *directories*). This is referred to as *logical file representation.* *Physical file representation* refers to how the files are physically stored on the storage medium.

Chapter Objective 2:
Name several general properties of storage systems.

MAGNETIC DISK SYSTEMS

Magnetic disk storage is most widely available in the form of hard disks and floppy disks.

Computer systems commonly include **floppy disk** *(diskette)* storage because it provides a uniform removable storage system at low cost. Each side of a floppy disk holds data and programs in concentric **tracks** encoded with magnetized spots representing 0s and 1s. **Sector** boundaries divide a floppy disk surface into pie-shaped pieces. The part of a track crossed by a fixed number of contiguous sectors forms a **cluster.** The disk's *file directory* or *file allocation table (FAT),* which the computer system maintains automatically, keeps track of the contents at each disk address. To use a floppy disk, you insert it into a *floppy disk drive.* A disk drive works only when the floppy disk is inserted correctly.

Today, floppy disks are facing challenges from other removable media with much higher storage capacities. *Superdiskettes* that can supplement or replace floppy disk systems include *Zip drives, HiFD drives,* and *SuperDisk (laser servo) drives.*

Hard disk systems offer faster access than floppy disks and much greater storage capacity. A hard disk system encases one or more rigid disk platters in a permanently enclosed case along with an *access mechanism.* A separate read/write head corresponds to each disk surface, and the access mechanism moves the heads in and out among the tracks to read and write data. All tracks in the same position on all surfaces of all disks in a hard disk drive form a disk **cylinder.**

Three events determine the time needed to read from or write to most disks: *seek time, rotational delay,* and *data movement time.* The sum of these three time components is called **disk access time.** A **disk cache** strategy, in which the computer fetches program or data contents in neighboring disk areas and transports them to RAM whenever disk content is retrieved, can speed up access time.

Three disk standards—*ATA/IDE, SCSI,* and *Fibre Channel*—dominate the hard disk market. Hard disks can be *partitioned* into more than one logical drive to reduce cluster size or facilitate multiple users or operating systems. If portability is required, removable hard disk systems are available. Hard disk systems for notebook PCs include internal and external hard drives, as well as PC card hard drives.

Chapter Objective 3:
Identify the two primary types of magnetic disk systems and describe how they work.

Disk drives on larger computers implement many of the same principles as PC-based hard drives. Instead of finding a single set of hard disks inside a hard drive permanently installed within a system unit, however, a refrigerator-sized cabinet separate from the system unit often encloses several removable racks of hard disk drives. **RAID** technology (for *r*edundant *a*rrays of *i*nexpensive *d*isks) can be used on larger systems to increase *fault tolerance* and performance.

OPTICAL DISCS

Optical disc systems, which work with laser read/write devices, are available in a wide variety of *CD* and *DVD* formats. **CD-ROM** (*c*ompact *d*isc *r*ead-*o*nly *m*emory) systems enable an optical drive to read from a CD-ROM disc an unlimited number of times but it cannot write to the disc. **Recordable CDs (CD-R)** and **rewritable CDs (CD-RW)** can both be written to, but only CD-RW can be erased and rewritten to, similar to a floppy disk or hard drive. *DVD* discs include **DVD-ROM** discs, which are similar to CD-ROM discs, but with a much greater storage capacity; **rewritable DVDs (DVD-RAM** or **DVD+RW,** depending on the manufacturer) will likely eventually emerge as the new optical disc standard.

Discs that use a combination of magnetic and optical technology are called *magneto-optical (MO) discs.*

OTHER TYPES OF STORAGE SYSTEMS

Other types of storage systems include **magnetic tape,** which stores data on a plastic strip coated with a magnetizable substance. Magnetic tapes are usually enclosed in cartridges and are inserted into a *tape drive* to be used.

Online storage is a newer type of storage system, where data is stored on a server available through the Internet or a private network. This type of storage is becoming increasingly important as workers need to access data from remote locations and diskless network PCs become more prominent in the home.

Smart cards and **flash memory** are newer types of storage systems becoming increasingly popular for use with digital cameras, portable PCs, and other portable devices, as well as for *e-commerce.* Smart cards are credit-card-sized pieces of plastic that contain a chip or other circuitry used to store data or money. Flash memory can be in the form of *flash memory sticks, flash memory cards,* or *flash memory drives.* Though originally intended for portable computers and devices, these media can be used with conventional PCs if the appropriate ports exists on the PC or if an appropriate adapter is used.

COMPARING STORAGE ALTERNATIVES

Most PCs today include a hard drive, floppy disk drive, and CD or DVD drive. The type of optical drive and any additional storage alternatives are often determined by weighing a number of product characteristics and cost factors. These characteristics include speed, compatibility, capacity, and removability.

Instructions: Match each key term on the left with the definition on the right that fits best.

1. CD-ROM

2. DVD-ROM

3. file

4. flash memory

5. floppy disk

6. folder

7. hard disk system

8. magnetic disk

9. nonvolatile

10. online storage

11. optical disc

12. recordable CD (CD-R)

13. rewritable CD (CD-RW)

14. rewritable DVD (DVD-RAM or DVD+RW)

15. smart card

16. storage

17. volatile

———— A storage medium that records data using magnetic spots on disks made of flexible plastic or rigid metal.

———— A credit-card-size piece of plastic containing a chip and other circuitry into which data can be stored.

———— A disc that is read and written to using a laser beam.

———— A high-capacity optical disc that can be read from, but not written to, by the user.

———— A logical named place on a storage medium into which files can be stored to keep the medium organized. Sometimes called a directory.

———— A low-capacity, removable magnetic disk made of flexible plastic permanently sealed inside a hard plastic cover.

———— A low-end optical disc that can be read from, but not written to, by the user.

———— A storage system consisting of one or more metal magnetic disks and an access mechanism typically permanently sealed inside its drive.

———— A type of CD that can be written to, as well as erased or rewritten to.

———— A type of CD that can be written to, but not erased or rewritten to.

———— A type of DVD that can be written to, as well as erased or rewritten to.

———— A type of nonvolatile memory that can be erased and reprogrammed; commonly implemented in the form of sticks or cards.

———— Saving data, results, or programs for future use.

———— Something stored on a storage medium, such as a program, document, or image.

———— Storage located on a network storage device, such as on a server accessible through the Internet.

———— Storage that retains its contents when the power is shut off.

———— Storage in which contents are erased when the power is shut off.

Self-Quiz

Answers for the self-quiz appear at the end of the book.

True/False

Instructions: Circle **T** if the statement is true or **F** if the statement is false.

T F **1.** A high-density 3½-inch floppy disk holds 1.44 MB.

T F **2.** The smallest amount of space a file on a disk can take up is one sector.

T F **3.** A computer system with a C and D drive must have two physical hard drives.

T F **4.** Iomega's Zip disks can be read by a Zip drive or a conventional floppy drive.

T F **5.** Most PCs today include a hard disk drive.

Completion

Instructions: Answer the following questions.

6. A storage medium is _____ if it loses its contents when the power is shut off.

7. A(n) _____ disc can be written to once, but not rewritten to.

8. TR-1, QIC-80, and DAT are types of _____ storage.

9. A(n) _____ looks similar to a credit card, but contains a chip and other circuitry into which data can be stored.

10. With _____ storage, data is stored and retrieved via a network, such as the Internet.

Exercises

1. Assume, for simplicity's sake, that a kilobyte is 1,000 bytes, a megabyte is 1,000,000 bytes, and a gigabyte is 1,000,000,000 bytes. You have a 10-gigabyte hard disk with the following usage characteristics:

APPLICATION	STORAGE SPACE USED
Operating system	27 MB
Other systems software	1.5 GB
Office suite	85 MB
Other software	250 MB
Documents	97 KB

Approximately how much room is left on the disk?

2. Match the PC component shown in each of the following pictures with the appropriate term.

A

B

C

D

E

_____ Removable hard disk
_____ Flash memory stick
_____ Floppy disk
_____ CD disc
_____ Smart card

3. On PC-compatible storage systems, what type of storage device would normally be assigned to the following drive letters?

    a. A: _____

    b. B: _____

    c. C: _____

    d. D: _____

4. Which storage media would be appropriate for someone who needed to exchange large (5 MB to 75 MB) files with another person? List at least three different types, stating why each might be the most appropriate under specific conditions.

5. For each of the following terms, indicate the type of storage medium they are related to (such as hard drive, floppy disk, superdiskette, optical disc, flash memory, smart card, etc.)

    a. SCSI _____

    b. RAID _____

    c. CompactFlash _____

    d. CD-R _____

Short Answer/ Research

1. **Smarter Cards** A smart card, as described in the chapter, is a credit-card-size piece of plastic that contains an electronic chip for storing data. These cards have gained wide acceptance in other countries, but have been slow to catch on in the United States. However, plans by many smart card companies to use these cards in new and exciting ways may boost the use of these cards in the U.S. In the last year, these cards have more than doubled in storage capacity and are now being produced with increasingly sophisticated capabilities, which will allow them to play an expanded role in Web-based transactions. For this project, summarize what smart cards are currently being used for, and what companies anticipate them being used for in the future. Would you be comfortable using one of these cards to purchase goods and services over the Internet? Are advertisers pushing this technology, or is the public asking for this technology in the U.S.? At the conclusion of your research, prepare a one-page summary of your findings and submit it to your instructor.

2. **Auto Backup?** For those of us who forget to back up our files on a regular basis, there is an alternative. The alternative involves using an automatic backup utility that performs this task for you on a regular basis. Several companies sell this type of software and it is not very expensive. In addition, many companies that sell storage devices with removable media include this software for free with the purchase of the device. Another option that has become very popular recently is backing up your files to a CD-R or CD-RW disc. This option continues to gain in popularity as the price of CD-R and CD-RW drives continue to decrease. For this project, research a few of the options that are available for performing automatic backups, and summarize the alternatives that you find. At the conclusion of your research, prepare a one-page summary of your findings and submit it to your instructor.

3. **Future Storage Plans** A few of the major companies that build storage systems are EMC, Compaq, IBM, Hitachi, Sun Microsystems, Seagate, and Hewlett-Packard. Each of these companies is betting that audio and video will dominate the Internet, and that the demand for storage will grow at least 20 percent per year, for the next five years. In addition, some analysts predict that storage-related sales will outpace server sales in the near future. For this project, research two of these companies and summarize what their strategy is for developing new storage solutions and capturing additional market share. At the conclusion of your research, prepare a one-page summary of your findings and submit it to your instructor.

Hands On

4. **Storage Evaluation** The computer you use on a regular basis has one or more forms of storage. For this project, identify each of them by type (floppy disk, CD, hard drive, DVD, tape drive, Zip drive, etc.) and specify the drive letter allocated to each of them. You should also determine the capacity for each device and the current amount of used and free space on all fixed storage devices. (*Hint:* Open a file management program, such as My Computer or Windows Explorer on Windows PCs, right-click the desired drive icon, and select a "Properties" option, if one exists, to see information about that drive, as shown in the accompanying image). At the conclusion of this task, prepare a one-page summary of your efforts and submit it to your instructor.

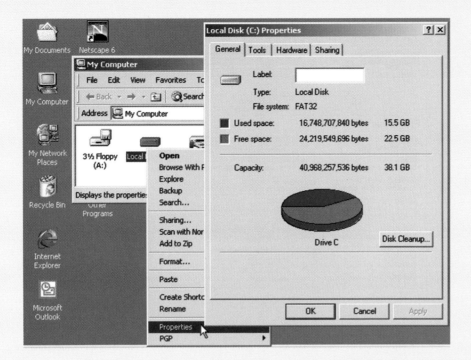

5. **Storage Service Providers** An alternative method to backing up your data is becoming fairly popular. It is generally referred to as online storage and is accomplished over the Internet. Several companies sometimes referred to as Storage Service Providers (SSP) offer this service for free to individuals and at modest prices to organizations. The revenue from this type of service is expected to reach $700 million by the year 2003. There are several advantages and disadvantages to this approach. For this project, visit several online storage Web sites and evaluate the services and options they offer. What are some the advantages and disadvantages to backing up business data using the online storage method? What additional services do these SSPs offer? Would you be interested in using one of these free services for your personal files? Submit this project to your instructor in the form of a short paper, not more than two pages in length.

6. **Music to the Web** The music industry is faced with the prospect of having to develop a new business model in order to deal with the Internet and the MP3 compression standard. MP3 compression allows you to store near-CD quality sound in 1/12 the disk space of the original storage requirement so, consequently, reduces the amount of time it takes to download high quality music files. For this project, describe how the MP3 format became so popular, the advantages of this format over the other formats (both online and offline), and what type of software you would need on your computer to play an MP3 file. Why is the music and recording industry concerned about this format? Has there been any legal action in regards to the MP3 format? Have you downloaded any MP3 files? (See the accompanying illustration on the next page.) Submit this project to your instructor in the form of a short paper, not more than two pages in length.

Writing About Computers

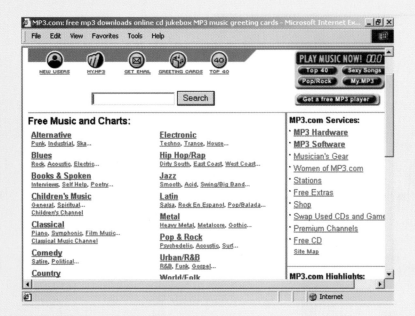

7. **Storage Options** The selection of an appropriate storage solution is based on the computer system and a set of defined storage requirements. For this project, form a group to discuss and define the storage requirements for each of the following three systems, and determine an appropriate storage solution for each one. The first system is for a home computer where several family members will be using the computer for homework, shopping, taxes, saving music, playing multimedia games, and surfing the Web. The second system is for a small accounting company that has only one computer and is using it to support all the administrative and information needs of the company. The third system is for a two-person video editing and multimedia production company that has two computers and specializes in weddings and other special occasions. Feel free to modify or clarify the three systems defined above in order to make your storage solutions match more closely with the diverse number of possibilities and storage options available today. Your group should submit this project to your instructor in the form of a short paper, not more than three pages in length.

Presentation/ Demonstration

8. **Burning a CD** The cost of CD-R and CD-RW drives has dropped significantly in the past few years and these are a good option if you need to store and distribute large files (such as photographs, video, or audio files). Before you go out and purchase one, however, you should take a few issues into consideration. These issues include compatibility, interface, speed, and cost. In addition, you should decide whether you want to have an internal or external drive. Several manufacturers make CD-R and CD-RW drives, and each one of them has its own set of performance characteristics and interface requirements. For this project, prepare a short presentation that evaluates at least three of these drives. You should assume that your budget is very tight, and make some recommendations based on your own preferences. Have you burned a CD before? If not, do you think this would be a very difficult task? Why are there multiple speeds (such as 4×/4×/24×) listed in the specifications for some of these drives? This presentation should not exceed 5 minutes and should make use of one or more presentation aids such as the chalkboard, handouts, overhead transparencies, or computer-based slide presentation format. You may be asked to submit a summary of the presentation to your instructor.

9. **e-Books** Both Microsoft and Adobe have developed technologies that claim to increase screen resolutions by 300 percent without raising the cost of the screens. The Microsoft version of the technology is called "ClearType" and the Adobe version is called "CoolType," but both are basically the same except for differences in the underlying technology. What makes this

technology exciting, beyond the fact that we may all save a little eye strain, is that Microsoft plans on using this technology on the their new e-Books. For this project, form a group to investigate e-Books and these new technologies. Your group should prepare a short presentation that explains your findings. Does this new technology really increase the resolution of screen without increasing the cost? Does it work on traditional monitors, or just certain types of screens? In addition, you should explain what an e-Book is and how these books are expected to create a new high-tech industry. This presentation should not exceed 10 minutes and should make use of one or more presentation aids such as the chalkboard, handouts, overhead transparencies, or computer-based slide presentation format. Your group may be asked to submit a summary of the presentation to your instructor.

10. **Optical Options** The number of optical storage formats available is amazing. These options include CD-R, CD-RW, DVD-ROM, DVD+RW, and DVD-RAM discs. Some of these formats have more capacity than others, and some are more compatible than others. The question of which format to choose is a matter of personal preference; however, you need to be aware of the different formats, capacities, and required system specifications for each of them, in order to make the best purchase decision. For this project, form a group to investigate the various options available and prepare a short presentation based on your findings. Be sure to explain some of the advantages and disadvantages of each format. Do any of you have any personal experience with any optical formats? If you needed to buy an optical drive today, which one would you choose and why? This presentation should not exceed 10 minutes and should make use of one or more presentation aids such as the chalkboard, handouts, overhead transparencies, or computer-based slide presentation format. Your group may be asked to submit a summary of the presentation to your instructor.

Interactive Discussion

11. **Information Overload** As the ability of the computer to process data and generate information continues to improve, and the number of systems that generate information continues to grow, we are going to be overwhelmed by information. It seems as though we are already generating more information than we can use to make a decision, and that additional information would only serve to confuse, or slow down the decision-making process. This is sort of analogous to a restaurant that produces a menu with too many selections. The more time customers spend looking at the menu trying to decide what they would like to eat, the less money the restaurant makes, because they end up with less time to serve additional customers. It could be argued that additional information leads to a better decision; however, at what point is the additional information counterproductive?

  Select one of the following positions, or make up your own, and express your point of view on the subject. Your instructor will indicate whether your response is to be posted to a class bulletin board, discussed in a class chat room, or discussed as an in-class activity. You may also be asked to submit a summary of your position and point of view to your instructor.

   a. You can never have too much information. The human information processing system is capable of discerning the relevant from the non-relevant information that a computer system generates and thus it is important to gather as much information as possible. If you limit the amount of information collected, you run the risk of being misinformed and this could lead to bad decisions.

   b. Too much information can be as bad as no information at all. We as humans will need to limit the amount and type of information that we consider in the decision-making process. As with the restaurant example, if we choose to consider too much information, we run the risk of failing to meet our objectives because we spent so much time analyzing and making the decision.

12. **Hardcopy: The End Is Near** Consider the following statement and establish your position, or point of view, on the subject. Your instructor will indicate whether your response is to be posted to a class bulletin board, discussed in a class chat room, or discussed as an in-class activity. You may also be asked to submit a summary of your position and evaluation of the statement to your instructor.

In 1970, Xerox founded the Palo Alto Research Center (PARC) to design the office of the future. Xerox did this partly out of concern for the up-and-coming digital age where Xerox feared that the sales of its photocopy machines might drop considerably, if people choose to store and transmit documents in an electronic format rather than a hardcopy form. This fear, of course, has not materialized to date; in fact, people do more copying and printing now than they have ever done in the past. Interestingly enough, one of the inventions to come out of Xerox's investment in PARC was the laser printer, which is now a multibillion dollar business. The question, however, still remains: Will we have a paperless office in the future? Will people stop printing everything they find on the Web and realize that they can simply store this information in a digital format? It seems that the immediate answer for the paperless office may be "No." However, what about the publishers of textbooks, newspapers, magazines, and the wide array of general interest books that can be found in bookstores? Many of these product could be delivered in a much more timely and cost-effective manner in a digital format. In fact, most news and magazine publications are currently available in both a digital and traditional format already. In the near future, we will be reading all our books, magazines, and newspapers in a paperless format.

Interactive Exercise

Understanding Storage. Let's see how much you remember about storage concepts! Go to the Interactive Exercise at www.course.com/parker2002/ch4 to complete this exercise.

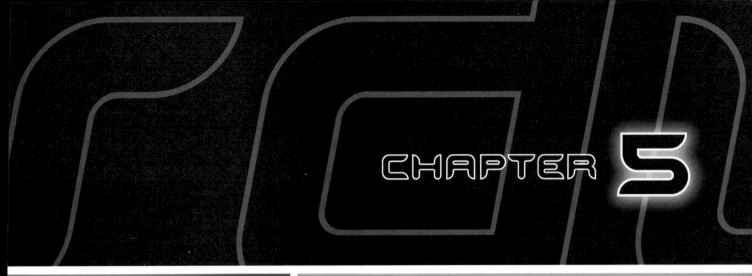

CHAPTER 5

Input and Output

LEARNING OBJECTIVES

After completing this chapter, you will be able to:

1. Identify several types of input and output devices and explain their functions.

2. Describe the characteristics of the input equipment that most users encounter regularly—namely, keyboards and pointing devices.

3. Explain what source data automation is and discuss how scanners and other devices can be used to accomplish it.

4. List several types of multimedia input devices and discuss their purpose.

5. Describe the characteristics of the output equipment that most users encounter regularly—namely, display devices and printers.

6. Discuss several types of multimedia output equipment.

7. Explain what a multifunction device is and list some advantages and disadvantages of using such a device.

In Chapter 4, we covered storage devices. Although some of those devices can also perform input and output functions, storage is their main function. In this chapter, we turn to equipment designed primarily for inputting data in a form the computer can process, or outputting results in a form that the user can understand.

We begin the chapter with a look at input. First up are keyboards and then pointing devices, such as the mouse. Most home and office users require these types of devices to enter commands or data into their computer systems. From there, we cover hardware designed for scanning images, text, and bar codes, as well as other devices used for fast, relatively error-free input for some applications. We also discuss multimedia input devices, such as those involving audio or video input.

Then we explore output, starting with display devices. Here, we highlight some of the qualities that distinguish one type of display device from another. Next, we turn to printers. In this section, you will learn about the wide variety of devices that place computer output on paper. We also discuss multimedia output and multifunction devices.

Keep in mind that this chapter describes only a sample of the input and output equipment available today. In fact, the marketplace offers thousands of hardware products, and they can work together in so many ways that you can create a computer system to fit almost any conceivable need. ■

INPUT AND OUTPUT

Input and output equipment allows people to communicate with computers. An **input device** converts data that humans can understand into a form that the computer can process. Such a device translates the letters, numbers, and other natural-language symbols that humans conventionally use in reading and writing into the binary 0s and 1s that the computer can process. Input devices can also be used to input other types of data, such as photographs, speech, and video.

Output devices, on the other hand, convert the processed 0s and 1s back into a form understandable to humans. These devices typically present output on the screen or paper. Output devices produce results in either hard-copy or soft-copy form. The term *hard copy* generally refers to output permanently recorded onto an easily portable medium such as paper. The term *soft copy* generally refers to output that appears temporarily in a form with limited portability, such as on a computer screen.

Some devices, such as a modem, can be used for both input and output.

>**Input device.** A piece of hardware that supplies input to a computer. >**Output device.** A piece of hardware that accepts output from the computer and presents it in a form the user can understand.

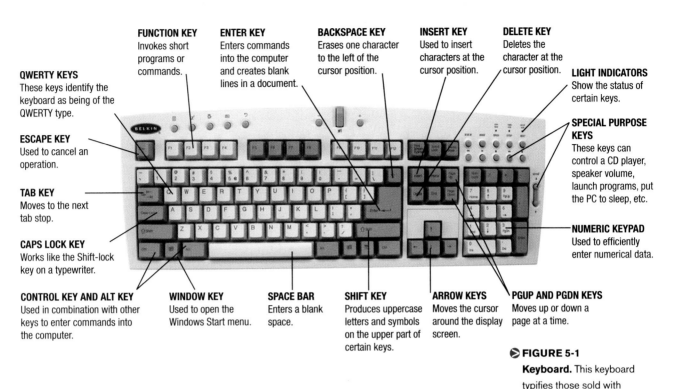

FUNCTION KEY
Invokes short programs or commands.

ENTER KEY
Enters commands into the computer and creates blank lines in a document.

BACKSPACE KEY
Erases one character to the left of the cursor position.

INSERT KEY
Used to insert characters at the cursor position.

DELETE KEY
Deletes the character at the cursor position.

LIGHT INDICATORS
Show the status of certain keys.

QWERTY KEYS
These keys identify the keyboard as being of the QWERTY type.

SPECIAL PURPOSE KEYS
These keys can control a CD player, speaker volume, launch programs, put the PC to sleep, etc.

ESCAPE KEY
Used to cancel an operation.

TAB KEY
Moves to the next tab stop.

NUMERIC KEYPAD
Used to efficiently enter numerical data.

CAPS LOCK KEY
Works like the Shift-lock key on a typewriter.

CONTROL KEY AND ALT KEY
Used in combination with other keys to enter commands into the computer.

WINDOW KEY
Used to open the Windows Start menu.

SPACE BAR
Enters a blank space.

SHIFT KEY
Produces uppercase letters and symbols on the upper part of certain keys.

ARROW KEYS
Moves the cursor around the display screen.

PGUP AND PGDN KEYS
Moves up or down a page at a time.

FIGURE 5-1
Keyboard. This keyboard typifies those sold with many PCs.

KEYBOARDS

Most computers are designed to be used with a **keyboard** (see Figure 5-1). A keyboard is one of the two main devices through which conventional computers receive user input. The large majority of keyboards follow a standard arrangement for letter keys called *QWERTY* (named for the first six letter keys at the top left of most typewriter keyboards). An alternative layout, purported to allow faster input, is the *Dvorak* keyboard, though this layout is not widely used.

Figure 5-1 shows a typical PC keyboard layout and describes the purposes of several keys. The Delete (Del) and Backspace keys, for example, are used to delete characters from the screen. The Enter key is used to enter commands into the computer, as well as to end paragraphs while creating written documents. Keyboards also feature several *function keys,* which are labeled F1, F2, F3, and so on (see the top of the keyboard in Figure 5-1). When the user presses one of these keys, the keystroke initiates a special command, dependent on the program being used. For example, pressing the F2 key in your word processing program may enable you to indent text, but the same keystroke in your spreadsheet program may let you edit what you've typed in a cell. Most keyboards also have a *numeric keypad* to allow you to easily and quickly enter numbers.

The number of special keys, as well as their capabilities and placement, varies among manufacturers. When buying a computer system, look carefully at the keyboard's key selection and the placement of keys. Common on newer keyboards are special keys to access favorite Web sites, control the volume of the CD/DVD player, and put the computer in standby mode. Notebook and handheld PC users should definitely try out the keyboard, whenever possible, before buying because these keyboards are smaller, contain less keys, and the keys are typically placed closer together than on a conventional keyboard. If desired, notebook users can connect and use a conventional keyboard, if their PC contains a keyboard port. Some

>**Keyboard.** An input device containing numerous keys, arranged in a configuration similar to that of a typewriter, that can be used to input letters, numbers, and symbols.

Handheld PC is
plugged in here.

FIGURE 5-2

Special-purpose keyboards. Special keyboards are available for specific uses, such as this folding portable keyboard designed for handheld PCs users (left), and this ergonomic keyboard, used to lessen wrist strain (right).

handheld PCs have the option of adding a portable folding keyboard, such as the Palm folding keyboard shown in Figure 5-2. The second type of special-purpose keyboard shown in Figure 5-2 is an *ergonomic keyboard,* used to lessen the strain on the hands and wrist.

POINTING DEVICES

The second main input device for most PCs is the **pointing device,** which can be used to move an onscreen pointer—usually an arrow or pointing hand—and select objects located on the screen. To move the pointer, the device is either moved along a surface or, alternatively, a ball on top of the device is rotated with a finger or thumb. To select objects, usually a button on the device is pushed. Some common types of pointing devices are the *mouse, electronic pen, touch screen, joystick, game pad,* and *trackball.*

Mouse

Most people supplement keyboard input with a **mouse** (see Figure 5-3). When you move the mouse along a flat surface, the onscreen pointer—usually called the *mouse pointer*—moves correspondingly. Older *mechanical mice* have a ball exposed on the bottom surface of the mouse to control the pointer movement; newer *optical mice* (such as the one in Figure 5-3) are completely sealed and track movements with light instead of ball movement. While mechanical mice are usually used in conjunction with a protective mouse pad and require regular cleanings to operate properly, optical mice typically don't.

Mice provide the capability to move rapidly from one location to another on a display screen, to make onscreen selections, to move and resize windows and other screen objects, to select hyperlinks, and to draw on the screen. A mouse usually accomplishes these tasks much faster or far more effectively than you could complete them by pressing combinations of keys on the keyboard.

As discussed in Chapter 2, when you use the mouse to activate a desktop icon or toolbar button, you point to it on the screen and press—or *click*—the left mouse button once or twice. To move an object from one part of the screen to another, you can point to the object, hold down the left mouse button, move the mouse to drag the object to its new position, and release the mouse button. This operation is commonly known as *dragging and dropping* and can be used to move paragraphs of text, images, or other objects to a new location. Many mice today have a scroll wheel or button on top, which can be used to more

---

>**Pointing device.** A piece of hardware that moves an onscreen pointer, such as an arrow or insertion point, to allow users to select objects on the screen. >**Mouse.** A common pointing device that you slide along a flat surface to move a pointer around the screen and make selections.

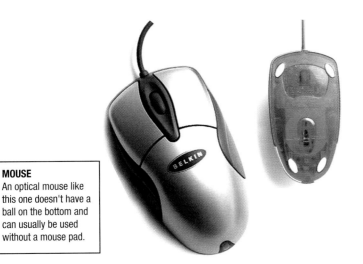

MOUSE
An optical mouse like this one doesn't have a ball on the bottom and can usually be used without a mouse pad.

MOUSE POINTER
When the mouse is moved along a flat surface, a pointer on the display screen moves correspondingly.

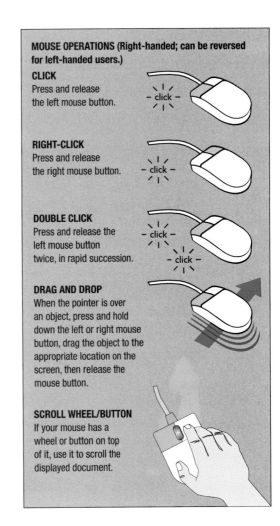

MOUSE OPERATIONS (Right-handed; can be reversed for left-handed users.)

CLICK
Press and release the left mouse button.

RIGHT-CLICK
Press and release the right mouse button.

DOUBLE CLICK
Press and release the left mouse button twice, in rapid succession.

DRAG AND DROP
When the pointer is over an object, press and hold down the left or right mouse button, drag the object to the appropriate location on the screen, then release the mouse button.

SCROLL WHEEL/BUTTON
If your mouse has a wheel or button on top of it, use it to scroll the displayed document.

FIGURE 5-3
Using a mouse.

easily *scroll* through the information displayed on the screen. These and other common mouse operations are summarized in Figure 5-3.

While most mice sold with PCs connect via the serial, USB, or PS/2 port on the computer's system unit, *cordless mice* are also available. These mice, powered by batteries, send wireless signals to a receiver usually plugged into the computer's serial port. Though earlier wireless mice used infrared signals and needed to be within line-of-sight to its receiver, newer models use radio waves and so don't need to use line-of-sight transmission, though there is a limit on the allowable distance between the mouse and the receiver. Conventional, cordless, and small travel mice can all be used with notebook PCs, if desired, as long as the appropriate port is present.

Electronic Pens

An **electronic pen** is used as an alternative to a mouse to select objects, draw, or write on the screen. A *light pen* (see Figure 5-4) is usually connected to the computer with a cable and senses marks or other indicators through a light-sensitive cell in its tip. When the tip of the pen is placed close to the screen, the display device can identify its position. Some light pens can be used with a standard monitor.

>**Electronic pen.** An electronic device, resembling an ordinary pen, used for computer input.

A cordless electronic pen that looks like a ballpoint pen and is used with pen-input devices—such as handheld PCs, tablet PCs, graphics tablets, and pen computers—is called a *stylus*. A stylus can be used to make selections from the screen, to draw on a screen or tablet, and to capture signatures or other handwriting, as shown in Figure 5-4. Some devices that use pen input are discussed next; pen-based PCs and *handwriting recognition*—capturing and attempting to recognize written words and numbers—will be discussed shortly.

Graphics Tablets

A **graphics tablet**—also called a *digitizing tablet*—is a flat, touch-sensitive tablet usually used in conjunction with a stylus (see Figure 5-4). Drawing directly on the tablet with the stylus or tracing over a design placed on the tablet transfers the drawing to the computer in digital form. When the drawing has been completed, it can be stored in digital format on the computer.

▶ FIGURE 5-4

Uses for electronic pens.

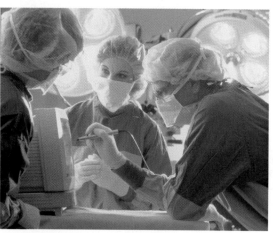

LIGHT PENS
A light pen allows precise onscreen selection down to a single pixel, allowing users in some applications to work much more efficiently.

GRAPHICS TABLET
A graphics tablet is used to draw or trace on; the resulting image is transferred to the computer.

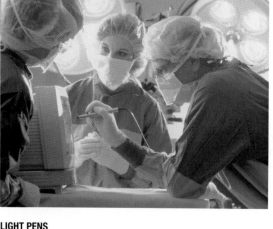

DIGITAL PORTFOLIOS
A digital portfolio contains both a PC and a writing surface that automatically transfers the written input to the PC.

SIGNATURE CAPTURE DEVICES
A signature capture device is used to input signatures, such as to authorize credit card purchases (as shown here) or record the delivery of merchandise.

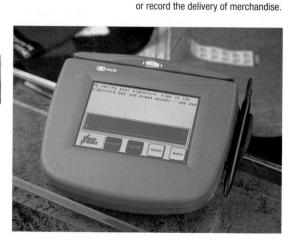

>**Graphics tablet.** An input device that consists of a flat board and a pointing mechanism that traces over it, storing the traced pattern in digital form.

Digital Portfolios

Similar to a graphics tablet, a *digital portfolio* includes a writing surface that can be used to input drawings or other handwritten data into the computer. There are digital portfolios available for a variety of types of PC, such as notebook and pocket computers (see Figure 5-4). Some portfolios are sold separately from the PC; others have the PC built in. Typically, a digital portfolio opens to reveal a notepad on one side and the PC on the other. Using either a special digital pen or a special notepad surface, everything written on the notepad is simultaneously, wirelessly, transmitted to the PC.

Signature Capture Devices

Another type of pen-based input device is the *signature capture device,* shown in Figure 5-4. These devices are commonly attached to point-of-sale equipment to electronically record signatures used to authorize credit card purchases. Delivery companies and other service businesses may use a special signature capture device to record delivery signatures. Signature capture may also be performed using a handheld or tablet PC with appropriate software.

Pen-Based Computers

Pen-based computers—whether they are palmtop, handheld, tablet, or some other type of PC—are one of the fastest-growing types of computers sold today. These devices usually use a stylus instead of a mouse or other pointing device to make selections from the screen and to input handwritten information. With some pen-based PCs, the pen is the only source of input; others use the pen to supplement keyboard input (see Figure 5-5).

Potential users of portable pen-based PCs include inspectors, factory workers, sales representatives, real-estate agents, police officers, doctors, nurses, insurance adjusters, store clerks, and truck drivers—in other words, anybody who would otherwise regularly carry around a clipboard or notebook to record information or fill out forms. Desktop PCs with pen input can be used by artists, children, or anyone else who wants or needs to enter pen-based data directly into the PC.

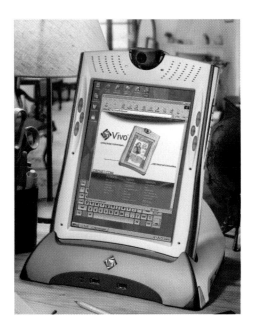

FIGURE 5-5

Pen-based PCs. Pen-based PCs use a stylus to select onscreen options instead of a mouse, as well as enter hand-written data. Pen-based PCs include pocket and handheld PCs, as well as tablet (left) and desktop (right) PCs.

TABLET PCS
Tablet PCs can often be inserted into some type of docking station, as shown here, to save battery life and to sometimes add additional capabilities, such as a keyboard, mouse, or printer connection.

DESKTOP PCS
Some desktop PCs incorporate pen input into a flat-panel display. This Sony unit has the additional advantage of being able to adjust the display for more comfortable writing, as needed.

If the pen-based PC needs to recognize pen input as actual text or commands instead of just graphical input, **handwriting recognition** technology is required. Depending on the device and technology used, the PC may be only capable of understanding commands, such as selecting options from a menu or checking particular check boxes on the screen (see Figure 5-6). Other pen-based devices accept handwritten input, such as notes, e-mail messages, and so forth, but have special requirements for the way the text is written, such as the special *Palm Graffiti* used with Palm handheld PCs. The newest types of systems can understand handwriting written in the users' own personal style. Though this type of handwriting recognition still has a way to go to be extremely accurate, it is available today and will continue to be refined and improved in the near future.

Handwriting recognition differs from *optical character recognition (OCR),* discussed shortly, in that handwriting recognition interprets writing performed directly on the screen of the device, while OCR involves interpreting scanned input.

Touch Screens

As PCs have become more and more integrated into the life of the consumer, **touch screens** have become increasingly prominent. With a touch screen, the user touches the

▶ FIGURE 5-6

Handwriting recognition and pen-based PCs. Users of pen-based PCs, such as the Fujitsu pen tablet shown here, can typically use their stylus to input handwritten data and instructions, as well as to tap on command buttons and boxes.

1. READING PEN INPUT
As the pen moves, the computer continually calculates its position, instructing the pixels it passes over to turn on.

2. PATTERN RECOGNITION
At the end of a pen stroke, the computer compares the pattern that was input to other patterns it has stored. It makes allowances within certain limits for imprecision.

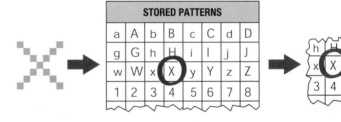

STORED PATTERNS

a	A	b	B	c	C	d	D
g	G	h	H	i	I	j	J
w	W	x	X	y	Y	z	Z
1	2	3	4	5	6	7	8

3. CONTEXT RECOGNITION
After a pattern is recognized, the computer looks at the context in which the pattern was made before it decides what to do. For instance, an "X" in a check box means selecting a certain action whereas an "X" over filled-in text implies a deletion operation.

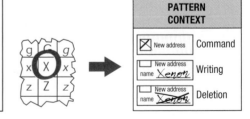

PATTERN CONTEXT

☒ New address	Command
☐ New address name *Xenon*	Writing
☐ New address name *Xenon*	Deletion

screen with his or her finger to select onscreen options (see Figure 5-7). People without much computer experience are generally more comfortable using a touch screen than a keyboard or a mouse—a definite advantage for touch-screen consumer applications. Touch screens are widely employed today in *kiosks* designed for specific purposes, such as accessing bridal registry information, creating greeting cards, withdrawing cash, looking up products, and so forth. Touch screens are also useful for factory applications and fieldwork, where users wear gloves or cannot otherwise operate keypads.

Other Pointing Devices

Joystick

A **joystick** (see Figure 5-8) provides input through a grip that looks like a car's gearshift. This input device is often used with computer games. The speed, direction, and distance at which the joystick is moved determine the movement of the onscreen pointer. Today, some electronic games replace joysticks with gloves containing built-in sensors, enabling the computer to detect hand movements directly, or a *game pad* that is held in the hand and contains buttons similar to those on a joystick. For driving games, a special *steering wheel* device can also be used.

Trackball

Similar to an upside-down mechanical mouse, a **trackball** (see Figure 5-8) has the ball mechanism on top, instead of the bottom. To move the on-screen pointer, the ball is rotated with the thumb, hand, or finger.

FIGURE 5-7

Touch-screen displays.

Touch-screen displays are ideal in settings where people may not be comfortable using a keyboard or mouse, as well as in places where using a key-board or mouse is impractical.

Pointing Stick

A *pointing stick,* which appears on the keyboard of many notebook computers (see Figure 5-8), is a pencil-eraser-shaped device that works similarly to a trackball. Instead of moving a ball, however, the thumb or finger pushes the stick in the appropriate direction.

Touch Pad

A **touch pad** is a rectangular pad that is sensitive to touch, similar to a touch screen. Sliding the fingertip or thumb across the pad moves the onscreen cursor. If the touch pad has accompanying buttons (as on the touch pad in Figure 5-8), the buttons can be used to perform the same actions as mouse buttons; if not, the pad is usually tapped instead. Though usually found on notebook computers, external touch pads (such as the one shown in Figure 5-8) and keyboards with built-in touch pads are available for use with desktop computers.

>**Joystick.** An input device that resembles a car's gear shift. >**Trackball.** An input device, similar to an upside-down mouse, that can be used to control an onscreen pointer and make selections. >**Touch pad.** A rectangular-shaped input device that is touched with the finger or thumb to control an onscreen pointer and make selections.

JOYSTICK
A joystick looks like a car's gear shift and is most often used with computer games.

POINTING STICK
Many notebook computers have a small keyboard stick that you push in different directions to move the onscreen pointer.

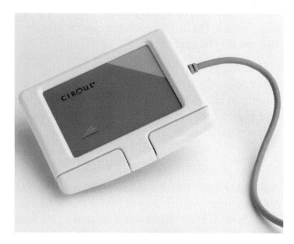

TRACKBALL
A trackball is essentially an upside-down mouse with the ball on top. A trackball requires less desk space to use than a mouse.

TOUCH PAD
Touch pads are commonly found on notebook PCs, keyboards, or as stand-alone devices, as shown here.

▶ **FIGURE 5-8**
Other pointing devices.

SCANNERS AND RELATED DEVICES

Applications often require the translation of data located on *source documents*—order forms, timecards, photographs, or other original forms of data—into digital form for electronic processing. This procedure sometimes consumes thousands of hours of wasteful, duplicated effort, and it can result in many mistakes and delays. *Source data automation* eliminates much of this wasted time and potential for error by either initially collecting data in digital form or capturing it directly from the original source document.

Source data automation has transformed a number of information-handling tasks. For example, workers who take orders over the phone today usually enter the order data directly into the computer, so they don't have to record the same data twice. Source data automation also speeds up checkout lines and inventory procedures at supermarkets, quality control operations in factories, and check processing at banks. In addition, source data automation allows the people who collect ready-to-process transaction data—those who know most about the events that the data represent—to check for accuracy during the data entry process. Many of the most common devices used in source data automation are *scanning devices*—devices that read printed text, codes, or graphics and translate the results into a form the computer can manipulate. This section discusses several different types of scanning devices.

Optical Scanners

An **optical scanner**—usually just called a **scanner**—converts flat images (a printed document, photograph, drawing, etc.) into digital form. After the digital image is input into the PC, the image can be manipulated as much as desired and then inserted into a document, posted on a Web page, or e-mailed to someone. With **optical character recognition (OCR)** software, many scanners are capable of recognizing standard typed text, as well as some handwritten text. Thus, the scanner can convert printed text into an electronic format that can later be edited using a standard word processing program. Without OCR, text documents are scanned as images, and the text cannot be edited. OCR software is an immense timesaver for users who have traditionally had to retype already typed documents in order to enter them into their computer system, such as office workers in the business and legal fields.

web tutor

For a tutorial on how scanners work, go to www.course.com/ parker2002/ch5

Scanners exist in a variety of configurations (refer to Figure 5-9). A *flatbed scanner* inputs one page at a time and works a lot like a photocopier—whatever is being scanned remains stationary while the scanning mechanism moves underneath it to capture the image. Most models can scan in color, and some even have attachments for scanning slides and film negatives. A *sheetfed scanner* functions similarly to a flatbed scanner, but documents are inserted into the top of the scanner instead, similar to a fax machine. This design reduces the scanner's cost and the amount of desk space required, as well as makes automatic sheet feeding possible. However, the feature also prevents the device from scanning bound-book pages or other items thicker or larger than a sheet of paper.

Handheld scanners are useful for inputting small amounts of data. The handheld scanner illustrated in Figure 5-9 can store about 20 pages of data and is designed to capture short articles and single lines of data, such as Web addresses, names, or telephone numbers.

Applications requiring the most professional results may require the use of a *drum scanner*. A drum scanner is much more expensive and more difficult to operate than the other types of scanners discussed here. When a drum scanner is used, the documents to be scanned are mounted on a glass cylinder, which is then rotated at high speeds around a sensor located inside the scanner. Multimedia applications may require the use of *three-dimensional scanners,* which can scan an image or person in 3D to input into a modeling or other type of computer graphics program. For example, when making the movie *Hollow Man,* in which the main character played by Kevin Bacon becomes invisible by losing layer by layer of skin, bones, and muscles, Kevin Bacon's body was scanned using a 3D scanner. This gave the animators the images they needed to begin creating the necessary digital effects and illusions.

The typical PC image scanner scans at a resolution of 300 or 600 dpi (dots per inch); professional scanners usually scan at 1,200 dpi or higher. As you might expect after the discussion at the beginning of Chapter 3 regarding storing bit-mapped images, a higher number of dots generates better quality, but also creates a larger file size, as illustrated in the bottom right image in Figure 5-9. The file size of a scanned image is also determined in part by the size of the image and the number of colors used. Many scanners have several color choices, such as black and white, grayscale, millions of colors, and so forth, in addition to

---

> **Optical scanner.** A device that reads hard-copy documents and inputs them into the computer in digital form. > **Scanner.** A term commonly used to refer to an optical scanner. > **Optical character recognition (OCR).** The ability of a scanning device to recognize written or typed characters and convert it to electronic form as text, not an image.

FLATBED SCANNER
A flatbed scanner looks and works
a lot like a photocopier, except
that it produces a computer file
instead of paper output.

HANDHELD SCANNER
Handheld scanners are
useful for inputting small
amounts of text and images.

SHEETFED SCANNER
Sheetfed scanners, such as this one
that attaches to an ordinary
keyboard, use a roller as opposed to
a flatbed mechanism to input images.

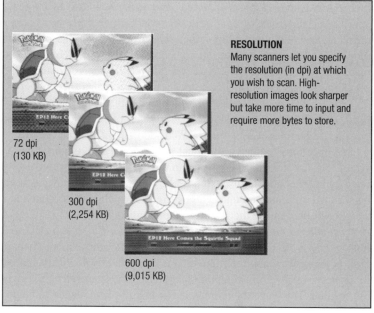

RESOLUTION
Many scanners let you specify
the resolution (in dpi) at which
you wish to scan. High-
resolution images look sharper
but take more time to input and
require more bytes to store.

72 dpi
(130 KB)

300 dpi
(2,254 KB)

600 dpi
(9,015 KB)

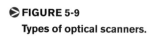

FIGURE 5-9

Types of optical scanners.

choice of resolution. When scanning an image, it is important to keep in mind the resolution of the output device to be used. Typically 72 to 150 dpi is used for images to be displayed on a monitor (such as on a Web page), and 300 dpi is used for images to be printed.

A final caution when evaluating different scanners is to watch for optical resolution measurements versus interpolated resolution. While *optical resolution* measures how many actual dots an image can contain, *interpolated* or *enhanced resolution* is software-enhanced resolution that is often about twice as high as the scanner's optical resolution. Interpolated resolution includes the actual dots, plus additional dots that are inserted between the actual dots—the scanner guesses at the appearance of the new pixels. When evaluating scanner quality, compare optical resolution.

Personal and business scanners can cost anywhere from one hundred to a few thousand dollars; professional-level models can cost tens of thousands of dollars.

Optical Readers

Optical reader technology encompasses a wide range of optical-scanning procedures and equipment designed for machine recognition of optical marks, characters, and codes. Optical readers use light to transform these symbols into digital input for a computer.

Optical Marks

One of the oldest optical reader applications is processing tests and questionnaires completed on special forms using *optical marks.* For example, most students have taken true-false or multiple-choice test questions by bubbling the correct answers with a number 2 pencil on a Scantron or similar form. You may have also filled out a survey, Census form, voting ballot, or other document using optical marks.

To tally the responses, a hardware device called an *optical mark reader* (refer to Figure 5-10) scans the form being used. Filled-in responses reflect the light, and the machine records that choice. If it is an exam or some other type of objective instrument, results can be printed on the exam form; surveys and other subjective forms are usually just tallied. In either case, results can be input to a computer system, if the reader is attached to a computer or allows the data to be stored on a disk or other storage medium.

Optical mark technology is also commonly used with voting systems, as discussed in the Trend box.

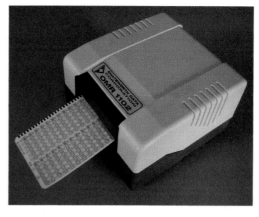

> **FIGURE 5-10**
> **Optical mark reader.**
> Readers such as these are commonly used to score tests and tally questionnaires.

Optical Characters

Optical characters are characters specially designed to be identifiable by humans as well as by some type of *optical character recognition (OCR)* device. Optical characters conform to a certain font design, such as the one shown in Figure 5-11. The optical reader shines light on the characters and converts the reflections into electronic patterns that the machine can recognize. The reader can identify a character only if it is familiar with the font standard used. Today, most machines are designed to read several standard OCR fonts, even when these fonts are mixed in a single document.

Optical characters are widely used in processing *turnaround documents,* such as the credit-card slips used for customer transactions in stores and restaurants. They also speed up processing of the monthly bills that are typically sent by credit card, utility, and cable-TV companies to their customers. Such documents are imprinted in certain places with optical characters to aid

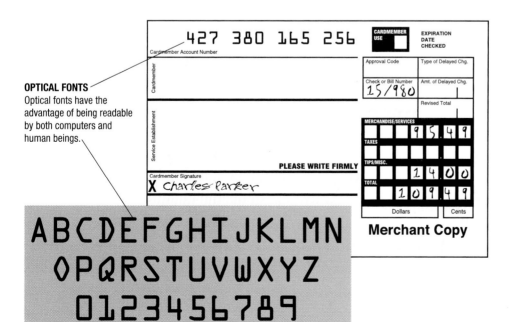

OPTICAL FONTS
Optical fonts have the advantage of being readable by both computers and human beings.

> **FIGURE 5-11**
> **Optical characters.** The most common use of optical characters is in turnaround documents, such as those used to support credit-card processing.

trend

No More Hanging Chads?

Alternative Voting Methods

Many people view the Florida 2000 presidential election as a complete breakdown of the voting process. The outcome of the election was delayed for over a month by voting discrepancies, forced recounts, and court battles over the ballots used in Florida. Most of the disputed ballots were punchcards—small cards in which openings are punched (with a supplied punch device) to represent the candidate or ballot issue choice. Punchcard ballots are read by a special machine that detects the light showing through the punched card.

The Florida controversy centered primarily on the cards that were not completely punched through and had a hanging "chad"—the small piece of paper that is supposed to be separated from the ballot when the hole is punched. Depending on whether or not the chad was blocking the punched opening when the ballot was read by the machine, the vote may or may not be tallied correctly.

Though punchcard voting systems are one of the most widely used, as a result of the 2000 election attention is shifting to alternative voting systems. *Optical voting systems,* which have been used for years, are considered to be much more accurate and consistent. These systems use optical mark technology where an empty rectangle, circle, oval, or an incomplete arrow is filled in by the voter to indicate his or her choice. The tabulating device reads the votes using "dark mark logic," whereby the computer selects the darkest mark within a given set area as the correct choice or vote.

The most recent configuration in the evolution of voting systems is known as *direct recording electronic devices,* or *DREs.* A DRE system enables the voter to directly enter his or her choices into electronic storage, typically using a touch-screen, rotary wheel, or push-button interface. A keyboard can be used in conjunction with the device to allow write-in votes, if needed. The voter's choices are stored in the machine and the final tallies are downloaded to the election's computer system when necessary.

Though reconfiguring America's voting system is a very expensive proposition, many companies are betting that the Florida debacle will lead to funds being allocated for improvements. High-tech heavyweights such as Unisys, Microsoft, Dell, and MicroTouch are jumping into the election product market feet first. Already common in countries such as Brazil and Italy, the prospect of multimillion dollar government contracts to implement electronic voting systems in cities and states across the nation is a very attractive inducement to product development. In fact, Florida has already announced that beginning with the 2002 election, it will completely eliminate paper and punchcard ballots in all 67 counties and move to an optical system.

To either eventually replace or supplement electronic voting systems, the next likely step will be *online voting* via the Internet. In actuality, Internet voting already exists. In March 2000, Arizona's Democratic Party held the first binding U.S. election in which voters could cast their ballots online. The response was startling—nearly half of the ballots cast in that election were cast online.

Online voting has several advantages and obstacles. The most obvious advantage is convenience. With more than half of all U.S. households having a computer, online voting could increase voter turn out significantly. For elderly individuals and people with limited mobility, it would be a tremendous convenience. Another consideration are the citizens in rural areas who now need to travel great distances to reach a polling place. Kelsey Begaye, President of the Navajo Nation, has had to drive four hours to reach a polling place and states that typically only about 40 percent of the people in his Navajo chapter can make it to the polls. He believes that "Internet voting will open up underrepresented minority sectors of the population to active participation in the voting process." Many believe online voting will also entice younger citizens to participate in the elections process.

Potential benefits aside, America is still not quite ready for Internet voting, according to recent studies. The main concerns seem to be security and privacy. How will the system prevent someone voting as another? What will prevent an individual's vote to be stored in a database to be used against them at a later time? Could individuals sell their vote to the highest bidder?

Nevertheless, online voting continues to be tested in a variety of locations. Perhaps in the future when smart cards, digital signatures, and other methods of uniquely authenticating an online user are perfected and more commonplace, e-voting will knock out punchcards and optical mark voting systems permanently.

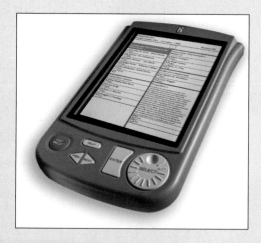

Touch screen, push button, and online electronic voting is likely the wave of the future.

processing when consumers send them back with payment—or "turn them around." Sometimes, as in the case of the restaurant bill in Figure 5-11, it's easy to spot the optical characters (see the top row of numbers). Today, however, many OCR fonts look so much like normal text that it's hard for an ordinary person to tell what parts the computer system can read.

Optical Codes

The most widely used type of *optical code* is the **bar code,** which represents data by arranging several bars of varying widths. Bar codes are typically read either by the operator passing a *handheld scanner* over the bar-coded label or sticker, or by passing the bar-coded item past a *stationary scanner* (see Figure 5-12). When read, the data being represented by the code is revealed.

HAND-HELD SCANNERS
Hand-held scanners are used for many manufacturing applications, as well as in many types of product-checkout environments. Portable units are particulary handy when the operator has to do scanning while on the move.

> **FIGURE 5-12**
Bar coding. Most bar-code readers are either handheld scanners or stationary scanners.

BAR CODE
The most widely known bar code is the universal product code (UPC) shown here, used on supermarket products. The numbers below the bars identify the manufacturer and products.

STATIONARY SCANNERS
Stationary scanners are found most often in supermarkets.

>**Bar code.** A machine-readable code that represents data as a set of bars.

The most familiar bar code is the *universal product code (UPC)* commonly found on packaged goods in supermarkets and in use since the early 1970s. Each UPC code identifies a particular product. The checkout system's bar code reader identifies the item so that the computer system can retrieve the necessary information about the item, such as the description and current price. While supermarket packaging probably represents the most common use of bar codes, codes similar to UPC support a variety of other applications. For instance, shippers such as Federal Express, United Parcel Service, and the U.S. Postal Service use their own bar codes to mark and track packages; hospitals use custom bar codes to match up patients with their charts and medicines; libraries and video stores use bar codes for checking out books and movies; researchers use bar codes to tag and track the migration habits of animals; and the police use bar codes to mark evidence. In fact, any business with a bar-code printer and appropriate software can create custom bar codes for use with their products.

Retail-based bar-coding systems that record sales transaction data at the point where the product or service is purchased are referred to as *point-of-sale (POS) systems*. When the store clerk scans each item, the associated computer performs all of the necessary arithmetic, prepares a customer receipt, and accumulates input for subsequent inventory and sales analysis. Not all POS systems use bar codes, however. For example, those at restaurants and hotels sometimes work exclusively with the magnetic strips on credit cards, supplemented with keyboard input.

Magnetic Ink Character Recognition Reader

Magnetic ink character recognition (MICR) is a technology confined primarily to the banking industry, where it supports high-volume processing of checks. Figure 5-13 illustrates

FIGURE 5-13

Magnetic ink character recognition (MICR).

MICR READER
This device that reads and sorts checks and other MICR-encoded documents can process around 600 documents per minute (dpm); faster units can process up to 2,000 dpm.

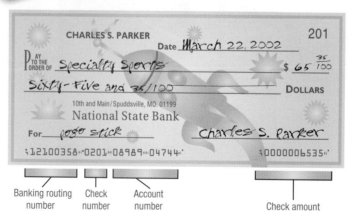

MICR-ENCODED CHECK
MICR characters on the bottom of the check respectively identify the bank, check numbers, account number, and check amount. The characters on the left are put on when checks are preprinted; those numbers representing the check amount are added when the check is cashed.

Banking routing number   Check number   Account number   Check amount

---

>**Magnetic ink character recognition (MICR).** A banking-industry technology that processes checks by sensing special characters inscribed in a magnetic ink.

a check encoded with MICR characters and a reader/sorter that processes such checks. The standard font adopted by the banking industry contains only 14 characters—the 10 decimal digits (0 through 9) and four special symbols. MICR characters are inscribed on checks with magnetic ink by a special machine. As people write and cash checks, the recipients deposit them in the banking system. At banks, reader/sorter machines magnetically sense and identify MICR-encoded characters, and the amount of the check is MICR-encoded on the check. This type of system also sorts so that they can be routed to the proper banks for payment.

MULTIMEDIA INPUT DEVICES

As multimedia becomes increasingly integrated into the computer and Web-based applications, multimedia input devices continue to grow in variety and importance. Some of the most common multimedia devices—*digital cameras, video cameras,* and *voice-* and *music-input systems*—are discussed next.

Digital Cameras

Digital cameras are much like regular cameras, but instead of recording images on film they record them on some type of digital storage medium. Most of the time the storage medium is removable, such as a disk or flash memory card (see Figure 5-14). As photos are taken, they are stored in digital form on the disk or card. Digital cameras are useful for many types of business and recreational applications. For instance, an insurance adjuster may need a quick picture of a damaged car, a home or business user may require a simple snapshot for a newsletter or a Web page, or a news photographer may need to capture an image immediately and send it over phone wires to an anxious editor. One of the most compelling advantages of digital cameras is that you can immediately see and use the photographs as you take them, without having to shoot an entire roll of film and wait to get it developed first. You can also often preview the image immediately after it is taken, so that a new photo can be shot if the image is not acceptable.

Digital cameras targeted for consumers use storage media that hold from a half dozen or so to 100 or more images. The number held depends both on the capacity of the medium and

▶ FIGURE 5-14
Digital cameras. Digital cameras resemble conventional cameras, but take images on digital media instead of on film.

STORAGE MEDIA
Digital cameras store images on reusable cards or disks. Either the media are inserted into the PC or printer, or the images are transferred to the PC by connecting the camera to the PC with a cable.

PREVIEWS
Most digital cameras let you display and erase images while shooting.

>**Digital camera.** A camera that records pictures as digital data (instead of film) images.

the image resolution being used. After taking photos, you can transfer them to your PC, if desired, by either connecting the camera to the appropriate port on your PC or inserting the storage medium into your PC, depending on the options available to you. You can then erase the disk or card so that you can take more pictures at a later time. After storing the images on your PC's hard drive, you can retouch them with image-enhancement software, if necessary, adjusting contrast, brightness, color, and focus or adding special effects or removing red-eye. You can then save them and print them, if desired. Some printers accept flash memory media directly, so uploading the images to your PC first isn't necessary.

Digital cameras for consumer use often cost anywhere from $50 to several hundred dollars; professional-level digital cameras can cost well over $10,000. Though earlier cameras could not match the quality of images produced by the conventional, 35-mm film camera, the newer *megapixel cameras* using multimillion-pixel-resolution do. One limitation of digital cameras is that they often require a lot of power, so batteries need to be replaced frequently.

You don't, however, need to go out and buy a digital camera in order to get digital photographs for use on a Web page or inclusion in a greeting card, newsletter, or other electronic document. As discussed in a previous section, you can scan processed traditional photographs using an optical scanner. Another alternative is requesting an entire roll of film to be processed onto a Kodak *PictureCD* instead of, or in addition to, your photos being processed onto photo paper. This option is available at most locations that process conventional film.

Video Cameras

Video camera use with PCs has been steadily increasing in recent years. They are currently being used primarily to send video images over the Internet (see Figure 5-15), such as during a *videoconference* or *video phone call*. Though video phone calls can be one-sided, usually during a videoconference each person has a PC video camera attached to his or her PC to transmit images to the other person. PC video cameras can also be used to continually broadcast images to a Web page, such as the cameras frequently found in zoo animal exhibits, on top of mountains, or other locations of interest to the general public. In this type of application, the video camera is often referred to as a *Webcam*. Some PC video cameras can take still images, as well.

Images from a PC video camera can either be displayed on the screen continuously, or can be static images taken at regular intervals, depending on the application and hardware being used. PC video cameras can also be used to capture video and store it in the computer for later use, though this application requires special software and a great deal of storage space. Stored video can be played again when needed, or inserted into a multimedia presentation. Short video clips can also be e-mailed to others.

To capture video from a traditional video camera, special hardware—such as a *video input board* or *video digitizer*—is required. As with live video, captured video can be stored on storage media to be used at a later time. Another application of video input use is a *TV tuner card* used to capture the video (and audio) from television signals and display them on your PC. Video cameras can also be used for identification

further exploration

For links to further information about digital cameras, go to www.course.com/parker2002/ch5

❯ **FIGURE 5-15**

PC video cameras. PC video cameras are commonly used to deliver video input over the Internet.

purposes, such as to authorize access to a secure facility or computer resource. This and other types of security applications are discussed in more detail in Chapters 8 and 15.

Audio Input Devices

Audio input is the process of entering audio data into the computer. Such input can include voice and music.

Voice-Input Systems

A hardware-and-software combination that can convert spoken words into digital data is known as a **voice-input system.** All voice-input systems consist of a microphone and appropriate software, such as IBM ViaVoice or Dragon Naturally Speaking (see Figure 5-16). Voice input can be recorded to be sent via e-mail or used in a multimedia presentation. It can also be used to dictate text or commands the computer will recognize, as an alternative to mouse or keyboard input. This type of voice-input system is more specifically called a *voice-recognition system.*

For example, with voice recognition you can dictate letters into your word processing program and dictate e-mail messages to your e-mail program. You may also be able to issue commands to your computer, such as to open a particular program or save a document. Specialty systems are even becoming available to assist in surgical procedures, such as to control robots, microscopes, and other electronic equipment.

As you may expect, there are distinct challenges in designing technology to interpret speech. Two people may pronounce the same word differently because of accents, personal styles of speech, and the unique quality of each person's voice. A single person may also pronounce words differently at various times—when eating, for example, or when suffering from a cold. Moreover, in listening to others, humans not only ignore background

▶ **FIGURE 5-16**

Voice-input systems. With appropriate software and a microphone, voice input can be used to dictate documents and give commands to the computer.

>**Voice-input system.** A system that enables a computer to recognize the human voice.

how it works

Voice Recognition

While each of the leading voice-recognition companies has its own proprietary methods, two primary processes are typically employed. First, after a microphone is used to input the spoken words into the PC, the sounds are broken into digital representations of phonemes. *Phonemes* are the basic elements of speech; the English language contains approximately 50 phonemes, such as *duh, aw,* and *guh* for the word "dog."

The second process involves interpreting the phonemes to convert them to words. The voice-recognition software being used analyzes the content of the speech. It compares the combinations of phonemes used to the words in its digital dictionary, a huge database of the most common words in the English language. Once the matching words are identified, they are displayed on the screen. If a match is questionable or a homonym is encountered (such as the choice between "their," "there," and "they're,") the program analyzes the context in which a word is

used in an attempt to identify the correct word. If the program inserts an inappropriate word, the user can usually override it.

In order to be reasonably effective, a user typically needs to train the speech-recognition software. This process typically involves reading passages displayed on the screen until the program gets a feel for the user's speech patterns, voice, accent, and pronunciation. Training usually takes at least an hour and can often be extended if the desired accuracy is not obtained.

The most widely used application for voice recognition is dictation. As discussed in earlier chapters, it is also being used as an alternative user interface for mobile devices and navigation/communications systems built into cars. For desktop PCs, the next major leap is expected to be natural language processing, which analyzes speech by looking at whole sentences, instead of the word-by-word approach. Far, far in the future may be sophisticated artificial intelligence systems that enable computers to understand what you mean instead of just what you say. Now if that could only work with people....

1. The user speaks into a microphone that cancels out background noise and inputs the speech into the computer.

2. An analog-to-digital converter inside the PC converts the spoken words to phonemes, the fundamental sounds in the language being used, and digitizes them.

The big black dog...

The big black dog...

3. Voice-recognition software matches up the phoneme combinations to determine the words spoken. Sentence structure rules are used to select one word if it is a questionable match or word with a homonym.

4. The spoken words appear on the screen in whatever application program (word processor, e-mail program, etc.) is being used.

noises but also decode sentence fragments. For a look at how voice recognition works, see the How It Works box.

Researchers have tried a number of tricks to overcome the obstacles for which humans naturally compensate. Many voice-input systems are designed to screen out background noises and to accept training from users, who repeat words until the system recognizes the patterns in their voices. The training often only requires a few minutes of time, though some systems have the option of longer training for increased accuracy. Older voice-input systems can recognize only limited numbers of isolated words. Newer *continuous-speech recognition systems* attempt to recognize whole sentences composed of continuous speech.

Continuous-speech-recognition products have dramatically increased in quality and dropped in price in recent years. You can pay less than $200 for a system that can recognize over 250,000 words, and speech recognition is beginning to be built into everyday products, such as word processing programs. The latest version of Windows—Windows XP—includes voice-input capabilities. Today's principal application for continuous-speech recognition is dictation.

Music-Input Systems

Musical input can be recorded for use in musical arrangements or to accompany a multi-media presentation. Music can be input into a PC via a CD or DVD player. For original compositions, a *MIDI—musical instrument digital interface*—device, such as a MIDI musical keyboard with piano-type keys instead of alphanumeric keys, can be used. Once the music is input into the computer, it can be saved, modified, manipulated, played, or inserted into other programs, as necessary.

Telephony

Telephony is the process of performing telephone-oriented tasks using the computer. Common telephony activities include using the computer as a dialing device for your regular telephone system, as well as placing telephone calls through the Internet. Internet telephony applications are discussed in more detail in a later chapter.

DISPLAY DEVICES

A **display device** is the most common form of output device. It is used to display output on a computer screen; for PCs, this device is usually called a **monitor.** Monitors are typically a separate piece of hardware, but are combined with the system unit into one piece of hardware in *all-in-one PCs* (such as the iMac shown in Figure 1-9 in Chapter 1), and most portable computers. Other display options are *flat-panel screens* and *high-definition television* sets.

Display devices are used to view output while working on the computer. To read a document away from the computer, however, another output device—the *printer,* discussed later in this chapter—would be used.

Monitors display the appropriate characters as keys are pressed on a keyboard, as well as display the appropriate mouse pointer in the appropriate location, as the mouse is moved on its mouse pad. The monitor generally displays a *cursor—*or *insertion point* as it is commonly referred to on PCs. This highlighted rectangle, highlighted underscore, or small vertical line indicates where the next character typed will be located or where your next edit will take place, unless the insertion point is moved first.

Many features differentiate the hundreds of display devices currently in the market. The following sections discuss a few of the most significant.

Size

Most monitors sold for desktop PCs today come with a screen size about 17 inches wide (measured diagonally), though both larger and smaller sizes are available. It is important to realize that the actual viewing area of a monitor is usually smaller than the screen size. For example, one 17-inch monitor might have a viewable area of 16 inches, while another 17-inch monitor might have a viewable area of 15.7 inches. Though 0.3 inches may not sound like much of a difference in size, small size variations can be noticeable and are important to keep in mind when comparing the quality and price of two monitors.

further exploration

For links to further information about input devices, go to www.course.com/parker2002/ch5

web tutor

For a tutorial on how display devices work, go to www.course.com/parker2002/ch5

>**Display device.** An output device that contains a viewing screen. >**Monitor.** A display device for a PC.

Pixels. Most monitors display images by lighting up pixels in the appropriate colors. The number of pixels (measured horizontally and then vertically, such as 640 × 480) is often referred to as the screen resolution.

Each dot (or square) on the screen is one pixel.

Resolution

A key characteristic of any display device is its *resolution,* or sharpness of the screen image. Most monitors form images by lighting up tiny dots on their screens called **pixels** (from the phrase "picture elements"), as illustrated in Figure 5-17. Because pixels are so finely packed, when viewed from a distance they appear to blend together to form continuous images. The density of the pixels, called the *dot pitch,* is measured by the distance between the pixels in millimeters. Many displays in use today have a dot pitch of .26 or .28. A smaller dot pitch results in a better, sharper image.

The term *resolution* is also frequently used when referring to the number of pixels used to display images on the screen. A display resolution of 640 by 480—usually referred to as 640 × 480—means that the screen consists of 640 columns by 480 rows of pixels. The higher the number of pixels displayed, the more data that can be displayed on the screen, but everything displayed on the screen is displayed smaller (refer to Figure 5-18). Higher resolutions also usually result in sharper images.

To accommodate the variety of screen sizes and users' personal preferences, most monitors allow the user to select from a few different resolutions, almost always 640 × 480 and 800 × 600; possibly also 1,024 × 768, 1,280 × 1,024, or more. At 800 × 600 resolution, the screen contains about half a million pixels. Very high-resolution monitors, such as those used for viewing digital X-rays and other specialized applications, can use more than 200 pixels per inch for a total of 9 million pixels or more on the screen.

Graphics Standards

Computer graphics standards specify such characteristics as the possible resolutions and number of colors that can be used. For example, the older *VGA* display (for *v*ideo *g*raphics *a*rray) uses a resolution of 640 by 480 pixels and allows a screen to display at most 256 colors. Most monitors today use the *SVGA* standard (for *s*uper *VGA*), which took over when Pentium computers and 17-inch monitors became popular. It allows for higher resolutions and *true color* (16.7 million colors).

>Pixel. A single small dot on a display screen that can be lit up to form images on the screen.

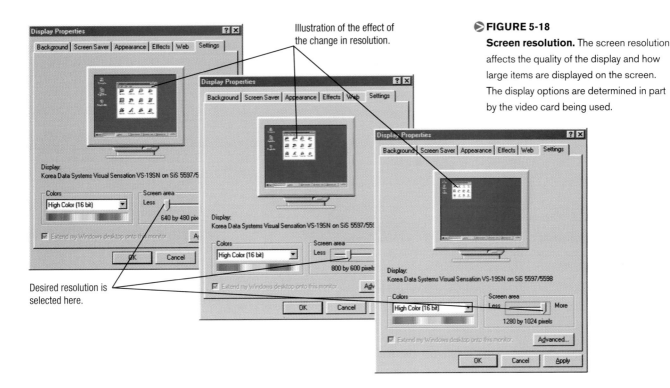

Illustration of the effect of the change in resolution.

Desired resolution is selected here.

⊘**FIGURE 5-18**

Screen resolution. The screen resolution affects the quality of the display and how large items are displayed on the screen. The display options are determined in part by the video card being used.

The system's *video card,* sometimes called a *graphics card,* connects the display to the system unit and will support a particular graphics standard. In addition, the card usually contains memory (frequently called *video RAM* or *VRAM*), though some systems use some of the PC's regular RAM instead for video RAM. The amount of memory located on the card must be enough to support the number of colors and resolution desired—usually about 32 MB today.

On Windows computers, the number of colors and screen resolution can be changed using the Display option in the Control Panel, as shown on the screens in Figure 5-18.

Color vs. Monochrome Displays

Display devices form text characters, graphics images, and video images alike by lighting up appropriate configurations of pixels. Color displays (by far, more common than *monochrome*—two-color—monitors) usually form all colors available on the screen by mixing combinations of only three colors—red, green, and blue (see Figure 5-19). For this reason, color monitors are sometimes referred to as *RGB* (for *r*ed, *g*reen, *b*lue) monitors. Three colors may not sound like much of a base, but when a monitor blends red, green, and blue light of varying intensities—for each of the hundreds of thousands of pixels on the screen—it can produce an enormous spectrum of colors.

Typical displays electronically manipulate and refresh (redraw) pixels at lightning-fast speeds on a regular basis. Pixels on the screen are refreshed—that is, redrawn so they remain bright—at a typical rate of 60 times per second.

CRT vs. Flat-Panel Displays

Monitors for most desktop systems project images on large picture-tube displays similar to standard TV sets. This type of monitor (shown in Figures 5-17 and 5-19) is commonly called a **CRT (cathode-ray tube)** display. CRT technology uses an electron gun that is fired at the screen, so CRT monitors have to be very deep. Over the years, CRTs have become

>**CRT (cathode-ray tube).** A display device that projects images onto a display screen using similar technology as conventional TVs.

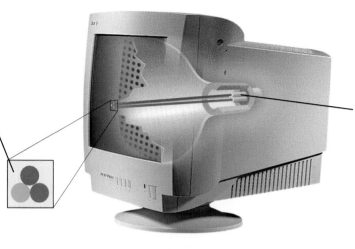

COLOR PIXELS
Each pixel on the screen is made up of some combination of red, green, and blue light. When red, green, and blue light of varying intensities are blended, a very wide range of colors is possible.

REFRESH RATE
Pixels on a typical desktop display screen are refreshed—that is, recharged with built-in electron guns so they will remain bright—at a rate of about 60 times each second.

FIGURE 5-19
A color CRT monitor.

further exploration

For links to further information about display devices, go to www.course.com/parker2002/ch5

very inexpensive and have gained capabilities for excellent color output. However, they also are bulky, fragile, and consume a great deal of power.

An alternative type of display device forms images by manipulating charged chemicals or gases sandwiched between thin panes of glass instead of firing a bulky electron gun. These much slimmer alternatives to CRTs are called **flat-panel displays.** Flat-panel displays take up little space, are lightweight, and require less power than CRT monitors. Because of these features, they are commonly found on portable computers and in a variety of consumer products, such as handheld video games, handheld television sets, and electronic photo frames (see Figure 5-20).

Most flat-panel displays on ordinary computer systems use *liquid crystal display (LCD)* technology. LCD displays light up charged liquid crystals located between two sheets of material, and special color filters manipulate this light to draw the appropriate images on the screen. Until recently, LCD screens for desktop computers have been too costly for many consumers compared to CRTs. The price gap is getting smaller, however, and it is largely expected that LCDs will overtake CRTs on the desktop in the not-too-distant future. In addition to the size and portability advantages already named, desktop LCDs provide a sharper picture than CRTs and emit less radiation. Large flat-panel displays use a similar technology called *gas plasma,* which uses a layer of gas instead of liquid crystals.

Many flat-panel displays use either *active-matrix* or *passive-matrix* color-display technology. Active-matrix displays provide much sharper screen images than passive-matrix screens—especially when viewed from an angle other than directly in front of the display—but they provide this benefit at a higher cost.

HDTV

HDTV (high-definition television) is a new type of television that supports high-resolution, digital broadcast signals. HDTVs can display digital broadcast images many times clearer and sharper than analog TVs. Many can also support the wider format commonly used with motion pictures (19:6 aspect ratio instead of 5:4).

Though there are some television shows currently being broadcast in high definition digital format, it is expected to be several years before such programming is widespread. According to government timetables, analog broadcasting will eventually be completely replaced by digital broadcasting, and analog TVs would need a special converter box to be able to display any television programming (though the quality would not be any better than the set can display with analog signals). The earliest this is expected to happen is around 2006.

>**Flat-panel display.** A slim type of display device.

DESKTOP MONITOR
Flat-panel displays provide sharper images and take up less desk space than conventional desktop CRTs, and they are now becoming cost competitive.

MOBILE WORKERS
People who have to move around with a computer to do their work need a display that is both lightweight and easy to carry.

TIGHT SPACES
In automobiles and forklifts, there is absolutely no room for a monitor that requires lots of space.

CONSUMER PRODUCTS
Consumer products, like the electronic frame shown here that displays digital photographs, commonly use flat-panel displays.

▶ **FIGURE 5-20**
Flat-panel displays.
These compact, lightweight, low-power-consumption displays suit a wide range of applications.

One advantage of high-definition broadcasting for the computer industry is that it is more compatible with interactive data services that the industry wants to deliver to television. HDTV is capable of receiving multiple input signals over the same channel and can also be used as a monitor for PCs. Because of this, HDTVs are expected to be used in the living room or family room for both television viewing and Internet access. They also will likely be used for other digital recreational activities, such as video-on-demand and interactive TV, once HDTV and fast Internet access become more commonplace.

PRINTERS

Monitors have two major limitations as output devices: (1) Only a small amount of data can appear on the screen at one time, and (2) their soft-copy output lacks portability. **Printers** overcome this limitation by producing hard copy—a permanent, printed copy of the output. This may not be the case in the future, however, as the possibility of *electronic paper* becomes closer to reality. This digital, erasable paper is currently made out of thin plastic embedded with millions of tiny black and white beads. When used in a printer, the beads are charged appropriately to form the desired printed image. When the printout is no longer needed, the paper can be reused. Current estimates put widespread electronic paper use at a minimum of five years away.

Characteristics of Printers

Printers differ in a number of important respects. One involves the technology through which they output images. Another is size; you can hold some computer printers in your hand, while others—like those that serve high-speed mainframe systems—can fill an entire room. Here, we briefly discuss some general printer characteristics.

Print Resolution

Most printing technologies today form characters as matrices of dots, similar to the way screen images are formed using a matrix of pixels. In contrast, if you look at the printing mechanism of an old typewriter, you'll notice that each character on the typewriter is embossed as a single solid image on a print head attached to a metal spoke. Many of the earliest computer printers used similar print heads to stamp output onto paper. However, virtually all of today's printers form images with dots instead, so that their output is much more versatile. Because all printed output is formed using an arrangement of dots printed on paper, both text and images can be printed, and text can appear in an almost unlimited number of appearances and sizes.

Print resolution is commonly measured in *dots per inch (dpi);* the higher the dpi, the better the quality of the printout. Print quality has become so good in recent years that the characters on paper can look like smooth, continuous strokes rather than collections of dots—even under close inspection (see Figure 5-21).

Impact vs. Nonimpact Printing

Printers produce images through either impact or nonimpact technologies. *Impact printing* is the older method of the two, mimicking the operation of the traditional typewriter. On such a typewriter, pressing a key activates the metal spoke containing that embossed character. The key then strikes an inked ribbon and transfers the character's image onto the paper. An impact *dot-matrix printer* for a desktop computer system works in a similar fashion, only the print head is comprised of pins—not fully formed characters—that strike the ribbon. As illustrated in Figure 5-22, the appropriate pins are extended to form the appropriate letter or design. When the pins press into the ribbon, dots of ink are transferred onto the paper.

Before 1995, most computer printers sold for personal use employed dot-matrix technology. In recent years, however, the popularity of these printers has been eclipsed by sales of *ink-jet* and *laser printers* (both nonimpact printers and discussed shortly). Today, dot-matrix printers are used mostly for producing multipart forms, such as invoices and credit-card receipts, since nonimpact printers cannot print multipart forms. Sometimes dot-matrix printers are also used in information systems departments for printing large computer printouts, because they are fairly inexpensive to operate.

Nonimpact printing does not depend on the impact of a print head on paper. In fact, the printing mechanism makes no physical contact at all with the paper. This, of course, makes

>**Printer.** An output device that records output on paper.

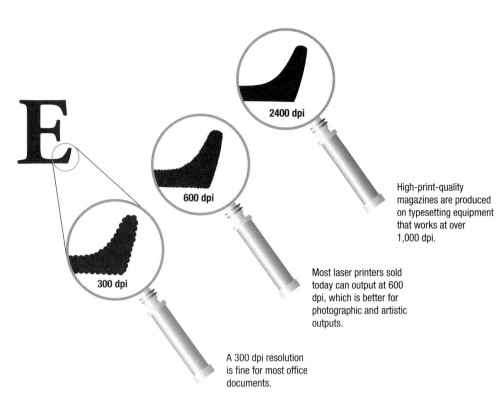

Print resolution. Print resolution is commonly measured in number of dots per inch (dpi). The higher the dpi, the harder it is to tell that dots were used to compose the image, so the better the appearance.

High-print-quality magazines are produced on typesetting equipment that works at over 1,000 dpi.

Most laser printers sold today can output at 600 dpi, which is better for photographic and artistic outputs.

A 300 dpi resolution is fine for most office documents.

for a quieter operation. Also, because nonimpact printers contain fewer moving parts than impact-based alternatives, they generally work much faster and more reliably with fewer breakdowns. They also produce better-looking output. Today, the vast majority of printers sold are nonimpact machines. Various nonimpact printers are discussed in the next section.

Both impact and nonimpact printers traditionally can print in permanent ink on various types of paper, transparencies, and other media.

Personal Printers

Most printers found in homes and many found in small businesses today are commonly referred to as *personal printers*—that is, printers connected to one computer and not shared with others. *Network printers,* in contrast, are printers shared by multiple users. Though some printers are capable of being used either as a personal or a network printer, smaller

Dot-matrix printing. Many dot-matrix printers today are high-speed printers used in manufacturing, shipping, or similar applications.

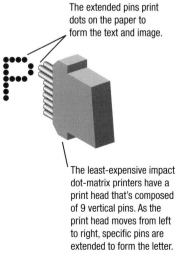

The extended pins print dots on the paper to form the text and image.

The least-expensive impact dot-matrix printers have a print head that's composed of 9 vertical pins. As the print head moves from left to right, specific pins are extended to form the letter.

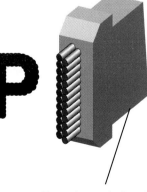

The most-expensive impact dot-matrix printers have a 24-pin head that can produce crisp-looking text.

printers designed primarily for personal use are discussed in this section; the more powerful printers designed for network use are discussed in the next main section.

The two printing technologies used most often by personal printers to create images are laser and ink-jet.

Laser Printers

Many PC systems rely on relatively inexpensive personal **laser printers** costing between $200 and $400 and printing 5 to 12 pages per minute (ppm). Most of these support resolutions of at least 600 dpi. At 600 dpi, every square inch of the output image is broken down into a 600-by-600 matrix of dots. That's 360,000 dots packed into every square inch. Laser devices are especially popular in businesses; in fact, they are the most common type of printer sold to that market segment.

Laser printers form images much as photocopying machines do—by charging thousands of dots on a drum with a very-high-intensity laser beam. The charged positions attract oppositely charged particles of ink toner from a *toner cartridge*. When the paper comes in contact with the drum, the toner is transferred to the paper to form the appropriate image. A heating unit then fuses the image permanently onto the paper (refer to Figure 5-23). As you might guess from this description, laser printers print an entire page at one time.

While most laser printers—like the one featured in Figure 5-23—produce only monochrome and grayscale outputs, some color laser printer models now cost only a few thousand dollars. Though often more expensive than other types of color printers, color laser printers typically print faster and have acceptable output quality for many purposes. A laser

⬥ FIGURE 5-23

Laser printing. Usually costing less than $400, personal laser printers are useful for routine business reports, correspondence, and other documents containing text and/or images.

1. As paper enters a laser printer it is covered with tiny electrically charged particles.

2. The printer's microprocessor decodes page data sent from the computer.

3. Instructions from the printer's microprocessor turn a laser beam rapidly on and off. The beam charges the appropriate locations on the drum so the toner will stick to it.

6. The paper exits the printer.

ABOUT LASER PRINTERS

Because of their speed and output quality, laser printers are by far the most popular type of printer for business applications.

Common speeds for personal laser printers are 4, 6, 8, and 12 pages per minute (ppm).

Many personal printers come with at least 1 MB RAM. While this is fine for text, at least 4 MB is better for intensive graphics work.

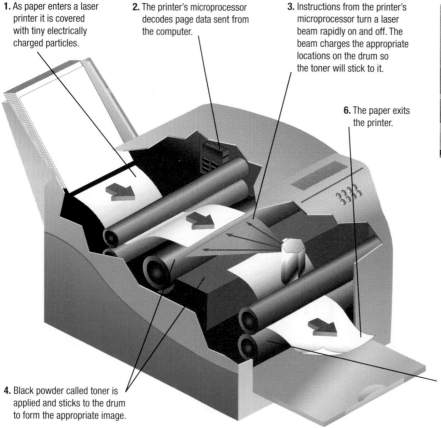

4. Black powder called toner is applied and sticks to the drum to form the appropriate image.

5. As the paper rolls over the drum, the toner is transferred to the paper, then the paper goes through the fusing unit, where toner is permanently affixed through heat and pressure.

>**Laser printer.** A printer that uses technology similar to that of a photocopier.

printer's toner cartridge (see Figure 5-24) is usually easily removed and replaced when empty. Toner cartridges can be purchased new or *recharged* (refilled); recharged cartridges typically cost about one-third less than new cartridges and last at least as long.

Ink-Jet Printers

Ink-jet printers produce images by spraying thousands of droplets of ink onto a page (see Figure 5-25). For the last several years, ink-jet printing has been the technology of choice for home users who want to produce affordable, hard-copy color output from their personal PCs. Most ink-jet printers sold today can print black-and-white, grayscale, and color outputs. Ink-jet printers print one line at a time, similar to dot-matrix printers, but they are nonimpact.

The principle advantage of ink-jet printing is its relatively low cost for color output. While some commercial-level ink-jet printers cost thousands of dollars, you can buy a respectable color ink-jet printer for your desktop PC for less than $100. Color printers using other technologies are generally more expensive. Ink-jet printers bring some disadvantages, however. They print more slowly than laser printers, and the hard copy may not look as crisp. To get good quality output, you may need to use special paper. What's more, ink-jet printers draw ink from replaceable color cartridges, and the cost of new cartridges can mount up over time if you print a lot of documents. However, the ability of being able

◗ FIGURE 5-24
Laser printer toner cartridges. Toner cartridges are removed and replaced when they are empty. They can be purchased either new or remanufactured (recharged).

◗ FIGURE 5-25
Ink-jet printing. The ink-jet printer is the printer of choice for home use, due to its low price (around $100), good quality, and ability to print in color.

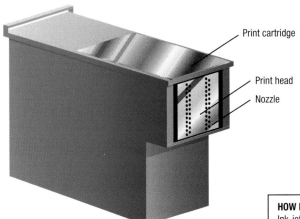

Print cartridge

Print head

Nozzle

HOW INK-JET PRINTING WORKS
Ink-jet printers create colors by mixing different combinations of four colors of ink—magenta, cyan, yellow, and black. The different colors can be in one or multiple cartridges. Each cartridge is made up of some 50 ink-filled firing chambers, each attached to a nozzle smaller than a human hair. To print images, the appropriate color ink is injected through the appropriate nozzles.

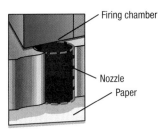

Firing chamber

Nozzle

Paper

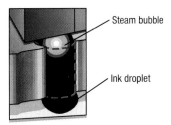

Steam bubble

Ink droplet

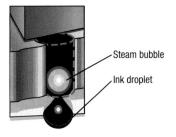

Steam bubble

Ink droplet

1. An electric current flows along the bottom of a firing chamber. This makes the ink boil and a steam bubble forms.

2. As a bubble expands, it pushes ink through the nozzle. The pressure of the bubble forces an ink droplet to be ejected onto the paper.

3. The volume of ink deposited is about one millionth that of a drop of water from an eyedropper. A typical character is formed by a 20-by-20 array of drops.

>Ink-jet printer. A printer that forms images by spraying droplets of ink onto a page.

to print color documents (Web pages, birthday cards, flyers, invitations, etc.), typically has great appeal for home users, especially for families with children.

As illustrated in Figure 5-25, the ink for an ink-jet printer is typically contained in a *print cartridge.* Most commonly, a printer will have one black ink cartridge and one color ink cartridge. When a print cartridge runs out of ink, it is replaced, similar to a laser printer's toner cartridge.

Network Printers

A *network printer* is a printer shared by several people over a local area network. The people are usually located in the same office, floor, or building. For a home or small office network, the printer may be a personal printer connected to one PC and shared through the network. For larger networks, the printers used are typically too big to fit on a desktop and are designed for network use, attaching directly to the network. These printers may work anywhere from twice as fast, to 100 or more times as fast, as their personal-system counterparts and cost anywhere from a few thousand dollars to more than $100,000. Network printers include both *line printers* and *page printers.*

Line printers get their name because they print one line of text at a time. Not long ago, virtually all printers for midrange and mainframe computer systems were line printers. Today, however, such devices are less common, except for possibly printing listings of computer programs and other informal printouts in information services departments. Though line printers are fast, their quality is typically much lower than page printers.

As the name suggests, a *page printer* produces a full page of output at a time, such as the personal laser printers discussed earlier. On office networks, the most common type of page printer is the *network laser printer.* Typically, these printers are bigger versions of personal laser printers, with several additional paper trays (see Figure 5-26). Network laser printers work much faster than personal laser printers, producing output at a rate of anywhere from 12 to 40 ppm. Many of the high-end models can collate and staple as well. A typical 24-ppm office printer is designed to handle workloads of up to 150,000 pages of output per month.

High-speed page printers for midrange and mainframe computer systems, such as the one shown in Figure 5-26, can print up to a hundred pages of output per minute or more. Such printers may cost $100,000 or even more. An organization that produces several hundred thousand or more pages of output per month may find one of these machines a cost-effective alternative.

FIGURE 5-26

Network page printers.

Network page printers include network laser printers (left) that can print about 12 to 40 ppm and high-speed page printers (right) that typically print between 50 and 100 ppm.

Special-Purpose Printers

There are a wide variety of printers designed for special purposes. Some of the most common are discussed next and illustrated in Figure 5-27.

Photo Printers

Photo printers (also sometimes called *snapshot printers*) are color printers specially designed to print photographs. Some photo printers use ink-jet technology. In fact, many regular ink-jet printers are capable of printing photographs. To achieve results closer to traditional photographic output, however, special photo paper is required. Photo printers have become increasingly popular as digital cameras have become more prominent. As mentioned earlier in this chapter, some photo printers accept the standard storage media used with digital cameras, such as flash memory sticks or cards.

> **FIGURE 5-27**
> **Special-purpose printers.**

PHOTO PRINTERS
Photo printers are used to print photos taken with a digital camera or scanned into the computer.

BAR-CODE PRINTERS
Bar-code printers can print a variety of bar codes, such as for price tags or stickers, document tracking, inventory control, and so forth.

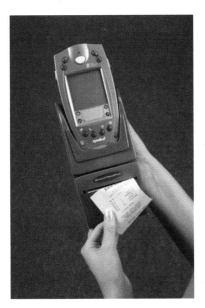

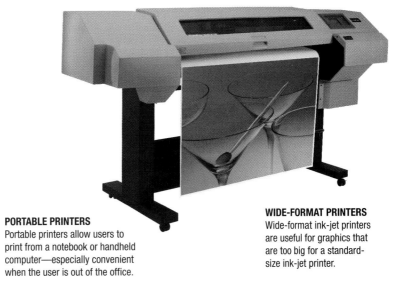

PORTABLE PRINTERS
Portable printers allow users to print from a notebook or handheld computer—especially convenient when the user is out of the office.

WIDE-FORMAT PRINTERS
Wide-format ink-jet printers are useful for graphics that are too big for a standard-size ink-jet printer.

For more professional applications, *thermal-transfer* photo printers, such as the one in Figure 5-27, are available. This technology uses heated wax or dye on special paper, which produces a better image than an ink-jet printer, but at a greater expense. Consequently, these types of printers are typically used only when professional-quality output is required.

Bar-Code and Label Printers

Retail stores often have the need to print custom bar codes on price tags, shipping labels, or other documents. *Bar-code printers,* such as the one shown in Figure 5-27, can usually print labels in a variety of bar-code standards. For other types of labels, such as for envelopes, packages, file folders, etc., regular *label printers* may come in handy. These types of printers vary from personal models to models appropriate for printing labels in an industrial environment. Some even can print *Internet postage* labels. These labels can be used the same as regular stamps and can be printed only after sufficient postage has been purchased and downloaded to an accompanying computer.

Portable Printers

Portable printers are small, lightweight printers that can be used with a notebook, handheld, or other portable computers. Some portable printers use a parallel cable or infrared port to communicate with the computer; others plug directly into the computer. The portable printer featured in Figure 5-27 is designed for printing receipts, bar codes, and other small items; many portable printers can print on regular-sized (8½-by-11-inch) paper.

Plotters and Wide-Format Ink-Jet Printers

A *plotter* is an output device that is designed primarily to produce charts, drawings, maps, blueprints, three-dimensional illustrations, and other forms of large documents. Though plotters are available using a variety of technologies, *electrostatic plotters* are the most common. These devices create images with toner similar to that of a photocopying machine or laser printer, but instead of drawing the image with a laser, they use a matrix of tiny wires to charge the paper with electricity. When the charged paper passes over the toner bed, the toner adheres to it and produces an image.

When a very large color image is needed for posters, signs, and other similar applications, an *ink-jet plotter*—more commonly called a *wide-format ink-jet printer* (see Figure 5-27)—would likely be used instead. Though typically used to print on some type of paper, some recent wide-format ink-jet printers can print directly on fabric and other types of materials.

One new type of printer expected to be available in the near future is the so-called "flavor printer"—printers used to experience taste over the Internet. This and a related application—Web-delivered smell—are explained in the Inside the Industry box.

MULTIMEDIA OUTPUT DEVICES

In addition to display devices and printers, computer systems often need hardware to generate several other kinds of output. In this section, we consider output devices appropriate for multimedia uses.

Speakers

Most computer systems sold today come with a set of **speakers.** Speakers provide audio output for such consumer-oriented multimedia applications as playing computer games, listening

>**Speakers.** Output devices that produce sound.

inside the industry

Point, Click, and ... Smell?

Scented and Flavored Web Content are Coming to a Printer Near You

First it was text and images. Next, came audio, video, and animation. The newest trend in Web content is taste and smell. Slightly reminiscent of the scratch-and-sniff movies of the '80s, scented and flavored Web pages are just about a reality.

Though many people find the idea of digital smell and taste generators amusing, there are many practical and commercial applications. For example, just imagine browsing a Web site about perfume and being able to smell the various scents without leaving your home. Or how about being able to taste a sample of that pizza or batch of chocolate chip cookies you're considering ordering online? Not to mention being able to send scented e-mail, or smell the gunpowder and sizzling flesh while playing a video game. It also lends an entirely new perspective to virtual travel.

One of the leading companies in the digital scents arena is DigiScents. The founders of DigiScents (see illustration) got the idea during a Florida vacation. While enjoying the flavors of tropical drinks, the fragrance of suntan lotion, and the soothing aroma of the ocean, they imagined being able to broadcast these scents over the Internet for others to enjoy. Their dream is rapidly becoming a reality.

The DigiScent system works as follows: Scents are digitized according to their chemical make up and their place in the scent "spectrum." This small file is sent as part of a Web page's content when the page is loaded or the scent is requested. At the user's end, the iSmell unit, which connects to the user's computer like a set of speakers, synthesizes the smell from a palette of "primary odors" according to the guidelines contained in the smell's digital file. The iSmell devices should eventually come in a variety of designs and use replaceable scent cartridges.

Soon to follow scented Web page capabilities are flavored Web pages. Though still in the development stages, most proposed products in this category dispense flavors onto edible wafers or chips, similar to the way ink-jet printers dispense ink onto paper. Earlier versions used flavored paper that the user licked to taste the sample, but those prototypes proved to be ineffective. The wafer idea seems to be much more promising but still has a long way to go until marketable products are realized. Companies in this area, such as Trisenx, bill their technology as delivering "multisensory simulations" that enable all of the senses to be a part of the Internet.

Though scent and taste Web delivery has some interesting potential, consider the potential downside—stinky spam and rotten egg computer viruses come to mind. Good thing most of these devices will come with an off switch!

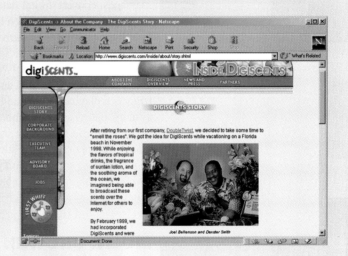

Joel Bellenson and Dexster Smith are co-founders of DigiScents.

to audio or video clips on the Internet, listening to background music from a CD, and watching television or a DVD movie in an onscreen window. Common business applications include video and multimedia presentations, as well as videoconferencing and telephony.

Computer speaker systems resemble their stereo-system counterparts and are available at a wide variety of prices. While an inexpensive speaker outputs the full frequency range through a single cone, a costlier model might include a special bass unit and separate output cones for different sound frequencies. Some computer sound systems are advertised as surround sound systems designed for near-theater-quality audio. Cases on speakers are often shielded to prevent magnetic interference with nearby storage devices. Also, speakers may come with brackets, stands, or other mounting devices to provide you flexibility in arranging them on your desk or wall; some speakers are built directly into, or permanently

◈ FIGURE 5-28

Data projectors. Most projectors today, such as the data/video projector shown here, can display both computer and video output.

attached to, the monitor. The port on a sound expansion card or a sound port integrated into the motherboard is used to connect speakers to a PC; these ports typically also include connectors for a microphone and headset.

Data and Multimedia Projectors

A *data projector* connects to a computer and projects any output sent to the computer monitor through the projector onto a wall or projection screen (see Figure 5-28). Most projectors today (usually referred to as *data/video projectors* or *multimedia projectors*) can project video, as well. In classrooms, conference rooms, and similar locations, projectors are often permanently mounted onto the ceiling. Portable projectors are also available, either as freestanding units or small panels that are used in conjunction with a standard overhead projector. Portable projectors are commonly used for business presentations that occur out of the office.

Voice-Output Systems

For a number of years, computers have been able to communicate with users by imitating human speech. How often have you dialed a phone number only to hear, "We're sorry, the number you are trying to reach, 555-0202, is no longer in service," or "The time is 6:15.... The downtown temperature is 75 degrees," or "Your current balance is $150.59?" **Voice-output systems,** the hardware and software responsible for such automated personalized messages, convert digital data into spoken output. These systems are used extensively by businesses to automate such customer service functions as relaying information about airline flight departures and arrivals, quoting the current price of stocks, and relaying current account balances and credit limits.

There are two types of voice-output systems. The first type digitizes voice messages, stores them electronically, and then converts them back to voice messages when the user triggers a playback command, such as with digital answering machines and the *voice mail* systems that answer telephone calls at many businesses. The second type of system produces synthetic speech by storing digital patterns of word sounds and then creating sentences extemporaneously, such as quoting a particular customer's account balance. Many of the systems that rely on synthetic speech have vocabularies of several hundred words and limited abilities to combine words dynamically to form intelligible sentences. As a result, these devices perform best in creating short messages.

MULTIFUNCTION DEVICES

A *multifunction device* (sometimes called a *multifunction printer* or *multifunction peripheral device*) is a device that offers some combination of printing, copying, scanning, and faxing capabilities. Most commonly, these types of devices are based on color ink-jet printer technology, though laser devices are also available.

The advantage of using a multifunction device is that it takes up less space and is less expensive than using multiple machines. The disadvantages include possibly not being able to find a multifunction device that has exactly the components you would get if you bought them separately, and the risk that when the device breaks down, you will lose all of its functions if the device needs to be repaired off site.

Though multifunction devices have traditionally been desktop units used in small offices and home offices, larger workgroup multifunction devices are now available that are designed for multiple users, either as standalone stations or as networked units.

>**Voice-output system.** A system that enables a computer to play back or imitate the human voice.

SUMMARY

Today's computer marketplace offers a wide and expanding variety of input and output devices.

INPUT AND OUTPUT

Input and output devices enable people and computers to communicate. **Input devices** convert data and program instructions into a form the CPU can process. **Output devices** convert computer-processed information into a form that people can comprehend.

Output devices produce results in either hard-copy or soft-copy form. The term *hard copy* refers to output that has been recorded in a permanent form onto a medium such as paper. The term *soft copy,* in contrast, generally refers to display output, which appears only temporarily. Hard-copy output is the more portable of the two, but it costs more to produce and creates waste.

Chapter Objective 1:
Identify several types of input and output devices and explain their functions.

KEYBOARDS

Most people use a **keyboard** as one of the two main sources of computer input. Keyboards typically include *function keys* and a *numeric keypad;* they may include special multimedia buttons, as well. For users with special needs, there are *ergonomic* and portable keyboards, among others.

Chapter Objective 2:
Describe the characteristics of the input equipment that most users encounter regularly—namely, keyboards and pointing devices.

POINTING DEVICES

Pointing devices are hardware devices that move an onscreen *mouse pointer* or similar indicator. The most widely used pointing device is the **mouse.** Some other common pointing devices are the **electronic pen** (used with special monitors, portable PCs, mobiles devices, and **graphics tablets**), **touch screen, joystick, trackball,** *pointing stick,* and **touch pad.** Some pen-based computers use **handwriting recognition** technology to recognize handwritten characters.

SCANNERS AND RELATED DEVICES

Source data automation involves collecting data in digital form at its point of origin. Many different input devices can be used for this purpose.

An **optical scanner**—usually just called a **scanner**—allows users to input printed data, such as photographs, drawings, and printed documents, into a computer system. Most scanners are of the *flatbed, sheetfed, drum,* or *handheld* type. Scanners are often accompanied by **optical character recognition (OCR)** software that enables a computer system to recognize scanned text characters and store them in a form that they can be manipulated. If not, the data is input as an image.

Optical reader technology refers to a wide range of optical-scanning procedures and equipment designed for machine recognition of entities such as *optical marks, optical characters,* and *optical codes* such as **bar codes.** Among the best-known uses of OCR are the *point-of-sale (POS) systems* used to record purchases at retail stores.

Magnetic ink character recognition (MICR) is an input technology confined almost exclusively to the banking industry; it enables automated systems to rapidly sort, process, and route checks to the proper banks.

Chapter Objective 3:
Explain what source data automation is and discuss how scanners and other devices can be used to accomplish it.

MULTIMEDIA INPUT DEVICES

There are several different devices that can be used for multimedia input.

Digital cameras work much like regular cameras, but instead of capturing images on conventional film, they record digital images on some type of digital storage medium. The images can later be

Chapter Objective 4:
List several types of multimedia input devices and discuss their purpose.

transferred to a PC for manipulation or printing, as desired. *Video cameras* are becoming more widely used with PCs to capture video images for videoconferencing, video phone calls, or as a *Webcam* to generate live video for a Web page. Related hardware includes *video input boards* used to capture video images taken with a conventional video camera, and *TV tuner cards,* used to display television broadcasts on a PC.

Systems that can be used to capture audio input include **voice-input systems,** which enable computer systems to recognize spoken words. Voice-input technologies offer tremendous work-saving potential, but they are only slowly reaching market acceptance. Other systems are *MIDI* devices and *telephony*—performing telephone-oriented tasks on a PC.

DISPLAY DEVICES

Display devices or **monitors**—hardware with a television-like viewing screen—are the most common type of output device. Monitors are available in a wide variety of sizes and are generally of the **CRT (cathode-ray tube)** or **flat-panel** type. Flat-panel displays generally use *liquid crystal display (LCD)* or *gas plasma* technology. The quality of a monitor can be measured by the *dot pitch* or distance between the **pixels** on the screen; the number of pixels on a screen is referred to as the *resolution*.

HDTV is a new television standard that uses high-resolution, digital broadcasts. HDTV should replace analog TV in the near future.

Chapter Objective 5:
Describe the characteristics of the output equipment that most users encounter regularly—namely, display devices and printers.

PRINTERS

Printers produce hard-copy output through either impact or nonimpact printing technology. In *impact printing,* the older of the two, metal pins or embossed characters strike ink ribbons and paper to form characters. *Nonimpact printing,* which is quieter and more reliable, is by far the most prevalent type of printing technology today. Nonimpact printing creates printed images through a wide variety of techniques. Most printers today form images as matrices of dots, though with many technologies, the dots are too small to be visible.

The most popular printers today for personal use are **laser printers** and **ink-jet printers.** Both employ nonimpact methods. Most laser printers do not print in color, though most ink-jet printers do.

Network printers today are commonly used in schools and larger businesses. They can be *line printers* or *page printers,* such as a network laser printer. Special purpose printers include *photo, bar-code,* and *portable* printers. *Plotters* are used to produce charts, maps, and other large illustrations; *wide-format ink-jet printers* can be used for posters and other documents too large for a conventional printer.

MULTIMEDIA OUTPUT EQUIPMENT

Chapter Objective 6:
Discuss several types of multimedia output equipment.

A large number of other output devices are used for multimedia applications. Among these are **speakers,** to output music or spoken voice; *data* and *multimedia projectors,* to project output from a PC's computer screen so that a large audience can view it; and **voice-output systems,** which enable computer systems to play back or compose spoken messages from digitally stored words, phrases, and sounds.

MULTIFUNCTION DEVICES

Chapter Objective 7:
Explain what a multifunction device is and list some advantages and disadvantages of using such a device.

A *multifunction device* is a single device that offers some combination of printing, copying, scanning, and faxing capabilities. While they can provide these functions at a lower total cost and space requirements, it may not be possible to find a device with your exact requirements and, if the device needs to be repaired, all functions will be unavailable during the repair period.

Instructions: Match each key term on the left with the definition on the right that fits best.

1. bar code

_____ A camera that records pictures as digital data instead of as film images.

2. CRT (cathode-ray tube)

_____ A display device for a PC.

3. digital camera

_____ A slim type of display device.

4. electronic pen

_____ A common pointing device that you slide along a flat surface to move a pointer around the screen and make selections.

5. flat-panel display

_____ A device that reads hard-copy documents and inputs them into the computer in digital form.

6. ink-jet printer

_____ A display device that can be touched with the finger to generate input.

7. input device

_____ A display device that projects images onto a display screen using similar technology as conventional TVs.

8. keyboard

9. laser printer

_____ A machine-readable code that represents data as a set of bars.

10. monitor

_____ A piece of hardware that accepts output from the computer and presents it in a form the user can understand.

11. mouse

_____ A piece of hardware that supplies input to a computer.

12. output device

_____ A printer that forms images by spraying droplets of ink onto a page.

13. pixel

_____ A printer that uses technology similar to that of a photocopier.

14. printer

_____ A rectangular-shaped input device that is touched with the finger or thumb to control an onscreen pointer and make selections.

15. scanner

16. touch pad

_____ A single small dot on a display screen that can be lit up to form images on the screen.

17. touch screen

_____ An electronic device, resembling an ordinary pen, used for computer input.

_____ An input device containing numerous keys, arranged in a configuration similar to that of a typewriter, that can be used to input letters, numbers, and other symbols.

_____ An output device that records output on paper.

Self-Quiz

Answers for the self-quiz appear at the end of the book.

True/False

Instructions: Circle **T** if the statement is true or **F** if the statement is false.

T F **1.** The function keys on a keyboard are used to more easily input numerical data.

T F **2.** Optical mark technology is used primarily in the banking industry.

T F **3.** The most widely known bar code is UPC.

T F **4.** Consumer kiosks located in retail stores commonly use touch screens for input.

T F **5.** A laser printer is an impact printer.

Completion

Instructions: Answer the following questions.

6. The term _____ generally refers to output that has been recorded on a permanent medium such as paper.

7. The small dots that comprise a screen image are called _____ .

8. A(n) _____ could be used to input a drawing or photograph into a computer system.

9. Handheld and pocket PCs typically use a(n) _____ for data input.

10. Portable PCs most always use _____ displays, while many monitors for desktop PCs still use the larger, more bulky _____ technology.

Exercises

1. For the following list of computer input and output devices, write the appropriate abbreviation (I, O, or B) to indicate whether each device is used for input, output, or both.

    a. Joystick _____
    b. Graphics tablet _____
    c. Speaker _____
    d. Photo printer _____
    e. Flat-panel display _____

2. For each printing application, select the most appropriate type of printer to be used. Note that all types of printers will not be selected.

    _____ To get inexpensive color printouts.
    _____ To print a large map.
    _____ To print all output for an entire office.
    _____ To print business documents at home.

    a. Personal laser printer
    b. Network laser printer
    c. Color laser printer
    d. Photo printer
    e. Bar-code printer
    f. Plotter
    g. Ink-jet printer

3. Why is voice recognition a difficult technology to perfect?

4. For each of the following hardware devices, state which terms apply to that device. Note that all terms may not be used and some devices may match more than one term (if so, list all appropriate terms).

_____ Digital camera
_____ Printer
_____ Monitor
_____ Scanner

a. Dots per inch (dpi)
b. Megapixel
c. 800×600 resolution
d. Pages per minute (ppm)
e. Dot pitch

5. If you could select only one type of input device to be used with an Internet appliance (a device to browser the Web and exchange electronic mail) you were marketing to senior citizens, which one would you choose? Why?

Short Answer/ Research

1. **New Keyboards** The design and capability of keyboards have improved in the past few years. Newer keyboards offer special features such as ergonomic design, Internet buttons, wireless connection, multimedia control buttons, and built-in fingerprint and smart card readers. For this project, research the various types of keyboards that are currently for sale. Select at least five different models and identify the special features and cost of each. At the conclusion of your research, prepare a one-page summary of your findings and submit it to your instructor.

2. **Access for Special Needs** Individuals with special needs (such as those who are visually impaired, hearing impaired, or who have limited use of their hands) may need special input and output devices to communicate with a computer. For this project, research the various types of alternative input and output devices currently available. For each type of device you discover, be sure to identify the manufacturer, the suggested retail price, the purpose of the device, and its target market. At the conclusion of your research, prepare a one-page summary of your findings and submit it to your instructor.

3. **Print Features** It seems as if a whole new line of printers is introduced into the market each year, featuring a variety of new features. These features may include improved resolution, more memory, photo printing capabilities, different interfaces, improved toner/ink cartridge life, ports for portable storage media, or better paper handling or performance. For this project, establish what you think are the most important printing features you, as a student, would need while going to college. Once you have done this, research printers currently on the market to identify which ones you feel would be the best printer for your needs. Be sure to take into consideration both the price of the printer and the price of consumables (paper, ink cartridge, toner, etc.) in your evaluation process. At the conclusion of your research, prepare a one-page summary of your findings and submit it to your instructor.

Hands On

4. **Properties and Settings** Each of the devices attached to a PC has an associated set of properties and settings. These properties and settings allow the device to be configured and managed by the user. For this project, identify the available properties and associated settings for the monitor, mouse, keyboard, and any other attached input or output device for a computer of your choice. Note: For Windows-based computers, you can access this information by opening the appropriate icon (Display, Mouse, Keyboard, Printer, etc.) for the particular device in the Control Panel, which can be opened using the Start menu. For each device, include such information as the speed, language used, manufacturer, and so forth. At the conclusion of this task, you should prepare a one-page summary of your efforts and submit it to your instructor. Note: Be sure not to change any of the settings for these devices while you are viewing them.

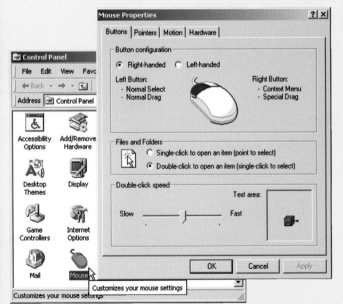

**Writing About
Computers**

5. **Color Scanners** Color scanners have become very popular peripheral devices in recent years for home and office use. As discussed in the chapter, scanners convert flat images into digital images that can be manipulated on your computer. For this project, assume that you work for a small company that needs to purchase a color scanner, and that your boss has asked you to survey the market in order to identify an appropriate product to purchase. Your boss would like you to prepare a short document stating which scanner you recommend and why. For the purposes of this project, you will need to establish what the scanning requirements of the small company are and make the selection based on these criteria (feel free to make any necessary assumptions about the company). Be sure to include both your assumed requirements and the related information about the scanner you select (manufacturer, model number, resolution, price, etc.) in your summary. Submit this project to your instructor in the form of a short paper, not more than two pages in length.

6. **Fast and Accurate** As described in the text, source data automation is the collection of data in digital format, directly from the original source document. The use of special devices for this purpose has resulted in significant cost savings to many organizations. For this project, prepare a short paper that identifies at least three different specific organizations or businesses located in your area and how they have implemented source data automation. Be sure to identify the type of source data automation technology used and what benefits you think the organization realized by using this technology. Do you think that source data automation technology will eliminate many of the entry-level jobs that are currently available at organizations? Do you see source data automation as a threat to future employment? Submit this project to your instructor in the form of a short paper, not more than two pages in length.

7. **All-in-One** Some printers today are marketed as multifunction devices. For this project, form a group to research and discuss them. Your group should identify three of the leading multifunction devices currently available and contrast them in terms of their cost, capability, functionality, and maintainability. In addition, your group should draw some conclusions about the advantages and disadvantages to purchasing a multifunction device for corporate, small business, and personal use. Your group should submit this project to your instructor in the form of a short paper, not more than three pages in length.

**Presentation/
Demonstration**

8. **Skinny Displays** Flat-panel desktop display screens may soon replace the traditional CRT monitor of the past. For this project, prepare a short presentation about the differences between traditional CRT and flat-panel monitors. Be sure to discuss the advantages and disadvantages of each in terms of cost, viewing angle, size, image quality, weight, power consumption, and compatibility with existing video cards. Be sure to include the specifications for at least one specific model of each type of monitor. In addition, identify which type of monitor you prefer and why. This presentation should not exceed 5 minutes and should make use of one or more presentation aids such as the chalkboard, handouts, overhead transparencies, or computer-based slide presentation format. You may be asked to submit a summary of the presentation to your instructor.

9. **Picture This** Digital cameras are now in the mainstream. The prices have fallen and the image quality for high-end digital cameras is almost indistinguishable from standard photographic image quality. For this project, form a group to prepare a short presentation about three of the best digital cameras on the market. The presentation should include image quality, cost, storage format, capacity, interface ability, and suitability for various tasks. Be sure to include some discussion about the advantages and disadvantages of a digital camera as compared to a traditional camera. This presentation should not exceed 10 minutes and should make use of one or more presentation aids such as the chalkboard, handouts, overhead transparencies, or computer-based slide presentation format. You may be asked to submit a summary of the presentation to your instructor.

10. **Ink-Jet or Laser** The selection of an ink-jet or laser printer is no longer black and white. The prices and capabilities of these two technologies have changed significantly in the past few years. For this project, form a group to research these two technologies. You should discover the differences between these two technologies and what criteria can be used to help select an appropriate printer. Your group should prepare a short presentation of your findings. The presentation should include specifications for at least one specific model of printer in each category, including the printer's speed, cost per page to operate, network compatibility, and ability to print text, graphics, and photos. You should also determine how long the ink or toner cartridge will last and how expensive it is to replace. If your group had to select a printer right now, which one would it choose and why? Do you think that the capability of these printers will continue to improve and drop in price as they have in the past? This presentation should not exceed 10 minutes and should make use of one or more presentation aids such as the chalkboard, handouts, overhead transparencies, or computer-based slide presentation format. Your group may be asked to submit a summary of the presentation to your instructor.

Interactive Discussion

11. **The Written Word** The use of computer input and output devices to facilitate written communication has had both positive and negative effects on our ability as humans to perform basic reading and writing tasks. On the positive side, computers can allow us to focus on the content of our communication independent of the final formatting of a document and spelling and grammatical errors, as these such tasks can be performed after the document content has been completed. In addition, most computers now have powerful tools for proofreading and formatting that will perform these tasks for you automatically. On the negative side, we as humans may not develop some abilities, or potentially lose our ability to perform some tasks, if we become too dependent on computers for one of our basic forms of communication.

    Select one of the following positions, or make up your own, and express your point of view on the subject. Your instructor will indicate whether your response is to be posted to a class bulletin board, discussed in a class chat room, or discussed as an in-class activity. You may also be asked to submit a summary of your position and point of view to your instructor.

    a. These skills are developed and maintained independent of computers and we have nothing to be concerned about. In addition, when voice activation becomes the standard way of communicating with the computer, we will still have nothing to worry about.
    b. We should each take positive steps to maintain our basic writing skills and be careful not to become too dependent on computers for our written communications. It has been long understood that if we do not use a skill, that skill will atrophy.

12. **Everything Is Automated** Consider the following statement and establish your position, or point of view, on the subject. Your instructor will indicate whether your response is to be posted to a class bulletin board, discussed in a class chat room, or discussed as an in-class activity. You may also be asked to submit a summary of your position and evaluation of the statement to your instructor.

    In the next few years companies will continue to use the concept of source data automation to make their business operations as fast, accurate, and reliable as possible. Unfortunately, humans will pay the price and businesses will reap the profits. This trend can been seen in the banking, insurance, and automotive industries, to just name a few. In the future, most transaction-based jobs will fall prey to source data automation and these individual will have to return to school in the hope of learning a skill that will not be taken over by technology. Those working in the retail industry will be hit the hardest, followed by the financial and manufacturing industries.

Interactive Exercise

Your New PC's Input and Output Devices and Screen Settings. Let's connect some input and output devices to a PC and change their settings! Go to the Interactive Exercise at www.course.com/parker2002/ch5 to complete this exercise.

MODULE SW

SOFTWARE

In Chapter 2, we looked at the software concepts with which you should be familiar in order to get up and

running on a computer system. We continue that focus in this module, discussing in more depth both the

software used to run a computer and *application software*–the software that performs the tasks for

which most people acquire a computer system.

Systems software, the subject of Chapter 6, encompasses the programs that enable the hardware of a

computer system to operate and run application software. Every computer user must in some way interact

with systems software to tell the computer what it is he or she wants the computer to do. Chapter 7 offers

a brief introduction to some of the most common applications or tasks that people use computers for.

SOFTWARE

OUTLINE

Systems Software

LEARNING OBJECTIVES

After completing this chapter, you will be able to:

1. Understand the difference between application software and systems software.

2. Explain the different functions of an operating system and discuss some ways that operating systems can differ from one another.

3. List several ways in which operating systems can enhance processing efficiency.

4. Name today's most widely used operating systems for desktop PCs and servers and highlight the strengths and weaknesses of each.

5. State several other devices besides desktop PCs and servers that require an operating system and list one possible operating system for each type of device.

6. Understand why several myths about operating systems are not correct.

7. Detail the role of utility programs and outline several duties that these programs can perform.

8. Speculate about what the operating systems of the future may be like.

Systems software consists of programs that control the various parts of a computer system and coordinate them to make the parts work together and run efficiently. These programs perform such tasks as translating your commands into a form the computer can understand, managing your program and data files, and getting your application software and hardware to work together, among other things.

Most users aren't aware of all the tasks that systems software is doing for them. For example, issuing a command for your PC to store a document on your hard drive requires that your PC's systems software first make sure that such a drive exists, then look for adequate space on the disk, then write the document onto this space, and finally update the disk's directory with the filename and disk location so the document can be retrieved again when needed. As users communicate with other computers over a network, they may not realize that systems software may perform such additional tasks as checking the validity of their user ID or password and ensuring they have been granted the right to access the data or programs they are requesting.

Systems software is usually divided into two categories: operating system software and utility programs. In this chapter, after taking a look at the difference between application software and systems software, we look closely at the *operating system,* the primary piece of systems software. Here we discuss what operating systems do and examine similarities and differences between them. Then, we cover *utility programs,* or utilities. Utilities typically perform support functions for the operating system, such as allowing you to perform maintenance on your computer, checking your PC for viruses, or recovering inadvertently erased files. The chapter closes with a look at what the future of systems software may be. Another category of software sometimes considered to be systems software—*language translators*—is discussed in Chapter 13. ■

SYSTEMS SOFTWARE VS. APPLICATION SOFTWARE

Computers run two general types of software: systems software and application software.

▼ *Systems software* consists of the "background" programs that allow your computer to start up and operate. They enable application software to run, and facilitate such important jobs as transferring files from one storage medium to another, configuring your computer system to work with a specific brand of printer or monitor, managing files on your hard drive, and protecting your computer system from unauthorized use.

▼ *Application software* provides the tools that allow a user to perform certain specific tasks on a PC, such as writing a letter, preparing an invoice, viewing a Web page, listening to an MP3 file, and so forth. Application programs are often referred to as *applications* and are discussed in detail in Chapter 7.

>**Systems software.** Programs, such as the operating system, that control the operation of a computer and its devices, as well as enable application programs to run on the computer system.

In practice, the difference between system and application software is not always clear-cut, because systems programs often contain application-software components. For example, the *Microsoft Windows* operating system contains such applications as a Web browser, calendar, and notepad. In addition, application programs typically allow you to do a small number of system tasks, such as deleting or renaming files on a disk. A program's classification as systems or application software usually depends on the principal task the program does.

THE OPERATING SYSTEM

A computer's **operating system** is the main collection of programs that manage its activities. The primary chores of an operating system are management and control. The operating system ensures that all actions requested by a user are valid and processed in an orderly fashion. It also manages the computer system's resources to perform those operations with efficiency and consistency.

    Most tasks that you do on the computer involve some work by the operating system. For example, when you want to finish the letter you started typing yesterday, the operating system must retrieve the appropriate word processing program and document from your hard drive and load them into memory. As the word processor carries out its processing tasks, the operating system acts as a supervisor, monitoring every step of the application to make sure it doesn't perform an illegal operation that would corrupt other computer-system resources. If that happens, the operating system tries to close the offending application with the least amount of impact on the rest of the system. Typically, the operating system does all these things and more as you issue commands.

    In effect, the operating system is the go-between that meshes you and your application's needs with the computer's hardware (see Figure 6-1). Because of its central role in coordinating all of the computer's work, many consider the operating system to be the

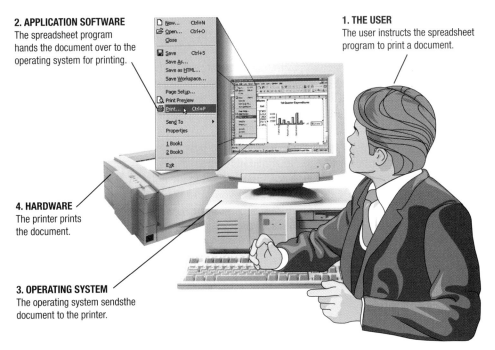

2. APPLICATION SOFTWARE
The spreadsheet program hands the document over to the operating system for printing.

1. THE USER
The user instructs the spreadsheet program to print a document.

4. HARDWARE
The printer prints the document.

3. OPERATING SYSTEM
The operating system sends the document to the printer.

▶ **FIGURE 6-1**

The intermediary role of the operating system.

The operating system acts as a gateway between the user and his or her computer, as well as between application programs and the computer system's hardware.

>**Operating system.** The main piece of systems software that enables the computer to manage its activities and the resources under its control, run application programs, and interface with the user.

most critical piece of software in the computer system. Without an operating system, no other program can run and the computer cannot function.

Differences Among Operating Systems

The marketplace offers a wide selection of operating systems, as this chapter illustrates. Because people's needs and preferences vary, there are often major differences among operating systems. Some of the major distinctions between operating systems include the type of user interface, whether the operating system is targeted to personal or network use, and what type of processing and CPU the operating system is designed for.

Command Line vs. Graphical User Interface

Most PC operating systems today use a *graphical user interface.* The older *DOS* operating systems and some versions of *Unix* and *Linux*—alternative operating systems to Windows that are discussed shortly—use a command line interface, though graphical versions of Unix and Linux are now available. Operating systems for larger computers, such as minicomputers and mainframe computers, tend to use command-line interfaces. With a *command-line interface,* commands are typed on the keyboard to give instructions to the computer (see the DOS screen in Figure 6-9); graphical user interfaces allow the user to issue commands by selecting icons, buttons, menu items, and other graphical objects with a mouse or other pointing device.

Personal vs. Network Operating Systems

About a decade or so ago, when PCs were far less powerful than today's machines, most operating systems accommodated either single users or multiple users, not both. Single-user products (such as DOS) served people working alone on their home or work PCs. Multiple-user products (such as Unix) served those working on larger computer systems and networks. Today, there are still single-user **personal** *(desktop)* **operating systems** and multiple-user **network** *(server)* **operating systems,** but the distinction between these two categories is blurring. Some personal operating systems, such as recent versions of Windows, can be used for home networking and other small networks. In addition, many operating systems—such as Windows, Unix, Linux, and *Mac OS*—can be purchased as either a personal or server version. These operating systems are discussed in more detail shortly.

When a network operating system is used, the network operating system is installed on the network server. Each PC attached to the network has its own personal operating system installed, just as with a stand-alone PC. The network operating system—*Novell NetWare,* for example—controls access to network resources, while the personal operating system controls the activity on the local PC. An example of how a typical session using this setup might unfold is described next and illustrated in Figure 6-2.

When you turn on a workstation or PC connected to the network, the network displays a log-on dialog box. To log on to the network, you must supply an appropriate user name and password. When the operating system accepts your input, it gives you access rights to the network and you are free to do any network operation within those assigned access rights. Possible operations include reading or writing to files, executing programs, and creating or deleting files. When you are working with a shared hard drive on the network, you generally treat it simply as another disk drive (such as F or G) on your own computer system. When you need access to other network resources, such as a printer as in Figure 6-2, the network operating system takes care of it for you.

If you ever choose to not work on the network or if the network is down and you have to work locally, you simply do not log onto the network. You then work just as you would

---

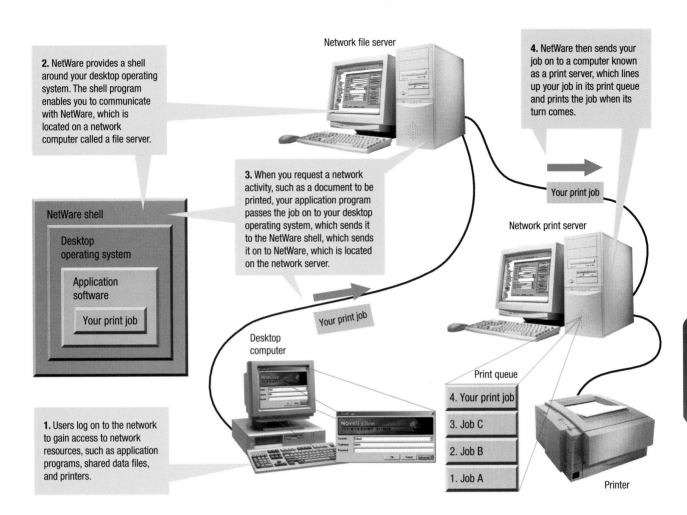

2. NetWare provides a shell around your desktop operating system. The shell program enables you to communicate with NetWare, which is located on a network computer called a file server.

Network file server

4. NetWare then sends your job on to a computer known as a print server, which lines up your job in its print queue and prints the job when its turn comes.

NetWare shell

Desktop operating system

Application software

Your print job

3. When you request a network activity, such as a document to be printed, your application program passes the job on to your desktop operating system, which sends it to the NetWare shell, which sends it on to NetWare, which is located on the network server.

Your print job

Network print server

Your print job

Desktop computer

Print queue

1. Users log on to the network to gain access to network resources, such as application programs, shared data files, and printers.

4. Your print job

3. Job C

2. Job B

1. Job A

Printer

FIGURE 6-2

Working with a network operating system. This figure illustrates how you would interact with a NetWare-controlled computer network. Many other network operating systems work in a similar fashion.

on an independent computer system. Keep in mind, however, that you can gain access to a program on the shared hard drive, save a document to the shared hard drive, or output to a shared printer only after you reestablish network access. Many other network operating systems work similarly to this NetWare example.

Whether or Not Multiple Processors or Shared Processing Is Supported

A big distinction between operating systems today is whether they support multiple processors or techniques that allow the CPU to be shared to speed up processing. These techniques are discussed shortly.

The Types of Processors Supported

Most operating systems today are geared for a specific type of processor, such as Intel, AMD, or a similar processor for IBM-compatible PCs; or Motorola chips for Apple computers. They also usually support CPUs that use either a 32- or 64-bit *instruction set*. As discussed in Chapter 3, most previous microprocessors, such as the Intel Pentium, used a 32-bit instruction set; newer 64-bit processors—such as the Intel Itanium—use a 64-bit instruction set.

Because their instruction capacity is twice as large, 64-bit processors can perform 64-bit operations at a much faster pace, though some 64-bit chips perform 32-bit instructions more slowly than a 32-bit machine because the 32-bit instructions must be translated into 64-bit instructions before processing. Newer chips, such as the AMD "Sledgehammer" chip scheduled to be available in late 2002, are expected to support both 32- and 64-bit instruction sets, so they can run either types of application equally efficiently. Operating systems that support 64-bit chips—such as some versions of Windows, *Solaris,* Unix, and Linux—often include other architectural improvements that together may result in a more efficient operating system, and, consequently, faster operations. Operating systems that support newer chips can also run the newest software designed for those CPUs.

Functions of an Operating System

Now that you have a general idea of what operating systems do and some of the differences between them, we can discuss their properties in greater detail. As we examine these properties, keep in mind that not all of them will apply to the operating system on your computer.

Booting Up the Computer and Configuring Devices

The first task your operating system performs when your PC is initially turned on is to assist in booting up the PC. During the **boot** process, certain parts of the operating system (called the *kernel*) are loaded into memory. Before the boot process ends and control is passed to the user, the operating system determines what hardware devices are attached, properly configured, and online. It also makes sure that its files tell it how to deal with those devices, and it reads an opening batch of instructions. These instructions—which the user can customize to some extent when necessary—assign chores for the operating system to carry out before the current session begins; for instance, checking for computer viruses or starting up a few programs to continually run in the background. In Windows, the system configuration information is stored in the *registry* files, which should be modified only by the Windows program itself and advanced Windows users.

When a computer system's hardware must communicate with input or output hardware such as a monitor, printer, or scanner, the operating system commonly works through a program known as a **device driver.** Newer operating systems are coming equipped with drivers to handle widely used hardware, and both computers and peripheral hardware are now supporting the universal serial bus (USB) standard to make installation even easier. With a true *plug-and-play* operating system, the operating system is able to automatically recognize and work with any device plugged currently into it. During the boot process, the operating system attempts to configure any new devices attached since the PC was last turned on. Most hardware products include an installation CD or disk that can be used to install the proper device drivers, if needed.

Once a device and its driver have been properly installed, they usually work fine. If the device driver file gets accidentally deleted or becomes corrupted, or if a new device has been connected to the PC, the operating system typically notifies the user during the boot process that the driver needs to be installed and attempts to install the driver and configure the device. When a device driver becomes corrupted, usually repeating the initial installation procedure for that piece of hardware corrects the problem. Device drivers are often offered as free downloads from the hardware manufacturer's Web site, in case the installation disk or CD can't be found or you need a new device driver after upgrading your operating system.

Interfacing with Users

One of the principal roles of every operating system, as Figure 6-1 suggests, is to translate user instructions into a form the computer understands. In the other direction, it translates any feedback from the hardware—such as a signal that the printer has run out of paper or the scanner is turned off—into a form that the user understands. In a previous chapter we saw

---

>**Boot.** To start up a computer. >**Device driver.** A program that enables an operating system to communicate with a specific hardware device.

that there were several ways that users can command a computer to take an action. Two of these—*typing* instructions that conform to a command syntax and *selecting* instructions from a graphical user interface—are the ways that most people interact with operating systems.

Managing Resources and Jobs

As a session begins and you start to request programs and data, the operating system retrieves them from disk and loads them into RAM. Once the operating system opens an application program, it relinquishes some control to that program. While a program such as a word processor or spreadsheet might accept keystrokes from users or conduct a spelling check on its own, it generally uses the operating system to monitor proper use of storage and availability of hardware. Thus, the operating system is in charge of managing system resources and making them available to devices and programs when they are needed.

Along with assigning system resources, the operating system performs a closely related process: scheduling user jobs to be performed using those resources. Scheduling routines in the operating system determine the order in which jobs are processed on hardware devices, such as shared drives and printers. An operating system serving multiple users does not necessarily assign jobs on a first-come, first-served basis. Some users may have higher priority than others or the devices needed to process the next job in line may not be available, among other factors.

The operating system also schedules operations throughout the computer system so that different parts of the system can work on different portions of the same jobs at the same time. Because input and output devices work much more slowly than the CPU itself, the CPU may complete billions of calculations for several programs while the contents of a single document are being printed or displayed. Using a number of techniques, the operating system juggles the computer's work in order to employ system devices as efficiently as possible. The methods that allow a computer to process a number of jobs at more or less the same time—such as *multitasking* and *multiprocessing*—are discussed in a later section.

Monitoring Activities

Another major function of the operating system is overseeing activities while processing is underway. For instance, the operating system may terminate any program that performs an illegal operation or demands more memory than is available. In doing so, it sends an appropriate message to the user. Similarly, the operating system informs the user of any equipment abnormalities that arise.

Besides apprising users when problems occur, many operating systems also monitor routine computer system performance and report on its status. Users and system administrators need to know information such as how much hard-drive space is used up, how much memory is free, and how response time changes as more network users try to access the same resources. Programs called *performance monitors* keep track of such activities.

File Management

One of the more important tasks of the operating system is *file management*—allowing a user to organize a disk and keeping track of the files stored there.

To simplify file management, operating systems commonly organize the files on a disk or hard drive hierarchically into **folders** or **directories.** As shown in Figure 6-3, operating systems allow you to see which folders are located on each drive and look inside the folders to see the other folders and documents stored there. Usually your operating system files are stored in one folder and each application program is stored in a separate

---

>**Folder.** A logical named place on a storage medium into which files can be stored to keep the medium organized. Sometimes called a directory.
>**Directory.** An older name for folder.

DRIVES AND FOLDERS
The left pane displays the available drives and the folders (directories) on those drives. Clicking an item selects it and displays its contents in the right pane.

DISK OR FOLDER CONTENTS
As disks or folders are selected in the left pane, their contents are displayed in the right pane.

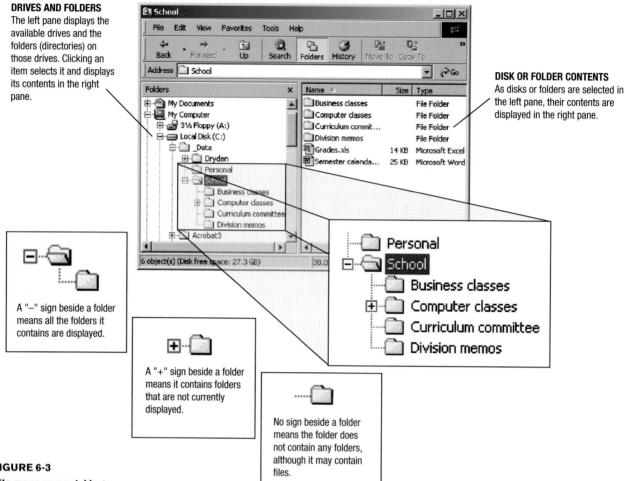

A "–" sign beside a folder means all the folders it contains are displayed.

A "+" sign beside a folder means it contains folders that are not currently displayed.

No sign beside a folder means the folder does not contain any folders, although it may contain files.

⬤ FIGURE 6-3

File management. Most operating systems have a file management system similar to the Windows Explorer program shown here.

folder. In addition, you will typically have one or more folders for your data files. As shown in Figure 6-3, for instance, you may want to have a separate folder for each college course or type of documents, such as memos, financial documents, photographs, personal documents, and so on.

When viewing the files on a storage medium in a hierarchy, as in the Windows Explorer screen shown in Figure 6-3, the top of the hierarchy for any disk is a "master" directory called the *root directory* for that disk (such as C:\ for the root directory of the hard drive C in Figure 6-4). The root directory usually contains several lower-level directories—called *subdirectories* or *subfolders*—in addition to files. When you want to access a file in any folder, you generally navigate to the folder where the document is stored by opening the appropriate subfolders, though you can specify the appropriate *path* to that file's exact location instead, if preferred. For example, as Figure 6-4 shows, the path

C:\My Documents\Letters\Mary

leads through the root directory of the C drive and the My Documents and Letters folders to a file named "Mary." A similar path can also be used to access the files *John* and *Bill.* As discussed in a previous chapter, users supply the desired filename for each file when the file is initially stored on the storage medium and there can be only one file with the exact same filename in any particular folder on a storage device. The rules for how files can be named vary with each operating system; files can be renamed, moved, copied, or deleted using the appropriate file management commands.

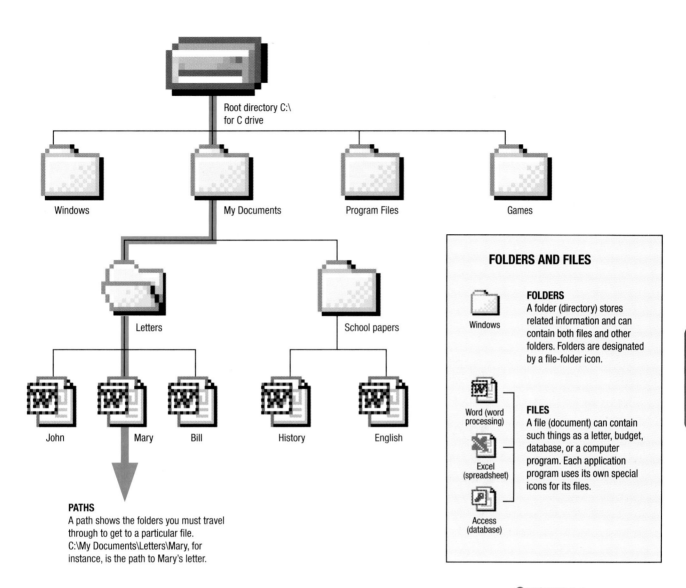

FIGURE 6-4
Organizing files into folders.

Another aspect of file management found in most operating systems is some type of search function. The search function is often used to find files located somewhere on your hard drive that meet a particular pattern, such as including certain characters in the filename or having a particular modification date (see Figure 6-5). The search functions of many operating systems also include locating people or devices on a network, or resources on the Internet.

Security

A computer's operating system can protect against unauthorized access by using *password* procedures to prevent outsiders from accessing system resources that they are not authorized to access. With almost all networks, access is protected by some type of log-on or password procedure. Stand-alone PCs can use password procedures, as well. In addition to protecting the PC against unauthorized use, some operating systems allow the use of user names and passwords to create personalized settings, such as desktop colors, desktop icons and toolbars, menu organization, and so forth. These settings are saved for each individual user who has access to the PC, such as a home PC used by both parents and their children. When an individual logs on with his or her user name and password, the appropriate desktop is displayed.

◈ **FIGURE 6-5**

Find/search capabilities.

Most operating systems have some option to help you locate files and other resources.

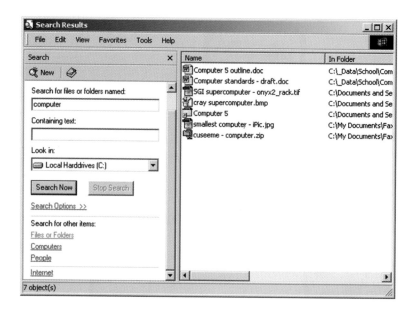

Many operating systems also provide some encryption procedures to protect valuable programs and data when they are transmitted to other computers. The subject of security is a lengthy one, and we consider it in depth in Chapter 15.

Processing Techniques for Increased Efficiency

Computers often take advantage of various processing techniques to operate more efficiently. These techniques enable computers to process many programs at the same time or almost at the same time. Consequently, these techniques—sometimes referred to as *interleaved processing techniques*—increase system efficiency and the amount of processing the computer system can perform in any given period of time. Some of these techniques are discussed in the next few sections.

Multitasking

Multitasking refers to the ability of an operating system to work with more than one program (called a *task*) at one time. For example, this feature would allow a user to edit a spreadsheet file in one program while loading a Web page in their Web browser in another window, or print one document while editing another document in a word processing program. Without multitasking ability, an operating system would require the user to close one program or document before opening another, as is the case with early operating systems like DOS. With multitasking, the CPU can technically only do one thing at the same time, so it rotates between the programs needing it, and spends a small fraction of time on one program's processing before moving to the next task. This is a type of *concurrent processing* (see Figure 6-6). Since today's CPUs work very fast, even though the operating system is rotating between processing tasks, executing part of one program, then part of another, and so on, to the user it appears as though all programs are executing at the same time. Virtually all recent operating systems are able to multitask.

Multitasking speeds processing because computers can perform thousands of computations during the short delays that occur in every session, such as the time it takes for a disk drive to load a single piece of data or for a user to respond to a question or menu choice. The

>**Multitasking.** The capability of an operating system to execute two or more program or program tasks concurrently for a single user.

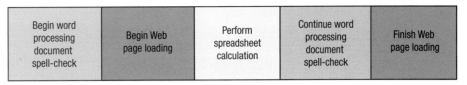

CONCURRENT PROCESSING
(multitasking, multithreading, and time-sharing)

| Begin word processing document spell-check | Begin Web page loading | Perform spreadsheet calculation | Continue word processing document spell-check | Finish Web page loading |

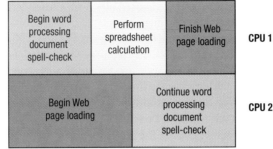

SIMULTANEOUS PROCESSING
(multiprocessing)

FIGURE 6-6

Concurrent vs. simultaneous processing. Concurrent processing techniques (such as multitasking, multithreading, and time-sharing) have to perform processing tasks one right after another; simultaneous processing techniques (such as multiprocessing) can perform multiple tasks at exactly the same time.

CPU usually decides when to rotate to the next program, based on what is happening with each task (program) at the moment. To further illustrate the concept of multitasking, think of the CPU as a waitress in a busy restaurant with several tables to attend to. The waitress *concurrently* attends to all of the customers within a given time period, but can only wait on one table at a time. She may take table 1's order, then move to table 3 to deliver the check, then move back to table 1 to bring the customers their appetizer, and so forth. As the waitress moves from table to table, assistants (such as a bus boy) may carry out minor tasks, such as bringing table 2 extra napkins or clearing the dishes from table 3.

Returning to multitasking, the CPU (like the waitress) works on only one program at a time. When it reaches a point at which peripheral devices or other elements of the computer system can take over some of the work, the CPU moves on to another program, returning to the first one when the situation requires further processing. While the computer waits for the hard drive to read data in one program, for example, it can perform calculations for another program. The systems software for the hard drive, like the bus boy, does background work; in this case, it retrieves the data stored on drive.

Users can fully appreciate multitasking when they need continuing access to their computers while performing time-intensive operations, such as performing a search through all the files on your hard drive to find the ones that meet a specified pattern or loading a Web page with lots of graphics or other slow-loading objects. With multitasking, you are allowed to use your computer to perform other tasks in the same or a different program while the search or Web page loading continues in the background. Without multitasking, you would have to wait for the task to be completely performed before exiting that application and beginning the alternate task.

The term *multitasking* is most commonly used in reference to single-user operating systems. Multitasking with a multiuser operating system is usually referred to as *multiprogramming*.

Multithreading

A *thread* is a sequence of instructions within a program that isn't dependent on other threads. Examples might include spell-checking, printing, and opening documents in a word processing program. *Multithreading* operating systems have the ability to process multiple threads within a program at one time, without opening multiple occurrences of the program, as long as the program was written to use multiple threads. This type of scheduling is more efficient, and helps speed up processing. Most current operating systems are multithreading, as well as multitasking.

Multiprocessing

Another way to speed up processing is by using **multiprocessing**—using two or more CPUs in a computer system to perform work on different jobs at the same time. Of course, the operating system must acknowledge multiple processors and assign processing tasks to them as efficiently as possible. In contrast with multitasking and multithreading, in which a single CPU processes several programs or tasks *concurrently* (taking turns), multiprocessing carries out multiple programs or tasks *simultaneously* (at precisely the same instant) on separate processors (refer again to Figure 6-6). Closely related to multiprocessing are coprocessing and parallel processing.

Coprocessing coordinates the functions of a primary CPU with those of "slave" processors that perform specialized chores, such as high-speed calculations for screen graphics. At any point in time, two or more processors may be performing work simultaneously, but the primary CPU still largely determines the time taken to perform an entire job.

In *parallel processing* (discussed in Chapter 3 and illustrated in Figure 3-24), there are several processors, each of which constitutes a full-fledged general-purpose CPU that operates at roughly the same level as the others. These tightly integrated CPUs typically work together on one job at the same time. The number of processors used, whether or not they share memory, and other characteristics vary with the design of the system. The concept of parallel processing may sound simple, but many practical problems complicate its implementation, and parallel processing often requires special software.

Multiprocessing is one way to implement *fault-tolerant computing,* in which a computer system includes duplicates of important components, such as the CPU. The duplicate components may or may not function together. In one example of fault-tolerant computing, such as the RAID disk mirroring discussed in Chapter 4, if a critical component fails, its identical backup component takes over. In another example, both components may be working side-by-side on the same task, comparing results at checkpoints. In either case, the computer switches to the duplicate component if one of the components fails. Fault-tolerant computing is used for systems that must be operational at all times.

Time-Sharing

Time-sharing is similar to multitasking in that it is a technique to share processing among many programs concurrently by allotting short, uninterrupted time periods to each. These techniques differ in the way they allot time, however. A time-sharing computer spends a fixed amount of time on each program and then goes on to another. A multitasking computer works on a program until it encounters a logical stopping point, such as a need to read more data, before going on to another program.

Time-sharing techniques are commonly used to allow a single computer system—usually a mainframe—to support numerous users at separate workstations. The operating system cycles through all the active programs in the system that need processing and gives each one a small time slice during each cycle. For example, say that users are currently using 20 programs and the system allocates a time slice of 1 second for each one. (However, time-sharing systems usually slice processing time in pieces much smaller than this, and the time allocated to each program is not necessarily the same.) In this example, the computer would work on program 1 for 1 second, then on program 2 for 1 second, and so forth. When it finishes working on program 20 for 1 second, it returns to program 1 for another second, program 2 for another second, and so on. Thus, if 20 programs run concurrently on the system, each program will get a total of 3 seconds of processing during each minute of actual

---

>**Multiprocessing.** A technique for simultaneous processing by multiple processors operating under common control in a single computer system.
>**Time-sharing.** A technique used in a multiuser environment in which the computer assigns a specific processing time allotment to each program and then rotates between the programs accordingly.

clock time, or 1 second in every 20-second period. As you can see, in a time-sharing system it is difficult for a single program to dominate the CPU's attention, thereby holding up the processing of other programs.

Memory Management

Another key function of the operating system is optimizing the use of RAM—often referred to as *memory management.* The operating system allocates RAM to programs as needed and then reclaims that memory when the program is closed. Sometimes programs don't release all the memory being used when the program is closed—a problem called *memory leakage.* If memory leakage occurs too many times during one session and the operating system can't reclaim the memory, eventually there won't be enough free memory for the computer to operate and the PC must be rebooted to reclaim all the available RAM once again.

Virtual memory is a memory management feature used by some operating systems to extend RAM by using portions of the hard drive as additional RAM capacity. It usually works like this: The operating system allocates a portion of the hard drive to function as extra RAM. Programs and data ready for processing are stored in the virtual-memory area of the hard drive (sometimes called the *swap file*). There, the contents of virtual memory are divided into either fixed-length *pages* or variable-length *segments.* (Whether programs are divided into pages or segments depends on the operating system's capabilities.) For example, a virtual-memory system might break a program requiring 400 kilobytes of storage space into 10 pages of 40 kilobytes each. As the computer executes the program, it stores only some of the pages in actual RAM. As it requires other pages during program execution, it retrieves them from virtual memory and writes over the pages in RAM that are no longer needed (see Figure 6-7). All the pages remain intact in virtual memory as the computer processes the program so, if the computer needs a page that was overwritten in RAM,

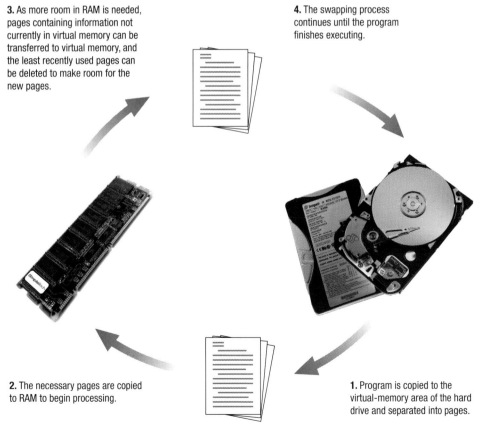

3. As more room in RAM is needed, pages containing information not currently in virtual memory can be transferred to virtual memory, and the least recently used pages can be deleted to make room for the new pages.

4. The swapping process continues until the program finishes executing.

2. The necessary pages are copied to RAM to begin processing.

1. Program is copied to the virtual-memory area of the hard drive and separated into pages.

❧ **FIGURE 6-7**

Virtual memory. With virtual memory, the operating system uses a portion of the hard drive as additional RAM.

it can be readily fetched from virtual memory again. If needed, the operating system can also transfer new pages from RAM to virtual memory to preserve them. This process—sometimes called *swapping* or *paging*—continues until the program finishes executing.

Not all operating systems offer virtual memory. Although this technique permits a computer system to get by with limited RAM, it can waste a lot of processing time swapping pages or segments in and out of RAM and reduce the overall processing efficiency of the computer.

Spooling

Some input and output devices work at extremely low speeds. Tape drives and printers, for example, work at a snail's pace compared to the CPU. If the CPU had to wait for these slower devices to finish their work, the computer system would face a horrendous bottleneck. For example, suppose that the computer has just finished processing a five-second print job that generated 100 pages of hard copy for the printer. A printer might output 8 pages per minute, requiring over 12 minutes to finish the job. If the CPU had to deal directly with the printer, memory would be tied up waiting for the printer to complete the job. As a result, other programs would have to sit unattended while this output was sent from memory to paper.

To avoid such a delay, many operating systems set up areas in RAM or on the hard drive for *spooling;* that is, storing output destined for the printer. These areas are often called *buffers* or *queues.* When the computer receives a Print command, the output is transferred to the spooling area. The computer is then free to use the memory just freed up to process another program, leaving it to the spooling program to transfer the output of the first program to the printer.

Spooling can also be used to hold, or *stage,* input on its way to the computer. As input enters the computer system, it is stored in a spooling area for the appropriate device, such as a keyboard buffer for keyboard input. When the operating system is ready for the input, it is retrieved from the appropriate spooling area.

COMMON OPERATING SYSTEMS FOR DESKTOP PCS AND SERVERS

web tutor

For a tutorial on the history and development of the various operating systems, go to www.course.com/parker2002/ch6

PC operating systems today are usually designed either for desktop PCs (personal operating systems) or network servers (network operating systems). As mentioned earlier, many new operating systems are available in versions for both uses. This section covers some widely used operating systems; the most recent versions of most of these are summarized in Figure 6-8 along with a few of their characteristics.

DOS

During the 1980s and early 1990s, **DOS** (for *D*isk *O*perating *S*ystem) was the dominant operating system for microcomputers. There were two primary forms of DOS: *PC-DOS* and *MS-DOS*. Both were originally developed by Microsoft Corporation, but PC-DOS was created originally for IBM microcomputers, whereas MS-DOS was used with IBM-compatible PCs. PC-DOS is now owned by IBM, which still updates the program. The latest version, PC-DOS 2000, works on both IBM PCs as well as those made by other manufacturers. Microsoft still owns MS-DOS, but the firm no longer updates the program; Version 6 was the last Microsoft update. A newer version of DOS called DR-DOS, originally developed by Digital Research, is currently being marketed for *thin client* use.

>**DOS.** The operating system designed for and on early IBM and IBM-compatible computers.

Operating System	Used Primarily on	Type of Interface	Versions Available
DOS	Intel (or compatible) PCs	Command-line	Personal only
Windows 2000	Intel (or compatible) PCs	GUI	Personal and server
Windows Me	Intel (or compatible) home PCs	GUI	Personal only
Windows XP	Intel (or compatible) PCs	GUI	Personal and server
Mac OS	Macintosh PCs	GUI	Personal and server
Unix	Servers and larger, multiuser computers; some PCs	Traditionally command-line, though GUI versions now exist	Personal and server
Linux	Intel (or compatible) PCs, servers, and larger, multiuser computers	Command-line or GUI	Personal and server
NetWare 6	Intel (or compatible) servers	GUI	Server only
OS/2 Warp 4	Business PCs and larger, multiuser computers	GUI	Personal and server

FIGURE 6-8
Recent versions of common computer operating systems.

DOS traditionally uses a command-line interface, as shown in Figure 6-9, though newer versions of DOS support a menu-driven interface. DOS is not widely used today because it does not use a graphical user interface and doesn't support modern processors and processing techniques. A sample of DOS commands is provided in Figure 6-9.

Windows

There have been a variety of different versions of Microsoft's **Windows** operating systems over the last several years. The next few sections chronicle the main developments of the Windows line.

Windows 3.x

Microsoft created *Windows 3.x* in an effort to meet the needs of users frustrated by having to learn and use DOS commands. Windows 3.x—the *x* stands for the version number of the software, such as Windows 3.0, 3.1, or 3.11—is an interconnected series of programs that provide a graphical user interface for DOS computers. By replacing the DOS command line with a system of menus, windows, and icons, Windows 3.x was much more user friendly.

Windows 3.x, however, was not a full-fledged operating system. It was instead an *operating environment*—a graphical shell that operated around DOS—designed to make DOS easier to use. Windows 3.x also allowed DOS to address more than 1 megabyte of RAM, perform multitasking, and run several built-in utility applications—such as a card file, calendar, and paint program. Still, the shortcomings of DOS limited the effectiveness of Windows 3.x and it is no longer widely used.

Windows 95 and Windows 98

In 1994, Microsoft announced that all soon-to-be-released versions of Windows after 3.11 would be full-fledged operating systems, not just operating environments. It also announced a new numbering system. Instead of calling the next upgrade Windows 4.0—as many had anticipated—it would number new versions of Windows with respect to the year of release. So, for instance, *Windows 95* refers to the 1995 version of Windows and *Windows 98* refers to the 1998 version.

>**Windows.** The primary PC operating system developed by Microsoft Corporation; common versions include Windows 95, Windows 98, Windows 2000, and Windows Me.

DOS. Even though DOS has become technologically obsolete, many PCs still use it. This table lists some of the most commonly used DOS commands, and the screen to the right shows DOS in action.

```
C:\WINDOWS>cd..

C:\>cd mydocu~1

C:\My Documents>dir

 Volume in drive C has no label
 Volume Serial Number is 1338-14DC
 Directory of C:\My Documents

.                <DIR>        07-19-01   1:34p .
..               <DIR>        07-19-01   1:34p ..
MYPICT~1         <DIR>        07-19-01   1:38p My Pictures
MYWEBS~1         <DIR>        07-26-01   8:59p My Webs
FAXTEM~1 DOC      20,480      08-21-01   7:37a Fax template.doc
COMPAN~1 JPG      12,009      08-27-01   6:46a Company logo.jpg
DIGITA~1 BMP      90,038      03-01-01  12:11p Digital signature Morley.bmp
MYMUSI~1         <DIR>        10-11-01   7:57a My Music
MYEBOO~1         <DIR>        10-24-01   1:46p My eBooks
HOMEWORK         <DIR>        10-24-01   3:54p Homework
          3 file(s)         122,527 bytes
          7 dir(s)       33,944.47 MB free

C:\My Documents>
```

Command	Description	Example	Explanation
COPY	Copies individual files	COPY BOSS A:WORKER	Makes a copy of BOSS and stores it on the A drive using the filename WORKER
DIR	Displays the names of files on a disk	DIR A:	Displays names of files on the A drive
DEL	Deletes individual files	DEL A:DOLLAR	Deletes the file DOLLAR from the A drive
REN	Renames individual files	REN SAM BILL	Renames SAM to BILL
CD	Changes to a new directory	CD HOMEWORK	Changes the current directory to HOMEWORK, located one level down from the current location on the current disk
FORMAT	Prepares a disk for use, erasing what was there before	FORMAT A:	Formats the disk in the A drive

Both Windows 95 and 98 employ a similar but easier-to-learn-and-use GUI than the one in Windows 3.x. Along with this improved interface and faster system response (the latter due to the fact that they are predominantly 32-bit operating systems), Windows 95 and 98 permit multitasking and long filenames. Windows 98 differs from Windows 95 in that it adds a higher degree of Internet integration, more options for customizing the desktop user interface, improved support for large hard drives, and support for both DVD and USB.

Windows NT

Windows NT (for *New Technology*) was Microsoft's standard networking operating system until the introduction of *Windows 2000* (discussed shortly). Windows NT is a multitasking operating system that uses a GUI similar to Windows 95 and Windows 98. The *Workstation* version is geared toward high-end single users, while the *Server* version is designed to run small LANs.

Windows 2000

Windows 2000—the upgrade to Windows NT—was released in 2000. Though primarily a network operating system geared toward business use and server computers, several different versions of Windows 2000 exist. The *Professional* edition is targeted to ordinary users

>**Windows NT.** The earlier version of the operating system designed by Microsoft Corporation for both high-end single user and network applications that was replaced by Windows 2000. >**Windows 2000.** The upgrade to Windows NT.

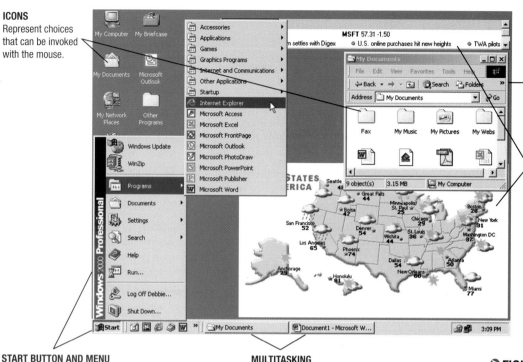

ICONS
Represent choices that can be invoked with the mouse.

FILE MANAGEMENT
Windows has two file management programs–Windows Explorer and My Computer–to allow you to view and organize the contents of your disks.

ACTIVE DESKTOP
Lets you add active Web content–such as weather, sports news, and stock prices–to your desktop. Content is continually updated when there is an active Internet connection.

START BUTTON AND MENU
Click for easy access to programs.

MULTITASKING
More than one program can be open at one time; the taskbar buttons can be used to switch the active window.

▶ **FIGURE 6-10**
Windows 2000. The interface used with Microsoft Windows 2000 is similar to the interface used in Windows 98 and Me.

working on powerful desktop computers, and the *Server* family of products is aimed at network administrators and network-management tasks. In addition, like most operating systems today, Windows 2000 supports multitasking and multiprocessing.

Windows 2000 is built using Windows NT technology, so it is more powerful and more stable than operating systems built on the Windows 9x kernel, such as Windows 95, Windows 98, and *Windows Me* (discussed next). And it is even more crash-proof than Windows NT. As with Windows NT, Windows 2000 uses an interface similar to previous versions of Windows (see Figure 6-10). One of the major disadvantages of Windows 2000 relative to Windows 95 or 98 is that its storage and RAM requirements are quite a bit more demanding. Consequently, many desktop users may choose to use a version of Windows based on 9x technology instead. The successor to Windows 2000—*Windows XP,* discussed shortly— was released in late 2001.

Windows Me

Windows Me (Millennium Edition) replaced Windows 98 as the Windows personal operating system designed for home PCs. Unlike Windows 2000, it is based on Windows 9x technology, not Windows NT, though on the surface it resembles Windows 2000 and the other recent versions of Windows. And, though it supports improved home networking and a shared Internet connection, it is a personal operating system, not a networking operating system. In addition to easier home networking, Windows Me features improved multimedia capabilities, better system protection, a faster boot process, and more Internet-ready activities and games. Windows Me is also the first operating system to support *Universal Plug and Play (UPnP),* which uses standard Internet protocols to connect PCs, intelligent appliances (smart coffee pots, refrigerators, etc.), and wireless devices over a network.

inside the industry

Project Code Names

When computer companies are developing new hardware and software products, they typically assign internal code names to the projects. For instance, Microsoft assigned the code names Chicago and Memphis, respectively, to the prerelease versions of Windows 95 and Windows 98. Less well-known code names for Windows products were Champaign (Windows NT 3.5), Cairo (Windows NT 4.0), Sparta (Windows for Workgroups), and Cleveland (Windows 4, which was never released). Some of the newest Microsoft code names are Whistler (for Windows XP) and Stinger (for Microsoft's introduction in the smart phone arena).

Often companies stick with standard themes for code names on related products. For Windows, Microsoft has gone with midwestern city names. Development of IBM's OS/2 operating system featured project names with a Star Trek theme, such as Warp, Borg, Q, and Ferengi. Other popular themes include beer, sushi, boats, Shakespeare, celebrities, animals, and mythical gods. Some code names stick—for instance, Macintosh and OS/2 Warp.

Some of the most interesting code names used over the years are Road Pizza (Apple's QuickTime software), Bladerunner (Borland's dBASE for Windows), Rolling Rock (Go Corporation's PenPoint for Hobbit), Shamu (the GUI for CompuServe), CyberDog (Apple browser), Dr. Pepper (an AppleTalk protocol), Big Foot (Borland's 32-bit DOS extender), and Bogart (Apple's Applesearch). One of the least interesting code names was P5 (Intel's Pentium chip).

Windows XP

Windows XP (for "experience") is the latest version of Windows and is designed to eventually replace both Windows 2000 (for business and server use) and Windows Me (for home use). It is based on Windows NT technology and is more stable and powerful than Windows Me, but also requires more memory—at least 64 MB. This new version (code-named "Whistler" during development, as explained in the Inside the Industry box) has a new user interface (see Figure 6-11), though the basic elements of Windows (Start menu, taskbar, etc.) are still present. In addition, users may choose to continue to use the classic Windows interface, featured in Windows 2000, Me, and 98, instead of the new interface. Some of the newest features of Windows XP are related to multimedia and communications, such as improved photo, video, and music editing and sharing; the ability to switch between user accounts without rebooting or even closing all open programs; and the use of real-time voice communications and application sharing. To cover both business and home applications, Windows XP is available in home, professional, and 64-bit editions.

Mac OS

Mac OS—previously called *Macintosh Operating System*—is the proprietary operating system for computers made by Apple Corporation. The Apple Macintosh, introduced in 1984, set the standard for graphical user interfaces. Many of today's new operating systems

>**Windows XP.** The latest version of Windows; designed to replace both Windows Me and Windows 2000. >**Mac OS.** The operating system for Apple's Macintosh line of computers.

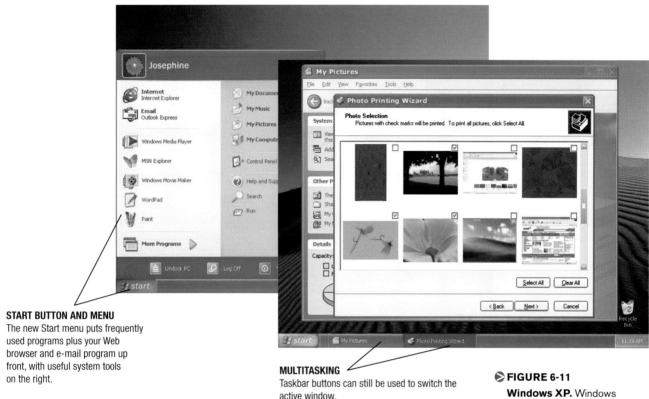

START BUTTON AND MENU
The new Start menu puts frequently
used programs plus your Web
browser and e-mail program up
front, with useful system tools
on the right.

MULTITASKING
Taskbar buttons can still be used to switch the
active window.

▶ **FIGURE 6-11**
Windows XP. Windows
XP—expected to replace previous versions of Windows for
both home and business use—
has a new interface to make it
even more usable than earlier
versions, though users have
the option of sticking with the
classic Windows interface
used in earlier versions
instead.

follow the trend that the Mac started and, in fact, highly resemble Apple's operating system
(see Figure 6-12).

Mac OS has grown with the times, keeping pace with increases in power brought by
each new CPU chip and Apple computer model. The latest version of the operating system is
Mac OS X (for version 10). Improvements include better multitasking, increased Unix compatibility and networking support, more stability, and better memory management. As with
the previous version—Mac OS 9—this version also includes the ability to save work settings
for multiple users and tools for Internet and e-commerce applications. On the downside,
OS X is memory-intensive, requiring at least 128 MB of RAM. Mac OS works almost exclusively on Apple computers and is available in both personal and server versions.

Unix

Unix was originally developed about three decades ago at Bell Laboratories as an operating system for midrange computers. Many properties of Unix make it a compelling choice
for high-end PCs.

First, Unix has established a long and relatively successful track record as a multiuser,
preemptive multitasking operating system. For desktop users who like Unix, there is a personal Workstation version available in addition to the normal Server version.

Second, Unix is flexible, so it can be used on a wide variety of machines. Unlike other
operating systems—such as Windows, which is designed for Intel-type chips, or Mac OS,
which is designed for PowerPC chips—Unix is not built around a single family of processors. Computer systems from microcomputers to mainframes can run Unix, and it can easily
integrate a variety of devices from different manufacturers through network connections.

>**Unix.** A long-standing operating system for midrange computers and high-end PCs.

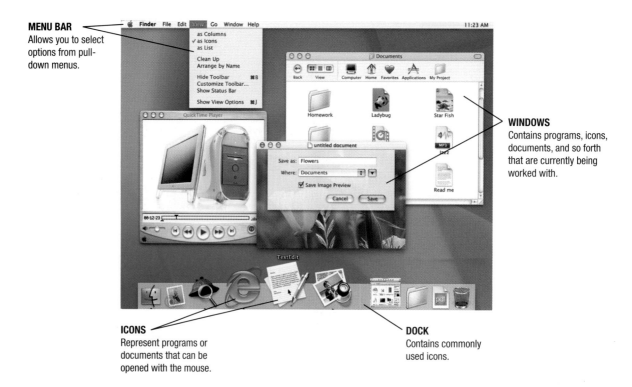

MENU BAR
Allows you to select options from pull-down menus.

WINDOWS
Contains programs, icons, documents, and so forth that are currently being worked with.

ICONS
Represent programs or documents that can be opened with the mouse.

DOCK
Contains commonly used icons.

◆ FIGURE 6-12

Mac OS. Mac OS remains very popular many years after emerging as the first commercially successful operating system with a graphical user interface.

This flexibility gives Unix a big advantage over competing operating systems for many types of applications.

But certain disadvantages have plagued Unix in the past. Its usual command-line interface makes it more difficult to use than GUI-based operating systems. What's more, the same features that give Unix its flexibility make it run more slowly than operating systems tailored around a particular family of microprocessors. This characteristic limits the benefits of applying Unix in an environment dominated by one type of PCs, such as Windows-based machines. Perhaps the greatest disadvantage of Unix is that the different versions of Unix on the market together are often incompatible with each other.

Today's newest versions of Unix sport a graphical user interface, instead of its traditional command-line interface. That, plus a new single Unix specification expected to be used with all upcoming versions of Unix to alleviate the incompatibility problems of the past, should help overcome the most prominent Unix limitations of the past.

One of the biggest competitors to Unix (as well as, recently, to Windows) is a variant called *Linux,* discussed next.

Linux

Linux (pronounced "*LINN-uks*") is a version of Unix that has achieved a loyal band of followers over the past few years. Originally created in 1991, some versions of Linux are available without charge over the Internet. Linux is *open-source software,* meaning the program's code is available to the public and can be modified to improve it or customize it to a particular application. Over the years, volunteer programmers from all over the world have collaborated to improve Linux, sharing their improved code with others over the Internet. In addition to being available for free, companies are permitted to sell Linux as a retail product. Some of the most widely known commercial versions of Linux are from Red Hat and Caldera.

Though Linux originally used a command-line interface, most recent versions of Linux programs use a graphical interface (see Figure 6-13). These interfaces are generally built

>**Linux.** A version of Unix that is available without charge over the Internet.

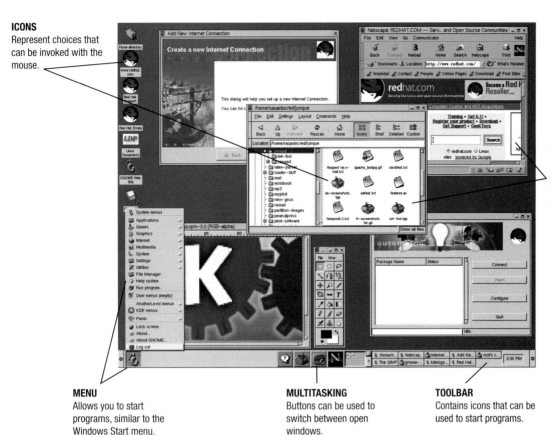

ICONS
Represent choices that can be invoked with the mouse.

WINDOWS
Contain programs, icons, documents, and so forth, that are currently being worked with.

MENU
Allows you to start programs, similar to the Windows Start menu.

MULTITASKING
Buttons can be used to switch between open windows.

TOOLBAR
Contains icons that can be used to start programs.

❧ FIGURE 6-13

Linux. Linux is a rapidly growing alternative to Windows and Mac OS that is available free of charge over the Internet. Purchased versions are also available, such as the Red Hat version illustrated here.

around either the *KDE* or *GNOME* desktop environments, products of the KDE Internet project and the GNOME project and foundation, respectively. Both organizations are committed to developing free, easy-to-use desktop environments and powerful application frameworks for Linux and other Unix-like operating systems. Purchased Linux operating systems usually come with more support materials than the versions downloaded for free.

Linux has grown from an operating system used primarily by computer techies who disliked Microsoft to a relatively widely accepted operating system in recent years. There is also an increasing amount of support from mainstream companies, such as Sun and IBM. This, plus the introduction of graphical interfaces to make it more user-friendly, will likely cause Linux acceptance and use to continue to grow in the future. It is expected that the biggest growth of Linux may be at the lower-end desktop, Internet appliance, and point-of-sale terminal use, though companies—such as IBM—are increasingly using Linux with their mainframes. Linux is even used on some supercomputers, usually on a group of Linux PCs linked together to form what is referred to as a *supercluster.* With the continued improvement and growth of Linux software such as Sun's *StarOffice*—a free desktop software suite available in both Linux and Windows versions and compatible with Microsoft documents—some predict Linux will give Windows a run for its money.

NetWare

NetWare—developed by Novell, Inc. during the mid-1980s—is the most widely used operating system today on PC-based local area networks (LANs). It is a direct competitor with the server versions of Windows 2000 and XP.

>**NetWare.** The most widely used operating systems for PC-based local area networks (LANs).

As discussed earlier and illustrated in Figure 6-2, NetWare provides a shell around your personal, desktop operating system through which you can interact with network resources, such as a shared printer or hard disk. The newest versions of NetWare include software for several specialty servers as well, including a Web server, FTP server, and multimedia server.

OS/2 and OS/2 Warp

OS/2 is an operating system designed by IBM for high-end PCs. The newest versions of OS/2 are called *OS/2 Warp*. OS/2 Warp supports true multitasking and multithreading and is capable of running programs written for DOS and Windows, in addition to programs written for OS/2. The *OS/2 Warp Server* version is geared primarily towards server use; a *Client* version can be used with client PCs.

OTHER OPERATING SYSTEMS

Though the majority of desktop and notebook computers run one of the operating systems discussed earlier (such as Windows, Mac OS, or Linux), some PC users choose to use an alternative operating system instead. In addition, Internet appliances and handheld PCs, as well as pagers, Web-enabled phones, and other mobile devices usually require a different operating system—either an operating system designed for mobile devices in general or a *proprietary* operating system designed solely for that one device in particular. Finally, larger computer systems often require a different operating system than desktop or server PCs. A variety of these alternative operating systems are discussed next.

Alternative PC Operating Systems

There are a variety of operating systems that can be used as an alternative to the operating systems already discussed. Two of the more common are *BeOS* and *Solaris*.

▼ *BeOS* is an operating system designed by a company called Be, Inc. Similar to Linux, the Personal Edition of BeOS is free to download via the Internet. BeOS can run on both Intel and PowerPC platforms, is geared toward multimedia applications, supports multiple processors, and is reputed to be faster and more crash-proof than other desktop operating systems. Though there is limited software to run on a BeOS system at the moment, new titles are being added all the time. A related software product—*BeIA*—is designed for Internet appliance use.

▼ *Solaris* is an operating system designed for *Sun* computers. The Solaris operating system can run on desktop systems and servers, as well as even on some supercomputers. There is also a Solaris operating environment that can be used to bring enhanced stability and functionality to Unix machines.

Operating Systems for Mobile Devices

For handheld PCs, the two most common operating systems are mobile versions of Windows and the *Palm OS* operating system. Web-enabled phones, pagers, and similar devices may use a proprietary operating system designed solely for that device instead. In many of the smaller devices, the operating system is embedded into the device using flash RAM chips or similar hardware. A few of the more widely used operating systems for mobile devices are discussed next.

Mobile and Embedded Versions of Windows

There are both mobile and embedded versions of Windows targeted for handheld PCs, smart phones, and other wireless devices. These versions of Windows have the look and feel of the larger desktop versions of Windows (see Figure 6-14), and typically support

further exploration

For links to further information about conventional operating systems, go to www.course.com/ parker2002/ch6

further exploration

For links to further information about alternative operating systems, go to www.course.com/parker2002/ch6

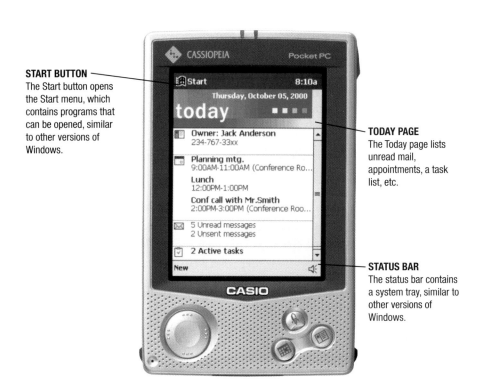

START BUTTON
The Start button opens the Start menu, which contains programs that can be opened, similar to other versions of Windows.

TODAY PAGE
The Today page lists unread mail, appointments, a task list, etc.

STATUS BAR
The status bar contains a system tray, similar to other versions of Windows.

FIGURE 6-14

Mobile Windows. Windows versions for portable devices resemble desktop Windows, but on a much smaller scale. For example, the Windows CE screen shown here includes a Start menu and taskbar.

handwriting recognition and such Internet components as e-mail and Web browsing. The most common mobile version of Windows is *Windows CE* (for *c*ompact *e*dition). Alternately, some devices may use a mobile or embedded version of another Windows, such as Windows 2000, instead.

There is a wide selection of software available for mobile devices running Windows, including portable versions of a variety of other Microsoft software products—such as Word, Excel, Explorer, Calendar, Media Player, and so forth.

Palm OS

Palm OS is the operating system designed for Palm handheld devices. It is also used by Palm-compatible devices, such as the Handspring Visor. The philosophy behind the Palm OS was to design an operating system specifically for information management on mobile devices, instead of trying to convert an entire desktop operating system into a smaller package. With Palm OS-driven devices, you can access e-mail and Web sites and exchange information with other devices, in addition to running the vast amount of software designed for Palm systems.

Some manufacturers—such as Nokia—are working on Palm OS-driven Web-enabled phones. Other phones may use the *Symbian* platform, discussed next.

EPOC and the Symbian Platform

A third contender in the mobile device operating system arena is *EPOC,* an operating system developed by a company called Psion. Psion joined with such mobile phone companies as Nokia and Ericsson to form the Symbian company to promote EPOC and the *Symbian platform* as the new industry standard for mobile devices, particularly smart phones. The Symbian platform uses a multithreaded, multitasking operating system, and has several different versions, such as one for keyboard-based devices, one for keyboardless devices,

>**Palm OS.** The operating system used with Palm handheld PCs.

and one for smart phones. Features include support for Web browsing, e-mail, handwriting recognition, synchronization, and applications written for the Symbian platform.

Operating Systems for Internet Appliances

Some Internet appliances run a standard desktop or mobile operating system, such as Windows CE. Others use a special embedded operating system, such as *QNX*. Still others use a special proprietary operating system created just for the device. Similar to operating systems for handheld devices, operating system for Internet appliances usually have more limited functionality than desktop operating systems.

Operating Systems for Larger Computers

Larger computer systems often use operating systems designed solely for that type of system. For example, the *OS/400* operating system is used with IBM AS/400 servers, and IBM's *VM/ESA* or *OS/390* operating system is designed for IBM mainframes. Most larger Sun computers are powered by the Solaris operating system. A growing trend of mainframes today, however, is to come Linux-ready as an alternative to a more traditional operating system. Supercomputers sometimes run completely different operating systems than other computers, though it is becoming increasingly common for supercomputing systems comprised of a collection of parallel servers to use a conventional operating system such as Windows, Unix, or Linux. Some supercomputer systems use multiple operating systems.

One additional device for which operating systems are being designed is the car. For a glimpse at current and future smart car applications, see the Trend box.

MYTHS ABOUT OPERATING SYSTEMS

Because many people don't fully understand the concept of what an operating system is and the functions that it performs, several myths about it exist.

Myth 1: One Computer Can Have Only One Operating System Installed

This first misconception stems from that fact that most PCs ship with just one operating system and many users never change it. What many people don't realize is that it is possible to install more than one operating system on a computer. When this is the case, the operating system to be used for the current session is selected when the computer is booted up. The most common reason for installing a second operating system on one PC is to experiment with another operating system (such as Linux or the newest version of Windows). Another possible reason is when the programs you must run on one PC require two different operating systems. As mentioned in an earlier chapter, one of the most common reasons for dividing your hard drive into partitions (multiple logical drives) is to install more than one operating system.

Myth 2: It Is Difficult to Change or Upgrade Operating Systems

The fact that many people are uneasy fiddling with their computer system has contributed to the spread of this myth. Many users never even consider the possibility of switching to a different operating system or upgrading to a different version. Upgrading to a new operating system—especially from one version to another of the same operating system—is usually fairly straightforward. It typically takes about an hour and in most cases all of the user's settings (menu structure, desktop icons, and so forth) are transferred from the older operating system to the new one. However, some hardware devices may require an updated drive for the new operating system and, occasionally, some of your older application software may not run under the newer operating system.

Smart Cars

The Emergence of the Digital Dashboard

Smart cars are here. Actually, there have been computers integrated into cars for years. High-end cars have a dozen or more computers to perform such tasks as regulating fuel consumption, controlling emissions, assisting with gear shifting, and remembering your seat position. The difference today is that we are beginning to see and use our cars' onboard computers more than in the past.

Without question, navigation systems are the most common smart car application. Virtually all auto manufacturers offer some type of GPS system in at least some models. Many car navigation systems are linked to maps and route information at a call center; newer systems are likely to obtain their information via the Internet. This integration will add tremendous capabilities, such as pairing up travel route data with information about restaurants, hotels, and attractions along the way.

Integrating computers and automobiles is referred to as *telematics*. In addition to GPS and navigation systems, the newest smart cars offer Web and e-mail access, and safety systems such as adaptive cruise control systems that slow your vehicle down when a driver in front of you slows down or pulls into your lane, and collision-avoidance systems. This latter type of safety system uses a camera in conjunction with the car's computer to monitor lane markings while tracking them to the speed of your vehicle. If the system detects that you are drifting into another lane, it sounds an alarm.

Other smart safety systems include bumper-based sensors to help drivers park cars more easily, smart air bags which determine the weight of the occupant and deploy the air bag with the minimum force necessary during a collision, and thermal windshield sensors that allow drivers to see up to five times farther on dark roads. In the future, telematics could also be used to automate such tasks as merging and lane changes—potentially making road rage a thing of the past.

One of the biggest challenges for smart car technologies is the safe use of all the smart gadgets being incorporated into cars. The concern stems mainly from the possibility that drivers won't pay enough attention to the road if they can surf the Web and read their e-mail while driving. If cell phone use is any indication, it is a valid concern—studies consistently show that drivers who use cell phones while driving are several times more likely to be involved in accidents than those drivers who don't. Voice controlled digital dashboards help because they are hands-free. Even better are systems that convert e-mail and other Web content into audio format, such as with the newest BMW system. Regardless of these concerns, like it or not, cars are getting smarter all the time with no signs of slowing down.

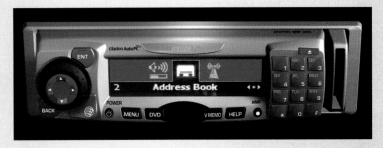

Clarion Joyride. This system, powered by Windows CE, incorporates music, navigation, and data storage into a single digital personal assistant located in your car's dashboard. Its hands-free voice interface increases user safety and data can be exchanged wirelessly with a PDA or via its CompactFlash port. Other features commonly found in these types of products include e-mail, telephone, and Web-browsing capabilities.

Some users don't change operating systems for fear that it will alter their data and other files stored on their PC. The truth is that operating system upgrades don't affect data files or program installations—just the operating system files. An exception to this rule is for some *beta* operating systems—prerelease versions of an operating system supplied to certain individuals to try out and test before the final operating system is released to the general public. With some beta operating system installations, if the beta version is uninstalled to revert to the previously installed operating system, any programs installed while the beta operating system was in place will need to be reinstalled. All data, however, should remain intact.

Myth 3: If You Don't Use Windows, You Can't Find Software

This misconception originated because there wasn't much software available for non-Windows PCs in the past. Though the availability of software designed for Apple, Linux, and other operating systems typically lags behind those for Windows, there still is an ample amount available for most applications. One benefit of Linux, for example, is that much of the software designed for that operating system is available free of charge, such as Sun's StarOffice suite.

UTILITY PROGRAMS

A **utility program** is a type of software that performs a specific task, usually related to managing or maintaining the computer system. Most operating systems include a variety of utilities. For instance, utility programs for finding files, diagnosing and repairing system problems, cleaning up your hard drive, and backing up files accompany virtually all operating systems. Utilities are also available as independent programs. These programs can be acquired to perform chores your operating system is incapable of doing, as well as do some types of operating-system tasks better.

Figure 6-15 briefly describes a variety of utility programs. A few of the more common utilities are discussed in more detail next; some—like *antivirus software* and *encryption software*—are discussed in later chapters of this text.

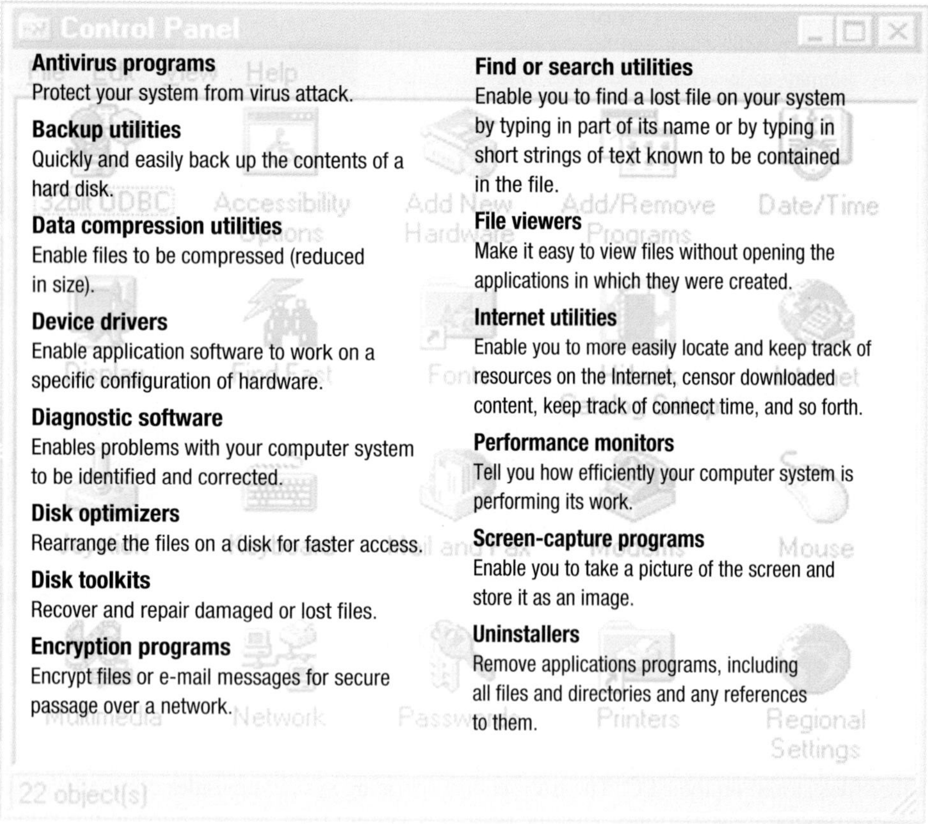

FIGURE 6-15

Utility programs. Utility programs extend the capabilities of a computer's systems software.

Antivirus programs
Protect your system from virus attack.

Backup utilities
Quickly and easily back up the contents of a hard disk.

Data compression utilities
Enable files to be compressed (reduced in size).

Device drivers
Enable application software to work on a specific configuration of hardware.

Diagnostic software
Enables problems with your computer system to be identified and corrected.

Disk optimizers
Rearrange the files on a disk for faster access.

Disk toolkits
Recover and repair damaged or lost files.

Encryption programs
Encrypt files or e-mail messages for secure passage over a network.

Find or search utilities
Enable you to find a lost file on your system by typing in part of its name or by typing in short strings of text known to be contained in the file.

File viewers
Make it easy to view files without opening the applications in which they were created.

Internet utilities
Enable you to more easily locate and keep track of resources on the Internet, censor downloaded content, keep track of connect time, and so forth.

Performance monitors
Tell you how efficiently your computer system is performing its work.

Screen-capture programs
Enable you to take a picture of the screen and store it as an image.

Uninstallers
Remove applications programs, including all files and directories and any references to them.

>**Utility program.** A program that performs some frequently encountered operation in a computer system, usually related to managing the computer's resources.

WINDOWS PROGRAMS
Diagnostic programs that come with an operating system typically include maintenance programs to check your hard drive and delete unnecessary files.

THIRD-PARTY PROGRAMS
There are a wide variety of third-party diagnostic and maintenance programs.

FIGURE 6-16
Diagnostic programs. Like many types of utility programs, diagnostic programs are usually available both as part of the operating system and as third-party packages.

Diagnostic Programs

Diagnostic programs deal primarily with diagnosing and repairing disk-related problems, such as recovering damaged or erased files, repairing damaged directories, and recovering from a disk crash (a crippling failure of the disk itself). Some diagnostic programs also include checking system software files for missing or duplicate files. At one time, virtually all diagnostic programs came from third-party vendors, but operating systems are increasingly including very adequate disk diagnostic programs. Still, vendors of third-party diagnostic programs seem to supply a continuing stream of useful disk-management routines beyond those of typical operating-system software. Some examples of diagnostic programs are shown in Figure 6-16.

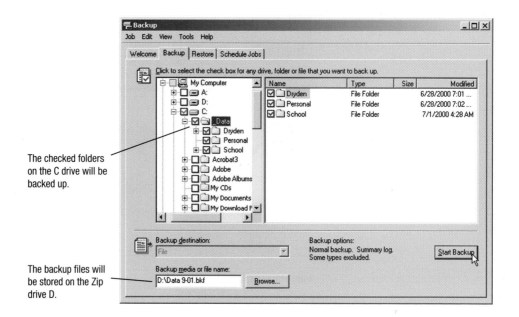

⊜ **FIGURE 6-17**

Backing up a hard disk.
Most backup utilities, such as
the Windows Backup program
shown here, allow you to back
up an entire hard drive or just
specific folders and files.

The checked folders
on the C drive will be
backed up.

The backup files will
be stored on the Zip
drive D.

Backup Utilities

Backup utilities are programs designed to back up the contents of a hard drive. You can back
up an entire drive or merely selected directories and files. Most serious backup systems
store the back-up copies on magnetic tape, rewritable optical discs, Zip disks, Jaz disks, or
some other removable high-capacity medium. Many users rely on the backup utilities supplied by their disk- or tape-drive makers; others use the back-up utility included with their
operating system, as in Figure 6-17. Using the Internet for backup is becoming another
popular option, especially for storing duplicates of important selected files.

Uninstall Utilities

When programs are *uninstalled* (removed from the hard drive), small pieces of programs
can be left behind on the hard drive or in system files. If programs are removed by deleting
the program's folder without using an *uninstall utility,* a huge amount of extraneous data can
accumulate on the hard drive over time. Uninstall utilities remove the programs themselves,
along with all references to those programs in your system files. Some uninstall capabilities
are built into most operating systems, uninstall utility programs are available as stand-alone
programs, and sometimes an uninstall routine is included in a program's folder when that
program is originally installed.

Occasionally, uninstall utilities can remove files that are also used by other programs
remaining on your system. Be cautious when uninstalling programs. If an uninstall utility
asks you whether to keep or delete a system file (such as a .dll file), it is safer to always
keep it.

Disk Defragmentation Programs

Disk defragmentation programs—also called *disk optimizers*—rearrange data and programs
on the hard drive so that they can be accessed faster. They do this primarily by consolidating
fragmented files, that is, rewriting related blocks of programs and data that have become
physically separated on the disk into contiguous (adjacent) sectors for faster access.

A file becomes fragmented when it's too large to be stored in contiguous clusters on a
disk. When this happens, the file is split and stored in noncontiguous locations, which
lengthens the time required to retrieve and save the file. When a disk becomes highly fragmented, a defragmentation utility can be used to rearrange the files and free space on your

**further
exploration**

For links to further information
about utility programs, go to
www.course.com/parker2002/ch6

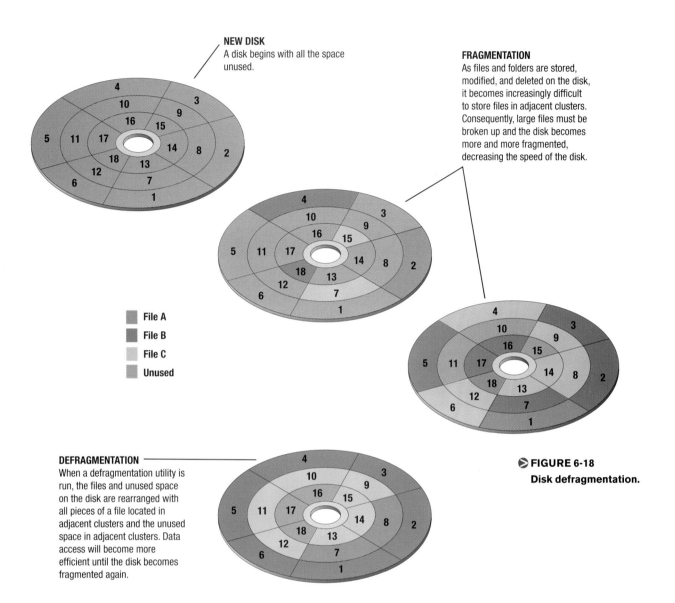

NEW DISK
A disk begins with all the space unused.

FRAGMENTATION
As files and folders are stored, modified, and deleted on the disk, it becomes increasingly difficult to store files in adjacent clusters. Consequently, large files must be broken up and the disk becomes more and more fragmented, decreasing the speed of the disk.

File A
File B
File C
Unused

DEFRAGMENTATION
When a defragmentation utility is run, the files and unused space on the disk are rearranged with all pieces of a file located in adjacent clusters and the unused space in adjacent clusters. Data access will become more efficient until the disk becomes fragmented again.

▶ **FIGURE 6-18**
Disk defragmentation.

disk, so that all files are stored in contiguous locations and free space is consolidated into a single block. Figure 6-18 shows how such a utility consolidates fragmented files. Many operating systems have their own defragmentation utilities.

File Compression Programs

File compression programs enable files to be stored in a smaller amount of storage space. This helps to free up disk space and to speed transmissions of files over networks, such as over the Internet. Sending compressed files over a network requires the receiver to run the appropriate decompression program to return the file to its original state. For convenience, some compression programs allow the file to be made executable to be decompressed automatically upon execution. Data compression is also commonly used as a space-saving strategy during system backups.

Data compression has become a relatively hot topic in recent years, largely because of two trends: the popularity of multimedia applications and the ever-increasing use of the Internet. Color graphics, sound, and video all consume a great deal of storage space. These types of files can be decreased tremendously in size by various compression algorithms. Image files often are *zipped* using such programs as *WinZip* (see Figure 6-19) for Windows

web tutor

For a tutorial on the file compression, go to www.course.com/ parker2002/ch6

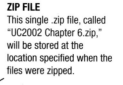

FIGURE 6-19

File compression. File compression can be used with both image and text files, though image files generally compress more efficiently.

ZIP FILE
This single .zip file, called "UC2002 Chapter 6.zip," will be stored at the location specified when the files were zipped.

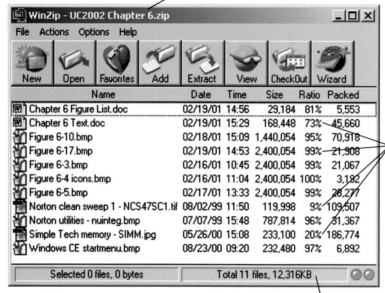

COMPRESSION RATIOS
Certain file formats (such as .bmp) compress more than others (such as .tif and .jpg). Text files (such as .doc) fall somewhere in between.

FILE SIZE
The 11 files, totaling over 12 MB, are zipped into a single 520 KB .zip file.

further exploration

For links to further information about compression programs, go to www.course.com/parker2002/ch6

users and *Stuffit* for Mac users. Typically, compression programs can compress either single or multiple files into a single compressed file. When multiple files are compressed, they are separated back into individual files when the file is decompressed.

Though compression programs are most commonly used with image, sound, video, or program files, large text files may benefit from compression, as well. For an explanation of how text compression works, see the How It Works box.

THE FUTURE OF OPERATING SYSTEMS

The future configuration of operating systems is anyone's guess, but it is expected that they will keep getting more user-friendly and, eventually, be driven primarily by a voice interface. They should also keep becoming more stable and self-healing, repairing or restoring system files as needed, and support multiple processors and other technological improvements.

With the pervasiveness of the Internet, operating systems in the future may be used primarily to access software available through the Internet or other networks, instead of accessing software on the local device. Operating systems in the future should also support on-the-fly networking, such as with the *Bluetooth* technology discussed in a later chapter, so all of the information devices a person uses in his or her life can communicate and be synchronized. Much of the progress in operating systems may evolve around mobile devices, such as smart phones and handheld PCs.

Text Compression

Even though storage capacities of ordinary desktop systems are now in the multigigabyte range—an unimaginable threshold until recently—many users still feel pinched by limitations on storage space. This is particularly the case when large files need to be transferred to a removable medium or sent over the Internet. MP3 compression for music files was discussed in Chapter 3 and image compression is discussed in some detail in Chapter 10. Here, we cover one other type of compression application: text files.

Though text files are generally smaller than multimedia files, and need to be compressed less frequently, the extra overhead added by word processing programs precludes placing more than a few large files on a conventional floppy disk. This, combined with the ease of transferring multiple files over the Internet if they are temporarily combined into one compressed file, has led text compression to be more widely used than ever before.

There are similarities between most types of compression. File compression programs typically try to eliminate redundant information, either by discarding unneeded information or substituting smaller size pieces of data for larger repeated chunks. For example, the phrase in the accompanying illustration contains 40 characters, with several repeated patterns. Substituting a single character for these patterns halves the number of characters needed to convey the phrase. To decode this message, the compression program also has to transmit some type of dictionary or key identifying the compression symbols and the character strings they are being substituted for. If this was the only phrase being compressed, the space saving would be minimal once the 16-character dictionary was added, but, assuming these strings could be used throughout the entire document, the space savings could be enormous.

Though some image formats compress more efficiently (think of a blue line being represented by a single blue pixel and the number 600 to indicate that the color should repeat for 600 pixels), in most languages, certain letters and words often appear together in the same pattern. This results in text files compressing relatively well. A reduction of 50 percent or more is typical—enabling a 3 MB file to fit on a single 1.44 MB floppy disk.

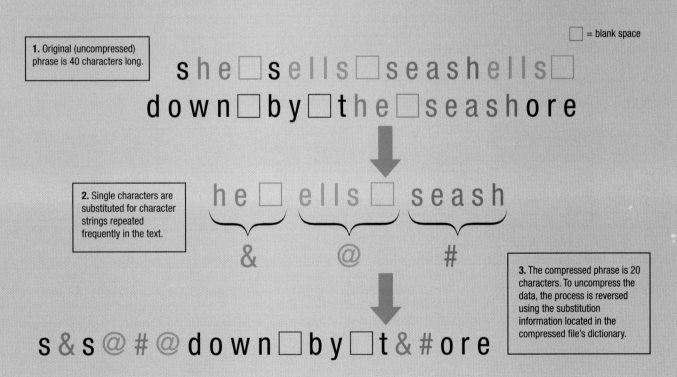

□ = blank space

1. Original (uncompressed) phrase is 40 characters long.

she□sells□seashells□ down□by□the□seashore

2. Single characters are substituted for character strings repeated frequently in the text.

he□ ells□ seash
&   @   #

3. The compressed phrase is 20 characters. To uncompress the data, the process is reversed using the substitution information located in the compressed file's dictionary.

s&s@#@down□by□t&#ore

SYSTEMS SOFTWARE VS. APPLICATION SOFTWARE

Chapter Objective 1:
Understand the difference between application software and systems software.

Systems software consists of the programs that coordinate the activities of a computer system. The basic role of systems software is to act as a mediator between application programs and the computer system's hardware, as well as between the PC and the user. In contrast, application software enables the computer to perform a specific task on the computer, such as word processing, playing a game, preparing taxes, browsing the Web, etc.

THE OPERATING SYSTEM

Chapter Objective 2:
Explain the different functions of an operating system and discuss some ways that operating systems can differ from one another.

A computer's **operating system** is the primary systems software program that manages the computer system's resources and interfaces with the user. The functions of the operating system include **booting** up the computer, configuring devices and **device drivers,** communicating with the user, making computer-system resources available for use, scheduling jobs for processing, monitoring activities, file management, and security.

Some of the differences between operating systems center around the type of interface used, whether it is a **personal operating system** designed for individual users or a **network operating system** designed for multiple users, and the types and numbers of processors supported.

To manage the enormous collection of files typically found on a hard drive, the operating system commonly allows the user to organize files hierarchically into **folders (directories).** To access a file in any directory, the user can specify the *path* that leads through intervening folders/directories to the file.

Chapter Objective 3:
List several ways in which operating systems can enhance processing efficiency.

Computers often enhance efficiency by implementing interleaved processing techniques. **Multitasking** allows concurrent execution of two or more programs from a single user; **time-sharing** is a technique in which the operating system cycles through all active programs currently running in the system that need processing, giving a small slice of time on each cycle to each one; and **multiprocessing** and *parallel processing* involve using two or more CPUs to perform work at the same time. *Virtual memory* strategies can be used to employ disk storage to extend conventional memory and *spooling* frees the CPU from time-consuming interaction with I/O devices such as printers.

OPERATING SYSTEMS FOR DESKTOP PCS AND SERVERS

Chapter Objective 4:
Name today's most widely used operating systems for desktop PCs and servers and highlight the strengths and weaknesses of each.

One of the original operating systems for PCs was **DOS,** which is still in existence, but not widely used. Some of today's more commonly operating systems for desktop PCs and servers include **Windows,** Mac OS, Unix, Linux, and NetWare.

Windows 3.x, an *operating environment,* added a GUI shell to DOS that replaced its command line interface with a system of menus, icons, and screen boxes called *windows. Windows 95, Windows 98,* and **Windows Millennium Edition (Me)**—all successors to Windows 3.*x*—free the user from the limitations of working with DOS and include an increasing number of enhancements, such as *multitasking;* a better user interface; and more Internet, multimedia, and communications functions. **Windows NT** and its successor, **Windows 2000,** are primarily network operating systems that can also be used with powerful desktop PCs. The successor to all desktop and server Windows versions is **Windows XP.**

Mac OS is the operating system native to Apple computers. **Unix** is a flexible, general-purpose network operating system that works on mainframes, midrange computers, PCs that act as network servers, graphics workstations, and even desktop PCs. A version of Unix called **Linux** has gathered popularity because it is distributed free over the Internet and can be used as an alternative to Windows. Linux has earned support as more of a mainstream operating system in recent years and is being used in all sizes of computer systems, from desktop PCs to supercomputers. **NetWare** is an operating system specifically designed to manage the activities of server computers on local area networks (LANs) and *OS/2 Warp* is an operating system designed by IBM for some high-end PCs.

OTHER OPERATING SYSTEMS

There are other operating systems for desktop and server PCs that can be used, instead of the ones already discussed. Two examples are *BeOS* and *Solaris*. In addition, devices other than desktop and server PCs—such as handheld PCs, PDAs, smart phones, Internet appliances, and larger computers— also require some type of operating system to function. These operating systems are frequently different than those used with desktop PCs.

For mobile devices, mobile versions of Windows, such as *Windows CE,* and **Palm OS** (the operating system designed for Palm handheld PCs) are two of the most widely used. Other possibilities for handheld PCs and smart phones include the *Symbian platform,* designed around the *EPOC* operating system, and proprietary programs designed for a specific device.

Internet appliances may run a standard desktop or mobile operating system or may use a proprietary system. Larger computers tend to use a version of Unix or an operating system designed for that specific computer, though many are beginning to use Linux as an alternative.

Chapter Objective 5:
State several other devices besides desktop PCs and servers that require an operating system and list one possible operating system for each type of device.

MYTHS ABOUT OPERATING SYSTEMS

There are several prevailing myths about operating systems, including that you can have only one operating system, that it is difficult to change operating systems, and that if you don't use Windows, there isn't much available software. These myths may have originated in part because people were intimidated by their PCs and operating systems and there was generally not much choice of operating systems for any one type of computer. With the increased use of a variety of operating systems for any one PC, these myths may become less prominent in the future.

Chapter Objective 6:
Understand why several myths about operating systems are not correct.

UTILITY PROGRAMS

A **utility program** is a type of systems software program written to perform specific repetitive processing tasks often involving some type of system maintenance. *Diagnostic programs* deal primarily with diagnosing and repairing disk-related problems. *Backup utilities* allow users to back up the contents of their hard drive. *Uninstall utilities* allow programs to be removed from a hard drive without leaving annoying remnants behind, *disk defragmentation* programs rearrange the contents of a hard drive to return all pieces of a single file to a contiguous section of the drive, and *file compression* programs reduce the stored size of files so they can be more easily archived or sent over the Internet.

Chapter Objective 7:
Detail the role of utility programs and outline several duties that these programs can perform.

THE FUTURE OF OPERATING SYSTEMS

In the future, operating systems will likely become even more user-friendly, voice-driven, and stable, repairing themselves when needed and causing errors and conflicts much less frequently.

Chapter Objective 8:
Speculate about what the operating systems of the future may be like.

Instructions: Match each key term on the left with the definition on the right that fits best.

1. boot

———— A type of operating system designed for single users.

2. folder

———— A type of operating system designed to support multiple users over a network.

3. Linux

———— To start up a computer.

4. Mac OS

———— A logical named location on a storage medium into which files can be stored to keep the medium organized.

5. NetWare

———— A long-standing operating system for midrange computers and high-end PCs.

6. network operating system

———— A program that performs some frequently encountered operation in a computer system, usually related to managing the computer's resources.

7. operating system

———— A version of Unix that is available without charge over the Internet.

8. Palm OS

———— Programs, such as the operating system, that control the operation of a computer and its devices, as well as enable application programs to run on the computer system.

9. personal operating system

———— The earlier version of the operating system designed by Microsoft Corporation for both high-end single user and network applications that was replaced by Windows 2000.

10. systems software

11. Unix

———— The latest version of Windows; designed to replace both Windows Me and Windows 2000.

12. utility program

———— The main piece of systems software that enables the computer to manage it activities and the resources under its control, run application programs, and interface with the user.

13. Windows

———— The most widely used operating systems for PC-based local area networks (LANs).

14. Windows 2000

———— The operating system for Apple's Macintosh line of computers.

15. Windows Millennium Edition (Me)

———— The operating system used with Palm handheld PCs.

16. Windows NT

———— The primary PC operating system developed by Microsoft Corporation; common versions include Windows 95, Windows 98, Windows 2000, and Windows Me.

17. Windows XP

———— The upgrade to Windows 98.

———— The upgrade to Windows NT.

Answers for the self-quiz appear at the end of the book.

True/False

Instructions: Circle **T** if the statement is true or **F** if the statement is false.

T F **1.** Microsoft Windows 2000 is an example of an application software program.

T F **2.** Multiprocessing techniques can help increase the efficiency of a computer system.

T F **3.** The principal reason so many people like Unix is that it is much easier to use than competing operating systems.

T F **4.** Windows 2000 is commonly used on handheld PCs and mobile devices.

T F **5.** A single computer can have more than one operating system installed.

Completion

Instructions: Answer the following questions.

6. Files can be stored inside _____ on a hard drive to keep them organized.

7. With _____, more than one task is processed concurrently, while with _____, more than one task is processed simultaneously.

8. _____ is the version of Unix available for free over the Internet.

9. When a file is _____, it is physically located in nonadjacent sections of the storage medium.

10. To decrease the size of a file, a(n) _____ utility program can be used.

1. List one operating system that uses a command line interface and one that uses a graphical user interface. Which type of interface would you expect most users to prefer and why?

2. Match up each of the following list of devices with the most appropriate operating system for each device.

_____ Home PC
_____ Mainframe computer
_____ Apple iMac
_____ Large business local area network
_____ High-end business computer
_____ Handheld PC

a. Mac OS
b. NetWare
c. Windows Me
d. Windows 2000
e. Palm OS
f. Unix

3. For the following path, identify the drive the document is located on, the name of the file, and whether or not the document is stored inside a folder. If the file is stored inside one or more folders, list the folder name(s).

   C:\My Documents\Resume

4. What type of devices is Palm OS designed for?

5. What type of utility program can be used to make a duplicate copy of your hard drive?

**Short Answer/
Research**

1. **Clear-Cut?** Many operating systems include a set of application software components as part of the operating system. These components are included to allow the user to perform some basic tasks without having to purchase an expensive application program. For this project, identify what application software components are included with the latest version of the personal versions of both Mac OS and Windows. Which of these components would be the most useful to you? Was a Web browser application component included with the operating system? At the conclusion of your research, prepare a one-page summary of your findings and submit it to your instructor.

2. **Cross Platform?** As discussed in the chapter, systems software enables application software to work with the computer system's hardware. Since application software depends on systems software, and systems software depends on the hardware configuration, not all applications run on all hardware platforms. In order to deal with this issue, some software vendors sell at least two versions of their software program: one designed to run under the Macintosh operating system, and one designed to run under Windows. For this project, identify at least four application programs and determine if each program is sold in a Mac OS, Windows, or cross-platform (can run on both operating systems) version. Be sure to indicate the version number of the software program and which specific operating systems version each program is compatible with. It might also be interesting to note the specific hardware requirements (CPU, RAM amount, hard drive space, etc.) during this task. At the conclusion of your research, prepare a one-page summary of your findings and submit it to your instructor.

3. **Compression** As described in the chapter, a compression program can be used to make more efficient use of disk space and speed up the delivery of files over networks (especially the Internet). The most common compression programs create files with the file extensions .zip, .sit, .tar, and .exe. These compression programs are operating system dependent and often allow you to create both compressed files and self-extracting compressed files. Self-extracting files automatically decompress when you download and open them, while compressed files must be decompressed by running a version of the program that compressed them. For this project, identify the compression programs associated with each of the file extensions listed above and determine which extensions represent a self-extracting format, and which extensions are associated with the Unix, Windows, and MacOS operating systems. In addition, you should determine how you would go about getting and installing a copy of the appropriate compression program for the type of computer you use most often. At the conclusion of your research, prepare a one-page summary of your findings and submit it to your instructor.

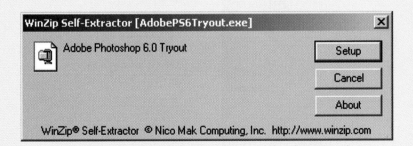

4. **Your System Properties** Before you purchase software or make a determination about upgrading your computer system, you should first find out about your current operating system and its performance settings. In most operating systems, the operating system settings can be viewed by

Hands On

opening the Control Panel (in Windows, it is available through the Settings option of the Start menu). For this project, investigate the operating system settings for the computer you use most often. Try to determine any network information (user name, computer name, etc.), name and version of the operating system being used, and any virtual memory settings. Also use the Device Manager option of the Control Panel to discover the name of the installed mouse. At the conclusion of this task, prepare a one-page summary of your efforts and submit it to your instructor.

Writing About Computers

5. **Time to Upgrade?** Assume that your computer currently has an operating system that is more than two years old and that you are considering upgrading to a newer version. In the process of determining whether or not to upgrade, you decide to do a little research on the hardware requirements and performance characteristics of the newest operating systems. During this research, you want to make sure that the newer version will run on your PC, work with your existing software and hardware, and have enough features to justify the purchase price. For this project, research the operating system upgrades available for the computer system that you use most often and determine if one of them would be appropriate for you. Submit this project to your instructor in the form of a short paper, not more than two pages in length.

6. **New and Improved** Newer versions of each of the popular operating systems are released on a regular basis (sometimes annually). When a software company makes significant changes to the functions and/or capabilities of an operating system it releases the program under a new version number or name. If the company wants to release a revised copy of the same version to resolve problems that have been identified and fixed, it keeps the version number the same and makes the software available under a different edition or release number. For example, Windows 98 is available in a second edition. For this project, identify the current release or edition number for three of the most popular operating systems currently sold today. In addition, you should visit the Web site for each of these operating systems and identify two of the latest software downloads that are designed to fix a problem discovered after the software was released. Are there any system software downloads that you need to download and install on the computer that you use most often? Submit this project to your instructor in the form of a short paper, not more than two pages in length.

7. **Is Linux for You?** As discussed in the chapter, Linux is a Unix-type operating system that you can download and install for free. It was originally developed by young student, Linus Torvalds (see accompanying photo), at the University of Helsinki in Finland, who released it to the public domain as open source freeware. Since that time, the operating system has become very powerful and picked up the support of many large software and hardware companies. This support has allowed Linux to make significant inroads into the mainstream operating system market. Some of the most common reservations about switching to the Linux operating system are that there are

very few application programs that currently run under this operating system, you may not be able to get support for the operating system if you have problems, and many hardware companies do not currently support this operating system. For this project, form a group to research the Linux operating system and determine if it is currently feasible for the average student to switch from one of the more popular Windows operating systems to Linux. What would the advantages be? The disadvantages? Be sure to address common reservations listed above, and well as the various options for obtaining Linux (a free version or a commercial version from a company such as Caldera or Red Hat). Also include any other issues your group feels are appropriate. Your group should submit this project to your instructor in the form of a short paper, not more than three pages in length.

**Presentation/
Demonstration**

8. **Plug-and-Play?** Newer operating systems are said to be true "plug-and-play." This means that you should be able to plug in a hardware device and it should play (work) without you having to load any special software or go through any special set-up procedure. Since this process does not always work, plug-and-play has been informally dubbed "plug-and-pray" by some. The plug-and-play concept works best when you are adding common hardware to your system that was developed and widely available prior to the purchase date of your computer. However, if you are trying to add a newer hardware device to an older operating system, or are updating to a newer operating system after you have added several peripheral devices to your existing system, you may be in situation where "plug-and-pray" would be the more appropriate phrase. For this project, assume that you are trying to add some additional hardware devices to the system and that the plug-and-play capability of the operating system is not recognizing the hardware. Form a group to discuss what you should do to resolve the problem. Be sure to discuss the possibility that you no longer have the original installation disks that came with the hardware devices and determine what options are available to you through the Internet. Your group should prepare a short presentation of your findings and recommendations. This presentation should not exceed 5 minutes and should make use of one or more presentation aids such as the chalkboard, handouts, overhead transparencies, or computer-based slide presentation format. Your group may be asked to submit a summary of the presentation to your instructor.

9. **O/S Bugs** No matter which operating system you have, it's likely you will eventually need to get some help resolving a system-related hardware or software problem. Support for most popular operating systems includes the following: searchable knowledge bases, download centers, technical support phone numbers and e-mail addresses, online support requests or chats, FAQs, and user discussion groups. For this project, research operating system support options and prepare a short presentation that explains each of the ones listed above, how you would use them, and where to start first. Be sure to include which options are currently available for the most recent personal version of Mac OS and Windows, and provide examples of how to use each of them. This presentation should not exceed 10 minutes and should make use of one or more presentation aids such as the chalkboard, handouts, overhead transparencies, or computer-based slide presentation format. You may be asked to submit a summary of the presentation.

10. **OS Evolution** From DOS in the early '70s to Windows 2000 and Mac OS X, personal operating systems have evolved from straightforward command-line interfaces to complex graphical user interfaces that can support a multiple-user network. For this project, form a group to research the development of personal operating systems to date. Your group should prepare a short presentation of your findings that highlight some of the important dates, people, companies, events, capabilities, and issues that have played a role in this development. Be sure to include some of the alternative operating systems in your presentation and the reasons your group thinks that some of these alternative systems will succeed or fail in the future. This presentation should not exceed 10 minutes and should make use of one or more presentation aids such as the chalkboard, handouts, overhead transparencies, or computer-based slide presentation format. Your group may be asked to submit a summary of the presentation to your instructor.

**Interactive
Discussion**

11. **Bundle, Integrate, or Neither** Microsoft was accused of unfair business practices when it integrated its Web browser into its operating system. Opponents of Microsoft felt it should not be permitted to bundle the browser with its operating systems, give it away for free, or integrate it into the operating system in ways that are unavailable to other firms, as this would lead to an unfair competitive advantage and eliminate the competition in the browser market. Proponents contended that the browser is in integral part of the operating system, not a separate application, and is a natural progression in the evolution of the operating system.

    Select one of the following positions, or make up your own, and express your point of view on the subject. Your instructor will indicate whether your response is to be posted to a class bulletin board, discussed in a class chat room, or discussed as an in-class activity. You may also be asked to submit a summary of your position and point of view.

a. Companies like Microsoft should not be permitted to bundle software with their operating systems, give it away for free, or integrate it with the operating system in ways that are unavailable to other firms, as this would lead to an unfair competitive advantage and eliminate the competition in the software market. The government was correct in labeling Microsoft a monopoly so that it can keep a closer watch on it in the future.

b. Companies like Microsoft should be allowed to bundle or integrate software with the operating system, as this is a natural progression in the evolution of the operating system and is necessary to remain competitive in a rapidly evolving market. The government had no business interfering and should not have labeled Microsoft a monopoly.

12. **OS Dominance** Consider the following statement and establish your position, or point of view, on the subject. Your instructor will indicate whether your response is to be posted to a class bulletin board, discussed in a class chat room, or discussed as an in-class activity. You may also be asked to submit a summary of your position and evaluation of the statement.

Microsoft Corporation has dominated the personal operating system market for many years and, because of this, enjoys a significant advantage over other software companies in the application software development market. The advantage Microsoft enjoys is based on its ability to tailor the operating system to work best with Microsoft applications, and limit the disclosure of its OS technology so that competitors could not make products that would work as smoothly with Microsoft's operating systems. In addition, Microsoft has been accused of taking actions that knowingly interfere with the performance of competitors' products. The dominance of Microsoft software (both application and operating system software) has both positive and negative effects on the consumers. It has been argued in a court of law that Microsoft should be split into two companies: One that would sell operating systems and another that would sell application software.

Interactive Exercise

Understanding System Software. It's time to practice using Windows and Windows utilities! Go to the Interactive Exercise at www.course.com/parker2002/ch6 to complete this exercise.

OUTLINE

Application Software

LEARNING OBJECTIVES

After completing this chapter, you will be able to:

1. Describe what application software is and some of the characteristics of a software suite.

2. Discuss word processing and identify the basic operations involved in creating, editing, and formatting documents.

3. Explain the purpose of spreadsheet software and identify the basic operations involved in creating, editing, and formatting worksheets.

4. Identify some of the vocabulary used with database software and discuss the basic operations involved with creating, editing, and retrieving information from a database.

5. Describe what presentation graphics are and how they are created.

6. List several other types of application software programs and discuss what functions they perform.

Overview

Today's computer users choose among thousands of software products that perform a wide range of different tasks. Users can buy software to write letters, keep track of their finances, send electronic mail and schedule meetings, learn a foreign language, entertain themselves, create music and movies, manage a business's inventory, create greeting cards and flyers, make business presentations, process orders, and hundreds of other applications. These types of software programs–those designed to carry out specific tasks–are classified as **application software.**

To begin, we explore the benefits of software suites and consider such topics as proprietary software, shareware, freeware, and how to get help while you are using a software program.

Next we briefly discuss the following four primary application programs.

▼ *Word processing software*–allows users to efficiently create, edit, and print the type of documents that would have been created on a typewriter in the past.

▼ *Spreadsheet software*–a convenient means of performing calculations that all businesspeople should be familiar with.

▼ *Database software*–allows users to store and organize vast amounts of data and retrieve information when needed.

▼ *Presentation graphics software*–designed to present business data in a visually oriented, easily understood way.

These application programs are sometimes referred to as *productivity software.* The chapter concludes with a look at a few other types of application software not previously discussed. ■

THE BASICS OF APPLICATION SOFTWARE

When you use any type of application software program, such as a word processor, to type a letter or a tax preparation program to prepare your taxes, there are some basic concepts and functions you need to be familiar with. These include common document-handling tasks, the concept of the software suite, ownership rights for the software you use, and how to get help while you work with the program. These topics are discussed in the next few sections.

Document-Handling Operations

While some document-handling operations are specific for a particular application program, some—such as the concept of opening a document, saving it, and printing it—are fairly universal. A few of the most common document-handling operations are described in Figure 7-1, with examples of the icons used to perform the operations in Windows' applications.

>**Application software.** Software programs that enable users to perform specific tasks or applications on a computer.

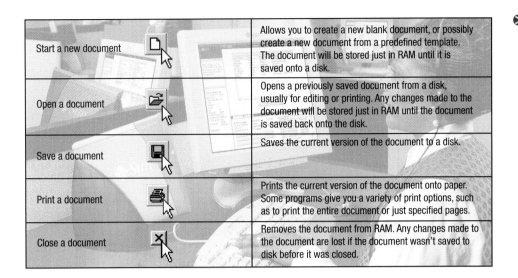

Start a new document		Allows you to create a new blank document, or possibly create a new document from a predefined template. The document will be stored just in RAM until it is saved onto a disk.
Open a document		Opens a previously saved document from a disk, usually for editing or printing. Any changes made to the document will be stored just in RAM until the document is saved back onto the disk.
Save a document		Saves the current version of the document to a disk.
Print a document		Prints the current version of the document onto paper. Some programs give you a variety of print options, such as to print the entire document or just specified pages.
Close a document		Removes the document from RAM. Any changes made to the document are lost if the document wasn't saved to disk before it was closed.

> **FIGURE 7-1**
> **Common document-handling tasks.**

In general, the commands to perform these operations are the same or very similar in all GUI programs. Because almost everyone needs fast access to document-handling commands, these operations are usually located on easy-to-reach menus or toolbars.

Software Suites

Most office-oriented programs, such as word processors and spreadsheets, are sold bundled together with other related application software in a **software suite.** The dominant leader in suite sales for office application is *Microsoft Office.* The high-end edition of this package bundles *Word* (for word processing), *Excel* (for spreadsheet work), *PowerPoint* (for presentation graphics), *Access* (for database management), together with several other programs such as *FrontPage* (for Web site development). Office is available for both Windows and Mac OS users. Similar suites are available from Corel (*WordPerfect Office* for Windows and Linux users) and Lotus (*SmartSuite* for Windows and OS/2 users). In addition, Sun's StarOffice suite gives Windows, Mac OS, Linux, and Solaris users a free alternative (see Figure 7-2).

Most software suites are revised continuously, with a new version being released every year or two, which can result in a high level of stress for those involved with the software development process. Both management and employees at high-tech companies like Microsoft often enjoy engaging in occasional on-the-job antics to let off stress, as described in the Inside the Industry box.

> **FIGURE 7-2**
> **Software suites.** The most common software suites are Microsoft Office, Corel Word-Perfect Office, and Lotus SmartSuite. A free alternative is the Sun StarOffice suite.

>**Software suite.** A collection of software programs bundled together and sold as a single package.

inside the industry

Lake Bill

Microsoft Corporation's headquarters is a campus of more than two dozen buildings located within easy reach of Seattle. On that campus is a small body of water that goes by the name of Lake Bill. Weird moniker? Not really. Bill is the first name of Microsoft's founder and chairman Bill Gates. We've got lakes named after presidents, animals, and birds, and even a bunch of pioneers who ate each other in the Sierra Nevada back in the 1840s. So why not one of the richest men in the world?

As you may have guessed, being surrounded by a lot of creative people who are regularly under deadline pressures, Lake Bill has occasionally been the site of manic merriment. Some few years ago, a manager in the Windows NT group bet another manager that his team would finish coding on time. If he lost, he promised to swim Lake Bill in a woman's swimsuit. While he did lose, he raised the ante by promising that his whole team would swim if a later date was missed. Fortunately for both the manager and his team, they finished the work on time.

If you think swimming Lake Bill is an activity confined to low-level personnel, think again. Several years back, Steve Ballmer—then a vice president and now CEO of Microsoft—

made a bet with another vice president that would have the loser swimming the lake. Both lost, so both had to swim. On the chilly day the two arrived at the lake, they discovered a bunch of thoughtful programmers had stocked it with large chunks of dry ice. Just so they wouldn't overheat going across, right?

Microsoft Corporation headquarters.

Closely related to suites are *integrated software programs*—such as *Microsoft Works*—which are similar to a full suite, but are less powerful with more limited functionality. Thus, instead of including a full-featured word processor or spreadsheet, an integrated software package incorporates smaller versions of each, providing only their main features in a single package. Users in the home market usually do not miss the omitted capabilities and, since they are usually less expensive and require less storage and fewer other system resources to run than the full suite, these types of programs are often a good choice for the home user. It is also common for these types of suites to be preloaded on home PCs, instead of their full-suite counterparts.

Some of the advantages of using a software suite are discussed next.

Common Interface

Though, as mentioned earlier, most programs written for the same GUI operating system (such as Windows) use similar interfaces and commands, a software suite goes one step further. Usually the menu and toolbar structure is very similar from program to program in the suite—not just the basic commands (such as Save and Print), but all commands the programs have in common (such as adding borders and shading or inserting a row or column). This arrangement makes it easier to learn a new program in a suite, once you have some experience working with any of the other programs in that suite.

Document-Centered Computing

With recent versions of GUI operating systems, the trend has moved towards *document-centered computing,* where work centers around the document to be used, rather than the program used to create or modify it. For example, if you open an icon representing a document on your hard drive, the computer will automatically open the appropriate program to display the document, without asking you to specify what that program is. This is usually accomplished by looking at which *file extension* is appended to the file's filename. File extensions are generally three characters preceded by a period and are automatically added to a filename by program in which that file was created. Some common file extensions are listed in Figure 7-3. If the file to be opened does not have a file extension that your operating system recognizes, you are prompted to select the appropriate program to use with that file.

Application Integration and OLE

One of the biggest advantages to using a software suite is being able to transport or share documents or parts of documents from one program to another. For instance, let's say you are writing a letter in your word processing program, and you want to insert a spreadsheet table. You can launch (start) your spreadsheet program, locate the particular table you want in a stored worksheet, and then copy and paste the table into your letter—all without ever closing the word processing program (see Figure 7-4).

In addition to copying and pasting part of a document from one program to another, many software suites also allow you to *embed* or *link* objects created in one program into a second document. The two documents can be the same type (such as both spreadsheet documents) or can be entirely different (such as one word processing document and one spreadsheet document). With embedding, the object is physically stored in the second document, though double-clicking on the object will edit the object in its original program. With linking, however, only a copy of the object is displayed in the second document—the data displayed is obtained from the original object file. Consequently, whenever the document containing the embedded object is opened (such as the letter in Figure 7-4), the most recent version of the object (the spreadsheet, in this case) is displayed. As with embedded objects, double-clicking a linked object opens it in the appropriate program (in this case, the spreadsheet program) to be edited. This process, commonly referred to as *object linking and embedding* or *OLE,* preserves the capabilities the original program gives to the document, such as formulas and automatic formula calculation when numbers change in a spreadsheet program, as explained in more detail shortly.

Online Help

Most people run into problems or need some help with a feature as they work with a software program. To provide help without forcing you to leave your computer screen, most application programs have an *online help* feature. Programs employ a variety of tools to provide online assistance. Some of the possible configurations are illustrated in Figure 7-5 and listed next.

- ▼ *Table of Contents.* A table of contents in a help program works similarly to the table of contents in a book: Topics are organized under main topics, and then subtopics. With most help systems, selecting a topic reveals the available subtopics. Selecting a help topic displays that information on the screen.

- ▼ *Index.* An index in a help program works similarly to an index in a book: Typing a term scrolls the *index* (an alphabetical list of available topics) to that term, if it is contained in the index. Selecting a term displays the appropriate information on the screen.

- ▼ *Search.* When a search option is available, it works similarly to an index with one exception: While searching through an index reveals only help topics listed in the index, a help search feature usually lists all help screens containing the terms searched for. Therefore, a help search generally returns more help screens than searching for the same term using a help index feature. Similar to the other types of help, selecting a help topic displays that information on the screen.

WIDELY USED EXTENSIONS

DOCUMENTS
.doc .txt .htm .html .xls .mdb .ppt .rtf

PROGRAMS
.bat .com .exe

GRAPHICS
.bmp .tif .jpg .eps .gif .png .pcx

AUDIO
.wav .au .mp3 .snd .aif .mid .swf .dcr

VIDEO
.mpg .mov .avi .mpeg .rm

COMPRESSED FILES
.ace .zip .rar .sit .tar

◗ **FIGURE 7-3**

File extensions. File extensions are automatically added by virtually all programs when a file is created. These extensions are used to associate the file with that program so that the proper program will be opened to view the file when needed.

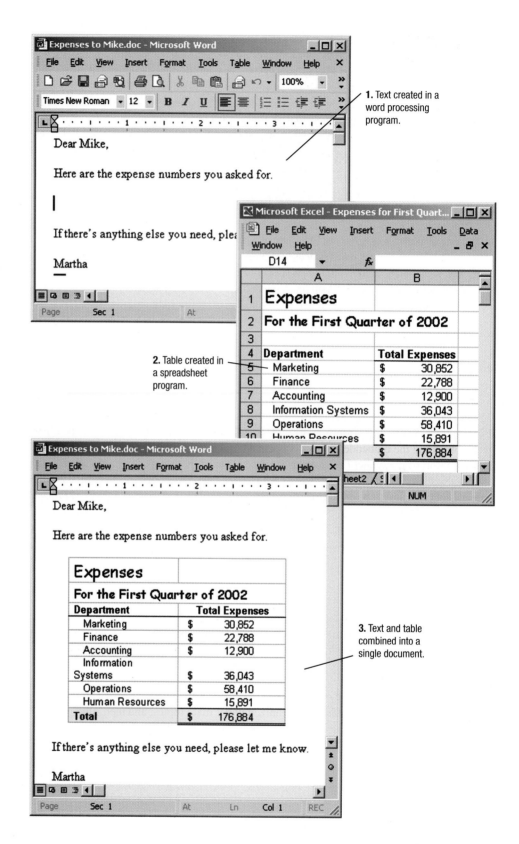

Application integration.
With a software suite, you
can create a single document
that contains information developed in two or more suite
applications—a process called
object linking and *embedding*.

1. Text created in a
word processing
program.

2. Table created in
a spreadsheet
program.

3. Text and table
combined into a
single document.

▼ *Natural-Language Help.* Many programs today supply a limited form of *natural-language help* to users—that is, help in which you type in a question and the help system tries to determine the topic for which assistance is required. For instance, in Microsoft Office, clicking the question-mark icon that's located on the standard

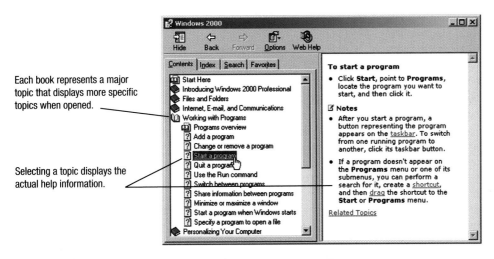

Each book represents a major topic that displays more specific topics when opened.

Selecting a topic displays the actual help information.

TABLE OF CONTENTS
A table-of-contents feature organizes help screens, into books by topic.

NATURAL LANGUAGE
Natural language help allows you to type questions in sentence format; appropriate help topics are then displayed.

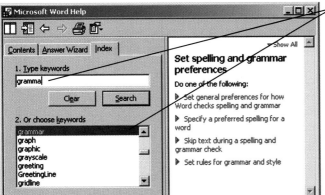

As you begin typing in a topic name, the list of topics changes correspondingly with each keystroke you press. When you see the topic you want, select it to display the matching information.

INDEX
An index feature lets you select a help topic from a large alphabetical list.

◗ FIGURE 7-5

Online help. Most application programs have online help available in one or more formats.

toolbar makes a text box pop up for you to type in a question. The help program then looks for keywords in the sentence you've entered and provides help topics based on what it believes may be the desired help topic.

▼ *Wizards.* A *wizard*—also called a *coach, assistant, tutor, expert,* and *advisor*—is a tool to guide you through a step-by-step procedure for completing a standard task, such as preparing a letter, invoice, report, fax, and the like. Wizards do this either by providing directed tutorials or by performing the difficult phases of a task automatically, using the input supplied by the user via some type of dialog box.

▼ *Tutorials and Tours.* Many software publishers provide tutorials or product tours that may be accessed from your hard drive, CD/DVD, or through a Web site, depending on the program used. These tutorials or tours enable you to do such things as learn how to use specific program features, as well as observe examples and demonstrations.

Ownership and Distribution Rights

Sensitive questions sometimes arise about ownership and user rights regarding software products. Typically, a software maker or publisher develops a program, secures a copyright on it, and then retains ownership of all rights to that program. The publisher then dictates who can use, copy, or distribute the program. The various classes of ownership and allowable use are discussed next.

Proprietary Software

Many of the systems software and application programs used today are *proprietary software.* This means that someone owns the rights to the program, and the owner expects users to buy their own copies.

Microsoft Office is a typical example. If you want to install this software on your PC, you must purchase a registered copy in a store, through a mail-order house, or over the Internet. In buying the software, you acquire a *license* that makes you an authorized user of the software. This license specifies such limitations as the number of PCs on which the software may be installed. Organizations such as businesses and schools, which may need software for use by several people, generally acquire *site licenses* or *network licenses* that allow the software to be installed on multiple computers or accessed by multiple users over a network.

If you buy a copy of Microsoft Office (or similar proprietary software) for your own use, you cannot legally make copies of it for your friends, nor can you install the software on their computer using your disks or CDs. You usually cannot even rent or lease the software to others. You have bought only the right to operate the software yourself and for its intended use—creating documents. Part of the price that you pay for the program becomes profit for the software publisher—such as Microsoft Corporation—for its efforts in bringing the product to the marketplace.

Instead of, or in addition to, offering proprietary software for sale, some software is available as Web-based applications. These applications can be accessed only via the Internet, and usually a monthly or yearly fee is charged for their use. One advantage to Web-based software is the programs and your files can be accessed from any PC with an Internet connection. Another is that the software may be updated on a regular basis for no additional cost to the user. For potential disadvantages, the cost may eventually exceed the cost of buying a similar shrink-wrapped package, and you can't access the program and your data when the server on which they reside goes down. Organizations that manage and distribute software over the Internet are referred to as *application service providers* or *ASPs.*

Along with its restrictions, licensed proprietary software generally brings many benefits, including quality, ongoing product support, and a large base of users. If, for instance, you buy a product from a well-known software maker such as Microsoft, Corel, or Lotus Development, you generally know that millions of dollars supported its creation, that the product will likely remain in use for several years, and that you can easily locate resources to help you learn more about that software, as necessary.

Usually to obtain product support or product updates, software publishers require you to register your software. An emerging trend for proprietary software vendors is to require software registration before the program can be used to ensure that only valid users are using their software.

Shareware

Some software is available as *shareware.* While you don't have to pay to install and try out shareware, most shareware specifies that you need to pay to continue to use the software after the trial period—often one month—expires. Your payment usually gives you access to any available support, such as written or online documentation, software updates, and technical help and advice. Though it is not illegal to use shareware past the specified trial period, it is ethical to either pay for the program or delete the program from your computer at that time.

Unlike proprietary software, it is usually permissible to make copies of shareware to distribute to your friends and colleagues. By allowing this, shareware authors hope that the people you share their programs with will like the program and pay for it—the more exposure their programs get, the better for the shareware authors. The Internet provides access to many shareware programs (see Figure 7-6).

Freeware

Freeware, or *public-domain software,* refers to programs that you can use and share with others free of charge. Who, you may ask, would want to give away software and not make so much as a dime off of it? Plenty of people, it so happens. College professors and graduate students are motivated to develop freeware because they are doing something academic institutions promote—advancing the state of the art of computer science and making new breakthroughs available as soon as possible to the public. Others may want to develop freeware just because it can be fun or because it provides excellent practice in honing one's

further exploration

For links to further information about application software, go to www.course.com/parker2002/ch7

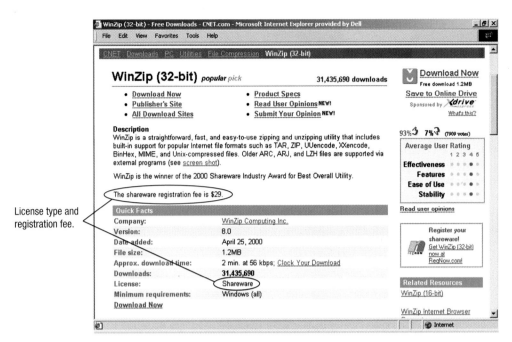

License type and registration fee.

Shareware. Both shareware and freeware are widely available via the Internet. Most shareware distribution sites disclose the allowable trial period and the registration fee, in any.

programming skills. Still others may want to encourage as many people as possible to test their software's marketability. If the freeware turns out to be popular, the developer may polish it up a bit and include documentation and support—and then turn around and sell the program for profit.

In recent years, even established software publishers have started embracing the freeware concept, giving it greater respectability with mainstream users. For example, Netscape and Microsoft both give away their browser software for free on the Internet. Also, users of office suites can often find several free applications that enhance working with suite components at their software publisher's Web site. The Sun StarOffice suite, as already mentioned, is a complete office suite currently available for free. Like shareware programs, freeware programs are widely available over the Internet.

A growing portion of the freeware available today is *open source software,* as the Trend box discusses.

WORD PROCESSING CONCEPTS

Word processing is one of the most widely used application programs today. Though the actual commands and features vary somewhat from program to program, it is important to be familiar with the basic features of word processing and the general concept of what word processing enables you to do. The following sections discuss these features and concepts, with illustrations from the Microsoft Word program.

What Is Word Processing Software?

Word processing refers to using computer technology to create, edit, save, and print written documents that generally contain a large amount of text, such as letters, legal contracts, manuscripts, newsletters, and reports. In general, word processing is used to do

web tutor

For a tutorial on word processing software, go to www.course.com/parker2002/ch7

>**Word processing.** A type of application program used to create, manipulate, and print written documents, such as letters, contracts, and manuscripts.

Open Source Software

The Software That Nobody Owns

Open source software is software for which the source code of the program is made available free of charge to the general public. The term *open source* came out of a strategy session held in 1998 in response to the announcement that Netscape was planning on giving away the source code to its browser. The individuals at this meeting coined the term and discussed strategies to take advantage of the window of opportunity following Netscape's announcement to sell the idea of open source software. This group led to the formation of the *Open Source Initiative (OSI),* a nonprofit corporation dedicated to managing and promoting the Open Source Definition. Software adhering to the definition must, among other things, allow everyone access to its source code, allow modifications of the source code, and not charge any royalties or fees if modified products are sold.

The rationale for the open source movement is that if a large group of programmers who are not concerned with financial gain work on the program, it will produce a more useful and bug-free product. These programmers read, redistribute, and modify the source code—a process that tends to eliminate bugs and improve the software at a much quicker rate than through the traditional commercial software development process.

Open source software has historically been very closely intertwined with both Unix and the Internet. In fact, the best known example of open source software is Linux—an operating system based on Unix and distributed through the Internet. The *GNU project,* started in 1983 by Richard Stallman at the Mass-

achusetts Institute of Technology, is another example. This project, which is pronounced "guh-NEW" and stands for "GNU's not Unix," is a Unix-compatible software system developed by the *Free Software Foundation (FSF).* Like Linux, GNU software is open source. Other examples of open source software include *Apache,* which runs over 50% of the world's Web servers; *FreeBSD,* another version of Unix; *GNOME* and *KDE,* Windows-like desktop environments for Unix workstations; and *Perl,* a scripting language commonly used with Web pages.

Though no one knows for sure the place of open source software in the future, all signs point toward its continued growing use and acceptance. Following the success of Linux, Netscape, Apple, Sun, Hewlett-Packard, and other large companies have released products with open source code. Who knows, there may come a day when virtually all software is owned by no one—or, consequently, everyone.

The stuffed penguin has become the mascot for Linux, the program that spearheaded the open source movement.

what was done on a typewriter before computers were commonplace, and then some. One of the greatest advantages of using word processing over a typewriter is that you can make changes without retyping the entire document, because the document is created and edited on the computer screen instead of typing it directly on paper. Consequently, it can be saved and retrieved from disk as many times as necessary, and can be modified, re-saved, and reprinted, as needed. Other advantages include the ability to insert drawings, photos, and other images into your documents, and add hyperlinks, video clips, and other multimedia items.

Virtually all formal writing today is performed using a word processing program. Among today's best-selling word processing programs are Microsoft's Word, Corel's WordPerfect, and Lotus's WordPro—all part of the software suites mentioned earlier in this chapter. Most word processing programs offer hundreds of features, but virtually all support a core group of features used to create, *edit,* and *format* documents. Some of these basic features are described in the next few sections.

Creating and Editing Documents

Every word processor contains an assortment of operations for creating and editing documents. Usually these operations allow for both text and graphic images to be inserted and moved, copied, or edited as needed.

Scrolling and Moving the Insertion Point

Virtually all word processors show a blinking vertical line character on the screen—called an **insertion point**—to designate where a newly entered character will appear (see Figure 7-7). To type new characters at that location, just start typing—the insertion point will move to the right as you type. To type characters at a different location, you must first move the insertion point (by pointing and clicking with the mouse or by using the arrow keys on the keyboard) to the appropriate location in the document. As the insertion point moves, the status bar at the bottom of the screen usually changes correspondingly to reflect the current position of the insertion point.

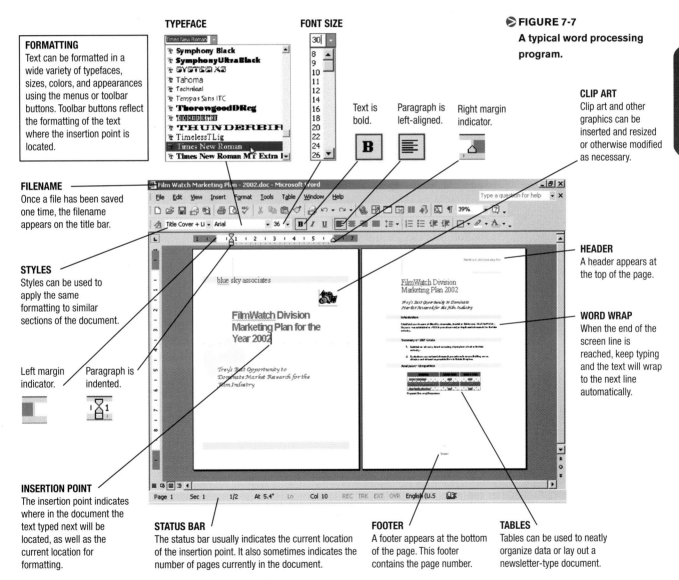

FIGURE 7-7
A typical word processing program.

TYPEFACE

FONT SIZE

FORMATTING
Text can be formatted in a wide variety of typefaces, sizes, colors, and appearances using the menus or toolbar buttons. Toolbar buttons reflect the formatting of the text where the insertion point is located.

Text is bold.

Paragraph is left-aligned.

Right margin indicator.

CLIP ART
Clip art and other graphics can be inserted and resized or otherwise modified as necessary.

FILENAME
Once a file has been saved one time, the filename appears on the title bar.

HEADER
A header appears at the top of the page.

STYLES
Styles can be used to apply the same formatting to similar sections of the document.

Left margin indicator.

Paragraph is indented.

WORD WRAP
When the end of the screen line is reached, keep typing and the text will wrap to the next line automatically.

INSERTION POINT
The insertion point indicates where in the document the text typed next will be located, as well as the current location for formatting.

STATUS BAR
The status bar usually indicates the current location of the insertion point. It also sometimes indicates the number of pages currently in the document.

FOOTER
A footer appears at the bottom of the page. This footer contains the page number.

TABLES
Tables can be used to neatly organize data or lay out a newsletter-type document.

Line Breaks and Paragraph Breaks

Typing on a conventional typewriter generally requires you to press the Return key to define the end of every line. Not so with a word processor. All word processors have a feature called **word wrap** that automatically returns the insertion point to the beginning of the next line when the end of the screen line is reached *without* the user pressing the Enter key (refer again to Figure 7-7). It is important to allow the computer to control these *line breaks* so that when changes are made to the document—such as adding or deleting text—the computer can continue to keep the appropriate amount of text on each line. If Enter is pressed (and a *paragraph break* is inserted) at the end of the screen line instead of allowing the computer to perform word wrap, there will always be a break at that location—even if more text is added to the line at a later time—until the paragraph break is deleted. Consequently, paragraph breaks should only be put in at the end of a paragraph or short line (such as the date or a closing), and to leave blank lines between paragraphs.

Editing Text

As mentioned earlier, to insert new text into a document, you need to move the insertion point to the appropriate location and then begin typing. To delete text one character at a time, either the Delete or Backspace key is used once the insertion point is properly positioned (the Delete key deletes one character to the right of the insertion point each time the key is pressed; the Backspace key deletes one character to the left each time it is pressed). Deleting a word, sentence, or block of text at a time can be done by first *selecting* the text to be deleted (by highlighting it with the mouse or holding the Shift key down and highlighting the text using the arrow keys on the keyboard) and then pressing either the Delete or Backspace key (see Figure 7-8).

Selecting text is also necessary when you want to move or copy text. *Moving* text physically moves some existing text to a new location in the document. *Copying* makes a duplicated copy at the new location, without removing the original text. To move or copy text, first select the text, then click either the Cut ✂ or Copy 📋 button on the toolbar. Move the insertion point to the desired new location, and then click the Paste 📋 toolbar button. You can also move text by selecting it and dragging it with the mouse.

The editing procedures discussed here apply to many other types of programs besides word processors.

Spell-Checking and Other Editing Tools

Most word processors have a variety of editing tools that allow you to check your spelling, compare two documents, and check your grammar, among other things. Some programs mark potentially misspelled words as you type; virtually all programs have an option to check the entire document for spelling. An important thing to realize is that words are considered misspelled if they are not in the program's dictionary. This means that a word may be spelled correctly (such as a proper name or technical term), may be marked as misspelled; or a word may not be marked as misspelled, but may be incorrect (such as "park" instead of "part"). To help correct these errors, many word processors include a grammar-checking feature. Another related feature incorporated into many word processors is a built-in thesaurus.

The find and replace features found in most word processing programs can also be extremely useful. The *find* operation lets you search automatically for all occurrences of a particular word or phrase. The *replace* operation gives you the option of changing that word or phrase to something else, such as one term or name in an entire document to another.

>**Word wrap.** The feature found in a word processing program that automatically returns the insertion point to the next line when reaching the end of the screen line, and keeps the proper amount of text on each line after the document is edited and formatted.

INSERTING TEXT

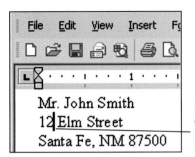

New text typed will appear at the insertion point's location.

DELETING TEXT

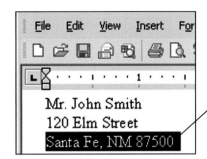

To delete text, select it with the mouse and press the Delete key on the keyboard.

MOVING TEXT

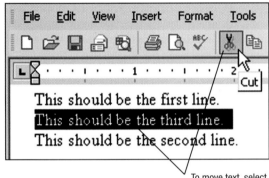

To move text, select it and click the Cut toolbar button.

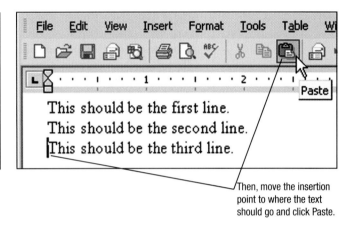

Then, move the insertion point to where the text should go and click Paste.

COPYING TEXT

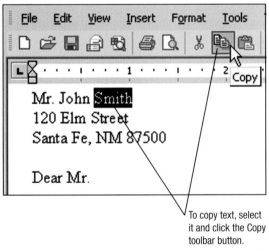

To copy text, select it and click the Copy toolbar button.

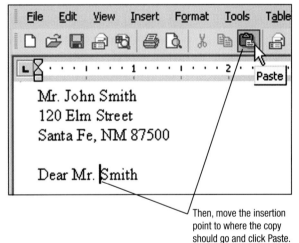

Then, move the insertion point to where the copy should go and click Paste.

> **FIGURE 7-8**
> **Editing text.**

Formatting Documents

While *editing* changes the actual content of a document, *formatting* changes the appearance of a document. Formatting can usually be applied at the character, paragraph, and document levels in word processing and other applications.

Character Formatting

Character formatting changes the appearance of individual characters. To format characters, they usually are first selected with the mouse, and then the appropriate format is applied. Common types of character formatting are *typeface, font size,* and *font style.*

A *typeface* is a named collection of text characters that share a common design, such as Arial or Times New Roman. The characters in a typeface are usually available in a wide variety of sizes called *point sizes*. All the characters in a particular typeface and point size are referred to as a *font;* for example, 12-point Times New Roman is a font. Figure 7-9 illustrates different typefaces and point sizes; changing the typeface and size was shown in Figure 7-7.

Paragraph Formatting

Paragraph formatting changes the appearance of entire paragraphs. Often it can be applied to the paragraph that the insertion point is in, without having to select the paragraph with the mouse first, though multiple paragraphs can usually be selected first to apply the formatting to all those paragraphs at one time. Common paragraph formats are *line spacing, margins, indentation, tabs, alignment,* and *styles.*

Line spacing controls the amount of blank space between lines of text. Usually it can be set to single-space or double-space, or to any fractional spacing supported by your printer. The left and right margins indicate how much blank space will be printed on the left and right edges of the paper. Most word processors allow you to view the margins either on the editing screen (as in Figure 7-7) or in a *preview mode.*

All word processing programs allow you to specify tabs and indention, usually applied on a paragraph-by-paragraph basis. Tab settings specify the locations that the insertion point will move to when the Tab key on the keyboard is pressed. Usually tabs are preset to every half inch across the document, though this setting can be changed by the user. With indentation, the left or right edge of the entire paragraph is moved over to the specified location. You can also indent just the first line of the paragraph, or indent all but the first line of the paragraph.

A paragraph's alignment or justification determines how the paragraph is aligned with the left and right margins of the document. Usually the options are left, right, center, or fully justified (flush with both the left and right edges of the document). For example, the document in Figure 7-7 is entirely left-justified and this textbook is fully-justified.

Paragraph *styles* are named format specifications that can be applied on a paragraph-by-paragraph basis to keep a uniform appearance for related sections in a document. For example, a report may include two levels of headings plus a variety of quotations. If a style (such as H1, H2, and QUOTE) is defined and applied to each occurrence of these parts of the report, they will have a consistent appearance. In addition, changing the specified format of a particular style (such as font, size, color, etc.) changes all text in the document identified as using that style.

Page and Document Formatting

Most word processors allow users to choose *page formatting* options, such as the top and bottom margins, the paper size being used, and whether you want the page to use the traditional *portrait* orientation (8½ inches wide by 11 inches tall on standard paper) or the wider *landscape* orientation (11 inches wide by 8½ inches tall on standard paper). You can also choose whether to include page numbers at the top or bottom of the page, usually as part of

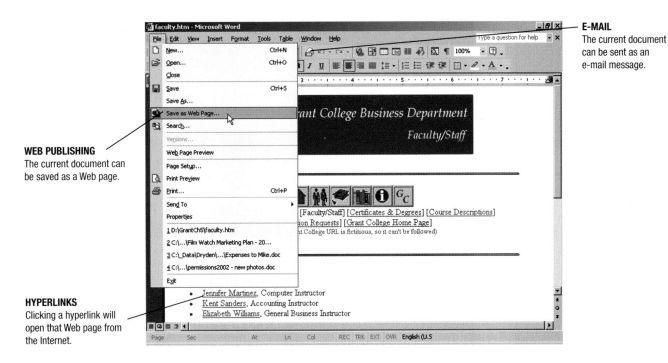

WEB PUBLISHING
The current document can
be saved as a Web page.

HYPERLINKS
Clicking a hyperlink will
open that Web page from
the Internet.

E-MAIL
The current document
can be sent as an
e-mail message.

a header or footer. A *header* prints automatically at the top of every page; a *footer* is printed at the bottom of every page (refer to Figure 7-7). When formats such as this are applied to all the pages of a document, it is referred to as *document formatting*. Other types of document formatting include generating end notes, a table of contents, or an index, as well as applying a background or theme to the document.

Graphics, Tables, and Templates

A word processor's graphics feature enables images to be inserted into a document, such as a photograph, a drawing from another program, or a *clip-art image* (refer to Figure 7-7). Usually after an image is inserted, it can be moved, resized, or otherwise modified.

A word processor's *tables* feature lets you organize page content into a grid of rows and columns. Once a table has been created, shading, borders, and other formatting can be applied. The widths and heights of the *cells* in a table can also be changed or the table can be set up to automatically adjust its size to fit the contents.

For common types of memos or reports, some word processors may have a template or wizard available to help you create a nice-looking document very quickly. A *template* is an already created and formatted document that fits a particular purpose, such as a fax cover sheet, memo, etc. Usually placeholder text is included for any text that should be customized, so all the user needs to do is fill in the blanks on the template document. A *wizard* goes beyond a template in that it consists of a series of screens that prompt you for the necessary information or actions to create a particular type of document; after completing all the screens, the appropriate document is generated.

Word Processing and the Web

The most recent versions of word processors and office suites include features that bring document preparation and the Web closer together. With a single mouse click, a document can be saved as a Web page or, conversely, a Web page can be opened and edited. In most word processors, when a Web address is typed, it is automatically created as a hyperlink, and clicking a hyperlink opens that Web page from the Internet in your Web browser program. Some word processors even allow you to create and send e-mail from within the word processing program (see Figure 7-10).

▶ FIGURE 7-10

Word processors and the Web. Common features found in a word processor include being able to create a Web page, open and edit an existing Web page, save a regular document as a Web page, automatically create hyperlinks as URLs are typed, and click hyperlinks to open the appropriate Web page. Some word processing programs also allow you to create and send e-mail messages.

further exploration

For links to further information about word processing software, go to www.course.com/parker2002/ch7

web tutor

For a tutorial on spreadsheet software, go to www.course.com/ parker2002/ch7

SPREADSHEET CONCEPTS

Today, one of the most important application programs that any businessperson should learn—whether he or she is a manager, an analyst, a secretary, or a sales representative—is the *electronic spreadsheet*. Spreadsheet software is to the current generation of business people what the pocket calculator was to previous generations—a convenient means of performing calculations. But while most pocket calculators can compute and display only one result each time new data are entered, electronic spreadsheets can present you with hundreds or even thousands of results each time you enter a single new value or command. Spreadsheet programs also typically allow you to create charts of, and do various types of analysis on, the data contained in a spreadsheet. Though the actual commands and features vary some from program to program, the basic features and concepts of spreadsheet programs discussed next remain the same. The spreadsheet program used in the illustrations in this section is Microsoft Excel.

What Is a Spreadsheet Program?

An electronic **spreadsheet** program produces computerized counterparts to the ruled paper worksheets associated with accountants. The advantages of using a computerized spreadsheet begin with the ability to save, modify, retrieve, and print the spreadsheet as often as necessary, the same as with a word processing program. Because spreadsheets tend to contain a great many numbers and mathematical calculations, however, there is a further benefit: The computer's mathematical ability and tremendous speed. These characteristics allow a computer to perform the calculations on the spreadsheet quickly and accurately, updating all calculations on the spreadsheet whenever a single value on the spreadsheet changes. This improves accuracy and saves the user from deleting and reentering the results of computations based on the value that needed to be changed.

Today's most common spreadsheet programs are Microsoft's Excel, Corel's Quattro Pro, and Lotus's 1-2-3—again, all part of the software suites mentioned at the beginning of this chapter. Some of the basic features supported by all spreadsheet programs are described in the next few sections.

The Anatomy of a Worksheet

In electronic spreadsheets, documents are generally called **worksheets.** Most spreadsheet programs allow multiple documents to be saved together in a single spreadsheet file, called a **workbook.** Worksheets are divided into **rows** and **columns.** Data is entered at the intersection of a row and a column—called a **cell.** Each cell can be accessed through a *cell address* comprised of the column letter followed by the row number, such as B4 or E22 (see Figure 7-11).

As you can see from Figure 7-11, a spreadsheet program screen contains a *formula bar* and *name box* below the toolbars at the top of the screen. The address for the current cell (the cell that the *cell pointer* is currently inside) is always displayed in the name box. The worksheet area in the middle of the screen contains the worksheet itself, and you can type or edit cell content directly on the worksheet itself or on the *formula bar.*

>**Spreadsheet.** A type of application program used to create documents that can be organized into rows and columns and typically contain a great deal of numbers and mathematical computations. >**Worksheet.** A document in a spreadsheet program. >**Workbook.** A collection of worksheets that are saved in a single spreadsheet file. >**Row.** A horizontal group of cells on a worksheet. >**Column.** A vertical group of cells on a worksheet. >**Cell.** The location on a worksheet into which data can be typed; the intersection of a row and column.

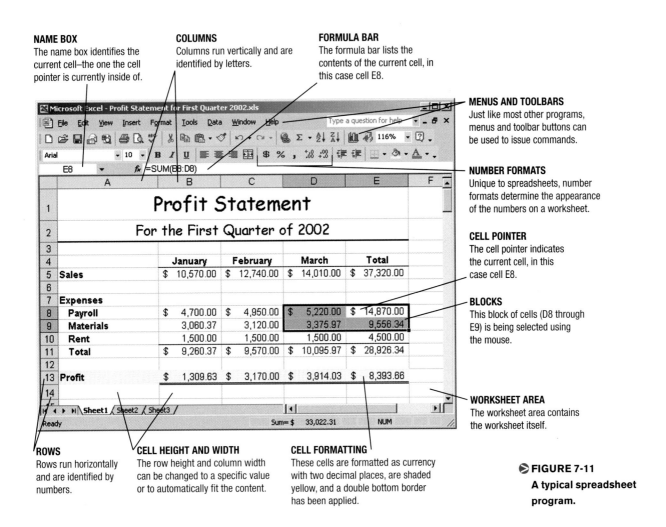

NAME BOX
The name box identifies the current cell–the one the cell pointer is currently inside of.

COLUMNS
Columns run vertically and are identified by letters.

FORMULA BAR
The formula bar lists the contents of the current cell, in this case cell E8.

MENUS AND TOOLBARS
Just like most other programs, menus and toolbar buttons can be used to issue commands.

NUMBER FORMATS
Unique to spreadsheets, number formats determine the appearance of the numbers on a worksheet.

CELL POINTER
The cell pointer indicates the current cell, in this case cell E8.

BLOCKS
This block of cells (D8 through E9) is being selected using the mouse.

WORKSHEET AREA
The worksheet area contains the worksheet itself.

ROWS
Rows run horizontally and are identified by numbers.

CELL HEIGHT AND WIDTH
The row height and column width can be changed to a specific value or to automatically fit the content.

CELL FORMATTING
These cells are formatted as currency with two decimal places, are shaded yellow, and a double bottom border has been applied.

➤ **FIGURE 7-11**
A typical spreadsheet program.

Blocks and Ranges

Often, users need to be able to manipulate more than one cell at a time, such as to format a group of cells or print just part of a worksheet. To do this in a spreadsheet program, a block of cells can be selected similarly to selecting text in a word processing program. A **block**—also called a *range*—is a rectangular-shaped group of cells (refer again to Figure 7-11). Blocks are usually specified with the mouse, though they can be typed as necessary by identifying two opposite corners of the block, such as D8 through E9 (usually typed as *D8:E9* or *D8..E9,* depending on the spreadsheet program being used). Once the block is defined, the appropriate formatting or command can be executed on just those cells.

Creating and Editing a Worksheet

To create a new spreadsheet (assuming a new, empty worksheet is displayed on the screen), the cell pointer is moved to the appropriate cell and the content of that cell is typed. Cell content can consist of a label, a constant value, or a formula or function. As in word processors, most spreadsheet programs have built-in templates to help users quickly create common types of business documents, such as balance sheets, income statements, and purchase orders.

>**Block.** A rectangular group of contiguous cells in a worksheet.

Entering Labels and Constant Values

Labels are words, column headings, and other nonmathematical data, such as *Profit Statement* and *January* in Figure 7-11. **Constant values** are numbers, such as *105* or *12740.25*. To enter a label or constant value into a cell, move the cell pointer to that cell, type the appropriate content (without any special formatting characters, such as a dollar sign or comma), and press the Enter key. Clip art, graphics, photographs, and other images can be inserted into a cell by using a menu option.

Entering Formulas and Functions

Formulas perform mathematical operations on the contents of other cells—such as adding or multiplying them together—and display the results in the cell containing the formula. To type a formula, most spreadsheet programs require that you begin with some type of mathematical symbol (usually the equal sign =), and then the appropriate cell addresses are typed using the mathematical operators listed in Figure 7-12. When typing formulas, it is important to always use the cell addresses of *where* the numbers you would like to include in the calculation are located (such as = B5 + C5 + D5 for the formula for cell E5 in Figure 7-11), rather than the numbers themselves (such as = 10570 + 12740 + 14010). If the actual numbers are used in the formula instead, the result of that formula (such as the total in cell E5) will not be correctly updated if one of the numbers (such as January sales in cell B5) is changed.

A **function** is a special type of named formula that invokes a preprogrammed formula (such as for computing the average of a group of cells or calculating a mortgage payment amount) or looks up information from other cells in the spreadsheet or from the computer itself (such as today's date). Spreadsheet programs normally contain a hundred or more built-in functions that can be used instead of writing complex formulas for a wide range of applications, including those in the fields of business, science, and engineering. Figure 7-13 describes some commonly used spreadsheet functions. Functions are typed, using the appropriate notation and inserting the appropriate cell addresses (in block notation), into the cell where the result should be displayed, similar to typing a formula. Many spreadsheet programs also include a function wizard to give you step-by-step instructions for using a function.

Symbol	Operation
+	Addition
−	Subtraction
*	Multiplication
/	Division
∧	Exponentiation

FIGURE 7-12

Mathematical operators.

The mathematical operators used in spreadsheet programs are universal operators used by most application programs that perform calculations.

FIGURE 7-13

Spreadsheet functions.

Like formulas, functions must begin with an equal sign (or other allowable formula symbol). In most functions (all but NOW in these examples), the cell addresses of the values to be used in the function must be specified in the listed order.

EXAMPLES OF FUNCTIONS	
= SUM (range)	Calculates the sum of all values in a range
= MAX (range)	Finds the highest value in a range
= MIN (range)	Finds the lowest value in a range
= NOW ( )	Inserts the current date and time
= COUNT (range)	Counts the number of nonempty cells in a range
= AVERAGE (range)	Calculates the average of values in a range
= ABS (cell or expression)	Calculates the absolute value of the argument
= PV (period payment, rate, number of payments)	Calculates the present value of an annuity at a specified interest rate
= IF (conditional expression, value if true, value if false)	Supplies to a cell a value that depends on whether the conditional expression is true or false

> **Label.** A primarily text-based entry entered into a worksheet cell that identifies data on the worksheet. **>Constant value.** A numerical entry entered into a worksheet cell. **>Formula.** An entry in a worksheet cell that performs computations on worksheet data and displays the results. **>Function.** A named formula that can be entered into a worksheet cell to perform some type of calculation or extract information from other cells on the worksheet.

Editing a Worksheet

Spreadsheet programs offer numerous options to help users edit the data contained on a worksheet. The following paragraphs review a sampling of the most important features.

Editing a Cell

To edit the contents of a cell, you move the cell pointer to the appropriate cell and then can either retype the contents or edit the contents on the formula bar. Notice that the formula bar always displays cell content as it was typed, so you see the actual formula that was typed in the cell, instead of the result of that formula as displayed in the cell. To delete the contents of a cell, most spreadsheet programs allow you to move to that cell and press the Delete key.

Inserting and Deleting Rows or Columns

All spreadsheet programs allow you to insert or delete columns or rows in a worksheet. Inserting or deleting involves moving the cell pointer to the appropriate position on the worksheet and issuing the proper command from either the Edit or Insert menu.

Moving and Copying Cells

Similar to a word processing program, a spreadsheet program permits a user to copy or move the contents of one cell (or several cells) to another location on the spreadsheet. Such commands require that you first specify the block of cells to be copied, then the Copy toolbar button or option on the Edit menu is used to copy that block. The cell pointer is moved to the appropriate destination location on the spreadsheet and then the Paste toolbar button is used to copy the data. The move procedure is similar, except the Cut toolbar button is used instead of the Copy button. Some spreadsheet programs have a shortcut for quickly duplicating a cell to adjacent cells, such as dragging the bottom right corner of the original cell in Microsoft Excel.

Relative vs. Absolute Cell Referencing

When you copy or move cells that contain formulas, you need to be aware of the difference between relative and absolute cell referencing to ensure that your formulas copy as intended. *Relative cell references* are used in most spreadsheet programs by default. With relative referencing, the cell addresses in the copied formula are adjusted to perform the same operation as in the original formula, just in the new location (instead of copying the cell addresses in the formula verbatim). In other words, the formula in the new location does the same relative operation as in the original location. For example, in the top screens in Figure 7-14, the copied formulas in cells C2 through C4 contain the result of subtracting the cell located two cells to the left of the formula cell, from the cell located one cell to the left of the formula cell.

With *absolute cell references,* in contrast, formulas are copied exactly as they are written (see the bottom screens in Figure 7-14). It is appropriate to use an absolute cell reference when you always want to add, subtract, multiply, or divide by a specific cell in all copies of the formula. That is, you don't want that cell address to change when the formula is copied. To make a cell reference in a formula absolute, a special symbol—usually a dollar sign—is placed before each row number and column letter that should not be changed. For example, to change both of the cell references in the formula $= A1 - B1$ located in cell C1 in Figure 7-14 to use absolute references, the formula would be rewritten as $=\$A\$1 - \$B\$1$.

Formatting a Worksheet

Similar to text in a word processing program, data in a worksheet is frequently formatted. In most spreadsheet programs, formatting can be applied at the cell, row or column, and worksheet levels.

COPYING WITH RELATIVE CELL REFERENCES. In most formulas, cell addresses are relative unless otherwise specified.

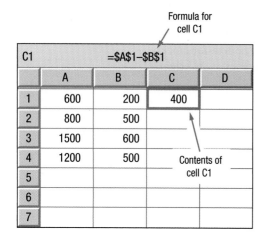

Before copy operation

After copy operation

COPYING WITH ABSOLUTE CELL REFERENCES. Using absolute cell references involves marking each column and row reference in the cell address with a dollar ($) sign. All absolute references will be copied exactly as they appear in the source cell.

Before copy operation

After copy operation

► FIGURE 7-14

Relative vs. absolute cell referencing.

Cell Formatting

Common types of *cell formatting* include changing the typeface, font size, font style, and alignment, similar to formatting characters in a word processing program. A difference is that the formatting is applied on a cell-by-cell basis, instead of character-by-character or paragraph-by-paragraph. For example, changing the font size while in cell A1 would change the size of all text located in cell A1, and clicking the center button while in cell B1 would center the contents of that cell just within the cell, not between the page margins. Multiple cells may usually be selected first (using the mouse or keyboard) to apply formatting to all of the selected cells using just one command.

One type of formatting that is unique to spreadsheet programs is numeric formatting. A variety of *number formats* are typically available in a spreadsheet program that can be used to change the way numbers on a spreadsheet look, such as how many decimal places are displayed, if the numbers are preceded by a dollar sign, and so forth. The default format in most spreadsheet programs displays no special symbols and as many decimals as will fit in the cell, if there is a decimal portion to the number. Because this results in an inconsistent appearance, most worksheet cells containing numbers will be formatted. This is usually accomplished by selecting a block of cells, and then clicking the appropriate number format toolbar buttons (refer back to Figure 7-11). After selecting the desired number format, such as *currency, percent,* or *comma,* most spreadsheet programs have toolbar buttons that can be used to increase or decrease the number of decimal places displayed, as needed. For example, a single click of the currency button might change "90000" to "$90,000.00", then two clicks on the decrease decimal button would change the display to "$90,000."

Other possible cell formatting includes changing the text color, changing the text direction or wrapping text within a cell, and adding borders or shading.

Row or Column Formatting

Row or column formatting generally includes just changing the height of a row or the width of a column. Similar to tables in a word processing program, most spreadsheet programs allow you to select a specific cell width or row height, or choose to have the width or height fit the contents of the cells.

Worksheet Formatting

Worksheet formatting includes changing the margins and adding headers, footers, and page numbers to a spreadsheet. Some spreadsheet programs also allow you to apply one of several different *autoformatting* styles. With autoformatting, the spreadsheet program analyzes your worksheet and automatically applies the color scheme and format you select based on the position of headings, borders, and data.

Charts and Sensitivity Analysis

Charts are commonly added to worksheets to better illustrate some of the numbers and computations included in the worksheet; sensitivity analysis is frequently used to help make better business decisions.

Charts

Most spreadsheet programs include some type of *charting* or *graphing* capability. Because the data used in business charts is often already located on a spreadsheet, using that program's charting feature eliminates reentering data. Instead, the cells containing the data to be charted are identified, then the type of chart, as well as titles and other customization, can be specified. The finished chart can usually be either inserted into a block of cells on an existing worksheet or placed on a blank worksheet by itself. Charts will be discussed in more detail later in this chapter.

What-If Analysis

Because they automatically recalculate all formulas on a worksheet every time a cell on the worksheet is edited, spreadsheet programs are particularly useful for *what-if analysis*— also called *sensitivity analysis.* For example, suppose you wish to know *what* profit would have resulted for January in Figure 7-11 *if* sales had been $15,000 instead of $10,570. You can simply enter the new value, 15000, into Cell B5, and the spreadsheet program automatically recomputes all formulas, allowing you to determine (from the new value in cell B13) that the profit would have been $5,739.63.

In seconds, electronic spreadsheets can perform recalculations that would require several hours to do manually. This allows business people to run through many times more possibilities before making decisions than in the past when all such calculations had to be performed by hand. Another type of sensitivity analysis involves having the spreadsheet compute the amount a constant value would need to be in order for the result of a particular formula to become a specified amount (such as the total sales required to obtain a profit of $5,000, if all of the expenses stayed the same).

further exploration

For links to further information about spreadsheet software, go to www.course.com/parker2002/ch7

Spreadsheets and the Web

As with recent word processors, recent spreadsheet programs also have built-in Web capabilities. Though they are less commonly used to create Web pages, many spreadsheet programs have an option on the File menu to save the current worksheet as a Web page, and hyperlinks can be inserted into worksheet cells. Blocks of cells can also be selected and copied to a Web publishing program to insert the spreadsheet into a Web page being created in that program.

DATABASE CONCEPTS

web tutor

For a tutorial on database software, go to www.course.com/parker2002/ch7

People often need to retrieve large amounts of data rapidly. An airline agent on the phone to a client may need to search quickly to find the lowest-cost flight from Tucson to Toronto for the client's vacation. The registrar of a university may have to scan student records swiftly to find all students who will graduate in June with a grade-point average of 3.5 or higher. A clerk in a video store may need to determine if a particular movie is available for rental. The type of software used for such tasks is a *database management system.* Computerized database management systems are rapidly replacing the paper-based filing systems that people have had to wade through in the past to find the information their jobs require. The basic features and concepts of PC-based *relational* database software are discussed next, using Microsoft Access as an example when needed. Other types of database programs are covered in Chapter 14.

What Is a Database Program?

A **database** is a collection of data that is stored and organized in a manner enabling information to be retrieved as needed. A *database management system (DBMS)*—also sometimes called just **database software**—enables the creation of a database on a computer and provides easy access to data stored within it.

Although not all databases are organized identically, most PC-based databases are organized into fields, records, and files. A **field** is a single type of data to be stored in a database, such as a person's name or a person's telephone number. A **record** is a collection of related fields—for example the ID number, name, address, and major of Phyllis Hoffman (see Figure 7-15). A *file*—frequently called a **table** in PC databases—is a collection of related records (such as all student address data, all student grade data, or all student schedule data). The resulting set of related files or tables (such as all student data) comprises the database.

The type of database software found on most PCs is the **relational database management system.** The most common relational database management systems include Microsoft's Access, Corel's Paradox, and Lotus's Approach—again, all part of their respective

---

>**Database.** A collection of related data that is stored in a manner enabling information to be retrieved as needed; in a relational database, a collection of related tables. >**Database software.** Application software that allows the creation and manipulation of an electronic database. >**Field.** A single category of data to be stored in a database, such as a person's name or telephone number. >**Record.** A collection of related fields in a database. >**Table.** In a relational database, a collection of related records. >**Relational database management system (RDBMS).** The most widely used database model in use today; can link data in related tables through the use of common fields.

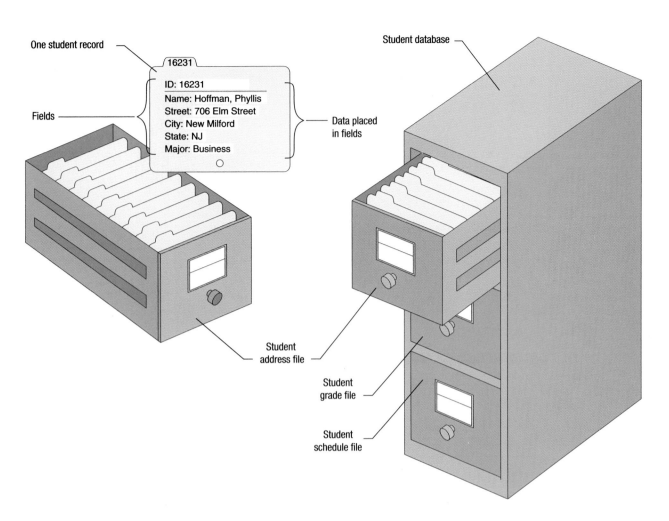

One student record

16231

ID: 16231
Name: Hoffman, Phyllis
Street: 706 Elm Street
City: New Milford
State: NJ
Major: Business

Fields

Data placed
in fields

Student database

Student
address file

Student
grade file

Student
schedule file

► **FIGURE 7-15**
**Fields, records, files, and
databases.** Fields, records,
and files (tables) organize the
data that are to be part of a
database.

software suites—as well as the Oracle database product from Oracle Corporation. Some of the basic features supported by database programs in general will be described in the next few sections.

Creating a Database

A database can contain a variety of *objects* (see Figure 7-16). The object created first in a new database is the table, then other objects can be created to be used in conjunction with that table as needed.

When creating a database, the number of tables to be included in the database should be determined. Then the data items to be stored in each table can be identified so that the appropriate field characteristics can be used. For each field, the following should be determined:

▼ Field name (an identifying name unique within the table)

▼ Type of data to be contained in the field (text, numbers, date, etc.)

▼ Field size (how many characters will be needed to store the data)

Once these specifications have been determined, the *structure* of each table containing the field specifications (see Figure 7-17) can be created.

After the table structure has been created, data may be entered into the table. Data entry can be performed in the regular table view—sometimes called the *datasheet view,*

DATABASE FILE
All of these objects are stored within the Inventory file.

MENUS AND TOOLBARS
Just as with most other programs, menus and toolbar buttons can be used to issue commands.

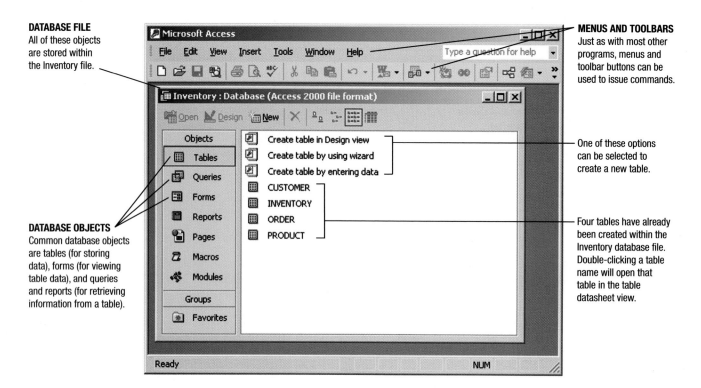

One of these options can be selected to create a new table.

DATABASE OBJECTS
Common database objects are tables (for storing data), forms (for viewing table data), and queries and reports (for retrieving information from a table).

Four tables have already been created within the Inventory database file. Double-clicking a table name will open that table in the table datasheet view.

▶ **FIGURE 7-16**

A typical database program. Common database objects include tables, forms, queries, and reports. Objects typically need to be created and opened before they can be viewed on the screen.

since the table looks similar to a spreadsheet—or a form can be created and used. A *form* allows you to view or edit table content in a more formal manner—usually just working with one record at a time, instead of a full page of records, as in the datasheet view. Figure 7-17 illustrates entering data using both methods once the table structure has been created.

Modifying a Database

Once a database table has been created, it may need to be modified. Changes may be made to the table structure or to the data located in the table as needed, as explained next.

Modifying the Table Structure

The table structure needs to be modified only when there are changes to the field properties. For example, a field may need to be widened to accommodate a name that is longer than anticipated, the wrong field type may have been initially selected, or a new field may need to be added. To modify a table, it is opened in the *design view* using the appropriate toolbar button or menu option, then any necessary changes can be made. The design view is the same view used initially to create the table structure (refer again to Figure 7-17).

Editing, Adding, and Deleting Records

To make changes to the actual data in a table, the table must first be opened (either using the table datasheet view or a form), and then the necessary changes can be made. To move to a particular record to edit its contents, either the arrows and other keyboard directional keys or the record buttons located at the bottom of the window, can be used (refer again to Figure 7-17). Since records are typically added to the end of a table, there is usually a *New Record* button in the group of record buttons that automatically moves you to a blank record at the end of the table.

To delete a record, either the Delete key on the keyboard or some type of *Delete Record* option on the menu bar is used. Since deleting a record by accident can be disastrous in a business database, most programs require the user to confirm the deletion in some manner before it is carried out.

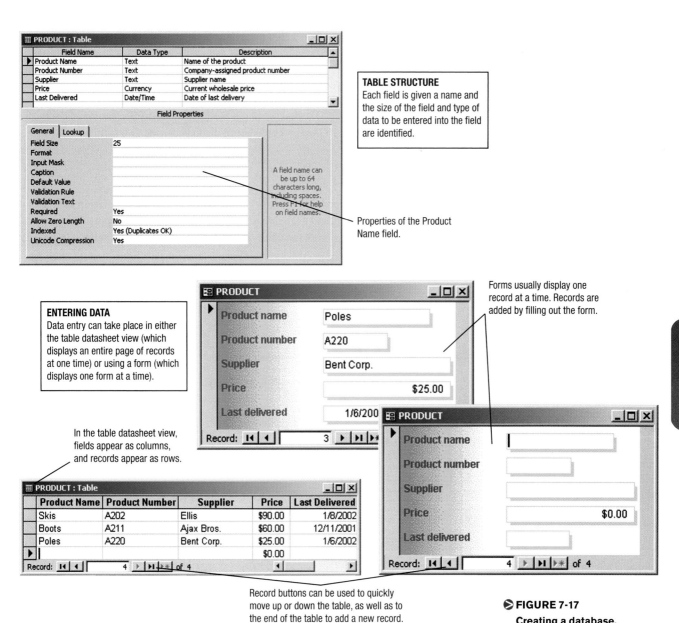

TABLE STRUCTURE
Each field is given a name and the size of the field and type of data to be entered into the field are identified.

A field name can be up to 64 characters long, including spaces. Press F1 for help on field names.

Properties of the Product Name field.

ENTERING DATA
Data entry can take place in either the table datasheet view (which displays an entire page of records at one time) or using a form (which displays one form at a time).

Forms usually display one record at a time. Records are added by filling out the form.

In the table datasheet view, fields appear as columns, and records appear as rows.

Record buttons can be used to quickly move up or down the table, as well as to the end of the table to add a new record.

▶ **FIGURE 7-17**
Creating a database.

Queries and Reports

To retrieve information from a database, *queries* and *reports* are used. A **query** is a question, or, in database terms, a request for specific information from the database. A query takes your instructions about what information you want to find and displays just that requested information. A report is a more formal printout of a table or query result.

Queries

When creating a query, you can specify both the fields and the records that you want to see in the query results. The desired fields are selected from a list of the fields in a specific table. The records to be displayed are selected by specifying *criteria*—specific restrictions that the data must meet in order for records to be included in the query results. For example, the criteria in the query screen in Figure 7-18 directs the computer to select all the products in

---

>**Query.** A question used to retrieve information from a database.

the Product table that cost less than $20. Though some database programs may require you to type the query request in sentence form, most programs include a screen similar to the one in Figure 7-18 for easier query requests. Queries can usually be saved under a name so that they can be redisplayed at a later time. When a query is opened and displayed, only the records meeting the specified criteria at the current time are displayed. Consequently, opening the query in Figure 7-18 after adding a new product costing less than $20 to the Products table would result in *three* records being displayed—the two in Figure 7-18 plus the new product.

Reports

Reports can be created for printing a more formal listing of a table or query result. Many database programs have a wizard available to assist users in creating a report. There is also usually an editing option available to enable users to create a report from scratch or modify a report that was initially created using a wizard.

▶ FIGURE 7-18

Queries and reports.

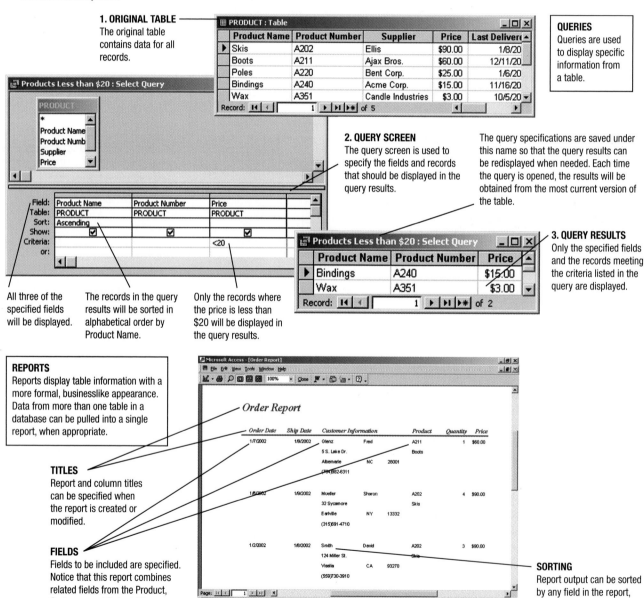

1. ORIGINAL TABLE
The original table contains data for all records.

QUERIES
Queries are used to display specific information from a table.

2. QUERY SCREEN
The query screen is used to specify the fields and records that should be displayed in the query results.

The query specifications are saved under this name so that the query results can be redisplayed when needed. Each time the query is opened, the results will be obtained from the most current version of the table.

All three of the specified fields will be displayed.

The records in the query results will be sorted in alphabetical order by Product Name.

Only the records where the price is less than $20 will be displayed in the query results.

3. QUERY RESULTS
Only the specified fields and the records meeting the criteria listed in the query are displayed.

REPORTS
Reports display table information with a more formal, businesslike appearance. Data from more than one table in a database can be pulled into a single report, when appropriate.

TITLES
Report and column titles can be specified when the report is created or modified.

FIELDS
Fields to be included are specified. Notice that this report combines related fields from the Product, Customer, and Order tables.

SORTING
Report output can be sorted by any field in the report, such as by name.

When a report object is created, the instructions for what the report should look like are saved under the report name. Whenever the report is opened, the appropriate table data is displayed in the specified locations on the report, as in the bottom part of Figure 7-18. Consequently, just as with queries, reports always display the data contained in a table at the time the report is run. Many database programs allow reports to be created in a variety of styles, and use text formatting, clip art, and other enhancements.

Though basic reports are often created from the data contained in just one table, reports can pull related data from more than one table. For example, in the report in Figure 7-18, the Order Date, Ship Date, and Quantity data came from the Order table; the Customer Information came from the Customer table; and the Product Information and Price data came from the Products table. In order for this to occur, the tables in a database must have common *key fields*—unique identifying fields, such as a customer number or product number—and the tables must be *related* together using those key fields. Different programs set up relationships between tables differently, but generally it just involves specifying which tables should be related and which field the tables have in common, such as the Customer Number field for the Customer and Order tables, and the Product number field for the Product, Order, and Inventory tables.

Databases and the Web

Databases and the Web are very closely related. Many Web sites use one or more databases to keep track of inventory; allow searching for people, documents, or other information; place real-time orders, and so forth. To try out a Web database yourself, go to a retail Web site that allows you to search for products (such as Amazon.com or Wal-Mart.com). After typing keywords in the search box displayed on the screen, the results of your search (query) are displayed on the screen. Though some Web sites may use one of the other types of database programs discussed in Chapter 14, a PC database can be linked to a Web site. For example Microsoft FrontPage—the Web publishing program included in some versions of Microsoft Office—can easily link an Access database to a site created in FrontPage.

further exploration

For links to further information about database software, go to www.course.com/parker2002/ch7

PRESENTATION GRAPHICS CONCEPTS

If you try to explain to others what you look like, it may take several minutes. Show them a color photograph, on the other hand, and you can convey the same information within seconds. The saying "a picture is worth a thousand words" is the cornerstone of presentation graphics.

What Is Presentation Graphics Software?

A *presentation graphic*—an image or electronic *slide* containing text, images, or other objects arranged on a screen-size page—visually enhances the impact of information communicated to other people. Presentation graphics objects can take many forms, a number of which are illustrated in Figure 7-19. Programs that allow you to create presentation graphics are called **presentation graphics software.** The most common form of presentation created with a presentation graphics program is the *electronic slide show*—a group of **slides** displayed on a large monitor or on a projection screen. Most programs also allow you to print out presentation graphics for handouts or overhead transparencies, or insert the graphics into a document in another program.

There are several compelling reasons to use presentation graphics in business. A person can often spot trends or make comparisons much more quickly by looking at a visual image

web tutor

For a tutorial on presentation software, go to www.course.com/parker2002/ch7

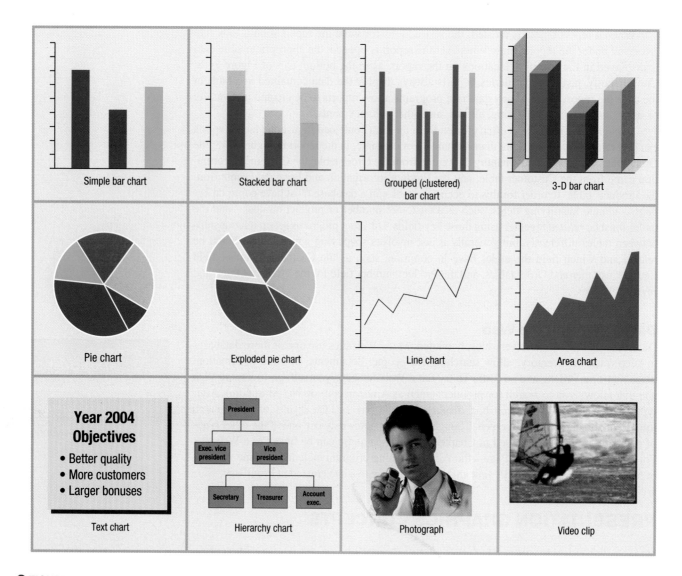

Simple bar chart · Stacked bar chart · Grouped (clustered) bar chart · 3-D bar chart

Pie chart · Exploded pie chart · Line chart · Area chart

Year 2004 Objectives
• Better quality
• More customers
• Larger bonuses

Text chart · Hierarchy chart · Photograph · Video clip

◗ **FIGURE 7-19**

Sample presentation graphics. Presentation graphics can include bar, pie, line, and text charts, as well as more complicated images.

than by reading text-only or number-only output containing the same information. Furthermore, a point can often be made far more dramatically and effectively by using pictures. Slide-show type presentations are frequently used to hold the interest of the audience while conveying the desired information. Studies have found that presentation graphics also make the presenter look more professional in the eyes of others. Often the design, colors, and type of graphic can determine how well your point will come across.

Some of today's most common presentation graphics programs are Microsoft's PowerPoint, Corel's Presentations, and Lotus's Freelance Graphics. The figures in the following sections illustrate the Microsoft PowerPoint program.

Creating a Presentation

Presentation graphics programs usually create new documents in the form of a group of slides, though some programs can be used to create stand-alone pieces to be printed or inserted into another program. To begin a slide presentation, a layout template that contains placeholders for the desired objects in the slide (such as text, images, or charts, as shown in Figure 7-20) is usually selected for the first slide. The placeholders located on the template slide are then selected and replaced with the proper content. The procedure is repeated until all slides are created.

Just as with the other application programs discussed so far, toolbar buttons can be used to format slide text to use the desired font face, size, style, and alignment. There are

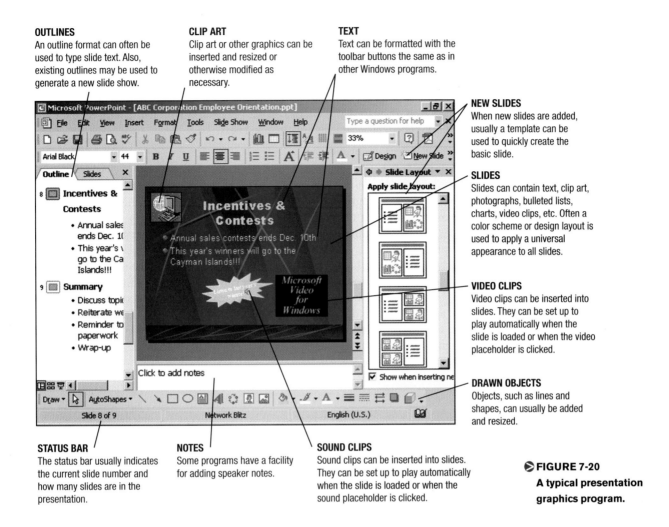

OUTLINES
An outline format can often be used to type slide text. Also, existing outlines may be used to generate a new slide show.

CLIP ART
Clip art or other graphics can be inserted and resized or otherwise modified as necessary.

TEXT
Text can be formatted with the toolbar buttons the same as in other Windows programs.

NEW SLIDES
When new slides are added, usually a template can be used to quickly create the basic slide.

SLIDES
Slides can contain text, clip art, photographs, bulleted lists, charts, video clips, etc. Often a color scheme or design layout is used to apply a universal appearance to all slides.

VIDEO CLIPS
Video clips can be inserted into slides. They can be set up to play automatically when the slide is loaded or when the video placeholder is clicked.

DRAWN OBJECTS
Objects, such as lines and shapes, can usually be added and resized.

STATUS BAR
The status bar usually indicates the current slide number and how many slides are in the presentation.

NOTES
Some programs have a facility for adding speaker notes.

SOUND CLIPS
Sound clips can be inserted into slides. They can be set up to play automatically when the slide is loaded or when the sound placeholder is clicked.

⟫**FIGURE 7-20**
A typical presentation graphics program.

also toolbar buttons and menu options to add other objects to the slide, such as images, video clips, and charts. Images can be photographs, graphics created in another program, arrows or other shapes, or clip art images. Video clips often use the .avi file format and can be set up to play automatically when the slide is displayed, or, alternatively, play when they are clicked with the mouse. Shapes are usually inserted using a toolbar button.

A variety of charts are typically available for insertion into slides when appropriate. Usually the data to be charted can either be entered in when the chart is created or can be imported from an existing spreadsheet. A description of the most common types of charts is included next (refer to Figure 7-19).

- ▼ *Bar charts*—also called *column charts*—are useful for comparing an attribute (sales, cost, etc.) for different items (such as products or months). The height of the bars in a bar chart corresponds to the size of the numbers being charted.

- ▼ *Pie charts* show how parts of something relate to a whole, such as monthly expenses or sales. Pie charts are often "exploded" to emphasize one piece of the pie.

- ▼ *Line charts* are usually used to show trends over time, such as sales or stock price for a year.

- ▼ *Text charts* contain a relatively small amount of text displayed in an easy-to-read format, such as short lines or a bulleted list.

- ▼ *Organizational charts* are used to illustrate a hierarchy, such as the employee organization within a company.

Enhancing a Presentation

While some presentations consist of simple visuals shown in slide show or overhead format, increasingly sound, video, and animated effects are being added alongside text and graphics to create fully featured multimedia presentations. As discussed earlier, video clips can be inserted into the appropriate locations on a slide and can either be played when that slide is initially displayed, or played when a placeholder is clicked with the mouse. Sound clips work similarly. Other enhancements are discussed next.

Animation and Transitions

Animated effects include animating existing text or other objects on a slide and using *transitions* between slides. When text is animated, a variety of effects can be used to display the text, such as *flying* the text in from the edge of the screen or *dissolving* the text in from a blank slide. Animation settings can also be specified to indicate the sequence chart objects will be displayed, whether a video will *loop* continuously or not, etc.

Transitions determine how one slide in a slide show leaves and the next slide is introduced. There are a wide variety of transitions that can be applied to individual slides or to an entire presentation. Many presentation programs have a random effects option that can be used to apply transitions at random to each slide in the slide show—a timesaving feature if specific transitions for each slide are not required. Sound effects can also be part of a transition in many presentation programs.

Slide Show Options

Once all of the slides in a slide show have been created and the desired animation and transition effects applied, the slide show is ready to be run. To view the order the slides will be displayed, presentation graphics programs typically have a special view, such as the *slide sorter view* shown in Figure 7-21. Using this view, slides can easily be rearranged as necessary. When the slide show is run, the slides are displayed in the stated order. Depending on the settings, the slides automatically advance after a specified period of time, or the speaker advances to the next slide by pressing the spacebar or clicking with the mouse.

As mentioned previously, most presentation software programs also include print options, which can be used in lieu of or in addition to viewing the slides as a slide show. The graphics themselves can be printed to make overhead transparencies and handouts; speaker notes or the presentation outline can also be printed for the speaker to use or to distribute to the audience as a handout.

further exploration

For links to further information about presentation graphics software, go to www.course.com/parker2002/ch7

Presentation Graphics and the Web

As with the other application programs discussed so far, presentation graphics programs can be used to generate Web pages or Web page content, and slides can include hyperlinks. Web-based presentations may include the same type of objects included in non-Web presentations, such as text, images, charts, video clips, and sound clips. When a slide show is saved as a series of Web pages and displayed using a Web browser, generally forward and backward navigational buttons are displayed on the slides to allow the user to control the presentation.

OTHER TYPES OF APPLICATION SOFTWARE

There are many other types of application software. Some are geared for business or personal productivity; others are for entertainment or educational purposes. Still others are designed specifically for a particular business application, such as a custom application program to generate one business's payroll or inventory reports. A few of the most common types of application software not previously covered are discussed next.

SLIDE SORTER VIEW
This type of view allows you to rearrange the order the slides in a presentation will be displayed.

SLIDE SHOW
When a slide show is run, it will usually be displayed full screen. Slides can be advanced at predetermined intervals or by clicking the mouse or pressing the spacebar.

⮞**FIGURE 7-21**
Slide shows. The slides in a slide show can be rearranged as necessary, then displayed as a full-screen slide show.

further exploration

For links to further information about desktop publishing software, go to www.course.com/parker2002/ch7

Desktop and Personal Publishing

Desktop publishing refers to using desktop PCs to combine and manipulate text and images to create attractive documents that look as if they came off a professional printer's press (see Figure 7-22). Though many desktop publishing effects can be produced using a word processing program, users who frequently create publication-style documents would likely find a desktop publishing program a more efficient means of creating those types of documents. *Personal publishing* refers to creating desktop-publishing-type documents for personal use—such as greeting cards, invitations, flyers, calendars, certificates, and so forth, as shown in Figure 7-22.

Multimedia Software

There is a vast amount of *multimedia software* available, from programs to create full-fledged multimedia applications, to programs that play, create, or edit audio or video clips (see Figure 7-22). For a look at how one type of multimedia software can be used to create personalized music CDs, see the How It Works box. Other types of multimedia software are discussed in Chapter 10.

DESKTOP PUBLISHING
Desktop publishing programs allow users to create publication-quality documents on their PCs.

PERSONAL PUBLISHING
Personal publishing programs allow users to create cards, calendars, newsletters, and other personal documents.

PERSONAL INFORMATION MANAGERS
Personal information managers (PIM) feature a variety of calendar and daily planner options, as well as to-do lists, phone book, and notepad.

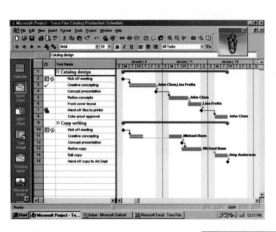

PROJECT MANAGEMENT
Project management software can provide timetables and graphs to show how the pieces of a project fit together.

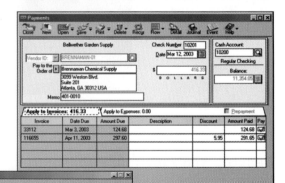

ACCOUNTING
Accounting programs, such as the Accounts Payable program, shown here, automate accounting tasks to save time.

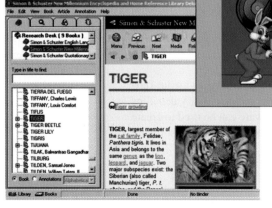

EDUCATIONAL
Educational software, such as the children's program shown here, often teach skills in a fun, entertaining manner.

REFERENCE
Reference software includes encyclopedias, atlases, dictionaries, and other helpful resources.

FIGURE 7-22
Other types of application software.

Personal Information Managers

Personal information managers (PIMs)—sometimes called *desktop organizers* or *desktop accessories*—are software programs that provide the electronic equivalents of the appointment calendars, Rolodexes, to-do lists, and other information management tools commonly found on an office desktop (see Figure 7-22). Desk accessory software varies among vendors, but most include at least an appointment calendar, address book, and notepad. Many handheld computers run similar software so that the data can be easily transferred between a user's desktop PC and his or her handheld PC.

Project Management Software

Project management software, illustrated in Figure 7-22, is used to plan, schedule, track, and analyze the tasks involved in a project, such as a construction project, installing a new manufacturing system, preparing a large advertising campaign for a client, and so forth. This software shows how project activities are related and when they must start and finish. Once created, schedules prepared by such software can be shared with others and updated as the project progresses.

Accounting and Personal Finance Software

Accounting software is used to automate some of the accounting activities that need to be performed on a regular basis. Common tasks include writing and printing checks, recording purchases and payments (refer again to Figure 7-22), creating payroll documents and checks, and preparing financial statements. *Personal finance software* is commonly used at home by individuals to write checks and balance their checking account, track personal expenses, manage stock portfolios, and prepare their income taxes. Some personal finance programs can be used in conjunction with the Internet, such as for online banking and investment tracking.

Education, Entertainment, and Reference Software

There are a wide variety of educational and entertainment application programs available. *Educational software* is designed to teach one or more skills, such as reading, math, spelling, a foreign language, world geography, or to help prepare for standardized tests. *Entertainment software* includes games, simulations, and other programs that provide amusement. A hybrid of these two categories is sometimes called *edutainment*—educational software that also entertains—such as the children's program illustrated in Figure 7-22.

Reference software is another common type of application software. Reference software includes encyclopedias, dictionaries, atlases, ZIP code directories, mapping/travel programs, and any other program designed to provide valuable information. An encyclopedia program is shown in Figure 7-22.

Computer-Aided Design Software

Computer-aided design (CAD) software enables designers to dramatically reduce the time they spend developing designs in such areas as manufacturing and architecture. For example, by using electronic pens and powerful PCs, engineers or architects can sketch ideas directly into the computer system and then instruct it to analyze the proposed design in terms of how well it meets a number of design criteria. Using the subsequent computer output, designers can modify their drawings until they achieve the desired results. Because drawings are typically displayed in 3D, CAD is especially helpful in designing automobiles, aircraft, ships, buildings, electrical circuits (including computer chips), and even clothing. Besides playing an important role in the design of durable goods, CAD is useful in fields such as art, advertising, law, architecture, and movie production.

how it works

Creating MP3 Files and Custom Music CDs

Creating customized music collections from an existing collection of CDs is a popular pastime today. Instead of having to carry around a bulky portable CD player and an assortment of discs, you can carry a small MP3 player instead. Or if you choose to use a CD player, you can at least use it with a single CD containing an assortment of your favorite songs.

Converting between music CDs (stored in the *.wav* format) to MP3 files, and from MP3 files to CD format requires a variety of multimedia software tools.

- ▼ *CD rippers* copy songs from a CD to a PC's hard drive.

- ▼ *MP3 encoders* compress songs stored on the hard drive in .wav format into the MP3 format.

- ▼ *MP3 decoders* convert MP3 files to the .wav format so they can be stored on a CD.

- ▼ *CD burners* store files on recordable or rewritable CDs. Usually a CD-R disc is used because it can be read by many newer CD and DVD players; CD-RW discs cannot be read by many CD and CD-R drives.

Many newer software programs—such as Windows MediaPlayer and the MusicMatch program shown in the accompanying illustration—perform most, if not all, of these tasks in one program.

The process for transferring songs from a CD to a PC in MP3 format and from a PC in MP3 format to a CD-R disc is illustrated in the accompanying figure. It is important to realize that most programs allow you to select the quality and corresponding compression levels for your MP3 files. Usually near-CD quality (93 Kbps) or CD quality (128 Kbps) is selected.

CD TO MP3

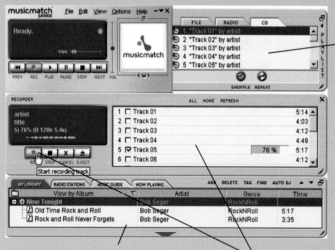

1. The CD to be used is inserted into the PC's CD drive and the appropriate software is opened.

3. Once the songs have been ripped and decoded, they usually appear in some kind of playlist or music library accessible from within the software program being used. They can then be played from the PC or transferred to an MP3 player.

2. The recorder controls are used to select the songs to be saved to the hard drive. Settings, such as where on the hard drive the files will be stored and the compression ratio to be used, are typically set up on an options or settings menu.

MP3 TO CD

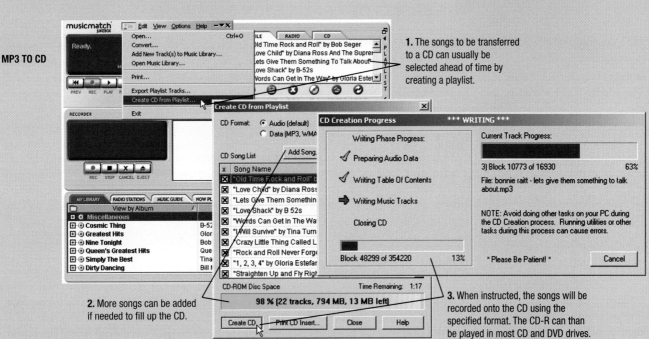

1. The songs to be transferred to a CD can usually be selected ahead of time by creating a playlist.

2. More songs can be added if needed to fill up the CD.

3. When instructed, the songs will be recorded onto the CD using the specified format. The CD-R can than be played in most CD and DVD drives.

THE BASICS OF APPLICATION SOFTWARE

Chapter Objective 1:
Describe what application software is and some of the characteristics of a software suite.

Application software is software designed to carry out a specific task. Though different in purpose, most application software programs share some of the same concepts and functions, such as similar document-handling operations and *online help* features. Most office-oriented programs are sold bundled together as a **software suite.** Within a suite, programs typically use a common interface, are *document-centered,* and allow *object linking and embedding (OLE).*

Many application software products on the market today are examples of *proprietary software.* Individual users purchase *licenses* authorizing them to use such software, while businesses often seek *site licenses.* Some software is also available as *shareware.* The shareware creator normally does not charge for use of the software, but requests payment from those users who like and want to continue to use the software after trying it. Still another class of software is *freeware*—programs that are available without restrictions of any sort. Organizations that provide Web-based software are referred to as *application service providers (ASPs).*

WORD PROCESSING CONCEPTS

Chapter Objective 2:
Discuss word processing and identify the basic operations involved in creating, editing, and formatting documents.

A **word processing** program uses computer technology to create, manipulate, and print written documents, such as letters, legal contracts, manuscripts, and so forth. Virtually all word processors use an **insertion point** to illustrate the current location in the document and a **word wrap** feature to automatically return the insertion point at the end of the screen line and keep the appropriate amount of text on each line, even after the document is later *edited* and *formatted.*

When editing text, text can be *selected* to be deleted, *moved,* or *copied.* Text is also frequently selected to apply *character formatting,* such as changing the *typeface, font size,* or *font style* used. Other types of formatting include *paragraph formatting,* (adjusting *line spacing, margins, indentation, tabs, alignment,* etc.) and *page/document formatting* (changing the top and bottom margins, paper size, adding *headers* and *footers,* etc.).

Other enhancements found in most word processing programs include the ability to include graphical images and *tables* in a document and to use *styles, templates,* or *wizards* for more efficient document creation. Documents can also include hyperlinks and be saved as Web pages in most programs. Most word processors also include a spell-checking feature and other types of editing tools.

SPREADSHEET CONCEPTS

Chapter Objective 3:
Explain the purpose of spreadsheet software and identify the basic operations involved in creating, editing, and formatting worksheets.

An electronic **spreadsheet** program produces computerized counterparts to the ruled paper worksheets that accountants frequently use. Documents created in a spreadsheet typically include a great deal of numbers and mathematical computations.

In electronic spreadsheets, documents are referred to as **worksheets;** a collection of worksheets stored in the same file is called a **workbook.** A worksheet is divided into **rows** and **columns** that intersect to form **cells,** each of which can be accessed through a *cell address,* such as B3. A rectangular group of cells is referred to as a **block** or *range.*

Content in a spreadsheet is typed into individual cells and may consist of labels, constant values, formulas, or functions. A **label** is a descriptive heading or other text that is not used in computations; a **constant value** consists of a numeric value; and a **formula** is a cell entry that performs a mathematical operation on other cells. A **function** is a special type of named formula that executes some type of prestored formula. Formulas in a cell can be typed using *relative cell references,* which change the formula when it is copied to perform the same computation relative to the new location, or *absolute cell references,* in which the formula is copied verbatim.

Once created, the contents of individual cells may be edited and formatted. *Number formats* are used to change the appearance of numbers, such as adding a dollar sign or displaying a specific number of decimal places. The width and height of a row or column can also be adjusted, as can the margins, page numbers, and headers and footers of the entire worksheet.

Spreadsheet programs commonly include a *charting* or *graphing* feature and the ability to perform *what-if analysis.* Some spreadsheet programs allow worksheets to be saved in the form of a Web page and the inclusion of hyperlinks in cells.

DATABASE CONCEPTS

A *database management system (DBMS)* or **database software** enables the creation of a **database**— a collection of data stored in a manner so that information can be retrieved as needed. **Relational database management systems** are the most common type found on PCs. These systems are so named because they relate data in various database files by common fields in those files. A file in a relational DBMS is commonly called a table. A **table** is a collection of related records; a **record** is a collection of related fields; and a **field** is a collection of characters that comprise a single piece of data, such as a name or phone number.

A relational database typically contains a variety of *objects,* such as tables; *forms* to be used to input or view data in a more formal manner; **queries** to be used to retrieve specific information from the database; and *reports,* which are used to print a more formal listing of the data stored in a entire table or the results of a query. When a table is first created, the fields to be included in the table are specified along with their characteristics, such as field name, size, and type of data. Then data can be entered into the table. Both the data in the table and the table structure can be modified, as needed.

Databases are commonly integrated into the Web, such as to keep track of inventory, store data to be retrieved, or to facilitate online ordering.

Chapter Objective 4:
Identify some of the vocabulary used with database software and discuss the basic operations involved with creating, editing, and retrieving information from a database.

PRESENTATION GRAPHICS CONCEPTS

Presentation graphics software is used to create images that visually enhance the impact of information communicated to other people. Most commonly, these programs are used to produce *online slide shows,* where each page in the presentation is referred to as a **slide.** Four of the most common types of presentation graphics are *bar charts, pie charts, text charts,* and *organizational charts.*

When the individual slides in a presentation are created, their content can be edited and formatted, as can the overall appearance of the slides. Multimedia elements, such as images, video clips, and audio clips, can also be included in a slide. After all slides have been created for a presentation, the order of the slides can be rearranged and *transitions* between the slides can be specified, as can any other type of animation.

It is becoming increasingly common to find these types of presentations available through the Web.

Chapter Objective 5:
Describe what presentation graphics are and how they are created.

OTHER TYPES OF APPLICATION SOFTWARE

Other types of application software include *desktop publishing* and *personal publishing* programs for creating professional-looking documents; *multimedia software* for creating, modifying, or playing multimedia items, such as animations, audio, and video files; *personal information managers (PIMs)* for keeping electronic calendars, address books, etc.; and *project management software* used to plan, schedule, and track the individual tasks included in a project. Businesses may also use *accounting software* programs; individuals may use *personal finance software* to manage their personal finances. *Educational, entertainment,* and *reference software* is very popular for home use. *Computer-aided design (CAD) software* is used to design products, buildings, and other items on a computer.

Chapter Objective 6:
List several other types of application software programs and discuss what functions they perform.

Instructions: Match each key term on the left with the definition on the right that fits best.

1. application software

2. cell

3. column

4. database

5. field

6. formula

7. insertion point

8. presentation graphics software

9. query

10. record

11. relational database management system

12. row

13. spreadsheet

14. table

15. word processing

16. word wrap

17. worksheet

_____ A collection of related fields in a database.

_____ A collection of related data that is stored in a manner enabling information to be retrieved as needed.

_____ A document in a spreadsheet program.

_____ A grid of rows and columns in a word processing document that can be used to organize page content; in a relational database, a collection of related records.

_____ A horizontal group of cells on a worksheet.

_____ A question used to retrieve information from a database.

_____ A single category of data to be stored in a database, such as a person's name or telephone number.

_____ A type of application program used to create documents that can be organized into rows and columns and typically contain a great deal of numbers and mathematical computations.

_____ A type of application program used to create, manipulate, and print written documents, such as letters, contracts, and manuscripts.

_____ A type of program used to create presentation graphics, including online slide shows.

_____ A vertical group of cells on a worksheet.

_____ An entry in a worksheet cell that performs computations on worksheet data and displays the results.

_____ An onscreen character that marks the current location in a document, which is where the next character typed will appear on the screen.

_____ Software programs that enable users to perform specific tasks or applications on a computer.

_____ The feature found in a word processing program that automatically returns the insertion point to the next line when reaching the end of the screen line, and keeps the proper amount of text on each line after the document is edited and formatted.

_____ The location on a worksheet into which data can be typed; the intersection of a row and column.

_____ The most widely used database model in use today; can link data in related tables through the use of common fields.

Answers for the self-quiz appear at the end of the book.

True/False

Instructions: Circle **T** if the statement is true or **F** if the statement is false.

T F **1.** Microsoft Works is the main office-oriented software suite offered by Microsoft Corporation for business use.

T F **2.** In a word processing document, the Enter key is always pressed at the end of each paragraph.

T F **3.** Changing the font size in a document is an example of an editing operation.

T F **4.** The cells referenced in spreadsheet formulas do not usually contain labels.

T F **5.** In a relational database program, a single database may contain more than one table.

Completion

Instructions: Answer the following questions.

6. _____ programs can be duplicated to give to others, but a payment is requested for continued use of the product.

7. Times New Roman is an example of a(n) _____; 12-point Times New Roman is an example of a(n) _____.

8. The location where a row and column meet in a spreadsheet program is called a(n) _____.

9. To retrieve specific information from a database, a(n) _____ is usually used.

10. A collection of pages created in a presentation graphics program designed to be displayed one after the other is usually called a(n) _____.

1. Would rearranging the paragraphs in a document using a word processing program use a move operation or a copy operation? Explain your answer.

2. Match each of the following with the description that fits best:

_____ =SUM(A1:A2)
_____ John Smith
_____ D4
_____ 150
_____ F18:F28
_____ =B6*C6

  a. An absolute cell address
  b. A formula
  c. A block
  d. A label
  e. A constant value
  f. A function

3. Referring to the table below, answer the following questions.

   a. How many records are there?

   b. How many fields are there?

   c. For a query requesting to see the records in which the State was "CO" and the Customer Balance was less than $10, how many customers would the query results contain?

Customer number	Name	Street	City	State	ZIP	Balance $
810	John T. Smith	31 Cedarcrest	Boulder	CO	80302	10.00
775	Sally Jones	725 Agua Fria	Santa Fe	NM	87501	0
690	William Holmes	3269 Fast Lane	Boulder	CO	80302	150.35
840	Artis Smith	2332 Alameda	Lakewood	CO	80215	3.50

4. For each of the following applications, select the most appropriate type of presentation graphic. Note that all graphic types will not be used.

_____ Illustrating the monthly sales for the past three months.

_____ Listing the corporate goals for the upcoming year.

_____ Illustrating the percent of sales coming from each sales territory.

   a. Pie chart

   b. Bar chart

   c. Line chart

   d. Text chart

   e. Organizational chart

5. For each of the following applications, select the most appropriate type of software. Note that all software types will not be used.

_____ Creating a custom music CD.

_____ Practicing your multiplication tables.

_____ Creating a child's birthday invitation.

_____ Looking up the capital of Brazil.

   a. Multimedia software

   b. Reference software

   c. Project management software

   d. Accounting software

   e. Educational software

   f. Personal publishing software

   g. CAD software

1. **WP Features** Most word processing programs offer a whole host of features to make your word processing tasks easier. These features include wizards, templates, macros, automatic spell checking, document tracking, support for other languages, a thesaurus, online collaboration, Web page creation, etc. For this project, identify and describe what you think are the five most important features offered by the word processing program installed on the computer you use most often. In addition, list and describe the wizards and templates available in that program for starting a new document. At the conclusion of your research, prepare a one-page summary of your findings and submit it to your instructor.

2. **SS and DB Features** Most spreadsheet and database programs include a set of templates to help you get started. The spreadsheet templates include built in formulas and formatting to save you time and effort. The database templates are predesigned to allow you to begin the task of data entry and report generation as soon as possible. For this project, identify what templates are available for the spreadsheet and database programs installed on the computer you use most often. Further investigate two of the spreadsheet templates and one of the database templates by opening them and discovering how they are set up and what they allow you to do. At the conclusion of your research, prepare a one-page summary of your findings and submit it to your instructor.

3. **3rd Party Documentation** Reading a book about how to use a particular application program that was written by an independent user rather than the company that produced the software can sometimes prove to be very helpful. It is generally assumed that a user who was not involved in the development of the software would tend to write a book about the software from the user's perspective, and, therefore, it would be easier to understand and use for learning purposes (but this is not always the case). For this project, visit a local or online bookstore and find at least one book about each of the application programs you will learn, or have already learned about, in this class. Write down the name of each book, the name of the author, the publisher, and the copyright date. In addition, write a one-paragraph description of each book that describes the level of the text (beginning or advanced) and topics covered. Do any of these books appeal to you? Have you used a book like one of these in the past? If so, did you like it? At the conclusion of your research, prepare a one-page summary of your findings and submit it to your instructor.

4. **Taking a Tour** Many application programs include built-in tours or tutorials that allow you to learn about the capabilities of the software. Some software companies even make these tours available over the Internet so that you can view them prior to purchasing the software. For this project, use a PC to take a tour of an application program that you would like to learn more about. If you don't have access to the program, or if the tour is not available on the computer, you should access the program's Web site to try to locate a tour or demonstration available over the Internet. During the tour, take some notes about those features that are of most interest to you. At the conclusion of this task, prepare a one-page summary of your efforts and submit it to your instructor.

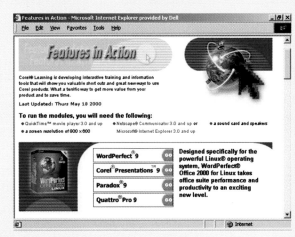

5. **Reference Software** As described in the chapter, reference software includes encyclopedias, dictionaries, atlases, ZIP code dictionaries, mapping/travel programs, and more. Many of these programs are available for purchase; some can be accessed over the Internet for free or with a paid subscription. For this project, visit your local software retailer or browse the Internet to identify at least five different reference programs of interest to you. Be sure to describe the type of information available to you by using each piece of reference software and if you think the software is worth the purchase price. Are any of these programs packaged together and sold as a suite? Submit this project to your instructor in the form of a short paper, not more than two pages in length.

6. **Educational Software** The amount of educational software available on the market has grown tremendously in the past few years. The advances in computer technology have made it possible to present concepts in a multimedia format and allow students of all ages to experience an interactive and self-paced approach to learning. Although it is not believed that this form of education will replace the traditional forms of instruction, it will certainly complement them and make the educational process more productive for both the student and the instructor. For this project, identify at least four categories of educational software that are of interest to you and investigate what programs are currently available in each category. What programs did you find? Which ones were of particular interest to you and why? Submit this project to your instructor in the form of a short paper, not more than two pages in length.

7. **Game Software** The amount of game software that can be played over the Internet, purchased as individual programs and played on your home PC, or purchased and played on a separate hardware device like the Sony PlayStation 2 or Sega Dreamcast is simply amazing. Some Web sites and traditional stores categorize the games by genres like action, adventure, role-playing, strategy, etc. In addition, many Web sites that sell game software will allow you to play online versions of these games and offer previews, reviews, and online tutorials for many of the most popular games. Traditional stores may allow potential purchasers to try out several games on one or more display computers or devices. For this project, form a group to investigate game software. Your group should visit a software store that sells game software, or visit a software game Web site and select at least three games that are of interest to the group members. After selecting the games, each member of the group should play each game and determine if the games meet, or exceed, their expectations. Be sure to identify the name of the game, version number, manufacturer, price, and reaction from the group for each game evaluated. Your group should submit this project to your instructor in the form of a short paper, not more than three pages in length.

8. **Software FAQs** Companies that sell application programs usually offer online support for their customers in order to reduce the number of telephone inquiries, and to improve customer service. The online support Web site will generally allow the customer to access a searchable knowledge base, submit a question to an online support person, or review a set of frequently asked questions (FAQs) by product. For this project, visit the customer support Web site for two of the software applications that you are learning in conjunction with this course and prepare a short presentation about the types of support available. In addition, summarize and present a few of the FAQs and answers that you found most helpful. This presentation should not exceed 5 minutes and should make use of one or more presentation aids such as the chalkboard, handouts, overhead transparencies, or computer-based slide presentation format. You may be asked to submit a summary of the presentation to your instructor.

9. **The New Standard** The traditional requirements and guidelines associated with the task of writing a news summary, report, or research paper have been consistent since these tasks were first assigned. However, the electronic tools, networking capabilities, and software at your disposal to accomplish these tasks have changed dramatically in the past decade. For this project, form a group to prepare a presentation that contrasts the research methods and preparation tools of a decade ago with the research methods and preparation tools available today. In the presentation, the group should identify how the content, format, and delivery of a news summary, report, or research paper created today might differ from one created just a decade ago. This presentation should not exceed 10 minutes and should make use of one or more presentation aids such as the chalkboard, handouts, overhead transparencies, or computer-based slide presentation format. Your group may be asked to submit a summary of the presentation to your instructor.

10. **Compatibility** Files created by an application program are often upward-compatible, but not always downward-compatible. In other words, if you create a file using the most recent version of Microsoft Word and attempt to open the file using Word 95, you may get an error message. However, you would be able to open a Word 95 file in Word XP. In addition, you may be able to open a document created in a different program, if the program is a similar type (such as opening a Word document in WordPerfect). Some application programs feature a "Save As" option to save the file in a format appropriate for an older version of the program or for a different program, but this is not always the case. When compatibility is a problem, more universal formats, such as .rtf (rich text format) and .pdf (portable document format) can be used.

For this project, form a group to investigate the compatibility issues discussed above for at least two popular programs and present your findings. In addition, your group should investigate what the .rtf and .pdf formats are, what company created the formats, how a file in each format is created, and in which programs it can be viewed. Do you have to pay for the program that creates the files? Do you have to pay for the program that views them? Can you edit documents that use those formats? Have any of the members of your group experienced one of the compatibility issues discussed above, and if so, how did you resolve the problem? This presentation should not exceed 10 minutes and should make use of one or more presentation aids such as the chalkboard, handouts, overhead transparencies, or computer-based slide presentation format. Your group may be asked to submit a summary of the presentation to your instructor.

11. **The Games We Play** In the past few years, games have become a large part the entertainment industry. They are now competing with TV, movies, and music as an entertainment medium of choice for today's youth. Fortunately, or unfortunately depending on your point of view, many of these games have evolved from what used to be action, adventure, and strategy, into hybrids that combine these categories around a central theme of violence. It seems like only a few years ago that we had games called Pac-Man, Frogger, and Mario Brothers, and now we have games called Street Fighter, Mortal Combat, and DOOM. In the future, as these games improve in their ability to engage us in an almost surreal world where we become both intellectually and emotionally evolved, we will need to think hard about restricting, controlling, or managing the access our youth have to these games.

Select one of the following positions, or make up your own, and express your point of view on the subject. Your instructor will indicate whether your response is to be posted to a class bulletin board, discussed in a class chat room, or discussed as an in-class activity. You may also be asked to submit a summary of your position and point of view to your instructor.

a. Man has been engaging in violent behavior for thousands of years. We have not been induced into engaging in acts of violence because of video games. Besides, we as humans have the ability to control our primal instincts and resolve confrontational situations in a manner which would not involve physical combat. In short, video games don't play a significant role in shaping the minds and actions of our youth and no regulation or control is warranted.

b. Our youth are very impressionable, and there is direct correlation between the violence enacted in video games and the potential for aggressive behavior in our youth. In the absence of some sort of regulation or control over this medium of entertainment, our youth will be affected by what they see and hear in these video games, which may lead to much heartache and tragedy in the future.

12. **An Application Education** Consider the following statement and establish your position, or point of view, on the subject. Your instructor will indicate whether your response is to be posted to a class bulletin board, discussed in a class chat room, or discussed as an in-class activity. You may also be asked to submit a summary of your position and evaluation of the statement to your instructor.

In the past few years many colleges and universities have started using application programs called *courseware* to automate some or most of the educational process for specific courses. These courseware programs focus on what is commonly referred to as the "student-driven" and "group-driven" learning models, as opposed to the "instructor-driven" models where the instructor lectures and the students participate in the traditional format. Courses offered in this format are called online or distance learning courses, and are usually offered in either a hybrid format where part of the course is online and part of the course is in the traditional format, or a completely online format where the entire course is conducted online. The automated portions of these courses deliver the course content in a digital format over the Web, on a CD, or both. In addition, students have the added benefits associated with most courseware programs such as online bulletin boards, chat rooms, e-mail, access to course grades, etc. Proponents of this type of education cite studies that focus on the positive aspects of the online approach, like the ability of students to engage in the instructional process on an anywhere, anytime basis, and the idea that student- or group-driven learning is more effective than instructor-driven learning. Opponents of this type of education cite studies that focus on the negative aspects associated with the online approach and claim that we are taking a step backwards by encouraging a mass-production and standardized approach to education with an eye toward commercial interests.

Interactive Exercise

Using Application Software. It's time to practice opening, closing, pasting, and other document-handling operations. Go to the Interactive Exercise at www.course.com/parker2002/ch7 to complete this exercise.

MODULE NET

COMPUTER NETWORKS

Computer networks play a critical role in society and business today. Without computer networks, it would be impossible for us to enjoy many of the modern conveniences that we depend on and that most businesses use to compete effectively.

Chapter 8 introduces the basic principles of communications and networks. Here you learn about many of the hardware, software, and communications–media products used to build networks, as well as common types of networks and transmission methods.

The Internet and its World Wide Web are the topic of Chapter 9. Though they were introduced in Chapter 2, Chapter 9 explains how the Internet and World Wide Web originated, and looks more closely at how to find information on the Web. Useful strategies, such as how to select an ISP and how to perform Internet searches, are some of the topics included in this chapter.

NETWORKS

CHAPTER 8

Communications and Networks

LEARNING OBJECTIVES

After completing this chapter, you will be able to:

1. Appreciate the changing nature of the communications industry and the effects of government legislation.

2. Describe several uses for communications technology.

3. Explain the difference between local area, wide area, and other types of networks.

4. Name specific types of transmission media and explain how they transmit messages from one device to another.

5. Identify the different protocols that can be used to connect the devices on a network.

6. Discuss some security issues involved with computer network usage.

7. List some employment opportunities and certifications available for networking professionals.

The term *communications,* when used in a computer context, refers to *telecommunications*–communications from one device to another using communications media. Such media can include phone lines, privately owned cables, and the airwaves. Communications usually take place over some type of communications *network* (a group of connected devices), such as a company network, the Internet, or a phone system. Communications applications have contributed to the essential role of the computer in the workplace and have boosted its popularity in the home.

In business, communications is an integral part of operations. Businesspeople throughout the world regularly use electronic mail and messaging systems to communicate with fellow employees and distant associates. Documents that companies once hand delivered from person to person now are delivered almost instantly at the click of a mouse. Computers allow ordering to take place in real time via the Internet or telephone, and shipping systems depend on computers that regularly communicate with other computers miles away to ensure on-time deliveries and allow real-time tracking of packages. The list of applications is endless.

In the home, the biggest communications development of recent years has been the whirlwind popularity of the Internet and World Wide Web. Almost overnight, the personal computer has evolved into a vehicle through which people communicate with faraway friends, work from remote locations, locate useful information, and obtain entertainment. Information on virtually any topic, stored on computers located almost anywhere on the globe, can be retrieved within seconds. With communications companies scrambling to bring faster transmissions into the home and with the Internet evolving to deliver new forms of services and entertainment, many industry experts predict that the best is yet to come.

In Chapter 8, we first profile the communications industry and discuss how government legislation has shaped its growth. Next, we look at several common communications applications. We then proceed to the major types of networks, including local area networks and wide area networks. From there, we touch on a number of technical issues, including the ways in which computers transmit data, the types of transmission media involved, and how networked devices connect to one another. The chapter closes with a discussion of some important network security issues and a brief look at some of the employment opportunities available in the rapidly growing field of computer networking. ■

THE COMMUNICATIONS INDUSTRY

The communications industry has been undergoing revolutionary changes over the past several years. Mergers between some of the industry's leading companies and vast technological improvements have added to this upheaval. In the next few sections, we look at the types of firms that make up the communications industry. We also consider the role government plays in shaping that industry's future.

The Major Players

At one time, the communications industry was synonymous with the phone company. While phone companies are still a major part of the communications scene, these days many other players participate as well. Keep in mind that the distinction between the following categories is blurring and some companies may fall into more than one category. For example, many phone companies are also Internet service providers.

Phone Companies

The phone companies own much of the mammoth telephone network that can connect virtually any two points on the globe. These companies not only provide regular phone service, but they also transmit data between businesses and handle a majority of Internet traffic. Some carriers provide just long-distance, local, or wireless service. Increasingly, firms are offering all these options, especially those that have merged with others to form national communications companies—a trend that regularly changes the players in the communications industry. Some of the biggest phone carriers are AT&T, MCI WorldCom, Sprint, Verizon (formed by the merger of Bell Atlantic and GTE), Verizon Wireless (consisting of GTE Wireless and AirTouch Cellular, among others), and SBC Communications (which provides comprehensive communications products and services through a global network of such brands as Southwestern Bell South, Pacific Bell, Ameritech, and Cellular One). The Germany-based Deutsche Telekom is one of the largest international phone carriers.

Many of the big phone companies provide and maintain the extremely fast, high-capacity, fiber-optic lines that are called *Internet backbones.* These lines are designed to carry data at very high speeds between regions of a country.

Cable-TV and Satellite Companies

At one time this industry sector operated almost exclusively to transmit television broadcasts. But the situation is dramatically changing. With cable now reaching into most major cities and towns and satellite dishes serving outlying areas, companies in this sector—such as AT&T Broadband, Time Warner Cable, and Comcast Cable—are well positioned to use their communications infrastructures to disseminate new information products such as electronic shopping and banking, video on-demand, and Internet services, in addition to traditional cable content. The largest satellite companies include Hughes Network Systems (DirecTV and DirecPC), EchoStar (DISH Networks and StarBand), and Gilat. While cable-TV and satellite firms have powerful transmission capabilities, until recently their systems were designed for one-way high-speed broadcasting. With this type of setup, a phone line was needed to transmit data back to the cable or satellite company. The two-way high-speed satellite and cable services now available don't require a phone line and should facilitate more interactive applications than were previously possible.

Service and Content Providers

The types of companies discussed thus far collectively own and operate the infrastructure over which information travels. Many of these companies also provide services along this infrastructure—such as phone, Internet, and television services—and are therefore also *service providers.* But you don't have to own part of the infrastructure to operate a service business. Service providers like America Online, for instance, rent capacity over a communications infrastructure and sell it to users. Since America Online also supplies content to the Internet (such as its own Web site and celebrity forums), it is also a *content provider.* The Internet has countless content providers—ranging from such familiar companies as Disney (entertainment) and CNN (news), to ordinary people who post personal information on their Web sites.

Software and Hardware Companies

Software companies—like Microsoft, IBM, and Oracle—contribute to the communications industry by building the necessary capabilities into the information software products of the future. Hardware firms such as Cisco Systems, Lucent Technologies, and Nortel Networks supply the communications hardware to the marketplace that allow national carriers and other companies to maintain and improve their networks.

further exploration

For links to further information about communications companies, go to www.course.com/parker2002/ch8

Throughout the communications industry, the wave of mergers, acquisitions, and partnering arrangements will determine the dominant players of the future. Firms that have traditionally operated in one sector are quickly expanding into other sectors to position themselves for success. A communications infrastructure needs content to deliver, and a content provider needs infrastructure to carry its product, so many firms are beginning to supply both ends to increase their product base and at the same time decrease their dependence on other firms. Furthermore, this activity requires the development of new software and the construction of new networks. To deliver the information products of the future, companies have to think beyond traditional markets and boundaries. Microsoft is one familiar company that's taken a plunge into this uncertain future by rapidly transforming itself from strictly a software company to a provider of hardware, Internet access, and online content.

The Government and Legislation

Not too long ago, AT&T was "the" phone company in the United States. It owned essentially all the phone lines and the phones used with those lines. At that time, the federal government believed that the survival of the phone system depended on protecting the interests of a single provider, though the government also tightly regulated AT&T.

The wheels of change began to turn in 1968, when the Federal Communications Commission (FCC) produced the *Carterfone Decision,* allowing a small company to connect its own two-way radios to the phone lines. This ruling opened the door for anyone to buy a non-AT&T phone and hook it up to the AT&T system. Later federal government rulings forced AT&T to divest its regional phone services—today's Baby Bells—and enabled companies like MCI and Sprint to compete with AT&T for long-distance phone business.

Despite the injection of competition, however, industry regulation was still relatively tight at the end of the 1980s. A license to operate in one sector of the industry often prohibited a company from entering another. Critics of government policy argued that this regulatory model would not serve the public well in the upcoming age of fast-paced technological change. They felt that if government tore down barriers to competition—so that companies were free to operate wherever they wanted—consumers would get better products at lower prices.

The *Telecommunications Act of 1996* essentially deregulated the entire communications industry. Telephone companies, cable-TV and satellite operators, and firms in other segments of the industry are now free to enter each other's markets. If telephone companies can compete with cable-TV operators, so the thinking goes, then perhaps the final result will be better television programming and service at lower prices. Similarly unconstrained cable-TV operators might also be able to produce better results with phone service.

Conventional wisdom may or may not prove correct, and you should expect turbulence in the future regulatory environment of the communications industry. Of course, it is not out of the realm of possibility that the government could reverse itself and return to a regulatory mode. A change in policy would be likely if deregulation produces monopolistic giants who keep prices high and thwart industry progress.

In addition to passing legislation regarding communications in general, the government has a distinct impact on the industry because of its ability to block potential mergers between communications companies. Generally, these blocks are justified on the basis of antitrust law to prevent new monopolies. The same antitrust justification is used to break apart companies—such as with the attempted break up of Microsoft in 2000 which, as of this writing, hadn't yet been resolved.

web tutor

For a tutorial on various uses of networks for communication, go to www.course.com/parker2002/ch8

COMMUNICATIONS APPLICATIONS

Today, a wide variety of important business applications involve communications, and the roster of uses is growing rapidly. Two of the most important applications are using the Internet and World Wide Web and exchanging e-mail, both of which were discussed in Chapter 2. Some other communications applications are mentioned briefly next.

Paging and Messaging

Two communications applications related to e-mail are *paging* and *messaging. Paging* is the term generally used for one-way communications, where short numeric or text messages are sent to a person's pager using his or her pager telephone number. The fastest-growing type of pager use today is two-way paging, generally referred to as *messaging.* These newer types of pagers usually allow you to send and receive text messages, as well as short e-mail messages. Some even allow downloading selected information—such as news, sports scores, and stock quotes—from the Internet. As shown in Figure 8-1, the newer two-way messaging devices usually have some type of built-in keyboard; traditional pagers don't. Both types of devices often communicate over special wireless networks. Messaging systems are extremely popular in other countries and their popularity is rapidly growing in the United States.

Wireless Phones

Cellular (cell) phones (see Figure 8-2) are the most common type of *wireless* or *mobile phones*—telephones that work without being connected to a standard phone outlet. Another, but less common, type of wireless telephone is the *satellite phone.* Though their use is similar, the technology driving each type of phone differs, as discussed later in this chapter. Both types of phones allow people to communicate with others from almost anywhere, and many of these phones can be used for messaging. Some phones can also be used for e-mail access and retrieving information from the Web, though their lack of or limited keyboard and small text-based screen limit the amount of Web activity many users wish to use their phone for. In countries where PC Internet access is not as prevalent, however, Internet telephone access is increasing dramatically. For instance, about 20,000 people a day are signing up for phone Internet access in Japan, where home PC Internet access is limited by expense and space.

Cellular phone use has increased at an astonishing rate: From 1.6 million users a decade ago, over 700 million users are expected by the year 2003. In fact, some people today have abandoned the conventional telephone entirely and use a cell phone exclusively. As cellular usage fees continue to decrease and as flat rates for local calls become more available, this will likely become more common. Cellular networks are a hit internationally too, especially in such countries as Poland, China, and Finland. And in countries with a poor traditional communications infrastructure, it is much easier to build new cellular networks than to fix current facilities or to install wired systems.

further exploration

For links to further information about mobile communications devices, go to www.course.com/parker2002/ch8

▶ FIGURE 8-1

Messaging devices. Unlike pagers which can be used to send very short numeric messages, many messaging devices can also send text-based messages, as well as download Web content and exchange e-mail and other types of messages.

NET

▶ FIGURE 8-2

Mobile phones. Types of mobile phones include cellular phones (left) and satellite phones (right). Mobile phones can frequently be used to access Internet resources, such as e-mail or Web page content, as well as their regular voice communications function.

Faxing

Fax (facsimile) technology resembles e-mail, except that it allows users to send images of documents to others over ordinary phone lines instead of sending an electronic copy of the actual text contained in the document, as in an e-mail file attachment. Faxed documents can contain text, photographs, or other images, as well as handwritten notations; since the document is sent as an image, all of the elements are transmitted just as they appear on the original document.

To fax documents, you can use a stand-alone *fax machine* or a computer with a *fax/modem board* and appropriate software. Both methods can send and receive faxed documents. Fax machines have the advantage of being able to rapidly transmit already printed documents. To send a printed document using a computer, the document would have to be input into the computer first (using some type of scanner) and then faxed. Consequently, computers are more frequently used to fax documents already in electronic form, such as word processing documents. In fact, many word processing programs now have faxing integrated into the program, so documents can be faxed about as easily as sending the document to a different printer.

Faxing capabilities are often combined with other mail and messaging technologies. For instance, free and paid *e-faxing* services are available on the Internet to allow a person to receive faxes via their e-mail address. Regardless of the type of fax device used, all fax technologies can communicate with each other. For example, a document sent by a stand-alone fax machine can be sent to another fax machine, a PC, or an Internet fax service.

Global Positioning Systems (GPS)

A **global positioning system** or **GPS** consists of a *GPS receiver* that can receive data sent by a specific group of 24 Department of Defense GPS satellites. The GPS receiver interprets the data to determine the receiver's exact geographic location. Though originally used solely by the military, GPS systems are now widely available for business and personal use. Today GPS systems are commonly used by hikers and motorists, surveyors, farmers, fishermen, and other individuals who want or need to know their precise geographical position at specific times. In the past, the government required consumer GPS receivers to be less accurate than they were technologically able to be. This practice was discontinued in 2000, leading to more accurate GPS receivers. Many systems now claim to be accurate within 3 meters (less than 10 feet).

Stand-alone GPS receivers are usually very portable (see Figure 8-3), often similar in size to a cell phone. GPS receivers are also beginning to become integrated into cars, as well as into mobile phones and other handheld devices. Using a GPS receiver attachment on a handheld PC, for example, allows the user to continuously determine his or her exact position while hiking or driving; downloaded maps could be used in conjunction with this information for navigational purposes. Some expect GPS systems to be a standard feature in new cars in the near future.

Satellite Radio

Another application that employs the use of satellites is *satellite radio*. Most often used in systems for the car, satellite radio offers delivery of radio stations across an entire country, instead of the usual limited broadcast area. This means one could drive from coast to coast without ever switching the radio station. One of the most prominent satellite radio providers is Sirius, which broadcasts 50 commercial-free radio stations that can be accessed across the entire United States. Most satellite radio services require a monthly subscription fee, usually $10 to $15 per month.

>**Global positioning system (GPS).** A system that uses satellites and a special type of receiver to determine the exact geographic location of the receiver.

> **FIGURE 8-3**

GPS. Global positioning systems can be used by anyone who needs to know their exact geographical location, such as for safety or navigational purposes.

Videoconferencing

Videoconferencing (also called *teleconferencing*) refers to the use of computer and communications technology to conduct face-to-face meetings between people in different locations. Using relatively inexpensive software and hardware, people can hear each other through their PC speakers and see each other on their PC screens (see Figure 8-4). Two of the most widely used programs for this purpose include *CUseeMe* and *Microsoft NetMeeting,* both available without charge. Microsoft Windows XP includes a newer program for this purpose called *Windows Messenger.* Some videoconferencing applications—such as distance learning classes and corporate videoconferences—may require a more sophisticated setup, such as a dedicated teleconferencing room set up with video cameras, large monitors, microphones, and other hardware. When teleconferencing is performed over the Internet (the norm today), it is sometimes referred to as *Web conferencing.*

> **FIGURE 8-4**
Videoconferencing.

Telecommuting

Telecommuting refers to people working at home, connected to their place of business using such means as the Internet, fax machines, personal computers, telephones, and pagers. With such tools, the employee can retrieve company database information and presentation materials, get phone calls, and exchange e-mail messages while working away from the office. Telecommuting enables a company to save on office and parking space and offers an

---

>**Videoconferencing.** Using computers and communications technology to carry on a meeting between people in different geographical locations.
>**Telecommuting.** Using a variety of computer and electronic devices to enable an individual to work from his or her home.

inside the industry

Internet Telephony

Packet Switching Is Making Calling Cheaper

Qwest Communications, MCI WorldCom, and Nokia are three companies betting on digital networks and packet switching for the phone system of the future.

Qwest was one of the pioneers. In the late 1990s, it began laying its own fiber-optic cable to offer voice subscribers in selected cities a faster, cheaper system than the traditional phone network. Customers often paid 5 cents a minute or less for calls. Qwest's network and those of its closest competitors deploy packet switching, a technology made famous by the Internet and its IP or Internet protocol. All messages traveling through the network—whether voice, text, graphics, or video data—are subdivided into units called packets. Packets travel independently across long distances and are assembled at the destination. When a private network is involved, this process is commonly referred to as "IP telephony" or "voice over IP."

For wireless users, the new General Packet Radio Service (GPRS), a faster version of the Global System for Mobile (GSM) communication network, is bringing mobile communications closer to the Internet experience. GPRS, like the Internet, is a packet-based wireless communication service. It can transmit data up to 114,000 bits per second, and promises a continuous—always-on—connection to the Internet for mobile phone and computer users.

While using broadband digital networks with packet switching like the Internet is still a viable possibility, placing calls over the Internet—referred to as Internet telephony—is expected to have phenomenal growth in the next few years. Services, such as Web2Phone, have allowed users to place free PC-to-PC or low-cost PC-to-phone calls over the Internet for several years now (or even phone-to-phone using a special device, such as the one in the accompanying photo). Recently, large businesses with PBX internal telephone systems have been looking at IP telephony as a replacement for their existing systems. Integrating voice traffic and data traffic on the same network has the advantages of lower cost to set up and maintain one instead of two separate networks; the ability to use an intuitive computer interface to set up conference calls, call-forwarding, retrieve voice mail, and other telephone activities; and remote access through the Internet for mobile workers. One estimate has projected IP telephony use for businesses growing from around 330 million minutes in 2000 to over 200 billion minutes in 2005.

The primary advantage of Internet-based telephone calls for individuals is the potential huge cost savings. Since the service is not distance dependent, it can be offered to customers at lower prices, especially on long-distance and international calls. It is even possible that, at some point in the future, your phone bill may change, looking more like the one from the electric company. Instead of being charged for the distance a call travels, you may be metered for the amount of time you are connected.

Yap Phone. Internet phone calls using the Yap Phone shown here in conjunction with Net2Phone service are free between Yap Phone users, and start at 1 cent per minute for domestic calls and 3.9 cents per minute for international calls otherwise.

employee considerable freedom in choosing when and where he or she wishes to work. As an environmental plus, it also helps cut down on the traffic and pollution derived from traditional work commuting.

The use of Internet technology to place telephone calls is the subject of this chapter's Inside the Industry box.

WHAT IS A NETWORK?

As discussed in Chapter 2, a **network** consists of a collection of computers and other hardware devices that are connected together to share hardware, software, and data, as well as to facilitate electronic communications. As discussed in Chapter 6, network communications require the use of a network operating system or a personal operating system with networking capabilities. A few specific uses for networks are listed in Figure 8-5.

Some of the characteristics of a network include its physical arrangement, its size, and the distance it spans, as discussed in the next few sections.

Topologies

Communications networks can be classified in terms of their physical arrangement or *topology*. Three common topologies are the star, bus, and ring (see Figure 8-6).

Star Networks

The **star network**—the oldest topology for computer networks—consists of a central computer as a *host* device to which all the computers and other devices in the network connect, forming a star shape. Sometimes, instead of using a central computer to connect the devices on a star network, a hub is used. A **hub** contains multiple ports to connect the devices in a network and acts as a central location where data arrives and then is transferred on in one or more directions. Star networks are common in traditional mainframe environments, as well as small office or home networks. In a star network, all data and other communications are sent through the host computer or hub.

Bus Networks

A **bus network** has no host computer. Instead, it consists of a central cable to which all network devices are attached in a linear fashion. For example, the bus network illustrated in Figure 8-6 contains three PCs and a printer attached to a single bus line. In a bus network,

Uses for Networks
Sharing expensive devices like network printers among several users
Sharing application software so it can be purchased less expensively than for each computer and only needs to be installed and updated on one computer
Sharing data, such as a company database
Facilitating electronic mail exchanges and Internet access

FIGURE 8-5
Uses for networks.

FIGURE 8-6
Basic network topologies.
Most networks use a simple star, bus, or ring shape.

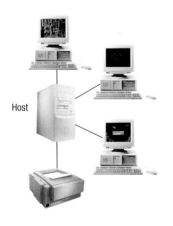

STAR NETWORK
A star network connects a single central host or hub directly to each device on the network.

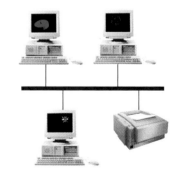

BUS NETWORK
A bus network uses a high-speed cable to which each device is connected in a linear fashion.

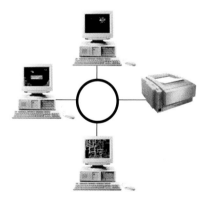

RING NETWORK
In a ring network, computers and other devices are connected in a loop.

Host

>**Network.** A collection of computers and other hardware devices that are connected together to share hardware, software, and data, as well as to facilitate electronic communications. >**Star network.** A communications network consisting of a host device connected directly to several other devices. >**Hub.** A device that acts as a central location where data arrives and is then transferred on in one or more directions. >**Bus network.** A communications network consisting of a central cable to which all network devices are attached.

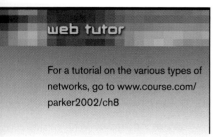

all data is transmitted down the bus line from one network device to another, and only one device can transmit at a time.

Ring Networks

A less common alternative to the star and bus topologies is the **ring network.** Like a bus network, ring networks don't have a host computer, but the computers and other network devices are connected in a ring formation (see the third illustration in Figure 8-6). In a ring network, data travels from one device to another around the ring in one direction only.

Combination Topologies

Networks often combine topologies, in effect turning several smaller networks into one larger one. Figure 8-7 shows two star networks connected together using a bus. Some networks, like the Internet, contain redundant links and so do not conform to a standard topology.

Local Area Networks (LANs)

Organizations often need networks to connect geographically close resources, such as PCs located in the same college classroom or business office. Such networks are known as **local area networks** or **LANs.** Most LANs are of the *client-server* or *peer-to-peer* variety.

> **FIGURE 8-7**
> **Combination topologies.**
> Many networks are formed by combining topologies, such as the bus and star topologies shown here.

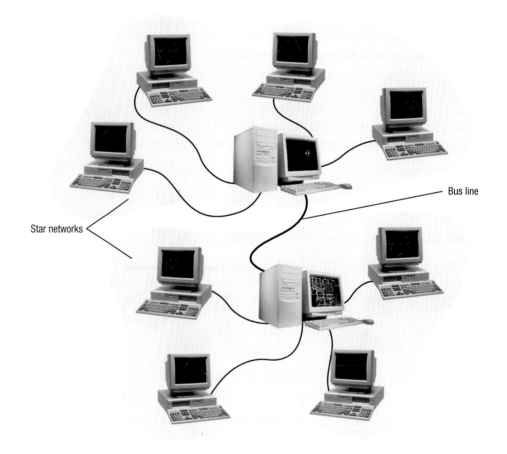

Bus line

Star networks

> **Ring network.** A communications network that connects devices in a closed loop. > **Local area network (LAN).** A network that connects devices located in a small geographical area, such as within a building.

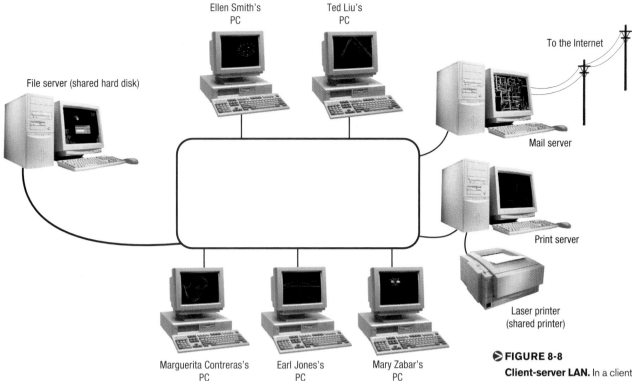

> **FIGURE 8-8**
> **Client-server LAN.** In a client-server LAN, each device that receives services is called a *client,* while the computers that manage requests for network services are called *servers.*

Client-Server LANs

Client-server LANs are so named because each workstation that receives network services is called a *client,* while the computers that manage the requests for network services are called *servers* (see Figure 8-8). For example, a *network server* manages network traffic and a *file server* manages shared files, enabling client computers to access the shared programs and data files stored on the network. Similarly, a *print server* handles printing-related activities, such as managing user output on a high-quality network printer. LANs can also incorporate such devices as *mail servers* and *Web servers,* which are dedicated to managing electronic mail and Web page requests, respectively.

Servers are typically powerful computers with lots of memory and a very large hard drive. In very large LANs, midrange and mainframe computers often function as servers. Frequently, instead of physically separate servers as illustrated in Figure 8-8, one server takes on the role of multiple servers, such as acting as both the file server and print server for the network. Retrieving files from a server is called *downloading;* transferring data from a PC back to a server is referred to as *uploading.*

Peer-to-Peer LANs

Applications that require very small networks may use a *peer-to-peer LAN.* These LANs do not predesignate computers as clients and servers per se. Instead, all the user computers and shared peripherals work on the same level, and users have direct access to each other's computers and shared peripherals. Peer-to-peer LANs were designed as a way to bring networking to small groups without the complexity and expense that normally accompany client-server systems. Peer-to-peer capabilities are built into many personal operating systems for small office or home networks.

A newer twist on peer-to-peer networking is peer-to-peer computing performed via the Internet. Instead of placing content on a Web server for others to view, content is exchanged directly with the other users of the peer-to-peer network. For instance, one user can copy a file located on another user's hard drive to his or her own PC. Another possibility is sharing a "virtual space" with others for online collaborations. Documents placed into the shared space are automatically opened on all the participants' PCs, and a shared whiteboard and instant messaging can be used for communication. To keep exchanges private, encryption software (discussed in Chapter 15) can be used. The most well-known uses of this *Internet peer-to-peer networking* are systems set up for exchanging MP3 files with others over the Internet. One such system—*Napster*—and the controversy it created is the topic of the next chapter's Inside the Industry box.

Wide Area Networks (WANs)

A **wide area network (WAN)** is a network that covers a wide geographical area. Many WANs link together two or more geographically dispersed LANs. The Internet, by this definition, is a very large WAN. Individual users connecting to a LAN from a distance is another way a WAN is created. WANs may be publicly accessible, like the Internet, or be privately owned and operated.

Most modern WANs send data in pieces or *packets*. The packets are sent individually over the WAN and then reassembled after they reach their destination. Because of this, and because WANs tie together so many different devices across such long distances, they need a number of special pieces of equipment. These devices are discussed next and several are illustrated in Figure 8-9.

FIGURE 8-9

Wide area networks (WANs). Wide area networks typically include a variety of types of devices and connecting hardware.

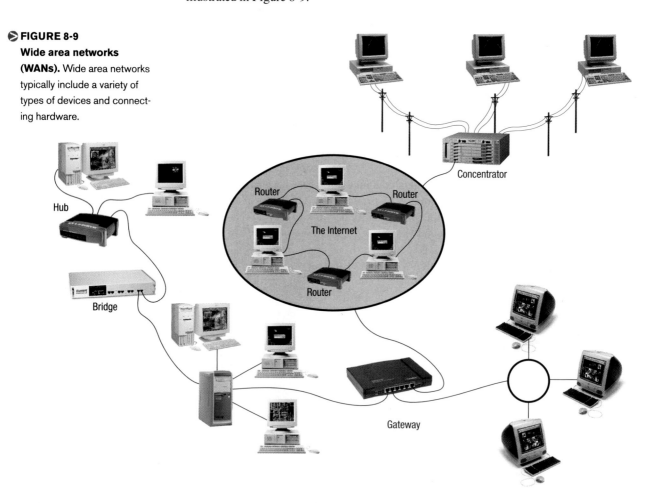

Concentrator

Router

Router

The Internet

Router

Hub

Bridge

Gateway

>**Wide area network (WAN).** A network that connects devices located in a wide geographical area.

Hubs, Switches, and Routers

As already mentioned, a hub provides a common connection point for a group of devices in a network. When a packet arrives at the hub, it is transmitted to all other network nodes connected to that hub. Similar, but more intelligent devices, are routers and switches. A *switch* transmits packets on a network, but instead of sending them to all nodes on the network like a hub, it sorts out the packets and only sends them to the proper node. This allows each node on the network to use the full capacity of the network channel; with a hub, the network capacity is shared among the nodes. *Routers* are used in large WANs—like the Internet—to pass packets along to their destinations. Most data is broken down into more than one packet and the individual packets may be routed over the same or different paths—the path taken is determined by the routers on the network. When a packet is received by a router, the router passes it along to the next router. The routers on a network work together to share information about the network. If one part of the network is congested or out of service, a router can choose to send a packet by an alternate route.

Some devices may contain the functions of two or more of these devices. For instance, a switch may include routing capabilities. Switches and routers are also often used in conjunction with *gateways* and *bridges,* discussed next.

Gateways and Bridges

Networks often must communicate with outside resources, such as those on other networks. Messages sent between two distinct networks reach their destinations via gateways and bridges.

A **gateway** is a collection of hardware and software resources that enable devices on one network to communicate with those on another, *dissimilar* network. Computers on a LAN, for instance, require a gateway to access the Internet. Two networks based on *similar* technology—such as a LAN in one city and similar LAN in another—communicate via a device called a **bridge.** Bridges can also be used to partition one large LAN into two smaller ones.

Repeaters

Repeaters are devices that amplify signals along a network. They are necessary on a WAN because signals often have to travel farther than would otherwise be possible over the wires or cables that carry them. Repeaters can also be used on LANs when longer than normal distances are required.

Multiplexers and Concentrators

High-speed communications lines are expensive and almost always have far greater capacity than a single device can use. Because of this, networks can run more efficiently if several low-speed devices share one line. A *multiplexer* makes this possible by combining the messages of several devices and sending them along a single high-speed path. When they reach their destination, the individual messages are separated from one another.

A *concentrator* is a type of multiplexer that combines multiple messages and sends them via a single transmission medium in such a way that all the individual messages are simultaneously active, instead of being sent as a single combined message.

Other Types of Networks

There are several other types of networks worth mentioning. A brief description of each follows next.

>**Gateway.** An interface that connects two dissimilar networks so they can communicate. >**Bridge.** An interface that connects two similar networks so they can communicate.

USES FOR INTRANETS
Facilitating electronic mail
Maintaining internal phone books
Storing procedure manuals
Posting training materials
Disseminating employee forms
Posting internal job listings
Providing electronic catalogs for ordering supplies
Facilitating workgroup computing
Scheduling meetings and appointments
Making available critical expertise
Disseminating newsletters
Posting reports and other types of information

▷ FIGURE 8-10

Uses for intranets. Companies can get an intranet up and running by following the standards and guidelines of the Internet and World Wide Web. Any or all of the applications listed here can become part of a company intranet.

Intranets and Extranets

An **intranet** is a private network—usually set up by a company for its employees—that implements the infrastructure and standards of the Internet and World Wide Web. Intranets today serve a variety of purposes, such as making company publications available to employees, disseminating forms, and enabling employees to communicate and work together on projects (see Figure 8-10). Because many company sites use very fast communications media, intranets can take advantage of rich, multimedia content.

In many ways, intranets provide the logical framework with which to build a company network. Many employees are already familiar with the Internet and its World Wide Web, so using their Web browser to access a similar-looking intranet virtually eliminates training requirements. Also, Internet technology (and therefore intranets) can be used with virtually any computer platform, and many companies have diverse mixtures of computers that need to communicate with one another. What's more, development costs are relatively small—no highly unique, proprietary system has to be designed.

Much newer to the scene than intranets are *extranets*—intranets that are at least partially accessible to authorized outsiders. Extranets provide such people as selected customers and suppliers access to some of a company's internal data and applications, usually via the Internet.

Storage Area Networks (SANs)

Another type of network becoming more widely implemented due in part to the rapid growth of *e-commerce* (performing business transactions over the Internet, as discussed in Chapter 11) and other Internet activities is the *storage area network* or *SAN*. A SAN is a high-speed, dedicated secure network of shared hard drives or other storage devices. It is similar to a file server, but on a larger scale because multiple storage devices are involved. And, instead of data being stored on one of the regular network servers, those servers just allow end users on the LAN or WAN access to the SAN for data retrieval. In addition to faster data access, there is the added potential benefit of overall faster network traffic resulting from the freeing up of the network task of storage retrieval.

SANs have become more important in recent years as companies have found their storage requirements increasing dramatically. It has been estimated that the storage needs of traditional businesses double annually—for some companies this amounts to several terabytes per year. An advantage to using a SAN system is that additional storage devices can be added to the SAN as more storage is required, without taking the server offline or otherwise disrupting the network.

In addition to storing data used by the company on a regular basis, SANs can also be used for backup and disaster recovery purposes. These topics are covered in Chapter 15.

Virtual Private Networks (VPNs)

A *virtual private network* or *VPN* is a network that transfers private information over a public communications system (such as the Internet) while still ensuring only authorized users have access to the information. A VPN is set up to be very secure at all times, encrypting every packet of data that flows over the network. The packets can only be decoded by users who can prove their identity.

The challenge of e-commerce has been to provide a secure environment at a manageable cost. Since using a public network is significantly cheaper than building a new private network, VPNs may very likely be the solution, at least for now. Encryption and e-commerce are discussed in more detail in later chapters.

Metropolitan Area Networks (MANs)

Short for *metropolitan area network*, a *MAN* is a network designed for a town or city. MANs usually fall between LANs and WANs in the size continuum and often are used to

---

>**Intranet.** A private network that is set up similar to the Internet's World Wide Web.

connect multiple LANs. Like WANs, most MANs are generally not owned by a single company or organization. Instead, a MAN is typically owned by either a consortium of users or by a single network provider who sells the networking service to its users.

Personal Area Networks (PANs)

A *personal area network* or *PAN* is a network of all the devices in one person's life. The PAN allows the devices to communicate and work together. The possibility of PANs is growing with the improvement of wireless technology (such as the *Bluetooth* standard discussed in a later section) that enables a collection of devices to automatically, wirelessly, communicate with each other when they get within a certain physical distance. PANs can keep portable devices synchronized with a desktop PC and coordinate Internet access and e-mail from remote locations. In a nutshell, PANs are intended to permit an individual's everyday devices to become smart devices that spontaneously network and work together.

HOW NETWORKS WORK

On a network, *transmission media* are used to send data over the network, and communications hardware is used to connect each device to the network. There are also specific characteristics about how networks send and receive data. These topics are discussed next. How the individual devices on the network communicate—called *communications protocols*—will be explored shortly.

Wired Transmission Media

Transmission media are used to transfer messages over a network. For instance, the transmission media used in a network may be a privately owned set of cables, the public phone lines, or a satellite system. Transmission media can either be wired or wireless. Wired media are discussed next; wireless media follow in a later section.

The three types of wired media most commonly used to carry messages are *twisted-pair wire, coaxial cable,* and *fiber-optic cable.*

Twisted-Pair Wire

Twisted-pair wire (two thin strands of insulated wire twisted together, as illustrated in Figure 8-11) is the transmission medium that has been in use the longest. Twisted-pair cable is used by older telephone networks, is the type of wiring used inside most homes for telephone communications, and is the least expensive type of LAN cable. Twisted-pair cable is rated by category. Category 3 twisted-pair cabling is regular telephone cable; higher speed Category 5, 6, or higher cable is frequently used for home or business networks.

In some instances, several thousand pairs of twisted-pair wire may be bound together into a single cable to connect telephone switching stations within a city. By contrast, only a few pairs are needed to connect a home phone to the closest telephone pole. Twisted-pair wire is twisted together to reduce interference and improve performance. To further improve performance it can be *shielded* with a metal lining.

Coaxial Cable

Coaxial cable, the medium pioneered by the cable television industry, was originally developed to carry high-speed, interference-free video transmissions. A coaxial cable (shown in Figure 8-11) consists of a relatively thick center wire surrounded by insulation and then a

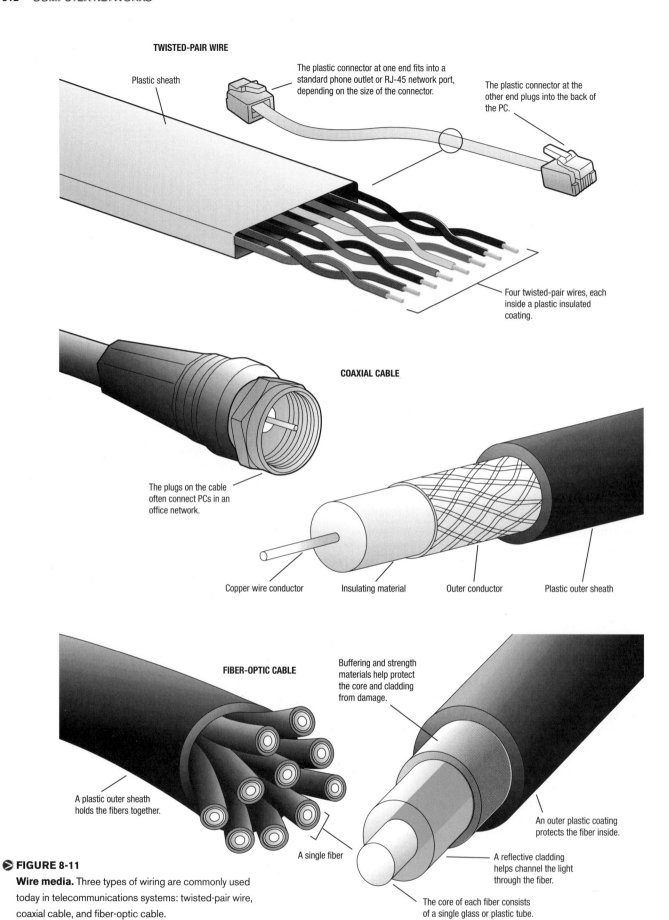

TWISTED-PAIR WIRE

Plastic sheath

The plastic connector at one end fits into a standard phone outlet or RJ-45 network port, depending on the size of the connector.

The plastic connector at the other end plugs into the back of the PC.

Four twisted-pair wires, each inside a plastic insulated coating.

COAXIAL CABLE

The plugs on the cable often connect PCs in an office network.

Copper wire conductor   Insulating material   Outer conductor   Plastic outer sheath

FIBER-OPTIC CABLE

Buffering and strength materials help protect the core and cladding from damage.

A plastic outer sheath holds the fibers together.

A single fiber

An outer plastic coating protects the fiber inside.

A reflective cladding helps channel the light through the fiber.

The core of each fiber consists of a single glass or plastic tube.

◐ **FIGURE 8-11**

Wire media. Three types of wiring are commonly used today in telecommunications systems: twisted-pair wire, coaxial cable, and fiber-optic cable.

grounded shield of braided wire (the shield minimizes electrical and radio frequency inter-ference). Coaxial cable is widely used today in computer networks. Additionally, phone companies rely heavily on coaxial cable. Although more expensive than standard telephone wire, it is much less susceptible to interference and can carry more data more quickly than twisted-pair wire.

Fiber-Optic Cable

One of the most successful developments in transmission media in recent years has been fiber optics. **Fiber-optic cable** uses clear glass or plastic fiber strands, each approximately the thickness of a human hair, to transfer data represented by light pulses (refer again to Figure 8-11). The light pulses are sent through the cable by a laser device at speeds of bil-lions or even trillions of bits per second. Each hairlike fiber has the capacity to carry data for several television stations or thousands of two-way voice conversations. Cables that link big cities often consist of several hundred fibers wrapped inside in a single cable.

Fiber-optic cable is commonly used for the high-speed backbone lines of a network, such as to connect LANs in separate buildings or for Internet infrastructure. In addition, telephone companies are steadily replacing traditional telephone lines with fiber-optic cables. In the future, it is expected that almost all communications will employ fiber optics to some extent.

The advantages of fiber optics over other traditional wire media include speed, size, weight, security, reliability, longevity, and *bandwidth* (the amount of data that can be carried at one time). In particular, enormous speed differences separate conventional wire and fiber-optic cable. While it may take a few seconds to transmit a single page of Webster's diction-ary over conventional wire, an entire 15-volume set of the *Encyclopedia Britannica* could be transmitted over fiber-optic cable in under one second. Another advantage is that data can be transmitted digitally, instead of in analog form like twisted-pair, coaxial cable, and most wireless media (discussed shortly).

The main disadvantage of fiber optics is the initial expense of both the cable and the installation. Since they are typically used for multiple purposes (such as carrying the telephone and network traffic for a college campus instead of for a single residence, for instance), fiber-optic setups often end up being less expensive when computed on a per use (per channel) basis. Another disadvantage is that fiber-optic cables are more difficult to work with than wire media.

Today most fiber-optic systems use a technology called *wave division multiplexing (WDM)* to combine 80 channels or more on the same fiber. *Dense WDM (DWDM)* is in the experimental stages, but can handle over 1,000 channels over a single fiber. DWDM is very fast, currently at about 3 terabits (3 trillion bits per second). At this speed, the entire contents of the Library of Congress could pass through a single fiber in a less than one minute.

Wireless Transmission Media

Wireless transmission media have become especially popular in recent years. They support communications in situations in which physical wiring is impractical or inconvenient (such as inside an existing home or over an ocean), as well as facilitate mobility. Wireless media are commonly used to connect devices to a network, to share information between com-puters, to connect wireless keyboards and mice to a computer, and for handheld PCs, wire-less phones, pagers, and other mobile devices. *Radio signals* transferred through the air are the heart of most types of wireless media. In addition to conventional *broadcast radio* applications, the *microwave, cellular,* and *satellite* transmission media discussed next also use radio signals to transmit data.

>**Fiber-optic cable.** A communications medium that uses hundreds of hair-thin, transparent fibers over which lasers transmit data as light.

Radio Technology

Radio transmissions (sometimes called *broadcast radio*) require the use of a *transmitter* to send the radio signals through the air. A *receiver* (usually containing some type of antenna) accepts the data at the other end. When a device functions as both a receiver and transmitter, it is commonly called a *transmitter-receiver* or *transceiver.*

Radio technology can transmit data over long distances. In addition to being used by radio and television stations to broadcast content, a special type of high-frequency broadcast radio is also used to provide high-speed Internet access in some areas to businesses and homes. In order to connect to the Internet in this manner, a roof-mounted antenna and a transceiver are required. Most of these setups are within a limited geographical area, such as within 100 miles of the ISP. The common term for this type of Internet service is *fixed wireless.*

Much of the radio technology used for networking and other types of personal communications is relatively short range. Short-range radio technology can be used to connect portable devices, such as a notebook computer, handheld computer, or other portable device, to a network. For example, it is common to have portable inventory devices located in a warehouse broadcast data to a transceiver located on the wall or ceiling of the warehouse. That transceiver, in turn, passes the data on to the network. Radio technology is also used with portable mice and keyboards, so the device doesn't have to be in line of sight of the receiver connected to the computer in order to function.

To respond to the increased use of short-range radio for transmitting data, radio capabilities are beginning to be built in to laptop and other portable computers. Radio-based wireless Internet access is available in public locations, such as airports, hotels, and restaurants. For example, Starbucks has an agreement with one wireless Internet provider to serve over 4,000 Starbucks locations. At most of these types of public Internet access points, customers are charged for their Internet time. Radio is also more commonly being used for home and small office networks.

Microwave and Satellite Technology

Microwaves are high-frequency, high-speed radio signals. All types of data (text, graphics, audio, video, etc.) can be converted to microwave impulses and transmitted through the air. Microwave signals can be sent in two ways: via *microwave stations* or via *satellites* (see Figure 8-12). Both can transmit data in large quantities and at high speeds, and are ideal for applications such as television and radio broadcasting and Internet downloads. They are also expected to be widely used in the near future for mobile telephone traffic, as well as for paging and messaging systems.

Terrestrial (earth-based) **microwave stations** can communicate with each other directly over distances of no more than about 30 miles or so. The stations use line-of-sight transmission, which means that the microwaves must travel in a straight line from one station to another with an unobstructed path. To avoid obstacles like mountains and the curvature of the earth, the stations are often placed on tall buildings and mountaintops. When one station receives a message from another, it amplifies it and passes it on to the next station.

Communications **satellites** are devices placed into orbit around the earth to receive and transmit microwave signals to and from terrestrial microwave stations. They were developed to facilitate microwave transmission when terrestrial stations were either not economically viable (such as over large, sparsely populated areas) or physically impractical (such as over large bodies of water). Traditional satellites maintain a *geosynchronous orbit,* 22,300 miles above the earth. "Geosynchronous" means that, because the satellites travel at a speed that keeps pace with the earth's rotation, they appear to remain stationary over a given spot on the globe. Such satellites are so far above the surface of the earth that it takes only two or three of them to blanket the entire planet.

> **Microwave station.** An earth-bound device that sends and receives high-frequency, high-speed radio signals. > **Satellite.** An earth-orbiting device that relays communications signals over long distances.

FIGURE 8-12

Microwave and satellite transmission. Microwave signals can move via terrestrial microwave stations or communications satellites.

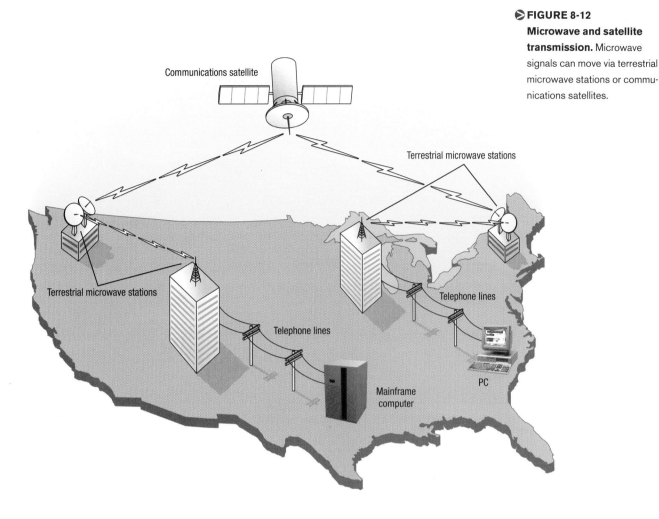

One example of a geosynchronous satellite system is *StarBand,* the first two-way satellite Internet service available for homes and businesses.

Though geosynchronous satellites are excellent for transmitting data, they are so far away that there is a slight delay while the signals travel from earth, to the satellite, and back to earth again. Though this delay—about a half-second—is very small for the distance involved and, though it doesn't really interfere with data communications, it makes geosynchronous satellite transmissions less practical for voice communications. To avoid this problem, *low earth orbit (LEO)* satellite systems were developed for telephone communications. These satellites typically are located 500 miles above the earth. LEO satellites are cheaper to build, and, because of their lower orbits, they provide faster message transmission than traditional satellites. *Teledesic* (which covers nearly 100% of the world's population and is billed as the "Internet-in-the-sky") and *Globalstar* (a satellite phone system designed as a replacement for cellular phones) are two current LEO projects. Other LEO projects—such as *Iridium*—failed soon after implementation. Whether or not telephone traffic alone can support the expense of an entire LEO system remains to be seen.

Cellular Technology

Cellular technology is a form of broadcast radio widely used for cellular phones. Cellular phones operate by keeping in contact with cellular antennae (see Figure 8-13). These antennae,

>**Cellular technology.** A form of broadcast radio that broadcasts using antennae located inside honeycomb-shaped cells.

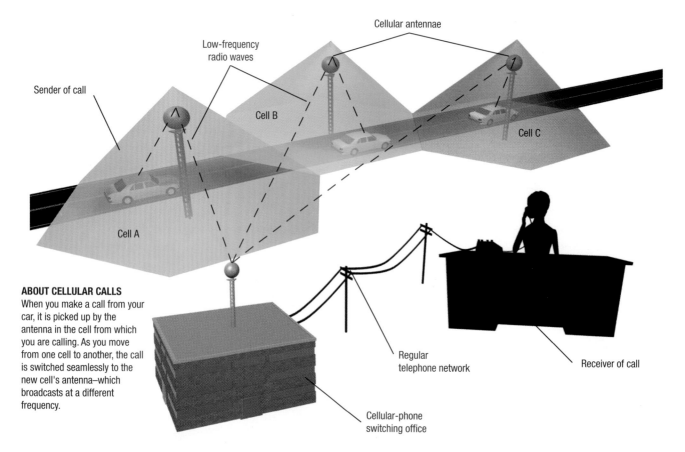

Cellular antennae

Low-frequency
radio waves

Sender of call

Cell B

Cell A

Cell C

ABOUT CELLULAR CALLS
When you make a call from your car, it is picked up by the antenna in the cell from which you are calling. As you move from one cell to another, the call is switched seamlessly to the new cell's antenna—which broadcasts at a different frequency.

Regular
telephone network

Receiver of call

Cellular-phone
switching office

FIGURE 8-13

Cellular transmission.

Most mobile telephones use cellular technology.

which resemble tall, metal telephone poles, are strategically placed throughout a calling area. Calling areas are divided into honeycomb-shaped zones called *cells,* each measuring 10 miles wide or so and containing its own antenna. The antennae perform two essential functions: (1) They enable a moving cellular phone to transmit and receive signals without interruption by passing signals from one antenna to another as the phone moves from one cell to another, and (2) they provide an interface with the regular public phone network via a switching office.

Cellular phone use has become incredibly popular. Those people who need to maintain constant contact with the office or clients but must be on the move as well—such as a busy executive, salesperson, truck driver, or real-estate agent—obviously benefit from the ability to carry cell phones. Farmers, refinery workers, and others who work outdoors also use cellular technology to stay in contact with others when they cannot afford the time it would take to get to a regular phone. In addition, the cell phone boom includes use by teenagers to stay in touch with friends, and by parents to keep in touch with each other and their children while on the go.

It is common to think of the cellular evolution in terms of generations. The original devices were analog. Newer second-generation cellular devices, such as *PCS* phones, are digital. The newest devices are referred to as *third generation (3G)* devices—devices that have been developed to provide enhanced data communication services within the cellular networks. Though currently in development, the 3G standard promises fast wireless access to a wide variety of rich multimedia content through your handheld PC, cell phone, or other mobile device.

Infrared Technology

Infrared (IR) technology has gained popularity in recent years as a way to set up wireless links between office PCs or between an office PC and a handheld device or printer. Infrared technology sends data as infrared light rays. Like your infrared television remote control, infrared technology requires line-of-sight transmission. Because of this limitation, many formerly infrared devices (such as wireless mice and keyboards) now use radio technology instead, as previously mentioned.

Some applications still using infrared technology include beaming data from a handheld PC, notebook, digital camera, or other device to a desktop computer, sending documents from a portable PC to a printer, and connecting a portable PC to a company network.

Sending Data Over Communications Media

Data travel over communications media in various ways. The following paragraphs describe basic data transmission characteristics.

further exploration

For links to further information about wired and wireless communications media, go to www.course.com/parker2002/ch8

Analog or Digital?

One of the most fundamental distinctions in data communications is the difference between analog and digital transmissions. The regular phone system, established many years ago to handle voice traffic, carries *analog* signals—that is, *continuous* waves over a certain frequency range (see Figure 8-14). Changes in the continuous wave reflect the myriad variations in the pitch of the human voice. Transmissions for cable TV and large satellite dishes also typically use analog signals, as do many wireless networks. Recent developments in telephone (such as PCS) and television (such as HDTV) have resulted in digital transmissions for some of these applications.

Virtually all business computing equipment, in contrast, transmits *digital* signals, which handle data coded in two *discrete* states: 0 and 1 bits. Your desktop computer is a digital device; so, too, are other types of personal computers. LANs transmit digitally encoded data transmissions, as well. Whenever communications require an interface between digital computers and analog networks, an adaptive device called a *modem* (covered in more detail shortly) is needed to translate between the two types of transmissions.

Bandwidth and Speed

Over an analog medium, data travel at varied frequencies. The difference between the highest and lowest frequencies is known as the medium's *bandwidth*. For example, many telephone transmission media have a bandwidth of 3,000 hertz (Hz), which is the difference between the highest (3,300 MHz) and lowest (300 MHz) frequencies at which it can send data. Transmissions of text data require the least amount of bandwidth; video data requires the most. Just as a wide fire hose permits more water to pass through it per unit of time than a narrow garden hose, a medium with a high bandwidth allows more data to pass through it than a small bandwidth medium in the same period of time.

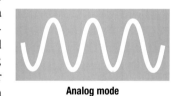

Analog mode

Conventional twisted-pair telephone wire can be called a "low-bandwidth" medium; faster-rated twisted-pair, coaxial cable, and fiber-optic cable are considered to be "high-bandwidth" or *broadband* media. Increasingly, high-bandwidth media are being installed in many homes and businesses to accommodate the growing number of multimedia information-related products coming into the marketplace. One of the world's most advanced fiber-optic data networks is used to transfer Hollywood movies during the production process, as discussed in the Trend box.

Digital mode

Transmission speed is often rated in *bits per second (bps), kbps* (thousands of bits per second), or *mbps* (millions of bits per second). Currently wired media are typically faster than wireless media, though the actual speed realized depends on the capabilities of the rest of the network hardware. For example, though coaxial cable can transmit data at speeds of 100 Mbps or higher, speeds for cable Internet service usually top out at 1.5 Mbps, with the speed degrading as more and more people use the network. Improvements in wireless technology are continually increasing data transfer speeds. 3G is expected to permit speeds up to 2 Mbps—as fast or faster than any consumer Internet access available today.

FIGURE 8-14

Analog and digital transmissions. Traditional telephone, cable TV, and satellite systems use analog transmissions; computer equipment and newer digital telephone and television broadcasting use digital transmission.

trend

The Making of *Chicken Run*

Broadband Comes to Hollywood

Chicken Run, a completely animated movie released in 2000, was a collaboration between DreamWorks Productions in L.A. and the British animation studio Aardman. Though the movie was produced in L.A., it was shot on location in Bristol, England, and special effects were added by a company in London. Though this collaboration brought together a vast collection of talent, the logistics of reviewing scenes and making decisions could have been a nightmare.

Enter Sohonet.

Sohonet is a high-speed, fiber-optic network linking Los Angeles and London. Instead of using couriers to shuttle the day's footage back and forth between London and L.A. (a time-consuming process considering the flight time and potential customs delays), as well as between the various facilities in England, *Chicken Run* footage was transferred over this network. Consequently, Sohonet enabled everyone involved in the production process to review scenes together instantly, dramatically reducing the production time.

Sohonet was built in 1995 by London's postproduction houses. Using fiber-optic cable and multiplexing, digital film footage can be transferred at speeds of 1 Gbps (gigabit per second) between London and Hollywood. This high speed (about a billion bits per second) is important because full-motion movie clips are huge. For example, there are 24 pictures in each second of film in *Chicken Run*—each picture contains a slightly different pose so that when they are played at full motion, the animation looks realistic, similar to a flip book. Just one second of this movie would require about 300 MB of storage space.

Super-high-speed networks, such as Sohonet, are becoming as much a part of the movie production process as cameras and microphones. Some production facilities are setting up private networks. *HollyNet*—a secure entertainment industry-wide initiative for building a high-speed, broadband network to serve as a common production platform for the industry in general—is another possibility. HollyNet has been tested successfully. For example, Ron Howard has used it to review pictures from his home on the East Coast, and Steven Spielberg used it to review parts of *Jurassic Park* while working on the set of *Schindler's List* in Europe. Recent security tests performed by the Entertainment Technology Center (ETC) of the University of Southern California School of Cinema-Television concluded that sensitive film production files can be transmitted safely over the network.

As the public's appetite for special effects grows and as more movies are shot 100% digitally, outsourcing will become even more important to help keep costs down. With outsourcing comes the transportation problem. As a result, it looks like broadband networks will become a permanent fixture in Tinseltown.

Bandwidth, plus the speed at which data travel over the media, determines the *throughput,* or how much data can be transferred over the media in a given period of time. As can be expected, higher bandwidth and higher speed result in a higher throughput.

Parallel vs. Serial Transmission

In most communications networks—especially where long distances are involved—data travel serially. In **serial transmission,** all of the bits in a message are sent one after another

>**Serial transmission.** Data transmission in which every bit in a byte must travel down the same path in succession.

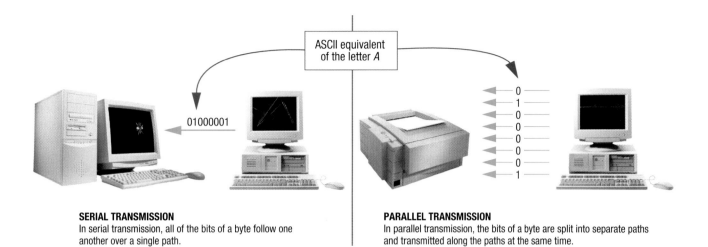

SERIAL TRANSMISSION
In serial transmission, all of the bits of a byte follow one another over a single path.

PARALLEL TRANSMISSION
In parallel transmission, the bits of a byte are split into separate paths and transmitted along the paths at the same time.

along a single path. On the other hand, **parallel transmission** sends an entire byte at one time with each bit in the byte taking a separate path, as illustrated in Figure 8-15.

As the figure suggests, parallel transmission is much faster than serial transmission. However, because it requires a cable with multiple tracks instead of one, its cables are more expensive. Thus, parallel transmission usually is limited to short distances, such as computer-to-printer communications. Most network traffic uses serial transmission.

▶**FIGURE 8-15**

Serial and parallel transmissions. Serial transmissions transmit one *bit* at a time; parallel transmissions transmit one *byte* at a time.

Transmission Directions

Another distinction between types of transmissions is the direction in which transmitted data move (see Figure 8-16).

Simplex transmission allows data to travel in a single, prespecified direction. An example from everyday life is a doorbell—the signal can go only from the button to the chime. Another example is television or radio broadcasting. The simplex standard is relatively uncommon for most types of computer-based communications applications; even devices that are designed primarily to receive information, such as printers, are able to communicate acknowledgment signals and send error messages back to the sending computer. In *half-duplex transmission,* messages can move in either direction, but only one way at a time. An example is a walkie-talkie or two-way radio—only one person can talk at a time. Some Internet telephony applications are half-duplex, as well.

▶**FIGURE 8-16**

Transmission directions. Transmissions can be simplex (one direction only), half-duplex (one direction at a time), or full-duplex (both directions at one time).

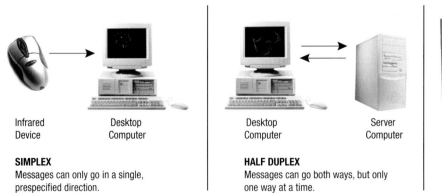

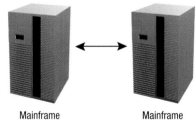

| Infrared Device | Desktop Computer | Desktop Computer | Server Computer | Mainframe | Mainframe |

SIMPLEX
Messages can only go in a single, prespecified direction.

HALF DUPLEX
Messages can go both ways, but only one way at a time.

FULL DUPLEX
Messages can go both ways, simultaneously.

>**Parallel transmission.** Data transmission in which each bit in a byte follows its path simultaneously with all of the other bits.

Full-duplex transmission works like a standard telephone—data can move in both directions at the same time. Full-duplexing is ideal for hardware devices that need to pass large amounts of data between each other. Most Internet connections are full-duplex.

Transmission Timing

As mentioned earlier, most data are transmitted serially in communications networks. When data is sent serially, a technique must be used to separate the bits into groups so that all the bits in one byte can be identified and retrieved together. Three ways of timing serial transmissions are *synchronous, asynchronous,* and *isochronous* (see Figure 8-17).

In *synchronous* (pronounced "SIN-kre-nuss") *transmission,* data is dispatched in blocks of characters—each block can consist of thousands of characters. The blocks are timed by both the sending and receiving devices and are sent at regular intervals; that is, the transmissions are synchronized. Synchronous transmission is faster, more efficient, and more accurate than *asynchronous transmission* (discussed next), though it requires more expensive and sophisticated equipment. Most communication within a computer is synchronous, timed by the computer's clock. Network transmissions are also usually synchronous.

In *asynchronous* (pronounced "A-sin-kre-nuss") *transmission,* the transmission is not synchronized. Therefore, as soon as the user strikes a key on a keyboard, the byte representation for that character can be transmitted. Striking a second key sends the byte for a second character, and so forth. To identify each byte, it is packaged with a "start bit" and "stop bit," which results in substantial transmission overhead. Because even the fastest typist can generate only a very small amount of data relative to what the line can accept, the line also sits idle a lot of the time, making it a less efficient transmission method. Asynchronous transmission is commonly used for communications between computers and peripheral devices.

A final consideration is *isochronous* (pronounced "eye-SOCK-ra-nuss") *transmission.* Isochronous—time-dependent—transmission refers to situations where data must be delivered within certain time constraints. For example, when sending multimedia data, the audio data must be received in time to be played along with the video data. When isochronous

◆ FIGURE 8-17

Transmission timing.

Synchronous (synchronized), asynchronous (not synchronized), and isochronous (time-dependent) transmissions can be used to transmit data. Most network transmissions use synchronous transmission.

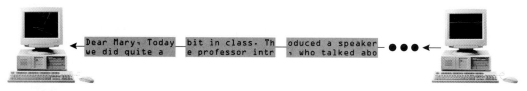

SYNCHRONOUS TRANSMISSION
In this type of transmission, data is sent in blocks of characters rather than one character at a time, and the blocks are timed so that the receiving device knows that it will be getting them in regular intervals.

ASYNCHRONOUS TRANSMISSION
In this type of transmission, one characer at a time is sent over a line, as it is entered.

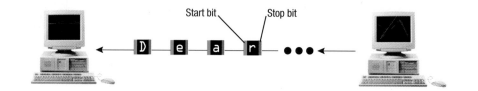

ISOCHRONOUS TRANSMISSION
In this type of transmission, the entire transmission is sent together after requesting and being assigned the bandwidth necessary for all the data to arrive at the correct time.

transmission is used, the entire necessary bandwidth is reserved for that transmission and no other device can transmit until the transmission is completed, to ensure that the data arrive within the required time period. Because its most common application is multimedia data, isochronous transfer is supported by the IEEE 1394 (Firewire) bus (discussed in Chapter 3).

Connecting to a Network

A computer needs special equipment to connect to a network or otherwise send messages over a communications medium. The type of equipment used depends on the medium, but some interface between the computer and the network—usually a *network interface card* or *modem*—is required. Connecting to a local area network usually requires a network interface card; connecting to a larger network (like the Internet) over media such as telephone lines, cable, or the airwaves, requires a modem or similar type of adapter.

Network Interface Cards

A **network interface card (NIC)** typically plugs into an expansion slot within the system unit of a desktop PC, or into a PC card slot on a notebook computer. The ports on the card accessible outside the PC are used to connect a coaxial cable, a twisted-pair cable, or both (see Figure 8-18). Some mobile devices may have a network interface integrated directly into the device; if so, the appropriate port is exposed through the case of the device like any other port. NICs for wireless network connections have no external ports because no cabling is used, though they often have an external antenna.

The purpose of a network interface card is to pass outgoing data from the PC to the network, and to collect all incoming data for the PC. Most network interface cards are designed for a particular *protocol,* such as *Ethernet* or *Token Ring.* Networking protocols are discussed shortly.

Modems

Because digital impulses—such as those sent by computers—cannot be transmitted over analog media, some means of translating each kind of signal into the other is required. Conversion of signals from digital to analog form is called *modulation,* and translation from

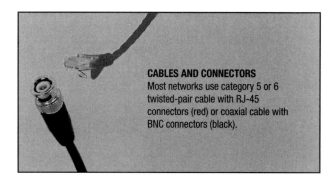

> **FIGURE 8-18**
> **Network interface cards (NICs).** NICs, used to connect PCs to a local area network, are available as expansion cards for both desktop PCs (top) and portable PCs (bottom).

Port for coaxial cable with BNC connector.

Port for twisted-pair cable with RJ-45 connector.

CABLES AND CONNECTORS
Most networks use category 5 or 6 twisted-pair cable with RJ-45 connectors (red) or coaxial cable with BNC connectors (black).

>**Network interface card (NIC).** An expansion card through which a computer can connect to a local area network.

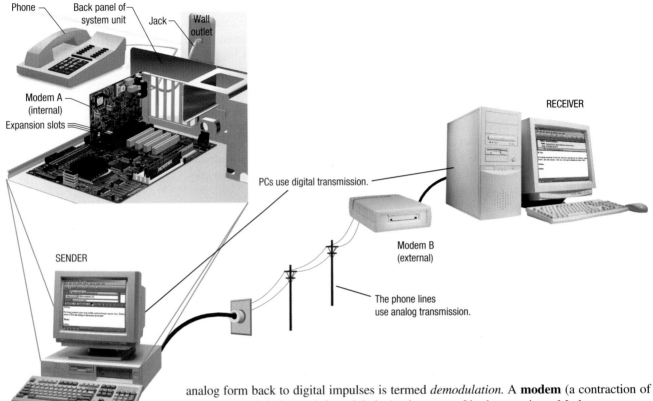

Phone — Back panel of system unit — Jack — Wall outlet

Modem A (internal)

Expansion slots

RECEIVER

PCs use digital transmission.

SENDER

Modem B (external)

The phone lines use analog transmission.

PC with internal modem

⊜ FIGURE 8-19

How modems work. A PC user types data that becomes digitally encoded. Modem A (inside the sender's PC in this figure) converts this digital data to analog form and sends it over the phone lines to Modem B. Modem B (attached to the receiving computer) reconverts the data to digital form and delivers it to the receiving PC. The latter PC can transmit back to the original PC by reversing these steps.

analog form back to digital impulses is termed *demodulation*. A **modem** (a contraction of the terms *mo*dulation and *dem*odulation) takes care of both operations. Modems are most often used to connect PCs to the Internet.

As Figure 8-19 shows, when a PC sends a message to a remote computer over an analog line (such as a phone line), the modem at the sending end converts the data from digital to analog. A modem at the receiving end then converts the data from analog to digital for the receiving computer to process. If the receiving computer belongs to an ISP, there would be a bank of modems instead of just one to allow multiple users to connect to the ISP's computer at one time.

There is a specific type of modem or similar adapter for each type of transmission media, as discussed next. Though the term *modem* technically applies only to devices that perform analog-to-digital and digital-to-analog conversion, the collection of transmission adapters discussed next are usually referred to as modems.

Conventional Dial-Up Modems

To dial up and connect to another computer using conventional telephone lines, a *conventional dial-up modem* is used. The modem is connected using regular twisted-pair telephone cable to the phone jack in your home, as illustrated in Figure 8-19.

Transmission rates for conventional dial-up modems are measured in thousands of bits per second or *kbps*. Older modems transmitted at 14.4, 28.8, and 33.6 Kbps; most dial-up modems today are rated as *56K modems,* for 56 Kbps. Most modems can function at any speed up to their maximum. In fact, under many dial-up conditions, the connection speed will be significantly slower than the theoretical maximum because of the condition of the telephone lines between the PC and the ISP, the amount of traffic on the ISP's system or the Web server being accessed, and other factors.

To achieve speeds faster than those achieved with a 56K modem, you need one of the higher-speed options discussed next. Most of these options are used to achieve higher-speed Internet access.

ISDN Modems

ISDN (for *integrated services digital network*) *modems* allow digital transmission of data over ordinary telephone lines. ISDN modems—sometimes called *ISDN adapters*—use the same twisted-pair wiring as dial-up modems, but by combining (multiplexing) signals, ISDN can transmit data faster. ISDN supports data transfer rates of 64 Kbps per line. Since two lines are used at one time, you can achieve a maximum transmission rate of 128 Kbps. To use an ISDN modem, the computer you are connecting to (such as your ISP) must support ISDN service.

DSL Modems

DSL (digital subscriber line) modems also allow faster transmission over your standard telephone line. DSL transmission is faster than ISDN and uses a technology that doesn't tie up your telephone line. There are two types of DSL: *ADSL* (for *a*symmetric *d*igital *s*ubscriber *l*ine) and *SDSL* (for *s*ymmetric *d*igital *s*ubscriber *l*ine). ADSL—by far the more common—uses faster transmission downstream (from the remote computer to the user) than upstream (from the user to the remote computer). In contrast, SDSL uses the same transmission rate for both directions. ADSL service and, consequently, ADSL modems, are frequently used for fast Internet service. A limitation of DSL transmission is distance: It can only be used within three miles of a telephone switching station, and the speed degrades as the distance gets closer and closer to the three-mile limit. This limitation may eventually be overcome by some type of repeating system to boost the signal over longer distances. DSL is also not available in all areas.

ADSL can transmit data up to about 8 Mbps downstream, though speeds of about 1.5 Mbps are pretty common; upstream speeds are about 640 Kbps. SDSL transfers data at approximately 3 Mbps in both directions. An upcoming new type of DSL is *VDSL* or *v*ery-high-speed *DSL*. Though not widely available at the present time, the VDSL standard supports speeds of around 52 Mbps, significantly faster than any other type of modem-based network access discussed in this section.

Cable Modems

Cable modems are used to connect a PC to cable Internet services and work similarly to the cable boxes used to obtain cable-TV service. Though cable transmissions were initially one-directional (simplex) transmissions (with a conventional dial-up modem being used for upstream transmissions), most cable providers have upgraded to two-way cable, which allows fast two-way (full-duplex) transmissions for very fast Internet access, though usually upload speed is slower than download speed. It is also fast enough to be used for digital TV and interactive TV applications.

Cable transmissions can be very fast—about 30 Mbps—but transmission speed is reduced as more and more people use it at one time. Because of this, the speed for cable Internet service is less consistent than other types of Internet service with rates around 1.5 Mbps—fairly comparable to ADSL—most of the time.

Satellite Modems

Satellite modems allow you to send and receive data using satellite technology. They are commonly used for high-speed Internet service, though at present some satellite Internet services use satellite technology for downstream data only (regular dial-up connections are used for upstream traffic for one-way satellite systems, as with one-way cable systems). Two-way satellite service is available from several providers, however, and is expected to be widely available soon. At the fairly high transfer rate of about 500 Kbps to 1 Mbps, satellite modems are a little slower than both DSL and cable transmissions, but have the advantage of being available for use in rural areas. Similar to cable transmissions, upload speed is generally slower than for downloads, and some satellite setups can be used to receive satellite television programs, in addition to Internet access.

Wireless Modems

Most handheld PCs, smart phones, and other mobile devices use *wireless modems* to wirelessly connect to the Internet. Wireless modems use radio technology and can be either attached to or built into the device. Though more commonly used with mobile devices (see Figure 8-20), wireless modems can also be used with notebook and desktop PCs for the *fixed wireless* networks and Internet access that are becoming increasingly common. Speeds for

▶ FIGURE 8-20

Wireless modems. Wireless modems are typically used with portable PCs and other types of mobile communications devices; they can also be used to connect desktop and notebook PCs to a wireless network, such as for fixed wireless Internet. A Palm PC is shown here being connected to a wireless modem.

fixed wireless data transmissions are comparable with satellite transmissions, except for perhaps slower upload speeds.

Cellular Modems

Instead of a wireless modem, many notebook users and some handheld PC users opt to connect to the Internet via their cell phone instead. To accomplish this, a *cellular modem* is used to connect to the notebook or other device to the cell phones.

COMMUNICATIONS PROTOCOLS

Because manufacturers have long produced devices that use a variety of transmission techniques, the communications industry has adopted standards called *protocols* to rectify the problem of conflicting procedures. A communications *protocol* is a collection of rules and procedures for establishing, maintaining, and terminating transmissions between devices. Protocols specify how devices physically connect to a network; how data is packaged for transmission; how receiving devices acknowledge signals from sender devices (a process called *handshaking*); how errors are handled; and so forth. Just as people need a common language to communicate effectively, machines need a common set of rules for this purpose.

Protocols are found in all types of networks. The following paragraphs discuss a few of the most common network protocols. As you will see, each protocol addresses a highly specific situation and determines the topology, speed, and other characteristics that may be used with the protocol. The most common LAN protocols are *Ethernet* and *Token Ring;* Internet computers use the *TCP/IP* protocol; and portable devices and appliances may use *WAP, Bluetooth,* or another wireless protocol.

web tutor

For a tutorial on communication protocols, go to www.course.com/parker2002/ch8

Ethernet

Ethernet refers to a collection of protocols that specify a standard way of setting up a LAN typically using a bus or star topology. It specifies the types and lengths of cables allowed, how the cables may connect, how devices communicate data, how the system detects and corrects problems, the speed at which data may be transferred, and so on. Networks using the Ethernet protocol are often referred to as *Ethernet networks.*

Data transmissions on an Ethernet network use a set of procedures collectively called *CSMA/CD,* which stands for *carrier sense multiple access* and *collision detection* (see Figure 8-21). *Carrier sense* means that when a computer on the network is ready to send a message, it first "listens" for other messages on the line. If it senses no messages, it sends one. *Multiple access* means that two computers might try to send a message at exactly the same time. *Collision detection* means that just after a computer transmits a message, it listens to see if the message collided with a message from another computer. When a collision takes place, the two sending computers wait for short, random periods of time and send their messages again. The chance of the messages colliding a second time is extremely small.

The traditional Ethernet network (also called a *10BaseT* network) can send data at a rate of up to 10 Mbps; newer versions transmit even faster. *Fast Ethernet* or *100Base-T* runs at 100 Mbps, and *gigabit Ethernet* is even faster at 1,000 Mbps (1 Gbps or 1 billion bits per second). Though most Ethernet networks are wired, *wireless Ethernet* is becoming a popular alternative, as discussed in a later section.

Token Ring

Like Ethernet, **Token Ring** is a common LAN protocol. It is usually used with a ring topology. Networks using the Token Ring protocol are often referred to as *Token Ring networks.*

>**Ethernet.** A collection of communications protocols that specify one standard way of setting up a LAN; also commonly called 10Base-T or 100Base-T. >**Token Ring.** A ring-based communications protocol that uses token passing to control the transmission of messages.

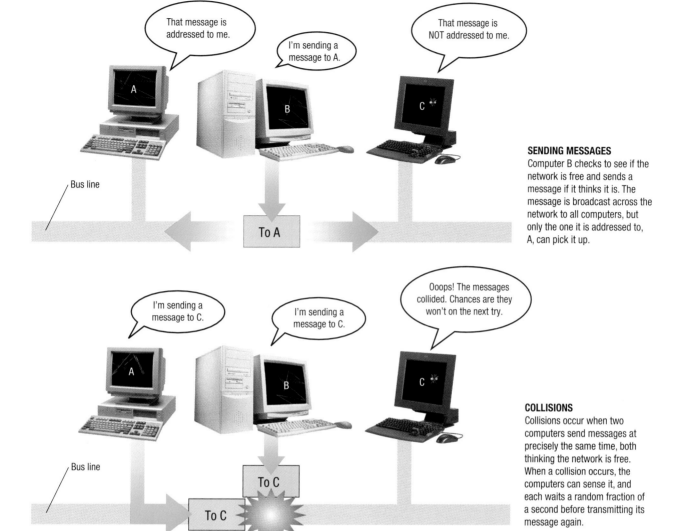

SENDING MESSAGES
Computer B checks to see if the network is free and sends a message if it thinks it is. The message is broadcast across the network to all computers, but only the one it is addressed to, A, can pick it up.

COLLISIONS
Collisions occur when two computers send messages at precisely the same time, both thinking the network is free. When a collision occurs, the computers can sense it, and each waits a random fraction of a second before transmitting its message again.

▶ **FIGURE 8-21**

Ethernet networks. Ethernet networks use the CSMA/CD access-control method.

An illustration of how a Token Ring network works appears in Figure 8-22. A small packet called a *token*—which has room for a message and the appropriate address—is sent around the ring. As the token circulates, the computers on the network check to see if the token is addressed to them; if so, they grab the token to retrieve the message. A token also contains a control area, which specifies whether the token is free or if it carries a message. When a token is free, any computer can take possession of it to attach a message. It does this by changing the status of the token from free to busy, adding the addressed message, and releasing the token. The message then travels around the ring until it reaches the receiving computer. The receiving computer retrieves the message, changes the status of the token back to free, and then releases the token.

Although the Token Ring protocol maintains more order than Ethernet because it eliminates collisions, sometimes a computer with a defective network interface card swallows a token. If the token is gone for too long, the LAN assumes it has vanished and generates another. Traditionally, Token Ring networks ran from about 4 to 16 Mbps. The newer second-generation Token Ring architecture can operate at 100 Mbps, 155 Mbps, or 1 Gbps, comparable with Ethernet networks.

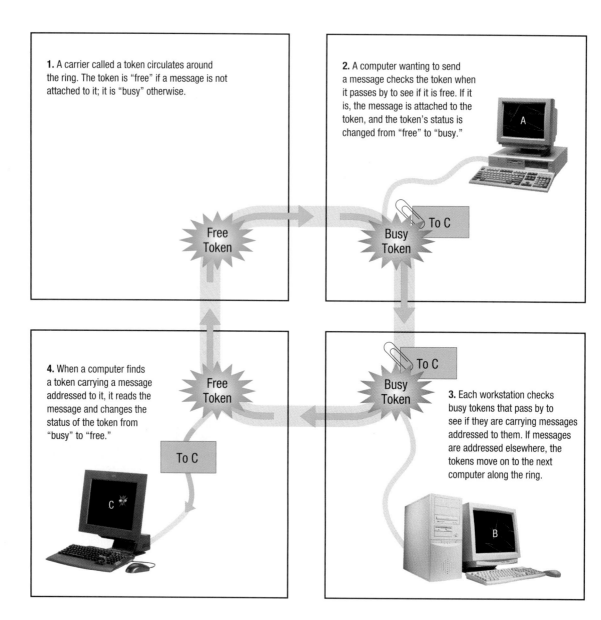

1. A carrier called a token circulates around the ring. The token is "free" if a message is not attached to it; it is "busy" otherwise.

2. A computer wanting to send a message checks the token when it passes by to see if it is free. If it is, the message is attached to the token, and the token's status is changed from "free" to "busy."

Free Token

Busy Token

To C

4. When a computer finds a token carrying a message addressed to it, it reads the message and changes the status of the token from "busy" to "free."

Free Token

To C

Busy Token

To C

3. Each workstation checks busy tokens that pass by to see if they are carrying messages addressed to them. If messages are addressed elsewhere, the tokens move on to the next computer along the ring.

To C

> **FIGURE 8-22**

Token Ring networks. Token Ring networks use token passing to control access.

TCP/IP

TCP/IP consists of two protocols: *Transmission control protocol (TCP)* and *Internet protocol (IP)*. Together, these protocols specify how to package and send messages among the hundreds of different types of computers connected to the Internet. TCP/IP relies on a procedure known as packet switching to do this. As briefly discussed in reference to WANs and as illustrated in Figure 8-23, *packet switching* divides messages into small units called *packets*. Packets travel along the network separately, based on the final destination and network traffic and other network conditions. When the packets reach their destination, they are reassembled in the proper order.

TCP/IP is also used with LANs and other company networks to implement an intranet. In recent years it has also begun to be used by telephone companies to provide faster, cheaper telephone transmissions.

>**TCP/IP.** The protocol used with Internet computers that uses packet switching to facilitate the transmission of messages.

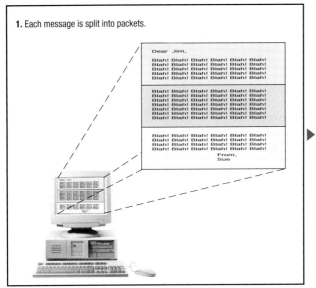

1. Each message is split into packets.

Dear Jim,

Blah! Blah! Blah! Blah! Blah! Blah!
Blah! Blah! Blah! Blah! Blah! Blah!
Blah! Blah! Blah! Blah! Blah! Blah!
Blah! Blah! Blah! Blah! Blah! Blah!
Blah! Blah! Blah! Blah! Blah! Blah!

Blah! Blah! Blah! Blah! Blah! Blah!
Blah! Blah! Blah! Blah! Blah! Blah!
Blah! Blah! Blah! Blah! Blah! Blah!
Blah! Blah! Blah! Blah! Blah! Blah!
Blah! Blah! Blah! Blah! Blah! Blah!

Blah! Blah! Blah! Blah! Blah! Blah!
Blah! Blah! Blah! Blah! Blah! Blah!
Blah! Blah! Blah! Blah! Blah! Blah!
                    From,
                    Sue

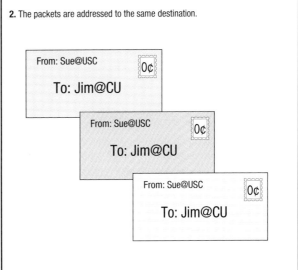

2. The packets are addressed to the same destination.

From: Sue@USC   0¢
To: Jim@CU

From: Sue@USC   0¢
To: Jim@CU

From: Sue@USC   0¢
To: Jim@CU

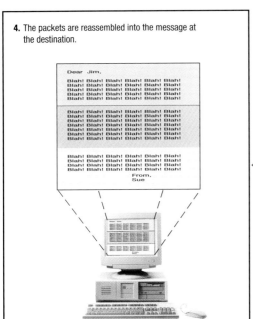

4. The packets are reassembled into the message at the destination.

Dear Jim,

Blah! Blah! Blah! Blah! Blah! Blah!
Blah! Blah! Blah! Blah! Blah! Blah!
Blah! Blah! Blah! Blah! Blah! Blah!
Blah! Blah! Blah! Blah! Blah! Blah!
Blah! Blah! Blah! Blah! Blah! Blah!

Blah! Blah! Blah! Blah! Blah! Blah!
Blah! Blah! Blah! Blah! Blah! Blah!
Blah! Blah! Blah! Blah! Blah! Blah!
Blah! Blah! Blah! Blah! Blah! Blah!
Blah! Blah! Blah! Blah! Blah! Blah!

Blah! Blah! Blah! Blah! Blah! Blah!
Blah! Blah! Blah! Blah! Blah! Blah!
Blah! Blah! Blah! Blah! Blah! Blah!
                    From,
                    Sue

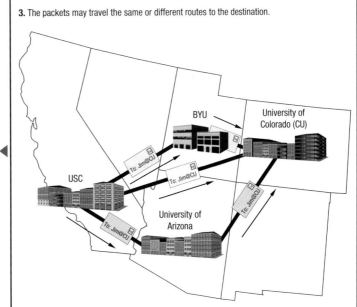

3. The packets may travel the same or different routes to the destination.

BYU

University of Colorado (CU)

USC

University of Arizona

NET

Wireless Application Protocol (WAP)

Wireless Application Protocol (WAP) is a standard for delivering content to mobile devices like mobile phones, pagers, and other wireless communication devices, using a wireless network. The content that can be delivered using WAP includes both consumer and corporate solutions, such as e-mail, corporate data, news, sports, entertainment, e-commerce transactions, and banking services. When WAP is used to deliver Internet content, a WAP-enabled browser—sometimes called a *microbrowser*—is needed on the device to view the Web pages. Already most Internet-enabled cell phone and pager manufacturers support WAP, enabling any WAP page to be displayed on these devices.

FIGURE 8-23
TCP/IP networks. TCP/IP networks (like the Internet) use packet switching.

>**Wireless Application Protocol (WAP).** A standard for delivering content to mobile devices.

campus close-up

Wireless in Wake Forest

Several years ago, Wake Forest University in Winston-Salem, North Carolina, began supplying its entire freshman class with notebook computers and high-speed, wired Internet access everywhere on campus. Now, Wake Forest has gone beyond the walls.

Beginning with the fall 2000 semester, all undergraduate students are now given the opportunity to subscribe to the university's wireless network, in addition to receiving an IBM ThinkPad notebook and Lexmark printer. Though all Wake Forest classrooms and dorm rooms have wired connections to the campus system, the new wireless network infrastructure extends that wired Ethernet backbone to 198 access points on campus. Now students can check their e-mail, research assignments, or access the campus intranet or the Internet from virtually anywhere on campus.

Students who subscribe to the service pay $250 per year and receive preloaded software and wireless LAN network interface cards in their PCs. To help students keep up with technology, the PCs are upgraded every two years and the students take them with them after graduation.

Though supplying students with computers as part of their tuition expense isn't a new idea, the wireless revolution on campuses is expected to increase Internet use and help create greater opportunities for communication between students and professors, as well as between students and students. By allowing students to work outside of traditional areas—such as a favorite table in the dining hall or library, or a bench in the quad—the entire campus is transformed into a learning environment.

Wireless Ethernet

Wireless Ethernet allows the Ethernet standard to be used with wireless network connections. It is also known as *Wi-Fi,* though technically the Wi-Fi label can only be used with wireless Ethernet products that are certified by the *Wireless Ethernet Compatibility Alliance (WECA).* Users of Wi-Fi certified products are assured that their hardware will be compatible with all other Wi-Fi certified hardware.

At its current maximum speed of approximately 11 Mbps, wireless Ethernet is slow compared to wired Ethernet. However, a newer version of this standard is expected to support speeds of up to 54 Mbps. As illustrated in the Campus Close-Up box, wireless Ethernet is a growing choice for organizations wishing to extend their wired Ethernet network.

Bluetooth

The **Bluetooth** standard is a low-cost, short-range, wireless radio solution for communications between handheld PCs, mobile phones, and other portable devices, as well as for connecting those devices to home and business equipment, such as PCs, telephones, printers, and more. Bluetooth wireless technology facilitates real-time voice and data transmissions

---

>Wireless Ethernet. A standard that allows the use of Ethernet with wireless network connections. **>Bluetooth.** A standard used to facilitate automatic communications between devices once they get within the allowable range.

between Bluetooth-enabled devices (devices containing a special Bluetooth transceiver chip). For example, a Bluetooth earpiece or headset can be used in conjunction with a cell phone left in a pocket or bag, or a PDA device can be instantly synchronized with a desktop PC on entering the office. Since Bluetooth devices automatically recognize each other when they get within transmission range—about 10 meters (approximately 35 feet) without an amplifier—handheld PCs, cell phones, and other portable devices can always be networked wirelessly when they are within range. Some industry experts predict that all household appliances will be Bluetooth-enabled in the future, resulting in an automatic, always connected smart home. For a closer look at Bluetooth, see the How It Works box.

Other Wireless Protocols

There are a variety of other up-and-coming networking protocols, mainly in the home networking or wireless networking arena. A few of the more common are:

▼ *Home Phoneline Networking Association (Home PNA) 2.0* is a standard allowing computers to be networked through ordinary phone wiring and phone jacks at speeds up to 20 Mbps. This standard is geared toward setting up quick and easy home networks for sharing files, peripherals, a single Internet connection, and facilitating multiplayer games over the network. A newer version is proposed to up the speed to 100 Mbps.

▼ *Powerline* network refers to PCs networked over existing power outlets. Though off to a slower start than Home PNA because of a delay in determining a single standard, powerline networking is expected to eventually compete with Home PNA networks. It also has great potential for other countries where phone jacks are not as prevalent as in the U.S. Current networking speeds are 10 Mbps.

▼ *Shared Wireless Access Protocol (SWAP)* is another standard aimed at home networking. It was developed to allow sharing voice and data between PCs, printers and other peripheral devices, PC-enhanced cordless phones, as well as sharing Internet access and allowing multi-player games over the network. SWAP works through existing cordless telephone and wireless LAN technologies; data transfer rates are currently no more than 2 Mbps.

NETWORK SECURITY ISSUES

So far in this chapter we've looked at the benefits and possibilities that computer networks provide. Unfortunately, there is also a dark side to this rosy picture. Because of the prolific nature of computers and networks today, an opportunity exists for criminals to commit acts that are not in the public interest. Such acts run the gamut from stealing money to intentionally destroying corporate data to stalking children over the Internet. While many of the legal, ethical, and other social issues involving computers are discussed in detail in Chapter 15, three issues that are very important with regards to network security—*computer viruses, unauthorized access,* and *firewalls*—are discussed next.

web tutor

For a tutorial on securing a network, go to www.course.com/ parker2002/ch8

Computer Viruses

A **computer virus** is a software program that is designed to cause damage to the system or some other malicious act. At best, a computer virus is annoying; at worst, it destroys your data or harms your system. Some viruses lay dormant for months and then destroy settings on a hard disk on a specific date or when a certain operator action is taken. Other viruses

---

>**Computer virus.** A software program designed to spread itself to other computers without the user's knowledge and, sometimes, to cause some harm to the system.

Bluetooth

Bluetooth is a communications standard for short-range, wireless radio transmissions. It can be used to connect PCs, peripherals, and mobile devices so they can easily communicate. In addition to being wireless, one of the most appealing factors of Bluetooth is that it is automatic—as soon as devices are in range, they are connected. So, for example, you can zap files from your PC, mobile device, or digital camera to a nearby printer. Or you can use your portable PC or mobile device to turn on the lights and unlock your door as you approach your home, or use a Bluetooth-enabled headset with your cell phone while it is located in your briefcase. Even better, you can use a Bluetooth-enabled pen to write on the screen of a PDA, cell phone, or other device and then have your information transmitted via a Bluetooth link back to the device being used.

Bluetooth works using radio waves in the frequency band of 2.4 GHz and can transmit voice and data at a theoretical maximum of 1 Mbps (a newer version of the Bluetooth standard is expected to support speeds of 54 Mbps). Once two Bluetooth-enabled devices (devices with Bluetooth chips installed) come within about 30 feet of each other, their software identifies each other (using their unique identification numbers) and establishes a link. Because there may be many Bluetooth devices within range, up to 10 individual Bluetooth networks (called *piconets*) can be in place within the same physical area at one time. Each piconet can connect up to eight devices, for a maximum of 80 devices within

any 10 meter (approximately 30 feet) radius. To facilitate this, Bluetooth divides its spectrum (2,400 to 2,483.5 MHz in the United States and Europe) into 79 channels of 1 MHz each. Each Bluetooth device can cover the entire range of frequencies, jumping randomly on a regular basis to minimize interference between Bluetooth devices, as well as between the Bluetooth device and other devices (such as garage-door openers and some cordless phones and baby monitors) that use the same frequencies. Since Bluetooth transmitters change frequencies 1,600 times every second automatically, it is unlikely that any two transmitters will be on the same frequencies at the same time.

For each piconet, there is a master device that continually emits requests for other devices to join the network. Any slave device wishing to network with the master device answers with its identification number.

Bluetooth isn't designed to compete with speedier local area networks. Instead, Bluetooth's promoters are positioning it as the technology for personal area networks (PANs) consisting of an individual's computing devices, as well as other electronic components, such as cell phones, entertainment systems, and appliances. At about $5 per device, it's inexpensive. It's also easy and doesn't require line-of-sight transmission. And with predictions of over 1 billion Bluetooth-compatible devices in use by 2005, it seems as if Bluetooth—named after Harald Bluetooth, a Viking and the king of Denmark between 940 and 981 who was known for his skill of making diversified people talk to each other and uniting Denmark and Norway—was aptly named.

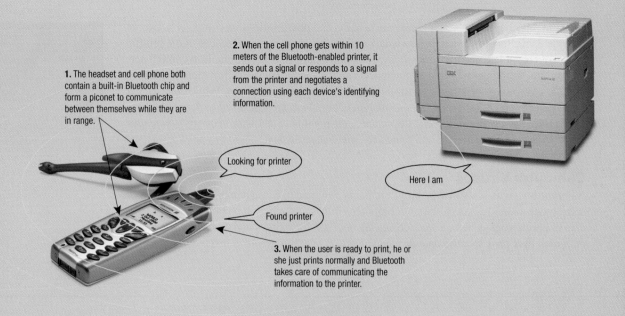

1. The headset and cell phone both contain a built-in Bluetooth chip and form a piconet to communicate between themselves while they are in range.

2. When the cell phone gets within 10 meters of the Bluetooth-enabled printer, it sends out a signal or responds to a signal from the printer and negotiates a connection using each device's identifying information.

Looking for printer

Here I am

Found printer

3. When the user is ready to print, he or she just prints normally and Bluetooth takes care of communicating the information to the printer.

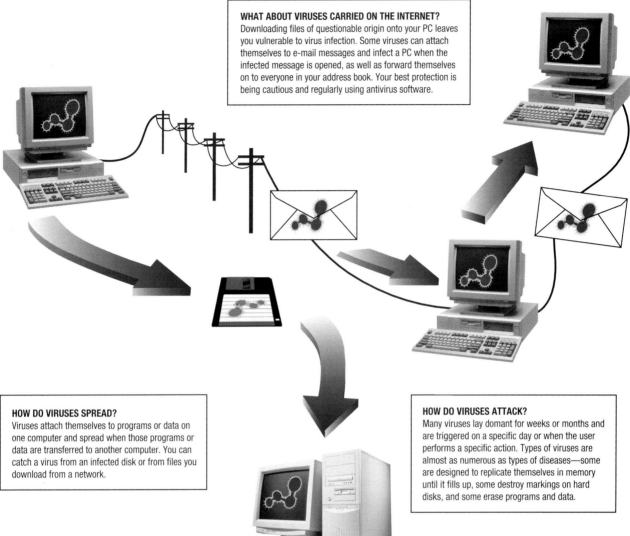

WHAT ABOUT VIRUSES CARRIED ON THE INTERNET?
Downloading files of questionable origin onto your PC leaves you vulnerable to virus infection. Some viruses can attach themselves to e-mail messages and infect a PC when the infected message is opened, as well as forward themselves on to everyone in your address book. Your best protection is being cautious and regularly using antivirus software.

HOW DO VIRUSES SPREAD?
Viruses attach themselves to programs or data on one computer and spread when those programs or data are transferred to another computer. You can catch a virus from an infected disk or from files you download from a network.

HOW DO VIRUSES ATTACK?
Many viruses lay domant for weeks or months and are triggered on a specific day or when the user performs a specific action. Types of viruses are almost as numerous as types of diseases—some are designed to replicate themselves in memory until it fills up, some destroy markings on hard disks, and some erase programs and data.

N E T

▶ **FIGURE 8-24**

Computer viruses. A computer virus is a harmful computer program or piece of a program that can alter programs or destroy data. Viruses can copy themselves onto legitimate programs and data, thereby spreading damage when the infected storage medium is used in another computer or the infected file is downloaded over the Internet or other network.

act immediately, duplicating themselves and clogging memory with garbage as soon as the computer is turned on, which usually renders the computer inoperable.

Computer viruses often replicate themselves onto new storage media on contact, infecting programs or data on those media that are then transferred to any other computer those media are inserted into (see Figure 8-24). Viruses are also commonly transferred today via the Internet or a company network, attaching themselves to downloadable files or being sent as attachments to e-mail messages. To protect your system from computer viruses, it makes sense to limit sharing disks and other removable storage media, to only download programs from reputable Web sites, and to only open e-mail attachments from people that you know. To further protect your PC, *antivirus* programs can be used to scan files before they are downloaded to your computer to be sure they are virus-free. They can also be used to detect and remove viruses from your system, when necessary. Using antivirus software is discussed in more detail in Chapter 15.

Unauthorized Access

Unauthorized access—the use of a computer, network, or network resource without permission—is a very important network security issue. To prevent unauthorized access, some type of identification procedure must be used. These vary from *passwords* to *physical access objects* (keys, access cards, etc.) to *biometric devices* that verify some type of personal characteristic, such as a fingerprint.

Some of the most secure access control systems address both identification and authentication. *Identification* involves verifying that the person's name or other identifying feature is listed as an authorized user; *authentication* refers to determining whether or not the person is actually who he or she claims to be.

Passwords

Passwords are commonly used to restrict access to programs and data. Passwords can be used to restrict access to the network in general, or just to certain resources. For example, a password might be required to access the system, then another password required to access any drive, folder, or document on a network file server that contains sensitive or confidential information. Once a document is opened, it may require an additional password to modify and save the document back to the network storage device, if only specific individuals with permission to read the document are authorized to edit it.

When using passwords, it is important to select good ones and to change them frequently. A few of the biggest disadvantages of password-only systems is that the passwords can be forgotten or guessed easily if good strategies are not applied. Supplying the correct password also just identifies the corresponding user as an authorized user, but doesn't authenticate the actual person using the password. Some strategies for selecting good passwords are listed in Figure 8-25.

Physical Access Objects

Common physical objects used to access a network are magnetic cards (similar to credit cards), smart cards, and encoded badges (see the top left image in Figure 8-26). Two disadvantages to using physical objects to restrict network access is that they can be lost or they can be used by anyone with the object in their possession, not by just the authorized individual (as

> **FIGURE 8-25**
> **Strategies for good passwords.**

PASSWORD STRATEGIES

- Make the password as long as you possibly can. A four- or five-character password can be cracked by a computer program in less than a minute. A 10-character password, in contrast, has about 3,700 trillion possible character permutations and could take a regular computer decades to crack.

- Choose an unusual sequence of characters for the password—for instance, mix in numbers and special characters with words from other languages or unusual names. The password should be one that you can remember yet one that doesn't conform to a pattern a computer can readily figure out.

- Keep a written copy of the password in a place where no one but you can find it. Many people place passwords on Post-it notes that are affixed to their monitors or taped to their desks—a practice that's almost as bad as having no password at all.

- Don't use your kids' or pets' names, your address, your birthdate, or other public information as your password.

- For Web site accounts that remember your settings or profile, such as online news, auction, shopping, or bookstore sites, use a different password than for your highly sensitive activities such as online banking or stock trading; passwords used on nonsensitive Web sites are usually more easily obtained by criminals than those on high-security sites.

- Change the password as frequently as you can. Sniffer programs that criminals frequently use can read passwords being entered into unsecured systems.

>**Password.** A combination of characters used to gain access to a system.

❯**FIGURE 8-26**

Network security devices.

Network security devices
include physical access
objects (such as the card
reader shown in the top left
image), as well as biometric
security devices that recognize
some unique physiological
characteristic of a person,
such as a fingerprint or hand
geometry, or some unique
learned characteristic, such as
a voice or signature.

with passwords, using physical access objects does not authenticate the user). These disadvantages can be reduced by using a password in conjunction with the object, or by using *biometric devices* instead (discussed next).

Biometric Devices

Biometric devices provide network access by recognizing a unique physiological characteristic of a person—such as a fingerprint or geometry of the hand—or a unique learned characteristic, such as a voice or signature. Since the access device (part of the body) cannot be lost or forgotten, and because it cannot be transferred to another individual or used without the authorized individual, biometric access systems can perform both identification and authentication.

In theory, biometric devices have great potential; in practice, they have had fairly good success. Hand geometry readers (see the top-right image in Figure 8-26) are being used instead of time cards to avoid "buddy punching" where one employee punches another employee in or out. Face recognition technology is being used to automate check-cashing services, and iris (eye) scanning is being used to authorize ATM withdrawals. Even ordinary computer hardware like mice and keyboards are getting in the action. Biometric mice and keyboards containing built-in fingerprint scanners can be used to allow network access or authorize transactions.

>**Biometric device.** A device that uses the recognition of some unique physical characteristic (fingerprint, voice, etc.) to grant access to a computer network or physical facility.

Alternatively, external fingerprint readers can be used instead. Fingerprint scanners built into notebook PCs can prevent unauthorized users from viewing the PC's contents; PC card fingerprint readers perform similar tasks (see the bottom image in Figure 8-26).

Because of its reliability and the amount of business beginning to be conducted over the Internet, biometric security is predicted to be a high-growth area in the future. According to IrisScan, a firm that uses the human eye's iris to verify people's identity, the chance of two different people's irises matching using their scanner is one in 10^{78}, which makes it more effective than DNA testing.

Firewalls

To ward off the threat of outside intruders into their network, more and more organizations are creating firewalls. A **firewall** is a collection of hardware and/or software intended to protect a computer or computer network from attack. In theory, firewalls are needed whenever a computer is continually connected to an outside network, such as the Internet. With the increased use of "always on" Internet connections in homes (such as DSL, cable, fixed wireless, and satellite connections), firewalls are becoming an important home PC necessity, as well.

Historically, network attacks usually originate outside the organization from hackers. As intranet creation has intensified, however, security experts are advising organizations to build internal firewalls, too, to keep nosy employees from browsing through data that they don't need to perform their jobs.

NETWORK EMPLOYMENT OPPORTUNITIES

Computer network employment opportunities abound. From the more structured network-related jobs found in the *information systems (IS) departments* of larger companies, to jobs in smaller businesses and network consulting firms, there are a variety of interesting, well-paying jobs for the networking professional to choose from. A number of *certifications* are also available to add to the networking professional's credentials.

The Information Systems Department

The information systems department—often called the *information technology department* or a similar name—varies in structure from one company to another. It often includes people who design and implement *enterprise-wide* (company-wide) systems, people who provide support services to PC users, and people who build and manage networks and databases. Many, but not all, IS jobs involve computer networking expertise. Figure 8-27 describes a number of network-related jobs often found within information systems departments.

Certifications

Certification is a way for potential employees to demonstrate a certain level of competency in a particular area while they are looking for a position. Existing employees can use certifications as justification for a raise or promotion, or just as a way of keeping their skills up to date. Some of the most common networking and other computer-oriented certification programs are listed next. Virtually all certification programs require some type of supervised test in order to be awarded certification; many require on-the-job experience, as well.

Microsoft Corporation

Microsoft has certification programs for both computer professionals (*Microsoft Certified Professional*) and end-users (*Microsoft Office User Specialist* or *MOUS*). Some of the specific technical certifications available through the Microsoft Certified Professional program

---

>**Firewall.** A collection of hardware and software intended to protect a computer or computer network from attack.

Network administrator
The person responsible for planning and implementing networks within an organization.

Network analyst/engineer
A person who manages the networks in an organization and determines what changes, if any, are needed to the current infrastructure.

Network installer
A person who installs or upgrades networks, often on a consulting (outsource) basis.

Network operator/troubleshooter
A person responsible for overseeing the day-to-day activities for a network, such as troubleshooting problems, documenting network events, and performing necessary duties to keep the network operating smoothly.

Network technician
A person who installs, maintains, and upgrades networking hardware and software.

Security specialist
The person responsible for seeing that an organization's hardware, software, and data are protected from computer criminals, natural disasters, accidents, and the like.

Trainer
A person who provides education to users about a particular program, system, or technology.

Webmaster
The person responsible for establishing and maintaining an organization's Internet presence.

Web page designer
A person who designs and develops Web pages or an entire Web site.

Web programmer
A person who writes the program code necessary for a Web site, such as to provide animation and database interactivity.

⬎ FIGURE 8-27
Networking jobs.

include Microsoft Certified Professional, Microsoft Certified Professional + Internet, Microsoft Certified Systems Engineer, Microsoft Certified Database Administrator, and Microsoft Certified Trainer. MOUS exams are available to show core and expert competence in the various Microsoft Office programs (Word, Excel, Access, PowerPoint, FrontPage, Project, and Outlook).

Novell

Each year, *Novell* certifies thousands of computer networking professionals. It has a variety of certification programs including the very well-respected *Certified Novell Administrator (CNA), Certified Novell Engineer (CNE),* and *Master CNE* certificates. There are also *Certified Novell Instructor (CNI), Certified Internet Professional,* and *Certified Novell Salesperson (CNS)* programs.

Cisco Systems

Cisco Systems has a certification program—Cisco Career Certifications—that offers several networking certificates in two areas: network support and network design. There are three possible levels of certificates: Associate, Professional, and Expert. The *Cisco Certified Internetwork Expert (CCIE)* certificate is the highest Cisco certification level and represents at least two years of on-the-job experience, in addition to the necessary expertise.

Institute for Certification of Computing Professionals (ICCP)

The *Institute for Certification of Computing Professionals* or *ICCP* has one of the most widely recognized and respected computer professional certification programs. The requirements for certification include passing a core exam, passing two specialty exams (such as Management, Business Information Systems, Communications, Programming, Systems Security, and Microcomputing and Networks), having two years of industry experience, and signing the "ICCP Codes of Ethics, Conduct and Good Practice" document. Though they have had separate certificates in the past for different areas of computer expertise, currently all certificates are referred to as the *CCP* for *Certified Computing Professional.*

further
exploration

For links to further information about networking certifications, go to www.course.com/parker2002/ch8

Communications, or *telecommunications,* refers to communications from one device to another over a distance—such as over long-distance phone lines, via privately owned cables, or by satellite.

THE COMMUNICATIONS INDUSTRY

Chapter Objective 1:
Appreciate the changing nature of the communications industry and the effects of government legislation.

The key players in the telecommunications industry include phone companies, cable-TV and satellite companies, service and content providers, and a wide variety of supporting software and hardware companies. Current deregulation and other types of government involvement and legislation are helping to create a telecom industry characterized by mergers and acquisitions, partnering arrangements, and shakeouts that will eventually determine the dominant players for the future.

COMMUNICATIONS APPLICATIONS

Chapter Objective 2:
Describe several uses for communications technology.

A wide variety of important business applications involve communications. Among these are *paging* or *messaging* (sending short text-based messages to a pager or similar device); *cellular (cell)* and *satellite phones; faxing;* **global positioning systems (GPS); videoconferencing;** and **telecommuting.**

WHAT IS A NETWORK?

Chapter Objective 3:
Explain the difference between local area, wide area, and other types of networks.

A **network** is a collection of computers and other hardware devices that are connected together to share hardware, software, and data, as well as to facilitate electronic communications. Networks can be classified in terms of their *topologies,* or geometrical patterns. Three common topologies are the **star network,** the **bus network,** and the **ring network.** Network topologies are often combined to combine smaller networks to make a larger one.

Many organizations use a **local area network (LAN),** which connects geographically close devices, such as within a single building. LANs fall into two categories. The first, *client-server LANs,* consist of *server* devices that provide network services to *client* computers. Services often include access to expensive printers and vast secondary storage, database access, and computing power. In the second type of LANs, *peer-to-peer LANs,* the user computers and the shared peripherals in the network operate at the same level. A **hub** is a device on a network that acts as a central location where data arrives and then is transferred on.

Wide area networks (WANs) are networks that span relatively wide geographical areas. Because they tie together so many devices over such long distances, they require a number of special pieces of equipment.

Repeaters amplify signals along a network. *Routers, switches,* and *hubs* work together to pass network messages along to their destinations. Devices on two dissimilar networks can communicate with each other if the networks are connected by a **gateway.** Devices on two similar networks can communicate with each other if they are connected by a **bridge.** A *multiplexer* enables two or more low-speed devices to share a high-speed line; a *concentrator* is a multiplexer with a store-and-forward capability.

Other types of networks include *metropolitan area networks (MANs); personal area networks (PANs);* **intranets** (private networks that implement the infrastructure and standards of the Internet and World Wide Web); *extranets* (intranets that are accessible to authorized outsiders); *virtual private networks (VPNs)* used to transfer private information over a public communications system, such as the Internet; and *storage area networks (SANs),* networks consisting of high-speed, shared storage devices.

HOW NETWORKS WORK

Transmission media are used to transfer messages over a network. Wiring, such as **twisted-pair wires, coaxial cable,** and **fiber-optic cable,** constitutes one major class of media. Messages also are commonly sent through the air in the form of *radio signals* (including *terrestrial* **microwave stations,** communications **satellites,** and **cellular technology** used for cellular phones). *Infrared (IR)* technology is another wireless medium.

Signals sent along a phone line travel in an *analog* fashion—that is, as continuous waves. Computers and their support equipment, however, are *digital* devices that handle data coded into 0s and 1s. Transmissions can be characterized by their *bandwidth, speed,* whether they use **serial transmission** or **parallel transmission,** whether they use *simplex, half-duplex, or full-duplex* transmission directions, and whether they are timed using *synchronous, asynchronous,* or *isochronous transmission.*

Computers are usually connected to a network through either a **network interface card (NIC)** or a **modem.** The type of modem depends on the type of connection to be used and will convert the signals between digital and analog mode as needed. Possibilities include *conventional dial-up modems,* as well as *ISDN, DSL, cable,* and *satellite modems.*

Chapter Objective 4:
Name specific types of transmission media and explain how they transmit messages from one device to another.

COMMUNICATIONS PROTOCOLS

A communications *protocol* is a collection of procedures to establish, maintain, and terminate transmissions between devices. Because devices transmit data in so many ways, they collectively employ scores of different protocols.

Two major protocols are **Ethernet** and **Token Ring.** Each of these architectures is specified in a detailed set of protocols. Ethernet LANs commonly use a protocol called *CSMA/CD* to exchange messages, whereas Token Ring LANs use a protocol called *token passing.* **TCP/IP** is the protocol used on Internet computers. Wireless network connections typically use the **Wireless Application Protocol (WAP), wireless Ethernet,** or **Bluetooth** standards.

Chapter Objective 5:
Identify the different protocols that can be used to connect the devices on a network.

NETWORK SECURITY ISSUES

Because computers and networks are so widespread, there is unprecedented opportunity for criminals and other individuals to commit acts that are not in the public interest. Three issues that especially pertain to computer networks are **computer viruses** (software programs designed to do some type of malicious act), *unauthorized access,* which can be prevented by using some combination of good **password** techniques, physical access objects such as badges and cards, and **biometric devices** (devices that recognize some type of physical characteristic, such as a handprint or face). To protect a computer always connected to an outside network, a **firewall** should be used.

Chapter Objective 6:
Discuss some security issues involved with computer network usage.

NETWORK EMPLOYMENT OPPORTUNITIES

There are many jobs available for the network professional, including positions in a corporate *information systems (IS) department.* To enhance an individual's marketability, a number of professional certificates are available from such companies as Microsoft, Novell, Cisco Systems, and the Institute for Certification of Computing Professionals (ICCP).

Chapter Objective 7:
List some employment opportunities and certifications available for networking professionals.

NET

Instructions: Match each key term on the left with the definition on the right that fits best.

1. biometric device

2. cellular

3. coaxial cable

4. computer virus

5. Ethernet

6. fiber-optic cable

7. global positional system (GPS)

8. intranet

9. local area network (LAN)

10. microwave station

11. modem

12. network

13. network interface card (NIC)

14. password

15. satellite

16. TCP/IP

17. twisted-pair wire

_____ A collection of communications protocols that specify one standard way of setting up a LAN; also commonly called 10Base-T or 100Base-T.

_____ A collection of computers and other hardware devices that are connected together to share hardware, software, and data, as well as to facilitate electronic communications.

_____ A combination of characters used to gain access to a system.

_____ A communications device that enables digital computers to communicate over analog media.

_____ A communications medium consisting of a center wire inside a grounded, cylindrical shield, capable of sending data at high speeds.

_____ A communications medium consisting of wire strands twisted in sets of two and bound into a cable.

_____ A communications medium that uses hundreds of hair-thin, transparent fibers over which lasers transmit data as light.

_____ A device that uses the recognition of some unique physical characteristic (fingerprint, voice, etc.) to grant access to a computer network or physical facility.

_____ A form of broadcast radio that broadcasts using antennae located inside honeycomb-shaped cells.

_____ A network that connects devices located in a small geographical area, such as within a building.

_____ A private network that is set up similar to the Internet's World Wide Web.

_____ A software program designed to spread itself to other computers without the user's knowledge and, sometimes, to cause some harm to the system.

_____ A system that uses satellites and a special type of receiver to determine the exact geographic location of the receiver.

_____ An earth-bound device that sends and receives high-frequency, high-speed radio signals.

_____ An earth-orbiting device that relays communications signals over long distances.

_____ An expansion card through which a computer can connect to a local area network.

_____ The protocol used with Internet computers that uses packet switching to facilitate the transmission of messages.

Self-Quiz

True/False

Instructions: Circle **T** if the statement is true or **F** if the statement is false.

T F **1.** If an individual posts some digital photographs on his or her Web site, he or she would be classified as a service provider.

T F **2.** GPS systems are used only by the government.

T F **3.** To connect a LAN to the Internet, a gateway would typically be used.

T F **4.** The type of cable used inside most homes for telephone service is twisted-pair wire.

T F **5.** A computer virus can only be transferred to another computer via a disk.

Completion

Instructions: Answer the following questions.

6. A(n) _____ is a private network set up and used similar to the Internet.

7. A(n) _____ is a network that transfers private information securely over the Internet or other public network.

8. A(n) _____ is an earth-orbiting device that sends and receives high-frequency, high-speed, radio signals.

9. Business computing equipment typically uses _____ transmission, whereas the regular phone system typically uses _____ transmission.

10. A(n) _____ device uses some type of unique physiological characteristic of a person to grant system access to only authorized individuals.

Exercises

1. For each of the following list of communication situations, select the most effective communications method from the list that follows. Note that all methods will not be used.

_____ To transmit a 15-page business report that has several handwritten comments on it.

_____ To conduct a meeting between the corporate headquarters in L.A. and a Miami-based clothing designer to decide which pieces to include in the final summer swimsuit line.

_____ To notify a person attending a wedding ceremony about the change in time for an important meeting that afternoon.

_____ To determine one's location while hiking in the mountains.

a. Fax
b. Telecommuting
c. GPS
d. Paging/messaging
e. Videoconferencing
f. Cellular phone

NET

2. For each of the following modems, indicate whether or not they allow for data transmission over ordinary telephone lines.

Type of Modem	Transmit Over Telephone Lines?
a. Conventional dial-up modem	_____
b. ISDN modem	_____
c. DSL modem	_____
d. Cable modem	_____
e. Satellite modem	_____

3. What topology does this network use?

4. Many types of communications software and Web pages with downloadable files will tell you how long you should expect to spend downloading a particular file. Assuming that you need to download a 350 KB file and have a 56 Kbps modem, how long should it take to download the file? What real-world conditions might affect this download time?

5. What communications protocol does the Internet use?

1. **Your Connection** In order for you to connect your PC to the Internet, you need both a service provider and a hardware device to act as the interface between your computer and your provider's network. The type of hardware device needed is dependent on the type of access used. The type of access used varies, depending on the types of service available in your area and your specific communication requirements. Your communication requirements include how important a fast upload and/or download data connection is, whether or not you can tie up your phone while you're online, and your budget for online access. It should be noted that not all types of services are available in all areas, and not all ISPs support all types of services. For this project, identify what types of Internet connections (conventional dial-up, ISDN, DSL, cable, satellite, wireless, etc.) are available in your specific neighborhood and which ISPs support those specific connections. Be sure to identify the pricing structure associated with each type of connection available. At the conclusion of your research, prepare a one-page summary of your findings, including which service provider you would select for home Internet access and why, and submit it to your instructor.

2. **The Geocaching Craze** GPS can be used to accomplish many tasks. One recent trend is *geocaching*—using GPS equipment to locate a hidden cache. Coordinates for a cache are first listed on the Internet, then GPS users use these coordinates to find the caches. Once found, successful hunters may take something out of the cache, but are supposed to leave something else in return. Many caches are stored in scenic locations that individuals and organizations would like others to experience.

   For this project, investigate what GPS equipment you would need to participate in geocaching, including the cost, features, size, and weight of at least two potential products. Find out what information the GPS receiver would need to provide you to find a cache, and try to locate that information about a cache near you on the Internet. Also find out how you would go about hiding a cache for others to find. At the conclusion of your research, prepare a one-page summary of your findings and submit it to your instructor.

3. **Getting the Message** Wireless messaging is a very convenient way to communicate with your colleagues, family, and friends. Communications companies are now offering these services, which allow you to send a text message directly to a wireless phone or other communications device and then check to see if the message has been delivered. You can even set up an account with these companies that allows you to create group lists which can be used to send the same message to a group of people at the same time. For this project, investigate which companies are offering these types of services, what the limitations are, and how much they cost. Do you currently use one of these services? In not, are you considering using one in the future? Why, or why not? At the conclusion of your research, prepare a one-page summary of your findings and submit it to your instructor.

4. **Lab Topology** A topology in the context of a computer network refers to the configuration or diagram of how the computers are connected to the network. For this project, determine what topology, LAN configuration (client-server or peer-to-peer), and protocol (Ethernet, Token Ring, TCP/IP, etc.) are currently being used in your school's computer lab. In addition, you

should determine what type of hardware device is being used to connect each computer to the network and what the maximum communications speed is. At the conclusion of this task, prepare a one-page summary of your efforts and submit it to your instructor.

Writing About Computers

5. **Biometric Legalities** As discussed in the chapter, biometric devices can be used to limit individuals' access to a network or physical facility. This form of security is now being implemented on a wider scale than in the past, but may run into a few snags as these products become mainstream. For example, when does taking a biometric measurement constitute a search? Can the information gathered for one purpose be used for another purpose? Which methods are OK and which methods invade our personal privacy? If an iris reading device is used in place of a time card punching machine and the device detects that you have been drinking, can this information be used against you? For this project, identify several biometric devices and discuss the potential impact on our societal and individual rights. Which U.S. Constitutional Amendments protect our privacy, due process, and prevention from unreasonable searches and seizures? Would you like to have your employer use biometric devices? Submit this project to your instructor in the form of a short paper, not more than two pages in length.

6. **The Satellite Connection** The creation of an "Internet-in-the-Sky" network is underway by a company called Teledesic. Some of the major investors in the company include Bill Gates, Motorola, and Boeing. The objective of the company is to provide a "fiber-like" telecommunications service to individuals and organizations that cannot be economically served using a terrestrial system. For this project, investigate the company and how it plans to build and offer this "Internet-in-the-Sky." Is Teledesic still in existence? When was the company founded and when is this system supposed to become operational? Who is the target market and what is the estimated pricing structure? Submit this project to your instructor in the form of a short paper, not more than two pages in length.

7. **The Major Players** The Telecommunications Act of 1996 has had a profound effect on the telecommunications industry. The goal was to lower prices and bring about a more diverse array of products and services for consumers by removing regulatory barriers and enforcing pro-competitive policies. In the past few years we have seen tremendous changes in this industry. These changes can be seen in the products and services offered and most notably in the mergers and acquisitions that take place between companies trying to remain competitive by acquiring smaller companies that offer supplementary or complementary products like voice, video, or data. For this project, form a group to investigate the three most recent mergers or acquisitions in the telecommunications industry and explain why the merger or acquisition was undertaken. Was the merger or acquisition in the best interest of the two companies, in the best interest of the public, or both? Do you think that excessive industry consolidation will threaten the development or maintenance of a competitive marketplace, which the Telecommunications Act was supposed to create? Your group should submit the results of your research and discussions to your instructor in the form of a short paper, not more than three pages in length.

Presentation/ Demonstration

8. **Personal Firewall** Firewalls are used by individuals and organizations to protect their computer systems from intruders while they are connected to a network (especially the Internet). Personal Firewalls or Desktop Firewalls are used for the same purpose, but are designed to protect a single Internet-connected computer. Several companies are currently incorporating firewall protection right into the chips that are used in cable and DSL modems. In addition, several major companies now offer firewall software that can be downloaded, and the latest versions of Windows include some firewall capabilities. For this project, present a summary of the software-based firewall applications available on the market, how they work, and how much they cost. If you had a computer at home and it was continually connected to the Internet, would you purchase this software?

Why, or why not? This presentation should not exceed five minutes and should make use of one or more presentation aids such as the chalkboard, handouts, overhead transparencies, or computer-based slide presentation format. You may be asked to submit a summary of the presentation to your instructor.

9. **Home Network** If you have two or more computers at home and want to share files, an Internet connection, or a printer, you will need to set up a local area network (LAN). A few years ago this would have been a difficult and expensive task, but not today. You can review straightforward directions available at many Web sites, or purchase a do-it-yourself LAN kit with all the necessary hardware, software, and directions in a box. For this project, form a group to prepare a presentation that identifies and explains the options available for setting up a home network. Be sure to include the basic tasks, equipment, software, and costs associated with the options available. Which option would be the best if you are planning for the construction of a new home? What about for an existing home? Do the options work equally well? Does anyone in the group currently have a home network or considered setting one up? Do you think that you could successfully accomplish this task? The presentation should not exceed 10 minutes and should make use of one or more presentation aids such as the chalkboard, handouts, overhead transparencies, or computer-based slide presentation format. Your group may be asked to submit a summary of the presentation to your instructor.

10. **Certification** Companies that purchase networking hardware and software products need qualified personnel to install and maintain them. In order to ensure that there are qualified individuals available for hire, most vendors offer a set of certification programs and exams, which are tied to the types of networking hardware and software products they sell. In the past few years the sales of networking products has skyrocketed and so has the demand for qualified individuals to install and maintain them. The demand for networking products can be filled by stepping up production, but the demand for qualified individuals is limited by the number of people wishing to get certified and willing to take the time needed to complete the training programs. The resulting demand for network certified individuals has allowed those individuals that are already certified to request a premium price for their services and caused some public and private educational institutions to begin their own certification programs. Some vendors like Cisco have even offered to team with some of these educational institutions to help them get more individuals trained and certified. A few of the private institutions that offer some of these certification programs on a condensed schedule are charging a premium for their programs and filling their classes. For this project, form a group to research the various certification programs available either locally or over the Internet. Your group should prepare a presentation about the five most popular certification programs you discover including who is offering the program, how long it takes to complete it, the program and exam costs, and what the employment prospects look like after completing the program. Do the jobs offered with this certification require any experience? Has anyone in your group already gone through or is considering going through one of these certification programs? The presentation should not exceed 10 minutes and should make use of one or more presentation aids such as the chalkboard, handouts, overhead

transparencies, or computer-based slide presentation format. Your group may be asked to submit a summary of the presentation to your instructor.

11. **Imagine Tomorrow** Imagine yourself 10 years from now. The telecommunications industry has continued to offer new products and merge with each other in hopes of capturing more market share and ensuring their future. The capability of the Internet has increased 10-fold and everyone has access to a high-speed connection. Your personal computer has the capability and capacity of today's fastest supercomputers.

Select one of the following positions about the future, or make up your own, and express your point of view on the subject. Your instructor will indicate whether your response is to be posted to a class bulletin board, discussed in a class chat room, or discussed as an in-class activity. You may also be asked to submit a summary of your position and point of view to your instructor.

a. My life will not be much different than it is right now, except that I will probably spend more time playing Web-based game software and watching TV on my personal computer.

b. My life and lifestyle will change dramatically. I will no longer drive to work each morning because my personal network communications device with holographic imaging capability allows me do my work while I am traveling the world.

12. **Too Much Access?** Consider the following statement and establish your position, or point of view, on the subject. Your instructor will indicate whether your response is to be posted to a class bulletin board, discussed in a class chat room, or discussed as an in-class activity. You may also be asked to submit a summary of your position and evaluation of the statement to your instructor.

With wireless technology, in the near future, no matter where you are or what you are doing, people will be able to access you and you will be able to access them. This capability is being developed and integrated along with a GPS into phones, pagers, and other wireless devices. With this technology, you will never be out of contact with work, family, and friends and you will always know where they are physically located on the surface of globe. The potential benefits of this new technology are tremendous. Imagine sailing across the ocean and not having to navigate by compass and stars, or visiting some new place you have never been before and not having to worry about getting lost, or being able to call your stockbroker at a moment's notice wherever you are when you hear some news that warrants immediate action. The benefits seem almost limitless, but what about the problems this technology might cause? Imagine trying to leave the office after a hard day's work, only to find that no matter where you go, your work goes with you, or dealing with the stress of knowing that your boss could potentially track where you are all day long. Sometimes too much information can be worse than no information at all.

Connecting Your PC to a Network. Your PC is about to be connected to a network! Go to the Interactive Exercise at www.course.com/parker2002/ch8 to complete this exercise.

The Internet and World Wide Web

LEARNING OBJECTIVES

After completing this chapter, you will be able to:

1. Discuss how the Internet has evolved into what it is today.

2. Identify the various types of individuals, companies, and organizations involved in the Internet community and explain their purposes.

3. Describe the device, connection, and provider options for connecting to the Internet, as well as some considerations to keep in mind when selecting an ISP.

4. Understand how to effectively search for information on the Internet, including search options, strategies, and how to properly cite Internet resources.

5. List several useful things that can be done using the Internet, in addition to basic browsing and e-mail.

6. Discuss censorship and privacy, and how it is related to Internet use.

7. Speculate as to the format, structure, and use of the Internet in the future.

It's hard to believe that before 1990 few people outside of the computer industry and academia had ever heard of the Internet. However, hardware, software, and communications tools were just not available back then to unleash the power of the Internet as it exists today. In fact, it is only in the last few years that technology has evolved enough to allow multimedia applications—such as downloading audio and video files and viewing animated presentations—to be an everyday activity.

What a difference a few years make. Today, *Internet* and *Web* are household words, and in many ways they have redefined how people think about computers and communications.

Despite the popularity of the Internet, however, many users cannot answer some important basic questions about it. What makes up the Internet? Is it the same thing as the World Wide Web? How did the Internet begin and where is it heading? What types of tools are available to help people make optimum use of the Internet? How do you find information on the Internet? This chapter addresses such questions.

Chapter 9 begins with a discussion of the evolution of the Internet, from the late 1960s to the present time. Then it looks into the many individuals, companies, and organizations that make up the Internet community. Next, the chapter covers the different options for connecting to the Internet, including the devices, types of connections, and types of service providers you can choose between. Then, it's on to one of the most important Internet skills you should acquire—efficient Internet searching. So you can appreciate the wide spectrum of resources and activities available through the Internet, we also take a brief look at some of the most common financial, entertainment, news, and research applications available via the Internet. The final sections of the chapter cover some of the important social issues that apply to Internet use and take a look at the Internet's future. ■

EVOLUTION OF THE INTERNET

The **Internet** is a worldwide collection of networks that supports personal and commercial communication and information exchange. It consists of thousands of separate, but interconnected, networks that are accessed daily by millions of people. Just as the shipping industry has simplified transportation by providing standard containers for carrying all sorts of merchandise via air, rail, highway, and sea, the Internet furnishes a standard way of sending messages and information across virtually any type of computer platform and transmission media. While *Internet* has become a household word only during the past few years, it has actually operated in one form or another for decades.

From ARPANET to Internet2
The Internet began in 1969 as an experimental project. The U.S. Department of Defense (DOD) wanted to develop a communications network that could withstand outages, such

>**Internet.** The largest and most widely used computer network in the world, linking millions of computers all over the world.

as those caused by nuclear attack or natural disaster. A principal goal was creating a system that could send messages along alternate paths if part of the network was disabled. With this purpose in mind, the DOD enlisted researchers at colleges and universities to assist with the development of protocols and message-packeting systems to standardize routing information, and *ARPANET* was born.

ARPANET

At its start and throughout many years of its history, the Internet was called **ARPANET** (pronounced *AR-pan-et*). ARPANET was named for the group that sponsored its development, the *A*dvanced *R*esearch *P*rojects *A*gency (ARPA) of the Department of Defense. At its inception, ARPANET connected four supercomputers. As it grew during its first few years, ARPANET enabled researchers at a few dozen academic institutions to communicate with each other and with government agencies on topics of mutual interest.

However, the Department of Defense got much more than it bargained for. With the highly controversial Vietnam War in full swing, ARPANET's e-mail facility began to handle not only legitimate research discussions but also heated debates about U.S. involvement in Southeast Asia. As students began to access ARPANET, other unintended uses—such as playing computer games—began.

As the experiment grew during the next decade, hundreds of college and university networks were connected to ARPANET. These local area networks consisted of a mixture of DOS and Windows-based computers, Apple Macintoshes, UNIX workstations, and so on. Over the years, protocols were developed to tie this mix of computers and networks together, to transfer data over the network, and to ensure that the data were transferred intact. Throw in the government networks also under development during that time—and add to that the decision to let friendly foreign countries participate—and you can see how ARPANET turned into a massive network of networks, which eventually evolved into the present-day Internet infrastructure, connecting millions of computers all over the globe.

The World Wide Web

Despite its popularity in academia and with government researchers, the Internet went virtually unnoticed by the general public and the business community for over two decades. Why? For two reasons—it was hard to use, and it was slow. Users had to type cryptic commands (see the first image in Figure 9-1), since attractive graphical user interfaces (GUIs) were still largely unknown.

As always, however, technology improved and new applications quickly evolved. First, communications hardware improved and computers gained speed and better graphics capabilities. Then, in 1989, a researcher named Tim Berners-Lee working at a physics laboratory called CERN in Europe, proposed the idea of the **World Wide Web.** The Web concept would organize information in the form of pages linked together through selectable text or images *(hyperlinks)* on the screen. Though the introduction of Web pages didn't replace other Internet resources (such as e-mail and file exchanges), it became popular with researchers as a means to supply information for others to read.

Matters really got rolling with the arrival of Microsoft Windows and the graphical user interface. In 1993, a group of professors and students at the University of Illinois National Center for Supercomputing Applications *(NCSA)* released *Mosaic*. Mosaic, the first graphically based Web browser, used a graphical user interface and allowed Web pages to include graphical images in addition to text. Soon after, use of the World Wide Web began to increase dramatically, because the graphical interface and graphical Web pages made surfing the World Wide Web both easier and more fun than in the past. Today's Web pages are a true

>**ARPANET.** The predecessor of the Internet, named after the Advanced Research Projects Agency (ARPA), which sponsored its development.
>**World Wide Web (WWW).** The collection of Web pages available through the Internet.

EARLY 1990s
Even at the beginning of the 1990s, using the Internet for most people meant learning how to work with a cryptic sequence of commands. Virtually all information was text-based.

FIGURE 9-1

Using the Internet: Back in the "old days" versus now.

TODAY
Today's Internet features the World Wide Web, which organizes much of the Internet's content into easy-to-read pages and replaces the cryptic command sequences with hyperlinks that you can activate with a mouse click. Web pages today can contain a wide variety of multimedia elements, such as on the Web page shown above.

multimedia experience. They can contain text, graphics, animation, sound, video, and three-dimensional virtual reality objects (refer to the second image in Figure 9-1).

Though the Web is only part of the Internet, it is by far one of the most popular and one of the fastest-growing parts today. As interest in the Internet snowballed, scores of companies began looking for ways to make it more accessible to customers, to make the user interface even more dazzling, and to make more services available over it. Today, most companies regard their use of the Internet as an indispensable competitive tool.

Internet2

The next significant improvements of the Internet infrastructure may be as a result of *Internet2,* a consortium led by over 180 universities working together with industry and the government. Internet2 was created to develop and implement advanced Internet applications and technologies—hopefully leading to improvements for tomorrow's Internet. One of the primary goals of the Internet2 project is to ensure that new network services and applications are quickly applied to the broader Internet community, not just to the Internet2 participants. It is important to realize that Internet2 does not refer to a new physical Internet that will eventually replace the Internet—it is just a research and development project geared to ensuring that the Internet in the future can handle tomorrow's applications.

A complementary project is the *Next Generation Internet (NGI).* While Internet2 is university sponsored, NGI is government sponsored. Internet2 is working in cooperation with the NGI project, as well as forming partnerships with similar projects in other countries, to ensure a cohesive and interoperable advanced networking infrastructure for the Internet of the future.

The Internet Community Today

The Internet community today is populated by individuals, companies, and a variety of organizations located throughout the world (see Figure 9-2). Virtually anyone with a computer that has communications capabilities can be part of the Internet, either as a user or as a supplier of information or services. Most members of the Internet community fall into one or more of the following groups.

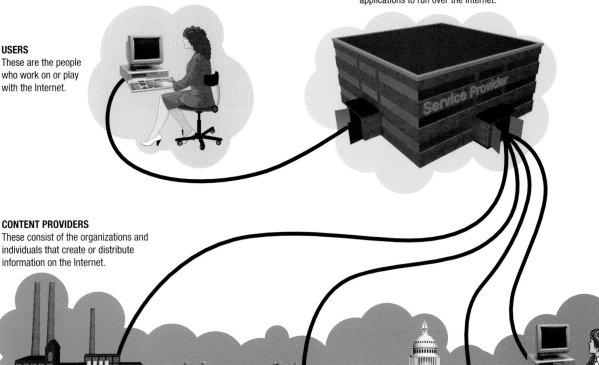

SERVICE PROVIDERS
Internet service providers connect individual users and user organizations to the Internet; application service providers supply users with applications to run over the Internet.

USERS
These are the people who work on or play with the Internet.

CONTENT PROVIDERS
These consist of the organizations and individuals that create or distribute information on the Internet.

COMPANIES   COLLEGES AND UNIVERSITIES   GOVERNMENT   INDIVIDUALS

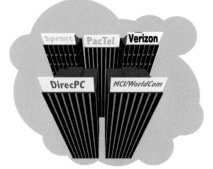

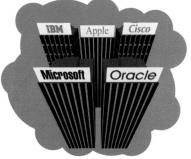

INFRASTUCTURE COMPANIES
These are the enterprises that own or operate the paths along which Internet data travel.

HARDWARE AND SOFTWARE COMPANIES
These companies make Internet-related programs and equipment.

GOVERNMENT AND OTHER ORGANIZATIONS
Several groups act as watchdogs on the Internet, make up the rules that govern it, and help manage sections of it.

Users

Users are people who avail themselves of the vast amount of resources available through the Internet at work or in their personal lives. There are well over a hundred million Internet users in the U.S. alone and they come from all walks of life. The U.S. *digital divide*—the disproportionate higher level of Internet use for certain groups of individuals (typically the more affluent and more educated)—is lessening as free Internet access is becoming more widespread in libraries, schools, and other public locations. That, plus the availability

▷ FIGURE 9-2
The Internet community.
Today's Internet community is composed of users; service, content, and application providers; infrastructure and other hardware and software companies; the government; and other types of organizations.

of cheap PCs and free dial-up Internet access in many areas today, has helped Internet use begin to approach the popularity of the phone and TV.

Internet Service Providers

Internet service providers (ISPs)—often called *service providers* or *access providers* for short—are organizations that provide Internet access to others. They operate very much like a cross between cable-television and phone companies in that they provide access to a communications service, usually for a monthly fee.

In addition to Internet access, ISPs furnish subscribers with e-mail addresses so they can exchange electronic mail. Many providers will also allow these individuals to post personal Web pages on the provider's Web site at no additional cost. A later section of this chapter covers the different types of ISPs available, plus factors to consider when selecting an ISP.

Internet Content Providers

Internet content providers, or *content providers,* are the parties that furnish the information available through the Internet. Here are some examples of content providers:

▼ A photographer creates electronic copies of some of her best work and places them along with her e-mail address and phone number on the Internet.

▼ A political-action group sponsors an online forum for discussions between people who share their opinions.

▼ A software company creates a Web site that users can access to both get product information and download trial copies of software.

▼ A national newspaper maintains an online site that anyone on the Internet can turn to for late-breaking news, feature stories, and video clips.

▼ A television network sponsors a site for its newest reality TV show, including statistics, photographs, and live video feeds.

▼ A music publisher creates a site where sample songs can be downloaded and custom CDs can be created, purchased, and downloaded.

▼ A film student releases his original short movies to be viewed on the Web.

Application Service Providers

Application service providers (ASPs) are companies that manage and distribute software-based services and solutions to customers across a network—usually the Internet. Instead of providing access to the Internet like ISPs do, ASPs provide access to software applications. In essence, ASPs rent software access to companies or individuals. Just as with Internet access, customers typically pay a monthly or yearly fee to use the applications. Advantages to customers over buying software outright include less up-front money, so small businesses may be able to afford the same state-of-the-art applications that larger companies use. It also may result in a reduction of computer support staffing, since the ASP can provide regular, automatic upgrades that all users see the next time they use the application; free or low-cost technical support and training may also be available from the ASP. Leasing applications in this manner also gives customers the flexibility of trying a different application whenever desired, without potentially wasting money purchasing software that may not fit the company's needs. Common ASP applications are office suites, groupware, and communications, accounting, and e-commerce software.

Though some Web sites provide access to online applications, such as mortgage calculators and games, and so could technically be referred to ASPs, major software companies—Microsoft, for example—are working on implementing ASPs on a much wider scale. It is speculated that these software companies' high level of interest is in response to the estimated huge level of software piracy that takes place at the small business level. While larger companies have systems and personnel in place to audit the programs installed on company computers to ensure compliance with licensing requirements, smaller companies rarely have either. Through the convenience and low per-computer cost for software rented through an ASP, software piracy could be significantly reduced.

Despite their motivations, industry experts—such as the CEOs of Sun Microsystems and Microsoft—predict that within a relatively short period of time, software purchasing as we know it today will not exist. Instead, all software will be delivered as a service and the option to purchase software outright just may not exist. In fact, though it later reversed its decision before Office XP became available, Microsoft had announced that it would be sold on a subscription basis. A twist on the ASP idea is converting Web page content for delivery via an alternative device. For example, companies that convert Web pages and Web applications for use with wireless devices such as Web-enabled phones and pagers sometimes refer to themselves as *wireless application service providers.*

Infrastructure Companies

Infrastructure companies are the enterprises that own or operate the paths or "roadways" along which Internet data travel. Included in this group are phone and Internet-backbone companies, cellular, satellite, and cable-TV companies, and the like, as discussed in the previous chapter.

Hardware and Software Companies

In addition to the types of companies covered thus far, a wide variety of hardware and software companies make and distribute Internet-related products. The firms that supply browser and e-mail software fall into this category. So, too, do the companies that make modems, routers, servers, PCs, server software, and Web-publishing tools. The customers of software and hardware companies are users, service and content providers, and infrastructure companies.

The Government and Other Organizations

Many other organizations influence the Internet and its uses. Governments have among the most visible impact; their local laws limit both information content and access in the Internet community. The *Internet Society* is another key organization. This professional membership society provides leadership in addressing the issues that affect the future of the Internet, and it also oversees Internet infrastructure standards, such as which protocols can be used and how Internet addresses should work. Also playing an important support role is the *Shared Registration System.* A competitive registration system developed by the Department of Commerce, *ICANN* (the *I*nternet *C*orporation for *A*ssigned *N*ames and *N*umbers), and Network Solutions, Inc., registrar companies included as part of the Shared Registration System are charged with registering Internet addresses and ensuring that no two are the same. Last but not least, many colleges and universities support Internet research and manage blocks of the Internet's resources.

Myths About the Internet

Because the Internet is so unique in the history of the world—and still a relatively new phenomenon—several widespread myths about it have surfaced.

Myth 1: The Internet Is Free

This falsehood has been perpetuated largely by the fact that people can access Web pages from anywhere in the world and freely engage in long-distance e-mail or chat exchanges without paying extra. It is true that the Internet's design never anticipated distance billing, and it is certainly also a fact that many people, such as students, employees, and consumers who opt for free Internet service, pay nothing to use the Internet. Yet it should also be obvious that someone, somewhere, has to pay to keep the Internet up and running.

Businesses, schools, public libraries, and home users often pay service providers flat monthly fees to connect to the Internet. The service providers—along with the phone companies—pay to keep the physical parts of the network running smoothly. Providers also pay software and hardware companies for the resources they need to support their users. Of course, most of these costs are eventually passed along to ordinary users in the way of higher costs. Free Internet access is usually supported by advertising revenue gained from onscreen ads, similar to regular TV broadcasting, or by selling personal or demographic data obtained from subscribers.

Though it may be a long while—or possibly never—that very fast, broadband access is available free to everyone, it is likely that free conventional dial-up service will remain. In the meantime, customers who need additional speed for multimedia and more interactive Internet content will be required to pay for it.

Myth 2: Someone Controls the Internet

The popularity of conspiracy theories in recent years has contributed to the spread of this myth. In fact, no one group or organization controls the Internet, although many would undoubtedly like to do so. Governments in each country have the power to regulate the content and use of the Internet within their borders, as allowed by their laws. However, legislators often face serious obstacles getting legislation passed into law—let alone getting it enforced. Making governmental control even harder is the bombproof design of the Internet itself. If a government tries to block access to or from a specific country, for example, users can establish links between the two countries through a third one.

Guidelines of watchdog groups such as the Internet Society have sometimes even given way before the tidal wave of people and organizations that have flocked to the Internet. Their policies that discouraged commercial use, for example, fell by the wayside many years ago. In the middle of 1994, only about 14 percent of Web sites were deemed to be commercial; today, commercial Web sites abound.

Myth 3: The Internet and World Wide Web Are Identical

Since you can use Web browser software to access almost all Internet resources today, many people think the Internet and the Web are the same thing. They're not. Technically, the Internet is the physical network and the Web is the collection of Web pages accessible over the Internet, though in everyday use, many people use the terms *Internet* and *Web* interchangeably. In fact, while the Web is the fastest-growing component of the Internet, it's not even the largest one. More people, for example, use e-mail. Helping this myth along is the ability of Web browsers today to access Internet resources other than Web pages, such as e-mail and collections of files.

INTERNET CONNECTIVITY ISSUES

Connecting to the Internet usually involves three decisions. The first is determining the type of device you will use to access the Internet. The second is selecting the type of connection desired. A final step is deciding on the type of Internet service provider required. Once these determinations have been made, an ISP can be selected and your computer can be set up to access the Internet.

Type of Device

The Internet today can be accessed by a variety of devices. The type of device used depends on a combination of factors, including the amount of portability needed and the desired content to be retrieved from the Web. Some possible devices are shown in Figure 9-3 and are discussed next.

PCs

Most users who have access to a PC at home, work, or school will use it to access the Internet, when needed. One advantage of using PCs for Internet access is that they are usually fast and can be connected to high-speed Internet connections, as discussed shortly. They also can be used to retrieve virtually any content from the Web, including pages with multimedia content, such as animation, music files, and video clips. A final advantage is that they

web tutor

For a tutorial on connecting to the Internet, go to www.course.com/ parker2002/ch9

FIGURE 9-3

Internet access devices.

A variety of devices, including (clockwise from top left) the PC, Internet appliance, smart phone, and handheld PC, can be used to access the Internet.

NET

usually have access to a printer and hard drive, so Web pages and e-mail messages can be printed, and e-mail and downloaded files can be saved when needed.

Internet Appliances

Internet appliances—devices that are designed specifically for accessing the Internet—are becoming increasingly common in homes, especially in homes that don't have a PC. Also known as *information appliances* and *Web pads,* these devices are typically very easy to use and can usually access both Web pages and e-mail. Web page graphics can be displayed, though not necessarily all other multimedia content. Disadvantages of Internet appliances include little or no storage space for saving e-mails or downloads (usually everything must be stored online); possibly not being able to connect the device to a printer; and usually not being able to use the device for tasks other than Internet activities. They also typically connect to the Internet through relatively slow connections, such as regular dial-up connections. In addition, many of these devices work only with a single specified provider, such as America Online, MSN, or a proprietary service just for that type of Internet appliance.

Mobile Devices

Mobile Web use—or *wireless Web,* as it is frequently referred to—is one of the fastest growing Web applications today. Notebook and handheld devices frequently use attached or built-in modems to access the Internet; most mobile phones and pagers have Internet connectivity built in. Notebook and other fully functioning portable PCs can usually access the Internet in the same manner as desktop PCs do—including multimedia Web pages and high-speed Internet connections. Handheld PCs, like the one in Figure 9-3, can usually access both Web pages and e-mail, though the display is small and often not in color, storage space is very limited, and not all Web pages can be viewed. With Web-enabled phones, pagers, and other small mobile devices, Web pages are often limited to text only and just a few lines can be displayed at one time, though some newer phones (like the one shown in Figure 9-3) open to provide access to a larger screen and keyboard. As with other handheld devices, storage is very limited and connection speeds may be slow.

Type of Connection

As discussed in the previous chapter, there are a variety of wired and wireless ways to connect to the Internet. In virtually all setups, the computer to which you connect is usually connected to a larger network called a *regional network;* regional networks are connected to the major high-speed networks within each country called *backbone networks.* Backbone networks within a country are connected together and to backbone networks in other countries to form the Internet.

The following sections discuss the most common types of Internet connections.

Dial-Up Connections

Dial-up connections usually work over regular telephone lines. To connect to the Internet, your modem (or other appropriate interface device) dials up and connects to a modem attached to your ISP's computer. While you are connected, your PC is assigned a temporary IP address for the current session. At the end of each Internet session, you disconnect from your ISP's computer to allow another user to connect in your place. One advantage to a dial-up connection is security. Since you are not continually connected, it is much less likely that anyone would gain access to your computer via the Internet, to either obtain information or mess with the data on your PC or, more commonly, to use your computer in some type of illegal or unethical manner. These types of *hacking* activities are discussed in Chapter 15.

>**Dial-up connection.** A type of Internet connection in which the PC or other device must dial up and connect to a service provider's computer before being connected to the Internet.

With a dial-up connection your telephone will be tied up while you are accessing the Internet, unless a second phone line is used. Some Internet call-waiting or call-forwarding services allow you to be notified when you get a telephone call while you are connected to the Internet. They are generally set up to allow the person to leave a short message; some newer systems give you a short window of time to disconnect from the Internet and pick up the telephone call, if desired. Newer dial-up modems are expected to facilitate some type of call-waiting service, as well.

Standard Dial-Up

As discussed in Chapter 8, standard dial-up Internet service uses a conventional dial-up modem rated at a maximum data transfer rate of 56 Kbps. These modems are commonly used with PCs and Internet appliances. Portable devices may also use a conventional dial-up modem; if so, they need to be connected to standard telephone jacks to access the Internet. Standard dial-up Internet service ranges from free to about $25 per month.

ISDN

Another dial-up option is *ISDN*. As discussed in Chapter 8, ISDN (*i*ntegrated *s*ervices *d*igital *n*etwork) allows digital transmission of data over ordinary telephone lines. It requires a special ISDN adapter or modem and can transfer data up to 128 Kbps, or almost three times as fast as a typical dial-up connection. Though fairly pricey for the speed at about $70 per month, ISDN is a faster Internet option for users who don't have access to a direct connection.

Direct Connections

Unlike dial-up connections that only connect to your ISP's computer when you need to access the Internet, direct connections keep you continually connected to the Internet. With a **direct** *(always-on)* **connection,** your PC is typically issued a *static* (nonchanging) IP address to be used to transfer data back and forth via the Internet. PCs connected to the network always have an Internet connection available—Internet access requires only opening a browser.

Types of direct Internet connections include connecting through a school or office LAN, as well as DSL, cable, satellite, and fixed wireless connections. Though, in theory, broadband Internet access can be up to 100 times as fast as a dial-up connections, actual speeds at the present time are more like 25 to 50 times as fast. Typical download speeds for DSL and cable are about 1.5 Mbps; satellite and fixed wireless usually download data between 500 Kbps to 1 Mbps. Virtually all of the these services use slower upload speeds. The most significant characteristics of each of these types of broadband Internet access are discussed next.

School or Office LAN

Most school or office LANs that offer a direct connection to the Internet lease a high-speed dedicated line (such as an ISDN or *T1* line) from the telephone company or an Internet provider. The speed of this type of Internet access depends on the speed of the connection between the school or office and their Internet provider, as well as the speed of the LAN itself.

DSL

As mentioned in Chapter 8, *DSL* (*d*igital *s*ubscriber *l*ine) is currently available only to users who are relatively close (three miles or less) to a telephone switching station with telephone lines capable of handling DSL, and long waits for installation are not uncommon. Nevertheless, DSL is a popular broadband option. DSL is sometimes offered at different speeds to fit different needs and budgets, such as a slower, less-expensive personal version and a faster business option. The monthly cost of standard DSL service is about $50.

Cable

A third type of direct Internet connection—*cable*—is the most widely used home broadband alternative. Cable connections are very fast and are available to anyone with cable access whose cable provider has upgraded the system to support Internet access. Just about all cable Internet access today is two-way (full-duplex), with the cable being used to transfer data in both directions. One disadvantage of cable is that all users in an immediate geographical area share the bandwidth of their local cable. Though this may not prove to be a problem all the time, during high-use times of day—such as early evening—the speed of cable Internet service can slow down dramatically as your neighbors go online. Cost is about $40 per month, in addition to regular cable fees.

Satellite

As discussed in Chapter 8, *satellite* Internet access is often the only broadband option in rural areas. It requires a satellite modem and a transceiver satellite dish mounted outside the home or building. The two-way satellite services available today, such as *StarBand,* are relatively reliable, though an unobstructed view of the southern sky is required and access may degrade during very heavy rainstorms. Typical cost is about $70 per month.

Fixed Wireless

One last type of broadband access that is relatively new for consumer use but shows great promise is *fixed wireless.* This type of service, such as *Sprint Broadband Direct,* is similar to satellite service in that it requires a modem and an outside-mounted transceiver, but is typically available only in larger metropolitan areas. A clear line-of-sight is required between the transceiver and the provider's radio transmission tower, which relays information between the user's transceiver and the Internet. Cost for service is about $50 per month.

Regardless of the type of connection used, a very important consideration for all users with a direct Internet connection is protecting the computer from unauthorized access or hackers. While most schools and offices are protected by some type of firewall, many home direct connections are not. Though it is unlikely that someone would access your home PC in this manner, the possibility will continue to increase as direct home connections become more common. To protect yourself, all computers using a direct connection should use a personal firewall program—especially those on a home network that allows file sharing. Firewall programs typically block access to your PC from outside computers, as well as allow you to specify which programs on your PC can access the Internet. Some firewall software, such as the ZoneAlarm software shown in Figure 9-4, are available free for home use. Some firewall protection is beginning to be incorporated into other programs, such as Windows XP.

Mobile Wireless Connections

Unlike satellite and fixed wireless connections, which use a cable to connect the modem to some type of fixed transceiver, *mobile wireless* connections allow the device to be moved from place to place. Consequently, most handheld PCs and other mobile devices (like Web-enabled cell phones) use a mobile wireless connection and access the Internet through the same wireless network as cell phones and messaging devices. Most mobile phones today capable of Internet access come "wireless Internet-ready" and can immediately be used to retrieve Web content, provided wireless Web service is included in the phone's service plan. Many handheld PCs also have Internet connectivity built in; if not, a wireless modem (such as the one shown in Figure 8-20) can be used. Alternately, a modem or other type of adapter can connect the device to a cell phone. Notebook PCs can connect to the Internet or a corporate network using either a wireless modem or cell modem. Some notebook computers today come with wireless capability built into the unit.

Type of Service Provider

There are traditionally two types of services providers: *basic ISPs,* and what used to be referred to as *commercial online services,* though that term is less commonly used today. The difference between them is the amount of services provided in addition to Internet

Shows programs that are allowed access to the Internet.

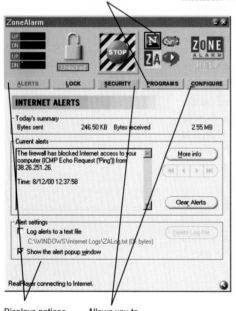

Displays notices of any blocking action that the program was required to take.

Allows you to select your desired level of security.

▶ FIGURE 9-4

Firewall software. Anyone using a direct Internet connection should use some type of firewall software to protect his or her PC from unauthorized access.

access. Most basic ISPs, whether they are local companies or large, national providers, supply Internet access and sometimes a *portal* page (a page designed to attract regular Web traffic by providing a broad array of resources and services), but that's about it. In contrast, commercial online services—such as *America Online (AOL)*—provide an interface geared toward easy use of online resources and activities (see Figure 9-5). They also usually provide specialized content not available to nonmembers. With increased competition for customers, such mergers as the one between AOL and Time Warner, and the availability of broadband connections to support multimedia content, there will likely be an increase in the amount of "members only" content in the future in an attempt to lure customers away from other providers. Some possibilities include proprietary downloads, on-demand movies, interactive TV, and other types of broadcasts.

Selecting an ISP and Setting Up Your System

Once the type of Internet access device, type of connection, and type of service provider is determined, the final steps to getting connected to the Internet are selecting a specific provider and setting up your system.

Selecting an ISP

Your geographical location, the type of device being used, and the desired type of connection may limit the choice of providers to just one or two; if multiple providers are available, the following criteria can be helpful when making the final selection.

Offerings

One of the most important steps in choosing an ISP is figuring out what you're getting. For instance, not all ISPs will give you full view to all parts of the Internet. On the Web, some ISPs may block access to certain types of Web sites. Other ISPs may or may not support instant messaging, buddy lists, e-mail filtering, e-mail attachments, and other specialized services. What's more, many of the large ISPs have special events to draw subscribers. You may be offered, for instance, a free subscription to the *New York Times* or *Wall Street Journal* Web sites, which nonsubscribers have to pay to see. Finally, you need to check what software is allowed for browsing and e-mail. Can you use the newest Internet Explorer or Netscape browser, or are you limited to a proprietary one? This is important, because

FIGURE 9-5

Proprietary Internet content. Commercial online services, such as America Online shown here, often provide specialized content for their members that is not available otherwise.

not all software is equal. For instance, the e-mail package you may be required to use may not support attachments.

Access Speeds and Connectability

An important consideration centers on how fast the service works. If you plan on using a 56K conventional or ISDN dial-up connection, make sure the ISP has a local access number that supports that speed. For other types of connections, compare both the upload and download speeds quoted by each of your possible ISPs to see if there is a difference between them.

Whether or not you can connect to your provider when you want to is another important issue for dial-up services. Before signing up with a dial-up service, ask the provider about the average number of people it has assigned to each modem or line. If that ratio exceeds 15:1 you may wind up getting a busy signal too often when you're trying to connect. A ratio of 10:1 is acceptable. For cable access, ask if there are any statistics available about the number of subscribers who will be using the same line as you will and the estimated effect on performance.

Service and Support

One of the most important service-related issues is reaching help when you have a problem with the service. Try calling the ISP's technical support number at the time you would most likely be using the Internet. Does anyone answer? Some understaffed providers have earned unsavory reputations for letting users linger on the line half an hour or more and for not returning phone calls or e-mails promptly. The quality of support help is important too. You want to talk to people who can solve your problems and get you back online fast when there is a problem with either the settings on your PC or with the ISP's hardware.

Cost

For most people, the bottom line in choosing a provider is cost. When comparing the cost for dial-up Internet service, be sure to find out whether it is a flat-rate plan with unlimited hours of *connect time* (the amount of online time allowed per month), or if only a certain number of hours are included in the monthly price. Unlimited service is by far the most common. With all types of connections, you should check if there is a one-time fee to set up your account, or if you have to sign a long-term service agreement. For broadband setups, other considerations include the cost of the necessary equipment (such as modem, satellite dish, transceiver, cable box, etc.), as well as installation fees. If special hardware is required, look into whether you can buy it more cheaply from someone other than your provider, or if your provider will throw it in with prepaid service for a certain period of time, such as six months or one year. To try out their service, many larger dial-up providers offer a free month or a set number of free hours of access; this may be a good way to test out a potential provider, as long as you already have the necessary hardware.

One final consideration for dial-up service is the price of calling up the ISP on a regular basis to get connected to the Internet. Virtually all providers have local phone numbers that subscribers can dial into so that they won't be billed for long-distance calls, but they aren't available in all areas. Before signing up with one, make sure that one of the numbers is in your local calling area, plus any other locations you will need to dial in from on a regular basis. For mobile wireless service, check into any type of roaming fees you may encounter.

Setting Up Your System

The specific steps that you must follow to connect to the Internet depend on the service provider you choose. Many will supply you with a startup CD; startup programs for several common dial-up ISPs are already installed on many new PCs. All you generally have to do is follow the directions on the CD or open the appropriate desktop icon to begin running the setup program. After the program begins, it will walk you through the sign-up process. Some sample screens of this process are shown in Figure 9-6. Instead of a setup program, smaller, local providers may just use a Web browser and phone dialing software instead, and will supply you with instructions on how to set them up properly.

further exploration

For links to further information about ISPs, go to www.course.com/parker2002/ch9

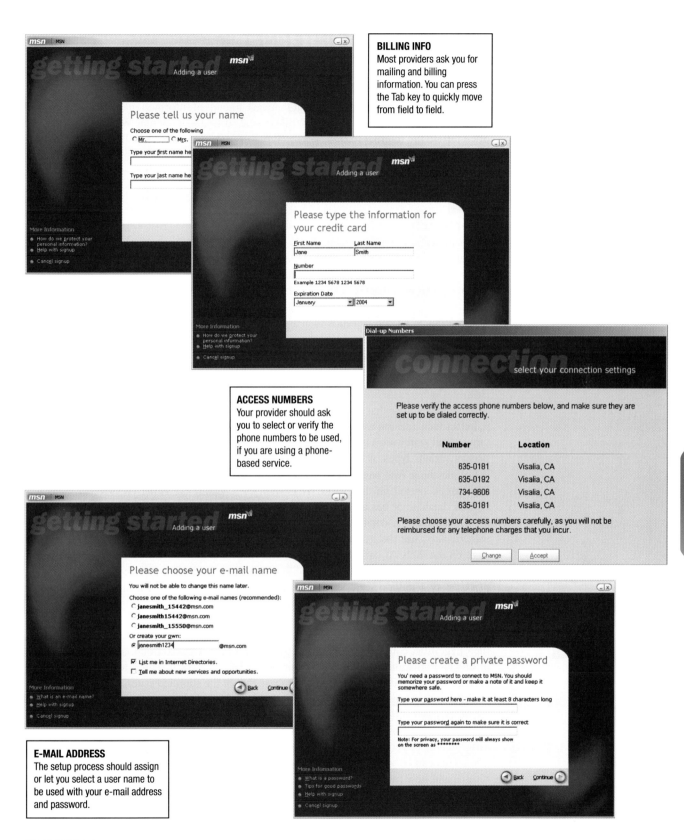

BILLING INFO
Most providers ask you for mailing and billing information. You can press the Tab key to quickly move from field to field.

ACCESS NUMBERS
Your provider should ask you to select or verify the phone numbers to be used, if you are using a phone-based service.

E-MAIL ADDRESS
The setup process should assign or let you select a user name to be used with your e-mail address and password.

FIGURE 9-6

Setting up Internet access. You can set up an account with many ISPs in just a few minutes by supplying information on a series of simple screens.

SEARCHING THE INTERNET

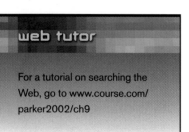

For a tutorial on searching the Web, go to www.course.com/parker2002/ch9

One of the most important skills an Internet user can acquire today is how to successfully search for and locate information on the Internet. The Internet is a huge storehouse of interesting and useful information, but that vast amount of information does you no good if you can't find it when you need it. While casual surfing is a popular Web pastime, people often turn to the Internet to find specific types of information as well. Basic searching was covered in Chapter 2, but to perform more successful Internet searches, you should also be familiar with the various types of search sites available, as well as some key searching strategies, as discussed next.

Search Sites

There are many different **search sites**—Web sites that enable users to search for and find information on the Internet—available. As discussed in Chapter 2, many of the most popular search sites, such as Yahoo!, AltaVista, Go.com, NorthernLight, HotBot, Google, Excite, and so on, can search using both *keywords* and a *directory*. Typically, these tools can be used interchangeably to find Web sites containing the information that you are seeking. With a few exceptions, search facilities such as these can be used free of charge. Since most search sites use some type of *search database* to locate appropriate Web pages as you search, it is important to understand a little about how such a database works.

Search Databases

While it may appear that a search site actually searches the Internet for you when you request it, in fact such a search would be entirely too time-consuming to perform in real time. Instead, virtually all search sites use a search database previously filled with millions of URLs classified by various types of keywords or categories and a **search engine** program to retrieve a list of matching Web pages from the database. Since there isn't a central database of all the Web pages located on the World Wide Web, each search site either creates and maintains its own database or has access to a search database created and maintained by another site. To maintain such a database, typically small, automated programs (often called *spiders* or *webcrawlers*) use the hyperlinks located on Web pages to continually jump from page to page on the Web. At each page the program records important data, such as the URL and descriptive information, into the database. These programs can be tremendously fast, visiting in excess of 1 million sites per day. Search databases also obtain information when people who create Web sites submit URLs and keywords to them through an option on the search site, as discussed more in Chapter 10.

Depending on the search site, pages can be classified based on such characteristics as their page title, content, supplied description from the organization that created the page, or any combination of these. When the search site receives a search request, it looks for and displays a list of the pages in its database that fit the supplied criteria.

The size of the search database varies with each particular search site. The Web is estimated to have over 4 billion Web pages. The search site with one of the largest databases—Google—claims to have indexed a billion or so of them to some extent. Search sites also differ in how close a match has to be before it is displayed as a matching Web page, called a *hit*. This can be good or bad, depending on the length of the list of matches the search returns and how much time you want to spend looking through the list of hits for something interesting enough to pursue further. To reduce the number of hits displayed, good search strategies (discussed shortly) can be used. Sites also differ regarding the order in which the hits are displayed. Some sites list the most popular sites (usually judged by the

>**Search site.** A Web site that allows users to search for Web pages that match supplied keywords or fit in particular categories.
>**Search engine.** A software program used by a search site to retrieve matching Web pages from a search database.

number of Web pages linked to it) first; others list Web pages belonging to organizations which pay a fee to receive a higher rank.

Searching with Keywords

When you know generally what you want but don't know at which URL to find it, one of your best options is to perform a *keyword search*. This type of search uses **keywords** (one or more key terms) that you supply to pull matching pages from its search database. (Performing a keyword search was explained in Chapter 2 and illustrated in Figure 2-20.) Once one or more keywords are typed in the appropriate location on the search site's Web page, the search engine will retrieve and display a list of matching Web pages.

Searching with Directories

Directories are usually a good choice if you want information about a particular category, but have less of an exact subject in mind. A directory also uses a database, but one that is usually screened by a human editor so it is much smaller, though often more accurate. For example, while a spider may classify a page about "computer chips" under the keyword "chips" together with information about potato chips, a human editor wouldn't. One of the largest directories—the Open Directory Project—claims to have indexed over 2 million Web pages using over 30,000 volunteer editors.

To use a directory located on a search site, categories are selected instead of typing keywords. After selecting a main category, a list of more specific subcategories for the selected main category is displayed. Eventually, after selecting one or more subcategories, a list of appropriate Web pages is displayed (refer again to Figure 2-20.)

Specialty Search Sites

A fairly new trend is the *specialty search site*. While some of the most popular search sites are general purpose, the database for a specialty search site contains Web pages only about a specific topic, such as flowers, movies, politics, music, astronomy, and so forth. Though the search database is smaller and the number of Web pages returned is much smaller, the results are usually much more relevant. To locate lists of specialty search sites, search any search site using the keywords "specialty search engines" or "specialty search sites."

Reference and Portal Sites

In addition to search sites, there are a number of *reference sites* on the Web, such as to generate maps, look up people or businesses, check the weather, etc. As mentioned earlier, *portal* sites include news and other popular information. They also typically contain links to reference sites, as well as other useful tools (stock quotes, free e-mail, shopping, etc.), in hopes of enticing visitors to return several times a day. The Yahoo! site shown in Figure 9-7 is one of the most popular portal sites; other search sites, and the home pages for large ISPs, news agencies, and television networks, are common portals, as well.

One additional type of feature common on many search and portal pages is a *shopping bot* feature. Shopping bots allow searching for specified products and return a summary of the prices, shipping, and delivery information found on a variety of sites, as explained in more detail in the Chapter 2 Trend box.

Metasearch Sites

Some search sites are *metasearch sites*—that is, they consult multiple databases, such as their own plus those of other search engines. Many metasearch engines, in fact, do not

---

>**Keywords.** Words typed on a search site to locate information on the Internet. >**Directory.** A collection of categories that is used to locate appropriate Web pages from a search database.

PORTAL PAGE
Links to maps and other reference tools, plus e-mail, a calendar, and other personalized content in addition to searching capabilities, has helped make Yahoo! a popular portal page.

SEARCH TOOLS
Both keywords and directory categories are available on this search site.

NATURAL LANGUAGE
This site allows search criteria to be phrased as a question instead of just keywords. Directory categories are also available for use.

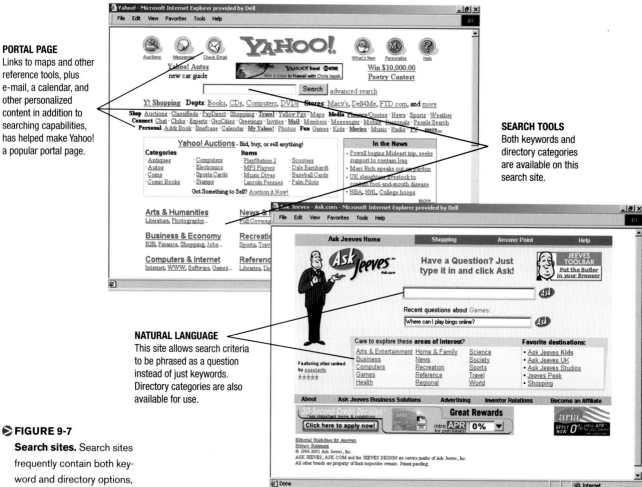

▶ FIGURE 9-7

Search sites. Search sites frequently contain both keyword and directory options, as well as reference tools and personalized content. They can also be a specialized or metasearch engine, as well as utilize a natural language interface.

even have their own search database. Instead, they act as a middleman, passing on the specified keywords to the various search sites they have access to, and then summarizing the results.

Natural Language Search Sites

A newer type of search site is the *natural language* search site, such as the Ask Jeeves site illustrated in Figure 9-7. Instead of typing keywords like for a keyword search on a conventional search site, natural language search sites allow you to type the search criteria in sentence form.

Hybrid Search Sites

Most major search sites employ a few of these various search options to make their sites more versatile and useful. For example, the Yahoo! site illustrated in Figure 9-7 uses both keywords and a directory, and contains a variety of reference tools. The Ask Jeeves site in this figure is a natural language search site that also includes directory categories. When there is more than one search option available, usually they can be used interchangeably, such as starting with the search engine and then selecting a directory category (as illustrated in Figure 2-20). Many sites automatically integrate their search options, such as displaying matching categories along with matching Web pages whenever keywords are used.

Search Strategies

There are a variety of strategies that can be employed to help whittle down the list of matching hits to a more manageable size (some broad searches can return thousands or even millions of Web pages). Some strategies can be employed regardless of the search site being used; others are available only on certain sites. Some of the more useful search strategies are discussed next.

Using Phrases

One of the most straightforward ways to improve the quality of the hits returned is to use *phrase searching* with a keyword search—essentially typing more than one keyword. Most search engines automatically return the hits that include all the keywords typed first, followed by the hits matching most of the keywords, continuing down to the hits that fit only one of the keywords typed. To force this type of sorting, virtually all search engines allow some type of character—such as quotation marks—to be used to indicate that you want to search for all the keywords. Sometimes quotation marks indicate that the keywords also need to appear in the same order as typed.

There are additional operators (such as the plus + and minus − symbols) that can be used in front of keywords to indicate that you want to find pages that include particular keywords, but not necessarily in the listed order, or pages that include some keywords, but not others. Because these options vary from site to site, it is best to look for a search tips link on the search site you are using; the search tips should explain the options available for that particular site.

Using Boolean Operators

To further specify exactly what you want a search engine to find, *boolean operators*—most commonly AND, OR, and NOT—can often be used in keyword searches. For example, if you want a search engine to find all documents that cover *both* the Intel and AMD microprocessor manufacturers, you can type *Intel AND AMD,* if the search engine supports boolean operators. If, instead, you want documents that discuss *either* (or both) of these companies, the boolean phrase *Intel OR AMD* can be used. On the other hand, if you want documents about microprocessors that are catalogued with no mention of Intel, *microprocessors NOT Intel* is what you would type in the search box. Just as with other operators, every search engine has its own way of letting you do a boolean search, so you should check out the preferred style before conducting a search. Some sites include an Advanced Search option using a fill-in form to walk you through using boolean operators; others allow the use of such symbols as plus (+) and minus (−).

Examples of using various phrase searching and boolean options are listed in Figure 9-8.

Using Multiple Search Sites

As illustrated in Figure 9-8, different search sites can return surprisingly different results. Though most users stick with one search site that they are comfortable using and are familiar with its allowable specific options, it's important to realize that other search sites may perform better under certain circumstances. If you are searching for something and aren't getting anywhere with one site, don't be afraid to try another. A variety of search sites you may want to try are listed in this module's Web Guide Window.

Using Appropriate Keywords, Synonyms, Variant Word Forms, and Wildcards

When choosing the keywords to be used with a search site, it is important to select words that represent the key concept you are searching for. Unless you are using a natural language site, leave off any extraneous words, such as "the," "a," "in," and so forth. For example, if you want to find out about bed and breakfasts located in the town of Leavenworth, Washington,

Search String Used	Search Site	Number of Pages Found	Title of First Two Pages Found (red entries indicate relevant Web pages)
dogs	AltaVista	2,223,900	Dogs in Canada Gone To The Dogs
	Google	3,170,000	I-Love-Dogs.com Guide Dogs for the Blind, Inc.
	Northern Light	4,247,080	411PETS - Dogs, dogs, Akitas, Rhodesian Ridgebacks... Linux Products - Yellow Dog Linux
hand signals	AltaVista	13,905	SimXtreme.com - Sim Gaming for Xtreme Gamers Maine Guides Online, Hunting, Fishing, Canoeing...
	Google	832,000	Soccer Hand Signals Cree Hand Signs
	Northern Light	703,740	Hand Signals Hand Signals
dog hand signals	AltaVista	2,345,664	The Deaf Dogs Web page Canine Agility of Central Minnesota Inc.
	Google	68,100	Cree Hand Signals Hunting Using Clicker for Training Dogs
	Northern Light	84,653	Dog Training: Sit/Stay Command Hand Signal How to Start Dog on Hand Signals
"dog hand signals"	AltaVista	12	Amazon.com: A Glance: 21 Days to a Trained Dog Training a Sick Dog
	Google	28	Training a Deaf Dog Training a Sick Dog
	Northern Light	31	Normal Aging and Expected Changes in Older (Senior, Geriatric) Dogs... Jump Heights
dog AND "hand signals"	AltaVista	2,544,363	The Deaf Dogs Web Page Canine Agility of Central Minnesota Inc.
	Google	4,740	Hunting Using Clicker for Training Dogs Cree Hand Signals
	Northern Light	3,914	Dog Training: Sit/Stay Command Hand Signal How to Start Dog on Hand Signals

> **FIGURE 9-8**

Examples of phrase searching and using boolean operations. Using a variety of phrase searching and boolean options can dramatically change the search results.

a keyword phrase such as *Leavenworth Washington bed and breakfast* should return appropriate results.

Another good strategy if your initial search didn't produce the results you were hoping for is to try the synonym approach. *Synonyms*—words that have similar meanings to others—can be typed as keywords in addition to, or instead of, the original keywords. For example, you could replace *bed and breakfast* with *hotel* or *lodging*. To use synonyms in addition to the original keywords, boolean operators can be used, such as the search phrase *"bed and breakfast" OR "hotel" OR "lodging" AND Leavenworth AND Washington.*

Variant—or alternate—word forms are another possibility. Try to think of a different spelling or form of your keywords, if your search still doesn't work as desired. For example, *bed and breakfast* could be replaced or supplemented with the variants *B&B* and *bed & breakfast,* and *hand signal* and *hand signaling* are variant word forms for the keywords *hand signals* used in Figure 9-8. Different capitalization or spelling is a form of this strategy, as well.

Another strategy that is sometimes used with keywords is the *wildcard* approach. A wildcard—usually represented by the asterisk symbol *—is used in conjunction with a part of a word that is required; any combination of letters are allowed in the wildcard location. For example, on many sites searching for *hand sign** would search for *hand signal, hand signals, hand signaling,* and any other keywords that fit this specific pattern.

Search String Used	Number of Pages Found	Title of First Two Pages Found	Page URL
title:"tax tips" (searches for Web pages containing "tax tips" in the page title)			
	1,838	Divorce Tax Tips Texas Trader status tax tips, online day trading, swing trading	www.raggiolaw.com/taxtips.htm www.traderstatus.com
url:taxtips (searches for Web pages containing "taxtips" in the page URL)			
	1,266	A Food Processor Conducting Business in Delaware Tip 26	www.state.de.us/revenue/obt/taxtips/ttfood_processor.htm www.tax-und-steuer.de/taxtips/1998/apr98.html
text:"tax tips" (searches for Web pages containing "tax tips" in the text of the page)			
	27,040	TipWorld: Free Daily Tips, Expert Advice, E-Mail News Retrieve Publications and Notices - IRS	www.tipworld.com www.irs.ustreas.gov/prod/forms_pubs/pubs.html
domain:gov (searches for Web pages located on government Web servers—domain ends in ".gov")			
	4,748,234	District of Alaska MISR Home	www.akd.uscourts.gov/akd/welcome.nsf www-misr.jpl.nasa.gov
title:"tax tips" domain:gov (searches for Web pages containing "tax tips" in the page title located on government Web servers—domain ends in ".gov")			
	2	News Release - April Tax Tips: Things You Should Know U.S. Senator Chuck Grassley - Word On - Tax Tips for Seniors	www.ftb.ca.gov/press/count.htm grassley.senate.gov/won/1999/wo902-15.htm

▶ FIGURE 9-9

Field searching. Using field searches can limit search engine results to just those pages with a specific title, page, or URL content, a specific top-level domain, or any combination of these. This figure illustrates various search results using the AltaVista search engine.

Using Field Searches

A more advanced search strategy that can be used when basic searching isn't producing the desired results is *field searching.*

A field search allows you to limit your search to a particular search characteristic (or *field*) such as the page title, URL, domain, and so forth. When a field search is performed, the specific text is searched for only in the specified field (see Figure 9-9). Many, but not all, search engines support some type of field searches. Check the search tips for the particular search site you are using to see if it has that option.

Evaluating Search Results

Once a list of potentially matching Web sites is returned as a result of a search, it is time to evaluate the sites to determine their quality and potential for meeting your needs. Two things to look for before clicking on a link for a matching page are:

▼ Does the title and listed description sound appropriate for the information that you seek?

▼ Is the URL from an appropriate company or organization? For example, if you want technical specifications about a particular product, you may want to start with information on the manufacturer's Web site. If you are looking for government publications, stick with government Web sites.

After an appropriate Web page is found, the evaluation process is still not complete. If you are using the information on the page for something other than idle curiosity, you will want to try to be reasonably sure the information can be trusted. Some general guidelines are listed in Figure 9-10.

Citing Internet Resources

According to the online version of the Merriam-Webster dictionary, the term *plagiarize* means "to steal and pass off the ideas or words of another as one's own" or to "use another's

FIGURE 9-10

Evaluating search results.
Before using information obtained from a Web page, use the following criteria to evaluate its accuracy and appropriateness.

Evalutate the source.	Information from the company or organization in question is generally more reliable than information found on an individual's Web site. Government and educational institutions are usually good sources for historical or research data. If you clicked on a link on a Web page to open the document in question, double-check the URL to make sure you still know what organization the page is from—it may be located on a completely different Web site than the page it was accessed from.
Evaluate the author.	Does the author have the appropriate qualifications for the information in question? Do they have a bias or is the information supposed to be objective?
Check the timeliness of the information.	Web page content may be updated regularly or posted once and forgotten. Always look for the publication date on online newspaper and magazine articles; check for a "last updated" date on pages containing other types of information you'd like to use.
Verify the information.	When you will be using Web-based information in a report, paper, Web page, or other document where accuracy is important, try to locate the same information from two different Web sources to verify the accuracy of the information.

production without crediting the source." To avoid plagiarizing Web page content, Web pages—as well as any other Internet resources—need to be credited appropriately.

The citation guidelines for Web page content are similar to that of written material. Citation guidelines for some Internet-based resources are listed next. Different style manuals may have different rules for citing Internet references—the following guidelines and examples in Figure 9-11 were obtained from the American Psychological Association Web site (http://www.apa.org). When in doubt, check with your instructor as to the style manual he or she prefers you follow and refer to that guide accordingly.

▼ *Web sites.* If you wish to cite an entire Web site (such as the APA citation above), instead of a specific document on the site, the site's URL can be listed next to the reference in the text.

▼ *Web pages.* To cite a specific Web page, list the information as you would for a print source, deleting the publication date and adding a "Retrieved by" date and the appropriate URL. If you are using the information verbatim, be sure to enclose it in quotation marks.

▼ *Web database article.* Citations should be similar to a CD-ROM or other database article, but include the date of retrieval and the database source, followed in parentheses by the name of the specific database used and any additional information needed to retrieve a particular item. This should be followed by the URL that can be used to enter the database.

▼ *E-mail correspondence.* E-mail messages are cited just as any other personal correspondence (such as a letter or memo) would be.

further exploration

For links to further information about electronic reference formats, go to www.course.com/parker2002/ch9

FIGURE 9-11

Citing Web sources. It is important to properly credit your Web sources. These examples are primarily from the American Psychological Association Web site (http://www.apa.org).

Type of Resource	Citation Example
Web site	The PBS Kids Web site has a variety of fun, educational, interactive activities for children of all ages (http://www.pbs.org/kids).
Web page	Electronic reference formats recommended by the American Psychological Association. (1999, November 19). Washington DC: American Psychological Association. Retrieved August 13, 2000 from the World Wide Web: http://www.apa.org/journals/webref.html
Web database article	Schneiderman, R. A. (1997). Librarians can make sense of the Net. San Antonio Business Journal, 11(31), pp. 58+. Retrieved January 27, 1999 from EBSCO database (Masterfile) on the World Wide Web: http://www.ebsco.com
E-mail	L. A. Chafez (personal communication, March 28, 2001).

BEYOND BROWSING AND E-MAIL

While many new Web users initially use the Web for access to specific Web sites and to exchange e-mail (as discussed in Chapter 2), as well as to look up information, there are a host of other activities that can take place using the Web. The next sections explore some of these activities.

Financial Transactions

Online financial transactions—a type of *e-commerce*, discussed in greater detail in Chapter 11—is a fast-growing Web activity. As more and more people have access to the Web from home and discover the convenience of shopping, banking, stock trading, and so forth on their home PCs, its popularity is likely to continue to grow. One of the major obstacles to online financial transactions is consumer concern for *online security*.

Online Security Considerations

When performing any type of financial transaction, it is very important to make certain that the Web page being used is *secure*, so that your private information (credit card number, bank account information, etc.) cannot be intercepted while it is being transmitted over the Internet. Most browsers display a locked padlock symbol such as 🔒 or 🔒 on the status bar to indicate a secure page. Be sure to never type any sensitive information (any information that you wouldn't want anyone else to see) on an insecure Web page. (A page containing a 🔓 icon in Netscape or a page containing no padlock icon in Internet Explorer indicates an insecure page). The URLs for most secure Web pages also begin with *https://* instead of *http://*. Some sites (such as the L.L. Bean site illustrated in Figure 9-12) do not switch to a secure server until the credit card information is requested.

Online Shopping

Online shopping is a fast-growing use of the Internet. You can buy products directly from large companies—like L.L. Bean, Dell Computer, Wal-Mart, Amazon.com, and Toys "R" Us—via their Web sites; a huge number of smaller retailers offer online shopping, as well. Many people also commonly buy items from **online auctions,** such as eBay. For a look at how an online auction works, see the How It Works box.

Typically, to buy items online you locate them on a Web site—often through a search feature or by browsing through an online catalog—and add the desired items to your online *shopping cart*. When you are finished shopping, you follow the checkout procedure to complete the sale, providing your billing and shipping information when requested (see Figure 9-12).

Today, you can buy items online using any of several different payment methods. The method you use depends on where you shop. While most online stores accept credit cards, other options may or may not be allowed. Some possible payment methods are listed next.

▼ *Credit card.* You can pay for online purchases with a credit card just as you can when buying goods or services over the phone. You simply select what you want to buy, type in your credit-card number, and the sale is either approved or rejected on the spot. On secure sites, your credit card data is encrypted (scrambled with a secret code) for safe passage over the Internet.

web tutor

For a tutorial on making purchases online, go to www.course.com/parker2002/ch9

>**Online shopping.** Buying products or services over the Internet. >**Online auction.** An online activity where bids are placed on items and the highest bidder wins.

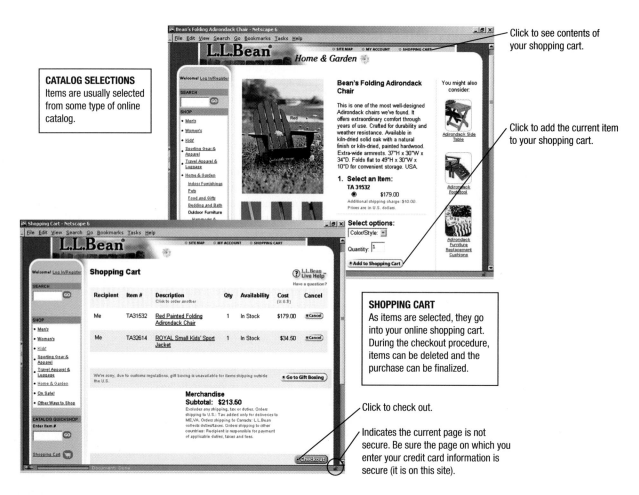

CATALOG SELECTIONS
Items are usually selected from some type of online catalog.

Click to see contents of your shopping cart.

Click to add the current item to your shopping cart.

SHOPPING CART
As items are selected, they go into your online shopping cart. During the checkout procedure, items can be deleted and the purchase can be finalized.

Click to check out.

Indicates the current page is not secure. Be sure the page on which you enter your credit card information is secure (it is on this site).

FIGURE 9-12

Online shopping. Online shopping can take place at large or small retail stores, as well as through online auctions. Be sure to only shop on secure Web sites.

▼ *Payment services.* This method is a twist on the credit-card payment system. For it to work, you need a valid checking account or national credit card (such as a VISA or MasterCard) and an e-mail address. You first need to set up an account with an online payment service, such as *PayPal, Billpoint,* etc., supplying it with the necessary account information and obtaining a user name and password. When you buy an item from a participating merchant or individual, you type your user name and password (on a secure Web page) to authorize the payment service to pay the merchant or individual a specific amount. The payment service then either charges your credit card or deducts the appropriate amount from your checking or payment service account; you usually receive confirmation of the transaction via e-mail. Many of these services can be used free of charge. A similar idea is the *digital wallet*—software that holds a user's payment information, a *digital certificate* to identify the user, and shipping information to speed transactions. The wallet usually resides on the user's PC. Digital wallets are built into the newest versions of the Netscape and Internet Explorer browsers, and are built into some ISPs' services, such as MSN and AOL. Digital certificates are discussed more in Chapter 11.

▼ *Smart card.* Smart card transactions are the opposite of credit card transactions. Instead of purchasing items on credit to be paid for at a later time, smart cards generally contain a prepaid amount of money that can be used like a debit card for retail purchases. Many individuals feel more secure using a smart card instead of a credit card over the Internet because of the limited amount of spending power available on it, as opposed to a credit

how it works

Online Auctions

Online auctions are big. Between eBay and Yahoo! Auctions, thousands of items are sold via this e-commerce model every day. An almost unfathomable variety of items are available—clothing, collectibles, sporting goods, toys, furniture, office equipment, and electronics. Even real estate and theater tickets can be auctioned off. Though many online auction sites are set up to sell goods and services between individuals, businesses can sell goods through a consumer site. There are also a huge number of specialty auction sites geared for business use.

A typical consumer auction is illustrated in the accompanying figure. After finding an item they would like to bid on, buyers place their bids and wait. Most auctions have a set minimum increment (such as 50 cents or $1) between bids. If desired, the seller can state a minimum opening bid.

As the auction progresses, the site is continually updated with new bids and bidders can rebid as often as necessary until the auction expires. At that time, the buyer with the highest bid wins the item. Most auction sites leave the payment and shipping details to the buyer and seller, though payment services and escrow services are available.

To support the auction services, the sellers usually have to pay a small fee to list their items, and then pay a percentage of the sale price as a commission to the auction site.

To attract bidders, auction sites employ a variety of techniques to make it easier than ever to bid on items. eBay, for example, allows a bidder to set a secret maximum bid and it will automatically bid for you, using the minimum increment, up to your maximum bid. You can also have a message sent to your pager or cell phone when another buyer places a higher bid.

For many auction buyers, it's not the low price they may—or may not—get, it's the excitement. For them, if their price beats all others, it's not like they just bought something—they won it.

card. Because of the proliferation of online shopping, some new keyboards and cell phones include a smart card reader (see Figure 9-13). Smart cards are discussed more in Chapter 11.

▼ *Conventional payment.* Many online merchants realize that consumers are wary of conducting business over the Internet. Consequently, they allow buyers to pay by conventional means. If this option is available on a site, there may be an option you can select on the final shopping cart page to have a person phone you about paying for the order by check or credit card. Or there may be a toll-free phone number for you to call to place your order instead of using the online form. While merchants usually welcome business of any sort, their costs rise when they have to hire staff to conduct business in this fashion. Because of this, some businesses charge a service fee for orders placed over the phone, or offer a discount for orders placed online without assistance. Like some mail-order businesses, it used to be common for online businesses to also charge a surcharge for orders charged to a credit card to offset the credit card fee; this practice is much less common today.

FIGURE 9-13

Smart cards. Smart cards are but one alternative for buying goods and services online.

Online Banking

A relatively new online financial application is **online banking.** Though it used to be available separately for a fee, now many conventional banks, such as Bank of America and Wells Fargo, offer free online banking services to supplement in-bank transactions. There are also Web-only banks, such as NetBank and Security First Network Bank. Because of their lower overhead, Web-only banks may offer higher interest rates.

As shown in Figure 9-14, online banking offers many options, like reviewing account activity, sending electronic payments, transferring funds between accounts, and viewing credit card balances.

Online Stock Trading

Getting online stock quotes is a common extra on many portal pages. Actually buying and selling stocks online, however, requires an online broker. Trading stocks in this manner is called **online stock trading**—a rapidly growing Internet application.

In addition to individual stock quotes, many portal and stock trading sites allow you to set up an *online portfolio.* An online portfolio allows you to specify the stocks you want to see quoted on a regular basis. That collection of stocks is displayed whenever the Web page containing your portfolio is accessed. Most stock quotes obtained through portal pages are delayed 20 minutes; real-time quotes are available on many brokerage Web sites.

Online brokers charge a fee for each transaction, but at roughly $10 to $15 per trade, online trading is generally much less expensive than comparable offline services. The brokerage firms that offer stock trades this inexpensively are sometimes referred to as *deep discount brokers; discount brokers* and *full-service brokers* usually charge higher fees, but provide a higher level of service or financial advice.

Once an online brokerage account is set up, you can order stock sales and purchases just as you would with an offline broker. Usually the history of your orders can be viewed online and open orders can be cancelled before they are executed, if desired (see the top image in Figure 9-15). Most brokerage and financial sites also have convenient access to a variety of performance history, corporate news, and other useful information for investors.

>**Online banking.** Performing banking activities over the Internet. >**Online stock trading.** Buying and selling stock over the Internet.

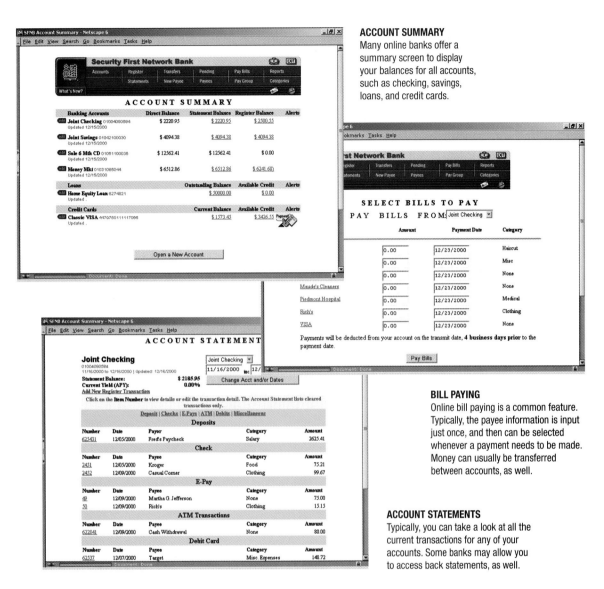

ACCOUNT SUMMARY
Many online banks offer a summary screen to display your balances for all accounts, such as checking, savings, loans, and credit cards.

BILL PAYING
Online bill paying is a common feature. Typically, the payee information is input just once, and then can be selected whenever a payment needs to be made. Money can usually be transferred between accounts, as well.

ACCOUNT STATEMENTS
Typically, you can take a look at all the current transactions for any of your accounts. Some banks may allow you to access back statements, as well.

> **FIGURE 9-14**
> **Online banking.** Online banking typically allows you to check your balances, authorize online payments, view your transaction history, and perform other useful activities.

Most portfolio and stock quote pages are static once the stock prices have been retrieved from the server. If so, it is important to realize that you need to reload the page to update the quotes. In contrast, the portfolio shown in the bottom part of Figure 9-15 is completely dynamic, using a *Java applet* (a type of Web-page animation discussed in more detail in Chapter 10) to continually refresh the screen for you.

The chapter Trend box contains some tips to help avoid falling victim to an online con artist, when performing financial transactions over the Internet.

Entertainment

Using the Web for entertainment purposes isn't a new idea, but some of the available options certainly are. Viewing online movies or TV, or playing games live against other Internet gamers were hard to imagine a few years ago when Web information crawled over the phone line at 14.4 or 28.8 Kbps. Some of the following applications can be accessed with virtually any type of connection; others require a broadband connection to make them worthwhile.

trend

Dot Cons

What Every Internet User Should Know About Online Fraud.

Unfortunately, Internet fraud is alive and well. The FTC received over 21,000 complaints of Internet-related crime in 2000 and the number is increasing every year. Using only secure Web pages can help avoid your credit card and other sensitive information from falling into a criminal's hand, but it doesn't protect you completely. More times than we'd like to remember, credit card lists have been stolen from online retailers—at least one of these hackers posted the numbers on the Web to show off his feat. *Identity theft, online auction scams,* and *investment hoaxes* are other possible swindles Internet users may encounter. A brief explanation of each of these types of illegal activity follows next.

▼ *Identity theft* involves someone obtaining enough personal information about you so that they can masquerade as you for online purchases and other activities. Though not widely performed today, identity theft will become more tempting as we continue to store increasingly valuable information online. The most important information a consumer should protect is his or her personal data (such as mother's maiden name, social security number, etc.), as well as financial data (credit card account numbers, bank account numbers and PIN numbers, brokerage account numbers and passwords, etc.). Online shoppers concerned about the security of their credit card data should consider using an online payment service, or low-limit credit card reserved just for online activities. Smart cards will likely give us secure alternatives in the near future.

▼ *Online auction scams*—where you pay for merchandise but it is never delivered—are the most prevalent type of online fraud today. Though auction sites reserve the right to ban sellers with complaints lodged against them, it is very easy for unscrupulous individuals to come back using a new e-mail address and identity. There have been some successful prosecutions of large-scale auction con artists, but they are frequently difficult to identify and locate. To protect yourself when bidding at an online auction, be wary of sellers with no or negative feedback, and consider using an *escrow service* for high-price items. On a similar note, be cautious when purchasing merchandise from a company you haven't heard of. Just because it has a professional-looking Web site doesn't automatically mean it is a legitimate business. Be skeptical if the site offers incredibly low prices or claims to have impossible-to-find items in stock. And always use a credit card or other payment method that gives you some type of recourse if the merchandise doesn't arrive.

▼ *Investment scams* include stock manipulation, where con artists use the Web to fraudulently promote their stocks to inflate prices, and then sell their shares for a big profit. Sometimes referred to as *pump-and-dump,* this technique often involves posting tips on investment message boards, sometimes under a variety of identities. To protect yourself, be wary of anyone on an investment message board who claims to have inside information—sharing that information even if it were valid would be illegal. Instead, do your own research before investing in any company.

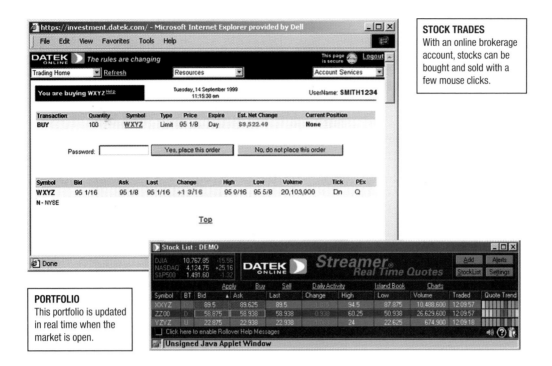

STOCK TRADES
With an online brokerage account, stocks can be bought and sold with a few mouse clicks.

PORTFOLIO
This portfolio is updated in real time when the market is open.

> **FIGURE 9-15**
> **Online stock trading.**
> Online stock transactions include buying and selling stocks. Brokerage sites can offer either delayed or real-time quotes.

Online TV and Movies

Online multimedia is still in the early stages, so what we have access to online today is likely just a drop in the bucket of what will be available a few years from now. The most common type of online TV and movie activity at the present time is viewing news clips, movie trailers, music videos, taped interviews, and similar short, prerecorded, videos. These clips can be found on specialty sites dedicated to providing multimedia Web content (as on the Film.com page shown in Figure 9-16); links to video clips are also widely found on news and entertainment sites.

Though some video files are played after they have been completely downloaded, because of the size of the files (and their corresponding long download times), it is becoming very common for multimedia files to use a *streaming* approach, where a small piece of the file is downloaded and *buffered* (temporarily stored on your hard drive), then the music or video begins playing while the remainder of the file downloads simultaneously. Video clips typically play using RealPlayer (see Figure 9-16), QuickTime, or Windows Media Player. Depending on the speed of your Internet connection and PC, some video files may be choppy, if the playing needs to stop for a moment to wait for more of the file to be downloaded and buffered.

In addition to the types of video mentioned so far, some sites host short original films that can be played, usually for free. There are also Web sites that offer old TV shows (such as *I Love Lucy*) that can be viewed on demand, as well as live TV broadcast over the Internet, though these applications are fairly limited at the current time. Television or movies delivered through your Internet connection are referred to as *Internet TV,* which is still in the infancy stages. However, it is expected to eventually become a very common Internet application, once broadband Internet connections become more widespread. Possibilities include receiving live broadcasts, movies on demand (paying for video downloads instead of physically renting videos at a video store), and *interactive TV.* This latter application—television synchronized with online activities—has been available on a very limited basis for several years. One example is shown in Figure 9-16.

NET

VIDEOS
Movie trailers, music videos, taped interviews, short movies, and more can be viewed online. Most videos are played using RealPlayer or Windows Media Player.

Click to see video clip.

INTERACTIVE TV
Interactive TV ties together the Web and broadcast television viewing.

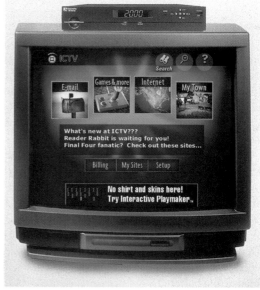

LIVE TV
Though available on a very limited basis, some live TV broadcasts are available over the Internet.

FIGURE 9-16

Online television and movies. Online TV and movie possibilities include viewing videos, previews, or short films, as well as taped TV shows, live TV broadcasts, and interactive TV.

INTERNET RADIO
Online radio station broadcasts, whether Internet or conventional station broadcasts, can be listened to live.

Click to select this station and start listening to the broadcast.

ON DEMAND MUSIC AND MUSIC DOWNLOADS
Many songs can be listened to for free or downloaded either for free or for a fee, depending on the site and the site's arrangement with the artist. Downloaded files can be listened to with a player program, such as MusicMatch, RealAudio, or Windows Media Player.

Click to download the file. Once the file is downloaded to your PC, it can be played with an appropriate player.

Click to just listen to the song or a sample of the song instead.

FIGURE 9-17

Online music. Music available online typically involves Internet radio broadcasts, music that can be listened to on demand, and music files that can be downloaded to your PC.

Online Music

Listening to and downloading **online music** are two of the hottest Web-based entertainment activities today. There are scores and scores of sites where music can be heard. For example, conventional radio programs are frequently broadcast over the Internet; there are also Internet radio sites that broadcast only over the Internet, like the NetRadio site shown in Figure 9-17. Many sites offer music that can be heard on demand or downloaded to your PC (see the bottom image in Figure 9-17). Once downloaded, the music can be played on your PC or transferred to a portable device, such as an *MP3 player*.

>**Online music.** Music played or obtained available over the Internet.

MP3 players play *MP3 files*—audio files that use MP3 file compression. MP3 compression takes high quality, large digital audio files (requiring about 10 MB per minute) and compresses them to about a twelfth of their size (less than 1 MB per minute). For example, a 30 MB three-minute song might compress to about 2.5 MB. When the files are played—either on a computer using appropriate software (as in Figure 9-17) or on an MP3 player (see Figure 9-18)—the song data is automatically decompressed with virtually no detectable loss in quality. MP3 capabilities are also beginning to be built into many regular CD and DVD players, so MP3 files—and custom CDs consisting of MP3 files burned on a CD-R disc (as explained in the How It Works box in Chapter 7)—can be played over home or car stereo systems.

To follow copyright laws, music downloaded from the Web should be either designated as a free download from the artist or recording company, or purchased from an appropriate download site. Some sites offer unlimited music downloads for a monthly fee; others allow you to purchase songs individually. The uproar from the recording industry about free unauthorized MP3 downloads from such sites as Napster and MP3.com and the resulting lawsuits has greatly affected the way music is available online, as discussed in the Inside the Industry box.

Online Gaming

Online gaming refers to playing games over the Internet. Many sites—especially children's Web sites—include games for visitors to play while visiting the site. There are also sites whose sole purpose is hosting games that can be played online. Some of the games can be played alone; others, such as Hearts, Backgammon, Quake, and so forth, can be played online against other gamers. The Backgammon games featured in Figure 9-19 can be played free of charge without special software; other games (such as Quake) require you to have the

> **FIGURE 9-18**
>
> **MP3 players.** Once online music is downloaded, it can be transferred to an MP3 player (such as this Diamond Rio player) for music on the go.

> **FIGURE 9-19**
>
> **Online gaming.** Many online games are multiplayer games that are played against other gamers that are online at the moment.

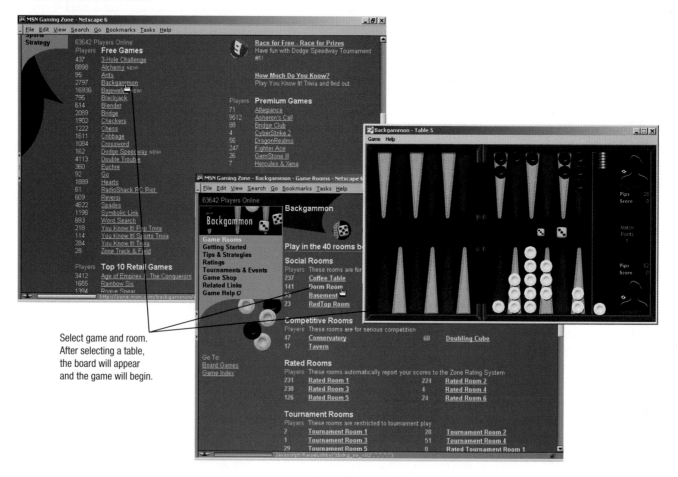

Select game and room. After selecting a table, the board will appear and the game will begin.

inside the industry

Napster

The Catalyst for Peer-to-Peer Computing?

Chances are you've heard of Napster, a music sharing service. It's been in the news the last several years because of its lawsuits with the recording industry. Just in case you're not familiar with it, Napster is a file-swapping service for music. Its Web site doesn't host any music files; instead, users log on to the service and are put in touch (automatically, via the Napster software) with other online users who have the song (usually as an MP3 file) that the user is looking for. After being presented with a list of users, their connection speeds, and their reliability ratings, the user looking for the music file can select a host user and begin downloading the file from that individual's computer.

Because, theoretically, one user could rip a song from his or her CD (as explained in the Chapter 7 How It Works box) and share it with an unlimited number of users via a music sharing service such as Napster, it's not surprising that the recording industry was not overjoyed by Napster's immense popularity. In fact Napster, as well as MP3.com and other sites involved with digital music, have been the subject of a blizzard of lawsuits. Most of these suits have since been settled. For example, MP3.com ended its legal dispute with Universal Music Group by paying over $53 million for a licensing agreement to use that record company's music. It is expected that Napster and other sources for online digital music will remain in business, but as a subscription service, where users pay a monthly or per-song fee to download music.

It should be noted, however, that not all recording artists are against Napster. Up and coming performers tend to like all the exposure they can get. Others like the idea of an international music community.

Despite, or perhaps because of, the Napster controversy, sharing files and communicating directly between Internet users—called *peer-to-peer computing* or *peer-to-peer networking*—is a hot topic. It differs from most Web activity in that there isn't a set server that always hosts the information for client computers to access. With peer-to-peer computing, any PC on the network could be a host or client, depending on whether they are seeking information or whether they have possession of information that someone else is seeking. It also includes straight peer-to-peer activities, such as sending e-mail and instant messages.

In original computer networks, all connected computers acted like equals, so the peer-to-peer idea has been around for a long while. With the introduction of the Internet, however, powerful servers were used to provide and process information rapidly, and desktop PCs assumed a client role. It wasn't until Napster that the idea resurfaced on a large scale and its potential examined in today's context. Many predict a new Internet revolution focusing on decentralized, peer-to-peer exchanges. And we'll owe it all to Napster.

appropriate program installed on your PC. Some gaming sites may offer additional premium games that are only available to paid subscribers.

E-Books

E-books or *online books* are plentiful online. From the entire works of Shakespeare to the newest Steven King novella, thousands of books can be read online or downloaded. There are online libraries that host online books (many in HTML format so they can be displayed on a Web page), and online bookstores where e-books can be purchased and downloaded (which usually requires special software). Depending on their format, e-books can be viewed on a desktop PC, a handheld PC, or a special device for storing and reading e-books, such as the RCA e-Book shown in Figure 9-20.

>**E-book.** A book in electronic format.

⬡ **FIGURE 9-20**

E-books. Electronic (online) books can either be read online or downloaded to your computer or special e-book reader (like the one shown here) to be read offline at your leisure.

further exploration

For links to further information about Web-based news, go to www.course.com/parker2002/ch9

News and Research

There is a plethora of news and research information available through the Internet. The following sections discuss a few of these opportunities.

News

Just about every large newspaper has an online site containing—at least—headline articles. Many newspapers have searchable archives to look for past articles, though often articles older than about a week require a fee to view. Network and cable news organizations also have Web sites that are updated several times a day (see Figure 9-21); as previously mentioned, many of these sites feature multimedia clips, in addition to written news. News *webcasts* can also be added to the desktop to display continually updated news headlines, as long as you have an active Internet connection.

Webcasting involves using the Internet to broadcast information. Unlike Web surfing, which relies on a *pull* method of transferring Web pages to the user's screen at the time the user requests it, Webcasting uses *push* technologies to deliver Web content to the user automatically on a regular basic. Once a webcast is selected, it will continually broadcast new information to your PC. Common types of webcasts include news tickers, stock tickers, and weather maps.

In addition to printed news, some news radio programs are broadcast over the Internet, similar to the music radio station illustrated in Figure 9-17. In addition, most portal pages contain up-to-the-minute headlines with links to the latest news articles, and commonly allow you to customize the page to display the news of your choice, such as sports, technology, weather, and national news, or local news.

Government Information

Government information is widely available on the Internet. Most state and federal agencies have Web sites to provide information to citizens, such as government publications, archived documents, forms, and so forth. You can also perform such tasks as downloading tax forms and filing your tax returns online. Soon you may be able to register your car, register to vote, and update your driver's license online, as well. Even voting over the Internet is coming. In the March 2000 primary, for example, Arizona's Democratic Party held the first binding U.S. election in which voters could cast their ballots online. The response was startling—nearly half of the ballots cast in that election were cast online.

Product and Corporate Information

Two types of sites related to online shopping and online investing are corporate and product information. Before buying an item online (or in a conventional *brick-and-mortar store,* for that matter), many people research product options online. By going to manufacturers' Web sites, as in Figure 9-21, specifications can be viewed or downloaded; you can sometimes also obtain special offers, rebate forms, and instruction manuals online.

Investors frequently wish to research companies before making an investment decision. As mentioned in an earlier section, many brokerage sites contain links to corporate information. There are also separate sites that specialize in providing this type of information, such as the Hoover's Web site shown in Figure 9-21. Depending on the site, some or all of the information may be available free of charge. For example, the Hoover's site allows you to view company summaries (called *capsules*) free of charge, but requires a fee for more in-depth information.

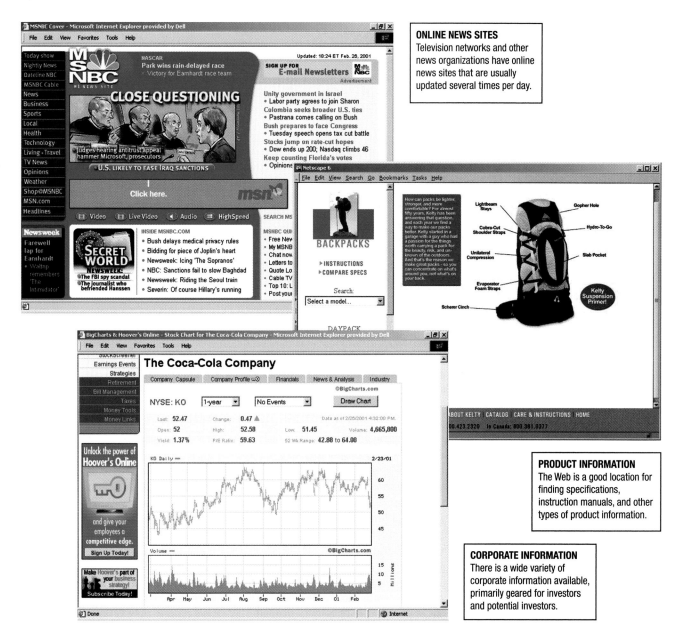

FIGURE 9-21

News, product, and corporate information. It is very common to find Web sites for newspapers and news agencies; product and corporate information is plentiful, as well.

Peer-to-Peer File Sharing

One of the earliest widespread application of *peer-to-peer file sharing*—sharing resources directly between users via the Internet—was Napster, the music-sharing service discussed in the Inside the Industry box. Unlike MP3.com and other music sites, when a music file was downloaded using Napster, it wasn't downloaded from the Napster server—it was downloaded from another Napster user.

Though Napster file sharing was not operational at the time of this writing and may not be in existence at the time you read this, the idea of peer-to-peer file sharing remains. One example is the *Scour* service, acquired by CenterSpan Communications after Scour shut down its exchange because of pending copyright infringement litigation. CenterSpan plans to use Scour to deliver a peer-to-peer digital distribution channel that enables members to publish, search for, and purchase digital content (such as music and video files, images, e-books, and so forth) in a secure and legal environment.

Many industry insiders believe peer-to-peer computing will have tremendous growth in the next few years. Companies such as CenterSpan, Intel, and Hewlett-Packard among others have joined the *Peer-to-Peer Working Group,* a consortium to create universal standards for peer-to-peer technologies.

CENSORSHIP AND PRIVACY

There are many important social issues related to the Internet. Two of the most important—censorship and privacy—are discussed next, in the context of Internet use. These and other social issues and how they relate to computer use in general are discussed in further detail in Chapter 15.

Censorship

The First Amendment to the U.S. Constitution guarantees a citizen's right to free speech. This protection allows people to say or show things to others without fear of arrest. People must observe some limits to free speech, of course, such as prohibitions of obscenity over the public airwaves and child pornography.

But how should the law react to alleged patently offensive or indecent materials on the Internet, where they can be observed by children and the public at large? A few years ago, the courts struck down the *Communications Decency Act,* which proposed making such actions illegal. The courts have so far had difficulty defining just what is "patently offensive" and "indecent." What's more, they have concluded that numerous self-policing mechanisms now available at the *client* level reduce the need for new laws that restrict content made available at the *server* level. For instance, a large selection of *blocking software* on the market allows users to block from view materials on the Internet that are objectionable to them or to family members. Organizations may also use this type of software on company PCs to prevent employees from accessing Web sites they deemed unacceptable.

Blocking-software packages work in a variety of ways. Some ISPs automatically censor portions of the Internet. Some provide tools that allow each user to turn blocking on or off for his or her individual PC. Users can also acquire blocking software on their own. The software may suggest a list of subjects or keywords that will automatically prevent access to a site; typically, you can modify this list. For instance, parents could block their home PC from displaying information on sex, drugs, bomb making, or hate literature.

Another option is to use your browser's built-in blocking feature. Many of the latest browsers allow users to block access in one way or another (see Figure 9-22). Momentum is also building within the Internet community to create a universal rating system—similar to the existing voluntary TV rating system—to help parents and other users who wish to use Internet filtering. For instance, a site might voluntarily rate its content on a scale of 1 to 9 on each of several dimensions—such as profanity, nudity, intolerance, and violence. Participating browsers would let users establish the maximum number on each dimension that they would tolerate and would place these controls in password-protected files. (Non-complying Web sites could be automatically assigned ratings of 9 on all dimensions.) When anyone was accessing the Internet from that PC, the software would read a site's rating before displaying it and block access if the rating exceeded the allowable rating.

Despite the controversial nature of and difficulty in implementing Internet content censoring, one area that has held up over the last few years is the distribution of *cyberporn* (pornographic material distributed over the Internet) involving children. There are various sting operations set up by the FBI and other law-enforcement offices to locate and arrest those involved with this type of material, as well as those who use the Internet to stalk children.

Privacy

Privacy, as it relates to the Internet, deals with what information about individuals is available, how it is used, and by whom. As more and more transactions and daily activities are being performed online, there is the potential for a huge amount of private information to be collected and distributed without the individual's knowledge or permission, if appropriate precautions are not taken. Thus, it is understandable that more public concern than ever exists regarding privacy and the Internet.

Though privacy will be discussed in more detail in Chapter 15, a few issues that are of special concern to Internet users are mentioned next.

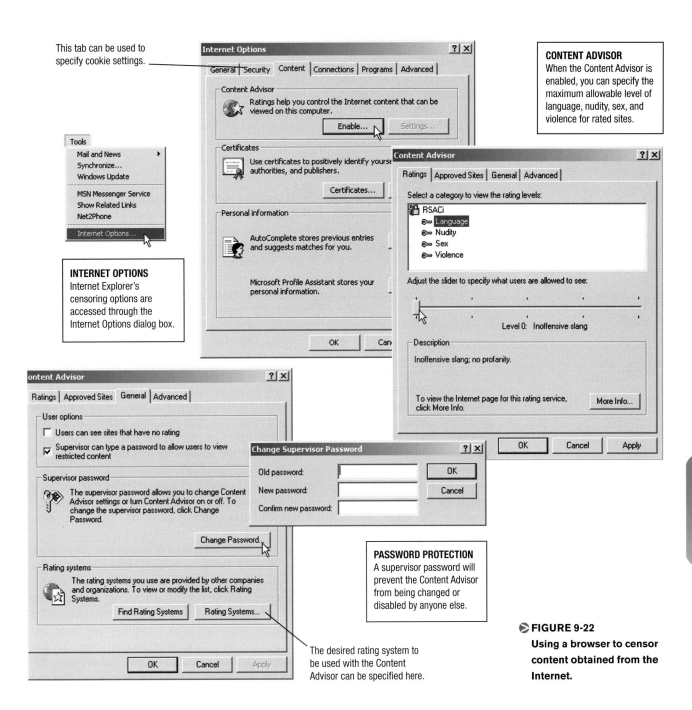

This tab can be used to specify cookie settings.

CONTENT ADVISOR
When the Content Advisor is enabled, you can specify the maximum allowable level of language, nudity, sex, and violence for rated sites.

INTERNET OPTIONS
Internet Explorer's censoring options are accessed through the Internet Options dialog box.

PASSWORD PROTECTION
A supervisor password will prevent the Content Advisor from being changed or disabled by anyone else.

The desired rating system to be used with the Content Advisor can be specified here.

FIGURE 9-22
Using a browser to censor content obtained from the Internet.

E-Mail Privacy

Many people mistakenly believe that e-mail is a private communications method. Since it is transmitted over public media, however, unless it is encrypted it *could* (though likely wouldn't) be intercepted and read by a party other than the intended recipient. There are e-mail encryption programs available for people who send sensitive or confidential e-mail messages; most of us, however, are more concerned with the privacy of our Web activity and transactions than securing the contents of our e-mail.

It is important to realize, however, that your e-mail provider (such as your company or your ISP) has access to your e-mail and can keep copies of it. There have been cases where e-mail sent by such crime suspects as computer hackers and stalkers has been used to prosecute the suspect. In addition, it has been ruled on in the courts that business e-mail is a company resource and businesses have the right to monitor it to ensure that company policies are being adhered to. Another interesting development in the world of Internet and crime-fighting is the FBI's *Carnivore* system—a wiretapping system for e-mail that enables the agency to intercept suspects' e-mails at the ISP level, as explained in the Chapter 15 Trend box. Though currently under attack, the result of this controversy will help form the future direction of e-mail privacy. In the meantime, it is wise to treat e-mail correspondence as closer to a postcard than a letter. If extreme privacy is required, *encryption software,* such as *Pretty Good Privacy (PGP),* can be used to encrypt files sent over the Internet; encrypted e-mail can be sent using such programs as *HushMail.* Encryption is discussed more in Chapter 15.

Web Activity Privacy

Another area of concern to many who browse the Web on a regular basis is the privacy of where they go and what they do at Web sites. Does anyone keep track of which sites you visit, how long you stay there, and what you download and buy? The answer is yes, but it may not be as much of a security concern as a nuisance.

When you first visit many Web sites, a **cookie**—a small electronic file—is stored on your hard drive. This cookie is used by the Web site to keep track of any information that your browser will need on a future visit, such as customized settings for a Web page displaying your weather and local TV listings on your portal page, for example. They can also be used to temporarily store the contents of your shopping cart, in case you don't finish shopping before closing the browser, as well as to remember your user name and password on a protected site so you don't have to type in that information every time.

Though there has been some concern about cookies being used to track your Internet activity, currently most cookies are used just for personalizing your Web browsing. An increasing trend, however, is using cookies for advertising purposes. Some advertising companies use cookies to track which ads you click to supply you with additional ads that fit your interests. There has been some demand for Congress or the FTC to legislate how this type of information can be used. Currently the advertising industry is pushing for voluntary adherence to usage standards, in lieu of legislation. The most recent set of standards—the *Network Advertising Initiative* or *NAI*—specifies such guidelines as notifying users if the data they are supplying will be "personally identifiable" data, obtaining permission before linking personalized data with data collected anonymously, and so forth. Collecting such data is known as *online profiling.*

To protect yourself against online profiling, there are several strategies you can employ, including browsing anonymously and not allowing cookies to be used. "Cloaking" software allows you to browse anonymously through a special Web server that hides your identity. Usually even that server doesn't know each user's identity. A less extreme option is to set up one browser program on your PC without any e-mail settings or other personal information to use for day-to-day browsing. This prevents Web sites from recording your name and e-mail address as you pass through the site. (A second browser program on the same PC can be set up for e-mail.) To control cookie use, every browser has an option to allow you to approve each cookie stored, or, alternatively, to deny access to all cookies entirely. You can also delete the cookies from your PC manually, when desired (see Figure 9-23).

Keep in mind, however, that despite what you do to prevent it, if you shop or do any other type of transaction online that requires your real identity, your information will eventually find its way into somebody's marketing database. And since many people find themselves frequently giving away their name and e-mail address in exchange for access to information on a site, free coupons and sample items, free newsletters, sweepstakes, etc., it is not surprising that the use of **spam**—junk, bulk e-mail—has dramatically increased.

>**Cookie.** A small file stored on your hard drive at the request of a Web server; used to preserve customized settings and keep track of a user's preferences.
>**Spam.** Unsolicited, bulk e-mail sent over the Internet.

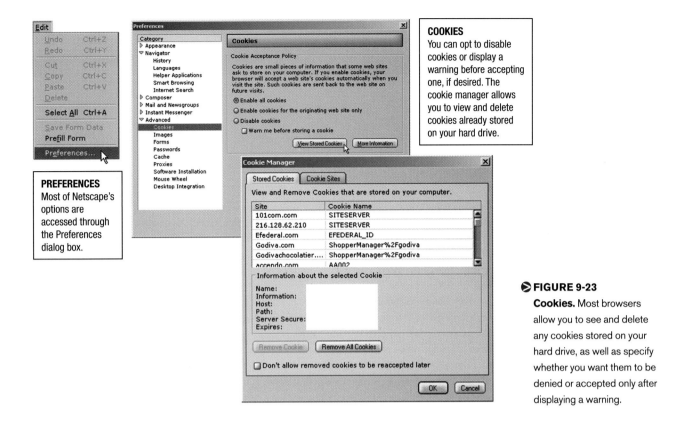

COOKIES
You can opt to disable cookies or display a warning before accepting one, if desired. The cookie manager allows you to view and delete cookies already stored on your hard drive.

PREFERENCES
Most of Netscape's options are accessed through the Preferences dialog box.

FIGURE 9-23

Cookies. Most browsers allow you to see and delete any cookies stored on your hard drive, as well as specify whether you want them to be denied or accepted only after displaying a warning.

THE FUTURE OF THE INTERNET

The Internet has changed a great deal since its inception in 1964. From only four supercomputers, it has evolved into a vast network connecting virtually every type of computer. The use of the Internet has changed dramatically, as well. As the structure of the Internet evolves and improves, it can support new types of activities. New desired types of applications also sometimes drive the technological improvements necessary to support them.

The exact composition of the Internet of the future is anyone's guess. It will likely be a very high-speed optical network with virtually unlimited bandwidth. It will be accessed by the PC of the day, which will probably be much smaller and less obtrusive than the standard PC today—possibly built directly into desks, refrigerators, and other objects, or carried around on your body or as some type of very portable device like a 3G cell phone. The primary interface will likely be the voice and most network connections will be wireless.

Chances are, the Internet will be used for a huge amount of day-to-day activities, such as shopping, phone calls, controlling home appliances, ordering and downloading TV shows or movies, and so forth. It will continue to be widely used for business purposes, and high bandwidth will allow a much higher level of real-time video communications facilitating even more use of telecommuting and home-based offices. A universal payment system for *micropayments*—small charges without prohibitive transactions fees—could pave the way for paying small fees for Web content, such as downloading music files or movies or placing telephone calls through the Internet. Ideally, all of an individual's micropayments would be combined into a single monthly bill.

This is an exciting time for the Internet. It is already firmly entrenched in our society, and it will be exciting to see how all the breathtaking new applications and technological improvements on the horizon pan out, and what the Internet evolves into next.

Internet has become a household word. In many ways, the Internet has redefined how people think about computers and communications.

EVOLUTION OF THE INTERNET

Chapter Objective 1:
Discuss how the Internet has evolved into what it is today.

The **Internet**—a worldwide phenomenon that consists of thousands of linked networks that are accessed by millions of people daily—dates back to the late 1960s. At its start and throughout many years of its history, the Internet was called **ARPANET.** It was not until the development of graphical user interfaces and the **World Wide Web** that public interest in the Internet began to soar. The next improvement of the Internet infrastructure may be as a result of projects such as *Internet2* and *Next Generation Internet (NGI).*

Chapter Objective 2:
Identify the various types of individuals, companies, and organizations involved in the Internet community and explain their purposes.

The Internet community is made up of individual *users,* companies such as **Internet service providers (ISPs), Internet content providers, application service providers (ASPs),** *infrastructure companies,* a variety of software and hardware companies, the government, and other organizations. Virtually anyone with a computer with communications capability can be part of the Internet, either as a user or supplier of information or services.

Because the Internet is so unique in the history of the world—and it remains a relatively new phenomenon—several widespread myths about it have surfaced. Three such myths are that the Internet is free, that it is controlled by some central force, and that it is equivalent to the World Wide Web.

INTERNET CONNECTIVITY ISSUES

Chapter Objective 3:
Describe the device, connection, and provider options for connecting to the Internet, as well as some considerations to keep in mind when selecting an ISP.

When connecting to the Internet, three decisions must be made. The type of device (PC, *Internet appliance,* or mobile device) must be selected, and you need to decide whether to use a **dial-up connection** (standard dial-up or ISDN), a **direct connection** (through a school or company LAN, or though a DSL, cable, satellite, or radio connection), or a *wireless connection.* You also need to decide on the type of Internet service provider to use *(basic ISP* or *commercial online service).* Next, the specific ISP can be selected and your system can be set up for Internet access.

SEARCHING THE INTERNET

Chapter Objective 4:
Understand how to effectively search for information on the Internet, including search options, strategies, and how to properly cite Internet resources.

Search sites—Web sites that enable users to search for and find information on the Internet—typically locate pages using **keywords** or **directories.** Both types of searches use a *search database* that contains information about pages on the Web and a **search engine** to retrieve the list of matching Web pages from the database. Databases that search sites use are generally maintained by automated *spider* programs; directory databases are typically maintained by human editors.

Keyword searches—where you type keywords in a search box and a list of matching Web pages are displayed—are useful when you know generally what you want, but you don't know at which URL to find it. Directory searches—where you select categories until a list of matching Web pages is displayed—can be used when you want information about a general topic, but you have less of a precise subject in mind. *Specialty search engines* and *metasearch engines* limit Web pages to specific topics and use multiple search engines, respectively. Some search sites are *natural language* sites; many use a combination of search options. Search sites commonly contain handy reference tools, as well; most are full-fledged *portal* pages.

There are a variety of search strategies that can be used, including typing phrases instead of single keywords; using *boolean operators;* trying the search at multiple search sites; and using *synonyms, variant word forms, wildcards,* and *field searches.* Once a list of matching pages is displayed, the hits need to be evaluated for their relevancy; if the information found on a Web page is used in a paper, report, or other original document, the source should be credited appropriately.

BEYOND BROWSING AND E-MAIL

The Web can be used for many different types of activities besides basic browsing and e-mail exchange. Common activities for individuals include a variety of consumer *e-commerce* activities, such as **online shopping, online auctions, online banking,** and **online stock trading.** When performing any type of financial transaction over the Internet, it is very important to use only *secure* Web pages.

Entertainment applications include online TV and movies, downloading *MP3* files and other types of **online music,** *online gaming,* and *online books* **(e-books).** A wide variety of news, government, product, and corporate information is widely available for consumer access as well. Having news or other information delivered to your desktop at regular intervals is referred to as *Webcasting.*

Chapter Objective 5:
List several useful things that can be done using the Internet, in addition to basic browsing and e-mail.

CENSORSHIP AND PRIVACY

Among the most important social issues relating to the Internet are censorship and *privacy.* Web content is not censored as a whole, so *blocking software* must be used by anyone wishing to prevent access to sites they deem objectionable. *Privacy* is a big concern for individuals, particularly about their Web activity. **Cookies** are used by Web sites to save customized settings for that site, but can also be used for advertising purposes and the potential to track Web activity exists. For individuals concerned about Internet privacy, they can send encrypted e-mail messages and files, not allow the use of cookies, and browse anonymously by using special cloaking software or by going through an anonymous Web server. As individuals are increasingly supplying personal information on the Internet, such as by signing up for free services or information, the use of **spam** (junk e-mail) has dramatically increased.

Chapter Objective 6:
Discuss censorship and privacy, and how they are related to Internet use.

THE FUTURE OF THE INTERNET

The Internet has evolved remarkably over the past few decades and will, no doubt, evolve in new ways that most people can't even dream of. The future Internet will likely be high-speed and accessed by wireless devices and appliances. Multimedia applications, such as real-time video communications and TV on demand, will likely be a reality in the near future.

Chapter Objective 7:
Speculate as to the format, structure, and use of the Internet in the future.

NET

Instructions: Match each key term on the left with the definition on the right that fits best.

1. application service provider (ASP)

2. ARPANET

3. cookie

4. dial-up connection

5. direct connection

6. directory

7. Internet

8. Internet service provider (ISP)

9. keywords

10. online auction

11. online banking

12. online music

13. online shopping

14. online stock trading

15. search engine

16. search site

17. World Wide Web

_____ A collection of categories that is used to locate appropriate Web pages from a search database.

_____ A small file stored on your hard drive at the request of a Web server; used to preserve customized settings and keep track of your preferences.

_____ A software program used by a search site to retrieve matching Web pages from a search database.

_____ A type of Internet connection in which the PC or other device must dial-up and connect to a service provider's computer before being connected to the Internet.

_____ A Web site that allows users to search for Web pages that match supplied keywords or fit in particular categories.

_____ An "always-on" type of Internet connection where your PC or other device is continually connected to the Internet.

_____ An online activity where bids are placed on items and the highest bidder wins.

_____ An organization that manages and distributes software-based services over the Internet.

_____ An organization that provides access to the Internet.

_____ Buying and selling stock over the Internet.

_____ Buying products or services over the Internet.

_____ Music played or obtained available over the Internet.

_____ Performing banking activities over the Internet.

_____ The collection of Web pages available through the Internet.

_____ The largest and most widely used computer network in the world, linking millions of computers all over the world.

_____ The predecessor of the Internet, named after the Advanced Research Projects Agency (ARPA), which sponsored its development.

_____ Words typed on a search site to locate information on the Internet.

Answers for the self-quiz appear at the end of the book.

True/False

Instructions: Circle **T** if the statement is true or **F** if the statement is false.

T F **1.** When the Internet was first developed back in 1969, it was called Mosaic.

T F **2.** On the Internet, an *access provider* and a *content provider* are essentially the same thing.

T F **3.** With a direct connection, you need only open your browser to start your Internet session.

T F **4.** All search sites allow you to type keywords.

T F **5.** When performing financial transactions on the Internet, make sure that your browser displays a locked padlock symbol, such as 🔒.

Completion

Instructions: Answer the following questions.

6. The physical network of the largest network in the world is called the _____.

7. A(n) _____ is a device specially designed for accessing the Internet.

8. MP3 files are used to compress _____.

9. A book that exists in electronic format is referred to as a(n) _____.

10. _____ deals with what information about an individual is available, how it is used, and by whom.

1. For each of the following situations, select the most appropriate Internet tool or application from the list that follows. Note that all tools and applications will not be used.

_____ To communicate with a friend in a different state.
_____ To have current national news displayed on your desktop on a regular basis.
_____ To play cards with a friend in a different state.
_____ To pay only as much as you specify for an item purchased through the Internet.
_____ To find Web pages containing information about growing your own Christmas trees.

a. Online banking
b. E-mail
c. Online shopping
d. Online auction
e. Searching
f. Interactive TV
g. Webcasting
h. Online gaming

2. Assume you want to find an ISP for a home Internet connection. Assuming that you don't want to tie up your phone when you're online and you plan to download multimedia files frequently, list two types of Internet services you could use. For each type of service, state one situation in which that type of service might be the best option and why.

3. List three different sets of keywords that could be used to search for the history of the U.S. Electoral College.

4. What would the following search look for?

text:"Internet privacy" domain:gov

5. List one advantage of and one disadvantage of the use of Web site cookies.

1. **Online Stock Trading** The business of trading online has continued to evolve in the past few years. Most online brokers offer multiplatform trading access (such as via the phone, PC, or wireless device), very low commissions (often $10 or less), and several investing resources (research, real-time quotes, stock reports, etc.). In addition, many of these companies will soon offer international trading on the major exchanges around the world. Some of the more popular brokers are Ameritrade, Datek, E*Trade, and Schwab. Several of these brokers offer a Web-based practice trading demonstration Web site where you can practice a few trades in order to get comfortable with this method of trading. For this project, research a few online brokers and determine what services they offer, what distinguishes them from their competition, and how you would go about opening an account. You should also review one of the online demonstrations and get a feel for how the trades are accomplished. Would you be comfortable using an online broker? Which broker would you choose if you were going to do online trading? At the conclusion of your research, prepare a one-page summary of your findings and submit it to your instructor.

2. **Client Censorship** The ability to limit or control what material children have access to on the Internet is of major concern to many parents. Several new software programs are now being sold that can accomplish this task (to a limited extent) on your home PC. Since these programs are designed to run on your personal computer rather than on your ISP's server, they are referred to as client-level blocking or filtering programs. These programs have several features and claim to be very user friendly. For this project, investigate a few of these programs and determine what features they offer and how much they cost. Would you use one of these programs if your children spent a lot of time online? Do you think that these programs can provide adequate protection for children who are real Web enthusiasts? What do these programs offer that aren't available through Web browser settings? At the conclusion of your research, prepare a one-page summary of your findings and submit it to your instructor.

3. **Travel Agent** Acting as your own travel agent can be a very appealing option these days. After all, travel arrangements are fairly straightforward and generally consist of just booking an airline seat, renting a car, and reserving a hotel room. Many Web-based travel sites do a great job of finding the lowest fares, allowing airline seat selection, providing information about weather conditions, booking rental cars, and finding affordable hotel rooms. Are you ready to be your own travel agent? For this project, review some of the most popular travel Web sites like Biztravel.com and Travelocity.com, to see what services they offer and how easy, or difficult, it is to become your own travel agent. Is there more to your traditional travel agent than just the tasks listed above? Can you have the best of both worlds? At the conclusion of your research, prepare a one-page summary of your findings and submit it to your instructor.

4. **You Can "Opt-Out"** Many organizations collect and store information about you. Some of them offer you the opportunity to "opt-out" of having this information shared with other organizations for promotional purposes. In order to accomplish this task you must contact them by traditional mail (snail mail) or e-mail to have your information protected. Some organizations that offer this option include credit bureaus (such as Equifax, Experian, and TransUnion), the Department of Motor Vehicles, and direct marketers. Not every DMV distributes personal information, but, if they do, Federal law (the *Driver's Protection Act*) requires that they provide

you with a means of opting out. The Direct Marketing Association (DMA) allows you to contact them by mail, e-mail, or telephone to opt-out of e-mail marketing (among other forms). For this project, visit the Federal Trade Commission's Sharing Your Personal Information Web page at www.ftc.gov/privacy/protect.htm and find out what kind of information you must provide these organizations in order for them to protect your personal information. Is there a "Sample Opt-Out Letter" available at this Web site? You may want to request that your information be protected at each of these organizations. At the conclusion of this task, prepare a one-page summary of your efforts and submit it to your instructor.

5. **Your Future Job** Preparing for your future job is something that can't wait until after you graduate. You should be thinking about what sort of job you would like to have or transition into during the educational process. What knowledge or skills will you have at graduation? What sort of job would you like to have in the future, and do the knowledge and skills you plan to have at graduation match that job? What is some trend data about the prospects for this job in the future (such as how much the job will pay, where you would have to live, the availability of positions, etc.)? Many Web sites provide job-related information and a good set of tools to help you search through current job listings, write a résumé, and research companies. For this project, summarize the skills or knowledge you plan to acquire during your educational program, and then make use of the available job posting Web sites to help you accomplish the following: Figure out what sort of job you are interested in having, determine if the skills or knowledge you plan to acquire match the type of job you are interested in having, and investigate the job prospects for this job in the future. Submit your findings to your instructor in the form of a short paper, not more than two pages in length.

6. **ASPs** The future of software in a box may be short-lived if application service providers (ASPs) have their way. Companies like Citrix are focused on "delivering any application to any device over any connection." Many ASPs are already hosting popular office suites, such as Microsoft Office. When you use an ASP, you don't have to purchase the software or have an expensive computer, because all the processing is done on the server. You could actually run Microsoft Office on an older computer using a conventional dial-up modem, as long as you are not using any graphics. For this project, determine what ASP companies are available, what programs they offer for use over the Internet, and how much they charge for their use. Would you be interested in using an expensive program over an ASP, rather than purchasing the program? What are the advantages of using the program over the Web besides saving the initial cost of purchasing the program? Submit this project to your instructor in the form of a short paper, not more than two pages in length.

7. **Searching the Web** An Internet search site is typically composed of three parts: a spider program that travels the hyperlinks of the Web classifying the Web pages it visits, a program that creates a catalog of these Web pages with associated keywords or directory categories, and a search engine program that returns matching Web pages when a person uses the search site. Most major search sites create huge catalogs and return many pages of results for each search request. Specialized search engines focus on specific topics and provide more targeted results. Metasearch engines provide results from multiple search engines. Other search sites allow you to ask a question in a natural language format. Each search site supports its own set of search strategies, such as using phrases, boolean operators, and specifying domains. For this project, form a group to identify a number of search sites. Visit each site and classify it based on the attributes discussed above. Your group should also identify the type of information each site is best at retrieving, the types of search strategies it supports, how you might submit a Web site to the search site, and some of the other features you feel are important about each of your selected search sites. Your group should submit this project to your instructor in the form of a short paper, not more than three pages in length.

**Presentation/
Demonstration**

8. Free Internet Several companies offer access to the Internet for free. One such company—NetZero—offers unlimited access to the Internet with all the benefits offered by most ISPs. These benefits include free customer support and a wide variety of local access numbers so you don't have to pay long-distance charges. They claim, "There are no catches, no contracts, and no commitments. There are no monthly bills or fees of any kind." For this project, investigate and prepare a presentation about a few of these companies. Do they really provide quality Internet access for free? What's the catch? If they also offer fee-based service, what is the different between that and the free access? How do these companies stay in business? This presentation should not exceed five minutes and should make use of one or more presentation aids such as the chalkboard, handouts, overhead transparencies, or computer-based slide presentation format. You may be asked to submit a summary of the presentation to your instructor.

9. Access to News and Information Our access to news and information has increased dramatically because of the Internet. Not only can we see and hear about events as they take place, but we can select the types of news and information we want to hear about 24 hours a day. This is a significant improvement over our traditional news and information sources that provide us with what they believe are important stories on their time schedule. For example, when the major U.S. networks decided not to televise the 2000 Summer Olympic Games live because of the large difference in time between Australia and the U.S., many individuals tuned in anyway, but did so through the Internet. Access to news and information is a very important feature of the Internet and allows you to see and hear about things that we might not have otherwise heard about. Another great feature of Web-based news is that we can access this information from multiple sources, which allows us to get different perspectives on the same news items to bypass any journalistic bias in the reporting of the news.

For this project, form a group to research available online news sources and the features they provide. Do any of you regularly access online news sources? If you want to read about some national news item, would the members of your group turn to their local newspaper or an online source? Do you think there may be a difference between the way stories are reported by U.S.-based news organizations and those of other countries? Your group should prepare a presentation of your findings. This presentation should not exceed 10 minutes and should make use of one or more presentation aids such as the chalkboard, handouts, overhead transparencies, or computer-based slide presentation format. Your group may be asked to submit a summary of the presentation to your instructor.

10. **"Pure-Play" Banking** Pure-play Internet banks are banks that offer banking services only over the Internet. These online banks offer all the services that a traditional bank offers, but at substantially reduced rates because they don't have the costs associated with a traditional bank. For example, The E*Trade bank offers free ATM withdrawals at over one-third of the ATMs operating in the United States. For this project, form a group to investigate a few online banks. For each bank, identify whether or not it is a pure-play bank, or just offers online banking to supplement its traditional physical presence. Prepare a presentation to summarize the banks, including the services they offer, how you would get started with one of them, and a summary of how their rates for savings, checking, and CDs compared to some of your local brick-and-mortar banks. Would the members of your group consider using a pure-play bank? Why or why not? Are pure-play banks doing well financially at the moment? Why or why not? This presentation should not exceed 10 minutes and should make use of one or more presentation aids such as the chalkboard, handouts, overhead transparencies, or computer-based slide presentation format. Your group may be asked to submit a summary of the presentation to your instructor.

11. **Your Privacy** When you surf the Web, you leave what is sometimes referred to as "click-stream data," "mouse droppings," or a "data trail." This information can be used to create a profile of your user activities. This profile, or collection of personal data, can then be sold as a commodity to others. Whoever buys your profile can then use it to target you with specific marketing materials in an effort to sell their products. Sometimes this data is collected through the use of cookies. After many years of relying on a self-regulatory approach to dealing with this problem, the Federal Trade Commission (FTC) is investigating its authority for regulating online privacy and is exploring the possibility of enacting baseline legislation to protect consumer privacy.

    Select one of the following positions, or make up your own, and express your point of view on the subject. Your instructor will indicate whether your response is to be posted to a class bulletin board, discussed in a class chat room, or discussed as an in-class activity. You may also be asked to submit a summary of your position and point of view to your instructor.

    a. We should avoid any sort of legislation with respect to the Internet. The companies that are guilty of collecting and using private information in an inappropriate way should be given additional time to amend their ways, and another chance to self-regulate their activities.

    b. Self-regulation is not the answer. If this were true, these companies would have resolved these problems several years ago. We have no choice but to enact legislation to deal with this issue.

12. **Online Shopping** Consider the following statement and establish your position, or point of view, on the subject. Your instructor will indicate whether your response is to be posted to a class bulletin board, discussed in a class chat room, or discussed as an in-class activity. You may also be asked to submit a summary of your position and evaluation of the statement.

    Will online shopping displace traditional brick-and-mortar stores any time soon? The number of products that can be purchased online grows each day. These products are sometimes offered at a significantly lower price than a traditional brick-and-mortar store could offer, and are shipped directly to your home with a return satisfaction guarantee. You can even plan a weekly meal menu online and have the grocery store deliver the necessary products to your home. Just about every business is considering setting up an e-commerce Web site, if they don't already have one. We even have virtual malls where you can walk around in a 3D virtual world and visit stores like Amazon, or

Interactive Discussion

NET

JCrew and purchase products at the click of a mouse (this requires a 3D browser available at www.activeworlds.com). Online shopping does have several advantages including an unlimited selection, convenience, price and lots of product information, but you cannot physically touch the product, get it immediately, or visit with your friends while shopping at the mall. The verdict on traditional brick-and-mortar vs. online stores is not in just yet.

Interactive Exercise

Using the Internet and the World Wide Web.   It's time to practice going online and searching the Web! Go to the Interactive Exercise at www.course.com/parker2002/ch9 to complete this exercise.

MODULE APPS

INTERNET APPLICATIONS

In the previous module, we took a look at how the Internet and World Wide Web work and some of the most common online activities. Two areas that were not discussed in as much detail as may be needed to fully grasp their significance in today's networked economy are *multimedia* and *e-business/e-commerce*.

This module introduces you to these two Internet-related topics. Chapter 10 delves into multimedia topics, such as advantages and disadvantages of using multimedia components, common multimedia applications, and issues involved with creating multimedia Web sites and other types of multimedia applications. Though non-Web-based multimedia applications are discussed in the chapter, the focus is on multimedia as an integral part of the World Wide Web. Chapter 11 explains in detail what e-commerce and e-business are and how they can be implemented over the Internet.

@ INTERNET

CHAPTER 10

Multimedia and the Web

LEARNING OBJECTIVES

After completing this chapter, you will be able to:

1. Describe what multimedia is and some advantages and disadvantages of using it.

2. Explain the difference between the following multimedia elements: text, graphics, animation, audio, and video.

3. List several Web-based and non-Web-based multimedia applications.

4. Briefly describe the basic steps and principles involved with multimedia and Web site design.

5. Discuss the various tasks involved with multimedia and Web site development.

6. Speculate about the format of multimedia in the future.

Multimedia involves integrating a variety of media, such as text, graphics, video, animation, and sound. Much of the time, the integration takes place using a computer. Today, many multimedia applications are also *interactive,* which means that the user is allowed to participate directly with the application. Multimedia applications are plentiful both on and off the Web.

In this chapter, we discuss elements found in multimedia applications and some advantages and disadvantages of using multimedia. Then we look at a variety of multimedia applications commonly found today. We also touch on the basic steps and principles involved with designing multimedia Web sites and other types of multimedia applications. Next, we cover multimedia and Web site development and the software that can be used during this process. The chapter closes with a brief look at the future of multimedia. ■

WHAT IS MULTIMEDIA?

As mentioned previously, multimedia refers to any type of application or presentation that involves more than one type of media. Though, technically, books such as this fit that definition since they use two types of media (text and graphics), typically applications aren't labeled "multimedia" unless they include sound, video, animation, or interactivity.

Interactivity refers to the ability of the user to control the flow, content, or other aspect of the application to some extent. It can be implemented using a variety of input methods, such as a touch screen, keyboard, mouse, or voice command. Typically, multimedia presentations today use some type of interactivity to allow multimedia applications to be customized to fit the interests of its users. The order of the information presented is determined by the options or topics the user selects or is determined based on the answers the user provides to questions. This customized content is usually a more effective means of presenting a user with the necessary information, instead of all users receiving the same information in the same linear order, as they would watching a videotaped or other noninteractive presentation.

In the past, multimedia was difficult to apply on a wide scale because the available technology wasn't sufficient to support it. With today's fast computers and Internet connections, however, multimedia implementation is much more feasible and its use is increasing exponentially. A growing number of Web sites incorporate multimedia, as do computer software and consumer interfaces, such as ATM machines and information kiosks. Multimedia presentations are also commonly used in business.

ADVANTAGES AND DISADVANTAGES OF USING MULTIMEDIA

Perhaps the biggest advantage of multimedia applications is that they appeal to a wide variety of people and can fit a variety of learning styles. Some people are *visual learners,* who learn best by seeing; others are *auditory learners,* who learn best by hearing. Still others are

>**Multimedia.** The integration of a variety of media, such as text, graphics, video, animation, and sound.

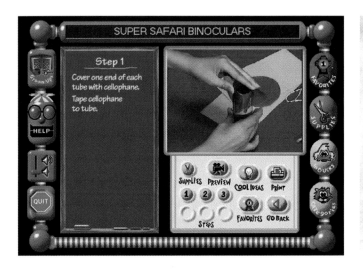

SUPER SAFARI BINOCULARS

YOU'LL NEED:
Two 4 1/2-inch cardboard tubes (toilet paper tubes)
Colored cellophane, cut into 3-inch circles
Tape
Construction paper, cut into two 4 1/2x6-inch pieces
Pencil
Two 24-inch pieces of yarn

STEP 1
Cover one end of each tube with cellophane.

And then tape cellophane to tube.

STEP 2
Cover each tube with a piece of construction paper. Tape paper to tubes.

Place tubes side by side. Tape tubes together.

With a pencil, poke a hole in outside edges of tubes about 1/2 inch from ends.

Use pencil to poke one end of yarn through each hole. Tie each end to prevent it from slipping out.

STEP 3
Finally, wrap the remaining yarn around other ends of tubes to cover tape and then tie it.

There's a super safari binoculars!

▶ **FIGURE 10-1**
Multimedia-based applications are often more interesting and more effective than their single-medium counterparts.

kinesthetic learners who learn best by doing. When a single medium is used, though it may be appropriate for some users, other users may be missing out on the full experience simply because the application or presentation doesn't match their learning styles. Multimedia has the advantage of presenting the material in multiple learning styles, which avoids this problem. For example, interactive exercises (such as the ones that are available through this text's Web site) using printed text and images, spoken narration, and activities that users perform cover all three types of learning. Studies have shown that when multiple learning styles are used, learning is enhanced.

Other advantages to multimedia use are that it usually makes the presented material more interesting and enjoyable, and many ideas are easier to convey in multimedia format. For an example, compare listening to the news on the radio to watching news on TV. The addition of the visual image of the newscaster combined with video clips, photographs, and other graphics typically makes watching the news a more enjoyable, informative experience than listening to a radio news broadcast. Another example is shown in Figure 10-1. This children's multimedia arts and craft program includes videos and photos to illustrate how to create each craft. Compare that medium to the printed directions shown in the figure; the multimedia version should be much more effective in teaching children how to perform the activity than the text-only version.

One disadvantage to multimedia applications is cost. They are usually quite a bit more expensive (though usually more effective) to create than a simple text-and-image format. Though multimedia presentations can be created in-house (if one or more employees have the necessary skills and experience with multimedia software), many businesses opt to outsource the development of their multimedia applications. Multimedia applications also require a great deal more storage space, which affects the deliverability of the finished product—this particularly affects Web-based applications. Web-based multimedia also has the added disadvantage of the wide variety of browsers, plug-ins, and Internet connection speeds that may be used to view a single Web page. Dealing with these limitations of Web-based applications is discussed in more detail later in this chapter.

MULTIMEDIA ELEMENTS

Multimedia applications can consist of a variety of different multimedia elements. The most common are discussed next.

APPS

web tutor

For a tutorial on the multimedia components found on a Web page, go to www.course.com/parker2002/ch10

FIGURE 10-2

Typefaces. Typefaces are collections of text characters that share a common design and can be either serif or sans serif.

SERIF TYPEFACES

Times New Roman

Rockwell Regular

SANS SERIF TYPEFACES

Arial

Middleton Regular

Text

Text is an important part of most multimedia applications. It can be used to supply basic content, as well as to add text-based menus, hyperlinks, and other navigational elements. As discussed in Chapter 7, text in application programs (including multimedia and Web development programs) can be displayed in a variety of typefaces, colors, sizes, and appearances. Remember that a typeface is a collection of text characters that share a common design, such as the Times New Roman, Rockwell Regular, Arial, or Middleton Regular typefaces illustrated in Figure 10-2. *Serif typefaces*—typefaces such as Times New Roman with small lines called *serifs* on the edges of the letters—tend to be more readable for large bodies of text, and so are traditionally used for this purpose. *Sans serif typefaces,* typefaces such as Arial that don't have serifs, are frequently used for titles, headings, and other text elements that usually are formatted larger or with a more distinctive appearance.

There are a huge number of typefaces available; one typeface can convey an entirely different feeling than another. For example, Times New Roman is a traditional, business-like typeface, where Middleton Regular is whimsical and fun. Selecting an appropriate typeface is important when planning a multimedia presentation or Web site. Another important factor is selecting the appropriate text size. Normal size is 12-point text—don't use a smaller size for any important text. Be sure not to make your text too large either; you want to make sure enough information fits on the screen at one time to avoid annoying your users. And watch your color combinations. A high degree of contrast between the text color and the screen's background color results in the most readable text.

When developing multimedia presentations for the Web, there is one additional important consideration: The computer and Web browser used ultimately determine the typeface and type size used to display the text on a Web page. Only the typefaces installed on the host computer can be used to display Web page text, unless the typeface is sent embedded in the Web page—a fairly new Web-development option. Another possibility is including alternative typefaces in the Web page instructions so they can be used if the specified typeface isn't available on the user's computer. Assuming that one of the typefaces will be available on the majority of host computers, this technique gives the Web page designer a little more control over the Web page text's ultimate appearance. It is important to remember, however, that when text is used there is the chance that it will not be displayed as intended, especially because most browsers give the user the option to override any specified typefaces on a page and use the ones he or she specifies.

For these reasons, when a consistent text appearance is required on a Web site—such as for a company logo or navigation buttons—an image is generally used instead. Unlike regular text, the typefaces used on images are displayed the same on all computers, since the item is displayed as a graphic, as illustrated in Figure 10-3. Graphics are discussed next.

Graphics

Graphics refer to digital representations of photographs, drawings, charts, and other visual images. Unlike *animation* or *video* (discussed next), graphic images are unmoving, static

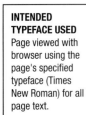

INTENDED TYPEFACE USED
Page viewed with browser using the page's specified typeface (Times New Roman) for all page text.

The typeface used to display the regular text can be different from user to user, depending on the typefaces installed on their computers and their browser settings.

Text created as part of an image is displayed as intended regardless of the user's fonts or browser setting.

BROWSER-SPECIFIED TYPEFACE USED
Page viewed with browser using Lucinda Handwriting as the display typeface for all text.

> **FIGURE 10-3**
>
> **Regular typed text vs. graphic text on a Web page.** Regular text on a Web page may appear differently on different computers, depending on the browser settings and the typefaces available on the PC. Graphics, however, appear the same.

images. Graphics can be created by scanning a photograph or document, taking a picture with a digital camera, or creating or modifying an image in an image-editing program (discussed later in this chapter). They can also be obtained as clip art or stock photograph images. *Clip art*—commercially prepared electronic images—and *stock photographs*—photos available for use in documents and presentations—can be purchased individually, in collections on CDs, or downloaded from the Internet. As shown in Figure 10-4, many images are available over the Internet. Often these images can be used free of charge, though there is sometimes a fee for commercial use.

Graphics are available in many formats, such as *TIF, BMP, GIF, JPEG,* and *PNG.* The TIF format is commonly used with scanned images, and the BMP format is used by Windows

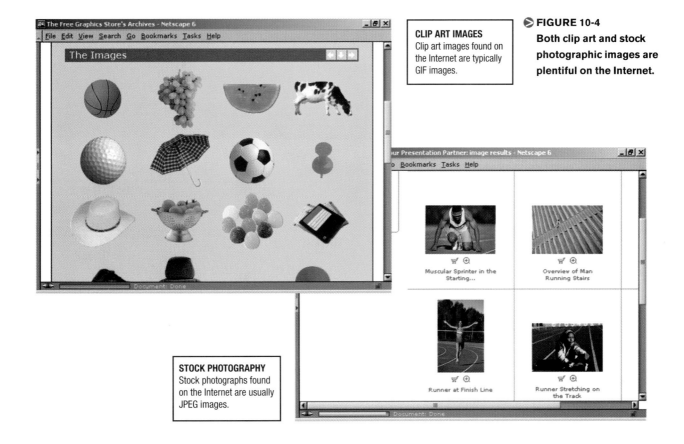

CLIP ART IMAGES
Clip art images found on the Internet are typically GIF images.

STOCK PHOTOGRAPHY
Stock photographs found on the Internet are usually JPEG images.

> **FIGURE 10-4**
>
> **Both clip art and stock photographic images are plentiful on the Internet.**

Paint and similar graphics programs. Web page images are usually saved in either the GIF, JPEG, or PNG format. These formats are explained in more detail next.

GIF

The *Graphics Interchange Format* (usually just referred to as **GIF** and saved with the file extension *.gif*) is the standard format for Web page images and is supported by all browsers that display images. It is an efficient, compressed format in which images can contain up to 256 colors. The GIF format uses *lossless* compression, so the quality of the image is not decreased when it is saved. GIF images are always rectangular, but can use a *transparent* background color to make the images appear to be nonrectangular (see Figure 10-5). GIF images can also be *interlaced,* which means that the image is displayed initially at low resolution and its quality is progressively increased until it appears at full quality; noninterlaced GIFs are drawn top to bottom at full quality instead. Even though an interlaced image doesn't actually load faster, interlacing enables the user to more quickly perceive what the image looks like; therefore, the image seems to load faster.

JPEG

The *Joint Photographic Experts Group* format (usually just referred to as **JPEG** and saved with the file extension *.jpg*) is supported by most Web browsers that display images. JPEG images are compressed using *lossy* compression, so image quality is lost during the compression process, and a compression amount from 0 to 100 percent is selected when the image is saved—the higher the compression, the smaller the file size, but more quality is lost in the

⬢ FIGURE 10-5
Transparent and interlaced GIFs.

TRANSPARENT GIFS

| Nontransparent (image's white background is visible) | | Transparent with white as the transparent color (page's yellow background is visible through the white text) | |

INTERLACED GIFS

JPEG - no compression (24 KB)   JPEG - 40% compression (5 KB)   JPEG - 80% compression (3 KB)

compression process, as illustrated in Figure 10-6. JPEG images can contain more than 16 million colors (called *true color*), so this format is often used for photographs and images that require more than 256 colors.

PNG

The *Portable Network Graphics* format (usually just referred to as **PNG** and saved with the file extension *.png*) is a newer format specifically created for Web page images. It is expected to eventually replace the GIF format, once the PNG format is widely supported by Web browsers. The PNG format uses lossless compression and the amount of compression cannot be specified, similar to GIF, but usually compresses more efficiently, resulting in slightly smaller file sizes. PNG images can use a specific color palette of 256 colors or less like GIF images, or can use true color like JPEG images; PNG images can also be interlaced and transparent.

When creating a Web page or multimedia application, it is important to use the most appropriate graphic format and keep the file size as small as possible to reduce loading time (for a Web page) or to conserve storage space (for a disk-based application). For Web pages, the GIF or PNG format is usually selected for *line art,* such as clip art, logos, and so forth. The JPEG format is usually used for photographs because true color and being able to select the amount of compression used often results in a higher-quality image at a smaller file size than if the GIF or PNG formats were used. A line art image and a photograph saved with each of these three formats is illustrated in Figure 10-7; for the JPEG images in this figure, varying amounts of compression were used and the one that had the smallest file size but that still had acceptable quality was selected.

When a Web page requires a large image, a *thumbnail image*—a small version of the image that can be clicked to display the full-sized image—can be used. This avoids increasing the page loading time for all users, when only some of the users may wish to view the full-sized image.

Animation

Animation is the term used to describe a series of graphical images that are displayed one after the other to simulate movement. Cartoons on television are one example of animation. Multimedia applications, both on and off the Web, generally use some type of animation. Types of animation commonly used in non-Web applications include *page transitions,* as discussed in Chapter 7, and animated objects, such as moving text or images. To add simple animation to a Web page, Java applets and animated GIFs are frequently used. A *Java applet*

▶ FIGURE 10-6
The amount of compression in a JPEG file affects both the file size and the display quality.

further exploration

For links to further information about graphics for multimedia applications, go to www.course.com/parker2002/ch10

>**PNG.** A newer graphics format designed for use with Web page images. >**Animation.** The process in which a series of graphical images are displayed one after the other to simulate movement.

| LINE ART The GIF or PNG format is usually used for line art images. |  GIF format - 3 KB |  JPEG format (10% compression) - 5 KB |  PNG format - 2 KB |

| PHOTOGRAPHS The JPEG format is usually used for photographs. |  GIF format - 12 KB |  JPEG format (50% compression) - 5 KB |  PNG format - 11 KB |

FIGURE 10-7

Graphic formats. Common graphic formats for Web page images include GIF, PNG, and JPEG.

is a small program downloaded with a Web page that can create such effects as scrolling text. An *animated GIF* is a group of GIF images stored in a special animated GIF file that display one after another to simulate movement, such as a rotating banner or a moving object or animal. For more complex animations, such as demonstrations or interactive games, *Shockwave, Flash,* or *ActiveX* animations are typically used instead. Animation can also be achieved using *Dynamic HTML (DHTML), JavaScript,* and *programming languages,* all discussed in more detail in Chapter 13. Some animation effects are illustrated in Figure 10-8.

When adding animation to a multimedia application, it is important to use it appropriately, so it adds to the overall quality of the application instead of being distracting. On Web pages, limiting the animated items to one per page is a good rule of thumb. In general, make sure there is a reason for using the animation—don't just include animations because you can.

Audio

Audio includes all types of sound, such as music, spoken voice, and sound effects. Most multimedia applications use sound to enhance the presentation or for content delivery. Audio for multimedia applications can be recorded using a microphone or MIDI instrument; audio can also be captured from CDs and downloaded from the Internet, as discussed in earlier chapters. Remember also from Chapter 4 that audio files take up a great deal of storage space, so compression methods are frequently used to reduce their file size.

Audio is often played automatically when a particular event happens, such as narration starting when the user gets to a particular page in a presentation or a sound effect playing when the mouse points to or clicks on a navigation button. Audio files on Web pages are commonly played with plug-ins or player programs, such as QuickTime, Windows Media Player, or RealPlayer (see Figure 10-9). Audio is also frequently incorporated into Shockwave and Flash animations.

As mentioned in Chapter 9, audio files on a Web page can be in the form of *streaming audio.* In this format, a small portion of the audio file is downloaded and buffered, and then begins playing while the remainder of the file downloads simultaneously. Because it allows the user to see or hear the file's contents significantly faster than if the entire file had to be downloaded first, it is recommended to use the streaming approach for all large audio and video files used with Web pages.

>**Audio.** Sound, such as music, spoken voice, and sound effects.

JavaScript is used to highlight the menu item when it is pointed to.

Animated GIF highlights the text.

Animated GIF displays several images one after the other to simulate a lightning strike.

> **FIGURE 10-8**
> **Animation.** Animated GIFs, Java applets, and JavaScript are frequently used for small Web site animations. More complex animations typically use Flash and Shockwave, though a plug-in is required to view them.

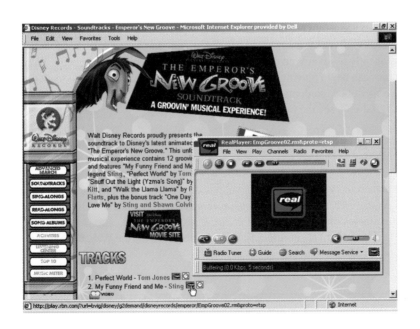

> **FIGURE 10-9**
> **Audio files.** Web page audio files typically play using a plug-in or a player program installed on the user's computer. Larger files should use streaming audio to avoid long delays before the audio file begins playing.

Some of the most widely used audio file formats are listed next.

▼ *.wav*—Waveform format; not compressed, so usually has large file sizes. Format CD music is stored in

▼ *.mp3*—Motion Picture Experts Group Audio Layer 3 format; very efficient, high-quality compressed audio. Waveform files can be converted to MP3 files to reduce their file size

▼ *.midi*—Musical Instrument Digital Interface format; used for files created with a MIDI device

▼ *.aif*—Audio Interchange Format; used for Macintosh waveform files

▼ *.dcr*—Shockwave Director Movie format; very compressed format that is played with the Shockwave player

▼ *.swf*—Flash format; very compressed streaming format that is played with the Flash player

further exploration

For links to further information about streaming audio, go to www.course.com/parker2002/ch10

Video

Video differs from animation in that it usually begins as a continuous stream of visual information that is broken into separate images or *frames* when the video is recorded. When the frames are projected—typically at a rate of 30 frames per second—the effect is a smooth reconstruction of the original continuous stream of information. As you might imagine, at 30 images per second, the amount of data involved in displaying a video during a multimedia presentation can require a substantial amount of storage space. Consequently, video data—like audio data—is often compressed. A variety of compression standards exist. Some of the most common video file formats are listed next.

▼ *.avi*—Audio-Video Interleave format; usually played using Windows Media Player

▼ *.mpeg*—Motion Picture Experts Group format; high-quality, compressed video

▼ *.mov*—QuickTime format; versatile format widely used to distribute video over the Web. Plays using Apple's QuickTime player

▼ *.rm*—Real format; highly compressed format used for streaming video files. Plays with the RealPlayer program

For multimedia presentations, video may be recorded using a standard (analog) video camera and then converted to digital form as it is input into a computer. Alternatively, the film can be recording digitally using a digital video camera. As already discussed, *streaming video* is frequently used on Web pages to reduce file size. Similar to streaming audio, streaming video files can begin playing once a portion of the video has been downloaded.

For a look at how students in the University of Akron's theater department used video to create digital sets, see the Campus Close-Up box.

further exploration

For links to further information about streaming video, go to www.course.com/parker2002/ch10

MULTIMEDIA APPLICATIONS

There are numerous types of multimedia applications. Web-based training and virtual reality are found on the Web. CD-based games, presentations, reference materials, and multimedia *kiosks* are examples of non-Web-based applications. Some applications (games, training and reference materials, etc.) are commonly found both on and off the Web. Common multimedia applications are discussed next.

>**Video.** A continuous stream of visual information broken into separate images or frames to be displayed one after the other to simulate the original information.

campus close-up

Digital Sets in Akron

When the University of Akron's New Media Center wanted to create innovative and exciting sets for the play "Fahrenheit 451," they didn't break out their paintbrushes. Instead, the theater group grabbed their cameras.

An impending visit from the play's author, Ray Bradbury, inspired the group to try something different. Beginning with a series of still images, a videotape of background scenery was created. During the play, the video was projected on a digital rear projection screen located behind the actors. In all, more than 10 different digital sets were created. Their biggest challenges? Timing, timing, and timing. Because the plays were performed live and could vary slightly from performance to performance, the set creators and the actors needed to work together to determine the proper timing for each sequence. To make this task even more difficult, the actors had their backs to the sets most of the time and couldn't see what was happening.

To have more control over the scenery changes, the group could have opted to control the sequences using a computer. Reluctant to do so because of the reliability factor, the group opted to stick with videotape. Remarkably, all six performances of the play went smoothly.

Non-Web-Based Applications

There is a wide variety of multimedia applications found off the Web. PowerPoint presentations, for example, are quite common for business presentations. CD-based games, reference materials, and other applications abound, as well. Some of these applications are discussed next and illustrated in Figure 10-10.

Business Presentations

As discussed in Chapter 7, presentation graphics programs such as PowerPoint are widely used business tools for creating fast, professional-looking, electronic slide shows. These presentations can include audio files, video files, sound effects, and transitions, and so are considered to be multimedia presentations. Though traditionally delivered in person, Power-Point presentations are increasingly found on the Internet, as well. Other business presentations, such as sales and marketing applications, may use Shockwave or Flash applications. If so, the appropriate player program must be included on the CD or other delivery medium.

Reference Materials

One of the most widely used multimedia-based reference materials is the multimedia encyclopedia (shown in Figure 10-10). Though the passages include text similar to a conventional encyclopedia, multimedia encyclopedias also feature video clips, sound clips, and animation to more easily convey information. Because of the size of these programs, they are usually run from a CD or DVD, instead of being completely installed on the hard drive.

APPS

CBT
Computer-based training commonly includes a variety of multimedia effects, including sound, video, and animations.

REFERENCE MATERIALS
Reference materials, such as the encyclopedia shown here, are commonly found in multimedia format.

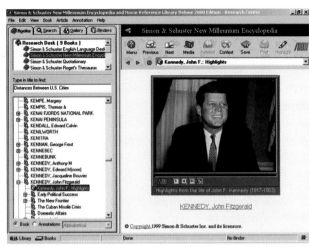

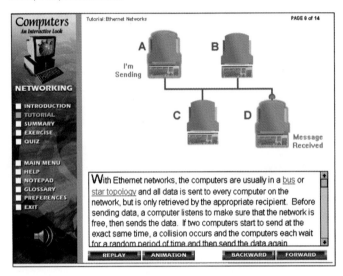

KIOSKS
Multimedia kiosks are commonly used to distribute information, sell products, provide Internet access, etc.

ENTERTAINMENT
Computer games for both kids and adults alike usually include multimedia components, such as background music, animation, and talking characters.

▶ **FIGURE 10-10**
Non-Web-based multimedia applications.

Virtual Reality

Virtual reality (VR) allows the computer to create three-dimensional views of objects, people, or locations that look like they do in the real world. Through VR, it is possible to take "tours" of buildings, museums, and vacation destinations, see all sides of a product

---

>**Virtual reality (VR).** A multimedia application that allows the computer to create three-dimensional views of objects, people, or locations that look like they do in the real world.

to be purchased, and so forth. VR applications have also arrived in full force in the entertainment industry, where illusion is the principal product. In many cities, amusement arcades feature virtual reality games in which players can battle enemies on realistic computer-generated landscapes. In some cases, the VR participant must wear special goggles, which project computer-generated images directly toward the eye, and wear gloves with built-in sensors, which change the visual images accordingly when the hands are moved. Feature-length movies and computer-game software also increasingly employ virtual-reality technology. Virtual reality is commonly used for training purposes, such as practicing new surgical techniques, learning how to fly an airplane, or performing repairs on expensive aircraft.

Computer-Based Training (CBT)

Computer-based training or **CBT** is an individual instruction method used to deliver contents via a computer. CBT is also called *computer-aided instruction,* or *CAI.* Many CBT applications are CD- or DVD-based, as in the example shown in Figure 10-10. Some programs are *mastery-based,* which means that the student is required to complete an exercise or test at a specific success rate or higher before moving on to the next exercise. CBT is commonly used to supplement curriculum for all levels of schooling, as well as for industry training.

Entertainment

It is very common for computer games designed for both adults and children to be multimedia-oriented (see Figure 10-10). Because of the amount of multimedia elements involved and their file sizes, most multimedia programs are run from a CD or DVD instead of being installed on the computer's hard drive, similar to reference materials. Common multimedia elements found in computer games include background music, sound effects, animated effects, narration, talking characters, and video clips.

Animation and multimedia special effects are also commonly used in motion pictures today, as discussed in the chapter How It Works box.

Information Kiosks

Information kiosks, such as the one shown in Figure 10-10, are self-service stations used for accessing information or requesting products or services. They are placed in public locations, such as stores, airports, and hotels. At a minimum, most information kiosks include text, graphics, and interactivity; animation is frequently included, as well.

Web-Based Applications

Multimedia elements can be added to virtually any Web page to add interest, to better deliver content, or to add functionality. There are some specific types of multimedia applications, however, where multimedia is an integral component of the Web site. The advantages of Web-based applications include:

▼ *Multiple platforms*—since Web pages can be viewed by many types of computers and platforms, multiple versions of the application (such as PC and Macintosh) don't need to be developed.

▼ *Familiar interface*—since Web-based applications are accessed with a Web browser, the user should feel somewhat familiar with the application the first time it is accessed.

>**Computer-based training (CBT).** Individual instruction delivered via a computer.

how it works

Creating the *Hollow Man*

Digital special effects are not new in Hollywood. The "blue screen" idea—where actors are filmed in front of a blue background and then footage and special effects are added behind them—has been around for quite a while. What was different about the *Hollow Man* movie, released in August 2000 by Columbia Pictures, was that the lead character—Sebastian Caine, played by Kevin Bacon—needed to be removed from most of the movie.

In the movie, Sebastian becomes invisible and reappears layer by layer. This presented a huge challenge to the development team that wanted the effects to look realistic. The process, which eventually took close to two years, began with extensive measurements and full body scans of Bacon. Working with this information and input from anatomy experts, a six-person model-ing team built one of the most complex geometric models ever made for film—essentially a digital Kevin Bacon. To create a map for the animation sequences, Bacon acted in the film wearing a variety of tools, such as a green suit with dots on his joints or a tight, glued-on latex mask. These objects enabled the developers to erase Bacon from the footage and replace him with a digital replica, or reconstruct the elements that should be showing through his invisible body instead. Though the process was somewhat tedious and time-consuming, being able to copy Bacon's movements and expressions helped the animators create realistic effects.

As an example of how difficult an undertaking this was, Bacon's model included a total of over 65,000 arteries, veins, and nerves; about 40,000 muscle fibers; 300 or so bones; and 20 organs.

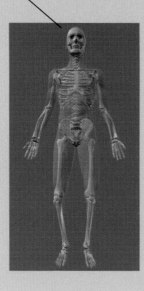

1. Precise measurements and digital scans were taken of Kevin Bacon. From the information, a digital model was created.

2. Scenes were shot with Bacon in a green suit and makeup or in a latex mask (below). The green suit allowed the animators to remove him later, for scenes where Sebastian is invisible or needs to be replaced with the digital model (when transforming). Below, painters were able to delete Bacon's eyes and mouth and rebuild and light the mask's interior.

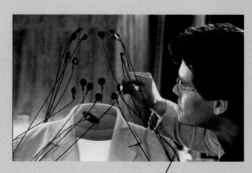

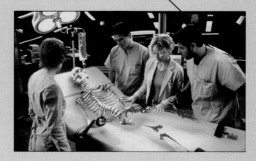

3. The result: Extremely realistic special effects.

▼ *Easily updated*—the content of a Web-based application can be updated as frequently as necessary and users always see the most recent version each time the Web site is accessed.

Some examples of Web-based multimedia applications are illustrated in Figure 10-11 and described next.

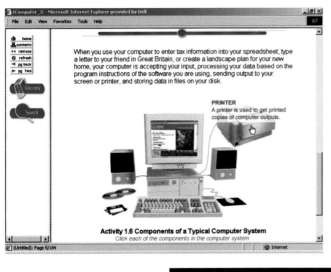

WEB-BASED TRAINING
Web-based training applications typically include online exercises and exams, as well as discussion groups, e-mail links, and other resources.

VIRTUAL REALITY
With VR, objects on a Web page can be viewed from any angle simply by rotating the object with the mouse.

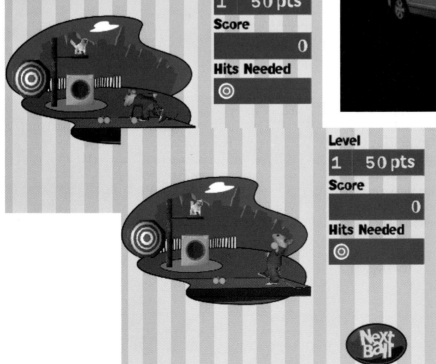

ENTERTAINMENT
With this Stuart Little game, you can control where Stuart throws the ball by using the mouse.

❯ **FIGURE 10-11**
Web-based multimedia applications.

Web-Based Training

Web-based training (WBT) is a type of individualized instruction delivered over the Internet using a Web browser (see Figure 10-11). The activities (training exercises, exams, animations, and so forth) are not downloaded, but are accessed in real time instead, just as other Web pages are.

Web-based training is a form of computer-based training (CBT), since the computer is used as the delivery medium. It is also a form of *distance learning,* because the learning can take place at multiple remote locations. Like other types of distance learning, Web-based training could be just for a specific topic—such as new employee training—or it could be an entire college course or program. With Web-based training, increasingly all instruction and evaluation take place over the Internet, though some schools require some in-person contact for credit courses, such as orientation and testing.

Some advantages of Web-based training include the following:

▼ *Self-paced instruction.* Students can usually work at any time of day or night at their convenience.

▼ *The ability to update material at any time.* Since all instructional material is hosted on a Web server, it can be updated whenever necessary simply by updating the server's content. Once updated, all users will see the newest version of the instructional material the next time they access the Web site.

▼ *Immediate feedback.* Web-based training systems can be set up to provide immediate feedback for exercises, practice tests, simulations, and so forth. The feedback can include automatically linking to review or supplementary material, as necessary, to provide adequate instruction for problem areas. It can also require mastery of the material before the student is allowed to move on to the next test or assignment.

Entertainment

Multimedia is widely used for online games and to distribute music, videos, and other items to the public. Music and videos can often be played on demand, or can be downloaded to play at a later time. Web-based games (see Figure 10-11) are usually played while the user is online to the Internet and commonly employ Flash or Shockwave technology. One new direction that has evolved in recent years is distributing the music of promising new artists over the Web in hopes that they will become popular, as discussed in the Inside the Industry box.

Virtual Reality (VR)

Virtual reality can allow users to explore three-dimensional environments on the Web, observing them from any number of views. If the interior of a house for sale is modeled in virtual reality, for example, you can walk through rooms, observing the objects in it closer or further away or from different angles. To explore virtual worlds, you need either a 3D browser program that supports *virtual-reality modeling language (VRML)* or a plug-in 3D package that works with your regular browser. For example, the VR automobile application shown in Figure 10-11 is displayed using the QuickTime VR program. The biggest problem today with viewing VRML sites on the Web is that virtual-reality applications require a lot of graphics, which in turn require a lot of bandwidth.

Another application of Web-based multimedia is the digital characters being used to deliver Web-based news and entertainment—the topic of this chapter's Trend box.

>**Web-based training (WBT).** Individual instruction delivered via the World Wide Web.

inside the industry

Using the Internet to Find the Next Musical Star

Move over Napster and MP3.com. We know where anyone can download a virtually unlimited number of free MP3 files. And guess what? It's legal.

Despite the copyright controversy and litigation involving Napster and MP3.com, there are still Web sites where musicians place their music in hopes it will be downloaded and distributed. One such site is Garageband.com.

Garageband.com was co-founded by former *Washington Post* music critic Tom Zito; Jerry Harrison, a music producer formerly of the Talking Heads; and Amanda Welsh, a former head of a research unit at Netscape. The idea for the business came about during a visit of Zito and Harrison. Looking at a staggering collection of CD and audiotape demos from aspiring artists in the corner of Harrison's office, the pair speculated about the possibility of creating a system to allow music fans to listen to and critique music via the Internet. The goal—using the listeners to spot the likely winners. Welsh thought the idea had enough possibility to leave Netscape to develop the system and Garageband.com was formed.

Garageband.com was officially launched in October 1999. In just four months bands uploaded 10,000 plus songs to the Web site—a feat that took MP3.com a year to accomplish. On the site, musicians from anywhere in the world can upload a track of its original material. Tracks are organized by genre. Reviewers pick a genre of music, listen to two anonymous tracks, and then complete a questionnaire about each track. Good reviews push tracks up Garageband.com's chart and, every two months, the top-ranked band plus four additional bands are invited to become "New Deal Artists" who can earn a $250,000 recording contract.

Garageband.com seems to be a good thing for everyone involved. Reviewers get free MP3 files and a free CD for every 20 reviews they complete. Bands get constructive feedback from musicians and fans around the world, professional feedback from an Advisory Board, free promotion to over 500,000 music lovers, not to mention an honest shot at a $250,000 recording contract. The company gets the opportunity to sign new talent with a good chance of making it, not to mention the huge marketing database generated from reviewer information. Created by musicians for musicians, Garageband.com may just make music company talent scouts obsolete.

garageband.com

MULTIMEDIA AND WEB SITE DESIGN

Design refers to the process of planning what your application or Web site will look like and how it will work. Though this chapter focuses on designing and developing multimedia Web sites, the process of designing multimedia applications is similar in many respects. In both instances, the importance of careful planning cannot be overemphasized. Time spent planning and designing an application or site on paper before jumping into the development process pays off in the long run. Some of the most important design considerations and guidelines are discussed next.

Basic Design Principles

When designing any type of multimedia application, it is important to keep two basic principles in mind: (1) Users like interesting and exciting applications; and (2) users have little patience with slow-to-load or hard-to-use applications.

A site or other application is *interesting* if it provides information of value to its target audience; users find it *exciting* if it rewards them with a stimulating experience. Unfortunately, interest and excitement wear off over time. On Web sites, if visitors see the same information at your site day after day or week after week, boredom sets in and they will stop coming. Therefore, it is important to refresh the content of your site regularly with new information.

Users—particularly Web users—generally don't have much patience. If they have a hard time figuring out how to navigate through the application or site to get the information

web tutor

For a tutorial on designing a Web site, go to www.course.com/ parker2002/ch10

APPS

Animated Anchors

Ananova, the world's first virtual newscaster, made her debut on the Internet on April 19, 2000 with the words "Hello World! Here is the news and this time it's personal!" Since then, the use of digital characters to deliver Web content has begun to catch on.

Ananova was designed from the start to deliver news over the Web. A great deal of thought when into her design: Male or female? Accent? What should her face look like? Hair color? After designers selected the desired features from hundreds of photographs of faces, a sketch and wire frame were developed. Over time, her animation was refined and Ananova grew more and more lifelike.

On the final model of Ananova, the different muscle groups of her face can be controlled to change her expression. Morphing allows an unlimited number of positions between, for example, her left eyebrow being fully raised and fully lowered. The final collection of expression sets is saved in a library to be accessed whenever Ananova is used.

To prepare a news story for Ananova to deliver, a team of editors mark up articles culled and edited from news sources. The general emotion of the story is tagged, as well as any particular parts of the story that require more emotion. Specific camera and lighting instructions are also included. When the story is run, specialized software generates Ananova to fit the marked up text, as well as to generate speech (with appropriate lip synching and facial animations) from the text.

The result? A realistic humanoid delivery of the news.

Ananova isn't the only game in town, however. The 1KTV Web site (named for its low bandwidth requirements of 1 Kbps) also uses animated characters. This site features selected news stories and a variety of TV shows. Instead of having live news broadcast on the Web site, 1KTV features selected news stories (as well as a variety of other shows) that can be viewed on demand. Another difference is that a viewer program is required.

The viewer contains some of the multimedia overhead, requiring less information to be downloaded. In addition to being available through its Web site, 1KTV content can be found on other Web pages. 1KTV uses photorealistic humans for its news broadcasts and incorporates actual voices in the broadcasts, in addition to animated characters and computer-generated voices. Video clips are frequently included, as well.

Though animated news anchors have their limitations (virtually everyone would rather hear about airplane crashes, bombings, and other such tragedies from a human instead of an animated character), their ability to deliver news live or on demand on devices ranging from your PC to your cell phone make them an appealing option for many.

they want, they often give up and may never return. To facilitate navigation and reduce frustration, you should design an intuitive site or application with clear, consistent navigational tools and information presented in a way that makes sense. For Web sites, the pages should load quickly and be easy to read. A good rule of thumb is to keep the total file size of all elements on a page to 30 KB to enable the page to load in 30 seconds or less for all users. For CD-based applications, it is best to fit the entire application on a single 650 MB CD whenever possible. To accomplish this, you need to select your multimedia elements carefully and modify them as necessary to be as efficient as possible, as discussed in a later section.

Another decision that impacts the design of a Web site is the device that your target audience will use to access the Web site. Since it can vary from a large screen TV to a handheld PC with a 2-inch screen, obviously a one-size-fits-all Web site is not an acceptable option. At a minimum, decide early on whether the site will be used for traditional PCs (with screen sizes ranging from about 12 inches on up), whether the site will be designed for a handheld or portable device, or whether content will be optimized for both delivery methods.

Even if a single delivery method is assumed (such as a conventional PC and Web browser), there are still many variations of platforms, browsers, and settings that could be used. Because of this, it is important to set up the site so it can be used on as many different PC configurations as possible. Careful consideration should be given to:

▼ *Features that require a specific browser.* Including snazzy animated effects for Internet Explorer users is wonderful for them, but ignores Netscape users. The standards for the two browsers are growing more closely together, which may help in the future. Presently, you have the option of not using browser-specific features, or using them for what should be your target audience's most widely used browser, as long as it doesn't inhibit the functionality of the application for other users. Or you can choose to identify the browser used for each visitor and display the version of your site that matches the visitor's browser. Identifying the browser used is usually performed by adding the appropriate JavaScript code to the home page of the site—an action sometimes called *browser sniffing.*

▼ *Features that require little used plug-ins.* Though it is annoying to have to download a plug-in before being able to use a Web page feature, most users tolerate downloading a few of the most widely used plug-ins. Try not to annoy your visitors by requiring unusual ones that they may not have or have no other reason to obtain.

▼ *The width of the page content.* Keep in mind that different browsers and screen resolutions allow different amounts of room to display Web page text. This affects how wide your images and columns of text should be. To be safe, keep banner images, image maps, and other full-width items to 550 pixels or less wide. Full-height items (such as an image map) should also be less than 300 pixels tall. This will ensure that the content is visible on virtually all PCs with the browser maximized to avoid the user having to scroll down or across the page. Assuming your users set their PCs to 800×600 screen resolution, you can make images a little larger when needed, but run the risk of annoying users with lower resolutions or nonmaximized windows.

▼ *High-bandwidth items.* Though an increasing number of users are using broadband Internet connections (such as cable, DSL, and satellite), there is still a huge installed base of dial-up modem users. If the intended audience of your site includes these users, pay extra close attention to the size of the images on the site, and use techniques to allow the user to decide whether to take the time to access certain features of the site. For example, instead of automatically downloading and playing a sound or video file, have a link to it (with an estimated download time listed). Also, provide streaming audio and video files and use thumbnail images whenever possible. Finally, be sure that all multimedia elements are consistent with the purpose of your site and add something significant. Don't add extra elements—particularly sound and video files—without a good reason. They just slow down your site and annoy your visitors.

Determining the Intended Audience and Objectives

One of first steps in designing a multimedia application or Web site should be to determine whom the intended audience is and what the primary objectives are. The intended audience must be considered because it greatly affects the appearance (style, colors used, etc.) you will select for the site. For example, four sites designed to appeal to distinctly different audiences are shown in Figure 10-12.

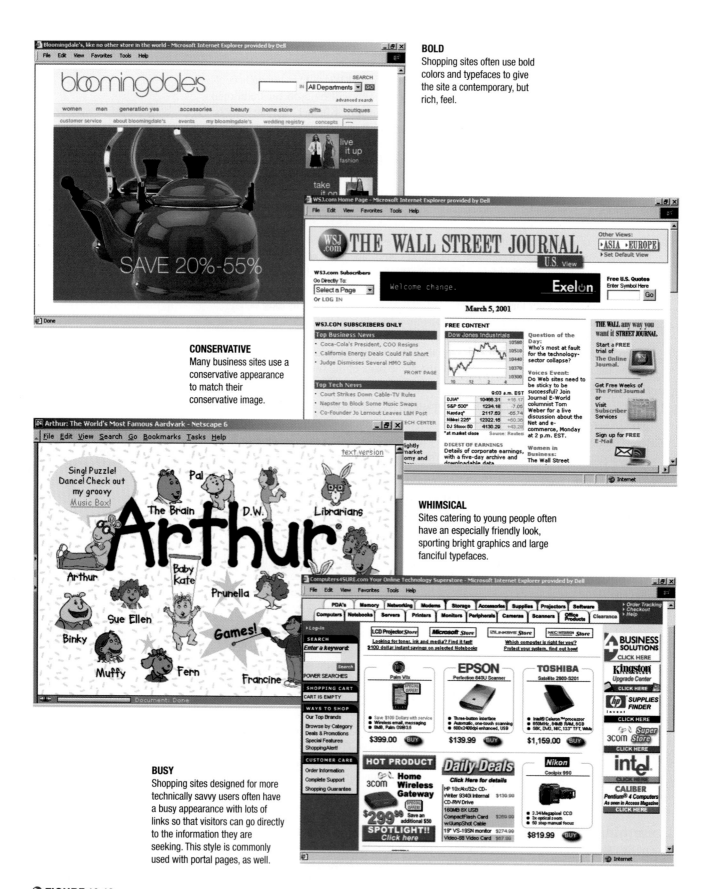

BOLD
Shopping sites often use bold colors and typefaces to give the site a contemporary, but rich, feel.

CONSERVATIVE
Many business sites use a conservative appearance to match their conservative image.

WHIMSICAL
Sites catering to young people often have an especially friendly look, sporting bright graphics and large fanciful typefaces.

BUSY
Shopping sites designed for more technically savvy users often have a busy appearance with lots of links so that visitors can go directly to the information they are seeking. This style is commonly used with portal pages, as well.

FIGURE 10-12

The intended audience affects the design of a Web site. Shown here are four sites designed for vastly different audiences.

The intended audience also affects the types of multimedia elements that can be included on a site. If you are designing a site to be accessed through an intranet, for example, you don't have to be as concerned about file size as someone designing a Web site to be accessed by the general public. When determining your target audience, give some thought to how users will access the site and how technologically savvy they are. Will they be using up-to-date browsers and have a variety of multimedia plug-ins installed? If your answer is "no," that impacts the types of multimedia elements you should include on the site.

The objectives of the site affect the content of the site, because you will want to make sure that the site includes the information needed to meet those objectives. Once the audience and objectives have been identified, you should have a good idea of the main topics that need to be included in the site. If you don't, don't go any further into the design process until you do. Rethink your audience and objectives, explore other sites on the Web, and talk to potential users until you understand what the site's content should include.

Using Flowcharts, Page Layouts, and Storyboards

After the intended audience, objectives, and basic content to be included in the application or site have been determined, the structure and layout can be designed. To this end, tools such as flowcharts, page layouts, and storyboards are often used.

A **flowchart,** when used with the design of a Web site or multimedia application, describes how the pages in the site or application relate to one another. The top part of Figure 10-13 shows a flowchart for a restaurant's Web site. Note that each box in the flowchart represents a separate Web page, and the lines between boxes show which pages logically relate to others. Remember, however, that you can hyperlink pages in any way you like. Though the lines between the flowchart boxes indicate logical hyperlinks, there would typically be additional links between the pages. For example, it is a good idea to place links to the main pages of the site (in this example, Home, Location, Menu, Reservations, and The Staff) on all pages of the site to facilitate navigation.

For designing the look of the pages in an application or Web site, either **page layouts** (for Web sites) or a **storyboard** (for multimedia applications) are typically used. Both tools are sketches—done by hand or with the help of a computer—that illustrate the layout and navigational structure of the site or application. For Web sites, typically two page layouts are created: one for the home page (see the bottom screen in Figure 10-13) and one to be used for all other pages on the site. For other types of multimedia applications, a storyboard—an ordered series of sketches of each page or screen in the application—might be used instead.

Navigational Design Considerations

As already mentioned, careful design of your navigational structure is extremely important. After drawing a preliminary flowchart of a site or application, take a look at the balance of the flowchart. You want enough main topics to keep the information organized, but not so many that users have difficulty finding what they are looking for. For Web sites, users should be able to get to most pages on the site within three mouse clicks. For large sites, navigational tools such as drop-down menus, *site maps* (table of contents pages for sites that contain links to all main pages on the sites), and search boxes can help accomplish this (see Figure 10-14). Other navigational options include text-based hyperlinks and navigation bars; image-based navigation bars; *image maps* (single images with separate areas linked to different locations); *frames* (with one frame always displaying the navigation bar and the

further exploration

For links to further information about multimedia resources, go to www.course.com/parker2002/ch10

APPS

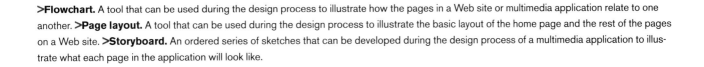

>**Flowchart.** A tool that can be used during the design process to illustrate how the pages in a Web site or multimedia application relate to one another. >**Page layout.** A tool that can be used during the design process to illustrate the basic layout of the home page and the rest of the pages on a Web site. >**Storyboard.** An ordered series of sketches that can be developed during the design process of a multimedia application to illustrate what each page in the application will look like.

FLOWCHARTS

A Web site flowchart describes how the Web pages on a site relate to one another. Each box represents a separate Web page, and the lines between them show which pages logically link.

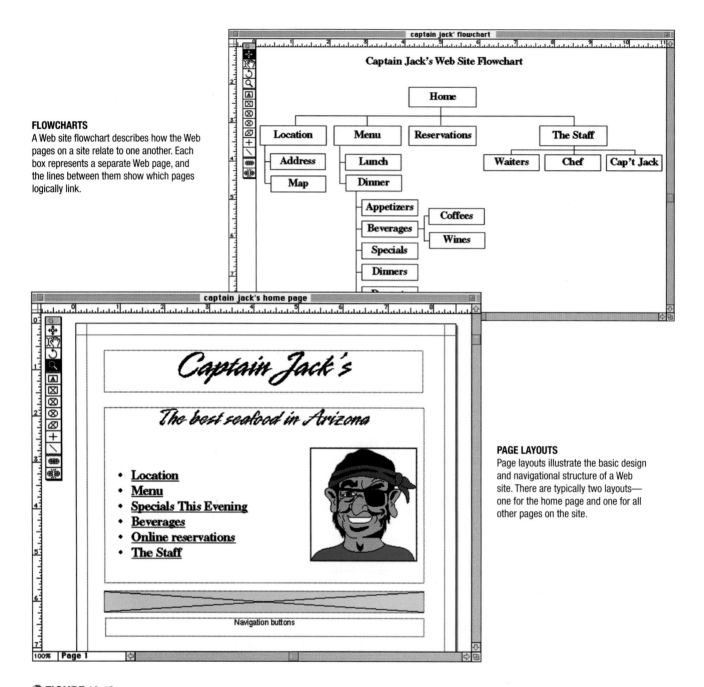

PAGE LAYOUTS

Page layouts illustrate the basic design and navigational structure of a Web site. There are typically two layouts— one for the home page and one for all other pages on the site.

> ➲ **FIGURE 10-13**
>
> **Web site flowcharts and page layouts.** A sample flowchart and page layout for a restaurant Web site is shown here.

other frame displaying the site contents as navigational links are clicked); and hyperlinks that display more options or a description of the link when pointed to. Some examples of these navigational elements are shown in Figure 10-14.

When designing your navigational structure, be sure to place the same navigational items in the same location on every page, so that users can easily find them. Also be sure that any icons or other graphics are easily understood. When in doubt, add a text name to the image, such as ▣ instead of ▣. In addition, if an image or text looks like it's a hyperlink, it should be one. For that reason, don't underline nonlinked text.

For long Web pages, consider separating the content into several pages to reduce scrolling and loading time. Similar to the pages in a linear section of a non-Web-based application, the separate pages would typically be linked with some type of "Back" and "Next" buttons (refer again to Figure 10-14). When you break a large document apart, consider including a link to view or download the entire document intact either as a Web page or in a common format, such as Word or PDF, so that users can read or print the entire document at one time.

SEARCH BOXES
Search boxes allow users to find
pages containing specific information.

IMAGE MAPS
Image maps contain links to
the main pages on the site.

DROP-DOWN MENUS
Drop-down menus allow quick access
to the main pages on the site.

PAGE TITLES
Descriptive page titles tell users
where they are within the site.

SITE MAPS
Site maps contain links to
all main pages on the site.

POP-UP MENUS
When a hyperlink on this image
map is pointed to, a pop-up menu
supplies additional choices.

MENU TABS
Menu tabs allow access to the main pages
of a site, as well as nicely indicate which is
the currently displayed page.

NAVIGATION BARS
Both text-based and image-
based navigation bars should
be in the same location on
every page in the site.

SECTION LINKS
The section links and the
Previous and Next buttons allow
users to move to the desired
section of a long document.

PRINT/SAVE LINKS
It is helpful to include an option to print or
save the entire document intact when a
document is broken into sections.

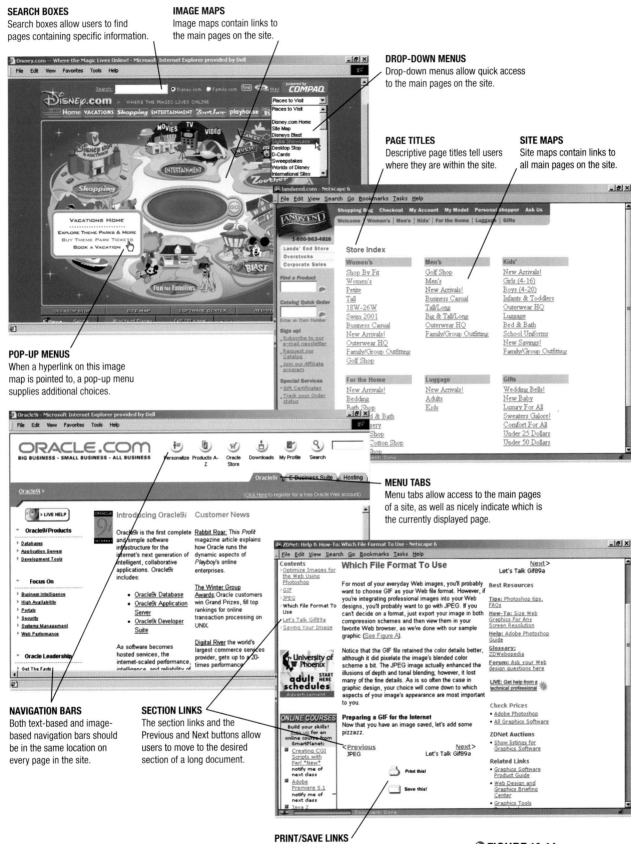

FIGURE 10-14
Navigational tools. A wide variety
of navigational tools exists to help you
make your Web sites easy to use.

For long Web pages that can't be broken into multiple pages, include a link that jumps users back to the top of the page periodically throughout the document so they don't have to scroll back up to the top of the page when they are finished reading it. It is also a good idea to include a table of contents at the top of a long page that allows users to jump down to a particular section of the document.

One final navigational hint: Be sure to include identifying information on each page of the site to indicate which page is currently being displayed, because not all users enter the site from your home page. This information can be text-based or reflected on your navigational structure, such as with a pushed-in navigation button, a different colored tab, an unlinked hyperlink on a text-based navigation bar, etc. You should also include the name of the organization and a link to the home page of the site on all pages.

Access Considerations

As already discussed, the device being used to access a Web site affects whether the site will be able to be accessed at all, as well as how functional it will be. For example, many portable devices used to access the Web cannot display regular HTML pages. Instead, they display pages that have been specifically modified for this type of access, typically using *wireless markup language* or *WML* instead of HTML. If you anticipate your intended audience wants to access your site with these devices, you need to plan on modifying the appropriate content into a mobile format. In addition, some browsers are not able to display all of the multimedia elements you may wish to include. It is a good idea to include links to download any plug-ins that are necessary for your site, as well as the newest version of your recommended browser for those users who may need to upgrade before exploring your site.

A second issue involves access for visually impaired people and others who require the use of an assistive product—such as a screen reader, which translates what's on a computer screen into audible output—to get information from the Internet. In order for information to be read with one of these devices, it needs to be in text form. Reading devices cannot read graphics, just text. In order for your navigational images to be usable for these visitors, they must be identified with an alternative text description. This description is easily added to an image and is displayed when the image is pointed to with the mouse or when image-display is turned off in a browser (see Figure 10-15).

The law only requires that federal Web sites follow the *Web Accessibility Initiative (WAI)* guidelines to provide individuals with disabilities (primarily visually impaired individuals) comparable access to content available to individuals without disabilities. However, it is a good idea to design your Web site to be accessible to the widest possible audience.

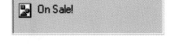

> FIGURE 10-15

Alternate text for images. An alternative text label for an image is displayed when the image is pointed to (top), as well as when image display is turned off (bottom), and can be read by a reading device.

MULTIMEDIA AND WEB SITE DEVELOPMENT

Once a site or other type of multimedia application has been carefully designed, it is time to create it. This process is called *development*. The development of a site or application can be performed in-house (if employees with the appropriate skills and appropriate software are available) or it can be outsourced to a professional developer. In either case, the development process includes three basic steps:

▼ Creating the multimedia elements

▼ Creating the application or Web site

▼ Testing the site or application

These three steps, along with the various types of software that can be used during each step, are discussed next.

Creating the Multimedia Elements

There is a tremendous selection of software that can be used to create the multimedia elements to be included in a multimedia application or Web site. Typically this process involves several programs, such as *graphics software* to create or modify the images, *animation software* to create animated elements, and *audio-* and *video-editing software* to create finished sound and video clips. A sampling of these software programs is included next.

Graphics Software

Graphic software is used to create or modify images; the finished images can then be used on Web pages or in multimedia presentations. Commercial graphics programs are commonly distinguished by whether they are primarily oriented toward painting, drawing, or image editing.

Painting and Drawing Programs

Painting programs enable you to create bit-mapped images and to color them pixel by pixel. Usually, the images you create cannot be resized without loss of resolution. Enlarging them may result in jagged edges, and reducing them may result in a blurry mess. In contrast, *drawing programs* enable you to create images that can be resized and otherwise manipulated without loss of quality. This is possible because the images are created using mathematical formulas, not by coloring pixels. Drawing programs also allow you to *layer* objects, so if you place one object on top of another, you can later separate the two images, if desired. In contrast, because a painting program colors the actual pixels in an image, if you move an object on top of another, the pixels are recolored and the objects cannot be separated.

Common painting programs include *Windows Paint* and *Jasc PaintShop Pro* (shown in Figure 10-16); widely used drawing programs include *Adobe Illustrator, Macromedia Freehand, CorelDRAW,* and *Microsoft PhotoDraw* (also shown in Figure 10-16).

Image-Editing Programs

Though painting and drawing programs can be used to edit images, *image-editing programs* are specifically oriented to touching up or modifying images. Editing options include correcting color, eliminating red-eye, cropping, resizing, and applying filters or other special effects. Most programs also include options for *optimizing* images to reduce the file size. Optimization techniques include reducing the number of colors used in the image and converting the image to a more appropriate file format. Perhaps the most widely used image-editing program is *Adobe Photoshop,* illustrated in Figure 10-17.

Audio and Video Software

For creating and editing audio and video files, special *audio-editing* and *video-editing* programs are used. To capture sound, a sound recorder can be used to capture input from a microphone or MIDI device; to capture sound from a CD, ripping software is used, as illustrated in the Chapter 7 How It Works box. Video is either captured using a video-capture card or is input directly in digital form from a digital camera's storage medium.

Once the sound or video file has been created or imported, it likely will need to be modified. Background noise or pauses may need to be removed, portions of the selection may need to be edited out, multiple segments may need to be spliced together, and special effects such as fade-ins and fade-outs may need to be applied. Remember that sound and video files tend to be extremely large, so editing a selection to be as short as possible is desirable for Web applications to minimize file size. Common audio-editing programs include *Windows*

>**Graphics software.** A type of program used to create or modify images.

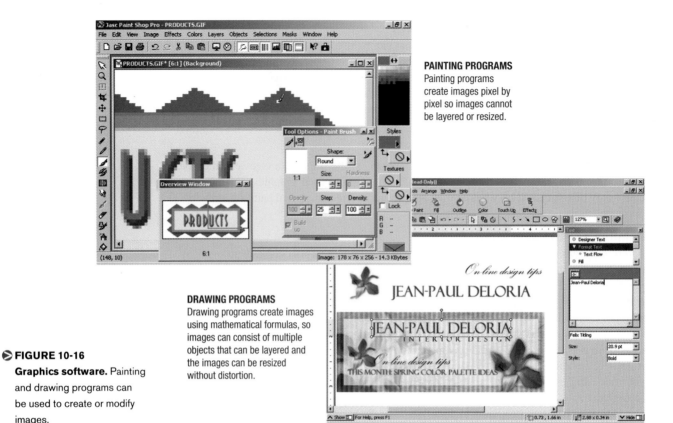

PAINTING PROGRAMS
Painting programs create images pixel by pixel so images cannot be layered or resized.

DRAWING PROGRAMS
Drawing programs create images using mathematical formulas, so images can consist of multiple objects that can be layered and the images can be resized without distortion.

FIGURE 10-16
Graphics software. Painting and drawing programs can be used to create or modify images.

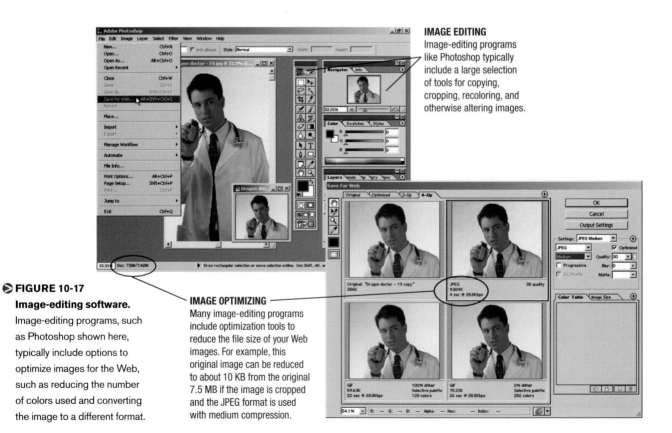

IMAGE EDITING
Image-editing programs like Photoshop typically include a large selection of tools for copying, cropping, recoloring, and otherwise altering images.

FIGURE 10-17
Image-editing software.
Image-editing programs, such as Photoshop shown here, typically include options to optimize images for the Web, such as reducing the number of colors used and converting the image to a different format.

IMAGE OPTIMIZING
Many image-editing programs include optimization tools to reduce the file size of your Web images. For example, this original image can be reduced to about 10 KB from the original 7.5 MB if the image is cropped and the JPEG format is used with medium compression.

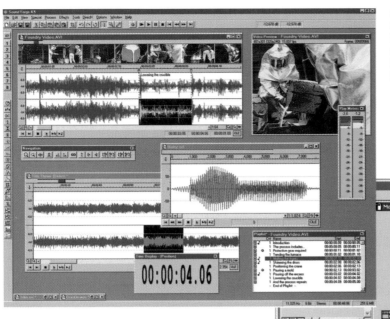

AUDIO EDITING

Audio-editing software allows audio files to be recorded, cropped, mixed with other sound clips, and otherwise edited. As with the example shown here, some programs include limited video editing, as well.

VIDEO EDITING

Video-editing software allows video files to be edited. As shown here, often a timeline can be used to assemble various clips into one finished product.

Sound Recorder, Peak, and Sonic Foundry's *Sound Forge* (shown in Figure 10-18). Common video-editing programs include *Apple QuickTime Pro, Avid Media Composer,* and *Adobe Premiere* (see Figure 10-18). Finished sound and video clips can be inserted into multimedia applications and Web pages, or incorporated into animations using animation software (discussed next).

Animation Software

Animation software is used to create animation to be used on Web pages or other multimedia applications. At the low end are animation programs used to create animated GIFs. These programs allow you to import the various images to be included in the animated GIF, rearrange them into the correct order, add transitions between them, and specify the display time for each image and the number of times the animation sequence should repeat. Once all settings have been selected, the entire animation is saved in a single animated GIF file.

For more complex animations, developers typically turn to a more powerful animation program, such as *Macromedia Fireworks, Macromedia Flash, Adobe LiveMotion,* or *Adobe After Effects* (illustrated in Figure 10-19). These programs enable developers to create Web animations complete with interactivity and sound. You can import or create a variety of still and moving objects, combine and layer them, as desired, and then add special effects, movement, and sound.

▶ FIGURE 10-18

Sound and video editing.

Once sound and video has been digitized, it often needs to be edited to make the finished product as efficient as possible, as well as to combine clips and add special effects.

APPS

>**Animation software.** A type of program used to create animations.

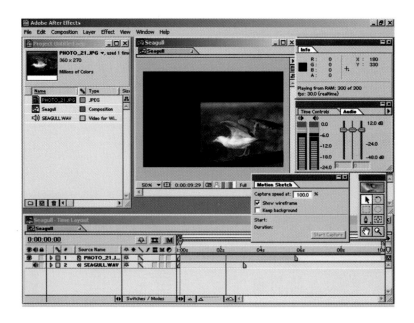

❷ **FIGURE 10-19**

Animation software.

Animation software ranges from simple GIF animators to more complex programs, such as the Adobe After Effects program shown here.

When choosing an animation program, be sure it can create images in a format you can use, depending on which program is going to be used to create the finished application. Some programs, such as After Effects and LiveMotion, are designed to be compatible with other specific programs, such as Illustrator and Photoshop. Some programs create finished elements in a standard format, such as Shockwave, Flash, or animated GIF, that can be inserted into various types of applications. Remember, however, that some formats—such as Flash and Shockwave files—require a special player to be viewed. For some types of animation, *Dynamic HTML (DHTML), virtual reality modeling language (VRML), JavaScript,* or *Java* may be more appropriate than an animation program. These tools are covered with programming languages in Chapter 13.

Creating the Application or Web Site

There are a variety of programs that can be used to create multimedia applications and Web sites. These are referred to as *authoring programs.* In general, authoring programs are used to create the basic site or application, and then to combine the multimedia elements to be used into one unified application. *Multimedia authoring programs, Web site authoring programs,* and *storefront software* are discussed next.

Multimedia Authoring Software

Multimedia authoring software consists of programs designed to create stand-alone multimedia applications. One of the most prominent companies in this area is Macromedia. Both *Director* and *Authorware* are widely used multimedia authoring programs. Director—recently renamed Director Shockwave Studio—is an *object-based authoring program,* where all objects are viewed as part of a movie production, such as cast members, a stage, and a score (refer to Figure 10-20). Finished Director movies can be viewed over the Web using the Shockwave player. Consequently, in addition to being used to create stand-alone multimedia applications, Director is frequently used to create Shockwave content to be incorporated into multimedia Web sites.

Macromedia Authorware is an *icon-based authoring program.* Icons representing the multimedia elements in an application (such as text, graphics, video, etc.) are placed on a

---

>**Multimedia authoring software.** Programs designed to create multimedia applications.

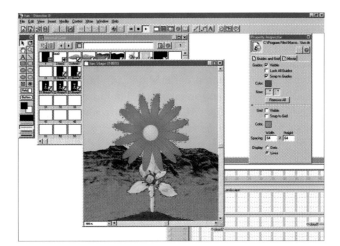

DIRECTOR
In Director, objects are viewed as cast members on a stage; the properties of each cast member can be specified.

◗**FIGURE 10-20**

Multimedia authoring programs. Two widely used authoring programs are Macromedia Director and Authorware.

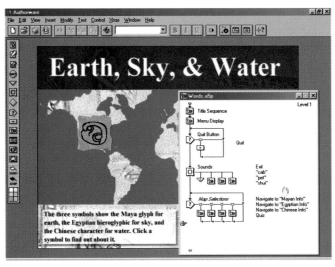

AUTHORWARE
In Authorware, elements are viewed as icons on a flowline.

flowline to indicate the sequence in which the elements should be displayed, as shown in Figure 10-20. Authorware is most often used for multimedia training and educational applications. Another widely used program for these types of applications is *Asymmetrix ToolBook*.

Web Site Authoring Software

The standard language for creating Web pages is *Hypertext Markup Language (HTML)*. HTML is a markup language, which specifies how text and other page elements should be displayed. These instructions are specified using *HTML tags*. HTML tags consist of paired symbols that indicate where an effect—such as larger text, bolded text, etc.—should begin and end. Tags are also used to specify where images, hyperlinks, video clips, and so forth are to be located on the page.

Web pages can be created in any word processor or text editor by inserting the appropriate HTML tags into the page content. Creating complex Web pages in this manner, such as those containing tables, frames, or input forms, is a very difficult task. **Web site authoring software** (also called *Web site development software*) makes the job of creating Web pages and complete Web sites much easier. Instead of entering the HTML tags directly, most Web site authoring programs automatically generate the appropriate HTML statements when

web tutor

For a tutorial on creating and publishing a Web site, go to www.course.com/parker2002/ch10

>**Web site authoring software.** Programs used to create Web pages and complete Web sites.

options are selected from menus, toolbar buttons are clicked, or the developer otherwise specifies what the Web page should contain and look like. Using HTML and other languages to create Web pages is discussed in more detail in Chapter 13.

Though there are very basic Web development tools built into Web browsers and many types of application programs today, to build a complex or multimedia Web site a dedicated Web site authoring program should be used. Some examples of popular Web site authoring programs are *Macromedia Dreamweaver, Allaire HomeSite* (now owned by Macromedia), *Claris Home Page, Hot Metal Pro, Adobe GoLive,* and *Microsoft FrontPage* (see Figure 10-21).

Web site development programs allow you to create an entire site—not just individual pages. This allows effects, styles, backgrounds, and navigational tools to be applied to an entire site at one time, saving time and increasing consistency in one fell swoop. These programs virtually always have the capability to include such multimedia elements as Shockwave and Flash animations, JavaScript, Java applications, animated GIFs, video and audio clips, and graphics. In addition, many Web site development programs allow you to easily include forms and database connectivity for more dynamic interactions with your visitors. Once the entire site is created, the program can be used to publish the entire site onto the appropriate Web server.

Storefront Software

In addition to creating the multimedia elements and basic Web site structure, e-commerce sites frequently may use **storefront software** to create an electronic storefront to facilitate ordering merchandise through the Web site. This software can be purchased in a variety of off-the-shelf packages; *Web-based storefront software* can be used via a Web site that offers that service.

Off-the-shelf software programs are known by several different names, such as *storefront, shopping cart, e-commerce builder, auction builder,* and *Web catalog software.* The exact features of each program vary from program to program. Some require the Web site or database to be created first, and then the purchasing capability can be added to the site (creating databases is discussed in more detail in Chapter 14). Other programs can be used to create an entire e-commerce system from scratch. Some ISPs offer free shopping cart software to Web sites hosted on their servers.

Web-based storefront software, also known as a *storebuilder,* allows you to create an online store using storefront software available through a Web site. These sites belong to application service providers that are sometimes referred to as *commerce service providers.* Typically, these software programs use templates or wizards for the basic site creation, as well as providing catalog, shopping cart, and secure purchasing capabilities. Some storebuilders are available free of charge; others require a processing fee, hosting fee, or commission on the sales generated through the site. Web-based storebuilding is becoming a very common option for small businesses.

Testing the Site or Application

Testing any type of multimedia application is extremely important. Each and every navigational item needs to be selected to ensure it takes the user to the proper place in the application. The testing should take place on a variety of computers and with a disparate selection of users. Be sure to select testers with a wide range of knowledge and abilities. If possible, an observer should discretely watch the testers and take note of any place in the application that users seem confused or end up somewhere they didn't intend to go. Finished applications should also be checked for spelling and grammatical errors. Your application should appear professional, so be sure to proofread each page or screen carefully.

>**Storefront software.** Software that can be used when developing e-commerce sites to facilitate the placement of orders.

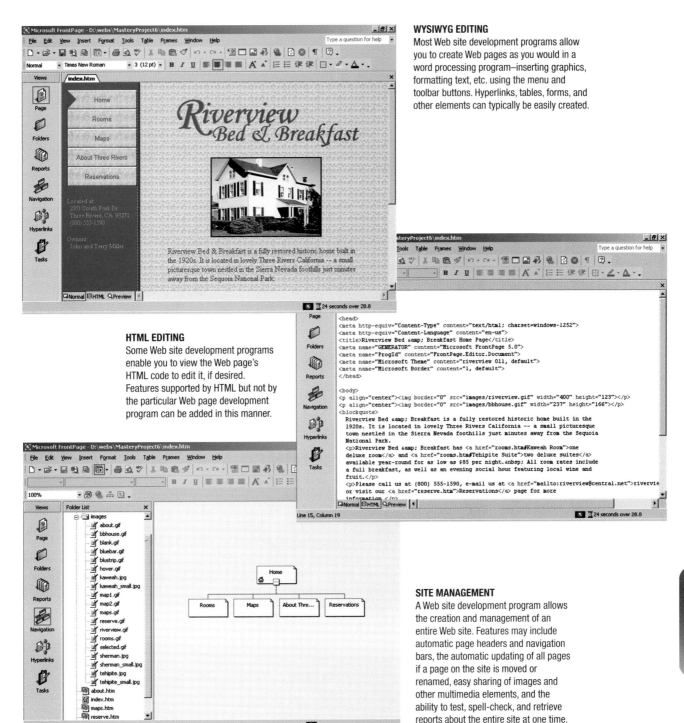

WYSIWYG EDITING
Most Web site development programs allow you to create Web pages as you would in a word processing program–inserting graphics, formatting text, etc. using the menu and toolbar buttons. Hyperlinks, tables, forms, and other elements can typically be easily created.

HTML EDITING
Some Web site development programs enable you to view the Web page's HTML code to edit it, if desired. Features supported by HTML but not by the particular Web page development program can be added in this manner.

SITE MANAGEMENT
A Web site development program allows the creation and management of an entire Web site. Features may include automatic page headers and navigation bars, the automatic updating of all pages if a page on the site is moved or renamed, easy sharing of images and other multimedia elements, and the ability to test, spell-check, and retrieve reports about the entire site at one time.

FIGURE 10-21

Web site authoring software. Web site authoring software is used to create an entire Web site, including tying together all of the multimedia elements on the site and publishing the site on the appropriate Web server.

For Web sites, you should also test the finished site for the following:

▼ *Browser and computer incompatibility*—Test your site on a variety of browsers, platforms, operating systems, and screen resolutions to ensure that your site works on as many different configurations as possible.

▼ *Download time*—Some Web site development programs indicate how quickly your pages will download over different Internet connection speeds. Remember, your goal should be 30 seconds or less for each page at the slowest conceivable connection speed (usually 28.8K or 56K).

▼ *Broken links*—Just as with other multimedia applications, you must test each and every hyperlink to make sure it goes to the correct location. Though some Web site development programs can test the site for broken links and generate a list of links that don't go to any page on the site, they can't test that the links go to the correct page on the site, so that must be done manually. Links to pages outside the site need to be tested on a regular basis to update any links to pages that have been deleted or moved, or are no longer appropriate.

After the mechanics of a Web site are tested, companies should consider subjecting their site to a "stress test." These tests are frequently performed by an outside agency and examine the capacity of the site and how many visitors and orders it can handle at one time. Though a fairly new type of service, it is important for large e-commerce sites. According to Amnon Landan, CEO of Mercury Interactive, a company that performs stress tests, the sites they test typically only handle about 20% of the traffic that the organization expects the site to handle. There are also software programs an organization can acquire to continuously monitor your site for problems and bottlenecks.

Once a site is up and running, the development process isn't over. As mentioned earlier, Web sites should be regularly updated to keep them current and interesting. Sites should also be evaluated on a regular basis to locate areas needing improvement, new problems that have become apparent, and so forth. If, at some point in time, it appears that the site needs a major overhaul, the design and development process will start over from the beginning.

THE FUTURE OF MULTIMEDIA

Though no one knows exactly what types of multimedia will be available in the future, it's a safe bet that it will be even more exciting and more embedded into everyday events than at present. As Internet users move to broadband, expect to see multimedia Web sites and television merge even more closely together. Options such as interactive TV and TV on demand (discussed in an earlier chapter) and Internet and multimedia capabilities built into Internet access devices and game boxes, such as the Sega Dreamcast 2 and Sony PlayStation 2, are all heading in that direction.

WHAT IS MULTIMEDIA?

Multimedia is the integrated use of a variety of media, such as text, graphics, video, animation, and sound. Multimedia applications are usually *interactive*. With today's fast computers and Internet connections, multimedia applications are widely found on the Internet, as well as in offline environments, such as information kiosks and ATM machines.

Chapter Objective 1:
Describe what multimedia is and some advantages and disadvantages of using it.

ADVANTAGES AND DISADVANTAGES OF USING MULTIMEDIA

One large advantage of multimedia applications is that they appeal to a wide variety of people and complement different learning styles. They also tend to hold users' interest more than single media applications. A disadvantage of multimedia is cost and the issue for Web-based applications of differing platforms and browsers, as well as slow Internet connection speeds which can hinder the usability of some multimedia content.

MULTIMEDIA ELEMENTS

Multimedia applications typically contain **text** in a variety of typefaces and appearances. Text is used to deliver content, as well as for instructions, menus, hyperlinks, etc. *Serif typefaces* are commonly used for large sections of text; *sans serif typefaces* are more frequently used with titles and headings. When a consistent text appearance is important for Web pages, the text is often rendered as a **graphic** image, so it will look the same for all users. Other types of graphics include photographs, drawings, charts, and other static images. Already created *clip art* and *stock photographs* are widely available for purchase or downloading via the Internet.

Common graphic formats include **GIF** *(Graphics Interchange Format)* and **PNG** *(Portable Network Graphics)* for line art images, and **JPEG** *(Joint Photographics Experts Group)* for photographs. Other possible formats include *TIF* for scanned images and *BMP* for Paint images.

Animation consists of a series of graphical images displayed one after the other to simulate movement. *Transitions* between pages in a presentation, as well as *Java applets, animated GIFs, Dynamic HTML (DHTL),* and *JavaScript* Web applications, are examples of animation. **Audio** includes all types of sound (music, spoken voice, sound effects, etc.), and **video** is a continuous stream of visual information captured by a series of separate images or frames. Audio, video, and graphics are frequently compressed to reduce the finished file size.

Chapter Objective 2:
Explain the difference between the following multimedia elements: text, graphics, animation, audio, and video.

MULTIMEDIA APPLICATIONS

Multimedia applications are widely found both on and off the Web. Non-Web-based applications include business presentations, reference materials, **virtual reality (VR)**, entertainment, **computer-based training (CBT),** and information kiosks. Web-based applications include **Web-based training (WBT),** entertainment, and virtual reality (VR), as well as being used to enhance Web sites.

Chapter Objective 3:
List several Web-based and non-Web-based multimedia applications.

APPS

MULTIMEDIA AND WEB SITE DESIGN

Chapter Objective 4:
Briefly describe the basic steps and principles involved with multimedia and Web site design.

When designing a multimedia Web site or other application, careful planning is essential to ensure an interesting and intuitive site that is attractive and easy to use. Web pages should also be efficient and versatile enough to be used with multiple browsers and platform configurations. Early steps in the design process include determining the intended audience, primary objectives, basic layout, and navigational structure for the site or application. Tools such as **flowcharts, page layouts,** and **storyboards** can be used during the design process.

MULTIMEDIA AND WEB SITE DEVELOPMENT

Chapter Objective 5:
Discuss the various tasks involved with multimedia and Web site development.

Once the site or application is designed, the development process can begin. Necessary tasks include creating the multimedia elements to be used in the site or application, creating the site or application itself, and testing the finished product. To create the multimedia elements, **graphics software** (such as *drawing, painting,* and *image-editing* programs), **animation software,** and *audio-* and *visual-editing* software can be used. Once the individual elements have been created, they can be inserted in the basic Web site or application created with **multimedia authoring** or **Web site authoring software.** E-commerce sites may also use **storefront software** to facilitate order placement. After the site or application has been completed, it must be thoroughly tested to ensure all features and links work, and that it is compatible with as many different types of computers, platforms, operating systems, and browsers as possible.

THE FUTURE OF MULTIMEDIA

Chapter Objective 6:
Speculate as to the format of multimedia in the future.

In the future, multimedia will likely be even more commonplace and integrated into our everyday life. Trends such as the convergence of TV and the Internet will lead us in that direction. How fast this evolves depends, in part, on how soon fast home broadband Internet access becomes the norm.

Instructions: Match each key term on the left with the definition on the right that fits best.

1. animation

2. animation software

3. audio

4. computer-based training (CBT)

5. flowchart

6. graphics

7. graphics software

8. multimedia

9. multimedia authoring software

10. page layout

11. storefront software

12. storyboard

13. text

14. video

15. virtual reality (VR)

16. Web site authoring software

17. Web-based training (WBT)

_____ A continuous stream of visual information broken into separate images or frames to be displayed one after the other to simulate the original information.

_____ A multimedia application that allows the computer to create three-dimensional views of objects, people, or locations that look like they do in the real world.

_____ A tool that can be used during the design process to illustrate how the pages in a Web site or multimedia application relate to one another.

_____ A tool that can be used during the design process to illustrate the basic layout of the home page and the rest of the pages on a Web site.

_____ A type of program used to create animations.

_____ A type of program used to create or modify images.

_____ Alphanumeric characters kept in a text, not image, format.

_____ An ordered series of sketches that can be developed during the design process of a multimedia application to illustrate what each page in the application will look like.

_____ Digital representations of photographs, drawings, charts, and other visual images.

_____ Individual instruction delivered via a computer.

_____ Individual instruction delivered via the World Wide Web.

_____ Programs designed to create multimedia applications.

_____ Programs used to create Web pages and complete Web sites.

_____ Software that can be used when developing e-commerce sites to facilitate the placement of orders.

_____ Sound, such as music, spoken voice, and sound effects.

_____ The integration of a variety of media, such as text, graphics, video, animation, and sound.

_____ The process where a series of graphical images are displayed one after the other to simulate movement.

Self-Quiz

Answers for the self-quiz appear at the end of the book.

True/False

Instructions: Circle **T** if the statement is true or **F** if the statement is false.

T F **1.** One advantage of multimedia presentations is that they are visual, and all people are visual learners.

T F **2.** Clip art images are predrawn graphics that can be inserted into multimedia applications or Web sites.

T F **3.** A Java applet can be used to add animation to a Web page.

T F **4.** Virtual reality applications can be delivered over the Web, but not in non-Web-based applications.

T F **5.** A painting program creates images by coloring pixels, so they cannot be resized without distortion or loss of quality.

Completion

Instructions: Answer the following questions.

6. The _____ graphic format is commonly used for photographs.

7. _____ is a form of distance learning where content is delivered over the Web.

8. _____ audio and video files, where the file begins playing before it has been completely downloaded, are frequently used on Web pages to make their delivery more efficient.

9. One of the first steps in designing a multimedia application or Web site is _____.

10. _____ software is commonly used to tie all of the components of a multimedia Web site together into the finished site.

Exercises

1. For each of the following descriptions, select the acronym or term from the list that follows that best matches the description. Note that all acronyms and terms will not be used.

_____ A type of animation where a series of images are displayed one after the other to simulate movement, and the entire set of images is saved together in one file.

_____ A format commonly used for audio files.

_____ A program used in conjunction with a Web browser that enables a multimedia element on the page to work.

_____ A tool frequently used during multimedia design.

   a. TIF
   b. animated GIF
   c. WBT
   d. Java applet
   e. MP3
   f. VR
   g. flowchart
   h. plug-in

2. Describe the difference between animation and video.

3. List one example of a non-Web-based multimedia application you have encountered recently. Explain whether or not you think the multimedia elements used added to the application's effectiveness.

4. List one example of a Web-based multimedia application you have encountered recently. Explain whether or not you think the multimedia elements used added to the application's effectiveness.

5. List three different types of software programs that might be used when creating a Web-based multimedia application. Explain what each program would be used for and list the name and publisher of one possible program for each type of software you selected.

For this project, form a group to investigate how you would go about building an online store using a Web-based storefront provider. Find a site that offers this service for free and begin the storebuilding process to see how it works (but don't finish the store and waste room on the site's server). Visit at least two other Web-based storefront providers and investigate their services. Prepare a summary of your group's research, including how you actually create a store, how the order, payment, and delivery are carried out, and what (if any) commissions or fees you have to pay the storebuilder site. Would the members of your group consider opening an online store using a Web-based storebuilder? If not, what method would they choose to use instead? Your group should submit this project to your instructor in the form of a short paper, not more than three pages in length.

Presentation/ Demonstration

8. **News Stream** Access to live streaming news over the Internet has expanded to beyond 4,000 sites. Each of these sites provides unique content and multimedia features. Most of the larger sites offer their own news search engines, stock quotes tools, and access to weather forecasts. For this project, present a summary of three major online news Web sites and the features they offer. Do the sites provide both local and national news? Do you have to download any special software to review stock quotes and company financial statements? Do the sites offer live streaming news in audio or video form, prerecorded streaming segments, or both? This presentation should not exceed five minutes and should make use of one or more presentation aids such as the chalkboard, handouts, overhead transparencies, or computer-based slide presentation format. You may be asked to submit a summary of the presentation to your instructor.

9. **Flash** Macromedia Flash is one of the most heavily used programs on the Web to deliver "high-impact, low-bandwidth Web sites that attract, engage, and retain site visitors." In June 2001, it was estimated that 98 percent of the Web population was already equipped with the Macromedia Flash Player. In other words, Macromedia Flash is for all practical purposes the industry standard for low-bandwidth animations delivered over the Web. For this project, form a group to learn more about the Flash program and prepare a presentation of your findings. Each member should visit the Macromedia Flash Web site, take the Web-based feature tour, and review the advertisement literature in order to become familiar with the program's capabilities. In addition, your group should determine how much this program costs and what the system requirements are to run it. Does anyone in your group have any experience with Flash or another animation program? Would anyone in your group be interested in learning this program, or is it too difficult? Does this program have any competition? If possible, the group should include a demonstration of a Flash animation located on a Web site in your presentation. This presentation should not exceed 10 minutes and should make use of one or more presentation aids such as the chalkboard, handouts, overhead transparencies, or computer-based slide presentation format. Your group may be asked to submit a summary of the presentation to your instructor.

10. **Winning a Webby** Just like winning an "Oscar" in the movie industry, you can win a "Webby" in the Web industry and it might make your site an overnight success. The Webby awards honor cyberculture in 27 categories and the winners are limited to a five-word acceptance speech. One May 2000 acceptance speech was "They said I could only...." In addition to the Webbys, many organizations offer awards for outstanding Web sites in various categories such as excellence in

design, content, browser compatibility, interactivity, and animation. When you win one of these awards, you can proudly display the Web badge (some type of graphic symbol or image) of the organization that declared your Web site a winner. The number of these Web badges seems to grow almost as fast as the Internet, but some are well recognized and offer the Web site a certain level of prestige. Some Web awards include Cyber Angels, Family-Friendly, Internet Content Rating Association, Argus Seal of Approval, Web Crawler Select, Snap Editor's Choice, and Internet Voyager 5-Star Site. For this project, form a group to research which sites won 5 of the last 27 Webby awards given, and why the Web site won the award. In addition, your group should present at least 3 Web badges that a Web site can be awarded and explain what the badge represents. For each badge, include an example of a winning Web site. This presentation should not exceed 10 minutes and should make use of one or more presentation aids such as the chalkboard, handouts, overhead transparencies, or computer-based slide presentation format. Your group may be asked to submit a summary of the presentation to your instructor.

Interactive Discussion

11. **Web Conquers All** It has been predicted that the Web will conquer all other forms of media and eventually dominate the media market. This trend is very much underway and can be seen in the print media with books and newspapers, in the radio industry with hundreds of online stations, and the television industry with live Webcasting. This prediction is based on two assertions. First, companies providing this media are profit oriented and will seek to increase revenues by using the interactive technologies available through the Web. These interactive technologies allow the media companies to develop more efficient business models that can effectively target consumers and thus generate additional revenue from increased advertising and direct sales. Second, consumers actually want the ability to control the media experience and will drive the market in this direction.

    Select one of the following positions, or make up your own, and express your point of view on the subject. Your instructor will indicate whether your response is to be posted to a class bulletin board, discussed in a class chat room, or discussed as an in-class activity. You may also be asked to submit a summary of your position and point of view to your instructor.

    a. The Web will not conquer all. Not all organizations are profit motivated and many would be reluctant to give up their traditional forms of media. Furthermore, consumers have little or no interest in controlling the media experience beyond changing the station when they are unhappy with the current content.

    b. The Web will conquer all. Media organizations are profit oriented and the opportunity for increased revenues will bring about the demise of traditional media. Besides, consumers really want to control the media experience and interact with the content.

12. **Netizen** Consider the following statement and establish your position, or point of view, on the subject. Your instructor will indicate whether your response is to be posted to a class bulletin board, discussed in a class chat room, or discussed as an in-class activity. You may also be asked to submit a summary of your position and evaluation of the statement.

    The convergence of multimedia, the Internet, and 3D software is leading toward the possibility of online virtual worlds where we can overcome the barriers of time and distance to satisfy our need for social interaction from the comfort of our own homes. With 3D modeling software we can create a visual "handle" of ourselves know as an *avatar* and visit these virtual worlds where we can shop, play games, watch movies, get an education, and interact with other avatars. The members of these virtual worlds are usually referred to as netizens who are sometimes required to apply for a tourist visa (requiring a name and e-mail address, plus possibly more information depending on the Web site) before being allowed to enter and browse the virtual environment. Our access to multimedia components such as text, graphics, animations, audio, and video components are almost unlimited and are a function of your virtual time and place. Some virtual malls are now leasing 3D stores that are strategically placed on imaginary roads that are complete with realistic textures and sounds. As our computers get more powerful and the speed at which we can connect to these virtual worlds improves, we, as humans, opt to meet our needs for entertainment, adventure, education, and social interaction, vicariously through our avatars, rather than in person.

Interactive Exercise

Designing and Creating Web Pages.   You've decided to design and create a Web site! Go to the Interactive Exercise at www.course.com/parker2002/ch10 to complete this exercise.

CHAPTER 11

E-Business and E-Commerce

LEARNING OBJECTIVES

After completing this chapter, you will be able to:

1. Explain what e-business and e-commerce are and some of their benefits and risks.

2. Describe the purpose of the following common e-business applications: EDI, ERP, EAI, CRM, and SCM.

3. Identify a variety of e-commerce business models and discuss their similarities and differences.

4. Discuss the types of Web sites that can be used to implement e-commerce.

5. List several strategies for implementing e-commerce using the Web, including some of the decisions that need to be made, the options available for accepting payments, and the process of designing and developing an effective Web site.

6. Outline some sales and marketing strategies that can be implemented using the Web.

7. Discuss some important security issues that are involved with performing financial transactions over the Internet.

The Internet and World Wide Web have greatly affected the way most of us live and do business. One of the biggest changes in the last year or two is the amount of business being transacted online. Frequently named as the fastest growing sector of the Internet economy, Web-based *e-commerce (electronic commerce)*—the act of doing business transactions over the Internet or similar technology—is redefining the way businesses operate and compete in the 21st century. It has been estimated that over 50,000 U.S. companies make some or all of their money online, and over a trillion dollars of Internet-based revenue annually is expected shortly. In addition, the Web influences offline sales, such as the scores of consumers who research purchases they eventually make offline.

This chapter initially examines the difference between *e-business* and *e-commerce* and some of the benefits and risks of using e-commerce. E-business applications, e-commerce business models, and types of e-commerce Web sites are discussed next. Among other things you learn the meaning of Internet buzz words such as "B2B" and "ERP." Then, we turn to issues a business needs to deal with as it begins to implement Web-based e-commerce. These issues include the type of business model and Web site to be used, how to handle the financial transactions generated from the site, and how to begin designing and developing an effective e-commerce Web site. The chapter closes with a discussion of sales and marketing strategies and e-commerce security issues. ■

WHAT IS E-BUSINESS AND E-COMMERCE?

E-business is the term used to describe any business with an online presence (Web site). The Web site may be used for marketing purposes, *e-procurement* (buying and selling goods and services over the Internet), servicing customers, collaborating with business partners, or otherwise using the Internet to conduct business. **E-commerce** is the term used specifically to describe performing financial transactions online. Though the terms are related, they are not interchangeable. For example, a business could have a Web presence but choose not to participate in e-commerce activities. And an individual can participate in e-commerce without being an e-business (see the How It Works box for a look at mobile e-commerce or *m-commerce*).

Though the terms *e-business* and *e-commerce* are fairly new and, today, are used in conjunction with the Internet, large corporations have been conducting e-commerce for decades using private networks. For example, the banking industry has carried out electronic funds transfers for many years. The collection of hardware, software, people, policies, and strategies used to perform and support e-commerce is referred to as an *e-commerce system*. There are many benefits and some risks involved with implementing an e-commerce system. Some of the more prominent are listed in Figure 11-1 and discussed in the next few sections. E-commerce is discussed in more detail later in this chapter.

>**E-business.** A business with an online presence. >**Electronic commerce (e-commerce).** The act of doing financial transactions over the Internet or similar technology.

how it works

Smart Vending Machines

Proponents of *m-commerce,* as in "mobile commerce," say it is what will finally lead us toward a cashless society. Though debit, credit, and check cards have helped move us in this direction, until recently it was tough to buy a soda or pay for a taxi without cash.

With m-commerce, consumers can use their mobile phone (or other wireless device, such as a pager, PDA, or WAP-enabled smart card) to pay for goods and services. The potential applications are enormous. Imagine buying a Coke with your cell phone, using your pocket PC to pay for your groceries, or using a smart tag to automatically pay for your fast-food order. Or how about your parking meter calling you up on your cell phone to ask if you want to add another hour to it while you're shopping? These activities are all part of the new mobile commerce market, estimated to soar to $200 billion by the year 2004 worldwide.

There are a few basic ways of implementing m-commerce. To buy a soda from a smart vending machine with your cell phone, for example, you would dial the number displayed on the vending machine and make your selection (see the accompanying illustration). The appropriate charge would appear on your phone bill at the end of the month. With a PDA, the charge could instead be deducted from your digital wallet. With a smart card, the amount would be deducted from the smart card balance.

Other examples of m-commerce are the Mobil Speedpass system, where a wand is waved at a gas pump to automatically pay for gasoline, and electronic toll collection, where cars can

drive the legal speed limit past an electronic toll booth and the toll is automatically deducted from their car's smart tag. Even fast-food restaurants are getting into the action. Customers at selected McDonald's restaurants can pay for their meal using a free small wand that fits on a keychain. When the wand is waved in front of an electronic sensor in the restaurants or drive-thru, the appropriate amount is deducted from the customer's Freedom-Pay account. Additional money can be added to the account either online or over the phone. Money can even be automatically transferred into the account when needed so customers are never caught without cash in their cashless account.

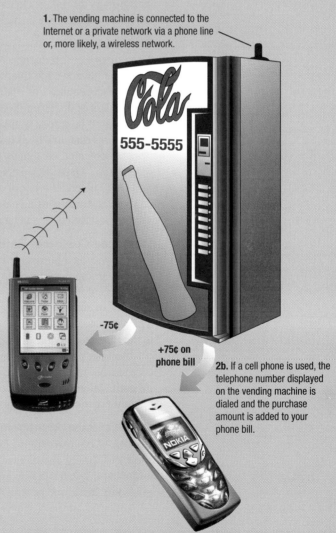

1. The vending machine is connected to the Internet or a private network via a phone line or, more likely, a wireless network.

2a. A PDA or other mobile device could either beam payment data to the vending machine, or a specific Web page could be opened to authorized payment. The amount would then typically be deducted from a digital wallet.

–75¢

+75¢ on phone bill

2b. If a cell phone is used, the telephone number displayed on the vending machine is dialed and the purchase amount is added to your phone bill.

FIGURE 11-1

Advantages and risks of e-commerce.

Advantages	Risks
To organizations • Reduced costs • Increased customer satisfaction • More effective management tools • Potentially higher sales *To customers* • Convenience • Easier comparison shopping • Higher degree of selection	• Have to have an effective, always-working Web site • Lost business, since some people will never perform online transactions • High rate of fraudulent transactions • Recurrent threat of new competitors offering lower prices

Benefits of E-Commerce

There are many benefits to both an organization and that organization's customers for implementing an e-commerce strategy. Most of these center around convenience and efficiency. A few of the most significant are listed next.

To Organizations

The primary advantages to an organization include reduced costs, increased customer satisfaction, more effective management tools, and potentially higher sales.

Reduced Costs

The primary cost reduction is due to smaller facility and staffing requirements. This is a particular advantage to Internet-only stores (frequently referred to as **dot-coms**) that don't have the expenditure of maintaining a physical storefront, like conventional **brick-and-mortar stores** do. Even though online stores need a company headquarters and possibly one or more inventory warehouses, these types of facilities are much less expensive than retail stores that may need to have a physical presence in multiple prime locations in order to reach potential customers. Many businesses have both brick-and-mortar stores and an online store. These organizations are sometimes referred to as *click-and-mortar stores.*

Other potential areas of cost reduction include eliminating middlemen and selling directly to customers, using electronic means for information disbursement and marketing to save on postage costs, and increased accuracy in order processing and pricing.

Increased Customer Satisfaction

Convenience is a big factor in determining whether or not a customer is satisfied. With a properly set up e-commerce system, the customer should find the process of shopping and obtaining information very convenient. Online stores are open *24/7* (24 hours a day/7 days a week), so customers can use the site at their convenience. They also don't have to drive to a physical location to pick up their purchases, since purchases are typically shipped directly to the customer's home or business.

Another possibility for increased customer satisfaction is the ability to send customers customized information, such as notices of specials on products they might be interested in, notification when an out-of-stock product becomes available, and updated information on their order's delivery status.

More Effective Management Tools

Because e-commerce transactions are performed electronically, the possibility of capturing an enormous variety of data exists. This data can be used in conjunction with an organization's information systems to give immediate feedback on sales and performance measures, as well as identify trends and patterns, as discussed in more detail later in the chapter.

>**Dot-com.** An Internet-only store with no physical presence. >**Brick-and-mortar store.** A conventional store with a physical presence.

Potentially Higher Sales

Because there are no geographical boundaries for e-commerce, there is enormous potential for increased sales. Instead of serving a specific geographical area, companies can now offer their goods or services worldwide. There are fewer physical restraints to growth, as well. When increased business strains the organization's sales department, instead of having to build new physical stores or other expensive, time-consuming solutions, e-commerce businesses can just add more electronic facilities (such as a more powerful server) and as many new internal employees as necessary to handle the resulting transactions.

To Customers

Benefits to customers include convenience, easier comparison shopping, a higher degree of selection, and potential cost savings.

Convenience

As already mentioned, e-commerce is a tremendous convenience for those customers who take advantage of it. They can shop from their home or office at any time of the day or night and have the products delivered to the appropriate location, usually within just a few days. If the appropriate online tools are in place, they can also check on the status of their order, track the delivery shipment, obtain reports of their past spending, and so forth.

Easier Comparison Shopping

Many customers like to comparison shop before purchasing products or signing on for certain services. With a brick-and-mortar business, this requires physically going to the store to look at the selections available, or at least calling and gathering information over the telephone. With e-commerce sites, however, information on a huge variety of products and services is available over the Internet. There are even *intelligent shopping agents* or *shopping bots* available that can gather prices, shipping, and delivery information from multiple sites for a particular product and summarize the results. Some portal pages offer this service; others are sites dedicated to this purpose, such as MySimon.com (featured in the Chapter 2 Trend box) and iBuyer.com (see Figure 11-2).

Higher Degree of Selection

Because of the enormous number of products and services available via the World Wide Web, consumers have the opportunity to shop from a much wider selection than can be provided by brick-and-mortar stores. Chances are that at least one online store will carry the item of interest, and it doesn't matter where that store is physically located.

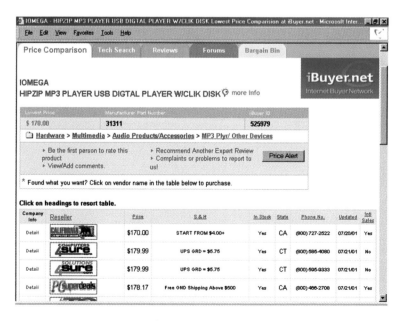

FIGURE 11-2
Shopping bots. Shopping agents can help consumers find the lowest prices on specific items they are looking for.

Are Internet Taxes on the Way?

Buying Online May Soon Cost You More

Increasingly, Americans are shopping online. When the buyer and seller are located in different states—which is often the case—the buyer can often escape without paying sales taxes. State and local governments want that to change.

Currently in the United States, there are more than 30,000 jurisdictions—states, counties, and cities—that have the authority to impose sales taxes. And each one that does would like a piece of every purchase transaction made by buyers living within its boundaries, in order to accomplish such worthy tasks as building roads, educating children, and fighting crime. In places that have sales taxes, local merchants back the states in taking a bite out of Internet commerce. Because local merchants are required to levy such taxes on consumers, they worry that un-taxed, out-of-state purchases will drive them out of business.

To a great extent, all of the furor over taxing Internet purchases is an online extension of old, offline battles. Examples abound. Consumers in New York City have for decades fled to nearby suburban New Jersey to do their clothes shopping, to avoid the onerous sales taxes on such items where they live. Also, for many years, U.S. consumers have found mail-order-catalog buying especially attractive because they similarly can avoid sales taxes.

Consumer shopping via the Internet has grown to a point where many state and local governments are getting alarmed. In 1997, only $8 billion in commerce was conducted online. Compare that with the estimated $1.6 trillion being spent on Internet commerce in 2003 (as predicted by International Data Corporation) and you can see what all the fuss is about.

The threat of Internet sales taxes has Internet merchants nervous. They fear that a free-for-all taxing environment could produce wild effects and turn consumers off of online commerce. Not to mention the logistical headaches of keeping track of how much tax you have collected for all of the possible jurisdictions.

To protect against Internet taxation being implemented without thorough review, the federal government has placed a temporary moratorium on Internet taxation. Originally intended to remain in place until the year 2001, it is expected to be extended for several more years. The idea is to give e-commerce a chance to become strongly established first, as well as to create an Internet sales taxation system that is fair and viable.

The issue has sparked controversy, and not even all consumers agree. Some worry that when a large number of people escape taxes, others wind up paying more. In the end, they feel, governments will get whatever funds they need from taxpayers, any way they can. One thing is for sure; the battle over whether to tax or not to tax will be a heated one and will likely last some time.

Online purchases. State and local governments are stepping up the pressure to charge consumers sales tax.

Potential Cost Savings

Though not all products available over the Internet are less expensive than those in their brick-and-mortar counterparts, online shoppers can frequently find items at bargain prices because of the increased number of merchants to choose from. As already mentioned, shopping bots can help locate the best buys from thousands of potential vendors. Another potential cost savings is the lack of sales tax on many online purchases. As discussed in the Trend box, however, the honeymoon period for Internet taxation may soon come to a close.

Limitations and Risks of E-Commerce

E-commerce is not without risks for an organization. For example, a business with an online presence is only accessible when its Web site is up and running. The "always open" nature of e-commerce puts enormous pressure on online businesses to have a solid, well-designed, and reliable Web presence. A Web site that isn't working properly or is simply too slow can drive potential customers away in a hurry. It is also important to realize that there are some folks who will choose to never perform financial transactions over the Internet. Without a brick-and-mortar store or some other acceptable alternative, those individuals' business can never be obtained. Similar to mail-order companies, online businesses also need to deal with the risk of fraudulent credit card transactions. One study found that Internet credit card transactions were 1,200% more likely to be fraudulent than conventional credit card transactions.

Another limitation for e-commerce companies is the ease of entry into the marketplace for competitors. While large brick-and-mortar businesses may not be threatened by a new "mom and pop" business opening in the area, small online businesses with low overheads may open up a storefront relatively cheaply and attract business away from other organizations by undercutting their prices. If the new business has a professional-looking, well-designed Web site, consumers may never realize how small or new the company is. Of course, from the perspective of the new businesses, this is an opportunity, not a risk.

Another risk is that many companies participating in e-commerce—particularly dot-coms—fail. As discussed in the Inside the Industry box, the year 2000 was a particularly bad year for dot-com companies.

For consumers, there are possible security and privacy risks, the disadvantage of not seeing and touching goods in person before purchasing them, as well as the expense of returning merchandise the consumer finds unacceptable. Some click-and-mortars eliminate this concern by allowing consumers to return merchandise they ordered online at a local store to avoid return shipping charges.

E-BUSINESS APPLICATIONS

There are numerous e-business applications and activities that can take place via the Internet. Probably the first activity to come to mind would be e-commerce, discussed in detail shortly. Though e-commerce is an important component for many e-businesses, there are other important e-business activities as well. Some of the most significant are discussed next.

web tutor

For a tutorial on e-business applications found on the Web, go to www.course.com/parker2002/ch11

Electronic Data Interchange (EDI)

Short for **electronic data interchange, EDI** refers to the transfer of data between different companies using networks, such as the Internet. EDI is a type of *interorganizational system (IOS),* which strategically links one organization's computers to the computers of key customers or suppliers. Many large companies today order sizable percentages of their supplies or raw materials through EDI.

EDI facilitates the exchange of standard business documents—such as purchase orders and invoices—from one company's computer system to the system of another company. The company doing the purchasing also often uses EDI to electronically track its orders' progress on the seller's computer system. A simplified example of how EDI might work compared to the traditional ordering processes is shown in Figure 11-3.

Some firms take EDI a step further. At giant companies like General Motors and DuPont, large suppliers of key items no longer even have to wait for purchase orders. When their suppliers see low stocks of materials on General Motors' or DuPont's computers, they automatically ship the goods and send corresponding electronic invoices.

>**Electronic data interchange (EDI).** The transfer of data between different companies using the Internet or another network.

inside the industry

The Dot-Com Fallout

The year 2000 was not good for dot-coms. With record declines in the stock market—particularly tech stocks—dot-com losses and layoffs abounded. Some dot-coms, such as eToys and Pets.com, didn't survive the fallout. Others barely hung on by a thread. Many of the companies that went under were so small that they didn't even make the news. Some were viewed as highly speculative right from the start, but even industry giants such as Amazon were affected.

To survive, failing dot-com companies are tightening their belts—particularly when it comes to marketing expenses. The 2001 Super Bowl was enlightening. Missing from the commercial lineup were 14 of the 17 dot-com companies that had shelled out big bucks for Super Bowl ads just the year before.

Part of the problem stems from the fact that many dot-com companies jumped into the business without a viable business plan. Though initially their stock may have skyrocketed as soon as they went public, companies that don't make any money have trouble staying in business. Some Web retailers simply underestimated how much infrastructure they would have to build and how much logistics work would be needed to get their e-commerce site up and running. Others just didn't have the business know-how needed—not surprising since many dot-com companies are started by young or inexperienced individuals.

As dot-coms began to go out of business, it became obvious that the bankruptcy process for dot-coms is different than for conventional businesses. Questions as to what a company with no inventory, property, or substantial staff can claim as an asset, as well as what dollar value can be placed on such resources as domain names and customer lists, have yet to be answered. Many of these companies simply didn't have the kind of assets

necessary to support a recovery. Instead of filing for reorganization under Chapter 11, Chapter 7—which is for liquidation—is the only option for some.

Though dot-com failure greatly affects investors, some view the shakeup as an opportunity. In much of the year 2001, tech stocks were selling for a bargain price. Some view the loss of the weakest members of the e-commerce community—while devastating for them—to be good for the industry as a whole. Consequently, the dot-coms that are able to remain in business will, hopefully, have a stronger base and the experience necessary to survive the next dot-com rollercoaster.

In addition to traditional EDI activities, new types are expected as electronic document submission becomes a more acceptable business practice. Facilitating this trend is the acceptance of **digital signatures** as legal signatures, based on the Electronic Signatures in Global and National Commerce Act of 2000. According to this federal law, online contracts have the same legal force as equivalent paper contracts. In addition to allowing companies to computerize the process of signing contracts for buying and selling products and services, digital signatures affect e-commerce from the consumer's standpoint. The law enables consumers to purchase cars or items that require a sales contract, get life insurance, or take out a mortgage without having to sign and mail paper documents. As discussed in Chapter 15, digital signatures use sophisticated encryption techniques to authenticate

>**Digital signature.** A unique digital code that can be attached to an e-mail message or document to guarantee the identity of the sender.

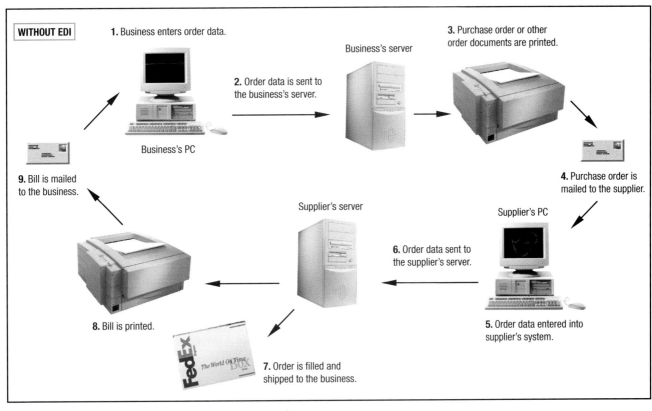

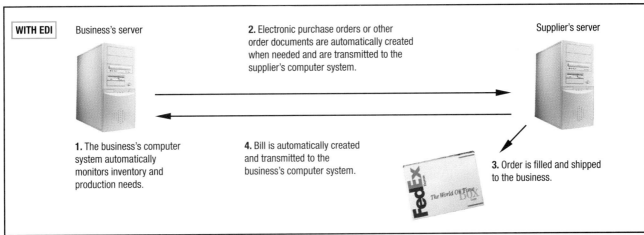

electronic documents. For example, the onSign digital signature shown in Figure 11-4 that can be inserted into Microsoft Word documents or e-mail messages changes its appearance if the document was altered after the digital signature was applied.

Enterprise Resource Planning (ERP) and Enterprise Application Integration (EAI)

Enterprise resource planning (ERP) is a special type of large, integrated system that ties together all types of a business's *(enterprise's)* activities, such as planning, manufacturing, sales, marketing, distribution, customer service, and finance. Instead of each department

> **FIGURE 11-3**
>
> **EDI.** Electronic data interchange (EDI) allows automated document processing and exchange, as well as automated ordering of parts and supplies as a business's products are being manufactured. Many EDI systems use multiple suppliers.

>**Enterprise resource planning (ERP).** A large, integrated system that ties together all a business's activities.

◆ **FIGURE 11-4**

Digital signatures. This digital signature changes its appearance to indicate whether or not the signed document was altered in any way after the signature was applied.

having its own computer system, as in the past, an ERP system combines them into a single, integrated application so the various departments can more easily share information and communicate with each other.

Today's ERP applications are commonly put on the Web so users inside and outside of the company can get easy access to ERP-generated data (refer to Figure 12-6 in Chapter 12). When information from an ERP or other type of internal system is exchanged between different applications and between organizations, it is called **enterprise application integration (EAI).** EAI tools can respond to and initiate events from multiple third-party applications and act as a common integration point for all of an organization's critical business processes. EAI is beginning to be viewed as a critical e-business tool, because it allows an organization to quickly extend any and all of its administrative systems to customers, suppliers, and other business partners over the Internet. Because of the importance of ERP and the way it ties together virtually all e-business applications, the terms *ERP* and *e-business* are beginning to be used interchangeably.

Customer Relationship Management (CRM)

All of a company's customer service programs together make up its **customer relationship management (CRM)** system. The goal of a CRM system is to build relationships with customers to increase customer satisfaction and loyalty, which, in turn, will lead to increased profits. CRM is an essential component of an e-commerce system and the use and improvement of CRM systems are growing—worldwide revenues in the CRM services markets are expected to exceed $125 billion by 2004. A CRM system can:

▼ Enable an organization's marketing department to generate quality leads for their sales teams.

▼ Assist an organization in improving sales and sales management.

▼ Allow the formation of individualized relationships with customers, with the aim of improving customer satisfaction and maximizing profits.

The Internet has created new ways to interact with and understand customers, which can improve customer service. Common Internet-enabled CRM (sometimes called *e-CRM*) activities include *data mining* (analyzing data collected from Web site visitors, as discussed later in this chapter); tracking Web site activity to identify customers and their needs; setting up product information and technical assistance on the Web site; providing order tracking; notifying customers by e-mail about product upgrades, specials, and service reminders; and so forth.

Supply Chain Management (SCM)

Supply chain management (SCM) is the oversight of materials, information, and finances as they move from the original supplier to the consumer. Its goal is to deliver the right product to the right place, at the right time, and at the right price. An effective supply chain management system shares information upstream to the organization's suppliers and downstream to the organization's customers, reduces inventory, and increases profits.

Three items flow through an organization's supply chain management system. The *product flow* includes the movement of goods from the supplier to the customer, or from the customer back to the supplier in the form of returned items. The *information flow* involves

further exploration

For links to further information about CRM software, go to www.course.com/parker2002/ch11

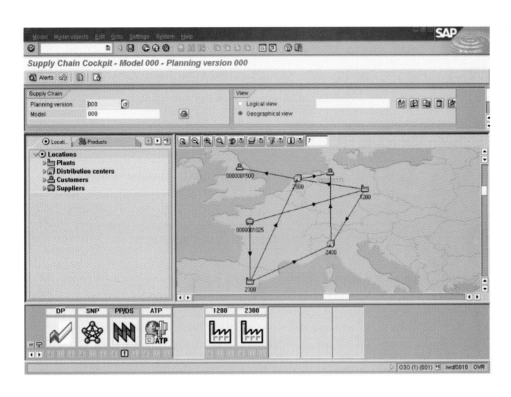

▶ **FIGURE 11-5**
Supply chain management software can help a business design, build, and run a successful supply chain.

processing orders and updating the order/delivery status. The *financial flow* consists of credit and payment information.

Related concepts are *value chain management* and *just-in-time systems,* discussed next. Most supply chain software (see Figure 11-5) ties in with a company's ERP system.

Value Chain Management

The *value chain* concept views a business or a network of businesses as a chain of business activities that add value to the resulting products or services. **Value chain management** is the process of maximizing the flow of products, services, and information from raw materials to the final consumer through a value-added network of suppliers. Each organization adds value to the product or service as it passes through the supply chain. Value chain management software can help companies find better ways to manufacture and distribute products by integrating the different areas of the value chain.

Just-in-Time (JIT) Systems

Just-in-time (JIT) systems are used in manufacturing to eliminate waste. With a just-in-time system, inventory, production resources, and finished products are limited to the right number at the right time as required to fill orders. By bringing production rates in line with market demand, JIT increases productivity and work performance and saves inventory and facility costs. Disadvantages include potential lost sales or delayed shipments if materials are unavailable due to supplier problems, defective materials, or materials ruined during manufacturing, because no extra materials are on hand in inventory.

The JIT concept is not new—it was introduced in Japan decades ago. The recent integration of the Internet with manufacturing and supply systems, however, has allowed just-in-time systems to be implemented on a much wider scale.

further exploration

For links to further information about SCM software, go to www.course.com/parker2002/ch11

E-Commerce

As already discussed, e-commerce involves performing financial transactions online. These transactions include, but are not limited to, buying and selling goods and services. E-commerce business models and types of Web sites are discussed next. Strategies for implementing effective e-commerce are covered later in this chapter.

E-COMMERCE BUSINESS MODELS

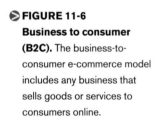

web tutor

For a tutorial on e-commerce business models for the Web, go to www.course.com/parker2002/ch11

A company's policies, operations, and technology define its **business model.** In essence, a company's business model describes how the company generates revenue. There are a number of standard *e-commerce business models,* including *business to consumer (B2C), business to business (B2B), consumer to consumer (C2C),* and *business to government (B2G).* Some of the most commonly used models are discussed next.

Business to Consumer (B2C)

With the **business-to-consumer (B2C) model,** businesses sell goods or services to individual consumers. The B2C model was one of the first major types of e-commerce business models to be defined and implemented using the Web. Some examples of B2C businesses include Amazon.com, L.L. Bean, Walmart.com, and Polo.com (see Figure 11-6). These businesses can be Internet-only stores, or click-and-mortar stores with both online and traditional storefronts.

Essentially, any business that sells goods or services online to consumers is a B2C business. For instance, service-oriented B2C sites include distance learning programs and online banking. Though initially expected to be the most prominent type of e-commerce business model, revenues from the *business-to-business (B2B)* model (discussed next) are now expected to far surpass the B2C marketplace. For example, one estimate puts 2004 B2C and B2B revenue at $204 million and $3.2 trillion, respectively.

FIGURE 11-6

Business to consumer (B2C). The business-to-consumer e-commerce model includes any business that sells goods or services to consumers online.

>**Business model.** A description of how a company does business, such as its policies, operations, and technology.
>**Business-to-consumer (B2C) model.** An e-commerce model where a business provides goods or services to consumers.

Business to Business (B2B)

Business-to-business (B2B) applications include any type of e-commerce transaction taking place between two businesses. B2B revenue is increasing and expected to continue to grow tremendously in the next few years. Several different estimates project 2004 B2B revenue in the United States alone to be over $3 trillion (compared to about $200 million for B2C). Worldwide B2B revenue is expected to exceed $6 trillion by 2004.

Many B2B activities focus on exchanging business information, such as to facilitate a business's supply chain. Others involve procuring goods and services needed for normal business activities.

Consumer to Consumer (C2C)

The **consumer-to-consumer (C2C)**—sometimes referred to as the *person-to-person* or *P2P*—business model almost solely consists of consumer *auctions* where consumers sell products to other consumers. With millions of products for sale every day, eBay (shown in Figure 11-9 later in this chapter) is one of the largest C2C e-commerce businesses today.

Business to Government (B2G)

With U.S. government spending exceeding $500 billion per year with no signs of slowing down, **business-to-government (B2G)** organizations are becoming more prominent. These organizations (see Figure 11-7) sell products and services to local, state, and federal government buyers.

In general, the government sector has been slower to embrace online buying than the private sector. Part of the reason may have been the preoccupation with *Y2K (Year 2000)* problems during the last few years. This may change, however, as a result of the recent *e-government initiative* geared toward shifting government procurement online. Though online bidding is likely to become a large part of the B2G system, many B2G businesses are finding a business niche supplying the millions of dollars worth of items purchased annually on items with prices too small to require a bid.

Related B2G activities include some states allowing citizens to make payments online, such as paying taxes, renewing driver's licenses, and so forth. This is sometimes referred to as *C2G* or *customer-to-government* e-commerce. The federal government's new Pay.gov Web site shown in Figure 11-7 is expected to allow transactions at the federal level.

Intermediary Hubs

Companies that follow the **intermediary hub model**—also called the *brokerage model*—don't sell goods or services directly to others, but instead bring buyers and sellers (usually both businesses) together within a specific industry or business process. The Internet has greatly eliminated the need for traditional intermediaries or middlemen—a trend called *disintermediation*. For example, individuals can now bypass a travel agent and purchase airline tickets directly from an airline online. New types of intermediaries are emerging as e-commerce evolves, however. This trend is called *reintermediation*. The use of these new types of intermediaries—sometimes referred to as *e-marketplaces*—can help businesses save time and money.

Some intermediaries bring an individual buyer and seller together. Others—called *buyer aggregators*—combine buyers so they can buy as a group and receive volume pricing to better compete with larger organizations. In either case, intermediary hubs usually receive a transaction fee from the seller, frequently based on the dollar amount of the sale.

further exploration

For links to further information about B2B Web sites, go to www.course.com/parker2002/ch11

APPS

>**Business-to-business (B2B) model.** An e-commerce model where a business provides goods or services to other businesses.
>**Consumer-to-consumer (C2C) model.** An e-commerce model where a consumer provides goods or services to other consumers.
>**Business-to-government (B2G) model.** An e-commerce model where a business provides goods and services to government organizations.
>**Intermediary hub model.** An e-commerce model where a business brings buyers and sellers together, instead of directly selling goods or services.

FIGURE 11-7

Business to government (B2G). B2G sites, such as the eFederal.com site shown here, sell products and services to local, state, and federal government organizations. Other sites, such as Pay.gov, allow citizens to pay various taxes, fees, and take care of other financial business. This latter type of site is sometimes referred to as a C2G site.

Intermediaries that provide additional services, such as payment settlement or order fulfillment services, are sometimes referred to as *metamediaries.* Two specific types of intermediary hubs are *vertical hubs* and *horizontal hubs.*

▼ *Vertical hubs* match buyers and sellers within a specific industry. Some vertical hubs offer more information and services than just facilitating purchases or exchanges; these sites are becoming known as *vertical portals* or *vortals.* Vortals typically provide news, research and statistics, discussion forums, newsletters, online tools, and other industry-specific services.

▼ *Horizontal hubs,* sometimes called *functional hubs,* focus on providing the same type of products or services or automating the same business process across different industries—a site that specializes in used office equipment or energy management, for example.

Some intermediaries (see Figure 11-8) match buyers and sellers within a specific industry and a specific product or service—essentially functioning as both a vertical and horizontal hub.

The term *intermediary hub* is generally used to refer to B2B transactions, though there are also other types of Web sites that closely fit this model. Some examples that involve consumers are *online auction sites* (where buyers bid for goods sold by sellers) and *financial brokerages* (for transactions such as buying and selling stock). These types of sites are discussed shortly.

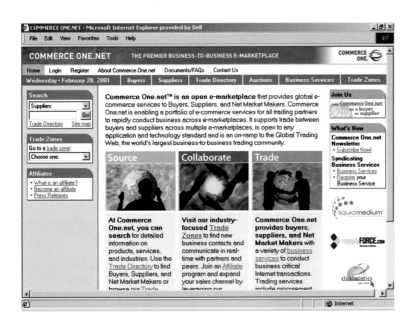

FIGURE 11-8

Intermediary hubs. Vertical hubs match buyers and sellers within a specific industry; horizontal hubs match buyers and sellers for a specific type of product or service. Some intermediaries—like the example shown here—function as both types of hubs.

TYPES OF E-COMMERCE WEB SITES

There is a variety of types of Web sites used for e-commerce activities. Some of the most widely used are manufacturer and *e-tailer* Web sites, *e-malls,* and brokerage sites.

Manufacturer and E-Tailer Web Sites

Both manufacturers and online retailers—often called **e-tailers**—can sell directly to customers. The customers may be consumers, businesses, or the government. Web sites that sell goods online are often referred to as *electronic storefronts.*

Most often, these sites feature an online catalog from which items are selected, and orders can be placed directly at the site. One example of an e-tailer—Ralph Lauren's Polo.com Web site—was illustrated in Figure 11-6. Increasingly, manufacturers are leaning toward not selling products directly on their sites, because of the conflict of interest with retail partners. To avoid this problem, many manufacturers are focusing on product information and customer service, leaving the actual selling of their products to their online and offline retailers.

E-Malls

Electronic malls or **e-malls** are collections of e-tailers organized into a virtual mall. There is usually a directory of some sort to help visitors select the online stores they would like to visit. Some e-malls assist businesses with creating a virtual storefront within the mall; others require the storefront to already be in existence and allow access to e-mall visitors through the e-mall structure. E-malls generate revenue by charging monthly "rent," charging a commission on the sales made through the online stores, or some combination of both.

Brokerage and Auction Sites

Brokerage sites bring buyers and sellers together and facilitate transactions. Instead of selling products or services directly to an individual or business, brokerage sites earn revenue in the form of commissions on sales made via the site. Three examples of brokerage sites are discussed next and illustrated in Figure 11-9.

further exploration

For links to further information about Web-based malls, go to www.course.com/parker2002/ch11

>**E-tailer.** An online retailer. >**E-mall.** A collection of e-tailers organized together into a virtual mall. >**Brokerage site.** A type of Web site used to bring buyers and sellers together to facilitate transactions, such as online stock trading and exchanging goods, services, and commodities.

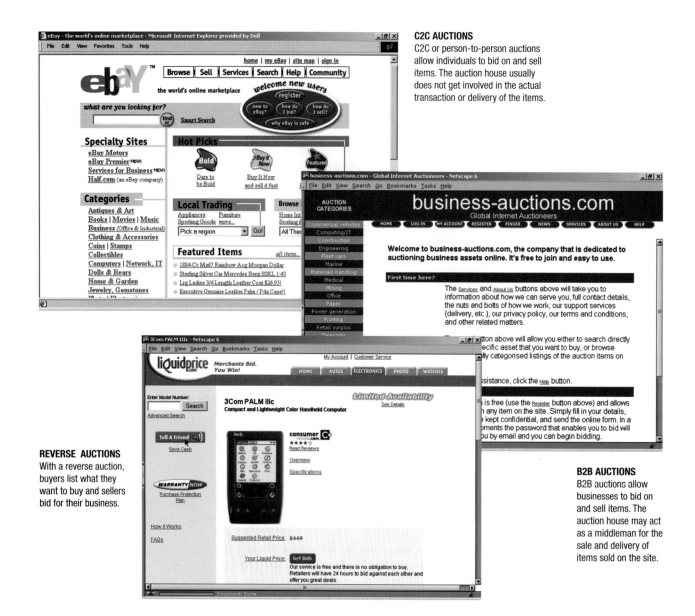

C2C AUCTIONS
C2C or person-to-person auctions allow individuals to bid on and sell items. The auction house usually does not get involved in the actual transaction or delivery of the items.

REVERSE AUCTIONS
With a reverse auction, buyers list what they want to buy and sellers bid for their business.

B2B AUCTIONS
B2B auctions allow businesses to bid on and sell items. The auction house may act as a middleman for the sale and delivery of items sold on the site.

⮞ **FIGURE 11-9**

Online auction sites.

Different types of auction sites include person-to-person (C2C) auctions, business-to-business (B2B) auctions, and reverse auctions.

Online Auctions

Person-to-person **online auction sites,** such as eBay (shown in Figure 11-9), provide individuals with a structured medium for selling goods and services to other individuals. These sites provide standardized rules so all bidders are treated equally. Many sites also collect comments about buyers and sellers from individuals to help others decide whether or not they want to do business with a particular buyer or seller. For a review of how an online auction works, refer to the How It Works box in Chapter 9.

An auction site usually obtains revenue when the items are initially listed for sale, as well as when the successful bidder purchases the item. For example, listing an item on eBay costs 30 cents to $3.30, depending on the opening bid, plus 1.25 to 5 percent of the final selling price. Though these auctions are designed for C2C transactions, some small businesses also sell their products at consumer auction sites, either in addition to, or instead of, maintaining an e-commerce Web site.

>**Online auction site.** A Web site where buyers bid on items and the highest bidder after a particular time period is allowed to buy the item.

In addition to person-to-person (C2C) auction sites, there are B2B auction sites designed for business-to-business auctions, and **reverse auctions** where buyers specify what they want and suppliers bid for the buyers' business. With a reverse auction, the buyer is sometimes allowed to select from all bids received (as on the LiquidPrice site illustrated in Figure 11-9); on some sites, the lowest bid automatically wins.

A similar type of site is the *dynamic pricing site.* Instead of a formal auction with a specific ending time and an automatic winner, these sites—such as the well-known Priceline.com—allow buyers to bid on items or services listed for sale and then the seller decides whether or not to accept each offer on an individual basis.

Financial Brokerages

Online stock trading (illustrated in Figure 9-15 in Chapter 9) is one example of a *financial brokerage site.* Other activities include buying and selling bonds, futures, and options. Brokerage companies generate revenue by charging commissions or transactions fees for each activity.

Market Exchanges

With a *market exchange,* organizations with goods or services to sell list those resources on the exchange site, which assists in matching up potential buyers to the sellers. Like a financial broker, the market exchange earns a fee for each transaction it facilitates. When commodities, such as natural resources and raw goods, are being sold, the term *commodity brokerage* is sometimes used. Common resources sold in this manner include energy, cattle, chemicals, and metals. These sites often specialize in a specific category of resources, such as the chemical exchange site shown in Figure 11-10. When these types of sites involve business-to-business transactions, they are commonly called *intermediary hubs,* as discussed earlier in this chapter.

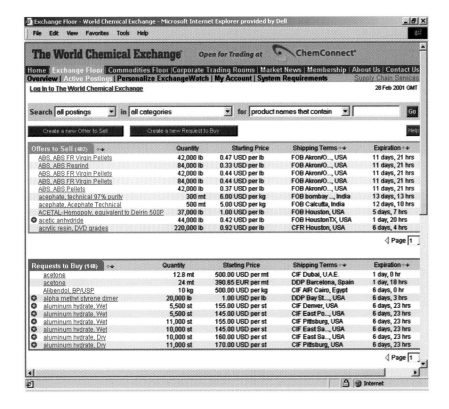

FIGURE 11-10
Market exchanges.

>**Reverse auction.** An auction where sellers bid for the a buyer's business; generally the seller with the lowest bid after a particular time period is allowed to sell the item to that particular buyer.

1. Select one or more appropriate business models and types of Web sites.

2. Select the desired e-commerce/ e-business applications.

3. Determine how to handle the electronic financial transactions generated at the site.

4. Design and develop an effective Web site.

5. Implement appropriate sales and marketing strategies.

> **FIGURE 11-11**

Implementing Web-based e-commerce. Implementing a Web-based e-commerce system usually involves the five steps listed here.

web tutor

For a tutorial on e-commerce implementation strategies, go to www.course.com/parker2002/ch11

IMPLEMENTING WEB-BASED E-COMMERCE

Several factors should be considered when an organization decides to use Web-based e-commerce. These include the type of Web site and software to be used and the means of handling financial transactions. Strategies for sales and marketing, as well as security issues, should also be considered. These issues are discussed in the remainder of this chapter.

Five basic steps are typically followed when implementing a Web-based e-commerce system. These steps are listed in Figure 11-11 and discussed next. Some companies perform some or all of these steps themselves; others hire a firm specializing in e-commerce implementation to carry out these tasks for them. Because the fine details involved with developing a Web-based e-commerce system are beyond the scope of this book, this discussion focuses on the general tasks involved in this process.

Step 1: Selecting Appropriate Business Models and Types of Web Sites

The first step a company should do is evaluate its business plan and determine which business models are currently being used and which models it would like to use with the new e-commerce system. These business models (B2B, B2C, intermediary hub, and so on) are not necessarily mutually exclusive. For example, one business could sell both to businesses and to end consumers.

Next, the company should decide what type of Web site it would like to use (e-tailer, auction site, exchange site, etc.). Just as with business models, some companies can choose to implement more than one type of site, though often multiple site models are phased in slowly. For example, Amazon.com was an e-tailer site long before it added its auction capabilities. When selecting business and Web site models, it is important to realize that some e-commerce business model features are protected by trademark law. For example, the buyer-driven commerce concept and functionality of Priceline.com and the one-click ordering method of Amazon.com are legally protected and cannot be used without permission.

Step 2: Selecting the Desired E-Commerce/ E-Business Applications

In addition to determining the desired business models and types of Web sites, a company should decide which e-commerce applications will be performed, such as online selling or buying, EDI, ERP, CRM, SCM, and so forth. Once the applications have been determined, the necessary software to implement those applications can be considered. Common vendors for e-business software include SAP, PeopleSoft, IBM, i2, and Oracle. Any specialty e-business or e-commerce software to be used is typically finalized during the Web site design process, discussed shortly.

Step 3: Determining How to Handle Electronic Financial Transactions

Successfully performing electronic financial transactions is the cornerstone of any e-commerce site. Therefore, a business should give careful thought as to which payment options it should offer, based on the type of site and the type of customers involved. The options range from standard credit cards to payment accounts to smart cards. Some of the most common ways of implementing electronic funds transfers for payment processing are discussed next. Typically, an e-commerce site would employ more than one of the following options.

Credit Card Processing

Credit card processing is the first thing that comes to mind when considering online payments. Though some people are hesitant to send their credit card information over the Internet, it is by far the most common payment method used for online purchases. Though it is possible to run an online business without accepting credit cards, for most B2C e-commerce sites, it is essential.

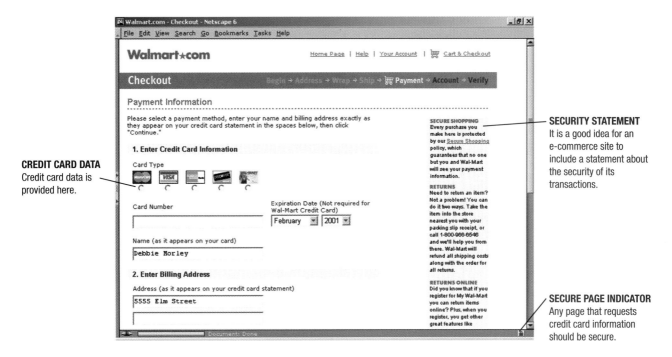

CREDIT CARD DATA
Credit card data is
provided here.

SECURITY STATEMENT
It is a good idea for an
e-commerce site to
include a statement about
the security of its
transactions.

SECURE PAGE INDICATOR
Any page that requests
credit card information
should be secure.

> **FIGURE 11-12**
Using credit cards online.
Most sites have a location on
their checkout page to supply
credit card data.

In order to accept credit cards, a business typically opens an *e-commerce merchant account,* also called an *Internet merchant account.* This account—issued through a bank—transfers money from the issuing credit card company to the merchant account each time an online transaction takes place. The bank usually is paid a monthly fee, plus a transaction fee or commission for each credit card sale. Internet merchant accounts can be set up at a traditional bank with an online presence or through a company that specializes in electronic funds transfers, such as CyberCash.

If a business is set up to accept credit cards online, its order form will include a place to type a credit card number (see Figure 11-12). As discussed previously, order forms should always be set up as secure Web pages and it is good practice to include a statement about it being a secure page to reassure your customers, as shown on the Walmart.com checkout page in Figure 11-12. Once the order form is completed and submitted, the credit card transaction is processed similarly to any other credit card transaction.

To avoid losing business to customers who don't feel comfortable sending credit card information over the Internet, many businesses include a toll-free number that can be used to place orders, if the customer prefers. To help increase consumer confidence, many credit card companies offer $0 liability for online purchases instead of the standard $50 liability, in an attempt to encourage skeptical shoppers to use a credit card for e-commerce transactions. In addition, it is becoming increasingly common for credit card companies to issue cardholders private codes or disposable account numbers to use with their credit card account to allow them to purchase online goods anonymously. Whenever desired, a new code or account number can be requested (and the old code or number cancelled) without having to change the credit card number. Some businesses may choose to include a mailing address where checks and money orders can be sent, if preferred.

Online Checks and Online Payment Transfers

Payment methods that transfer money from a buyer's checking account, credit card account, or online payment account have become increasingly popular for small business's transactions—especially for online auction payments. These options are commonly referred to as *digital cash.*

APPS

Online Checks

An **online check** works as a paper check does, except that the check is created on a Web page and the appropriate bank account and routing information is supplied, along with the payee and payer information (see the sample online check in Figure 11-13). Online checks transfer money directly from a checking account and are significantly faster than waiting for conventional checks to be received through the mail. Consequently, using an online check instead of a conventional check speeds up the delivery process, because the waiting period for the check to clear is reduced.

Online Payment Accounts

As discussed in Chapter 9, **online payment accounts** allow individuals to deposit funds from their checking accounts into the payment account or to charge payments to their credit cards. In either case, when an item is purchased at an online store or auction, funds are sent from the payment account to the recipient after a password or other verification process is completed. The funds are then deducted from the payment account. The recipient typically collects the money by logging onto the online payment service's Web site. While there are usually no fees for either the buyer or the seller on personal transactions, online stores usually pay a nominal fee (less than 2% of the sale up to a maximum of $10, for instance) for each online sale. This fee is typically less than most credit card transaction fees.

One of the leading online payment companies is PayPal, shown in Figure 11-13. As shown, a user first sets up an account and deposits funds, and can then transfer money from that account to anyone else's account using the recipient's e-mail address. Alternatively, he or she can have the sent funds charged to a credit card. Services such as PayPal and eBay's Billpoint are extremely popular with online auction sellers (refer to the bottom screen in Figure 11-13), because it is a fast, safe way to finalize auction payments.

Many online payment accounts can be used to send funds to anyone for any reason, not just to settle an online purchase.

Other Types of Digital Cash

Other forms of digital cash include *virtual* (online) *gift certificates, InternetCash cards,* and *Flooz.* Typically, these payment methods occur completely electronically, identified and secured with a login name or password. However, some—like InternetCash cards—can be purchased in physical form to be more easily given to others, such as college students to use for online purchases.

These types of digital cash are usually limited to specific Internet merchants. E-commerce businesses should determine which (if any) of these other types of digital cash they wish to accept on their Web sites.

Smart Cards

Another type of electronic funds transfer method is the **smart card,** discussed in earlier chapters. Though perhaps the biggest potential for e-commerce smart card use is with point-of-sale card readers installed on vending machines, inside taxis, and other locations where cash transactions take place (as illustrated in this chapter's How It Works box), smart cards are also used for online purchases. As discussed in Chapter 4 and illustrated in Figure 4-20, smart cards have an embedded computer chip that holds more information than the magnetic strip on the back of a credit card. Unlike a magnetic strip, the information in the chip can be updated when appropriate. For e-commerce purposes, the smart card stores some amount of prepaid money and is read by a smart card reader attached to the buyer's PC as an external device or built into a keyboard or pointing device. Advantages to

>**Online check.** An electronic check written and submitted via the Internet. >**Online payment account.** A type of payment account accessed via the Internet used to make electronic payments to other, either from funds deposited into the account or by charging the appropriate amount to a credit card. >**Smart card.** A credit-card-sized piece of plastic containing a chip and other circuitry into which data can be stored.

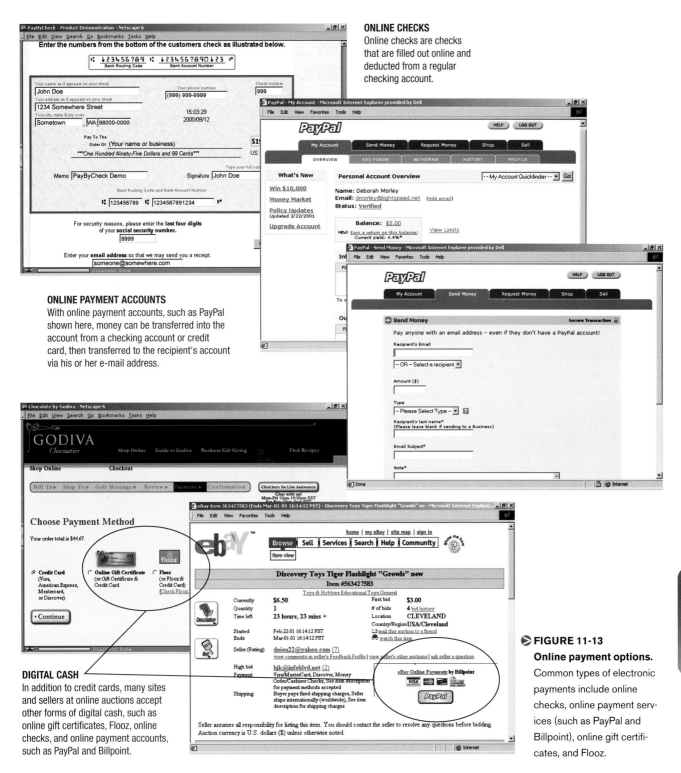

ONLINE CHECKS
Online checks are checks that are filled out online and deducted from a regular checking account.

ONLINE PAYMENT ACCOUNTS
With online payment accounts, such as PayPal shown here, money can be transferred into the account from a checking account or credit card, then transferred to the recipient's account via his or her e-mail address.

DIGITAL CASH
In addition to credit cards, many sites and sellers at online auctions accept other forms of digital cash, such as online gift certificates, Flooz, online checks, and online payment accounts, such as PayPal and Billpoint.

> **FIGURE 11-13**
> **Online payment options.**
> Common types of electronic payments include online checks, online payment services (such as PayPal and Billpoint), online gift certificates, and Flooz.

consumers for using smart cards include a limited amount of liability, since the card contains a preset amount of money, and the password protection that can be used with some smart cards. Advantages to merchants include a low charge-back rate for fraudulent charges as compared to credit cards and lower transaction fees. Smart cards can also contain *digital signatures* for use with transactions that require one.

The Campus Close-Up box takes a look at the growing use of smart cards on college campuses.

campus close-up

Penn State ID+ Smart Cards

At Pennsylvania State University, the traditional school ID card has become much more than just an ID card. Built into the card is a chip that can hold "LionCash"—digital cash values loaded onto the card. The smart card can then be used in designated laundry, vending, and copy machines, as well as a variety of retail stores and restaurants located both on and off campus. When the cash stored in the card is used up, the card can be reloaded at a card value center using cash or a credit card.

In addition to the chip, the Penn State ID+ card also contains a magnetic stripe. The card can be used to identify students for exams and meal service, and provides access to secure areas, such as labs and residence halls. It even can be used as a long-distance phone card and ATM card.

Smart card ID systems like this are not unique on college campuses today. More than 40 universities across the country have either switched to or augmented their magnetic stripe cards with smart card technology. The convenience of smart ID cards is a good fit with college students. They need to carry it around anyway and can buy lunch, a soda, or make copies without having to worry about how much cash they have on hand.

And the storage capability of the chip on the typical smart card—up to 500 times more than traditional magnetic stripe cards and growing all the time will lead to new applications being created for college smart cards in the near future. Possibilities include using the card to access school records, check test scores, register for classes, tally customer loyalty points at stores and restaurants, store medical information, and make travel arrangements—not to mention online shopping. Using any computer with Internet access and a smart-card reader, students could even access their school information from anywhere in the world.

The biggest drawback of smart cards is security, since losing a preloaded card is the same as losing cash. However, colleges report that card loss is generally fairly low. Because of the variety of uses for the card, students tend to take them with them everywhere they go and keep good track of them. And when a lost card is turned in, remarkably it usually has the cash value still on it.

The Penn State University ID+ card can be used for a wide variety of on and off campus activities.

Digital Wallets

Digital wallets (sometimes referred to as *e-wallets*) offer customers a convenient way of storing purchasing information, such as an online payment account number, smart card information, Web site passwords, a digital signature, and shipping and billing information. There are independent digital wallets, such as the First USA digital wallet shown in Figure 11-14. In addition, some sites offer a digital wallet for use with that site and digital wallets are becoming integrated in Web browsers and operating systems.

Digital wallets are accepted by a variety of vendors and allow the customers' shipping and billing information to be automatically supplied when they reach the checkout page of an online store. E-commerce sites wanting to offer their customers digital wallet services need to decide whether to accept an existing type of digital wallet or offer a custom digital wallet just for their particular site.

>**Digital wallet.** An encrypted electronic file that holds information to speed up online purchase transactions, such as electronic payment, billing, and shipping information.

Special Considerations for B2B Financial Transactions

Though some of the payment methods already discussed can be used with B2B financial transactions, due to the size of B2B purchases, some other considerations are often necessary.

B2B Transaction Processing

Though some of the companies mentioned earlier—such as CyberCash—offer merchant services, larger businesses may benefit from using an electronic payment company specializing in *business-to-business transaction processing* instead. These companies—a type of horizontal intermediary hub—usually allow merchants to customize their payment-processing plans to fit their needs. They commonly offer many of the following services:

▼ Credit card, debit card, checks, and digital cash settlement

▼ Credit checking for new customers

▼ Online expense tracking

▼ Electronic billing

▼ Payment settlement services that are compatible with ERP systems

▼ Consolidation and reconciliation of business transactions, such as order processing, invoicing, and settlement

▼ Secure storefront hosting

Instead of a complete payment-processing system, some companies may opt to use an *online escrow company* to handle their B2B and B2G monetary transactions. Instead of transferring money directly to the seller, the buyer transfers money to the escrow company, which holds onto the money until it is notified by the buyer that the merchandise was received. At that point, the money is released to the seller.

Order-Fulfillment Companies

Order-fulfillment companies (sometimes also called *e-fulfillment companies*) are companies that provide a distribution network for merchants who can't, or choose not to, process their own orders. Though these companies can be used with all e-commerce models, they are most commonly used for B2B and B2G transactions. Because of their higher volume, these transactions may be difficult for a small merchant to warehouse and process alone.

An order-fulfillment company's Web site is shown in Figure 11-15. Some of the services such a company may offer include the following:

▼ *E-fulfillment strategic planning*—consulting and development services in such areas as the business's supply chain, database, and e-commerce Web site.

▼ *Integration with existing systems*—seamless integration with the business's e-commerce site. Ideally the order fulfillment system is integrated with the business's existing ERP system.

▼ *Order management*—real-time online ordering, ideally integrated with purchasing and inventory services.

▼ *Distribution services*—services such as shipping, inventory management, and returns processing.

▼ *Customer relationship management services*—a professional customer response system that is integrated with the distribution process to provide such services as order tracking and designed to help build effective customer relations.

▼ *Marketing tools*—reports and other tools to assist in planning and forecasting for the future.

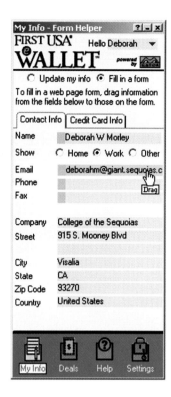

◐ FIGURE 11-14

Digital wallets. Digital wallets can hold billing, payment, and shipping information for fast online shopping transactions. This wallet allows the contents to be dragged to the appropriate locations on an onscreen order form.

APPS

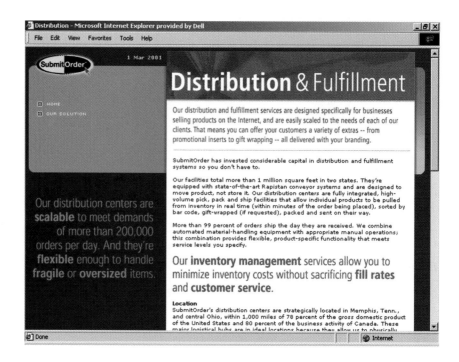

FIGURE 11-15

Order-fulfillment companies. Order-fulfillment companies, such as SubmitOrder.com shown here, can provide warehousing and shipment processing services for e-commerce companies.

Step 4: Designing and Developing an Effective Web Site

Web site design refers to the process of planning what a Web site will look like and how it will work. *Web site development* refers to the actual creation, testing, and implementation of the Web site. E-commerce Web sites can be designed and developed in-house, though it is common for a business to outsource these tasks to a professional Web development company.

It is extremely important that an e-commerce site be attractive, fast loading, easy to use, and secure. Guidelines to ensure an effective Web site design, as well as the steps involved in developing a Web site, were covered in Chapter 10.

Step 5: Implementing Appropriate Sales and Marketing Strategies

There is a variety of strategies that a business can use to increase sales and use of its Web site. One important topic—designing an effective Web site—has already been discussed. A few other strategies are discussed next.

Include Adequate Customer Service Features

Every e-commerce Web site should include adequate customer service features to increase customer satisfaction and begin to build loyalty in new customers. Good features to include are online order tracking, online versions of product instruction manuals, and an e-mail link to a customer service technician who replies to all e-mails quickly—definitely within 24 hours. A toll-free number that customers can call if they prefer is also an important feature. Some sites offer a live chat option, as well.

Collect Taxes from Customers Only If Required by Law

Currently, e-commerce firms are not required to collect sales tax from customers unless the customer and the merchant are located in the same state, or the merchant has a physical presence (such as a brick-and-mortar store or shipping facility) in the customer's state. Though *Internet taxation* has being hotly debated over the last few years and may eventually be imposed for all online sales (as discussed in this chapter's Trend box), the appeal of avoiding sales tax lures many customers to make online purchases. Collecting sales taxes only when you are required to can be a draw for your Web site.

Display a Privacy Policy and Security Statement

Many online consumers are very concerned about their online privacy and security when purchasing items over the Internet. To reassure these customers, all e-commerce sites should develop and display a *privacy policy* stating how collected information will be used. One of the most recognized privacy certification organizations is *TRUSTe*. Web sites displaying the TRUSTe *trustmark* (see Figure 11-16) have privacy policies approved by TRUSTe.

FIGURE 11-16

TRUSTe. Web sites displaying the TRUSTe trustmark have privacy policies approved by the TRUSTe organization.

As mentioned earlier in this chapter, all exchanges of financial information should take place on a secure Web page. A *security statement* (refer to the Walmart.com checkout screen in Figure 11-12) should be used to reassure customers that their transactions are secure and their information cannot be intercepted by a third party when it is transferred over the Internet.

Use an Appropriate Domain Name and URL

Because many customers will type the URL of the e-commerce site to shop or to return for customer service, it is important that the URL be easy to remember and easy to type. Try to register an intuitive domain name and be sure the home page of your site is set up so that the customer need not type anything other than the domain name and ".com" to access the site. Domain names are unique and are registered with an official domain name registrar. You can visit any of these company's Web sites (such as networksolutons.com) to see if a domain name that matches your organization's name is available. If not, you can try variations of the name—many registration sites automatically help by displaying available names that are similar to the one typed, if that name is unavailable. Keep in mind, however, that if you own the trademark to your business name, the *Anticybersquatting Consumer Protection Act of 1999* protects your trademark in cyberspace. According to the law, domain names similar to a trademarked name cannot be registered, unless the person has a legitimate claim to that name (such as it is his or her last name) or if the domain name was registered prior to the use of the registered trademark. Registering a domain name to cause confusion, to dilute the established trademark, or with the intent of reselling the trademark (called *cybersquatting*) has been ruled illegal.

Promote Your Web Site Sufficiently

Promotion of your site—that is, advertising its existence, purpose, and URL—provides a critical connection to the people you want to find you. One of the best ways to promote your site is by listing it with as many search sites as you can—such as Yahoo!, Excite, AltaVista, NorthernLight, AskJeeves, and Lycos. Most search sites allow you to fill out online forms on which you list your site's URL and describe your site to them (see Figure 11-17). There are also sites that allow you to fill out one form that they submit to several search sites at one time, usually for a reasonable fee of about $200 or less. Most businesses find using such a submission service is the most efficient means of promoting a new site. In addition to submitting your site to the general-purpose search sites, if one or more specialty search sites exist for your industry, be sure to submit your site to them as well.

When submitting your URL to a search site, the submission page usually asks you to provide keywords—usually nouns—that you expect people to enter when looking for a site like yours. If you've developed a Web site for a fishing-tackle-and-outfitter business in Boise, Idaho, for instance, you want to make sure that people can find it through such informative words as *fish, fishing, trout, tackle, hobby, outfitter, recreation, Boise,* and *Idaho*.

As another useful form of promotion, you might pursue listings at any trailblazer sites that deal with the subject of your site. A *trailblazer site,* or *supersite,* provides a comprehensive list of Web resources on a given subject. These sites are frequently created and maintained by individuals or by organizations related to the subject area. Returning to the fishing-tackle-and-outfitter-business example, you would want to locate trailblazer sites devoted to fishing, trout, and related subjects. If a link doesn't exist to submit your page to the list, e-mail the administrators of those sites to request the addition of your URL. The easiest way to locate trailblazer sites is through a search site.

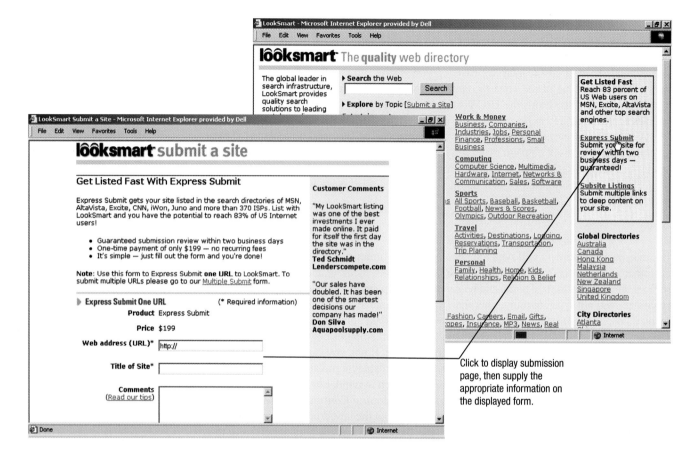

Click to display submission page, then supply the appropriate information on the displayed form.

➲ FIGURE 11-17

Search site submission.

Virtually all search sites have a link to a page where you can suggest a Web page to be added to the site's database, though sometimes a fee is required for faster service. Third-party submission services can be used to submit your site to a large number of search sites at one time.

Consider also several other promotional options. You might arrange to rent a storefront in a cybermall or purchase *banner ads* on other sites. Banner ads can appear in a wide variety of shapes and sizes (see Figure 11-18) and are commonly found on news sites, reference sites, search sites, and other high-traffic Web pages. Most banner ads act as hyperlinks to the advertised company's Web site. There are also several free link or banner exchanges on the Web in which you display links or banner ads for other sites on your Web site in return for your link or banner ad being displayed on other sites—this is a good alternative for companies with a limited advertising budget. You can also hire a Web promotion firm to publicize your site for you. A definite must is using your site's URL on all offline advertising and print material, such as letterhead, business cards, and television, radio, and print ads.

A final important promotional strategy is regularly updating your site with new content. Visitors will come back to your Web site on a regular basis if you constantly refresh it with interesting or exciting information, or the chance to win freebies. Sweepstakes and contests are especially popular.

To help build your customer database to target promotions and marketing materials to your customers, as discussed in the next section, you may want to include some type of form that users can fill out to supply vital facts or voice their opinions. Most sites require a minimum of an e-mail address when registering for a prize or contest; some sites require that or additional information in order to access certain information on a site.

Data Warehousing and Mining

Two marketing concepts that all e-businesses should be aware of are data warehousing and data mining. A **data warehouse** is a comprehensive collection of data about a company and

---

>**Data warehouse.** A comprehensive collection of data about a company and its customers.

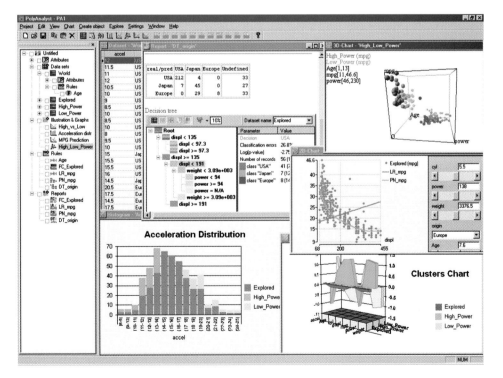

its customers. In a data warehouse, data from transaction processing and other operations are reorganized and put into a form that is optimized for queries. For e-businesses, data about customers' activities on the company Web site (sometimes called *clickstream data*) may be included, as well.

Data mining makes use of a data warehouse by applying intelligent software to scan its contents for subtle patterns that may not be evident to management (see Figure 11-19). Put another way, data mining finds hidden patterns and relationships between data. For example, data in one data warehouse may suggest that when a new home is purchased, 50 percent of the time a new refrigerator is bought within a month. Data mining can be a useful sales and marketing tool to help retail companies match up customers with products that they would be likely to purchase—a type of customer *profiling*.

FIGURE 11-19

Data mining. The goal of these tools is to find patterns in data that management never imagined existed.

>**Data mining.** Intelligent software used to analyze data warehouses for patterns that management may not even realize exist.

Both data warehousing and data mining are common in large enterprises. The amount of data that can be collected via a Web site, however, makes these activities an exciting opportunity for e-businesses. Online businesses can use data to entice customers to return to the Web site by offering free shipping for return customers or by notifying customers of new products or specials on products that they might be interested in. It can also be used to encourage customers to buy products by using personalized content, such as displaying banner ads that match the customer's interest. Personalized shopping experiences are a powerful way to satisfy customers and keep them coming back to a Web site. Data mining used in conjunction with Web site data is sometimes referred to as *Web mining*.

As you may have already guessed, the amount of data in a data warehouse can be enormous. Recent estimates put the amount of customer data for the average online enterprise by 2004 to be over 100 terabytes; some companies—such as Wal-Mart—are already there. If that data was printed out on regular $8\frac{1}{2} \times 11$ sheets of paper and laid end to end, it would reach to the moon and back nine times. Managing this vast amount of data and retrieving useful information to increase sales and improve customer relations is one of an e-business's greatest challenges.

Security Issues

Security issues are covered in more detail in other chapters, but it is such an important topic for e-commerce that some of the key points are reemphasized here. An e-business must:

▼ *Secure financial transactions*—All financial transactions should take place on a secure Web server. As mentioned in Chapter 8, *virtual private networks* or *VPNs* can be used to transfer private information over the Internet and ensure only authorized users have access to the information. *Encryption*—scrambling data through a coding method so it is unreadable unless you have the appropriate means or *key* to unscramble *(decrypt)*—is explained in detail in Chapter 15.

▼ *Secure sensitive documents and files*—Sensitive business documents should be encrypted when sent. They can then be decrypted when received by the authorized party.

▼ *Authenticate online business partners*—Systems such as *public key infrastructure (PKI)*, which uses *digital certificates* and digital keys, can be used to verify and authenticate the validity of each party involved in an Internet transaction. This is especially important when contracts and other important documents are signed and exchanged electronically. Digital certificates and keys are discussed in more detail in Chapter 15.

The Internet and World Wide Web have greatly affected the way most of us live and do business. One of the biggest changes in the last year or two is the amount of *e-commerce (electronic commerce)* being transacted.

WHAT IS E-BUSINESS AND E-COMMERCE?

E-business is the term used to describe any business with an online presence. The term **e-commerce** is used to describe performing financial transactions online. A **brick-and-mortar store** is a traditional store with a physical presence; online stores that also have a physical presence are sometimes called *click-and-mortar stores.*

The benefits of e-commerce to organizations include reduced cost, increased customer satisfaction, more effective management tools, and potentially higher sales. For consumers, the benefits include convenience, easier comparison-shopping, and a higher degree of selection. An e-commerce organization runs the risk of losing business when its Web site is down, as well as from customers not comfortable performing transactions online. Consumers accept security and privacy risks with e-commerce activity.

Chapter Objective 1:
Explain what e-business and e-commerce are and some of their benefits and risks.

E-BUSINESS APPLICATIONS

Numerous e-business activities can take place via the Internet, in addition to e-commerce. One of the oldest is **EDI (electronic data interchange),** which refers to the transfer of data between different companies using networks, such as the Internet. EDI facilitates the exchange of standard business documents—such as purchase orders and invoices—from one company's computer system to the system of another company, and is frequently used for ordering supplies and raw materials.

Enterprise resource planning (ERP) is a special type of large, integrated system that ties together all types of a business's activities, such as planning, manufacturing, sales, marketing, and finance, instead of each department having its own computer system, as in the past. When information from an ERP or other type of internal system can be exchanged between different applications within and between organizations, it is called **enterprise application integration (EAI).**

The goal of **customer relationship management (CRM)** is to build relationships with customers to increase satisfaction and loyalty, which, in turn, leads to increased profits. The goal of **supply chain management (SCM)** is to deliver the right product to the right place, at the right time, and at the right price, by overseeing materials, information, and finances as they move from the original supplier to the consumer. **Just-in-time (JIT) systems** are a form of SCM used in manufacturing to eliminate waste. With a just-in-time system, inventory and other production resources, as well as finished products, are limited to the right number at the right time as required to fill orders. **Value chain management** is the process of maximizing the flow of products, services, and information from raw materials to the final consumer through a value-added network of suppliers. Each organization adds value to the product or service as it passes through the supply chain.

Chapter Objective 2:
Describe the purpose of the following common e-business applications: EDI, ERP, EAI, CRM, and SCM.

E-COMMERCE BUSINESS MODELS

A company's **business model** defines its policies, operations, and technology in the generation of revenue. *E-business models* typically define the types of buyers and sellers involved. Some of the most common e-commerce business models include the **business-to-consumer (B2C), business-to-business (B2B), consumer-to-consumer (C2C),** and **business-to-government (B2G)** models. The

Chapter Objective 3:
Identify a variety of e-commerce business models and discuss their similarities and differences.

APPS

intermediary hub model is used by companies that bring buyers and sellers together within a specific industry *(vertical hub)* or business process *(horizontal hub)* but don't sell products or services directly to their customers.

TYPES OF E-COMMERCE WEB SITES

Chapter Objective 4:
Discuss the types of Web site models that can be used to implement e-commerce.

There is a variety of types of Web sites that can be used for e-commerce activities. Some of the most common are manufacturer sites, **e-tailer** (online retail) Web sites, and *electronic malls* **(e-malls)**—groups of e-tailers organized together with access through one location. **Auction** and **reverse auction** sites allow companies or individuals to bid on merchandise. Other **brokerage** sites that facilitate transactions in addition to the auction site include *financial brokers* and *market exchanges.*

IMPLEMENTING WEB-BASED E-COMMERCE

Chapter Objective 5:
List several strategies for implementing e-commerce using the Web, including some of the decisions that need to be made, the options available for accepting payments, and the process of designing and developing an effective Web site.

When implementing Web-based e-commerce, five basic steps are usually followed. First, the types of business models and Web sites to be used are selected. Then, the desired e-commerce and e-business applications are determined. The business must also decide how to handle the electronic financial transactions that occur via the site. Some possibilities include accepting credit cards, **online checks, online payment accounts,** and **smart cards.** Some customers may want to use a **digital wallet** to supply shipping and billing information—online businesses must decide whether to support each payment possibility. B2B sites may want to consider using a *B2B transaction processing service* or *order-fulfillment company* to assist with their transactions.

The design and development of the e-commerce Web site are extremely important. An intuitive, easy-to-use site is a must. In addition, the site must be secure so that potential customers feel confident performing financial transactions online. After the site is completed, some of the strategies a business can use to increase sales and the use of its Web site include adequate customer service features, collecting sales tax only if required by law, displaying privacy and security statements prominently on the site, using an appropriate domain name and URL, and promoting the Web site sufficiently. In addition, data warehousing and data mining can be used. A **data warehouse** is a comprehensive collection of data about a company and its customers. **Data mining** consists of intelligent software that can analyze data warehouses for patterns that management may not even realize exist.

Chapter Objective 6:
Outline some sales and marketing strategies that can be implemented using the Web.

Some of the key security issues that all businesses conducting e-commerce activity should consider are using a secure Web server for all financial transactions, *encrypting* sensitive documents and files sent over the Internet, and authenticating online business partners. Some authentication procedures include using *public key infrastructure* and digital certificates.

Chapter Objective 7:
Discuss some important security issues that are involved with performing financial transactions over the Internet.

Instructions: Match each key term on the left with the definition on the right that fits best.

1. brick-and-mortar store

2. brokerage site

3. customer relationship management (CRM)

4. data mining

5. data warehouse

6. digital wallet

7. e-business

8. electronic commerce (e-commerce)

9. electronic data interchange (EDI)

10. enterprise application integration (EAI)

11. enterprise resource planning (ERP)

12. just-in-time (JIT) system

13. online auction site

14. order-fulfillment company

15. smart card

16. supply chain management (SCM)

17. value chain management

_____ A business with an online presence.

_____ A company that provides a distribution network for merchants who cannot or choose not to process their own orders.

_____ A comprehensive collection of data about a company and its customers.

_____ A conventional store with a physical presence.

_____ A credit-card-size piece of plastic containing a chip and other circuitry into which data can be stored.

_____ A large integrated system that ties together all of a business's activities.

_____ A type of Web site used to bring buyers and sellers together to facilitate transactions, such as online stock trading and exchanging goods, services, and commodities.

_____ A Web site where buyers bid on items and the highest bidder after a particular time period is allowed to buy the item.

_____ An encrypted electronic file that holds information that can speed up online purchase transactions, such as electronic payment, billing, and shipping information.

_____ An inventory system in which inventory, other production resources, and finished products are limited to the right number at the right time as required to fill orders.

_____ Exchanging information from an ERP or other internal system between different applications and organizations.

_____ Intelligent software used to analyze data warehouses for patterns that management may not even realize exist.

_____ The act of doing financial transactions over the Internet or similar technology.

_____ The oversight of materials, information, and finances as they move from the original supplier to the consumer.

_____ The process of building and managing good relationships with customers.

_____ The process of maximizing the flow of products, goods, services, and information through a value-added network of suppliers.

_____ The transfer of data between different companies using the Internet or another network.

Self-Quiz

Answers for the self-quiz appear at the end of the book.

True/False

Instructions: Circle **T** if the statement is true or **F** if the statement is false.

T F **1.** All e-businesses sell products or services via their Web site.

T F **2.** Because most users shop online during the daytime, e-commerce sites can shut down for maintenance during the middle of the night without losing sales.

T F **3.** Online auction sites are available for both C2C and B2B applications.

T F **4.** The transfer of data between different companies using the Internet is referred to as supply chain management.

T F **5.** A business can use more than one type of business model.

Completion

Instructions: Answer the following questions.

6. A company selling parts to NASA is using the _____ e-commerce business model.

7. At a(n) _____ site, sellers place bids and the lowest price gets the buyer's business.

8. A brokerage site uses the _____ e-commerce business model.

9. A(n) _____ can help speed up online purchases by storing a buyer's payment, shipping, and billing information so it can be supplied electronically.

10. _____ is a marketing tool that attempts to uncover hidden patterns and relationships between data about a company and its customers.

Exercises

1. For each of the following descriptions, select the acronym from the list that follows that represents the most appropriate e-business application. Note that not all applications will be used.

_____ An inventory system in which only the right amount of materials and finished products are kept on hand at any given time.

_____ A large integrated system that ties together all of a business's activities, such as planning, manufacturing, sales, marketing, and finance.

_____ An organization's customer service solution.

   a. EAI
   b. EDI
   c. ERP
   d. CRM
   e. SCM
   f. JIT

2. List two potential advantages to an organization of using e-commerce.

3. List two potential risks to an organization of using e-commerce.

4. For each of the following descriptions, select the most appropriate type(s) of payment from the list that follows. Note that some applications may match more than one payment type (if so, list all appropriate payment methods), and some payment types may not be used.

———————— A parent wishes to supply their college student with a small amount of money for online purchases.

———————— A person purchases an expensive painting from an individual at an online auction site.

———————— A person purchases an inexpensive item from an online auction, but needs to receive the item in three days or less.

———————— A person makes a lot of online purchases and wishes to avoid entering in shipping, billing, and payment information each time a purchase is made.

———————— A person buys a book from Amazon.com.

  a. smart card

  b. credit card

  c. online payment account

  d. online check

  e. online escrow company

  f. digital wallet

5. Describe the difference between data warehousing and data mining.

SYSTEMS

Information Systems and Systems Development

LEARNING OBJECTIVES

After completing this chapter, you will be able to:

1. Explain what information systems are and who uses them.

2. Describe several types of information systems commonly found in organizations.

3. Explain what system development is and who is responsible for it.

4. Identify and describe the different steps of the systems development life cycle (SDLC).

5. Discuss several approaches used to develop systems.

In previous chapters of this textbook we looked at different types of hardware and software. Here we turn to the process of putting these elements together to form complete *computer systems*.

Systems are found in all organizations. For example, systems attend to accounting activities such as sending out bills and processing payrolls, they provide information to help managers make decisions, they help run factories efficiently, and they enable workers to exchange information and collaborate on projects. Such systems require considerable effort to design, build, and maintain. Unfortunately, since no two situations are exactly alike, there is no single, surefire formula for successful *systems development*. A procedure that works well in one situation may fail in another. These facts notwithstanding, there is a set of general principles that, if understood, will enhance the likelihood of a system's success. Those principles are the subject of this chapter.

The chapter opens with a discussion of *information systems*—systems that are used to generate information—and how they are used by different levels of employees in an organization. Then we cover the most common types of information systems. From there we turn to the process of systems development, beginning with the computer professionals who develop systems and their primary responsibilities. We then look at the *systems development life cycle*—the set of activities that are at the heart of every serious systems-building effort. This chapter concludes with a discussion of the major approaches to systems development. ■

WHAT IS AN INFORMATION SYSTEM?

A **system** is a collection of elements and procedures that interact to accomplish a goal. A football game, for example, is played according to a system. It consists of a collection of elements (two teams, a playing field, referees) and procedures (the rules of the game) that interact to determine which team is the winner. A transit system is a collection of people, buses or trains, work rules, fares, and schedules that get people from one place to another. Similarly, an **information system** is a collection of people, hardware, software, data, and procedures that interact to generate information to support users in an organization. Although most information systems within organizations serve employees, increasingly information systems are expanding to support the needs of customers and suppliers, as well.

The function of many systems, whether manual or computerized, is to keep an organization well managed and running smoothly. Systems are created and altered in response to changing needs within an organization and shifting conditions in its surrounding environment. When problems arise in an existing system or when a new system is needed, systems development comes into play. *Systems development* is the process of analyzing a work environment, designing a new system or making modifications to the current system to fit the needs of the work environment, acquiring any needed hardware and software, training users, and getting the new or modified system to work.

>**System.** A collection of elements and procedures that interact to accomplish a goal. >**Information system.** A system used to generate information to support users in an organization.

Systems development may be required for many reasons. New laws may call for the collection of data never before assembled. The government may require new data on personnel, for example. The introduction of new technology, especially new computer technology, may prompt the wholesale revision of a system. Or, as is the trend today, a company may decide to convert certain applications into a global networked environment or modify an information system to enable customers and suppliers to access it via the Internet. These and other kinds of requirements prompted by new regulations or the need to stay abreast of the competition often bring about major changes in an organization's systems.

In the early days of commercial computing, businesses purchased computers almost exclusively to perform routine transaction processing tasks. Used in this way, the computers cut clerical expenses considerably. As time passed, however, it became apparent that the computer could do much more than replace clerks. It could also provide information to assist managers in their decision-making role.

WHO USES INFORMATION SYSTEMS?

Since information systems are used to generate information for organizational decisions, much of the time they are used by decision makers, such as management employees. With an information system, managers can spend less time gathering facts and use more information when making their decisions. As a result, managers have more time to do the things they do best—thinking creatively and interacting with people.

Managers are usually classified into three categories: *executive, middle,* and *operational.* These positions are often pictured as a pyramid to illustrate their number and ranking (see Figure 12-1) with executive managers on top and organizational managers on the bottom. Middle managers usually fall in between the other two types, though with the increased use of information systems and other technological advances, the middle-management level is becoming less essential and has begun to disappear in some organizations. This trend is referred to as the *flattening* of the organizational structure.

Managers most often manage the employees one level below them on the pyramid. For example, executive managers are in charge of middle managers. Operational managers (at the bottom of the management pyramid) supervise nonmanagement workers.

What classifies a user into one of these categories are the job functions performed, as well as the types of decisions made. The most common types of information systems used by each level of management are discussed next.

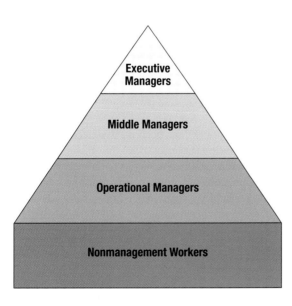

FIGURE 12-1
The management pyramid.
Management positions are generally classified as executive, middle, or operational.

Executive Management

Executive managers, also called *senior managers* or *top-level managers,* are the highest management positions in an organization. They include the president, vice-president, CEO, and so forth. Executive managers spend a great deal of time on long-range planning and use information systems to make *strategic decisions,* though their decision-making process tends to be fairly unstructured.

Middle Management

Middle managers use information systems to make *tactical decisions* that affect the firm's activities approximately one to five years in the future. Some examples of middle-management positions are a human resources or purchasing manager. The decisions made by middle management are moderately structured.

Operational Management

Operational managers supervise nonmanagement workers. They include various types of supervisors, foremen, office managers, and so forth. Operational managers use information systems to make decisions about meeting short-term objectives, usually within the current fiscal year. These decisions tend to be highly structured decisions.

Nonmanagement Workers

Nonmanagement workers, such as office workers, accountants, or engineers, use information systems as necessary to perform their jobs. Nonmanagement workers today have more information available to them than in previous decades and, consequently, make more on-the-job-type decisions than in the past.

TYPES OF INFORMATION SYSTEMS

web tutor

For a tutorial on selecting an information system, go to www.course.com/parker2002/ch12

Undoubtedly, you've already encountered many types of systems in organizations. When you go into the supermarket, you generally see electronic cash registers and scanning devices that are part of the supermarket's inventory and pricing system. Or when you've registered for college classes, perhaps you've observed someone at a PC checking to see whether a certain class you want to take is still open and whether you've paid your bills—all part of a registration system.

While hundreds of specific types of information systems are in existence today, many fall into one or more of five categories: *office, transaction processing, management information, decision support,* and *enterprise-wide systems.* These systems and the workers who use them are summarized in Figure 12-2. We look more closely at each of these systems, plus one additional type of system—*artificial intelligence systems*—next.

Office Systems

In recent years, computer technology has been used widely to increase productivity in the office. The term **office automation (OA)** describes this phenomenon. Office automation can be achieved through a wide variety of technologies and processing techniques, as described in this section. These combinations of hardware, software, and other resources used to facilitate communications and enhance productivity are collectively referred to as **office systems.** Office systems are used by all levels of management and by nonmanagement employees.

>**Office automation (OA).** Computer-based office-oriented technologies, such as word processing, e-mail, workgroup computing, and the like.
>**Office system.** A type of system in which office automation hardware, software, and resources are used to facilitate communications and enhance productivity.

Nonmanagement Workers (job-related decisions)	Operational Managers (operational decisions)	Middle Managers (tactical decisions)	Executive Managers (strategic decisions)
Office Systems			
Transaction Processing Systems			
		Management Information Systems	
		Decision Support Systems	
Enterprise Systems			

FIGURE 12-2

Types of information systems and the people who use them. Each level of management generally makes specific types of decisions and, consequently, requires different types of information.

Document-Processing Systems

The cornerstone of most organizations is the document—memos, letters, reports, manuals, forms, and the like. Consequently, a major focus of office automation relates to the creation, distribution, and storage of documents. Sometimes the catchall phrase *document processing* is used to collectively refer to such office technologies as word processing, desktop publishing, and other types of electronic document handling. Though the predicted *paperless office* has yet to materialize, there are an increasing number of electronic document management software programs available to help store, organize, and retrieve documents once they have been created electronically or scanned into a PC.

Communications Systems

Various types of *communications systems* in place in many organizations include electronic mail (discussed in Chapter 2); faxing, teleconferencing, and telecommuting (discussed in Chapter 8); and *workgroup computing.*

   Workgroup computing—also called *collaborative computing*—allows several people to use their PCs to collaborate on job tasks, without ever leaving their offices (or other work location). Special *workgroup-computing software* (also called *groupware*) incorporates a variety of tasks, such as e-mail, shared calendars, project scheduling, document sharing, and so forth (see Figure 12-3). Some programs even have built-in teleconferencing abilities so users can see each other as they collaborate on shared documents, carry on real-time voice or typed conversations, or draw on a shared whiteboard application.

   The insurance industry provides a good example of why workgroup computing can be effective and increase efficiency. Years ago, clerks would have processed an accident claim by filling out forms by hand and manually walking file folders around from desk to desk for approvals and signatures. Today, such claims are processed electronically using groupware. The groupware software generates electronic forms for workers to fill out, review, and approve payment at their desktop PCs. The software can automatically route and monitor the progress of forms as well. Consequently, insurers can process claims more rapidly and more reliably and with far fewer errors than they could before groupware was available. Better service is often provided too, since an adjuster can keep claimants informed

---

>**Workgroup computing.** Software that allows individuals to use their PCs to collaborate on job tasks and projects.

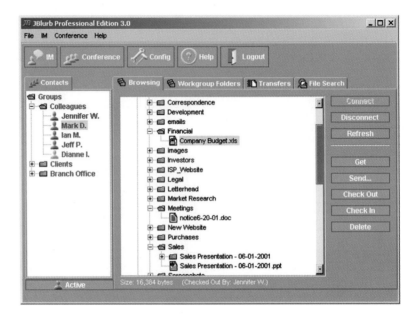

For links to further information about office systems software, go to www.course.com/parker2002/ch12

⊗ FIGURE 12-3

Workgroup computing. Collaborative software can consist of instant messaging, chatting, and videoconferencing capabilities, in addition to document sharing and shared calendaring/scheduling capabilities.

about a claim's progress immediately upon request. Alternatively, claimants can get reports themselves over the Internet with some systems.

Workgroup-computing software is getting attention wherever people collaborate on their jobs. For example, engineers and architects commonly use this type of software to collaborate on designs. Newspapers and publishing companies use it to circulate pieces among writers and editors, and advertising firms use it to share ideas and client proposal documents.

Transaction Processing Systems

Virtually every company carries out a number of routine, structured accounting operations, most of which involve some form of tedious record keeping. These operations, such as payroll and accounts receivable, inspired some of the earliest commercial applications for computers and are still among the most important. Because these systems involve processing business transactions—paying employees, recording customer purchases and payments, and vendor receipts and payments—they are called **transaction processing systems** (see Figure 12-4).

Transaction processing systems are typically used to provide information to operational managers. Some of the functions commonly performed by transaction processing systems are discussed in the following paragraphs.

Order-Entry Systems

Many organizations handle some type of order processing on a daily basis. Customers submit orders by phone, by mail via the Internet, or in person. The systems that record the data generated from these transactions, and help staff members manage them, are called **order-entry systems.** Specific types of order-entry systems are *e-commerce systems* (used for financial transactions performed over the Internet) and *point-of-sale systems* (used to record purchases at the point where the customer physically purchases the product or service, such as at a cash register).

>**Transaction processing system.** A type of information system that handles data created by an organization's business transactions.

>**Order-entry system.** A system that helps staff record and manage order processing.

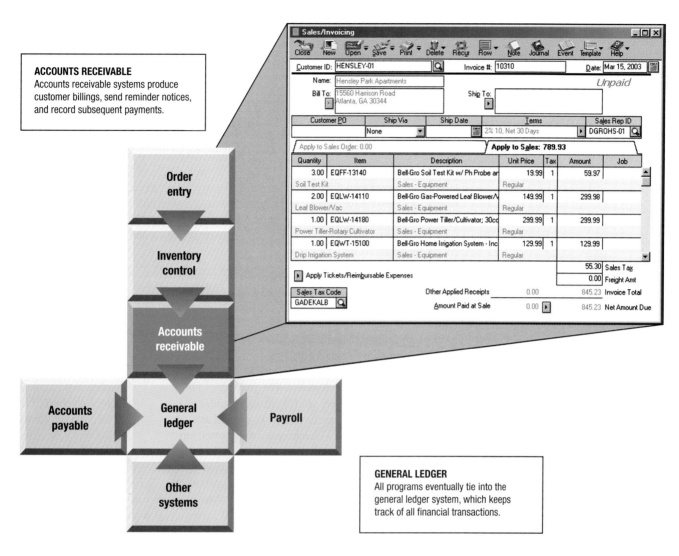

ACCOUNTS RECEIVABLE
Accounts receivable systems produce customer billings, send reminder notices, and record subsequent payments.

GENERAL LEDGER
All programs eventually tie into the general ledger system, which keeps track of all financial transactions.

FIGURE 12-4

Transaction processing systems. Programs in a transaction processing system typically include accounts receivable programs—which keep track of money coming into a company—and general ledger programs—which keep track of all financial transactions.

Inventory Control Systems

The units of product that a company has in stock to use or sell at a given moment make up its inventory. An **inventory control system** keeps track of the number of units of each product in inventory and ensures that reasonable quantities are on hand.

Payroll Systems

Payroll systems accept input about employee pay rates or salaries, hours worked, and deduction amounts, and then compute deductions, subtract them from gross earnings, and issue paychecks to employees for their net pay. These systems also contain programs that prepare reports for management and for tax purposes for the federal, state, and local governments.

Accounting Systems

Accounting systems refer to the variety of systems in place to record the details of financial transactions, such as payments and purchases. A few specific types of accounting systems are:

>**Inventory control system.** A system that keeps track of the number of each product in inventory. >**Payroll system.** A type of transaction system that generates employee payroll amounts and reports. >**Accounting system.** A system that deals with the financial transactions and financial record keeping for an organization.

▼ *Accounts receivable systems*—to keep track of customers' purchases, payments, and account balances. They also produce invoices and monthly account statements and provide information to management. Other output includes sales analyses, which describe changing patterns of products and sales and reports on current and past-due accounts. Figure 12-4 includes an example of an accounts receivable program.

▼ *Accounts payable systems*—to keep track of bills to be paid, and often generate checks to pay them. It records who gets paid and when, handles cash disbursements, and advises managers about whether they should accept discounts offered by vendors in return for early payment.

▼ *General ledger systems*—to keep track of all financial summaries, including those originating from payroll, accounts receivable, accounts payable, and other sources (refer again to Figure 12-4). It also ensures that a company's books balance. A general ledger system typically produces income statements, balance sheets, and other accounting documents.

Management Information Systems (MIS)

Management information systems (MIS)—sometimes called *information reporting systems*—evolved from transaction processing systems. They provide decision makers with preselected information, usually in the form of computer-generated reports. An MIS produces information that managers need to perform their jobs. The types of information produced from an MIS are often preplanned, just like the information you see on your monthly checking account statements. The individual *values* on your statements (such as check numbers, check amounts, and deposit amounts) change from month to month, but the *types* of information you receive (checks cashed and deposits made) remain the same. Every other person receiving a checking account statement from your bank receives virtually the same type of information.

Many management information systems provide decision makers with information generated from the data obtained from transaction processing. For example, a manager in the accounts receivable department regularly receives a report listing overdue accounts, and a sales manager gets regular sales reports. This information is most frequently used to make moderately structured, middle-management-type decisions.

Decision Support Systems (DSS)

A **decision support system (DSS)** helps people organize and analyze the information they need to consider when making decisions. It is useful to anyone whose requirements for information are unpredictable and unstructured. Instead of the more structured transaction processing and management information systems, decision support systems provide information on demand whenever a decision-making situation arises. DSSs may incorporate data from internal (within the company) and external (outside of the company) sources. External data includes interest rates, consumer confidence index numbers, and other economic indicators.

Decision support systems are tailored around the needs of an individual or group and are designed to help with specific types of decisions. Thus, "Sales support system" is the name typically given to a DSS aimed at the special decision-making needs of sales or marketing personnel. Likewise, a "Fire-suppression support system" might be a DSS targeted to helping a forest supervisor develop specific strategies for fighting wildfires. Two different types of decision support systems at work are shown in Figure 12-5.

>**Management information system (MIS).** A type of information system that provides decision makers with preselected type of information that can be used to make middle-management-type decisions. >**Decision support system (DSS).** A type of information system usually used by upper management that provides people with the tools and capabilities to organize and analyze their decision-making information.

FLOOD DAMAGE DSS
Some DSSs come with routines that overlay decision-making information on maps. In the application shown here, disaster-relief planners can pull up and analyze flood data to help minimize property damage. Flood insurance companies also use this data to set premium rates.

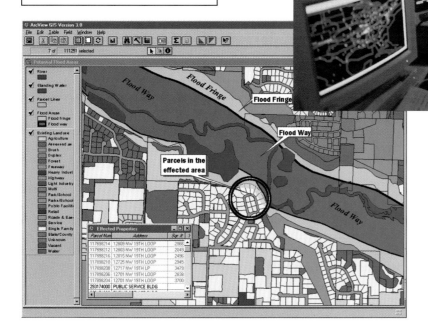

TRANSPORTATION DSS
The DSS used at the FedEx control tower shown here helps employees monitor plane activity. Other DSSs provide FedEx employees with up-to-the minute information about shipments, as well as weather and other factors that can affect delivery time.

◆ FIGURE 12-5
Decision support systems.

Let's put DSSs into perspective with an example. To assist with product pricing decisions, a sales manager uses a DSS that has been set up on his or her PC. Using the displayed menus, the manager first accesses the price of an item. Then he or she asks for the average price of other items, and then for the inventory turnover of yet a different item. Next, a financial model may be used to predict the sales volumes for specific items five years into the future. As the example suggests, the manager can pose questions as needs arise and receive answers immediately. At the end of the interactive session, the manager uses the DSS to prepare a summary of his or her findings and several charts for a meeting to propose repricing the item.

Decision support systems are typically used by middle and upper managers, though there are some types of DSSs that are used by others, such as a customer. A special type of DSS specifically targeted to upper management is called an *executive information system* or *EIS*. As many executives see it, the business world today is so competitive and fast paced that they need instant access to the freshest information. These systems typically demand powerful computers to run the appropriate software and handle the extremely large databases that must be accessed, such as the data warehouses discussed in Chapter 11. In fact, a growing trend is the use of supercomputers to support executive decision making.

Enterprise-Wide Systems

As discussed in Chapter 11, *enterprise resource planning (ERP)* is a special type of large, integrated system that ties together all types of a business's activities, such as planning, manufacturing, sales, marketing, and finance, using special e-business software. In a nutshell, ERP attempts to integrate all departments and functions across a company into a single resource that can serve all those different departments' particular needs. Instead of each department having its own computer system, as in the past, they are all combined together into a single, integrated software environment so that the various departments can more easily share information and communicate with each other. Because it is a system that integrates the entire company or *enterprise,* it is referred to as an *enterprise-wide system.* These systems are also sometimes called *e-business systems.*

For example, when an order is placed, the employee who takes the order from a customer has all the information necessary to complete the order (such as the customer's credit information and history, the company's inventory levels, and the shipping schedule). Throughout the order fulfillment and billing process, everyone in the company who deals with the order in some manner has access to the same information regarding the customer's order. When one department finishes with the order, the ERP system automatically routes it to the next department. At any point in the process, the order status can be determined by anyone in the company.

Some of the most successful ERP software developers are SAP, Oracle, and People-Soft. Most of today's e-business applications are structured to work over the Internet—making them accessible anytime, anywhere, via a Web browser (see Figure 12-6). As mentioned in Chapter 11, when information from an ERP or other internal system is exchanged between different applications or organizations, it is called *enterprise application integration (EAI).*

Design and Manufacturing Systems

Computers are widely used in organizational systems to improve productivity at the design stage—through *computer-aided design (CAD)*—and at the manufacturing stage—through *computer-aided manufacturing (CAM).*

Computer-Aided Design (CAD)

As discussed in Chapter 7, **computer-aided design (CAD)** is used by designers to reduce the time they spend developing products. CAD software, such as *AutoCAD,* is available for such applications as architecture and manufacturing (see Figure 12-7).

further exploration

For links to further information about enterprise-wide system providers, go to www.course.com/parker2002/ch12

● FIGURE 12-6

E-business software. Many e-business systems today are integrated with the Internet. A single integrated e-business or enterprise-wide system can be used for such activities as creating sales, purchase, and production orders; creating invoices; channeling and incorporating customer feedback; procuring raw materials; controlling distribution logistics; and collaborating on product designs.

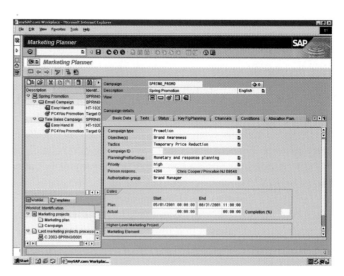

>**Computer-aided design (CAD).** A general term applied to the use of computer technology to automate design functions.

Computer-Aided Manufacturing (CAM)

Computers have been used on the factory floor for more than 40 years, long before engineers used them interactively for design. **Computer-aided manufacturing (CAM)** refers to the use of computers to help manage manufacturing operations and control machinery used in those processes. One example is a system that observes production in an oil refinery, performs calculations, and opens and shuts appropriate valves accordingly. Another system, commonly used in the steel industry, works from preprogrammed specifications to shape and assemble steel parts automatically. Increasingly, *robots* (discussed shortly) are used to carry out processes that were once performed by humans. CAM is also widely used to build cars and ships, monitor power plants, manufacture food and chemicals, and perform a number of other functions.

FIGURE 12-7
Computer-aided design (CAD).

Artificial Intelligence Systems

A computer can perform work at extremely fast speeds. It can also be programmed with a set of rules or guidelines, thereby enabling it to draw certain types of conclusions based on the input it receives. When computer systems combine these two abilities to perform in ways that would be considered intelligent if observed in humans, it is commonly referred to as *artificial intelligence (AI)*. Systems that use artificial intelligence are called **artificial intelligence systems.**

Four main types of artificial intelligence systems are *expert systems, natural language systems, neural network systems,* and *robotics.*

Expert Systems

Expert systems are programs that provide advice that is normally obtained from a human expert. In medicine, expert systems are used to incorporate the knowledge and decision-making guidelines of some of the world's best physicians. For example, the symptoms exhibited by a patient might be entered into an expert system. The program may then ask the attending physician questions about details to obtain more information. Through questioning and checking the responses against a large database of successfully diagnosed cases, the program may draw the same conclusion that an attending physician might—though much more quickly—or it may reach additional conclusions that the physician may not have thought of because the expert system has access to a wider base of knowledge. Some expert systems are designed to take the place of human experts, while others are designed to assist them. A list of several possible applications for expert systems is provided in Figure 12-8.

Most expert systems consist of two parts: data and software (see Figure 12-9). The data part is commonly called a *knowledge base,* and it contains specific facts about the expert area and any rules that the expert system should use to make decisions based on those facts. For instance, an expert system used to authorize credit for credit card customers would have in its knowledge base facts about customers as well as a set of *rules,* such as

>**Computer-aided manufacturing (CAM).** A general term applied to the use of computer technology to automate manufacturing functions.
>**Artificial intelligence system.** A system in which a computer performs actions that are characteristic of human intelligence.
>**Expert system.** A computer system that provides the type of advice that would be expected from a human expert.

FIGURE 12-8

Some expert system applications.

Applications area	Example application
Credit authorization	Deciding whether to grant credit to individuals and companies based on both their past histories and other similar credit cases.
E-commerce	Determining how to personalize the Web pages used by consumers visiting commercial sites.
Insurance sales	Helping an insurance agent tailor an insurance package to a client, given the client's insurance, investment, financial planning, and tax needs.
Manufacturing	Finding the best way to design, produce, stock, and ship a product.
Medical diagnosing	Presenting possible diagnoses based on supplied symptoms and other patient data.
Portfolio planning	Determining the best securities portfolio for a client, given the client's growth and equity objectives.
Repair/maintainence	Assisting machine repairpeople by providing expert diagnosis of malfunction.
Tax accounting	Assisting tax accountants by providing advice on the best tax treatment for an individual or corporation.
Training	Putting newly hired employees into computer-simulated situations in which their performance is aided by or compared with experts.

"Do not automatically authorize credit if the customer has already made five transactions today." Generally, the knowledge base is jointly developed by a human expert and a specialized *systems analyst* (discussed shortly) called a *knowledge engineer*.

The software part of an expert system often consists of several different programs. A program called an *inference engine* is used to apply rules to the knowledge base to reach decisions. Other programs may enable users to communicate with the expert system in a natural language such as English or Spanish, provide explanations to users about how the expert system reached a particular conclusion, and allow computer professionals to set up and maintain the expert system.

Expert systems can be built from scratch or acquired as packages that have all the software components in place but lack a knowledge base. This latter type of package is called an *expert system shell*. Shells represent the most common and inexpensive way to create an expert system.

FIGURE 12-9

An expert system at work.

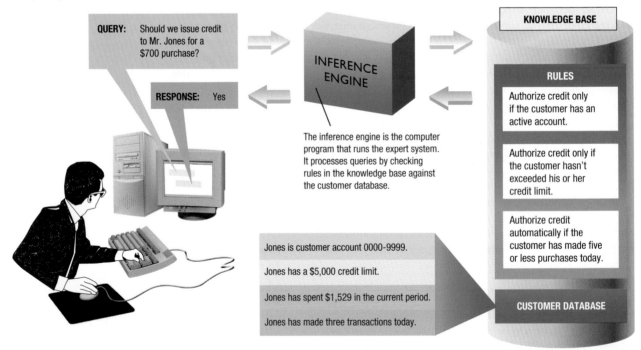

Sometimes, specialized systems are used in conjunction with an expert system. One example of these is a *vision system.* Vision systems enable computer-controlled devices to "see" and interpret what they see based on data from an accompanying expert system. A vision system might work as follows: Parts produced in a manufacturing process are sent along an assembly line for inspection. A vision system located at a station along the line takes a digital snapshot of each part as it passes by. The picture is broken down into vital pieces of data that are compared to data showing how the part would look if it were produced correctly. An accompanying expert system applies rules to judge whether the part has been made correctly or is flawed. If flawed, the system determines the nature of the flaw and the necessary corrective action.

Natural Language Systems

One of the greatest challenges that scientists in the field of AI face is giving computer systems the ability to communicate in *natural languages*—such as English, Spanish, French, and Japanese. Unfortunately, this challenge is not easy to meet. People have personalized ways of communicating, and the meanings of words vary according to the contexts in which they are used. Nonetheless, researchers have made some major strides toward getting computers to listen to and respond in natural languages. Systems in which the computer can understand natural languages are called **natural language systems.**

Neural Network Systems

Today, many expert systems use *neural-net computing*—a technology in which the human brain's pattern-recognition process is emulated by a computer. **Neural network systems** (also called *neural nets*) are designed to learn by observation and by trial and error—the way people learn. Neural nets are typically used to recognize patterns in data. They are employed in such areas as handwriting-, speech-, and image-recognition; credit-risk assessment; stock-market analysis; and crime analysis (see Figure 12-10).

For a look at how a computer system can recognize faces for identification purposes, see the How It Works box.

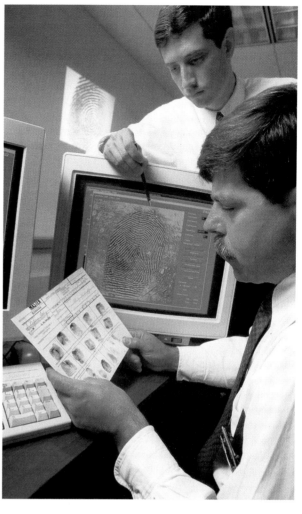

FIGURE 12-10
Neural network systems. Neural network systems specialize in analyzing patterns. In fingerprint identification, a computer can be taught to match similarities that human experts look for, and to do so in a matter of minutes or seconds.

Robotics

Robotics—the field devoted to the study of robot technology—plays an integral role in computer-aided manufacturing (CAM) systems. *Robots* are machines that, with the help of a computer, can mimic a number of human motor activities to perform jobs that are too monotonous or dangerous for their flesh-and-blood counterparts—welding and painting cars, mining coal, defusing bombs, exploring the bottom of the ocean, and so on. Many robots can even "see" by means of embedded cameras and "feel" with sensors that permit them to assess the hardness and temperature of objects. Robots can represent substantial savings to a company, because they don't go on strike and don't need vacations.

Some companies, such as Honda, Sony, and NEC, are working toward creating human-looking robots to carry out common household tasks, as well as to be electronic playmates. For a look at how far they've come, see the Trend box.

>**Natural language system.** A system in which the computer can understand natural languages. >**Neural network system.** An expert system in which the human brain's pattern-recognition process is emulated by the computer system. >**Robotics.** The study of robot technology.

Face Recognition

A variety of biometric techniques exists to identify individuals. Fingerprint identification has been used for several years and has the advantage of being very affordable and accurate. Hand scanning is a similar possibility. Iris scanning (scanning the eye) is very accurate but significantly more expensive. Voice-identification has great potential for the future. One newer biometric technique that is getting a lot of attention lately is face recognition.

With face recognition, one or more cameras scan the individual's face. The data is then digitized and compared with a database of photos (see the accompanying illustration). Face recognition has been used to verify the identify of ATM users, to admit individuals to secure areas, and to look for fugitives or terrorists at public locations. London, for example, uses a network of over 240 surveillance cameras to continuously look for previously convicted criminals in high crime areas. Future possibilities include being used to validate e-commerce transactions and distance learning testing.

Because face recognition can perform one-to-many matching (which locates one specific individual from a database of many photographs), instead of just one-to-one authentication (where the system needs to know the person's identity first by the individual entering his or her name, ID number, or swiping a smart card, and then can authenticate that the person is truly the stated individual), face recognition can be used in a broad range of applications. It also has the advantage of requiring no direct contact with the reading device. Cameras can take photos and identify individuals as they walk past, such as was the case during the Super Bowl XXXV in 2001. Dubbed the "Snooper Bowl" by critics, law enforcement agents used cameras to snap photos of the 100,000 or so fans as they stepped through the turnstiles. The photos were then compared to a police database of known criminals. Though the surveillance system only picked out 19 people (all petty criminals) from the database, the system pushed face recognition and privacy issues into the public spotlight.

Proponents and law enforcement argue that face recognition systems are no different than the scores of video surveillance systems in place today in a wide variety of public locations. They view it as just one more tool to be used to protect the public, similar to scanning luggage at the airport. Privacy advocates fear being put in a perpetual police lineup. How accepting the public will be about being in a digital lineup at the grocery store or while pumping gas remains to be seen, though the terrorist attack of September 11, 2001 changed many U.S. citizens' attitudes about these types of identification tools. Immediately following the attacks, face recognition technology companies were flooded with inquiries from private companies, the government, airports—even the Olympics.

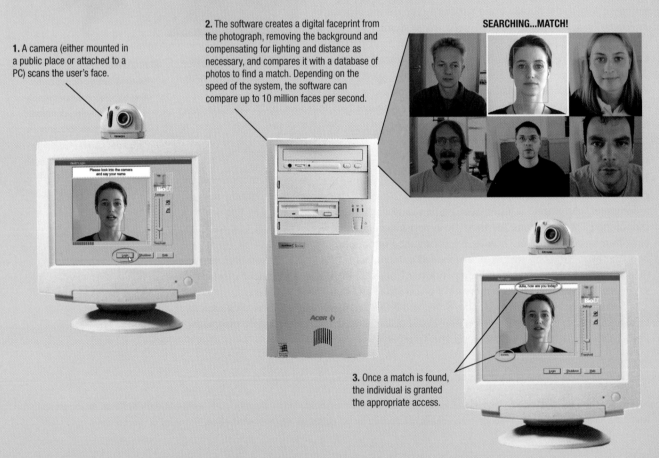

1. A camera (either mounted in a public place or attached to a PC) scans the user's face.

2. The software creates a digital faceprint from the photograph, removing the background and compensating for lighting and distance as necessary, and compares it with a database of photos to find a match. Depending on the speed of the system, the software can compare up to 10 million faces per second.

SEARCHING...MATCH!

3. Once a match is found, the individual is granted the appropriate access.

trend

Robot-Happy

In the last few years, there's been a lot of robot activity in the toy market. Sony received a great deal of attention with its Aibo robot dog. Following on that success are a number of new robot toys from Hasbro that make the original robots look like wind-up toys. These new toys can tell jokes, sing rounds with their robotic pals, and make appropriate facial expressions. At least one even plugs itself in to recharge when its battery is running low.

But electronics companies aren't just stopping with toys. Industrial engineers all over the world, but particularly those in Japan, are working on more humanoid robots that do more than just entertain. Honda, for example, has the child-sized ASIMO (which stands for Advanced Step in Innovative Mobility). While, at the moment, this 4-foot, 95-pound creation can't do more than dance and wave, Honda expects its robot to be welcoming visitors at showrooms in a year or two. Honda says it is studying ways to give the robot voice-recognition capabilities and the ability to identify faces and other functions, before making it a commercial product.

Voice and image recognition in robots is already here, at least in a limited sense. Sony's 20-inch SDR-3X humanoid robot—based on the same technology as the Aibo robot dog—can be verbally controlled through two microphones in the ear section. It can recognize about 20 prerecorded words and can respond to specific verbal instructions. It can speak about 20 words as well. In addition, the robot can distinguish specific color areas from visual data captured by a camera in the head area. Based on this ability, the SDR-3X can perform such feats as dance, pick out a particular colored ball from a group of balls, or kick a soccer ball and recognize whether or not the ball landed in the net.

NEC's new Personal Robot PaPeRo (from Partner-type Personal Robot) isn't exactly humanoid but sure is cuddly (see the accompanying photo). The PaPeRo has the capability to talk and play, and perform such activities as making small talk,

playing games, sending and receiving audio and video messages, acting as a TV remote control, and accessing messaging via the Internet. It has two cameras equipped as its eyes to capture real-time images and recognize them. Because of the cameras and its built-in sensors, it walks smoothly, and avoids furniture and obstacles. It can also recognize human faces and tries to follow the face of the person talking to it. Microphones on its head are used to locate people and for speech recognition. PaPeRo remembers information about family members and previous interactions and talks and responds to each individual based on this information. It even responds when you pat it on the head, takes a nap if it can't find anyone to play with, and searches for individuals it needs to deliver messages to.

For household chores, there are robotic lawn mowers and robotic vacuum cleaners. A long way from the Jetsen's Rosie washing the dishes, but it's a start.

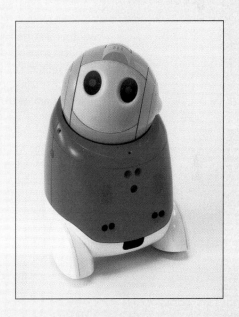

RESPONSIBILITY FOR SYSTEMS DEVELOPMENT

As mentioned earlier, the process that includes planning, building, and maintaining systems is called *systems development*. Systems can be developed in-house or *outsourced* to external companies. Organizations with thousands of employees and thousands of details to keep track of use hundreds of systems, ranging from personal systems to systems that operate at an enterprise-wide level. Deciding which systems best support the direction of the organization, and how much attention to give each one, is where the job of systems development begins. A variety of individuals are responsible for one or more parts of the systems development process, as discussed next.

A company's *chief information officer (CIO)* has primary responsibility for systems development. Often this position is at the level of vice president. One of a CIO's duties is to develop a strategy that defines the role of information technology within the organization. Another duty is to develop a plan that maps out which systems are to be studied and possibly built or revamped now and over the next several years.

Because information technology plays such a pervasive role within most companies, *steering committees* comprised of top-level executives normally approve technology plans and set broad guidelines for performing computer-related activities. These committees do not involve themselves with technical details or administer particular projects. Such functions are the responsibility of the organization's *information systems department.*

The Information Systems Department

The *information systems (IS) department*—sometimes called the *information technology (IT) department*—varies in structure from one company to another. It often includes people who design and implement enterprise-wide systems, people who provide support services to PC users, and people who build and manage networks and databases. Figure 12-11 describes a number of jobs often found within information systems departments.

The pillar of most information systems departments is the *data processing area,* whose primary responsibility is to keep mission-critical transaction-processing-oriented systems within the company running smoothly. These systems, by and large, control the money coming into and going out of the organization. The data processing area predates all other areas within the information systems department and is still considered by many to be the most important. After all, if their computers stopped processing high volumes of business transactions, most large organizations would have to shut down.

Within the data processing area, the *system analysis and design group* analyzes, designs, and implements new software and hardware systems. The *programming group* codes computer programs from design specifications. The *operations group* manages day-to-day processing once a system has become operational.

The person most involved with systems development is the **systems analyst.** Generally speaking, the systems analyst's job is to plan, build, and implement the large systems that use the computers the organization has or will acquire. When such a system is needed, the systems analyst interacts with current and potential users to create one. The analyst generally is involved in all stages of the development process, from beginning to end.

Most large projects use a team of people. A systems analyst is often appointed as a *project manager* to head up the team. Other people on the team might include users, programmers, an outside consultant, a cost accountant, and an auditor. Users are especially vital to any team because they are the people who know the practical side of the application, and, also, they are the people who must work with any new system on a day-to-day basis.

Outsourcing Companies

When an organization lacks the staff to build or operate a system it needs, it often chooses an outsourcing option. *Outsourcing* involves turning over certain information systems functions to an outside vendor—usually one that specializes in outsourcing. For instance, many smaller banks outsource check-processing and customer-statement operations to companies that are skilled at this type of high-volume processing. It is also common for a business to outsource the development of its ERP or e-commerce system.

>**Systems analyst.** A person who studies systems in an organization in order to determine what work needs to be done and how this work may be best achieved.

Application programmer
A programmer who codes application software.

Computer operations manager
The person who oversees the computer operations area in an organization.

Computer operator
A person who is responsible for the operation of large computers and their support.

Control clerk
The person who monitors all work coming in and out of a computer center.

Database administrator
The person responsible for setting up and managing large databases within an organization.

Data-entry operator
A member of a computer operations staff responsible for keying in data into a computer system.

Data processing director
The person in charge of developing and/or implementing the overall plan for transaction processing in an organization and for overseeing the activities of programmers, systems analysts, and operations personnel.

Help-desk troubleshooter
A person who, by phone or computer, assists users in solving software and hardware problems.

Knowledge engineer
The person responsible for setting up and maintaining the base of expert knowledge used in expert system applications.

Network administrator
The person responsible for planning and implementing networks within an organization.

Programmer/analyst
A person, usually found in smaller companies, with job responsibilities that include both application programming and systems analysis and design.

Security specialist
The person responsible for seeing that an organization's hardware, software, and data are protected from computer criminals, natural disasters, accidents, and the like.

System administrator
The individual responsible for maintaining a large, multiuser system.

System librarian
The person in the computer operations area who manages files stored offline on tapes, disks, microfilm, and so on.

Systems analyst
A person who studies systems in an organization to determine what work needs to be done and how this work may best be achieved with computer resources.

Systems programmer
A person who codes systems software, fine-tunes operating-system performance, and performs other system-sofware-related tasks.

Trainer
A person who provides education to users about a particular program, system, or technology.

Vice president of information systems
The person in an organization who oversees routing transaction processing and information systems activities as well as other computer-related areas. Also known as the *chief information officer* (CIO).

Webmaster
The person responsible for establishing and maintaining an organization's Internet presence.

FIGURE 12-11
Information systems jobs.

Why do companies outsource? A small firm might find it too expensive to keep specialized personnel or equipment on hand. A large company might not have the capacity or capital to expand its operations in-house, so it may outsource some of them temporarily. Also, many firms have found it easier to outsource operations in areas where it's too hard to find or too expensive to hire new personnel. Firms often turn to an outsourcer when they think that the outsourcer can do the job better or at a lower cost than they can. An acute shortage of computer skills in recent years (see the Inside the Industry box), combined with high domestic labor costs and advances in networking technology, have led to explosive growth in global outsourcing. In the United States, program maintenance, data entry, and system conversion tasks are often sent to India and the Caribbean.

Along with the benefits of outsourcing come serious drawbacks. Some firms simply hand over their work to an outsourcer and then expect miracles. This is not effective because leadership needs to come from the client firm, not from the outsourcer. Also, when in-house personnel have to mix with the outsourcer's personnel, conflicts can arise. The in-house personnel may feel their jobs are threatened by the outsourcer's personnel, or they may disagree about who is in charge. Finally, the matters of control and security

inside the industry

IT Perks

Despite the recent dot-com fallout, the IT industry is still complaining about the shortage of qualified workers, particularly programmers. With studies showing that the best programmers are as much as 10 times as productive as the weakest ones, it is understandable that companies would want to try to find—and keep—the best employees. While the "finding" part is sometimes difficult, many companies find the "keeping" part the harder challenge.

In an attempt to lure and keep high-quality workers, many companies are becoming innovative. High salaries, lucrative stock options, and rewards (such as free food and free massages) during crunch times are still viable perks. However, newer approaches include limiting the workweek to 40 hours (to prevent burnout and losing employees who want to have a personal life outside of the office), allowing flexible hours, and having a variety of perks available at the office.

For example, basketball courts, punching bags, and nap rooms (complete with bunk beds or camping tents), child care centers, and wellness areas staffed with a fitness expert are working their way into many high-tech companies. Some organizations sponsor a variety of "idea rooms" to foster creativity. These may use a variety of themes and related decor to meet the employee's mood at the moment, such as a Zen room with a garden and water fountains, and a retro room with shag carpeting and lava lamps. iXL, an Internet consulting firm, goes a step further with its wild conference room complete with black lights, purple beanbag chairs, and Velcro walls that engineers can fling themselves onto during brainstorming sessions.

At MWW/Savitt, a Seattle public relations firm, the director of human resources (purportedly titled "the HR Goddess and Director of Cool") kicks off happy hour every Friday afternoon with a red wagon full of drinks. Salt Lake City's Campus Pipeline has a 180-hole golf course winding its way around the fifth-floor office. And at Excite@Home, executives use two big, red, winding slides instead of stairs to zip between floors. Now, that's a fun job!

This rooftop basketball court high atop DoubleClick's New York office building is just one type of perk available to IT employees today.

further exploration

For links to further information about information system developers, go to www.course.com/parker2002/ch12

need to be considered. Although an outsourcer provides some assistance in these areas, a company achieves the most control over its information processing and the best security when it keeps its work on site with its own people. When work goes outside, anything can happen.

Despite these drawbacks, outsourcing appears to be an unstoppable trend. Companies are eliminating many in-house jobs because of the high overhead involved in maintaining them. Among the leading suppliers of computer outsourcing services are Electronic Data System (EDS), Computer Sciences Corporation, and Andersen Consulting.

THE SYSTEMS DEVELOPMENT LIFE CYCLE (SDLC)

There are many specific tasks involved with systems development. Though the arrangement and order of these tasks may vary from organization to organization, a systems development project often contains six steps or phases.

- ▼ Phase 1: Preliminary investigation
- ▼ Phase 2: System analysis
- ▼ Phase 3: System design
- ▼ Phase 4: System acquisition
- ▼ Phase 5: System implementation
- ▼ Phase 6: System maintenance

Collectively, these phases make up the **systems development life cycle (SDLC).** As illustrated in Figure 12-12, the SDLC describes the development of a system from the time it is first studied until the time it is put into use. When a new business pressure necessitates a system change, the steps of the cycle begin anew.

web tutor

For a tutorial on the systems development life cycle, go to www.course.com/parker2002/ch12

◆ **FIGURE 12-12**

The systems development life cycle (SDLC). Each phase of the systems development life cycle produces some type of documentation to pass on to the next phase.

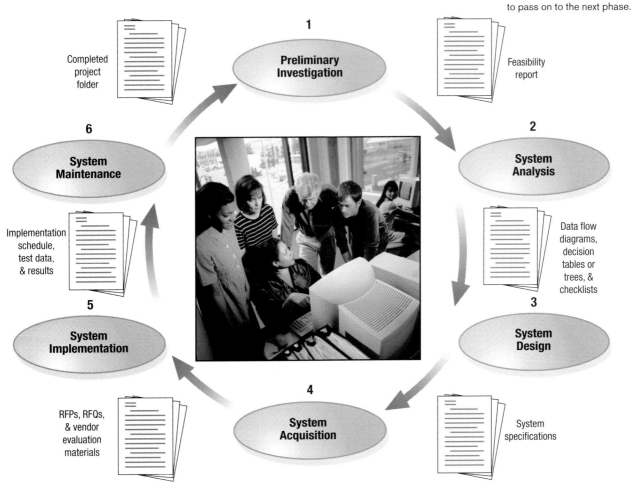

Completed project folder

1 Preliminary Investigation

Feasibility report

6 System Maintenance

2 System Analysis

Data flow diagrams, decision tables or trees, & checklists

Implementation schedule, test data, & results

5 System Implementation

3 System Design

RFPs, RFQs, & vendor evaluation materials

4 System Acquisition

System specifications

SYS

>**Systems development life cycle (SDLC).** The process consisting of the six phases of system development: Preliminary investigation, and system analysis, design, acquisition, implementation, and maintenance.

Duties of the Systems Analyst
Preliminary investigation During this phase the analyst studies a problem briefly and suggests solutions to management.
System analysis If management decides that further development is warranted, the analyst studies the applications area in depth.
System design The analyst develops a model of the new system and prepares a detailed list of benefits and costs.
System acquisition Upon management approval of the design, the analyst decides which vendors to use in order to meet software, hardware, and servicing needs.
System implementation After system components have been acquired, the analyst supervises the lengthy process of training users, converting data, and the like.
System maintainence The analyst evaluates the system on an ongoing basis, to determine any corrections or modifications that should be considered.

FIGURE 12-13

The role of the systems analyst in the six phases of systems development.

The six steps of the SDLC define in principle the process for building systems for multimillion-dollar information systems used in large corporations, as well as for information systems developed for a home office PC. As shown in Figure 12-12, each step results in some type of *documentation* that moves on to the next step in the cycle. The activities that may occur in each step of the SDLC will be discussed shortly. The role of the systems analyst during each step of the SDLC is illustrated in Figure 12-13.

Before taking a look at each of the steps in the SDLC, it is important to realize that these six steps do not always follow one another in a strict sequence. For example, analysis and design are frequently interwoven. Compare this process with an example from everyday life—vacation planning. People don't always design the whole plan as the first step and then execute it, without modification, as the second step. They might design a plan ahead of time but, when the first day of the vacation is over, they might use that day's experiences as a basis for modifying the plan for the second day. Many systems are designed this way as well. Smaller systems in smaller companies may also follow a less formal process of development, skipping or condensing some of the activities discussed next.

Preliminary Investigation

When a proposal for a new system or system modification is submitted, one of the first steps is to conduct a **preliminary investigation,** or *feasibility study.* The purpose of this investigation is to define and evaluate the problem area at hand relatively quickly, to see if it is worthy of further study, and to suggest possible courses of action. Accordingly, the investigation examines such issues as the nature of the problem, the scope of the work involved to solve it, possible solutions, and the approximate costs and benefits of each proposed solution.

The systems analyst must take care to distinguish *symptoms* from *problems* at the outset. For example, suppose an analyst is talking to a warehouse manager who complains that inventories are too high. This may be so, but this fact in itself is not enough to warrant corrective action. It's a symptom, not a problem. There is a problem, however, if these high inventories force the company to build an expensive new warehouse or if it is unnecessarily drawing on funds or other resources that could be used more productively. Note that even if a serious problem is identified, an organization may not be able to do anything about it. For instance, the high-inventory problem may be due to a strike somewhere else.

Documentation: Feasibility Report

The main output of the preliminary investigation is the *feasibility report,* which includes the systems analyst's findings on the status of the existing system, and the benefits and feasibility of changing to a new system. Feasibility is commonly measured using a few different perspectives, such as whether the organization has, or can acquire, the hardware, software, and personnel needed to implement the new system; whether the new system would fit well with the other systems in the organization; whether the estimated benefits of the new system outweigh the estimated costs; and so forth. The feasibility report also contains the system analyst's recommendations about whether or not the project should move on to the next stage in the SDLC: *system analysis.*

System Analysis

System analysis is the phase of systems development in which the problem area is studied in depth and the needs of system users are assessed. The main activities conducted during system analysis are *data collection* and *data analysis.*

Data Collection

The objective of *data collection* is to gather information about the work being performed in the system under study. The data collection process attempts to ascertain what resources users need to better perform their jobs. Later in this phase, the data collected should suggest some possible solutions. Which data is collected depends largely on the problem being studied. Some data-gathering tools that can be used include reviewing documents that show how the application is supposed to work, sending questionnaires to users, observing current activities, and interviewing those who use the system or the information produced by it.

An *organizational chart* that covers the functions being studied and the people in charge of those functions is an especially useful document to anyone studying a system. The chart gives an overview of the decision-making chain and how areas of responsibility are organized. Because people often don't do what they say they do, however, the only way an analyst can really determine if a system operates the way it is supposed to is by going to where people work and observing what they do.

Data Analysis

As information about the system is gathered, it must be analyzed so the requirements for a new system can be determined. Three useful tools for performing *data analysis* are diagrams, tables, and checklists.

Figure 12-14 shows a data flow diagram for the order-entry operation of a mail-order firm. *Data flow diagrams* show the relationships between activities that are part of a system as well as the data or information flowing into and out of each activity. In essence, they provide a visual representation of data movement in an organization.

Decision tables are useful for identifying procedures and summarizing the decision-making process for one step of a system. For example, the decision table in Figure 12-14 summarizes the decisions involved with the "Verify order is valid" process on the data flow diagram in that same figure. By using the table, it can be unequivocally determined which action to take during this process. The process of creating the table helps to ensure that all possible conditions have been considered. When the data in a decision table is expressed in a tree format, it is called a *decision tree.*

Checklists are often developed for important matters such as the goals of the system and the information needs of key people in the system. An accounts receivable system, for example, should have such goals as getting bills out quickly, informing customers about late payments, and cutting losses due to bad debts. On the other hand, a decision support system that helps teachers advise students should increase the quality of course-related information and decrease the time it takes to develop suitable curricula for students.

Common sense must dictate which type of checklist, table, or diagram is most appropriate for the situation at hand. The principal purpose of these tools is to help the analyst organize his or her thoughts so that he or she may draw conclusions about what the system under study should do.

Documentation: Data Flow Diagrams, Decision Tables, Decision Trees, and Checklists

The documentation resulting from the system analysis phase includes any instruments (questionnaires, interview questions, etc.) used in the data gathering stage, as well as the resulting diagrams, tables, trees, checklists, and other tools used to summarize and analyze the data.

System Design

System design focuses on specifying what the new system will look like. The system design phase primarily consists of developing a model of the new system and performing a detailed analysis of the expected benefits and costs.

>**System design.** The phase of the systems development life cycle in which a model of the new system and how it will work is formally established.

RULES

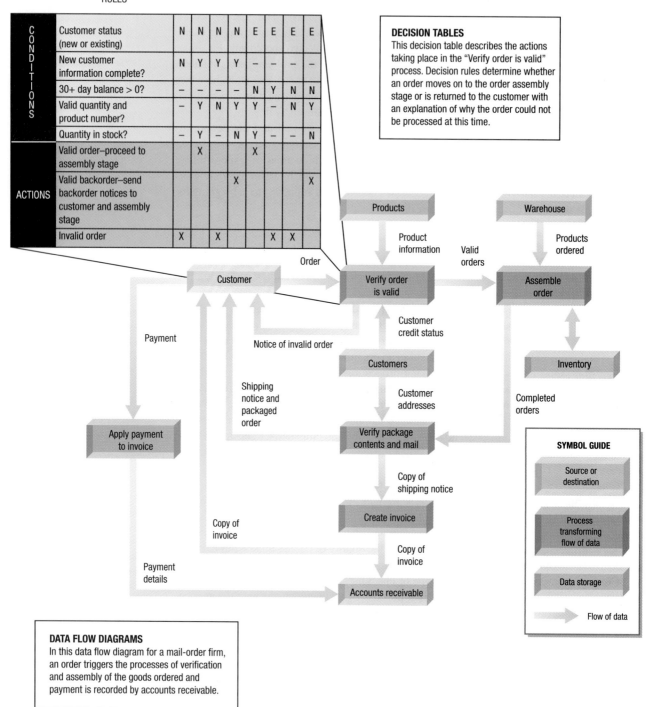

CONDITIONS		N	N	N	N	E	E	E	E
	Customer status (new or existing)	N	N	N	N	E	E	E	E
	New customer information complete?	N	Y	Y	Y	–	–	–	–
	30+ day balance > 0?	–	–	–	–	N	Y	N	N
	Valid quantity and product number?	–	Y	N	Y	Y	–	N	Y
	Quantity in stock?	–	Y	–	N	Y	–	–	N
ACTIONS	Valid order–proceed to assembly stage		X			X			
	Valid backorder–send backorder notices to customer and assembly stage				X				X
	Invalid order	X		X			X	X	

DECISION TABLES
This decision table describes the actions taking place in the "Verify order is valid" process. Decision rules determine whether an order moves on to the order assembly stage or is returned to the customer with an explanation of why the order could not be processed at this time.

SYMBOL GUIDE

Source or destination

Process transforming flow of data

Data storage

Flow of data

DATA FLOW DIAGRAMS
In this data flow diagram for a mail-order firm, an order triggers the processes of verification and assembly of the goods ordered and payment is recorded by accounts receivable.

⬤ **FIGURE 12-14**

Data flow diagrams and decision tables. These tools are frequently used to analyze a system during the system analysis phase of the systems development life cycle.

Developing a Model of the New System

Once the systems analyst understands the nature of the problem or situation under study, it is helpful to draw a number of diagrams of the new system. For example, the data flow diagrams discussed earlier show how data flows through the existing system; new data flow diagrams would be necessary to show how data would flow through the new system.

When designing a system, the analyst must take into account output requirements; input requirements; data access, organization, and storage; processing; system controls; and per-

Output Considerations

- Who are the system users and what types of information do they need?

- How often is this information needed? Annually? Monthly? Daily? On demand?

- What output devices and storage media are necessary to provide the required information?

- How should output be formatted or arranged so that it can easily be understood by users?

Input Considerations

- What data need to be gathered and who will gather them?

- How often do data need to be gathered?

- What input devices and media are required for data collection and input?

Storage Considerations

- How will data be accessed and organized?

- What storage capacity is required?

- How fast must data be accessed?

- What storage devices are appropriate?

Processing Considerations

- What type of functionality is required in the software?

- What type of processing power is required? A mainframe? A midrange server? A PC?

- What special processing environments must be considered? A communications network? A database processing environment?

System Controls

- What measures must be taken to ensure that data are secure from unauthorized use, theft, and natural disasters?

- What measures must be taken to ensure the accuracy and integrity of data going in and information going out?

- What measures must be taken to ensure the privacy of individuals represented by the data?

Personnel and Procedures

- What personnel are needed to run the system?

- What procedures should be followed on the job?

> **FIGURE 12-15**
>
> **Issues to cover during the system design stage of the SDLC.** System design ultimately addresses all major elements of a computer system: hardware, software, data, people, and procedures.

sonnel and procedure specifications. Figure 12-15 covers some of the issues that the analyst must address during the design stage.

Some of the tools a system analyst can use to model the new system are *system flowcharts, input/output designs,* and a *data dictionary.* System flowcharts illustrate operations that occur throughout the system—similar to a data flow diagram, but much more specific regarding each individual process. Input and output (I/O) designs show in what form input to, and output from, the system will appear—for example, input screens or printed reports. Both flowcharts and I/O designs are discussed in more detail and illustrated in Chapter 13.

A *data dictionary* is used to describe the characteristics of data used in a database or other type of computer system. It includes such information as a name and description for each piece of data, as well as the files that data will be found in; what type and size of data is allowed; any restrictions on the format of input (within a certain range of numbers, just certain characters of the alphabet, etc.); as well as who has the authority to update that data's specifications. Data dictionaries are discussed and illustrated in Chapter 14.

Cost/Benefit Analysis

Most organizations are acutely sensitive to costs, including computer system costs. The cost of a new computer system includes the initial investment in hardware, software, and training, as well as ongoing expenses such as personnel and maintenance. Some benefits can be computed easily by calculating the amount of labor the new system will save, the reduction in paperwork it will allow, and so on. These gains are called *tangible benefits,* because they represent quantifiable dollar amounts.

Other benefits, such as improvements in customer service or better information supplied to decision makers, are significantly more difficult to express as dollar amounts. These gains are called *intangible benefits.* Clearly, the existence of intangible benefits complicates management efforts to make cost/benefit decisions. Yet some of the most important systems projects undertaken in a company involve strategic opportunities that are difficult to quantify. On a project with a large number of intangible benefits, management must ask questions such as "Are the new services that we can offer to customers worth the $3 million they will cost us?"

Documentation: System Specifications

The system specifications developed during the system analysis phase consist of all the documentation necessary to illustrate the new system. This documentation includes data flow diagrams, system flowcharts, input and output designs, a data dictionary, and so forth, for the new system.

System Acquisition

Once a system has been designed and the required types of software and hardware have been specified, the analyst must decide where to obtain the necessary components. This decision lies at the heart of the **system acquisition** phase. While hardware is usually purchased from outside vendors, software can be either developed in-house or obtained from an outside vendor, depending on the alternative that works out best for the company. This decision is referred to as the *make-or-buy decision.*

The Make-or-Buy Decision

One of the first steps in the system acquisition phase it to determine whether the programs needed for the new system should be created in-house or acquired from a software vendor.

The "Make" Alternative

If an organization decides to develop its own application software, it moves into the *program development* process. As will be described in Chapter 13, this process has a life cycle that begins with the *problem analysis stage*—which takes a look at the documentation generated by the system design phase in the SDLC—through writing, testing, and maintaining the program. Once the *program development life cycle* has been completed, the software development life cycle continues, just as it would if the software had been purchased, as discussed next.

>**System acquisition.** The phase of the systems development life cycle in which hardware, software, and necessary system components are acquired.

The "Buy" Alternative

A choice often made by organizations is to select products that require virtually no in-house programming. During the past couple of decades, prewritten application programs for such tasks as payroll, accounting, financial planning, project management, and scores of others have become more widely available from software publishers. These packages usually consist of an integrated set of ready-to-run programs and documentation; training modules may be included, as well. Because they provide immediate results at a cost far lower than that of developing similar software from scratch, application packages are quite popular. However, it is not always possible to find an application package that exactly meets an organization's specific needs—in which case, the "make" alternative is preferable.

RFPs and RFQs

Once it has been determined that specific types of hardware or software must be purchased for the new system, many organizations prepare a document called a *request for proposal (RFP)*. This document contains a list of technical specifications for equipment, software, and services determined during the system design phase. The RFP is sent to all vendors who might satisfy the organization's needs. In the proposal they send back to the initiating organization, vendors recommend a solution and specify their prices for providing that solution.

In some cases, an organization knows exactly which hardware, software, and service resources it needs from vendors and is interested only in a quote on that specific list of items. In this case, it sends vendors a document called a *request for quotation (RFQ)*, which names the desired items and asks only for a quote. Thus, an RFP gives a vendor some leeway in making system suggestions, while an RFQ does not. Sometimes after the responses to an RFP have been received, the organization will then send out an RFQ for the system best determined to fit the organization's needs.

Evaluating Bids

Once vendors have submitted their bids or quotes in response to an RFP or RFQ, the acquiring organization must decide which one to accept. Two useful tools for making this choice are vendor rating systems and benchmark tests.

In a *vendor rating system,* important criteria for selecting computer system resources are identified and each is given a weight. For example, if the weights of 60 and 30 are given for hardware and documentation, respectively, it may be loosely interpreted to mean that the organization considers hardware twice as important as documentation. Each vendor that submits a bid is rated on each criterion (such as from 0 to 60 for its hardware). The buyer then totals the scores and, all other things being equal, chooses the vendor with the highest total. Although such a rating tool does not guarantee that the best vendor will always have the highest point total, it has the advantage of being simple to apply and relatively objective. If several people are involved in the selection decision, individual biases tend to average out.

After tentatively selecting a vendor, some organizations make their decision conditional on the successful completion of a **benchmark test.** Such a test normally consists of running a pilot version of the new system on items to be purchased from the vendor under consideration. To do this, the acquiring organization usually visits the vendor's testing center and attempts to determine how well the winning hardware/software configuration will work. Benchmark tests, however, are expensive and far from foolproof. It's quite possible that the pilot system will perform admirably at the benchmark site but the real system,

---

>**Benchmark test.** A test used to measure computer system performance simulating conditions of typical use prior to purchase.

when installed, will not. If the hardware to be used in the new system is already in place, another alternative is installing a demo or trial version of the proposed software to see how the software performs on the organization's hardware.

Documentation: RFPs, RFQs, and Vendor Evaluation Materials

The RFP or RFQ sent to potential vendors, the proposals received, and any documentation produced during the evaluation of the bids (vendor rankings, benchmark test results, etc.) comprise the documentation gathered during the system acquisition stage.

System Implementation

Once arrangements for the delivery of the ordered hardware and software have been made, the **system implementation** phase begins. This phase includes the tasks necessary to make the system operational. Implementation consists of converting programs and data files from the old system to the new one, preparing any existing equipment to work in the new systems environment, testing the system, and training personnel.

Converting to a new system can take place using one or more strategies (see Figure 12-16). With a *direct conversion,* the old system is completely deactivated and the new system is immediately implemented—a fast, but extremely risky, strategy. With a *parallel conversion,* both systems are operated in tandem until it is determined that the new system is working correctly, and then the old system is deactivated. With a *phased conversion,* the system is implemented modularly, with each module being implemented with either a direct or a parallel conversion. With a *pilot conversion,* the new system is used at only one location within the organization. After it is determined that the new system is working correctly, it is installed at the other locations. It is not unusual for an organization to implement a new system using some combination of these conversion options.

To ensure that the system will be working by a certain date, the system analyst prepares a timetable. One tool for helping with this task is *project management software* (illustrated in Chapter 7 in Figure 7-22), which shows how certain implementation activities are related and when they must start and finish. Once created, schedules prepared by such software can often be shared over a company network or the Internet and fine-tuned through feedback, as necessary. The schedule should include adequate time for testing the new system to make certain it is working properly.

When the system is tested, the data used in the testing process and the results obtained are usually saved in case they are needed at a later time. The data can be used to retest the system in the future, if modifications are made to the system. The data and corresponding results are also useful for determining if problems that occur with the system at a later time were tested for during this phase. That determination can indicate if the new problem is a result of a situation that was not taken into consideration during the system design process, or if there is another origin of the problem. When selecting test data, using copies of real data is preferred.

Documentation: Implementation Schedule, Test Data, and Results

The schedule and type of implementation used, as well as the test data and results, should all be saved for future reference.

System Maintenance

System maintenance is usually viewed as an ongoing process, beginning when the system is fully implemented and continuing on until the end of the system's life. One of the first

>**System implementation.** The phase of the systems development life cycle that encompasses activities relating to making the system operational.
>**System maintenance.** The phase of the systems development life cycle in which minor adjustments are made to the finished system to keep it operational until the end of the system's life or the time that the system needs to be redesigned.

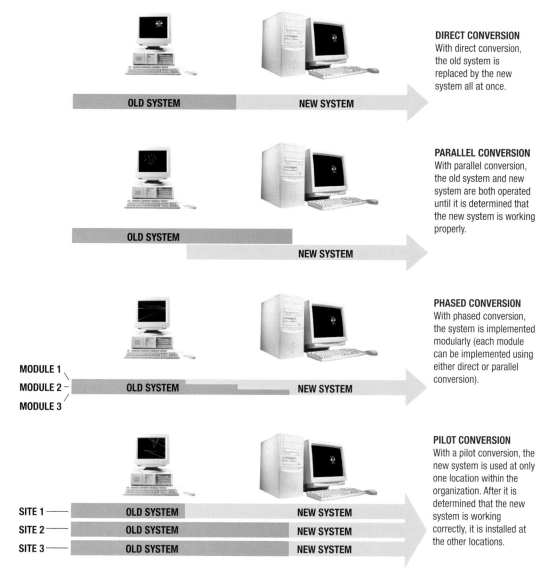

DIRECT CONVERSION
With direct conversion, the old system is replaced by the new system all at once.

OLD SYSTEM | NEW SYSTEM

PARALLEL CONVERSION
With parallel conversion, the old system and new system are both operated until it is determined that the new system is working properly.

OLD SYSTEM
NEW SYSTEM

PHASED CONVERSION
With phased conversion, the system is implemented modularly (each module can be implemented using either direct or parallel conversion).

MODULE 1
MODULE 2 — OLD SYSTEM | NEW SYSTEM
MODULE 3

PILOT CONVERSION
With a pilot conversion, the new system is used at only one location within the organization. After it is determined that the new system is working correctly, it is installed at the other locations.

SITE 1 —— OLD SYSTEM | NEW SYSTEM
SITE 2 —— OLD SYSTEM | NEW SYSTEM
SITE 3 —— OLD SYSTEM | NEW SYSTEM

FIGURE 12-16
System conversion.
Converting from an old system to the new one often follows one of these four approaches.

activities that takes place after the system has been implemented is some type of *post-implementation review.* This is basically a follow-up evaluation that is intended to correct any glitches that may have arisen in the system so far, and to provide feedback on the systems development process in general, so that the organization can continue to improve in this area as needed. The postimplementation review checks into whether or not the system is meeting its intended goals, whether costs are within expectations, and whether users are adapting favorably to the new systems environment.

System maintenance that may be required includes other software and hardware that need to be added to a system, either to update what's already in place or to add new features. It also includes correcting any problems or situations that have arisen and that were not addressed in the current system design. Maintenance can be costly to an organization, and it's not unusual to spend several dollars in maintenance over time for every dollar that was originally put into building the system.

A well-designed system should be flexible enough to accommodate changes over a reasonable period of time with minimal disruption. However, if a major change eventually becomes necessary, the organization must develop another system to replace the current one. At this point, the systems development life cycle—from preliminary investigation to implementation—begins all over again.

Documentation: Completed Project Folder

After the postimplementation review has been completed, its results are added to the documentation accumulated from the other stages of the SDLC. Since the system is fully implemented at this point, it is a good time to ensure all documentation has been gathered and organized in some manner, such as inside a *project folder*. This documentation is useful for auditors who may need to assess that proper procedures were followed during the system development process, as well as for systems analysts who may need to modify the system in the future.

APPROACHES TO SYSTEMS DEVELOPMENT

web tutor

For a tutorial on selecting a systems development strategy, go to www.course.com/parker2002/ch12

In this section, we examine the three main approaches to systems development: the *traditional approach, prototyping,* and *end-user development.*

The Traditional Approach

In **traditional systems development,** the phases of systems development are carried out in a preset order: (1) preliminary investigation, (2) analysis, (3) design, (4) acquisition, (5) implementation, and (6) maintenance. Each phase begins only when the one before it has been completed. Often, the traditional approach is reserved for the development of large transaction processing systems. Because the traditional approach is usually expensive, extensive, and time-consuming, knowledgeable professionals—systems analysts—normally carry it out.

Traditional systems development requires users to consider proposed plans for the new system by looking at detailed diagrams, descriptive reports, and specifications of the proposed new system. The entire system is planned and built before anyone gets to use it or test it. As each phase of development is completed, users "sign off" on the recommendations presented to them by the analyst, indicating their acceptance.

Many organizations have lost faith in the traditional approach to systems development. First, this approach often takes too long to analyze, design, and implement the new system. By the time a system finally begins operating, important new needs that were not part of the original plan may have already surfaced. Second, the system developed may turn out to be the wrong one. Managers frequently have difficulty expressing their information needs, and it is not until they begin to use a system that they discover what they really need.

These problems notwithstanding, traditional development is useful when the system being developed is one with which there is a great deal of experience, where user requirements are easy to determine in advance, and where management wants the system completely spelled out before giving its approval.

Prototyping

To avoid the potential problem of a system being incompatible with the system user, instead of developing the entire system before users ever lay their hands on it, many systems analysts have advocated prototyping. In **prototyping,** the focus is on developing a small model, or *prototype,* of the overall system. Users work with the prototype and suggest modifications. Then the prototype is enhanced. As soon as the prototype is refined to the point where upper management feels confident that a larger version of the system will succeed, either

---

>**Traditional systems development.** An approach to systems development where the six phases of the systems development life cycle are carried out in a predetermined sequence. >**Prototyping.** A systems development alternative where a small model, or prototype, of the system is built before the full-scale systems development effort is undertaken.

the prototype can be expanded into the final system or the organization can go full steam ahead with the remaining steps of systems development.

In prototyping, analysis and design generally proceed together in small steps that finally result in a completed system (see Figure 12-17). Prototyping is highly applicable in situations where user needs are difficult to precisely define, the system must be developed quickly, and some experimentation is necessary to avoid building the wrong system.

Prototyping and traditional development sometimes are combined in building new systems—for instance, by following the traditional approach but using prototyping during the analysis and design phases to clarify user needs.

End-User Development

End-user development is a systems development effort in which the user is primarily responsible for the development of the system. This is in contrast to the other types of development discussed here, in which a qualified computer professional, such as a systems analyst, takes charge of the systems development process.

As you might guess, end-user development is feasible only when the system being developed is relatively small and inexpensive. A good example is when a user purchases a PC and develops applications on his or her own. In developing the system, the user might follow a prototyping approach or a method similar to traditional development.

Certain dangers exist when users develop their own systems. Among these are users who do not incorporate proper security measures in their systems, who create systems that interfere with other systems within the organization, and who build systems that cannot effectively be supported. Nonetheless, when computer professionals within an organization are too overloaded to build small important systems to help users, end-user development may be the only alternative.

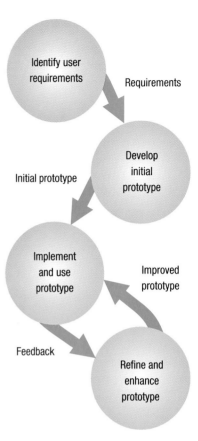

FIGURE 12-17

Prototyping. Prototyping is an interactive process. After each prototype is built, the user and analyst try it out together and attempt to improve on it.

Types of *systems* and how organizations build them are the principal subjects of this chapter.

WHAT IS AN INFORMATION SYSTEM?

Chapter Objective 1:
Explain what information systems are and who uses them.

A **system** is a collection of elements and procedures that interact to accomplish a goal. The function of many systems, whether manual or computerized, is to keep an organization well managed and running smoothly. An **information system** is a system used to generate information to support users in an organization.

Systems development is the process that consists of all activities needed to put a new system into place. Systems development may be required for many reasons—for example, changes in government regulations or the availability of new computer technology.

WHO USES INFORMATION SYSTEMS?

Information systems are used by decision makers, who are most commonly management employees. Managers are usually classified as *executive, middle,* and *operational* managers and typically manage the employees one level below them on the management pyramid. Operational managers typically manage *nonmanagement workers.* Executive managers generally use information systems to help them make relatively unstructured *strategic decisions;* middle managers typically use them to make relatively structured *tactical decisions;* and operational managers use them to help make operational decisions. Nonmanagement workers may access information systems to make on-the-job decisions.

TYPES OF INFORMATION SYSTEMS

Chapter Objective 2:
Describe several types of information systems commonly found in organizations.

Many types of information systems are used by businesses and other organizations. The term **office automation (OA)** refers to a wide variety of technologies and processing techniques, including *document processing* and *communications systems.* Together, the combination of hardware, software, and other resources used to facilitate communications and enhance productivity are collectively referred to as **office systems. Workgroup computing** is a type of communication system that allows several individuals to use their PCs to collaborate on job tasks. Office systems are frequently used by nonmanagement workers, as well as by managers.

Transaction processing systems perform tasks that generally involve the tedious record keeping that organizations handle regularly. Among these are **payroll, order-entry, inventory control,** and **accounting systems.** These types of systems are most commonly used by operational managers.

Management information systems (MIS) evolved from transaction processing systems and provide decision makers—primarily middle managers—with preselected types of information. A **decision support system (DSS)** helps middle and executive managers organize and analyze their own decision-making information. *Executive information systems (EISs)* are DSSs customized to meet the special needs of executive managers.

Enterprise-wide systems (such as *enterprise resource planning* or *ERP*) are integrated throughout the entire company or *enterprise.*

Computers are widely used in industry to improve productivity both at the design stage—through **computer-aided design (CAD)**—and at the manufacturing stage via **computer-aided manufacturing (CAM).**

The ability of some computer systems to perform in ways that would be considered intelligent if observed in humans is referred to as **artificial intelligence (AI).** Currently, the four main applications areas of AI techniques are **expert systems, natural-language systems, neural network systems,** and **robotics.** Most expert systems consist of a *knowledge base* as well as several programs, one of which is called an *inference engine.*

RESPONSIBILITY FOR SYSTEMS DEVELOPMENT

The *chief information officer,* or someone with a similar title, typically holds primary responsibility for the overall direction of systems development. The technical details are the responsibility of individual areas—such as the *data processing area* within the *information systems department.* **Systems analysts** are the people involved most closely with the development of systems from beginning to end. Often, the systems analyst acts as the *project manager* on the team assigned to the systems project. When a company lacks the in-house expertise, time, or money to do its own computer processing, it often turns to an *outsourcing* company to provide system services.

Chapter Objective 3:
Explain what systems development is and who is responsible for it.

THE SYSTEMS DEVELOPMENT LIFE CYCLE (SDLC)

Systems development often proceeds through six phases: preliminary investigation, system analysis, system design, system acquisition, system implementation, and system maintenance. These phases are often collectively referred to as the **systems development life cycle (SDLC),** because they describe a system from the time it is first studied until the time it is put into use. When a new business pressure necessitates a change in a system, the steps of the cycle begin anew.

Chapter Objective 4:
Identify and describe the different steps of the systems development life cycle.

The first thing the systems analyst does when confronted with a new project assignment is conduct a **preliminary investigation,** or *feasibility study.* This investigation addresses the nature of the problem under study, the potential scope of the systems development effort, the possible solutions, and the costs and benefits of these solutions. By the end of this phase, a *feasibility report* discussing the findings of the feasibility study is prepared.

Next, the **system analysis** phase begins. During this phase, the main objectives are to study the application in depth (to find out what work is being done), to assess the needs of users, and to prepare a list of specific requirements that the new system must meet. These objectives are accomplished through *data collection* and *data analysis.* A number of tools can help with analysis, including *data flow diagrams, decision tables, decision trees,* and *checklists.*

The **system design** phase of systems development consists of developing a model of the new system and performing a detailed analysis of benefits and costs. Various tools, such as *system flowcharts, input/output diagrams,* and a *data dictionary* can be helpful during this phase.

Once a system has been designed and the required types of software and hardware have been specified, the analyst must decide where to acquire the necessary components. This decision lies at the heart of the **system acquisition** phase. The *make-or-buy decision* determines whether the necessary components will be purchased or developed in-house. For the components to be purchased, many buying organizations use a *request for proposal (RFP)* or a *request for quotation (RFQ)* to obtain input from vendors. Vendors submitting bids are then commonly evaluated through a *vendor rating system* and then, possibly, a **benchmark test.**

Once arrangements have been made with one or more vendors for delivery of computer resources, the **system implementation** phase begins. This phase includes all the remaining tasks that are necessary to make the system successfully operational, including conversion of data, preparing any equipment to work in the new systems environment, and training. System implementation can use *direct conversion, parallel conversion, phased conversion,* or *pilot conversion. Project management software* may be used to create and maintain a schedule for the implementation.

System maintenance is an ongoing process that begins when the system is fully implemented and continues until the end of the system's life.

APPROACHES TO SYSTEMS DEVELOPMENT

Chapter Objective 5:
Discuss several approaches used to develop systems.

In **traditional systems development,** the phases of the SDLC are carried out in a predetermined order: preliminary investigation, analysis, design, acquisition, implementation, and maintenance. The focus in **prototyping** is on developing small models, or prototypes, of the target system in a series of graduated steps. *End-user development* is a systems development approach in which the user is primarily responsible for building the system. This is in contrast to other types of development, in which a qualified computer professional, such as a systems analyst, takes charge of the systems development process.

Instructions: Match each key term on the left with the definition on the right that fits best.

1. computer-aided design (CAD)

2. computer-aided manufacturing (CAM)

3. decision support system (DSS)

4. information system

5. management information system (MIS)

6. preliminary investigation

7. prototyping

8. robotics

9. system

10. system acquisition

11. system analysis

12. system design

13. system implementation

14. system maintenance

15. systems analyst

16. systems development life cycle (SDLC)

17. transaction processing system

_____ A collection of elements and procedures that interact to accomplish a goal.

_____ A general term applied to the use of computer technology to automate design functions.

_____ A general terms applied to the use of computer technology to automate manufacturing functions.

_____ A person who studies systems in an organization in order to determine what work needs to be done and how this work may be best achieved.

_____ A system used to generate information to support users in an organization.

_____ A systems development alternative whereby a small model, or prototype, of the system is built before the full-scale systems development effort is undertaken.

_____ A type of information system that handles data created by an organization's business transactions.

_____ A type of information system that provides decision makers with preselected types of information that can be used to make middle-management-type decisions.

_____ A type of information system usually used by upper management that provides people with the tools and capabilities to organize and analyze their decision-making information.

_____ The phase of the systems development life cycle in which a brief feasibility study is performed to assess whether or not a full-scale project should be undertaken.

_____ The phase of the systems development life cycle in which a model of the new system and how it will work is formally established.

_____ The phase of the systems development life cycle in which a problem area is thoroughly examined to determine what should be done.

_____ The phase of the systems development life cycle in which hardware, software, and other necessary system components are acquired.

_____ The phase of the systems development life cycle in which minor adjustments are made to the finished system to keep it operational until the end of the system's life or the time that the system needs to be redesigned.

_____ The phase of the systems development life cycle that encompasses activities relating to making the system operational.

_____ The process consisting of the six phases of system development: preliminary investigation, system analysis, design, acquisition, implementation, and maintenance.

_____ The study of robot technology.

Self-Quiz

Answers for the self-quiz appear at the end of the book.

True/False

Instructions: Circle **T** if the statement is true or **F** if the statement is false.

T F **1.** Executive managers tend to make highly unstructured decisions.

T F **2.** A decision support system would be most likely to be used by a nonmanagement worker.

T F **3.** An expert system is an example of an office system.

T F **4.** A data flow diagram would most often be created during the system analysis phase of the systems development life cycle.

T F **5.** Users are only involved in the systems development life cycle if the end-user approach is being used.

Completion

Instructions: Answer the following questions.

6. A(n) _____ provides decision makers with preselected, preplanned types of information typically generated through transaction processing and is most commonly used to make relatively structured, middle-management-type decisions.

7. A(n) _____ holds primary responsibility for systems development within an organization.

8. The program used in an expert system in conjunction with the knowledge base to reach decisions is called the _____.

9. Benefits that are easy to quantify in dollars are called _____ benefits.

10. Turning over specific tasks to an outside company is referred to as _____.

Exercises

1. For operational managers, indicate what type of employees they typically manage and what type of information systems they would most commonly use.

2. In the list below are several descriptions of activities performed by computer systems or by people working with computer systems. For each activity, indicate to which of the following information system categories the activity best belongs using the notation: Office system (O), transaction processing system (T), management information system (M), decision support system (D), enterprise-wide system (E), design and manufacturing systems (DM), and artificial intelligence systems (A). Note that categories may be used more than once and not all categories may be used.

Activity	Type of Information System
a. An employee creating a budget using a spreadsheet program	_____
b. Accounts receivable	_____
c. A manager receiving the same type of report every month	_____
d. A person buying a software package on the World Wide Web	_____

	Type of
Activity	**Information System**
e. A group of bank personnel collaborating on the approval of a personal loan on their desktop computers	_____
f. ERP	_____
g. An architect using a computer system to plan the layout of an office building	_____

3. For each of the following descriptions, select the most appropriate phase of the systems development life cycle (SDLC).

_____ The final phase of the SDLC.
_____ The phase of the SDLC that involves studying the system environment in depth.
_____ The phase of the SDLC in which the old system is converted to the new system.
_____ The phase of the SDLC that involves RFP or RFQ preparation, vendor rating systems, and benchmark tests.
_____ The first phase of the SDLC.
_____ The phase of the SDLC that follows system analysis.

   a. design
   b. implementation
   c. preliminary investigation
   d. analysis
   e. maintenance
   f. acquisition

4. Explain the difference between a request for proposal (RFP) and a request for quotation (RFQ).

5. Assume that a company is ready to install a new system at a single location. If they have a reasonable amount of time in which to implement the new system, select the two most appropriate conversion methods for the company to consider and explain under what circumstances they may wish to select one method over the other.

**Short Answer/
Research**

1. **Election 2000** Are information systems solely responsible for the information they generate, or do the humans that input and interpret this information assume some of the responsibility? Computer-based information systems have been used in the process of electing the President of the United States since 1952 when UNIVAC was used to predict the outcome of the Eisenhower, Stevenson election. The interpretation of the information generated by UNIVAC during the election and the eventual aftermath of a decision made about publicizing the information was very controversial and made U.S. history. The use of computer-based information systems to predict and determine the outcome of the 2000 presidential election also made history. The events and near national crisis of the 2000 election are significantly different from those of the 1952 election, but both involve humans and the interpretation of information generated by computer-based information systems. For this project, review the events, timing, and appropriateness of the prediction decisions made during both the 1952 and 2000 elections. Do you think humans have a tendency to rely too much on the information generated by information systems? Are the results of information systems always subject to interpretation? At the conclusion of your research, prepare a one-page summary of your findings and submit it to your instructor.

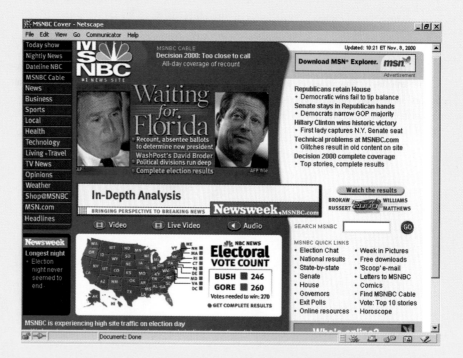

2. **Chatterbots** A *chatterbot* (coined from the terms *chatter* and *robot*) is a program that attempts to simulate the "chat" of another human. These programs have been available since the early 1960s, and can be experienced on multiple sites over the Internet. One use of a chatterbot is to interact with game players on the Web while they are waiting for their turn to play the game. Another more recent and much more exciting use is to have them act as a virtual interface to your Web site. In this case you would call them "verbots" instead of chatterbots and they would appear in a small picture on your screen and allow you to interact with them. One company called Virtual Personalities, Inc., is creating these "highly intelligent user interfaces featuring

verbally interactive characters called Verbots," and plans to revolutionize the way people relate to technology. For this project, research the history of chatterbots and communicate with a few of them over the Internet. In addition, you should visit the Virtual Personalities Web site and experience its "highly intelligent user interface" and have a verbal conversation with one, if that option is available. What chatterbots did you communicate with? Do you think that they responded to your comments in a human-like fashion? What do you think of the verbot at Virtual Personalities? Are verbots the wave of the future? At the conclusion of your research, prepare a one-page summary of your findings and submit it to your instructor.

3. **Robonaut** At the NASA Johnson Space Center program, scientists are developing robonauts to accompany humans in future space exploration programs. A *robonaut* is an advanced humanoid system that can go through a series of motions directed by an astronaut located in a space station. The robonauts will be about the size of a human and are configured with two arms, two five-fingered hands, a head, and a torso. The purpose of a robonaut is to minimize the danger and fatigue associated with space exploration by using the robonaut to accomplish certain tasks. Many such robotic-type devices have been used in the past to accomplish tasks in conjunction with surgery, the Chernobyl cleanup, deep-sea exploration, volcanoes, and recovering items from the *Titanic,* to name just a few. For this project, research at least three past, current, or planned uses of robots to perform tasks normally associated with humans. Why were robotics used in place of humans in each case? Were the tasks accomplished successfully? If so, what was accomplished? Would you be comfortable working with a robotic device? At the conclusion of your research, prepare a one-page summary of your findings and submit it to your instructor.

4. **Your Decision** The construction of a decision table is beneficial during the systems development life cycle. This tool can be used during the analysis phase to document how a decision is currently being made, during the design phase to document how the decision will be made in the new system, and during the actual coding of the new programs to assist the programmer in determining what actions to take, based on the identified rules and conditions. The utility of this tool is not limited to the analysis, design, and coding of information systems, however. It can just as easily be used to clarify and add structure to a decision about your future career plans. In this case, the analysis involved in identifying the rules and conditions that lead to the alternative actions may prove to be as productive and meaningful as the resulting table. For this project, construct a "Career Options" decision table that defines what actions you will need to obtain a job based on a set of conditions and rules. At the conclusion of this task, prepare a one-page summary of your efforts and submit it to your instructor along with your decision table.

Hands On

5. **NORAD** The development and implementation of information systems goes beyond the traditional business environment. One such example is the North American Aerospace Defense Command (NORAD) complex, which was originally designed to deter a massive nuclear attack, but now meets the aerospace needs of both Canada and the United States. These informational needs are based on the proliferation of cruise and ballistic missiles, which have made the post–Cold War threats more, rather than less dangerous. Over the past half-century NORAD has continued to improve its information systems to meet the changing needs of our political and military environment. On the humorous side, NORAD also acts as the worlds international "Santa Tracking Website" and has received more than 45 international Internet awards for Web site excellence. For this project, visit the NORAD Web site

Writing About Computers

SYS

at www.norad.org and review the proposed vision that information systems will have to support in the year 2010. Submit this project to your instructor in the form of a short paper, not more than two pages in length.

6. **Weather Systems** Can reliable weather forecasting information increase a company's revenues or reduce its costs? Many large companies are now examining the long-range forecasting data generated by supercomputers and including this information in their decision-making processes. Some of these companies download the raw data available from the U.S. government and develop their own information system to process the data and support their decision-making processes; others pay private forecasting companies to accomplish this task. In any case, it has been suggested that approximately 20 percent of our economy is vulnerable to the effects of the weather. For example, a company called Duraflame saved hundreds of thousands of dollars in distribution and buyback costs associate with the sale of its fabricated fireplace logs by using predicted weather data to more accurately estimate the sales of its products around the country. Other examples can be seen in the entertainment, sports, and utility industries. For this project, read about or visit the online Climate Prediction Center Web site located at www.nnic.noaa.gov/cpc and review the information available. In addition, you should identify at least three different situations in which you think that a company or industry could make use of this data to increase revenues or reduce costs. Submit this project to your instructor in the form of a short paper, not more than two pages in length.

7. **CIO or CTO** The role of the Chief Information Officer (CIO) at most large corporations is either being retired, augmented, or supplanted by a new position called Chief Technology Officer (CTO). The traditional role of the CIO is to oversee the strategies, policies, and operations of the companies information systems. The primary goal of the CIO is to ensure that the company's internal needs for strategic, tactical, and operational information are met on a timely basis. In the past few years, however, companies have been under great pressure to expand beyond the information provided by traditional information systems, and to develop strategies to implement e-commerce business models, e-commerce Web site models, and e-business applications—not typically a CIO's tasks. This pressure has lead to the new Chief Technology Office position at many corporations. The specific goals and responsibilities of a

CTO are not clearly defined at this point and will most likely overlap those of the traditional CIO. For this project, form a group to review several job announcements and news articles related to this subject and determine what the current roles and responsibilities are for a CTO and how they are differentiated from a CIO. How much does a CIO or CTO of a large corporation or emerging dot-com get paid on an annual basis? Will CTOs replace CIOs, or is this the big wake-up call for CIOs to get educated with respect to the Internet and e-commerce? Is anyone in your group interested in becoming a CIO or CTO? Your group should submit this project to your instructor in the form of a short paper, not more than three pages in length.

Presentation/ Demonstration

8. **IT and Wine** The process of making wine seemingly could not be simpler. All it requires is some grapes, your feet, a barrel, and, eventually, some bottles. This age-old tradition has been going on since biblical times and is considered more of an art, or a tradition, than a science. This being the case, why have most large wine companies decided to develop information systems and use them during the course of business? The answer to this question can be found in examining just how complicated the wine production process has become, and how much money is at stake. For this presentation, investigate the wine-making business, get a feel for the processes involved, and present a summary of the information systems that have been developed to ensure a quality and safe product, without hurting profit margins. This presentation should not exceed five minutes and should make use of one or more presentation aids such as the chalkboard, handouts, overhead transparencies, or computer-based slide presentation format. You may be asked to submit a summary of the presentation to your instructor.

9. **Staffing IT** The number of Information Technology (IT) jobs left unfilled at the end of 2000 exceeded 850,000, which was more than twice the number of jobs left unfilled in 1999. The demand for Internet-related and Java programming abilities were among the most sought after skills. As a result, companies have started offering tuition reimbursement and sign-on bonuses to attract new employees. For this project, form a group to investigate the current IT job situation and present a summary of the various IT job classifications, which areas offer the most opportunity for employment, what the educational and experience requirements are, where the majority of these jobs are available, and how much you can expect to earn if you get one of these jobs. Is anyone in your group interested in any of these jobs? If so, which ones? This presentation should not exceed 10 minutes and should make use of one or more presentation aids such as the chalkboard, handouts, overhead transparencies, or computer-based slide presentation format. Your group may be asked to submit a summary of the presentation to your instructor.

10. **Your Predictions** The future of technology and how it will impact information systems and their ability to make businesses more competitive is anybody's guess. The only sure bet is that things will not remain constant as businesses continue to incorporate the Internet and e-commerce into their business plans. Will we continue to have Chief Information Officers (CIOs), or will this position transition into Chief Technology Officers (CTOs) as businesses choose to take advantage of the Internet and implement e-commerce strategies? Will companies choose to manage data and information systems on internal computers and networks, or choose to outsource these services? How will your personal information on company systems be collected, managed, used, and protected? Will the information systems and basic structure of companies change? For this project, form a group to research each of the questions posed above and arrive at your own conclusions. How could any of the predictions you have made affect your future career plans? This presentation should not exceed 10 minutes and should make use of one or more presentation aids such as the chalkboard, handouts, overhead transparencies, or computer-based slide presentation format. Your group may be asked to submit a summary of the presentation to your instructor.

11. **Accountability** Many companies are producing information systems that track human productivity and accountability. These systems are generally sold as labor management systems and track such things as performance, productivity, and quality of work preformed by individuals. In addition, this information can be tracked for years and used to produce reports on a daily, weekly, monthly, or yearly basis. As the competition between companies in our new computerized and networked economy continues to intensify, organizations will increasingly use this software to differentiate between the employees they keep and those that they layoff.

Select one of the following positions, or make up your own, and express your point of view on the subject. Your instructor will indicate whether your response is to be posted to a class bulletin board, discussed in a class chat room, or discussed as an in-class activity. You may also be asked to submit a summary of your position and point of view.

a. Labor management systems will indeed be implemented. However, they will not be used to differentiate between employees for the purpose of employment. They will be used to enhance the employee's performance and reward outstanding productivity.

b. Labor management systems will be implemented. However, they will be abused by management to monitor and eliminate the least productive members of an organization. In addition, the implementation of these systems will serve to lower the moral and productivity of all employees.

12. **E-Sourcing** Consider the following statement and establish your position, or point of view, on the subject. Your instructor will indicate whether your response is to be posted to a class bulletin board, discussed in a class chat room, or discussed as an in-class activity. You may also be asked to submit a summary of your position and evaluation of the statement.

A company's ability to make use of information technology (IT) to streamline its business model and maximize its shareholders value will play a key role in the success or failure of most organizations over the next few years. Several factors influence a company's ability to implement information technology, including their in-house ability to develop and deploy these systems, the willingness of existing employees to accept these systems, the costs associated with the hardware, software, and development efforts, and the time it takes to implement these systems. Some companies realize that these tasks are beyond the capability of their in-house personnel and are opting to outsource and "e-source" much of this development and implementation. Outsourcing, as described in the text, is when an organization turns over certain information systems development tasks to an outside organization. *E-sourcing* takes outsourcing to the next level by contracting with outside organizations to provide both the information technology, and the access to this technology by using the Internet. Both of these approaches are very attractive to organizations because it allows them to meet their information needs without hiring specialized employees, reduce the number of existing employees quickly and easily as the organization becomes streamlined, rent access to existing information technology software rather than purchasing it, and allow for rapid expansion or adjustments in the companies business model. The increasing ability of organizations to outsource or e-source their information needs spells the end of long term job security for lower and middle level management employees. We will eventually have flat organizations made up of the individuals that do the work, and the owners of the companies that make the decisions.

Understanding Information Systems and Systems Development.   Let's see how much you remember about system development! Go to the Interactive Exercise at www.course.com/parker2002/ch12 to complete this exercise.

CHAPTER 13

Program Development and Programming Languages

LEARNING OBJECTIVES

After completing this chapter, you will be able to:

1. Identify and describe the activities involved in the program development life cycle (PDLC).

2. Understand what constitutes good program design.

3. Describe several tools that can be used by computer professionals when designing a program.

4. Explain the three basic control structures and how they can be used to control program flow during execution.

5. Explain some of the activities involved with coding, debugging, maintaining, documenting, and ensuring the quality of programs.

6. List tools that can be used to speed up or otherwise facilitate the program development process.

7. Identify programming language options available to code programs.

8. List some Web-based languages that can be used instead of, or in addition to, programming languages to create Web content.

If you wanted to build a house, you'd probably begin with some research and planning. You might speak to people about home design, draw up some floor plans, estimate the cost of materials, and so on. In other words, you wouldn't start digging a hole and pouring concrete on the first day. Creating successful application programs for a computer system also requires considerable planning.

Computer professionals need to develop new applications from time to time. They do this by using either a traditional programming language or a Web-based language, depending on the particular application. In the previous chapter we spent a great deal of time looking at developing entire computer systems. In this chapter we look specifically at practices for developing the application programs used within systems. Therefore, we discuss the activities that take place in the systems acquisition stage of the systems development life cycle, if the decision is made to create the necessary programs in-house. These same steps would occur, but possibly in an abbreviated manner, if an existing program is to be modified in-house to better fit the needs of the system. If the software to be used with the new system is to be purchased from an outside vendor, the activities described in this chapter are executed by the outside vendor as it develops the requested program, not by the organization purchasing the software.

The chapter opens by discussing the *program development life cycle*–the steps involved when a new program needs to be created or an existing program needs to be modified. This process includes program design, coding, debugging, testing, and maintenance. We then turn to *programming languages,* discussing what they are and some of the most popular languages. The chapter closes with a brief discussion of other types of languages frequently used in Web page development. ■

THE PROGRAM DEVELOPMENT LIFE CYCLE (PDLC)

Creating application programs is referred to as *application software development* or **program development.** Program development often begins with the system specifications that are developed during the analysis and design phases of the systems development life cycle (SDLC), which we discussed in Chapter 12. The steps involved in program development are referred to as the **program development life cycle (PDLC)** and consist of the following (see Figure 13-1).

▼ Step 1: Problem analysis

▼ Step 2: Program design

▼ Step 3: Program coding

▼ Step 4: Program debugging and testing

▼ Step 5: Program maintenance

web tutor

For a tutorial on program development, go to www.course.com/
parker2002/ch13

>**Program development.** The process of creating application programs. >**Program development life cycle (PDLC).** The process containing the five steps of program development: Analyzing, designing, coding, debugging and testing, and maintaining application software.

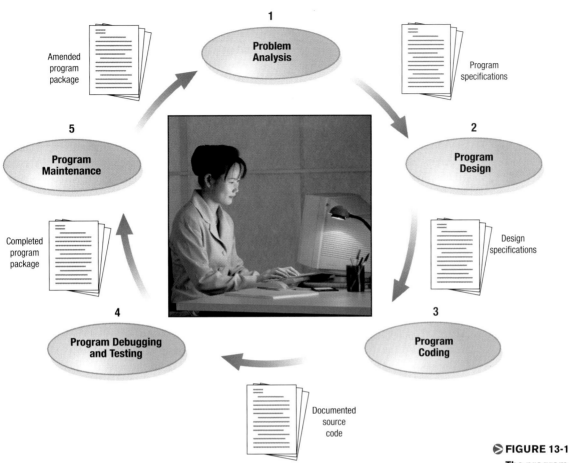

FIGURE 13-1

The program development life cycle (PDLC). Each step of the program development life cycle produces some type of documentation to pass on to the next step.

The activities that take place during each step of the program development life cycle are discussed in the next few sections. As each critical development activity is taking place, documentation is generated. The documentation consists of details about what the program does and how it works.

Problem Analysis

As discussed in the previous chapter, during the first few steps of the systems development life cycle the systems analyst develops a set of specifications indicating exactly what the new system should do and how it will work. During **problem analysis**—the first step of the PDLC—these specifications (data flow diagrams, system flowcharts, input and output designs, data dictionary, etc.) are reviewed by the systems analyst and the **programmer**—the person who will code the program to these specifications using a *programming language*. During this stage, the systems analyst and programmer may meet with the users of the new system to fully understand what functions the software they are creating for the new system must perform.

Documentation: Program Specifications
The end result of this first step in the program development life cycle is a set of program specifications outlining what the program must do, the timetable for completing the program, which programming language will be used, how the program will be tested, and what documentation is required.

>**Problem analysis.** The step in the program development life cycle in which the problem is carefully considered and the program specifications are developed. >**Programmer.** A person whose job it is to write, maintain, and test computer programs.

Program Design

In the **program design** stage of program development, the specifications developed during the problem analysis step are used to spell out as precisely as possible the nature of the required program. The design, or plan, derived from these specifications expresses the *algorithm*—set of steps—needed to solve the problem in question. This algorithm must address all the tasks that programs must do, as well as how to organize or sequence these tasks when coding programs. Only when the design is complete does the next stage—the actual program coding—begin.

Good program design helps the development process go more smoothly and makes revisions easier in the future. Just as with Web site design (discussed in Chapter 10), careful planning and design is extremely important and pays off in the long run. Some program design considerations are discussed next.

Structured Programming and Object-Oriented Programming

There have been various approaches to program design over the years. The approach used is partially determined by the actual *programming language* to be used. It also affects which *program design tools* may be used during the design process. Two of the most significant approaches—*structured programming* and *object-oriented programming*—are discussed next.

Structured Programming

Beginning in the 1960s, a number of researchers began to stress program planning and design and the merits of separating the design process from the actual program coding. Such a division of labor is a natural one. For example, architects design buildings and construction crews work from those specifications to build them. Many of the proposed ideas of the researchers caught on, and methods evolved that made program design more systematic and the programs themselves easier to understand and maintain. These methods are usually grouped together under the term **structured programming.**

In structured programming, programs are separated into smaller programs (called *modules* or *subprograms*). Prior to structured programming, programs were written as one large set of instructions containing statements such as "GOTO 100," which sends program control to line 100 of the code to execute commands from that point on until another GOTO statement is reached. This jumping from one part of the program to another with these and similar statements continued until the program ended. To overcome the problem of understanding, following, and modifying this type of program (sometimes referred to as "spaghetti code," because it was a disorganized, intertwined, jumble of statements), structured programs send control out to a subprogram whenever it is necessary to perform a small or repeated task, instead of sending control to a different location in the main program. Program control then returns to the main program to continue down the lines of code once the subprogram has finished executing. Tasks in a structured program usually follow one of the three types of *control structures,* illustrated in a later section.

Object-Oriented Programming (OOP)

A newer approach to program design is called **object-oriented programming (OOP).** While OOP technology has been around for nearly two decades, only recently has it become widely used. One of the principal motivations for using OOP is to handle multimedia and Web-page applications. Another is writing program code that's more intuitive and reusable in other words, code that can significantly shorten program-development time.

>**Program design.** The step in the program development life cycle in which the program specifications are expanded into a complete design of the new program. >**Structured programming.** An approach to program design in which a program is separated into smaller subprograms, and step-by-step instructions are executed one after the other, accessing the subprograms when needed. >**Object-oriented programming (OOP).** An approach to program design in which a program is comprised of a collection of objects.

OOP is a style of programming in which real-world objects—buttons, windows, employees, cars, etc.—are modeled using software *objects.* Though this modeling can be done with conventional programming languages, *object-oriented programming languages* provide direct support for objects, making it significantly easier to do. An *object* is a software bundle containing *variables* (data about the state of the object) and related *methods* or *functions* (instructions to be used with the data to control or illustrate the current behavior of the object). For example, possible variables for a button object would include one to hold the coordinates of the display rectangle and one to hold the color of the button (see Figure 13-2). The button object would also include methods for any actions that may be taken, such as to display, hide, or dim the button. The bundling of an object's variables and methods into a single package so that the details are hidden from the user's view is called *information hiding* or *encapsulation.*

In addition to variables and methods, objects also contain information that defines how the object can exchange *messages* with other objects. When an object receives a message, it invokes the appropriate response. The same message can be sent to different objects and each object deals with the message using its appropriate method. This OOP principle is called *polymorphism.* For instance, a *Display* message sent to the button object would cause the button to be displayed on the screen, whereas the same Display message sent to an employee object might cause the employee's information (name, address, photo, etc.) to be displayed. How each object reacts to each message is determined by the corresponding method (*Display* method, in this example) stored in the object.

The data contained within an object can be in a variety of formats, such as numeric, text, image, video, audio, and so forth. This, combined with the ability to manipulate different types of objects with the same message, leads to new applications that were difficult, or impossible, to create with traditional programming languages. For example, the statement

$$c = a + b$$

is a typical statement in most programming languages. It would generally be used to combine (add) numbers together. In an OOP language, however, the same statement could be used to combine two strings of data to display a first and last name next to each other. It could also be used to combine two music clips, or one video clip and one soundtrack, to play them at the same time. In an OOP, there is no limit to the complexity of an object.

Objects in an OOP are organized into classes. A *class* is a blueprint that defines the unique characteristics common to all objects of a certain kind. For example, all buttons have things in common and the class describes these common characteristics. There may also be *subclasses* below a class, such as for round buttons and polygon buttons. In addition to the characteristics of the subclass, all objects in a subclass automatically possess—or *inherit*—all characteristics of the class from which it was derived. Classes and objects are illustrated in Figure 13-9 later in this chapter.

One advantage of OOP is that objects can be accessed by multiple programs. When objects are accessed, the program determines which methods or procedures are available, depending on the current state of the object. Therefore, objects can be reused without having to alter the code contained in the object.

Designing an object-oriented program differs somewhat from designing a structured program. Some design tools that can be used with OOP are discussed shortly.

Program Design Tools

Program design tools are planning tools. They consist of diagrams, charts, tables, and models that outline the organization of program tasks, the steps the program will follow, or the characteristics of an object. Once a program has been coded and implemented, program design tools serve as excellent documentation. Three program design tools widely used with structured programming are *structure charts, flowcharts,* and *pseudocode.* A fourth tool sometimes used with object-oriented program design is *data modeling.* We cover each of these tools next.

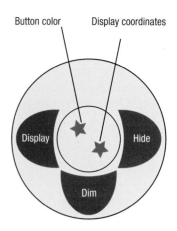

Button color   Display coordinates

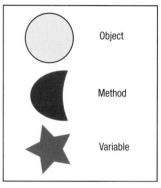

Object

Method

Variable

◈ FIGURE 13-2

Objects. Objects in an object-oriented program contain both data and instructions. The Button object shown here contains two variables to hold data about the current state of the button and three methods (sets of instructions) to be used to react to messages the object receives.

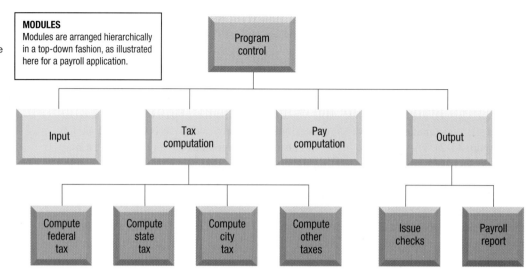

Structure charts.
Structure charts illustrate the individual modules contained within a program; each module represents a specific processing task.

MODULES
Modules are arranged hierarchically in a top-down fashion, as illustrated here for a payroll application.

Start or stop program

Processing

Input or output

Decision

Flowline

Connector

Offpage connector

◉ **FIGURE 13-4**
Program flowchart symbols.

Structure Charts

Structure charts (sometimes called *hierarchy charts*) depict the overall organization of a program. They show how program segments, or modules, are defined and how they relate to one another. Figure 13-3 illustrates a structure chart for a payroll application.

A typical structure chart, with its several rows of boxes connected by lines, resembles a corporate organization chart. Each box on the chart represents a program module—that is, a set of logically related operations that perform a well-defined task. The modules in the upper rows serve as control functions, directing the program to process modules under them as appropriate. The modules in the lower boxes perform specific processing functions. These latter modules do the majority of the program work and may be further broken down into submodules, if necessary. The lines connecting the boxes indicate the relationship between higher-level and lower-level modules.

Structure charts embody a *top-down design* philosophy—that is, modules are conceptualized first at the highest levels of the hierarchy and then at progressively lower levels. Put another way, the broad functions that are first defined at the highest levels are broken down further, level by level, into well-defined subfunctions with specific tasks to be carried out. This stepwise refinement is similar to what happens in a corporate organization chart—broad functions such as marketing, production, and information systems are defined at higher levels on the chart than the job areas falling underneath those functions. For example, under information systems might fall operations, programming, and systems analysis and design; under programming, responsibilities may be further divided into application programming, systems programming, and Web programming.

Logically speaking, establishing how a program is organized is the first step in program design. Once all functions of the program are carefully laid out in a structure chart or equivalent tool, the next step of design—showing the step-by-step logic that is to take place in each module—starts. This is where program flowcharts and pseudocode are useful.

Program Flowcharts

Program flowcharts use geometric symbols, such as those in Figure 13-4, and familiar *relational operators,* such as those in Figure 13-5, to graphically portray the sequence of steps involved in a program. The steps in a flowchart occur in the same logical sequence that their corresponding program statements follow in the program. To help you understand what the symbols and operators mean and how they are used, let's consider an example.

A common activity in information processing is scanning a file to locate people with certain characteristics. Suppose a company's human resources department wants a printed list of all employees with computer experience and at least five years of company service. A flowchart that shows how to accomplish this task and also totals the number of employees who meet these criteria is shown in Figure 13-6.

This particular flowchart uses five symbols: start/stop, processing, decision, connector, and input/output. The lines with arrows that link the symbols are called *flowlines* and they indicate the flow of logic.

Every flowchart begins and ends with an oval-shaped *start/stop symbol*. The first of these symbols in the program contains the word *Start,* and the last contains the word *Stop.*

Operator	Meaning
<	Less than
<= or ≤	Less than or equal to
>	Greater than
>= or ≥	Greater than or equal to
=	Equal to
≠ or <> or ><	Not equal to

◉ FIGURE 13-5
Relational operators used in flowcharts.

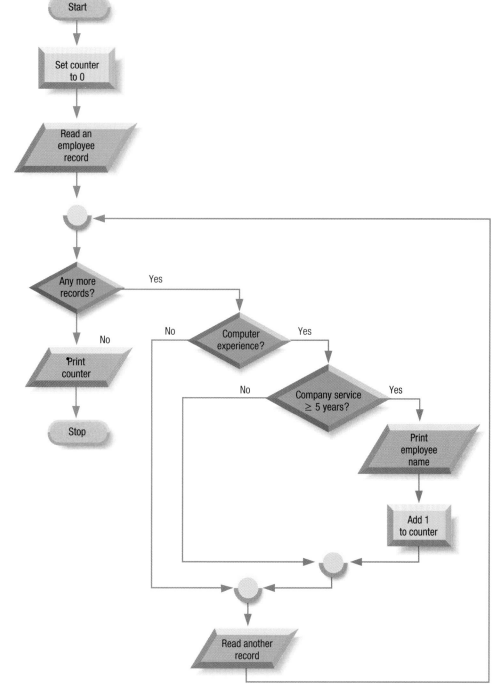

◉ FIGURE 13-6
A flowchart example: Scanning an employee file. This flowchart represents scanning an entire employee file to determine all people who have computer experience and at least five years of company service. When those individuals are located, their names are printed out. When the scan has been completed, the running count of the number of people matching the criteria is printed out.

The diamond-shaped *decision symbol* indicates a question, generally with only two possible answers—yes or no (or true or false). Decision symbols always have one flowline entering and two flowlines (representing each of the two possible outcomes) exiting.

The rectangular *processing symbol* contains an action to be taken—for example, "Set counter to 0" and "Add 1 to counter." The *connector symbol* provides a meeting point for several flowlines. The *input/output symbol* enables the process depicted in the flowchart to either accept or output data.

The flowchart in Figure 13-6 involves a *looping* operation. We read a record, inspect it, and take an action; then read another record, inspect it, and take another action; and so on until the file is exhausted. (This and other possible types of *control structures* are discussed in more detail shortly.) When the computer reads a record, as indicated by the input/output symbol, it brings it into memory. If the record meets both search criteria, the employee's name is printed and a counter is incremented by 1. After the last record is read and processed, the value of the counter is printed and then the program ends.

For easier flowchart development and modification, flowcharting software (shown in Figure 13-7) can be used.

Pseudocode

An alternative to the flowchart is **pseudocode.** This structured technique uses English-like statements in place of the flowchart's graphic symbols.

As shown in Figure 13-8, pseudocode looks more like a program than a flowchart. In fact, it's often easier to code a program from pseudocode than from a flowchart, because the former provides a codelike outline of the processing to take place, though pseudocode isn't necessarily tied to a particular programming language. As a result, the program designer has more control over the end product—the program itself. Also unlike a flowchart, pseudocode is relatively easy to modify and can be embedded into the program as comments. However, flowcharts, being visual, are sometimes better than pseudocode for designing logically complex problems and are usually faster to create.

No formal set of standard rules exists for writing pseudocode, but Figure 13-8 follows some common conventions. Note that all words relating to a control structure (to be discussed shortly) are capitalized and the processing steps contained within those structures are indented. Indentation can also be used to enhance readability. The keywords *Start* and *Stop* are often used to begin and end pseudocode.

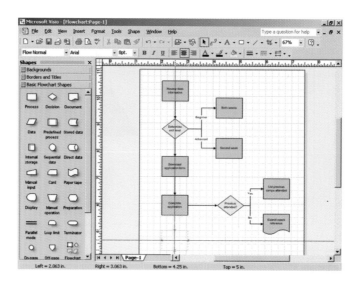

◗ FIGURE 13-7

Flowcharting software can make it easier to create and modify program flowcharts.

>**Pseudocode.** A program design tool that uses English-like statements to outline the logic of a program.

Data Modeling

Data modeling is a technique to illustrate the data in an application and is often used when designing an application to be implemented using object-oriented programming (OOP). With an OOP application, all the objects in the program are identified, along with their corresponding class, properties, and variables. The relationships between the objects are also illustrated in the data model. For example, Figure 13-9 contains a data model for a bicycle object that might be used in an OOP program to model a bike controlled by a user in a video game or bikes for sale in a bike shop. As shown in the figure, the bicycle class specifies the properties that all bicycles have in common. Each individual object in the bicycle class (called an *instance*) contains variables to indicate the current value for the number of gears, and current gear, speed (in mph), and pedal cadence (in rpm) for each bike. The bicycle object also includes appropriate methods, such as for braking, changing the pedal cadence, and changing gears, but those methods are not illustrated in this diagram. Note that each instance inherits the characteristics of the class but has its own values for each variable. When appropriate, a single class can be broken into subclasses. For example, the single class in Figure 13-9 could be broken down into racing, mountain, and regular bikes, if appropriate for the application.

Control Structures

A **control structure** is a pattern that controls the order in which instructions in a computer program are performed. Advocates of structured programming have shown that any program can be constructed from three fundamental control structures: *sequence, selection,* and *iteration.* These control structures are illustrated in Figure 13-10 and discussed next.

```
Start
Counter = 0
Read a record
DOWHILE there are more records to process
    IF computer experience
        IF company service ≥ 5 years
            Print employee name
            Increment Counter
        ELSE
            Next statement
        END IF
    ELSE
        Next statement
    END IF
    Read another record
END DO
Print Counter
Stop
```

◗ FIGURE 13-8

Pseudocode example: Scanning an employee file. The problem (the same as illustrated in the flowchart in Figure 13-6) requires printing the names of all people in an employee file with computer experience and at least five years of company service. A count of the number of such people is also included as output.

◗ FIGURE 13-9

Data model for an object-oriented program.

| Class |
| Property |
| Instance |
| Variable |

CLASSES
A class defines the common properties for all subclasses and instances below it in the hierarchy.

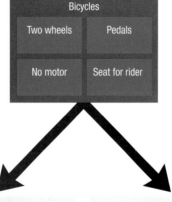

Bicycles

| Two wheels | Pedals |
| No motor | Seat for rider |

INHERITANCE
The class properties are inherited by all subclasses and instances of the class.

Bike 1

| CurrentSpeed = 15 | CurrentCadence = 90 |
| NumberGear = 10 | CurrentGear = 2 |

Bike 2

| CurrentSpeed = 10 | CurrentCadence = 60 |
| NumberGear = 15 | CurrentGear = 5 |

INSTANCES
Instances are the specific objects in a class. Though they inherit all properties of the class and any subclass above it in the hierarchy, they also contain variables for properties that are not common among all class instances. Each instance also includes methods to be used with this data.

>**Control structure.** A pattern for controlling the flow of logic in a computer program.

The Sequence Control Structure

A *sequence control structure* is simply a series of procedures that follow one another. After the first instruction has been carried out completely, the program control moves to the next step.

The Selection Control Structure

With a *selection control structure,* the direction that the program control takes depends on a certain condition. The most common type of selection control structure is the *if-then-else structure* shown in Figure 13-10, where the condition can only result in two possibilities—true or false (yes or no). *If* a certain condition is true, *then* the program follows one procedure; *else,* if false, the program follows a different procedure.

Another possible selection control structure is used when there are more than two possibilities. This structure—known as the *case control structure* and shown in Figure 13-10—allows for as many possible results of the specified condition as needed. For example, in the flowchart in Figure 13-6, the two individual choices—"Computer experience?" and "Company service ≥ 5 years?"—result in the following four possibilities, or cases:

▼ Case 1: No computer experience, company service < 5 years

▼ Case 2: No computer experience, company service ≥ 5 years

▼ Case 3: Computer experience, company service < 5 years

▼ Case 4: Computer experience, company service ≥ 5 years

To use the case control structure instead of the two nested if-then-else structures in the flowchart in Figure 13-6 would result in a case structure with four choices; the only actions (printing the employee's name and incrementing the counter) would be listed under Case 4.

The Iteration Control Structure

The *iteration control structure* (also called the *repetition* or *looping control structure*) is used when one or more instructions are to be repeated until a particular condition is reached. This control structure can take one of two forms: do-while or do-until.

With the *do-while structure,* a loop is executed as long as a certain condition is true ("do *while* true"). Therefore, if the condition is not true to begin with, the instructions within the loop are never executed (notice that the decision is at the top of the do-while structure in Figure 13-10). With the *do-until structure,* the loop continues as long as a certain condition is false ("do *until* true"). With do-until, the loop procedure is always executed at least once, because the procedure appears before any test is made about whether or not to exit the loop (refer to the do-until structure in Figure 13-10).

Good Program Design

Good program design is essential. If a program is not well planned out before the coding process begins, it usually results in a more time-consuming, and, potentially, a lower-quality result than if the design process had been carried out properly. Just as when designing Web sites, as discussed in an earlier chapter, time spent planning is time well spent. A few principles that should be kept in mind to help facilitate good program design are discussed next.

Be Specific

When illustrating the instructions that the computer will follow, *all* things that the computer must do or consider must be specified. Though the instruction "Please make me a piece of toast" would be a clear enough request for another person to follow, a computer would be lost with that lack of specificity. To properly instruct a computer, every step the computer must perform and every decision the computer must make has to be stated exactly. For example, the instructions that would be required for a computer to understand how to make a piece of toast are listed in Figure 13-11.

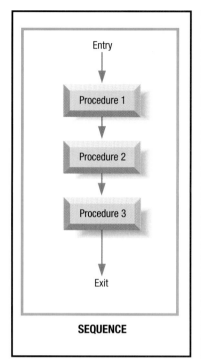

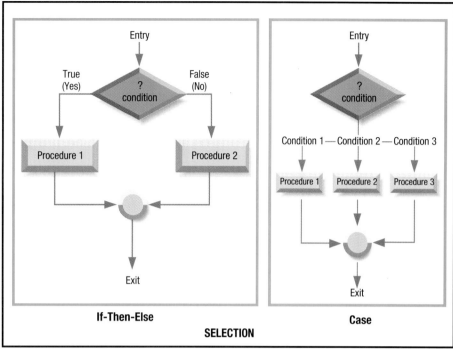

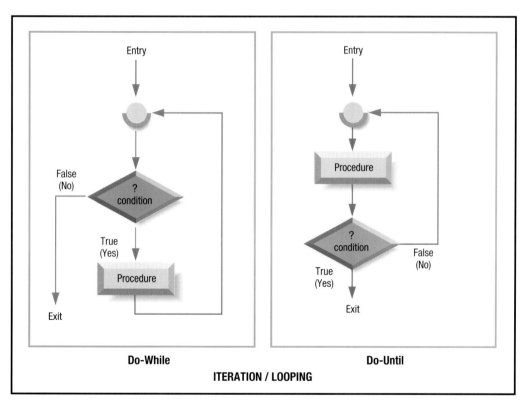

One-Entry-Point, One-Exit-Point Rule

An extremely important characteristic of the control structures previously discussed is that each permits only one entry point into and one exit point out of any structure. This property is sometimes called the *one-entry-point/one-exit-point rule*. Observe the marked entry and exit points in the control structures in Figure 13-10. The one-entry-point/one-exit-point convention makes programs much more readable and easier to maintain.

> **FIGURE 13-10**
>
> **Examples of the three fundamental control structures of structured programming.** Note that each structure has only one entry point and only one exit point.

FIGURE 13-11

Example: Writing instructions for a computer versus a person. A computer requires step-by-step instructions.

Directions for Human	Directions for Computer
1. Please make me a piece of toast	1. Take one slice of bread out of the bag of bread.
	2. Put the bread into the slot on the toaster, narrow edge first with the widest part of the bread fitting into the widest part of the slot.
	3. Push the start lever on the toaster down.
	4. When the toast pops up, remove the toast from the toaster.
	5. Place the toast onto a plate.
	6. Open the silverware drawer, take out a knife, then close the silverware drawer.
	7. Open the refrigerator, remove the margarine, and shut the refrigerator.
	8. Take the lid off the margarine.
	9. Scoop out one teaspoon of margarine with the knife.
	10. Spread the margarine on the top side of the toast, evenly covering that surface of the toast.

No Infinite Loops

An *infinite loop* is a set of instructions that repeats forever. An infinite loop occurs when a do-while condition never becomes false or a do-until condition never becomes true. This can happen when the statement to increment a counter is forgotten; when the wrong operators are used—such as less than (<) instead of greater than (>); or when a similar error in logic is made. To test for infinite loops and other logic problems, it is a good idea to walk through your finished flowchart, keeping track of the values of any loop counters and other values that affect the direction of the program to ensure the program will do what you intended it to do. Examples of testing a flowchart and some common errors that might occur are shown in Figure 10-12.

Documentation: Design Specifications

The documentation resulting from the design step of the program development life cycle is a set of design specifications illustrating the set of steps needed to solve the problem in question. This algorithm can be expressed using one or more design tools, such as flowcharts and pseudocode.

Program Coding

Once the program design is complete, the *programming language* to be used is chosen and then the program is coded. **Coding** is the actual process of creating the program in a programming language. During the coding process, computer professionals often take advantage of a number of special techniques to help make them more productive. The purpose of these techniques is to ensure that programmers produce code rapidly while creating programs that are both easy to maintain and as error-free as possible. Some techniques that are useful in this regard are selecting the most appropriate programming language and using consistent *coding standards, reusable code,* and *data dictionaries.* These coding techniques, along with how finished code is prepared for execution, are discussed in the next few sections.

Choosing a Programming Language

When a program is in the design stage, it is not necessary to know which programming language will be used to code the program. At the coding stage, however, the programming language must be selected. Various programming languages to choose from are discussed later in this chapter, but a quick overview of several factors that may affect this decision is listed next.

further exploration

For links to further information about program design, go to www.course.com/parker2002/ch13

>**Coding.** Writing the actual programming language statements to create a computer program.

Tracing Results for Correct Flowchart

Flowchart stage	Counter	Decision test results (counter < 2)	Number	Sum
Initialization	0	—	—	0
First decision test	0	T (enters loop)	—	0
After first loop	1	—	6	6
Second decision test	1	T (enters loop)	6	6
After second loop	2	—	3	9
Third decision test	2	F (exits loop)	3	9
Printed Results: Sum = 9				

Tracing Results for Incorrect Flowchart

Flowchart stage	Counter	Decision test results (counter < 2)	Number	Sum
Initialization	1	—	—	0
First decision test	1	T (enters loop)	—	0
After first loop	2	—	6	6
Second decision test	2	F (exits loop)	6	6
Printed Results: Sum = 6				

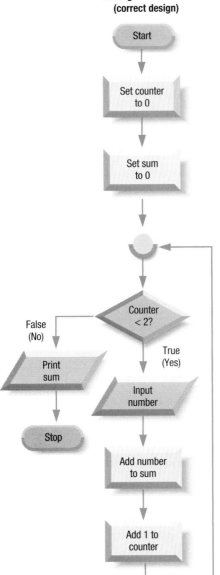

Adding two numbers (correct design)

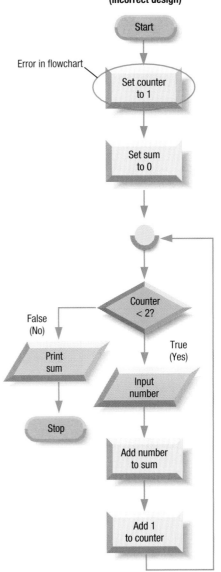

Adding two numbers (incorrect design)

> **FIGURE 13-12**

Tracing a flowchart to look for logic errors. These flowcharts are supposed to input two numbers and compute their sum, but only one flowchart is correct. The numbers 6 and 3 are being used for test data.

▼ *Suitability* Probably the most important selection criterion is the suitability of the language for the application under consideration. For instance, *Java* is a natural choice for creating programs to be used on the Web. Also, object-oriented programming languages, such as Java or *C++*, should be used when using OOP.

▼ *Integration* If the application is going to mesh with others that are already coded in a certain programming language, it should probably be coded in the same language. This is why *COBOL* is still a widely used programming language, even though many people consider it old-fashioned.

▼ *Standards* Many information systems departments have standards that dictate using a specific language in a given applications environment—such as *COBOL* for transaction processing.

▼ *Programmer availability* Both the availability of in-house programmers fluent in the language and the market for new programmers need to be considered. Choosing a widely used language means programmers can more easily be hired and may not even have to be trained.

▼ *Portability* If the application is to run on different computers or operating systems—such as Windows, Macintosh, and Unix computers—the ability of those platforms to collectively handle the language becomes a key factor.

▼ *Speed* The faster an application is coded, the sooner it can be put into use to generate benefits. Programs that reuse large chunks of code already in existence, or that use a language that is easier to code and test (as discussed later in this chapter), go faster.

Coding Standards

Back in the early days of computers, programmers were largely left to code programs in their own style. The result was often a confusing jumble of statements that, while producing correct results, were difficult for anyone except the original programmer to understand. To avoid this problem, many organizations today follow a set of *coding standards*—a list of rules designed to standardize programming styles. These rules help make programs more universally readable and easier to maintain. When programs consistently use the same set of conventions, anyone making changes to the program knows what to expect.

Comments or *remarks* are one of the most important but often one of the least adhered to coding standards in organizations. Comments are notes within the actual program code that identify key features and steps of the program but that are written in such a way that the computer knows to ignore them when the program is executed (see Figure 13-13). Usually there is a comment section at the top of the program that identifies the author, date the program was written or last modified, and the names and descriptions of the *variables*—the named entities that contain values during a program, such as Counter, Sum, First_name, and so on—used in the program. Comments also typically appear at the beginning of each main step of the program, such as "Initialize variables," "Compute taxes," "Calculate net amount due," and so forth. Comments are also called *internal documentation*.

Reusable Code

Related programs often use some of the same blocks of code. For example, a company may have a dozen or more payroll programs—programs that print checks, report all checks issued, collect payments for taxing agencies, and so on. Rather than having programmers code each program or program piece from scratch, most organizations maintain libraries of reusable code. *Reusable code,* as you might guess, refers to generic code segments that can be used over and over again with minor modifications. Thus, reusable code enables portions of new programs to be created by copying and pasting pretested, error-free code segments from existing programs, greatly reducing development time. Both structured programming and object-oriented programming lend themselves to reusable code.

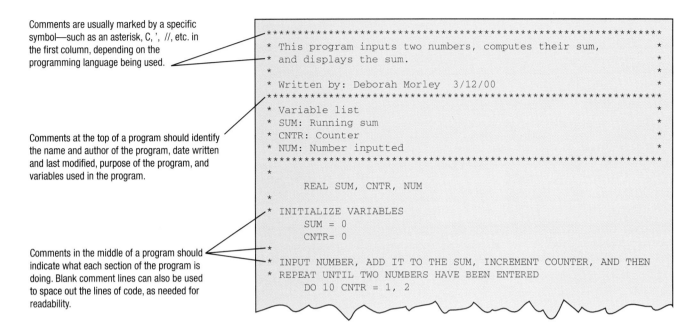

Comments are usually marked by a specific symbol—such as an asterisk, C, ', //, etc. in the first column, depending on the programming language being used.

Comments at the top of a program should identify the name and author of the program, date written and last modified, purpose of the program, and variables used in the program.

Comments in the middle of a program should indicate what each section of the program is doing. Blank comment lines can also be used to space out the lines of code, as needed for readability.

```
****************************************************************
* This program inputs two numbers, computes their sum,        *
* and displays the sum.                                       *
*                                                             *
* Written by: Deborah Morley  3/12/00                         *
****************************************************************
* Variable list                                              *
* SUM: Running sum                                           *
* CNTR: Counter                                              *
* NUM: Number inputted                                       *
****************************************************************
*
        REAL SUM, CNTR, NUM
*
* INITIALIZE VARIABLES
       SUM = 0
       CNTR= 0
*
* INPUT NUMBER, ADD IT TO THE SUM, INCREMENT COUNTER, AND THEN
* REPEAT UNTIL TWO NUMBERS HAVE BEEN ENTERED
       DO 10 CNTR = 1, 2
```

Data Dictionaries

A *data dictionary* contains information about the data that are encountered in the company's information processing environment. In an organization's data dictionary, there would be, for example, the names, descriptions, and rules of usage for the fields, records, and files used in the organization's systems. Most data dictionaries are *active*, meaning they are online to the applications that they support. If, for example, a programmer attempts to use a field name improperly or inconsistently, the active data dictionary immediately warns the programmer and prohibits the alleged infraction from being part of the finished application. Data dictionaries are illustrated in Chapter 14.

Translating Coded Programs into Executable Code

There is a difference between the code a programmer writes and the code a computer can execute. The collection of program statements that you write using a programming language is referred to as the **source code** or *source module*. Source code is the only type of code easily read by humans. To run a program on a computer, however, source code needs to be converted into the bits and bytes the computer can understand. This machine-language version of the program is called the **object code** or *object module*. Code is converted from source code to object code using a language translator.

A *language translator* is a software program that converts the programmer's application program into machine language. Three common types of language translators are *compilers*, *interpreters*, and *assemblers*. Each one performs translations in its own way.

Compilers

A **compiler** translates an entire program into machine language before executing it. Every compiler-oriented language requires its own special compiler. For instance, a *COBOL* program needs a COBOL compiler; it cannot be converted into object code using a *BASIC* compiler.

Normally, before the object code actually begins execution, it is combined with other object modules the CPU needs to process the program. For example, most computers can't compute square roots directly. Instead, they rely on small object modules stored on the system. If your program calls for a square root calculation, the operating system temporarily binds the

FIGURE 13-13

Comments. Good comments in a program make a program much more easily understood; this is especially important when the program needs to be revised at a later time.

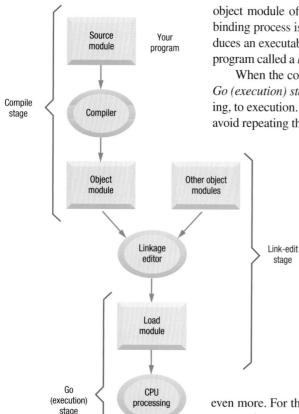

Compile stage

Go (execution) stage

Link-edit stage

◐ FIGURE 13-14

Compiler and linkage editor. A compiler and a linkage editor convert a source module into a load module for processing by the CPU.

object module of your program together with a copy of the square root routine. The binding process is referred to as *linkage editing,* or the *link-edit stage;* this activity produces an executable package called a *load module.* Systems software includes a special program called a *linkage editor* that automatically carries out this binding.

When the computer is ready to execute or run the load module, it has reached the *Go (execution) stage.* Figure 13-14 shows the process from compiling, to linkage editing, to execution. You can save both the object module and load module for later use to avoid repeating the compilation and linkage editing every time you want to execute the program. Filenames for object and load modules often carry the extensions .obj and .exe, respectively.

Interpreters

An **interpreter** translates programming language statements in a different way than a compiler. Rather than creating a complete object module for a program, an interpreter reads, translates, and executes the source program one line at a time. It performs the translation into machine language at the same time the program is run, every time the program is run.

Interpreters offer advantages and disadvantages compared with compilers. Two major advantages are that interpreters are easier to use, and—because the execution usually stops at the point where an error is encountered—they help programmers discover program errors more easily. The interpreter program itself requires relatively little storage space, and because it does not generate an object module, the required storage space is reduced even more. For these reasons, interpreters provide ideal tools for beginning programmers and nonprogrammers.

The major disadvantage of interpreters is that they work less efficiently than compilers do, so interpreted programs run more slowly. Because an interpreter must translate each program statement into machine language just before executing it, it wastes a lot of time. This is especially true when the program must repeatedly execute the same statements thousands of times, reinterpreting each one every time. In contrast, a compiler translates each program statement only once. By storing the object module of a compiled program on disk, the programmer avoids retranslating the source program every time the program runs. Compiled programs need to be recompiled only when the source code is modified.

Some programming-language packages include both interpreter and compiler software, giving the programmer the best of both worlds. He or she can work with the interpreter to discover and correct any program errors and then compile the error-free program, saving the object code to run whenever it is needed.

Assemblers

The third type of language translator, an *assembler,* converts assembly-language statements into machine language. *Assembly language,* discussed later in this chapter, is used almost exclusively by professional programmers to write efficient code. An assembler works like a compiler, producing a stored object module. Each type of computer system can typically use only one assembly language; thus, only one assembler is required.

Documentation: Documented Source Code

The program coding stage results in finished, executable source code, written in the desired programming language. The source code should implement the logic illustrated by the program design specifications and include enough internal documentation (comments) to make the source code understandable and easy to update.

>Interpreter. A language translator that converts program statements line by line into machine language, immediately executing each one.

inside the industry

The Original Program "Bug"

As discussed in the chapter, a program bug is an error that causes a program to malfunction. The first official recorded use of the word *bug* in the context of computing is associated with the temporary failure of the Mark II computer, which was in service at the Naval Weapons Center in Dahlgren, Virginia, on September 9, 1945. The problem was traced to a short circuit caused by a moth caught between two contacts in one of the computer's relays. The offending moth was taped into the log book with the notation, "First actual case of a bug being found" (see the accompanying photograph).

Legend has it that Grace Hopper, a naval officer and mathematician who is often referred to as the mother of computing, actually discovered the moth. Hopper led the committee that invented COBOL, is credited with developing the first compiler, and became the first woman to achieve the rank of rear admiral in the United States Navy.

Though some say the wording implies that the term *bug* was already in existence at the time and that this was the first instance of an actual bug being found in a computer, many prefer to believe that this was the origin of the term. Regardless, it is certainly the most widely known "bug" story that will likely be repeated for decades to come.

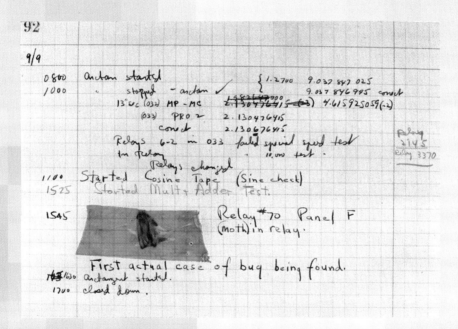

The dead moth that caused the temporary failure of the Mark II computer in 1945, thought to be the origin for the computer term *bug,* was taped into the actual log book for that computer.

Program Debugging and Testing

Debugging is the process of ensuring that a program is free of errors, or *bugs* (for a look at the origin of the term *bug,* see the Inside the Industry box). Debugging is usually a lengthy process, sometimes amounting to more than 50 percent of a program's development time. The more careful one is designing a program, testing the logic of a program's design, and writing the actual code, the less debugging time is needed.

>**Debugging.** The process of ensuring a program is free of errors.

Preliminary Debugging

The debugging process begins after the program is initially entered into the computer system. Rarely is any program error-free the first time the programmer attempts to execute it. A very long program may have hundreds or thousands of errors of one sort or another at the outset. Errors rooted out during debugging often are of two types: *syntax errors* and *logic errors*.

Syntax Errors

A **syntax error** occurs when the programmer has not followed the proper *syntax* (rules) of the programming language being used. For example, a computer won't be able to understand what you're trying to do if you misspell PRINT as PRNT or if you type END OF IF STATEMENT instead of the correct phrase END IF. The language's interpreter or compiler usually provides the programmer with an error message indicating the source of syntax error (see Figure 13-15).

> **FIGURE 13-15**
>
> **Syntax and logic errors.**
> Syntax errors occur when the syntax, or grammar rules, for a program is not followed precisely; logic errors are more difficult to identify. Good debugging techniques, such as using dummy print statements to display the values of key variables, can help locate the errors in a program.

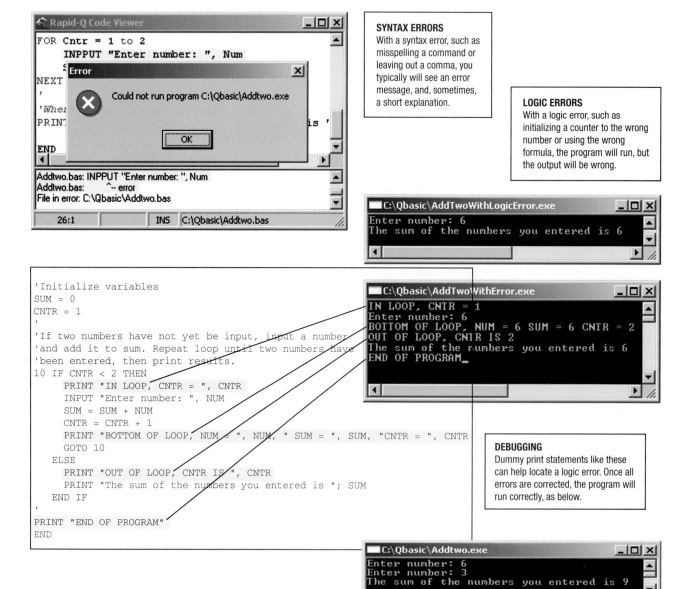

SYNTAX ERRORS
With a syntax error, such as misspelling a command or leaving out a comma, you typically will see an error message, and, sometimes, a short explanation.

LOGIC ERRORS
With a logic error, such as initializing a counter to the wrong number or using the wrong formula, the program will run, but the output will be wrong.

DEBUGGING
Dummy print statements like these can help locate a logic error. Once all errors are corrected, the program will run correctly, as below.

```
'Initialize variables
SUM = 0
CNTR = 1
'
'If two numbers have not yet be input, input a number
'and add it to sum. Repeat loop until two numbers have
'been entered, then print results.
10 IF CNTR < 2 THEN
      PRINT "IN LOOP, CNTR = ", CNTR
      INPUT "Enter number: ", NUM
      SUM = SUM + NUM
      CNTR = CNTR + 1
      PRINT "BOTTOM OF LOOP, NUM = ", NUM, " SUM = ", SUM, "CNTR = ", CNTR
      GOTO 10
   ELSE
      PRINT "OUT OF LOOP, CNTR IS ", CNTR
      PRINT "The sum of the numbers you entered is "; SUM
   END IF
'
PRINT "END OF PROGRAM"
END
```

Logic Errors

Logic errors, or *execution-time errors,* stem from a logic problem in the program's design and are often difficult to detect. Such an error results when the command syntax is correct but the program produces incorrect results. This may happen if you've expressed a formula incorrectly, if you've made a mistake on a decision condition (as in the incorrect flowchart shown in Figure 13-12), or if you've misdefined the problem entirely. To identify logic errors, the programmer often uses temporary *dummy* output statements. These statements can be inserted at various locations to show how a program is branching (such as "Inside loop, counter is COUNTER," where the current value of the counter will be printed where the COUNTER variable name is listed). Knowing the values of certain key variables (such as loop counters) and how many times the program looped before exiting can help identify the location of the logic error. For example, if running the program to add up two numbers resulted in an incorrect sum, as shown in the first logic error screen in Figure 13-15, inserting temporary print statements to trace where the program control goes and what the values of the counter and sum variables are during the course of the program can help identify the problem, as shown in the second logic error screen in Figure 13-15. These temporary print statements make it relatively easy to determine that only one number is being input because the counter is being initialized to 1, instead of 0.

If a logic error is serious enough, it may involve going back to the program design step—a costly mistake that emphasizes how important good program design the first time through is.

Most compilers today include built-in debugging tools to help locate bugs and analyze the behavior of the programs. Debuggers typically provide tracing of executed statements to help locate the source of the error; color-code comments, command statements, and variables to assist readability; and allow the programmer to choose between line-by-line execution and full speed execution, among other features. These tools help programmers quickly track down and correct errors. After making the necessary corrections, the programmer recompiles and reexecutes the program to see if all errors have been eradicated. This "execute, check, and correct" process is repeated until the program is free of bugs.

Testing

At some point in the debugging process, the program will appear to be correct. At this time, the original programmer—or, preferably, someone else—runs the program with extensive *test data.* Good test data should be real data generated by the system's users to subject the program to the conditions it will encounter when it is finally implemented. The test data should also check for likely sources of coding omissions. For example, will the program issue a check or a bill in the amount of $0.00? Does the program provide for leap years when dating reports? Will it accept a product quantity less than 0? Although rigorous testing significantly decreases the chance of malfunctioning when a program is implemented, there is no foolproof guarantee that the completed program will be bug-free.

Proper debugging and testing is vital, because an error that costs only a few dollars to fix at this stage in the development process may cost many thousands of dollars to correct after the program is implemented.

Beta Testing

Tests done on-site by a company are frequently referred to as *alpha tests.* Programs created for mass distribution—such as new revisions of software made by companies like Microsoft, Netscape, and Corel—also undergo several rounds of testing outside the company. With the possible configurations of PC hardware in use so large that it is impossible to fully anticipate many problems that may occur, hundreds or thousands of potential users are sent preliminary versions of a program to evaluate its suitability. For their participation, beta testers are usually given a free copy of the finished program, or, occasionally, a nominal fee or freebie.

>Logic error. A programming error that occurs when running a program produces incorrect results.

Documentation: Completed Program Package

When the program debugging and testing step is finished, a copy of the test data, results, and finished program code should be added to the program package. This data is useful if the program is modified in the future, as well as to see if the program was tested for particular situations, if a problem develops in the future.

So far, virtually all the documents in the collected program documentation could be referred to as *developer documentation*—tools that may be useful when a programmer needs to look at or modify the program code in the future. To finish up the *program package,* the necessary *user documentation* should be developed. User documentation normally consists of a user's manual containing such information as instructions for running the program, a description of software commands, and a troubleshooting guide to help with difficulties. Since users may have widely differing levels of computer expertise, user documentation must be written to be comprehensible to all users. User documentation can be either paper based or in an electronic format.

Program Maintenance

Virtually every program, if it is to last a long time, requires ongoing maintenance. *Program maintenance* is the process of updating software so it continues to be useful. For instance, if new types of data are added to a database, program maintenance is necessary so that the program can use the new data. Software revisions, new equipment announcements, and changes in the way business is conducted also commonly trigger program maintenance.

Program maintenance is costly to organizations. It has been estimated that many organizations spend well over half—some estimates put it closer to 80%—of their programming time maintaining existing application programs. A major reason such tools as coding standards, object-oriented programming, reusable code, and data dictionaries are so popular is because they can result in lower maintenance costs.

Documentation: Amended Program Package

As program maintenance takes place, the program package should be updated to reflect what problems occurred and what changes to the program were necessary to alleviate them. If a problem is too serious for routine program maintenance, the program development cycle should begin again.

TOOLS FOR FACILITATING PROGRAM DEVELOPMENT

If you ask most managers when they need to get programs delivered to users, you'll get an answer such as "yesterday." The sad truth in business today is that developers are typically under tremendous time pressure to get finished work out the door. In extreme cases, getting product into the user's hands is not just a priority—it is *the* priority.

Rapid development techniques and tools are needed now more than ever because there is a serious shortage of skilled workers in the information-technology area. Thus, departments developing systems and programs often have to get by with fewer people, all of whom are then under greater pressure to produce. *Program development tools* can be used to facilitate the program development process. Program development tools include *application generators, CASE tools,* and *rapid development.*

Application Generators

An *application generator* is a software product that enables programmers, as well as end users, to code new applications quickly. A simple example is a wizard program. Wizards, which commonly appear in word processors, spreadsheets, and other application programs, allow you to quickly and easily create such things as fax cover sheets, database reports, and Web pages. More complex generators can create the code for a complete application. Some specific types of application generators are described next.

web tutor

For a tutorial on software engineering tools, go to www.course.com/parker2002/ch13

Macro Languages

Many application programs—particularly word processing and spreadsheet programs—allow you to create macros. A *macro* is a sequence of keystrokes saved in a special file that can be replayed whenever you wish within the application program in which it was created. These simple programs can be created by the application or may come prewritten as part of the program. In either case, the macros can be used to automate repeated or difficult tasks. For example, users could create a macro to type a standard closing to a letter whenever they press a key combination, such as Ctrl+Y, or use the built-in Date macro to type the current date whenever Ctrl+D is pressed.

Macros are written in some type of *macro programming language* (such as *Visual Basic for Applications* for Microsoft Word or Excel macros) and can be difficult to write and understand. Consequently, most programs that use macros allow users to record them instead of having to write them. Macro recorders work similarly to tape recorders or video cameras in that you turn the macro recorder on and it records everything that happens until the recorder is turned off. The primary difference is that a macro recorder records keystrokes and mouse clicks, instead of audio or video. After a macro has been recorded, the code generated by the macro recorder can be edited to make minor modifications, as needed.

Report Generators

A *report generator* enables you to prepare reports quickly and easily. Report generators packaged with database management systems allow you to create reports by declaring which data fields are to be represented as report columns and how you wish the data to be sorted. As discussed in the next chapter, the report is then generated automatically.

Form Generators

Form generators are similar to report generators, except that they create the forms or screens used to input data into a program or database. Most database programs contain some type of form generator capability, as discussed in the next chapter.

Graphics Generators

Graphics generators are tools that help you prepare business graphics. When you invoke a typical graphics generator, it asks you a number of questions about your graph—what type you would like it to be, where to find the data from which the graph should be generated, what colors and titles you want, and so on. After you respond to all the questions, the graph is automatically created. Spreadsheet programs almost always include a graphics generator, as discussed in Chapter 7.

Code Generators

Code generators are programs that allow applications to be created by automatically translating them from one programming language into another, or from some other format (such as pseudocode or text) to source or object code. Code generators are commonly used to translate documents written with a word processing program into HTML-coded Web pages. Also, several code generators exist that translate shortcut instructions into standard COBOL statements.

Computer-Aided Software Engineering (CASE)

CASE (computer-aided software engineering) tools—sometimes called *business modeling tools*—refer broadly to products designed to automate, manage, and simplify one or more stages of program development. Like a carpenter's workbench that has numerous carpentry tools—hammers, saws, chisels, drill bits, and the like—CASE systems contain a number of design, programming, and maintenance tools to help develop software products faster. Tools can be included to perform activities such as developing data flow diagrams, flowcharts, or other design tools; scheduling development tasks; preparing and storing project

⟩**FIGURE 13-16**

A CASE package. CASE
products make it possible to
develop applications faster
with fewer coding mistakes.
As shown here, many CASE
products can automatically
generate code from the design
diagrams and specifications.

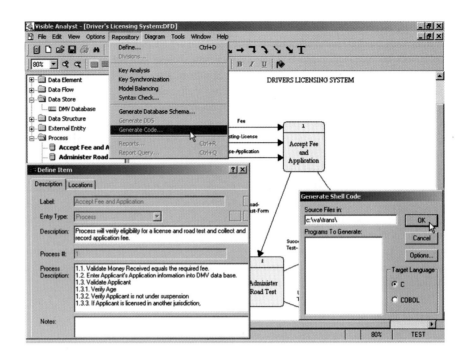

**further
exploration**

For links to further information about
CASE tools, go to www.course.com/
parker2002/ch13

documentation; developing user interfaces and menus; and generating program code from
the design specifications. The specific CASE tools included vary from one vendor to another.
One example of a CASE program is shown in Figure 13-16.

One of the principal advantages to CASE tools, besides their speed in application
development, is their ability to maintain consistency. For example, if program code is generated from an online design diagram, the two will be consistent. Also, if someone later tries
to change the program without changing the diagram, the CASE tool can flag the inconsis-
tency. On the downside, there is very little standardization from one vendor to another, and
many of the CASE tools currently in the marketplace are targeted only to solving highly
specific problems.

Rapid-Application Development (RAD)

Rapid-application development (RAD) refers to a group of program-development methods
in which a major goal is to meet an extremely tight timetable. Using RAD tools, software
development often takes place during the entire program development process, instead of
just during the program-coding step. RAD is often used in conjunction with object-oriented
programming.

RAD tools, used by both analysts and programmers, provide CASE-like assistance for
developing user interfaces and for preparing code for reuse. RAD programs typically include
wizards to generate applications quickly, screen painters that generate graphical user interfaces, libraries of objects that can be easily stitched together into applications, groupware to
manage team development efforts, debugging and prototyping utilities, and so forth. Three
widely used RAD products are Microsoft's *Visual Basic* (discussed later in this chapter),
Powersoft's PowerBuilder, and Borland's Delphi.

PROGRAMMING LANGUAGES

As discussed earlier, an important decision to make during the development of a program
is the programming language to be used. There are several general categories of programming languages and many widely used ones to choose from. In addition, there are also
other types of languages and tools that can be used to create applications. These topics are
discussed in the remainder of this chapter.

What Is a Programming Language?

A **programming language** is a set of rules used to write computer programs. To write a program, a software program whose principal purpose is to enable users to develop computer programs in a given language is used. The program contains the language translator necessary to convert the program into machine language and may also include tools that make it easier to develop, maintain, and manage programs.

Categories of Programming Languages

Programming languages are commonly divided into three classes: *low-level, high-level,* and *very-high-level (fourth-generation) languages.* They can also be *natural* or *visual* programming languages.

Low-Level Languages

The earliest programming languages—machine language and *assembly language*—are called **low-level languages.** They are so named because the programmers who code in them must write instructions at the lowest level, such as in binary code, so the computer's hardware can easily and quickly understand them. In both machine languages and assembly languages, each line of code corresponds to a single action of the computer system. Both types of languages are *machine dependent,* which means that they are usually not transportable between different brands or kinds of computers. For example, assembly-language code written to instruct a particular mainframe at one organization cannot be used on one of the organization's PCs. Machine and assembly languages were respectively developed during the first and second product generations that define computer history.

Virtually no one writes machine-language programs, which consist of strings of 0s and 1s, anymore. Nonetheless, all programs must be converted into machine language by a language translator before they are executed, as discussed earlier in this chapter.

Assembly languages were developed to replace some of the 0s and 1s of machine language with names and other symbols that are easier to understand and remember. The big advantage of assembly-language programs today is executional efficiency: They're fast and require little storage compared with their higher-level counterparts. Unfortunately, assembly-language programs take longer to write and maintain than programs written in higher-level languages, and they are not transportable to other types of computers. An example of the program of adding up two numbers (illustrated with the flowchart in Figure 13-12) written in assembly language for one type of computer system is shown in Figure 13-17. Also illustrated in that figure are some machine-language statements that correspond to the assembly-language statements in the program.

High-Level Languages

High-level languages differ from their low-level predecessors in that they are closer to natural languages than machine language, require less coding detail, and make programs easier to write. These languages are typically machine independent, freeing programmers from knowing the fine details about the hardware on which programs run. Included in this class of languages are what have come to be known as *third-generation programming languages,* such as *BASIC, COBOL, Pascal, C, FORTRAN,* and others that are discussed shortly. Ultimately, programs written in a high-level language must be translated into machine language by a compiler or interpreter before they can be executed.

web tutor

For a tutorial on the different types of programming languages, go to www.course.com/parker2002/ch13

SYS

>**Programming language.** A set of rules, words, symbols, and codes used to write computer programs. >**Low-level language.** A highly detailed, machine-dependent class of programming languages. >**Assembly language.** A low-level programming language that uses names and symbols to replace some of the 0s and 1s in machine language. >**High-level language.** A programming language that is closer to natural language and easier to work with than a low-level language.

MACHINE LANGUAGE
Machine language instructions are typically in binary form, and the memory address locations, as well as the instructions themselves, need to be specified.

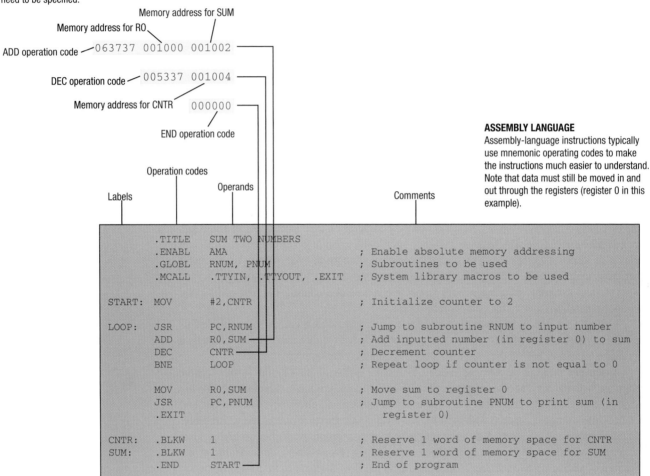

Memory address for SUM

Memory address for R0

ADD operation code — 063737 001000 001002

DEC operation code — 005337 001004

Memory address for CNTR 000000

END operation code

Operation codes

Labels   Operands   Comments

ASSEMBLY LANGUAGE
Assembly-language instructions typically use mnemonic operating codes to make the instructions much easier to understand. Note that data must still be moved in and out through the registers (register 0 in this example).

```
        .TITLE   SUM TWO NUMBERS
        .ENABL   AMA                        ; Enable absolute memory addressing
        .GLOBL   RNUM, PNUM                 ; Subroutines to be used
        .MCALL   .TTYIN, .TTYOUT, .EXIT     ; System library macros to be used

START:  MOV      #2,CNTR                    ; Initialize counter to 2

LOOP:   JSR      PC,RNUM                    ; Jump to subroutine RNUM to input number
        ADD      R0,SUM                     ; Add inputted number (in register 0) to sum
        DEC      CNTR                       ; Decrement counter
        BNE      LOOP                       ; Repeat loop if counter is not equal to 0

        MOV      R0,SUM                     ; Move sum to register 0
        JSR      PC,PNUM                    ; Jump to subroutine PNUM to print sum (in
        .EXIT                               ;    register 0)

CNTR:   .BLKW    1                          ; Reserve 1 word of memory space for CNTR
SUM:    .BLKW    1                          ; Reserve 1 word of memory space for SUM
        .END     START                      ; End of program
```

⊗ **FIGURE 13-17**

Assembly language and machine language. Though all programs are converted to machine language before they are executed, virtually no one programs in it anymore. Occasionally, a program may be written in assembly language to make it extra efficient.

Fourth-Generation Languages (4GLs)

Fourth-generation languages (4GLs) are also sometimes called *very-high-level languages.* Though there is no precise definition of a 4GL, more people agree that they are closer to natural language than third-generation languages and are much easier to use. Because they often allow both programmers and users to get by with very little coding, if any, they also result in increased productivity. A disadvantage to 4GLs is that they can result in a greater number of program statements and less time-efficient object code when they are compiled into machine language. Because they use more storage space and execute more slowly, professional programmers may choose to use a third-generation or assembly language instead of a fourth-generation language in some instances.

The property that makes 4GLs easier to use is that they are *declarative,* rather than *procedural,* as the third-generation languages are. This means that you tell the computer

> **Fourth-generation language (4GL).** A programming language that is closer to natural language and easier to work with than a high-level language.

what to do without telling it *how* to do it. For instance, to draw a bar chart in a *procedural language,* you must tell the computer pixel by pixel how to draw bars and where to place them. In a *declarative language,* you point to the data you want graphed, select a graph type, and supply some titles to get the same results. Coding in a declarative language is reduced to simple commands or mouse clicks that select instructions. However, if you want a highly customized program to do something well beyond the ordinary, you will probably need a procedural language. To provide more flexibility, some software packages have both declarative and procedural components.

Fourth-generation languages are commonly used to access databases. For example, *query languages,* which allow users to retrieve information from a database (as discussed in more detail in the next chapter), are usually fourth-generation languages. A typical 4GL query is:

FIND ALL RECORDS WHERE LASTNAME = "SANCHEZ"

Another example are *decision support system tools,* which provide computing capabilities to help people make decisions. Application generators and some of the programs discussed earlier as tools to help facilitate program development are also usually considered to be fourth-generation languages.

Natural and Visual Languages

Some recent programming languages can be classified as *natural* or *visual languages.* Programs with either of these characteristics help to make programming easier.

Natural Languages

Software that uses a *natural-language interface* enables humans to communicate with the computer system in their native language—English, Spanish, Japanese, and so on. The user of a natural-language interface does not have to learn the rules, or syntax, of a particular computer language. Instead, the user enters requests on a keyboard or uses voice commands that the computer can understand.

Natural-language processing is still in its infancy. It is most frequently employed to request information or generate reports from a database. As each request is typed or spoken, the natural-language subsystem determines how it corresponds to a command that can be processed by the main program and then hands over the deduced command to the program for execution. The natural-language subsystem extracts key nouns from sentences and then looks for instances in its database where the words it extracts appear. Fourth-generation languages are the closest things we have to natural programming languages at the present time. Some believe that the fifth-generation of programming languages will be pure natural languages.

Visual Languages

A *visual language* is one that uses a graphical programming environment for developing graphical user interfaces. Instead of worrying about syntax details, programmers using a visual environment can create a substantial amount of code simply by dragging and dropping objects, and then defining their appearance and behavior. Visual languages are also sometimes referred to as *event-driven* languages, since the program continually checks for and reacts to messages or events, like a click on a button or icon. The first programming language that used a visual environment was *Visual Basic.* Since then, visual environments have been created for many programming languages, including *C++, Pascal,* and *Java.* These programming languages are described in the next section.

Popular Programming Languages

The most popular programming languages today are third- and fourth-generation languages. Some of the most widely used are discussed and illustrated next.

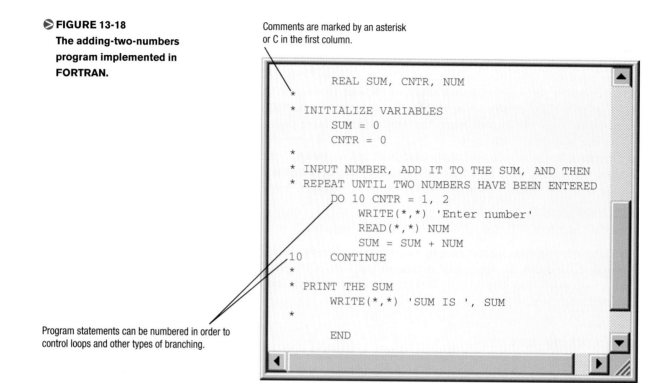

⊗ **FIGURE 13-18**

The adding-two-numbers program implemented in FORTRAN.

Comments are marked by an asterisk or C in the first column.

```
        REAL SUM, CNTR, NUM
*
*  INITIALIZE VARIABLES
        SUM = 0
        CNTR = 0
*
*  INPUT NUMBER, ADD IT TO THE SUM, AND THEN
*  REPEAT UNTIL TWO NUMBERS HAVE BEEN ENTERED
        DO 10 CNTR = 1, 2
            WRITE(*,*) 'Enter number'
            READ(*,*) NUM
            SUM = SUM + NUM
 10     CONTINUE
*
*  PRINT THE SUM
        WRITE(*,*) 'SUM IS ', SUM
*
        END
```

Program statements can be numbered in order to control loops and other types of branching.

FORTRAN

FORTRAN (*FOR*mula *TRAN*slator), which dates back to 1954, was designed by scientists and is oriented toward manipulating formulas for scientific, mathematical, and engineering problem-solving applications. Because of the numerous computations and frequent looping that characterize such applications, execution speed is a primary concern. Most FORTRAN compilers are so effective at producing fast object code for "number crunching" applications that they are superior in this respect to the compilers of most modern languages. The reasons for this date back to the 1950s when FORTRAN was first developed. It had to compete with assembly languages for execution efficiency, and this quality has remained an important factor in its development.

A FORTRAN program to add two numbers (as illustrated in the flowchart in Figure 13-12) appears in Figure 13-18. Note the short comments above each main section in the program.

COBOL

COBOL (*CO*mmon *B*usiness-*O*riented *L*anguage) is a widely used transaction processing language. It is a structured programming language and makes extensive use of *modules* and *submodules*. That is, most COBOL programs are made up of smaller subprograms, each of which is itself a structured program (see Figure 13-19). This modular building-block approach makes it easier to develop large programs.

Currently, the majority of mainframe transaction-processing applications in large organizations are coded in COBOL. COBOL programs are lengthy and take a long time to write and maintain. Some complain that COBOL is old-fashioned and cumbersome, but with billions of dollars invested in COBOL programs and thousands of programmers versed in COBOL use, the language will likely endure.

In addition to its traditional uses, COBOL is evolving to support new applications. The language now supports the creation of object-oriented COBOL programs; COBOL

Comments are marked by an asterisk in the first column.

Most COBOL programs use a number of modules to break down the program into manageable pieces. These modules are called from a main control module.

Three submodules are used in this program.

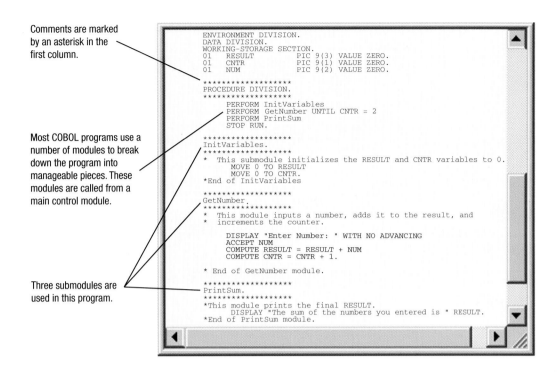

```
                    ENVIRONMENT DIVISION.
                    DATA DIVISION.
                    WORKING-STORAGE SECTION.
                    01    RESULT          PIC 9(3) VALUE ZERO.
                    01    CNTR            PIC 9(1) VALUE ZERO.
                    01    NUM             PIC 9(2) VALUE ZERO.

                    *******************
                    PROCEDURE DIVISION.
                    *******************
                         PERFORM InitVariables
                         PERFORM GetNumber UNTIL CNTR = 2
                         PERFORM PrintSum
                         STOP RUN.

                    *******************
                    InitVariables.
                    *******************
                    *  This submodule initializes the RESULT and CNTR variables to 0.
                            MOVE 0 TO RESULT
                            MOVE 0 TO CNTR.
                    *End of InitVariables

                    *******************
                    GetNumber.
                    *******************
                    *  This module inputs a number, adds it to the result, and
                    *  increments the counter.

                          DISPLAY "Enter Number: " WITH NO ADVANCING
                          ACCEPT NUM
                          COMPUTE RESULT = RESULT + NUM
                          COMPUTE CNTR = CNTR + 1.

                    * End of GetNumber module.

                    *******************
                    PrintSum.
                    *******************
                    *This module prints the final RESULT.
                          DISPLAY "The sum of the numbers you entered is " RESULT.
                    *End of PrintSum module.
```

> **FIGURE 13-19**
> **The adding-two-numbers program implemented in COBOL.**

statements can be embedded in Web pages, as well. Because of this, COBOL is enjoying a resurgence in popularity. Instead of retraining COBOL developers and rewriting COBOL programs in *Java* or another newer language, both new and legacy COBOL programs can be converted and restructured in other formats as needed, such as *Active-X controls* or *Java bytecode* (discussed later in this chapter).

The adding-two-numbers problem implemented as a COBOL program is shown in Figure 13-19.

Pascal

Pascal, named after the mathematician Blaise Pascal, was created to fill the need for a teaching tool to encourage structured programming. Most versions of Pascal contain a rich variety of control structures with which to manipulate program modules in a systematic fashion. Pascal also supports an abundance of data types and is especially appropriate for math and science applications.

See Figure 13-20 for a sample Pascal program.

BASIC and Visual Basic

BASIC (*B*eginner's *A*ll-purpose *S*ymbolic *I*nstruction *C*ode) was designed to meet the need for an easy-to-learn beginner's language that would work in a friendly, nonfrustrating programming environment. Over the years, it has evolved into one of the most popular and widely available programming languages. Because it is easy to learn and use, and because the storage requirements for its language translator are small, BASIC works well on almost all PCs and is one of the most widely used instructional languages for beginners. Figure 13-21 shows the BASIC version of the adding-two-numbers program.

BASIC is often used for interactive programs, enabling programmers to write instructions that pause a program so that the user can take a specific action. When such an instruction is

Comments are enclosed in { } braces.

The symbol := is used instead of the equal sign, and semicolons mark the ends of command statements.

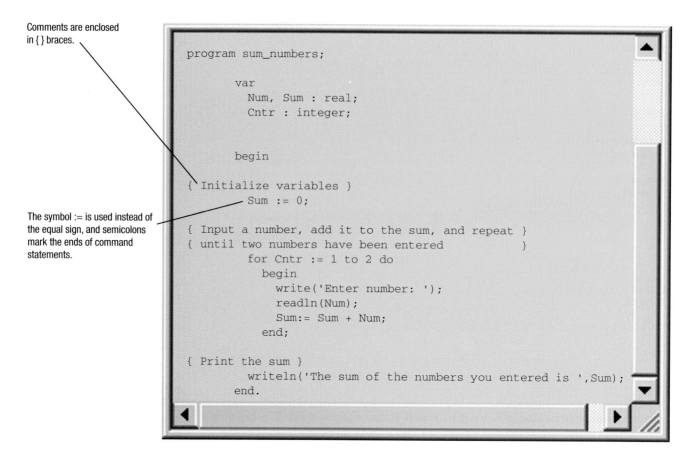

```pascal
program sum_numbers;

      var
        Num, Sum : real;
        Cntr : integer;


      begin

{ Initialize variables }
        Sum := 0;

{ Input a number, add it to the sum, and repeat }
{ until two numbers have been entered            }
        for Cntr := 1 to 2 do
          begin
            write('Enter number: ');
            readln(Num);
            Sum:= Sum + Num;
          end;

{ Print the sum }
        writeln('The sum of the numbers you entered is ',Sum);
      end.
```

◗ **FIGURE 13-20**
The adding-two-numbers program implemented in Pascal.

Comments are marked by a single quote in the first column.

```basic
'Clear the screen
CLS
'
'Initialize variables
SUM = 0
CNTR = 0
'
'Input number and add it to sum until two numbers have been
'entered.
DO
    INPUT "Enter number: ", NUM
    SUM = SUM + NUM
    CNTR = CNTR + 1
LOOP UNTIL CNTR = 2
'
'When done looping, display Sum on screen
PRINT "The sum of the numbers you entered is "; SUM
END
```

◗ **FIGURE 13-21**
The adding-two-numbers program implemented in BASIC.

encountered during program execution, the program expects an event—such as the user making a selection or typing some input—to take place before it proceeds.

Visual Basic is an object-oriented, fourth-generation version of BASIC designed to create sophisticated applications that run under the Microsoft Windows operating system. On the front end, Visual Basic has drag-and-drop tools that enable a programmer to quickly develop screens for graphical user interfaces; on the back end, it has a code generator that can supply the underlying programming code. For a look at how Visual Basic can be used to create a program, see the How It Works box.

Visual Basic has become widely used in recent years, and there are now nearly as many Visual Basic programmers as there are COBOL programmers.

C, C++, and C#

C combines the best features of a structured high-level language and an assembly language—that is, it's relatively easy to code (at least compared to assembly language) and it uses computer resources efficiently. Although originally designed as a systems programming language (in fact, the first major program written in C was the UNIX operating system), C has proven to be a powerful and flexible language that can be used for a variety of applications. It is used mostly by computer professionals to create software products.

Although it is a high-level language, C is closer to an assembly language than are most other high-level languages. This allows C programmers to write very efficient code, but can also make the language difficult to use.

A newer object-oriented version of C is called **C++** (see Figure 13-22). C++ includes the basic features of C, making all C++ programs understandable to C compilers, but has

FIGURE 13-22

The adding-two-numbers program implemented in C++.

Comments are preceded by two slashes //.

The instructions in a function or loop are enclosed in { } braces.

```
#include <iostream.h>

void main ()
{

// Declare and initialize variables
      float fSum = 0;
      float fNum;
      int iCntr = 0;

// Input a number, add it to the sum, and repeat
// until two numbers have been entered
      do
         {
         cout << "Enter number: "; // Prompt for input
         cin >> fNum;
         fSum = fSum + fNum;
         iCntr = iCntr + 1;
         }
      while(iCntr < 2);

// Print the sum
      cout << "The sum of the numbers you entered is " << fSum;
}
```

>**Visual Basic.** A object-oriented, fourth-generation version of the BASIC programming language. >**C.** A high-level structured programming language that has the executional efficiency of an assembly language. >**C++.** A newer, object-oriented version of the C programming language.

how it works

Visual Basic

Programming in Visual Basic begins as with any other language. You first need to define and understand the problem, then develop your solution and logic. Design tools such as flowcharts and pseudocode can be used to represent logical sections of the program. In addition, the interface (such as the red box with the buttons and text boxes in the accompanying illustration) should be designed.

Once the design has been completed, the first task using the Visual Basic program is to build the GUI. Programs in Visual Basic are referred to as projects and contain at least two files: The *project file* that contains the names and locations of all other files that make up the application, and at least one *form file* that contains the user interface window plus the underlying code.

When a new project is started, a blank form (called "Form1") is displayed. The form can then be resized, renamed, and so forth using the Properties window, as shown in the first screen below. As command buttons, labels, text boxes, and more are added using the toolbox shown on the left edge of the screen, their properties can be adjusted as well. Common property changes for a text box, for example, include the object's name (to be used when addressing that object in the code), what text (if any) should be displayed in the box, the font and border to be used, etc.

To specify what should happen when the user performs a specific action (called an *event*), such as clicking on a command button or changing the text in a box, the appropriate code is entered into the code window (double-clicking any object on the form opens the appropriate section of the code for that object). Once all events have been specified, clicking the Run toolbar button starts the program so it can be tested and debugged. As with any other good program, the final code should contain appropriate comments.

1. The user creates the interface object and changes the design and properties, as needed.

2. As properties are assigned, the appropriate code is generated. The code can also be edited as needed.

3. When the program is run, the objects behave according to the instructions in the objects' code. For example, clicking the Get Sum button here totals the two numbers located in the boxes and displays the sum in the appropriate box (see the GetSum part of the code shown in step 2).

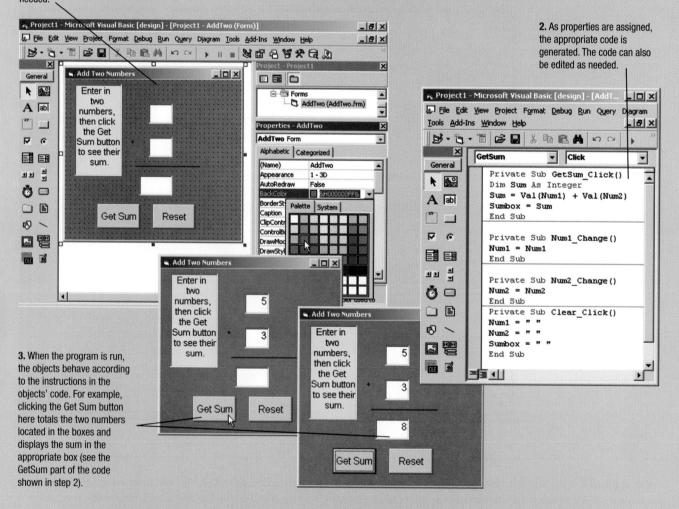

additional features for objects, classes, and other components of an OOP. There is also a visual version of the C++ language. All in all, C++ is one of the most popular programming languages for graphical applications.

The newest version of C is C# (pronounced "C sharp"). A hybrid of C and C++, **C#** is Microsoft's newest programming language developed to compete directly with Sun's *Java* language, discussed next. C# is an object-oriented programming language designed to improve productivity in the development of Web applications. In essence, C# is a simplified and more modern version of C++ designed to make the development of the next generations of applications much easier.

Java

Java is a high-level programming language developed by Sun Microsystems. Java is an object-oriented language similar to C++, but is simplified to eliminate features that cause common programming errors. Java is a general purpose programming language that can be used to write complete stand-alone applications (see Figure 13-23) or smaller programs called *Java applets.*

Java programs can be run using any operating system or Web browser that understands Java bytecode. *Bytecode* is the compiled format of a Java program that usually has the .class extension. Once a Java program has been converted to bytecode, it can be run on any platform—Windows, UNIX, Mac OS, Web browser, etc.—as long as that platform includes the *Java Virtual Machine (Java VM)*. Bytecode's general-purpose platform independence is significantly different than the platform-specific object code generated by traditional programming languages.

Platform independence is one of Java's biggest advantages. Because of it, programs can be written once and then run on any number of computer configurations, without special

◗ FIGURE 13-23

The adding-two-numbers program implemented in Java.

The java.io package will handle the user input; * indicates all classes will be available.

Comments within the code are preceded by two slashes //.

The *println* method and variable *out* in the System class of the java.io package is used to output the results.

```
import java.io.*;
public class AddTwo {
        public static void main(String[] args) throws IOException {
        BufferedReader stdin =
            new BufferedReader ( new InputStreamReader( System.in ) );
        String inData;
        int iSum = 0;
        int iNum = 0;
        int iCntr = 0;

// Input a number, add it to the sum, and repeat
// until two numbers have been entered
    do
        {
        System.out.println("Enter number: ");
        inData = stdin.readLine();            // get number in character form
        iNum = Integer.parseInt( inData );    // convert inData to integer
        iSum = iSum + iNum;
        iCntr = iCntr + 1;
        }
    while (iCntr < 2);

// Print the sum
    System.out.println ("The sum of the numbers you entered is " + iSum);
        }
    }
```

>C#. The newest, object-oriented version of the C programming language. **>Java.** A high-level, object-oriented programming language frequently used for Web-based applications.

accommodations. This unique characteristic has led Java to become the cornerstone of applications that run over the Internet, instead of from the local PC. Some expect the use of Java programming to explode as more and more applications are written specifically to be delivered via the Web.

Java applets are written by Java programmers. They are similar to Java applications but run using a Java-enabled Web browser. Many Java applets are written using allowable variables (called *parameters*) that enable the applet to be customized when it is used on a Web page, such as to specify the colors to be used, the text to scroll, the text size, etc. (see Figure 13-24). To use a Java applet on a Web page, the applet's .class files containing the applet's code must be stored in the Web site's folder. Then the applet can be inserted by typing or generating the appropriate HTML statements; parameter values are included in the HTML statements used to display the applet on the Web page. When the Web page is displayed in a Java-compatible browser, the applet is downloaded and run on the viewing computer. Applets that run on the server instead of on the client computer are called *servlets*.

Other High-Level Languages

In addition to the languages already mentioned, other languages are commonly found in programming environments. Several of these are listed and described next.

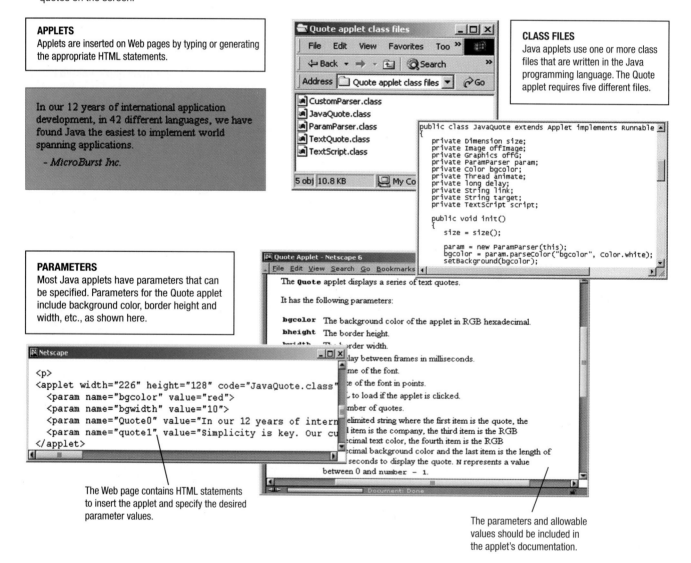

◉ FIGURE 13-24

Java applets. Java applets are displayed on Web pages and typically add some type of animation, such as the Quote applet featured here that displays a series of quotes on the screen.

APPLETS
Applets are inserted on Web pages by typing or generating the appropriate HTML statements.

In our 12 years of international application development, in 42 different languages, we have found Java the easiest to implement world spanning applications.

- MicroBurst Inc.

CLASS FILES
Java applets use one or more class files that are written in the Java programming language. The Quote applet requires five different files.

```
public class JavaQuote extends Applet implements Runnable
{
    private Dimension size;
    private Image offImage;
    private Graphics offG;
    private ParamParser param;
    private Color bgcolor;
    private Thread animate;
    private long delay;
    private String link;
    private String target;
    private TextScript script;

    public void init()
    {
        size = size();

        param = new ParamParser(this);
        bgcolor = param.parseColor("bgcolor", Color.white);
        setBackground(bgcolor);
```

PARAMETERS
Most Java applets have parameters that can be specified. Parameters for the Quote applet include background color, border height and width, etc., as shown here.

```
<p>
<applet width="226" height="128" code="JavaQuote.class"
  <param name="bgcolor" value="red">
  <param name="bgwidth" value="10">
  <param name="Quote0" value="In our 12 years of intern
  <param name="quote1" value="Simplicity is key. Our cu
</applet>
```

The Web page contains HTML statements to insert the applet and specify the desired parameter values.

The **Quote** applet displays a series of text quotes.

It has the following parameters:

bgcolor The background color of the applet in RGB hexadecimal.
bheight The border height.

The parameters and allowable values should be included in the applet's documentation.

▼ *Ada*—a superset of Pascal. Ada is a structured language developed and used by the U.S. Department of Defense.

▼ *APL*—stands for *A P*rogramming *L*anguage. APL is an extremely compact language that uses a special keyboard and facilitates rapid program coding.

▼ *LISP*—stands for *LIS*t *P*rocessor. LISP is used to develop applications in the field of artificial intelligence.

▼ *Logo*—an easy-to-use language that is primarily used to teach children how to program computers.

▼ *PL/1*—stands for *P*rogramming *L*anguage/1. PL/1 is a structured programming language that combines the capabilities of FORTRAN and COBOL.

▼ *Prolog*—stands for *Pr*ogramming *log*ic. Prolog is used to develop applications in the field of artificial intelligence.

▼ *RPG*—stands for *R*eport *P*rogram *G*enerator. RPG is a report generator that uses special forms to enable programmers to quickly specify what a report should look like.

▼ *SmallTalk*—the first successful object-oriented language commercially available; still in use today.

further exploration

For links to further information programming languages, go to www.course.com/parker2002/ch13

MARKUP, SCRIPTING, AND OTHER TYPES OF LANGUAGES

There are languages other than programming languages that are used in conjunction with application development. The majority of these are Web related, as discussed in the next few sections.

HTML and Other Markup Languages

Most Web pages today are written in a **markup language.** Markup languages are designed to make it possible to transmit documents over a network using minimal line capacity. Instead of sending exact specifications regarding the appearance of a Web page, markup languages define the structure and layout of a Web page by using a variety of *tags.* The most common markup language for Web pages is **HTML (Hypertext Markup Language).** HTML uses *HTML tags.*

When a Web page is created—using either a word processor, text editor, or a special Web site development program (as discussed in Chapter 10 and illustrated in Figure 10-21)—HTML tags are inserted in the appropriate locations within the Web page's text. Some tags are used alone; others are used in pairs. For example, ** turns bolding on for the text that follows up until a tag ** is reached, so the following HTML statement

<b> This text is bolded. </b>

would produce the following when viewed with most Web browsers.

This text is bolded.

It is important to realize that with a markup language like HTML, the Web browser and computer being used to display the Web page ultimately determine what the Web page will look like. Text that looks like 36-point boldfaced text on a Web page as it is being developed might be transmitted over the Internet in regular type *marked* as "very large" and "bolded"

Web page as displayed
in browser.

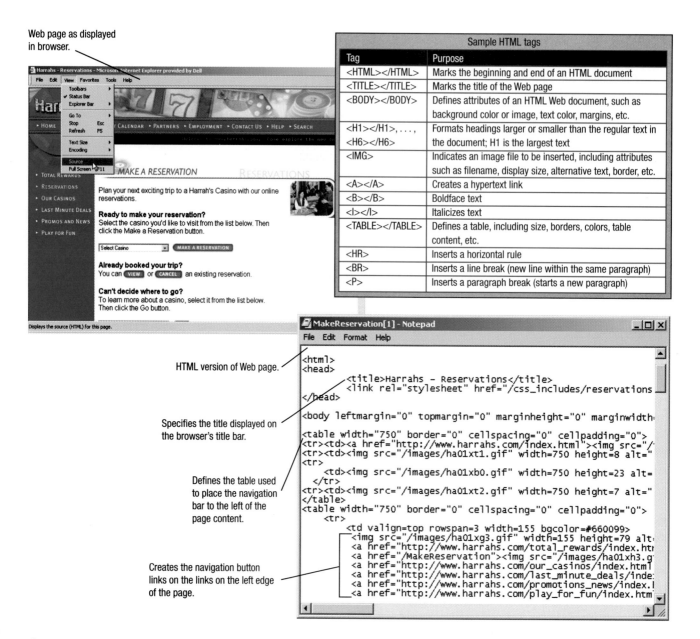

Sample HTML tags	
Tag	Purpose
<HTML></HTML>	Marks the beginning and end of an HTML document
<TITLE></TITLE>	Marks the title of the Web page
<BODY></BODY>	Defines attributes of an HTML Web document, such as background color or image, text color, margins, etc.
<H1></H1>, . . ., <H6></H6>	Formats headings larger or smaller than the regular text in the document; H1 is the largest text
<IMG>	Indicates an image file to be inserted, including attributes such as filename, display size, alternative text, border, etc.
<A></A>	Creates a hypertext link
<B></B>	Boldface text
<I></I>	Italicizes text
<TABLE></TABLE>	Defines a table, including size, borders, colors, table content, etc.
<HR>	Inserts a horizontal rule
 	Inserts a line break (new line within the same paragraph)
<P>	Inserts a paragraph break (starts a new paragraph)

HTML version of Web page.

Specifies the title displayed on
the browser's title bar.

Defines the table used
to place the navigation
bar to the left of the
page content.

Creates the navigation button
links on the links on the left edge
of the page.

● **FIGURE 13-25**

HTML.

text. The receiving PC's browser then determines the particular font to be used to display the text, bolds the text if possible, and figures out how large "very large" type should be. A Web page and its corresponding HTML code are shown in Figure 13-25, with some common HTML tags.

The strength of markup languages is also their main weakness. Because they simplify pages to send them rapidly, they can also produce some unexpected surprises. Small text that looked acceptable on your screen might look like an unreadable mess on another, because of the browser or computer being used or the size or resolution of the display screen. As HMTL evolves and as other markup languages become available, Web authors are gaining more control over the look of screen documents. For example, Web authors can specify alternative fonts to be used if the desired font isn't available on the Web site visitor's PC, and it is beginning to be possible to embed fonts into a Web page so they are available to all client computers. As Internet connection speeds improve, an increasing amount of text—especially logos, headlines, and other customized text—is being inserted into Web pages as images. As discussed in Chapter 10, this alleviates much of the uncertainty of the text's appearance but can significantly increase display time.

HTML tags can be used to perform such tasks as:

▼ Declaring titles for pages

▼ Identifying the sizes of headings (e.g., first-level head, second-level head, and so on)

▼ Marking the ends of paragraphs

▼ Establishing such text styling as italic and boldfaced type

▼ Setting up hyperlinks to other documents

▼ Identifying complex elements to be inserted into a document, such as images, video clips, and sound files

▼ Specifying the layout of tables and frames

HTML is widely considered a very easy language to learn and use when creating simple Web pages without a lot of advanced features. Markup languages that can be used as a replacement for, or in conjunction with, HTML as necessary to create Web page content are listed next.

Dynamic HTML

Dynamic HTML (DHTML) adds some dynamic capabilities to static HTML Web pages, such as objects that move, grow, shrink, appear, disappear, or change color depending on the user's mouse actions. It enables Web page developers to create pages that change in layout and content without the user having to retrieve any new information from a remote server, making the page more exciting. Versions 4 and higher of Netscape and Internet Explorer support some forms of DHTML. Some DHTML features are expected to be built into future versions of HTML.

XML

XML (for e*x*tensible *M*arkup *L*anguage) is a set of rules for how one might define data to be shared on the Web. It's called "extensible" because the markup can be customized for one or more particular purposes, such as being displayed with a variety of types of PCs or other access devices. XML can be looked at as a method of exchanging data over the Web.

Very closely interrelated with XML is Microsoft's *.NET* strategy to increase the convergence of personal computing with the Web. In a nutshell, .NET is Microsoft's platform to implement XML-based Web services. These services allow applications to communicate and share data over the Internet, regardless of the operating system or programming language being used. Microsoft products that support the .NET platform include the most recent versions of Windows and Visual Studio .NET. Other .NET-compatible consumer products and developer tools are expected in the near future. For a more complete description of .NET, see the chapter Trend box.

XHTML

XHTML (for e*x*tensible *H*yper*t*ext *M*arkup *L*anguage) is a particular application of XML for expressing Web pages. Therefore, it is sometimes referred to as a hybrid between HTML and XML. XHTML is commonly used with Internet appliances and similar devices and is similar to HTML but is stricter and more portable. Some believe that a future version of HTML may just be a version of XHTML.

WML

WML or *W*ireless *M*arkup *L*anguage is a language similar to XML that is used with pages to be displayed on a WAP-enabled wireless device, such as a cell phone. WML is supported by almost all mobile phones found around the world.

trend

.NET

The Microsoft *.NET Framework,* introduced in 2000, is a new platform for building integrated, service-oriented applications. These applications—built from reusable chunks of code—can communicate and share data over the Internet, regardless of the operating system or programming language being used. In essence, .NET is a way of tying together different operating systems and programming languages to rapidly create XML-based *Web services;* that is, specific services accessed from a Web page. Similar to Java applets, Web services can be incorporated into multiple Web pages.

.NET introduces a completely new model for developing and delivering applications. It is the first development platform designed from the ground up with the Internet in mind. This makes Internet functionality and interoperability easier and more transparent. Many of these applications will be hosted on the Web, enabling end users to use them with their own personal data from anywhere with any Web-enabled device (PC, Web tablet, smart phone, etc.).

Some of the key features of .NET are listed next.

▼ *Code reuse.* A set of base components provide various standard, routine functions. Programmers can also create their own components and add them to the code library.

▼ *Easier deployment.* .NET provides an application execution environment that takes care of managing memory, addresses versioning issues, and improves the reliability, scalability, and security of the application. Necessary application components are loaded with the application so the application should always run and conflicts with other applications are avoided. This also makes programming, installing, and uninstalling applications much less complicated than traditional applications.

▼ *Multiplatform support.* .NET applications can execute on a wide variety of hardware configurations and operating systems.

▼ *Language integration.* .NET allows the use of a variety of languages and they can be integrated with one another in a single application. For example, it is possible to create a class in C++ that derives from a class implemented in Visual Basic. This is possible because each language is complied into the .NET *common language runtime.* Consequently, .NET allows developers to program in whatever language they are comfortable with, using the most appropriate tool for each application.

JavaScript and Other Scripting Languages

HTML is principally designed for laying out Web pages that have no moving elements, much as a desktop-publishing program is designed for laying out printed pages. Thus, HTML has minimal tools to create Web pages that change as the user looks at them or to enable users to interact with Web pages on their screens, other than some capabilities with DHTML and recent HTML enhancements. If you want to develop pages with a great deal of dynamic content, a *scripting language,* such as JavaScript, may be appropriate. Such languages enable you to build program instructions, or *scripts,* directly into a Web page's code to add dynamic content. For example, JavaScript is commonly used to display submenus or new images when a menu item is pointed to (see Figure 13-26).

JavaScript was originally developed by Netscape to enable Web authors to implement interactive Web sites. Although it shares many of the features and structures of the full Java language, it was developed independently. When using JavaScript, it is important to realize

---

>**JavaScript.** A scripting language widely used to add dynamic content to Web pages.

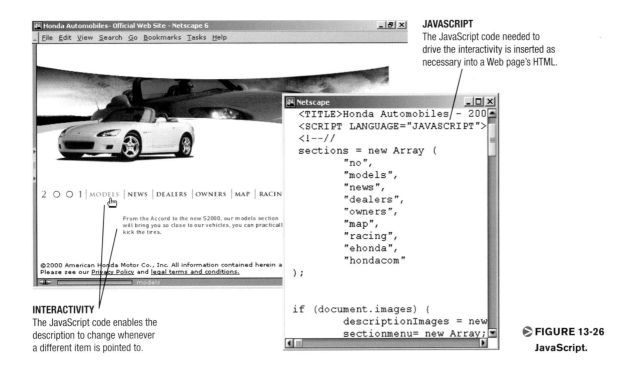

JAVASCRIPT
The JavaScript code needed to drive the interactivity is inserted as necessary into a Web page's HTML.

INTERACTIVITY
The JavaScript code enables the description to change whenever a different item is pointed to.

> **FIGURE 13-26**
> **JavaScript.**

that not all scripting commands work with all browsers. Because of this, make sure that the important features you add to your site with JavaScript are not browser specific.

VBScript

Another scripting language in use today is Microsoft's *VBScript* (which is part of the Visual Basic development environment). VBScript is based on the Visual Basic programming language but is simpler. In many ways, VBScript is similar to JavaScript—it enables Web developers to include interactive elements, such as buttons and pop-up content, on their Web pages. Individuals already familiar with Visual Basic can easily incorporate VBScript content into their Web pages.

Perl

Short for *Practical Extraction and Report Language*, *Perl* is a programming language designed for processing text. Because of its strong text processing abilities, Perl has become one of the most popular languages for writing *CGI scripts*—scripts that are often used to process data entered into Web page forms, as discussed in the next chapter. Perl is an interpretive language, which makes it easy to build and test simple programs.

Technology Tools and Modeling Languages

Two content development tools not yet discussed are *ActiveX* and *VRML*. These tools are commonly used in Web environments and are briefly introduced next.

ActiveX

ActiveX, developed by Microsoft Corporation, is a set of controls that provides an alternative to Java for creating interactive Web pages. In a nutshell, ActiveX extends *object linking and embedding (OLE)*—also developed by Microsoft and adopted widely as a standard by the software industry—to work on the Web. OLE permits you to take such actions as launching a spreadsheet from your word processor and vice versa. It also lets you copy and paste spreadsheet objects such as charts and tables into your word-processed document. Put in a more general way, OLE is a method of nesting any OLE-supported applications inside

further exploration

For links to further information about scripting languages, go to www.course.com/parker2002/ch13

SYS

of each other as you are preparing a document. ActiveX, in implementing OLE on the Web, allows you to do such things as launch your word processor or spreadsheet from your Web browser and share objects among applications. It also enables your Web browser to play special content on Web pages; for instance, the Shockwave ActiveX control can play interactive multimedia presentations that are created in the popular Shockwave format.

ActiveX content can be virtually any type of object—a Java applet, a C++ program, an animation, or a PowerPoint presentation. Software that supports ActiveX sets up any such object as an interactive component on the Web page; ActiveX is essentially the "glue" that holds the different page components together. What ActiveX in effect allows Web publishers to do is grab files from their hard disks that are suitable for the Web and drop them directly into HTML documents. Such a capability is especially useful for office intranets, where a lot of potential Web page content already exists in office documents.

To view ActiveX content, your browser must either directly support it or have access to an appropriate plug-in.

Virtual Reality Modeling Language

Short for *Virtual Reality Modeling Language*, *VRML* is a specification for displaying three-dimensional objects on the World Wide Web. You can think of it as the 3-D equivalent of HTML. Files written in VRML have the extension .wrl (short for "world"). To view these files, you need a VRML browser or a Web browser with a VRML plug-in. VRML objects, such as cars, homes, and other photo-realistic 3-D objects, can be rotated as desired, to be viewed from any angle. An example of a VRML application was shown in Figure 10-11 in Chapter 10).

Like building a house, creating a successful application program requires considerable planning.

THE PROGRAM DEVELOPMENT LIFE CYCLE

Creating application programs is referred to as **program development.** The steps involved with program development are called the **program development life cycle (PDLC).** These steps begin with **problem analysis,** where the system specifications are reviewed by the systems analyst and **programmer** to understand what the proposed system—and corresponding new program—must do. In the next step—**program design**—the program specifications from step one are refined and expanded into a complete set of design specifications.

Good program design is essential. Some key design principles include being very specific, using only one *entry point* into and one *exit point* out of any structure, and ensuring that there are no *infinite loops* in your programs.

Two common approaches to program design are **structured programming,** in which programs are written in an organized, modular form, and **object-oriented programming,** where programs are comprised of a collection of *objects.* Many *program design tools* are available to help the analyst design programs, including structure charts, flowcharts, and pseudocode.

Structure charts depict the overall hierarchical organization of program modules. *Top-down design* indicates that modules are defined first at the highest levels of the hierarchy and then at successively lower levels. **Program flowcharts** use geometric symbols and familiar relational operators to provide a graphic display of the sequence of steps involved in a program. The steps in a flowchart follow each other in the same logical sequence as their corresponding statements will follow in a program. **Pseudocode** is a structured technique that uses English-like statements in place of the graphic symbols of the flowchart.

Data modeling is a technique used in designing an application to be developed using object-oriented programming. A data model identifies the *classes* and *subclasses* in an application, as well as their unique characteristics.

Advocates of structured programming have shown that any program can be constructed out of three fundamental **control structures**—sequence, selection, and looping. A *sequence control structure* is simply a series of procedures that follow one another. The *selection* (or *if-then-else*) *control structure* involves a choice: *If* a certain condition is true, *then* follow one procedure; *else,* if false, follow another. When more than two conditions are used, the resulting structure is known as the *case control structure.* A *looping* (or *iteration*) *control structure* repeats until a certain condition is met. A loop can take two forms: *do-while* and *do-until.*

Once analysts have finished the program design for an application, the next stage is to code the program. **Coding,** which is the job of programmers, is the process of writing a program from scratch from a set of design specifications. Programs are written in an appropriate *programming language.* Among the techniques that have been developed to increase programmer productivity are coding standards, *reusable code,* and *data dictionaries.* Completed programs require a *language translator* to convert the application program's **source code** into machine language or **object code.** A **compiler** translates the entire program into machine language before executing it; an **interpreter** translates and executes program statements one line at a time. An *assembler* is used to convert an assembly-language program into machine language.

Debugging, part of the fourth step in the program development life cycle, is the process of making sure that a program is free of errors, or "bugs." Debugging is usually a lengthy process, sometimes amounting to significantly more than half of the total development time for an in-house program. Most bugs can be classified as being either **syntax errors** or **logic errors.** Once preliminary debugging is complete, programs will also have to be *tested.* Good test data will subject the program to all

Chapter Objective 1:
Identify and describe the activities involved in the program development life cycle (PDLC).

Chapter Objective 2:
Understand what constitutes good program design.

Chapter Objective 3:
Describe several tools that can be used by computer professionals when designing a program.

Chapter Objective 4:
Explain the three basic control structures and how they can be used to control program flow during execution.

Chapter Objective 5:
Explain some of the activities involved with coding, debugging, maintaining, documenting, and ensuring the quality of programs.

SYS

the conditions it might conceivably encounter when finally implemented. Mass-distributed commercial programs are also *beta tested.*

Program maintenance, the final step in the program development life cycle, is the process of updating software so that it continues to be useful. Program maintenance is costly.

TOOLS FOR FACILITATING PROGRAM DEVELOPMENT

Chapter Objective 6:
List tools that can be used to speed up or otherwise facilitate the program development process.

Program development tools can be used to facilitate the program development process. *Application generators,* such as *macros, report generators, authoring software,* etc. enable programmers and end users to code new applications quickly.

CASE (computer-aided software engineering) tools refer broadly to products designed to automate one or more stages of applications software development. To provide CASE-like assistance with such tasks as developing user interfaces and reusable-code libraries, some vendors provide *rapid applications development (RAD)* tools for programmers.

PROGRAMMING LANGUAGES

Chapter Objective 7:
Identify several programming language options available to code programs.

An important decision that must be made during the design phase is the selection of a **programming language.** Programming languages are **low-level languages,** such as machine and **assembly languages; high-level languages,** such as **BASIC, Pascal, COBOL, C, C++, C#, Java,** or **FORTRAN;** or *very-high-level languages,* which are also called **fourth-generation languages (4GLs).** 4GLs are predominantly *declarative languages,* whereas 3GLs are mostly *procedural languages.* Programming languages can also use a *natural-language interface,* as well as be a *visual language,* such as **Visual Basic.**

MARKUP, SCRIPTING, AND OTHER TYPES OF LANGUAGES

Chapter Objective 8:
List some Web-based languages that can be used instead of, or in addition to, programming languages to create Web content.

Most Web pages today are written in a **markup language,** where the appearance of text is *marked up* with *tags,* instead of being absolutely specified. **Hypertext markup language** or **HTML** is a widely used mark up language for Web pages. For more dynamic applications, *dynamic HTML* or a *scripting language,* such as **JavaScript** can be used. For more versatile or portable applications, *XML, XHTML,* and *WML* are possibilities.

Two additional important content development tools that are not programming or scripting language are *ActiveX,* used as an alternative to Java for creating interactive Web pages, and *VRML,* used to create three-dimensional objects on Web pages.

Instructions: Match each key term on the left with the definition on the right that fits best.

1. assembly language

_____ A high-level programming language developed for transaction processing applications.

2. BASIC

_____ A high-level programming language used for mathematical, scientific, and engineering applications.

3. C

_____ A high-level structured programming language that has the executional efficiency of an assembly language; newer versions are called C++ and C#.

4. COBOL

5. FORTRAN

_____ A high-level, object-oriented programming language frequently used for Web-based applications.

6. HTML (HyperText Markup Language)

_____ A type of language that uses symbols or tags to describe what a document should look like when displayed.

7. Java

_____ A low-level programming language that uses names and other symbols to replace some of the 0s and 1s in machine language.

8. JavaScript

_____ A markup language widely used for creating Web pages.

9. markup language

_____ A person whose job it is to write, maintain, and test computer programs.

10. Pascal

_____ A scripting language widely used to add dynamic content to Web pages.

11. problem analysis

_____ A set of rules, words, symbols, and codes used to write computer programs.

12. program design

_____ A structured, high-level programming language that is often used to teach structured programming, as well as for math and science applications.

13. program development

14. program development life cycle (PDLC)

_____ An easy-to-learn, high-level programming language that was developed to be a beginner's language.

_____ An object-oriented, fourth-generation version of the BASIC programming language.

15. programmer

_____ The process containing the five steps of program development: Analyzing, designing, coding, debugging and testing, and maintaining application software.

16. programming language

_____ The process of creating application programs.

17. Visual Basic

_____ The step in the program development life cycle in which the problem is carefully considered and the program specifications are developed.

_____ The step in the program development life cycle in which the program specifications are expanded into a complete design of the new program.

Self-Quiz

Answers for the self-quiz appear at the end of the book.

True/False

Instructions: Circle **T** if the statement is true or **F** if the statement is false.

T F **1.** A systems analyst is an individual who writes the actual code for a program.

T F **2.** The terms *class* and *inheritance* refer to the object-oriented programming approach.

T F **3.** With a do-until structure, the program statements in the loop are always executed at least once.

T F **4.** Pascal is an example of a fourth-generation language.

T F **5.** FORTRAN is an example of a scripting language.

Completion

Instructions: Answer the following questions.

6. Program flowcharts and pseudocode would most likely be developed during the _____ step of the program development life cycle.

7. A(n) _____ converts an application program to machine language one line at a time.

8. Using an incorrect formula is an example of a(n) _____ error.

9. A(n) _____ programming language uses a graphical programming environment, allowing programmers to create code by dragging and dropping items with the mouse instead of actually typing code.

10. _____ is the most widely used language for business transaction processing applications.

Exercises

1. List at least three types of information that should be included in a program's internal documentation (comments).

2. For each of the following descriptions, select the most appropriate phase of the program development life cycle (PDLC).

_____ The step of the PDLC that generates the program's source code.
_____ The step of the PDLC that continues until the program is retired or needs redesigning.
_____ The step of the PDLC in which a beta test may take place.
_____ The first step of the PDLC.
_____ The step of the PDLC in which a structure chart might be developed.

a. program design
b. program maintenance
c. program coding
d. problem analysis
e. program debugging and testing

3. For each of the following descriptions, select the most appropriate language. Note that all languages will not be used.

_____ A programming language used to write applets for use with Web pages.
_____ A low-level programming language.
_____ A markup language used to display Web pages on cell phones and other portable devices.
_____ A set of controls used to add interactivity to Web pages.
_____ A markup language widely used to display Web pages on PCs.

a. assembly language   **e.** C++
b. HTML   **f.** ActiveX
c. Java   **g.** WML
d. COBOL   **h.** BASIC

4. Follow the accompanying flowchart, completing the included tracing table as you go, to see if the flowchart does what is intended (use any numbers for your input). If not, identify what the program would do instead and how it could be corrected.

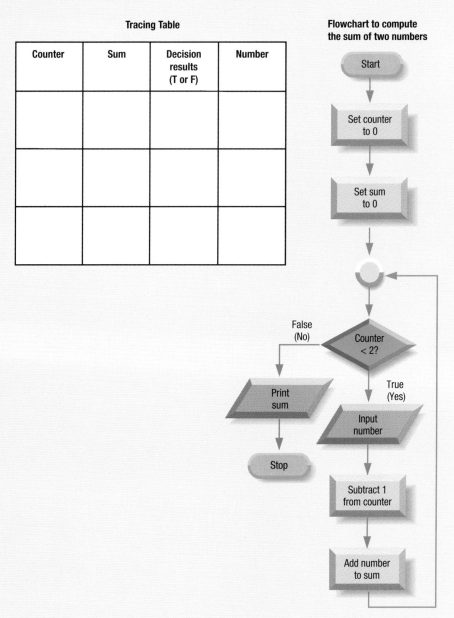

Tracing Table

Counter	Sum	Decision results (T or F)	Number

Flowchart to compute the sum of two numbers

Start

Set counter to 0

Set sum to 0

Counter < 2?

False (No) → Print sum → Stop

True (Yes) → Input number → Subtract 1 from counter → Add number to sum

5. Draw a flowchart for the following situation: Input a person's age. If the person is less than 21 years old, the message "You are underage" should be displayed. For individuals 21 or older, display the message "You are 21 or older." Be sure to test your flowchart to make sure it illustrates the proper logic.

1. **Alpha Beta** Before software is released for purchase by the general public, it is typically subjected to alpha and beta testing. Alpha (the first letter of the Greek alphabet) testing is generally the first phase of testing and is performed by the company developing the software. Beta (the second letter of the Greek alphabet) testing is generally the second phase of testing and is performed by a select set of "real-world" users. The goal of beta testing is to discover problems or errors in the code prior to its actual release, and to provide users with a preview of the new software. For this project, read computer journals, do a search on the Web, or check major software company Web sites to determine some of the beta tests that are currently being conducted. Do the current articles indicate that the beta testers are pleased with the new software? Have you been or ever considered being a beta tester? Of the beta tests currently being conducted, are there any that you could become involved in? If so, how would you go about getting involved? If not, do any of them have instructions for signing up for the next beta test? At the conclusion of your research, prepare a one-page summary of your findings and submit it to your instructor.

2. **A Cup of Oak?** The story behind the Java platform dates back to 1990 and is filled with several aspiring software engineers, a few top executives at Sun Microsystems, a sudden realization that the Internet was the future software medium, and a strong desire to beat HP, IBM, and Microsoft to the punch. For this project, research the history of the Java (originally named "Oak") programming language from its inception through the present. Be sure to include the major events, people, decisions, strategies, and challenges that were faced by Sun Microsystems to date. Will Java be the de facto standard for the Web in the future? Have you considered learning the Java programming language? At the conclusion of your research, prepare a one-page summary of your findings and submit it to your instructor.

3. **The Other Interface** Computers have at least two notable interfaces. The one most commonly referred to is the interface between the user and the computer. This interface is called the graphical user interface (GUI) and is generally credited for making computers more usable by the average person. Although this interface usually receives most of the press, the second interface is perhaps the more important of the two, from the programmer's point of view. The second interface is called the *application program interface (API)* and is only seen by the programmer in the process of writing the source code. This interface allows the application programs to talk with each other and the operating system in the course of processing. It has been suggested that the invention and evolution of APIs actually drive the computer industry and define the limits of the application software. For this project, investigate the evolution of APIs and determine what their impact has been on the computer industry. Do you believe that APIs drive the computer industry? Do you think that APIs will drive the computer industry in the future? At the conclusion of your research, prepare a one-page summary of your findings and submit it to your instructor.

4. **Pass or Fail** As described in the text, a program flowchart is a graphical representation of the sequence of steps involved in a program. For this project, draw a flowchart that depicts the sequence of steps involved in passing the course for which you are using this textbook. To simplify the diagram, you may assume that you will either pass or fail this class (no grade will be issued). The flowchart should print the names of all students on the instructor's roster who have met the requirements of the course by achieving a score of at least 70 percent on all graded components (refer to your specific course syllabus for this information). In addition, you should print the total number of students on the roster, as well as the number that passed the class. Be sure to trace the flowchart to verify your logic, then write a pseudocode version

of this situation. When you have completed this task, submit a copy of the flowchart and pseudocode to your instructor, as verification of your efforts.

5. **Who's to Blame?** When humans and computers are both involved in accomplishing a task and something goes wrong, we tend to blame the computer program. There is little question about the existence of software bugs or glitches, but can all errors we read about in the newspapers or see on the television be attributed to the software program? For this project, investigate at least two publicized problems in which a computer was involved (erroneous bank transactions, military training incident, delayed paychecks, etc.) and determine if the fault of the incident rests with a human, the computer program, or both. Be sure to summarize the events and provide some basis for your conclusion. Have you experienced any software problems? If so, what were they, and how were they resolved? Submit this project to your instructor in the form of a short paper, not more than two pages in length.

6. **Nonobvious** The term *nonobvious* is used in software patent law during the determination of patentability. If a programmer wants to patent a software program, the program must not be an obvious extension to an existing program as determined by "one of ordinary skill." If you pass this test, you still have several other issues to resolve but may be granted a patent for your software. The whole idea of getting a copyright or patent on software can be a bit confusing but may be worth the price, as shown by Stac Electronics' $120 million patent infringement award against Microsoft in 1994. For this project, investigate what the requirements are for getting a copyright or patent on a software program. In addition, investigate at least two cases involving copyright or patent infringement and the results of each case. After completing this investigation, would you be willing to apply for a copyright or patent? Why, or why not? Submit this project to your instructor in the form of a short paper, not more than two pages in length.

7. **BASIC History** The history of the BASIC programming language goes back to 1964 when Dartmouth College needed a very simple language that could be learned and translated easily. They were successful at developing a version of this language and it was implemented on the G.E.225 computing device. A few years later, Bill Gates and Paul Allen decided to develop of version of the BASIC language for the Altair computer, which was being developed by a company called Micro Instrumentation and Telemetry Systems (MITS). Their efforts paid off and MITS became the first commercial customer of Microsoft. Since that time, the BASIC program and various compilers have been at the heart of many commercial ventures. Since 1964, the program was ported (modified to run) under several different platforms and distributed under such names as BASICA, GW-BASIC, Quick-Basic, Visual Basic, TurboBasic, and PowerBasic.

For this project, form a group to learn more about the history of the BASIC programming language and prepare a summary of the people, companies, and events that have been involved in the development of one or more versions of the BASIC programming language and compiler. In addition, you should contrast at least three versions of the program available today and explain the differences. Are any of the versions shareware? Has anyone in your group written a BASIC or Visual Basic program? Do you think that the current version of the Visual Basic program today meets the needs of the beginning-programming student? Should a student start with BASIC or Visual Basic as the first programming language? Your group should submit this project to your instructor in the form of a short paper, not more than three pages in length.

8. **Bug Hunters** Many security freelance programmers in the software industry (sometimes referred to as bug hunters) like to search for security flaws in their spare time and make this information public. The goal is to make the unsuspecting users aware of the possible security problem and encourage the producer of the software to write a security patch. Unfortunately, some of these bug hunters like to go public with the security flaw immediately in order to get

public recognition for their efforts and end up compromising the security of more users than if they had not found the flaw in the first place. For this project, research two recent major security flaws discovered in a widely used software program and present a summary about who found them, how the information was made public, what the security problem was, and how the problem was resolved (or is being resolved). This presentation should not exceed five minutes and should make use of one or more presentation aids such as the chalkboard, handouts, overhead transparencies, or computer-based slide presentation format. You may be asked to submit a summary of the presentation to your instructor.

9. **Hot Languages** It seems like we have one or two hot new development languages every year. Some of the latest of these include Perl, ActiveX, XML, and C#. Why do we need new languages? What is wrong with the languages that already exist? If this trend continues, we will end up with more programs than programmers can handle, and the resulting mix of code and platforms will become more difficult to maintain than it is right now. For this project, form a group to present a summary of the currently hot new programming languages and figure out if they are really new languages or just different versions of existing programs with new names and great packaging. Your group should also attempt to summarize and present the direction languages are headed in the future. Will component-based development become more popular in the future? This presentation should not exceed 10 minutes and should make use of one or more presentation aids such as the chalkboard, handouts, overhead transparencies, or computer-based slide presentation format. Your group may be asked to submit a summary of the presentation to your instructor.

10. **Extreme Programming** A relatively new software development methodology called "extreme programming" can be used in place of the traditional method when the requirements of the system are likely to change dynamically, and the system must be up and running in a very short period of time. This approach to programming has been used successfully at many companies like Daimler-Chrysler and First Union National Bank and is gaining acceptance as a solid alternative to the traditional approaches to system development. For this project, form a group to prepare a short presentation that explains what extreme programming is, when it might be appropriate to use, and how the methodology could be used to achieve greater success than with the traditional approach. This presentation should not exceed 10 minutes and should make use of one or more presentation aids such as the chalkboard, handouts, overhead transparencies, or computer-based slide presentation format. Your group may be asked to submit a summary of the presentation.

Interactive Discussion

11. **Open Source** The software industry of the future will be based on *open source* code—in which the source code is available free of charge to the public to be used and modified—rather than a proprietary approach. The advantages and disadvantages to this approach are often debated, but several programs have already been developed and distributed in this format and more are on the way. One of these programs is the free Linux operating system, which is a very powerful O/S used on both personal computers and network servers. You can also download a significant number of high-quality free software programs to run under Linux, including word processing, spreadsheets, database, and multimedia. Some of the disadvantages to using open source software are that it often requires a higher level of technical knowledge to install and use than the common-off-the-shelf (COTS) software, and it is not always compatible with existing hardware.

   Select one of the following positions, or make up your own, and express your point of view on the subject. Your instructor will indicate whether your response is to be posted to a class bulletin board, discussed in a class chat room, or discussed as an in-class activity. You may also be asked to submit a summary of your position and point of view to your instructor.

   a. Open source code will never become the standard. People will continue to purchase all their software from the major software companies that have established a track record of good products. They will not be swayed by the opportunity to download free software because of concerns about compatibility, capability, and support.

b. Open source code will continue to gain ground against proprietary software. People will try the free downloads and find that the software works as well, if not better, than the program they currently have on their computers. Finding this to be true, they will refuse to pay for a proprietary program when they can download a better one for free.

12. **Program Literacy** Consider the following statement and establish your position, or point of view, on the subject. Your instructor will indicate whether your response is to be posted to a class bulletin board, discussed in a class chat room, or discussed as an in-class activity. You may also be asked to submit a summary of your position and evaluation of the statement to your instructor.

It has been suggested that people should become more program literate, and not be so dependent on the software developers for everything they would like to accomplish on a computer. The task of creating a simple program to accomplish a procedure is not all that difficult, and should be part of the basic skills learned while getting an education. The inability of the average person to program in today's computer based society can be compared to the average person's inability to read in the year 1450, when Gutenberg invented the printing press (the Chinese had in fact developed this ability before Gutenberg). It took a while, but eventually people learned to read and participate in the intellectual life that was the exclusive domain of the church and courts of that time. Reading literacy actually became a necessity of urban existence in the late 1400s, just like programming skills will become a necessity of the 21st century. Programming should not be the exclusive domain of the software companies, we need to empower ourselves with these skills in order to actively participate in today computer based society.

**Interactive
Exercise**

Understanding Program Development and Programming Languages. It's time to review programming steps and see examples of programming code! Go to the Interactive Exercise at www.course.com/parker2002/ch13 to complete this exercise.

CHAPTER 14

Databases and Database Management Systems

LEARNING OBJECTIVES

After completing this chapter, you will be able to:

1. Explain what a database is, including common database terminology and some of the advantages and disadvantages of using databases.

2. Discuss some basic concepts and characteristics of data, such as hierarchy, entity relationships, keys, etc.

3. Identify some basic database classifications and discuss the differences between them.

4. List four types of database models.

5. Understand how a relational database is designed, created, and used.

6. List some ways databases are used on the World Wide Web.

7. State four key personnel involved with database systems.

People often need to sort through a large amount of data rapidly to retrieve some piece of information. One of the easiest and most widely used way of organizing data is in a *database*. Databases range from a small address book created and used by an individual, to a company-wide database consisting of product and customer data used by company employees, to a search engine database consisting of data about millions of Web pages accessed by anyone around the entire world.

In this chapter, we cover *database management systems,* the type of software used to specifically create, maintain, and use databases. We set the stage by taking a look at what a database is and some important database concepts and vocabulary. We then turn to key concepts about data itself. Next, we go into a brief discussion of how databases evolved, followed by an explanation of database classifications and models. The chapter then continues with a discussion of how databases are used on the Web, and closes with a look at the people who use databases. ■

WHAT IS A DATABASE?

As discussed in Chapter 7, a **database** is a collection of related data that is stored and organized in a manner enabling information to be retrieved from the database as needed. Though not all databases are organized identically, databases often consist of interrelated **tables** consisting of **fields** and **records.** In non-PC environments, the term *file* is frequently used instead of *table.* Though this chapter discusses more than just PC database systems, to avoid confusion we stick with the term *table* instead of *file* when referring to a collection of records. The term *file* is used only when what we are referring to is a physical file that can be stored on a storage medium, such as a physical file used to store the contents of a database.

For example, there are three tables in Figure 14-1—one for product data, another for inventory data, and another for data about products on order. Each table consists of several records (which appear as rows). The Product table, for example, contains five records—one each for skis, boots, poles, bindings, and wax. Each record consists of distinct fields (which appear as columns). The Product table stores four fields for each record—product name, product number, supplier, and price. The Inventory table contains five records and three fields, and the Uncommitted-order table contains six records and three fields.

Relational Databases: A Simple Example

The best way to understand how a database works is by example. The type of database illustrated in this section is a *relational database*—the type found on most PCs and one of the easiest to understand. The example shown in Figure 14-1 is a simplified one. Real-world databases often consist of scores of tables, each containing thousands of records.

web tutor

For a tutorial on database fundamentals, go to www.course.com/parker2002/ch14

>**Database.** A collection of related data that is stored in a manner enabling information to be retrieved as needed; in a relational database, a collection of related tables. >**Table.** In a relational database, a collection of related records. >**Field.** A single category of data to be stored in a database, such as a person's name or telephone number. >**Record.** A collection of related fields in a database.

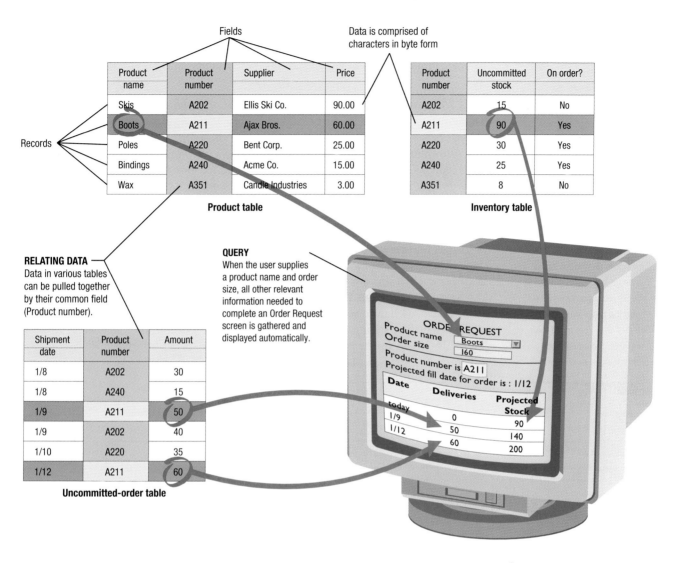

Fields

Data is comprised of characters in byte form

Product name	Product number	Supplier	Price
Skis	A202	Ellis Ski Co.	90.00
Boots	A211	Ajax Bros.	60.00
Poles	A220	Bent Corp.	25.00
Bindings	A240	Acme Co.	15.00
Wax	A351	Candle Industries	3.00

Product table

Product number	Uncommitted stock	On order?
A202	15	No
A211	90	Yes
A220	30	Yes
A240	25	Yes
A351	8	No

Inventory table

Records

RELATING DATA
Data in various tables can be pulled together by their common field (Product number).

QUERY
When the user supplies a product name and order size, all other relevant information needed to complete an Order Request screen is gathered and displayed automatically.

Shipment date	Product number	Amount
1/8	A202	30
1/8	A240	15
1/9	A211	50
1/9	A202	40
1/10	A220	35
1/12	A211	60

Uncommitted-order table

ORDER REQUEST
Product name   Boots
Order size   160
Product number is A211
Projected fill date for order is : 1/12

Date	Deliveries	Projected Stock
today		
1/9	0	90
1/12	50	140
	60	200

> **FIGURE 14-1**
Using a relational database management system.

For this example, imagine that you're a sales manager at a ski-equipment warehouse and an order comes in for 160 pairs of ski boots. You first need to find out if the order can be filled from stock in inventory. If it can't, you need to know how long it will be before enough stock is available. You have an impatient client on the phone who wants an immediate response.

This type of task is especially suited to a database. In Figure 14-1, the Inventory table is used to store current stock levels, the Uncommitted-order table is used to keep track of future shipments of stock that have not yet been promised to customers, and the Product table is used to store the product descriptions. Though this database contains three tables, it is important to realize that the structure of a database is often transparent to the user, who knows only that the information is "somewhere in the database system" and usually has no idea from where the system is extracting it.

The following scenario would be ideal for you. From the PC on your desk, you execute the appropriate command to display an Order Request screen and enter the product description, "Boots," and the order size, 160. The computer system responds with a screen that shows the current level of uncommitted stock in inventory as well as information about stock arriving soon from suppliers that has not yet been committed to other customers. It also provides an estimate as to when the order can be filled: January 12. Thus, within seconds, right in front of you, you have the information you need to respond to the client's request and close the order.

Data from several tables are combined quickly by a *relational database management* system through the fields that the tables have in common. The name *relational database* implies that the software relates data in different tables by common fields in those tables. In the example we just covered, data from the three tables were pulled together through a common Product-number field (the green shaded columns in Figure 14-1).

File Management Systems vs. Database Management Systems

The software programs that can be used to create and use databases can be classified as *file management systems* and *database management systems*.

A **file management system** (sometimes called a *file manager*) is a program that allows the creation of individual database tables (often referred to as *flat files*). Each table is stored in its own physical file and the program can only work with one file at a time. Put another way, file managers cannot interrelate tables. In contrast, a **database management system (DBMS)** allows more than one table to be stored in a single database file and it can access data from any of the tables as needed, just as more than one worksheet can be stored in one workbook file in most spreadsheet programs. For example, the database illustrated in Figure 14-1 contains three tables. To create the data shown on the screen in that figure, the DBMS must retrieve information from all three of the tables that collectively form the company database—this would not be possible using a file management system. With a file management system, each table would have to contain all the data that may need to be retrieved at one time (such as storing the Product name and Supplier in all three tables), as shown in Figure 14-2. This results in a much higher level of redundancy, which can lead to errors in

FIGURE 14-2

A file management system.

This figure shows the same tables as in Figure 14-1 set up as a file management system. Since the program cannot retrieve data from more than one table, there is a much higher level of redundancy.

Shipment date	Product number	Product name	Supplier	Price	Amount
1/8	A202	Skis	Ellis Ski Co.	90.00	30
1/8	A240	Bindings	Acme Co.	15.00	15
1/9	A211	Boots	Ajax Bros.	60.00	50
1/9	A202	Skis	Ellis Ski Co.	90.00	40
1/10	A220	Poles	Bent Corp.	25.00	35
1/12	A211	Boots	Ajax Bros.	60.00	60

Uncommitted-order table

REDUNDANT FIELDS
Instead of just having one field duplicated like in a DBMS (green shaded columns), file management systems require many more fields to be duplicated (yellow shaded columns). Notice that the yellow shaded columns shown here appear only in the Product table in Figure 14-1.

Product name	Product number	Supplier	Price
Skis	A202	Ellis Ski Co.	90.00
Boots	A211	Ajax Bros.	60.00
Poles	A220	Bent Corp.	25.00
Bindings	A240	Acme Co.	15.00
Wax	A351	Candle Industries	3.00

Product table

Product number	Product name	Supplier	Price	Uncommitted stock	On Order
A202	Skis	Ellis Ski Co.	90.00	15	Yes
A211	Boots	Ajax Bros.	60.00	90	Yes
A220	Poles	Bent Corp.	25.00	30	Yes
A240	Bindings	Acme Co.	15.00	25	Yes
A351	Wax	Candle Industries	3.00	80	No

Inventory table

>**File management system.** A program that allows the creation of individual databases, but only one file can be accessed at a time.
>**Database management system (DBMS).** A type of software program used for data management in which data can be retrieved from more than one file at a time.

inside the industry

One Tech Company . . . and Hold the Fries

The computer industry is full of interesting characters, and a few were also the visionaries who created some of its most successful corporations. One such person is Phillipe Kahn, a multi-talented individual who founded Borland International, once one of the largest software companies in the world. With its Paradox and dBASE product lines–the former now licensed to Corel Corporation–Borland was once the undisputed leader in desktop database software, though their first product was Turbo Pascal. Today, Borland is a leading provider of high-performance e-business implementation solutions with such products as Delphi/C++ (a RAD toolset for client/server and distributed computing) and InterBase (an embedded relational database).

When Kahn came to the United States from France he had very little money, but he had a lot of imagination. In 1983, he attended Las Vegas's Comdex convention, the largest computer trade show in the United States. At Comdex, he hoped to get his fledgling company, Borland, a room for a press conference on credit. When he talked to the convention's manager, however, he was curtly told to go to McDonald's to entertain the press if he couldn't afford Comdex's rates.

Surprisingly, that's exactly what Kahn did. Six journalists showed up, and Kahn received reviews from all but one of them, thrusting Borland into the public's eye.

McDonald's. The first Borland press conference was a fast-food affair.

the database and storage issues. It also requires additional work. For example, performing the task illustrated in Figure 14-1 would take the following successive steps:

1. Access the Product table to get the product number.

2. Check the Inventory table for that product number to see if the company can fill the order from current stock.

3. If current stock is inadequate, check the Uncommitted-order table to see when enough stock will be available to fill the order.

What's more, the date on which the order could be filled would have to be hand calculated. Because this file-management method would be much slower than having the tables automatically integrated, in a manner transparent to the user, both service to clients and efficiency would suffer.

It is important to realize that it is possible to choose not to interrelate tables or to choose to have only a single table in a database file when using a DBMS, even if the program has the capability to relate multiple tables. Database management systems available for use on PCs include Microsoft's Access, Borland's Paradox (which is sold by both Borland and Corel), and Lotus Development's Approach. Of these, Access is the most widely used. For an interesting look at the beginning of Borland Corporation, see the Inside the Industry box.

SYS

Not all database programs are as equally easy to use or have all of the same features. Some key features found most often in a DBMS are:

1. The ability to link related data between tables.

2. The existence of a *data dictionary* to standardize the structure of data used in the system.

3. A *query language* or similar feature to enable retrieval of selected data from the database.

4. A *programming-language facility* to permit integration of the database and software programs.

5. *Fourth-generation application development software* to facilitate the creation of forms, reports, and other items.

6. Security and management features to protect access to data.

These topics are discussed throughout the remainder of this chapter.

Interacting with a Database Management System

Users interact with a database management system through an easy-to-use retrieval/update facility that accompanies the database program or an application program written in a programming language.

Retrieval/Update Facility

A typical database program's *retrieval/update facility* presents a graphical user interface that lets users pose *queries* (questions) onscreen and interact with the database. The graphical user interface is designed primarily to satisfy the needs of ordinary users. Among the most critical of these needs are creating databases, updating data from time to time, and retrieving information, usually by making simple queries or by requesting more formal reports.

A database environment for a typical PC is illustrated in Figure 14-3. The DBMS serves as an interface between the user at one end and data and programs at the other. As users develop applications and input data, DBMS utility programs, such as the *data dictionary* (discussed later in this chapter), ensure that the applications and data are appropriate for the database. Other utility programs, such as a rich assortment of wizards, templates, and a help facility, can be summoned when the user needs assistance creating a form or report or help with executing a command. Query languages, such as *SQL* discussed later in this chapter, can also be used.

FIGURE 14-3

Database environment.
The DBMS serves as an interface between users at one end and data and programs at the other.

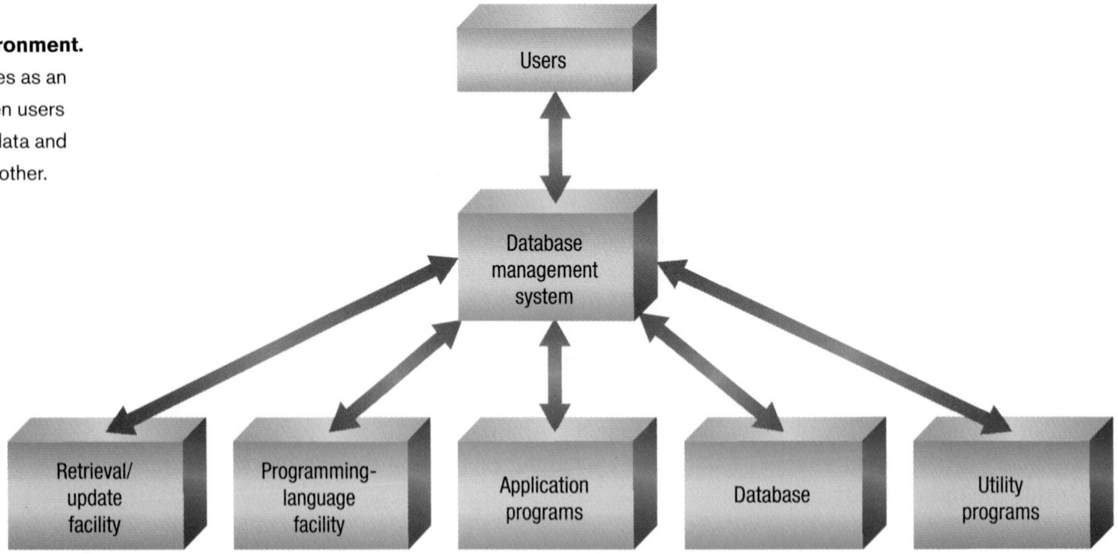

Programming-Language Facility

A database program's *programming-language facility* allows relatively sophisticated users to develop complex database applications. This feature is targeted to users and programmers who want to design custom menus or screens or to create applications that go well beyond the standard ones offered with the database package. Most PC-oriented DBMSs come equipped with a proprietary programming language, such as Microsoft's Visual Basic for Applications.

Database management systems on large computer systems often need to be able to be accessed by programs coded in widely used programming languages, such as C++ and COBOL. Millions of dollars have been invested in such programs, and many of the programs were in use well before DBMS technology became a fixture in organizations during the last couple of decades. An interfacing feature known as a *data manipulation language (DML)* is used to handle this problem. The DML is simply a set of commands that enables the language the programmer normally works with to function in a database environment. For example, if the programmer writes programs in COBOL—the most widely used language in business transaction-processing systems—a COBOL DML must be used.

Thus, a COBOL program in a database environment consists of a mixture of standard COBOL statements and COBOL DML statements. The program containing this mixture of statements is then fed to the DBMS's COBOL *precompiler,* which translates this program into a standard COBOL program. This program can then be executed with the regular COBOL compiler available on the computer system, as discussed in Chapter 13.

High-level languages supported by their DMLs are called *host languages.* Several host languages may be available on any particular system. Languages that a DBMS commonly uses as hosts are COBOL, C, C++, PL/1, and BASIC.

Advantages and Disadvantages of the Database Approach

Using a DBMS offers several advantages:

▼ *Better information.* Because data are integrated in a database environment, information that otherwise might be difficult or impossible to pull together can be collected.

▼ *Faster response time.* Because data are integrated into a single database, complex requests can be handled much more quickly.

▼ *Lower operating costs.* Because response time is faster, users can do more work in less time.

▼ *Lower storage requirements.* In a database system, integration often means that the same data need not appear over and over again in separate tables (refer to Figures 14-1 and 14-2), thereby saving valuable disk space.

▼ *Improved data integrity.* In a database system, integration and the subsequent lower level of redundancy mean that a data update need be made in only one place to be reflected throughout the system automatically. This avoids the errors that can easily occur when the same update has to be made manually in multiple tables. With a file management system, the data could be typed incorrectly in one of the tables or one table could easily be missed and the data not updated. Either way, this would result in erroneous data in the database.

▼ *Better data management.* Central storage in a single database gives a DBMS better control over the *data dictionary* (discussed shortly), security, and standards.

The database approach also has a downside that a company or an individual should consider. Some of the major problems involve cost, though there are other risks as well:

▼ *Higher cost of software.* Relative to other types of file-management software, a DBMS is expensive. On large computer systems, database packages can cost several thousand dollars.

▼ *New hardware.* A DBMS often requires a great deal of processing power, memory, and hard disk space, and accessing records can be time consuming. Thus, some users find it necessary to upgrade to a bigger, more powerful computer system—with some type of removable backup system—after acquiring a DBMS.

▼ *Higher training costs.* PC-based database management systems are often considerably more difficult to master than file managers, spreadsheets, and word processors. Relating data in different tables can be tricky at times. Also, users who want to custom-design their applications with the programming-language facility must prepare for a substantial investment in learning time.

▼ *Increased vulnerability.* Database processing can increase a system's vulnerability to failure. Because the data in the database are highly integrated, a problem with a key element might render the whole system inactive, and the potential loss is much greater. Also, the limited redundancy can create problems if records in one table are deleted accidentally or the table becomes unusable. Consequently, backup procedures are an extremely important responsibility for anyone using a DBMS.

Despite the disadvantages, however, DBMSs have become immensely popular with both organizations and individuals.

DATA CONCEPTS AND CHARACTERISTICS

Data is frequently considered to be one of an organization's most valuable assets. Without it, businesses would find it impossible to perform some of their most basic activities. Data is also the heart of a database. Consequently, its concepts and characteristics need to be understood in order to successfully design, create, and use a database. Some of the most important concepts and characteristics are discussed in the following sections.

Data Hierarchy

Data in a database has a definite hierarchy. At the lowest level, there are the bits and bytes that comprise the *characters* used in the database. Next up the hierarchy are *fields*—single pieces of data in the database made up of individual characters, such as product name or quantity. *Records* are groups of related fields (such as all the fields for a particular product), *tables* are made up of related records, and *databases* or *database files* consist of related tables (refer back to Figure 14-1).

Data Definition

Data definition involves describing the properties of the data that go into each database table. During the data definition process, the types of information that are supplied include:

▼ The name of each field

▼ The type of data (text, numeric, date, etc.) each field will store

▼ The maximum length of each field

▼ Any allowable range or required format for the data

▼ Whether or not a particular field is required

▼ Any initial value to appear in the field of all new records (the value can be overwritten by the user, when needed)

>**Data definition.** The process of describing the characteristics of data that are to be included in each file in a database.

These finished specifications are commonly referred to as the *table structure.* For example, the data definition of the Inventory table from Figure 14-1 might be as follows:

FIELD NAME	DATA TYPE	WIDTH	REQUIRED FIELD?
Product number	Text	4	Yes
Uncommitted stock	Number	Integer	No
On order?	Logical (Yes/No)	1	No

Roughly translated, this table structure declares that three fields will be present in the Inventory table: *Product number, Uncommitted stock,* and *On order?* The Product number field will store text (character) data. The width of 4 means that product numbers will consist of four characters. The Uncommitted stock field will consist of numeric data that will have no decimal places (integers). Instead of a maximum width specified in characters, this program specifies numeric values in terms of how much storage space (in bytes) can be used. The field size *Integer,* for instance, allocates 2 bytes of storage and can hold any number from −32,768 to 32,767. An integer field was used in this instance because stock is counted in units of product and no decimal places are needed. If larger integers were possible for this field, a different field size, such as *Long Integer,* would be selected. If the data to be entered into this numeric field could contain a decimal portion, still other sizes, such as *Decimal* or *Double* would be used instead. The On order? field in this table is specified as a *Yes/No,* or *logical,* field. A logical field often contains either the value *T,* for true (sometimes represented instead by a *Y,* for yes, or a checked box), or *F,* for false (sometimes represented instead by an *N,* for no, or an unchecked box). A product that was on order might be given the value *T;* a product not on order, the value *F.*

This table structure and corresponding table developed in one DBMS are shown in Figure 14-4. Notice that in addition to the specifications listed above, the Product number field (whose definition is displayed in the field properties section of the top screen in the figure) has been specified to be one letter followed by three numbers. If the data typed in that field do not fit the specified pattern (sometimes called the *input mask*), it will not be accepted. This field is also specified as required, so it cannot be left blank.

> **FIGURE 14-4**
>
> **Data definition.** Before a database table can be created, the fields to be contained in that table must be defined.

Desired fields and type.

Field size.

Pattern data must follow (one letter followed by three numbers).

Field is required and cannot be left blank.

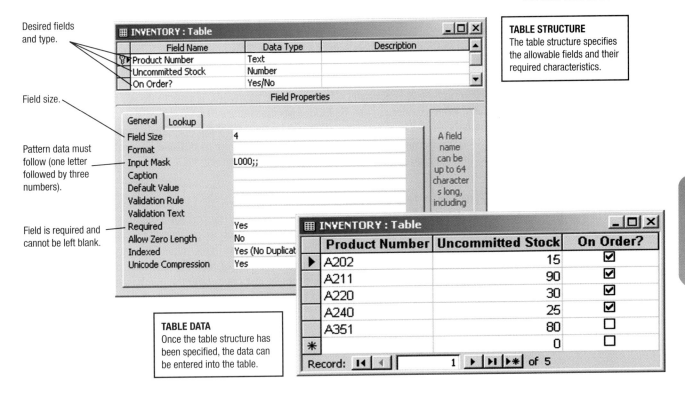

TABLE STRUCTURE
The table structure specifies the allowable fields and their required characteristics.

TABLE DATA
Once the table structure has been specified, the data can be entered into the table.

DATA TYPES	
Text	Text (character) fields store data that are not manipulated arithmetically, such as Johnson or 182-45-7782. You can, however, sort, index, or compare these fields.
Number	Numeric (Number) fields, which store integer numbers and numbers that contain decimal points, are those that must be arithmetically manipulated. Usually subcategories, such as integer and decimal, are available.
Currency	Many database programs have a special field type for numeric data that are to be output in a currency format, with dollar signs, decimal points, and commas.
Logical	Logical (Yes/No) fields are used for fields that can contain only one of two values—for instance, a "Y" (for "yes") and an "N" (for "no").
Date/Time	Date/time fields store dates and times as values. Usually they can be sorted, added, or otherwise manipulated. Several formats, such as short date (e.g., 12/13/02) and medium time (e.g., 3:34 PM) are available.
Memo	Memo fields are used to store large blocks of text. They cannot be arithmetically manipulated or compared, but they can be edited and output.
Hyperlink	Some database programs have hyperlink fields, which store hyperlinks as descriptive names and URL addresses.

FIGURE 14-5

Selected data types.

Each field in a table must be declared a specific data type.

In database management systems, arithmetic computations can be performed on data that have been declared as numeric, but not on data declared as text or logical. Many database packages also have additional data types. Some examples are *Date/Time* and *Memo* (see Figure 14-5).

DBMS packages targeted to large computer systems usually include a special language component dedicated to the data definition function. Such languages have generically come to be known as *data definition languages (DDLs).* Besides simply defining data, a major function of the DDL in these large packages is security—protecting the database from unauthorized use.

Because a large database management system is typically used by numerous people, its databases are particularly vulnerable to security problems. For example, unscrupulous employees may attempt to alter payroll data, access privileged salary or financial account data, or even steal or erase data. To circumvent such possibilities, the DDL may assign passwords to limit which users access which data. This practice gives users only restricted views of the full database. For example, in an airline's passenger reservation database, a regular clerk or agent may not be allowed to rebook a special-rate passenger on an alternate flight, but a high-level supervisor, who knows the password, is able to do so. Similarly, sensitive data, such as salaries, can be hidden so that only certain users of the database, furnished with the proper password, are authorized to retrieve them or modify them.

The overall description of a database's structure as defined by the DDL is referred to as the database's *schema.*

The Data Dictionary

The **data dictionary** is a repository of all data definitions for a database. Such definitions include table structures, security information (such as passwords), relationships between the tables in the database, and so on. Also included in the data dictionary is basic information about each table, such as its current number of records. The data dictionary does not store any of the data in the database tables, just data *about* the database tables. Usually the data dictionary file is hidden from users, since it is accessed only by the DBMS when the database is being used.

>Data dictionary. The repository of all data definitions in a database.

A database's data dictionary is usually kept active to the application. This means that when data is being entered into a table or the data are otherwise being accessed, the data dictionary is monitoring the application environment and will not permit data to be entered or used in any conflicting way. For example, you couldn't enter a seven-character product number if the dictionary expected all product numbers to be a maximum of four characters long. Nor would the dictionary let you type text data into a numeric field or leave a required field blank. And without the proper password, the system would not allow you to view password-protected data.

Data Integrity and Security

Because data is so vital to organizations, data integrity and security are important issues for database designers and users.

Data Integrity

Data integrity refers to the accuracy of data. A longstanding computer saying—"garbage in, garbage out" or "GIGO"—is still appropriate. The quality of the information generated from a database is only as good as the accuracy of the data. Though it is possible to generate poor information from quality data by making poor assumptions or using poor data analysis, it is virtually impossible to generate quality information from inaccurate data. Because so many important decisions are made based on information generated by information systems (which generally use some type of database), data integrity is a vital concern for organizations. Responsible, reliable employees at the data entry level, teamed with good *data validation* methods, can increase the accuracy of the data in a database.

Data validation refers to the process of ensuring that the data entered into a database match the specified type, format, and allowable values. As previously discussed, the data dictionary is responsible for comparing all data entered into a table with these requirements and only allows data to be entered into the database table if it follows the specified rules. If not, a message is displayed on the screen and the record is not entered into the database table until all fields are deemed valid.

Data Security

Data security refers to protecting data against destruction and misuse. Because redundancy is minimized in a database management system, any loss of data or erroneous altering of data can have extremely grave consequences. As mentioned earlier, security precautions are usually incorporated into the data dictionary and enforced by the DBMS to ensure only authorized individuals have access to view and change data. To prevent against data loss, stringent backup procedures should be implemented. Backup software was illustrated in Figure 6-17 in Chapter 6, and is discussed in more detail in Chapter 16.

Entity Relationships

An **entity** in a database system is something (person, object, place, or event) of importance to the organization. If an entity is something that the organization wants to store data about, it typically becomes a database table. There are three basic relationships between entities; these relationships are useful when discussing *database models*. Database models will be covered shortly.

One-to-One Relationships

One-to-one relationships exist when one entity is related to only one other entity of a particular type, so knowledge of one of the two entities is enough information to determine the second entity. In this type of relationship, each record in the first table can have only one matching record in the second table. This type of relationship is not common, because all the information would typically be located in a single table instead.

One-to-Many Relationships

One-to-many relationships are the most common and exist when one entity can be related to more than one other entity of a particular type. Knowledge of one of the "many" entities is enough information to determine the "one" entity, but not vice-verse. For example, an individual supplier would have just one entry in a supplier information table, but the supplier could appear multiple times in the product table, if the supplier supplied more than one product to the company. If one product is identified, its supplier can be determined, but if the supplier is known, there are several choices for the product.

Many-to-Many Relationships

Many-to-many relationships exist when one entity can be related to more than one other entity of a particular type, and those entities can be related to multiple entities of the same type as the original. With this type of relationship, knowledge of one of the many entities is not enough information to determine the corresponding entity. For example, there could be a many-to-many relationship between orders and products. Since one order can contain multiple products and each product can appear on many orders, knowing an order number is not enough information to determine a single corresponding product, and knowing a product number does not identify a single corresponding order that the product appears on. This type of relationship requires a third table—such as an order details table—to tie the two tables together.

Data Organization

Virtually all databases are organized in some manner to facilitate the retrieval of information. Arranging data for efficient retrieval is called *data organization*. The access method used most frequently depends on whether the data must be accessed sequentially (as with tape storage), directly (as with disk storage), or both. In addition, the speed and frequency with which data must be retrieved should also be considered to select the best data organization method, which minimizes the time needed to retrieve data.

Data may be organized in many ways. For any method of organization, typically one or more key fields must be declared. Key fields are explained next, followed by three types of data organization: *sequential, indexed,* and *direct*.

Key Fields

A *key field* is a particular field in a table that is used to identify specific records in a table. A **primary key** uniquely identifies each record in that table. Consequently, no two records can have the same value in the primary key field. To ensure the uniqueness of the primary key, it usually consists of some sort of identifying number, such as Social Security, customer, or product number. For example, in Figure 14-1, the Product number field is the key field for the Product table. When picking a primary key, it is important to pick a field that is unique and is not likely to change. Consequently, names, telephone numbers, and addresses are poor choices for a primary key.

Once a primary key is designated for a table, the key can be used to relate that table to other tables. For example, the Product number key field in the Product table of Figure 14-1 was used to relate, or tie, that table to the other two tables in the database so the data could be re-

---

>**Primary key.** A specific field in a database table that uniquely identifies the records in that table.

trieved from the other tables as needed. To create the screen shown in that figure, for instance, the Product table was accessed to print the Product name, then the Inventory table was used to print the stock on hand, and then the Uncommitted-order table was used to print the estimated quantities and their delivery dates until the required number of boots were listed.

In addition, key fields are used to identify the location of records so they can be located when requested. Typically, the records are organized in one of the three methods discussed next.

Sequential Organization

Sequential organization is used when only sequential access is required. The data in physical files using sequential organization are arranged in a particular order by the contents of a key field. Needless to say, sequential organization is very slow if you are accessing a large database file and you need to access the records in random order, such as locate account information when a customer calls in with a question. Consequently, sequential organization and sequential access are used primarily with batch processing. With *batch processing,* transactions are batched together and processed at one time, such as a company updating customer balances at the end of each day or week, or processing the payroll at the end of each month. Batch processing often takes place at night, when computing demands are unlikely to disrupt other uses of the computer.

As illustrated in Figure 14-6, two physical data files—a master file and a transaction file—are frequently used in batch processing. The *master file* normally contains relatively permanent information, such as a customer's account number, name, address, and phone number. For this example, let's say it also contains data about the customer's outstanding balance. The records in the master file are arranged in ascending order based on the value of the key field (account number, in this case). The *transaction file* contains data about all transactions (purchases, payments, etc.) that have occurred since the last update and is ordered the same as the master file.

FIGURE 14-6

Sequential organization is frequently used for batch processing.

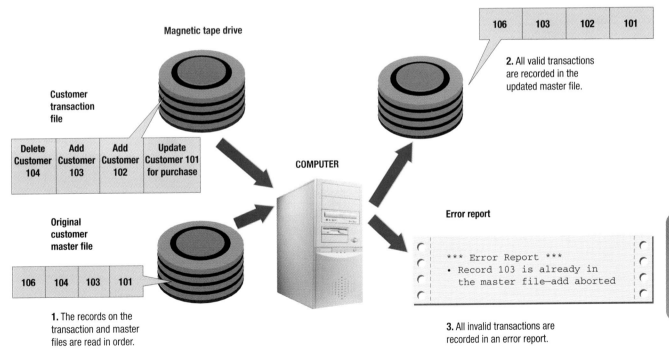

1. The records on the transaction and master files are read in order.

2. All valid transactions are recorded in the updated master file.

3. All invalid transactions are recorded in an error report.

>**Sequential organization.** A method for organizing data on a storage medium in either ascending or descending order by the contents of some key field, so that the data can be accessed sequentially.

Whenever the data is to be processed, the update program reads the first record in each file. If the key fields match (meaning the current record in both the transaction file and the master file are for the same customer), it performs the operation specified in the transaction file (such as recording the purchase or payment). If the current record in the transaction file is for a customer not in the master file, the program creates a new record for that customer in the updated master file. If an error occurs, such as trying to add a new customer using an account number already in place, the information is sent to an error report. The processing continues in this manner until the program processes the last record in the transaction file.

Indexed Organization

Indexed organization provides a way of arranging data for direct access, though data can also be accessed sequentially for batch processing, if needed. An **index** is a table consisting of a list of one key field for each record coupled with location information for that record. For example, the index in Figure 14-7 contains the key field *Customer number* plus

⬤ **FIGURE 14-7**

Indexed organization is often used for real-time transaction processing.

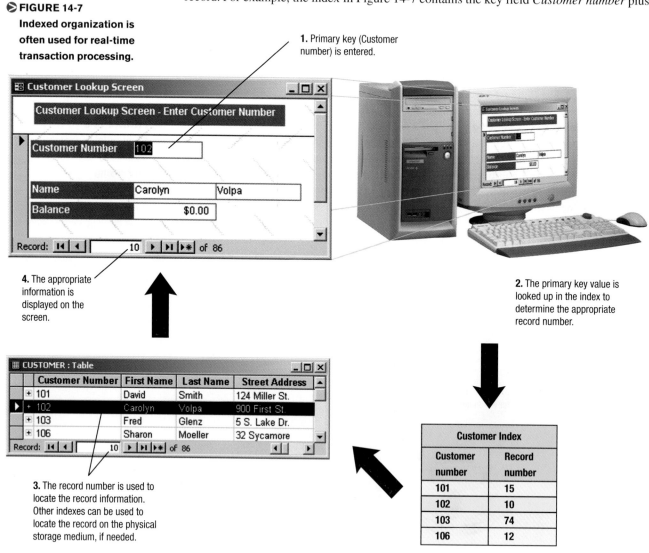

1. Primary key (Customer number) is entered.

2. The primary key value is looked up in the index to determine the appropriate record number.

4. The appropriate information is displayed on the screen.

3. The record number is used to locate the record information. Other indexes can be used to locate the record on the physical storage medium, if needed.

Customer Index	
Customer number	Record number
101	15
102	10
103	74
106	12

>**Indexed organization.** A method for organizing data on a storage medium or in a database so they can be located using an index. >**Index.** A small file containing a primary key and the location of the record belonging to that key; used to locate records in a database.

the record number for each record. As shown in the figure, indexes are sorted in order by the key field to allow records to be looked up in the index very quickly and their location determined. In addition to a record number index, as in Figure 14-7, there can also be indexes that indicate the physical location of the record on the disk, such as track or cylinder number. Databases may use as many indexes as necessary; the indexes are usually viewed just by the program, not the user.

Indexed organization permits *real-time* transaction processing—accessing records and updating transaction data as they occur in random order. For instance, a teller in a bank's lobby may need to find out how much money is in Sandy Patz's checking account. Seconds later, a customer named Karen Jones is at an ATM machine withdrawing cash. Then a question comes up about Maria Castillo's account. In each case, the computer must move back and forth through the checking-account records to obtain information.

Direct Organization

Although indexed files are suitable for many applications, finding information through index searches is potentially more time-consuming than is appropriate for some real-time applications. **Direct organization** was developed to provide faster access.

Direct organization eliminates the need for an index by using each record's key field to determine a unique address where the record is physically stored in the database file. The computer does this by applying mathematical formulas called *hashing algorithms.* Several hashing algorithms have been developed. One of the simplest involves dividing the key field by a particular prime number. This number is determined by the number of records to be stored or the number of storage areas to be used. The *remainder* of this division procedure (see Figure 14-8) becomes the address at which the record will be stored.

Hashing procedures are difficult to develop, and they pose certain problems. For example, it is possible for the hashing procedure to result in two or more records being assigned the same disk address. When this occurs, one record is placed in the computed address location and assigned a "pointer" that chains it to the other, which typically goes into an available location closest to the hashed address. Good hashing procedures result in few collisions.

While direct organization has the advantage of very rapid access, it has a disadvantage. Because records are not stored in sequence, programs usually cannot process them sequentially. Therefore, direct organization should be used only in applications that do not require batch processing.

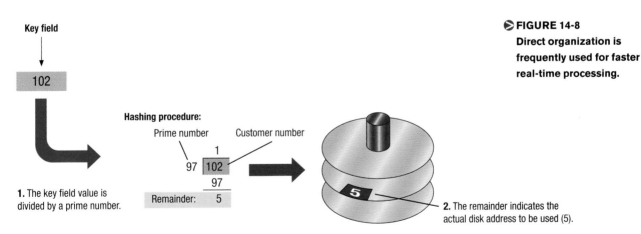

FIGURE 14-8
Direct organization is frequently used for faster real-time processing.

Key field

102

Hashing procedure:

Prime number   Customer number

1
97 | 102
97
Remainder: 5

1. The key field value is divided by a prime number.

2. The remainder indicates the actual disk address to be used (5).

>**Direct organization.** A method of arranging data on a storage medium so it can be accessed directly (randomly).

DATABASE CLASSIFICATIONS

Database systems can be classified in a variety of manners. Three of the most common classifications are discussed next.

Single-User vs. Multiuser Systems

Single-user databases are located on a PC and designed to be accessed by one user. Single-user systems are widely used for personal applications and very small businesses. Most business database systems today are designed for multiple users. This is generally accomplished using a computer network with one of the classifications discussed next.

One important issue multiuser systems have to address is controlling access to data, since potentially two or more users may try to access and modify the same data at the same time. For example, assume that a program is tallying a series of customer balances in a database. When it is halfway finished, another program controlled by someone else transfers $5,000 from Account 001 (which the first program already has updated) to Account 999 (which it hasn't). This will result in erroneous account balances.

To prevent such problems, most database systems allow users to place temporary locks on certain blocks of data while they are being accessed to ensure that no other modifications to these data are made during processing.

Client-Server Systems

Recall from Chapter 8 that *client-server systems* usually consist of computer networks using powerful server computers to supply resources to PCs, which function as client devices. One of the biggest application areas of client-server systems is database processing, in which the principal resource being managed is a database.

In a typical client-server database application, the client is called the *front end.* Typically, the PC at the front end runs a desktop relational DBMS such as Access or Paradox. This program determines the user interface and the format for information retrieval on the client computer.

At the *back end,* a database server program from such companies as Oracle, Sybase, Informix, Microsoft, or IBM runs on the server. The back end manages the database itself, and it translates any commands coming from the front end into a form that the back end can understand. A typical client-server scenario is illustrated in Figure 14-9.

Client-server systems have many compelling benefits, perhaps the most important of which are lower hardware cost and *scalability* to meet future needs. PCs are easier to use and much less expensive than larger computers—you can put a network in place for a fraction of the cost of a mainframe. Also, when you need extra capacity, you can add a new server or add more power to an existing one.

On the downside, client-server networks do not have nearly the successful track record of centralized mainframe systems, which have been around much longer and are discussed next. Hardware costs may not prove especially significant, either, since they often represent

> **FIGURE 14-9**
>
> **Client-server database systems.** A typical client-server arrangement consists of "front-end" clients that input transactions and a "back-end" server computer—with the database—that processes transactions.

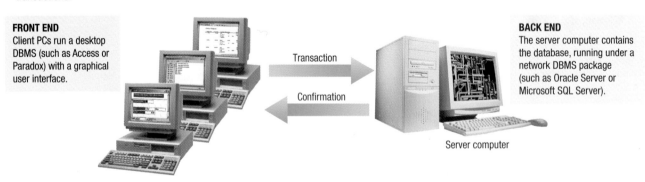

FRONT END
Client PCs run a desktop DBMS (such as Access or Paradox) with a graphical user interface.

Transaction

Confirmation

BACK END
The server computer contains the database, running under a network DBMS package (such as Oracle Server or Microsoft SQL Server).

Server computer

Client PCs

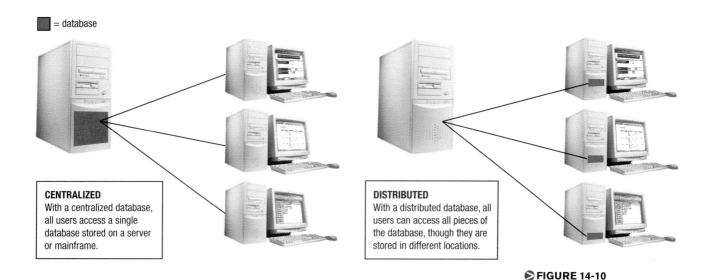

■ = database

CENTRALIZED
With a centralized database, all users access a single database stored on a server or mainframe.

DISTRIBUTED
With a distributed database, all users can access all pieces of the database, though they are stored in different locations.

❯ **FIGURE 14-10**
Centralized vs. distributed databases.

only a small part of the total cost of a system. Software for centralized mainframe sites is easier to develop and support, and data are more secure. The cost to an organization if its data get corrupted or its computers go down for a day can easily dwarf the purchase cost of a new system.

Drawbacks notwithstanding, client-server networks are a growing trend. Many industry experts feel that—once some of the implementation problems are worked out—the client-server approach will be the main way that database data are delivered over computer networks.

Centralized vs. Distributed Database Systems

With a *centralized database system,* a database is located in its entirety on a single computer, such as a server or mainframe computer. On large computer systems, a DBMS may be distributed instead. A *distributed database* divides the data among several computers connected through a network. The data is considered to belong to a single database and can be accessed by any authorized user through the network, regardless of which computer the data is stored on. For example, customer addresses may be stored at the corporate office while customer credit histories are stored in the credit department located in another building across town, but employees in the credit department can access the customer-address information.

In a distributed DBMS, data are divided to optimize performance measures, such as communications cost, response time, storage cost, and security. Moreover, data can be placed at the sites at which they are most needed and best managed. A user accessing the database typically has no idea where the data is physically coming from.

When the user makes a request to a distributed DBMS, it is up to the DBMS to determine how to best get the data; how it does this is transparent to the user. Ideally, a consistent interface among member systems is used so that a user needs to learn only one set of rules to get information from any server hooked into the network.

Distributed DBMS are not widely used because of the complexity involved with distributed database processing.

DATABASE MODELS

Databases have evolved significantly since the early 1960s. This evolution has occurred in response to our increased reliance on information systems, advances in programming languages, and the need to represent complex data, such as multimedia objects. The significant advances in databases can be summarized primarily in terms of their organization of data and access to data.

► **FIGURE 14-11**

The evolution of data-bases. Databases have evolved over the years, becoming more flexible, capable, and easier to work with.

Model	Flat Files	Hierarchical	Network	Relational	Object-Oriented
Year began	1940s	1960s	1960s	1970s	1980s
Data organization	Flat files	Trees	Trees	Tables and relations	Objects
Data access	Low-level access	Low-level access with a navigational language	Low-level access with a standard navigational language	High-level, nonprocedural languages	High-level, nonprocedural, object-oriented languages
Skill level required to access data	Programmer	Programmer	Programmer	User	User
Entity relationships supported	One-to-one	One-to-one, one-to-many	One-to-one, one-to-many, many-to-many	One-to-one, one-to-many, many-to-many	One-to-one, one-to-many, many-to-many
Data and program independence	No	No	No	Yes	Yes

The Evolution of Databases

The organization of data has evolved from a collection of independent flat files with tree or branching structures and high levels of data redundancy, to a collection of tables and objects that support interrelated multimedia objects with a minimum of data redundancy. Newer types of databases also have much easier-to-use interfaces, allowing use by programmers and nonprogrammers alike.

A summary of this evolution is shown in Figure 14-11; the models listed in the figure are discussed in the following sections.

The Hierarchical and Network Database Models

The relational database model, discussed earlier in this chapter, is particularly useful in managerial (decision-support) retrieval situations in which users are free to pose almost any query to the database. For example, a user might first ask for the price of an item, then request a sales total on a group of items, then see how many units of another item are in stock. Thus, the database must be designed to be flexible. In other situations, however, the types of queries that users make are highly predictable and limited. For example, in banking, tellers usually only need such facts as current customer account balances, deposits, and withdrawals. In such transaction processing environments, *hierarchical* and *network database models*—which are designed more for speed and security than flexibility—are sometimes used instead of relational ones. These models are explained next and illustrated in Figure 14-12.

web tutor

For a tutorial on database models, go to www.course.com/parker2002/ch14

Hierarchical Databases

A *hierarchical database management system* stores data in the form of a tree, with typically a one-to-many relationship between data entities. For example, each professor in the top part of Figure 14-12 is assigned to one and only one department. If Professor Schwartz was a member of two departments—such as marketing and information systems (IS)—she would have to be represented twice in the database to maintain the hierarchical structure, once under marketing and once under IS. The database system would treat Professor Schwartz as two distinct individuals. She might even get two separate graduation invitations from the school's computer. Such inefficiency can be tolerated, however, if it's relatively rare. One of the leading hierarchical database management systems is IBM's IMS (Information Management System).

Network Databases

In a *network database management system,* the relationship between data elements is usually either one-to-many or many-to-many. The solid lines in Figure 14-12 depict one-to-many relationships; for example, one professor and one grader can each handle many courses. The

HIERARCHICAL
Hierarchical databases are in the form
of a tree, with one-to-many
relationships between entities.

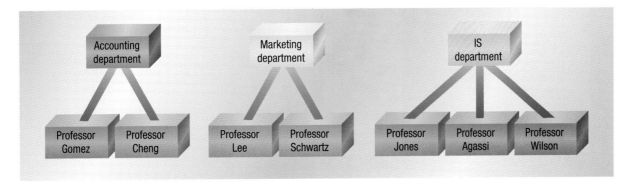

NETWORK
Network databases also use a tree
format and can have both one-to-many
and many-to-many entity relationships.

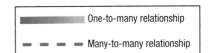

One-to-many relationship

Many-to-many relationship

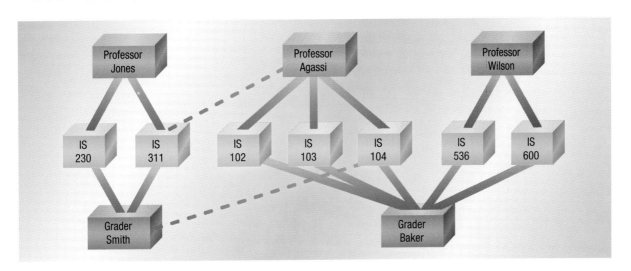

> **FIGURE 14-12**
> **The hierarchical and net-work database models.**

dotted lines, on the other hand, represent many-to-many relationships, where classes can be cotaught by two or more professors or have multiple graders. Networks with many-to-many relationships are harder to model, but they can always be converted into simple networks consisting of only one-to-many relationships. Sometimes this is done when, as in the earlier case of Professor Schwartz, some minor duplication can be tolerated.

Although further explanation of how hierarchical and network models work goes beyond the scope of this book, suffice it to say that these models make access faster for predefined types of queries. In large systems with thousands of requests a minute, the speed of processing requests can be very important. Hierarchical and network databases have been around longer too, so the security on these types of database systems is better than security on relational systems. Because hierarchical and network databases are harder to set up and use, professionals known as *database administrators (DBAs)* are commonly hired to assist. Most databases created today do not use the hierarchical or network models; these models are generally used with existing older—*legacy*—systems that are still operational and must be maintained.

Professor file (table)

Course	Professor
IS 230	Jones
IS 311	Jones
IS 311	Agassi
IS 102	Agassi
IS 103	Agassi
IS 104	Agassi
IS 536	Wilson
IS 600	Wilson

Grade file (table)

Course	Grader
IS 230	Smith
IS 311	Smith
IS 102	Baker
IS 103	Baker
IS 104	Baker
IS 104	Smith
IS 536	Baker
IS 600	Baker

Department file (table)

Professor	Department
Jones	IS
Agassi	IS
Wilson	IS

FIGURE 14-13
The relational database model.

The Relational Database Model

The **relational database management system (RDBMS)** is the most widely used database model today. As discussed earlier in this chapter and illustrated in Figure 14-13, relational databases organize data using tables. Because the tables are independent, they can be linked through common key fields by the user whenever necessary to respond to a request for information. This is in contrast to hierarchical and network databases, where data relationships are predefined, data are prelinked, and only linked data can be accessed. Having to create links while a query is taking place, of course, takes time, which is why relational databases are relatively slow.

Before a relational database can be created, it should be properly designed and the table structure created. Then the process of adding data into the database or otherwise using the database in some hands-on fashion—called *data manipulation*—can be carried out. These topics are discussed next.

Designing a Relational Database

The first step in designing a relational database is to identify the purpose of the database and what data (fields) need to be included in the database. Sketching a diagram of the reports and other desired database output can be helpful in identifying the necessary fields. Next, the fields should be organized into tables, grouping the fields that logically belong together in the same tables. Before continuing, it is important to evaluate the proposed table structure to ensure that it is the most appropriate for the data to be collected. At this point, the tables can be restructured, if necessary, to minimize the redundancy of the data. This process is called *normalization.*

During normalization, one of the most important things to do is ensure that redundant fields from table to table are kept to a minimum. Fields should only be repeated as necessary to relate the tables together; then data can be retrieved from the other tables as needed. Other factors to look at when finalizing the basic structure of each table is to break down fields as needed for the type of information that will need to be extracted from the database. For example, if you want to be able to generate a listing of people by just their last name, then their full name should be entered as two separate fields (*Last_name* and *First_name,* for example) instead of just a single field called *Name.*

>Relational database management system (RDBMS). The most widely used database model today; can link data in related tables through the use of common fields.

Once the tables and the data to be stored in each table have been determined, the structure of each table should be developed. As discussed in the Data Definition section earlier in this chapter, the structure should specify a unique field name, as well as data type, field size, any restrictions on input format, and whether or not a field is required for each field in the table. A primary key for each table can also be specified, if needed. These steps are summarized below.

1. Identify the purpose of the database and what output is wanted (sketch sample reports on paper).

2. Determine the tables and fields to include in the database.

3. Assign the fields to the appropriate table and restructure as needed (normalization process).

4. Finalize the structure of each table, listing each field's name, type, size, and so on (data definition process).

Creating a Relational Database

To create a relational database, first the structure of each individual table is created (based on the design already determined), and then the actual data can be entered into each table in the database. Once data has been entered into a table, records can be modified, deleted, or added as needed using an input form or the regular table view, as shown in Figure 14-14. (Entering records using a form was illustrated in Figure 7-17 in Chapter 7.) Figure 14-14 illustrates creating a table, entering and modifying the data in the table, and relating multiple tables together. Whenever necessary, the table structure can be modified to accommodate unexpectedly large values or to fix minor problems encountered during data entry.

Retrieving Information from a Relational Database

Information retrieval usually takes the form of a query or a report. A *query* feature refers to extracting specific information from a database by specifying particular conditions (called *criteria*) about the data you would like to retrieve, such as retrieving all names for customers who live in Tennessee, or all products whose inventory level is below 100 units. An important fact to keep in mind is that if you can manually pull together the database data you need, you should be able to design a query to get your database management system to pull these same data together *automatically*—and a lot faster too. *Reports* provide more formal listings of an entire table or the result of a query. A query and a report were both illustrated in Figure 7-18 in Chapter 7.

Every database management system provides its own tools through which users query the database for information. One such tool is a *query language.* The query example shown in Figure 14-15 is based largely on **structured query language (SQL),** which is recognized as today's de facto standard for information retrieval in relational databases. There have been several versions of SQL over the years—the latest is *SQL3.* A number of graphical-user-interface tools are available from database vendors to make it easy for users to construct database queries without having to learn a language like SQL. One of the most widely used of such tools is **query by example (QBE).**

Rather than entering complicated commands, users of QBE can illustrate their information needs by filling in requirements on a QBE screen. Figure 14-16 illustrates filling in a QBE screen on a Web site to search for a DVD movie to purchase. Shoppers enter their search criteria into a form, and a search program at the site looks through its database

further exploration

For links to further information about relational DBMS software, go to www.course.com/parker2002/ch14

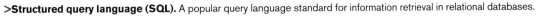

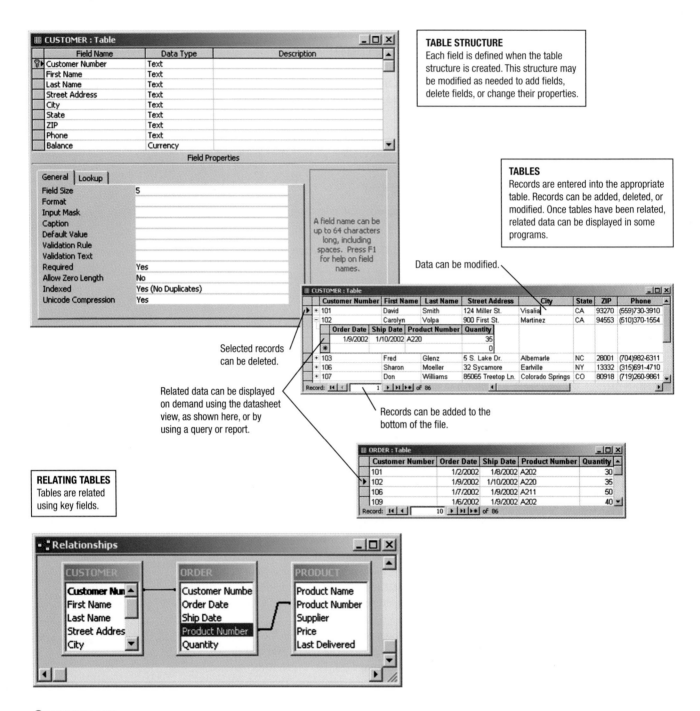

◗ **FIGURE 14-14**
Creating and using related tables.

of products to find matches. The query example shown in Figure 7-18 in Chapter 7 is another example of using QBE. As you can see from this figure, the specific fields to be output are specified on the query screen along with the criteria for the records to be displayed. The query results can also be sorted by a particular field. All these specifications are entered on the query screen and then the appropriate information is displayed. Most desktop DBMSs—such as Access, Paradox, and Approach—include QBE as a standard feature.

When SQL or QBE cannot be used to extract the wanted information in the desired format, a final option is to use database programming techniques to write more specific instructions. This is a fairly difficult task that is best performed by experienced database programmers.

The Object-Oriented Database Model

Traditionally, data management software has dealt with *structured* types of data, that is, primarily text-based data that can be organized neatly into rows (records) and columns (fields). Structured data are the type you've mostly been reading about in this chapter and probably the type you've been working with on your PC. However, user needs and technologies have led to a new type of database that is putting an entirely different face on data management. In addition to handling conventional record data, computer databases are now being used to store documents, diagrams, still photographs, video, animation, and sound. The World Wide Web has certainly been a big factor in pushing database developers to cater to these new data types. So have the rising number of computer users who clamor for data to be presented in a natural-looking way that resembles experiences from real life. This growing interest in other data types and the need to include them in a multimedia format have given rise to **object-oriented database management systems,** abbreviated as *OODBMS.* The stakes in the object-oriented-technology-development race are huge, since it will eventually be critical that companies establish friendly and exciting interactive environments in which to conduct electronic commerce and other Web-based applications.

Objects in an OODBMS are similar in concept to the objects in an object-oriented programming application, discussed in the previous chapter. An object can be made from

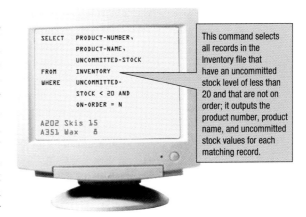

This command selects all records in the Inventory file that have an uncommitted stock level of less than 20 and that are not on order; it outputs the product number, product name, and uncommitted stock values for each matching record.

▶ **FIGURE 14-15**

Querying a database using structured query language (SQL). This example pulls information from the database illustrated in Figure 14-1.

▶ **FIGURE 14-16**

Using query by example (QBE) on the Web. At Amazon.com's video site, you can hunt for DVD movies by filling information into a form. Here a search is made for all DVD movies starring both Tom Cruise and Nicole Kidman that cost $25 or less.

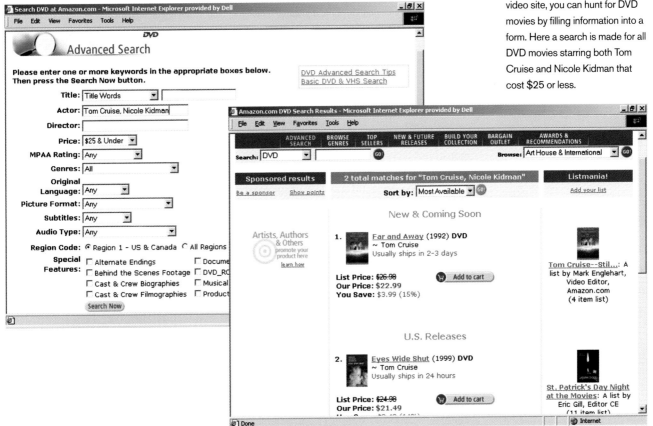

> **Object-oriented database management system.** A database in which multiple types of data—text, graphics, video, sound, etc.—are represented as objects with methods describing how the different types of data in an object are combined.

virtually anything—a video clip, a photograph with a narrative, text with music, and so on. For example, a recorded speech consists of two types of data: voice and a moving image of someone talking. Thus, the speech can form an OODBMS object made up of voice, moving-image data, and a set of *methods* (procedures or instructions) describing how to combine the two.

You can also combine other objects with the speech. If the speech is on the environment, for example, pollution statistics and photographs of defoliated areas may be useful to include. These, too, would exist as objects in the database, each with its own set of methods. For example, the pollution statistics would be accompanied by program instructions telling how the data should be displayed on screen. Unlike a traditional relational database in which each record has a similar format, little similarity may exist among the data elements that form the objects.

An object-oriented database management system makes it possible to store objects in an object-oriented database, as well as copy and paste them into applications, where people can access them and manipulate them as needed. Because all stored objects are reusable, new applications can be developed in a fraction of the time it took before these databases existed.

There is not a single standard for the object-oriented database model, but its key characteristics (objects, methods, encapsulation, polymorphism, classes, inheritance, etc.) are similar to the object-oriented programming principles discussed in Chapter 13. Object-oriented databases are generally accessed using an object-oriented programming language, such as Java or C++, or an *object query language (OQL)*, essentially an object-oriented version of SQL. The ability to directly manipulate data stored in an object-oriented database using an object-oriented programming language is called *transparent persistence.*

Though it is not expected that object-oriented databases will replace relational databases any time soon, the use of object-oriented database fundamentals is expected to grow in popularity as more existing traditional databases need to include more complex, non-traditional content, such as multimedia elements. An OODBMS is faster, more efficient, and more appropriate for some applications than other database models. OODBMS are becoming more prominent on Java servers and databases accessed via the Internet.

A new type of the relational DBMS, referred to as *object-relational database management systems,* allow some type of object orientation. These hybrid systems are DBMSs that combine object and relational technology. One such example is Oracle, Version 8. Many industry observers speculate that object-relational databases will supplant relational databases as the standard for ad hoc queries on desktop PCs. It is also expected that the interface used to access information from databases will continue to become easier and less technical to use—perhaps even voice driven in the not too distant future.

DATABASES AND THE WEB

Databases are extremely common on the World Wide Web. Virtually all companies that offer products or corporate information, online ordering, or similar activities through a Web site use a database. The most common applications involve client-server database transactions, where the user's browser is the client software. The use of peer-to-peer information exchange, however, is increasing, as discussed in the Chapter 9 Inside the Industry box.

Examples of Web Databases in Use

There are scores of examples of how databases can be used on the Web. Databases facilitate information retrieval and processing, as well as allow more interactive, dynamic content. A few specific examples of the context with which Web-enabled databases may be encountered are covered next. Following these sections is a discussion and example of how a Web database might work and a brief look at other Web-database-related issues.

web tutor

For a tutorial on accessing data over the Web, go to www.course.com/parker2002/ch14

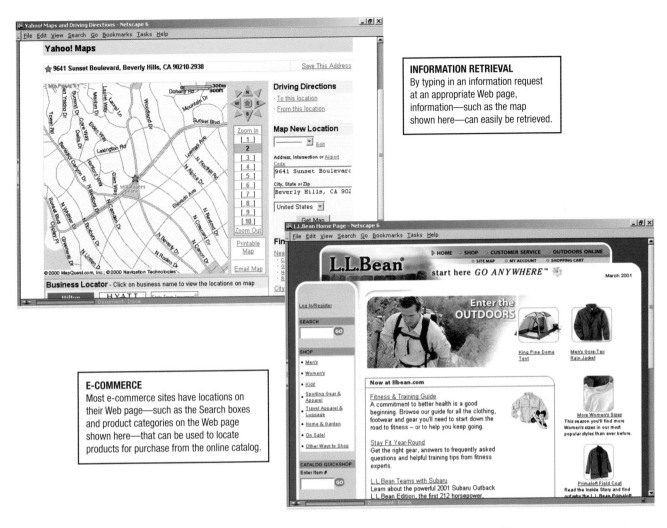

INFORMATION RETRIEVAL
By typing in an information request at an appropriate Web page, information—such as the map shown here—can easily be retrieved.

E-COMMERCE
Most e-commerce sites have locations on their Web page—such as the Search boxes and product categories on the Web page shown here—that can be used to locate products for purchase from the online catalog.

▶ **FIGURE 14-17**
Information retrieval and e-commerce. Databases are widely used on the Web for information retrieval and ordering products.

Information Retrieval

By their very nature, databases lend themselves to information retrieval on the Web, which is, in essence, a huge storehouse of data waiting to be retrieved. Data is stored in the database, and Web site visitors can request and view it (see Figure 14-17). The information can be product information, Web pages, press releases, maps, photographs, documents, and so forth. Information retrieved from organizations, as well as search sites and reference sites, fits into this category. A growing trend is to enable customers to look up information directly about the status of their order or shipment—even the status of new home construction, as discussed in the Trend box.

E-Commerce and E-Business

Another widely used database application on the Web is to support and facilitate *e-commerce.* Catalog information, pricing, customer information, shopping cart contents, and more can be stored in a database to be retrieved on demand using an appropriate script or program to link the database with the Web site (refer again to Figure 14-17). Related business uses for databases, such as *supply chain management* and *data mining,* are discussed in Chapter 11. For a look at one further example—package tracking via the Web—see the How It Works box.

Dynamic Web Pages

Static Web pages display the same information for everyone, every time the page is displayed, until the Web page file is modified. In contrast, the appearance and content of *dynamic* Web

SYS

Web-Based Customer Service

Web-based customer service (sometimes referred to as *eCRM*) is a rapidly growing trend. Either to supplement or to replace telephone-based customer support, many organizations are offering customers information through the company's Web site. After a customer places an order, for example, he or she can use the Web site to track it, see when the order was shipped, and use the shipper's package tracking system to find out when it will be delivered (refer to this chapter's How It Works box for a discussion about online package tracking systems).

An example of an innovative use of Web-based customer service is the MyCentexHomes.com Web site. This Web site enables buyers to monitor the progress of their new home's construction online, whenever they want. Using his or her user ID and password, a homeowner can access floor plans and status reports, as well as view photos of the home as it is being constructed. In addition, the site is used as a communication tool, allowing the home buyers to contact their sales managers or field managers via e-mail.

To keep the site up-to-date, construction managers input updates directly from the field and the information is immediately available to the customer. Once the home is completed, homeowners can continue to use the site to review warranty information and request repairs.

This application illustrates the power of the Internet as a tool to communicate with and service customers regardless of

their location. Centex customers can feel they are supervising the construction of their new homes without setting a foot on the property. Web-based customer support systems such as this one can result in happy customers and lower customer service cost—a good combination for any organization.

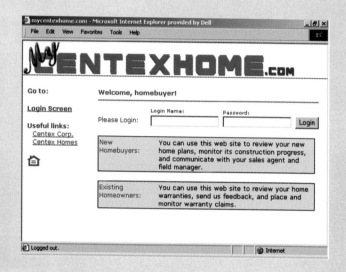

This Web site allows Centex home buyers to monitor the progress of their home construction 24/7.

pages change based on a user's input. This input can be based on selections specified on a form located on the page or controlled by some other aspect, such as a Java applet, ActiveX control, or the activities that the user has already performed on the site, such as clicking a displayed ad or a product's hyperlink.

Databases facilitate dynamic Web pages, allowing more types of activities to alter the content, as well as to simplify the task itself. Usually this results in much faster delivery of information and a more engaging experience for the user.

How Web Databases Work

To further illustrate more about how databases and the Web can work together, let's look at an example.

Web Databases: A Simple Example

The request to retrieve information from or store data into a Web database is usually initiated by the user. Filling out a Web page form, selecting an option from a menu displayed on a Web page, or clicking an onscreen ad are common ways database requests are made. The request

further exploration

For links to further information about Web-based databases, go to www.course.com/parker2002/ch14

Web-Based Package Tracking

Package shipment companies, such as FedEx and United Parcel Service (UPS), have had tracking services for some time now. Data about all shipments are recorded periodically during the shipping process, such as when packages enter or leave a facility or vehicle. Using the package's reference number (provided by the sender), the sender or would-be package recipient can call an 800 number and find out the status of the shipment. With the explosion of e-commerce and Internet use, however, package tracking systems have gone online.

To track a shipment via the Internet, a tracking number link located on an electronic receipt, such as on an order page or e-mailed receipt, is clicked to load the appropriate tracking Web page on the shipping company's Web site. If a tracking link is not available, the tracking number can be entered into the shipping company's Tracking section of its site (see the accompanying illustration). The tracking information displayed indicates where the package has been scanned, so its approximate location can be determined. Once the package has arrived, the delivery date and time are recorded.

In addition, UPS and FedEx allow you to track packages via e-mail; FedEx has a Netscape sidebar so your tracking information can be continually available while your browser is open; and virtually all services offer signature confirmation—copies of the electronic signature captured at the time of delivery—upon request.

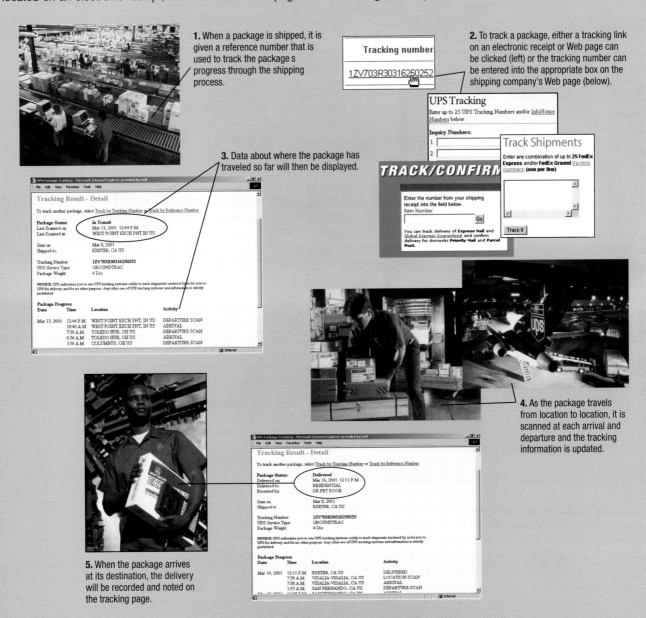

1. When a package is shipped, it is given a reference number that is used to track the package's progress through the shipping process.

2. To track a package, either a tracking link on an electronic receipt or Web page can be clicked (left) or the tracking number can be entered into the appropriate box on the shipping company's Web page (below).

3. Data about where the package has traveled so far will then be displayed.

4. As the package travels from location to location, it is scanned at each arrival and departure and the tracking information is updated.

5. When the package arrives at its destination, the delivery will be recorded and noted on the tracking page.

is received by the Web server, which then converts the request into a database query and passes it on to the database server with the help of intermediary software called *middleware,* discussed in the next section. The database server retrieves the appropriate information and returns it to the Web server (again, via middleware) where it is displayed on the user's screen as a Web page. These steps are illustrated in Figure 14-18.

Middleware

Software that connects two otherwise separate applications—such as a Web server and a database management system, as in Figure 14-18—is referred to as **middleware.** The most common types of middleware used to interface between a database and a Web page are *CGI* and *API scripts.* A newer scripting language becoming increasingly more popular is *PHP.*

⊖ **FIGURE 14-18**

A Web database in action.

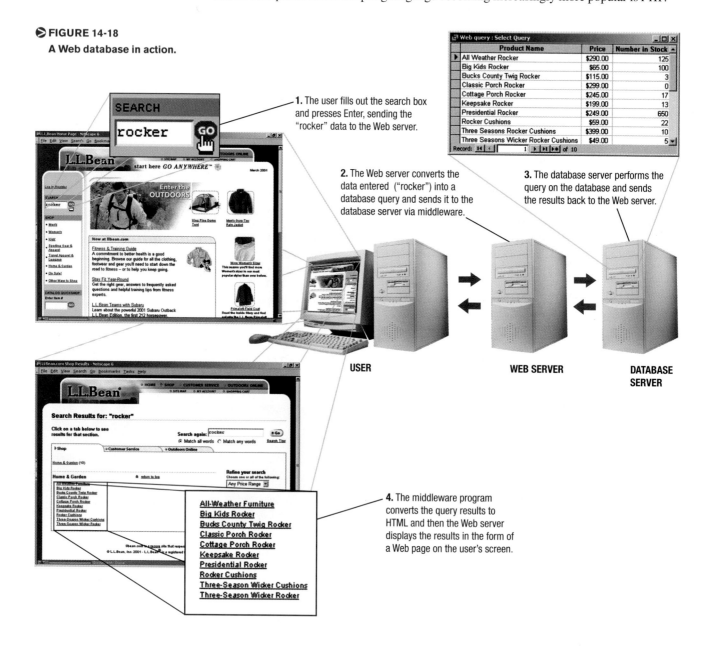

1. The user fills out the search box and presses Enter, sending the "rocker" data to the Web server.

2. The Web server converts the data entered ("rocker") into a database query and sends it to the database server via middleware.

3. The database server performs the query on the database and sends the results back to the Web server.

4. The middleware program converts the query results to HTML and then the Web server displays the results in the form of a Web page on the user's screen.

USER   WEB SERVER   DATABASE SERVER

>**Middleware.** Software used to connect two otherwise separate applications, such as a Web server and a database management system.

CGI

A *CGI (common gateway interface) script* is a set of instructions written in a programming language (such as C++, Perl, Java, or Visual Basic) that is designed to accept data from and return data to a Web page visitor. CGI scripts usually reside on the Web server and handle such tasks as processing input forms and information requests. On very busy sites, CGI can slow down server response time significantly because it processes each request individually.

API

To alleviate the inefficiency problems with using CGI on busy Web sites, the server's *API (application program interface)* can be used. An API is designed for a particular operating system or application program and can be used to make requests of that operating system or program. Common APIs include *ISAPI (Internet Server Application Program Interface)* for Windows-based Web servers and *NSAPI (Netscape Server API)* for Netscape's Web servers. On the Web, API applications are increasingly being used instead of CGI applications because they run faster.

PHP

PHP is a scripting language that can be used to create dynamic Web pages. It uses code similar to Perl or C that is inserted into the HTML code of a Web page using special PHP tags. This allows Web page authors to jump between HTML and PHP when they are creating the page. PHP is a server-side script, so the client PC can't view the PHP code. PHP is typically used to perform tasks similar to CGI and API but has the advantage of high compatibility with many types of databases. It is also an open-source program, available free to all users.

As Web-site publishing programs mature, capabilities to generate the appropriate scripts for dynamic Web pages are being incorporated into the programs. For example, FrontPage and ColdFusion both include features to connect Web pages to databases without the developer having to write any scripts to tie the two elements together. Custom programs can also be written to act as middleware to tie Web pages and databases together. Another option for Web developers familiar with Visual Basic is creating *active server pages (ASPs)*. Active server pages are dynamically created Web pages with an .asp extension that uses ActiveX scripting—usually in VB Script or JavaScript code—to deliver dynamic content.

DATABASE MANAGEMENT SYSTEMS PERSONNEL

A final topic to discuss are the individuals within an organization who are involved with creating and using databases. These personnel include:

▼ *Database designers* who are responsible for designing the new and modified databases in an organization. These individuals are also called *database architects* or *database engineers.*

▼ *Database programmers* who write the programs that allow access to the database. When the access is from a Web page, these individuals are sometimes called *Web programmers,* though Web programmers typically do other programming, as well.

▼ *Database administrators* who are the people responsible for setting up and managing the large databases within an organization.

▼ *End users* who are the individuals who access and use the database on a regular basis.

further exploration

For links to further information about DBMS certification exams, go to www.course.com/parker2002/ch14

Database management systems are widely used to manage large banks of data.

WHAT IS A DATABASE?

A **database** is a collection of related data that is stored and organized in a manner that allows information to be retrieved as needed. Most databases consist of one or more **tables;** each table contains a collection of related **records,** which, in turn, is a collection of related **fields.**

A *relational database* is the most common type of database found on PCs. This type of database is so named because it relates data in various database tables by common fields in those tables. It is created with a relational version of a **database management system (DBMS)**—a software program used to create database applications and information to be stored into or retrieved from more than one table at a time. In contrast, **file management systems** allow the use of only one table at a time, so relating tables is not an option.

A database is usually accessed through an easy-to-use retrieval/update facility or an application program. Complex database applications may require custom programming via a *data manipulation language (DML)* and a standard programming language.

A DBMS can offer several advantages. Among these advantages are better information, faster response time, lower operating costs, fewer data storage requirements, improved data integrity, and better data management. The biggest disadvantages are cost and a greater vulnerability to failure.

DATA CONCEPTS AND CHARACTERISTICS

Data in a database has a definite hierarchy. At the lowest level, data—such as a name or phone number—is a collection of bytes or characters; this data is entered into fields in the database. Related fields form records, related records form files, and a group of related files comprises the database.

One task performed by anyone setting up a database is **data definition**—the process of describing data to the DBMS prior to entering them. The descriptions of these data are used to create a *table structure* for each table. This structure contains a description of the data to be entered into the table, and a **data dictionary,** which contains information about all data in the application.

Because data is so vital to an organization, **data integrity, data validation,** and **data security** are important issues to ensure the quality of information retrieved from the database and the safety of the database.

Different databases may relate their **entities** differently. Common types of entity relationships include *one-to-one, one-to-many,* and *many-to-many.* Databases typically use **primary keys** to relate files together and **indexes** to more easily locate data when it is requested. In addition to **indexed, sequential** and **direct organization** provide for sequential and rapid direct access, respectively. Sequential organization is used for *batch* processing; indexed and direct organization can be used for *real-time* transaction processing.

DATABASE CLASSIFICATIONS

Database systems can be classified as single-user or multiple-user systems, depending on how many users need to access the database. In addition, *client-server systems* are accessed by client computers and their desktop DBMSs at the *front end,* and are managed by the server computers at the *back end.*

Many applications are set up on *distributed databases*. Instead of a single *central database system* existing on a large centralized mainframe—the most widespread practice for storing database data in large companies—the database is divided among several smaller computers that are hooked up in a network.

DATABASE MODELS

Database models have evolved over time. Traditionally, database systems have conformed to one of three common types: relational, hierarchical, and network. A *hierarchical database management system* stores data in the form of a tree, where the relationship between data elements is usually one-to-many. In a *network database management system* the relationship between data elements is typically either many-to-one or many-to-many. The **relational database management system** is the most widely used database model today. The growing interest in other data types and the need to combine them into multimedia formats for applications have given rise to **object-oriented database management systems.** These databases combine disparate data types into storable entities called *objects*.

To create a relational database, the structure of the database is first designed and then created. The data can then be entered into the database and information can be retrieved using *queries* and *reports*. Two common types of queries are using **structured query language (SQL)** and **query by example (QBE).**

Chapter Objective 4:
List four types of database models.

Chapter Objective 5:
Understand how a relational database is designed, created, and used.

DATABASES AND THE WEB

Database applications are plentiful on the Web. When information is retrieved via an input form or other interactive element on a Web page, a database is used. In addition to information retrieval, *e-commerce* and *dynamic* Web pages are database oriented.

When a request for information is transferred from a Web page to a database, it is converted—using **middleware** software—to a request the database can process. The retrieved information is then passed back to the Web server and displayed in the form of a Web page.

Chapter Objective 6:
List some ways databases are used on the World Wide Web.

DATABASE MANAGEMENT SYSTEMS PERSONNEL

The individuals in an organization involved with creating and using databases include *database designers, programmers, administrators,* and *end users.*

Chapter Objective 7:
State four key personnel involved with database systems.

Instructions: Match each key term on the left with the definition on the right that fits best.

1. data definition

_____ A query procedure in which an onscreen query form is used to indicate what information should be retrieved.

2. data dictionary

_____ A collection of related data that is stored in a manner enabling information to be retrieved as needed; in a relational database, a collection of related tables.

3. data integrity

4. data validation

_____ A collection of related fields in a database.

5. database

_____ A collection of related records, in relational database terminology.

6. database management system (DBMS)

_____ A database in which multiple types of data—text, graphics, video, sound, etc.—are represented as objects with methods describing how the different types of data in an object are combined.

7. field

_____ A popular query language standard for information retrieval in relational databases.

8. file management system

_____ A program that allows the creation of individual databases, but only one file can be accessed at a time.

9. index

_____ A single category of data to be stored in a database, such as a person's name or telephone number.

10. middleware

_____ A small file containing a primary key and the location of the record belonging to that key; used to locate records in a database

11. object-oriented database management system

_____ A specific field in a database table that uniquely identifies the records in that table.

12. primary key

_____ A type of software program used for data management in which data can be retrieved from more than on file at a time.

13. query by example (QBE)

_____ Software used to connect two otherwise separate applications, such as a Web server and a database management system.

14. record

_____ The accuracy of data.

15. relational database management system (RDBMS)

_____ The most widely used database model in use today; can link data in related tables through the use of common fields.

16. structured query language (SQL)

_____ The process of describing the characteristics of data that are to be included in each file in a database.

17. table

_____ The process of ensuring that data entered into a database match the data definition.

_____ The repository of all data definitions in a database.

Answers for the self-quiz appear at the end of the book.

True/False

Instructions: Circle **T** if the statement is true or **F** if the statement is false.

T F **1.** A file management system can pull information from more than one table at a time.

T F **2.** In a distributed database, all of the data is physically located on one computer.

T F **3.** In a relational database, more than one table can be included in a database file.

T F **4.** The network database model is the most widely used model today.

T F **5.** With query-by-example, it is not necessary to learn a query language.

Completion

Instructions: Answer the following questions.

6. In a student information database, the Name column would be considered a(n) _____, while all of Jennifer Mitchell's information would be called a(n) _____ .

7. The _____ stores all the data definitions for a database.

8. _____ refers to the process of ensuring that the data entered into a database matches the required specifications.

9. A(n) _____ can contain a wide variety of data types stored in the form of objects.

10. Software used to connect two otherwise separate applications, such as a Web server and a database management system, is called _____ .

1. List one disadvantage to using a database management system and explain at least one procedure that can be used to reduce the risks of that disadvantage.

2. Would the data type text, numeric, or logical be the most appropriate for a telephone number field that needs to store data in the format (123)456-7890? Explain your answer, including why the data types you did not select would not work or are not as appropriate.

3. Of the following fields, which would be the most appropriate for the primary key in a customer information table? Explain your answer.

Customer name
Customer number
Phone number
Customer address

4. Explain the difference between a static Web page and a dynamic Web page. Which one typically uses a database? For what purpose?

5. Refer to the two relational database tables below and answer the following questions:

   a. Which employees work in the Accounting department and make at least $60,000 per year?

   b. Which employees have Jonas as their manager?

   c. In which of the preceding questions did you have to relate data in both tables to get an answer? Through what field(s) did you relate tables?

Employee Table

Name	Location	Department	Salary
Doney	Phoenix	Accounting	$58,000
Black	Denver	Sales	$71,000
James	Cleveland	Sales	$44,000
Giles	San Diego	Accounting	$62,000
Smith	Miami	Accounting	$73,000
Fink	San Diego	Sales	$54,000
. . .	. . .	. . .	. . .

Office Table

Location	Manager
San Diego	Hurt
Cleveland	Holmes
Miami	Jonas
Phoenix	Alexis
. . .	. . .

1. **Data Recovery** Several companies specialize in recovering data from failed hard drives. If your company's database is not backed up and the hard drive fails, don't give up hope. You can always call one of these data recovery companies and, in most cases, retrieve at least some of your data. This service is not cheap, but if you have no other choice, it is the way to go. Several of these companies advertise that they have a 100% success rate in recovering the data, if the organization has not tried to use a commercial utility program first, and a 95% success rate if it has. For this project, research a few of these types of companies and summarize the information you find. Be sure to view any articles they have written and any frequently asked questions (FAQ) list on their Web page. At the conclusion of your research, prepare a one-page summary of your findings and submit it to your instructor.

2. **Schema** The methods used to design information systems and databases are constantly evolving. Organizations are now taking a closer look at their information systems in terms of their ability to support their informational requirements, and to see if their underlying databases can be better designed to support these systems. In order to better understand the informational requirements and arrive at improved database designs, a three-schema approach is now being used. For this project, define what a schema is and how the three-schema approach is used to define a database. Has someone already defined a fourth and a fifth schema approach? At the conclusion of your research, prepare a one-page summary of your findings and submit it to your instructor.

3. **Normalization** The process of normalizing the data for a database was first proposed by Dr. E. F. Codd in 1972, when President Nixon was in the process of normalizing relations with China (so-named because of Nixon's efforts). The overall objective of normalization is to reduce the redundancy of data in a database and to ensure that update errors do not occur. For this project, name the six normal forms and describe the process required to achieve the first normal form. At what normal form are database designers usually satisfied? Can a database be fully normalized, or is this impractical? What is the difference between unnormalized data, normalized data, and denormalized data? At the conclusion of your research, prepare a one-page summary of your findings and submit it to your instructor.

4. **Dialing 411** When you dial 411, you get the local information operator who has access to all the listed businesses and residential telephone number in your area. For this project, identify and write down each of the questions a 411 operator would ask you, if you need the telephone number for a person who lives within your local area code, but not in your specific city; runs a business under their full name; and has a very common first and last name. After completing this task, you should explain how each of the questions asked by the operator corresponds with a database concept you learned in this chapter. Is the operator actually using a computerized database to answer your question? Why do you think the operator will not tell you the telephone number of a person who lives outside your area code? If you have access to the Internet, look up a telephone number using a service such as Switchboard.com (see the accompanying image). How does this service differ from that provided by your local information operator? At the conclusion of this task, prepare a one-page summary of your efforts and submit it to your instructor.

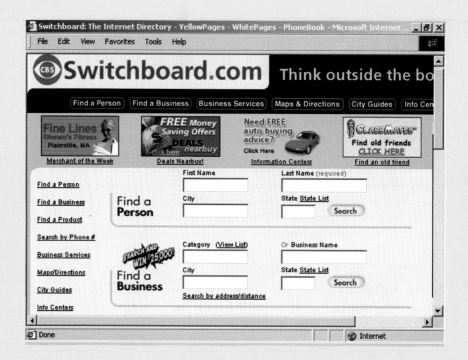

Writing About Computers

5. **Database Protocol** In order for an application program to access a specific database without the programmer having to write code that is unique to that database, the programmer could use an application programming interface (API), as discussed in the chapter. A few of these interfaces are called ISAPI, NSAPI, ODBC, JDBC, and OLE-DB. For this project, determine what these acronyms stand for, who created them, when they would be used, and their relationship to SQL. Do you need a special driver to use these interfaces? If you were a Web programmer, would you be using these protocols? Submit this project to your instructor in the form of a short paper, not more than two pages in length.

6. **Book 'Em** Many criminal investigation organizations have implemented the database approach to automate the paperwork involved in apprehending, booking, and tracking criminals through the legal and incarceration processes, as well as sharing information between county, state, and federal systems. Some systems have names like ViCAP, HITS, HALT, and HEAT. For this project, investigate at least two systems currently being used by a criminal investigation organization and summarize what the system was designed to accomplish. Do you think these systems should share information with private organizations? Do you think private organizations should share information with these systems? Submit this project to your instructor in the form of a short paper, not more than two pages in length.

7. **Future DB Plans** Several large database companies like Oracle, IBM, and Sybase have Web sites where they release the latest company news and information about their database software, as well as their plans for the future. For this project, form a group to investigate each of these companies (or three other similar companies), and explain what database products the company has available, and any future products that information is available for. Your group should also identify any plans the company has to team with another provider of hardware or software in order to make their products more appealing to potential customers. Have any of these companies considered becoming an application service provider (ASP)? Do any of these companies sell other software that could be used in combination with their database software to make it easier for a company to implement an e-commerce strategy? Was there an employment link at each of these Web sites? Would anyone in your group consider working for any of these companies? Your group should submit this project to your instructor in the form of a short paper, not more than three pages in length.

8. **ERIC** The world's largest collection of educational information is organized and available though a database called the Educational Resources Information Center (ERIC). The database was established in 1966, and is supported by the U.S. Department of Education, Office of Educational Research and Improvement, and the National Library of Education. For this project, present a summary of what is actually available in the ERIC database, how you would go about getting access to the documents and journals, and the terms *digest, component,* and *clearinghouse* as they relate to ERIC. This presentation should not exceed five minutes and should make use of one or more presentation aids such as the chalkboard, handouts, overhead transparencies, or computer-based slide presentation format. You may be asked to submit a summary of the presentation to your instructor.

9. **Example Database** Designing a small relational database is not extremely difficult. For this project, form a group to design a relational database for the students, instructors, and class offerings at your school. The database should consist of three tables (one each for students, classes, and instructors) and each table should have at least four fields. Be sure to select an appropriate primary key for each table. Your group should design one input screen, one query screen, and one report (design these on paper) and determine if any tables need to be related to each other in order to obtain the necessary information. Annotate each of the three designs with the table and field names for each piece of information to be included. Be sure to include at least one sample record for each table in your design documentation. Your group will present your design to the class. The presentation should not exceed 10 minutes and should make use of one or more presentation aids such as the chalkboard, handouts, overhead transparencies, or computer-based slide presentation format. Your group may be asked to submit a summary of the presentation to your instructor.

10. **Certifications** Companies that make database software need to ensure that employers have an established standard from which to measure an individual's competence for specific jobs relating to the database software they have purchased. In order to accomplish this, the software companies generally develop and offer certification exams in one or more core competencies for each of their database products. The larger database companies like Oracle and Sybase offer several certification exams. Aside from the proprietary database programs, you can also get certified in SQL by a number of different organizations, including IBM. For this project, form a group to research and prepare a presentation about the three most popular database certification programs. Be sure to include the organization offering them, how long it takes to complete them, how much the program/exams cost, and what the employment prospects look like after passing the exam. Do the jobs offered with this certification require experience, as well? Is anyone in your group interested in taking one of these certification programs? The presentation should not exceed 10 minutes and should make use of one or more presentation aids such as the chalkboard, handouts, overhead transparencies, or computer-based slide presentation format. Your group may be asked to submit a summary of the presentation to your instructor.

11. **Privacy at Stake** Many people hold the opinion that we should have the right to know when any data about us is being collected and stored. In addition, we should have the right to get our data removed from any database we don't want our information stored in, unless it is for official federal, state, or local purposes. Some feel laws should be passes about this issue, since the companies participating in this behavior do not police themselves.

    Select one of the following positions, or make up your own, and express your point of view on the subject. Your instructor will indicate whether your response is to be posted to a class bulletin board, discussed in a class chat room, or discussed as an in-class activity. You may also be asked to submit a summary of your position and point of view to your instructor.

    a. This issue is of paramount importance and we should act as soon as possible to get some laws passed to protect our privacy. The companies that prey on our every mouse click should be put under a microscope themselves and pay a heavy price for their unscrupulous behavior.

b. This issue is of great concern, but passing laws is not the answer. The problem was created by technology and should be solved with technology. At this point, we should simply set our browsers to not accept cookies and wait until the markets react by stopping this behavior, or technology solves the problem by allowing us to surf the Web anonymously.

12. **Where Will It End?** Consider the following statement and establish your position, or point of view on the subject. Your instructor will indicate whether your response is to be posted to a class bulletin board, discussed in a class chat room, or discussed as an in-class activity. You may also be asked to submit a summary of your position and evaluation of the statement to your instructor.

Consumer information has been tracked and stored in databases since databases were first developed, but not to the extent and in the level of detail that it is today. In addition, there used to be informal limits with respect to the type and amount of information a company would share about its customers. Today, however, most companies seem to be willing to sell your private information without giving it a second thought. Furthermore, companies like DoubleClick have gone way beyond what the average person would consider reasonable in their efforts to track and store information about individuals. They use small programs called cookies to track your Web surfing habits and compile an online profile about you. Though the cookies don't track your activities on Web sites without DoubleClick banners, the banners are prevalent enough to enable the company to compile immense amounts of data. It has been reported that DoubleClick has collected over 100 million files on consumers using this method. This in itself may constitute an invasion of your privacy, but what makes it worse is that companies like DoubleClick now hope to combine your online information with offline data, such as your name and street address. Some privacy advocates see this as a horrendous invasion into our private lives. On the other hand, companies like DoubleClick argue that they are simply providing a service that is in the best interest of the consumer. They say that consumers prefer to get targeted advertisements, and that they are doing nothing wrong. In fact, DoubleClick commissioned a survey that found "of Internet users surveyed, 61 percent are interested in receiving banner advertisements that are tailored to their personal preferences."

Interactive Exercise

Understanding Databases and Database Management Systems.   Let's see how much you remember about database concepts! Go to the Interactive Exercise at www.course.com/parker2002/ch14 to complete this exercise.

COMPUTERS IN OUR LIVES

No study of computers is complete without a look at the growing impact of these devices on daily life. From home offices to company desktops, more and more people are operating computer systems. Children are routinely exposed to PCs through home and school use. News bureaus regularly report about computer-related issues–hackers breaking into computer systems, the Internet's potential for changing our lives, privacy problems, viruses attached to e-mail messages, and so forth.

Chapter 15 looks at the problems computers can create, including new ethical dilemmas, computer crime, potential invasions of personal privacy, and the impact of computers on the physical and emotional health of users.

Chapter 16 addresses issues that arise in developing one's own personal computer system. It covers many of the facts about **PCs** that you should understand if you decide to buy your own system. Today, with unprecedented numbers of people purchasing their own **PCs** or participating in computer-buying decisions at work, knowledge in this area has become essential for virtually everyone.

COMPUTERS IN OUR LIVES

Ethics, Computer Crime, Privacy, and Other Social Issues

LEARNING OBJECTIVES

After completing this chapter, you will be able to:

1. Explain what is meant by ethics and provide several examples of unethical behavior in computer-related matters.

2. Give several examples of types of computer crime.

3. List some ways computer crime can be prevented.

4. Discuss how computer technology can encroach on people's privacy and describe some of the legislation enacted to prevent such abuses.

5. State why it is important for computer users to be aware of intellectual property rights.

6. Describe some of the impact computers may have on health and the environment.

Since the era of commercial computing began about 50 years ago, computers have rapidly woven their way into the fabric of society. In the process, they've created opportunities and problems. Consequently, they've been both cursed and applauded—and for good reason.

So far in this text, we've focused on the opportunities more than the problems. We've examined the impact computers have had in organizations and on people. Throughout the text, you've seen how these devices are used to speed up routine transaction processing tasks, to provide managers with better information for decision making, to design and manufacture better products, to provide access to the vast resources available through the Internet, and to improve the overall quality of people's lives. The Ubiquitous Computing window in this module summarizes some of the ways computers have become integrated into our lives.

Although the computer revolution has brought undeniable benefits to society, it has also produced some troubling side effects. Like any fast-paced revolution, it has been disruptive in many ways. Some jobs have been created, others lost, and still others threatened. Computers have immensely increased access to sensitive information, creating new possibilities for crime and compromised personal privacy. In addition, an increasing variety of health-related concerns have surfaced that affect people who work with computers and related technologies. Clearly some controls to limit the dangers that these awesome devices pose will always be needed.

In this chapter, we highlight four key problem areas: ethical uses of technology and computers, computer crime, computers and privacy, and health and environmental issues. We'll also touch on what is meant by *intellectual property rights* and why this issue is something that computer users need to be aware of. ■

ETHICS

web tutor

For a tutorial on ethical considerations, go to www.course.com/parker2002/ch15

Ethics refers to standards of moral conduct. For example, telling the truth is a matter of ethics. An unethical act isn't always illegal, but sometimes it is. For example, purposely lying to a friend is unethical but normally is lawful, but perjuring oneself as a courtroom witness is a crime. Whether or not criminal behavior is involved, ethics play an important role in shaping the law and our interpersonal relationships.

Ethical Issues Regarding Computers
Today, computers present a number of ethical concerns. Several examples of these are covered in the following list.

▼ Some people regularly use a software package that they aren't licensed to use for personal purposes, claiming they are doing so just to get the feel of it. Although many vendors encourage limited experimentation with their products, they frown on someone who hasn't bought the software using it regularly. Such use is, at a minimum, ethically questionable and possibly illegal, as discussed shortly.

>**Ethics.** A term that refers to standards of moral conduct.

▼ A computer professional working for one software company leaves to take a job for a competing company. Almost immediately, the professional divulges product secrets that were entrusted in confidence by the former employer, putting the new employer at an unfair competitive advantage.

▼ A medical programmer is assigned to code a software program that is to be part of a system that monitors the heart rate of hospital patients. Before the program can be fully tested, the programmer is ordered to hand it over so that the system can meet its promised deadline. The programmer tells the project supervisor that the code may contain serious bugs. The supervisor responds, "It's not our fault if the program fails because the deadline is too tight."

▼ A large software company, hearing that a small competitor is coming out with a new product, spreads a rumor that it is working on a similar product. Although the large company never provides a formal release date for its product, it leaves potential users with the mistaken impression that they will be taking a major risk by adopting the small competitor's product. Software such as this that is not ready to be shipped on or close to its announced ship data is referred to as *vaporware*.

Why Study Ethics?

Why has ethics become such a hot topic? Undoubtedly, ethics has taken on more significance in recent years because the proliferation of computers in the home and workplace provides many more possibilities for unethical acts than in the past. From individuals using their companies' PC for personal e-mail and Web surfing, to companies attempting to monitor the activities of their Web site visitors after they leave the company Web site, to teenagers making copies of software and music to share with their friends, the sheer number of ethically questionable acts has increased tremendously. In addition, some believe that the overall ethical climate in our country is deteriorating.

Many scholars think that the focus on ethics has been pushed aside in the rush to achieve measurable results. A movement is afoot to try to reverse this, however. In recent years, professional computer organizations and the vast majority of the largest U.S. corporations have established *codes of conduct* covering unauthorized uses of software, hardware, and communications networks to educate their employees, as well as warn them of the consequences of performing acts the company has deemed unacceptable (see Figure 15-1). Many schools—especially colleges—have followed suit. Ethics is also frequently a topic in computer journals and at professional conferences today.

COMPUTER CRIME AND SECURITY

Computer crime—sometimes referred to as *cyber-crime*—is defined as the use of computers to commit criminal acts. Both state and federal governments have been slow to pass computer crime legislation in the past. Some legislation that exists is discussed shortly. In general computer crime is hard to pin down and technology changes so fast that it is difficult for the legal system to keep pace with the expanding types of computer crimes. In addition, there are jurisdictional issues domestically and internationally, since many computer crimes affect areas other than the one in which the computer criminal is located.

Another issue that makes legislation and prosecution difficult is that is often difficult to decide when a questionable act is really a crime. No one doubts that a bank employee who uses a computer system to embezzle funds from customers' accounts is committing a crime. But what about an employee who uses a company computer to balance his or her

---

>**Computer crime.** The use of a computer to commit a criminal act.

FIGURE 15-1

Codes of conduct. Codes of conduct are prevalent in a wide variety of industries, as well as schools and government agencies.

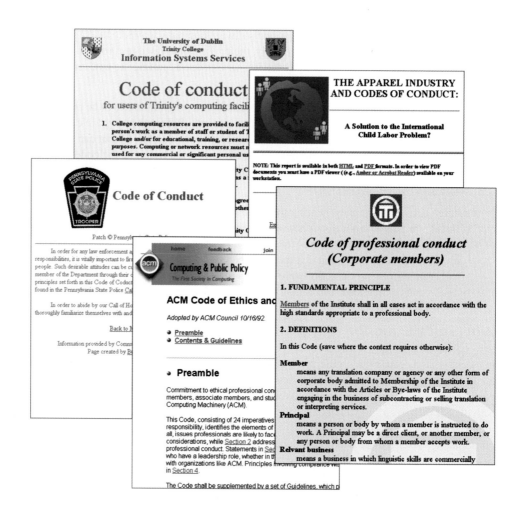

personal checkbook, or someone who e-mails jokes to friends while on the clock? Aren't those acts also unauthorized? Where does one draw the line?

An additional problem in pinning down computer crime is that judges and juries—not to mention law-enforcement personnel—sometimes have difficulty understanding the technical issues involved in such cases. Thus, many companies lack confidence that computer crimes will be investigated and prosecuted successfully, and so they don't report them. Also, companies that discover computer crime performed by their employees are reluctant to press charges because they fear adverse publicity. Why get clients worried or drive the price of the corporate stock down?

Types of Computer Crime

Computer crime takes many forms. Some cases involve the use of a computer for theft of financial assets, such as money. Others concern copying information or other resources, such as programs or data. Still other cases involve manipulating data, such as grades, for personal advantage. Increasingly, computer crimes have involved acts of sabotage using *computer viruses,* as discussed a little later in this chapter. Insiders commit a huge amount of the computer crimes inflicted on businesses.

The cost of computer crime to individuals and organizations is estimated at billions of dollars annually. No one knows for sure what the exact figure is, because so many incidents are either undetected or unreported. Just one virus incident can be extraordinarily expensive. For example, the Melissa computer virus in 1999 resulted in an estimated $80 million minimum in damage, and damage from the Love Bug virus in 2000 was estimated to cost billions of dollars. Most of this expense was the time required by companies to remove the virus from their computers and lost productivity of workers whose PCs were unusable until the virus was eliminated.

A sampling of some broad categories of computer crime along with some examples of specific forms that computer crime can take is contained in the next few sections.

Computer Viruses

A **computer virus** is a software program—often transmitted to a computer system via the Internet or other network—that is designed to be spread automatically from one computer to another, without the knowledge or consent of the individuals involved. Viruses can be attached to program files, data files, or e-mail messages. When an infected file or e-mail is opened, the virus is spread to that PC. As illustrated in Figure 8-24 in Chapter 8, viruses can also be distributed by sharing disks or other writable storage media between PCs.

Attaching viruses to e-mail messages seems to be the favorite method of infection used lately. Often this type of virus is set up to spread by e-mailing itself to all the people in the new computer's e-mail address book file, once the e-mail attachment is opened. For an example of how fast these types of viruses can spread, the Melissa virus, released on Friday, March 26, 1999 by David Smith (see Figure 15-2) infected over 100,000 machines by the end of the weekend.

Some viruses are designed to cause damage to the computer systems they are transmitted to. Others—so-called "benign" viruses—are just designed to be distributed but don't contain malicious code. Typical malicious virus activity is to clog the PC's memory with garbage as soon as the computer is turned on, or to overwrite or delete data on the hard drive. "Benign" viruses bog down networks by the increased e-mail activity, require enormous amounts of time to get rid of, and disrupt communications for the organizations involved. Once a computer is infected and the virus is stored on the computer, it remains until it is specifically removed. At that time, the damage can be assessed. Some damage may be reversible (such as filled-up memory, which will return to its original state once the virus is removed and the PC is rebooted); other damage (such as erased or altered data) may be permanent, unless the data was backed up and can be restored—often an expensive process. If no damage occurred to the computers and data involved, then the total damage results in lost time, potentially lost revenue, and the expense of the computer personnel needed to eradicate the virus.

Protecting a computer system from viruses, as well as detecting and removing a computer virus, is discussed later in this chapter.

Unauthorized Access and Use

Many computer crimes include *unauthorized access.* Sometimes unauthorized access is used as a means to perform a specific crime; occasionally achieving the access itself is the only goal. *Unauthorized use* involves using a computer for unapproved activities. These activities may be illegal, as well as unethical. Some specific examples are discussed next; ways of preventing unauthorized access are discussed later in this chapter.

> **FIGURE 15-2**
> **David Smith, creator of the Melissa e-mail virus, is known as the first individual in the U.S. to receive jail time for unleashing a computer virus.**

>**Computer virus.** A software program designed to spread itself to other computers without the user's knowledge and, sometimes, to cause some harm to the system.

Hacking

Hacking is a computer term most often used to refer to the activities of people who use computers to crack the security of remote computer systems. Usually this action is performed to steal or corrupt data, but sometimes it is done to prove one's computer expertise or at the request of an organization to test the security of its system. Once a hacker has gained access to a system, there are numerous computer crimes that can be committed, such as altering data or programs, planting a computer virus, shutting down the system, stealing programs or information, and so forth. These crimes are discussed in more detail shortly. Among computer professionals, the term *hacker* was originally used in a complimentary fashion for a computer enthusiast, but now the word has a derogatory connotation. See the Inside the Industry box for more jargon from the computer industry.

Hacking has become a serious problem, with new reports of hacking attempts into private or government computers occurring almost daily. For example, U.S. Department of Defense computers are attacked by hackers hundreds of thousands of times a year, with probably many more times that number of attacks going undetected. Many feel, in fact, that hacking is one of the most serious threats to our nation's security. For example, in 1997 the National Security Agency hired 35 professional hackers to perform simulated attacks on the U.S. electronic infrastructure. During that exercise, the hackers achieved access to 36 of the Department of Defense's 40,000 networks, turned off sections of the U.S. power grid, shut down parts of the 911 network in Washington, D.C., and gained access to systems aboard a Navy cruiser at sea. Another example of the potential threat of hackers to our defense occurred during the Gulf War when it was reported that Dutch hackers stole information about U.S. troop movements from U.S. Defense Department computers and tried to sell that information to the Iraqis. Fortunately, the Iraqis thought it was a hoax and turned it down. Hacking also poses a serious threat to vulnerable business computer systems.

In the early days of PCs, the typical profile of a hacker was a nerdy teenager who was in it purely for the excitement that came from snooping and bragging about it. Today's hacker is more likely to be a well-trained professional with strong computer skills. With the proliferation of hacking programs and Web sites, hacking is unfortunately becoming easier and easier to do. A favorite target these days are credit card numbers and other sensitive financial information located on Internet computers.

Information Theft

Information theft includes stealing proprietary corporate information, as well as credit card and other personal information. For businesses, loss of corporate information can have a devastating effect. For consumers, loss of personal information—especially credit card numbers—can be equally problematic. One recent example that affected consumers was the hacker who stole 300,000 credit card numbers from an online music site and posted them on the Internet for anyone to see. Because the current credit card system allows purchases over the Internet or telephone with only a name, credit card number, and expiration date, it is expected to hasten the development of other payment options. Some possibilities for online purchases include *smart cards*. As discussed in Chapters 9 and 11, smart cards have the advantage of needing to be physically inserted into a smart card reader, as well as usually having lower available monetary amounts associated with the card.

Spoofing and Denial of Service Attacks

Spoofing refers to fooling or tricking a computer system, such as making it appear that a message came from somewhere else. Lately, spoofing has been used in a type of crime called a *denial of service attack*. As illustrated in the How It Works box later in this chapter, a denial of service attack attempts to flood a computer system with so many requests for action that it shuts down or simply cannot handle legitimate requests any longer. For example, a hacker might set up a large number of computers to continually *ping* a server

---

>Hacking. Using a computer to penetrate the security of a remote computer system. **>Information theft.** The theft of information, usually from a company, via a computer crime.

inside the industry

A Technobabble Miniglossary

A Combat Guide to Tech Talk

Many years ago, computer jargon was spoken with confidence only at staff meetings of technical specialists. But now that computers have entered the mainstream, everyone seems to want to belong to their growing subculture. One key to membership is *technobabble*–a dialect for digital conversations that splices computer and networking terminology into everyday speech. Here's a smattering of technobabble terms to use or avoid at your pleasure.

Alpha Geek   The person in a group who is most respected for his or her technical proficiency. *Sample technobabble:* "The one with the pointy head must be their alpha geek."

Bandwidth   Brain power. *Sample technobabble:* "She's a high-bandwidth woman."

Betazoid   A person who lives to test prereleases, termed *beta copies,* of software. *Sample technobabble:* "The betazoids will go wild when they see this new interface."

Big Iron   Mainframe computer. *Sample technobabble:* "We replaced the big iron with a client-server network."

Cyberspace   The Internet world. *Sample technobabble:* "We met in cyberspace."

Digerati   Computer professionals. *Sample technobabble:* "The digerati says the server's going down at 3 P.M."

E   To send someone electronic mail, or e-mail. *Sample technobabble:* "E me on that, would you?"

Flame Mail   Electronic mail that is critical, rude, or abusive. *Sample technobabble:* "I got some flame mail from my supervisor this morning about my handling of that situation."

Meatspace   The "real" or physical world, as opposed to the Internet. *Sample technobabble:* "We've just met through e-mail; meatspace is still months away."

Newbie   A new user to an online computer group. *Sample technobabble:* "Those know-nothing newbies are really slowing the system down today."

Random   Illogical or nutty. *Sample technobabble:* "His ideas on that subject are totally random."

Rumorazzi   The people who write industry-insider columns for the computer journals. *Sample technobabble:* "The rumorazzi tells us that Company XYZ is going to miss its shipping deadline."

Scud Memo   A misguided or poorly conceptualized e-mail message, memo, or letter. *Sample technobabble:* "He sent me his usual scud memo on it."

Shovelware   Extra, poorly integrated software or documentation that is hastily dumped by a software publisher onto a CD or DVD to fill any space on the disk left over from the main application. *Sample technobabble:* "Ninety percent of this disk is pure shovelware."

Snail Mail   Mail sent via the traditional Postal Service. *Sample technobabble:* "I'll send those contracts to you via snail mail."

Sneakernet   Transferring electronic information by manually carrying disks or tapes from one machine to another. *Sample technobabble:* "Not only does that company rely on snail mail, it's a sneakernet outfit, too."

Spam   Junk e-mail. *Sample technobabble:* "Don't use your real e-mail address on that newsgroup unless you like getting spammed."

Speeds and Feeds   The technical specifications of a product. *Sample technobabble:* "Give me the speeds and feeds of that new system, will ya?"

Taking It Offline   Resolving an issue after a meeting. *Sample technobabble:* "I'll get back to you on that offline."

Vaporware   Software that doesn't exist. *Sample technobabble:* "I think that rumored next release is just vaporware."

Web Surfing   Casually browsing the Web. *Sample technobabble:* "You won't believe what I found Web surfing last night."

Zorch   Raw power. *Sample technobabble:* "Does this machine have plenty of zorch, or what?"

(contact it with a request to send a responding ping back) with a false return address, or continually request nonexistent information. If enough computers are used, the server has no resources left to deal with legitimate requests.

It is common for hackers to gain unauthorized access to a large number of individuals' computers and plant a program to cause that computer to participate in the denial of service attack without the individuals' knowledge. This is one reason that *firewalls*—hardware or software that prevents use of a computer over a network by an unauthorized source, as discussed in Chapter 8—are important for PCs that are continually connected to the Internet.

Software Piracy

Software piracy, the unauthorized copying or use of a computer program, is usually a crime. It is definitely a crime to copy a program and then attempt to sell it for profit. If one uses an illegitimate copy that was made by someone else, that usage can be a crime as well, although it is rarely prosecuted. Anyone knowingly involved with pirated programs can be found guilty of breaking copyright laws. A number of companies have been successfully prosecuted for buying one or a few copies of a software package and then using that software on more PCs than they are authorized for.

In an attempt to prevent professional software pirates from duplicating and selling bootleg CDs and DVDs, *holograms* that change the text or images displayed on the disc when the disc is tilted and other difficult to reproduce features are becoming more common on discs, software packaging, and licenses. Potential new antipiracy tools include DNA marking and molecular tagging.

Eavesdropping

There are scores of examples involving the use of technology to *eavesdrop* on information intended for others. One of the earliest types of eavesdropping, and still one of the most common today, is wiretapping. Recent technology has made it possible to eavesdrop in new ways. For example, by having access to a user's password, an unauthorized user can look at confidential files. Intercepting and reading e-mail messages intended for others is another example. For a look at the federal government's Carnivore program designed to intercept e-mail messages and other Internet traffic sent to and from criminal suspects, see the Trend box.

Physical Theft

Physical theft includes stealing hardware and software from businesses or homes. Ways a business can help prevent physical theft are discussed shortly.

Data or Program Alteration

Some computer crimes involve hacking into a system and then changing the data (such as a grade or an account balance) stored there or modifying a computer program to make it behave differently.

Data Diddling

Data diddling is one of the most common computer crimes. It involves altering data located on a computer system in some unsanctioned way. Data diddlers often are found changing grades in university files, falsifying input records on bank transactions, making unauthorized changes to Web pages, or other similar acts.

The Trojan Horse

A *Trojan horse* is a procedure for adding concealed instructions to a computer program so that it will still work but will perform prohibited duties. For example, a bank worker who subtly alters a program containing thousands of lines of code by adding a few more program instructions to instruct the program not to withdraw money from his or her specified account would be using the Trojan horse method. Other examples are the computer viruses that are embedded in seemingly legitimate files.

>**Software piracy.** The unauthorized copying or use of computer programs.

trend

FBI's Carnivore

Legitimate Law Enforcement or Invasion of Privacy?

The FBI's relatively new e-mail sniffing system commonly known as Carnivore, but subsequently renamed DCS1000, has many privacy advocates up in arms. The idea behind the system is to monitor the e-mail traffic sent from a criminal suspect.

Carnivore is apparently the third generation of online detection software used by the FBI (there hasn't been a great deal of information released on this system). Although earlier versions were specifically for intercepting e-mail messages, the newest version is reportedly capable of intercepting and recording all types of Web activity (such as Web pages viewed and files downloaded), in addition to e-mail activity.

Carnivore is a *packet sniffer*—a program that can see all the information passing over the network with which it is being used. As data passes through the network, the program looks at, or "sniffs," each packet. To use Carnivore, the FBI and the suspect's ISP work together to identify an access point that contains all traffic involving the suspect, with as little other traffic as possible—that's the location the Carnivore system is installed. These specific packets are then bypassed through the Carnivore system, which copies them and then sends them back on their way. A filter is used to ensure only the packets meeting the specifications of the court order are stored on a removable hard drive; all other packets are discarded (see figure).

Though the FBI stresses that the Carnivore system is to be used only under a court order, similar to a wiretap, and only the communications sent by the suspect are looked at by agents, privacy advocates are concerned. They argue that Carnivore differs from a wiretap in that the system has access to all messages passing through the ISP, not just those going to or coming from the suspect's PC, so the potential for abuse is huge. The FBI counters that using Carnivore in any way other than as specified in the court order is illegal. It plans to use Carnivore to gather evidence regarding suspects in specific areas, such as terrorism, child pornography, espionage, and fraud—crimes that routinely use communications networks.

All of these concerns have made implementation of Carnivore an uphill battle for the FBI. Making the task even more difficult are programmers and cryptographers who work on projects designed to help individuals to encrypt their data and e-mail messages in a manner that cannot be understood (even by the FBI) if intercepted. Needless to say, the FBI must work continuously to break any encryption code that criminals may use to disguise their electronic communications. Because uncrackable encryption allows terrorists and other criminals to communicate without outside intrusion, attempts have been made to pass legislation that requires backdoor entrances for the federal government on all encryption products, but none have made it into law yet.

Some speculate that the September 11, 2001 bombings may reduce the resistance to systems like Carnivore, though whether this system—used within hours of the attack—will help identify and prosecute the individuals responsible remains to be seen.

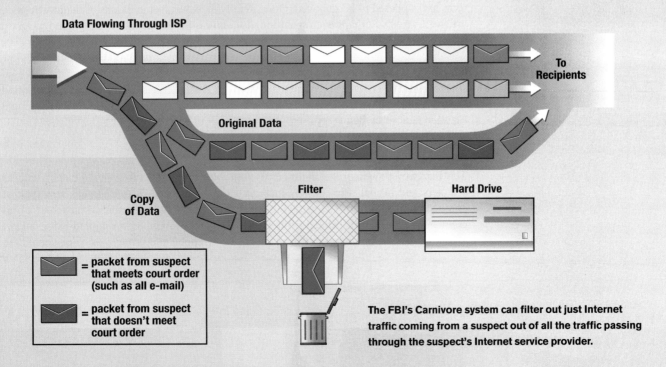

The FBI's Carnivore system can filter out just Internet traffic coming from a suspect out of all the traffic passing through the suspect's Internet service provider.

Salami Shaving

Salami shaving involves manipulating programs or data so that many small dollar amounts—for example, a few cents' worth of interest payments in a bank account—are shaved from a large number of transactions or accounts and accumulated elsewhere. The victims of a salami-shaving scheme generally are unaware that their funds have been accessed, because the amount taken from each individual is trivial. The recipient of the salami shaving, however, benefits from the aggregation of these small amounts, often substantially. Supermarkets have been occasionally accused of salami shaving at the checkout counter by not conscientiously updating prices in their computer system to reflect lower shelf prices.

Logic and Time Bombs

Logic bombs are programs or short code segments designed to commit a malicious act as soon as the unsuspecting program user performs a specific operation. In one documented case, a programmer inserted a logic bomb to destroy the company's entire personnel file if his name was removed from it. A *time bomb* works just like a logic bomb, except that a date or time triggers the criminal activity. Logic and time bombs are also sometimes built into computer viruses, such as the Michelangelo virus, which erases important system files from the hard drive of any infected computer that boots up on Michelangelo's birthday (March 6).

Sabotage

Sabotage is the act of damaging aspects of a system (data, equipment, procedures, etc.) so that the system can no longer functions normally. As it relates to computers, sabotage can include erasing data or programs from a computer system, physically damaging a computer system, and otherwise making a computer system crash or become nonfunctioning. One example was the denial of service attack in 2000 that crippled several top e-commerce sites, such as eBay, Yahoo!, Amazon.com, and E*TRADE, preventing them from being able to perform their normal business activities. (For a look at how a denial of service attack works, see the How It Works box.) Computer viruses can also be used for sabotage; the Michelangelo virus just discussed is one example.

Trapdoors

Trapdoors are diagnostic tools used to develop programs that enable programmers to gain access to various parts of a computer system. Before the programs are marketed, these tools are supposed to be removed. Occasionally, however, some blocks of diagnostic code are overlooked—perhaps even intentionally. Thus, a person using the associated program may be provided unauthorized views of parts of a computer system. In the past, a trapdoor was discovered in a well-known Web browser that enabled individuals to remotely view the hard-disk contents of the browser users. In 1998, several trapdoors traced to foreign sources were discovered in computer systems in Air Force and Navy bases in the United States, legitimizing the fear that computer-system break-ins may become a new battlefield between nations in the twenty-first century.

Digital Counterfeiting

The increasing availability of low-cost, full-color computer imaging products, such as scanners and ink-jet printers, has increased the occurrence of a relatively new type of computer crime—**digital counterfeiting.** It has been estimated that almost half of all counterfeit currency distributed in the United States was printed or copied using ink-jet technology. Most commonly, the bills are either scanned and printed, or color-copied. To

---

>**Digital counterfeiting.** The use of computer hardware and software to make illegal copies of currency, checks, collectibles, and other paper-based items.

how-it works

Denial of Service Attack

One by one, leading sites on the Web have been brought to their knees by the flood of *denial of service attacks* occurring during the last few years. Virtually no big organization, including Microsoft, Yahoo!, eBay, cNet, Amazon, and CNN, have been spared.

A denial of service attack, or *DoS,* floods a Web server with so many requests for information that the system is overwhelmed and slows to a crawl or ultimately crashes. Though a denial of service attack can originate with one hacker, the hacker often employs the use of many computers in the attack (referred to as a *distributed denial of service attack* or *DDoS*). These computers participate in the attack by sending specified requests to the target server, though the owners of those PCs typically do not realize that their PCs are involved. Hackers gain control of the PCs by hacking into unprotected PCs—education, business, or home PCs alike—through the Internet.

When the attack begins, the server is typically either bombarded with requests for nonexistent information or is given false return information so that when the server tries to respond back to authorize access to the server, the PC cannot be found. In either case, the server wastes time and computing resources trying to fulfill the requests (see the accompanying illustration).

Though one such bogus request wouldn't bring down a server, multiply it by hundreds or thousands of requests at the same time (either by utilizing multiple PCs or sending multiple bogus requests at one time) and it's easy to see how the server may become overwhelmed.

Denial of service attacks are difficult to protect against, since the offending PC is doing the same thing legitimate PCs do—requesting access to the system—but is just doing it with false information. One of the more common methods of trying to block this type of attack is to set up a filter, or *sniffer* program, on the network in front of the site's Web server. The filter is set up to look for attacks by noticing patterns in the supplied information, such as repeated requests from the same IP address on a regular basis. If a pattern comes in frequently, the filter would begin to block messages containing that pattern. To prevent their organization from unwittingly participating in a DoS attack, companies can set up their system to only allow packets to leave their network if they have a valid source IP address belonging to the network. This will minimize the chance that the network will be used in a *spoofed* (bogus ID) DoS attack. It won't, however, prevent being used in an attack using valid source address information. For that purpose, both businesses and individuals with continuous (always-on) Internet connections should utilize firewall protection.

1. PC sends several requests asking to establish a regular connection to the server, but supplies false return information. In a distributed DoS attack, multiple PCs would send multiple requests at one time.

4. The server becomes so overwhelmed that legitimate requests can't get through and, eventually, the server usually crashes.

Hello? I'd like some info...

2. Server tries to respond back, but can't locate the PC. Often waits for a minute or so before closing the connection.

I can't find you, I'll wait and try again...

3. As a connection closes, PC continues to send in new requests, typing up the server indefinitely.

Hello? I'd like some info...

Hello? I'd like some info...

I'm busy, I can't help you right now.

Hacker's PC   **Web server**   **Legitimate PC**

prevent counterfeiting, the Treasury Department has released new currency that is more difficult to duplicate (see Figure 15-3). The government is continually working on technological means to prevent currency from being copied, as well as to track the devices used in the counterfeiting process. For example, many color copiers now print invisible codes on copied documents, making counterfeit money copied on those machines traceable. In fact, Canon has been incorporating anticounterfeiting technologies into its products since 1992 but is prohibited from disclosing any information about them.

⬤ **FIGURE 15-3**

New U.S. currency is designed to help reduce digital counterfeiting. These new features are much more difficult to reproduce using current imaging products than older currency.

A thread embedded in the paper contains several items that can be seen when held up to the light or placed in front of an ultraviolet light.

Enlarged portrait has more detail and is harder to duplicate.

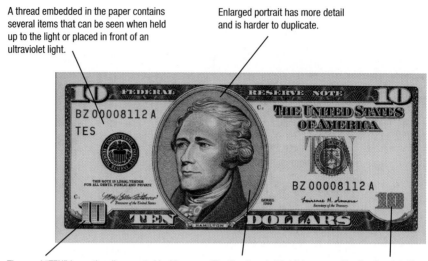

The word "TEN" is continually repeated inside the "10" in extremely small print called microprinting that is very difficult to reproduce.

The fine lines behind this image are hard to duplicate.

Number is printed in color-shifting ink that changes color when viewed from different angles.

Counterfeiting isn't limited to currency, however. By using a scanner to read in a corporate logo and then using a standard desktop publishing program, producing forged business checks that look genuine is something that, unfortunately, is not all that difficult to do. Printed collectibles, such as Pokémon trading cards and celebrity autographs, are other possible sources of revenue for the digital counterfeiter. As already discussed, making counterfeit (unauthorized) versions of software—software piracy—is another common computer crime.

Online Scams and Fraud

A booming area of Internet crime involves online scams, fraud, and related activities. The anonymity of the Internet makes it very easy for con artists to appear to be almost anyone they want to be, including a reputable-looking business with a professional-looking Web site. Scams include selling merchandise that is never delivered, selling nonexistent items on an online action site, and using *spam* (junk e-mail) to sell potentially worthless products or services. Online auction scams are one of the fastest-growing areas of this type of computer crime. According to the Federal Trade Commission, consumer complaints regarding online fraud increased from about 1,000 in 1997 to more than 25,000 in 2000. Online auction scams and other types of online fraud were discussed in the Chapter 9 Trend box.

Cover-Ups

In recent years, technology has been used to cover up criminal activity—which in itself is a crime. For example, many criminals booby-trap PCs containing potential evidence so that the data is destroyed if the computer is confiscated by the authorities. For example, a program could be written to erase the contents of the entire hard disk when a particular command is executed or an invalid password is supplied more than once. Another trick is rigging the door frame in a computer room with magnetic strips, so that a computer's disk storage is demagnetized (and the disk contents destroyed) as soon as someone tries to cart the computer outside.

Computer Crime Legislation

Federal law has had mixed results deterring computer crime. The main piece of legislation regarding using computers in criminal ways—the *Computer Fraud and Abuse Act*—has been regularly amended to broaden its scope and to clarify its intent (see the list of selected federal computer crime laws in Figure 15-4). The law currently outlaws unauthorized access to data stored in federal government computers and federally regulated financial institutions. It also outlaws the deliberate implantation of computer viruses in those computers. Actions taken with intent to harm are classified as felonies, while actions performed merely with reckless disregard are considered to be misdemeanors. Critics say the law doesn't go far enough in that a hacker who is merely curious may not be found guilty of a crime at all. At the time of this writing, more stringent computer crime legislation was being considered and was likely to be implemented in the near future.

The rapid growth of the Internet has recently pushed the issue of computer crime legislation into the forefront. There have long been laws addressing such offenses as sending indecent material through the mail, libel, harassment, inciting hatred, and the like, but how should those laws apply to computer networks?

One problem is jurisdictional. Because networks can be global and hackers can make it appear that activity is coming from a different location than it really is, it can be hard to determine where a crime is being committed and whose laws apply. A second problem is that many existing laws do not transfer well to networks. For example, should inflammatory comments over a network be treated like casual chat in a telephone conversation or like carefully crafted words sent through the mail? A third problem deals with responsibility and enforcement issues. Whose job is it to monitor the massive number of messages sent over computer networks daily? Will the right to personal privacy be compromised? Will the public be willing to pay for the potentially exorbitant cost of having networks policed? These issues need to be resolved to enact just legislation.

Computer Security and Safeguards Against Computer Crime

It's impossible to achieve 100 percent protection from criminal activity; consequently, the emphasis is on minimizing its occurrence and the associated losses. To achieve this end, organizations can combat computer crime in many ways, as we discuss next.

further exploration

For links to further information about computer crime legislation, go to www.course.com/parker2002/ch15

❯ FIGURE 15-4
Some important computer crime legislation.

DATE	LAW AND DESCRIPTION
1984	**Computer Fraud and Abuse Act of 1984** Makes it a crime to break into computers owned by the federal government.
1986	**Computer Fraud and Abuse Act of 1986** Amends the 1984 law to include federally regulated financial institutions.
1991	**Telephone Consumer Protection Act** Requires telemarketing companies to respect the rights of people who do not want to be called and significantly restricts the use of recorded messages.
1994	**Computer Abuse Amendments Act** Extends the Computer Fraud and Abuse Act to include computer viruses.
1996	**National Information Infrastructure Protection Act** Amended the Computer Fraud and Abuse Act to punish information theft crossing state lines and crack down on network trespassing.
1996	**Anticounterfeiting Consumer Protection Act of 1996** Expands counterfeit law to include computer programs, documentation, packaging, and other audio-visual works, as well as the ability of law enforcement to seize counterfeiting property and equipment.
1997	**No Electronic Theft (NET) Act** Expands computer piracy laws to include distribution of copyrighted materials over the Internet.

LIV

Assess Risks

The most important way an organization can minimize crime is by having a good plan for security, and the centerpiece of any such plan is an assessment of which operations are most vulnerable to attack. Once the key areas are identified, procedures can be implemented to try to protect against attacks, as discussed in the next few sections.

Take Caution with Employees

Studies have consistently shown that insiders commit most computer crimes. Consequently, it pays to be cautious with your employees, such as following the precautions listed next.

Hire Trustworthy People

Employers should carefully investigate the background of anyone being considered for sensitive computer work. Some people falsify résumés to get jobs. Others may have criminal records. One embarrassing mistake made by Rutgers University was to hire David Smith, the author of the Melissa virus, as a computer technician when he was out on bail for that crime.

Beware of Malcontents

The type of employee who is most likely to commit a computer crime is one who has recently been terminated or passed over for a promotion, or one who has some reason to get even with the organization. Whenever an employee is terminated, the former employer should update its records immediately to show that the person involved is no longer employed and remove that employee's company computer access.

Separate Employee Functions

An employee with many related responsibilities can commit a crime more easily than one with a single responsibility. For example, the person who authorizes adding new vendors to a file should not be the same one who authorizes payments to those vendors. Generally the more people who would have to be involved to commit a crime, the less likely it will happen and, if it does, the more likely it is that it will be discovered.

Devise Staff Controls

After-hours work should be carefully monitored, because computer crimes often occur at times when the criminal thinks he or she is unlikely to be interrupted. Sensitive documents that are no longer needed should be shredded. Access to computer facilities and read/write access to the programs and sensitive data on the network server should be strictly limited to authorized personnel only.

Monitor Important System Transactions

The systems software in use should include a program for maintaining a log of every person gaining, or attempting to gain, access to the system. The log should contain information about the computer used, the data files and programs accessed, and the time at which the work began and ended. Such a log allows management to isolate unauthorized system use.

Conduct Regular Audits

Unfortunately, many crimes are discovered by accident. Key elements of the system should be subjected to regular **audits**—inspections that verify that the system is working as expected—to ensure that there is no foul play. Auditing often involves two components: looking for security loopholes and inspecting system-activity logs to ascertain that nothing unusual is taking place.

Educate Employees

One of the best ways to prevent computer crime is to educate employees about security matters. People should be told about computer crime and the conditions that foster it, informed

---

>**Audit.** An inspection used to determine if a system or procedure is working as it is supposed to.

of the seriousness and consequences of computer crime, and instructed on what to do when they suspect a computer crime is taking place or is about to occur.

Restrict System Access and Use

People who use a computer system should have access only to the resources they need to do their jobs. A data entry clerk, for example, should be told only how to enter data into the system and not what all of the programs on the system do and how they work. Also, users who need only to retrieve information should not also be given updating privileges. In addition to controlling what computer system resources an employee has access to, there should be stringent controls in place to restrict access to the system to start with. Strategies for restricting system access were discussed in Chapter 8 and are summarized next.

▼ *Passwords* can be used to restrict access to the network in general, as well as to certain resources, such as accounting files and confidential personnel files. Strategies for selecting good passwords were listed in Figure 8-25.

▼ *Physical access objects* (common physical objects used to access a network) include keys, magnetic and smart cards, and encoded badges (refer to Figure 8-26).

▼ *Biometric devices* provide network access by recognizing some unique physiological characteristic of a person—such as a fingerprint or hand geometry (see Figure 15-5), or some unique learned characteristic, such as a voice or signature.

▼ *Callback devices,* which hang up on and call back people phoning in from remote locations, can be used for employees telecommuting or otherwise accessing the network from a consistent telephone number.

▼ *Firewalls*—collection of hardware and/or software intended to protect a computer network from outside access or attack—can be used to prevent hackers penetrating the network from a remote computer or using a computer on the network as a participant in an illegal activity, such as a denial of service attack.

❂ **FIGURE 15-5**
Fingerprint readers. Fingerprint readers and other types of biometric devices can be used to protect systems from unauthorized use, as well as identify users for remote access, e-commerce, and other Internet activities.

Companies should also use such commonsense precautions as keeping doors locked, when appropriate, and securing valuable PCs and other hardware with locks. This includes storing backup hard drives or media away from the computer system's immediate area. As illustrated by the disappearance of removable hard drives from a storage facility during a fire at the Los Alamos National Laboratory, security precautions for extraneous components of a computer system should not be overlooked.

Secure Transmissions

Files and e-mail messages sent over a network can be intercepted and read or altered, unless that has been prevented in some manner. It is also virtually impossible to know for sure who actually sent you a message or file just from looking at the "From:" information on an e-mail message, since that information is specified by the sender. When securing the contents of a message or file or authenticating the originator of a message is important, digital security methods—such as *digital certificates, encryption,* and *digital signatures*—can be used.

Digital Certificates

A **digital certificate** (also called a *digital ID*) is a group of electronic data that verifies that the person or organization sending a message or about to process a transaction is who he or she claims to be (see Figure 15-6). Digital certificates can be obtained from any *Certificate*

>**Digital certificate.** A group of electronic data, often used in conjunction with a public key and private key, that can be used to verify the identity of a person or organization.

🔵 **FIGURE 15-6**

Digital certificates. Digital certificates, which authenticate an individual or business, are available from any certificate authority.

Authority, such as VeriSign or PrivacyX. Digital certificates are often used in conjunction with *encryption* and *digital signatures,* discussed next.

E-Mail and File Encryption

Encryption—or *cryptography*—involves scrambling data and program contents through a coding method so they are unreadable unless you have the means to unscramble or *decrypt* them. If e-mail or files distributed over the Internet or another network are not encrypted in some manner, it is possible—though unlikely—that someone could intercept them and access their contents. With an encrypted file or e-mail, the contents would be unreadable if intercepted, as shown in Figure 15-7.

There are two basic forms of encryption: private key and public key. With either type of encryption, *keys*—special passwords—are used for coding and decoding the e-mail or file. One key locks the message at the sending end to make it unreadable during transit. Only a person who is authorized to see the message can decrypt it with the second key at the receiving end. With *private key encryption,* both the sender and the receiver have the exact same key. With *public key encryption* (sometimes referred to as *public key/private key encryption*), one public key and one private key are used, as described next and illustrated in Figure 15-7.

To send a message to a person using public key encryption, you need to have access to his or her public key (he or she can send it to you if you don't already have it). Most encryption programs have a *key ring* feature that stores the public keys you frequently use, just like an e-mail program's address book feature stores commonly used e-mail addresses. After encrypting the e-mail message or file, it is sent to the receiver. If the e-mail or file is intercepted, the contents are unreadable, as shown in Figure 15-7. Only after the recipient types the matching private key password (sometimes called a *passphrase*) will the unscrambled contents of the e-mail or file be revealed.

For another example, let's see how this might work in electronic banking: Customers' *public keys* are kept in the bank's directory and authorized employees can access them when an encrypted message needs to be sent to a customer. Each customer has access to a *private key,* known only to him or her, which is used to decrypt the message coming from the bank. When a customer sends a message back to the bank, he or she uses the bank's public key; the bank then uses its own private key to decrypt the message.

Encryption is starting to become integrated into e-mail and other programs. Separate encryption programs, such as the *Pretty Good Privacy (PGP)* program illustrated in Figure 15-7, can also be used. Many of these programs are compatible with at least some office suites and e-mail programs, so the documents or messages can be encrypted by simply selecting that option from the program's menu or toolbar button. If an encryption option is not available in the program being used to create the document, the encryption program is opened to encrypt the file or message instead.

Encryption algorithms and key sizes vary from program to program, which affects their ability to be cracked. It is generally believed that keys that are 128 bits or longer are virtually uncrackable—at least without the assistance of an extremely powerful supercomputer.

Digital Signatures

Though encrypted files and digital certificates can be used to verify that the person sending you a file or e-mail is who you expect it to be, sometimes using a **digital signature** is more appropriate and efficient. Like a written signature, the purpose of a digital signature—some-

---

>**Encryption.** A method of protecting data or programs so they will be unrecognizable if intercepted by an unauthorized user.
>**Digital signature.** A unique digital code that can be attached to an e-mail message or document to guarantee the identity of the sender.

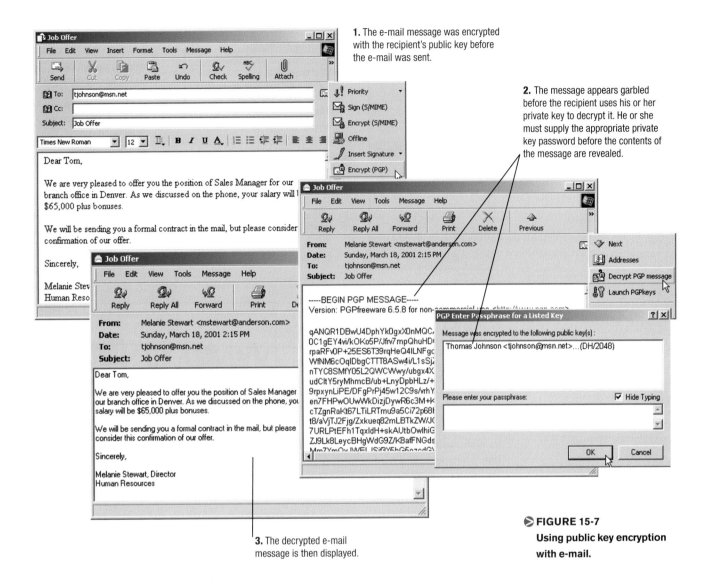

1. The e-mail message was encrypted with the recipient's public key before the e-mail was sent.

2. The message appears garbled before the recipient uses his or her private key to decrypt it. He or she must supply the appropriate private key password before the contents of the message are revealed.

3. The decrypted e-mail message is then displayed.

⊜ **FIGURE 15-7**

Using public key encryption with e-mail.

times called an *e-signature*—is to guarantee that the individual sending the message really is who he or she claims to be. Instead of being handwritten, digital signatures are comprised of a unique digital code, though some digital signatures may use a scanned image of the individual's signature along with the code, as shown in Figure 15-8.

Digital signatures can be used with documents in widely used file formats, such as Microsoft Word and Adobe Acrobat files, to verify that the document was not altered since it was signed. As shown in Figure 15-8, digital signatures can also be used to authenticate the sender of an e-mail message. In this figure, Outlook Express has two separate digital signatures programs (OnSign and PGP) available through its toolbar. Digital signatures are extremely important for electronic commerce and contract business being carried out over the Internet. The Federal Electronic Signatures in Global and National Commerce Act, signed in 2000, makes e-signatures as legally binding as handwritten signatures for e-commerce transactions.

Secure Web Servers

As discussed in Chapters 9 and 11, sensitive Internet transactions such as online shopping, banking, stock trading, or other financial transactions should only be performed via Web pages that use encryption or some other appropriate security method. Most browsers display a locked padlock such as 🔒 on the status bar when a secure Web page is being viewed, and usually the URL for a secure page begins with *https* instead of *http*. When performing a sensitive transaction, if you notice that the page is not secure (some browsers display a message

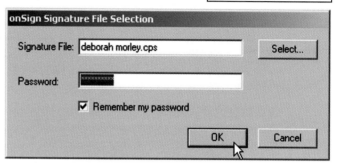

FIGURE 15-8

Using digital signatures. Digital signatures can be added to e-mail messages and other documents to authenticate the sender and ensure the file or message was not altered since it was signed.

SIGNATURE COMMAND
Many digital signature programs work in conjunction with your regular office suite and e-mail program, so an option to sign the file or e-mail can be found on a menu.

ADDING SIGNATURE
To add your signature, you must select the desired signature and then supply the appropriate password or passphrase.

VALID SIGNATURES
The file or e-mail message will display the signature, as well as a notice stating whether or not the signature is valid. The signature will be marked as invalid if the content of the file or e-mail was changed since it was signed.

to warn you), think very carefully before continuing—virtually all reputable companies doing business on a regular basis over the Internet use secure Web pages, so you should be able to find a secure site offering the service or merchandise you are looking for.

Use Antivirus and Other Crime-Prevention Software

A variety of software products are available to help in the fight against computer crime. For example, **antivirus software** is available to help detect and eliminate the presence of computer viruses (see Figure 15-9). Because computers are often used to file false claims, computer programs using artificial intelligence techniques have been deployed by businesses and government agencies to analyze suspicious claims, access logs for suspicious break-in attempts, and the like.

Have a Recovery Plan

Since no security plan can guarantee 100 percent safety, one should assume that the worst can happen. Organizations should specifically take steps to make sure they have recent backups at all times, in case disruptive events such as fires, floods, viruses, or computer outages occur. Backup provisions should include having copies of important programs and data stored at another physical location, as well as making arrangements for resuming normal day-to-day operations at a backup site. A plan that spells out what an organization will do to prepare for and recover from disruptive events is called a *disaster-recovery plan*. This plan should include such information as who will be in charge, how employees will communicate, what alternate facilities and equipment can be used, the priority of getting each operation back online, and so forth. The importance of this was made obvious following the collapse of the World Trade Center towers, which housed numerous large financial companies, in 2001. Minutes following the first airplane hitting the towers, corporate executives,

>**Antivirus software.** Software used to detect and eliminate computer viruses.

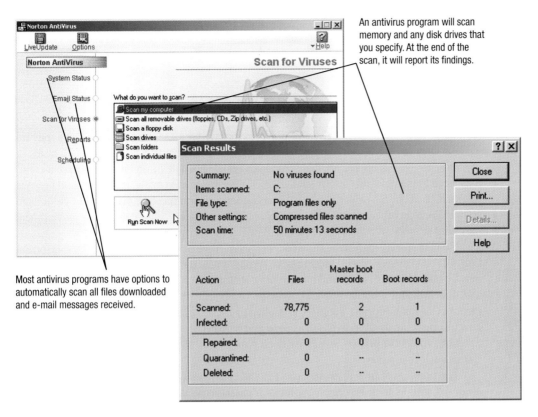

An antivirus program will scan memory and any disk drives that you specify. At the end of the scan, it will report its findings.

Most antivirus programs have options to automatically scan all files downloaded and e-mail messages received.

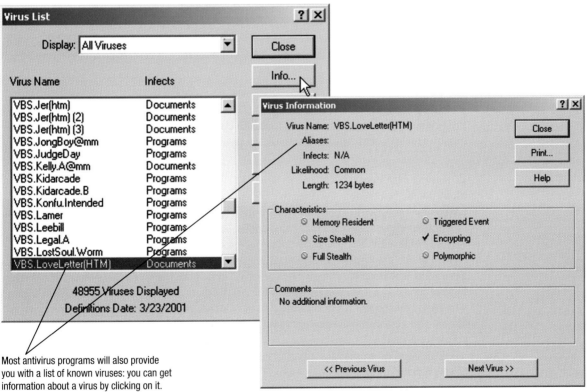

Most antivirus programs will also provide you with a list of known viruses: you can get information about a virus by clicking on it.

▶ **FIGURE 15-9**

Antivirus software. Antivirus programs can detect and remove virtually all viruses, but to work with the most recent viruses, they need to be updated on a regular basis.

disaster recovery firms, and backup companies began arranging for employees and backup data to be moved to temporary offices. As a result, many businesses were operational within a day or so of the attacks, despite the complete destruction of their facilities.

COMPUTERS AND PRIVACY

Almost all of us have some aspects of our lives that we prefer to keep private. These may include a sorry incident from the past, sensitive medical or financial facts, or certain tastes or opinions. Yet we can appreciate that sometimes selected people or organizations have a legitimate need for some of this information. A doctor needs accurate medical histories and lifestyle information about his or her patients. Financial information must be disclosed to credit card companies, loan officers, and college scholarship committees. A company or the government may need to probe into the lives of people applying for unusually sensitive jobs.

For a tutorial on privacy issues, go to www.course.com/parker2002/ch15

No matter how legitimate the need, however, there is always the danger that information will be misused. Stored facts may be wrong. Facts may get to the wrong people. Facts may be taken out of context and used to draw distorted conclusions. Facts may be collected and disseminated without one's knowledge or consent. Victims can be denied access to incorrect or inappropriate data. As it applies to information processing, **privacy** refers to how information about individuals is used and by whom.

For a look how privacy issues are dealt with by one college's computer system, see the Campus Close-Up box.

The problem of how to protect privacy and ensure that personal information is not misused was with us long before electronic computers existed. But today's computer systems, with their ability to store and manipulate unprecedented quantities of data and to make those data available to virtually anyone through the Internet, have added new wrinkles to the privacy issue. The trend for a long time has been for more and more sensitive data to be put online and for such data to be packaged and sold to others. Thus, it is not unusual that public concern exists regarding privacy rights. Much of this concern centers around electronic mail and marketing databases.

Privacy and Electronic Mail

Privacy and e-mail were discussed from the consumer's point of view in Chapter 9. This topic is revisited next, with an emphasis on its effect on companies.

Company Electronic Mail

Many people believe that the objective of e-mail within companies is to facilitate communication among workers. They claim that e-mail should be viewed as the modern-day version of informal chatting around the water cooler, and that e-mail messages should not in any way be confused with official company records. Others claim that any business document created on the premises of an organization is not the property of the individual but of the organization. The issue has largely been resolved in favor of the latter viewpoint; what you say in your company e-mail can be legally seized by others and used against you. What's more, you can be prosecuted for destroying e-mail evidence if you deliberately do it to avoid retribution, and your company can get into legal trouble for not taking proper precautions with employee e-mail.

The issue of employees creating potentially damaging e-mail messages has reached crisis proportions in many companies. The widespread use of e-mail has made it easier for anyone—clients, employees, disgruntled people, and regulators—to file a lawsuit against a company. Charges already filed have ranged from sexual and racial discrimination to stolen secrets and uncompetitive practices.

>Privacy. How information about an individual is used and by whom.

campus close-up

Gettysburg College, Wired for Information

Gettysburg College, listed as one of *Yahoo! Internet Life* magazine's 100 Most Wired Colleges for two years running, is a pioneer in distributing college information via a campus network. The college's campus network system, CNAV, provides many different groups of individuals access to college-related information. For example, faculty members can edit course information and access student and budget information. College advisors can track appointments, access student records, and monitor student academic progress. Students can access information about campus events, view the college catalog, make electronic course reservations, access personal financial information, update their student information, and obtain information about their current courses.

Other groups that can access CNAV are alumni, prospective students, and parents. Allowing outsiders to access such a system can raise privacy and security issues. If outsiders can access the system in general, is there a higher risk of security and privacy breaches? How do you protect confidential records? Who should decide what personal information about students should be available over the network?

Since its development began in the summer of 1995, privacy and security have been a very important consideration for the college. Deciding what information each group of individuals should be entitled to see was one step. Protecting the system so that information cannot be accessed by unauthorized individuals was another.

To ensure privacy, CNAV includes a detailed privacy subsystem that allows each user to carefully control who can see each item of their "public" information (photo, campus address, campus phone, home address, home phone, class schedule, etc.). There is a separate level of access control for students, college employees, and outside individuals. For example, a student could decide to grant all students access to his or her photo and campus contact information, to deny outsiders access to any personal information, and to give his or her parents access to all of his or her public information plus transcripts. Another student may choose to give everyone access to the public information and his or her parents additional access to financial information but not transcripts. Giving the students control of who can access their personal information resolves much of the privacy issues associated with such a system.

The system has not been without problems, however. For example, one semester when final grades became available on CNAV once they were submitted by instructors, students who had already received their final grades flooded faculty offices demanding attention while instructors were still trying to administer exams to other students. This illustrated that having so much information available so quickly may not be in the best interest of the college all the time.

Despite the small snags encountered along the way, CNAV is viewed as a success. About 76 percent of the entire campus (faculty, staff, and students) have used CNAV, and more than 50 percent of students and faculty use it frequently. Provided adequate security and privacy controls remain in place, CNAV should continue to be a useful tool for the college community, as well as an information bridge to parents, alumni, and prospective students.

To protect themselves, companies often rely on a formal e-mail policy and software to help enforce it. For example, at Amazon.com, the policy is that all nonessential documents "should be destroyed when they are no longer current or useful." To help enforce policies, the software industry has responded with products that range from *e-shredders* (software programs that claim to completely obliterate e-mail messages) to filtering/monitoring programs. Some of these programs alert workers with onscreen warnings when the contents of incoming or outgoing e-mail may be in violation of a company's e-mail policy; others surreptitiously monitor all computer activity and record it so it can be reviewed by the company, if needed.

Precautions notwithstanding, a large part of the problem is that companies aren't sure what is expected of them. What type of e-mail is appropriate and what's not? What constitutes being prudent and careful in the eyes of the law? How long must e-mail legally be kept?

The matter of whether or not companies should be allowed to eavesdrop on their employees' e-mail messages is a matter of heated debate. Companies are quick to point out that they have to protect themselves from unauthorized use of their e-mail systems. After all, a careless comment in a memo could make the company liable. Privacy-rights advocates often counter that companies don't casually rifle through people's desks or file cabinets, so why should they peek at their computer files? Also, the advocates point out, e-mail monitoring can be used for political purposes.

Presently, eavesdropping by companies on their e-mail systems is totally legal, and the law doesn't require that employees be informed that their messages are monitored. Nonetheless, it makes good business sense to have a computer-resource-usage policy in effect that informs all employees that such monitoring may be taking place.

Spam

Spam refers to unsolicited, bulk electronic mail sent over the Internet. The electronic equivalent of junk mail, spam most often originates from commercial sources. At best, it is an annoyance to recipients and can clog a mail network and slow down the delivery of important messages. At worst, it can disable a mail network completely.

Internet service providers such as America Online often have millions of pieces of spam clogging its network each day, and the problem is growing worse. Many people use *e-mail-filtering programs* that automatically discard incoming messages if they appear to contain spam, and some service providers automatically block or discard incoming spam. Currently, legislation is being drafted at both federal and state levels to curb spam abuse. As a minimum today, all unsolicited e-mail messages are required to have a working e-mail address included in the message that can be used to *unsubscribe* to future e-mails.

Privacy and Marketing Databases

Marketing databases are repositories that contain information about the consuming public. They record where people live, what they are inclined to do, and what they buy. Using such facts, companies attempt to determine the best way to promote specific products to specific types of people. Virtually anytime you leave traceable information about yourself anywhere—either online or offline—there's a good chance that it eventually finds its way into somebody's marketing database and to a company that wants to sell to you (see Figure 15-10).

When you buy a house, for example, your name, address, and the sales price are recorded in county records. These records are available to the public, including micromarketers. *Micromarketers* are companies that specialize in creating marketing databases and selling information to companies that sell products or services to others. The micromarketer typically breaks down the neighborhoods in a region into several dozen categories. Consumers are placed into

---

>Spam. Unsolicited, bulk e-mail sent over the Internet. **>Marketing database.** An electronic repository containing information useful for product marketing.

HOW MARKETING DATABASES WORK

When you make an electronic transaction, information about who you are and what you buy is recorded.

The identities of people and what they buy are sold to a micromarketer.

The micromarketer uses its computers to reorganize the data in a way that might be valuable to others.

Companies buy the reorganized data and use it for their own purposes.

► FIGURE 15-10
Marketing databases.

one of these categories according to their addresses, which indicates their approximate income levels. There are also categories for urban professionals, the elderly, and so on.

Each category is correlated in the micromarketer's computer system with certain buying preferences, a profiling technique known as *geodemographics.* The wealthier categories are more likely to buy expensive cars and take trips to places such as Aspen and St. Thomas. Those in another category may be more inclined to buy minivans and children's products. This information helps companies customize a direct-mail campaign to consumers' specific tastes. Some consumers, of course, look at unsolicited direct or electronic mail as junk mail and resent it as an intrusion on privacy.

In addition to geodemographic data, micromarketers also collect data showing consumers' past purchasing behavior. Every time you make a computerized purchase, valuable data about your purchasing tastes can be gathered and entered into a computer system. Records kept by stores, credit card companies, banks, the companies whose magazines you subscribe to, and other organizations may be sold to the micromarketer.

Privacy Legislation

Since the early 1970s, the federal government has sought to protect citizens' rights by passing legislation to curb privacy abuses. Some important laws enacted for this purpose are described in Figure 15-11.

Many people inside and outside of the computer industry feel that privacy legislation is woefully out of date and due for an overhaul. The major privacy laws were enacted more than two decades ago and largely apply to the conduct of the federal government and the organizations to which it supplies aid. A lot has changed since then. Twenty-five years ago, most information was centralized on mainframes and available only in hard-copy form; today it is much more common for data to be accessed though the Internet.

further
exploration

For links to further information on privacy legislation, go to www.course.com/parker2002/ch15

INTELLECTUAL PROPERTY RIGHTS

Intellectual property rights refer to the ability to legally use the creations of others. They include such restrictions as when a property can or cannot be used without permission, how long the individual retains full rights to the property, and so forth. Three main areas of intellectual property rights are *copyrights, trademarks,* and *patents.*

Copyrights

Copyrights protect intellectual property such as books, movies, music, and artwork. Just by creating a personal piece of property, the creator automatically claims the copyright to that work and has the right to make a statement such as "Copyright © 2001 by XYZ, Inc. All

DATE	LAW AND DESCRIPTION
1970	**Freedom of Information Act** Gives individuals the right to inspect data concerning them that are stored by the federal government.
1970	**Fair Credit Reporting Act** Prevents private organizations from unfairly denying credit to individuals and provides individuals the right to inspect their credit records for truthfulness.
1974	**Education Privacy Act** Stipulates that, in both public and private schools that receive any federal funding, individuals have the right to keep the schools from releasing such information as grades and evaluations of behavior.
1974	**Privacy Act** Stipulates that the collection of data by federal agencies must have a legitimate purpose.
1978	**Right to Financial Privacy Act** Provides guidelines that federal agencies must follow when inspecting an individual's bank records.
1984	**Cable Communications Policy Act** Limits disclosure of customer records by cable TV companies.
1986	**Electronic Communications Privacy Act** Extends traditional privacy protections to include e-mail, cellular phones, and voice mail.
1988	**Video Privacy Protection Act** Limits disclosure of customer information by video-rental companies.
1988	**Computer Matching and Privacy Act** Limits the use of government data in determining federal-benefit recipients.
1991	**Telephone Consumer Protection Act** Requires telemarketing companies to respect the rights of people who do not want to be called and significantly restricts the use of recorded messages.
1992	**Cable Act** Extends the Cable Communications Policy Act to include companies that sell wireless services.
1998	**Telephone Anti-Spamming Amendments Act** Applies restrictions to unsolicited, bulk commercial e-mail.

FIGURE 15-11

U.S. laws relating to privacy.

rights reserved." To be legally enforceable, however, copyrights should be registered with the U.S. Copyright Office. Copyrights generally last until 70 years after the creator's death.

In particular, Web developers should be aware of copyright law so that they do not include any copyrighted content (images, text, videos, etc.) without the proper permission, credit, and fee. There has been a flurry of cease and desist requests and lawsuits pertaining to removing copyrighted material (comic strips, music, images, and TV clips, for example) from Web sites. There have even been claims of copyright infringement when Web sites link to pages within another Web site in a manner (such as with frames) that made it appear the page on the other site belonged to the current site.

Trademarks

further exploration

For links to further information about trademarks and logos, go to www.course.com/parker2002/ch15

A *trademark* is any word, name, symbol, or other device that identifies one organization's goods or services from another's. Trademarks that are claimed, but not registered with the U.S. Patent and Trademark Office, can use the mark ™; registered trademarks can use the symbol ®. There have been a number of claims of trademark infringement in the last few years, such as organizations claiming the exclusive right to a particular domain name because it was a trademark, and organizations not wanting their trademarks (the "K" in Kmart or the Lego logo, for instance) displayed on unauthorized Web sites.

Patents

A *patent* is the exclusive right to an invention for the period of 20 years. Computer-related patents—particularly Internet-related patents—have skyrocketed in recent years. There are even patent claims for a variety of business methods and models, including CoolSavings.com's Internet coupon distribution method, Amazon.com's one-click purchase, and Priceline.com's name-your-own-price business model. When an item or business model is patented, no other organization can use it during the patent period without risking prolonged patent litigation or paying an agreed-on royalty to the patent holder.

HEALTH, ERGONOMICS, AND THE ENVIRONMENT

Computers have been said to pose a threat to our mental and physical well-being. Although the body of scientific evidence supporting this claim is far from conclusive and is likely to be that way for many more years, we should all be aware of the major concerns raised about the possible effects of computers on our health.

Stress-Related Concerns

Emotional problems such as financial worries, feelings of incompetence, and feelings of being overworked often produce emotional *stress.* Stress may also be triggered by a computer-related event, such as those discussed next.

Layoff or Reassignment

One of the first criticisms leveled at computers on their entry into the workplace was that their very presence resulted in job-related stress. When computers were introduced, many people were no longer needed and were subsequently laid off and forced to find new jobs. Workers at the lowest rungs worried most about job security. Many feared the full potential of computers in the office or in the factory and spent much of their time never knowing if machines might replace them. Such fears still exist today.

Even people who were not laid off found that their jobs had changed significantly and that they required new skills. Airline agents, for example, had to learn how to manipulate a database-retrieval language and to work with computers. Secretaries and other office employees were pressured into learning word processing and office-related software to keep in step. Many workers never made the transition successfully.

A growing fact of life is that, because of computers, fewer people are needed to do many types of work today. Computers also change the way work is done, often in ways that are difficult to predict. For example, modern computer networks are posing a new threat to workers in that companies no longer have to staff as many physical locations as in the past. Networks also mean that work can be transferred to foreign countries more easily. And the Web is threatening to put many small travel agencies, real estate agents, and booksellers out of business.

Fear of Falling Behind

The microcomputing boom that has taken place since the early 1980s has put computing power of awesome dimensions at almost everyone's fingertips. Many researchers perceive a widespread fear that failure to learn how to use PCs will make one fall behind. One example is the numerous noncomputer-oriented executives, managers, and educators who see themselves being upstaged by computer-savvy colleagues. There are so many big advances occurring on so many new technology fronts these days that the pace of change is fast enough to make even computer experts feel they are falling behind.

Fear of Being Out of Touch

One benefit of our communications-oriented society is that one never has to be out of touch. With the use of personal cell phones and pagers, as well as the ability to access e-mail and

web tutor

For a tutorial on health, ergonomic, and environmental concerns, go to www.course.com/parker2002/ch15

company networks from virtually anywhere, workers can be available around the clock, if needed. Though this is an advantage to some, it is also a cause of great stress to others. Workers who fear being out of touch may lose the distinction between personal time and work time and end up being always on the job. This can affect their personal lives, emotional health, and well-being. On the flip side, some employees may not be able to enjoy their down time if they have no means of being in touch, for fear that they are missing out on something important that may affect their career.

Burnout

Burnout is caused by overuse of computers. The infusion of such technologies as PCs, e-mail, pagers, mobile phones, and the Web in the home and office has raised new concerns about emotional health. What will happen to children who withdraw into their computer systems, to managers who are inadvertently swept into the tide of the computer revolution and its relentless pace, or to families whose relationships are threatened by overuse of computers and related devices in their homes? Little research has been done on computer burnout, and the long-term effects, if any, remain to be seen.

Ergonomics-Related Concerns

Ergonomics is the science of fitting jobs to the people who work in them. It typically focuses on making products and work areas more comfortable and safe to use. With respect to technology, ergonomics covers the effects on workers of such things as display devices, keyboards, and workspaces.

Display Devices

For more than a decade, large numbers of PC users have reported a variety of physical problems purportedly stemming from their interactions with display devices. The complaints have centered on visual and muscular disorders resulting from long hours of continuous computer use. These disorders include blurred eyesight, eyestrain, acute fatigue, headaches, and backaches. In response to these problems, hardware vendors have redesigned their products with features such as antiglare screens that fit over the monitor screen (see Figure 15-12), and monitors that tilt and swivel to enable them to be placed at a more comfortable angle.

Because humans are part of the equation too, some companies have passed computer-usage rules requiring mandatory short breaks from computer use at regular intervals. Other operator-induced factors that play a large part include poor posture, poor exercise habits, bad placement of the monitor on the desktop, and the like.

Keyboards

A condition known as *carpal tunnel syndrome,* a painful and crippling condition affecting the hands and wrists, has been traced to the repetitive finger movements routinely made when using a keyboard. It is an example of a *repetitive stress injury,* in which hand, wrist, shoulder, and neck pains can result from performing the same physical movements over and over again. Physicians recommend that to minimize the chance of such injuries you should take breaks every hour or so and relax or stretch your body. Recently, a number of innovatively designed keyboards have become available that claim to reduce stress in the hands and wrists. An ergonomic keyboard was shown in Figure 5-2 in Chapter 5; a supportive wrist pad is shown in Figure 15-12.

further exploration

For links to further information about ergonomic accessories, go to www.course.com/parker2002/ch15

>**Ergonomics.** The field that studies the effects of things such as computer hardware and work environment on people's comfort and health.

► FIGURE 15-12
Ergonomic equipment.
A variety of ergonomic computer accessories are available, such as the antiglare screen (left) and supportive wrist pad (right) shown here.

Workspace Design

Monitors and keyboards are not the only culprits in an uncomfortable work environment. The furniture may be nonadjustable, forcing the user into awkward postures that are guaranteed to produce body kinks. Or bright lighting or sun shining through a nearby window may cause a headache-producing glare on the display screen. Even disconcerting noise levels, due to poorly designed office equipment or acoustics, may be the culprits. Ergonomics researchers are constantly studying such problems, and the results of their efforts are becoming apparent in the consumer products now being offered to the ergonomics-conscious buyer. Figure 15-13 illustrates some principles of good workspace design.

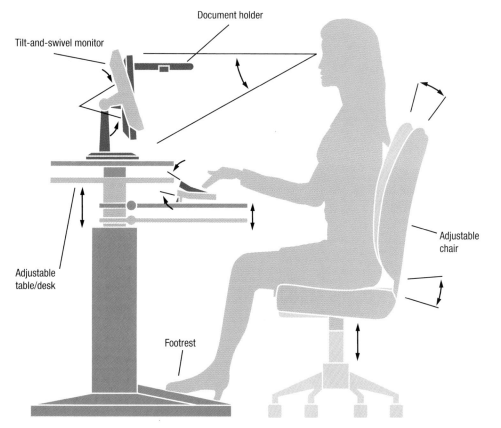

Tilt-and-swivel monitor

Document holder

Adjustable table/desk

Footrest

Adjustable chair

► FIGURE 15-13
Workspace design.
Features and equipment such as adjustable desks and chairs, footrests, document holders, and tilt-and-swivel monitors can all work together to help workers work more comfortably.

⏵ **FIGURE 15-14**

Assistive hardware. Assistive hardware includes extra large monitors, Braille keyboards and other alternative input devices, screen readers and other voice output systems, etc. This blind Michigan newspaper reporter uses a Braille notetaker, keyboard, and scanner for input; and headphones and screen reader software for output.

Workplace comfort is not the only reason that computer hardware has been redesigned in recent years. The increased diversity of the workforce has created the need for *adaptive* or *assistive* input and output devices, such as Braille keyboards, specialized mice, large monitors, and screen readers, as well as wheelchair-compatible work stations, as shown in Figure 15-14.

Environment-Related Concerns

The surge in personal computer use during the past several years has caused a variety of environmental concerns. Take power use, for example. The U.S. Environmental Protection Agency (EPA) estimates that home and office PC systems consume billions of dollars worth of electricity annually. This indirectly has resulted in the discharge of tons of pollutants into the atmosphere. The PC industry has responded by adding a variety of energy-saving devices to computer hardware. Among these devices are power-management software programs that put the computer system into a sleep mode when it is not being used, low-power-consumptive chips and boards, and flat-panel displays. In addition, most computer hardware today is *Energy Star* compliant, which means it exceeds the minimum federal standards for reduced energy consumption. To see if a piece of hardware is Energy Star compliant, look for the label shown in Figure 15-15.

The environmental threat goes much deeper than just the higher electrical use. For example, the so-called paperless office that many visionaries predicted for the computer age has become largely a myth. Because computer output is so easy to produce, more paper than ever is now consumed. It is estimated that U.S. businesses generate about a trillion pages a year—an amount that would stack more than 50,000 miles high.

⏵ **FIGURE 15-15**

Energy Star logo. The Energy Star logo affirms that the product meets or exceeds the government's energy efficiency requirements for that device.

Since the early 1950s, when the era of commercial computing began, computers have rapidly woven their way into the fabric of modern society. In the process, they have created both opportunities and problems.

ETHICS

Ethics refers to standards of moral conduct. Today one of the most important ethical concerns regarding computers is using someone else's property in an improper way. Another is being dishonest with others when it works to one's advantage. It is becoming increasingly common for businesses to establish *codes of conduct* to address what behavior is considered ethical and unethical at that particular organization.

Chapter Objective 1:
Explain what is meant by ethics and provide several examples of unethical behavior in computer-related matters.

COMPUTER CRIME AND SECURITY

Computer crime is defined as the use of computers to commit criminal acts. In practice, even though there are laws that deal with computer crime, it is sometimes difficult to decide when a questionable act is really a crime, companies are often reluctant to press charges, and it is difficult for legislation to keep pace with the changing technology.

Computer crime may take many forms. Computer crimes include **computer viruses** (computer programs spread via disk or over a network that are designed to replicate themselves and possibly cause damage to a system); *unauthorized access and use* (including such acts as **hacking, information theft,** *spoofing, denial of service attacks,* **software piracy,** *eavesdropping,* and *physical theft*); data or program alterations *(data diddling, Trojan horses, salami shaving, logic and time bombs,* and *sabotage);* **digital counterfeiting;** online scams and fraud; and cover-ups. A *trapdoor* intentionally left in a program can also be considered a computer crime.

There is some amount of computer crime legislation in place, but the rapid growth of the Internet and jurisdictional issues have contributed to the lack of sufficient legislation.

Organizations can attempt to minimize computer crimes in many ways: Assessing risks, hiring trustworthy people, taking precautions with malcontents, conducting regular **audits,** separating employee functions, and other employee-management precautions are a good start. In addition to physically securing computer hardware, restricting system use with *passwords, physical access objects, biometric devices,* and *firewalls* can help prevent unauthorized access. All sensitive transmissions, e-mail, and files should be secured with **encryption** methods and can be authenticated using **digital certificates** and **digital signatures.** All sensitive transactions should take place via a secure Web server. Using **antivirus software** can help protect against computer viruses, as well as remove a virus from the system once it has been detected.

Chapter Objective 2:
Give several examples of types of computer crime.

Chapter Objective 3:
List some ways computer crime can be prevented.

COMPUTERS AND PRIVACY

Most people want some control over the kinds of facts that are collected about them, how those facts are collected and their accuracy, who uses them, and how they are used. Modern computer systems, with their ability to store and manipulate unprecedented quantities of data and make those data available to many locations, have added new dimensions to the personal **privacy** issue. Recently, electronic mail, junk e-mail or **spam,** and **marketing databases** have created further concerns about invasion of privacy. Privacy legislation exists but needs updating to reflect current issues and technology.

Chapter Objective 4:
Discuss how computer technology can encroach on people's privacy and describe some of the legislation enacted to prevent such abuses.

L I V

INTELLECTUAL PROPERTY RIGHTS

Chapter Objective 5:
State why it is important for computer users to be aware of intellectual property rights.

Intellectual property rights refer to the ability to legally use the creations of others. *Copyrights* protect intellectual property such as books, movies, music, artwork, and other original creations. *Trademarks* identify an organization's goods or services and can be either claimed or registered. *Patents* grant an exclusive right to an invention for 20 years. Computer users need to be aware of these rights so they don't use the works of others improperly.

HEALTH, ERGONOMICS, AND THE ENVIRONMENT

Chapter Objective 6:
Describe some of the impact computers may have on health and the environment.

One of the first criticisms leveled at the entry of computers into the workplace was that their presence resulted in stress. Stress-related concerns triggered by the so-called computer revolution include fear of layoff or reassignment, fear of falling behind, fear of being out of touch, and job burnout. In addition to these problems, concerns related to **ergonomics** issues, such as monitor and keyboard usage, as well as workspace design, have surfaced. Many people also worry about environment-related issues such as the energy usage and the massive amounts of paper our computer systems generate.

Instructions: Match each key term on the left with the definition on the right that fits best.

1. antivirus software

2. audit

3. computer crime

4. computer virus

5. digital certificate

6. digital counterfeiting

7. digital signature

8. encryption

9. ergonomics

10. ethics

11. hacking

12. information theft

13. marketing database

14. privacy

15. software piracy

16. spam

_____ A group of electronic data, often used in conjunction with a public key and private key, that can be used to verify the identity of a person or organization.

_____ A method of protecting data or programs so they will be unrecognizable if intercepted by an unauthorized user.

_____ A software program designed to spread itself to other computers without the user's knowledge and, sometimes, to cause some harm to the system.

_____ A term that refers to standards of moral conduct.

_____ A unique digital code that can be attached to an e-mail message or document to guarantee the identity of the sender.

_____ An electronic repository containing information useful for product marketing.

_____ An inspection used to determine if a system or procedure is working as it is supposed to.

_____ How information about an individual is used and by whom.

_____ Software used to detect and eliminate computer viruses.

_____ The field that studies the effects of things such as computer hardware and work environment on people's comfort and health.

_____ The theft of information, usually from a company via a computer crime.

_____ The unauthorized copying or use of computer programs.

_____ The use of a computer to commit a criminal act.

_____ The use of computer hardware and software to make illegal copies of currency, checks, collectibles, and other paper-based items.

_____ Unsolicited, bulk e-mail sent over the Internet.

_____ Using a computer to penetrate the security of a remote computer system.

LIV

Self-Quiz

Answers for the self-quiz appear at the end of the book.

True/False

Instructions: Circle **T** if the statement is true or **F** if the statement is false.

T F **1.** All unethical acts are illegal.

T F **2.** As long as a business owns one legal copy of a software program, it can install it on as many computers as desired without fear of retribution.

T F **3.** Firewalls should be used to protect any computer, business or personal, continually connected to the Internet.

T F **4.** A digital signature is as legal as a written signature for many e-commerce transactions today.

T F **5.** Carpal tunnel syndrome can be developed by using a computer keyboard.

Completion

Instructions: Answer the following questions.

6. Using a computer to break into a remote computer system is called _____ .

7. To protect sensitive e-mail and files, they should be _____ before transmitting them over a network.

8. _____ software can be used to detect and remove a computer virus.

9. A(n) _____ identifies one organization's goods or services, while a(n) _____ is the exclusive right to an invention for a period of time.

10. Products that are _____-compliant exceed the minimum federal standards for reduced energy consumption.

Exercises

1. Several situations regarding the use of computers follow. In the space provided, indicate whether each act is unethical (U), criminal (C), or neither (N). The "neither" category can include both ethical acts and acts that, while not morally wrong, may not be commendable.

Situation	Type of Situation
a. A company spokesperson tells employees that the company doesn't monitor e-mail messages, knowing full well it does.	_____
b. A teenager hacks into a federal government computer. Once inside the system, the teenager looks around for a few minutes and then leaves, disturbing nothing. When asked, he stated that he just wanted to see if he could do it.	_____
c. A systems analyst is given the job of building a system that will deliver a new computer service to consumers, signing a legally binding agreement to not disclose facts about it to outsiders. She is so fascinated by the service that she immediately quits her job and interests a competitor to hire her on at twice her former salary in order to develop a competitive service.	_____
d. A fund-raiser at a hospital has access to a database that reveals the recent deaths of people who were able to afford expensive medical care. The fund-raisers uses the database to target bereaved family members for contributions.	_____

2. For each of the following cases, select the type of computer crime involved from the list that follows. Note that all types of computer crimes will not be used.

   _____ A person working for the Motor Vehicle Division deletes a friend's speeding ticket from a database.

   _____ An individual attaches a file to an e-mail message that will automatically send itself to the first 10 people on the recipient's e-mail address book when the file is opened.

   _____ A person uses a desktop publishing system to create phony checks.

   _____ A systems programmer leaves in some code in a finished program to allow him to access the program and computer system after it is installed.

   a. Unauthorized access and use
   b. Computer virus
   c. Trapdoor
   d. Digital counterfeiting
   e. Data or program alteration

3. List two ways of protecting yourself from a computer virus.

4. Assume that you have created a Web site to display your favorite original photographs. Explain whether or not that site would be protected by copyright law. If not, explain what steps, if any, you could take to ensure it was protected.

5. List three negative physical effects of working on a computer and describe one way to lessen each effect.

Short Answer/ Research

1. **Is It Just a Hoax?** Computer virus hoaxes have been around as long as the viruses themselves, and can sometimes be as damaging as an actual virus. It turns out that people spend so much time reading and forwarding these hoaxes that businesses lose out in productivity, and this can hurt them just as much as an actual virus. In order to take some of the guesswork out of determining if the virus warning is real or not, the U.S. Department of Energy has set-up a "Hoax-busters" Web site that divides hoaxes into categories and provides information about how to recognize and deal with them. In addition, this site provides a history of interesting hoaxes. For this project, visit the Hoaxbusters Web site at hoaxbusters.ciac.org and summarize some of the content provided about the categories of hoaxes, how to recognize them, and how to deal with them. Have you received any virus warnings via e-mail or from a colleague or friend? If so, did you know if they were hoaxes or not? If you received a warning e-mail, did you forward the message? At the conclusion of your research, prepare a one-page summary of your findings and submit it to your instructor.

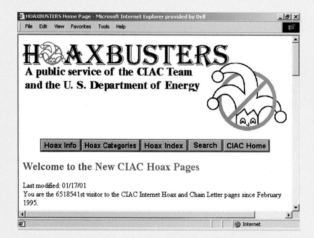

2. **Stressful** Computers are amazing tools that can help you accomplish tasks that used to take days, or even weeks, in a matter of minutes. However, they can also cause an inordinate amount of stress in the process. It seems like these devices know when you are most susceptible to stress and they somehow choose those times to refuse communication with the printer, or they generate a system error that you cannot recover from. There are, however, some ways that you can learn to manage the stress of working with technology and maintain your sanity. For this project, research and summarize a few of the ways an individual can learn to manage stress on a regular basis. At the conclusion of your research, prepare a one-page summary of your findings and submit it to your instructor.

3. **"Hacktivism"** A whole new approach to the political and social "sit-ins" of the 1960s, called "Hacktivism," has gained widespread appeal and is expected to become one the more popular ways that a group can make its concerns known to organizations and the public at large. Groups with names like the "Electrohippies" and "Electric Disturbance Theater" are using programs with names like "Hacktivismo" and "Flood Net" to orchestrate their Hacktivisms, or what could also be referred to as denial-of-service attacks. In addition, most of the groups that write these programs are making their software available for free over the Internet. You can now download the above-mentioned programs, as well as a newer one called the "Disturbance Developer's Kit," right over the Internet. For this project, research a few of these groups and the software they use

to commit hacktivism. You should also report on a few of the latest attempts by these groups to commit hacktivism, and just how successful they were in bring media attention to their cause. Can these groups be held liable for their actions? Do you think this is an appropriate way to advance a group's cause? Would you be inclined to get involved with one of these groups? At the conclusion of your research, prepare a one-page summary of your findings and submit it to your instructor.

Hands On

4. **Ergo Me** Lots of companies sell ergonomic office furniture and often set up sample workspaces to illustrate what is ergonomically correct. For this project, visit a few of these stores and test-drive their ergonomic office arrangements. Take some notes about the types of office equipment and accessories you like best. What was the arrangement like? Did you actually feel more comfortable? What did the salesperson tell you about the equipment that you were trying on for size? Finally, what was the cost of all this ergo stuff? At the conclusion of this task, prepare a one-page summary of your efforts and submit it to your instructor.

Writing About Computers

5. **"The Code"** The Computer Society and Association of Computing Machinists (ACM) has a widely known code of ethics called "The ACM Code of Ethics and Professional Conduct." The code includes eight general moral imperatives intended to serve as a guide to academia and industry. For this project, look up these principles and examine each one to prepare a short summary of the document (go to the ACM Web site at www.acm.org and visit the Public Policy section to find the text of the code). Do you understand and agree with each principle? Do you think that industry will abide by each principle? If not, which one do you think they will fail to follow? Submit your findings and opinions to your instructor in the form of a short paper, not more than two pages in length.

6. **Top 10 "Dot Cons"** A whole new cottage industry, sometimes referred to as Internet "no-service" providers (INSP's) or "dot cons," has developed on the Web in recent years. Some of the most profitable of these companies are the ones that manage to slip charges onto your phone bill without your authorization—sometimes called *Web cramming*. All these companies have to do is call you up on the phone and offer to provide you some service, and then send your name to a clearinghouse know as a "billing aggregator." Whether you decline the service does not seem to be a factor in determining whether you actually get billed for their services. The problem is that most people don't realize how easy it is to add a charge to your phone bill, and don't scrutinize their phone bill for erroneous charges on a regular basis. For this project, investigate online fraud and scams and come up with at least three examples that have occurred in the United States. You may want to visit the Federal Trade Commission (FTC) Web site at www.ftc.gov and review their ten top dot cons (use the site's Search link and search for the term *dot con* to find the most current list of the top 10 dot cons; on that Web page, also look for a link to the Top Ten Dot Con Web site). When you have finished your research, prepare a summary of the information you find. Have you been targeted by a "dot con" yet? How do you avoid getting "dot conned"? Does the FTC allow you to file a complaint at its Web site? Submit this project to your instructor in the form of a short paper, not more than two pages in length.

7. **E-Mail Policy** As it stands now, employees have no reliable defense against employers violating their privacy by monitoring their incoming and outgoing office e-mail. There are, however, a few legal documents that may help you mount a very good defense, until such time as a

high-ranking judge decides to resolve one of these cases in favor of the defendant (the person whose e-mail was compromised) and set a new precedent. These documents include the United States Constitution, the individual state constitutions, and individual state statutes. Each of these documents contain sections that could be used in your defense if a company should decide to take action against you by using information they found in one of your e-mail messages. For this project, form a group to determine what sections of each of these documents for your individual state might be of some help in mounting a person's legal defense with respect to a violation of e-mail privacy. Do the members in your group feel that employers should be able to freely monitor e-mail that goes through the company server? Would any actions or potential actions taken by the employee more easily justify monitoring their e-mail? Your group should submit this project to your instructor in the form of a short paper, not more than three pages in length.

Presentation/ Demonstration

8. **Computer Forensics** Most law enforcement agencies either have a computer forensics expert within the agency, or contract the services of a computer forensics company to help investigate crimes where a computer may contain some evidentiary data. The task of collecting this data involves special skills that require the investigator to capture it in a manner that is acceptable in a court of law. Some of the companies that assist law enforcement agencies break their services into separate areas such as investigation services, forensic services, and evidential systems. For this project, take a look at a few of these companies and summarize the services they offer. Are you interested in this line of work? Did the companies that you researched have job openings? Do all the companies you researched offer the same services? This presentation should not exceed five minutes and should make use of one or more presentation aids such as the chalkboard, handouts, overhead transparencies, or a computer-based slide presentation. You may be asked to submit a summary of the presentation to your instructor.

9. **Online Rip-Off** Imagine this: You have just been ripped of by an unscrupulous online vendor and you want to know what your can do about it. The situation surrounding the rip-off was not common. You were surfing the Web about two weeks ago and found this great e-book for sale at one-third the price that you have seen them for sale elsewhere, and you decided to use your credit card to purchase it over the Internet. When it was delivered today, the package contained a cardboard version of the e-book consisting of a scrolled piece of paper with two thumb wheels and a cheap pen. You start to panic and one of your friends reminds you of a few organizations that may come to your aid. These organizations are the Consumer Information Center (CIC), the Direct Marketing Association (DMA), and the Federal Trade Commission (FTC), not to mention your credit card company. For this project, form a group to discuss this scenario and prepare a short presentation about what each of these organizations could do to help. In addition, your group should present a few general guidelines to follow when purchasing products over the Web and give some suggestions for how this rip-off could have been avoided in the first place. This presentation should not exceed 10 minutes and should make use of one or more presentation aids such as the chalkboard, handouts, overhead transparencies, or computer-based slide presentation format. Your group may be asked to submit a summary of the presentation to your instructor.

10. **DMZ** Just when you thought that your company's e-mail system was impervious to hackers and viruses, you get a virus and your e-mail system turns into the angel of death by spreading the virus to every computer in the company. It does not seem to matter that you have spent months of effort and thousands of dollars building a demilitarized zone (DMZ); you will always be susceptible to viruses transmitted via e-mail. This is not to say, however, that you shouldn't invest in such things as e-mail filtering software, firewalls, virus protection software that is updated on a regular basis, and e-mail safety training for your employees, because you should. However, these things will not ensure that your company's computers and data are safe.

For this project, form a group to investigate and explain each of the concepts and terms introduced in the preceding paragraph to the class in the form of a short presentation. Why are our computers still not safe from viruses even after implementing each of the possibilities listed above? Has anyone in your group ever received a virus? If so, did it cause any damage and how did the group member deal with the issue? This presentation should not exceed 10 minutes and should make use of one or more presentation aids such as the chalkboard, handouts, overhead transparencies, or computer-based slide presentation format. Your group may be asked to submit a summary of the presentation to your instructor.

Interactive Discussion

11. **Economics of Ergonomics** Each time the Occupational Safety and Health Administration (OSHA) announces a new ergonomic standard for industry, businesses foot the bill and worker's compensation insurers save a fortune. For example, one of the latest ergonomic standards imposed by OSHA cost businesses $4.2 billion, but saved worker's compensation insurers an estimated $20 billion. This sounds like quite a deal for the insurance industry, but what about the small companies that cannot afford to spend the estimated $150 per workstation for ergonomic equipment, as well as provide 90% of an employee's regular pay while they recover from whatever injury or condition with which they were inflicted?

    Select one of the following positions, or make up your own, and express your point of view on the subject. Your instructor will indicate whether your response is to be posted to a class bulletin board, discussed in a class chat room, or discussed as an in-class activity. You may also be asked to submit a summary of your position and point of view to your instructor.

    a. The cost of providing ergonomic equipment is part of doing business. If a small company cannot afford this expense, it should not be in business. Employees have a right to work in a safe environment.
    b. Small businesses should not have to conform to OSHA standards since they cannot afford the expense. Small businesses should only be required to educate the employees about ergonomic issues and show them how to avoid problems but should not have to purchase specially designed ergonomic equipment.

12. **It's a Digital World** Consider the following statement and establish your position, or point of view, on the subject. Your instructor will indicate whether your response is to be posted to a class bulletin board, discussed in a class chat room, or discussed as an in-class activity. You may also be asked to submit a summary of your position and evaluation of the statement to your instructor.

    Since 1951, when Remington Rand introduced the first electronic digital computer called UNIVAC, companies have been in a rush to take advantage of their speed, accuracy, and reliability. Because of this, computers have worked their way into almost every facet of our economic and social lives. We have reached a point where we can no longer make the decision not to interface with a computer, since almost everything we do is somehow influenced by them. The dominance of computers in our lives has both positive and negative aspects, but one thing is certain, you are going to have to deal with them because they are here to stay. It is likely that older generations will attempt to avoid computer technology as much as possible; however, many will be forced to communicate or interface with a computer in one form or another. The ones that end up using some of the technology may initially resent the imposition, but will eventually accept and even begin to prefer the new technological approach. The current generation will be in a constant struggle to keep up with the changing technology and resent the fact that they must learn a new way of doing business almost every year in order to keep their jobs or advance their careers. The younger generations will immediately accept technology and view the changing aspects as a positive rather than negative influence on their daily lives.

Interactive Exercise

Safeguarding Your Computer. You'd like to practice some basic PC security measures, such as checking for viruses and backing up your files! Go to the Interactive Exercise at www.course.com/parker2002/ch15 to complete this exercise.

OUTLINE

You and Your PC

LEARNING OBJECTIVES

After completing this chapter, you will be able to:

1. Identify the key components of a computer system to be acquired and discuss some factors to keep in mind when you are deciding on the type of system needed.

2. List several alternatives for acquiring PC products.

3. Explain how to select and install a PC for home or office use.

4. Name some computer maintenance practices designed to protect software, hardware, and data resources from damage.

5. List some important guidelines for troubleshooting problems and seeking assistance.

6. Describe some of the ways to upgrade a PC and explain the conditions that prompt an upgrade.

7. Name several sources for learning more about PCs.

I t is very common today for a person to own a PC or to use one at work. Consequently, more people than ever before are involved with buying a PC, installing new hardware and software, maintaining and upgrading a PC system, and other tasks that used to be left to computer professionals. The purpose of this chapter is to help you become an informed computer consumer, able to deal with the issues that are involved with being a PC owner.

Chapter 16 opens with a discussion of the vendors who make the important pieces of a computer system that you need to know about when acquiring a PC. Next, we look at some of the things you should know and do when acquiring a PC for home or work. We also discuss the various purchasing options available to the PC buyer. From there we turn to several operational and maintenance issues, including setting up a new system, installing new hardware and software, system maintenance, trouble-shooting problems, and obtaining product support. Next, we cover upgrading a computer system. Finally, we discuss some of the resources that are at your disposal for learning more about PCs. ▓

PC SYSTEM COMPONENTS

Whether acquiring a PC for home or business use, it is important to be familiar with the manufacturers of the most important components of a PC system. Though the actual components and how they worked were explained earlier in this text, we have yet to discuss much about the different manufacturers you will need to decide among. That discussion takes place next.

System Units

IBM, Compaq, Hewlett-Packard, Dell, Sony, Gateway, NEC, and Apple are among the big names in PC system units. Most of these companies produce PC-compatible computers, the vast majority of PCs sold. Most of the system units sold are of the desktop variety, but note-books, tablets, pockets, and other portable PCs are gaining fast and some analysts predict that they may eventually overtake desktop systems for business use. Among the most common manufacturers of handheld PCs are Palm, Handspring, Hewlett-Packard, and Casio.

While some PC manufacturers actually manufacture some of the components that go inside the system unit, most purchase individual components and just assemble the finished PCs. For this reason, when you buy a PC from a particular company—for example, Dell—you will be told (or should ask) which brand of hard drive, CPU, CD or DVD drive, monitor, etc. will be included in the system.

Vendors of system units are often ranked in tiers. The top-tier vendors include long-standing industry firms like IBM and Compaq whose equipment commands premium prices. Top-tier companies often are involved in extensive research and development efforts, and their equipment is usually top quality and an all-around safe purchasing bet. Second-tier vendors are less well known and often sell at prices of about 10 to 20 percent less than their top-tier counterparts. Second-tier companies often do little research and development, use less-expensive components, and frequently farm out service and support to third-party firms. Nonetheless, the equipment coming out of second-tier companies is usually high quality, service and support are very good, and one's purchase risk is low.

You might save yet another 10 percent on the purchase price of hardware by going to a third-tier vendor. These companies usually have no name recognition and many have been in business only a very short period of time. They are typically local vendors or companies that sell their PCs at discounted prices over the Internet and mail order. Because of the increased risk involved, many organizations have policies forbidding them to do business with any computer vendor below what they consider the second tier.

Monitors, Printers, and Other Peripheral Devices

With the exception of a few U.S. companies such as IBM, Hewlett-Packard, ViewSonic, and Xerox, the monitor and printer markets are dominated by Japanese manufacturers. Major players include Sony, Epson, Toshiba, Seiko, Brother, Fujitsu, Canon, and Okidata. Drive manufacturers include Sony, Iomega, Seagate, Imation, Philips, Western Digital, and many others. For input and output peripheral devices, the manufacturers vary more widely: Microsoft and Logitech are popular keyboard and mouse manufacturers; MicroTouch is a widely used touch screen manufacturer; and Creative Labs and Harmon Kardon are popular speaker manufacturers.

CPUs

The CPU market is ruled largely by Intel, Advanced Micro Devices (AMD), and Motorola. Intel and AMD make CPU chips for most of the leading PC-compatible system units, whereas Motorola makes chips for Macintosh compatibles. There are other lesser-known manufacturers, such as Cyrix and Transmeta, that produce Intel-compatible chips. Transmeta chips are geared primarily for portable computers, because of their lower power requirements.

Software

Many application programs today are sold as part of software suites, which bundle together several full-featured software programs for sale at lower prices than the separate programs would collectively command. Among the largest PC software producers (and their leading products) are Microsoft Corporation (Windows and the Office suite of applications), IBM (OS/2, Lotus Notes, and Lotus SmartSuite), and Corel Corporation (the WordPerfect Office suite of applications and CorelDRAW!).

SELECTING A PC SYSTEM

Chances are good that at some point in your life, you will need to select a PC for home or work. There are a number of steps to follow when acquiring a PC, as discussed next, though these steps may not always be followed formally.

Analyzing Needs

With regard to a computer system, a *need* refers to a functional requirement that the computer system must be able to meet. For example, at a video rental store, a computer system must be able to enter bar codes automatically from videos or DVDs being checked in and out, identify customers with overdue movies, manage movie inventories, and do routine accounting operations. Requiring portability—a computer that you can take with you "on the road"—is another example of a need. For example, sales personnel working out of the office can often justify purchasing a notebook computer simply on the basis of its usefulness as a sale-closing tool during presentations at their clients' offices.

Selecting a PC for home or business use must begin with the all-important question "What do I want the system to do?" Once you've determined what tasks the system will be used for, you must choose among the software and hardware alternatives available. Making a list of your needs in areas discussed in the next few sections can help you get a picture of what type of system you are shopping for. If you're not really sure what you want a system to do, you should think twice about buying one. Computer systems that are configured to

further exploration

For links to further information about CPUs, go to www.course.com/parker2002/ch16

web tutor

For a tutorial on selecting a PC, go to www.course.com/parker2002/ch16

FIGURE 16-1

Office suites for the most
popular operating systems.

Operating System	Most Common Application Suites
Microsoft Windows	Microsoft Office
	Corel WordPerfect Office
	Lotus SmartSuite
	Microsoft Works
Mac OS	AppleWorks
	Microsoft Office
Linux	Sun StarOffice

match the requirements of certain applications (such as preparing a novel) often perform poorly at others (playing power-hungry multimedia games, for example). You can easily make expensive mistakes if you're uncertain about what you want a system to do.

Operating Systems and Application Software

Determining what functions you want the PC system to perform will help you decide which application software is needed. Most users start with an application suite containing a word processor, spreadsheet, and other programs. In addition, specialty programs, such as tax preparation, drawing, home publishing, reference software, games, and more may be needed or desired.

As shown in Figure 16-1, not all of the popular application suites are available for all operating systems. If a specific piece of software is needed, that choice may determine which operating system you need to use. Alternatively, if your documents need to be compatible with those of another computer (such as other office computers or between a home and office PC), your operating system decision may be already made for you.

Application software is usually selected first. For example, if you want a computer system to do commercial art, it would be wise to first look at the various programs available in this area. It makes no sense to choose hardware first and then possibly discover that your selected system is not the best choice for the type of art package you need to use. Many artists, for example, prefer a Macintosh platform and may be disappointed if they buy a PC-compatible computer and then discover later that the Mac is better suited for the work that they want to do and the software they need to use. The platform decision is discussed next.

Platforms and Configuration Options

If your operating system has already been determined, that is a good start in deciding the overall platform you will be looking for. As mentioned in an earlier chapter, most users will choose between the IBM-compatible and Apple Macintosh platform. IBM and compatible PCs usually run either Windows or Linux; Apple computers almost always use Mac OS.

Configuration decisions involve primarily determining the size of the machine desired. For nonportable solutions, you have the choice between tower, desktop, or all-in-one configurations. For any of these PCs, you should determine how large a monitor is needed. Portable, fully functioning PCs can be notebook or tablet PCs. If a powerful fully functioning PC is not required, you may decide to go with a more portable option, such as a handheld or pocket PC.

You should also consider any other specifications that are important to you, such as the size of the hard drive, type of removable storage needed, amount of memory required, and so forth. As discussed in the next section, these decisions often require reconciling the features you want with the amount of money you're willing to spend.

Power vs. Budget Requirements

As part of the needs analysis, you should look closely at your need for a powerful system versus your budgetary constraints. Most users don't need a state-of-the-art system. Those who do should expect to pay more than the average user. For most users, a system that was top of the line six months or a year ago is now an affordable business system that would be more than adequate for their needs. Users who just want a PC for basic tasks, such as using the Internet and word processing, can likely get by with a low-end, inexpensive, home or family multimedia PC.

When determining your requirements, be sure to identify the features and functions that are absolutely essential for your primary PC tasks (such as a large hard drive and lots of memory for multimedia applications, a fast video card for gaming, a fast Internet connection for stock traders or individuals with a high level of Internet use, and so forth).

Listing Alternatives

After you establish a set of needs, you should make a checklist of the features you've determined are absolutely necessary in your new system. Desirable options that would be nice to have if the price isn't prohibitive can be listed separately to be included if possible. The next step is to look through advertisements, configure systems online via manufacturers' Web sites, call or visit stores, etc. to get enough information to compare and contrast a few alternative systems that satisfy your stated needs. A comparison sheet listing your criteria and the systems you are considering, such as the one included with other PC buying hints in the Inside the Industry box, can be helpful to summarize your options.

When you select potential vendors, you should keep in mind that there are three basic systems you can acquire:

▼ *Off-the-shelf systems*—Complete "turn-key" system, already put together with accompanying software installed. You typically cannot custom configure the features, such as hardware options and software (the most common type of system offered at large retail stores, such as Best Buy, CompUSA, Circuit City, Wal-Mart, and Costco).

▼ *Custom systems*—Systems that are built to your specifications, with your desired hardware and software components that are selected from available options (a common option when purchasing from computer specialty stores and over the Internet or telephone).

▼ *Build-your-own systems*—Systems that you put together yourself with components you buy separately (an option generally considered only by computer professionals or individuals who like to build computers as a hobby).

The categories of vendors these systems may be purchased from are described in the next few sections.

Brick-and-Mortar vs. Online Stores

When selecting an actual establishment from which to buy your PC system, the two most common options are local *brick-and-mortar stores* and *online stores* (see Figure 16-2). Purchasing at a brick-and-mortar store gives you the advantage of being able to see (and possibly try out) the system before purchasing it; you also typically can bring the system home the same day. In addition, it may be easier to return items, though many computer product returns require a restocking fee. Local stores may, however, have higher prices, less variety, and a lower degree of customizability than online stores. Advantages of online stores include potentially lower prices, greater selection, and home delivery—a definite plus for customers in small towns without many computer stores. A disadvantage of ordering a system online is the time it may take to get to you, as well as the potentially high cost of delivery.

Many organizations, such as Circuit City, CompUSA, and Costco, have both brick-and-mortar stores and an online presence. When this is the case, you have the option of buying locally or ordering a system.

inside the industry

Buying a PC

When buying a new PC, be sure to consider the following:

▼ *Size and type:* If you need portability, you'll need a notebook or handheld computer. Notebook buyers should expect to pay about $500 more than they would for a comparable desktop model, even though the processor and hard disk are usually slightly less capable.

▼ *Platform and operating system:* Choose between PC-compatible and Macintosh. PC users need to select a version of Windows, unless they choose to go with Linux or another alternative OS.

▼ *Speed and power:* Try to buy enough power, memory, and disk space to last you for a few years. The amount you need will be determined by the type of applications you need to run.

▼ *Storage systems:* Decide whether you'll need a high-capacity drive, such as a Zip drive, as well as what type of optical drive you prefer (CD-R, CD-RW, DVD, etc.). Internal drives are typically faster and it's easier to have them installed when you buy the machine than to add them yourself later.

▼ *Printer type:* If you need color, select an ink-jet; if business-quality black and white is what you need, pick a personal laser printer. Be sure to also consider multifunction machines. If you also need a copier or scanner, it may be less expensive to buy a printer with those features built in, instead of acquiring multiple machines.

▼ *Modem and Internet connection:* Be sure to get a modem that is compatible with the Internet service you will be using. Remember that dial-up, cable, DSL, and satellite connections all require different modems. If you know you will be using a large provider such as AOL or MSN, look for systems that include a rebate for new subscribers.

▼ *Service and support:* Be sure to get a system with at least a one-year warranty and find out if problems will be fixed on site or if you have to mail the PC somewhere (an expensive and inconvenient requirement).

COMPONENT	DESIRED SPECIFICATIONS	SYSTEM #1 Vendor:	SYSTEM #2 Vendor:
Operating System	Windows XP		
Manufacturer	HP or Compaq		
Style	Tower		
CPU	AMD 1 GHz or higher		
RAM	128 MB or higher		
Hard drive	60 GB or higher		
Removable storage	Floppy drive and Zip 250 drive		
Optical drive	CD-RW		
Monitor	Flat-panel 17		
Video card and video RAM	must have at least 16 MB dedicated video RAM		
Keyboard	would like sleep key		
Mouse	with scroll wheel		
Sound card/speakers	Harmon-Kardon preferred		
Modem	Cable		
Network card	10/100Base-T Ethernet		
Printer	ink-jet if get deal on price with complete system		
Scanner	don't need		
Included software	Microsoft Office or Works		
Warranty	3 years min. (1 year onsite if not a local store)		
Other features			
Price			
Tax			
Shipping			
TOTAL COST			

Comparing PC alternatives. A checklist such as this can be helpful to organize your criteria and specs for the systems you are considering.

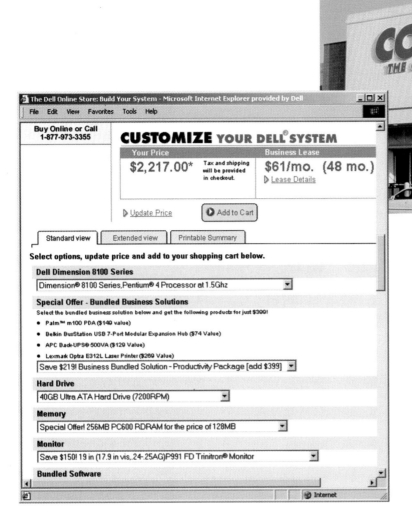

Regardless of whether it's through a brick-and-mortar store or an online storefront, most PC hardware and software products are purchased through computer stores, discount and department stores, manufacturers, value-added resellers, or alternative outlets (see Figure 16-3). These options are discussed in the next few sections.

Computer and Other Retail Stores

When buyers need strong local support in selecting and using PC products, they often turn to *computer stores* such as Computer City and CompUSA. Generally, the salespeople are relatively knowledgeable about computers and help buyers try out products before making a purchase. In addition to hardware, software, and advice on purchasing a new system, computer stores also offer consulting, repair, and other support services.

Computer stores come in many varieties. Most are national or multistate chain stores, but some serve only regional areas, such as a single town or a state. Large chains, because they can buy in volume, are likely to have better prices. Many regional stores try to compete by providing superior support. Virtually all computer stores are *resellers*—that is, they sell the hardware and software products made by another company. While many computer stores are as large as the average mall store, massive *computer superstores* have also become popular. Most consumer electronics stores, such as Circuit City, also carry an extensive line of PCs.

During the past several years, PC hardware and software have become so popular that many other types of retail stores have added these items to their showroom floors. Today,

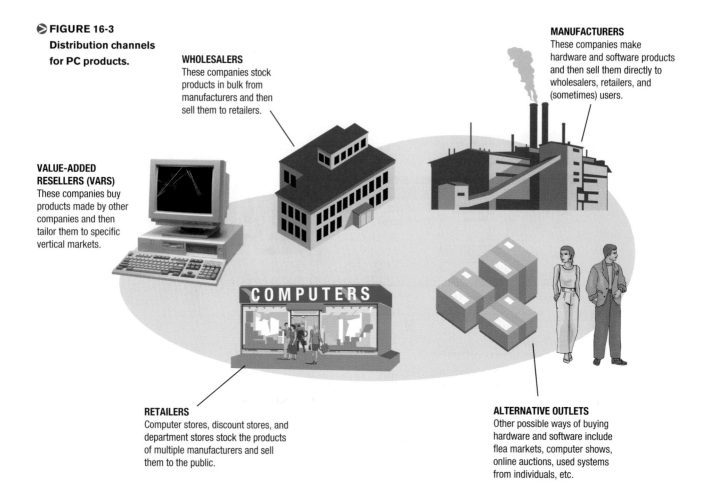

FIGURE 16-3
Distribution channels for PC products.

WHOLESALERS
These companies stock products in bulk from manufacturers and then sell them to retailers.

MANUFACTURERS
These companies make hardware and software products and then sell them directly to wholesalers, retailers, and (sometimes) users.

VALUE-ADDED RESELLERS (VARS)
These companies buy products made by other companies and then tailor them to specific vertical markets.

RETAILERS
Computer stores, discount stores, and department stores stock the products of multiple manufacturers and sell them to the public.

ALTERNATIVE OUTLETS
Other possible ways of buying hardware and software include flea markets, computer shows, online auctions, used systems from individuals, etc.

you can buy hardware and software at discount stores (such as Target and Wal-Mart), warehouse clubs (such as Price Club and Costco), department stores (such as Sears), office supply stores (such as Office Depot and Staples), and bookstores (such as Amazon.com and Waldenbooks).

As a general rule, discount stores and warehouse clubs have the best prices but typically offer a smaller selection and little or no technical support. The smaller selection is often due to deals the store gets on volume purchases and on inventory closeouts—for example, stock of a printer model the manufacturer wants to get rid of because a replacement model has just come out. If the store has what you are looking for, however, the combination of low prices and immediate availability makes this an attractive option.

Some retail stores that specialize in computer equipment primarily sell products through the Internet or by phone (see Figure 16-4). These stores frequently offer relatively low prices, some technical advice, and quick delivery.

Manufacturers

Yet another alternative for buying hardware and software is going straight to the manufacturer of the product, such as Apple, IBM, Compaq, Dell, or Gateway. Many PC companies today sell directly to the public, usually through their Web sites or 800 numbers. Many of these companies do not maintain finished inventories of computers; instead, they build each system to suit the buyers' tastes as they receive each order. Consumers enjoy the advantage of ordering exactly the computer system they want from a single source and usually get free support and service for a limited period of time. Whether or not they make their own components, companies that put their own brand names on hardware devices such as computer systems and peripheral devices and sell the hardware directly to the public are called *direct manufacturers*.

FIGURE 16-4
Online and catalog sales.
Some computer retailers sell mainly through their catalogs or Web sites.

Many *software manufacturers*—known as *software publishers*—also sell directly to the public. Similar to hardware manufacturers, buyers generally reach software publishers through the publisher's toll-free number or Web site. Some software publishers allow you to download copies of their products over the Internet for trial purposes; an increasing number are selling their software via download, as well.

Value-Added Resellers

Value-added resellers (VARs) are companies that buy computer hardware and software from others and make their own specialized systems out of them. For example, many of the computer systems used in the video- and DVD-rental-store business, in medical and dental offices, and in certain other types of *vertical markets* come from VARs. The VAR essentially packages together the custom hardware and software needed to run operations in the area in which it specializes and often provides full service and support as well. Although going through a VAR is usually more costly than configuring a system on one's own, it is definitely a compelling choice for a small business owner who is not computer savvy or who is too busy with other matters to design and create a specialized system.

Alternative Outlets

Alternative sources of computer products include flea markets, computer shows, and online auctions. These options are usually much riskier than the other sources discussed, because they almost never include any type of return policy. In addition, the merchandise may not be exactly as described or not in new condition. With online auctions, there is also the risk that the merchandise will never be shipped to you—online auction fraud is a growing problem, as discussed in the Chapter 9 Trend box. Another option is buying a used system from an individual through the newspaper or flyer on a college campus.

Computer Leases

When looking for a new computer system, you may want to consider leasing one instead of buying outright. Many direct manufacturers—among them Compaq, Dell, and Gateway—both sell and lease computer systems. Over the long run, leasing is usually more expensive than buying, but provides greater flexibility since you can often switch out of your current system into a newer model on a regular basis to keep pace with changes in technology. Many leasing plans run for two or three years and some provide the lessee the option to buy the system after the lease runs out, instead of trading up to a newer model, if preferred.

"Free" PCs and Other Products

Some users may want to look into the "free" PCs that are becoming increasingly popular in advertisements. As you would suspect, none of these PCs are free outright; instead they are usually free with a prepaid subscription to an Internet service provider. For example, you pay for two years of Internet service up front and get a free PC. Alternatively, you may be given a gift certificate for other merchandise equal to or less than the value of your PC's purchase price. These offers are worth considering if you would want to purchase additional items or want to purchase Internet service through that provider anyway. You should always compare the price and components of the entire system with your other alternative systems—don't just look at the free items.

For a look at the types of free computer goods and services frequently available, see the Trend box.

further exploration

For links to further information about manufacturers and hardware buying sites, go to www.course.com/parker2002/ch16

>**Value-added reseller (VAR).** A company that buys hardware and software from others and makes computer systems out of them that are targeted to particular vertical markets.

LIV

trend

Free Stuff

There is a definite trend of using the Web to distribute free goods and services. First came shareware and freeware. Then came free e-mail. Next were free PCs and Internet access. Now there's free advice, free shipping, free newspapers and magazines, and free merchandise. However, some free offers aren't worth the time and trouble. For example, if you don't like seeing onscreen advertisements, forget free ISPs. If you aren't willing to have your information entered into marketing databases and distributed, forget coupons and rebates. If you can tolerate some onscreen advertising, however, many free Web services aren't too obtrusive.

Though some free items are distributed out of the goodness of someone's heart (like some freeware authors who write programs for satisfaction or noteriety), the vast majority of free offers have strings attached—usually conveying some type of advertising or obtaining marketing data. A sampling of free Web-related offers is listed next.

▼ *Freeware.* Can be downloaded from such sites as Download.com and Shareware.com, as well as from the offering organization's Web site.

▼ *Internet access.* Can save you lots of money, but usually display a lot of banner ads. Two providers are NetZero and Juno.

▼ *E-mail.* Free e-mail accounts, such as those provided by Excite, Yahoo!, Hotmail, MSN, and virtually all portal sites, are useful if you switch ISPs frequently, so you can have a consistent e-mail address. For users on the go, many free e-mail services are Web based, so you can access your e-mail from any PC without having to change that PC's e-mail settings.

▼ *Web searching and reference tools.* As mentioned throughout the textbook, there is a huge variety of free search and reference tools on the Web. In addition to traditional sites—such as phone lookup and mapping services—other tools are online encyclopedias (Britannica.com) and do-it-yourself guides (Doityourself.com). In addition, online magazines, journals, and newspapers are plentiful.

▼ *Coupons and rebates.* Electronic coupons are available through sites such as CoolSavings.com; free samples and products that are free after rebate are itemized on the scores of Web sites dedicated to sharing these links,

such as TheFreeSite.com (search for "free stuff" on any search site to find them).

▼ *Free hardware and software.* A growing trend is to supply free PCs or Internet access devices with a subscription to an ISP, application for a loan, or some other type of financial commitment. It is also extremely common for hardware and software manufacturers to offer rebates on their products. Many work out to be completely free after rebate and may be available from both on and offline stores. Search for rebate sites and watch newspaper circulars to find these offers.

▼ *Financial tools.* Free stock quotes can be obtained through portal sites, such as Yahoo! and AltaVista, as well as brokerage sites, such as Datek.com. Some sites allow you to create your own free online portfolio for easy checking on a regular basis.

▼ *Multimedia.* Scores of clip-art images, video clips, and audio clips can be accessed and often downloaded from the Web. Also available are online electronic greeting cards (BlueMountain.com). Though downloaded music has been the subject of numerous legal challenges, free music is still available, typically as sample tracks from a CD (MP3.com) or from online radio stations.

▼ *Office tools.* Tools such as free electronic faxing (eFax.com) and free clip art (The Free Graphics Store) are widely available.

Evaluating Alternatives

You can begin evaluating your alternatives once you have listed what you think are your best options, such as by completing a checklist like the one in this chapter's Inside the Industry box. You can also read reviews of software and hardware products from the many computer journals available at newsstands, libraries, and online. Many of these journals also periodically describe the best and worst features of products, rate and compare products, and have industry analysts address product trends (look ahead to Figure 16-14). Such information can be useful when evaluating your purchasing alternatives.

Prospective buyers can evaluate alternative PC systems most effectively by "test driving" them, though this is not always possible. If you do get to test drive a system, keep in mind that you are observing the performance of certain software programs on a given configuration of hardware. A program that runs smoothly on a Gateway 1 GHz computer system with 256 MB of RAM likely won't run as well on a Packard Bell 500 MHz PC with 32 MB RAM, because the varying components used by different manufacturers can affect performance, and because of the different CPU chips and amount of memory used in these two systems. Also, the look, feel, and performance of a computer in the Apple Macintosh line are often noticeably different than they are in a PC-compatible machine. Sometimes it's quite difficult, when selecting a configuration of hardware and software, to see the entire system together, but it's certainly advisable to do this whenever possible. As discussed in Chapter 12, when purchasing a large system consisting of multiple computers plus software, some vendors will set up the exact system for you to test before finalizing the purchasing decision; this is less possible with an individual purchase.

As you evaluate software and hardware products, a number of criteria will help you to make your final selection. The most important selection criterion is *functionality*—the type of work the product does. For many people, ease of learning, ease of use, and the availability of phone support follow closely behind. Also, most people prefer widely used products to unknown ones, because the larger user base of the more popular products ensures that support will be available for a long time. Good documentation showing how to use the hardware or software is also important. When a helping hand isn't readily available, documentation is often the best alternative for answering a tough question. Figure 16-5 lists some important general criteria for selecting a particular PC.

In acquiring hardware, one of the most common mistakes people make is not thinking enough about the future. You should buy as much processing speed and storage capacity in your initial purchase as you can afford. New software updates—which come out about every year or two—usually require more speed and storage space for effective operation, though many users may opt not to upgrade to a newer version if the current one is sufficient for their needs. However, if you buy a bottom-of-the-line system and do upgrade to the next version of your favorite software program, you may find it crawls at a snail's pace. If you buy a system for business use, expect your hardware to last about two to three years before new software or hardware needs may force you to buy a new system; personal PCs can often be used for four to five years or more before they need to be replaced.

☑ Product functionality
☑ Ease of learning and use
☑ Cost
☑ Vendor reputation
☑ Support and warranty
☑ Expandability
☑ Meets industry standards
☑ Performance
☑ Favorable reviews
☑ Delivery time and cost
☑ Included documentation

▶ FIGURE 16-5

General selection criteria.

In addition to specific system needs, criteria about the product or vendor in general should be considered.

Purchasing the PC System

After you have considered the available alternatives, it's time to choose a system and purchase it. People choose among system alternatives in a number of ways. For example, some people use a checklist of features similar to the one in this chapter's Inside the Industry box and, from the systems that meet their basic needs, rate each option or extra feature with a value representing importance or dollar amount. They then select the alternative that scores the highest total importance value or highest value per dollar when the ratings are added up.

Others prefer to make their choices less formally. After thinking about their needs and the criteria they apply to evaluate alternatives, they select the first computer system they see that "feels right." Although such an acquisition process could be criticized for lack of thoroughness, many people claim that their busy schedules leave no time to spend researching choices with greater care. Of course, rushing to make a selection has a negative side. Just as a car owner can go through years of disappointment driving around in the wrong type of car, a computer buyer can also wind up with the headaches resulting from a poor choice.

SETTING UP A NEW SYSTEM

When you take possession of a new computer system, you should find that most of the hardware and software you need are already in place, as long as you evaluated your needs appropriately and picked a system that met those needs. You'll need to connect the components and start the system up; then, you'll be off and running. If your system does not include a piece of hardware or software that you want it to have, you can usually buy and install it yourself relatively easily, as discussed shortly.

Setting up a new system involves four primary tasks:

1. Unpacking the components

2. Connecting the devices

3. Adding any additional hardware and software

4. Customizing the system

Unpacking the Components

When unpacking the components that came with your system, be sure to look for small items (power cords, cables, warranty cards, user's manuals, and so forth) inside the packing materials. Carefully remove each item and keep it together with any other hardware that came inside the box. After emptying a box, it is a good idea to repack it with all of the original packing material and save it, in case the unit needs to be returned for service at a later time.

⊜ **FIGURE 16-6**

New system setup quick reference. Many PC manufacturers include labeled or color-coded ports on the system unit, as well as a quick setup guide to get your PC up and running fast.

Connecting the Devices

Each device in a PC system needs to connect to the system unit; most peripheral devices also need to connect to a power outlet. To protect your equipment against power fluctuations, you should plug the devices into a *surge suppressor* (discussed later in this chapter), instead of directly into the wall outlet. To hook up a device, connect one end of the cable that came with the device into the device itself (if it's not permanently attached), then plug the other end into the appropriate port on the system unit. To help you locate the proper port for each device, many PCs come with labeled or color-coded ports; many manufacturers also include a setup reference card to help you get up and running quickly (see Figure 16-6). If not, just match the shape and size of the connector with the PC's ports—there is usually just one that will match exactly. Also, be sure to turn the connector the appropriate direction—most of the time they only fit into the port one way.

For a closer look at setting up a new system, see the How It Works box.

how it works

Setting Up a New PC

After you unpack the components for your new PC, locate the installation manual or reference card. It should contain specific directions for your system. That, in conjunction with the color-coding or labeling system for the ports and plugs included on your system should help you get all the components connected correctly. Be sure to use a surge protector and plug that into the wall outlet as the last step to avoid the PC booting up before you're ready.

Don't forget to give some thought to the location of your PC. It should be close enough to a power outlet so the surge protector can reach the PC. It should also be close to a phone jack, if one is needed. In addition, the location should have enough room for ventilation and not be in direct sunlight.

After your system is up and running, be sure to make a *boot disk* or *startup disk* so your PC can be started up if there is ever a problem with your operating system setup or your hard drive. Most operating systems have an option in the Control Panel (such as under the Add/Remove Programs option in some versions of Windows) to create the disk for you.

1. Unpack all components and locate the installation guide to refer to during the setup process.

2. Plug in all cables (for the monitor, mouse, keyboard, printer, speakers, etc.) into the appropriate port on the system unit. For speakers, usually just one speaker is connected to the system unit; the second speaker connects directly to the first speaker. For conventional modems, the cord from the telephone wall jack is plugged into the appropriate jack on the system unit; the second telephone jack can be used for a telephone, if desired.

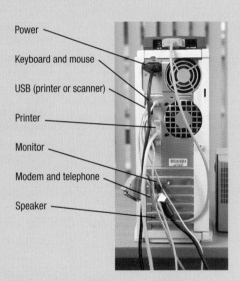

Power
Keyboard and mouse
USB (printer or scanner)
Printer
Monitor
Modem and telephone
Speaker

3. Plug all power cords (for the system unit, monitor, printer, scanner, powered subwoofer, etc.) into a surge suppressor, then turn the power on.

4. Turn on the power to the system unit and monitor and wait for the PC to boot up.

5. Be sure to make a boot disk and back up any application software that was preinstalled on your PC but not supplied on disc. You can then customize your desktop, set up your Internet connection, and have fun!

Adding Additional Hardware

Historically, users have not had an easy time installing new equipment on their computers. The cover of the system unit had to be carefully taken off and an expansion card inserted correctly. Then the device driver software had to be correctly installed. From start to finish, the process was time consuming and stressful. Something could easily go wrong—a circuit could get damaged, the expansion card could crack, or the new hardware might not be compatible with other hardware in the system. When a problem cropped up, users wasted hours trying to figure out what was causing it.

Fortunately, the scenario just described is gradually disappearing. A great deal of hardware today uses a USB port, which doesn't involve opening up the system unit and can connect an enormous number of devices (using a USB hub, if needed), so there is always an available port on the PC. The *plug-and-play* approach has also helped make it easier than ever for PC owners to install hardware on their own. With plug-and-play, theoretically all users of such systems need only plug in any new equipment into the system unit (with the power to the computer turned off, unless it's a USB or Firewire device, as discussed in Chapter 5), and then they're almost ready to go. When the computer is turned back on after installing the new hardware, the operating system recognizes the new device and automatically locates and installs the proper driver for it. If the operating system does not have the appropriate driver, it requests that the user insert the installation disk or CD that came with the device. In actuality, sometimes plug-and-play doesn't work this ideally, though it is a big improvement over past situations. If a newly installed device isn't recognized for some reason, it can be installed via the Windows Control Panel, or similar operating system feature.

Installing Additional Software

Generally, software of any type is relatively easy to install today. When you buy a new program, the package usually contains one or more installation disks or CDs. To install the program, you insert the first of the disks into the proper drive and, if instructed, enter a command (most installation programs on CDs start automatically without needing any typed commands). Then it's just a matter of following a set of usually straightforward instructions on the screen. In most cases, there is very little you have to do beyond entering some identifying information about yourself and specifying the location on your hard drive where the new program should be installed, if you don't want to use the default location.

Sometimes, the type of installation you would like to do, such as a typical install or a custom install, can be selected. A *typical install* places most of the files you need onto your hard disk in the default location. A *custom install* enables you to select such options as the location where the program will be installed, whether or not to keep older versions of the program, which optional components to install, whether to run the program or optional components from the CD, and so forth. Recent versions of Microsoft Office, for example, require about 250 MB of hard-disk space for a typical install, whereas a custom install can require significantly more or less, depending on the programs and options installed.

In addition to installing any additional software that was purchased separately from the system, some users may need to install software to set up their Internet connection. Some PCs come with preinstalled installation programs for various ISPs with icons conveniently located on the desktop; an installation CD can frequently be ordered for other ISPs. Still others may just require certain operating system components (such as dial-up networking or Internet connection sharing software) to be installed from the operating system CD. Setting up an Internet connection was discussed in detail in Chapter 9.

Customizing a New System

A final, but optional, step in setting up your new system is customizing the settings. Most PCs include options for background images, color schemes, themes, screen savers, screen resolution, the order of items on the menus, and so forth. In Windows, the desktop options are accessible through the Control Panel, as shown in Figure 16-7. You can also use the Control Panel to set up your network and Internet settings.

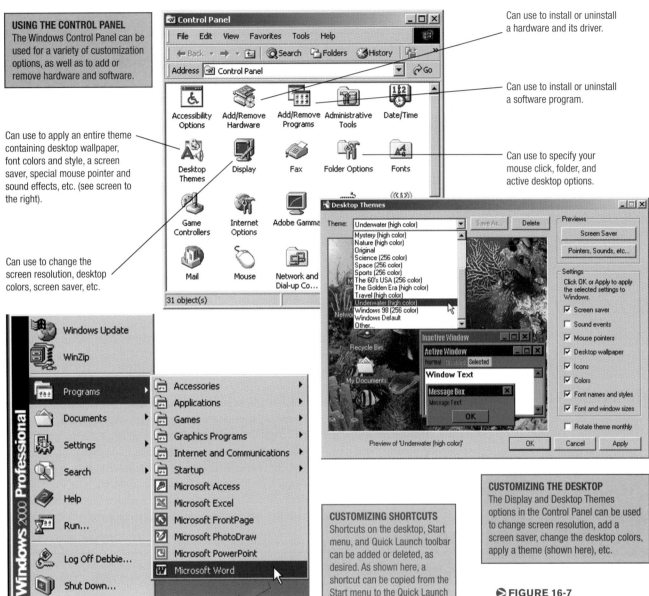

Can use to install or uninstall a hardware and its driver.

Can use to install or uninstall a software program.

Can use to apply an entire theme containing desktop wallpaper, font colors and style, a screen saver, special mouse pointer and sound effects, etc. (see screen to the right).

Can use to specify your mouse click, folder, and active desktop options.

Can use to change the screen resolution, desktop colors, screen saver, etc.

CUSTOMIZING SHORTCUTS
Shortcuts on the desktop, Start menu, and Quick Launch toolbar can be added or deleted, as desired. As shown here, a shortcut can be copied from the Start menu to the Quick Launch toolbar by dragging.

CUSTOMIZING THE DESKTOP
The Display and Desktop Themes options in the Control Panel can be used to change screen resolution, add a screen saver, change the desktop colors, apply a theme (shown here), etc.

▶ **FIGURE 16-7**
Customizing your PC. In Windows, you can specify the display options and folder options that you prefer using the Control Panel, as well as rearrange the desktop, menu, and Quick Launch toolbar shortcuts, as desired.

As shown in the bottom part of Figure 16-7, the shortcut items on the desktop, menu, and Quick Launch toolbars can also be customized. You can drag these menu items around, as desired, to move them or make new shortcuts in new locations. To delete an item, right-click on it and select the Delete option.

SYSTEM MAINTENANCE

Once you acquire a PC, you should develop a set of careful practices to protect your software, hardware, and data from damage and costly mistakes. Three important areas in this regard are system *backup,* maintenance and protection of hardware, and problem detection and correction.

web tutor

For a tutorial on maintaining your PC, go to www.course.com/ parker2002/ch16

Backup Procedures

Virtually every computer veteran will warn you that, sooner or later, you will lose some critical files. Maybe a storm will knock down power lines, erasing the document you're creating in RAM. Perhaps a small brownout will cause the heads on your hard disk to drop out of orbit and crash onto the disk surface, carving a miniature canyon through the electronic version of a 45-page term paper that's due tomorrow. Or, more likely, you'll accidentally delete or overwrite an important file or the file just won't open properly anymore. Computer veterans will also tell you that file losses always seem to happen at the worst possible times—perhaps because when we're tired, stressed, or overworked, we are more likely to make a mistake such as deleting or overwriting a file.

Fortunately, there is a solution to most of these problems—backing up important data and programs. Creating a **backup** means making a duplicate copy of any file you can't afford to lose so that when a problem occurs, you're confronted with only a minor irritant rather than an outright catastrophe. Theoretically, you can back up any file on your computer system. The backups you create—by copying individual files or the contents of an entire drive—can be on a regular or superfloppy disk, removable hard disk, recordable CD, tape, or virtually any other removable storage medium. The backup copy should then be stored in a different physical location (or a fire-resistant safe) to protect against loss due to a fire or natural disaster. A variety of accidents that can destroy programs and data—all of them good reasons to back up data stored on disk—are listed in Figure 16-8.

One practice that everyone should follow is frequently saving to disk a long file that is being developed in RAM (essentially creating a backup of the RAM contents). For example, suppose you are word processing a paper for a class. About every five minutes or so you should make sure that you save the current version of the document onto the hard disk or whatever storage medium you are using. Each time you save the document, the older version on the disk is overwritten with the newer version. If something happens later during the session, the most you will have lost would be five minutes of work. After completing the document and saving the final version, it can then be backed up on another medium, if desired.

For backing up several files at the same time, many different strategies exist. Some users perform *full backups,* storing all files from their hard disks onto tapes or disks at the end of a day or a week. The advantage to a full backup is that it is relatively straightforward. On the downside, a full backup takes up more storage space and takes longer than a backup

◢ FIGURE 16-8

Reasons for file backup.

Why back up?

- A disk sector goes bad, destroying part of a file.
- A file that you thought you no longer had a need for and erased turns out to be important.
- You modify a file in an undesirable way, and the damage done is irreversible.
- You accidentally reformat a disk containing an important document.
- The disk suffers a head crash.
- A power brownout or failure at the time of saving a file causes "garbage" to be saved.
- You save a file to the wrong folder, overwriting a different file that has the same name.
- While rushing your work, you make a mistake that causes the wrong files to be erased.
- You unwittingly destroy a file while working on it—such as by deleting parts of it erroneously and then saving the file.
- Malfunctioning hardware or software causes files to be erased or destroyed.
- A computer virus enters your system and destroys files.
- Your disk is physically destroyed—for instance, a diskette is left in the sun or the hard disk is given a jolt. Alternatively, a fire or flood may destroy the PC.
- Someone steals your diskette or computer.

>**Backup.** A procedure that produces a duplicate version of files on a computer in case the original version is destroyed.

in which only selected files are targeted for copying. An alternative to the full backup is a *partial backup* in which you copy only the files that you have created or altered since the last backup.

When doing either a full or partial backup, users may choose to back up only document files, since program files could be reinstalled from the original installation disks, if needed. Instead of backing up all document files, some individuals choose just to back up the most important documents. These are usually backed up as they are finished, or at regular intervals for long, ongoing projects. The folder containing an individual's e-mail Inbox should also be backed up for those individuals with important e-mail messages that they can't afford to lose. Though individuals vary widely on when (or if) they backup their data, businesses should perform backups on a regular basis—many perform a full backup every night. Using a backup program was illustrated in Figure 6-17 in Chapter 6.

Equipment Maintenance and Protection

PCs consist of sensitive electronic devices, so users must treat them with appropriate care. In this section we discuss protecting your computer system with a surge suppressor or UPS unit; caring for disks; protecting your computer system from dust, heat, and static; and protecting your PC from damage or theft.

Surge Suppression

One of the best devices to have on your computer system to minimize the chance of unexpected damage is a surge suppressor. A **surge suppressor,** which is installed between your computer system and the electrical outlet being used to provide power to the PC, is a hardware device that prevents random electrical power spikes from impacting your system (see Figure 16-9). All components connected to the PC that require power (powered speakers, printer, scanner, etc.) should be plugged into a surge suppressor.

Probably the most common problem caused by a spike is loss of data in RAM. Cases have also been reported, however, of loss of data stored on disk and destruction of equipment, so it's important to realize that a surge suppressor cannot fully guarantee complete electrical protection. If lightning strikes your house, a surge suppressor will probably fail to protect your data or equipment, though some surge protectors do claim to be able to withstand a direct lightning hit. To be on the safe side, if you are working on your computer system when an electrical storm hits, you should save to disk what you've been working on and turn off your PC. You should also turn off the power to your PC if it is on when a power failure occurs, so it won't go back on until you determine that the power problems have stabilized.

Instead of a plain surge suppressor, some users have an **uninterruptible power supply (UPS)** unit (see Figure 16-10). This device is a surge suppressor with a built-in battery, the latter of which keeps power going to the computer when the main power goes off due to a lightning storm, a brownout, damage to an outside cable, or other reason. UPS units are much more frequently used by businesses than individuals. UPSs designed for the average PC often run for a few minutes without outside power before they have to be recharged; UPSs for larger computers may run for several hours. In either case, it gives the user a chance to save all open documents, back up important files onto a removable storage device, if necessary, and properly shut down the system.

Storage Media Care

User precautions with disks, hard disks, CDs, and DVDs to safeguard any programs and data stored on them. Disks may look like inert slabs of plastic, but they are actually extremely sensitive storage media that work well over time with appropriate care. You should never touch the actual surface of a disk or optical disc. Also, keep magnetic media, such as floppy disks,

⊘ **FIGURE 16-9**
Surge suppression. The system unit and all powered peripheral devices should be plugged into a surge suppressor. The surge suppressor is then plugged into a standard wall outlet, and all of the equipment can typically be turned on or off by a single switch.

>**Surge suppressor.** A device that protects a computer system from random electrical power spikes. >**Uninterruptible power supply (UPS).** A surge suppressor with a built-in battery, the latter of which keeps power going to the computer when the main power goes off.

FIGURE 16-10

Uninterruptible power supply (UPS) units, such as these made by American Power Conversion, use batteries to provide power to a computer system for a limited amount of time during a power failure.

Zip disks, and removable hard drives, away from magnetic objects including stereo speakers. Avoid extreme temperatures (hot or cold) with any storage media.

The most important precaution for a hard disk is placing it in a location where it is not likely to be bumped or subjected to electrical interference. As far as CDs and DVDs go, make sure that the side containing data (usually the bottom, unprinted side for a one-sided disc) remains free of dirt, fingerprints, and scratches, all of which may impair laser reading. Keep the discs in their storage cases when not in use.

Dust, Heat, and Static

Each of the tiny processors and memory chips in your hardware units are packed tightly with thousands or millions of circuits. Dust particles circulating in the air can settle on a chip, causing a short circuit. Some people and businesses use dust covers that fit snugly over each of their hardware devices when the computer is turned off to prevent foreign particles in the air from causing hardware failure. For those users who leave their PCs on all the time, try to avoid placing the PC in a dusty area; small handheld vacuums made for electrical equipment can be used periodically to remove the dust from the keyboard and inside the system unit.

Desktop and tower system units also generate lots of heat and require cooling fans. When placing your system unit on a desktop or on the floor, make sure it is in a place where the ventilation is adequate, especially around the fan outlet.

Static electricity is especially dangerous because it can damage chips, destroy programs and data in storage, or disable your keyboard. If you have a lot of static electricity at your location, you might consider buying an antistatic mat for under your workstation chair or an antistatic pad to put under your keyboard so that the electrical discharges from your fingertips don't get transferred to your PC. Static electricity is more likely in dry areas and in the wintertime, when there's less humidity in the air. To discharge the static electricity from your fingers before touching any components inside the system unit when installing or removing a component, most experts recommend first turning off the PC and unplugging the PC, then removing the cover, and then touching the outside of the power supply module inside the system unit before touching any other components. An antistatic wristband can be used as an extra precaution.

Security

Security refers to protecting a computer system's hardware, software, and data from unintentional damage, malicious damage, or any type of tampering. Ways of protecting a computer system from hackers and other security violations were discussed in previous chapters. There are also many ways to physically secure a computer system, including locks on doors, lockplates on equipment, and protecting access to your computer with a *screen saver password,* as shown in Figure 16-11.

No matter what type of security strategy you decide to go with, it is important to realize that no strategy can give you 100 percent protection. Nonetheless, giving a little thought to some of the things that can go wrong and taking a few simple precautions can save you big headaches later on.

Troubleshooting and Technical Assistance

If you work with computers for any length of time, at some point you will probably have an experience when your hardware or software does not work properly. You may turn on your

>**Security.** A collection of measures for protecting a computer system's hardware, software, and data from damage or tampering.

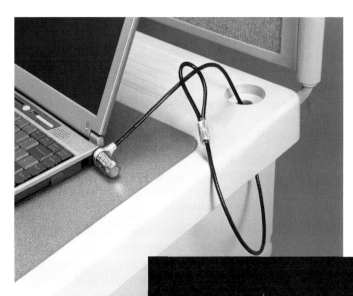

LOCKS
Computer locks are available to secure both desktop and notebook computer to desks or tables.

FIGURE 16-11
Securing your PC.

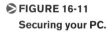

SCREEN SAVER PASSWORDS
Screen saver passwords can be used to prevent anyone from using your computer or looking at the contents of your screen while you are away from your desk.

computer system one day and get no response. Perhaps your screen will begin flickering badly every few seconds. Or maybe you will issue a familiar command in a software package that you work with regularly and the keyboard will lock up or the command will remain unexecuted. When such an event takes place, you will need to troubleshoot to isolate the underlying problem. If the problem is serious enough, assistance from an outside source may be necessary.

Troubleshooting

Troubleshooting refers to actions taken to diagnose or solve a problem. Unfortunately, many problems are unique to specific types of hardware and software, so no simple troubleshooting remedy works all of the time. Nonetheless, the following simple steps and guidelines can help you to identify and correct a number of common problems.

▼ Try again. A surprising number of procedures work when you try a second or third time. You may have pressed the wrong keys the first time, not pressed the keys hard enough, or have a special function turned on (such as by accidentally pressing the Caps Lock, Num Lock, or Insert key on the keyboard). If you've accidentally turned on such a function by accident, pressing the key again should turn the feature off and correct the problem.

▼ Check to see that all the equipment is plugged in and turned on and that none of the cables are detached or loose.

▼ Reboot the system. Many software problems are corrected after the computer is restarted and the program is opened again. Some operating systems—such as Windows—will also try to reconfigure problem devices when the system is restarted, as well as give you the option of temporarily disabling certain devices if your system crashed, to help you determine the problem device. If for some reason the system doesn't boot at all, use your system startup disk (most systems either come with one or suggest you make one using a system option and keep it in a safe place).

▼ Recall exactly what happened between the time the system was operating properly and the time you began to encounter problems. You may have just deleted a large group of files or programs and possibly deleted a part of the systems software by accident. Or perhaps you installed a new piece of hardware or software during your last session, and it is affecting the way your current application works.

▼ Be observant. If strange noises came out of the disk drives when you unsuccessfully tried to boot the system up, those noises might be important. Even though solving the problem may be beyond your capabilities, you may be able to supply important facts to the people who will assist you in getting your system up and running again.

▼ Check the **documentation,** or descriptive instructions, that came with the system. Many products come with a hard-copy manual with a troubleshooting checklist; software programs usually have an online help feature that can help you solve many of your own problems.

▼ Use diagnostic software. *Diagnostic software* (discussed in Chapter 6 and illustrated in Figure 6-16) enables you to test your system to see if parts of it are malfunctioning or are just giving you poor performance. Sometimes, when new equipment is added, problems arise with existing equipment or software. Also, hard disks can get fragmented with use over time (refer to Figure 6-18) and may need to be sped up with defragmentation software.

You should weigh the time that it takes to solve a problem yourself against the cost of outside help. It's not a personal failure to give up if the problem is more than you can handle. It is simply an admission that your time is valuable and that you are wise enough to know when to call in a professional for assistance.

Technical Assistance with Hardware and Software

One of the most important items in working with hardware or software products is getting technical assistance when you need it. Three such sources of assistance are discussed next.

The Manufacturer

One of the best prospects for support is turning to the company that made the hardware or software with which you are working. Probably nobody knows more about correcting problems than the people who may have created the device or program in the first place. It's that very thought that often leads people to contact the hardware manufacturer or software publisher first whenever something bad happens.

Many manufacturers provide toll-free phone numbers, fax numbers, e-mail addresses, and Web sites for users to contact to get help with technical problems. To reach others, you will have to make a toll call or, worse yet, dial a 900 number where you get charged by the minute. Some vendors are notorious for keeping users on hold. If you can't get through on the regular technical support line and are in a hurry to get your problem fixed, check to see if some type of premium service is available where you can get a faster and perhaps higher level of response. Also check if phone support is still covered under your system warranty.

>**Documentation.** A description of how a program, procedure, or system works.

FIGURE 16-12

Web-based technical
support. Gateway's Web
site provides a wide variety of
customer support, such as
product technical information,
driver downloads, and tutorials, as well as a variety of
contact options, such as chat,
e-mail, faxable documents,
and telephone.

With the cost of support escalating, hardware and software makers are increasingly devising more ways to provide assistance over the Web (see Figure 16-12). IBM, for example, has placed a vast storehouse of technical-support knowledge on the Web that used to be available only to its support staff. Other systems, such as Intel's Troubleshooting Assistant, include interactive wizard-type screens to help you locate the appropriate information. Gateway offers an automatic driver update utility, in addition to its other support options. Some Web sites include a feature to have a technician call or e-mail you if you are unable to find the solution using their Web resources. Others have certain times you can join in a live chat session with a technician. Commonly, software manufacturers place *patches*—small software program updates that correct known bugs in the program—on their Web sites. These patches can usually be downloaded for free and easily installed.

Third-Party Support

Products are sometimes supported through third-party firms that specialize in giving assistance. You can contact one of these firms yourself, or you may be put in touch with them by a hardware or software maker. Many of the latter, incidentally, do not have in-house technical support groups but outsource customer support to third-party firms.

Third-party firms often have toll-free or 900 telephone numbers that you call to get help. In the case of the 900 numbers, many firms cap charges at a limit—often $25 or $50— so your bill doesn't become outrageous. When dealing with anyone who charges for support, check to see if any follow-up calls you make once a problem is theoretically corrected will incur an additional charge. There are also third-party support Web sites that offer free or paid support. For a list of these sites, search for "free technical support" on a search site or visit a site such as www.techsupportalert.com, which contains information about and links to a large number of third-party support sites. Some of the paid support sites have a group of technicians who bid a price to answer your question.

User Support

If you don't know anyone personally who can give you help, take solace in the fact that many users post problems on Internet discussion groups. To find an appropriate group, check the manufacturer's Web site to see if it has a link to a discussion group for the product in question, or locate an appropriate group from a third-party technical support Web site. The message you post might be read by literally hundreds of other users, and there's a good

further exploration

For links to further information about technical support sites, go to www.course.com/parker2002/ch16

possibility that someone out there has encountered and solved the problem you are now wrestling with. While you may get the answer you are seeking without paying a dime, don't be surprised if you have to wait for a few days or more to have your plea for help read by the right person.

With the more widely used products, you may also find formal user groups. As discussed more later in this chapter, *user groups* enable you to meet other users in person and to talk about common problems and creative ways to use the hardware or software.

Equipment Repairs

In some cases, a problem is so simple that no equipment repair is necessary. When a repair is necessary that is beyond the scope of your capabilities, however, you will need to seek professional help. Likely sources of such help are the party that sold you the problematic hardware, computer stores in your area, and computer repair technicians listed in the Yellow Pages of your local phone book.

Keep the following questions in mind when asking someone else to diagnose or repair your system:

▼ Is it better to repair old equipment or to buy new equipment? For example, if the estimated repairs are more than a few hundred dollars, it may be cheaper to buy a replacement for the problematic component. For older systems, it may be cheaper in the long run to replace the entire system, depending on the type of problem and the expense of getting it repaired.

▼ Will the repair work be done under **warranty**? Most new equipment is sold with a warranty stating that the manufacturer will pay for certain repairs if the equipment fails within a given number of days or months after purchase. If the warranty hasn't expired, the repair may cost you nothing (except possibly return shipping of the bad part for PCs purchased via mail order or over the Internet). Be aware that many manufacturers state in their warranties that the warranties become void if you attempt to repair the equipment yourself or if a repair is attempted by an unauthorized person or shop.

▼ Can you get an estimate before proceeding with the work? In many cases, repair technicians can provide a free estimate of what the repair will cost. If they can't, you might want them to diagnose the problem first and to call you when they are able to provide an estimate. You never, ever want to put yourself in a situation in which you are presented with an unexpected, outrageously expensive repair bill.

▼ Is priority service available? People who use their computers as part of their jobs often need repairs immediately. Many repair shops realize this and provide same-day or next-day turnaround for an extra fee. Some will even loan you equipment while repairs are being made.

When you buy a computer system, you can often choose to buy an extended maintenance contract to cover certain repairs beyond those stated in the warranty, though often these are not worth the expense involved. Regardless of whether or not an extended warranty or maintenance contract is purchased, be sure your warranty clearly states the length of time the product is covered for both parts and labor, any additional time that parts are covered, and where the service will take place (such as on site, at a local store, or by mail to the manufacturer).

>**Warranty.** A conditional pledge made by the manufacturer of a product to protect consumers from losses due to defective products.

UPGRADING

Hardware and software generally need to be upgraded over time. **Upgrading** a computer system means buying new hardware or software components that extend the life of your current system. The question you must ask when considering an upgrade is the same one that you would ask when considering costly repairs to a car: Should I spend this money on my current system or start fresh and buy a completely new system?

When you acquire a new PC, it is important to formulate an upgrade strategy. Ideally, you should buy a PC that adheres to a well-supported standard. This and other considerations, such as making sure there is room for additional expansion cards, storage devices, and memory, will give you flexibility to upgrade it to meet reasonable future needs over the course of its lifetime. Of course, you cannot anticipate all your future needs, but you invite unnecessary and expensive upgrades later on by spending no time thinking about system growth.

web tutor

For a tutorial on upgrading your PC, go to www.course.com/parker2002/ch16

Functional vs. Technological Obsolescence

As suggested in earlier paragraphs, PC products can serve user needs for several years before they must be replaced. A product becomes **functionally obsolete** when it no longer meets the needs of an individual or business. Functionally obsolete products should be upgraded or replaced. Improvements to hardware and software products are continuous, however, and often a product is replaced in stores with a newer version or release well before it is functionally obsolete. A product in this latter class is said to be **technologically obsolete.** Technologically obsolete systems do not need to be upgraded or replaced until they are also functionally obsolete.

How long a computer will last before it becomes functionally obsolete depends on a number of factors, such as what features were included in the system when it was purchased and what applications the computer is being used for. Many businesses plan on replacing their PCs about every two or three years; home PCs typically last significantly longer before they need to be replaced.

In upgrading, a common problem is that users believe the product they are using is functionally obsolete when it is merely technologically obsolete. Because of the rapid pace of technology, virtually anyone buying a computer system today will have at least one technologically obsolete component within a matter of months. What's more, it's often smart not to jump into a new version of a product immediately but instead to wait for the initial bugs in it to be fixed.

The term **legacy system** is often used for technologically obsolete products. Most companies have a variety of legacy systems on their hands today, and many of these systems are capable of years of further use before they have to be replaced.

Upgrading Hardware

Some common hardware upgrades include adding more RAM or an additional storage device to a system, installing a faster modem or additional memory, adding expansion boards to provide new types of functionality, and adding new peripheral equipment such as an image scanner or color printer. Unless your system is powerful enough to handle growth, many upgrades are not possible. For example, if you have the old Intel 80486-based processor and you want to do a serious upgrade, you should just purchase a new

---

>**Upgrading.** The process of buying new hardware or software to add capabilities and extend the life of a computer system. >**Functionally obsolete.** A term that refers to a product that no longer meets the needs of an individual or business. >**Technologically obsolete.** A term that refers to a product that still meets the needs of an individual or business, although a newer model, version, or release is available. >**Legacy system.** A system that is technologically obsolete.

PC, since you can't bring a 486 computer up to the level of today's desktop computers without replacing the motherboard and virtually every other item inside the system unit. The same situation may apply if you have a tiny hard drive and a very small amount of memory. With some new PCs selling for $500 or less, it may cost less to buy an entirely new machine that meets your new requirements than to perform a major upgrade to a low-end PC.

Today, some PCs sold in the marketplace are touted as *upgradable PCs.* These devices are designed with modest and predefined types of replacement in mind, making it possible to swap out components like the CPU chip as more powerful ones become available.

Upgrading Software

Many PC software vendors enhance their products in some major way every year or two, prompting users to upgrade. Each upgrade—called a **version**—is assigned a number, such as 1.0, 2.0, 3.0, and so on. The higher the number, the more recent and more powerful the software is. Minor versions, called **releases,** typically increase their numbers in increments of 0.1—such as 1.1, 1.2, and 1.3—or .01. For example. release 3.11 might follow release 3.1, and release 7.1 might follow 7.0. Releases are usually issued in response to bugs or shortcomings in the version and are often free. Recently, the versions and releases of many software products began being assigned numbers that correspond exactly or approximately to the year of issue—such as Office 97 (for the 1997 version of Microsoft Office) and Office 2000 (for the 2000 version, which actually came out in 1999). Others, such as Windows XP and Office XP, are given names instead.

With the increased use of the Internet, many software companies are making upgrades available to users as free downloads. Like the patch programs discussed earlier, between official versions and releases of a product you may be able to take advantage of free enhancements for only the effort it takes to download them.

Virtually all software products tend to be *upward compatible.* This means that applications developed on earlier versions or releases of the software also work on later versions or releases. *Downward compatibility* is also possible, though often the files need converting to the lower version format. For example, WordPerfect 9 enables users to save files in either WordPerfect 9 or any of several earlier formats, such as the once-popular WordPerfect 6.1. All of the latest versions of Microsoft Office use the same file format, so that documents created in any version of Word can be opened in any other version of Word. *Cross compatibility* is also widely found today. This feature enables you to open documents in one program (such as Microsoft Word) that were created in a different program (such as WordPerfect). When translating documents from one vendor's software format to another, you should be aware that certain details can get lost in the translation. For example, sometimes bold-facing and italicizing may not be picked up. Another possibility is using a nonproprietary format, such as *RTF* (*rich text format*), *PDF* (*portable document format*), or *HTML* (*hypertext markup language*).

Generally, software upgrades are offered to current users at a lower price than buying a new complete package of the program to make the upgrade more attractive. The potential user has to weigh the benefits of changing to the new version against its costs. The costs include the sticker price of the software, additional training, setting up new standards for use, and, possibly, equipment upgrades due to the increased requirements of the software. Each version of a software product is virtually guaranteed to be more sophisticated and complex than the previous one, which may result in needing more RAM, hard drive space, and a faster processor.

LEARNING MORE ABOUT PCS

A wide range of resources fulfill the needs of those who want to learn more about PCs and their uses. There are a variety of sources of this type of information that can be obtained in person, in print, through videos or television, or via the Web.

In Person

Some resources you can access in person include computer classes, computer clubs, and computer shows.

Computer Classes

A good way to learn any subject is to take an appropriate class. Many four-year colleges, universities, and community colleges offer PC-oriented courses for undergraduate, graduate, and continuing education students. Your local computer stores and Internet-enabled coffeehouses (cybercafés) may also organize classes. Some stores provide classroom support as part of system purchases.

Computer Clubs and User Groups

Computer clubs—sometimes called user groups—are an effective way to get an informal education in computers. They are also a good place to get a relatively unbiased and knowledgeable viewpoint about a particular product or vendor. Generally clubs are organized by region, product line, or common interests. For example, Apple computer enthusiasts join clubs such as Apple-Holics, Apple Pie, or Apple Core. Many clubs also function as buying groups, obtaining software or hardware for members at reduced rates. Computer clubs range in size from two or three members to several thousand.

Computer Shows

A computer show gives you a firsthand look at leading-edge hardware and software products. Such shows typically feature numerous vendor exhibits as well as seminars on various aspects of computing. Every November, Las Vegas hosts one of the largest trade fairs in the world, the Computer Dealer Expo (COMDEX) show (see Figure 16-13). This weeklong event commonly attracts hundreds of vendors and around 200,000 visitors, many of them from foreign countries. COMDEX is a spectacular event; the number of COMDEX shows worldwide has grown to at least 20 per year. For those individuals that prefer smaller, more specialized shows, local computer shows are frequently offered in larger cities.

FIGURE 16-13

Computer shows. The weeklong Computer Dealer Expo (COMDEX) in Las Vegas attracts hundreds of thousands of enthusiasts from around the world. There are smaller weekend shows held in many other cities about once a year.

In Print
Print resources include a variety of periodicals and books.

Periodicals
Periodicals (newspapers, magazines, and journals) are a good source of information about PCs. Scores of them fill newsstands, collectively catering to virtually every conceivable interest area. You can generally browse through a variety of computer-related publications at your local bookstore, computer store, and public or school library; many are also available in online versions on the Web. Online periodicals have the advantage of enabling users to electronically search for information on specified topics and often giving users access to back issues.

Books
One of the best ways to learn about any aspect of personal computing is to read a book on the subject. A host of books are available, covering topics ranging from the simple to the highly sophisticated. Included are how-to books on subjects such as using the more widely known productivity software packages, programming in PC-based languages, creating Web sites, and the technical fundamentals of PCs. You can find such books in your local library, computer stores, and bookstores. Some books are also published on the World Wide Web. Always check the copyright date of a book before you use it; computer technology moves along rapidly, and books in the field can go out of date just as fast.

Videos or TV Shows
One easy way to learn a subject in our electronic age is to pick up a training videotape or watch a television show devoted to the subject. Today, videotapes are plentiful for basic computer literacy, as well as for demonstrating how to use specific software programs. In addition, many television shows—especially on public television, cable, and satellite—are oriented to computer education and knowledge.

On the Web
The World Wide Web is a veritable treasure trove for all sorts of free information about computers. Sources include news and technology sites, manufacturer sites, and educational sites. You may also be able to gain information via newsgroups, e-mail, and chat.

News and Technology Sites

further exploration

For links to further information about PC news and reviews, go to www.course.com/parker2002/ch16

There are a large number of sites that feature computer-related news and information. One of the largest is CNET.com, shown in Figure 16-14. Other good sites include the technology sections of the CNN and MSNBC news sites, as well as online computer journals, such as *PC World* and *Smart Business*. In addition to technology news, these sites often contain downloads and product reviews. Some Web sites not affiliated with any particular manufacturer or news organization can also offer valuable information about a particular area of technology. One example is Tom's Hardware Guide (www.tomshardware.com), which features news, reviews, and technical information about a wide range of hardware products.

Manufacturer Sites
As already discussed, you can often get information about specific products and technologies from manufacturers' Web sites. Many sites include specifications for products you may wish to purchase, as well as technical support for products you already own. Still other sites include information about the particular technology used in their products and how it works.

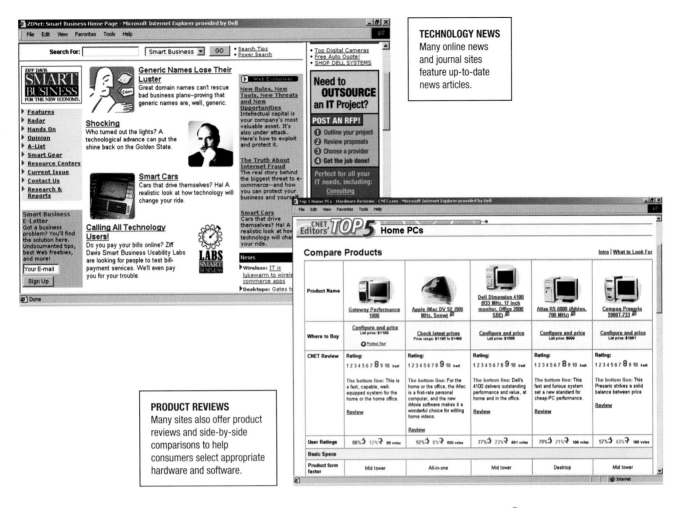

TECHNOLOGY NEWS
Many online news and journal sites feature up-to-date news articles.

PRODUCT REVIEWS
Many sites also offer product reviews and side-by-side comparisons to help consumers select appropriate hardware and software.

Educational Sites

Educational sites include sites that accompany college courses, sites sponsored by nonprofit organizations, and educational sites provided by the government. Some of these sites feature free online tutorials and demonstrations.

Newsgroups, E-Mail, and Chat

If you can't find the information you are looking for on a Web site, you may need to turn to newsgroups, e-mail, or chat to get the information from another individual. As previously discussed, many manufacturers sponsor these services for their customers. Other possibilities include public newsgroups about a particular type of product or technology.

▶ **FIGURE 16-14**

Learning about computers on the Web. Scores of useful Web sites provide news items and articles about computers. Many are either online computer journals or news sites and frequently include product reviews, as well as current technology news.

Chapter 16 covers such related activities as users acquiring their own computer systems, maintaining and upgrading their PC, and educating themselves about PCs.

PC SYSTEM COMPONENTS

Chapter Objective 1:
Identify the key components of a computer system to be acquired and discuss some factors to keep in mind when you are deciding on the type of system needed.

Whether acquiring a PC for home or business use, it is important to be familiar with the various manufacturers of the important components of a PC system, such as the monitor, printer, CPU, and other hardware. The PC marketplace is composed of a wide variety of firms that make hardware and software products.

SELECTING A PC SYSTEM

Chapter Objective 2:
List several alternatives for acquiring PC products.

Steps for selecting a computer system include analyzing needs, listing system alternatives, evaluating alternatives, and choosing a system. When selecting a PC system, a business or individual should first analyze its needs to identify exactly what the PC is needed for. That helps determine the application software to be used, and then the desired operating system, platform, and system configuration can be selected. Selecting PC components is often a balance between features a user might like to have and the amount of money he or she is willing to spend.

Most users get their hardware and software products from computer stores or other retail stores, directly from the manufacturer, from a **value-added reseller (VAR),** or some type of alternative outlets. Many of these businesses exist as both traditional *brick-and-mortar stores,* as well as *online stores.* Some stores may offer a PC discounted or "free" after a rebate of some sort; leasing a computer is another possible option.

SETTING UP A NEW SYSTEM

Chapter Objective 3:
Explain how to select and install a PC for home or office use.

When you buy a computer system today, most of the hardware and software you need will probably already be in place, with the exception of plugging in power cords and the cables to connect the devices. To make it easier than ever for PC owners to install any additional hardware on their own, both hardware and software vendors have moved to a *plug-and-play* approach. Most new hardware can be purchased in USB versions to avoid the problem of not having an available port of the proper type, as well as having to open up the system unit.

Additional software can usually be installed by just inserting the installation CD into the appropriate drive, and custom operating system settings—such as colors, screen savers, menu option, etc.—can be specified as desired.

SYSTEM MAINTENANCE

Chapter Objective 4:
Name some computer maintenance practices designed to protect software, hardware, and data resources from damage.

Typical system maintenance activities include system backup, hardware maintenance and protection, and problem detection and correction. **Backup** refers to procedures for making duplicate copies of valuable files. Two types of backup methods are *full backup* and *partial backup.* Backup files should optimally be stored in a different physical location than the PC.

PCs contain sensitive electronic devices, so they need careful treatment and protection from damage. A **surge suppressor** prevents most random electrical spikes from entering your system and causing damage. An **uninterruptible power supply (UPS)** unit lets you operate your computer when the main power to your home or office fails. Your disks and other storage media should also be carefully treated. **Security** measures protect a computer system's hardware, software, and data from unintentional and malicious damage and tampering. Computers can be physically secured with computer locks, and *screen saver passwords* can be used to deter another person from accessing your PC while you are away from your desk.

Although no two problems with a computer system are ever totally alike, some useful guidelines can be followed when *troubleshooting* problems or when seeking outside technical assistance. For example, just trying a procedure a second time or checking the **documentation** that comes with a product often solves the problem. Three sources of technical assistance are support from the manufacturer, third-party support, and user support. This support is typically offered over the telephone or Web. When considering an equipment repair, you should check first to see what protection the manufacturer offers under **warranty.**

Chapter Objective 5:
List some important guidelines for troubleshooting problems and seeking assistance.

UPGRADING

You can **upgrade** your computer system by buying new hardware or software components that add capabilities and extend its useful life. When planning a hardware upgrade, you must consider such things as your current system's storage capacity, the number of expansion slots, and the power of the system unit. You need to ask yourself whether upgrading is better than starting fresh and buying a new computer system. You also must consider whether you are planning to replace a product that's only **technologically obsolete** instead of **functionally obsolete.** Technologically obsolete systems are sometimes called **legacy systems** and do not have to be replaced until they become functionally obsolete. Software upgrades are often accomplished by acquiring a new **release** or **version** of the program that you are currently using.

Chapter Objective 6:
Describe some of the ways to upgrade a PC and explain the conditions that prompt an upgrade.

LEARNING MORE ABOUT PCS

A wealth of resources is available to those who want to learn more about PCs and their uses. Classes, computer clubs, computer shows, magazines, newspapers, books, and videos or TV shows are all sources of information about PCs. The Web hosts a wide variety of resources, including news and technology sites, newsgroups, and information from manufacturers.

Chapter Objective 7:
Name several sources for learning more about PCs.

Instructions: Match each key term on the left with the definition on the right that fits best.

1. backup

2. documentation

3. functionally obsolete

4. legacy system

5. release

6. security

7. surge suppressor

8. technologically obsolete

9. uninterruptible power supply (UPS)

10. upgrading

11. value-added reseller (VAR)

12. version

13. warranty

_____ A term that refers to a product that no longer meets the needs of an individual or business.

_____ A collection of measures for protecting a computer system's hardware, software, and data from damage or tampering.

_____ A company that buys hardware and software from others and makes computer systems out of them that are targeted to particular vertical markets.

_____ A conditional pledge made by the manufacturer of a product to protect consumers from losses due to defective products.

_____ A description of how a program, procedure, or system works.

_____ A device that protects a computer system from random electrical power spikes.

_____ A major upgrade of a software product.

_____ A minor upgrade of a software product.

_____ A procedure that produces a duplicate version of files on a computer in case the original version is destroyed.

_____ A surge suppressor with a built-in battery, the latter of which keeps power going to the computer when the main power goes off.

_____ Another name for a system that is technologically obsolete.

_____ A term that refers to a product that still meets the needs of an individual or business, although a newer model, version, or release is available.

_____ The process of buying new hardware or software in order to add capabilities and extend the life of a computer system.

Answers for the self-quiz appear at the end of the book.

True/False

Instructions: Circle **T** if the statement is true or **F** if the statement is false.

T F **1.** Iomega is a popular printer manufacturer.

T F **2.** A fast video card would likely be considered a "need" for a computer artist.

T F **3.** Most PCs come out of the box with all cables connected to the appropriate hardware.

T F **4.** Surge suppressors protect your PC against power fluctuations.

T F **5.** If you buy a USB scanner, you will have to open the system unit and install a USB card in order to connect the scanner to your PC.

Completion

Instructions: Answer the following questions.

6. With a(n) _____ device, you theoretically need only connect a new piece of hardware and your operating system will take care of configuring it for you the next time the PC is turned on.

7. _____ refers to making, for security purposes, a duplicate copy of a file.

8. To prevent your computer from being turned off when the power fails, a(n) _____ can be used.

9. A(n) _____ password can be used to deter others from accessing your PC when you are away from your desk.

10. _____ obsolete equipment should be replaced, whereas _____ obsolete equipment may continue to be used for a while longer.

1. For each description, select the company name that fits best. Note that all companies will not be used.

_____ A large, U.S.-based maker of PC-compatible computers
_____ A manufacturer of primarily storage products
_____ The maker of Windows as well as a wide variety of other software products
_____ A manufacturer of CPU chips for PC-compatible computers
_____ The biggest producer of microcomputers that are not PC-compatible

a. Apple
b. Compaq
c. Corel
d. Intel
e. Microsoft
f. Motorola
g. Seagate

2. For each of the following situations, indicate which type(s) of vendors would be the most appropriate. Choose from computer store or other retailer (R), manufacturer (M), value-added reseller (V), or alternative outlet (A). Note that some situations may match more than one type of vendor.

Situation	Type(s) of Vendor
a. You're nervous about buying a home PC and want to see it before you buy it.	————
b. You want a cheap printer and you don't care if it's technologically obsolete or has a good warranty.	————
c. You just opened a taco restaurant and need a computer system that specializes in fast-food operations.	————
d. You want a system that has your exact desired components.	————

3. Assume your new PC was just delivered. In order, list four steps you need to follow to get it up and running.

4. Assume you are writing a novel that you expect will take three to four months to write. Explain what, if any, backup procedures you think you should adhere to. Be specific with respect to what drives or files should be backed up and how often the procedure will take place.

5. Briefly explain what is meant by the term *legacy system*. Is such a system still useable?

1. **Buying a Desktop PC** The accompanying figure shows an ad for a desktop PC. To demonstrate your knowledge of computer terms and components, answer the following questions.

   a. What types of storage devices come with the PC? What is the capacity of each storage device?

   b. What CPU chip comes with this system? How fast is it? Who makes it?

   c. Is the system PC compatible? What operating system is installed?

   d. Besides the operating system, is any other software included?

   e. Does a printer come with this system? If so, what type is it and who makes it?

   f. What are the available ports on this PC for adding new hardware components? If the needed port isn't available, is there room to add an expansion card?

   g. How much memory comes with the PC? Can more be added?

   h. What options would you have if the DVD drive fails after one year of use?

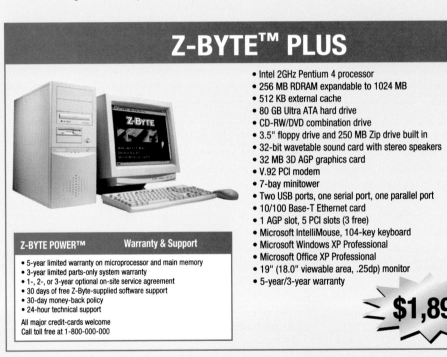

Z-BYTE™ PLUS

- Intel 2GHz Pentium 4 processor
- 256 MB RDRAM expandable to 1024 MB
- 512 KB external cache
- 80 GB Ultra ATA hard drive
- CD-RW/DVD combination drive
- 3.5" floppy drive and 250 MB Zip drive built in
- 32-bit wavetable sound card with stereo speakers
- 32 MB 3D AGP graphics card
- V.92 PCI modem
- 7-bay minitower
- Two USB ports, one serial port, one parallel port
- 10/100 Base-T Ethernet card
- 1 AGP slot, 5 PCI slots (3 free)
- Microsoft IntelliMouse, 104-key keyboard
- Microsoft Windows XP Professional
- Microsoft Office XP Professional
- 19" (18.0" viewable area, .25dp) monitor
- 5-year/3-year warranty

$1,899

Z-BYTE POWER™   **Warranty & Support**

- 5-year limited warranty on microprocessor and main memory
- 3-year limited parts-only system warranty
- 1-, 2-, or 3-year optional on-site service agreement
- 30 days of free Z-Byte-supplied software support
- 30-day money-back policy
- 24-hour technical support

All major credit-cards welcome
Call toll free at 1-800-000-000

2. **"Free" PCs** Not too long ago, PCs cost several thousand dollars and the likelihood of an individual having a home PC was very low. However, you can now get a free PC from one of many major ISPs. How can this be? What's the catch? Is the PC really free when the ad says, "Three years of Internet access and a free PC for just $29.95 monthly"? So what's to keep you from getting the free PC and dropping the Internet service after the first month? For this project, research a free PC advertisement and read the fine print (check the ads in your local paper or visit ISP and consumer electronic store Web sites to get you started). Is the PC really free? Do you have any obligation to the company after receiving the free PC? What type and configuration of PC do you get for free? Would you be interested in getting this free PC? Why, or why not? At the conclusion of your research, prepare a one-page summary of your findings and submit it to your instructor.

3. **School Discounts** Most computer system vendors like Dell, Compaq, Toshiba, Hewlett-Packard, and IBM offer significant discounts to students purchasing their computer systems through a campus bookstore. For this project, visit your campus bookstore and inquire about the purchase

of a computer system. You should determine which systems they sell, the cost of the "standard" systems, how warranty issues are dealt with, and how long it takes to get the computer delivered. If your bookstore does not offer this service, find out if it can facilitate this through another campus' bookstore. At the conclusion of your research, prepare a one-page summary of your findings and submit it to your instructor.

Hands On

4. **A Custom Desktop** Customizing your desktop is a fun and straightforward task. In the process of customizing the desktop you can set a desktop background (one of your photos in digital format or any of several preinstalled images), select a screen saver, select a desktop theme, view your desktop as a Web page, and change your monitor's color and resolution settings. For this project, experiment with your PC's various desktop setting options and determine which settings are most appropriate for you. (Windows users will access these options through the Control Panel.) If you are doing this task on a school computer, be sure to not change the settings permanently; if your instructor indicates temporary changes are permitted, be sure to change them back after experimenting. At the conclusion of this task, prepare a one-page summary of your efforts and submit it to your instructor.

Writing About Computers

5. **Join the Club** There are lots of computer clubs and user groups across the country. Most of these clubs can be located by performing an Internet search. Many of these clubs have online cyber meetings, maintain Web sites with bulletin boards and chatrooms, have newsletters, get involved in local events, and even have elected club officers. For this project, investigate a few of the online and local computer clubs in your area. Do they hold regular meetings? Do they have elected club officers? Do they maintain a Web site with information about events and programs you could get involved in? Are you interested in joining a computer club? Why, or why not? Submit this project to your instructor in the form of a short paper, not more than two pages in length.

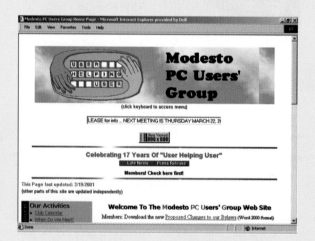

6. **Today's Standard** Most computer manufacturers generally advertise between three and five standard computer configurations, in three or more categories with names such as Home & Home Office, Business, and Government. Within each of these categories, the standard systems are targeted at the low-end user, average user, and high-end user. For this project, visit the Web sites of at least three computer manufacturers (such as Dell, Gateway, and Hewlett-Packard) and compare the standard home system that is targeted at the average user. How do these systems compare in terms of price, speed, memory, storage, included software, and included hardware? Which of these systems do you think is the best deal and why? Are the capabilities of all these systems approximately the same? If so, what do you think would cause a person to choose one system over another? Submit this project to your instructor in the form of a short paper, not more than two pages in length.

7. **The Lease Option** Leasing a computer, as described in the text, is usually more expensive than buying the computer outright, but does have a few advantages. With a lease, you don't have to pay the total cost of the system up front, and you have the flexibility of exchanging the system when it no longer meets your needs. Several click-and-mortar companies, and most of the top-tier computer manufacturers, offer leasing programs. For this project, form a group to investigate computer-leasing programs. Locate and obtain specifications from at least one local store and at least one large computer manufacturer. During the course of your investigation you should identify the types of leases available; what kinds/brands of computer equipment can be leased; the terms of the buyout option, if one exists; what types of upgrades are allowed during the leasing period; what is required to qualify for a lease; and how long the lease process takes. Be sure to compute the total cost of the system for the entire lease period and what equity, if any, you would end up with when the lease expired. After doing the research, would anyone in your group be interested in leasing a computer? Why, or why not? How does the lease option compare to taking out a loan and buying a new system up front? Your group should submit this project to your instructor in the form of a short paper, not more than three pages in length.

8. **Swap Meet Experience** If you have never attended a computer swap meet, you should consider it. It is quite an experience, and it will give you an opportunity to put some of the PC jargon you learned in this class to work. For this project, attend a local computer swap meet or show and prepare a short presentation about your experience. When you visit the swap meet or show, be sure to make some notes about your experience and share them with the class during your presentation. Visit as many booths as possible and ask a lot of questions about which components you should purchase and how to properly configure your system to achieve the best performance. How knowledgeable do the sellers appear? Also check out some of the prices for components; do they seem high, reasonable, or lower than you expected? Look for a low-priced hard drive and question the vendor about why the price is so low. Did he or she give a plausible answer? What types of components were being sold at the swap meet? Would you consider purchasing any components at the swap meet? Why, or why not? This presentation should not exceed five minutes and should make use of one or more presentation aids such as the chalkboard, handouts, overhead transparencies, or computer-based slide presentation format. You may be asked to submit a summary of the presentation to your instructor.

9. **Build-Your-Own** A popular, but not necessarily recommended, option to consider when purchasing a computer system is to build your own PC from individual components you purchase on your own. For this project, form a group to compare the price of two manufacturers' off-the-shelf computers (use reliable vendors like Dell, Compaq, Gateway, or IBM and select comparable systems), and then attempt to determine the cost of putting together a comparable version of the two computers using the build-your-own approach. Your group should be careful to select comparable components in the build-your-own version, so that the capabilities and quality of the three systems are as close as possible. After completing this task, your group should then evaluate the three systems in terms of their cost, warranties, and any other advantages or disadvantages you think are appropriate. What conclusions can you draw from this effort? Do the members in your group think the brand-name computers will be any more stable than the one you could put together? How should the warranty issue be considered between these systems? Is anyone in your group inclined to build his or her own computer? Your group should prepare a presentation of your findings. This presentation should not exceed 10 minutes and should make use of one or more presentation aids such as the chalkboard, handouts, overhead transparencies, or computer-based slide presentation format. Your group may be asked to submit a summary of the presentation to your instructor.

10. **Your Recommendations** In this chapter you learned that it was important to analyze your needs and list the available alternatives as part of the PC-selection process. For this project, form a group to summarize the computing needs of two different group members (make sure the needs won't be too similar), and then research possible systems to meet their needs. Your group should be sure to take into consideration the operating system, application software, platform/configuration options, necessary computing power, and budgetary constraints (for simplicity, assume that one

student has an unlimited source of funds, and the other student has a very limited budget). After reviewing the summarized needs and potential systems, select a recommended system for each of the two students. After that, your group should determine how satisfied the two individuals would be with the group's recommendation. Do any members of the group have a differing opinion about the recommendations made? If so, what is at issue?

This presentation should not exceed 10 minutes and should make use of one or more presentation aids such as the chalkboard, handouts, overhead transparencies, or computer-based slide presentation format. Your group may be asked to submit a summary of the presentation to your instructor.

Interactive Discussion

11. **Do the Ends Justify the Means?** One of the important decisions that should to be assessed in the process of purchasing a computer is whether you will ultimately purchase the computer from a brick-and-mortar, click-and-mortar, or Internet-only company. There are advantage and disadvantages associated with each option, but in the short run you could probably get the best deal by exploiting the knowledge and personal assistance of a brick-and-mortar store, researching the alternative options for a specific brand through a click-and-mortar, and ultimately purchasing the system for the best price from the Internet-only outfit. We have already seen the reverse of this process take place in the auto industry. Investors spent a lot of money setting up elaborate Web sites to assist consumers in the process of purchasing a vehicle and ended up being very disappointed when the consumers exploited the sites for information about the products, options, and pricing, but then returned to their local dealerships to make the actual purchase. In this scenario, the Web sites were exploited and the local auto dealers reaped the profits. In the previous scenario, the brick-and-mortars would be exploited, and the Internet-only companies would reap the profits.

Select one of the following positions, or make up your own, and express your point of view on the subject. Your instructor will indicate whether your response is to be posted to a class bulletin board, discussed in a class chat room, or discussed as an in-class activity. You may also be asked to submit a summary of your position and point of view to your instructor.

a. The markets have their own way of resolving these issues. We as consumers can, and should, make the best use of our options. The fate of local brick-and-mortars is a function of their ability to adapt to the changing business environment, not the allegiance of a few local patrons.

b. Exploiting the knowledge and personal service of a local business, when you know that you will ultimately make the purchase online, is unconscionable. These businesses are part of your local community and are providing you with a service that deserves your patronage.

12. **Faster Is Better** Consider the following statement and establish your position, or point of view, on the subject. Your instructor will indicate whether your response is to be posted to a class bulletin board, discussed in a class chat room, or discussed as an in-class activity. You may also be asked to submit a summary of your position and evaluation of the statement to your instructor.

When purchasing a computer, the clock speed of the microprocessor should not be the primary factor in determining which computer to purchase. Every few months or so the processor speeds make a big jump from, for example, 800 MHz to one gigahertz or more, but this should not cause you to select the system with the faster megahertz rating. In other words, a higher speed does not always mean that you are purchasing a faster computer. Unfortunately, the majority of money spent on advertising the available systems is focused on just the microprocessor, without giving the public a balanced view of the other factors, such as the amount of RAM, bus size, cache, hard drive size and speed, and other included components. Some people have been down this path before and would disagree with this approach. They feel that they can upgrade just about everything but the microprocessor, and believe we should always purchase the machine with the fastest megahertz rating. It might be interesting to note that some computer analysts feel we have now reached a point where the processing speeds of current systems have out-paced the software manufacturers' demands, and we should be willing to trade higher speeds for a lower prices.

Understanding Your PC.   It's time to make sure you're ready to buy a new PC. Go to the Interactive Exercise at www.course.com/parker2002/ch16 to complete this exercise.

Interactive Exercise

OUTLINE

INTRODUCTION

The world of computers is continually changing and evolving. Although the computer concepts covered in the *Understanding Computers 2002* text are still applicable today, there have been some improvements in technology and some new products made available since the *Understanding Computers 2002* edition was published. Bringing you up to date on the latest advances in these areas is the purpose of this enhancement update.

Update 2003 has three main sections. First, a two-page spread for each chapter covers new developments related to content covered in the *Understanding Computers 2002* text, followed by a look at new and emerging trends not covered in that edition. Next, a new Inside the Industry box takes a look at the history of computers, focusing on the characteristics of each computing generation. Update 2003 concludes with a collection of exciting new video projects. These projects, titled Tech News Video Projects, are structured around TechTV news video clips (located on the Online Companion site). As directed by your instructor, you will watch the video clip and then express your opinion on the issue detailed in the video either in class, via an online discussion group or class chat room, or in a written paper.

UPDATE

Some recent changes in overall computer use include the increased use and capabilities of mobile devices and portable PCs, new styles of desktop PCs, and a new world's fastest computer.

Changes in Mobile Devices and Portable PCs

The past year has seen an increased use of mobile devices and portable PCs for personal use, as well as for business and school purposes. New applications designed for these devices and built-in or slip-on keyboards have made both mobile devices and handheld PCs increasingly more practical for day-to-day tasks. In fact, these two types of devices have begun to converge, with many smart phones offering PDA features and some PDAs now including telephone capabilities (see Figure U-1). These *hybrid devices* typically offer features such as scheduling, e-mailing, text messaging, Web browsing, telephoning, and note taking. Many PDAs include either a built-in speakerphone or a headset jack so the PDA can be used to take notes or look up information during telephone calls placed through that device.

Also growing more common today are watches with built-in computing capabilities. Although not as powerful or versatile as a fully-functioning PDA, new *wrist PDAs* expected to be available in mid-2003 are smart watches that run the same operating system as the popular *Palm PC* handhelds. They can synchronize data with other PCs to keep a contact list, calendar, and other stored data up-to-date, and are compatible with all Palm PC software. For input, a stylus integrated into some watchbands can be used to enter data in the Palm *Graffiti* format; buttons and switches on the edge of the watch can be used to select items on the screen; and an infrared port incorporated into some wrist PDAs can be used to beam data between the PDA and another Palm-compatible computer.

Changes in notebook PCs include swivel screens for easier reading or easier business presentations, and notebooks that fold a second time to make them pocket-sized. With the recent arrival of *convertible tablet PCs*—many based on the new *Windows XP Tablet PC* operating system—the notebook and the tablet PC have also begun to converge, allowing for a combination of pen, mouse, and keyboard use. Although some tablet PCs are still available only in the original *slate* (non-foldable) format, convertible tablet PCs can be used as both a notebook and a tablet (see Figure U-2). In the notebook format, the keyboard and mouse can be used, just as they can with any other notebook PC; when the screen is rotated and then closed with the screen facing out, the device resembles a slate tablet PC and just pen input is used. Both notebook and tablet PCs today usually come with communications capabilities built in, so the PCs can be easily connected to an office network or the Internet.

▶ FIGURE U-1

Hybrid mobile devices.

New "hybrid" devices combine mobile phone and portable PC capabilities.

▶ FIGURE U-2

Convertible tablet PCs.

Can be used as a regular notebook PC, a notebook PC with the screen rotated for a client presentation, or a tablet PC with the screen rotated and folded shut.

Changes in Desktop PCs

Desktop PCs over the past year have gotten smaller, usually to fit more efficiently on a desk. Instead of the traditional beige system unit box, several different PC vendors have released units where the system unit is completely integrated into the monitor or the keyboard. And at least one PC maker has created a complete Windows XP PC that is slightly larger than a handheld PC.

World's Fastest Computer

The trend to create less expensive supercomputers by connecting hundreds of smaller computers or processors—typically midrange computers (now commonly referred to as *midrange servers*)—into a *supercomputing cluster* that acts as a single computer has continued. This past year, NEC's *Earth Simulator* surpassed IBM's ASCI White as the world's fastest supercomputer. The Earth Simulator contains a total of 640 computers containing 8 CPUs each for a combined total of 5,120 CPUs. It cost approximately $400 million, can perform about 40 trillion calculations per second, requires the floor space of four tennis courts, and is used primarily to simulate various global environmental phenomena such as global warming, the El Niño effect, and atmospheric and marine pollution, as well as to predict environmental changes on Earth.

New and emerging computing trends over the past year include alternate power for PCs and mobile devices, and an expected use of more *smart objects*.

Alternate Power for PCs and Mobile Devices

Alternate power generators are now available to run a cell phone, pager, GPS device, or portable PC to either reduce electricity costs or to allow the use of the device in situations where dependable electricity isn't available, such as in developing countries, while traveling, or while outdoors (see Figure U-3). Common options are *solar power* (where panels that are connected to the device and are carried or attached to a car or bike recharge the device's batteries using the sun); *hand power* (where a handle is cranked or squeezed to keep the batteries in an attached device charged); and *pedal power* (where a device attached to a regular or exercise bike charges the device's batteries whenever the bike is ridden). Since limited battery life is an issue with portable cell phones and PCs, users may find alternate power more convenient and environmentally-friendly than frequently replacing batteries or recharging batteries using an electric charger. For use in the home or office, a *foot power* charger (in which a device is stepped on to recharge the batteries used in an attached device) is expected to be available soon. Solar and pedal power generators are also being used in developing countries to provide remote villages that have no electricity or telephones with communication and computing tools. One project in Laos is supplying villages with alternate powered PCs that are networked to other nearby villages and to the Internet.

Smart Objects

A step beyond personal computers and smart appliances are *smart objects* or *smart gadgets*—a possibility for the near future. Bill Gates recently revealed Microsoft's new *Smart Personal Objects Technology (SPOT)*, which is being designed to enhance the core functionality of everyday objects to make them smarter, more personalized, and more useful. One example of a future product expected to become available within the next year or so is the smart travel alarm clock; capabilities are expected to include adjusting itself for time zone changes, automatically setting itself according to the owner's schedule for that day as entered into his or her PC, and waking up the owner with his or her favorite music and any urgent messages or news reports.

NEW AND EMERGING TRENDS

Solar-powered charger

FIGURE U-3
Alternate power. This solar-powered charger can power a cell phone, GPS device, or portable PC.

tech news video project

To complete the Chapter 1 "High Tech Climbing" video project, go to page U-36.

UPDATE

Changes over the past year include the new *Windows XP* interface appearing on most PCs sold today, new browser versions and features, and an increased use of instant messaging for both business and personal communications.

The Windows XP Interface

While the overall interface of the most recent versions of Windows (such as windows, menus, hyperlinks, and icons) work the same as in earlier versions, there are some functional differences with the new Windows XP desktop, as shown in Figure U-4 and discussed next.

▼ *Desktop*—is less cluttered, with fewer desktop icons by default, although desktop icons can be added by the user.

▼ *Start menu*—puts the most frequently used programs on the left pane; items such as the My Documents folder, Help, and the Control Panel are listed on the right pane; the Shut Down and Log Off options are located at the bottom; and all programs are listed under the *All Programs* option.

▼ *Taskbar*—now uses *taskbar grouping* to combine all windows for the same program into a single task button when there isn't room on the taskbar to display a task button for each open window; clicking a grouped task button allows you to select the desired window from a list. To provide more room on the taskbar, icons in the system tray on the right edge are automatically hidden from view when they haven't been used in a while.

▼ *Icons and windows*—have a different appearance in such Windows utilities as the Control Panel and Help.

Web Browser Update

The most commonly used Web browser is Microsoft Internet Explorer, although Netscape Navigator is expected to make somewhat of a gain in market share with its newest version. The most recent versions of these browsers (*Internet Explorer 6* and *Navigator 7*) have some new and interesting features. For instance, Internet Explorer 6 has a new *Media* toolbar button which displays a *Media Explorer bar* that can be used to play music, video, or multimedia files, as well as to select an Internet radio station to listen to. Navigator 7 includes a *tabbed browsing* interface and a new *click-to-search* feature, as described next.

◗ **FIGURE U-4**
The Windows XP desktop.

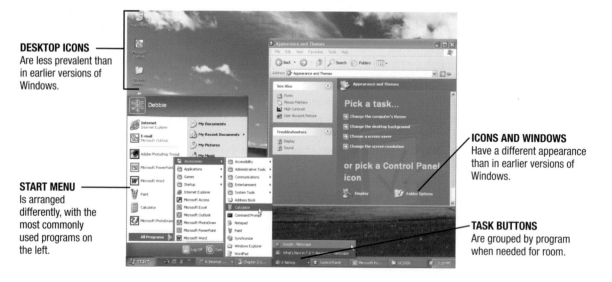

DESKTOP ICONS
Are less prevalent than in earlier versions of Windows.

START MENU
Is arranged differently, with the most commonly used programs on the left.

ICONS AND WINDOWS
Have a different appearance than in earlier versions of Windows.

TASK BUTTONS
Are grouped by program when needed for room.

▼ *Tabbed browsing*—enables users to switch between open browser windows using the tabs at the top of the screen; an entire set of tabs can be bookmarked together for easy retrieval in future sessions.

▼ *Click-to-search*—allows users to perform a quick search for any word displayed on a Web page by selecting it, right-clicking it, and choosing the *Web search for...* option on the displayed shortcut menu.

Instant Messaging Update

Popular instant messaging services for PCs today include *AOL Instant Messaging*, *MSN Messenger*, and *Yahoo! Messenger*. Instant messaging use has grown over the past year and so has the problem of incompatible systems (people using different IM systems can't exchange messages unless they are using a third-party service). As IM use for business has grown, there has been increased pressure for IM providers to work together to create compatible systems. In the meantime, most IM providers are adding secure, *encrypted* IM services to attract more corporate business. According to the consulting firm IDC, currently 80 million office workers worldwide are using IM; other analysts predict that IM use will surpass e-mail use for internal corporate communications by 2005. In addition to being used on PCs, instant messaging is extremely popular with mobile phone users.

NEW AND EMERGING TRENDS

One emerging trend is the increased use of smart phones for e-mail, Web browsing, and other activities. Another is *video e-mail*.

Smart Phones

As with instant messaging, exchanging e-mail using smart phones and other types of mobile devices is growing in the U.S. and in many other countries; many smart phones now have large enough screens to facilitate increased Web browsing. In response to this trend, some mobile devices have begun to incorporate a keyboard into the device; there are also slip-on or attachable keyboards that can be used with most devices. Microsoft has expanded into the smart phone arena with its recent release of the *Smartphone* version of Windows. Phones that adhere to the Smartphone standard (see Figure U-5) include full Web access, easy-to-use e-mail and instant messaging, day-planners, and other PDA-type applications. In addition, attachable cameras, games, and other software are available.

Video E-mail

Although off to a slow start, primarily due to slow Internet connections and the large file size video recordings require, *video e-mail* (see Figure U-6) is currently available and expected to grow in popularity in the near future. E-mail providers, such as Yahoo! Mail and AT&T WorldNet, offer free video e-mail as part of their service. There are also third-party services that can be used to attach video e-mail messages to any regular e-mail message; normally these services charge a monthly fee for a set number of minutes which are used for recording and viewing e-mail videos. Today's video e-mails are typically stored and delivered from the provider's server, which both frees up storage space on the sender's and recipient's PCs, and speeds up delivery time. Videos are typically played using a standard media player program, such as Windows Media Player, installed on the recipient's PC.

▶ **FIGURE U-5**
A Smartphone.

▶ **FIGURE U-6**
Video e-mail.

UPDATE

Some of the most significant changes in the areas of processing and memory over the last year have involved faster and more powerful processors and improved chip technologies; most PCs today also come with a greater amount of memory than a year ago. An emerging technology of past years—nanotechnology—has also moved more into the mainstream.

Faster and More Powerful Processors

The most common CPUs for desktop computers today are the Intel® Pentium® 4 and the AMD *Athlon™ XP,* although lower-end, home PCs may use a Celeron® CPU instead. The newer *Athlon MP* CPU processor is designed for multiprocessing servers and workstations. Most processors today run at a clock speed of between 1.8 and 3 GHz.

Three new 64-bit processors include the Intel® *Itanium® 2 Processor* (see Figure U-7) and AMD's *Opteron™,* both designed for server and workstation use, and a 64-bit version of AMD's Athlon CPU (named the *Athlon 64* and shown in Figure U-7) designed for desktop and portable PC use. The Itanium® 2 was released in 2002 and both AMD processors are expected to be available in early 2003. Another new CPU expected to be released in 2003 is Intel's low-power *Pentium® M Processor* (originally code-named *Banias*) that is part of Intel's new *Centrino™* mobile technology designed for portable PCs.

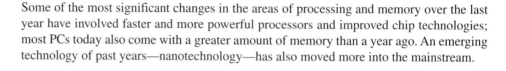

FIGURE U-7

New CPUs. The Intel Itanium 2 Processor (top) and the AMD Athlon 64 CPU (bottom).

Improved Chip Technologies

Researchers are continually working on developing chip technologies that add new capabilities and increase processing speed while at the same time try to control the amount of heat generated. Techniques that insulate transistors—such as the SOI (silicon on insulator) process used in some chips the last year or two—are expected to continue to grow in importance. New cooling technologies are being tested; some possibilities for the future include liquid-filled tubes that act as radiators to draw heat away from processors and misters that spray a fine mist of liquid onto chips when they become too hot.

A new technique in the area of multiprocessing and parallel processing is *hyperthreading,* which enables software to treat a single processor as two processors. Since it utilizes processing power in the chip that would otherwise go unused, this new technology lets the chip operate far more efficiently, resulting in faster processing, provided the software being used supports hyperthreading.

Memory Update

Because the cost of RAM has been decreasing, most PCs today come with significantly more of it than a year ago. Very low-end PCs may come with 128 MB of RAM, but 256 or 512 MB is much more common. Servers and workstations typically have between 1 and 4 GB of RAM. Since today's 32-bit CPUs can only address up to 4 GB of RAM, once 64-bit processors become more widely available much more RAM will likely be utilized in high-end PCs. Much of the advances in memory the past year—such as *film memory* and *phase-change memory*—has been in the area of non-volatile flash memory, which is discussed in Chapter 4.

Nanotechnology

In the last year, there has been more progress made in the field of nanotechnology—working at the individual atomic and molecular levels to create computer chips and other components that are thousands of times smaller than conventional technologies permit. Using newly developed technologies, such as *extreme ultraviolet (EUV) light,* transistors as small as 15 nanometers have been created in lab settings. In addition to computer applications, nanotechnology has been applied to consumer products, such as stain-resistant fabrics and long-life tennis balls. Future applications include improved military uniforms that protect against bullets and germ warfare, and molecular structures that can be injected into the bloodstream and instructed to destroy cancer cells or perform another important medical task. The federal government has also demonstrated increased interest in nanotechnology this past year, holding Senate hearings, forming a *National Nanotechnology Research Program*, and introducing legislation to increase funding for nanotechnology research and development.

New and emerging trends for processors and memory include *quantum computing, optical computing,* and *3-D chips.*

NEW AND EMERGING TRENDS

2003

Quantum Computing

The idea of *quantum computing* emerged in the 1970s, but has received renewed interest lately along with nanotechnology. Quantum computing applies the principles of quantum physics and quantum mechanics to computers, going beyond traditional physics to work at the subatomic level. Quantum computers differ from conventional computers in that they utilize atoms or nuclei working together as quantum bits or *qubits*; qubits function simultaneously as both the computer's processor and memory. Each qubit can represent much more than just the two states (one and zero) available to today's electronic bits; a qubit can even represent many states at one time. Because of this, theoretically quantum computers can perform calculations exponentially faster than conventional computers. Quantum computers in the future may consist of a thimbleful of liquid whose atoms are used to perform calculations as instructed by an external device.

While quantum computers are still in the pioneering stage, working quantum computers do exist. For instance, in 2001 the researchers at IBM's Almaden Research Center in San Jose, California, created a seven-qubit quantum computer (comprised of the nuclei of seven atoms, which can interact with each other and be programmed by radio frequency pulses) that can factor the number 15 successfully (see Figure U-8). Although this is not a complicated computation for a conventional computer, the fact that it was possible for a person to supply a quantum computer with the problem and have it compute the correct answer is viewed as a highly significant event in the area of quantum computer research. A primary application area for quantum computers is expected to be encryption and code-breaking.

Optical Computing

Optical chips, which use light waves to transmit data, are currently in development. A possibility for the future is the *optical computer*—a computer that uses light, such as from laser beams or infrared beams, to perform digital computations. Because light beams don't interfere with each other, optical computers can be much smaller and faster than electronic PCs. For instance, according to NASA senior research scientist Hossin Abduldayem, an optical computer could solve a problem in one hour that would take an electronic computer 11 years to solve. While some researchers are working on developing an all-optical computer, others believe that a mix of optical and electronic components—or an *opto-electronic computer*—may be the best bet for the future. In fact, the first chips that have both optical and electrical functions combined on a single silicon chip—a feat that was thought to be impossible until recently—are expected to be available in 2003.

FIGURE U-8
Quantum computers. The vial of liquid shown here contains the seven-qubit computer used by IBM researchers in 2001 to perform the most complicated quantum computing computation to date—factoring the number 15.

3-D Chips

Three-dimension (3-D) chips are an alternative to nanotechnology to solve the problem of trying to pack an increasing number of components onto small chips. With 3-D chips, either multiple layers of circuitry are used or the circuitry stands vertically, rather than horizontally. In either case, a successful 3-D chip design is predicted to increase power and speed by a factor of 10 at no additional cost, as well as to extend Moore's Law for up to 30 years beyond its theoretical limits. One company—Matrix Semiconductors—has announced it should have a 3-D memory chip on the market by early 2003.

tech news video project

To complete the Chapter 3 "Toxic PCs" video project, go to page U-36.

UPDATE

◈ FIGURE U-9

Portable hard drives. This USB portable hard drive can be used with both desktop and portable PCs and holds up to 120 GB.

◈ FIGURE U-10

Flash memory drives. The Trek ThumbDrive Touch shown here holds 128 MB of data and uses biometric technology to allow its data to be accessed only by authorized users.

Not surprisingly, removable storage trends over the past year are continuing to move away from floppy disks towards optical discs and flash memory media. Hard drives remain necessary and have become faster with a higher storage capacity.

Faster and Larger Hard Drives

The hard drive is still the primary storage device for desktop and portable PCs, housing the operating system, application programs, and data. Most desktop PCs today come with a hard drive that can hold between 40 GB and 120 GB of data, although hard drives as large as 200 GB are available. Portable hard drives, such as the USB version of Iomega's new HDD product line shown in Figure U-9, are becoming increasingly popular for backing up or exchanging large amounts of data.

Hard drives for notebook computers have also seen improvements in speed and capacity this past year. Speeds of some drives are approaching common desktop hard drive speeds, and a capacity of 80 GB has recently been announced by IBM using its new *Pixie Dust* technology, which sandwiches three atoms of the precious metal ruthenium between two magnetic layers. Instead of a hard drive, handheld PCs, smart phones, and other small portable PCs and mobile devices often rely on flash memory media.

Changes in Removable Storage

As expected, the floppy disk and drive are becoming less important; in fact, some new PCs sold today don't include a floppy disk drive. Replacing the floppy disk on these PCs are optical discs and flash memory media. Some superdiskette options (such as HiFD, SuperDisk, and Peerless drives) have been discontinued by their original manufacturers; however, the Iomega Zip drive—now available in a 750 MB disk format—is still on the market.

The biggest news of late in optical discs is the rewritable DVD. Although the rewritable DVD first became available in 2001, it has now hit the mainstream. Unfortunately, the DVD format wars have not been resolved, so there are still a confusing collection of rewritable disc formats, such as *DVD-RW*, *DVD-RAM*, and *DVD+RW*. Luckily, many DVD drive manufacturers are introducing new drives that support more than one standard, such as one drive from Sony that is compatible with DVD+RW, DVD+R, DVD-RW, DVD-R, CD-RW, and CD-R discs. Because of the format controversy, recordable and rewritable DVD have taken off more slowly than originally anticipated. However, just as CD-R and CD-RW drives have virtually replaced CD-ROM drives, it still seems likely that rewritable DVD drives will eventually replace CD drives. And a new *Blu-ray* technology—which uses blue-violet lasers instead of red to record data more compactly than on conventional DVD discs—is expected to increase the storage capacity of an optical disc to 27 GB. Consumer products based on Blu-ray technology are expected to begin to become available in 2003.

Flash memory cards are still the most common storage media for handheld PCs, digital cameras, smart phones, and other types of mobile devices. Flash memory use with both desktop and portable PCs has grown and many vendors are now offering these tiny, key-chain-size drives that plug into a USB port and are automatically recognized as a new drive. Capacity for both flash memory cards and flash memory drives is currently up to about 1 GB, with 4 GB versions expected in the near future. Some flash drives are beginning to come with built-in fingerprint readers for extra security to ensure the data on the drive can be accessed only by an authorized user (see Figure U-10).

NEW AND EMERGING TRENDS

New and emerging trends for storage include the increased use of storage devices in consumer products and *network attached storage (NAS)*. An additional emerging issue—*mandatory copy protection* for storage products—is featured in the Inside the Industry box.

inside the industry

Mandatory Digital Copy Protection

Citing millions of dollars in estimated losses due to copyright-infringement activities such as copies of movies and songs being exchanged via the Internet, the movie and music industries are backing legislation–such as the *Consumer Broadband and Digital Television Act* introduced by Senator Ernest Hollings in 2002–that would require mandatory copy protection built into future hardware such as CD, DVD, and MP3 players. Intended to prevent individuals from sharing movies and music with others, if it passes this legislation would also prevent consumers from exercising their "fair use" rights to use the media they buy on any device of their choosing for personal use, such as copying a song from a purchased CD to a PC in order to make a custom CD for his or her personal enjoyment. In fact, it would make that act illegal since the *Digital Millennium Copyright Act (DMCA)* passed in 2000 forbids the circumvention of any copyright protection method built into a product. In addition to supporting the legislation introduced by Senator Hollings, the movie industry is pushing for a law or FCC regulation to include mandatory copy protection systems in all devices that accept digital input (such as TV sets, PCs, and digital video recorders) to prevent the transfer of digital video over a TCP/IP network like the Internet.

Proponents of mandatory copy protection believe that it will reduce the potential for piracy, which, in turn, will reduce the reluctance of media companies to make entertainment content available through the Internet. Opponents counter that while professional pirates will likely figure out a way to bypass any security measures adopted, copy-protection schemes will only prevent innocent consumers from exerting their fair use rights to use the music CDs and other digital content that they acquire legally. In fact, some CDs being sold today cannot be played in a PC's CD drive, angering some consumers. The outcome of the push for mandatory copy protection is as of yet uncertain, but it will likely have an important impact on the future direction of digital media, as well as on PC and Internet technologies.

Increase in Consumer Product Storage Applications

Once just a computer-related product, storage hardware has been increasingly incorporated into consumer products. Toys, cell phones, digital cameras, MP3 players, and many other consumer products utilize flash memory technology, and *digital video recorders (DVRs)*—such as TiVo—and *game boxes*—such as Xbox and PlayStation—contain internal hard drives. Although growth in the computer storage industry has been slowing, demand for storage products for consumer applications is on the rise.

Network Attached Storage (NAS)

With the huge amounts of data that many companies need to manage and store today—for instance, Yahoo! needs to store more than a petabyte of data generated by Yahoo! e-mail users—network-based storage has become increasingly important this past year. An emerging alternative to storage area networks (SANs) for smaller applications is *network attached storage (NAS)*. Although similar in idea to a SAN, there are some technical differences. For instance, NAS devices are typically connected individually to a network and use ordinary network connections to exchange data. SAN units, on the other hand, are usually connected using faster Fibre Channel connections and so can be added without having to conform to the size restrictions of the network. With the recent improvements in networking speed, however, the functional distinction between a SAN and a NAS is blurring.

UPDATE

Recent changes in input and output devices have centered on making them smaller, more conducive to portable use, and more compatible with devices that are growing in importance, such as digital cameras.

Changes in Input Devices

As the use of portable PCs and mobile devices has increased, there has been a proliferation of new keyboards designed for these devices. Portable keyboards designed for handheld PC use typically fold or roll up; *thumb pads* slip over the bottom of a handheld PC or smart phone and are pressed with the thumbs instead of the fingers (see Figure U-11). Some PDAs now come with built-in thumb pads. Electronic pens have also evolved in the last year. In addition to being used with tablet and handheld PCs, new types of digital pens can be used to transfer data written on special paper to a PC—either by transferring the data to the PC in real time or by storing it inside the pen to be transferred later via a docking station attached to the PC.

◆ **FIGURE U-11**
Portable keyboards and thumb pads.

Photos can be previewed and edited here

Flash memory media can be inserted here

◆ **FIGURE U-12**
A photo printer.

Changes in Output Devices

For output devices, flat-panel desktop displays have become more common, both for their smaller footprint and lower power consumption. Flat plasma televisions are now available for consumer use, although they are expensive. In the printer area, increased photo printing capabilities are common, such as slots for a variety of flash media cards and USB ports being located on the outside of the printer so that digital photos can be printed without first being transferred to a PC. Some specialty photo printers also have built-in preview screens for viewing and editing photos before printing (see Figure U-12).

NEW AND EMERGING TRENDS

Two new output trends are *electronic paper* and *smart displays.* An emerging trend—the use of *radio frequency identification (RFID)* as a possible replacement for bar codes—is discussed in the Trend box.

Electronic Paper (E-Paper)

Similar to *e-books,* which display the contents of books in an electronic format on a special book-sized device, *electronic paper (e-paper)* displays written content in electronic form, but on thinner, more paper-like plastic displays. Still in the early stages of development, electronic paper is expected eventually to become a viable replacement for some traditional paper and ink applications, such as newspapers and retail display signs. Currently, conventional newspapers and retail signs have to be physically exchanged for new ones on a regular basis with the old ones being discarded. Using e-paper, however, these documents could be erased and then the e-paper reused. One way of displaying text and images on e-paper involves the use of millions of tiny half black and half white colored beads sealed with some liquid inside individual tiny pockets created from two sheets of very thin transparent plastic. Each bead rotates within its pocket only when directed by an electrical signal; to change the text or images displayed on the "paper," these signals—usually sent to the paper through a wireless transmission—instruct the beads to rotate to display either their black sides or white sides to form the proper text and images.

RFID: Smart Bar Codes

Radio frequency identification (RFID) tags contain tiny *RFID chips* used in conjunction with a tiny radio antenna and transponder to store data in and transmit data from the chip. RFID tags can be attached permanently to items such as product packaging, product labels, badges, wristbands, and key ring tags (see the accompanying photo). RFID applications used in recent years include tracking inventory pallets in warehouses, authorizing payment for gas or fast food (such as the Mobil *SpeedPass* system), and facilitating automatic highway toll collection. RFID tags are beginning to be used on product labels in conjunction with a unique identifying product code referred to as an *electronic product code* or *ePC* and are expected to eventually replace UPC bar codes.

Advantages of RFID tags over conventional bar codes include the ability to store more data and update it throughout the life of the product and the use of ePC codes in conjunction with the Internet to provide product data, menu suggestions, and other useful information for consumers, as well as by manufacturers and retailers to streamline the supply chain, identify recalled or expired products, and products that need reordering. RFID tags are also read by radio waves which do not require line of sight, can be read from a distance of up to 15 feet, and can pass through materials such as cardboard and plastic. Although RFID tags are beginning to be used on expensive products, at about 5 cents each they are still too costly to put on a soda can, pack of gum, or other low-price item. Many experts predict that once the cost reaches 1 cent or less apiece, they will be a viable replacement for all product bar codes.

A key ring RFID tag.

One of the first areas in which e-paper has been applied is department store signs. These *e-signs* look like ordinary paper signs, but their text can be changed electronically. Future applications include e-paper shelf price tags that always match the price in the store's database and e-paper books and newspapers that feel like real paper but their content can be wirelessly downloaded from the Internet. One day the technology may also be used on billboards, T-shirts, and even wallpaper and paint for easy redecorating—the message on your billboard or T-shirt and the colors and patterns on your walls could be updated using your portable PC.

◆ **FIGURE U-13**
Smart displays can be moved around the home while still accessing their designated PC.

Smart Displays

Smart displays are portable monitors that are wirelessly connected to a desktop PC so that they can remotely access the PC from anywhere within a home or office. Although similar in appearance to a tablet PC (see Figure U-13), an important difference is where the computing hardware is located. Unlike a tablet PC, which contains all processing hardware inside the tablet, a smart display does not contain processing hardware and is instead always used in conjunction with its associated PC. The first smart monitors are expected to be available in early 2003.

**tech news
video project**

To complete the Chapter 5 "DirecTV Pirates" video project, go to page U-37.

UPDATE

Over the past year, there have been some changes in the popularity of various operating systems and a possible settlement in the Microsoft antitrust case.

⊘ **FIGURE U-14**

Windows XP Media Center Edition. This version of Windows XP is currently available only on new Media Center PCs–computers billed as "complete PCs enhanced for home entertainment".

Changes in Operating Systems

The predominant operating system for desktop PCs is still Windows. Windows XP is the most current release and there are now five different versions: Professional, Home Edition, *Media Center Edition*, *Tablet PC Edition*, and *64-bit Edition*. The Media Center Edition incorporates additional features for watching live TV, recording television shows, watching DVDs, and managing music, video, and photo collections on a PC (see Figure U-14). The Tablet PC Edition is designed specifically for use with tablet PCs, and the 64-bit Edition is designed to be used with high-end workstations using a 64-bit processor, such as the Itanium. There are also versions of Windows designed for the Pocket PC, smart display, and Smartphone platforms. Palm OS is still widely used, and Palm recently acquired Be, Inc.—the maker of the BeOS alternative operating system—and plans to integrate Be's technology into its Palm OS operating system. The delayed server version of Windows XP has now been renamed *Windows .Net Server 2003* and is expected to ship in the first half of 2003. The next major upgrade to Windows—code-named *Longhorn*—isn't expected until at least late 2004.

Support for the Linux operating system has continued to grow. It has become increasingly more user-friendly, although some tasks still require the use of typed commands. As discussed in the Inside the Industry box, the emergence of new free or low-cost application programs for Linux PCs has helped make Linux a viable option for businesses.

Update on Microsoft Antitrust Case

Microsoft's *antitrust* problems began in 1998 when the Justice Department sued Microsoft for antitrust violations for such actions as (1) preventing computer manufacturers from installing some competing software if they also chose to install Microsoft products, and (2) integrating Windows and Internet Explorer components into many other Microsoft programs. At one point during the proceedings, the original trial judge ordered Microsoft to be split into two companies—one for their operating system software and one for their application software. That decision was eventually reversed and a tentative settlement was reached in late 2001; that settlement was finally approved in November 2002. Although a few states are still arguing for tougher sanctions, many experts believe the case is just about over. The settlement prevents Microsoft from participating in exclusive deals that could hurt competitors and requires Microsoft to release some technical information so that software developers can write programs for Windows that work as well as Microsoft's own products work. In fact, Microsoft has already released *Windows XP Service Pack 1* which enables PC makers and consumers to hide access to several programs included with Windows XP, including Internet Explorer. The settlement is expected to allow Microsoft rivals more flexibility to offer competing software features on computers running Windows.

NEW AND EMERGING TRENDS

New and emerging trends for systems software include new types of utility programs and *autonomic computing*.

New Types of Utility Programs

Utility programs that have become available or more widely used during the past year include those programs that help you more easily recover data when a computer problem develops, move your data and program settings to a new PC, or synchronize the data on

inside the industry

Linux Desktops: The Wave of the Future?

Although Linux has been around for many years and is now commonly used for business servers and mainframes, it has only recently spread to mainstream desktop PC use. The primary reason companies are switching to Linux and other open-source software is cost. For example, Burlington Coat Factory reported saving one-half million dollars due to its recent switch to Linux desktops for its stores. Linux supporters also assert that Linux desktops crash less often, are less prone to viruses and other security hazards, and are easy to run on older equipment.

The move to Linux for desktop PC use is occurring in a wide range of companies, from small retail outfits that need only a limited number of applications to companies employing programmers, engineers, and other technical workers who are already familiar with Linux or Unix servers. One reason for the increased use of Linux on desktop PCs is the recent availability of adequate application software. Using free or low-cost office suites compatible with Microsoft Office documents paired with a Linux-compatible Web browser and e-mail program can enable a business to work competitively while at the same time saving several hundred dollars per machine (see the accompanying table). Although most of these programs do not incorporate as many features as Microsoft Office, many users find them adequate for their needs. Most experts predict that use of Linux and other open source software will continue to grow.

Type of Software	Program	Approximate Cost
Operating System	Microsoft Windows XP	$200–300
	Linux	Free–$60
Office Suite	Microsoft Office XP	$450–550 ($130–250, Academic edition)
	OpenOffice.org 1.0	Free
	StarOffice 6.0	$75 (Free, Education users)

Cost of Microsoft software vs. alternative software.

two or more PCs. For instance, *disk-imaging* programs enable users to back up their entire PC once all software programs have been installed and all user settings have been adjusted. If a problem occurs at a later time, the PC can quickly be restored to the imaged configuration. Figure U-15 illustrates a new Web-based application program that allows users—after supplying the proper name and password—to access and use their PCs from remote locations, such as to read, edit, or print files located on their office PCs from their homes or from Internet cafés while traveling. Similar programs allow the files on two or more PCs to be automatically synchronized at all times, using the computers' Internet connections. Utility programs to burn rewritable DVDs have also recently become available.

Autonomic Computing

Autonomic computing is a term coined by IBM to refer to computers that can operate on their own with little need of attention from a person. To facilitate this, autonomic computers of the future are expected to have built-in self-diagnostics and other types of utilities, as well as other appropriate software. According to Nick Donofrio, senior vice president of technology and manufacturing at IBM, "The end game is to deliver a computing environment that is online all the time as a utility." Autonomic computers will likely be designed with built-in abilities to recognize, isolate, and recover from problems, with as little human intervention as possible. Some see autonomic computing as a natural progression for computing, similar to the way the telephone system evolved from using a human switchboard operator to a system that automatically routes calls on its own; others are more skeptical.

FIGURE U-15

Remote PC access software. After supplying the appropriate logon information, the remote desktop shown here can be manipulated over a secure Internet connection, just as if the user were seated at that PC.

UPDATE

Recent changes to application software include new features added to the newest versions of Microsoft Office and an increase in the amount of legal action for business *software piracy*.

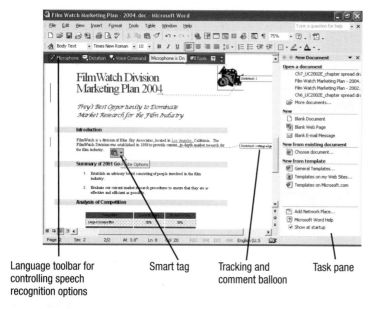

Language toolbar for controlling speech recognition options   Smart tag   Tracking and comment balloon   Task pane

◗ **FIGURE U-16**

New Office XP features.

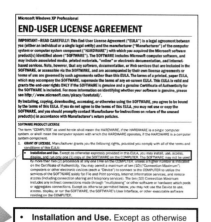

◗ **FIGURE U-17**

Software licenses. An end-user software license agreement specifies conditions such as how many PCs the program may be installed on, if it can be resold, and more.

Office Suite Update

Microsoft still remains the industry leader, having a total of 94% of the office suite market, according to the Giga Information Group. New features included in the most recent version of Microsoft Office—*Office XP*—include the following (see Figure U-16); the next version of Office (code-named *Office 11*) is expected to be released in mid-2003.

▼ *Smart tags*—appear as needed (such as when you are pasting data in a document or when you need to correct an error in a spreadsheet formula) to provide options for completing that task quickly.

▼ *Task panes*—display on the edge of the application window when appropriate and enable users to access specific tasks (such as searching, opening documents, and inserting clip art).

▼ *Speech recognition*—allows the use of spoken commands and dictation.

▼ *Handwriting support*—permits notes taken on a handheld PC to be uploaded to an Office document as text.

▼ *Balloons*—show edits and comments in a tracked, collaborative document without disturbing the current text.

Crackdown on Illegal Software Installations

As discussed in Chapter 15, *software piracy* is the unauthorized copying or use of a computer program. Although most people might think the term applies only to people who copy and sell software illegally, it also applies to businesses that install software on more PCs than allowed for by their software licenses. Prosecution of this type of software piracy is increasing.

Investigations for business software piracy are usually performed by the *Business Software Alliance (BSA)*—an organization formed by a number of the world's leading software developers including Adobe, Apple, Microsoft, and Symantec. The BSA estimates that approximately 40% of all business application software globally (and about 25% of all business application software in the U.S.) is installed illegally for a worldwide monetary loss to the software industry for 2001 of nearly $11 billion. To investigate a company suspected of software piracy, the BSA conducts a court-ordered audit of software installed on company PCs; most companies found to be in violation of their software licenses end up settling with the BSA, routinely paying $100,000 or more in penalties in addition to agreeing to purchase the correct number of software licenses. Although the BSA does encounter situations where the problem is a result of poor recordkeeping and asset management, they also see companies who knowingly break the law to save money. The ease at which installation CDs can be copied has fueled this problem. To avoid unintentional software piracy, both businesses and individuals should pay close attention to the terms of their software licenses (see Figure U-17).

One type of software that is receiving considerable attention is *spyware*. An emerging new consumer application is the *smart ATM machine*.

Smart ATM Machines

New software and technologies are in the works to make ATMs smarter and friendlier than ever before. Some anticipated features are geared towards generating more ATM activities (such as being able to buy theater or plane tickets through an ATM); others are geared towards assisting customers with special needs or increasing customer trust and security. Possibilities include ATMs that can:

▼ *Talk*—use speech output to assist visually-impaired customers.

▼ *See*—use cameras to authenticate users (see Figure U-18) or to customize the display based on the customer's facial expression, such as rephrasing instructions if the customer appears confused or enlarging the screen text if the customer appears to be squinting.

▼ *Scan*—use imaging technology to scan deposited checks inserted without an envelope to start processing the deposit faster as well as to output a scanned image of the check on the customer's receipt.

▶ FIGURE U-18
Smart ATMs. Iris scanners may soon become standard features on ATM machines to verify the identities of customers performing ATM transactions.

Spyware

Spyware is the term used for any software that is installed without the user's knowledge, secretly gathers information about the user, and transmits that information through his or her Internet connection to advertisers or other interested parties—usually for marketing purposes. Spyware programs are often installed unknowingly at the same time another program is installed on a user's computer. Once a spyware program is installed on a PC, it typically does not show up on any list of installed programs, making it difficult for users both to realize that the spyware program has been installed and to uninstall it.

One example of spyware that became known to the public recently involved the popular *Kazaa* file-sharing program. The millions of people who downloaded and installed the program during the past year or so also installed several third-party software programs, including one program intended to be used for a new peer-to-peer network. The new peer-to-peer service—called *Altnet*—went online in mid-2002 and works within the Kazaa service to disseminate music and other content available from different companies. It also has the capability of using the processing power of individual PCs for distributed computing, such as performing complicated research-oriented computing tasks for clients. As a result of the backlash from outraged customers, Kazaa has since made most of its third-party software programs optional, though at least one—an ad server program—must remain installed in order to use the Kazaa service.

Privacy advocates object to spyware because it collects and transmits data about individuals to others, as well as uses up users' system resources and Internet bandwidth, all without the users' consent. As an additional annoyance, many spyware programs are not removed if the original hosting program is uninstalled.

**tech news
    video project**

To complete the Chapter 7 "NASA Robot Crews" video project, go to page U-37.

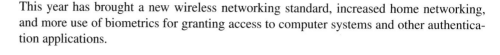
UPDATE

This year has brought a new wireless networking standard, increased home networking, and more use of biometrics for granting access to computer systems and other authentication applications.

Wireless Networking Update

Wireless networking has a number of advantages—for instance, surfing the Web on your notebook PC from anywhere in your house; accessing the Internet while traveling just by being close to a public access point in a restaurant, park, or airport; and creating a home network without having to run wires between your PCs. Consequently, the use of wireless networking has continued to grow rapidly over the past year in both private and public locations.

A new possibility for wireless networking is *802.11a*. At up to 54 Mbps, this new standard (also called *Wi-Fi5*) is about five times faster than the original Wi-Fi (also known as 802.11b). Because it is more expensive and is not compatible with 802.11b products, however, home users are expected to stick with the original Wi-Fi standard for the time being, although some business travelers may switch to Wi-Fi5. Just as with other types of networking standards, Wi-Fi5 requires the use of a network interface card or adapter (see Figure U-19) but, unlike wired networking connections, no cable is plugged into the card. A newer Wi-Fi version named *802.11g* that runs at 54 Mbps, but is compatible with 802.11b products, is expected to be available sometime in 2003.

⊜ FIGURE U-19

Wi-Fi5 network adapters for desktop (top) and notebook (bottom) PCs.

Home Networking Update

The use of home networks has continued to increase over the past year. The research firm Parks Associates estimates that over 7 million U.S. households are networked and expects that number to increase to over 20 million by 2006. Although wired Ethernet is still less expensive and faster than wireless networks, the ability to set up a network without pulling cables throughout the home, as well as to connect to the network from anywhere within the home via a portable PC, make wireless home networks increasingly attractive to consumers. Alternatively, more home network users are turning towards phoneline (such as the HomePNA standard) and powerline (such as the HomePlug standard) networks as their speed and dependability continue to increase.

Increased Use of Biometrics

Perhaps due to increased interest and attention being focused on security as a result of the terrorist attacks of 9/11 and the increased amount of Internet activity consumers perform today, use of biometrics has increased. Fingerprint readers are beginning to replace access cards and passwords to log on to PCs and Web sites, as well as to access resources such as transportation tickets and welfare benefits. Hand geometry readers are commonly used to control access to facilities and to punch employees in and out of work. Iris scanners and face recognition are used to control access to secure areas in hospitals, prisons, and nuclear power plants, as well as to identify suspects being booked by law enforcement agencies (see Figure U-20). In addition, face recognition at airports and other public locations has increased in the last year or so. For instance, video cameras and face recognition systems are in place at border crossings, in airports, and in many public locations in the Washington, D.C. area; portable setups have also been used during high-alert times, such as to screen ferry passengers going to the Statue of Liberty during the Fourth of July holiday in 2002. Although public use of video surveillance and biometric identification systems was not widely supported originally, public sentiment has changed following the 9/11 terrorist attacks.

⊜ FIGURE U-20

Biometric ID systems. Use of face recognition technology, such as this system used to identify suspects being booked at the Pinellas County Sheriff's Office in Florida, is increasing.

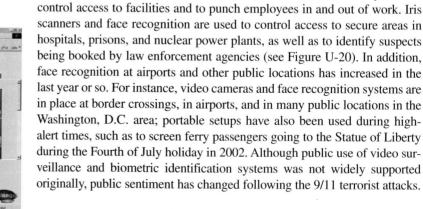

A recent study by Saflink Corporation found that over 80% of Americans supported the use of biometric devices to enhance airline security and approximately 60% were accepting of their use at public events.

New and emerging communications applications include *telemedicine* and *presence technology*.

Telemedicine

The improved nature of the Internet and networking has made *telemedicine*—the use of communications technology to provide medical information and services—a viable possibility. It exists today in the form of telephone consultations and videoconferences, remote monitoring and diagnosis of patients, and the emergence of *telesurgery* (see Figure U-21). Telemedicine has enormous potential for providing quality care to individuals who live in areas without access to sufficient medical care. It will also be necessary for future long-term

space exploration—such as a trip to Mars and back that may take three years or more—since astronauts will undoubtedly need medical care while on the journey. And any type of robotic surgery (whether the robotic device is controlled by a surgeon from a control console or by voice command within the operating room or is controlled remotely via the Internet) has the advantage of working with much smaller incisions than are possible by human surgeons. These smaller incisions allow for less invasive surgery (for example, not having to crack through the rib cage to access the heart), resulting in less pain for the patient, a faster recovery time, and fewer potential complications.

NEW AND EMERGING TRENDS

2003

FIGURE U-21
Telemedicine applications.

REMOTE DIAGNOSIS
At remote locations, such as the New York child care center shown here, trained employees provide physicians with the real-time data (sent via the Internet) they need for diagnosis.

TELESURGERY
Using voice and computer commands, surgeons can now perform surgery via the Internet; a robotic system actually operates on the patient, according to the surgeon's commands.

Presence Technology

Presence technology refers to the ability of one computing device (such as a desktop PC, PDA, or smart phone) on a network (such as the Internet) to locate and identify another device on the same network and determine its status. In theory, it can be used to tell when someone on the network is using his or her computer or mobile phone, as well as where that device is physically located at any given time. For example, when an employee at a company using presence technology (sometimes called *presence management* when used in a business context) has a question that needs answering, he or she can check the directory displayed on his or her PC or mobile phone to see which team members are available for a quick telephone call or instant message, regardless of where those team members are physically located (see Figure U-22). Presence technology is also expected to eventually be used on regular Web pages, so that visitors—usually potential or current customers—can see which salespeople, service representatives, or other contacts are available. Another possible application is including dynamic presence buttons in e-mail messages—the presence button would display one message (such as "I'm online") if the sender is online at the time the e-mail message is read, and a different message (such as "I'm offline") if the sender is not signed in at that time.

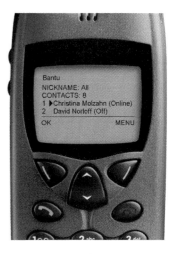

FIGURE U-22
Presence technology in use.

UPDATE

Over the past year, Internet use has slowly evolved to a higher level of wireless and broadband Internet access and Napster finally admitted defeat, although other peer-to-peer file-sharing networks are still in existence.

Generation	Analog/ Digital	Designed For	Maximum Speed
1	Analog	Voice	2.4 Kbps
2	Digital	Voice/Data	14.4 Kbps
3	Digital	Voice/Data (including high-speed Internet and multimedia)	2 Mbps (fixed setting)
4	Digital	Data (including high-quality full-motion video)	100 Mbps (estimated)

FIGURE U-23

Generations of cellular service.

Internet Access

The past year has seen increased broadband use—according to a 2002 Dataquest study, 28% of all U.S. online households use broadband connections. Most commonly access is via cable or DSL, although satellite remains the only broadband option for many rural areas. ISDN is rapidly losing ground to other types of broadband access and now has only about an 8% market share. To attract cost-conscious customers, some cable service providers are offering tiered pricing plans, similar to DSL providers.

Mobile wireless Internet has also continued to grow and now third-generation (3G) networks are finally becoming a reality. Although speeds haven't yet reached the estimated maximum of 144 Kbps while driving in a car or 2 Mbps in a fixed setup, 3G is significantly faster than conventional mobile wireless services which usually top out at about 14.4 Kbps (see Figure U-23). However, it is also quite a bit more expensive (such as $50 per month for 400 voice minutes and 1 MB of data on one plan) and so may be used primarily by business travelers at the present time. The faster 3G service can be used with 3G cell phones, as well as with PDAs and notebook PCs. *Fourth-generation (4G)* cellular services, expected to move data significantly faster than 3G (some expect speeds of 100 Mbps or more), may arrive as soon as 2006. A future possibility may be aircraft-based Internet, as discussed in the Trend box.

Napster and Peer-to-Peer File-Sharing Update

Although Napster had plans to reorganize with the help of a German media company, those plans fell through in September 2002 and the Napster name and other assets were acquired by multimedia software company Roxio in November 2002. Other peer-to-peer file-sharing services—such as Kazaa, Morpheus, and Madster—still remain. Because most of these services are used to some extent to transfer copyrighted material (such as music files), they are facing the same legal issues that Napster did. For instance, is the company responsible if users violate copyright restrictions? Or, is the company violating copyright law just by providing the service? Is it the company's responsibility to make sure no copyright violations occur? Because they are not actually distributing copyright-protected material to others since the files are transferred directly from one user's hard drive to another's—not from the P2P's server—some peer-to-peer services argue that they cannot be held responsible if users violate copyright laws. However, that argument hasn't been supported by the courts. Pirated copies of movies are also increasingly being shared via the Internet and, in response, the music and motion picture industries have filed lawsuits against popular file-sharing services that they believe are being used to share copyrighted material.

NEW AND EMERGING TRENDS

New trends for the Internet include new online security and privacy tools and increased broadband content.

New Online Security and Privacy Tools

Credit card companies are continuing to develop programs and procedures to help alleviate consumer hesitations about shopping online. They recommend using a credit card for online payments so that any fraudulent activities can be disputed and most now offer a zero liability program for online transactions. Disposable account numbers are also becoming

Aircraft-Based Internet: Broadband of the Future?

Instead of providing Internet access via cables, satellites, or radio towers, a new possibility is *aircraft-based Internet*, which uses aircraft to transmit signals between end users and their ISP. The aircraft—officially called a *High Altitude Platform Station (HAPS)*—would fly over a specific area to provide service to that area.

One such service, expected to be available by the end of 2004, is AeroVironment's *SkyTower*, developed in conjunction with NASA. The SkyTower program uses solar-powered (with hydrogen fuel cell power backup), unmanned aircraft flying at 65,000 feet (see the accompanying photo). Each aircraft can remain airborne for up to 6 months and is expected to cover an area of about 50 miles in diameter. To receive fixed Internet service, each end user needs a small outside-mounted transceiver dish; mobile wireless services for both telephones and portable PCs are also expected to become available. SkyTower service is predicted to be implemented at a much lower cost than cable, DSL, and satellite service since there are no cables to run to end-user locations (like cable and DSL service) and the aircraft are much less expensive to deploy than satellites launched into space. The SkyTower platform is also scalable; that is, aircraft

can be added or moved as needed to meet demand. Similar programs are being tested by other companies using manned aircraft and blimps. Whether or not aircraft-based Internet becomes a viable alternative remains to be seen. It does, however, offer an intriguing solution to the "last-mile" problem of providing broadband access to each customer's location.

An unmanned SkyTower aircraft.

---

more widely available and easier to use. For instance, the *Discover Card Deskshop* program runs in the background while the registered Discover cardholder surfs the Web; it can automatically fill in the appropriate billing and shipping information and generate a single-use credit card number when a shopping checkout page is reached. Typically, these disposable credit card numbers—sometimes called *virtual credit cards*—expire after a short time, have a maximum credit limit of the purchase amount, and can only be used with the specified retailer, which means they cannot be reused if intercepted by an unscrupulous individual.

A new tool for individuals concerned about online privacy is the free AT&T *Privacy Bird* browser plug-in. Once the user specifies his or her desired level of privacy (such as whether or not the company may share health information or contact the user by phone or e-mail), then the bird—located on the Web browser's title bar—indicates whether or not each site visited meets the user's privacy restrictions (see Figure U-24). The Privacy Bird program makes its determination based on the site's *Platform for Privacy Preferences (P3P)* policies—a standardized way of disclosing how a visitor's personal information is collected and used, recently developed by the *World Wide Web Consortium (W3C)*. If a visited site doesn't have a posted P3P policy, then the bird cannot make a judgment on that site.

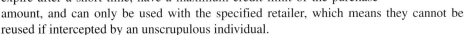

Yellow indicates that privacy information cannot be accessed.

Green indicates that privacy information matches the user's specifications.

Red indicates that privacy information does not match the user's specifications (clicking the icon displays a detailed summary of the site's privacy policy).

◈ FIGURE U-24
Privacy Bird. The Privacy Bird title bar icon notifies a Web surfer whether or not the site being viewed meets his or her privacy specifications.

Increased Broadband Content

Increased broadband Internet access has brought about the addition of broadband content to many Web sites. Webcasts, video clips, and 3D virtual reality tours are becoming increasingly common. Although some broadband content is free—such as news clips on many news sites and entertainment clips on movie and television sites—a growing trend is to offer broadband content for a fee. Revenue from paid Internet content is expected to grow to $5.8 billion by 2006, according to a recent market forecast from Jupiter Media Metrix.

tech news
video project

To complete the Chapter 9 "Rural Broadband" video project, go to page U-38.

UPDATE

Recent changes in multimedia and Web site creation include easier ways to create a special form of Web site called a *Weblog*, royalty issues surrounding Internet radio, and increased access considerations.

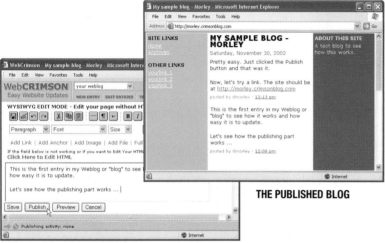

THE PUBLISHED BLOG

CREATING THE BLOG

◆ **FIGURE U-25**

Creating a blog with a free Web-based service.

◆ **FIGURE U-26**

Access considerations.

The increased use of mobile devices (left) and assistive hardware (right) needs to be taken into consideration by today's Web developers.

Weblogs

A *Weblog* or *blog* is a publicly-accessible Web page often used as a personal journal for an individual. Weblogs have been around for several years but couldn't be implemented on a wide scale because creating and publishing Web pages was fairly complicated. Today's new *blog tools* make updating a blog as easy as typing a new entry on a form and pressing a Publish button (see Figure U-25), so blog use is now on the rise. In mid-2002, the *New York Times* estimated that over one-half million Weblogs were in existence, with that number growing all the time. Today, blogs are used to express personal opinions, for work-related collaborations, and in writing classes.

Internet Radio Royalty Update

One Web-based multimedia application that continues to gain popularity as the use of broadband Internet access has increased is *Internet radio*—Web sites that broadcast songs over the Internet. It has been estimated that there are approximately 25 million listeners to the 10,000 or so different online stations. Historically, radio stations have been exempt from paying royalties on the songs they play because they provide promotional value for songs. However, the recording industry has long opposed the exemption and the Digital Millennium Copyright Act enacted in 1999 included a clause granting record companies and artists the right to be paid an additional royalty whenever their recordings are played over the Internet.

The proposed royalty rate was originally set at $1.40 per song per 1,000 listeners and was later cut in half to 70 cents per song per 1,000 listeners to be paid beginning in late 2002. However, the fee was still too high for many independent Internet radio stations with low revenues and began forcing them off the air. For instance, the popular SomaFM.com station shut down in June 2002 to avoid paying approximately $15,000 per month in royalties (the site was supported by listener donations, which brought in approximately $3,000 per month in revenues). The controversy continued until the end of 2002 when Congress passed legislation allowing smaller Internet radio broadcasters to pay lower royalty fees (the actual rate is set on an individual basis depending on the radio station's revenue). Assuming the bill is signed into law, this may resolve the Internet radio controversy once and for all—in fact, SomaFM.com had just gone back online at the time of this writing.

Access Update

The increased use of smart phones and other mobile devices, as well as the increased use of assistive input and output devices, has affected Web designers to a greater extent this past year. As shown in Figure U-26, Web content for mobile phones and other portable devices displays differently than Web content for PCs—namely, images and multimedia content are limited and the screen size is much smaller. Web developers also need to consider users of assistive output devices, such as the Braille display shown in Figure U-26 that translates all screen output into Braille that can then be read by the fingers. Web developers must be aware of the fact that these devices usually cannot understand images or multimedia content so they must design Web pages to accommodate these restrictions.

One multimedia-oriented trend is the *smart classroom.* An emerging trend for the future is *ultra wideband (UWB) communications.*

NEW AND EMERGING TRENDS

Smart Classrooms

As a result of the trend to incorporate multimedia technology into the classroom, *smart classrooms* have become more common (see Figure U-27). At a basic level, a smart classroom may contain an instructor station with a desktop or notebook PC connected to a data projector so that software can be demonstrated, Internet resources can be accessed, and PowerPoint presentations can be displayed for the entire class at one time. An even smarter classroom might also include

FIGURE U-27
Smart classrooms.
Smart classrooms can range from small classrooms with individual PCs and a projection system (left) to large teleconferencing auditoriums (right).

a videotape and DVD player, a document camera, and a sound system. High-end smart classrooms can include two-way audio and video conferencing capabilities; either built-in PCs or network connections at all student desks so students can plug in their portable PCs for immediate access to the campus intranet, class Web content, and Internet resources; and the ability for the instructor to send images (for instance, the image on his or her monitor, an image on a student's monitor, or a video frame) to all student PCs. Some setups are used for distance learning, as well as for traditional classroom meetings. The idea behind the smart classroom is to provide instructors immediate access to all the multimedia resources they might need for effective class meetings. Typically, these resources are available through a central control panel located at the instructor's station, although future smart classrooms may be voice controlled.

Ultra Wideband (UWB) Communications

Ultra Wideband (UWB) communications is a wireless technology that was originally developed for the military in the 1960s; today, it is in the initial stages of experimentation for consumer use. UWB can be used both indoors and outdoors and currently transmits data at speeds up to 60 Mbps, although that is expected to increase eventually to 1 Gbps. Applications currently in development focus on consumer multimedia. For example, BE LABS' *Wireless Multimedia System (WMS)* is a within-the-home, Ultra Wideband wireless delivery system for multiple high-quality streaming video, data, and audio sources. Recent tests indicate that an HDTV-quality signal can be transmitted anywhere within a house within a range of about 300 feet. BE LABS is positioning their WMS product as a multimedia gateway to replace wired set-top boxes for cable and satellite TV services, as well as to centralize the delivery of high speed Internet access, cordless phone services, video on demand, and other multimedia services into one comprehensive platform.

To develop standards for networking personal multimedia devices using systems such as UWB, nine leading technology companies recently formed the *WiMedia Alliance.* This non-profit organization will adopt standards and establish a certification program to accelerate widespread consumer adoption of wireless multimedia solutions.

UPDATE

The past year has seen growth in the use of e-commerce and m-commerce, increased attention paid to CRM, and the emergence of *Web services.*

E-Commerce and M-Commerce Update

Despite the economic slowdown and national security concerns, e-commerce in the United States has continued to grow at a steady pace. According to comScore Networks, total consumer online sales for 2002 through September 30 was $52.5 billion, up 41% over the same period in 2001. Many expect this trend to continue, such as Michelle David Adams, comScore Networks vice president, who recently predicted "E-commerce will continue to outgrow traditional retail, as the Internet appeals to growing numbers of consumers in search of the best deals, convenience, and breadth of offerings." A recent report titled "E-Commerce and Development Report" issued by the U.N. Conference on Trade and Development (UNCTAD) estimates that around 18% of all purchasing by firms and individuals could be done over the Web by 2006.

The UNCTAD report also estimated that m-commerce will generate worldwide revenues of almost $50 billion in 2002 and grow to $225 billion by 2005. According to the report, difficulties in making electronic payments and concerns over the security and privacy of transactions are currently limiting the m-commerce market. A new *u-commerce* trend (see the Inside the Industry box) being strongly supported by Visa may help eliminate these problems.

Increased Emphasis on CRM

Despite the tight economy, U.S. companies spent almost $10 billion on customer relationship management (CRM) systems in 2001 and the research firm Jupiter predicts that CRM spending will exceed $16 billion by 2006. New online CRM tools such as those that add an *e-community* to the company Web site for customer use are becoming more widely prevalent. These CRM tools allow customers to exchange ideas, ask questions, and provide feedback on products, as well as chat online live with technical support who provide instant answers to questions (see Figure U-28).

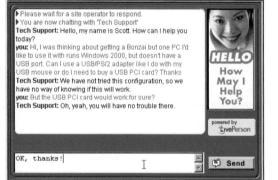

▶ FIGURE U-28

Customer service or technical support live chat accessible through the company Web site is becoming more widely used as an e-CRM tool.

Web Services

The term *Web services* refers to a way of allowing organizations to communicate data with each other and with clients. Building on the idea of interorganizational systems, such as EDI, Web services provide a standardized way of integrating Web-based applications over the Internet. The real value of Web services is that they can help a variety of individual systems work together. Use of Web services is expected to grow rapidly over the next year and help facilitate integration between companies. They can also speed up the delivery of products and services, and help build faster and stronger customer and partner relationships.

NEW AND EMERGING TRENDS

New and emerging trends regarding e-business and e-commerce include a variety of new *enterprise computing* tools—tools that support company operations. Two examples are *product life cycle management (PLM)* and *price optimization systems.*

Product Life Cycle Management (PLM)

The goal of *product life cycle management* is to organize and correlate all information about a product (such as specifications, quality history, customer feedback, research and testing results, and sales history) to help companies improve products, more efficiently create and manage the production of products, and better track costs and profits. PLM software—often available as a Web-based application—links electronically all facets and

inside the industry

U-Commerce: Another Step Towards a Cashless Society?
E-commerce (buying goods and services electronically) and m-commerce (performing e-commerce using a mobile communications device) has helped move us towards a cashless society, but we're not there yet. The management at Visa is looking towards *u-commerce* to help move us another step closer. U-commerce or *universal commerce* is thought by many to be the next natural step for e-commerce and m-commerce, continuing to move these activities from the "point of sale" to "point of convenience"—wherever and whenever a financial transaction needs to occur. With u-commerce, transferring funds electronically via your PC, PDA, smart phone, or other electronic device is expected to continue to get easier and easier, facilitating activities such as instructing your PC to pay a bill on its due date; transferring funds to your secretary for your share of an office gift; ordering lunch and paying the taxi fare electronically during the cab ride to a restaurant; or buying a movie or concert ticket from an ATM machine or public kiosk (see the accompanying illustration). With u-commerce, these types of transactions can take place seamlessly regardless of the time of day, physical location, or currency and payment device being used.

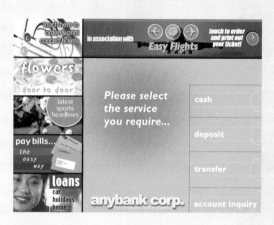

members of a project team, regardless of their locations, making new information available to the entire team as it becomes known. PLM is credited for dramatically reducing the amount of time needed to implement design changes and get products to market. For instance, Cannondale Bicycle credits PLM for enabling their first-ever ATV product to be released on time, after just 14 months of development. Cannondale estimates their motorsport group spends 40% less time on communications while old problems—such as delayed production due to out-of-date schematics and wasted days test-driving old versions of components—have virtually been eliminated. According to a recent survey by AMR Research, managers selected PLM as their most needed new software.

Price Optimization Systems

Price optimization is the practice of maximizing revenues and profits through determining the optimal price for products to maximize profitability. It relies on computer analysis of sales data to set the optimal price of a product and its competing products to maximize a retailer's overall profit. Until recently, the complex calculations required for this type of analysis demanded sophisticated computers that were out of the price range of many businesses. With today's cheaper and more powerful computers, price optimization is now a powerful business tool available to many.

Price optimization software is most commonly used by grocery and drug stores; a similar type of software—*markdown optimization*—can be used by clothing, electronics, and other retailers of non-perishable goods to time markdowns of products towards the end of their lifecycle to maximize revenue. Forrester Research estimates that the move from "gut instinct" pricing to a price optimization software system will increase a company's gross margin anywhere from 2% to 10% in the first three months. To eliminate the problems of employees mismarking shelf prices, some retailers are turning towards *electronic shelf labels (ESLs),* such as the one shown in Figure U-29, which use radio technology to communicate wirelessly with the supermarket pricing computer so that shelf prices always match the optimized price.

FIGURE U-29
An electronic shelf label (ESL).

tech news video project

To complete the Chapter 11 "Telesurgery" video project, go to page U-38.

UPDATE

Over the past year, there has been an increase in the use of online collaboration tools, such as workgroup computing and videoconferencing. In the field of artificial intelligence, *chatterbots* have emerged and a number of new robot products have become available.

Increased Use of Online Collaboration Tools

Immediately following the attacks of 9/11, interest in videoconferencing and other types of online collaboration tools soared. With the airports closed, many meetings scheduled for the remainder of that week were held electronically; some World Trade Center businesses also used online collaboration tools to keep in touch with the families of the missing and to connect employees scattered at remote offices. PlaceWare, an Internet collaboration service provider, saw the market steadily growing prior to 9/11 but says that usage increased 38% following the attacks. Although business travel has since resumed, improvements in collaboration technology and the troubled economy have led an increasing number of firms to continue to use videoconferencing and collaboration tools.

► FIGURE U-30
A chatterbot.

Chatterbots

A *chatterbot* is a natural language artificial intelligence system—often represented visually by an animated character—that is capable of carrying on written "conversations" with humans. Often chatterbots respond both verbally and with appropriate physical gestures to create the illusion that the exchange is taking place between two thinking, living beings. Chatterbots are beginning to appear on Web sites (see Figure U-30), such as to answer basic customer questions or to deliver Web-based news and entertainment. Although some chatterbots are able to provide human-like responses to questions, true artificial intelligence has not been reached, as discussed in the Inside the Industry box.

► FIGURE U-31
Packbot entering a cave on its first mission in Kandahar, Afghanistan.

Robotics Update

There are a number of new robotic products that have recently become available. The iRobot company has several new robotic devices, including *CoWorker* (a 3-foot tall teleconferencing robot that can transmit video and audio to individuals at remote locations via their Web browser, enabling them to participate in meetings, tour facilities, etc.); *Roomba* (a robotic vacuum cleaner that can vacuum a room on its own); and *Packbot* (a battlefield robot that can be used to check out trails, buildings, caves, and other structures before soldiers enter them—see Figure U-31).

NEW AND EMERGING TRENDS

Not surprisingly, many new and emerging trends in AI and robotics are developed on behalf of the military or national security. For instance, work on the *exoskeleton suit* is progressing and a new smart airline passenger screening system is being developed.

Smart Airline Passenger Screening Systems

The push for more effective airline passenger screening systems escalated following the tragic events of 9/11. As a result, the government has been developing a second generation of the *Computer-Assisted Passenger Prescreening System (CAPPS)* now in use—the new system is referred to as *CAPPS II*. In place since the mid-1990s, the original CAPPS system attempts to spot potential hijackers by examining such details as whether a ticket was paid for in cash, whether it was a one-way ticket, and how long before the date of departure it was purchased. Although information about the new system is closely guarded, it is expected to use AI software, data mining techniques, and biometric technology to predict who might be a potential terrorist. The software will likely make predictions by analyzing a variety of personal information and spotting predictors—such as social associations with known terrorists or unusual bank account activity—that might otherwise go unnoticed.

inside the industry

The Turing Test and Loebner Prize

According to John McCarthy, who coined the term artificial intelligence (AI) in 1956 and is considered by many to be one of its fathers, AI is "the science and engineering of making intelligent machines." In other words, AI is concerned with creating intelligent devices controlled by intelligent software programs—machines that think and act like humans. At the present time, AI systems tend to mimic human intelligence instead of display pure intelligence. In 1950, Alan Turing—one of the first AI researchers—argued that if a machine could successfully pretend to be human to a knowledgeable observer then it should be considered intelligent. To illustrate this idea, Turing developed a test—later called the *Turing Test*—in which one observer interacts with both a computer and a human being electronically (originally by teletype and later by computer). During the test, the observer asks both the computer and the human questions in writing, evaluates their written responses, and tries to identify which answers came from the computer and which came from the human. Turing argued that if the computer could repeatedly fool the observer into thinking it was human, then it should be viewed as intelligent.

Many Turing Test contests have been held over the years, and in 1990, Dr. Hugh Loebner initiated the Loebner Prize, pledging a grand prize of $100,000 and a solid gold medal (see the accompanying photo) for the first computer whose responses to a Turing Test were indistinguishable from a human's. A contest is held every year, awarding a prize of $2,000 and a bronze medal to the most human computer, but so far the gold medal has not been awarded.

The Loebner Prize gold medal.

Information to be analyzed may include personal information taken from passenger manifests and data culled from numerous government databases and private databases belonging to banks, credit-reporting agencies, and other companies that collect detailed personal information. Although some experts believe that such a system could be highly effective in increasing our personal safety, privacy advocates are concerned about the amount of personal data being aggregated, as well as the possibility of certain groups of people being unfairly targeted by the system.

Exoskeleton Suits

The term *exoskeleton* refers to a hard protective or supportive outer structure. Currently being researched and developed by several organizations—such as MIT, Oak Ridge National Laboratory (ORNL), and Sarcos—under grants from the Defense Advanced Research Projects Agency (DARPA), *exoskeleton suits* are wearable robotic systems designed to give soldiers additional physical capabilities and protection (see Figure U-32). For instance, an exoskeleton suit could give a soldier the ability to run faster, lift and carry heavier items, and leap over large obstacles. For protection, the exoskeleton suit would likely be made of light, protective material—possibly molecular-based chain mail—that would be bulletproof and could solidify on demand to form a shield or turn into a medical cast if a soldier got injured. Other possible features of the suit include changing its color automatically for camouflage purposes; relaying information via sensors about a soldier's health, injuries, and location to field headquarters; and administering painkillers or applying pressure to a wound when directed by a physician. Most of the proposed exoskeleton components are based on nanotechnology or robotics. Although they hope to deliver some usable exoskeleton components within the next five years, most researchers project that a true exoskeleton suit is many years from reality.

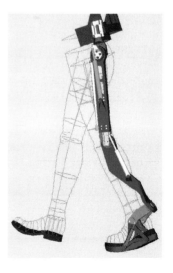

FIGURE U-32
One of ORNL's concepts for a lower-limb exoskeleton.

UPDATE

Over the past year, programming has continued to evolve to meet current needs. This year also saw changes in markup languages and application development tools.

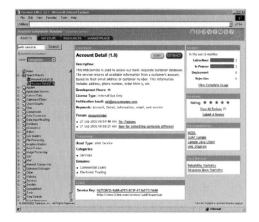

FIGURE U-33

A software-asset management program.

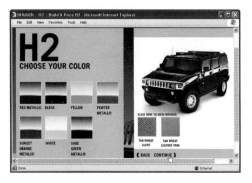

FIGURE U-34

Flash. This Web site uses Flash extensively; for instance, when you choose a color on this page, Flash redraws the car in that color.

Programming Languages Update

The Java programming language remains one of the most popular modern programming languages. In fact, beginning in the spring of 2004, Java will replace C++ as the programming language used for the Advanced Placement exam in Computer Science taken by high school students to earn college credit. Reusable code is still an important consideration for many developers and new *software-asset management programs* are available to act as central repositories of tested software components that can be used in new applications quickly and effectively. For instance, the Flashline CMEE program (see Figure U-33) can be used to manage many types of software assets, such as a company's Java and .NET components and Web services. Asset management can take place anywhere from an individual project level to an enterprise level and search features allow easy retrieval of appropriate assets. The goal in using software-asset management software is to build new applications and support new business processes more quickly and reliably.

Markup Languages and Application Development Tools Update

This year brought the beginning of the next generation of HTML, called *XHTML 2.0.* The XHTML 2.0 standard includes new tags for line breaks, embedded objects, and headings, as well as a new forms model expected to be a large improvement for businesses maintaining Web-based applications. In addition, developers are looking towards other alternatives—such as Flash—to create Web content. Although Flash has been used consistently to create opening *splash* pages for Web sites and for individual animated components, it is beginning to be viewed as a viable development tool for overall Web development (see Figure U-34) and as an interface builder for rich corporate software applications. There is increased interest in improving the quality of the interfaces used for Web page visitors and other end users to make them more attractive, user-friendly, and useful—Macromedia hopes to fill that niche with Flash.

Additional .NET development tools have become available recently, such as Microsoft *Visual J#.NET*—a development tool for Java-language developers who want to build applications and services using the Microsoft .NET Framework. Attention has also focused on providing content and Web services for wireless devices. For instance, Microsoft's *.NET Compact Framework* is available for developers wanting to implement Web services on mobile devices.

While many developers are looking ahead to the future, some are preserving the past, as discussed in the Inside the Industry box.

NEW AND EMERGING TRENDS

New and emerging programming trends include *aspect-oriented programming* and a new alternative to the .NET platform.

Aspect-Oriented Programming

Aspect-oriented programming (AOP) is an emerging type of software development tool, based on more than a decade of research at Xerox's PARC, IBM, Boston's Northeastern University, and the Netherland's University of Twente. AOP is able to encapsulate critical policies such as security, error handling, and data caching as aspects of a program that can be woven into the code wherever they are needed.

inside the industry

Antique Software

Software developed before about 1990–called *antique software* by some–is not widely used today, but there are a few individuals who have never left it behind. While the computer industry pushes businesses and consumers to continually upgrade to the next version of each software program, some *software preservationists* want people to remember the programs developed at the beginning of the PC era. For instance, Dave Winer, the current CEO of UserLand Software, has recently posted downloadable versions of three of his early applications from the 1980s on his Web site (with permission from his former publishers).

Another software preservationist is Dan Bricklin, co-creator of VisiCalc, the first spreadsheet program designed for the PC, which was released in 1979 (see the accompanying illustration). Bricklin has placed a downloadable version of the original VisiCalc program on his Web site (with permission from copyright holder Lotus) so that people can download and try out

the program. One of the most amazing things about VisiCalc is that while it was considered to be one of the first "killer apps" for PCs at the time it was released, the entire program is only 27 KB–less than a typical one-page Microsoft Word document.

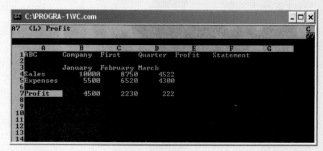

This original version of VisiCalc requires only 27 KB of disk space.

Today's object-oriented systems don't do this well, so policies may end up being located in hundreds or thousands of places scattered throughout a program's code, making it very difficult to update them when needed. Aspect-oriented programming's ability to cut across the typical divisions of responsibility in a given programming model—such as across multiple classes in an object-oriented program—is called *crosscutting* and helps to avoid this problem, improving software quality and lowering IT development and maintenance costs.

One aspect-oriented programming tool recently released is *AspectJ,* an aspect-oriented extension to the Java programming language; IBM is reported to have a similar product under development. Some AOP advocates view it as the next logical step after object-oriented programming, continuing the trend of making software programs smaller and more manageable by sharing and reusing more code across their parts. In fact, John Seely Brown, director emeritus of Xerox PARC, views AOP as "the next generation of software engineering."

IBM's .NET Alternative

Although Microsoft would like people to think of Web services and .NET hand-in-hand, IBM recently announced a new software solution—called *IBM WebSphere Studio Version 5* and shown in Figure U-35—designed to make it easier to create Web services from new and existing applications across multiple platforms, languages, legacy applications, and vendors. Instead of forcing companies to rewrite applications to fit a particular model (such as .NET), the program allows the use of Java and traditional assets (such as COBOL code) in a single development environment for Web services—an industry first. Consequently, developers can integrate older software assets into Web services, while writing needed new applications in Java. The development tools included in the WebSphere Studio suite include performance analysis and tracing tools, legacy asset analysis, automatic code generators, integrated debuggers, and built-in test environments to detect bugs early in the development process.

FIGURE U-35
IBM's WebSphere Studio Version 5 is positioning itself as a viable alternative to .NET for developing Web services.

tech news video project

To complete the Chapter 13 "Homeless Hacker" video project, go to page U-39.

UPDATE

Recent changes in databases include increased emphasis on data protection and moving towards *multi-tiered* database systems.

Increased Emphasis on Data Protection

Although data integrity and security have always been high priority database issues, since the terrorist attacks of 9/11 (see Figure U-36) there has been increased attention paid to this aspect of data protection. The total destruction of the computer housing a crucial database, as well as the threat of unauthorized access and data alteration of a vital system, are being viewed as much more realistic than just a few years ago. Consequently, many businesses and government organizations are evaluating their computer access control methods and improving them, if needed. When warranted, general access to the system can be protected by an access card or biometric system; typically access to data and files is controlled by user names and passwords and the allowable activities (such as read, add, update, and delete) can be specified down to the individual column level. To protect against disasters, such as hard drive failure or the total destruction of the computer, possible precautions include keeping a redundant copy of the database on a mirrored drive, backing up the data at frequent intervals, and having a comprehensive *disaster-recovery plan,* as discussed in more detail in Chapter 15.

FIGURE U-36

System destruction. The 9/11 attacks killed nearly 3,000 people and destroyed hundreds of business offices, including critical cables located at this Verizon building adjacent to Ground Zero.

Multi-Tiered Database Systems

Client-server database systems—where a front end client accesses the database located on the back end server—have become the most commonly implemented database model. A growing trend is to use an *n-tier database system,* in which there is at least one middle piece of software—referred to as middleware—between the client and the server, instead of having just two components (the client and the server) as in the typical 2-tier system (see Figure U-37). The additional tiers—such as the middle tier in a *3-tier database system*—provide caching and other functionality to improve performance. In addition, because the programming for a tier can take place in languages different from the other tiers and can be changed or relocated without affecting the other tiers, the n-tier model makes it easier for the database system to be modified as new needs and opportunities arise. N-tier systems are most commonly found in e-commerce applications.

FIGURE U-37

A 2-tier vs. an n-tier database model.

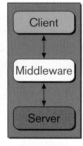

2-TIER MODEL

N-TIER MODEL (the middleware section can be one or more programs)

NEW AND EMERGING TRENDS

New and emerging database trends include data warehousing growth and the emergence of *in-memory* database systems. The use of DNA and biometric databases for criminal and terrorist identification is discussed in the Trend box.

Data Warehousing Growth

As discussed in Chapter 11, a data warehouse is a comprehensive collection of data belonging to a company. Both the use of data warehousing and the size of data warehouse databases have been increasing lately. For instance, Wal-Mart's data warehouse has been expanded to hold over 200 terabytes of data and some experts predict the first data warehouse with a petabyte of storage space will emerge in 2004. These huge leaps in size complicate information retrieval and are requiring database vendors to improve their software; many are developing new database tools to support petabyte-sized databases.

DNA and Biometric Databases

Today's databases can contain more than just photos and fingerprints—for example, they can contain DNA and voice clips. Two such database systems are the FBI's *Combined DNA Index System (CODIS)* and the military's *Biometrics Automated Toolset (BAT)*.

The CODIS system is a national DNA database containing DNA data about criminals (state law governs who is required to provide DNA samples, but typically sampling is limited to convicted criminals or criminals convicted of violent crimes). The DNA profiles (more than 1 million are currently in the system) are uploaded to the database and analyzed using computers (see the accompanying photo). Law enforcement officials can search the CODIS system when investigating unsolved crimes to try to find a match with a criminal whose DNA profile is already in the database—a match made in this way is called a "cold hit". Many states have begun offering financial assistance to counties to enter DNA data from old unsolved cases into the system and it has begun to produce results. For instance, California's old cases are being solved at the rate of about one per day, and Virginia has produced over 1,000 cold hits to date. Prosecutors and law enforcement agencies view the CODIS system as a powerful law enforcement tool. Although some privacy advocates dislike the idea of a national DNA database, DNA evidence can work both ways—already over 100 people in the U.S. have been cleared of the crimes they were convicted of due to the subsequent use of DNA testing.

The military's BAT system, in use since early 2002, is used to collect and store biometric data gathered from prisoners apprehended during the Afghanistan conflict. It is also expected to be used to gather information about potential terrorists encountered during any future military actions in other countries. Data is gathered for the terabyte-sized BAT database using a collection of laptop computers equipped with biometric scanners. Other data that can be entered into the database include surveillance photos, anonymous fingerprints gathered during investigations, text and sound clips from prisoner interrogations, and digital images of scanned items seized during a search. The idea behind the BAT system is to be able to identify terrorists when they are detained or at checkpoints, even if they have changed their identity papers or appearance. The database can be accessed by soldiers in the field via satellite telephone.

Crime lab computers, such as this one in the Massachusetts State Police Crime Laboratory's DNA Unit, analyze and compare DNA evidence.

In-Memory Databases

With the recent reduction in the cost of RAM this past year, there has been increasing interest in *in-memory databases (IMDBs)*—databases that are designed to hold all data in the main memory of the computer, rather than on disk. In-memory databases can perform dramatically faster than disk-based databases, however backing up data or otherwise periodically storing the data on a nonvolatile medium is extremely important since data in RAM is lost if the computer goes down or power goes out. Most IMDBs today can synchronize two or more database copies for non-stop operation, as well as include some type of capability to copy data from memory to a nonvolatile medium to protect against data loss—although user backups are still critical. IMDBs are beginning to be used both in high-end systems where performance is crucial (such as in e-commerce applications) and in small-footprint, embedded applications (such as set-top boxes and other smart consumer electronic devices).

UPDATE

Many of the recent changes in societal issues such as ethics, computer crime, and privacy have been in response to recent events; for example, the increased occurrence of illegal corporate behavior and the war on terrorism. A brief look at noteworthy changes follows.

Ethics Update

The large number of corporate scandals occurring during 2002 has brought personal and business ethics into the public eye. The scandals—such as the ones surrounding Enron, Tyco International, WorldCom, and Martha Stewart—involved lies, fraud, deception, and other illegal and unethical behavior, which forced both Enron and WorldCom into bankruptcy proceedings and threatened many individuals with jail time. When asked to comment on the scandals, 3Com chief executive officer Bruce Claflin said on CNBC that "I would argue we don't have an accounting problem—we have an ethics problem."

As a result of these scandals, the *Sarbanes-Oxley Act of 2002*, also called the *Corporate Responsibility Act*, was passed. This law increases penalties for corporate wrongdoing and requires CEOs and CFOs personally to vouch for the truth of their company's disclosures. The scandals have also caused many business schools to evaluate their curriculum and consider balancing the traditional emphasis on profit maximization with ethics and social responsibility. To bring attention to the unethical nature of cheating on assignments or exams, many schools are also developing *academic honor codes*. At the University of Denver, for instance, all incoming students are asked to publicly sign the school's honor code (see Figure U-38). Regardless of whether or not students choose to sign the honor code, they are required to abide by it, and research shows that having an academic honor code effectively reduces cheating.

◆ FIGURE U-38

Academic honor codes.
The honor code at the University of Denver is signed by virtually all incoming students.

Computer Crime Update

The ever-growing amount of data being stored on computers connected to the Internet has led to growing concerns about unauthorized access, identity theft, credit card fraud, and other related computer crimes. And these crimes seem to be occurring more often and on a wider scale. For instance, in late 2002, the FBI and the U.S. Attorney charged three men with running an identity theft ring that impacted more than 30,000 consumers and cost nearly $3 million in losses—the largest identity theft case in U.S. history to date. In another recent example, two hackers calling themselves the *Deceptive Duo* broke into secured databases and published selected information onto government Web sites, purportedly to bring attention to these systems' vulnerabilities. To help prevent these types of acts, it is becoming increasingly important for businesses to strongly secure the computers housing their customer data and for consumers to use sensible precautions, such as only performing e-commerce transactions on secure Web servers.

Two other emerging types of computer crime are *cyberstalking*—the use of repeated threats or harassing behavior via e-mail or another Internet communications method—and *cybervandalism*—defacing or otherwise changing Web sites via hacking (see Figure U-39).

◆ FIGURE U-39

Cybervandalism. The Stanford Cardiology Web site (left image) was defaced by hackers in 2002 (right image).

Computers and Privacy Update

Although there has been a shift since 9/11 in how much personal freedom and privacy individuals are willing to trade for increased national security, concerns surrounding personal privacy still exist. Programs that help individuals filter out potential spam and control or identify the use of cookies, spyware, and *Web bugs* (tiny images located on

Web pages that transmit data about Web page visitors back to the Web page's server) are very popular.

Although *computer monitoring software* that records keystrokes or otherwise monitors computer activity is considered by many to be an invasion of privacy, it is being used more commonly by both employers (to ensure employees are performing only work-related activities and are not participating in any activities that might make the company legally vulnerable) and by the government (for law enforcement purposes). The federal government's use of keystroke monitoring software has increased dramatically because terrorists and other types of criminals are using sophisticated encryption software to protect their data and transmissions. Without the appropriate passwords, encrypted computer files intercepted during transit—such as by using the FBI's Carnivore program—are essentially useless, since it can take a long time for a supercomputer to crack today's strong encryption methods. However, using keystroke monitoring programs—such as the new *Magic Lantern* program—government agencies can obtain encryption passwords to decrypt and read encrypted files. Instead of having to be installed in person on the suspect's PC, Magic Lantern is designed to be installed using a computer virus sent over the Internet. Programs such as Magic Lantern are supported by the recent *USA Patriot Act,* which grants federal authorities expanded surveillance and intelligence-gathering powers.

New and emerging societal trends include increased use of *computer hoaxes* and *digital manipulation* and the increased occurrence of *computer* and *Internet addiction.*

NEW AND EMERGING TRENDS

Computer Hoaxes and Digital Manipulation

Computers and the Internet are being used frequently today to perform two types of acts that can be ethically questionable: *computer hoaxes* and *digital manipulation.* Computer hoaxes—inaccurate statements or stories—are commonly spread through e-mail today. Common hoax subjects include nonexistent computer viruses, serious health risks of a particular product, impending terrorist attacks, chain letters, and free prizes or give-aways (see Figure U-40). Because hoaxes are so common, regardless of how realistic or frightening the information appears to be, it is a good idea to double-check any warning you receive by e-mail or read on a Web site before passing that warning on to another person. One reliable source to use is the government's Hoaxbusters site found at hoaxbusters.ciac.org.

Digital manipulation usually consists of altering photographs using a PC. While there are some beneficial, ethical, and noncontroversial applications of digital manipulation—such as aging photos of missing children to show what they may look like at the present time—the matter of altering photos to be published is the subject of debate. Some publications and photographers see no harm in altering photographs to remove an offending item (such as a telephone pole behind someone's head), to make someone look more attractive, or for entertainment purposes; others view any change in content as unethical and a disservice to both the general public and our history. For example, fifty years from now, will anyone know that a staged or altered photograph of a historical event wasn't an actual depiction of the event? Adding to the problem is digital camera use by professional photographers, which virtually eliminates any concrete evidence—such as negatives—that show what photos looked like at the time they were taken.

Computer and Internet Addiction

Although experts disagree about whether it should be called an *addiction* or a *compulsion,* the problem of not being able to stop using a computer or the Internet—or the overuse of computers or the Internet creating problems in your personal or professional life—is increasingly being viewed by mental health professionals as a true psychophysiological disorder. And as such, computer addiction is a growing societal issue. Computer addiction can afflict people of any age and can take a variety of forms. The most common forms today are online chatting/instant messaging and online multiplayer games. Computer addiction can be treated, typically with therapy, support groups, or medication.

FIGURE U-40

Computer hoaxes. In late 2002, the Applebee's Web site added a pop-up message for Web site visitors in response to a hoax being widely distributed via e-mail.

tech news video project

To complete the Chapter 15 "Washington, D.C. Security Camera Network" video project, go to page U-39.

UPDATE

Many of the recent changes regarding buying and maintaining a PC center around the type of PC to buy and essential maintenance practices and security precautions.

FIGURE U-41
The NEC PowerMate Eco.

FIGURE U-42
A USB flash drive.

Update on Selecting a PC

One important decision to consider when selecting a PC today is choosing between a desktop PC and a portable PC. If the computer is to be used in a stationary position at all times, a desktop PC is the most practical and economic choice. Today's desktop PCs, such as the one shown in Figure U-41, tend to be smaller and more environmentally friendly than in the recent past. Although they are not meant to be portable, they do take up less room on the desktop and have an attractive, sleek appearance. Users who opt for a portable PC will have to decide if a notebook PC, a slate tablet PC, or one of the new convertible tablet PCs best meets their needs. In any case, all users should select a computer that contains at least a 1.8 GHz processor, a minimum of 256 MB RAM (512 MB is better), a DVD or CD drive, and at least two USB ports (many new PCs are using USB instead of serial, parallel, and PS/2 ports for most peripheral devices). Another option growing in popularity—especially for those individuals who will use a digital camera, digital music player, PDA, or other device that uses flash memory cards for storage—is a built-in slot or an external reader for flash memory cards. For transferring files from one PC to another, flash memory drives that plug into the computer's USB port (see Figure U-42) are becoming the standard.

Update on Maintaining and Safeguarding a PC

To protect their PCs from unauthorized access and computer viruses, all users should have an antivirus program running in the background at all times. Users with direct Internet connections should also use a firewall program. Performing routine maintenance—such as periodically deleting old Internet files and e-mail messages and running a disk defragmentation program—can also help keep your system running smoothly. Finally, creating a full backup of your system once all programs and settings are in place, as well as backing up your data files on a very regular basis, is an essential precaution. Remember, unless it is inside a fire-resistant safe, backup media should not be located in the same place as your PC.

NEW AND EMERGING TRENDS

New and emerging database trends include new trends in wearable PCs and new proposed programs to help facilitate computer recycling.

Trends in Wearable PCs

Although wearable computers for the workplace have been available for a few years, they are just beginning to take off as a viable business tool, as well as a personal computing option. Today's wearable PCs are used on the job in situations where hands-free computing is necessary or beneficial. One of the hottest new applications for wearable computing is sending wearable PC-equipped employees into a customer line to process orders more quickly—a technique called *line busting*. Because the orders are entered directly into the system by the line-busting employee, they can be processed more quickly than if that employee had to relay the message via a headset or walkie-talkie to another employee inside the establishment who would then place the order.

For personal computing, a tiny consumer wearable PC, designed to slip into a pocket, has recently been released. A head-mounted eyepiece display and a small pointing device are used in conjunction with the device. Until the time when personal electronics are more integrated into our clothing or jewelry, *e-garments* (such as the one shown in Figure U-43), can be used to help individuals more easily carry and use their personal electronics while on the go. Typically, these jackets or vests have built-in compartments to run cables inside the jacket to connect components, hide earbuds when not in use, and more.

One future application for wearable PCs includes displaying personalized information on the display screen in reaction to your current location and what you are currently looking at. This application (sometimes referred to as *augmented reality*) could provide directional information, data about restaurant and store hours as you look at those establishments—possibly even to provide personal information about the individuals that you pass on the street. In fact, a similar product—called a *smart badge*—is being developed for conference participants. These badges exchange information with other smart badges about their wearers to aid the communication and networking that occurs at conferences. Some pervasive computing advocates believe that the ultimate wearable computer will be the one embedded within the user's body. Needless to say, not everyone views that as a viable or desirable possibility.

Computer Recycling

When a computer becomes functionally obsolete or damaged and needs to be replaced, the issue of what to do with the old system arises. Unfortunately, most of it ends up in landfills (see Figure U-44). Compounding the problem of the amount of *electronic waste* or *e-waste* is the fact that conventional PC hardware contains a variety of toxic and hazardous materials, and nontoxic components may be made of material that is difficult to recycle. For instance, the average CRT monitor alone contains about eight pounds of lead and a single computer may contain up to 700 different chemical elements and compounds, many of which (such as arsenic, lead, mercury, and cadmium) are hazardous and expensive to dispose of properly.

In addition to more environmentally friendly components—such as flat-panel displays and system units made out of recyclable plastic—becoming more common, various programs have emerged to encourage recycling and the safe disposal of e-waste to try to protect people and the environment from future contamination from electronic waste. For instance, the *National Electronics Product Stewardship Initiative*—a coalition of computer companies, government agencies, and recycling centers—was recently formed to develop a plan to accept old computers, recycle any possible components, and safely dispose of the rest. The initiative is based on the concept of *product stewardship*, in which all parties who have a role in producing, selling, or using a product also have a role in managing it at the end of its useful life. The plan is expected to be financed through a fee added to the cost of new computers, gradually taking effect over the next few years. In the meantime, some recycling centers will accept computer equipment, but many charge a fee for this service. Another option is a manufacturer's program, such as the ones offered by IBM and Hewlett-Packard. If the manufacturer of your obsolete or broken computer equipment has such a program, typically you send the equipment—along with a processing fee—to the company and the company makes sure it gets to a recycling facility.

Expired toner cartridges and ink cartridges can sometimes be returned to the manufacturer (using the supplied shipping label included with some cartridges) or exchanged when ordering new cartridges; the cartridges are then *recharged* (refilled) and resold. (Cartridges that cannot be refilled can be sent to a recycling facility.) In addition to helping to reduce e-trash in landfills, using recharged printer cartridges saves the consumer money, since they are less expensive than new cartridges. Other computer components—such as CDs, DVDs, and computer disks—can also be recycled through some organizations. Older equipment that is still functioning can often be donated to schools and nonprofit groups.

FIGURE U-43

E-garments. Specialized jackets and vests with multiple pockets and compartments for housing PDAs, cell phones, MP3 players, and other personal electronics and for managing their cables are becoming available.

FIGURE U-44

E-trash. The vast majority of the 40 million or so computers that become obsolete each year end up in landfills, often in other countries such as China, India, and Pakistan.

inside the industry

A Look at Computer Generations

The computer, in the form we recognize today, is a fairly recent invention. In fact, personal computers have only been around since the 1970s. But the basic ideas of computing and calculating are very old, going back thousands of years. The history of computers is often referred to in terms of *generations,* with each new generation characterized by a major technological development. This box takes a look at early calculating devices and the different computer generations.

Pre-Computers and Early Computers (Before Approximately 1945)

Ancient civilizations demonstrated a desire to count and compute, as illustrated by archeological finds such as notched bones, knotted twine, and hieroglyphics. The *abacus* is considered by many to be the earliest recorded calculating device. Believed to have been invented by the Babylonians sometime between 500 B.C. and 100 B.C., it and similar types of counting boards were used solely for counting.

Other early computing devices include the *slide rule,* the *mechanical calculator,* and Dr. Herman Hollerith's *Punch Card Tabulating Machine and Sorter.* This device (see the accompanying photo) was the first electromechanical machine that could read *punch cards*—special cards with holes punched in them to represent data. Hollerith's machine was used to process the 1890 U.S. Census data and was able to complete the task in two and a half years, instead of the decade it usually took to process the data manually.

First Generation (Approximately 1945-1957)

First-generation computers were powered by *vacuum tubes* and were enormous, often taking up entire rooms. The vacuum tubes—glass tubes that look similar to large cylindrical light bulbs—needed replacing constantly, required a great deal of electricity, and generated a lot of heat. These computers could only solve one problem at a time, and needed to be physically rewired to be reprogrammed. Usually paper punch cards and paper tape were used for input, and output was printed on paper.

Two of the most significant examples of first generation computers were *ENIAC* and *UNIVAC*. ENIAC (see the accompanying photo) was the world's first large-scale, general-purpose computer and was developed for the U.S. Army. UNIVAC was the first computer to be mass produced for general commercial use and was used to analyze votes in the 1952 U.S. presidential election. Interestingly, its correct prediction of an Eisenhower victory only 45 minutes after the polls closed wasn't publicly aired because the results weren't trusted.

▷ **Computer history generations.**

PRE-COMPUTERS
Dr. Herman Hollerith's Punch Card Tabulating Machine and Sorter is an example of an early computing device. It was used to process the 1890 U.S. Census in about one-quarter of the time usually required to tally the results by hand.

FIRST GENERATION
First-generation computers, such as ENIAC shown here, were large and bulky, used vacuum tubes, and had to be physically wired and reset to run programs.

Second Generation (Approximately 1958-1963)

The *second generation* of computers began when the *transistor* started to replace the vacuum tube. Transistors—devices made of semiconductor material that can act like switches to open or close electronic circuits—allowed computers to be physically smaller, more powerful, cheaper, more energy-efficient, and more reliable than before. Typically data was input on punch cards and magnetic tape, output was on punch cards and paper printouts, and magnetic tape and disks were used for storage (see the accompanying photo). *Programming languages* (such as *FORTRAN* and *COBOL*) were also developed and implemented during this generation.

Third Generation (Approximately 1964-1970)

The replacement of the transistor with *integrated circuits (ICs)* marked the beginning of the *third generation* of computers. Integrated circuits incorporate many transistors and electronic circuits on a single tiny silicon *chip*, allowing computers to be even smaller and more reliable than in earlier generations. Instead of punch cards and paper printouts, keyboards and monitors were introduced for input and output; magnetic disks were typically used for storage. The introduction of the computer operating system during this generation meant that operators no longer had to reset relays and wiring manually. An example of a third-generation computer is shown in the accompanying photograph.

Fourth Generation (Approximately 1971-Present)

The ability to place an increasing number of transistors on a single chip led to the invention of the *microprocessor* in 1971, which ushered in the *fourth generation* of computers. In essence, a microprocessor contains the core processing capabilities of an entire computer on one single chip. The original IBM PC (see the accompanying photo) and Apple Macintosh, and most of today's modern computers, fall into this category. Computers in this generation typically use a keyboard and mouse for input; a monitor and printer for output; and magnetic disks and optical discs for storage. This generation also witnessed the development of computer networks and the Internet.

Fifth Generation (Now and the Future)

Although some people believe that the *fifth generation* of computing has not yet begun, most think it is in its infancy stage. This generation has no precise classification and some experts disagree with one another about its definition, but one common opinion is that fifth-generation computers will be based on *artificial intelligence*, where computers can think, reason, and learn. Voice recognition will likely be a primary means of input, and computers may be constructed differently than they are today, such as in the form of optical computers that can compute at the speed of light.

SECOND GENERATION
Second-generation computers, such as the IBM 1401 mainframe shown here, used transistors instead of vacuum tubes so they were physically smaller, faster, and more reliable than earlier computers.

THIRD GENERATION
The integrated circuit marked the beginning of the third generation of computers. These chips allowed the introduction of smaller computers, such as the DEC PDP-8 shown here, which was the first commercially successful minicomputer.

FOURTH GENERATION
Fourth-generation computers (such as the original IBM PC shown here) are based on microprocessors. Most of today's computers fall into this category.

tech news
video projects

These eight Tech News Video Projects, which are new to this enhanced edition of Understanding Computers, are designed to be used in conjunction with selected TechTV news clips (located on the Online Companion site at www.course.com/parker2002/videos).

Instructions: Following your instructor's directions, watch the video either individually or as a class, and then express your opinion on the issue detailed in the video in a class discussion, via an online discussion group or class chat room, or in a written paper. Although they are designed to be completed after every other chapter in the Understanding Computers text, the projects may be assigned at any time during the course—check with your instructor if you are unsure when you are expected to complete these projects.

Chapter 1: Introduction to the World of Computers

tech news
video project

To view the "High Tech Climbing" video clip, go to www.course.com/parker2002/videos

1. **High Tech Climbing** Pervasive computing has found its way into the world of sports via the increased number of technological devices and gadgets available for sportspeople. The accompanying video clip features professional mountain climber Ed Viesturs who brings a variety of high-tech gear (such as a notebook computer, digital video camera, satellite phone, solar panels to recharge the equipment, and an all-in-one digital barometer, thermometer, altimeter, and wind gauge) on his climbs.

After watching the video, think about the impact of technology on sporting and recreational activities. Viesturs' ability to get updated weather reports on his satellite phone as he is climbing unarguably keeps him safer, but is there a chance that this type of technology may endanger others? Could high-tech gadgets lead individuals into participating in potentially dangerous activities—such as mountain climbing and long-distance sailing and kayaking—that require expert knowledge, physical strength, and special skills to perform successfully? Could high-tech gadgets give individuals who are not properly prepared for an activity enough of a false sense of security so that they participate in the activity anyway, assuming that their technological devices will protect them? Will even experienced sportspeople rely too much on technology and ignore their good sense? Think of an outdoor sporting activity that you enjoy. Do you think bringing high-tech gear along would enhance or detract from the whole experience?

Form an opinion: What impact does the use of high-tech gadgets have on professional and personal sports?

According to your instructor's directions, either be prepared to discuss your position on this issue (in class, via an online class discussion group, or in a class chat room), or write a short paper stating and supporting your opinion. Use the video clip and the questions previously asked as the foundation for your response; you may also be asked to do research and provide additional resources to support your opinion.

Chapter 3: The System Unit: Processing and Memory

tech news
video project

To view the "Toxic PCs" video clip, go to www.course.com/parker2002/videos

2. **Toxic PCs** PC hardware—including the CPU and other chips, the motherboard, and the monitor—contains a variety of toxic and hazardous materials. As more and more computers are replaced by newer models, the problem of how to dispose of obsolete—and potentially dangerous—computer equipment, known as *e-waste*, grows. E-waste is also generated by the manufacturing of computer chips and other components. The accompanying video clip takes a look at the issue of e-waste and features resolutions by the Calvert Group, a self-proclaimed leader in the area of socially responsible investing.

After watching the video, think about the impact of e-waste on the environment. According to a press release by the Calvert Group, one computer may contain up to 700 different chemical compounds—such as arsenic, lead, mercury, and cadmium—many of which are hazardous. If the materials used in a PC are hazardous, should manufacturers be allowed to continue to use those materials or should they be forced to find alternatives? What if a restriction on these compounds severely limited the types of computer equipment that could be manufactured? Or, are landfills full of discarded equipment just the price we pay for being a technological society? What efforts should be made to recycle discarded PCs? Who should bear the cost of the recycling—the manufacturers, the consumers, the government? Would you be willing to pay more for a PC that was manufactured in an environmentally-friendly manner or that used more recyclable materials?

Form an opinion: What impact does e-waste have on society and who is responsible for reducing the amount of e-waste being generated?

According to your instructor's directions, either be prepared to discuss your position on this issue (in class, via an online class discussion group, or in a class chat room), or write a short paper stating and supporting your opinion. Use the video clip and the questions previously asked as the foundation for your response; you may also be asked to do research and provide additional resources to support your opinion.

3. **DirecTV Pirates** At least one type of satellite TV system—DirecTV—uses input from a special type of smart access card to tell the system which channels the user has paid to see. As discussed in the accompanying video, hackers can alter these cards to allow them to be used to steal satellite TV service. The cards are sold to individuals—usually through the Internet and newspaper ads. Once the altered card is inserted into the DirecTV receiver, the individual using the card is recognized as an authorized user.

After watching the video, think about the ramifications of depending on input contained on a hackable medium to identify who users are or what services they are entitled to receive, as well as the use of altered input cards to steal services. The U.S. Justice Department is actively pursuing distributors of these altered cards, but not individual buyers at the moment. DirecTV periodically sends out a signal that identifies altered access cards and destroys them. Is this procedure sufficient or should users of altered cards be prosecuted? In Canada, DirecTV doesn't have a license to broadcast its signals. For those Canadians who live in an area where the U.S. signal spills over the border, the only way they can get DirecTV is to steal it, although it isn't illegal, according to the video. If an individual can use false input—such as someone else's password or a hacked access card—to steal services or obtain products that are not illegal in the place they are located, does that make it ethically acceptable to do so? Does the growing ability of hackers to crack security measures built into smart cards and other physical access media make you wary of storing your personal information on a smart card?

Form an opinion: What is the impact of using hacked access and identity cards on our society?

According to your instructor's directions, either be prepared to discuss your position on this issue (in class, via an online class discussion group, or in a class chat room), or write a short paper stating and supporting your opinion. Use the video clip and the questions previously asked as the foundation for your response; you may also be asked to do research and provide additional resources to support your opinion.

4. **NASA Robot Crews** Robotics research is continuing to make smarter and more capable robots. NASA researchers have even developed software that enables a crew of robots to work together to grasp, lift, and move heavy loads across rough, varied terrain. The accompanying video clip takes a look at these new robots and some of their expected future uses.

After watching the video, think about the impact of programming robots to become more intelligent and capable of performing more complicated or more critical tasks. According to the video, the difference between the new NASA robot crews and other robots is special software that allows the robots to "share a brain," so that each robot knows what the rest are doing and can compensate or react accordingly. This technology enables the robots to work together to develop plans, such as how to maneuver around a rock or other obstacles the crew may encounter. Some worry that this technology provides the potential for a "super robot", such as the Borg enemy portrayed in the "Star Trek: The Next Generation" television show. Can robots

Chapter 5: Input and Output

**tech news
video project**

To view the "DirecTV Pirates" video clip, go to www.course.com/parker2002/videos

Chapter 7: Application Software

**tech news
video project**

To view the "NASA Robot Crews" video clip, go to www.course.com/parker2002/videos

and other software-driven devices get too smart? Is it the programmer's responsibility to ensure that his or her programs are not used in a socially-irresponsible manner? What steps should our society take to ensure that robotic devices cannot become physically dangerous? What roles do you envision robots assuming in the near future and five or ten years from now?

Form an opinion: What is the potential impact of continuing to make robots that are smarter and more capable than their previous versions?

According to your instructor's directions, either be prepared to discuss your position on this issue (in class, via an online class discussion group, or in a class chat room), or write a short paper stating and supporting your opinion. Use the video clip and the questions previously asked as the foundation for your response; you may also be asked to do research and provide additional resources to support your opinion.

Chapter 9: The Internet and World Wide Web

5. **Rural Broadband** Citizens who live in rural areas typically have less access to broadband Internet than those in more highly populated areas. Maryland's Speaker of the House Casper R. Taylor views this as the real digital divide. Without broadband, he believes that "our kids are not going to have the advantage of urbanized society going into the future if we're disconnected from the rest of the world...If we don't accomplish this, we are clearly creating a second-class society." The accompanying video clip discusses bringing broadband Internet access to his home town of Cumberland, Maryland.

After watching the video, think about the importance of broadband Internet and whose responsibility it is to provide it. If a region has only 56K dial-up service, does that really put it at a disadvantage? Is the digital divide more about separating those who have access to technology such as the Internet and those who don't, or is it about the quality of that technology? What about the government's role? Should the government provide the necessary infrastructure (as in Cumberland) to ensure an appropriate level of Internet access to all U.S. citizens? If not, how will the digital divide within the U.S. be eliminated? Will it ever be eliminated? What about your personal experience—if you have no Internet access at home or just dial-up service, do you feel you are at a competitive disadvantage for school or job success?

Form an opinion: What impact does access or lack of access to broadband Internet have on individuals, and is it the government's responsibility to make sure it is available to all?

According to your instructor's directions, either be prepared to discuss your position on this issue (in class, via an online class discussion group, or in a class chat room), or write a short paper stating and supporting your opinion. Use the video clip and the questions previously asked as the foundation for your response; you may also be asked to do research and provide additional resources to support your opinion.

tech news
video project

To view the "Rural Broadband" video clip, go to www.course.com/parker2002/videos

Chapter 11: E-Business and E-Commerce

6. **Telesurgery** The Internet, telecommunications technology, and robotics have advanced enough in recent years to allow for a new type of Internet application: *telesurgery* or operating on patients via a PC. The accompanying video clip features Dr. Louis Kavoussi of Johns Hopkins Bayview Medical Center, who performs surgery on patients all over the world from his home office instead of in the actual operating room. He uses his PC to control robotic surgical tools and cameras, as well as to give attending surgeons written and verbal instructions.

After watching the video, think about the impact of using remote technologies, such as those involved in telesurgery, to provide services in our society. There are obvious benefits to using remote technologies in military and space exploration applications, but will the average citizen go along with having surgery or other services performed via communications technology? What types of precautions will need to be taken to overcome concerns about software and hardware malfunctions, as well as privacy and security breaches? What other types of services may possibly be delivered via remote technology in the near future? Have you ever utilized a service delivered using remote technology, such as having a technician troubleshoot your PC

tech news
video project

To view the "Telesurgery" video clip, go to www.course.com/parker2002/videos

by accessing it remotely? Would you be willing to have telesurgery performed on you or utilize any other type of service delivered using remote technology?

Form an opinion: What impact does the use of remote technology to deliver services have on our society and on individuals' personal safety and privacy?

According to your instructor's directions, either be prepared to discuss your position on this issue (in class, via an online class discussion group, or in a class chat room), or write a short paper stating and supporting your opinion. Use the video clip and the questions previously asked as the foundation for your response; you may also be asked to do research and provide additional resources to support your opinion.

7. **Homeless Hacker** Hackers who try to gain access to business and government computers are a growing problem. Some hackers do it for monetary gain, others supposedly to bring attention to system and programming vulnerabilities or other, purportedly more noble, purposes. The accompanying video clip features 21-year-old Adrian Lamo, a freelance security consultant who regularly tries to hack into systems without authorization, looking for their security holes.

After watching the video, think about the impact of hackers breaching the security of business and government computers. If hackers like Lamo continue to use real networks and Web servers to practice and improve their hacking skills, what are the implications? Will it expose the data located on those networks to greater danger? Or will this type of hacking force programmers to tighten system security, improve firewall software, and, ultimately, create more secure systems? Lamo says that, while he is an intruder, he is guided by a sense of curiosity and he is helping corporations and consumers understand the limits of Internet and system security. Should these types of hacks be treated any differently than hackers who break into systems to steal data or other resources? Or, as Lamo charges, are companies at fault by leaving their networks unprotected? What responsibility, if any, do hackers who make their hacking programs available to others via the Internet have if those programs are used to access a system without authorization? If someone hacked into a computer system containing your personal information and read through your files but didn't change anything or use that information for any other purpose, would you want the hacker prosecuted?

Form an opinion: What impact does hacking have on businesses, the government, and individuals and how should it be treated?

According to your instructor's directions, either be prepared to discuss your position on this issue (in class, via an online class discussion group, or in a class chat room), or write a short paper stating and supporting your opinion. Use the video clip and the questions previously asked as the foundation for your response; you may also be asked to do research and provide additional resources to support your opinion.

8. **Washington, D.C. Security Camera Network** Individual live surveillance cameras are being used in an increasing number of public locations. Washington, D.C. is going one step further—it is building what will be the nation's largest network of surveillance cameras. The system is expected to include hundreds of cameras to watch over mass transit stations, public schools, traffic intersections, shopping malls, national monuments, and more. The accompanying video takes a look at the system and some of the objections to it from privacy groups.

After watching the video, think about the impact of live public video surveillance on our society. Is it a valid crime prevention tool or an invasion of privacy? Does the government have the responsibility to use every means possible to protect the country and its citizens? Or do citizens have the right not to be watched in public? What if it was a live police officer that was stationed at each video camera location instead of a camera? Is that more acceptable from a privacy standpoint? If people don't plan to commit criminal acts in public, should they be concerned that law enforcement personnel may see them? Would you object to being captured on a public surveillance tape?

Chapter 13: Program Development and Programming Languages

tech news video project

To view the "Homeless Hacker" video clip, go to www.course.com/parker2002/videos

Chapter 15: Ethics, Computer Crime, Privacy, and Other Social Issues

tech news video project

To view the "Washington, D.C. Security Camera Network" video clip, go to www.course.com/parker2002/videos

Form an opinion: What impact does public video surveillance have on our society and who should have the final say regarding how (or if) it will be used?

According to your instructor's directions, either be prepared to discuss your position on this issue (in class, via an online class discussion group, or in a class chat room), or write a short paper stating and supporting your opinion. Use the video clip and the questions previously asked as the foundation for your response; you may also be asked to do research and provide additional resources to support your opinion.

CREDITS

2003 Update

Throughout the 2003 Update: Screen shots of Microsoft Word and Windows reprinted with permission from Microsoft Corporation.

Internet Interfaces: Copyright Netscape Navigator. All rights reserved.; Copyright Microsoft Explorer reprinted with permission from Microsoft Corporation.

Figure U-1, Courtesy of Handspring, Inc.; **Figure U-2,** Courtesy Acer America; **Figure U-3,** Courtesy of iSun; **Figure U-5,** Courtesy of Orange SA; **Figure U-6,** Courtesy of Talkway, Inc.; **Figure U-7a,** Courtesy of Intel Corporation. Intel and Itanium are trademarks or registered trademarks of Intel Corporation or its subsidiaries in the United States and other countries.; **Figure U-7b,** © 2002 Advanced Micro Devices, Inc., Reprinted with permission. AMD, the Arrow AMD logo, AMD Athlon, AMD Opteron and combinations thereof are trademarks of Advanced Micro Devices, Inc.; **Figure U-8,** Courtesy: IBM Research, Almaden Research Center. Unauthorized use not permitted.; **Figure U-9,** Photo courtesy of Iomega Corporation. Copyright (c) 2002 Iomega Corporation. All Rights Reserved. Iomega, the sylized "i" logo and product images are property of Iomega Corporation in the United States and/or other countries.; **Figure U-10,** Courtesy Trekstor USA; **Figure U-11a,** Courtesy Logitech, Inc.; **Figure U-11b,** Courtesy of Seiko Instruments Austin, Inc.; **Figure U-12,** Courtesy of Sony Electronics Inc.; **Figure Chapter 5 Trend box,** Courtesy of Texas Instruments RFID Systems; **Figure U-13,** Courtesy of Microsoft Corporation; **Figure U-14,** Courtesy of Microsoft Corporation; **Figure U-17,** Courtesy of Microsoft Corporation; **Figure U-18,** Courtesy Diebold, Incorporated; **Figure U-19a,** Courtesy of NETGEAR; **Figure U-19b,** Courtesy of Proxim Inc.; **Figure U-20,** Courtesy of Pinellas County Sheriff's Office and Viisage Technology; **Figure U-21a,** Courtesy, University of Rochester; **Figure U-21b,** Courtesy of Computer Motion, Inc.; **Figure U-22,** Courtesy of Bantu, Inc.; **Figure Chapter 9 Trend box,** Courtesy of SkyTower, Inc.; **Figure U-26a,** Courtesy of Palm, Inc.; **Figure U-26b,** Courtesy of Freedom Scientific, Inc.; **Figure U-27a,** Courtesy of National Technical Institute for the Deaf; **Figure U-27b,** Courtesy of The Sextant Group, Inc.; **Figure Chapter 11 Inside the Industry box,** Courtesy of NCR Corporation; **Figure U-29,** Courtesy of NCR Corporation; **Figure Chapter 12 Inside the Industry box,** Courtesy of Dr. Hugh Loebner; **Figure U-31,** Courtesy of iRobot Corporation; **Figure U-32,** Courtesy of Oak Ridge National Laboratory; **Figure U-33,** Courtesy of Flashline, Inc.; **Figure U-35,** Courtesy of IBM Corporation; **Figure U-36,** Courtesy of Verizon Communications; **Figure Chapter 14 Trend box,** Photo courtesy of Massachusetts State Police Crime Lab; **Figure U-38,** Courtesy of University of Denver; **Figure U-41,** Courtesy of NEC Solutions (America), Inc.; **Figure U-42,** Courtesy of KTI Networks Inc.; **Figure U-43,** Courtesy of SCOTTeVEST, www.scottevest.com; **Figure U-44,** Courtesy of Silicon Valley Toxics Coalition; **Figure History of Computers Inside the Industry box: a,** Courtesy of IBM Archives; **b,** Courtesy U.S. Army; **c,** Courtesy of DEC; **d,** Courtesy of IBM Archives; **e,** Courtesy of IBM Archives.

Windows–History New Photos

a, Courtesy of Intel Corporation. Intel and Itanium are trademarks or registered trademarks of Intel Corporation or its subsidiaries in the United States and other countries.; **b,** Photo courtesy of Ericsson.

Windows–Web Guide New Photos

a, Courtesy of Microsoft Corporation; **b,** Courtesy of Motorola; **c,** Courtesy of Simply Internet Ltd.

Windows–Ubiquitous New Photos

a, Courtesy of NEC Solutions (America), Inc.; **b,** Courtesy of Motorola; **c,** Courtesy of Electrolux; **d,** Courtesy of Microsoft Corporation; **e,** Caourtesy of Handspring; **f,** Courtesy of Motorola; **g,** Photo courtesy Xybernaut Corporation; **h,** Courtesy of Microsoft Corporation.

Overview
The Decimal and Binary Numbering Systems
The Hexadecimal Numbering System
Converting Between Numbering Systems
Computer Arithmetic
Using a Scientific Calculator

This appendix covers fundamental characteristics of numbering systems. First the two primary numbering systems—the decimal numbering system (used by people) and the binary numbering system (used by computers)—that were discussed in Chapter 3 are reviewed, followed a discussion of the hexadecimal numbering system. The latter system is a shorthand way of representing long strings of binary numbers so they are more understandable to people. The appendix also covers conversions between numbering systems and principles of computer arithmetic. Instructions for using the Microsoft Windows scientific calculator to perform conversions are also provided.

The Decimal and Binary Numbering System

As discussed in Chapter 3, a numbering system is a way of representing numbers. The system we most commonly use is called the *decimal,* or *base 10,* system and uses 10 symbols—the digits 0, 1, 2, 3, 4, 5, 6, 7, 8, and 9—to represent all possible numbers. The *binary,* or *base 2,* system is used extensively by computers to represent numbers and other characters. This system uses only two digits—0 and 1. As illustrated in Figure 3-4 in Chapter 3, the place values (columns) in the binary numbering system are different than in the decimal system. For example, the right-most column has a value of 1, just like the decimal system, but the second column is the 2s column (instead of 10s), the third column is the 4s column (instead of 100s), and so on.

The Hexadecimal Numbering System

Computers often output diagnostic and memory-management messages to programmers and technically oriented users in *hexadecimal* (or *hex*) notation. Hex is a shorthand method for representing the binary digits stored in the computer system. Because large binary numbers—for example, 11010100010011101—can easily be misread by programmers, hexadecimal notation groups binary digits into units of four, which, in turn, are represented by other symbols.

Hexadecimal means *base 16,* implying that there are 16 different symbols in this numbering system. Because there are only 10 possible digits, hex uses letters instead of numbers for the extra 6 symbols. The 16 hexadecimal symbols and their decimal and binary counterparts are shown in Figure A-1.

FIGURE A-1

Hexadecimal characters and their decimal and binary equivalents

Hexadecimal Character	Decimal Equivalent	Binary Equivalent
0	0	0000
1	1	0001
2	2	0010
3	3	0011
4	4	0100
5	5	0101
6	6	0110
7	7	0111
8	8	1000
9	9	1001
A	10	1010
B	11	1011
C	12	1100
D	13	1101
E	14	1110
F	15	1111

Hexadecimal is not itself a code that the computer uses to perform computations or to communicate with other machines. This numbering system does, however, have a special relationship to the 8-bit bytes of ASCII and EBCDIC that makes it ideal for displaying messages quickly. As you can see in Figure A-1, each hex character has a 4-bit binary counterpart, so any combination of 8 bits can be represented by exactly 2 hexadecimal characters. Thus, the letter A (represented in EBCDIC by 11000001) has a hex representation of C1.

Let's look at an example to see how to convert from hex to decimal. Suppose you receive the following message on your display screen:

PROGRAM LOADED AT LOCATION 4F6A

This message tells you the precise location in memory of the first byte in your program. To determine the decimal equivalent of a hexadecimal number such as 4F6A, you can use the procedure shown in Figure A-2.

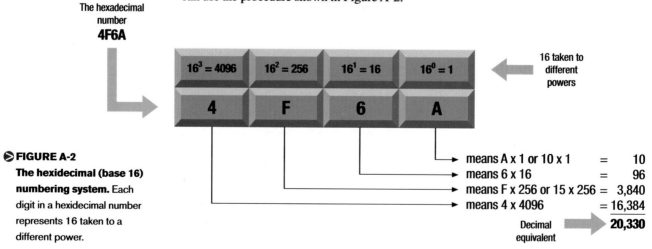

The hexadecimal number **4F6A**

$16^3 = 4096$	$16^2 = 256$	$16^1 = 16$	$16^0 = 1$
4	F	6	A

16 taken to different powers

means A x 1 or 10 x 1   =   10
means 6 x 16   =   96
means F x 256 or 15 x 256 = 3,840
means 4 x 4096   = 16,384

Decimal equivalent **20,330**

FIGURE A-2

The hexidecimal (base 16) numbering system. Each digit in a hexidecimal number represents 16 taken to a different power.

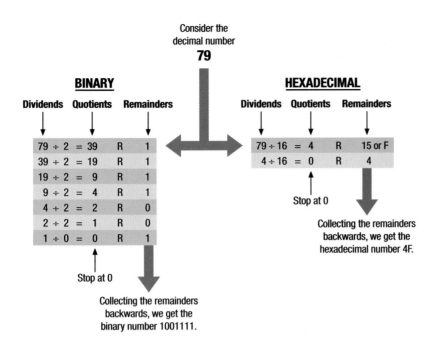

The remainder method.
The remainder method (dividing a decimal number by 2 or 16, and then repeating the process with the quotient until the quotient is 0) can be used to convert the number to binary or hexidecimal format. The remainders written backwards are the equivalent binary or hexidecimal representation.

Converting Between Numbering Systems

In Figure 3-4, we illustrated how to convert from binary to decimal; so far in this appendix, we've shown how to convert from hexadecimal to decimal. To convert the other way—from decimal to either binary or hex, we can use the remainder method. To use the remainder method, the number is divided by 2 (to convert to a binary number) or 16 (to convert to a hexadecimal number). The remainder of the division operation is recorded and the process is repeated using the quotient as the next dividend, until the quotient becomes 0. At that point, the collective remainders (written backwards) represent the equivalent binary or hexidecimal number (see Figure A-3).

To convert from base 16 to base 2, we convert each hex digit separately to 4 binary digits (using the table in Figure A-1). For example, to convert F6A9 to base 2, we get

F	6	A	9
1111	0110	1010	1001

or 1111011010101001 in binary representation. To convert from base 2 to base 16, we go through the reverse process. If the number of digits in the binary number is not divisible by 4, we add leading zeros to the binary number to force an even division. For example, to convert the binary number 1101101010011 to base 16, we get

0001	1011	0101	0011
1	B	5	3

or 1B53 in hexadecimal representation. Note that three leading zeros were added to make this conversion. A table summarizing all the numbering system conversion procedures covered in this text is provided in Figure A-4.

Computer Arithmetic

To most people, decimal arithmetic is second nature. Addition and subtraction using decimal numbers is introduced in kindergarten or first grade. Addition and subtraction using binary

> **FIGURE A-4**
>
> **Summary of conversions.**

From Base	To Base		
	2	**10**	**16**
2		Starting at right-most digit, multiply binary digits by 2^0, 2^1, 2^2, etc., respectively. Then add products.	Starting at right-most digit, convert each group of four binary digits to a hex digit.
10	Divide repeatedly by 2 using each quotient as the next dividend; then collect remainders in reverse order.		Divide repeatedly by 16 using each quotient as the next dividend; then collect remainders in reverse order.
16	Convert each hex digit to four binary digits.	Starting at right-most digit, multiply hex digits by 16^0, 16^1, 16^2, etc., respectively. Then add products.	

and hexadecimal numbers are not much harder than the same operations with decimal numbers. Practically the only difference is in the number of symbols used in each system.

Figure A-5 provides an example of addition and subtraction with decimal, binary, and hexadecimal numbers. Note that with binary and hexadecimal, as in decimal arithmetic, you carry to and borrow from adjacent positions as you move from right to left. Instead of carrying or borrowing 10, however—as you would in the decimal system—you carry or borrow 2 (binary) or 16 (hexadecimal).

Using a Scientific Calculator

A scientific calculator can be used to convert numbers between numbering systems, or to check conversions performed by hand. Many conventional calculators have different numbering system options; scientific calculator programs can be used for this purpose, as well. For example, using the Windows Calculator program to convert numbers is illustrated in Figure A-6 (the Scientific option must be selected using the View menu to display the options shown in the figure). Arithmetic can also be performed in any numbering system on a calculator, once that numbering system is selected on the calculator.

> **FIGURE A-5**
>
> **Adding and subtracting with the decimal, binary, and hexadecimal numbering systems.**

	Decimal	Binary	Hexadecimal
Addition	142 +47 ——— 189	10001110 +101111 ——— 10111101	8E +2F ——— BD
Subtraction	142 −47 ——— 95	10001110 −101111 ——— 1011111	8E −2F ——— 5F

1. After entering a number (such as the decimal number shown here), select the numbering system to which the number should be converted (hex in this example).

2. The number is now displayed in hex notation. To convert it to binary, select that mode.

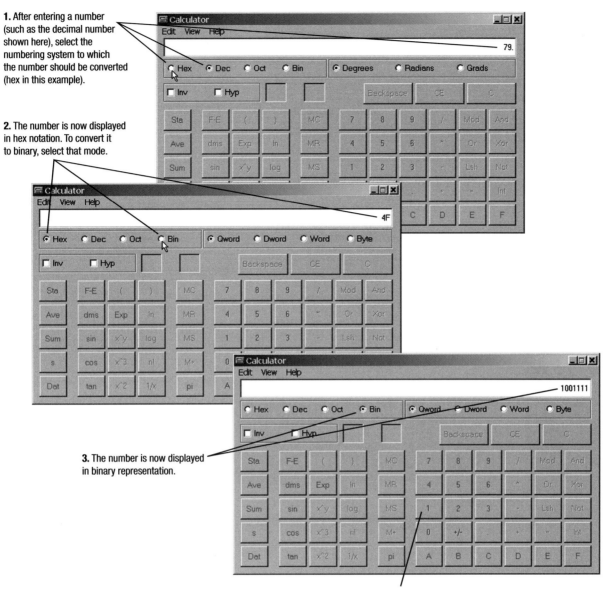

3. The number is now displayed in binary representation.

In any mode, numbers and operators can be selected to perform arithmetic using that numbering system.

FIGURE A-6

Using a scientific calculator.

A physical or computerized calculator (such as the Windows Calculator program shown here double checking the hand calculations performed in Figure A-3) can be used to convert numbers between numbering systems, as well as to perform arithmetic in different systems. The Calculator program is typically located under Accessories on the Windows Start menu; select the Scientific option using the Calculator's View menu.

REVIEW ACTIVITIES

Self-Quiz

Answers for the self-quiz appear at the end of the book.

True/False
Instructions: Circle **T** if the statement is true or **F** if the statement is false.

T F **1.** Most computations inside the CPU are performed using the decimal numbering system.

T F **2.** A base 5 numbering system would use only the digits 0 through 4.

T F **3.** The decimal equivalent of the largest hexadecimal character (F) is 16.

T F **4.** To convert binary numbers to decimal numbers, you must use the remainder method.

T F **5.** Most scientific calculators should have options to convert numbers between various numbering systems.

Completion
Instructions: Answer the following questions.

6. The sum of the binary numbers 11011001 and 1011101 is _____.

7. The numbering system that represents all numbers using 16 digits is called the _____ numbering system.

8. Adding the hexadecimal numbers 8E and 5D yields _____.

9. The _____ method can be used to convert decimal numbers to hexadecimal representation.

10. The "Bin" option on a scientific calculator will switch the calculator to _____ mode, whereas the "Oct" option should switch it to base _____.

1. Convert the following binary numbers to decimal numbers:

   a. 1011
   b. 101110

2. Convert the following decimal numbers to binary numbers:

   a. 51
   b. 260

3. Convert the following binary numbers to hexadecimal numbers:

   a. 101
   b. 11010

4. Convert the following hexadecimal numbers to binary numbers:

   a. F2
   b. 1A8

5. Convert the following hexadecimal numbers to decimal numbers:

   a. B6
   b. 5E9

ANSWERS TO SELF-QUIZ

Chapter 1
1. F **2.** T **3.** T **4.** F **5.** F **6.** output **7.** storage **8.** network computer or thin client
9. information **10.** personal computer or PC

Chapter 2
1. F **2.** T **3.** T **4.** F **5.** F **6.** File **7.** radio buttons **8.** Web browser **9.** bookmark or favorite
10. browser plug-in

Chapter 3
1. T **2.** F **3.** F **4.** T **5.** T **6.** 13 **7.** cache **8.** motherboard or system board **9.** port
10. pipelining

Chapter 4
1. T **2.** F **3.** F **4.** F **5.** T **6.** volatile **7.** CD-R **8.** magnetic tape **9.** smart card **10.** online

Chapter 5
1. F **2.** F **3.** T **4.** T **5.** F **6.** hard copy **7.** pixels **8.** scanner **9.** electronic pen/stylus
10. flat-panel; CRT

Chapter 6
1. F **2.** T **3.** F **4.** F **5.** T **6.** folders/directories **7.** multitasking; multiprocessing **8.** Linux
9. fragmented **10.** file compression

Chapter 7
1. F **2.** T **3.** F **4.** T **5.** T **6.** shareware **7.** typeface; font **8.** cell **9.** query **10.** slide show

Chapter 8
1. F **2.** F **3.** T **4.** T **5.** F **6.** intranet **7.** virtual private network (VPN) **8.** satellite
9. digital; analog **10.** biometric

Chapter 9
1. F **2.** F **3.** T **4.** F **5.** T **6.** Internet **7.** Internet appliance **8.** music **9.** e-book or online
book **10.** privacy

Chapter 10
1. F **2.** T **3.** T **4.** F **5.** T **6.** JPEG **7.** Web-based training (WBT) **8.** streaming **9.** identifying
the intended audience and primary objectives **10.** Web site authoring

Chapter 11
1. F 2. F 3. T 4. F 5. T 6. business-to-government (B2G) 7. reverse auction
8. intermediary hub 9. digital wallet 10. data mining

Chapter 12
1. T 2. F 3. F 4. T 5. F 6. management information systems (MIS) 7. systems analyst
8. inference engine 9. tangible 10. outsourcing

Chapter 13
1. F 2. T 3. T 4. F 5. F 6. program design 7. interpreter 8. logic 9. visual 10. COBOL

Chapter 14
1. F 2. F 3. T 4. F 5. T 6. field; record 7. data dictionary 8. data validation 9. object-oriented database 10. middleware

Chapter 15
1. F 2. F 3. T 4. T 5. T 6. hacking 7. encrypted 8. antivirus 9. trademark; patent
10. Energy star

Chapter 16
1. F 2. T 3. F 4. T 5. F 6. plug-and-play 7. backup 8. uninterruptible power supply (UPS)
9. screen saver 10. functionally; technically

Appendix
1. F 2. T 3. F 4. F 5. T 6. 100110110 7. hexadecimal 8. EB 9. remainder 10. binary; 8

CREDITS

Throughout the modules: Screen shots of Microsoft Access®, Excel®, Paint®, PowerPoint®, Publisher®, Virtual Basic®, Word®, and Windows® reprinted with permission from Microsoft Corporation.

Internet Interfaces:
Copyright © Netscape Navigator. All rights reserved.
Copyright © Microsoft Explorer® reprinted with permission from Microsoft Corporation.

Chapter 1

Figure 1.1a, © Comstock Photography; **Figure 1.1b,** Courtesy Alcatel; **Figure 1.1c,** Courtesy Scientific-Atlanta; **Figure 1.1d,** © Corbis Images; **Figure 1.2a,** Courtesy International Business Machines Corporation; **Figure 1.2b,** Courtesy InFocus/Proxima; **Figure 1.2c,** Courtesy Intermec; **Figure 1.2d,** © Mark Richards/PhotoEdit; **Figure 1.3a,** Courtesy Seagate Technology; **Figure 1.3b, c,** Courtesy Iomega Corporation; **Figure 1.3e, f,** Courtesy Acer America; **Figure 1.3h,** Courtesy International Business Machines Corporation; **Figure 1.4a,** Courtesy Iomega Corporation; **Figure 1.4b,** Courtesy Backroads.com; **Figure 1.5,** © Photopia; **Figure 1.6f,** Courtesy Backroads.com; **Figure 1.7a,** Courtesy International Business Machines Corporation; **Figure 1.7b,** Courtesy Acer America; **Figure 1.7e,** Courtesy International Business Machines Corporation; **Figure 1.8a,** Reproduced with permission of Motorola, Inc.; **Figure 1.8b,** Courtesy Kyocera Wireless Corporation; **Figure 1.8c,** Courtesy Nokia Corporation; **Figure 1.9a1,** Courtesy International Business Machines Corporation; **Figure 1.9a2,** Courtesy Acer America; **Figure 1.9a3,** © Don Couch Photography; **Figure 1.9b1,** Courtesy Casio Corporation, Cassiopeia EM-500 Pocket PC; **Figure 1.9b2,** Courtesy Hewlett-Packard Company; **Figure 1.9b3,** Courtesy Microsoft Corporation; **Figure 1.9b4,** Courtesy Acer America; **Figure 1.10,** Courtesy Honeywell; **Figure 1.11,** © Comstock Photography; **Figure 1.12,** Courtesy Sun Microsystems; **Figure 1.13,** Courtesy Lawrence Livermore National Laboratory; **Box 1.campus,** Courtesy Stanford University Medical Center; **Box 1.how,** Courtesy Kyocera Wireless Corporation; **Box 1.trend,** Courtesy Xybernaut Corporation; **Project 1.3,** Courtesy Diebold, Inc.; **Project 1.7a,** Courtesy Apple Computer, Inc.; **Project 1.7b,** Courtesy Roxio; **Project 1.7c,** Photo of Quicken 2001 Deluxe courtesy of Intuit, Inc.

Chapter 2

Figure 2.1, © PhotoDisc/Getty Images; **Figure 2.12a,** Courtesy MSN.com; **Figure 2.12b,** Courtesy MyOperaNetwork.com; **Figure 2.12c,** Courtesy Netscape Communications Corporation; **Figure 2.13c,** Courtesy Sonymusic.com; **Figure 2.15a,** Courtesy Microsoft.com; **Figure 2.15b,** Courtesy Netscape Communications Corporation; **Figure 2.16a,** Courtesy Microsoft.com; **Figure 2.16b, c,** Courtesy SanDiegoZoo.com; **Figure 2.17a,** Courtesy MySeasons.com; **Figure 2.17b,** Courtesy Smithsonian.gov; **Figure 2.17c,** Courtesy CBS.com; **Figure 2.18a,** Courtesy CBS.com; **Figure 2.18b,** Courtesy MySeasons.com; **Figure 2.19a,** Courtesy PBSKids.org; **Figure 2.20,** Courtesy AltaVista.com; **Figure 2.22a,** Courtesy Polo.com; **Figure 2.26a,** Courtesy Adobe.com; **Figure 2.26b,** Courtesy IRS.UStreas.gov; **Box 1.trend,** Courtesy MySimon.com; **Box 2.how,** Courtesy Alcatel; **Project 2.4,** Courtesy Congress.org; **Project 2.9,** Courtesy CNET.com.

Chapter 3

Figure 3.2a, Courtesy International Business Machines Corporation; **Figure 3.2b,** Courtesy Intel Corporation; **Figure 3.9a,** Courtesy Intel Corporation; **Figure 3.9b,** © 2001 Advanced Micro Devices, Inc. Reprinted with permission; **Figure 3.14,** Courtesy Xircom; **Figure 3.15,** Courtesy Handspring; **Figure 3.16a,** Courtesy Acer America; **Figure 3.16b–l,** Courtesy Belkin Components; **Figure 3.17,** Courtesy Acer America; **Figure 3.20b,** Courtesy Simple Tech, Inc.; **Figure 3.21,** Courtesy Symantec Corporation; **Figure 3.22,** Courtesy International Business Machines Corporation; **Figure 3.24a,** Courtesy NCSA, University of Illinois at Urbana-Champaign; **Exercise 3.4a,** © 2001 Advanced Micro Devices, Inc. Reprinted with permission; **Exercise 3.4b,** Courtesy Simple Tech, Inc.; **Project 3.7,** Courtesy Intel Corporation; **Project 3.12,** Courtesy Intel Corporation; **Box 3.how b,** Courtesy MusicMatch; **Box 3.inside,** Courtesy Intel Corporation; **Box 3.trend,** Courtesy ChampionChip.

Chapter 4

Figure 4.1, Courtesy AcerAmerica; **Figure 4.7a,** Courtesy Iomega Corporation; **Figure 4.7b,** Courtesy Dell Computer Corporation; **Figure 4.8,** Courtesy International Business Machines Corporation; **Figure 4.11a,** Courtesy SimpleTech, Inc.; **Figure 4.11b,** Courtesy Intel Corporation; **Figure 4.11c,** Courtesy Seagate Technology; **Figure 4.12a, c,** Courtesy Iomega Corporation; **Figure 4.12b,** Courtesy Castlewood Systems, Inc.; **Figure 4.13a, b,** Courtesy Simple Tech, Inc.; **Figure 4.13c,** Courtesy International Business Machines Corporation; **Figure 4.14a, b,** Courtesy International Business Machines Corporation; **Figure 4.16b,** Courtesy Imation Corporation; **Figure 4.16c,** Courtesy Maxell Corporation; **Figure 4.17,** Data Play, Inc., 2001; **Figure 4.18,** Courtesy Imation Corporation; **Figure 4.19,** Courtesy Xdrive; **Figure 4.20a,** The smart Visa card image has been reprinted with permission from Visa USA, Inc. (Visa). Permission to reprint does not constitute Visa's endorsement of Parker & Morley or Harcourt College Publishers/Thomson Learning's products, services, or publication. Any other use of the smart Visa card image is expressly prohibited without written permission from Visa. VISA, Comet Design, Bands Design, and Dove Design are all registered trademarks of Visa International Service Association; **Figure 4.20b,** Courtesy SchlumbergerSema; **Figure 4.21a–c,** Courtesy Sony Electronics, Inc.; **Figure 4.21d–f,** Courtesy Simple Tech, Inc.; **Figure 4.21g,** Courtesy Agate Technologies, Inc.; **Exercise 4.2a,** Courtesy Iomega Corporation; **Exercise 4.2c,** Courtesy Sony Electronics, Inc.; **Exercise 4.2d,** The smart Visa card image has been reprinted with permission from Visa USA, Inc. (Visa). Permission to reprint does not constitute Visa's endorsement of Parker & Morley or Harcourt College Publishers/Thomson Learning's products, services, or publication. Any other use of the smart Visa card image is expressly prohibited without written permission from Visa. VISA, Comet Design, Bands Design, and Dove Design are all registered trademarks of Visa International Service Association; **Project 4.6,** Courtesy MP3.com; **Box 4.how a,** GemPC Touch440 smart card reader and fingerprint match device used in conjunction with smart card will provide secure network authentication, Gemplus International, S.A.; **Box 4.how b,** The smart Visa card image has been reprinted with permission from Visa USA, Inc. (Visa). Permission to reprint does not constitute Visa's endorsement of Parker & Morley or Harcourt College Publishers/Thomson Learning's products, services, or publication. Any other use of the smart Visa card image is expressly prohibited without written permission from Visa. VISA, Comet Design, Bands Design, and Dove Design are all registered trademarks of Visa International Service Association; **Box 4.inside,** Courtesy Lucent Technologies.

Chapter 5

Figure 5.1, Courtesy Belkin Components; **Figure 5.2a,** Courtesy Targus, Inc.; **Figure 5.2b,** Courtesy Microsoft Corporation; **Figure 5.3a, b,** Courtesy Belkin Components; **Figure 5.4a,** Courtesy Fastpoint & Eclyptis, Inc.; **Figure 5.4b,** © Wacom Technology; **Figure 5.4c,** Courtesy Seiko Instruments, USA, Inc.; **Figure 5.4d,** Courtesy NCR Corporation; **Figure 5.5a,** Courtesy Aqcess Technologies, Inc.; **Figure 5.5b,** Courtesy Sony Electronics, Inc.; **Figure 5.6,** Courtesy Fujitsu PC Corporation; **Figure 5.7,** MicroTouch capacitive touchscreen monitor; **Figure 5.8a, b,** Courtesy Kensington Technology Group, www.kensington.com; **Figure 5.8c,** Courtesy Toshiba; **Figure 5.8d,** Used with permission of Cirque Corporation; **Figure 5.9a,** Courtesy Microtek Lab, Inc.; **Figure 5.9b,** Courtesy Siemens, AG; **Figure 5.9c,** Courtesy Hewlett-Packard Company; **Figure 5.10,** Courtesy Chatsworth Data Corporation; **Figure 5.12a, b,** Courtesy Intermec; **Figure 5.12c,** Courtesy NCR Corporation; **Figure 5.13a,** Courtesy NCR Corporation; **Figure 5.14,** Courtesy Lexar Media; **Figure 5.15,** Courtesy Intel Corporation; **Figure 5.16a, b,** Courtesy Dragon Systems; **Figure 5.17a,** Courtesy Acer America; **Figure 5.19b,** Courtesy Acer America; **Figure 5.20a,** Courtesy Hewlett-Packard Company; **Figure 5.20b,** © The Stock Market/Corbis Images; **Figure 5.20c,** Courtesy Intermec; **Figure 5.20d,** Courtesy Ceiva Logic, Inc.; **Figure 5.22a,** Courtesy Printek, Inc.; **Figure 5.23b,** Courtesy Hewlett-Packard Company; **Figure 5.24,** Courtesy Static Control, Inc. and AMS Laser Supply; **Figure 5.25a,** Courtesy Hewlett-Packard Company; **Figure 5.26a, b,** Courtesy Hewlett-Packard Company; **Figure 5.27,** Courtesy Eastman Kodak Company; **Figure 5.27b, c,** Courtesy Monarch; **Figure 5.27d,** Courtesy MacDermid ColorSpan; **Figure 5.28,** Courtesy InFocus Corporation; **Project 5.7,** Courtesy Hewlett-Packard Company; **Box 5.how a,** Courtesy Dragon Systems; **Box 5.how b,** Courtesy Acer Americaid; **Box 5.inside,** Courtesy Digiscents; **Box 5.trend,** Courtesy Hart InterCivic.

Chapter 6

Figure 6.2, Screen shots courtesy Novell, Inc.; **Figure 6.7a,** Courtesy Simple Tech, Inc.; **Figure 6.7b,** Courtesy Seagate; **Figure 6.12,** Courtesy Apple Computer, Inc.; **Figure 6.13,** Courtesy Red Hat; **Figure 6.14,** Courtesy Casio Corporation; **Box 6.trend,** Courtesy Clarion Sales Corporation; **Project 6.7,** © Charles Bennett/AP Wide World Photos.

Chapter 7

Figure 7.1, Courtesy Sun Microsystems; **Figure 7.2a,** Box shot reprinted with permission from Corel Corporation; **Figure 7.2b,** Courtesy Microsoft Corporation; **Figure 7.2c,** Courtesy Lotus Development Corporation; **Figure 7.2d,** Courtesy Sun Microsystems; **Figure 7.6,** Courtesy CNET.com; **Figure 7.19a,** Courtesy Dragon Systems; **Figure 7.22a,** Courtesy Adobe Systems, Inc.; **Figure 7.22b,** Courtesy Learning Co.; **Figure 7.22c,** Courtesy Lotus Development Corporation; **Figure 7.22d,** Courtesy Microsoft Corporation; **Figure 7.22e,** Courtesy Peachtree Software, Inc.; **Project 7.4,** Courtesy Corel Corporation; **Project 7.7,** Courtesy Sega of America, Inc.; **Box 7.inside,** Courtesy Microsoft Corporation; **Box 7.trend,** Courtesy Linux Online, Inc.

Chapter 8

Figure 8.1, Courtesy Motorola, Inc.; **Figure 8.2a,** Courtesy Ericsson; **Figure 8.2b,** Courtesy Globalstar, L.P.; **Figure 8.3,** Courtesy Magellan Corporation; **Figure 8.3b,** © Corbis Images; **Figure 8.4,** © Zigy Kaluzny/Stone; **Figure 8.18a, b,** Courtesy Linksys, © 2001; **Figure 8.18c, d,** Courtesy Belkin Components; **Figure 8.20,** Courtesy OmniSky Corporation; **Figure 8.26a,** Courtesy Diebold, Inc.; **Figure 8.26b,** Courtesy Recognition

Systems; **Figure 8.26c,** Courtesy Ethentica, Inc.; **Project 8.3,** Courtesy Nokia Corporation; **Project 8.9,** Courtesy Linksys, © 2001; **Box 8.campus,** Courtesy Wake Forest University; **Box 8.how a,** Courtesy Ericsson; **Box 8.how b,** Courtesy International Business Machines Corporation; **Box 8.inside,** Courtesy Net2Phone, Inc.; **Box 8.trend,** © Dreamworks/Neal Peters Collection.

Chapter 9

Figure 9.1a, b, Courtesy Acer America; **Figure 9.1b,** Screen courtesy NBCOlympics.com; **Figure 9.3a,** Courtesy Acer America; **Figure 9.3b,** Courtesy Qubit Technology, Inc.; **Figure 9.3c,** Courtesy Hewlett-Packard Company; **Figure 9.3d,** Courtesy Nokia Corporation; **Figure 9.5,** Courtesy Netscape.com; **Figure 9.7a,** Courtesy Yahoo.com; **Figure 9.12,** Courtesy LLBean.com; **Figure 9.13,** Courtesy Gemplus International, S.A.; **Figure 9.14,** Courtesy SecurityFirstNationalBank.com; **Figure 9.15,** Courtesy Datek.com; **Figure 9.16a,** Courtesy Film.com; **Figure 9.16b,** Courtesy ScientificAtlanta.com; **Figure 9.16c,** Courtesy MSNBC.com; **Figure 9.17a,** Courtesy NetRadio.com; **Figure 9.17b,** Courtesy RollingStone.com; **Figure 9.18,** Courtesy SONICblue, Inc.; **Figure 9.19,** Courtesy MSNGamingZone.com; **Figure 9.20,** Courtesy Nuvomedia/Gemstar; **Figure 9.21a,** Courtesy MSNBC.com; **Figure 9.21b,** Courtesy Kelty.com; **Figure 9.21c,** Courtesy HooversOnline.com; **Box 9.inside,** © Ken Krauss/AP Wide World Photos; **Box 9.how,** Courtesy eBay.com; **Project 9.8,** Courtesy NetZero.com; **Project 9.12,** © PhotoDisc/Getty Images.

Chapter 10

Figure 10.3, Courtesy ESPN.com; **Figure 10.4a,** Courtesy TheFreeGraphicsStore.com; **Figure 10.4b,** Courtesy Corbis.com; **Figure 10.8,** Courtesy PumpkinMasters.com; **Figure 10.9,** Courtesy Disney.com; **Figure 10.10d,** Courtesy Kiosk Information Systems; **Figure 10.11b,** Courtesy Audi.com; **Figure 10.11c,** Courtesy StuartLittle.com; **Figure 10.12a,** Courtesy Bloomingdales.com; **Figure 10.12b,** Courtesy WSJ.com; **Figure 10.12c,** Courtesy PBSKids.org; **Figure 10.12d,** Courtesy Computers4sure.com; **Figure 10.14a,** Courtesy Disney.com; **Figure 10.14b,** Courtesy LandsEnd.com; **Figure 10.14c,** Courtesy Oracle.com; **Figure 10.14d,** Courtesy ZDNet.com; **Project 10.2,** Courtesy RoseArt Multimedia, Inc.; **Project 10.9,** Courtesy Macromedia; **Box 10.campus,** © Stephen Allen, The University of Akron; **Box 10.how,** © Neal Peters Collection; **Box 10.inside,** Courtesy Garageband.com; **Box 10.trend,** Courtesy Ananova.

Chapter 11

Figure 11.1a, b, Courtesy Intermec; **Figure 11.2,** Courtesy iBuyer.com; **Figure 11.5,** Courtesy SAP; **Figure 11.6,** Courtesy Polo.com; **Figure 11.7a,** Courtesy Pay.gov; **Figure 11.7b,** Courtesy eFederal.com; **Figure 11.8,** Courtesy CommerceOne.net; **Figure 11.9a,** Courtesy eBay.com; **Figure 11.9b,** Courtesy Business-auctions.com; **Figure 11.9c,** Courtesy LiquidPrice.com; **Figure 11.10,** Courtesy ChemConnect.com; **Figure 11.12,** Courtesy Walmart.com; **Figure 11.13a,** Courtesy PayByCheck.com; **Figure 11.13b,** Courtesy PayPal.com; **Figure 11.13d,** Courtesy Godiva.com; **Figure 11.13e,** Courtesy eBay.com; **Figure 11.15,** Courtesy SubmitOrder.com; **Figure 11.16,** Reprinted with permission of TRUSTe; **Figure 11.17,** Courtesy LookSmart.com; **Figure 11.19,** Courtesy Megaputer; **Project 11.4,** Courtesy Yahoo.com; **Project 11.8,** Courtesy MySimon.com; **Box 11.how a,** Courtesy Hewlett-Packard Company; **Box 11.how c,** Courtesy Nokia Corporation; **Box 11.campus,** Courtesy Penn State University.

Chapter 12

Figure 12.3, Courtesy Ordia; **Figure 12.4a,** Courtesy Peachtree Software, Inc.; **Figure 12.5a,** Courtesy FedEx Corporation; **Figure 12.5b,** Graphic image supplied courtesy of ESRI. © ESRI. All rights reserved; **Figure 12.6a, b,** Courtesy SAP; **Figure 12.7,** Courtesy Sun Microsystems; **Figure 12.10,** Courtesy TRW, Inc.; **Figure 12.12,** © PhotoDisc/Getty Images; **Project 12.1,** Courtesy MSNBC.com; **Project 12.5,** Courtesy NORAD.gov; **Box 12.how a, c, d,** Courtesy of BioID, AG Biometric Authentication Technologies; **Box 12.how b,** Courtesy Acer America; **Box 12.trend,** Courtesy NEC Corporation; **Box 12.inside,** © Joshua McHugh Photography.

Chapter 13

Figure 13.1, © PhotoDisc/Getty Images; **Figure 13.7,** Courtesy Microsoft Corporation; **Figure 13.16,** Courtesy Visible Systems Corporation; **Figure 13.25a, c,** Courtesy Harrahs.com; **Figure 13.26,** Courtesy AmericanHondaMotorCo.com; **Box 13.inside,** Courtesy U.S. Navy; **Box 13.trend,** Courtesy Microsoft Corporation; **Project13.2,** Java and the Java Coffee Cup logo are trademarks or registered trademarks of Sun Microsystems, Inc. in the United States and other countries; **Project 13.7,** Courtesy Microsoft Corporation.

Chapter 14

Figure 14.7b, Courtesy Acer America; **Figure 14.16a, b,** Courtesy Amazon.com; **Figure 14.17a,** Courtesy Yahoo.com; **Figure 14.17b,** Courtesy LLBean.com; **Figure 14.18a, d,** Courtesy LLBean.com; **Project 14.4,** Courtesy Switchboard.com; **Project 14.8,** Courtesy ERIC.com; **Box 14.inside,** © Sandy Felsenthal/Corbis Images; **Box 14.how a, d, e, f,** UPS and UPS shield design are registered trademarks of United Parcel Service of American, Inc. Used by permission; **Box 14.how b, c, g,** Courtesy UPS.com; **Box 14.trend,** Courtesy MyCentexHome.com.

Chapter 15

Figure 15.1a, Courtesy University of Dublin, Trinity College; **Figure 15.1b,** Courtesy DOL.gov; **Figure 15.1c,** Courtesy Pennsylvania State Police; **Figure 15.1d,** Courtesy ACM.com; **Figure 15.1e,** Courtesy Institute of Translation and Interpreting; **Figure 15.2,** © Daniel Hulshizer/AP Wide World Photos; **Figure 15.3,** Courtesy U.S. Treasury Department; **Figure 15.5,** Courtesy Digital Persona, Inc.; **Figure 15.12a, b,** Courtesy Kensington Technology Group, www.kensington.com; **Figure 15.14,** © Dina Rudick; **Figure 15.15,** Courtesy U.S. Environmental Protection Agency; **Project 15.1,** Courtesy Hoaxbusters.ciac.org; **Project 15.5,** The ACM logo appears courtesy of AMC, Inc.; **Box 15.how a, b, c,** Courtesy Acer America; **Box 15.campus,** Courtesy Gettysburg College.

Chapter 16

Figure 16.2a, Courtesy of CompUSA, Inc.; **Figure 16.2b,** Courtesy Dell.com; **Figure 16.4,** Courtesy Zones, Inc.; **Figure 16.6,** © Rodney Collins Photography; **Figure 16.8b,** Courtesy Iomega Corporation; **Figure 16.9,** Courtesy Kensington Technology Group, www.kensington.com; **Figure 16.10,** Courtesy American Power Conversion; **Figure 16.11a,** Courtesy Kensington Technology Group, www.kensington.com; **Figure 16.12,** Courtesy Gateway.com; **Figure 16.13,** Courtesy of Key3 Media Group/COMDEX Fall 2000; **Figure 16.14a,** Courtesy ZDNet.com; **Figure 16.14b,** Courtesy CNET.com; **Project 16.5,** Courtesy Modesto PC Users Group; **Box 16.how a, b, d,** © Rodney Collins Photography; **Box 16.how c,** Courtesy Kensington Technology Group, www.kensington.com.

Windows-History

1, Courtesy International Business Machines Corporation; **2,** Courtesy Jim Bready; **3, 4, 5, 6,** Courtesy International Business Machines Corporation; **7,** Courtesy Iowa State University; **8,** Courtesy International Business Machines Corporation; **9,** Courtesy U.S. Army; **10,** Courtesy AT&T; **11,** Courtesy Unisys Corporation; **12,** Courtesy U.S. Navy; **13,** Courtesy Bootstrap Institute; **14, 15,** Courtesy International Business Machines Corporation; **16, 17,** Courtesy Intel Corporation; **18,** Courtesy Cray Computer Corporation; **19, 20,** Courtesy Microsoft Corporation; **21,** Courtesy Apple Computer, Inc.; **22,** Courtesy Texas Instruments; **23,** Courtesy Dan Bricklin; **24,** Courtesy International Business Machines Corporation; **25,** © TimePix, Inc.; **26,** Courtesy Compaq Computer; **27,** Courtesy Microsoft Museum; **28,** Courtesy Apple Computer, Inc.; **29,** Fabian Bachrach, courtesy W3C; **30,** Courtesy Intel Corporation; **31,** Courtesy Microsoft Corporation; **32,** Courtesy Netscape Communications Corporation; **33,** Courtesy Microsoft Museum; **34,** © Adam Nadel/AP Wide World Photos; **35,** Courtesy RCA; **36,** © Don Couch Photography; **37,** Images of Palm handhelds provided by Palm, Inc. Palm is a trademark of Palm, Inc.; **38,** Courtesy Intel Corporation; **39, a, b, c,** Courtesy Microsoft Corporation; **40,** Courtesy Intel Corporation; **41,** Courtesy Nokia Corporation; **42,** Courtesy Microsoft Corporation.

Windows-Web Guide

1, 2, Courtesy Nokia Corporation; **3, 4,** Courtesy Intel Corporation.

Windows-Ubiquitous

1, Courtesy Symbol Technologies, Inc.; **2,** Courtesy Hewlett-Packard Company; **3,** Courtesy Nokia Corporation; **4,** Courtesy WideRay; **5,** Courtesy Honeywell; **6,** Courtesy Nokia Corporation; **7,** Courtesy Fastpoint/Eclypsis; **8,** Courtesy Merinta; **9,** Courtesy Electrolux; **10,** Courtesy Symbol Technologies, Inc.; **11,** Courtesy Intermec; **12,** Courtesy Microtouch; **13,** Courtesy Optobionics; **14,** © Shizuo Kambayashi/AP Wide World Photos; **15,** © William Mercer McLeod; **16,** Courtesy IDMicro, Inc.; **17,** Courtesy Friendly Robotics, Inc.; **18,** Courtesy WebTV; **19,** Courtesy Kyocera Wireless Corporation; **20,** Courtesy RCA; **21,** Courtesy Scientific-Atlanta; **22,** Snapstream pocketpvs application allows users to watch their favorite TV shows on their pocket PC device, www.snapstream.com; **23,** Courtesy Casio Corporation; **24,** Courtesy RCA; **25,** Courtesy Hewlett-Packard Company; **26,** Courtesy Inviso, Inc.; **27,** Courtesy SGI; **28,** Courtesy Fujitsu; **29,** Courtesy Garmin Group; **30,** Courtesy BEELINE Technologies; **31, 32,** Courtesy Lockheed Martin; **33,** Courtesy Garmin Group; **34,** Courtesy Globalstar; **35,** Courtesy Garmin Group; **36,** Courtesy Starband.

GLOSSARY

The following terms are presented in the text as key terms. Numbers in parentheses after the definitions of terms indicate pages on which the terms are boldfaced and defined in the text.

Accounting system. A system that deals with the financial transactions and financial record-keeping for an organization. (p. 483)

ALU. *See* Arithmetic/logic unit. (p. 108)

Animation software. A type of program used to create animations. (p. 421)

Animation. The process where a series of graphical images are displayed one after the other to simulate movement. (p. 401)

Antivirus software. Software used to detect and eliminate computer viruses. (p. 622)

Application service provider (ASP). An organization that manages and distributes software-based services over the Internet. (p. 350)

Application software. Software programs that enable users to perform specific tasks or applications on a computer. (pp. 11, 252)

Arithmetic/logic unit (ALU). The part of the CPU that contains circuitry to perform arithmetic and logical operations. (p. 108)

ARPANET. The predecessor of the Internet, named after the Advanced Research Projects Agency (ARPA), which sponsored its development. (p. 347)

Artificial intelligence system. A system in which a computer performs actions that are characteristic of human intelligence. (p. 487)

ASCII. A fixed-length, binary coding system widely used to represent text-based data for computer processing on many types of computers. (p. 87)

ASP. *See* Application service provider. (p. 350)

Assembly language. A low-level programming language that uses names and symbols to replace some of the 0s and 1s in machine language. (p. 539)

Audio. Sound, such as music, spoken voice, and sound effects. (p. 402)

Audit. An inspection used to determine if a system or procedure is working as it is supposed to. (p. 618)

Backup. A procedure that produces a duplicate version of files on a computer in case the original version is destroyed. (p. 658)

Bar code. A machine-readable code that represents data as a set of bars. (p. 181)

BASIC. An easy-to-learn, high-level programming language that was developed to be a beginner's language. (p. 543)

Benchmark test. A test used to measure computer system performance simulating conditions of typical use prior to purchase. (p. 501)

Binary numbering system. The numbering system that represents all numbers using just two symbols (0 and 1). (p. 86)

Biometric device. A device that uses the recognition of some unique physical characteristic (fingerprint, voice, etc.) to grant access to a computer network or physical facility. (p. 333)

Block. A rectangular group of contiguous cells in a worksheet. (p. 267)

Bluetooth. A standard used to facilitate automatic communications between devices once they get within the allowable range. (p. 328)

Boot. To start up a computer. (pp. 39, 216)

Brick-and-mortar store. A conventional store with a physical presence. (p. 440)

Bridge. An interface that connects two similar networks so they can communicate. (p. 309)

Brokerage site. A type of Web site used to bring buyers and sellers together to facilitate transactions, such as online stock trading and exchanging goods, services, and commodities. (p. 451)

Browser plug-in. A program that supplies a browser with additional capabilities. (p. 69)

B2B. *See* Business-to-business model. (p. 449)

B2C. *See* Business-to-consumer model. (p. 448)

B2G. *See* Business-to-government model. (p. 449)

Bus. An electronic path on the motherboard or within the CPU or other computer component along which bits are transmitted. (p. 101)

Bus network. A communications network consisting of a central cable to which all network devices are attached. (p. 305)

Business model. A description of how a company does business, such as its policies, operations, and technology. (p. 448)

Business-to-business (B2B) model. An e-commerce model where a business provides goods or services to other businesses. (p. 449)

Business-to-consumer (B2C) model. An e-commerce model where a business provides goods or services to consumers. (p. 448)

Business-to-government (B2G) model. An e-commerce model where a business provides goods and services to government organizations. (p. 449)

Byte. A group of 8 bits that represents a single character of data. (p. 88)

C. A high-level structured programming language that has the executional efficiency of an assembly language. (p. 545)

C++. A newer, object-oriented version of the C programming language. (p. 545)

C#. The newest, object-oriented version of the C programming language. (p. 547)

CAD. *See* Computer-aided design. (p. 486)

CAM. *See* Computer-aided manufacturing. (p. 487)

Cathode-ray tube. *See* CRT. (p. 189)

CBT. *See* Computer-based training. (p. 407)

CD-R. *See* Recordable CD. (p. 146)

CD-ROM. A low-end optical disc that allows a drive to read data on the disc, but not write to it. (p. 146)

CD-RW. *See* Rewritable CD. The most widely used database model in use today; can link data in related tables through the use of common fields. (p. 146)

Cell. The location on a worksheet into which data can be typed; the intersection of a row and column. (p. 266)

Cellular technology. A form of broadcast radio that broadcasts using antennae located inside honeycomb-shaped cells. (p. 315)

Central processing unit (CPU). The chip located inside the system unit of a computer that performs the processing for a computer and communicates with its peripheral devices. (pp. 9, 93)

Cluster. The part of a track on a disk that crosses a fixed number of contiguous sectors and the smallest addressable area of a disk. (p. 135)

Coaxial cable. A communications medium consisting of a center wire inside a grounded, cylindrical shield, capable of sending data at high speeds. (p. 311)

COBOL. A high-level programming language developed for transaction processing applications. (p. 542)

Coding. Writing the actual programming language statements to create a computer program. (p. 528)

Column. A vertical group of cells on a worksheet. (p. 266)

Compiler. A language translator that converts an entire program into machine language before executing it. (p. 531)

Computer. A programmable, electronic device that accepts data input, performs operations on that data, and presents and stores the results. (p. 8)

Computer-aided design (CAD). A general term applied to the use of computer technology to automate design functions. (p. 486)

Computer-aided manufacturing (CAM). A general term applied to the use of computer technology to automate manufacturing functions. (p. 487)

Computer-based training (CBT). Individual instruction delivered via a computer. (p. 407)

Computer crime. The use of a computer to commit a criminal act. (p. 607)

Computer network. A collection of computers and devices that are connected together to share hardware, software, and data, as well as to electronically communicate with one another. (p. 16)

Computer virus. A software program designed to spread itself to other computers without the user's knowledge and, sometimes, to cause some harm to the system. (pp. 330, 609)

Constant value. A numerical entry entered into a worksheet cell. (p. 268)

Consumer-to-consumer (C2C) model. An e-commerce model where a consumer provides goods or services to other consumers. (p. 449)

Control structure. A pattern for controlling the flow of logic in a computer program. (p. 525)

Control unit. The part of the CPU that coordinates its operations. (p. 108)

Cookie. A small file stored on your hard drive at the request of a Web server; used to preserve customized settings and keep track of a user's preferences. (p. 382)

CPU. *See* Central processing unit (CPU). (pp. 9, 93)

CRM. Customer relationship management. (p. 446)

CRT (cathode-ray tube). A display device that projects images onto a display screen using similar technology as conventional TVs. (p. 189)

C2C. *See* consumer-to-consumer model. (p. 449)

Customer relationship management (CRM). The process of building and managing good relationships with customers. (p. 446)

Cylinder. The collection of tracks located in the same location on a set of hard disk surfaces. (p. 139)

Data. Raw, unorganized facts. (p. 11)

Database. A collection of related data that is stored in a manner enabling information to be retrieved as needed; in a relational database, a collection of related tables. (pp. 272, 566)

Data definition. The process of describing the characteristics of data that are to be included in each file in a database. (p. 572)

Data dictionary. The repository of all data definitions in a database. (p. 574)

Data integrity. The accuracy of data. (p. 575)

Data mining. Intelligent software used to analyze data warehouses for patterns that management may not even realize exist. (p. 463)

Data security. Protecting data in a database against destruction and misuse. (p. 575)

Data validation. The process of ensuring that data entered into a database match the data definition. (p. 575)

Data warehouse. A comprehensive collection of data about a company and its customers. (p. 462)

Database management system (DBMS). A type of software program used for data management in which data can be retrieved from more than one file at a time. (p. 568)

Database software. Application software that allows the creation and manipulation of an electronic database. (p. 272)

DBMS. *See* Database management system. (p. 568)

Debugging. The process of ensuring a program is free of errors. (p. 533)

Decision support system (DSS). A type of information system usually used by upper management that provides people with the tools and capabilities to organize and analyze their decision-making information. (p. 484)

Desktop. The background work area displayed on the screen when using Microsoft Windows. (p. 40)

Device driver. A program that enables an operating system to communicate with a specific hardware device. (p. 216)

Dialog box. A box that requires the user to supply information to the computer about the task being requested. (p. 44)

Dial-up connection. A type of Internet connection in which the PC or other device must dial-up and connect to a service provider's computer before being connected to the Internet. (p. 354)

Digital camera. A camera that records pictures as digital data (instead of film) images. (p. 183)

Digital certificate. A group of electronic data, often used in conjunction with a public key and private key, that can be used to verify the identity of a person or organization. (p. 619)

Digital counterfeiting. The use of computer hardware and software to make illegal copies of currency, checks, collectibles, and other paper-based items. (p. 614)

Digital signature. A unique digital code that can be attached to an e-mail message or document to guarantee the identity of the sender. (pp. 444, 620)

Digital wallet. An encrypted electronic file that holds information to speed up online purchase transactions, such as electronic payment, billing, and shipping information. (p. 458)

Direct connection. An always-on type of Internet connection where your PC or other device is continually connected to the Internet. (p. 355)

Direct organization. A method of arranging data on a storage medium so it can be accessed directly (randomly). (p. 579)

Directory. A collection of categories that are used to locate appropriate Web pages from a search database; also an older name for folder. (pp. 217, 361)

Disk access time. The time it takes to locate and read data from (or position and write data to) a storage medium. (p. 140)

Disk cache. A disk-management scheme that directs a drive to read additional data adjacent to the required data during a disk fetch to reduce the number of disk fetches. Also used to refer to the part of RAM used to store this data. (p. 141)

Display device. An output device that contains a viewing screen. (p. 187)

Documentation. A description of how a program, procedure, or system works. (p. 662)

Domain name. A text-based address used to uniquely identify a computer on the Internet. (p. 53)

DOS. The operating system designed for and on early IBM and IBM-compatible computers. (p. 224)

Dot-com. An Internet-only store with no physical presence. (p. 440)

Downloading. The process of copying a file from one computer to another over the Internet or other network. (p. 69)

DSS. *See* Decision support system. (p. 484)

DVD-RAM. *See* Rewritable DVD. (p. 148)

DVD-ROM. A low-end optical disc that can be read from, but not written to, by the user. (p. 148)

DVD+RW. *See* Rewritable DVD. (p. 148)

EAI. *See* Enterprise application integration. (p. 446)

EBCDIC. A fixed-length, binary coding system widely used to represent text-based data on IBM mainframe computers. (p. 87)

E-book. A book in electronic format. (p. 377)

E-business. A business with an online presence. (p. 438)

E-commerce. *See* Electronic commerce. (p. 438)

EDI. *See* Electronic data interchange. (p. 443)

Electronic commerce (e-commerce). The act of doing financial transactions over the Internet or similar technology. (p. 438)

Electronic data interchange (EDI). The transfer of data between different companies using the Internet or another network. (p. 443)

Electronic mail (e-mail). Electronic messages sent from one user to another over the Internet or other network. (p. 63)

Electronic pen. An electronic device, resembling an ordinary pen, used for computer input. (p. 171)

E-mail. *See* Electronic mail. (p. 63)

E-mail address. An address consisting of a user name and computer domain name that identifies a person on the Internet. (p. 54)

E-mall. A collection of e-tailers organized together into a virtual mall. (p. 451)

Encryption. A method of protecting data or programs so they will be unrecognizable if intercepted by an unauthorized user. (p. 620)

Enterprise application integration (EAI). Exchanging information from an ERP or other internal system between different applications and organizations. (p. 446)

Enterprise resource planning (ERP). A large integrated system that ties together all a business' activities. (p. 445)

Entity. Something in a database system (person, place, object, event, etc.) that is of importance to the organization. (p. 575)

Ergonomics. The field that studies the effects of things such as computer hardware and work environment on people's comfort and health. (p. 630)

ERP. *See* Enterprise resource planning. (p. 445)

E-tailer. An online retailer. (p. 451)

Ethernet. A collection of communications protocols that specify one standard way of setting up a LAN; also commonly called 10Base-T or 100Base-T. (p. 324)

Ethics. A term that refers to standards of moral conduct. (p. 606)

Expansion card. A circuit board that can be inserted into a slot on a PC's motherboard to add one or more functions or attach a peripheral device. (p. 104)

Expert system. A computer system that provides the type of advice that would be expected from a human expert. (p. 487)

Fiber-optic cable. A communications medium that uses hundreds of hair-thin, transparent fibers over which lasers transmit data as light. (p. 313)

Field. A single category of data to be stored in a database, such as a person's name or telephone number. (pp. 272, 566)

File management system. A program that allows the creation of individual databases, but only one file can be accessed at a time. (p. 568)

File. Something stored on a storage medium, such as a program, document, or image. (p. 132)

Firewall. A collection of hardware and software intended to protect a computer or computer network from attack. (p. 334)

Flash memory. A type of nonvolatile memory that can be erased and reprogrammed; commonly implemented in the form of sticks or cards. (pp. 101, 153)

Flat-panel display. A slim type of display device. (p. 190)

Floppy disk. A low-capacity, removable magnetic disk made of flexible plastic permanently sealed inside a hard plastic cover. (p. 134)

Flowchart. A tool that can be used during the design process to illustrate how the pages in a Web site or multimedia application relate to one another. (p. 415)

Folder. A logical named place on a storage medium into which files can be stored to keep the medium organized. Sometimes called a directory. (pp. 132, 217)

Formula. An entry in a worksheet cell that performs computations on worksheet data and displays the results. (p. 268)

4GL. *See* Fourth-generation language. (p. 540)

FORTRAN. A high-level programming language used for mathematical, scientific, and engineering applications. (p. 542)

Fourth-generation language (4GL). A programming language that is closer to natural language and easier to work with than a high-level language. (p. 540)

Function. A named formula that can be entered into a worksheet cell to perform some type of calculation or extract information from other cells on the worksheet. (p. 268)

Functionally obsolete. A term that refers to a product that no longer meets the needs of an individual or business. (p. 665)

Gateway. An interface that connects two dissimilar networks so they can communicate. (p. 309)

GB. *See* Gigabyte. (p. 88)

GIF. A graphics format that supports 256 colors and is commonly used for Web page images and line art. (p. 400)

Gigabyte (GB). Approximately 1 billion bytes. (p. 88)

Global positioning system (GPS). A system that uses satellites and a special type of receiver to determine the exact geographic location of the receiver. (p. 302)

GPS. *See* Global positioning system. (p. 302)

Graphical user interface (GUI). A graphically-based interface that allows a user to easily communicate instructions to the computer. (p. 40)

Graphics. Digital representations of photographs, drawings, charts, and visual images. (p. 398)

Graphics software. A type of program used to create or modify images. (p. 419)

Graphics tablet. An input device that consists of a flat board and a pointing mechanism that traces over it, storing the traced pattern in digital form. (p. 172)

GUI. *See* Graphical user interface. (p. 40)

Hacking. Using a computer to penetrate the security of a remote computer system. (p. 610)

Handwriting recognition. The ability to identify handwritten characters. (p. 174)

Hard disk system. A storage system consisting of one or more metal magnetic disks and an access mechanism typically permanently sealed inside its drive. (p. 138)

Hardware. Physical equipment in a computer system, such as the computer and its peripheral devices. (p. 9)

High-level language. A programming language that is closer to natural language and easier to work with than a low-level language. (p. 539)

Home page. The main starting page for a Web site. (p. 51)

HTML (Hypertext Markup Language). A markup language widely used for creating Web pages. (p. 549)

Hub. A device that acts as a central location where data arrives and is then transferred on in one or more directions. (p. 305)

Icon. A small picture or other type of graphical image that represents a program or document and invokes some action when selected. (p. 44)

Index. A small file containing a primary key and the location of the record belonging to that key; used to locate records in a database (p. 578)

Indexed organization. A method for organizing data on a storage medium or in a database so they can be located using an index. (p. 578)

Information. Data that have been processed into a meaningful form. (p. 14)

Information system. A system used to generate information to support users in an organization. (p. 478)

Information theft. The theft of information, usually from a company, via a computer crime. (p. 610)

Ink-jet printer. A printer that forms images by spraying droplets of ink onto a page. (p. 195)

Input. What is supplied to a computer to process. (p. 8)

Input device. A piece of hardware that supplies input to a computer. (p. 168)

Insertion point. An onscreen character that marks the current location in a document, which is where the next character typed will appear on the screen. (p. 261)

Intermediary hub model. An e-commerce model where a business brings buyers and sellers together, instead of directly selling goods or services. (p. 449)

Internet. The largest and most widely used computer network in the world, linking millions of computers all over the world. (pp. 16, 50, 346)

Internet address. What identifies a computer, person, or Web page on the Internet. (p. 53)

Internet appliance. A specialized network computer designed primarily for Internet access and e-mail exchange. (p. 23)

Internet content provider. An organization that provides Internet content. (p. 350)

Internet Service Provider (ISP). An organization that provides access to the Internet. (pp. 53, 350)

Interpreter. A language translator that converts program statements line by line into machine language, immediately executing each one. (p. 532)

Intranet. A private network that is set up similar to the Internet's World Wide Web. (p. 310)

Inventory control system. A system that keeps track of the number of each product in inventory. (p. 483)

IP address. A numeric address used to uniquely identify a computer on the Internet. (p. 53)

ISP. *See* Internet service provider. (p. 53, 350)

Java. A high-level, object-oriented programming language frequently used for Web-based applications. (p. 547)

JavaScript. A scripting language widely used to add dynamic content to Web pages. (p. 552)

JIT. *See* Just-in-time. (p. 447)

Joystick. An input device that resembles a car's gear shift. (p. 175)

JPEG. A graphics format that supports true color and is commonly used for photographs. (p. 400)

Just-in-time (JIT) system. An inventory system in which inventory, other production resources, and finished products are limited to the right number at the right time as required to fill orders. (p. 447)

KB. *See* Kilobyte. (p. 88)

Keyboard. An input device containing numerous keys, arranged in a configuration similar to that of a typewriter, that can be used to input letters, numbers, and symbols. (p. 169)

Keywords. Words typed on a search site to locate information on the Internet. (p. 361)

Kilobyte (KB). 1,024 bytes. (p. 88)

Label. A primarily text-based entry entered into a worksheet cell that identifies data on the worksheet. (p. 268)

LAN. *See* local area network. (p. 306)

Laser printer. A printer that uses technology similar to that of a photocopier. (p. 194)

Legacy system. A system that is technologically obsolete. (p. 665)

Linux. A version of Unix that is available without charge over the Internet. (p. 230)

Local area network (LAN). A network that connects devices located in a small geographical area, such as within a building. (p. 306)

Logic error. A programming error that occurs when running a program produces incorrect results. (p. 535)

Low-level language. A highly detailed, machine-dependent class of programming languages. (p. 539)

Mac OS. The operating system for Apple's Macintosh line of computers. (p. 228)

Machine cycle. The series of operations involved in the execution of a single, machine-level instruction. (p. 110)

Machine language. A binary-based programming language that the computer can execute directly. (p. 92)

Macintosh. A type of personal computer manufactured by Apple. (p. 23)

Magnetic disk. A storage medium that records data using magnetic spots on disks made of flexible plastic or rigid metal. (p. 133)

Magnetic ink character recognition (MICR). A banking-industry technology that processes checks by sensing special characters inscribed in a magnetic ink. (p. 182)

Magnetic tape. A plastic ribbon with a magnetizable surface that stores data as a series of magnetic spots. (p. 149)

Mainframe computer. A large computer that performs extensive business transaction processing. (p. 24)

Management information system (MIS). A type of information system that provides decision makers with preselected type of information that can be used to make middle-management-type decisions. (p. 484)

Marketing database. An electronic repository containing information useful for product marketing. (p. 626)

Markup language. A language that uses symbols or tags to describe what a document should look like when displayed. (p. 549)

MB. *See* Megabyte. (p. 88)

Megabyte (MB). Approximately 1 million bytes. (p. 88)

Memory. A temporary holding place for the computer to store data and program instructions awaiting processing, intermediate results, and processed output. (p. 10)

Menu. A set of options (usually text-based) that can be displayed on the screen to enable the user to issue commands to the computer. (p. 41)

MICR. *See* Magnetic ink character recognition. (p. 182)

Microcomputer. A computer system based on a microprocessor, designed to be used by one person at a time. (p. 20)

Microprocessor. Another name for CPU. (p. 93)

Microsoft Windows. The most common operating system for IBM and IBM-compatible PCs. (p. 40)

Microwave station. An earth-bound device that sends and receives high-frequency, high-speed, radio signals. (p. 314)

Middleware. Software used to connect two otherwise separate applications, such as a Web server and a database management system. (p. 592)

Midrange computer. An intermediate-size and medium-price computer. (p. 23)

MIS. *See* Management information system. (p. 484)

Mobile device. A very small device, usually based on a wireless phone or pager, that can perform a limited amount of computing. (p. 18)

Modem. A communications device that enables digital computers to communicate over analog media. (p. 322)

Monitor. A display device for a PC. (p. 187)

Motherboard. The main circuit board of a computer, located inside the system unit, to which all computer-system components connect. (p. 93)

Mouse. A common pointing device that you slide along a flat surface to move a pointer around the screen and make selections. (p. 170)

Multimedia. The integration of a variety of media, such as text, graphics, video, animation, and sound. (p. 396)

Multimedia authoring software. Programs designed to create multimedia applications. (p. 422)

Multiprocessing. A technique for simultaneous processing by multiple processors operating under common control in a single computer system. (pp. 116, 222)

Multitasking. The capability of an operating system to execute two or more program or program tasks concurrently for a single user. (p. 220)

Natural language system. A system in which the computer can understand natural languages. (p. 489)

NC. *See* Network computer. (p. 22)

NetWare. The most widely used operating systems for PC-based local area networks (LANs). (p. 231)

Network. A collection of computers and other hardware devices that are connected together to share hardware, software, and data, as well as to facilitate electronic communications. (p. 305)

Network computer (NC). A PC designed to access a network for processing and data storage, instead of performing those tasks locally. (p. 22)

Network interface card (NIC). An expansion card through which a computer can connect to a local area network. (p. 321)

Network operating system. A type of operating system designed to support multiple users over a network. (p. 214)

Neural network system. An expert system in which the human brain's pattern-recognition process is emulated by the computer system. (p. 489)

NIC. *See* Network interface card. (p. 321)

Nonvolatile. Storage that retains its contents when the power is shut off. (p. 131)

OA. *See* Office automation. (p. 480)

Object code. The machine language version of a computer program generated after the program's source code is compiled. (p. 531)

Object-oriented database management system. A database in which multiple types of data—text, graphics, video, sound, etc.—are represented as objects with methods describing how the different types of data in an object are combined. (p. 587)

Object-oriented programming (OOP). An approach to program design in which a program is comprised of a collection of objects. (p. 520)

OCR. *See* Optical character recognition. (p. 177)

Office automation (OA). Computer-based office-oriented technologies, such as word processing, e-mail, workgroup computing, and the like. (p. 480)

Office system. A type of system in which office automation hardware, software, and resources are used to facilitate communications and enhance productivity. (p. 480)

Online auction. An online activity where bids are placed on items and the highest bidder wins. (p. 367)

Online auction site. A Web site where buyers bid on items and the highest bidder after a particular time period is allowed to buy the item. (p. 452)

Online banking. Performing banking activities over the Internet. (p. 370)

Online check. An electronic check written and submitted via the Internet. (p. 456)

Online music. Music played or obtained available over the Internet. (p. 375)

Online payment account. A type of payment account accessed via the Internet used to make electronic payments to other, either from funds deposited into the account or by charging the appropriate amount to a credit card. (p. 456)

Online shopping. Buying products or services over the Internet. (p. 367)

Online stock trading. Buying and selling stock over the Internet. (p. 370)

Online storage. Storage located on a network storage device, such as on a server accessible through the Internet. (p. 150)

OOP. *See* Object-oriented programming. (p. 520)

Operating system. The main piece of systems software that enables the computer to manage its activities and the resources under its control, run application programs, and interface with the user. (pp. 39, 213)

Optical character recognition (OCR). The ability of a scanning device to recognize written or typed characters and convert it to electronic form as text, not an image. (p. 177)

Optical disc. A disc read and written to using a laser beam. (p. 146)

Optical scanner. A device that reads hard-copy documents and inputs them into the computer in digital form. (p. 177)

Order-entry system. A system that helps staff record and manage order processing. (p. 482)

Output. The results of computer processing. (p. 8)

Output device. A piece of hardware that accepts output from the computer and presents it in a form the user can understand. (p. 168)

Page layout. A tool that can be used during the design process to illustrate the basic layout of the home page and the rest of the pages on a Web site. (p. 415)

Palm OS. The operating system used with Palm handheld PCs. (p. 233)

Parallel processing. A computing system that uses two or more CPUs to share work and simultaneously perform necessary processing. (p. 116)

Parallel transmission. Data transmission in which each bit in a byte follows its path simultaneously with all of the other bits. (p. 319)

Pascal. A structured, high-level programming language that is often used to teach structured programming, as well as for math and science applications. (p. 543)

Password. A combination of characters used to gain access to a system. (p. 332)

Payroll system. A type of transaction system that generates employee payroll amounts and reports. (p. 483)

PC. *See* Personal computer. (p. 20)

PC card. A small card that fits into a slot on the exterior of a portable computer to provide new functions. (p. 105)

PC compatible. A personal computer based on Intel microcomputer or compatible CPUs. (p. 23)

PDLC. *See* Program development life cycle. (p. 518)

Personal computer (PC). Another name for microcomputer. (p. 20)

Personal operating system. A type of operating system designed for single users (p. 214)

Pipelining. A CPU feature designed to begin processing a new instruction as soon as the previous instruction reaches the next stage of the machine cycle. (p. 116)

Pixel. A single small dot on a display screen that can be lit up to form images on the screen. (p. 188)

PNG. A newer graphics format designed for use with Web pages images. (p. 401)

Pointing device. A piece of hardware that moves an on-screen pointer, such as an arrow or insertion point, to allow users to select objects on the screen. (p. 170)

Port. A socket on the exterior of a PC's system unit to which a device may be connected (p. 105)

Preliminary investigation. The phase of the systems development life cycle in which a brief feasibility study is performed to assess whether or not a full-scale project should be undertaken. (p. 496)

Presentation graphics software. A type of program used to create presentation graphics, including online slide shows. (p. 277)

Primary key. A specific field in a database table that uniquely identifies the records in that table. (p. 576)

Printer. An output device that records output on paper. (p. 192)

Privacy. How information about an individual is used and by whom. (p. 624)

Problem analysis. The step in the program development life cycle in which the problem is carefully considered and the program specifications are developed. (p. 519)

Processing. The conversion of input to output. (p. 8)

Program. A set of instructions that command a computer system to perform specific actions. (p. 14)

Program design. The step in the program development life cycle in which the program specifications are expanded into a complete design of the new program. (p. 520)

Program development. The process of creating application programs. (p. 518)

Program development life cycle (PDLC). The process containing the five steps of program development: Analyzing, designing, coding, debugging and testing, and maintaining application software. (p. 518)

Program flowchart. A visual program design tool showing step by step how a computer program will process data. (p. 522)

Programmer. A person whose job it is to write, maintain, and test computer programs. (pp. 15, 519)

Programming language. A set of rules, words, symbols, and codes used to write computer programs. (p. 539)

Prototyping. A systems development alternative where a small model, or prototype, of the system is built before the full-scale systems development effect is undertaken. (p. 504)

Pseudocode. A program design tool that uses English-like statements to outline the logic of a program. (p. 524)

QBE. *See* Query by example. (p. 585)

Query by example (QBE). A query procedure in which an onscreen query form is used to indicate what information should be retrieved. (p. 585)

Query. A question used to retrieve information from a database. (p. 275)

RAID. A storage method that uses several small hard disks in parallel to do the job of a larger disk. (p. 145)

RAM. *See* Random access memory. (p. 98)

Random access memory (RAM). Chips located on the motherboard that provide a temporary holding place for the computer to store data and program instructions while it is needed. (p. 98)

RDBMS. *See* Relational database management system. (pp. 272, 584)

Read-only memory (ROM). Nonerasable chips located on the motherboard that usually store program instructions. (p. 100)

Record. A collection of related fields in a database. (pp. 272, 566)

Recordable CD (CD-R). A type of CD that can be written to, but not erased or rewritten to. (p. 146)

Register. A high-speed staging area within the CPU that temporarily stores data during processing. (p. 100)

Relational database management system (RDBMS). The most widely used database model in use today; can link data in related tables through the use of common fields. (pp. 272, 584)

Release. A minor upgrade of a software product. (p. 666)

Reverse auction. An auction where sellers bid for the a buyer's business; generally the seller with the lowest bid after a particular time period is allowed to sell the item to that particular buyer. (p. 453)

Rewritable CD (CD-RW). A type of CD that can be written to, as well as erased or rewritten to. (p. 146)

Rewritable DVD (DVD-RAM or DVD+RW). A type of DVD that can be written to, as well as erased or rewritten to. (p. 148)

Ring network. A communications network that connects devices in a closed loop. (p. 306)

Robotics. The study of robot technology. (p. 489)

ROM. *See* Read-only memory. (p. 100)

Row. A horizontal group of cells on a worksheet. (p. 266)

Satellite. An earth-orbiting device that relays communications signals over long distances. (p. 314)

Scanner. A term commonly used to refer to an optical scanner. (p. 177)

SCM. *See* Supply chain management. (p. 446)

Scroll bar. A horizontal or vertical bar that appears along an edge of a window when the window is not large enough to display the entire content contained within the window; the scroll bar can be used to view the rest of the information in the window. (p. 49)

SDLC. *See* Systems development life cycle. (p. 495)

Search engine. A software program used by a search site to retrieve matching Web pages from a search database. (p. 360)

Search site. A Web site that allows users to search for Web pages that match supplied keywords or fit in particular categories. (pp. 61, 360)

Sector. A pie-shaped area on a disk surface. (p. 135)

Security. A collection of measures for protecting a computer system's hardware, software, and data from damage or tampering. (p. 660)

Sequential organization. A method for organizing data on a storage medium in either ascending or descending order by the contents of some key field, so that the data can be accessed sequentially. (p. 577)

Serial transmission. Data transmission in which every bit in a byte must travel down the same path in succession. (p. 318)

Slide. A one-page presentation graphic that can be displayed in a group with others to form an online slide show. (p. 277)

Smart card. A credit-card-sized piece of plastic containing a chip and other circuitry into which data can be stored. (pp. 150, 456)

Software. Computer programs. (p. 10)

Software piracy. The unauthorized copying or use of computer programs. (p. 612)

Software suite. A collection of software programs bundled together and sold as a single package. (p. 253)

Source code. A computer program before it is compiled. (p. 531)

Spam. Unsolicited, bulk e-mail sent over the Internet. (pp. 383, 626)

Speakers. Output devices that produce sound. (p. 198)

Spreadsheet. A type of application program used to create documents that can be organized into rows and columns and typically contain a great deal of numbers and mathematical computations. (p. 266)

SQL. *See* Structured query language. (p. 585)

Star network. A communications network consisting of a host device connected directly to several other devices. (p. 305)

Storage. Saving data, results, or programs for future use. (pp. 8, 130)

Storefront software. Software that can be used when developing e-commerce sites to facilitate the placement of orders. (p. 424)

Storyboard. An ordered series of sketches that can be developed during the design process of a multimedia application to illustrate what each page in the application will look like. (p. 415)

Structured programming. An approach to program design in which a program is separated into smaller subprograms, and step-by-step instructions are executed one after the other, accessing the subprograms when needed. (p. 520)

Structured query language (SQL). A popular query language standard for information retrieval in relational databases. (p. 585)

Supercomputer. The fastest, most expensive, and most powerful type of computer. (p. 25)

Supply chain management (SCM). The oversight of materials, information, and finances as they move from the original supplier to the consumer. (p. 446)

Surge suppressor. A device that protects a computer system from random electrical power spikes. (p. 659)

Syntax error. A programming error that occurs when the programmer has not followed the rules of the programming language. (p. 534)

System. A collection of elements and procedures that interact to accomplish a goal. (p. 478)

System acquisition. The phase of the systems development life cycle in which hardware, software, and necessary system components are acquired. (p. 500)

System analysis. The phase of the systems development life cycle in which a problem area is thoroughly examined to determine what should be done. (p. 496)

System board. Another name for motherboard. (p. 93)

System clock. The timing mechanism within the computer system that synchronizes the transmission of instructions and data through the computer's circuits. (p. 110)

System design. The phase of the systems development life cycle in which a model of the new system and how it will work is formally established. (p. 497)

System implementation. The phase of the systems development life cycle that encompasses activities relating to making the system operational. (p. 502)

System maintenance. The phase of the systems development life cycle in which minor adjustments are made to the finished system to keep it operational until the end of the system's life or the time that the system needs to be redesigned. (p. 502)

Systems analyst. A person who studies systems in an organization in order to determine what work needs to be done and how this work may be best achieved. (p. 492)

Systems development life cycle (SDLC). The process consisting of the six phases of system development: Preliminary investigation, and system analysis, design, acquisition, implementation, and maintenance. (p. 495)

Systems software. Programs, such as the operating system, that control the operation of a computer and its devices, as well as enable application programs to run on the computer system (pp. 11, 212)

System unit. The main box of a computer that houses the CPU, motherboard, memory, and other devices. (p. 93)

Table. In a relational database, a collection of related records. (pp. 272, 566)

TB. *See* Terabyte. (p. 88)

TCP/IP. The protocol used with Internet computers that uses packet switching to facilitate the transmission of messages. (p. 326)

Technologically obsolete. A term that refers to a product that still meets the needs of an individual or business, although a newer model, version, or release is available. (p. 665)

Telecommuting. Using a variety of computer and electronic devices to enable an individual to work from his or her home. (p. 303)

Terabyte (TB). Approximately 1 trillion bytes. (p. 88)

Text. Alphanumeric characters kept in a text, not image, format. (p. 398)

Thin client. Another name for network computer. (p. 22)

Time-sharing. A technique used in a multiuser environment in which the computer assigns a specific processing time allotment to each program and then rotates the between the programs accordingly. (p. 222)

Token Ring. A ring-based communications protocol that uses token passing to control the transmission of messages. (p. 324)

Toolbar. A set of icons or buttons displayed horizontally or vertically on the screen that can be used to issue commands to the computer. (p. 44)

Touch pad. A rectangular-shaped input device that is touched with the finger or thumb to control an onscreen pointer and make selections. (p. 175)

Touch screen. A display device that can be touched with the finger to generate input. (p. 174)

Track. A concentric path on a disk where data are recorded. (p. 135)

Trackball. An input device, similar to an upside-down mouse, that can be used to control an onscreen pointer and make selections. (p. 175)

Traditional systems development. An approach to systems development where the six phases of the systems development life cycle are carried out in a predetermined sequence. (p. 504)

Transaction processing system. A type of information system that handles data created by an organization's business transactions. (p. 482)

Twisted-pair wire. A communications medium consisting of wire strands twisted in sets of two and bound into a cable. (p. 311)

Unicode. A coding system for text-based data in any written language. (p. 88)

Uniform resource locator (URL). An address, usually beginning with *http://*, that identifies a Web page on the Internet. (p. 54)

Uninterruptible power supply (UPS). A surge suppressor with a built-in battery, the latter of which keeps power going to the computer when the main power goes off. (p. 659)

Unix. A long-standing operating system for midrange computers and high-end PCs. (p. 229)

Upgrading. The process of buying new hardware or software to add capabilities and extend the life of a computer system. (p. 665)

UPS. *See* Uninterruptible power supply. (p. 659)

URL. *See* Uniform resource locator. (p. 54)

User. A person who uses a computer system. (p. 15)

User name. A name that uniquely identifies a user on a particular network. (p. 54)

Utility program. A program that performs some frequently encountered operation in a computer system, usually related to managing the computer's resources. (p. 236)

Value chain management. The process of maximizing the flow of products, goods, services, and information through a value-added network of suppliers. (p. 447)

Value-added reseller (VAR). A company that buys hardware and software from others and makes computer systems out of them that are targeted to particular vertical markets. (p. 651)

VAR. *See* Value-added reseller. (p. 651)

Version. A major upgrade of a software product. (p. 666)

Video. A continuous stream of visual information broken into separate images or frames to be displayed one after the other to simulate the original information. (p. 404)

Videoconferencing. Using computers and communications technology to carry on a meeting between people in different geographical locations. (p. 303)

Virtual reality (VR). A multimedia application that allows the computer to create three-dimensional views of objects, people, or locations that look like they do in the real world. (p. 406)

Visual Basic. An object-oriented, fourth-generation version of the BASIC programming language. (p. 545)

Voice-input system. A system that enables a computer to recognize the human voice. (p. 185)

Voice-output system. A system that enables a computer to play back or imitate the human voice. (p. 200)

Volatile. Storage whose contents are erased when the power is shut off. (p. 131)

VR. *See* Virtual reality. (p. 406)

WAP. *See* Wireless application protocol. (p. 327)

WAN. *See* Wide area network. (p. 308)

Warranty. A conditional pledge made by the manufacturer of a product to protect consumers from losses due to defective products. (p. 664)

WBT. *See* Web-based training. (p. 410)

Web-based training (WBT). Individual instruction delivered via the World Wide Web. (p. 410)

Web browser. A program used to view Web pages. (p. 51)

Web page. A document, usually containing hyperlinks to other documents, located on a Web server and available through the World Wide Web. (p. 50)

Web server. A computer that hosts Web pages so they can be accessed through the Internet. (p. 51)

Web site. A related group of Web pages usually belonging to an organization or individual. (p. 51)

Web site authoring software. Programs used to create Web pages and complete Web sites. (p. 423)

Wide area network (WAN). A network that connects devices located in a wide geographical area. (p. 308)

Window. A rectangular area appearing on the screen of a computer using a GUI operating system such as Windows; windows can contain icons, documents, and other information. (p. 41)

Windows. The primary PC operating system developed by Microsoft Corporation; common versions include Windows 95, Windows 98, Windows 2000, and Windows Me. (p. 225)

Windows Millennium Edition (Me). The upgrade to Windows 98. (p. 227)

Windows NT. The earlier version of the operating system designed by Microsoft Corporation for both high-end single user and network applications that was replaced by Windows 2000. (p. 226)

Windows 2000. The upgrade to Windows NT. (p. 226)

Windows XP. The latest version of Windows; designed to replace both Windows Me and Windows 2000. (p. 228)

Wireless Application Protocol (WAP). A standard for delivering content to mobile devices. (p. 327)

Wireless Ethernet. A standard that allows the use of Ethernet with wireless network connections. (p. 328)

Word processing. A type of application program used to create, manipulate, and print written documents, such as letters, contracts, and manuscripts. (p. 259)

Word wrap. The feature found in a word processing program that automatically returns the insertion point to the next line when reaching the end of the screen line, and keeps the proper amount of text on each line after the document is edited and formatted. (p. 262)

Workbook. A collection of worksheets that are saved in a single spreadsheet file. (p. 266)

Workgroup computing. Software that allows individuals to use their PCs to collaborate on job tasks and projects. (p. 481)

Worksheet. A document in a spreadsheet program. (p. 266)

World Wide Web (WWW). The collection of Web pages available through the Internet. (pp. 50, 347)

WWW. *See* World Wide Web. (pp. 50, 347)

INDEX